THE
ENCYCLOPEDIA
OF
PROTESTANTISM

THE
ENCYCLOPEDIA
OF
PROTESTANTISM

VOLUME 4
S–Z
Index

HANS J. HILLERBRAND
EDITOR

Routledge
New York   London

Published in 2004 by

Routledge
29 West 35th Street
New York, NY 10001-2299
www.routledge-ny.com

Published in Great Britain by
Routledge
11 New Fetter Lane
London EC4P 4EE
www.routledge.co.uk

Routledge is an imprint of Taylor & Francis Books, Inc.

10 9 8 7 6 5 4 3 2 1

Printed on acid-free, 250-year-life paper
Manufactured in the United States of America

Library of Congress Cataloging-in-Publication Data

Encyclopedia of Protestantism / Hans J. Hillerbrand, editor.
    p. cm.
Includes bibliographical references and index.
  ISBN 0-415-92472-3 (set)
  1. Protestantism—Encyclopedias. I. Hillerbrand, Hans Joachim.
BX4811.3.E53 2003
280′.4′03—dc21
                                                    2003011582

Contents

S

SABATIER, AUGUSTE (1839–1901)

French theologian. Born in Vallont-Pont-d'Arc in 1839, Louis-Auguste Sabatier was a French Reformed Protestant theologian and philosopher of religion. He first lectured on reformed dogmatics in the Protestant Faculty of Theology at Strasbourg (1867–1872), and later helped to found the Protestant Faculty of Theology at Paris (1877), where he remained professor of THEOLOGY until his death, and from 1895 served as dean. Amid the religious and political complexities of the Third Republic, he proudly affirmed his allegiance to Huguenot traditions (see HUGUENOTS), his antipathy to the Catholic Church of FRANCE, and his objection to the absolutization of science within Positivism. Sabatier died in Paris in 1901.

He was a prolific writer of theology who combined studies in biblical theology, psychology, and philosophy with the critical study of the history of religions and the history of Christianity. His works included *L'Apôtre Paul, esquisse d'une histoire de sa pensée* (1870), *Les origines littéraires et la composition de l'apocalypse de Saint Jean* (1888), *La doctrine de l'expiation et son évolution historique* (1903), and *Les religions d'autorité et la religion de l'esprit* (1904), as well as the work that brought him fame, *Esquisse d'une philosophie de la religion d'après la psychologie et l'histoire* (1897). All were translated into English, extending his influence, with the most powerful book being *Outlines of a Philosophy of Religion Based on Psychology and History* (tr. 1897).

Sabatier is usually classified as a liberal theologian whose influence reached both Protestant and Catholic modernists. He is also called a symbolist because of the role he grants to metaphor and nonfixity in the formulation of theological doctrine. The labels are inadequate to indicate his theological program, however. In *Esquisse d'une philosophie,* he emerges as a staunch advocate of both the Reformed Church of France and Protestant doctrines. To reach these positions, however, he does not start with the creed or orthodox doctrine or ecclesiastical institutions or the BIBLE. He starts instead with what he calls "the instinct of every being to persevere in being," that is, the religious impulse inside every person. The impulse, rightly followed, results in PRAYER as the filial movement of the soul to live in relation with God the Father. This Sabatier knows through what he calls psychology, something like study of the soul. Then, through historical study, he discovers that amid all the religions of the world Christianity emerges as the only one within which reconciliation with God is complete. Likewise he detects within the history of Christianity a clear progression from an initial Messianic form to the later Catholic form and finally to the higher Protestant form, which alone brings the original inner impulse of religion to fulfillment. Protestants successfully unite the promptings of the inner spirit with the authority of Scripture, the doctrines of SALVATION, and the common life of the CHURCH.

See also Catholicism, Protestant Reactions; Liberal Protestantism and Liberalism; Modernism

References and Further Reading

Primary Sources:

Sabatier, Auguste. *The Doctrine of the Atonement and its Historical Evolution.* London: Williams & Norgate, 1904.

Sabatier, Auguste, and Emmanuel Christen. *The Vitality of Christian Dogmas and Their Power of Evolution.* London: A. & C. Black, 1898.

Sabatier, Auguste, and Louise Seymour Houghton. *Religions of Authority and the Religion of the Spirit.* New York: McClure, Phillips, 1904.

Secondary Sources:

Reymond, Bernard. *Auguste Sabatier et le procès théologique de l'autorité.* Lausanne, Switzerland: L'age d'homme, 1976.

Silkstone, Thomas. *Religions, Symbolism, and Meaning: A Critical Study of the Views of Auguste Sabatier.* London: Faber, 1968.

C. T. McIntire

SABATIER, PAUL (1858–1928)

French theologian. Born in 1858 at Saint-Michael-de-Chabrillanoux, Ardèche, Sabatier served one Reformed Church pastorate in Strasbourg until being forced to leave in 1889 for not relinquishing his French citizenship, and a second at St-Cierge-la-Serre in the Cévennes until resigning in 1893 because of poor health. He then spent long periods in ITALY, especially Assisi, where he engaged in research on medieval spirituality and became a historian of St. Francis of Assisi. In 1919 he became professor of church history at the Protestant Faculty of Theology at Strasbourg. He died in Strasbourg in 1928.

His book *La vie de St. François d'Assise* (1893), written while serving his pastorate in Cévennes, became a standard study of St. Francis of Assisi in his day. He depicted St. Francis as something like a Protestant who followed the pure Gospel of Jesus Christ, distanced himself from the Roman Curia, and stimulated a reformation of the church. The Vatican placed the book on the Index of Prohibited Books (1894). Unusual for a Protestant, he was an active leader in international and national societies of Franciscan studies, and a rigorous researcher after documents relevant to medieval religious themes. He was also fluent in Latin and Italian. His Franciscan interest boosted his own reputation as a mystic.

Within FRANCE he was a avid commentator on the religious condition of the nation. His book *L'orientation religieuse de la France actuelle* (1911), following upon *À propos de la separation des eglises et de l'état* (1905), and *Les modernistes, notes d'histoire religieuse contemporaine* (1909), provided an analysis of the religious history of France during the Third Republic, especially since the Law of Separation (1905). His works played down the evident polarization of religious partisanship and aimed to persuade Protestants to accept the new realities. He showed immense sympathy for Catholic Modernists (see MODERNISM), whom he interpreted as devoted Catholics desiring to help their church, and for Free Thinkers, whom he saw as authentic searchers after truth and not antireligious. He criticized his fellow Protestants for in-fighting and squandering their opportunities for timely leadership. His eye focused on the new generic *morale laïque,* which the government had established in the public schools of France, displacing Catholic teachings. He regarded this action as not antithetical to Catholic or Protestant traditions. The *morale laïque* was, he urged, the clearest expression of the new religious orientation of France. It tapped a universal morality common to society as a whole, and harmonized with the best elements of Protestantism.

References and Further Reading

Primary Sources:

Sabatier, Paul. *Life of St. Francis of Assissi.* New York: Scribner's Sons, 1894.

———. *Modernism.* New York: Scribner's Sons, 1908.

Secondary Sources:

Colwell, H. J. *Two French Protestant Pastors and Mystics: J. F. Oberlin and Paul Sabatier.* London: Spottiswoode, Ballantyne, 1944.

Little, A. G. *Paul Sabatier, Historian of St. Francis.* Manchester, UK: University Press, 1943.

C. T. McIntire

SABBATARIANISM

An often misunderstood movement that cut across denominational boundaries, Sabbatarianism is best considered under two rubrics, the restorationist and the reformist. Advocates of the former type sought a return to the Old Testament Sabbath, and therefore set aside Saturday, the seventh day of the week, for WORSHIP and rest. Most prominent among restorationists are the SEVENTH-DAY ADVENTISTS and Seventh-Day Baptists. Advocates of the reformist brand of Sabbatarianism, on the other hand, maintained that the Sabbath was transferred to Sunday when Christ rose from the dead on that day. They sought through measures both coercive and persuasive to ensure that Sunday was properly observed as a Sabbath. Although each type of Sabbatarianism was evident in the sixteenth century, it was not until industrial and commercial rhythms and styles of work, rest, and worship remade societies in Western Europe and North America that they flourished. This process occurred in various communities at different times, following different paces and mandates, but it was most accelerated and pronounced in ENGLAND, colonial America, and later the UNITED STATES. This entry primarily focuses on reformist Sabbatarianism because the restorationist type, now institutionalized in a variety of Seventh-Day denominations, is addressed elsewhere.

The early Protestant reformers, above all JOHN CALVIN and MARTIN LUTHER, cast Sunday as a day for religious assembly and PRAYER, but did not seek to abolish restful and harmless sports from the day. It is well known, for instance, that Calvin played bowls on Sundays, as did many of his prominent followers on the Continent and in England. As part of their larger efforts to eradicate the superstition that they felt corrupted the Catholic Church, the early reformers taught that the Fourth Commandment applied exclusively to the Jews, and that Christians were only obligated to set aside a convenient day for rest and religious duties. Perhaps spurred by the Catholic Church's Council of Trent's publication of a treatise on the Fourth Commandment in 1567, Protestants in England and on the Continent began to closely consider Christ's actions and words in relation to the Old Testament law of the Sabbath. Out of this close reading emerged a great variety of sentiments about the Sabbath, including the restorationist and the reformist brands of Sabbatarianism.

Restorationist Sabbatarianism

Before 1617 no Christian congregations observed the seventh day (Saturday) as the Sabbath. The emergence among a handful of Protestant congregations of the seventh-day Sabbath was an aspect of the larger impulse to return to the practices of the apostolic church and to rid Christianity of papist innovations. Many of the early Sabbatarians, who could be found in small numbers from Silesia to WALES and were known to their peers as Jews, believed that Sunday worship violated God's command, and was one of the many errors imposed on Christians by the Roman Catholic church. They argued that the Sunday-Sabbath was as tainted as the many red letter days that bled into one another on the Roman calendar. Most zealous about the Saturday-Sabbath were BAPTISTS, some of whom restored the seventh-day Sabbath along with foot washing (see FEET, WASHING OF), abstinence from unclean meats, and the laying on of hands. Chief among the radical critics of the Sunday-Sabbath was the English theologian Theophilus Brabourne (1590–1661), who wrote the first seventh-day Sabbatarian treatise, *A Discourse Upon the Sabbath Day* (1628). In it and in a subsequent, more influential publication titled *A Defence of . . . the Sabbath Day* (1632), Brabourne made the case for observance of the Mosaic Sabbath. In the following decades several independent congregations formed with the intention of observing the Saturday-Sabbath, most prominently the Lothbury Church and the Mill Yard Church, and their leaders were often tried, and on occasion executed, for hewing too closely to the Old Testament, the Mosaic code, and the seventh-day Sabbath. Led by the nonconformist Francis Bampfield (1615–1684) the "seventh-day men" sought to radically

reform the calendar by abolishing all saints days and the Sunday-Sabbath too.

Puritan Sabbatarianism

The majority of Protestants in the seventeenth century as in our own, however, were content to leave the Sunday-Sabbath intact. The Puritan brand of Sabbatarianism, the best-known and most lampooned type, developed in England during the seventeenth century (see PURITANISM). It too was part of the broader reforms of popular culture and of the Roman calendar. In seeking to regularize the rhythm of work and rest by abolishing all saints days and holidays such that on six days men and women could and would work without interruption, Puritans infused the Sunday-Sabbath with much more importance than it had held previous to the REFORMATION. For medieval and early modern Europeans there were many opportunities for revelry, worship, and rest, and for completing the irregular, seasonal, syncopated work that characterized the largely agricultural and subsistence economy. However, with the parallel rise of Protestantism, mercantile capitalism, and industrialism, pressures to regularize rhythms of work and rest accelerated (see INDUSTRIALIZATION). Thus the Fourth Commandment, "thou shalt work six days and rest on the seventh," resonated deeply with other currents in the culture and economy such that Sunday became the site of all that was meant to be restful and worshipful. This was first evident in Great Britain.

Under the reigns of ELIZABETH I and James I, Puritan divines and Anglican authorities clashed over the observance of Sunday (see ANGLICANISM). Although the crown forbade the performance of plays on Sunday in London (1680) it also vetoed a Parliamentary bill promoting strict observance of Sunday (1684). All agreed that church attendance should be mandatory, but it was over amusement, trade, and work that conflict developed. Puritans sought to abolish the fairs, games, frolics, and mayhem that erupted after morning services in favor of religious education and public and private prayer. The crown and its bishops, however, sanctioned church in the morning and play in the afternoon, which James I's "Book of Sports" (1618) codified. James I was concerned that without Sunday "the poorer sorts" would have no chance for recreation at all. Near mid-century, Parliamentary law established one Tuesday a month as a day of "recreation and relaxation," but it did not take long for this ruling to fall into abeyance. The crown's revision and enforcement of moderate Sunday codes irked Puritans and other reformers on both sides of the Atlantic. Thus, many treatises about the Sunday-Sabbath were penned and published, including Nicolas Bownde's

The Doctrine of the Sabbath (1595), Gilbert Ironside's *Seven Questions of the Sabbath* (1637), Thomas Shepard's *Theses Sabbaticae* (1649), and William Pynchon's *Holy Time, or, the True Limits of the Lords Day* (1654). The Restoration by no means resolved the debates over the meanings and obligations of Sunday. However, fierce theological parries diminished in power and frequency, the rationalization of the yearly calendar continued its course, Sunday observance was firmly understood as a matter for both religious and civil law, and many parties in the divided English church cherished Sunday as a day of rest and worship.

Sabbatarianism in the Nineteenth and Twentieth Centuries

So it is out of the collapse of medieval Europe's variegated and elaborate calendar that pressures on and hopes for Sunday coalesced. In eighteenth- and nineteenth-century Britain and North America, Sunday was the safety valve for many communities during a time when work days extended beyond twelve hours and religious duties remained rigorous. An array of expectations and disappointments split the large numbers of Christians, both Protestant and Catholic, who treated Sunday as the day of rest, and out of these hopes and frustrations arose a number of Sabbatarian organizations and leaders who tried to mold Sunday into their ideal of the Sabbath. These ideals changed over time, of course, such that early Sabbatarians condemned all reading but that of the BIBLE, whereas later ones actively worked in support of opening on Sundays libraries stocked with a full range of secular works. Sabbatarian goals and issues were defined far more deeply by contemporary understandings of the meaning and nature of rest than by beliefs about worship, the sacred, and biblical injunction. By charting the history of the meaning of rest, one can predict with a fair degree of surety the contours of the Sabbatarian crusade in the nineteenth and twentieth centuries.

It is no surprise then that the great Sabbatarian crusades began in both the United States and Great Britain at the beginning of the nineteenth century, gained momentum at mid-century, and spread to the Continent before the turn of the twentieth century. This was the age when industrial rhythms of work and rest permeated the countryside as well as the city, with railroads, telegraphs, and electricity remaking all aspects of everyday life. Societies to suppress Sunday trading, established in London in 1809 and 1810, inaugurated the practices of publishing and distributing Sabbatarian tracts and pamphlets. At about the same time in the United States a nationwide controversy over the transportation and distribution of mails erupted, eventually giving rise to the first American Sabbatarian organization, the General Union for Promoting the Observance of the Christian Sabbath (1828). In addition to publishing tracts, this organization took the novel step of petitioning the federal congress and senate in favor of a strict Sunday law prohibiting the distribution and transportation of mails. (This law was not passed until 1913.) Across the Atlantic the newly formed and long-lived Lord's Day Observance Society (1831) sounded the alarm that the nation faced immediate ruin if its people continued to desecrate Sunday. Although its successes were few, and the General Union failed in its campaign and disbanded, their formation heralded a century of Sabbatarian activity on the local, national, and international levels.

In both the United States and England, Sabbatarian organizations formed through the 1840s and 1850s with the intention of preventing the running of trains on Sundays, the sale of goods, and sundry other activities that characterized market economies and cultures. In 1843 American-born TEMPERANCE activist Justin Edwards founded the American and Foreign Sabbath Union, an umbrella organization for a variety of Sabbatarian groups and causes. Members and leaders of Sabbatarian organizations tended toward ORTHODOXY and conservatism, but came out of the great variety of Protestant denominations. In the 1850s the old question of Sunday amusements again became chief among Sabbatarian concerns. In Britain controversy about opening the Crystal Palace on Sunday afternoons caused a deluge of pamphlets, tracts, and editorials on the question, which only prepared the public for the widespread protests against a bill limiting the Sunday hours of public houses and another bill restraining Sunday trade. One witness to the demonstrations in Hyde Park during the summer of 1855, Karl Marx, was convinced that the English revolution had finally begun. Later that year a bill proposing the opening of the British Museum on Sunday afternoon to provide uplifting entertainment divided the nation. Robert Morrell, a member of England's Radical Party, formed the National Sunday League (1855) in favor of Sunday opening. Two years later opponents countered by forming the National Lord's Day Rest Association (1857), which recruited members from the working classes and dissenting churches (see DISSENT). At the end of the tumultuous decade John Stuart Mill attacked Sabbatarianism in his laissez-faire statement of political philosophy, *On Liberty*.

Although the 1850s was not as active a decade for American Sabbatarians as for those in Britain, in 1857 the influential New York Sabbath Committee (NYSC) formed in reaction to the "Continental Sabbath" activities—beer drinking, concert going, excursion taking—of the large numbers of German and Irish immigrants. As in Britain, recreation, amusements, and, above all, drinking, were at the heart of the controversy. With the outbreak of the CIVIL WAR, the NYSC lobbied President ABRAHAM LINCOLN and Union general George McClelland, urging them to ensure Sabbath observance among the troops. Troops, trains, and supplies moved on many Sundays during the Civil War, and some of the bloodiest battles were also fought on that day, despite Sabbatarian pleas for restraint. For the most part Sabbatarians were quiet during the 1860s and 1870s. Their twin successes in keeping the Boston Public Library and the 1876 World's Fair in Philadelphia closed on Sundays were temporary. By 1893 the Chicago World's Fair, along with nearly all public libraries, art museums, and public parks in the United States and Great Britain, were open Sundays.

During the last quarter of the nineteenth century, Sabbatarians formed hundreds of organizations, including the National Sunday League (England), the American Sabbath Association (United States), and the Lord's Day Alliance (United States). Led by career reformers and ministers like Londoner Frederick Peake, Canadian J. G. Sherarer, and Americans Wilbur F. Crafts, William Wallace Atterbury, Alexander Jackson, and Martin D. Kneeland, these groups mostly campaigned against Sunday opening and worked to have their convictions written into civil law. On the local level Sabbatarian laws proliferated, but as the economy became more and more diversified, so did the laws legislating what could and could not be done Sunday. In the 1890s more than thirteen million Americans petitioned the United States Senate to pass a federal Sunday law enjoining it as a day of worship and rest. NATURAL LAW, historic precedent, and biblical mandate were all invoked in support. Sabbatarianism was one of the leading topics of the time, and sermons, pamphlets, editorials, short stories, and tracts concerning Sunday observance were widespread and frequent. Despite the widespread disagreement over the particulars, consensus was that Sunday was and should remain the day of rest.

During this same period the first Sabbatarian organizations began to form in Continental Europe, but unlike their Anglo-American brethren, these associations were animated by concern over Sunday work. Between 1876 and 1915 a series of international congresses on Sunday rest were held, usually in conjunction with world's fairs. The proceedings of these conferences highlight the tremendous variety, and at times conflict, within Sabbatarianism. Biblical injunctions against Sunday amusement and recreation animated the more conservative Anglo-American Sabbatarians. A broad and liberal interpretation of Mark 2:27 ("The Sabbath was made for man, not man for the Sabbath") characterized the more heterodox Sabbatarians. A concern with the conditions of working people motivated the nonreligious Sabbatarians, many of whom were Continental Europeans. By the twentieth century many European countries had passed labor legislation limiting the hours and days of work, and in these places Sabbatarianism all but disappeared. In the United States and England, too, Sabbatarianism as a movement slowly disappeared. Controversies over the popularity of concerts, motion pictures, spectator sports, and automobile driving on Sundays continued through the 1930s. Sabbatarianism lived on in the courts, as men and women were occasionally prosecuted for violating a Sunday law. In one case that went to the United States Supreme Court in 1961, *McGowan v. Maryland,* the justices decided that although Sunday laws may have had religious origins, they had been sufficiently secularized so as not to violate the constitutional guarantee of a separation between CHURCH AND STATE. Nevertheless, in the 1970s and 1980s Sunday laws were widely repealed.

The inability, and at times refusal, of Sabbatarians to address the most significant and widespread form of "Sabbath breaking"—work—compromised the movement's success. Throughout the nineteenth century Sabbatarians agitated for Sunday closing of cultural and recreational sites, but at the same time trains set and followed Sunday schedules, factories ran continuously, and even in homes domestic laborers ran to and fro preparing large dinners and sewing buttons on church pants. This hypocrisy was glaringly obvious to many contemporaries, who sought to fashion movements of their own against Sunday work or in favor of healthful and uplifting activities on Sundays for those who worked tirelessly through the week. However, because those who gladly took the name "Sabbatarian" were on the one hand committed to preventing all amusements, excursions, and diversions from tainting Sunday, and on the other hand turned a blind eye to the steam and smoke pouring forth from factories, some of which they owned, the movement for a Sunday-Sabbath was doomed. To be sure, Sunday is the day of worship for most Protestants, but the aspirations and ideals of the earliest Sabbatarians have been lost in the tides of industrialism and commercialism. So the legacy of Sabbatarianism is mixed: in more conservative congregations a strict regard for Sunday as the Sabbath holds sway, but most Protestant Sundays are similar in their essentials to pre-Reformation Sundays—a little church, a little revelry or sport, and some shopping.

References and Further Reading

Ball, Bryan W. *The Seventh-day Men: Sabbatarians and Sabbatarianism in England and Wales, 1600–1800.* Oxford, UK: Clarendon Press, 1994.

Dennison, James T. *The Market Day of the Soul: The Puritan Doctrine of the Sabbath in England, 1532–1700.* Lanham, MD: University Press of America, 1983.

Hill, Christopher. "The Uses of Sabbatarianism." In *Society and Puritanism in Pre-Revolutionary England.* New York: Schocken Books, 1964.

Katz, David S. *Sabbath and Sectarianism in Seventeenth-Century England.* New York: E. J. Brill, 1988.

McCrossen, Alexis. *Holy Day, Holiday: The American Sunday.* Ithaca, NY: Cornell University Press, 2000.

McMillan, Duncan, ed. *Sunday, the World's Rest Day.* New York: Doubleday, Page, and Co., 1916.

Parker, Kenneth L. *The English Sabbath: A Study of Doctrine and Discipline from the Reformation to the Civil War.* Cambridge: Cambridge University Press, 1988.

Solberg, Winton. *Redeem the Time: The Puritan Sabbath in Early America.* Cambridge, MA: Harvard University Press, 1977.

Wigley, John. *The Rise and Fall of the Victorian Sunday.* Manchester, UK: Manchester University Press, 1980.

ALEXIS MCCROSSEN

SACRAMENTS

A sacrament (from the Latin *sacramentum*) is defined in Protestantism as visible sign of an inward GRACE. Traditionally sacraments denote those rites which the church understands to be "means of grace" for the recipient. Protestant churches have recognized two such rites, both of which are explicitly ordained by Christ in the New Testament: BAPTISM and the LORD'S SUPPER (or Eucharist or Holy Communion). In this, they rejected the Catholic affirmation of seven sacraments, insisting that a sacrament required the specific institution by Jesus and the promise of the conveyance of grace. Protestant churches affirming the former, but not the latter, prefer the term "ordinance."

Seeking to correct a perceived overemphasis on the externality of sacramental performance in the medieval Catholic church, the reformers of the sixteenth century stressed the FAITH of the believer as a prerequisite for sacramental efficacy. Thus the Protestant doctrine of the sacraments came to be regarded as a corollary of the doctrine of JUSTIFICATION by faith alone. While MARTIN LUTHER and JOHN CALVIN retained the sacraments as a visible means of grace, and continued to emphasize the ecclesial significance of their outward practice, they placed preeminent importance on the sacraments' role in the strengthening of the faith of the believer. HULDRYCH ZWINGLI sought to redefine a "sacrament" as an "oath" between the believer and God, and as a public demonstration of the believer's allegiance to the church.

The seventeenth and eighteenth centuries with their stress on interior faith had several lasting effects on Protestant sacramental practice, ranging from significant changes (such as the shift from infant to adult believer's baptism by the BAPTISTS) to a moderation of the ceremonious aspects of sacramental worship (PURITANISM and PIETISM). In some cases, the result was the elimination of sacramental ceremony from the liturgical order altogether (see FRIENDS, SOCIETY OF). While some countercurrent sacramental movements arose within Protestantism, such as the largely communal practices of early METHODISM, and although the aesthetic concerns of ROMANTICISM provided a catalyst for the renewal of ceremony in Protestantism, the individual notion of sacramental WORSHIP remained pervasive through the nineteenth century.

The ecumenical movement of the twentieth century restored the importance of the communal church to Protestant sacramental worship. United by the perceived common mission of all Christians in the world, churches (both Protestant and Catholic) witnessed remarkable convergence in their understanding and use of the sacraments, especially as attested to in the WORLD COUNCIL OF CHURCHES report on *Baptism, Eucharist, and Ministry*. These developments have done much to address the practical concerns of sacramental worship, but doctrinal divergences, both within Protestantism and between Protestants and Catholics, remain points of serious contention. This is due in large part to the fact that questions of practice have not as readily led Protestant theologians to propose the sacraments themselves as doctrinal loci. Where such work has occurred, the way forward appears to depend on the extent to which the role that the sacraments played in constituting the liturgical life of the church in the early REFORMATION could be recovered today.

See also Catholicism, Protestant Reactions; Ecumenism

References and Further Reading

Gerrish, Brian. *Grace and Gratitude: The Eucharistic Theology of John Calvin.* Minneapolis, MN: Fortress Press, 1993.

Thurian, Max, ed. *Ecumenical Perspectives on Baptism, Eucharist and Ministry.* Geneva, Switzerland: World Council of Churches, 1983.

White, James F. *The Sacraments in Protestant Practice and Faith.* Nashville, TN: Abingdon Press, 1999.

NATHAN R. KERR

SAINTS

The figure of the saint is found in all world religions. Saints embody ideals of personal transformation, or holiness, which is common to all religious traditions. However, the meaning of holiness, the functions of saints, and forms by which saints are recognized and honored vary among and within religions. In all religious traditions, however, the recognition of saints is narratively constructed; that is, individuals are identified as saints through the stories told of them, for imitation and celebration, by communities of faith. Although the Protestant reformers rejected the medieval Christian cult of the saints, especially their veneration and their role as intercessors with God, the churches of the REFORMATION continue to emphasize the Christian call to holiness. Moreover, reverence for and even devotion to certain saints of the pre-Reformation church persists, most notably in ANGLICANISM. Distinctions must be made, therefore, between the veneration of saints and their intercession, as found in the Roman Catholic and Orthodox traditions (see ORTHODOXY, EASTERN), and the memorializing of certain martyrs and champions of faith, which is manifest in various Protestant traditions.

Saints in World Religions

Outside of Christianity, where official sainthood is conferred posthumously in the Roman Catholic and Orthodox traditions, veneration of saints includes both the living and the dead. Buddhists venerate their *arahants,* their *bodhisattvas.* Hindus revere a wide range of divinely human and humanly divine figures, including their personal gurus or spiritual teachers. Muslims acknowledge various *alwailya Allah* (close friends of God) and assorted Sufi masters. Even in JUDAISM, which discourages the veneration of individuals, one can find popular devotion to the Biblical prophets, particularly Moses and Elijah, to assorted Jewish martyrs, and to beloved rabbis and other *tsaddikim* (just men), primarily among the Hasidim.

However, if the saint is a familiar figure in world religions, the meaning of sainthood and the functions of the saint differ according to traditions. Although all saints inspire admiration, some are considered so extreme in behavior, or so extraordinary in their manifestation of holiness, as to be inimitable. On the other hand, whereas not everyone is a saint, in most traditions the expectation is that all should aspire to holiness. Thus, in every tradition there are various schools of spirituality that have as their goal the achievement of holiness, variously understood, which constitutes sainthood.

Functionally a saint is an exemplar of holiness. In their capacity as paradigms, saints embody the mode of personal transformation that every religion puts forward as the goal of human existence. Thus the Hindu saint is one who realizes in his own life the divinity of the Self; that is, the realization that within him or her is the Atman that is identical with the Brahman. The Buddhist saint is one who realizes the emptiness of self and true compassion. In monotheis-

tic traditions, God alone is holy. Yet saints are said to achieve a kind of holiness of their own through Divine GRACE, usually manifest through PRAYER, exceptional virtue, austerities, and other spiritual disciplines. Typically, saints are seen as charismatic figures. In all traditions saints work miracles; in Hinduism and Buddhism, miracles are regarded as supernormal powers that the saint acquires in the course of attaining progressively higher levels of spiritual liberation from the attachments of normal human existence. In the monotheistic religions, miracles ascribed to the saints are generally regarded as the work of the Holy Spirit acting through the agency of the saint. There is also in each tradition an intimate connection between personal holiness or transformation and the power to work miracles. In classic rabbinic Judaism, for example, the goal of every Jew is not simply to study the Torah but to "become" the Torah. Thus in the Talmudic literature we find exceptional sages whose holiness also included the power to work miracles. In certain Hasidic traditions the rebbe is regarded as a figure whose soul is rooted in God; in this capacity, he functions as a mediator between God and the members of his Hasidic circle. In Islam sainthood is mostly identified with Sufi mysticism; that is, miracles are attributed to those who have drawn close to Allah through mystical practices.

In sum we can say that in all traditions, a saint is someone who has been transformed, who is often credited with working miracles as the sign of that transformation, and who embodies to an exceptional degree the holiness or spiritual liberation that is held out as the perfection of human existence. It is not surprising, therefore, that saints (as charismatic figures) are often in tension with the protectors of ORTHODOXY. This has been particularly evident in the history of Christianity, Judaism, and Islam. At the same time, saints are also figures whose appeal bridges the gap that often exists between popular religion and religion's intellectual elites.

Saints in Christianity

From a sociological perspective a saint is anyone who is recognized as such by others. The Christian cult of the saints, therefore, began as a process of recognizing certain individuals who have conformed their lives to Christ in an extraordinary manner. Theologically speaking, a Christian cannot be a Christ in the way a Buddhist, for example, can become a Buddha. However, through the power of the Holy Spirit, a Christian's life can be transformed—a "new creation," as the Apostle Paul declared—so that Christ can be recognized through the members of His body.

For the early Christians what mattered most about Christ was his DEATH and resurrection. Therefore, those who were martyred for Christ were those whose witness (in Greek, *martys* means "witness") was considered complete. Although the first Christians referred to all baptized believers as saints (in Greek, *hagioi*), before the first century was out the term was reserved for MARTYRS: just as BAPTISM signified incorporation into the body of Christ, so martyrdom signified a dying with Christ and a rising again into the fullness of everlasting life.

All this is evident from the story of the protomartyr in the Book of Acts. There we see that the story of Stephen's arrest, testimony to Christ, his forgiveness of his enemies, and his death replicates the passion and death of Jesus. Here we have the first example of what was to become a tradition: to be recognized as a saint was to have one's death remembered and told as the story of Jesus all over again. Put differently, the only way the Christian community was able to recognize Stephen as a saint was to see in him the story of Jesus. To this day, in fact, wherever saints are formally canonized or informally recognized by a community of Christians, that recognition takes the form of constructing the saint's story so that it reveals—in new and individual ways—the transformation that occurs in those who allow Christ to live in them.

The martyr, then, was the first model for the Christian saint, and martyrdom remains the privileged form of sainthood to this day, although other models were soon added. One of the earliest was the confessor—individuals who confessed their willingness to die for Christ but whose lives, for various reasons, were spared. Once Christianity became the religion of the Roman Empire, anchorites and hermits who fled to the desert wastes of Syria and Egypt were shown the deference usually accorded to martyrs. Just as the martyrs were purified by their suffering and death, so, it was thought, these ascetics were purified by the rigors of their self-denial—and by the temptations of Satan (see DEVIL). Thus to the "red martyrdom" of those who shed their blood was added the "white martyrdom" of the ascetics.

The cult of the saints developed out of the cult of the martyrs. Their stories were recited as examples to the faithful. Their feast days were celebrated not on the day of their birth, but on their *dies natalis,* the day of their rebirth into everlasting glory. Because Christians believed in the resurrection of the body, saints' bones were preserved as relics. Altars were built over their tombs, which later became places of pilgrimage. Moreover, because the martyrs were with God in heaven, they could, it was believed, intercede with God on behalf of the faithful still on earth (see HEAVEN AND HELL). Believing as they did in the "communion of saints," Christians prayed to those in heaven for help, protection, cures, and other favors. In this way miracles attributed to the saints while they were alive were extended to include those that they could work posthumously through their relics. As historian Peter Brown has observed, the cult or veneration Christians gave to their martyrs challenged the "accepted boundaries" in the Greco-Roman world between the realm and role of the living and the realm and role of the dead.

In later centuries the list of recognized saints came to include missionaries and bishops and other nonmartyrs who were considered holy for the way they lived. It also came to include biblical figures like John the Baptist and Anne, the mother of Mary, as well as figures of legend like Christopher "the Christ-bearer" and even nonhuman figures like the archangel Michael. In short, the cult of the saints brought the dead to life, breathed life into legend, and provided every community of Christians with their own heavenly patrons.

Seeing that the cult of the saints was rivaling the worship of Christ, several early church fathers took pains to distinguish between the veneration *(latria)* accorded to saints and the worship *(dulia)* reserved for God alone, although this abstract distinction had little practical effect.

Canonization: The Transformation of Lives into Texts

To "canonize" means to place a name in a canon or list of saints. The earliest lists were "martyrologies" or lists of local martyrs. Gradually these lists were expanded to include local calendars with the names and burial places of the saints. Whatever else it was, the veneration of the saints was a liturgical act: on their feast days, their stories were read out for the community. In a few cases, like the martyrdom of Perpetua and Felicitas, the local churches possessed the Roman notary's actual transcript of the dialogue between the magistrate and the accused. More often, these dialogues were apocryphal texts composed by the community, to which were attached *libelli* or stories of the miracles ascribed to the saint as further proof of Divine approbation. In some cases, these texts became full-blown hagiographic biographies like the hugely popular Life of St. Martin of Tours. By the fifth century, therefore, all the key elements existed that would eventually be codified in the formal canonization procedures of the Catholic church. Saints were identified as such by their reputations for holiness among the people; by their stories and legends into which their lives were transmuted as exemplars of heroic Christian virtue; and by their reputation for producing miracles, especially those worked posthumously at shrines containing their relics. On this last point, the fourth-century discovery of the relics of the proto-martyr Stephen played an important role. After collecting stories of the miracles produced by the relics, Augustine proclaimed them proof of the resurrection of the body—and divine confirmation that saints are truly with God in heaven and therefore worthy of veneration. Luxuriant in its growth, the cult of the saints took on a life of its own. Detached from the body and separate from the tomb, relics assumed a thaumaturgic power that confirmed the triumph of the concept of the saint as source of miraculous power over the saint as an example of the imitation of Christ. Clearly some form of quality control was required lest Christianity become a Hinduism of the West.

Initially saints were recognized by popular acclamation of the local Christian community. In the early Middle Ages, however, bishops began to assume control over the cult of the saints. In the first phase residential bishops required petitioners to prove a saint's reputation for holiness by providing them with written accounts (called *vitae*) of the saint's life and virtues, together with accounts of miracles he or she performed. Later the bishops demanded to hear from eyewitnesses to these events. Still later tribunals were established to investigate the lives and miracles claimed on behalf of candidates for sainthood. Eventually, as the institution of the papacy developed, the authority to investigate lives and to canonize those found worthy passed into the hands of the pope and his curia. One result is the process of canonizing saints became more fastidious and—more bureaucratic. Another is that the number of officially recognized saints radically declined. Today the Roman Catholic Church regards as official only those saints canonized since 1234, when Pope Gregory XI published his *Decretals* (in which he asserted the papacy's universal jurisdiction over the canonization process), although the church regards as valid the cult of many saints recognized before this date.

Even so, throughout the later Middle Ages many local bishops resisted handing over canonization to Rome, and on the popular level, Christian communities continued to recognize and venerate their own local patron saints. As Andre Vouchez has shown, the popular interest in saints focused on their miracles and especially their power to answer prayers, whereas the church's elites were interested in recognizing only those who manifest exemplary virtue. Either way, the saint was perceived as someone whose life was far beyond the capabilities of all but a few Christians. Nevertheless humble sinners could take hope: the perfect few, the church taught, had produced a "treasury" of vicarious "merits" that the church could dispense through indulgences practiced by the masses. It was this spiritual economy that was effectively challenged by Martin Luther. In the name of a purer Gospel he would reject both the spiritual athletes put forward by Rome and the panoply of wonder-working patron saints invoked by the common believer.

The Reformation

Luther was hardly the first to question the cult of the saints. Medieval figures and movements, such as the Cathars and Waldensians, vigorously denied the intercession of the saints. However, Luther's criticisms carried a personal edge. He had become a monk in part because he had promised St. Anne that he would do so if she saved him from a thunderstorm. As a monk he gave himself over to the penances and ascetic disciplines exemplified by many of the saints, hoping thereby to merit saving grace, although these practices only intensified his sense of personal Sin and never gave him the certainty of personal Salvation that he sought. Thus, having found devotion to the saints useless in his own life, he rejected them in the Reformed practices he laid down for others.

The immediate object of Luther's criticism was the system and its cash nexus whereby the papacy conferred indulgences for sins in return for payment, although it was his mature theological convictions that caused him to reject the cult of the saints. Because salvation is through personal faith alone, no one—not even the saints—can merit salvation through his/her own good works, much less assign that merit to others. Because Luther could find no support in scripture for invoking the saints, he rejected their veneration, mediation, and supplication for favors as pagan practices. God alone, he insisted, is deserving of a Christian's worship and devotion. Luther did retain belief in "the communion of saints," but by that he meant the mutual edification and support that all true Christians ought to give each other. Because Luther believed that even Christians justified by faith remain sinners, he rejected the notion that grace might bring a believer to the perfection of a saint.

Huldrych Zwingli, John Calvin, and the other leaders of the Protestant Reformation, none of whom had been monks like Luther, were even firmer—and terser—in rejecting the cult of the saints as unscriptural. Thus, wherever the Reformation churches took root in continental Europe, saints, their cults, their statues, and their stories gradually disappeared. Since the Reformation, the cult of the saints has largely disappeared from Protestant Christianity, although even among conservative Evangelicals special reverence is attached to the prophets of the Old Testament and the apostles of the New. Something like the cult of the saints continues among Anglicans and Lutherans, who maintain feast days and calendars of saints (see LUTHERANISM). Thus, besides acknowledging biblical and later classic figures as saints, Lutherans from time to time recommend new, more contemporary names (for example, DIETRICH BONHOEFFER and Dag Hamarskjold, are recent additions) for special thanksgiving and remembrance by the faithful. Formal theological conversations between Roman Catholics and various Protestant churches in the late twentieth century suggest that the role and function of saints represent a permanent difference in religious imagination, but not a barrier to ecumenical reconciliation. This optimistic view, however, was somewhat chastened by the offer of indulgences by Pope John Paul II during the Roman Catholic Church's celebration of Jubilee year 2000, which expressed the important role saints play in the Catholic understanding of the economy of salvation.

See also Catholicism, Protestant Reactions

References and Further Reading

Primary Sources:

Athanasius. "The Life of Antony and the Letter to Marcellinus." In *The Classics of Western Spirituality*. New York: Paulist Press, 1980.

Calvin, John. *Institutes of the Christian Religion*. Edited by John T. McNeil. Translated and indexed by Ford Lewis Battles. vol. XXI, 878–887. The Library of Christian Classics. Philadelphia, PA: The Westminster Press, 1960.

Zwingli, Huldrych. *Commentary on True and False Religion*. Edited by Samuel Maculey Jackson and Clarence Nevin Heller. Durham, NC: The Labyrinth Press, 1981.

St. Augustine. *City of God*. Translated by Henry Bettenson, 1033–1049. New York: Penguin Classics, 1985.

Secondary Sources:

Brown, Peter. *The Cult of the Saints: Its Rise and Function in Latin Christianity*. Chicago: University of Chicago Press, 1982.

———. *The Body and Society: Men, Women, and Sexual Renunciation in Early Christianity*. New York: Columbia University Press, 1988.

Bynum, Caroline Walker. *Holy Feast, Holy Fast: The Religious Significance of Food to Medieval Women*. Berkeley: University of California Press, 1987.

Delehaye, Hippolyte, S. J. *The Legends of the Saints*. New York: Fordham University Press, 1962.

Delooz, Pierre. *Sociologie et canonizations*. Liège, Belgium: Faculté de Droit, 1969.

Duffy, Eamon. *The Stripping of the Altars: Traditional Religion in England 1400–1580*. New Haven, CT: The Yale University Press, 1992.

Geary, Patrick J. *Furta Sacra: The Theft of Relics in the Middle Ages*. Princeton, NJ: Princeton University Press, 1978.

Hawley, John Stratton, ed. *Saints and Virtues*. Berkeley: University of California Press, 1987.

Heffernan, Thomas J. *Sacred Biography: Saints and Their Biographers in the Middle Ages*. New York: Oxford University Press, 1988.

Huizinga, J. *The Waning of the Middle Ages: A Study of the Forms of Life, Thought and Art in France and the Netherlands in the Dawn of the Renaissance*. Garden City, NY: Doubleday Anchor, 1954.

Kieckhefer, Richard, and George E. Bond, eds. *Sainthood: Its Manifestations in World Religions*. Berkeley: University of California Press, 1988.

Raitt, Jill, ed. *Christian Spirituality: High Middle Ages and Reformation*. New York: Crossroad, 1987.

Reames, Sherry L. *The Legenda Aurea: A Reexamination of Its Paradoxical History*. Madison: University of Wisconsin Press, 1085.

Vouchez, Andre. *La Sainteté en Occident aux derniers siècles du moyen age, d'apres les croces de canonization et les documents hagiographiques*. Rome: Ecole Française de Rome, 1981.

Ward, Benedicta. *Miracles and the Medieval Mind*. Philadelphia: University of Pennsylvania Press, 1987.

Wilson, Stephen, ed. *Saints and Their Cults: Studies in Religious Sociology, Folklore and History*. Cambridge: Cambridge University Press, 1983.

Woodward, Kenneth L. *Making Saints: How the Catholic Church Determines Who Becomes a Saint, Who Doesn't and Why*. New York: Simon & Schuster, 1990.

———. *The Book of Miracles: The Meaning of the Miracle Stories in Christianity, Judaism, Buddhism, Islam*. New York: Simon & Schuster, 2000.

KENNETH WOODWARD

SALT, TITUS (1803–1876)

English businessman. In mid-Victorian Britain, Titus Salt was much admired as the paragon of the virtuous, Christian capitalist who both cared for his workers and sought to reduce class tensions. It was for this reputation he was made a baronet in 1869.

Born at Morley in Yorkshire September 20, 1803, his parents raised him in the region's Independent dissenting tradition (see DISSENT). His father, Daniel Salt, was a farmer and wool merchant who relocated to the town of Bradford, Yorkshire, in 1822. After an apprenticeship in the wool trade, Titus joined the family firm, and by the mid-1830s had established himself as an owner of wool textile mills. He pioneered the production of blended, especially alpaca, wool fabrics, benefited from the mechanization and expansion of Bradford's textile industry, and so accumulated a large personal fortune.

He was a civic-minded man of liberal, reformist opinions who supported the extension of the franchise to working men but opposed factory legislation limiting hours of work. Although a poor public speaker he served as Mayor of Bradford (1848–1849), president of its chamber of commerce (1855–1856), and its member of Parliament (1859–1861). He was a lifelong, devout supporter of the Congregational Church (see CONGREGATIONALISM), which he generously patronized with large donations. He also helped other denominations and steadfastly declined to support anti-Catholic organizations (see CATHOLICISM, PROTESTANT REACTIONS).

Salt's great legacy was his planned industrial community of Saltaire near Bradford, which opened in 1853 and was under construction until 1872. Its large mill employed 3,000 people and the model town was provided with superior housing, churches, educational institutes, and recreational facilities. To both British and foreign dignitaries who toured the site, Saltaire was an exceptionally advanced urban environment for its time.

Titus Salt, who died December 29, 1876, is now seen as an exemplar of the paternalist employer whose career demonstrated for many Victorians that capitalism could be consistent with Christian virtue. He left little in the way of letters, personal papers, or writings that reveal his inner thoughts. Instead his permanent bequest to posterity is Saltaire, which has become a UNESCO world heritage site.

References and Further Reading

Reynolds, Jack. *The Great Paternalist: Titus Salt and the Growth of Nineteenth-Century Bradford.* New York: St. Martin's Press, 1983.

FRED DONNELLY

SALVATION

The term salvation corresponds, via the Latin *salus,* to the Greek *soteria,* which suggests both physical and spiritual wholeness. It is with the latter that Christians most often associate "salvation." Salvation refers to God's restoration of the world to the life appointed for it through the life, death, and resurrection of Christ. The precise nature of this restoration and its benefits—the subject of the discipline of *soteriology*—is construed in various ways throughout the history of Christian theology, and this variation is an irreducible part of the idea of salvation. That is, no "neutral" or "official" soteriology exists to which various expressions are given (see CHRISTOLOGY, which does have an orthodox formulation). Rather, the variety in formulations of the human problem with which God is concerned, the way in which that problem is addressed, and the manner in which human beings appropriate the divine assistance is intrinsic to the doctrine and reflects the several Christian renderings of salvation in the New Testament and in its Hebraic and Greek backgrounds. The discipline of soteriology is a close relative to theological and moral anthropology,

and the notion of salvation is a close companion to those of HEAVEN AND HELL, GRACE, and ATONEMENT.

Salvation in the New Testament

Early Christian views of salvation developed against the background of Jewish and Hellenistic thought. The Jewish commitment to the observance of the law as participation in the life-giving covenant with God envisioned right relation to God as the primary end of humanity. The Greek mystery religions contemporaneous with early Christianity aimed at participation in the divine life of the gods, usually through ritual initiation practices. Not a few of the gods associated with these practices were given titles that included the term *soter* (savior). Christian views of salvation were direct descendants of neither of these approaches but were affected by both, as well as by the forms of thinking labeled (somewhat erroneously) as "gnosticism," which tended on the whole to devalue the body. New Testament notions of salvation reflect the classical moral anthropology found in Plato, Aristotle, and others in which the soul, rather than the body, is fundamental to human identity. At the same time, lying somewhat uneasily alongside this classical model is a more Hebraic reverence for the body and a confidence that salvation will somehow involve the body as well as the soul; thus, the Gospel accounts of Jesus's resurrection as a glorified state inclusive of some form of physical presence, and Paul's account of the resurrection of the saints in which their bodies, too, will rise.

There are several lines of thinking about Christian salvation in the New Testament, none mutually exclusive. In various texts, salvation is seen as deliverance from coming judgment, forgiveness of SIN, the remedy of ignorance, release from captivity to the powers of this world, the gift of immortality, or the intrinsic blessing of the just life. Arguably four models of salvation emerge as the most prominent and well-formed among these ideas. The earliest is probably the identification of salvation with "the day of the Lord" in which the just will be rewarded and those who have been wronged will be vindicated. Salvation on this model is awaited as a future event. It is especially visible in the early writings of Paul and is rooted, at least in part, in Jewish apocalyptic thinking. In this model the shape of the salvation that is to come is manifested in Jesus Christ.

Alongside this future-oriented model of salvation is the idea of atonement for past sins. Also rooted in Jewish practice, the precision that we associate with this idea awaits later theological developments. In the New Testament the death of Christ simply brings the forgiveness of sins in which the church participates by forgiving others as Christ did in his ministry, taught in the Lord's prayer, and modeled on the cross. Salvation as atonement draws vigorously on the Hebraic sacrificial system and on the Isaian imagery of the suffering servant found in the gospel of Luke.

Salvation is also seen in the New Testament as deliverance from DEATH. Although mortal life may be subject to extinction, the life that is given through Jesus will not be extinguished—a life that, in the gospel of John, begins in the present time and survives our physical demise. In the epistles the victory of Jesus over death is frequently depicted in battle imagery, in which Satan or the ruler of this world is vanquished by Jesus's incarnation and passion. It is this model of salvation that will capture the imagination of such later theologians as Athanasius and Gregory of Nyssa; Gregory did not shy from describing salvation as a victory achieved by a divine deception in which the life of humanity is ransomed from the DEVIL.

A fourth prominent model of salvation in the New Testament is the flourishing that comes from a personal relationship with God. Through Jesus, the way is opened for a return to COVENANT (alternatively, a new covenant) with God, whose Spirit is poured out on those who believe and from whom one is no longer separated by sin. This model focuses not so much on salvation from the conditions of existence (e.g., mortality) as salvation within them.

Development of the Second through Fourth Centuries

New Testament models of salvation combined and recombined in the theology of early church writers, often existing in tension within the thought of a single writer. Many worked within the classical Greek moral anthropology in which the soul is composed of reason, will, and the appetites: reason, rightly oriented, provides will its object of the good while ordering and chastening the appetites accordingly. For the early writers who worked within this model, salvation remedies not so much a defect in the will but a failure of knowledge. This knowledge may be moral in character, as in the Didache's contrast of the "two ways" that lead to life or death, or it may tend toward the mystical, as in Clement of Alexandria's rendering of Christ as the true gnosis through whom "our darkened understanding springs up to the light" (*I Clement* 59). Justin Martyr also inclined toward the identification of right knowledge as the content of salvation: he referred strikingly to candidates for baptism as "illuminands" (Justin Martyr, *First Apology*, 61).

Whereas Justin, Clement, and others focused on the intellective defect of the human person, other models

of salvation continued to thrive in the second century as well. The *Epistle of Barnabas,* written around the turn of the second century, lauds the deliverance of Christ's flesh to corruption so "that we should be sanctified by the remission of sin, that is, by his sprinkled blood" (*Ep. Barnabas*, 5.1). Ignatius of Antioch, in his *Letter to the Ephesians,* referred to the Eucharist as the "medicine of immortality," connecting the SACRAMENTS and work of Christ through the notion of salvation from mortality and death. Gregory of Nyssa, writing two centuries later, offered a similar interpretation of the Eucharist in its connection to salvation.

It is in the context of this theological diversity that one must evaluate the claim of the Swedish Lutheran Gustav Aulén that the soteriology of the early church was mainly a ransom theory of atonement aimed at deliverance of humanity from death. Aulén's classic study, published in English as *Christus Victor* in 1931, overstates the predominance of this theory as a coherent system of thought, but accurately points to an important fourth-century trend. The ransom theory reckons humanity in debt to Satan as a result of the fall; through Christ, God deceives the devil by concealing divinity under the form of flesh and "catches" the devil as a fish is caught on a hook. Thus, humanity is released from the power of death. This version of the ransom theory is that of Gregory of Nyssa, although the idea originated with Origen. It is not without soteriological alternatives, even in the fourth century. Gregory of Nazianzus, although accepting immortality as the primary benefit of salvation, rejected both the idea that God was compelled to pay a ransom and that God would engage in deception to achieve salvific ends. Gregory of Nazianzus held a position closer to that of Athanasius who, writing earlier in the fourth century, proposed that in death Christ is our substitute. Because the divine Son takes on humanity and dies the death that human beings merit by their fall, humanity is thus taken up by adoption into the divine life, receiving incorruption. Athanasius's position lies somewhere between the idea of salvation as the conferral of immortality and the forgiveness of sin. His notion of substitution laid the groundwork for the theory of satisfaction that, with important differences from Athanasius, would be developed in the eleventh century by Anselm of Canterbury.

Before turning to such later developments, one must take note of Augustine's writing, which gives a strong account of the role of grace in salvation. Sharing the classical moral anthropology through which earlier writers identified the illumination of reason as the focus of salvation, Augustine shifted the emphasis in thinking about salvation to the entrapment of the will. Through the Fall it is no longer possible for the human being not to sin *(non posse non peccare)*; even if one identifies and desires the good, one is unable to choose it because the ability to will the good is fundamentally compromised by the Fall (original sin). Although Augustine seeks the illumination of the intellect, he is clear that the grace of God must liberate the will for one to choose rightly and order all goods in light of what God reveals. John Cassian, Pelagius, and others proposed a more cooperative relationship between divine grace and the human will, but the Augustinian account of the problem of the will and the paradoxical interaction of grace and human freedom would later combine with Anselm's atonement theory in the views of the major reformers.

As noted above, the doctrine of salvation is closely related to the doctrine of heaven/hell and no less variety of thinking about this doctrine existed in the early period than on the idea of atonement or grace. Augustine's own position, shaped by the pressure of conflict with Pelagius and others who felt that Augustine's strong version of grace threatened human freedom, implied a predestination of some to damnation, although he did not teach this directly. Gregory of Nyssa, on the other hand, assumed the invincibility of God's saving intent, providing a strong connection between salvation and the moral life. Offering an extremely nuanced account of the conditions under which some are able more easily to choose the good than others, Gregory suggests that salvation is ultimately intended for all, although some will enter into this blessed state more quickly than others. Ultimately all will be saved, but the morally vicious may not do so until "cleansed" by the fire of hell and judgment, which are not the emblems of the failure of salvation but are tools by which God achieves it, even beyond this life. The contrast between possible damnation and universal salvation set the two extreme ends of the spectrum in subsequent Christian soteriology, although the latter is arguably a minority position.

Medieval Developments in Christian Soteriology

The formulation of salvation in the Middle Ages turns again to the theory of the atonement, although reflection on the operation of divine grace and the role of the human moral action is never far in the background. In the context of a feudal social system Anselm shifts the focus of the fourth-century view on the debt by which human beings are bound: our obligation, as the result of the Fall, is to God, not to the devil, yet our predicament is insurmountable because in our sin and our finitude we cannot repay the infinite debt we owe. Our salvation is achieved by Christ who takes the form of sinful humanity, yet does not sin, and dies paying a debt he does not owe for those who owe the debt but cannot pay. This was necessary so that God's honor is reaffirmed and humanity is saved from payment for sin. This theory of "satisfaction" for sin is not accepted by all—Abelard offers a nontransactional moral theory of salvation whereby we are saved in our response to the death of Christ whose love inspires us to right action—but the shift in focus to a debt owed to God, rather than to the devil, predominates in subsequent theology. The position is considerably modified by Thomas Aquinas who, anxious to maintain a sense of God's freedom, suggests that this manner of salvation was not a necessary action but a gift of superlative grace because the mortal debt we owed was satisfied by an action of infinite worth. At the same time, Aquinas refashions Aristotelian moral theory as a component of his view of salvation: human beings are sinful yet God causes in them both the inclination to good and, cooperatively, the grace to develop dispositions toward virtue. Simultaneously, supernatural virtues are also infused in the soul. The grace God gives to empower the human enjoyment of God as the highest good is one that blesses human nature with a capacity beyond its natural state.

Reformation and Modern Developments

The classic reformers focused on the forgiveness of sin as the primary aim of salvation and tended, like Augustine and Paul, to identify the human will as flawed. Thus, MARTIN LUTHER proclaims that the law commands but we are unable to do anything; yet, by acceptance of grace offered in Christ, we can do all. Luther's theology of salvation fleshed out his criticism of medieval theology's excessive valuation of the human contribution to the state of blessedness. For Luther, God acts in Jesus Christ who substitutes for us as a sinner; his death is our JUSTIFICATION by divine grace, despite our sin. What actions we take toward God and the good of the neighbor are construed primarily as a response to this grace rather than as an active contribution to our salvation because nothing we do can earn salvation that is already freely given. The response we make is, as with Augustine, by virtue of the grace of God that sets the will free to act. In similar fashion JOHN CALVIN understood Christ to incur by his death the penalties of the law that were due to sinners, but combined this with a high view of the instructive use of the law, by which we are tutored in the commands of God toward right action. Consistent with this the judgment we incur for our continuing sin is, by virtue of Christ's sacrifice, no longer punitive but rehabilitative. Yet Calvin's emphasis on the sovereignty of God in acting toward humanity's salvation led him, like Augustine, to pose a doctrine of predestination that somewhat downplayed the capacities of human freedom to contribute to the enjoyment of the blessed state. All the reformers—Lutheran, Calvinist, English, and Swiss—were largely united in viewing Christ's death as a sacrifice with saving effect, to which human effort added nothing substantial; in this, the reformers both recovered the singular significance of the cross for salvation and struggled, at times, to connect salvation with the moral life (SANCTIFICATION).

The resistance once exemplified by Abelard to Anselm's view of salvation as satisfaction for sin continued to live in the REFORMATION in the new forms of SOCINIANISM and ARMINIANISM. The former, largely condemned by other reformers, was associated with two Siennese theologians, Lelio and FAUSTO SOZZINI. Socinianism denies the idea of original sin and, as a result, any sense in which the death of Christ was a satisfaction. Salvation is found, by contrast, in the response to his death as a moral example and with trust in that death as a pledge of forgiveness. Arminianism is less a rejection of a transactional view of salvation by the death of Christ, but insists that this gracious and sovereign act of God is more compatible with human freedom than allowed for by Calvin's strong sense of grace. Both Socinian and Arminian ideas still exercise some influence in modern reformed theology through the continuing influence of Unitarianism (see UNITARIAN UNIVERSALIST ASSOCIATION).

The modern period has seen the modification of these classical positions in various forms. In the climate of the ENLIGHTENMENT and the scientific revolution, objective or transactional soteriologies fell out of favor for a time; preferred alternatives were versions of Abelardian exemplarism or, as in PAUL TILLICH's fully developed version in the twentieth century, renderings of Christ as the living symbol of human capacity to transcend the stresses and anxieties of existence. However, the enormity of the human capacity for evil and our awareness of it kept the classic approach alive, in which salvation is an objective reality wrought through Christ who enacts God's freedom to unite the human to the divine (e.g., KARL BARTH). Of equal significance in the twentieth century has been the attention of biblical studies to Jesus's teaching on the *basileia tou theou,* the reign of God. The corresponding soteriology is eschatological: the blessed life is one lived in practical anticipation of the coming reign and conformed to it. This eschatological soteriology comes to its fullest expression in the work of JÜRGEN MOLTMANN and in both Catholic and Protestant Liberation Theologies. Here, soteriological force is shifted to the life of Jesus, whereas his death and resurrection are a vindication of his teaching and a source of hope.

The horizons of soteriology in the twentieth century were set by a number of other critiques of the classic approaches. Feminist theologians raised productive questions about the soteriological significance of "sacrifice" that may undermine the ability of women and children to resist victimization in situations of abuse. The encounter of Christian theology with work of René Girard raised questions in a similar vein about the integral role of violence in theories of atonement. African American theologians have criticized traditional accounts of salvation for being insufficiently attentive to ethical practice. Finally the increased cross-cultural encounters between Christian theology and other religions revived attention to the internal relationships within traditions between their models of salvation and their conception of the *telos* of human life.

See also Feminist Theology; Liberation Theology; Theology

References and Further Reading

Aulén, Gustav. *Christus Victor.* New York: Macmillan, 1931.

Brock, Rita Nakashima, and Rebecca Ann Parker. *Proverbs of Ashes: Violence, Redemptive Suffering, and the Search for What Saves Us.* Boston: Beacon, 2001.

Cone, James H. *God of the Oppressed.* San Francisco: Harper San Francisco, 1975.

Dillistone, Frederick W. *The Christian Understanding of Atonement.* London: SCM, 1968.

Dubose, William Porcher. *The Soteriology of the New Testament.* New York: Macmillan, 1892.

McGrath, Alister E. *Iustitia Dei: A History of the Christian Doctrine of Justification.* 2 vols. Cambridge: Cambridge University Press, 1987.

McIntyre, John. *The Shape of Soteriology.* Edinburgh: T. & T. Clark, 1992.

Sykes, Stephen, ed. *Sacrifice and Redemption.* Cambridge: Cambridge University Press, 1991.

Weaver, J. Denny. *The Nonviolent Atonement.* Grand Rapids, MI: Wm. B. Eerdmans, 2001.

JAMES W. FARWELL

SALVATION ARMY

The Salvation Army was founded in 1865 by WILLIAM (1829–1912) and CATHERINE (1829–1890) BOOTH as a mission to England's urban, working-class communities (see REVIVALS, HOLINESS MOVEMENT). It drew upon METHODISM, revivalism and holiness theologies, the women's rights movement, the emerging urban commercial culture, and the neighborhood culture of England's working class to create a distinctive religious organization. In the 1880s, its evangelizing reached into Europe, North America, and parts of the British Empire. In the 1890s, a social service wing was established that offered shelter to the homeless, programs for the unemployed, and homes for unmarried mothers. By the early twentieth century it was best known as a provider of social services, but its evangelical mission remained at the core of its work.

The Origins of the Salvation Army

The religious census of 1851 revealed that ENGLAND's urban working class had the lowest rate of religious attendance of any social group. Christians, motivated by both compassion and fear, reacted with alarm to these statistics. Religion was associated by many with respect for the authority of the crown and government. Social commentators noted that many continental revolutionary movements attacked the church as well as the government. Working-class indifference to religion therefore posed a serious threat.

It was commonly believed that cities, with their crowding, filth, and the temptations of the public house and theaters, made urban dwellers more subject to disease and immorality than those who lived in the countryside. East London was regarded as an especially difficult neighborhood to evangelize because it was so vast and uniformly poor and it was not well served by the existing parish structure. Beginning in the 1850s, this area grew dramatically. Thousands of people moved to East London seeking work in the burgeoning industries there. It was also home to many Irish immigrants and after 1880, the majority of Jewish immigrants. Because they were neither English nor Protestant, these immigrants seemed doubly foreign. The term "heathen masses" was often used to describe these seemingly irreligious people. Anglicans and nonconformists responded by creating various agencies to bring working-class people into the churches (see ANGLICANISM; CHURCH OF ENGLAND; NON-CONFORMITY). The London City Mission, the Open Air Mission, Ranyard's Biblewomen, the Mildmay Mission, and the Metropolitan Tabernacle of CHARLES M. SPURGEON were all examples of organizations designed to bring Christianity to the urban working class with methods developed particularly for them. The Salvation Army was one part of that wider mission to the urban working class.

William Booth was particularly concerned with the state of England's "heathen masses." He felt a call to bring them into the church. He was ordained by the Methodist New Connexion in 1855 and worked as a circuit preacher and itinerant evangelist. His wife, Catherine Mumford Booth, was also a preacher. In 1859 she published a widely read pamphlet in support of female PREACHING and soon after began to preach herself. She proclaimed the "women's right" to preach the gospel and, unlike most of her contemporaries, did not believe women required a special call to preach nor did they need to cast themselves as the weak and

low. She believed women's preaching was sanctioned in Scripture and was an absolute necessity given the dire state of England, and the world's, people. She preached by invitation with her husband and alone. Her unusual work gained her considerable attention and criticism, but she was not permitted to preach in many churches and chapels.

In 1861 William Booth resigned from the Methodist New Connexion because he felt its restrictions impeded his ability to do soul-saving work. For four years the Booths preached in Cornwall, Wales, the midlands, and north, finally coming to London in 1865.

The Establishment of the Christian Mission

William Booth was engaged by the editors of the evangelical weekly, *The Revival,* to conduct services in the East of London for three weeks in July 1865. He drew substantial crowds and with the encouragement of London evangelicals and philanthropists, William Booth agreed to continue the work. Catherine also received invitations to preach in London, and the couple determined to make the city the focus of their efforts. With the financial support of wealthy philanthropists and members of several evangelical organizations, William Booth began the East London Christian Mission, soon renamed the Christian Mission. He preached in the streets and rented halls for weeknight and Sunday services. He slowly drew a following of evangelists and volunteer workers to assist in him this work. By 1868 a London newspaper estimated that between 7,000 and 14,000 people attended the 140 weekly services. In that same year, William Booth began publishing a monthly magazine, *The East London Evangelist,* renamed the *Christian Mission Magazine* in 1870. It included reports on the mission's activities, biographies and autobiographies, and articles on religious questions. The mission continued to grow and by 1872 had twelve London stations and eight outside London.

The mission was modeled on the Methodist structure with class meetings, elders meetings, circuits, and annual conferences. William Booth was the general superintendent. Membership in the mission required active participation in both worship services and the work of running the organization. The mission's doctrines were essentially Methodist with a strong emphasis on holiness. Members were to abstain from alcohol, could not work in any aspect of the drink trade, and were to shun wasteful and cruel pastimes like betting, boxing, and animal sports.

Creating an Army

In 1879 the Christian Mission was reorganized into the Salvation Army. The committees, conferences, and voting procedures were disbanded and William Booth appointed himself general of this army, with direct control over the organization. It had grown into a dynamic, national organization with mission stations along the south coast, the midlands, the north, the northeast, and Wales. It employed 127 paid evangelists and another 700 worked part-time without salary. There is little evidence to explain the abandonment of a Methodist style of organizing and the adoption of a military style structure except the leaders' own assertion that the committees and annual conferences were too awkward, slow, and inefficient for a growing organization. The Deed Poll gave William Booth "oversight, direction and control" of the organization. He could expend all money donated and was required to publish an annual balance sheet. He was also to appoint his successor. This gave Booth greater authority over this organization than that of most Protestant leaders and some criticized him for enjoying greater powers than the pope. The name Salvation Army was adopted in 1879 and was intended to capture its aims as well as the dedication, faith, and obedience required of its members.

The Salvation Army created an organizational structure with a series of ranks and duties assigned to each. A corps was a town, or portion of a town, and it included all soldiers who lived in that area. It was run by a paid officer, usually a captain, assisted by a lieutenant, with a group of volunteers each with their own rank and duties. Corps were grouped into districts under the command of a major, and several districts formed a division under the command of a colonel. As the army moved outside Great Britain, it created territories that were a country or group of countries with a marshal in command. This structure provided a clear, unequivocal chain of command and division of responsibility. The duties and beliefs of each individual member were described in the *Orders and Regulations* (first published in 1878 and regularly updated) and the *Doctrines and Discipline* (first published in 1881). In 1880 uniforms were first introduced. The dark blue, military style uniform allowed officers and soldiers to be recognized instantly, but were criticized by some journalists and social commentators because they appeared to presume the authority and dignity of the British military. The sight of uniformed women particularly offended the army's critics.

Beginning in 1882 the Salvation Army required all soldiers to sign the Articles of War. This document listed the Army's principle beliefs and the requirements of membership. Every soldier had to promise that "Believing solemnly that The Salvation Army has been raised by God, and is sustained and directed by Him, I do here declare my full determination, by God's help, to be a true soldier of The Army until I die."

William Booth remained general of the Salvation Army until his death in 1912. His eldest son, Bramwell Booth, succeeded him. He served until 1929 when he was deposed and the Deed Poll altered to allow a council of leading officers to select a general. That system, with some modifications, has continued to the present day.

Holiness Theology

Holiness was the distinguishing feature of the movement's theology. The doctrine was the most frequently explained and advocated in Christian Mission, and later Salvation Army, publications. JOHN WESLEY (1703–1791), in *A Plain Account of Christian Perfection,* had stated that holiness could be attained by Christians in this life but was not required. In the 1820s and 1830s, some theologians reinterpreted this doctrine and asserted that it was the duty and privilege of all Christians to attain holiness. The Booths were fervent advocates of that position. Holiness meant that any Christian could be delivered from sin. William Booth wrote in *Doctrines and Discipline* (1881), "Entire sanctification supposes complete deliverance. Sin is destroyed out of the soul and all the powers, faculties, possessions, and influences of the soul are given up to the service and glory of God." Holiness was an absolute necessity for office in the Salvation Army. Salvationists also believed it was the only assurance of heaven.

This theology meant that the usual education required for clerical office was far less important than a sanctified soul. Salvationists believed the experience of entire sanctification empowered them to do God's work far better than the performance of religious ritual or memorizing a creed. Many clergy, journalists, and social critics denounced the Salvation Army because it allowed previously dissolute men and women with none of the education or knowledge usually required of clergy to preach and even to question the work of learned clerical men.

Women's Work

This doctrine was particularly important for WOMEN. Because holiness was believed to remove sin, the burden of Eve's transgression was lessened and distinctions between men and women were diminished. It also allowed converts to justify unconventional behavior when called by the Holy Spirit. This doctrine also relied heavily on the events described in the Acts of the Apostles, where women figured prominently. The Christian Mission authorized women to preach, hold any office, and to vote at all meetings. In 1875 Annie Davis was the first woman to take charge of a mission station, which gave her authority over both spiritual and practical matters. This degree of responsibility and authority was matched in virtually no other denomination or voluntary organization at that time. The women who joined the army were predominantly working class and many had little formal education or other qualifications usually required for ministry. They learned to preach by addressing meetings, visiting homes, and speaking to people in the streets. There is evidence of some resistance within the organization to women's work; an 1875 conference resolution affirmed that the conference could not "obstruct the admission of females to any work or office in the Mission." Some converts also recalled their initial horror at the sight of female preachers. Still, the women preachers, dubbed, "Hallelujah Lasses," drew considerable crowds and many credited their conversion to a woman. In the early years, women's wages were equal to men's, but there was no set scale and wages were determined by the individual's family circumstances and experience. By 1882, however, male captains earned twenty-one shillings per week and female captains only fifteen shillings.

Salvationists were expected to make all aspects of their lives part of an effort to evangelize the world. In 1882 the army adopted the Articles of Marriage. All Salvationists who wished to marry had to sign the document promising that "we do not seek this marriage simply to please ourselves, but that we believe it will enable us to better serve the interests of the Salvation Army." Officers were not permitted to marry anyone who was not a member of the Salvation Army until 2000 when that particular regulation was dropped.

Until 1883 the Salvation Army offered communion. It was given monthly by the corps officers, male and female alike. This was among the first instances of women offering communion in Britain. Even denominations that allowed women to preach, such as the Methodists, still distinguished between lay ministers and ordained clergy, allowing only the latter to perform sacraments. Salvationist women who offered communion received strong criticism from clergy. The practice of communion was given up in 1883 because Salvationists feared it might be mistaken as a means to salvation. In her book, *Popular Christianity* (1887), Catherine Booth warned, "What an inveterate tendency there is in the human heart to trust in outward forms, instead of inward grace! And when this is the case, what a hindrance rather than help have these

forms proved to the growth, nay to the very existence, of that spiritual life which constitutes the real and only force of Christian experience." The theology that allowed women to offer communion also justified abandoning the practice. The army's refusal to regard outward, physical distinctions between men and women as meaningful also meant that material means to receive the Holy Spirit were not deemed necessary.

In 1880 the Salvation Army instituted formal training for officers. Two training homes, one for women, one for men, were opened. Basic accounting and record keeping were taught along with theology, preaching, and singing. Women made up nearly half of all those trained prior to World War I. By 1881 the Salvation Army employed just over fifteen percent of all the women in England listed by the census as missionaries, scripture readers, and preachers.

Evangelizing

The Salvation Army created a battle plan especially suited to the urban geography and culture of working-class communities. Mass commercial culture was new; in the 1870s working-class Britons began to have enough leisure and disposable income to enjoy music halls or trips to the seaside, as well as traditional pleasures like the public house and local sporting events. Salvationists borrowed aspects of popular entertainment to draw crowds and to transform the culture they believed fostered sin. They held services in music halls, sang hymns in front of public houses, and appropriated the language and much of the style of commercial entertainment. The services were lively and audiences were encouraged to join in the hymn singing, shout out responses to the preacher, and stand and testify to their own experience of sin and salvation. The Salvation Army copied advertisements from the music halls or circuses so closely that sometimes the audience was not aware they had come to a religious service. Salvationists took popular music hall tunes and wrote new words. "Champagne Charlie" was among the most popular of the Victorian music hall songs and the Salvation Army published their own version of the song in 1882, entitled "Bless His Name He Set Me Free." It became a popular song with Salvationists, but one Anglican clergyman complained in a church newspaper about the shocking impropriety of crowds singing sacred words to this music hall tune, voicing a concern shared by many (see MUSIC, POPULAR; HYMNS AND HYMNALS).

Salvationists wanted to draw a crowd and eagerly seized on sensational methods to attract attention. A preacher might dive off the platform, making swimming motions, to demonstrate the sea of God's love, or tear a hymn book into shreds to show how the devil attacks sinners. They adopted special titles like the Hallelujah Fishmonger. In 1880 Eliza Haynes hung a sign around her neck saying "I am Happy Eliza" and marched through the streets of London's Marylebone neighborhood handing out invitations to a service while playing a fiddle. Her antics got written up in the London papers, she was followed by the police, and a music hall song was written about her. These techniques, decried as sensationalism, earned the Salvation Army criticism from many other denominations. The *Primitive Methodist Quarterly Review* in 1883, for example, opined that the effect of the army's activities was to make people incapable of any religious life "as they destroy the very foundation of religion in the human soul—reverence."

Salvationists were also the focus of local, neighborhood opposition from the earliest years through the 1890s. In some locales, gangs of young men attacked Salvationists when they marched through the streets and the police arrested Salvationists for disturbing the peace. Some communities passed bylaws forbidding marches on Sunday in an effort to contain the army's work. Eastbourne and Torquay witnessed street frays that included more than 1,000 people in the early 1890s. The army's leaders succeeded in overturning the laws restricting their use of the streets and affirmed their right to march in the public thoroughfares.

The Salvation Army's uniformed preachers, dramatic techniques, and energetic evangelism drew converts. The army never published regular statistics on its membership and it is difficult to assess with any certainty. In 1883 the Salvation Army had 528 corps and 1,340 officers in the United Kingdom. By 1886 that number had grown to 1,006 corps and 2,260 officers, but it is impossible to know how many people attended the services or joined the Salvation Army. In 1886 and 1902, religious censuses were conducted in London indicating that fewer than one percent of London's population attended a Salvation Army hall on a given Sunday. But in 1902 the army accounted for eighteen percent of all nonconformist attenders in London. Some scholars have suggested the Army was more successful in provincial towns. It is difficult to make any strong claims about membership. Salvationists were, however, very successful at getting and keeping public attention, and certainly by the 1880s, they were well-known figures in working-class communities throughout the country as well as stock figures of fun in comic magazines and music halls.

International Expansion

The Salvation Army sent a group of officers to begin evangelizing in the UNITED STATES in 1880, to AUSTRALIA in 1881, and to CANADA in 1882. These largely Protestant countries were, it was hoped, fertile ground for the kind of work the army had pioneered in Britain. The army did succeed in establishing strong national organizations in these countries, which continue to the present day. In FRANCE and SWITZERLAND the army's officers were not welcomed. The Booth's eldest daughter was jailed and expelled from Switzerland in 1882; even after she obtained permission to evangelize there the Swiss were not sympathetic to these foreign evangelists. In 1882 the Salvation Army commenced work in INDIA. They focused their efforts on the non-Christian population and found some success with the lowest caste peoples. In 1883 the army began work in Cape Town, SOUTH AFRICA, by 1886 the army was active in nineteen countries with 1,932 officers at work outside Britain. Again, it is difficult to ascertain how many people attended army services or joined the movement, but the army has remained active in various countries in North and South America, Europe, AFRICA, Asia, Australia, and NEW ZEALAND up to the present day.

Social Services

In 1890 William Booth published *In Darkest England and the Way Out.* England's "submerged tenth," its poorest citizens, needed help. Booth likened the "cannibals and pygmies" of darkest Africa to these citizens of "Darkest England." His solution, he claimed, would be "as wide as the scheme of Eternal Salvation set forth in the Gospel.... If the scheme ... is not applicable to the Thief, the Harlot, the Drunkard, and the Sluggard, it may as well be dismissed without ceremony." Existing charitable programs and state assistance helped too few and were ineffective. He proposed to establish city, farm, and overseas colonies. The city colonies would gather together the destitute, provide for their immediate needs, and commence with moral regeneration. They would then proceed to farm colonies, where they would restore their health and character. Finally they would find work either at home or in an overseas colony. In addition, Booth proposed to extend the army's already established network of shelters for the homeless and cheap food depots. Booth stated that it was his goal to bring the clothing, food, and shelter of everyone up to the standard of those provided to the London cab horse, a graphic comparison mentioned by many reviewers.

Scholars have debated why Booth proposed this scheme at this time. Historian Norman Murdoch (1939–) argues that Booth realized he had failed to reach England's very poorest and hoped that social services would attract them. Murdoch regards this program as an important departure from the army's previous work. Others, notably Jenty Fairbank, instead emphasize the continuity of the darkest England scheme with earlier programs. Fairbank notes that only three of the ten social services did not begin before 1890. In 1883 the army had, for example, opened a home for "fallen women," a category that included unmarried, pregnant women and prostitutes. Under the direction of Florence Booth, daughter-in-law of William Booth, the program grew to include 117 homes for women in Britain and overseas by 1914. It was one of the largest, and some argued, the most innovative of the rescue programs in Britain. The work extended to maternity hospitals, homes for women awaiting birth, adoption services, and programs for new mothers and infants. The stated goal of all these programs was to bring about the CONVERSION and salvation of these "fallen women."

The army's social services grew very quickly to include a large number of full-time officers, a publication devoted to their activities, and a strong public presence. The Salvation Army ran shelters for the homeless; distributed soup to the unemployed; provided homes for orphaned or abandoned children; established a farm colony, Hadleigh, beginning in 1891; and created a service to locate missing persons. By the time of the 1909 Royal Commission on the Poor Law, some experts who addressed the committee advocated providing state subsidies to the Salvation Army to extend its social service work with the poor. During World War I, the army offered food and shelter to refugees; setup canteens for military men, where they first introduced doughnuts to many soldiers; and provided services for those who lost their livelihoods or homes due to war. These programs were well regarded. It offered similar services during World War II. In both wars, the army offered services to all, regardless of nationality, but their programs were far more extensive in the Allied nations because of the army's English origins and the difficulty of any religious organization operating independently under the Nazis. An enormous variety of people came into contact with the army's services during the war, greatly enhancing the army's public profile and support after 1945.

The Salvation Army Today

In 1999 the Salvation Army worked in over 100 countries. There were over 14,000 corps worldwide and social service programs operated in more than 140 languages. The army ran 152 centers for alcoholics, 200 children's homes and day nurseries, 13 holiday camps for children, 800 shelters for the homeless, and 130 centers for refugees. The army ran 2,000 food distribution centers and 450,000 prisoners in jail were

visited that year. It is among the world's largest providers of social services.

References and Further Reading

Ervine, St. John. *God's Soldier: General William Booth.* London: Heinemann, 1934.

Fairbank, Jenty. *Booth's Boots: Social Service Beginnings in the Salvation Army.* London: The Salvation Army, 1983.

McKinley, Edward H. *Marching to Glory: The History of the Salvation Army in the United States.* Grand Rapids, MI: William B. Eerdmans, 1995.

Murdoch, Norman. *Origins of the Salvation Army.* Knoxville, TN: University of Tennessee Press, 1994.

Sandall, Robert, et. al. *The History of the Salvation Army.* Reprint, London: The Salvation Army, 1979.

Taiz, Lillian. "Applying the Devil's Works in a Holy Cause: Working-Class Popular Culture and the Salvation Army in the United States, 1879–1900." *Religion and American Culture* 7, no. 2 (1997): 195–223.

Walker, Pamela J. *Pulling the Devil's Kingdom Down: The Salvation Army in Victorian Britain.* Berkeley: The University of California Press, 2001.

Winston, Diane, *Red Hot and Righteous: The Urban Religion of the Salvation Army.* Cambridge, MA: Harvard University Press, 1999.

PAMELA J. WALKER

SANCTIFICATION

Sanctification is the process of making something or someone holy. (Biblical Greek and Hebrew have no separate words for sanctification and holiness.) In Protestantism, the doctrine of sanctification refers to believers being made holy. In Protestant theology, sanctification occurs after religious CONVERSION, or JUSTIFICATION. "Entire sanctification" is the distinguishing doctrine of the Protestant HOLINESS MOVEMENT.

MARTIN LUTHER's sixteenth-century Protestant insight reversed the assumed order of justification and sanctification in Christian SALVATION. In Luther's understanding, Catholicism taught that sanctification preceded justification. Believers had to make their lives holy (sanctify themselves) before God would declare them righteous (justify them). Luther believed that placing sanctification before justification promoted righteousness by works and that justification by faith could be preserved only by placing justification before sanctification.

For Luther, justification was a judicial process whereby God declared sinners righteous apart from any righteousness of their own. In justification, God imputed Christ's righteousness to sinners on the basis of faith. Sanctification, the attainment of holiness, followed justification, but the believer's holiness was always alien to the believer because justification was always God's gift to sinners. For Luther, therefore, sanctification could not result in moral transformation.

Believers were always sinners and could never possess holiness of their own. Sanctification was the ever deeper awareness of one's sinfulness. At the same time, however, Luther also insisted that the Christian was called upon to live a godly life.

JOHN CALVIN accepted Luther's understanding of imputed righteousness, but made holiness the goal of Christian life. In the Calvinist tradition, therefore, a believer's quest for holiness posed no threat to justification by FAITH. The believer's holiness, although always a gift of grace and incomplete before death, was not entirely alien. CALVINISM allowed for genuine moral transformation as Christians were sanctified.

The eighteenth-century Anglican cleric JOHN WESLEY taught the doctrine of Christian perfection, which optimistically asserted that Christians could experience perfect love toward God and human beings before death. Among Wesley's followers, this doctrine became identified as "entire sanctification." The qualifier "entire" distinguished Wesleyan sanctification from the less-optimistic Calvinist sanctification. For Wesleyans, to be "entirely sanctified" was to love God and neighbor perfectly.

Although Wesley founded the Methodist Church in America and led the Methodist movement in Britain, by the mid–nineteenth century entire sanctification was primarily taught in interdenominational North American settings under the auspices of the National Camp Meeting Association for the Promotion of Holiness (later the Christian Holiness Association). Most "holiness" denominations (e.g., CHURCH OF THE NAZARENE, FREE METHODIST CHURCH OF AMERICA, and WESLEYAN CHURCH) originated from this American holiness movement.

Nineteenth-century evangelical preachers like CHARLES GRANDISON FINNEY and DWIGHT LYMAN MOODY also preached sanctification and equated sanctification with spirit BAPTISM (e.g., Acts 2). Such doctrines of sanctification emphasized the believer's empowerment for witness and service without espousing perfectionist themes ("sanctification" rather than "entire sanctification"). The charismatic tradition often follows this evangelical doctrine of sanctification and emphasizes the gift of speaking in tongues as the evidence of one's sanctification.

See also Evangelicalism; Methodism; Methodism, England; Methodism, United States; Sin; Tongues, Speaking in

References and Further Reading

Alexander, Donald, ed. *Christian Spirituality: Five Views of Sanctification*. Downers Grove, IL: InterVarsity Press, 1988.

Bassett, Paul M., and William M. Greathouse. *Exploring Christian Holiness, Vol. 2: The Historical Development*. Kansas City, MO: Beacon Hill Press, 1985.

THOMAS E. PHILLIPS

SANKEY, IRA DAVID (1840–1908)

Gospel hymn singer and composer. Sankey joined preacher DWIGHT LYMAN MOODY to form one of the most popular evangelistic teams in nineteenth-century America. Born in 1840 in Edinburg, Pennsylvania, Sankey joined the Methodist Episcopal Church in 1856 (see METHODISM, NORTH AMERICA) and sang at SUNDAY SCHOOL gatherings throughout Pennsylvania and Ohio. He met Moody at a Young Men's Christian Association (see YMCA, YWCA) convention in Indianapolis in 1870.

After witnessing Sankey's ability to move an audience through song, Moody asked him to be his partner. Sankey's text-driven, emotion-filled renderings of old Sunday school songs complemented Moody's PREACHING style. The pair found initial success in a Revival campaign in Britain from 1873 to 1875 (see REVIVALS). Upon returning to the UNITED STATES, the pair established evangelistic crusades in major cities that won thousands of converts.

For his own compositions and hymn collections, Sankey chose lyrics focused on testimony rather than DOCTRINE. In his songs, humans passively receive God's grace in an emotional, intimate experience with Jesus. Several of Sankey's settings became widely popular, particularly "The Ninety and Nine."

Audiences urged Sankey to publish the songs he performed. In 1873 he issued a sixteen-page pamphlet, *Sacred Songs and Solos*. Sankey eventually added 1,200 songs to this collection, which sold more than 80 million copies. Sankey also joined with composer Philip Bliss to compile a six-volume series, *Gospel Hymns and Sacred Songs,* released from 1874 to 1891. These volumes became the standard gospel hymn collection in America. Sankey died in Brooklyn in 1908.

See also Evangelicalism; Evangelism; Hymns and Hymnals; Music, American

References and Further Reading

Primary Source:

Sankey, Ira D. *My Life and the Story of the Gospel Hymns*. New York: Harper & Brothers, 1928.

Secondary Sources:

Sizer, Sandra S. *Gospel Hymns and Social Religion: The Rhetoric of Nineteenth Century Revivalism*. Philadelphia, PA: Temple University Press, 1978.

Wilhoit, Mel R. " 'Sing Me a Sankey': Ira D. Sankey and Congregational Song." *Hymn* 42 (1991): 13–19.

JENNIFER GRABER

SATTLER, MICHAEL (c.1490–1527)

Swiss Anabaptist leader. Sattler was a former prior of a Benedictine monastery and the short-lived leader of the Swiss Anabaptist movement in the Zurich *Unterland*. Little is known of his early life beyond the fact that he was born in Staufen in the Breisgau near Freiburg in about 1490. He likely did not have university training, although he was fluent in Latin. Appointed prior at the Benedictine monastery of St. Peter's northeast of Freiburg sometime between 1518 and 1525, Sattler left that position—probably in May of 1525 amid the religious and economic unrest associated with the Peasants' War—and moved to the area around Waldshut-Schaffhausen, a region noted for its radical religious DISSENT. In November of 1525 Zurich authorities arrested Sattler for his association with Anabaptists, and extracted an oath of loyalty before expelling him from the territory.

It is probable, though not certain, that Sattler was baptized as an Anabaptist in the summer of 1526 (see ANABAPTISM). He next appeared in Strasbourg, where he had friendly encounters with the reformers MARTIN BUCER and WOLFGANG CAPITO, both of whom he addressed as "beloved brothers in Christ" in a farewell letter to them written early in 1527. The letter to Bucer and Capito contained the essential features of Sattler's theological position, features that found fuller expression a few weeks later in his most important writing—the so-called SCHLEITHEIM CONFESSION *(Bruderliche Vereinigung)*. Ratified on February 24 by a gathering of leaders in Schleitheim am Randen, this brief affirmation of Anabaptist distinctives became a foundational reference point for Swiss Anabaptist THEOLOGY as it took shape in subsequent decades. The christocentrism and ecclesiological separatism central to the CONFESSION—rooted in believer's BAPTISM, the practice of mutual aid and CHURCH DISCIPLINE, and a rejection of the oath, violence, and magisterial offices—show clear traces of Sattler's Benedictine background and underscore the debt owed by the Swiss Anabaptist movement to late medieval Catholic piety as well as to evangelical Protestantism.

In late February of 1527 Sattler, his wife Margarethe, and several other Anabaptists were arrested in Horb (Württemberg). After some two months of imprisonment—during which time Sattler wrote a lengthy letter of encouragement to the persecuted Anabaptist congregation at Horb—the group was transferred to a prison in Rottenburg, a territory under the jurisdiction of ARCHDUKE Ferdinand of Austria. On May 20, 1527, after a HERESY trial of several days,

Rottenburg authorities tortured, then executed Sattler by burning. His wife was drowned in the Neckar river on the following day.

Despite the abbreviated nature of his leadership, Sattler gave the fledgling Swiss Anabaptist movement a theological coherence—sealed with the authority of his martyrdom—that helped to ensure its viability even amid persistent persecution in subsequent decades.

References and Further Reading

Primary Sources:

Yoder, John Howard, trans. and ed. "The Legacy of Michael Sattler." In *Classics of the Radical Reformation,* vol. 1. Scottdale, PA: Herald Press, 1973.
———, trans. and ed. *The Schleitheim Confession.* Scottdale, PA: Mennonite Publishing House, 1977.

Secondary Sources:

Haas, Martin. "Michael Sattler: Auf dem Weg der Täufer in die täuferische Absonderung." In *Radikale Reformatoren,* edited by H.-J. Goertz, 115–124. Munich: C. H. Beck, 1978.
Snyder, C. Arnold. "The Life and Thought of Michael Sattler." In *Studies in Anabaptist and Mennonite History,* vol. 26. Scottdale, PA: Herald Press, 1984.

JOHN D. ROTH

SCHAFF, PHILIP (1819–1893)

American church historian. Schaff was born in Chur, SWITZERLAND, on January 1, 1819. His piety led him to a religious career, not in ministerial service but rather in academic studies. While studying at universities in Tübingen (1837–1839) and HALLE (1839–1840), he came under the influence of FERDINAND C. BAUR, whose ideas about the historical development of Christian thought and practice became a permanent part of his thinking. Finishing his studies in Berlin (1840–1841), Schaff obtained a licentiate in THEOLOGY and began teaching as a *Privatdozent* (lecturer). While there he was befriended by JOHANN AUGUST NEANDER, another seasoned scholar of the history of Christianity, who greatly affected the young instructor's religious and intellectual life. In 1844 he accepted an invitation to become professor of church history and biblical literature at a fledgling institution in the New World. Arriving at the German Reformed Seminary in Mercersburg, Pennsylvania, he quipped that he was Swiss by birth, German by education, and American by choice.

At the seminary the newcomer became associated with JOHN W. NEVIN, a vigorous theologian in the Reformed tradition, and during Schaff's tenure there (1844–1863) the two developed the "MERCERSBURG

THEOLOGY," a distinctive emphasis on broad confessionalism based on historical continuity. The CIVIL WAR interrupted normal activities in central Pennsylvania, and so Schaff moved to a place of greater safety, serving from 1864 to 1869 as secretary for the New York Sabbath Committee and lecturing occasionally (1868–1871) at Andover, Drew, and Union Theological Seminaries. Beginning in 1870 he occupied various professoriates at Union, lecturing on theology, scripture, and history until retirement in 1893. Vigorous and energetic throughout his career Schaff remained active up to the last month of his life, dying on October 20, 1893 at his home in New York City.

Schaff's most important contribution lay in historical studies of Christianity, lectures, and publications that ranged from biblical times to his own age. His efforts for a half century were sustained by a conception of developmental change that resembled a broadly Hegelian process, one that drew strength from positive, although often conflicting, forces in past times and pointed to future possibilities for improvement. As soon as he arrived in this country Schaff began articulating ideas about dialectical processes in history, patterns familiar to him but startlingly novel to many new compatriots. Most Americans in the Reformed tradition held a much more static view of church history, suspicious of the idea that they had departed from earlier precedent and resentful of any charitable thought that regarded Roman Catholicism as a valid form of Christianity (see CATHOLICISM, PROTESTANT REACTIONS). In 1845 such Nativists (see NATIVISM) charged the young German professor with HERESY, hinting also that he leaned toward "popery." Schaff defended himself in open debate and in two classic books: *The Principle of Protestantism, As Related to the Present State of the Church* (Chambersburg, 1845) and *What is Church History? A Vindication of the Idea of Historical Development* (Philadelphia, 1846). In the end Schaff was completely exonerated, and, reassured by that overt vindication, he continued to disseminate attitudes about broad ecclesiastical cooperation and ideas about dynamic progress in historical experience.

Breadth of Interests

Although primarily a historian, Schaff was interested in an impressively wide range of topics in religion studies. In the area of primary concentration his work culminated in his six-volume *History of the Christian Church* (New York, 1882–1892) and in his successful coordination of other scholarly efforts in a thirteen-volume collection of denominational histories known as *The American Church History Series* (New York,

1893–1897). Schaff's warm, perennial interest in theology yielded many academic reflections, notably *Theological Propaedeutic* (New York, 1892), whereas cumulative liturgical studies eventuated in *Bibliotheca Symbolica Ecclesiae Universalis: The Creeds of Christendom* (New York, 1877). All in all, more than eighty publications bore his name, and these finished products plus his continuing example helped create a greater appreciation in this country for critical scholarship, especially that which displayed dispassionate and open-minded attitudes about all forms of religious expression.

During a lifetime of variegated academic and ecclesiastical activities Schaff was sustained by an abiding ecumenical vision (see ECUMENISM). Indeed, his view of historical development led him to expect that Protestantism and Catholicism would eventually progress to a higher level of institutional life, an "evangelical catholicism" that moved beyond current malpractices while retaining the present-day benefits of each form. Pursuing that end he lectured, wrote, and organized to promote better understanding among various branches of Christianity. He served, for example, as a key figure in the EVANGELICAL ALLIANCE and worked from 1866 to 1873 to organize an American chapter of that group, hoping also to convene one of its international conferences in New York City. Most of Schaff's historical research was based on an irenic ecumenical perspective, and his instrumental presence in founding the AMERICAN SOCIETY OF CHURCH HISTORY in 1888 served as another expression of this conviction that future growth stemmed from an adequate grasp of the past. Other pivotal activities such as committee work on creedal revision and on new biblical translations were also characterized by the hope that greater mutual understanding among churches would facilitate greater toleration and cooperation.

In 1893 the city of Chicago hosted a Columbian Exposition, and a WORLD PARLIAMENT OF RELIGIONS was held in conjunction with it. Schaff was determined to attend the meetings and present a paper there, entitled "The Reunion of Christendom." Doctors advised against such strenuous activity, but he pursued his objective with the same dogged persistence that he had exhibited for more than five decades. Travel by train so exhausted the old American professor that he was forced to remain seated on the rostrum while a colleague read his address for him. The return trip further depleted Schaff's strength, but he was glad to have articulated his vision one last time, even though the effort shortened his life. Emotionally and physically drained, he died less than a month later.

References and Further Reading

Primary Sources:

Schaff, Philip. *America: A Sketch of its Political, Social, and Religious Character.* Cambridge, MA: Belkap Press of Harvard University Press, 1961.

———. *The Principle of Protestantism.* Philadelphia, PA: United Church Press, 1964.

———. *Church and State in the United States.* New York: Arno Press, 1972.

Secondary Sources:

Graham, Stephen R. *Cosmos in the Chaos: Philip Schaff's Interpretation of Nineteenth-Century American Religion.* Grand Rapids, MI: Eerdmans, 1995.

Penzel, Klaus. *Philip Schaff, Historian and Ambassador of the Universal Church: Selected Writings.* Macon, GA: Mercer University Press, 1991.

Schaff, David. *The Life of Philip Schaff, In Part Autobiographical.* New York: Charles Scribner's Sons, 1897.

Shriver, George H. *Philip Schaff: Christian Scholar and Ecumenical Prophet.* Macon, GA: Mercer University Press, 1987.

HENRY W. BOWDEN

SCHELLING, FRIEDRICH WILHELM JOSEPH VON (1775–1854)

German philosopher. Born in Württemberg, GERMANY, in 1775 Schelling was a leading representative of German Idealism. Some of his major works are *Ideas towards a Philosophy of Nature* (1797), *System of Transcendental Idealism* (1800), and *Philosophical Inquiries into the Nature of Human Freedom* (1809). He also left behind a considerable body of lectures, published posthumously as the *Philosophy of Mythology* and *Philosophy of Revelation.* He died in Ragaz, SWITZERLAND, in 1854.

Schelling's main contribution to nineteenth-century Protestant theology was to provide an alternative to GEORG W. F. HEGEL. Schelling's emphasis on God's freedom contrasted favorably with Hegel's tendency to make creation a matter of logical necessity. An indication of the anxiety about the pernicious effect of Hegel's philosophy was the decision by the Prussian government to bring Schelling to Berlin as professor of philosophy in 1841. The express purpose of this appointment was to combat the influence of Hegel.

In the twentieth century Schelling's influence on Protestant thought is best seen in the theology of PAUL TILLICH. Tillich was attracted to several aspects of Schelling's philosophy. First, he credited Schelling with recognizing the importance of the unconscious as a philosophical principle. Second, he found Schelling's understanding of the divine presence within NATURE appealing. Third, he found valuable resources for existential philosophy in Schelling's later thought.

Fourth, his doctrine of God corresponds roughly to Schelling's. For both, God is the ideal harmony of polar opposites. Both represented God as a dialectical movement between identity and difference.

See also Boehme, Jakob; Theology

References and Further Reading

Primary Sources:

Schelling, Friedrich Wilhelm Joseph von. *Clara, or, On Nature's Connection to the Spirit World.* Albany: State University of New York Press, 2002.

Schelling, Friedrich Wilhelm Joseph von, and Peter Lauchlan Heath. *System of Transcendental Idealism (1800).* Charlottesville: University Press of Virginia, 1978.

Schelling, Friedrich Wilhelm Joseph von, and Karl Friedrich August Schelling. *Friedrich Wilhelm Joseph von Schellings sämmtliche Werke.* Stuttgart, Germany: J. G. Cotta, 1856–1861.

Schelling, Friedrich Wilhelm Joseph von, and James Gutmann. *Schelling, Of Human Freedom.* Chicago, IL: Open Court, 1936.

Secondary Sources:

Beach, Edward Allen. *The Potencies of God(s): Schelling's Philosophy of Mythology.* Albany: State University of New York Press, 1994.

Brown, Robert F. *The Later Philosophy of Schelling: The Influence of Boehme on the works of 1809–1815.* Lewisburg, PA: Bucknell University Press, 1977.

Tillich, Paul. *Perspectives on 19th and 20th Century Protestant Theology.* Edited by Carl E. Braaten. New York: Harper & Row, 1967.

SAMUEL M. POWELL

SCHILLER, JOHANN CHRISTOPH FRIEDRICH (1759–1805)

German playwright. Schiller (von Schiller after 1802) was born on November 11, 1759 in Marbach, and died on May 10, 1805 in Weimar. From 1767 to 1773 he attended grammar school in Ludwigsburg. On the order of Duke Carl Eugen von Württemberg he entered the Karlsschule, a military preparatory academy. He began studying law in 1774 and medicine in 1776, and in 1780 he served as an army physician in Stuttgart.

His play *Die Räuber (The Robbers)* premiered in 1782, which prompted the duke to prohibit him from further writing. Schiller fled to Mannheim, where in 1783 he secured a position as a playwright. In 1787 he traveled to Weimar and met JOHANN GOTTFRIED VON HERDER and Christoph Martin Wieland. In 1789 he moved to Jena and became a professor of philosophy. In 1790 he married Charlotte von Lengefeld. In 1791 he was gravely ill, and it was at this time that he began his study of the work of IMMANUEL KANT. He became close friends with JOHANN WOLFGANG VON GOETHE in 1794, and in 1796 he met the philosopher FRIEDRICH WILHELM JOSEPH VON SCHELLING. He moved to Weimar in 1799.

Schiller grew up in the setting of what was known as Württemberg Protestantism, which characterized by the moderate PIETISM influenced by JOHANN ALBRECHT BENGEL, and he originally wanted to become a minister. In the last hours of his life he is said to have called out many times for a *Judex* (judge). Schiller is considered the most important dramatist of German classicism. After the tragedies *Die Räuber* (1781) and *Kabale und Liebe* (1784), his dramas portray historical situations of crises in different European countries and address the problem of freedom: *Die Verschwörung des Fiesco zu Genua* (1783), *Don Karlos: Infant von Spanien* (1787), *Wallenstein* (three parts, 1798–1799), *Maria Stuart* (1800), *Die Jungfrau von Orleans* (1801), *Die Braut von Messina* (1803), *Wilhelm Tell* (1804), and *Demetrius* (1805; posthumous fragment). In his philosophical treatises, especially *Philosophische Briefe* (1786), *Über die tragische Kunst* (1792), *Über die Ästhetische Erziehung des Menschen* (1795), and *Über naive und sentimentalische Dichtung* (1795–1796), he provides a theoretical foundation and justification for his art.

See also Literature, German

References and Further Reading

Primary Source:

Schiller, J. C. F. *Nationalausgabe*. Edited by Julius Petersen et al. Weimar, Germany: Hermann Böhlaus, 1943–.

Secondary Sources:

Hammer, Stephanie B. *Schiller's Wound: The Theater of Trauma from Crisis to Commodity*. Detroit, MI: Wayne State University Press, 2001.

Pugh, David. *Schiller's Early Dramas: A Critical History*. New York: Camden House, 2001.

ULRICH KARTHAUS

SCHLEIERMACHER, FRIEDRICH DANIEL ERNST (1768–1834)

German theologian. Friedrich Daniel Ernst Schleiermacher, Reformed theologian and pastor in Prussia (at that time an independent German state), was the founder of a new epoch in Protestant THEOLOGY. He proposed a distinctive theological method based on the centrality of Christian experience that took seriously ENLIGHTENMENT criticisms and understandings and moved beyond them to articulate a Protestant

vision in a new framework. He is widely regarded as the founder of "modern" or "liberal" Protestant theology. Schleiermacher's recasting of Protestant theology in this-worldly, existential terms has led some to hail him as a renewer of faith and theology and others to condemn him for having sold out the faith to the intellectual and cultural currents of his day. Such diversity of evaluation has continued since his own lifetime.

Schleiermacher was born on November 21, 1768 in the city of Breslau into a family of Reformed CLERGY; his father and both grandfathers were pastors, and an uncle was a professor of theology. Although he is known to posterity for his theological contributions, he was also a pastor. He preached weekly for almost forty years and was pastor of the 12,000-member Trinity Church in Berlin from 1810 until his death there on February 12, 1834. In his pastoral role, he was a participant in the creation of the Prussian Union Church in 1817 that brought Lutheran and Reformed traditions together in one church. Schleiermacher supported the Union because he recognized the commonalities between the two versions of Protestantism. At the same time, he resisted King Friedrich Wilhelm III's imposition of a common LITURGY. He and eleven other pastors (the "twelve apostles") held out against the King for seven years before finally succumbing when threatened with losing their pastorates. Throughout his career, Schleiermacher advocated for the independence of the church from the state in a period when state control of all aspects of life in Prussia was on the increase (see CHURCH AND STATE, OVERVIEW).

Schleiermacher's Theology in Historical Context

At the beginning of the nineteenth century, Schleiermacher pioneered an approach that moved Protestant theology beyond the rationalism, ORTHODOXY, and PIETISM of the previous century into a new era. Schleiermacher's theology resonated with such Protestant themes as the centrality of GRACE of Christ in SALVATION, the church enlivened by the Spirit as the means by which salvation is made known, and the experiential accent in the theology of MARTIN LUTHER and JOHN CALVIN. Self-consciously Protestant, Schleiermacher also participated in the ongoing reformation of church and theology. His theology evidenced significant material continuity with REFORMATION concerns, even as it recasts the theological enterprise so that it makes sense in the post-Enlightenment world. Particularly in his magnum opus, *The Christian Faith,* Schleiermacher set forth a theological vision grounded in Christian experience and explicating the faith in organic, naturalistic, and this-worldly terms.

The new epoch that Schleiermacher inaugurated is variously termed the New Protestantism (see ERNST TROELTSCH) or, more commonly, modern or liberal theology. Academic theology in the nineteenth century was dominated by thinkers who took important clues from Schleiermacher, although he had few disciples. Figures as diverse as JOHN CAMPBELL, Wilhelm Hermann, ADOLPH VON HARNACK, HORACE BUSHNELL (the "American Schleiermacher"), ALBRECHT RITSCHL, Ernst Troeltsch, and WALTER RAUSCHENBUSCH belong to the liberal tradition and show the influence of Schleiermacher. None of these figures follows him slavishly, however.

Liberal theology in general and Schleiermacher in particular came in for deep suspicion by the dialectical theology, or NEO-ORTHODOXY, of KARL BARTH and EMIL BRUNNER in the early twentieth century. Brunner accused Schleiermacher of psychologism and mysticism that obscure the way that the word of God comes to the self from beyond. Barth's interpretation is more nuanced than Brunner's, and he recognized potential in Schleiermacher for a theology of the Holy Spirit. Still, Barth concluded that Schleiermacher's anthropological starting point ends up selling out revelation for religion and the Word for cultural accommodation.

The negative verdict of dialectical theology dominated Schleiermacher interpretation well into the 1960s. Beginning in the 1970s and continuing into the twenty-first century, there has been a Schleiermacher renaissance led in GERMANY by scholars including Martin Redeker, Heinz Kimmerle, Kurt-Victor Selge, and Hans-Joachim Birkner and in the UNITED STATES by Richard R. Niebuhr and B. A. Gerrish. These thinkers called for a reassessment grounded in careful analysis of Schleiermacher's theological method and the results that it produced. They demonstrated the connections between Schleiermacher and classical Protestantism and extolled the depth and creativity of his work without seeking to obscure his departures from traditional theology.

The Young Rebel and the Speeches on Religion

While a student at the Moravian seminary in Barby from 1785 to 1787, Schleiermacher experienced a community at once joyous in its assurance of salvation and rigidly disciplined, as "worldly pleasures" such as swimming, skating, card games, and board games were prohibited and rigorous educational and religious practice were required. Schleiermacher received a solid biblical and classical education at Barby even as his doubts about traditional theological claims came to the fore. He became a leader in a small group of "independent thinkers" that read banned books, such as the works of JOHANN WOLFGANG GOETHE and IMMANUEL KANT. The group was found out by seminary leaders and commanded to desist. Schleiermacher, meanwhile, wrote his father and shared his doubts about the divinity of Christ, Christ's death as vicarious ATONEMENT, and eternal damnation of unbelievers. Father Gottlieb wrote back a letter full of sorrow, admonition, and pleading. In the end Schleiermacher was asked to leave the seminary. He had no place to study and no place to live, but his father agreed to support him for a year of study at the University of HALLE.

Schleiermacher completed his study, passed his ordination examinations, and worked as a tutor and a pastor for several years before being assigned to the Charité hospital in Berlin. In the Prussian capital from 1796 until 1802, Schleiermacher moved in fashionable but countercultural society. He became a member of the Romantic circle of poets and thinkers that included FRIEDRICH SCHLEGEL, A. W. Schlegel, and the poets Novalis, Ludwig Tieck, Friedrich Hölderlin, and Jean Paul. The Romantics rebelled against the Enlightenment and its focus on reason and science, order, morality, and universality, instead focusing on feeling and art, mystery, intuition of the infinite, and individuality (see ROMANTICISM). Schleiermacher was both a full member of the circle and unique. He was no poet or aesthete and would lead persons beyond ART to religion, although, to be sure, his conception of religion was cast in Romantic, aesthetic terms.

Schleiermacher also became part of Berlin's "salon society," gatherings of cultured folk and intellectuals who met in the homes of the growing bourgeoisie to hear presentations on artistic and scientific topics and discuss the cultural issues of the day. The salons were scandalous in their day for the mixing of Jews and Gentiles, commoners and nobility, and men and women. They were part of the "new Berlin," moving beyond some of the strictures that kept folk of different status separated. Schleiermacher thrived in this atmosphere, as he was with people who stimulated his mind and heart and provided the community so necessary to his life and work.

Schleiermacher burst on the cultural scene in 1799 with the publication of *Speeches On Religion (Über die Religion. Reden an die Gebildeten unter ihren Verächtern)*. The book caused a tremendous stir with its unorthodox interpretations of Jesus and the Bible and the surprising and unconventional way it spoke about religion. Although the book was published anonymously, soon everyone knew the author to be Schleiermacher, the thirty-one-year-old minister serving as a chaplain at the Charité hospital.

The style of *Speeches* is conversational and confessional—a breezy, informal tone with the cultured "despisers" and a critical, even biting tone when talking about the status quo in religion and society. Questions are addressed to the cultured despisers; the speaker goes so far as to join them at the point of their contempt for religion. And sharp criticism is leveled against the dominant understandings and practices of contemporary religion, even as the speaker clings firmly to religion in its pure state. Confessing that "religion was the maternal womb in whose holy darkness my young life was nourished," the speaker says,

> Religion helped me when I began to examine the ancestral faith and to purify my heart of the rubble of primitive times. It remained with me when God and immortality disappeared before my doubting eyes (Schleiermacher 1988:84).

The key distinction operative in the *Speeches* is that between "intuition" on the one hand and knowledge or action, on the other hand. The *Speeches* insist that religion in its essence is a matter of inward, lived experience; religious knowledge and action are secondary, derivative, a step removed from true religious experience. In this way Schleiermacher connected with the emphasis on FAITH in classical Protestantism. Although his conception was strikingly different, the focus on the passive and receptive character of religion resonated with conceptions of faith in Luther and Calvin. For them, faith is a gift given by God; for Schleiermacher in the *Speeches,* religion is intuitive reception of the universe. Echoes of and striking differences from REFORMATION formulations are evident.

The *Speeches* also proposed startling interpretations of Revelation, the BIBLE, the visible church, and Jesus. In place of the supernaturalism of traditional theology, the *Speeches* proposed a naturalistic understanding of such concepts as "miracle" and "revelation." The speaker states that " 'Miracle' is merely the religious name for event . . . To me, everything is miracle." "Revelation" is similarly defined in a naturalistic and personalistic way: "Every original and new intuition of the universe is [a revelation], and yet all individuals must know best what is original and new for them" (Schleiermacher 1988:131).

The Bible and Jesus are also subject to critique and reconstruction. The *Speeches* emphasize oral communication and see written forms, including the Bible, as secondary and derivative. Personal, communal, living communication is valued over written expression. Here the young minister departed from the Reformation affirmation of *sola scriptura*—the Bible as the only norm for faith and life.

The *Speeches* also articulated what PAUL TILLICH was later to call the "Protestant Principle"—the call for ongoing reform and searching self-criticism. When the *Speeches* reflected critically on Jesus, it concludes that Jesus never claimed to be the only Savior. To be true to itself and to Jesus, Christianity must remain essentially free and open, imposing no restrictions, allowing no narrowness. True Christianity is always expansive, anticipating further disclosures of the Christian principle manifest in Jesus. In the *Speeches,* Schleiermacher claimed the reform dynamic of Protestantism, and it led him to conclusions notable for their discontinuity with traditional Protestant theology.

Halle and Christmas Eve

Schleiermacher left Berlin in 1802 under pressure from his ecclesiastical superiors. Between the furor caused by the *Speeches,* his deep friendship with the controversial poet Friedrich Schlegel, and his public courting of Eleanore Grunow, a married woman, scandal had mounted to the point where it was deemed that Schleiermacher had to leave his beloved Berlin. From 1802 to 1804 he was miserable in his pastorate at Stolp on the Baltic Sea, but the following years in Halle (1804–1809) were a turning point for him in terms of his ecclesial career and theological development. In Halle, he wrote his *Christmas Eve: Dialogue on the Incarnation (Weihnachtsfeier).* This work marked a move away from the *Speeches,* wherein Schleiermacher began with religion in general and only at the conclusion of the work moved to consider Christianity in particular. In *Christmas Eve* Schleiermacher began from within the standpoint of Christian faith.

Christmas Eve portrays a conversation among friends about the meaning of Christmas set in the parlor of a middle-class home on Christmas Eve. What emerges in the course of the dialogue is the insight that the Christian experience of a new and higher life may be found in and through the community, its remembrance and ritual. A prime example of this is the celebration of Christmas itself. As the originator of the Christian community and the experiences it mediates, Christ must be the possessor of a unique and powerful consciousness of God in which Christians now share. This is a "CHRISTOLOGY from below" that starts not with creeds or scripture, but rather with the Christian experience of new life, then works backward to who Christ must be. This shift in method—focusing not on religious experience, but rather on Christian experience—was to be decisive for the further development of his theology. This approach was continued in Schleiermacher's great work, *Der Christliche Glaube (The Christian Faith).*

The University of Berlin and the *Brief Outline*

Upon his return to Berlin in 1809, Schleiermacher earned his way onto the planning committee for the new university by writing an independent essay on the character that a modern German university ought to have. This work so impressed Wilhelm von Humboldt that he made Schleiermacher his chief collaborator in the project. Other contributions made by Schleiermacher include selecting the university's original theological faculty, serving as its dean for four terms, and teaching a wide array of courses in theology and philosophy. In this connection he also wrote his *Brief Outline on the Study of Theology,* a programmatic work that sets forth a plan for a theological curriculum. This work conceived of theology as comprising subdisciplines that come together to form an organic whole. Theology is an academic enterprise with a practical goal. Theological work brings together the results of biblical, historical, and dogmatic study informed by insights from all of the secular sciences. What holds all of this disparate knowledge together, infusing it with unity and life, is its orientation toward the upbuilding of the church and faith. The community of the faithful is at once the ground and goal of theology. Theology does not seek to prove faith, but rather seeks to understand its meaning and significance for human life and to explicate how faith lives in the world. This makes practical theology the "crown and goal" of all of the theological disciplines, for it connects most directly with the life of the church, delineating methods to be used for leadership.

The *Brief Outline* made two signal contributions to its vision of theology as a discipline. On the one hand, it oriented theology toward the practical goal of leadership for life in the church. It made explicit the role of theology in service in the church. On the other hand, it affirmed the historical character of theology in a new way. Faith and theology are manifest in the lives of real human beings, persons limited by concrete circumstances of their lives. There can be no absolute formulation of truth that transcends the limits placed on people by their location in history. Theology is always limited by being historically conditioned. For Schleiermacher, there was a relativity to all theological claims, and this opened the door to his "revisionist" program in theology. As the faithful in the past have expressed the faith in ways that spoke to their particular situations, so the contemporary person of faith is called to theological revision for the sake of the credibility of the faith in the contemporary world. The historical character of theology comes to the fore in a new way.

The Christian Faith

Schleiermacher's magnum opus, the *Christian Faith,* is a comprehensive dogmatics comparable to St. Thomas Aquinas's *Summa Theologiae* or Calvin's INSTITUTES OF THE CHRISTIAN RELIGION, but distinctive in its theological method by making faith as experienced by contemporary Christians the dominant center. Where older dogmatics had typically begun with the dogmas of the church and/or Scripture, the *Christian Faith* begins with Christian piety. Indeed, the work has been aptly called "a theology within the limits of piety alone" (Gerrish 1982:163). Schleiermacher once again stood in a relationship of continuity and discontinuity with Protestant forebears, especially Calvin. Schleiermacher appropriated Calvin's insight that piety is the crucial touchstone for authentic theology. But for Schleiermacher, piety also became the limiting principle beyond which theology may not go, in this way departing significantly from Calvin. The *Christian Faith* argues that claims about origins (e.g., of the world or of SIN) and about the future (especially traditional Christian eschatological claims) are not, properly speaking, theological, for they go beyond what can be known on the basis of Christian piety or feeling. Theology is to explicate the contents of Christian piety, and while claims about God and the world can be made, theology most fundamentally deals with states of consciousness. Claims about God and the world have a secondary, derivative status. Theology is reconceived in terms that are strictly experiential, naturalistic, and this-worldly.

The structure of the *Christian Faith* also parallels that of Calvin's *Institutes* in its attention to a twofold knowledge of God as creator and redeemer. This twofold knowledge provides the organizational principle for both works. Of course, in Schleiermacher's work this knowledge is rendered in terms of Christian consciousness, and so knowledge of God as creator is expressed in terms of an immediate self-consciousness of absolute dependence. That is, Christian piety includes a sense of oneself (and the world) as not being self-caused. Underlying feelings of relative freedom and relative dependence is the sense of utter dependence on an other. This feeling of utter dependence resonates with the emphasis on the sovereignty of God articulated by Calvin and the Reformed tradition generally. Knowledge of God as redeemer is the other aspect of Christian consciousness. This is the sense that one has been delivered to a higher form of life in which one's consciousness of God is pervasive in a way it had not been previously. This higher life includes a sense of newness and joy; it derives from and participates in the perfect God consciousness of Jesus, mediated to people in the present by means of the

Christian community. Christian piety then includes these two moments bound together inextricably: a higher and living awareness of absolute dependence on God made known through Jesus as He lives on in the community that He founded.

The Christian naturalism of Schleiermacher's system is evident in his treatment of the twin doctrines of Christ and CHURCH, which together stand at the very heart of his theology. Christian consciousness includes within itself the awareness that all blessedness is "grounded in the new divinely-effected corporate life" (Schleiermacher 1928:358).

The church is a natural, living organism. To be sure, it is enlivened by Christ, but it is also caught up in the flux of social and historical life like every other human movement or institution. This conception of the church as a living organism reclaims the organic images of the New Testament. There the church is imaged as the living branches of the one true vine and as the living members of the body of Christ. The church is a true community of persons united by a common spirit that is more than the individuals who make up the community. This common spirit that Schleiermacher identifies as the spirit of Christ or the Holy Spirit, at once the community's source and the one made known in and through the community. This means that the church can be comprehended and analyzed as a natural historical entity in many ways similar to any other human movement. For believers, it is the source of the new and higher life in Christ.

Schleiermacher's christology in the *Christian Faith* has much more substance than is found in the *Speeches*. In the mature dogmatic work focus is on the humanity of Christ. Christ is the sinlessly perfect human one and thereby the culmination of God's intention for humanity. Here is the one remaining "supernatural" element in Schleiermacher's otherwise seamlessly "naturalistic" system. Jesus's perfection cannot be explained by his historical context. He was born into a sinful world. Still, Christ is only relatively supernatural, for he manifests what is possible in theory for any human being—a perfect consciousness of God.

Schleiermacher's method in this christological reflection was consistent with his usual approach. He began with the new and higher form of life that the believer receives in and through the Christian community and then moved archeologically, tracing backward to the origin. The immediate source of the experience of salvation is the Christian community. The community in turn traces its origin to its founder, Jesus Christ, and attributes all its blessedness to the founder. Schleiermacher's method, then, was to retrace steps and discover who Jesus must have been to communicate this new and higher life to believers. He concluded that Jesus must be the possessor of a unique and unblemished consciousness of God, the human ideal in whose blessedness the believer participates. Schleiermacher cannot achieve a literal restatement of orthodox views of the person of Christ—"two natures in one person"—or the Trinity—three persons in one being. He asserted that such claims are beyond our ken. But as the ultimate source of the reality of salvation in believers' lives, Jesus must be perfect in his God-consciousness, and divine and human in that sense. And Schleiermacher can affirm a trinity of God, Christ, and Spirit in the church. Here the revisionist character of Schleiermacher's enterprise is again evident: He refuses to take traditional formulas at face value. Instead, he crafts revised understandings that resonate with the spirit of the tradition even as views of God and Christ are significantly reconceived.

Schleiermacher's companion to the *Christian Faith* was his similarly mammoth work, the *Christian Ethics*. This work, pulled together posthumously from Schleiermacher's lecture notes and those of students, is the complement to and completion of the *Christian Faith*. The *Ethics* provides a comprehensive analysis of actions in the church and the wider society, and sets forth the teleological drive of Christian faith: transformation of life in this world.

See also Calvinism; Ecclesiology; Liberal Protestantism and Liberalism; Moravian Church

References and Further Reading

Primary Sources:

Schleiermacher, Friedrich. *Brief Outline on the Study of Theology*. Translated by Terrence N. Tice. Richmond, VA: John Knox Press, 1966.

———. *Christmas Eve: Dialogue on the Incarnation*. Translated by Terrence N. Tice. Richmond, VA: John Knox Press, 1967.

———. *The Christian Faith*. Edited by H. R. Mackintosh and J. S. Stewart. Edinburgh, UK: T. & T. Clark, 1928.

———. *On Religion: Speeches to its Cultured Despisers*. Translated by Richard Crouter. Cambridge, UK: Cambridge University Press, 1988.

Secondary Sources:

Blackwell, Albert L. *Schleiermacher's Early Philosophy of Life: Determinism, Freedom, and Phantasy*. Chico, CA: Scholars Press, 1982.

Brandt, James M. *All Things New: Reform of Church and Society in Schleiermacher's Christian Ethics*. Louisville, KY: Westminster/John Knox Press, 2001.

Gerrish, B.A. *Continuing the Reformation: Essays on Modern Religious Thought*. Chicago, IL: University of Chicago Press, 1993.

———. *The Old Protestantism and the New*. Chicago, IL: University of Chicago Press, 1982.

———. *A Prince of the Church: Schleiermacher and the Beginnings of Modern Theology*. Philadelphia, PA: Fortress Press, 1984.

———. *Tradition and the Modern World: Reformed Theology in the Nineteenth Century*. Chicago, IL: University of Chicago Press, 1978.

Lamm, Julia A. *The Living God: Schleiermacher's Theological Appropriation of Spinzoa*. University Park, PA: The Pennsylvania State University Press, 1996.

Niebuhr, Richard R. *Schleiermacher on Christ and Religion*. New York: Charles Scribner's Sons, 1964.

Redeker, Martin. *Schleiermacher: Life and Thought*. Translated by John Wallhausser. Philadelphia, PA: Fortress Press, 1973.

Spiegler, Gerhard. *The Eternal Covenant: Schleiermacher's Experiment in Cultural Theology*. New York: Harper and Row, 1967.

Thandeka. *The Embodied Self: Friedrich Schleiermacher's Solution to Kant's Problem of the Empirical Self*. Albany, NY: State University of New York Press, 1995.

Williams, Robert R. *Schleiermacher the Theologian: The Construction of the Doctrine of God*. Philadelphia, PA: Fortress Press, 1978.

JAMES M. BRANDT

SCHLEITHEIM CONFESSION

Often referred to as the Schleitheim Articles or Brotherly Union, the Schleitheim Confession was adopted by Swiss Anabaptists in the town of Schleitheim, in the area of Schaffhausen on February 24, 1527. Originally entitled *Brüderlich vereinigung etlicher Kinder Gottes, sieben artickel betreffend (Brotherly Union of a Number of Children of God Concerning Seven Articles)*, the confession did not influence ANABAPTISM as a whole, but it did come to play a formative role in the development of the Swiss Anabaptist tradition, to which present-day AMISH, HUTTERITES, and some MENNONITES are related.

Scholars assume that a former Benedictine monk, MICHAEL SATTLER, drafted the CONFESSION, including the prefatory letter and concluding postscript. Sattler had likely been prior at Saint Peter's monastery in the Black Forest near Freiburg. In the mid-1520s he joined the Anabaptist movement, and his missionary activities took him to the vicinities of Zürich and Strasbourg. After conversations with reformers MARTIN BUCER and WOLFGANG CAPITO in Strasbourg, Sattler led the conference at Schleitheim. Soon after, he was arrested, tried by Austrian authorities, and then executed on May 21, 1527.

The confession was polemical in tone and sought to demarcate the boundaries of Swiss Anabaptism over against other expressions of belief. Some scholars have concluded that the confession was directed against mainline reformers, while others have asserted that the confession represents an internal Anabaptist discussion. Whatever the immediate occasion, the confession did serve the purpose of distinguishing Swiss Anabaptist practice from that of Catholicism, mainline Protestantism, as well as other Anabaptist streams.

The Schleitheim Confession takes for granted the essential beliefs of Christian orthodoxy such as belief in the triune God, the ATONEMENT, and the ongoing activity of the Holy Spirit. Attention in the confession is given to concerns that highlight the distinct beliefs of the Swiss Anabaptism community: BAPTISM, CHURCH DISCIPLINE, the LORD'S SUPPER, the relationship between the CHURCH and the world, church leadership, the sword, and the oath.

The article on baptism rejects the practice of infant baptism and emphasizes that before the rite can take place, there must be genuine repentance and amendment of life. Baptism is given to those who truly understand, believe, and have a desire to be buried with Christ, and who want to "walk in the resurrection." It is a practice that links the inner desire of repentance with an outer practice of walking in Christ's footsteps.

The article on church discipline focuses on the ban and assumes that the members of the Christian community are accountable to one another, having been baptized into the body of Christ, and having committed themselves to a life of discipleship. In cases where Christians have fallen into error and SIN, the pattern set in Matthew 18 is in force. Christians may be warned twice in private, and a third time admonished before the community of believers. This is to be done before Christians can participate in the Lord's Supper, to ensure that unity of the community is maintained.

The theme of unity continues in the third article dealing with the Lord's Supper, which is a commemorative rather than sacramental event. The community of faith that gathers to participate in the breaking of bread according to the command of Christ must before hand be united through baptism. The validity of the Supper is dependent on the character of the community whose head is Christ. For this reason, only the true children of God have a rightful place at the table.

The emphasis on separation is given attention in article four, which makes a strong distinction between the faithful community and the sinful world. By rejecting all worldly associations, and by highlighting the radical dualism between the church and the world, the Swiss Anabaptists underscore their resolve to maintain a sectarian ECCLESIOLOGY.

The fifth article attends to the various responsibilities of leaders within the Christian community. Pastors must have a good reputation outside of the church; they are called by the local congregation and must be accountable to it. If they are driven away or killed, another pastor is to be ordained that same hour—an arrangement that not only highlights the context of persecution, but also indicates the importance of church leadership among the Swiss Anabaptists.

The final two articles are concerned with how Christians are to relate to civil authorities. In the article on the sword, the role of government is affirmed and seen as ordained of God. Yet, the article's main point is that the sword is "outside the perfection of Christ." Government is necessary in the world to protect the good and to punish evildoers, but among true Christians only the ban is used as a disciplinary measure. While the world is armed with steel and iron, Christians are armed with the Word of God. Christians cannot take up the sword because of Christ's teachings and example.

The final article is concerned with the swearing of oaths, which the civil authorities often demanded of its subjects on an annual basis. Again, the Anabaptists point to Christ as the basis for their point of view: Christians cannot swear the oath, because Christ forbids it.

As to the question of the confession's theological nature and origins, there is no scholarly consensus. Mid–twentieth-century historiography tended to see the confession as representing a continuation of Zürich Anabaptist beginnings. Since then, scholars have asked whether the confession may ostensibly represent some continuation of peasant aspirations, a continuation of late medieval ascetic traditions, a continuation of a Benedictine communal tradition, or perhaps some combination of these influences.

See also Free Church; Grebel, Conrad; Hubmaier, Balthasar; Martyrs and Martyrologies; Mathiis, Jan; Pacifism; Sectarianism; Switzerland; War

References and Further Reading

Fast, Heinhold, ed. *Quellen zur Geschichte der Täufer in der Schweiz.* Vol. 2. Zürich, Switzerland: Theologischer Verlag, 1973.

Goertz, Hans-Jürgen. *The Anabaptists.* Translated by Trevor Johnson. London and New York: Routledge, 1996.

Haas, Martin. "The Path of the Anabaptists Into Separation: The Interdependence of Theology and Social Behaviour." In *The Anabaptists and Thomas Müntzer.* Translated and edited by James M. Stayer and Werner O. Packull, 72–84. Toronto, Canada: Kendall/Hunt, 1980.

Snyder, C. Arnold. *The Life and Thought of Michael Sattler.* Scottdale, PA: Herald Press, 1984.

———. "The Schleitheim Articles in Light of the Revolution of the Common Man: Continuation or Departure?" *The Sixteenth Century Journal* 16 (1985): 419–430.

———. "The Influence of the Schleitheim Articles on the Anabaptist Movement: An Historical Evaluation." *Mennonite Quarterly Review* 63 (1989): 323–344.

Yoder, John H., ed. *The Legacy of Michael Sattler.* Scottdale, PA: Herald Press, 1973.

KARL KOOP

SCHMALKALD ARTICLES

This confessional document, penned by MARTIN LUTHER in December 1536, is a series of interrelated doctrinal statements ("articles"). It became known by the town (Schmalkald, in Thuringia, GERMANY) where the SCHMALKALD LEAGUE met in February 1537. A testamentary document, it was written under the pressure of the reformer's supposed imminent death and summarized Luther's mature Reformation Theology, as well as his critique of the sixteenth-century Catholic Church.

In May 1536, when Pope Paul III called a general council of the church to meet the following spring, Luther's ongoing bouts with illness made death seem near. Therefore Luther's ruler, elector John Fredrick of Saxony, took the proposed council as the occasion to commission the reformer to write a summary of his theological priorities—and thereby dampen the smoldering doctrinal disagreements of second-generation reformers and also provide a theological statement for the council. The elector's concerns over Luther's health were well founded—not only did Luther suffer numerous illnesses in the early and mid-1530s, he suffered an apparent heart attack while composing the document itself, forcing him to dictate the last few articles from his sick bed.

Secondarily John Fredrick wanted a doctrinal statement that could serve as the basis of the Schmalkaldic League's response to the papal council. When the League met at Schmalkald, in February 1537, the articles did not come to the floor of the meeting—the princes decided not to attend the council and Luther became deathly ill, preventing his participation in the deliberations.

After Schmalkald, Luther regained his health, made some changes in the document, added a preface, and had it published at Wittenberg in 1538. Later it was incorporated into various Lutheran *corpora doctrinae* ("bodies of doctrine"), designed to summarize Lutheran teaching. These local *corpora* were eclipsed by the definitive collection of Lutheran confessional writings published as the BOOK OF CONCORD in 1580, which gives prominent place to *The Schmalkaldic Articles.*

Luther organized the content of the articles into three sections. Part I, "The Lofty Articles of the Divine Majesty," briefly summarizes Western Trinitarian, creedal doctrine. In four short articles Luther quotes and refers to the three catholic creeds, as well as his own Small Catechism, as he demonstrates the Catholic starting point of evangelical teaching. He ends with a summary: "These articles are not matters of dispute or conflict, for both sides confess them.

Therefore, it is not necessary to deal with them at greater length now."

Part II, "The Office and Work of Jesus Christ, or Our Redemption," contains four articles. The "First and Chief Article" delineates Luther's understanding of JUSTIFICATION by GRACE alone through FAITH alone. Significantly he constructs this article with biblical citations designed to demonstrate the Scriptural foundation of Lutheran DOCTRINE.

On the basis of this statement of his central doctrinal conviction, Luther criticized various churchly practices and their underlying theologies, thereby pointing to the heart of his reform agenda. Article Two critiques prevailing understandings of the Mass—"a human invention, not commanded by God." Article Three critiques "foundations and monasteries"—they are not "better than everyday Christian walks of life." Article Four critiques the papacy—the pope is "not the head of all Christendom 'by divine right'."

In Part III Luther integrates the catholicity of Part I with the evangelicalism of Part II, providing a constructive outline of "catholic-evangelical" doctrine for discussion "with learned, reasonable people." The key is article four, "Concerning the Gospel." The first three articles (Sin, Law, and Repentance) lead to the Gospel and the succeeding articles (Baptism, Holy Communion, the Keys, and Confession) flow from it. The concluding six articles deal with various matters of church practice (Marriage of Priests, Good Works, "Human Regulations," etc.).

This document was to Luther himself one of his most significant works, serving as a confessional capstone to his REFORMATION career. However, a number of factors (e.g., polemical tone, appearance late in Luther's career, etc.) have kept it from receiving the attention it deserves. Nevertheless, it is ecumenical and evangelical in scope, clearly schematizing the main doctrinal features of Martin Luther's reform initiatives.

See also Baptism; Catholicism, Protestant Reactions; Clergy, Marriage of; Lord's Supper; Lutheranism; Sin

References and Further Reading

Primary Source:

Luther, Martin. "The Smalcald Articles." In *The Book of Concord,* edited by Robert Kolb and Timothy Wengert. Minneapolis, MN: Fortress Press, 2000.

Secondary Sources:

Haile, H. G. *Luther*. Princeton, NJ: Princeton University Press, 1983.

Russell, William R. *Luther's Theological Testament: The Schmalkald Articles*. Rev. 2nd ed. St. Louis, MO: Concordia Publishing, 2003.

WILLIAM R. RUSSELL

SCHMALKALD LEAGUE

This defensive military alliance of REFORMATION-era German Protestant princes was formally organized in February 1531 at Schmalkald (in Thuringia, GERMANY). The League was established as a political response to imperial and pro–Catholic moves (e.g., Regensburg Alliance in 1524, the Recess of the Diet of Speyer in 1529), culminating in the Recess of Augsburg (1530), which gave Protestants six months to acquiesce to the Catholic Church or face legal and military action from the emperor. It was meant as a defensive alliance.

From the beginning, the twenty-three cities and territories that joined the League confronted enormous internal differences. Politically questions of finances and leadership dogged the alliance. Theologically disagreement arose over the fundamental question of propriety of armed resistance to defend the gospel (with MARTIN LUTHER initially opposed to such action), as well as over various theological issues.

These disagreements inhibited development of a coherent strategy in response to imperial incursions during the Schmalkald War (1546–1547). With the victory of Charles V's forces at Mühlberg and the surrender of Wittenberg in 1547, the League disbanded. However, the League was an important part of the religious and political dynamics of the era, which culminated in the Peace of Augsburg in 1555. This agreement codified the principle "*cuius regio, eius religio*," granting Protestant princes the right to determine the religious practices within their jurisdictions. In sixteen years of existence the League provided the nascent Protestant movement with a degree of protection from Imperial attack.

See also Catholicism, Protestant Reactions; Pacifism; Schmalkaldic Articles; War

References and Further Reading

Brady, Thomas. "Schmalkald League." In *The Oxford Encyclopedia of the Reformation*. Vol. 4, 12–15. New York: Oxford University Press, 1996.
Dueck, A. J. "Religion and Temporal Authority in the Reformation: The Controversy among the Protestants prior to the Peace of Nuremberg, 1532." *Sixteenth Century Journal* 13 no. 2 (1982): 55–74.

WILLIAM R. RUSSELL

SCHMUCKER, SAMUEL SIMON (1799–1873)

American Lutheran theologian. Schmucker was an influential Lutheran American in the early nineteenth century. He was a revivalist who made significant contributions in EDUCATION and ECUMENISM.

Schmucker was born in February 28, 1799 in Hagerstown, Maryland. After serving as a pastor for several years, in 1826 he became the first professor of the Lutheran Theological Seminary in Gettysburg, Pennsylvania, an institution whose founding Schmucker had encouraged. The seminary quickly established a classical school or prep school, which in 1831 became Gettysburg College.

Among Lutherans, Schmucker's revivalist tendencies evoked controversy. Antirevivalists, called Old School, favored retention of the German language, and they embraced confessionalism and the CATECHISM. Schmucker and other New School Lutherans preferred English and methods associated with CAMP MEETINGS, including emotion and spontaneous conversion, although Schmucker kept the most exuberant worship at arm's length. Old School conservatives charged that revivalists distorted LUTHERANISM, but New School Lutherans cited the Pietist heritage within their tradition. Among Lutherans the tide ran against Schmucker, and had he not retired in 1865, his continued service at Gettysburg might have been difficult.

Schmucker exemplified the marriage of heartfelt faith and interdenominational reform that typified eighteenth-century Pietists and nineteenth-century revivalists on both sides of the Atlantic. He participated in a variety of reform societies, including those promoting SUNDAY SCHOOL, TEMPERANCE, Sabbath-keeping, and social work. He was particularly active in the EVANGELICAL ALLIANCE movement, which encouraged Christian unity and ecumenism.

Schmucker died of a heart attack on July 26, 1873.

See also Christian Colleges; Ethnicity; Evangelicalism; Higher Education; Pietism; Revivals; Seminaries

References and Further Reading

Primary Sources:

Schmucker, S. S. *Elements of Popular Theology.* New York: Leavitt, Lord, 1834.
———. *The Lutheran Manual on Scriptural Principles.* Philadelphia: Lindsay & Blakiston, 1855.
———. *The American Lutheran Church.* New York: Arno Press, 1969.
Schmucker, Samuel Simon. *The American Lutheran Church, Historically, Doctrinally, and Practically Delineated, in Several Occasional Discourses.* Springfield, IL: D. Harbaugh, 1851.
———. *Elements of Popular Theology, with Special Reference to the Doctrines of the Reformation, as Avowed before the Diet of Augsburg, in MDXXX.* Andover, MA: Gould and Newman, 1834.

Secondary Source:

Wentz, Abdel Ross. *Samuel Simon Schmucker: Pioneer in Christian Unity.* Philadelphia: Fortress Press, 1967.

STEPHEN LONGENECKER

SCHÖN, JAKOB FRIEDRICH (LATER, JAMES FREDERICK) (1803–1889)

German missionary. Schön was born in Baden, GERMANY in 1803 and died in Chatham, ENGLAND on March 30, 1889. He offered for mission service through the BASEL MISSION and attended their seminary, but like many of his contemporaries received his commission through the (Anglican) CHURCH MISSIONARY SOCIETY. He attended their college in Islington and was ordained in the CHURCH OF ENGLAND (deacon 1831, priest 1832). In 1832 he was appointed to SIERRA LEONE and spent the next fifteen years based in Freetown and the villages of "liberated Africans" taken from intercepted slave ships. Unlike many missionaries in Sierra Leone, such as HANNAH KILHAM, Schön studied African languages, both local vernaculars and the languages of the "liberated African" communities. Stationed at the village of Kent, he made studies of the grammar and vocabulary of Bullom, spoken in the area, and made some translations. (Gustav Nylander, 1776–1825, the pioneer translator of Bullom, was the father of Schön's first wife.)

As he changed stations, Schön essayed languages spoken by large numbers of the liberated, notably Igbo and Hausa. In 1841 he was appointed, together with the Yoruba teacher SAMUEL ADJAI CROWTHER, to represent the missionary interest on the British expedition to the Niger. This was inspired by the ideas of Thomas Fowell Buxton (1786–1845) about producing an economic alternative to the slave trade that would allow Christianity and economic and technological development to spread in the African interior. The disastrous loss of life on the expedition (some forty members died, all Europeans) discredited these ideas and cooled any public interest in AFRICA. Schön's report, however, insisted that the evangelization of inland Africa was still possible, provided it was based on African rather than European missionaries. These would be people of Crowther's type, recruited and trained in Sierra Leone, where, among the liberated slaves, all the main languages of West Africa were already in use, despite predictions that they would die out and be replaced by English. During the expedition the interpreters, almost all from Sierra Leone, had been impressive, and Crowther's Yoruba useful; and although his own Igbo had been too rudimentary to be much use, Schön had preached in Hausa and been understood.

So far as circumstances allowed, Schön's recommendations formed the core of the CMS West African policy for the next two decades. For Schön, Hausa became his life's work. The French scholar Maurice Delafosse called Schön the "discoverer" of Hausa, in that he made the language known to science and revealed the vast numbers who spoke it. Schön, whose literary output was enormous, translated most of the BIBLE and composed a major grammar and dictionary.

Schön left Africa through ill-health in 1847 and became chaplain of the Melville Hospital at Chatham naval base, taking British nationality in 1856. His duties allowed him time for his linguistic studies. Besides working on Hausa he acted as an honorary linguistic adviser to the CMS, revising in particular—not always to their satisfaction—the work of the missionaries of the Niger Mission. The mission and its African staff came under heavy fire in the 1880s, and Schön's competence was also questioned by people who had no means of assessing it. He was defended, however, by the redoubtable writer on languages, R. N. Cust (1821–1909), who opened the way for Schön to receive an honorary doctorate from Oxford. The Institut de France also awarded him their gold medal for his linguistic studies.

Although neither a trained linguist nor an encyclopedic scholar like SIGISMUND W. KOELLE, Schön was tireless and thorough. He did much to improve the standard of missionary translation and laid the foundation for the study of Hausa, West Africa's most spoken language. He was the father and grandfather of CMS missionaries.

See also Bible Translation; Missions; Missionary Organizations

References and Further Reading

Primary Source:

Schön, J. F., and Samuel Crowther. *Journal of an Expedition up the Niger in 1841*. London: Church Missionary Society, 1843.

Secondary Sources:

Church Missionary Society Register of Missionaries and Native Clergy. London: CMS, 1904.
Hair, P. E. H. *The Early Study of Nigerian Languages*. Cambridge: Cambridge University Press, 1967.
Stock, Eugene. *History of the Church Missionary Society*. London: 1899.

ANDREW F. WALLS

SCHÜTZ, HEINRICH
(1585–1672)

Composer. Heinrich Schütz, also known as Henricus Sagittarius, was a Lutheran composer and church musician who wrote MUSIC for the whole church. He was one of the finest composers of the seventeenth century and one of the most important composers in the church's history. He linked the evangelical and the catholic, the Renaissance and the Baroque, the Italian and the German. He wrote for large and small forces, pieces of tonal splendor and ones with a more archaic and delicate flavor. He set Latin texts skillfully, but also broke open German texts with remarkable musical capacity.

Born in Köstritz, GERMANY, on October 8, 1585 and baptized the next day, he and his family moved to Weissenfels in 1590. Eight years later Landgrave Moritz of Hessia convinced his parents to send him to the court at Kassel. There, in 1599, Schütz became a choirboy who sang and studied well.

In 1608 he went to Marburg to study law. Landgrave Moritz intervened again and paid his way to Venice to study with Giovanni Gabrieli from 1609 to 1612, when Gabrieli died. Back to Germany in 1613 his parents urged him to study law, but Moritz gave him the position of second court organist at the court in Kassel.

Johann Georg I, elector of Saxony, then intervened. He first got Moritz to lend Schütz to him and then in 1617 got him officially released from the Kassel court and employed as music director in Dresden, the largest and most significant Protestant musical enterprise in Germany. Until his death in 1672 Schütz remained with the Dresden court, although his conducting responsibilities ended in 1657. Because the Thirty Years War (1618–1648) severely limited musical resources in Germany, Schütz took three leaves: from 1628 to 1629 he went to Venice to study with Monteverdi; from 1633 to 1635 and from 1642 to 1644 he worked at the court in Copenhagen.

In 1619 Schütz married Magdalene Wildeckin, who was eighteen. The union was apparently an unusually happy one, but it abruptly ended in 1625 when Magdalene became ill and died. Her death was a great blow to Schütz; he never remarried.

Works

In *The Psalms of David* of 1619 Schütz brought to Germany Gabrieli's Venetian technique, with polychoral and instrumental splendor. In 1625 forty Latin four-voice motets called the *Cantiones sacrae* were published. If these two works exhibit a Lutheran and Catholic spirit, a harmonized set of German metrical versions of the Psalms (1628, revised and enlarged in 1661) might be seen with the Calvinist Genevan Psalter in the background. Called the "Becker Psalter" after the Leipzig theologian Cornelius Becker who prepared the texts, some of these were originally conceived for the morning and evening devotions of his choirboys for whom Schütz also wrote table graces.

Three *Symphoniae sacrae* ("spiritual concerts") appeared in 1629, 1647, and 1650—the first twenty Latin biblical texts, mostly from the Old Testament; the second in German with reduced musical forces because of the war; and the third in the Italian polychoral style of *The Psalms of David* again. All three sets were influenced by Monteverdi, whom Schütz greatly admired. Two sets of *Kleine geistliche Konzerte* ("Little Spiritual Concerts") on generally biblical texts were published in 1636 and 1639 with modest forces dictated by the war. *The Musikalische Exequien,* which influenced Johannes Brahms's *German Requiem,* also was published in 1636. It contains a Missa Brevis (*Kyrie* and *Gloria*), a motet for two choirs, and a *Nunc Dimittis* with a superimposed text that Brahms would later employ, "Blessed are the dead which die in the Lord."

Schütz set the core of the New Testament in several works: *The Resurrection History* in 1623, *The Seven Words of Jesus Christ on the Cross* in 1645, *The Christmas Story* in 1664, and three *Passions* according to Luke, John, and Matthew in 1665 and 1666. The Passions, especially the one according to Matthew, are among the most remarkable of Schütz's output, although written in his eighties. Unlike the Christmas and Resurrection histories that use instruments, the Passions followed Dresden's traditional practice of not using instruments during Holy Week and are unaccompanied. They are vernacular liturgical works modeled after the Gregorian Passions, with newly composed modal recitatives for each individual influenced by Florentine operatic monody and German Lied. Each individual has a characteristic flavor and range. The groups (*turba*) are given to a chorus, mostly in four parts. The text is simply the Passion narrative from the respective gospel with an introductory announcement and a stanza of a hymn as a conclusion, both for the choir. The *St. John Passion* alone uses the hymn's cantus firmus. The *St. Matthew* and *St Luke* employ musical material totally from Schütz's hand, his more usual practice.

Death

Schütz died on November 6, 1672. Martin Geier, first court preacher at Dresden, delivered the funeral sermon on November 17. Biographical details were appended, but the sermon itself, at Schütz's request, was

about a Lutheran understanding of music in the life of the church.

Schütz was an orthodox Lutheran who regularly went to CONFESSION, heard the Word, and received the LORD'S SUPPER until September 15 of his last year when illness confined him to his house. He lived out his faith by charitable concern for his neighbors, including support for needy musicians, and through his VOCATION of composing music for the church. For his funeral he chose Psalm 119:54, "Your statutes have been my songs in the house of my pilgrimage." Geier treated that as both generally applicable and representative of Schütz's outlook: the whole understanding of God's will was to be put into devout and edifying songs for the congregation in its public WORSHIP, at home, and in travels. Geier also worked from Ecclesiasticus 43:30, which Schütz had inscribed on his music cabinet: "Glorify the Lord and exalt him as much as you can, for he surpasses even that." Geier took this to mean that the church musician, exemplified by Schütz, was to exercise the finest craft for the praise of God as a joyous, holy, laborious, and endless work of delight.

See also Lord's Supper; Music, Northern European; Vocation

References and Further Reading

Baron, Stephen, Kurt Gudewill, Derek McCulloch, and Joshua Rifkin. "Schütz, Heinrich." In *The New Grove Dictionary of Music and Musicians,* edited by Stanley Sadie, vol. 17, 1–37. London: Macmillan Publishers Limited, 1980.
Leaver, Robin. *Music in the Service of the Church: The Funeral Sermon of Heinrich Schütz (1585–1672).* St. Louis, MO: Concordia, 1984.
Moser, Han Joachim. *Heinrich Schütz: His Life and Work.* Translated by Carl F. Pfatteicher. St. Louis, MO: Concordia, 1959.
Schalk, Carl. *Music in Early Lutheranism: Shaping the Tradition (1524–1672).* St. Louis, MO: Concordia, 2001.
Smallman, Basil. *Schütz, the Master Musician.* Oxford: Oxford University Press, 2000.
Website: http://www.grovemusic.com/schütz

PAUL WESTERMEYER

SCHWEITZER, ALBERT (1875–1965)

German biblical scholar and medical missionary. Born on January 14, 1875 in Kaysersberg (Alsace), Schweitzer grew up in Günsbach, a town in the Alsatian Münstertal. Here his father administered the parish of the Lutheran community. Having attended school in Günsbach and Mühlhausen in Alsace, Albert Schweitzer studied THEOLOGY and philosophy at the University of Strasbourg from 1893. In 1894 and 1895 he did his military service in the Prussian Army (Alsace then belonged to the German Empire). A man of many talents, Schweitzer also took organ lessons from Charles-Marie Widor in Paris. In the Whitsun holidays of 1896, Schweitzer made a vow that as of his thirtieth birthday he would serve his fellow humans, but until then would concentrate on scholarly activities. He did so with great academic success: in 1899 he obtained his doctorate with a dissertation on *Die Religionsphilosophie Kants* (Kant's Religious Philosophy). After this Schweitzer passed both theological examinations and became a vicar at St. Nicolai in Strasbourg, an office he occupied until 1912. In 1901 he qualified as a lecturer at the theological faculty with his study *Das Messianitäts- und Leidensgeheimnis. Eine Skizze des Lebens Jesu* (The Mystery of Messiahship and Suffering. A Sketch of the Life of Jesus) and in 1902 began teaching as an outside lecturer at the University of Strasbourg.

During this period Schweitzer managed a remarkable amount of work in a day. After intensive studies on Johann Sebastian Bach (1903–1904) and during his preoccupation with research on the life of Jesus (*Von Reimarus zu Wrede;* From Reimarus to Wrede, 1906), in 1905 he began to study medicine at the faculty of medicine in Strasbourg. He successfully completed these studies in 1913, obtaining a medical degree with his work *Die psychiatrische Beurteilung Jesu. Darstellung und Kritik* (The Psychiatric Study of Jesus. Exposition and Criticism).

His interest in medicine was linked to the decision that he had already made in 1904 to enter the service of the Paris Missionary Society. However, this Missionary Society mistrusted the liberal theologian, and Schweitzer looked to find a meaningful field of occupation independently in AFRICA as a doctor rather than a theologian. Having been appointed as a professor in the meantime, Schweitzer gave up his position as a vicar and his university career, married Helene Breslau, a nurse (1879–1957), studied tropical medicine in Paris for a further year, and in 1913 went to Lambaréné in Equatorial Africa (Gabon). There he established a hospital with personal funds. The hospital had to be closed in 1917, however, because Schweitzer and his wife were interned by the French authorities for being citizens of the German Empire. In 1918 Schweitzer returned to Alsace, again took up his service as vicar in St. Nicolai, and sought to pay off the debts he had incurred in Africa by giving numerous organ concerts and lectures. In 1920 he decided to continue his work in Lambaréné and in 1924 he emigrated to Africa for the second time. There he spent a total of thirty years in his jungle hospital. In 1957 and 1958 Schweitzer, who kept out of day-to-day politics, spoke out in three radio addresses on Radio Oslo—as the holder of the Nobel Prize for peace, which he had been awarded in 1952—against the dangers of a nuclear war. These addresses attracted much criticism of Schweitzer and contributed, along with the increasing reproaches of COLONIALISM, to his loss of popularity in the 1950s and 1960s. In 1959 Schweitzer left Europe for good and died on September 4, 1965 in Lambaréné.

Range of Interests

Schweitzer's multifaceted works cover the areas of theology, cultural philosophy, and MUSIC. His activities in the field of medicine, for which he was renowned and on the basis of which many are still aware of him today, can be regarded as an integral part and consequence of his theological and philosophical research. Committed to liberal theology, Schweitzer emphasized his support of the school of thought of consistent ESCHATOLOGY: Jesus is the future Messiah whose expectation that upon his sacrifice on the cross the KINGDOM OF GOD would set in immediately was, however, disappointed. Thus, he believed, for today's faith only the spirit of the historical Jesus counted, which came from his word and would conquer the world. Schweitzer also remained true to eschatological ETHICS in his studies on Paul, who is consistently interpreted on the basis of early Jewish writings on the Apocalypse. For Schweitzer, his theological achievement lay in developing an eschatological ethic from an ethic of readiness for the heavenly kingdom to an ethic of being delivered *(Mystik des Seins in Christo).* As a philosopher of CULTURE Schweitzer, who imposed on philosophy the decline of culture that he had diagnosed, was seeking the basic principle of morality. He found this in his ethic of reverence for life. The key phrase of this was "I am life that wants to live in the midst of other life that wants to live." He came to the conclusion from this that it was good to preserve life but bad to destroy life (*Werke V,* 158). This "reverence for life" also includes reverence for all animals and plants; for the ethic of reverence, every life is sacred. Schweitzer was fully aware that the development of conflicts from this position was absolutely inevitable: life can exist only at the cost of other life. Yet in this ever-recurring situation of conflict between life and DEATH only the individual can make subjectively justifiable decisions. According to Schweitzer there are no objective criteria for these decisions. In the area of music Schweitzer dedicated his attention to Johann Sebastian Bach and organ playing. He not only produced *Kritisch-Praktische Ausgabe des gesammten Orgelwerkes von Bach* (New York 1912–1967), but with his study *Johann Sebastian Bach* (1908) Schweitzer produced a standard work for Bach research.

Schweitzer's impact on today's Protestantism is limited. Whereas his work in Lambaréné is continued in the Albert-Schweitzer Hospital, there is—with few exceptions (Erich Gräßer for example)—little attention paid to Schweitzer in contemporary theology. References to his cultural philosophy have also been marginal. However, a change appears imminent. Schweitzer broke the traditional restrictions of anthropocentric ethics and cleared the way for a global ethic of responsibility, the basic principle of which is "reverence for life." With a worldwide ecological crisis and unrestricted possibilities in gene technology, Schweitzer's ethical guidelines are receiving increased attention.

See also Colonialism; Ecology; Jesus, Lives of; Liberal Protestantism and Liberalism; Missions

References and Further Reading

Primary Sources:

Schweitzer, Albert. *Gesamtausgabe.* Tokyo: 1956–1961.
Schweitzer, Albert. *The Psychiatric Study of Jesus.* Boston: Beacon Press, 1948.
———. *Memoirs of Childhood and Youth.* New York: Macmillan, 1949.
———. *The Philosophy of Civilization.* New York: Macmillan, 1949.
———. *Paul and His Interpreters.* New York: Macmillan, 1951.
———. *J. S. Bach.* New York: Dover, 1966.
———. *Reverence for Life.* New York: Harper & Row, 1969.
———. *Out of My Life and Thought.* New York: Henry Holt, 1990.
Schweitzer, Albert, and Norman Cousins. *The Words of Albert Schweitzer.* New York: Newmarket Press, 1984.
Schweitzer, Albert, and John Henry Paul Reumann. *The Problem of the Lord's Supper According to the Scholarly Research of the Nineteenth Century and the Historical Accounts.* Macon, GA: Mercer University Press, 1982.
Werke aus dem Nachlaß. vols. I–VIII. Munich, Germany: 1995 ff.

Secondary Sources:

Buri, Fritz. *Ehrfurcht vor dem Leben. Albert Schweitzr. Eine Freundesgabe zum 80 Geburtstag.* Bern, Switzerland: Haupt, 1955.
Gräßer, Erich. *Albert Schweitzer als Theologe.* Tübingen, Germany: JCB Mohr, 1979.
———. *Albert Schweitzer. Gesammelte Aufsätze.* Edited by Andreas Mühling. Bodenheim, Germany: Philo-Verlag, 1997.
Griffith, Nancy S., and Laura Person. *An International Bibliography.* Boston: G. K. Hall, 1981.
Günzler, Claus. *Albert Schweitzer. Einführung in sein Denken.* Munich, Germany: C. H. Beck, 1996.
Pojman, Louis P., ed. *Life and Death. A Reader in Moral Problems.* Boston: Jones and Bartlett, 1993.
Seaver, George. *Albert Schweitzer. The Man and His Mind.* London: Adam and Charles Black, 1947.

ANDREAS MÜHLING

SCHWENCKFELD, CASPAR (1489–1561)

German spiritualist reformer. Schwenckfeld was a noble and a courtier in his native Silesia. He became a follower of MARTIN LUTHER in 1519. In 1525 he broke with Luther over the Eucharist (see LORD'S SUPPER). Pressured by Lutheran and Catholic authorities, in 1529 Schwenckfeld went into lifelong exile. Schwenckfeld was distressed by the splintering of the church into competing confessions, and he argued that a visible true church had not existed since the death of the Apostles and that only divine intervention, a new Pentecost, could reestablish it. He denied the CHURCH, the CLERGY, the SACRAMENTS, or even the BIBLE any role in producing saving faith. His followers in South Germany were primarily of the upper classes. The Silesian Schwenckfelder movement, however, embraced entire communities and still survives in Pennsylvania.

Schwenckfeld was born in 1489 at his family's estate in Ossig. He attended university at Cologne (1505) and Frankfurt/Oder (1507), although he left without a degree, as was usual for students of his rank, and in 1510 began his career at court. Responding to Luther's teaching, the young courtier underwent in 1519 the first of several "divine visitations" *(Heimsuchungen)*. These events combined revelation or illumination with a wrenching CONVERSION experience. Schwenckfeld became an important lay leader of the Silesian Lutheran movement. However, Schwenckfeld was disappointed by the lack of moral improvement brought by Luther's REFORMATION. This provoked his second *Heimsuchung.*

The Eucharistic controversy pitting Luther against ANDREAS KARLSTADT and HULDRYCH ZWINGLI drew Schwenckfeld's attention to the Lord's Supper. Schwenckfeld blamed the missing improvement on confidence in the Lord's Supper to save souls because of Luther's teaching that Christ was present in the bread and wine. Schwenckfeld agreed that if Christ were really present in the bread and wine, the Lord's Supper should in fact bring SALVATION, given that participation in the body and blood of Christ could not fail to cleanse and transform the believer. It was clear, however, that not everyone who received the Lord's Supper manifested such a change. After all, the DEVIL entered into Judas after Judas partook of the bread at the Last Supper. Christ could not be in the Outer Supper, but must be received directly in an Inner Supper. At Schwenckfeld's request and as the result of divine revelation, the humanist Valentin Crautwald provided a new exegesis of the applicable biblical texts using his knowledge of Greek and Hebrew. A 1525 visit to Wittenberg failed to procure Luther's agreement to Schwenckfeld's Eucharistic theology and Crautwald's biblical interpretation. Instead Luther and PHILIPP MELANCHTHON began to warn against the Silesians.

During 1525 and 1526, influenced by Crautwald, Schwenckfeld developed a thoroughgoing SPIRITUAL-ISM. Schwenckfeld's third *Heimsuchung* (1527) ratified his repudiation of "external" Christianity that he identified with Luther. Schwenckfeld's symbolic interpretation of the Lord's Supper was quite similar to the position of Swiss and South German Reformers such as JOHANNES OECOLAMPADIUS and MARTIN BUCER, although Schwenckfeld also applied similar reasoning to BAPTISM, the church, and the Bible. The Christian did not only commune directly with Christ through the Spirit in the Lord's Supper; the Spirit also inspired saving FAITH directly, not through PREACHING or the Bible. Only after faith was infused could the Christian use the Scriptures with profit. The Outer Word, the Outer Baptism, and Outer Supper merely reflected the Inner Word, Inner Baptism, and Inner Supper that the Christian received directly and that created a new human capable of leading a visibly Christian life. Reliance on the Outer Word and Sacraments produced a dead faith that neither changed the inner person nor produced newness of life.

Schwenckfeld's emphasis on participation in the body and blood of Christ in the Inner Eucharist made his CHRISTOLOGY his most distinctive teaching. He and his followers often described themselves as Confessors of the Glorified Christ. Schwenckfeld taught that God was Father to Christ both in his divinity and humanity. After Christ's death and glorification, his humanity became fully one with the Godhead. Participation in that humanity, and through it the divinity, saved and divinized Christians.

Condemned by both Lutherans and Catholics, Schwenckfeld was forced to leave Silesia in 1529. Despite an initially warm welcome in Strasbourg, he was soon at odds with the clergy. Schwenckfeld's Spiritualism led him to advocate religious TOLERATION and to oppose state churches as unchristian. When combined with his dismissal of the outward church, Schwenckfeld's position made him a threat to the new Protestant churches in the cities of GERMANY and SWITZERLAND. He was asked to leave Strasbourg in 1533. The vehemence of the clergy of Ulm also led that city to expel him. For the rest of his life he remained peripatetic, spending varying periods of time in cities and in the castles of nobles sympathetic to him. He died in Ulm in 1563.

Schwenckfeld built a network of landed nobles and urban patricians throughout South Germany. With them he conducted an extensive correspondence, much of which survives. WOMEN were especially prominent recipients of his letters, and often were the leaders of Schwenckfelder groups. He seemed especially popular with physicians and lawyers. Because of his many powerful supporters, he was also able to publish extensively, much to the chagrin of his clerical opponents. His books won him disciples among the middle classes in the cities, and this put him in direct competition with Anabaptist groups. Although often categorized with the Anabaptists, Schwenckfeld's controversy with PILGRAM MARPECK made clear the differences separating ANABAPTISM and Schwenckfeld's Spiritualism.

See also Lutheranism, Germany

References and Further Reading

Primary Sources:

Schwenckfeld, Caspar. *Corpus Schwenckfeldianorum.* Leipzig, Germany: Breitkopf & Hartel, 1907–1961.
———. *Commentary on the Augsburg Confession.* Pennsburg, PA: Schwenkfelder Library, 1982.
———. *The Correspondence of Caspar Schwenckfeld of Ossig and the Landgrave Philip of Hesse, 1535–1561.* Leipzig, Germany: Breitkopf & Hartel, 1908.

Secondary Sources:

Erb, Peter E., ed. *Schwenckfeld and Early Schwenkfeldianism.* Pennsburg, PA: Schwenkfelder Library, 1986.
McLaughlin, R. Emmet. *Caspar Schwenckfeld: Reluctant Radical.* New Haven, CT: Yale University Press, 1986.
———. *The Freedom of the Spirit, Social Privilege, and Religious Dissent: Caspar Schwenckfeld and the Schwenckfelders.* Baden-Baden, Germany: Éditions Valentin Koerner, 1996.
Schantz, Douglas. *Crautwald and Erasmus. A Study in Humanism and Radical Reform in Sixteenth Century Silesia.* Baden-Baden, Germany: Éditions Valentin Koerner, 1992.
Weigelt, Horst. *The Schwenkfelders in Silesia.* Translated by Peter C. Erb. Pennsburg, PA: Schwenkfelder Library, 1985.

R. EMMET MCLAUGHLIN

SCIENCE

The origins of modern science are usually traced to seventeenth-century Europe. The fact that the rise of science follows closely upon the Protestant REFORMATION has led to considerable speculation about the impact of Protestantism on the emergence of modern science, and on the ways in which Protestant doctrines and practices may have encouraged the development of the sciences. The Protestant work ethic, theological voluntarism, Protestant anthropology, biblical literalism, and antisacramentalism are aspects of Protestantism that have been plausibly linked to the emergence of modern science in the seventeenth century. The subsequent relationship between Protestantism and science throughout the eighteenth and early nineteenth centuries was mostly positive, largely because of a strong tradition of natural theology that informed the natural sciences. From the middle of the nineteenth century, however, the advent of evolutionary theory and the growing influence and prestige of the sciences together provoked diverse reactions from different sectors within Protestantism. The historical interactions of Protestantism and science are an important aspect of the history of modernity.

The Merton Thesis

As early as the seventeenth century, figures associated with the new sciences drew attention to possible connections between Protestantism and the new forms of natural philosophy. In the seminal work *The Advancement of Learning* (1605), FRANCIS BACON maintained that the reformation of the Christian church was part of a more comprehensive reformation of knowledge that had been ordained by providence to take place at this time. Arguments suggesting a common origin in divine providence for parallel reformations in religion and learning were not uncommon among Protestant thinkers in the seventeenth century. Not until the twentieth century, however, were formal attempts made to establish more direct causal connections between Protestantism and the emergence of modern science. In the 1930s the sociologist Robert Merton identified a strong link between Puritan commitment and scientific achievement. Merton argued that Protestants, and Puritans in particular, were disproportionally represented in the ranks of seventeenth-century scientists, pointing out that of the ten figures who formed the nucleus of the Royal Society in its formative stages, seven were Puritans. By 1663, he observed, almost two-thirds of the Society were Puritans at a period during which Puritans constituted a minority in the general population. To account for this apparently remarkable correlation, Merton invoked the "Weber–Tawney" thesis, which associated the rise of capitalism with the "Protestant work ethic" (see MAX WEBER). Merton suggested that the same "this-worldly asceticism," which inspired Puritans to more energetic economic activity, also promoted an engagement with the natural world and motivated diligent, scientific enquiry.

The Merton thesis has not proven convincing to all historians. The term "puritan" is problematic, and it has often been pointed out that a number of the individuals Merton identified as "puritans" had broader religious commitments than those suggested by this narrow designation. Moreover, many of the pioneers of early modern science—JOHANNES KEPLER, Galileo Galilei, René Descartes, and William Harvey—had made their most important contributions well before the ascendancy of PURITANISM, a movement that was in any case typically English. Galileo and Descartes, of course, were Catholics, as were other leading figures in the new sciences. Such criticisms allow for a more general link between Protestantism and science, and even for the possibility that Protestantism might have provided fertile ground for the development of science once it had been established, but they cast some doubt on the nexus of the Calvinist doctrine of ELECTION, the Protestant work ethic, and scientific activity.

Voluntarism, Original Sin, and Experimental Science

Another widely held view that links Protestantism with the development of empirical science is the "voluntarism and science" thesis. Theological voluntarism is generally understood as the DOCTRINE according to which God's will is his primary attribute, and is prior to his reason and goodness. For the voluntarist none of God's acts is necessitated by such considerations as wisdom and goodness. In the moral realm this means that what is good is so only because God wills it. In the physical realm voluntarism is thought to entail the view that all events that occur in NATURE do so contingently, and it follows that nature must be investigated empirically. To put it another way, for the voluntarist, God could have instituted any one of an infinite range of natural orders. To determine which of these God actually chose, recourse must be had to observation of nature. Moreover, because God's choices in this regard were not driven by reasons, rational speculation can provide no insights into the particular laws that God chose to institute in the physical realm. Voluntarism is said to have originated among certain late medieval thinkers, and is associated with the Protestant reformers. It is commonly asserted that the promotion of a voluntarist conception of God on the part of Protestant theologians provided one of the metaphysical foundations for the development of empirical science.

Aspects of this view have also been subjected to criticism. Whether voluntarism can be characterized as a typically Protestant theological position is open to question, not least because such prominent Catholic natural philosophers as Pierre Gassendi and Descartes were also voluntarists. The case of Descartes further complicates the issue, given that not only was he an extreme voluntarist but, unlike Gassendi and most other voluntarists, he was famously committed to rationalism. Thus, for Descartes, at least some fundamental laws of nature could be known through reason alone, without empirical investigation of natural states of affairs. The case of Descartes weakens any thesis of an exclusive connection between Protestantism, voluntarism, and empiricism. Yet there is little doubt that voluntarism played an important role in the early modern development of the concept of laws of nature, a concept of central importance in modern science. The Aristotelian science of the Middle Ages typically sought explanations in terms of the inherent properties of physical objects. It tended, moreover, to be qualitative rather than quantitative. During this period the domain of "natural laws" had been the moral rather than the physical realm. Laws of nature were then typically understood as universal moral principles that could be known through the exercise of reason (see NATURAL LAW). The early modern period witnessed the extension of the idea of natural laws to the physical world, and voluntarism was central to this development. The notion that God directly exercised control over nature through the external imposition of mathematical laws replaced the older view of a natural world that was ordered according to the intrinsic properties of self-governing matter. Inasmuch as science now concerns itself with the discovery of laws of nature, it is indebted to the voluntarist conception of a divine legislator who imposed laws on the physical universe. Although it is clear that such Protestant thinkers as ROBERT BOYLE and ISAAC NEWTON played a key role in this transition, voluntarist contributions to this new science of nature were not confined to Protestant thinkers, as the cases of Gassendi and Descartes illustrate.

Another explanation for the rise of experimental science that finds a special place for the role of Protestant thought relates to the reformers' stress on the limited capacities of the fallen human mind. MARTIN LUTHER and JOHN CALVIN both argued that the human mind had been corrupted as a consequence of the Fall—a view that differed from the standard Thomist position according to which Adam's mind had merely suffered a privation of supernatural gifts. This stance also contrasted with that of Aristotle, who had assumed that the mind and the senses were generally reliable, and that science could therefore be premised on commonsense observations of nature in its normal state. The more pessimistic assessments of human cognitive capacities that the reformers promoted informed the mitigated skepticism of what came to be known as "the experimental philosophy," championed by Francis Bacon, Robert Boyle, and the Royal Society. This inductive approach eschewed the certainty and confidence that characterized both the uncritical empiricism of Aristotelian science and the optimistic rationalism of Descartes. For the experimentalists, knowledge of nature would come as the end result of long and laborious procedures and the cumulative labors of many generations. Even then, it would produce knowledge that was probable at best. Related to this approach was the conviction that because nature itself had fallen, it was no longer transparent to human investigators in the way it had been for Adam in the Garden of Eden—hence, again, the need to manipulate nature experimentally and to probe its secrets more actively than had previously been thought necessary. In this manner the renewed emphasis on the Fall and on its cognitive effects that followed in the wake of the Reformation helped shape the experimental approach to nature that plays so important a role in the history of the natural sciences.

Science, Scripture, and the Symbolic View of Nature

It is often supposed that an emphasis on the AUTHORITY of scripture, particularly when combined with a preference for literalism, will inevitably give rise to conflicts with scientific conceptions of nature. In the sixteenth and seventeenth centuries, however, literal approaches to the interpretation of scripture actually made an important contribution to the revolution that was taking place in the sciences. From the time of the Church Fathers, and for most of the Middle Ages, the literal sense of scripture formed the foundation on which figurative or allegorical readings were constructed. Although in principle the literal sense enjoyed primacy, in practice allegorical readings of scripture often displaced the literal. This tendency to elevate the importance of nonliteral readings was vigorously opposed during the Renaissance by both humanist scholars and Protestant reformers, who insisted that scripture be interpreted primarily in its grammatical or literal sense.

The relevance of this for the rise of science lies in the fact that the allegorical mentality of medieval scholars was premised on a particular view of nature. Allegory entailed the view that natural objects bore moral and theological meanings. As both Augustine and Thomas Aquinas had explained, determination of the literal sense of scripture lay in identifying the objects to which the words referred. The allegorical meaning, however, had to do with the meanings of the objects. In the literal sense words referred to objects; in the allegorical sense objects referred to other objects. Allegorical readings thus extended to the natural world, which was at that time regarded primarily as a locus of transcendental truths. Nature was scrutinized primarily for its meanings, rather than being understood in terms of causal or mathematical relations. The demise of allegory in the sixteenth and seventeenth centuries—a situation to which the Protestant preference for the literal sense was a major contributing factor—was thus accompanied by the need to reorder a natural world now evacuated of its rich symbolic theological and moral associations. The mathematical sciences along with new classificatory schemes of natural history that we associate with the new sciences came to fill the vacuum left by the collapse of the symbolic world of the Middle Ages. The rise of biblical literalism was thus one of the factors that paved the way for a scientific understanding of nature.

Other features of Protestantism, in particular a suspicion of images and of the visual realm, further contributed to the decline of the symbolic understanding of nature. Central to medieval WORSHIP had been the spectacle of the mass, and religious experience was mediated by additional sacramental performances, along with images, statuary, and VESTMENTS. The reformers had not only vested authority in the literal words of a single text, but had changed the emphasis of worship to the PREACHING of the word. As a further consequence of their elevation of word over visual representation, "idolatrous" images and statues were replaced by inscriptions of the Decalogue or other passages of scripture. Protestant reforms thus utterly transformed the sensory context of religious worship, and arguably revolutionized religious experience generally. In all of this Protestant reformers evinced a profound distrust of the visual sense, which was held responsible for idolatry in religion and illicit curiosity in matters of the sciences. This suspicion of all things visual was inevitably felt in the empirical sciences, and complemented the general skepticism about the possibility of knowledge that arose out of the more pessimistic anthropology of the reformers. Experimentation, the use of magnifying instruments, the development of protocols for judging observation reports, communal witnessing, emphasis on the corporate nature of the scientific enterprise, and the development of formal theories of vision were all part of a response to the crisis of visual representation precipitated by the Protestant Reformation.

Biblical literalism also promoted the new sciences of the early modern period in another way. New, purely historical readings of the creation narratives in Genesis provided seventeenth-century thinkers with powerful motivating images for pursuing the natural sciences. Adam was thought to have possessed a perfect knowledge of all sciences, a knowledge lost to posterity when he fell from grace and was expelled from the Garden of Eden. Seventeenth-century scientists such as Bacon and his successors in the Royal Society saw as their goal the regaining of the scientific knowledge of the first man. Indeed, for these individuals the whole scientific enterprise was an integral part of a redemptive endeavor that, along with the Christian religion, was to help restore the human race to its original perfection. The biblical account of the creation, shorn of allegorical elements, provided these early scientists with an important source of motivation, and in an age still thoroughly committed to traditional Christianity the new science was to gain social legitimacy on account of these religious associations.

The Age of Physico-Theology

Throughout the Middle Ages, plants, animals, and stones had served the human race not merely for practical purposes but had represented moral and theological truths. All of this had been part of the symbolic and sacramental view of medieval Catholicism. The denial of symbolic functions to natural objects, which came in the wake of the Reformation, brought with it a renewed emphasis on the practical uses of the creatures. It was still held that God had made the creatures for human use, but these uses were increasingly understood in terms of how they might be exploited for practical purposes rather than what they might have represented symbolically. Throughout the eighteenth century and well into the nineteenth, an important justification for scientific investigation was that these practices enabled human investigators to discern the practical uses of natural objects that God had intended for God's human creatures.

At the same time, some theological truths were still held to be apparent in nature. If animals and plants no longer symbolized theological and moral truths, they nonetheless constituted evidence of God's wisdom and goodness. The study of nature thus served not merely to minister to physical human needs, but remained in some sense a theological activity. This was particularly so in ENGLAND, where a strong tradition of natural theology flourished. The study of nature was thought to demonstrate the wisdom and power of God, and natural theology and natural history were virtually indistinguishable. To investigate the natural world was to study God's providential handiwork, and the discipline of natural history consisted largely of the enumeration of instances of divine design or contrivance. So intimate was the connection between theology and the study of nature that a new hybrid discipline known as "physico-theology" emerged at this time. WILLIAM PALEY's *Natural Theology* (1801) is the best known example of the genre. It became one of the standard texts at CAMBRIDGE UNIVERSITY, and influenced the young Charles Darwin during his student days there. For their part, Catholic thinkers, too, contributed to this tradition, although not perhaps with the same enthusiasm as English clergymen. Relations between Protestantism and science throughout the eighteenth century and for much of the nineteenth thus tended to be congenial and close.

The Conflict Myth

Two developments in the latter half of the nineteenth century and one in the early twentieth century were to disturb the happy alliance represented by the discipline of physico-theology. First, the appearance in 1859 of Darwin's *Origin of Species* seemed to challenge both biblical authority and theological claims about the uniqueness of human beings. Second, the nineteenth century witnessed the emergence of the professional scientist and the beginnings of a concerted campaign to improve the social standing of the sciences. Attempts were made to give science a central place in the university curriculum, to establish mechanisms for its public funding, and through the formation of professional societies, generally to enhance its social prestige. The final development, which took place early in the twentieth century, was the emergence in the UNITED STATES of a conservative form of evangelical Protestantism that became known as FUNDAMENTALISM. Together, these factors led to a new phase in the relationship between Protestantism and science.

With regard to DARWINISM, it must be pointed out that nineteenth-century criticisms came from a variety of sources, not all of them religious. As was the case with Galileo's advocacy of the heliocentric hypothesis, there were significant disputes within the scientific community itself over the merits of the theory. Two issues proved controversial: the mechanism of natural selection, and the method that Darwin had used to arrive at his theory. By the third decade of the twentieth century, however, most scientists had come to accept both natural selection and the Darwinian hypothetico-deductive method. To a degree, the reactions of both Catholics and the major Protestant denominations mirrored those of the scientific community. Genesis was interpreted in ways that could be reconciled with evolutionary theory, and it was argued that the special status of human beings was unaffected by a common ancestry with apes. Up until the 1930s many conservative Protestants regarded the "days" of creation set out in the first Genesis creation narrative as long periods of time, and were thus able to give qualified support to evolutionary thought.

As for the nineteenth-century attempts to raise the profile of the sciences, one common strategy called for the complete elimination of all religious and moral elements from the sphere of the natural sciences. Science was to be a secular discipline, and its methods were to be informed by methodological agnosticism. This development coincided neatly with Darwinism,

which had made the alliance between natural religion and natural history superfluous. Some went further in prosecuting this agenda to make the additional claim that science and religion were, in fact, inimical. Andrew Dickson White's *History of the Warfare between Science and Religion* (1896) and John Draper's *History of the Conflict between Religion and Science* (1875) famously advanced the thesis that throughout history religion had been a regressive force that had obstructed scientific progress. Thus was the myth of an ongoing warfare between science and religion born. Although its historical merits are dubious, its legacy is pervasive, and it continues to attract adherents. Subsequent fundamentalist rejections of science also fueled the perception of conflict. Equally significant is the fact that the improved fortunes of the sciences—the consequence of these nineteenth-century developments—effected a subtle inversion of the power relations between science and religion. Scientists assumed the mantle of authority that once had rested on the CLERGY. By the end of the nineteenth century science had become a cultural force to be reckoned with.

Twentieth-Century Developments

The newly established independence of science, along with its growing prestige, led to a number of reactions within the Christian church. On the one hand, over the course of the twentieth century, Protestant and Catholic thinkers alike have sought to reconcile theological doctrines with the findings and methods of the sciences. WOLFHART PANNENBERG is perhaps the most prominent Protestant theologian to attempt such a rapprochement. The beginning of the twenty-first century has seen the development of a burgeoning field of "science and theology" that has attracted the attention of theologians and theologically inclined scientists. This development represents not only a defensive apologetic strategy on the part of some theologians, but a genuine rekindling of interest in theological issues on the part of some within the scientific community. In certain instances, the primacy of the sciences has led to major reformulation or even abandonment of fundamental Christian doctrines. PROCESS THEOLOGY might be regarded as an instance of the latter.

On the other hand, the perceived displacement of religion from the center of the cultural life of the West has provoked an entirely different response from some conservative Protestants, particularly in North America. Fundamentalist groups, to some degree correctly, regard science as having been responsible for the increasing marginalization of Christianity in the modern West and for its waning influence in public life.

For such groups science, and more specifically the teachings of evolutionary scientists, represent a threat to the literal truths of Scripture and to important Christian beliefs, and as a consequence must be vigorously resisted. By the same token fundamentalists have also rejected the "liberal" theological positions of fellow Protestants who, in their view, have too easily capitulated to the sciences and have underplayed genuine areas of conflict. Paradoxically, even fundamentalists have tacitly acknowledged the cultural prestige of the sciences, representing themselves as adhering to an alternative scientific thesis—CREATION SCIENCE. If biblical literalism helped to pave the way for the emergence of scientific culture in the early modern period and provided motivations for its first practitioners, the same cannot be said for the twentieth century.

Some Qualifications and Concluding Remarks

General claims about purported relationships between Protestantism and science need to be viewed in the light of four important qualifications. First, caution needs to be exercised in taking at face value the claims of contemporary historical actors for the positive influence of Protestantism on the development of science. In the seventeenth century, when tension between rival modes of Christianity in Europe was at a high point, utterances about some supposed connection between Protestantism and the advancement of knowledge could function as anti-Catholic polemic. It suited the purposes of Protestant apologists to portray Catholicism as dogmatic, authoritarian, and backward looking. Similarly polemical motives are apparent in the distorted historical treatments written by the nineteenth-century progenitors of the warfare model, although in this instance, criticism was extended to religion generally. It is important, in short, to consider likely sources of historical bias in accounts of the historical relations between science and religion.

Second, although this article has alluded to possible positive influences of Protestantism on the development of early modern science, its silence with regard to Catholicism should not be interpreted to mean that no contribution was forthcoming from that quarter. Mention has already been made of Descartes and Gassendi. A comprehensive account of the relations between science and Christianity would include a more complete account of Catholic contributions.

Third, "Protestantism" is not now, if it ever was, a monolithic phenomenon. The range of attitudes toward science exhibited by Protestants from the end of the nineteenth century is sufficient testimony to this principle. Ideally, claims about relationships between Protestantism and science should specify which Protestants, in what place, and during which historical period. Moreover, in seeking to identify possible historical influences it is important to distinguish Protestant doctrines from Protestant practices. With respect to the Reformation, likewise, the social and political conditions that ensued in its wake need to be considered separately from the explicit intentions of its principal architects. To speak of the impact of Protestantism, then, is to have regard to its doctrines, its practices, and the conditions that it generated. These are not the same and may have different and even contrary consequences.

Fourth, similar considerations apply to science. There is a popular image of "science" as a unitary entity that endures over time, and that generates reliable knowledge through the application of "the scientific method." However, the cultural institution "science," as we currently understand it, is really the product of the nineteenth century. It was then that the term "scientist" first appeared, that professional associations were formed, that the sciences began to consolidate their place in the university curriculum, and that the study of nature became a genuinely secular enterprise. This is not say that the seventeenth-century developments usually referred to as "the scientific revolution" are not central to the genealogy of modern science. However, inasmuch as scientific and religious concerns were inextricably bound together at this time, the study of nature was of necessity a somewhat different activity from the secular sciences of late modernity. In addition, now more than ever, there is a plurality of sciences each with a distinct subject matter and range of methodologies. Indeed, it is these differences that account for the fact that it is evolutionary biology that generates the most conflict in science–religion discussions, whereas cosmology tends to be cordially embraced as a useful ally—almost the reverse of the situation of the eighteenth century.

With these qualifications in mind, three broad conclusions can be drawn about Protestantism and science. First, there are good reasons to suppose that Protestantism played a significant role in the emergence of modern science, both because of its doctrines and practices, and as a consequence of the social conditions that it generated. Second, cordial relations between Protestantism and science persisted through the eighteenth century and into the nineteenth. Third, current diversity within both Protestantism and the sciences is reflected in a diversity of relationships.

See also Biblical Inerrancy

References and Further Reading

Brooke, John Hedley. *Science and Religion: Some Historical Perspectives.* Cambridge: Cambridge University Press, 1991.

Cohen, I. Bernard, ed. *Puritanism and the Rise of Modern Science: The Merton Thesis.* New Brunswick, NJ: Rutgers University Press, 1990.

Harrison, Peter. "Original Sin and the Problem of Knowledge in Early Modern Europe." *Journal of the History of Ideas* 63 (2002): 239–259.

———. "Voluntarism and Early Modern Science." *History of Science* 40 (2002): 63–89.

———. *The Bible, Protestantism and the Rise of Natural Science.* Cambridge: Cambridge University Press, 1998.

Klaaren, Eugene. *Religious Origins of Modern Science.* Grand Rapids, MI: Wm. B. Eerdmans, 1977.

Lindberg, David, and Ronald Numbers, eds. *God and Nature: Historical Essays on the Encounter between Christianity and Science.* Berkeley: University of California Press, 1986.

Livingstone, David N., D. G. Hart, and Mark A. Noll, eds. *Evangelicals and Science in Historical Perspective.* New York: Oxford University Press, 1999.

Merton, Robert K. *Science, Technology and Society in Seventeenth-Century England.* New York: Harper, 1970.

Osler, Margaret. *Divine Will and the Mechanical Philosophy: Gassendi and Descartes on Contingency and Necessity in the Created World.* Cambridge: Cambridge University Press, 1994.

Russell, Colin A. "The Conflict Metaphor and its Social Origins." *Science and Christian Belief* 1 (1989): 3–26.

Turner, Frank. "The Victorian Conflict between Science and Religion: A Professional Dimension." *Isis* 49 (1978): 356–376.

Webster. Charles. *The Great Instauration: Science Medicine and Reform 1626–1660.* London: Duckworth, 1975.

PETER HARRISON

SCIENTISM

Scientism in the strongest sense is the view that everything could and should be understood in terms of science. Science is then typically interpreted in a narrow way, referring only to the natural sciences. A weaker version of scientism holds that as much as possible could and should be understood in terms of science. It is assumed that there is something problematic, inferior, or even irrational about activities or enterprises that could not be understood in such a way.

In what follows a background to scientism is given, different versions of scientism are distinguished, and the criticism that scientism has received especially from Protestant thinkers is presented.

Background

The overwhelming intellectual and practical successes of SCIENCE have led some people to think that there are no real limits to the competence of science, no limits to what can be achieved in the name of science. There is nothing outside the domain of science, nor is there any area of human life to which science cannot successfully be applied. A scientific account of anything and everything constitutes the full story of the universe and its inhabitants. Or, if there are limits to the scientific enterprise, the idea is that science at least sets the boundaries for what we humans can ever know about reality. This is the view of scientism.

The historical roots of scientism can probably be traced to the ENLIGHTENMENT with its ideology of progress and perfectibility. Perhaps its most well-known historical advocate is the French social philosopher Auguste Comte (1798–1857) and his attempt to create a religion based on science: the "Religion of Humanity." Another interesting and far-reaching attempt to have science take over many of the functions of religion and thus itself become a religion was made by the German chemist and Nobel Prize-winner Wilhelm Ostwald (1853–1932). He argued for science as an "Ersatzreligion"—a substitute religion. Yet many different forms of scientism have emerged over the last three centuries.

During the last three decades, an increasing number of distinguished natural scientists, including Peter Atkins, Richard Dawkins, Carl Sagan, and Edward O. Wilson (as well as philosophers like Daniel D. Dennett and Michael Ruse), have advocated scientism in one form or another. Besides receiving a number of prestigious scientific prizes and awards, these scientists have sold an enormous number of books. Their views have been discussed in newspapers and have been broadcast on radio and television. If scientism has been around for a while, the great impact these advocates of scientism have had on popular Western CULTURE is new. They have brought not only science, but also scientism, into the living room of ordinary people.

Different Versions of Scientism

All advocates of scientism believe that the boundaries of science (i.e., the natural sciences) could and should be expanded in such a way that something not previously understood as science can become a part of science. Thus a possible synonym for scientism is *scientific expansionism*. How exactly the boundaries of science should be expanded and what more precisely it is that is to be included within science are issues on which there is disagreement, and for this reason, scientism cannot immediately be equated with scientific naturalism or materialism (although such an equation is often correct). *Scientific naturalism* or *materialism* is roughly the view that all genuine knowledge about reality is to be found through science and science alone, and that matter (or matter and energy) is the fundamental reality in the universe.

The most common way of defining scientism, however, is to say that it is the view that science tells us everything there is to know about reality. The epistemological version of scientism is an attempt to expand the boundaries of science in such a way that all genuine (in contrast to apparent) knowledge must either be scientific or at least be reducible to scientific knowledge. Everything outside science is therefore taken as a matter of mere belief and subjective opinion. Consequently, the agenda of the scientists who accept this form of scientism is to strive to incorporate many other areas of human life within the sciences, so that rational consideration and acquisition of knowledge can be made possible in these fields as well. This is a part of the mission of the scientistic faith: In a demon-haunted world, science is the candle in the dark. *Epistemic scientism* raises an obvious challenge to Christianity (or any other religion). Christianity could give us knowledge about God, human beings, and the world only if those knowledge claims could be confirmed by the methods of the natural sciences, because genuine knowledge—according to this version of scientism—could be obtained only through such methods.

Another way of expanding the boundaries of science is to maintain that science not only can fully explain morality, but also can replace traditional ETHICS and tell us how we ought to behave. Science, contrary to what we previously have thought, can justify ethical norms and beliefs and provide us with a new, scientific ethic. However, for a claim to be scientistic in this sense, it must maintain more than that science is relevant to ethics. Nobody would deny that. Rather, it must state that science is the sole (or at least by far the most important) source for developing a moral theory and explaining moral behavior. To the extent that advocates of *normative scientism* offer an account of morality that contradicts a Christian understanding of morality, it creates a challenge to Christianity. So, for instance, if science (as some evolutionary biologists claim) can show that morality is an illusion and ultimately about selfishness or maximizing one's reproductive success, then genuine altruism of the Mother Teresa kind seems not to be possible or at least irrational. But, according to Christians, altruistic people such as Mother Teresa behave rather in the most rational way, because they actually reflect the unselfishly loving character of God.

Perhaps the most astonishing kind of scientism is the one that expresses a belief in the salvific mission of science. The idea is that because we have modern science, we no longer have to resort to superstition when faced with such deep problems as "Is there a meaning to life?", "What are we here for?", and "What is human nature?", because science is capable of dealing with all these questions and constitutes in addition the only alternative to superstition. Science can be our new religion and answer our existential questions. Indeed, we ought to become "science believers" and leave our traditional religions behind. Scientism in this form is the idea of SALVATION through science alone. *Salvific scientism* is the view that science alone cannot only fully explain traditional religion and but also replace it.

Criticism of Scientism

Scientism (including scientific naturalism) has been severely criticized by many Protestant thinkers, including Ian Barbour, Alvin Plantinga, Huston Smith, Mikael Stenmark, and Keith Ward, as well as by other groups of scientists and scholars. The critical responses have differed, depending on what form of scientism is being analyzed and what understanding of Christianity is being defended. The main criticism, however, is that the advocates of scientism, in their attempt to expand the boundaries of science, base their arguments not merely on scientific, but also on philosophical premises, and thus scientism is not science proper, but rather naturalism or atheism disguised.

Perhaps the most embarrassing problem for spokespersons for scientism is that one of its central claims seems to be self-refuting. The difficulty is that the scientistic belief that we can only know what science can tell us (epistemic scientism) seems to be something that science cannot tell us. How can one set up a scientific experiment to demonstrate the truth of that claim? It seems impossible. But we cannot *know* that scientific knowledge is the only mode of knowledge unless we are able to determine this by scientific means. This is so simply because science—according to epistemic scientism—sets the limits for what we can possibly know. Hence the claim that we can only know what science can tell us falsifies itself. If it is true, then it is false.

See also Natural Law

References and Further Reading

Atkins, Peter. "The Limitless Power of Science," in *Nature's Imagination: The Frontiers of Scientific Vision*. Edited by John Cornwell. Oxford: Oxford University Press, 1995.

Dawkins, Richard. *The Selfish Gene*. 2nd ed. Oxford, Oxford University Press, 1989.

Midgley, Mary. *Science as Salvation*. London: Routledge, 1992.

Smith, Huston. *Why Religion Matters: The Fate of the Human Spirit in an Age of Disbelief*. San Francisco: HarperCollins, 2001.

Sorell, Tom. *Scientism: Philosophy and the Infatuation with Science*. London: Routledge, 1991.

Stenmark, Mikael. *Scientism: Science, Ethics and Religion.* Aldershot, UK: Ashgate, 2001.

Ward, Keith. *God, Change and Necessity.* Oxford, UK: Oneworld Publications, 1996.

Wilson, Edward O. *On Human Nature.* Cambridge, MA: Harvard University Press, 1978.

MIKAEL STENMARK

SCOFIELD REFERENCE BIBLE

The *Scofield Reference Bible* emerged as one of the most influential texts in twentieth-century evangelicalism and fundamentalism shortly after Oxford University Press published the first edition in 1909. Conceptualized and compiled by the Reverend Cyrus Ingerson Scofield (1843–1921), the BIBLE contained a series of connected topical references known as "chain links," extensive annotations, attractive paragraphing, and supplementary material aimed at explaining and clarifying the KING JAMES VERSION text for average readers. Theologically, Scofield's commentary supported, reflected, and somewhat modified the views associated with John Darby and the Plymouth Brethren, dividing the Bible into seven historical periods known as dispensations and arguing for the pre-tribulation secret rapture of the true Christian church. The reference bible proved extraordinary popular and has sold tens of millions of copies since its initial appearance. Scofield himself revised and prepared a second edition in 1917, and Oxford issued a third edition in 1967 under the supervision of an editorial board that consisted of leading evangelical and fundamentalist scholars.

Cyrus Ingerson Scofield

Details concerning Scofield's life remain somewhat sketchy and controversial. Supporters and detractors have contested various biographical facts and drawn deeply contrasting portraits of the man, but several common themes and elements emerge from their accounts. Scofield was born on August 19, 1843, in Lenawee County, Michigan, not far from the Ohio border, where his parents farmed and operated a sawmill. At some point, probably in the late 1850s, Scofield migrated to Wilson County, Tennessee, and at the outbreak of the CIVIL WAR, enlisted in the Confederate army, serving one year with the Tennessee infantry. By the late 1860s, he had relocated to St. Louis, married into a prominent local family, and commenced the study of law under the patronage of his wealthy in-laws. Politics and legal work occupied Scofield for the next decade as he moved his family to Kansas, earned election to the state legislature as a Republican, and was appointed U.S. attorney for Kansas. Personal problems, legal troubles, and continual

bouts with alcohol apparently cut short his political career in the early 1870s, and Scofield subsequently moved back to St. Louis, leaving his family behind. His wife ultimately secured a final divorce decree in 1883, retaining custody of the couple's two children.

At some point in 1879, Scofield apparently underwent a conversion experience in St. Louis. He began studying Christianity under the prominent Presbyterian minister and ardent dispensationalist James Hall Brookes, assisted in DWIGHT L. MOODY's urban evangelistic campaign, joined the Pilgrim Congregational Church, and became acting director of the St. Louis YMCA. Within a very short time, Scofield earned a considerable reputation with the growing pandenominational coalition of conservative Protestants that would eventually coalesce into the fundamentalist movement. In 1882 the Congregationalist Church's American Home Missions Board for the Southwest called Scofield to Dallas, Texas, where he remarried and spent the next twelve years slowly transforming a struggling congregation into the influential First Congregational Church, subsequently renamed Scofield Memorial Church. After pastoring Moody's Trinitarian Congregational Church in East Northfield, Massachusetts from 1895 through 1902, Scofield returned to Dallas and served basically as an absentee pastor while working on his reference Bible project. Scofield severed his connection with the Dallas church and with congregationalism generally in 1909, perhaps owing to his conviction that the denomination had grown too liberal and modernist in its sympathies. He affiliated with the Southern Presbyterian Church at Paris, Texas, and relocated to Long Island shortly thereafter. Scofield launched a popular correspondence course and night school in New York City and successfully completed his second edition of the *Reference Bible*. Plagued by ill health for the last several years of his life, Scofield died at Douglaston, New York, on July 24, 1921.

Scofield's prominence in evangelical and fundamentalist circles owed principally to his cultivation of, and participation in, a growing network of conservative Christian institutions that began to take shape in the late nineteenth century. He participated regularly in the annual Bible conferences that drew together a national evangelical cohort interested in exploring prophecy belief and debating premillennial themes each summer in pleasant resort settings. Scofield also developed his own correspondence courses based on his interpretations of biblical text. Indeed, he proved instrumental in conceptualizing, founding, and/or managing several important Protestant institutions, including: Lake Charles College, Northfield Bible Training School, New York Night School of the Bible, Central American Mission, and Philadelphia School of the Bible. His writings reflect a consistent commitment to dispensational premillennialism; his career pattern illustrates his effort to forge a broad Christian coalition that transcended denominational boundaries. The publication of *The Scofield Reference Bible* in 1909 most clearly articulated his theological views and proved to be a critical document in both coalescing conservative Christian sentiment and providing coherence to the somewhat inchoate fundamentalist movement.

First Edition

Scofield's closest friends and associates recalled that he began formulating his plan for a reference bible during the early years of his Dallas pastorate, but that he did not thoroughly commit himself to the endeavor until July 1901, while attending a summer Bible conference at Sea Cliff on Long Island. Evangelical colleagues enthusiastically embraced the concept and encouraged him to persist. Initial financial support came from Alwyn Ball, Jr., a wealthy New York City real estate broker attending the Bible conference, and from John T. Pirie, the Chicago-based department store magnate whose Sea Cliff estate hosted the Christian gathering. Recognizing the need to minimize pastoral responsibilities, Scofield returned to First Congregational Church in Dallas in December 1902 and negotiated a protracted sabbatical. He spent the next several years working on the Bible project, primarily in Europe, where he also established a connection with Henry Frowde, the head of Oxford University Press. Frowde promoted the reference Bible to officials at Oxford's American Branch, and the first edition appeared in 1909.

Several core principles, reflected both in the introduction to the 1909 edition and in discussions with colleagues, undergirded Scofield's work. First, and perhaps foremost, he committed himself to using the King James text rather than the Revised Version of 1885. Although he acknowledged the significance of nineteenth-century biblical scholarship and the discovery of ancient monastic manuscripts in the 1840s and 1850s, Scofield believed that these developments confirmed the essential accuracy of the Authorized Version and that minor corrections might be addressed through emendations and textual notes. The reference Bible thus both confirmed and contributed to the general popularity of the King James Version and, in Scofield's view, allowed him to combine up-to-date scholarly viewpoints with the perceived literary merit of the 1611 translation.

Second, he sought to base his book on the soundest contemporary scholarship, while avoiding interpretations that he viewed as representing mere novelties.

"The Editor disclaims originality," he proudly announced in his introduction, and Scofield clearly intended the reference bible to reflect evangelical orthodoxy rather than to offer interpretive breakthroughs. Accordingly, he assembled an impressive list of consulting editors in order to lend broader credibility to the project, and their names constituted many of the leading conservative voices in early twentieth-century Protestantism: Arno C. Gaebelein (1841–1945), ARTHUR T. PIERSON, James M. Gray, William J. Erdman, Henry G. Weston, Elmore Harris, and W. G. Moorehead. Scofield composed much of the text abroad, working at Oxford, England, and Montreaux, Switzerland where he claimed to have consulted several leading European biblical scholars and have used the most sophisticated academic libraries.

Third, Scofield's distinctive method of linking topical references and concepts throughout the Bible remained in his mind a significant advance over older "unscientific" methods. His chain links allowed readers to systematically trace keywords and themes throughout the Scriptures, thereby creating a sense of unity, consistency, and coherence across the entire text. Scofield especially emphasized prophetic beliefs, carefully linking their exposition in the Hebrew Bible to their fulfillment in the New Testament. Further, Scofield intended the topical references to provide readers with a holistic view of Scripture that discouraged them from drawing hasty generalizations and from quoting material out of context.

Other editorial decisions also differentiated his work from the growing body of biblical commentaries, study helps, and exegetical literature that flooded the early twentieth-century Christian book market. Scofield offered simple and straightforward definitions of such controversial concepts as sin, grace, and justification. Brief introductory notes preceded each book of the Bible, and italicized subheads guided the reader topically through the subsequent text. Explanatory notes appeared on the same page as the concepts under review, thus facilitating ready reference. Difficult and obscure words received pronunciation aids. Throughout his introduction Scofield repeatedly emphasized the average reader as his intended audience and his principal aim involved making the Bible more accessible and understandable to a broader reading public.

In the final analysis, the most distinctive feature of *The Scofield Reference Bible,* and the characteristic that ultimately proved most influential and controversial, involved his incorporation of dispensational beliefs into the annotations. Scofield believed wholeheartedly in the verbal, literal inerrancy of Scripture, and argued that the Bible contained a series of progressive divine revelations that articulated and explained God's dealings with humankind. He divided biblical history into seven broad chronological periods, known as "dispensations." Each dispensation constituted a period of time during which human beings were tested by some specific revelation of God's will and each could be traced to a particular biblical passage that inaugurated a new dispensation. Scofield defined the seven dispensations as follows: Innocence (Genesis 1:28), Conscience (Genesis 3:22), Human Government (Genesis 8:20), Promise (Genesis 12:1), Law (Exodus 19:8), Grace (John 1:17), and Kingdom (Ephesians 1:10).

Subsequent History

Critics initially greeted *The Scofield Reference Bible* with mixed reviews; liberals rejected its intellectual assumptions while some conservatives felt that it relied excessively on good works as a means of salvation and that it suffered from theological inconsistency. Still, after modest but promising initial sales, the volume quickly gained considerable popularity. The prominent consulting editors aggressively promoted the book and it proved especially attractive to participants at Bible conferences and evangelistic campaigns. In 1911, Oxford issued a 300th anniversary commemorative edition of the King James Bible containing Scofield's chain links along with a "carefully corrected text" scrutinized by prominent biblical scholars.

Within a few years, Scofield decided that a completely new and improved revision of his 1909 compilation seemed necessary, and Oxford agreed to issue a second edition in 1917. One major change involved the incorporation of exact dates into the text, based on Archbishop James Ussher's (1581–1656) chronology and pinpointing the date of creation at 4004 B.C. Scofield also incorporated a new section, entitled "A Panoramic View of the Bible," that sought to emphasize unifying themes throughout the Bible and present the compiler's understanding of the relationship between various textual elements. For Scofield, Christ remained at the center of the Bible, and all sixty-six books could be grouped under five thematic concepts: preparation for Christ, constituting the entire Old Testament; manifestation of Jesus in the world, explicated through the Gospels; propagation of Jesus's message, contained in the Acts; explanation of Christ's ministry, described in the Epistles; and consummation of God's work through Christ, revealed in the Apocalypse.

The reference bible remained a best-seller for Oxford into the mid-twentieth century. Oxford University Press offered a complete Scofield product line and numerous foreign language translations appeared. Oxford even contracted with E. Schuyler English (1899–1981), former president of Philadelphia School of the Bible and editor of *Our Hope* magazine, to abridge the annotations into a popular *Pilgrim Edition* (1948), which employed the King James text and was designed primarily for young readers. By 1954 Oxford concluded that recent archaeological discoveries, exegetical advances, and changes in the English language justified a revision of Scofield's work. Accordingly, the press commissioned a third major edition of the reference bible and selected English to chair the editorial committee. The eight other committee members represented the leading fundamentalist and evangelical scholarly institutions in mid-twentieth century America: John F. Walvoord (1910–) of Dallas Theological Seminary, William Culbertson (1905–1991) of Moody Bible Institute, Wilbur M. Smith (1894–1976) of Fuller Theological Seminary, Frank E. Gaebelein of The Stony Brook School, Alva McClain (1888–1968) of Grace Theological Seminary, Clarence E. Mason, Jr., of Philadelphia College of the Bible, Charles L. Feinberg of Talbot Theological Seminary, and Allan MacRae of Faith Theological Seminary.

The 1967 edition retained Scofield's dispensational system, revelatory outlook, and pretribulationist stance. The editors did change the sixth dispensation from "Grace" to "Church Age" and attempted to clarify a related doctrinal issue by carefully noting that salvation in every dispensation depended upon grace through faith. This modification sought to combat critics' claims that Scofield had implied that humanity might be saved through good works rather than faith, and that he limited salvation by grace to one particular dispensation. Other alterations attempted to place the 1967 volume more in conformity with contemporary textual and critical scholarship, as well as with twentieth-century developments in Bible prophecy. The revisers abandoned Ussher's chronology, for example, acknowledging that no date earlier than 2000 B.C. could be accurately fixed and that subsequent dates could only be approximated in most instances.

The editorial committee continued to rely on the King James Version as its biblical text, but it introduced numerous changes designed to make the language more intelligible to a late twentieth-century public. English and his colleagues altered obsolete and archaic words, modernized spellings, changed relative pronouns, and occasionally clarified questionable translation decisions, carefully noting modifications in the text. They also greatly expanded the editorial apparatus, nearly doubling the number of notes to over 1,500, and providing approximately 50,000 cross-references in contrast to the 27,000 in the 1917 edition. The committee also included new maps drawn in accordance with contemporary archaeological and cartographical advances, a concise concordance especially prepared for the revision, revised subheadings that more clearly differentiated editorial commentary from biblical text, and expanded introductions to each book. Sales figures indicate that the 1967 Scofield proved popular, though not as revolutionary or influential as its early twentieth-century predecessors. Oxford estimates that the third edition has sold millions of copies since its appearance, and sales numbered in the tens of thousands annually through the late 1990s. Clearly, *The Scofield Reference Bible* continued to satisfy a loyal audience of theologically conservative Protestants who remained devoted to the King James Version and who sought interpretive aids that remained faithful to dispensationalist teachings.

References and Further Reading

Canfield, Joseph M. *The Incredible Scofield and His Book.* Vallecito, CA: Ross House Books, 1988.

Gaebelein, Arno C. "The Story of *The Scofield Reference Bible,*" *Moody Monthly.* (October 1942 and serially through March 1943).

Gaebelein, Frank E. *The Story of The Scofield Reference Bible, 1909–1959.* New York: Oxford University Press, 1959.

———. *The New Scofield Reference Bible: Its Background and Making.* New York: Oxford University Press, 1967.

Scofield, C. I., ed. *The Scofield Reference Bible.* New York: Oxford University Press, 1909.

———, ed. *The New Scofield Reference Bible.* New York: Oxford University Press, 1967.

Trumbull, Charles Gallaudet. *The Life Story of C. I. Scofield.* New York: Oxford University Press, 1920.

PETER J. WOSH

SCOTLAND

Contempt and Scottish Protestantism seem to have gone hand in hand. Viewed from the eighteenth century, arguably Scotland's finest hour, the CHURCH OF SCOTLAND and its clergy appear almost to deserve the same opprobrium as the Catholic church, complete with its prelatic hierarchy and indulgences, from which Protestantism had dramatically removed itself at the time of the REFORMATION. The professor of divinity at Aberdeen, Alexander Gerard, in a series of "Theological Prelections" published in 1799, under the title *The Pastoral Care,* cited the oft-repeated list of contemptible practices of the clergy as both an admonition to his students and as a historical reminder. In timely fashion Gerard's instruction was also intended as a corrective to the "misrepresentation" not just of "abuses" but, more important, of the relation of Protestantism's official church in Scotland to the national character itself, and indeed of "religion itself."

The "disrespect" and "detestation of mankind" fell on ministers purportedly guilty of "hypocrisy, super-stition, ambition, vanity, party-spirit, rancour, and revenge." As enthusiastic in its "malicious eagerness and exultation" as some of those religious parties were themselves, this mischief converted "imaginary faults" into "real vices," and "small failings" into "atrocious crimes." Moreover, throughout all of these "great blemishes" it made no allowance for the "weakness of human nature, or the temptations of the world." Significantly, Gerard makes reference here to his countryman DAVID HUME's "Essay on National Characters," recognizing perhaps that this Scottish Trojan horse threatened to "confound" the "natural and primary tendency" of Scotland's national church and to fell the "city," this great "Athens of the North" (Edinburgh, the eventual seat of the combined Church of Scotland's Assembly Hall). But what was that "tendency," that the Orkney poet and critic Edwin Muir should, on traveling through the Borders region and encountering Melrose Abbey, also muse that after the Reformation something of "transcendent loveliness" should have passed out of Scotland's life?

Protestantism and Scottish Nationalism

Protestantism in Scotland has ever been tied inextricably to the nation's character and its fortunes. The nineteenth-century historian H. T. Buckle went so far as to charge that the Scotch church had "dwarfed and mutilated" the national character in the seventeenth century, thereby making the work of Scotland's "Enlightenment" thinkers all the more difficult, in their attempt to wrest from what some have called that "glacial age of Calvinism" a society and an economy worthy of its people. However, mutilation can infect all those who would tamper with, or confound, the body. As he reflected on the patronage that had sustained the reign of the so-called Moderates in eighteenth-century Scotland, a youthful Dr. THOMAS CHALMERS, whose sheer oratory later helped to bring about the Disruption from which emerged the Free Church of Scotland in 1843, proclaimed utter distaste. A student still at St. Andrews, and a contemporary of James Mylne who earned a reputation as a radical "sensationalist" after he left a curacy at Paisley Abbey to become Glasgow's professor of moral philosophy, Chalmers admitted that he and his fellow students had "inhaled not a distaste only, but a positive contempt, for all that is properly and peculiarly gospel" (McCosh 1875:394).

Their contempt had the ring of earlier cries of disdain not, however, as the young Chalmers then supposed, for things "peculiarly gospel," but for the empty rhetoric as well as practices that had come to distort and malign the "everlasting Gospel" of the "true Church of Scotland," in the words of his friend and fellow "Disrupter," James McCosh. It was the same ring that two centuries before had been heard in the voices of JOHN KNOX and ANDREW MELVILLE, in successive stages the catalysts, if not strictly the founders (that "Headship" belonged, of course, to Christ, as Covenanters and Free Church ministers never failed to remind their flocks) of Protestantism in Scotland. The object of Knox's and Melville's contempt had rather been popery, episcopacy, and kings (see BISHOP AND EPISCOPACY). If these three objects were the seeds of PRESBYTERIANISM, the contempt born against them planted itself deep in the Scottish mind. Its issue, a creature of ironic form, was no less than the flowering of a spirit of national liberty and the fruit of a fanatical intolerance.

That intolerance has sometimes had its share of almost comical twists. Although antipapistical, antiliturgical, and antiepiscopal invective may be regarded as extreme rebukes of other persons' forms of WORSHIP, under the shifting, acrimonious, high-stakes, and frequently destructive tides of political maneuvering, especially in the seventeenth century, the installation of a bishop or prelate here, the imposition of "popish words" such as "CLERGY" and "LAITY" there, and "anti-christian" liturgical forms everywhere (so said JOHN BAILLIE, the Presbyterian preacher and principal of Glasgow University, of the "beautiful prayers" of the Scottish Prayer Book forced on them by Charles I and the archbishop of Canterbury WILLIAM LAUD, in 1636), were enough to turn blood and sea red. Tit for tat, Scottish Covenanters hit back with their own peculiar logic. Unlike the fairly evenly balanced forces of Catholicism and Protestantism then in ENGLAND,

> "in Scotland it was not so; nearly all (for the Catholics were mere Ishmaelites) were then Presbyterian. When the Covenanters insisted that Charles I and when the protesters insisted that Charles II should force Presbyterianism on England and Ireland, they returned, unconsciously, to Tudor principles. If it was wrong for the king to compel Scotland to accept the Liturgy [however slightly modified, in deference to the Scots], it was right for him to compel England and Ireland to accept Presbyterianism. Such was Covenanting logic" (Lang 1904: 28).

The niceties of this logic notwithstanding, Lang was under no illusions about the temper that fueled and fired it time after time during the same century. Protestantism in Scotland, he recounts, like its counterpart in England, owned a "savage religious temper." THOMAS HOBBES had attested as much, and had built an argument for political authoritarianism on the basis of just such a ruthless intolerance of anyone standing in one's way, yet with a zeal and a relish for blood not in the converted, but in the natural human soul.

H. T. Buckle, who has earned his own share of Scottish nationalist wrath, described the Presbyterian body that grew out of the sixteenth- and seventeenth-century conflicts as a "restless and unscrupulous body, greedy after power, and grossly intolerant of whatever opposed their own views" (Buckle 1970:110). The fearlessness of religious intolerance made even kings and nobles want to ally themselves to this energy, if not strictly to its principles. As Buckle noted, albeit with his own disdain, the Scotch clergy "covered with contempt" the "great ones of the earth" and "cast down" all "who were above them." Those bitterly and cruelly divisive conflicts to which many historians have alluded had arisen in large measure out of Presbyterian concerns to reclaim ecclesiastical properties seized by the Crown with the help of self-interested nobles; to ensure the democracy (the system of equality insisted on by Knox and his leadership successor Andrew Melville, as early as 1575) of the elect against the almost irresistible tides of hierarchical thinking; and to discipline (to "inure," in a word much favored by Scottish educationalists in the eighteenth century) the soul not only against political restorations, which would eventually lead to such torments for the Scots as the Act of Union of 1707, but also against the *instauratio,* the celebration of new beginnings predicted by FRANCIS BACON, which would bring about the advancement at once of learning and of luxury. Buckle himself had to concede that even when the Church of Scotland fostered a feeling "almost . . . of disgust," its most fanatical adherents were nevertheless to be admired for having "kept alive the spirit of national liberty."

Change

Ironically, that same spirit has among modern Scots succeeded in hoisting Buckle with his own petard. The guiding principles of his historical reading of the Scots—ignorance and fear—have seemed to thinkers such as George Davie rather to cover, and to color, himself. Fear leads to all sorts of excesses, none more so than in contagiously colorful historical accounts. Buckle had taken the servile and ignominious fear, with which he claimed the Scots clergy had crushed all the noblest feelings of human nature, and had splashed it over the entire Scots character, painting the latter, under the name of "Scottish Calvinism," as now permanently "dwarfed and mutilated." This virtual defacement of the Scots character, ironically by its own Presbyterian and egalitarian ethos, survives in spite of, or paradoxically because of, the winds of metaphysical, educational, scientific, jurisprudential, and indeed cultural change that blew across Scotland during the eighteenth century and made it, a worthy companion to FRANCE itself, one of the bastions of the new, distinctly modern and secularist age. Davie recognizes a certain restraint in Buckle's, as also in the historian F. W. Maitland's, judgment, tempered as they are by an acknowledgment of the dramatic changes in post-1707 Scotland, but he expresses chagrin that other historians, such as Hugh Trevor-Roper and even the Scottish Gordon Donaldson, have taken up the cudgel of mutilation to beat the excesses of Scottish EVANGELICALISM into the less repugnant, more moderate, conformity of Scottish with English forms of Protestantism that the Act of Union (a political, not a religious settlement) supposedly made possible.

If there is such a thing as a religious monopoly in Scotland, a CALVINISM so deeply branded into the Scots character as to "dwarf" all other features, then a historical decision of considerable moment comes to the fore. Either pre-Union Scotland was a pure backwardness of austerity and fanaticism that even the long shadow of the post-Union eighteenth century was only gradually able to erode (as Scottish historians such as H. G. Graham and James Young have urged), or not even the civilizing force of political union with England nor the dynamics of Scotland's own great enlightenment could quite efface the savagery, the dogmatic tone, the inflexibility, and the ignorance of this largely middle- to lower-class religious outlook. (If the Moderate Presbyterianism of the eighteenth century seems positively genteel by comparison, the reason lies in the fact that the Church of Scotland was for a sustained period under the sway of the cultured and intellectual upper classes.) The idea that Scotland might have evolved a "distinctive blend," as George Davie puts it, of the "secular and the sacred," that Protestantism in Scotland might over time have actually transformed itself from within into an entity combining disciplines of mind with those of soul and body, has until quite recently not been taken as seriously as it might be. Among others, more recent thinkers such as Craig Beveridge and Ronald Turnbull have endeavored to change the religious face of Scotland, as it were, uniting it more positively, less on the long-held note of "inferiorization," with the real cultural and political forces at work in the Scottish nation.

Even Edwin Muir characterized his own people as "a dull drove of faces harsh and vexed." The blame rested squarely on the shoulders, or rather in the "preaching palms," of Knox and Melville. Scottish Calvinism had created a joyless countenance; the faces of its children, according to others, are those of the starving and culturally destitute. Beveridge and Turnbull counter "this mindless endorsement of metropolitan prejudice" by citing what they regard as the strengths, not weaknesses, of Knox's legacy or rather of Scotland's Calvinist inheritance more generally—"moral seriousness, distrust of complacency [and] passion for theoretical argument" (Beveridge and Turnbull 1989:10). To their modern list might be added, perhaps more judiciously, the insights of the Rev. Hugh Blair, a Moderate preacher as well as professor of rhetoric and belle lettres at Edinburgh, and thus very much a product of that age of transformation that one might rather call, in deference to Davie's principle of a distinctive blend in Scottish culture, the age of "polite Calvinism." In a sermon entitled, "On the Mixture of Joy and Fear in Religion," Blair achieves his own blend of religious discipline with practical fulfillment, the rigors of "duty" and "obedience" with the "cheerfulness" of "performance." Wanting this combination, he asserted, "our religion discovers itself not to be genuine in principle, and in practice it cannot be stable. Religious obedience, destitute of joy, is not genuine in its principle." It is possible that Buckle could not see the "joy" behind the faces of ignorance and fear in the children of Knox and Melville. It is also possible that the *Books of Discipline,* as they were called, could not see the joy within themselves.

The Reign of Discipline

The physical face of Scottish Protestantism had never shown itself to be a thing of aesthetic grandeur or even comeliness. It, too, bore the marks, it seems, of austerity, or perhaps only of neglect, whether truly spiritual or simply zealously indifferent. In the *First Book of Discipline,* preserved in Knox's *History of the Reformation,* a series of "recommendations," between April 1560 and January 1561, to "the lords" (a provisional governing body of Protestant nobles and lairds), the principles of austerity had been enunciated. They were directed, of course, primarily against the legacy of "idolatry" that had led to the "holy Sacraments" being "[wrongly] ministered" in buildings as diverse as abbeys, nunneries, cathedral kirks, and colleges. Significantly, the only exceptions to this "suppression" of idolatry were to be the "parish Kirks or Schools" which had found a home in the properties confiscated after the Reformation. Nevertheless, however austere might have been the recommended "doors, close windows of glass, thatch or slate able to withhold rain, a bell to convocate the people together, a pulpit, a basin for baptism, and tables for the ministration of the Lord's Supper," repairs were to be made in the event that "unseemliness of the place [should] come in contempt."

In spite of this attempt to put distance between Scottish Protestants and such "contempt," Andrew Lang notes a description of St. Giles' Church in 1627 as telling of a colorless, if not joyless, setting for worship, but also of a spiritual discipline run amok in the growing capitalism of the day: "Bare walls and pillars all clad with dust, sweepings and cobwebs . . . and on every side the restless resorting of people treating of their worldly affairs; some writing and making obligations, contracts, and discharges, others laying counts or telling over sums of money" (Lang 1904:iii,25). Part of the resistance in 1638 to the infliction on the Scottish Church of an orderly or "decent" LITURGY, one that was as uniform throughout the churches as it was free of "barbarisms" or political jibes, was that it lacked "conception" or the free springing to mind of inspired thoughts or radical opinions. The General Assembly at Perth in 1618 had enjoined that "everie minister . . . sall make choice of severall [sic] and pertinent texts of Scripture, and frame their doctrine and exhortation thereto, and rebuke all superstitious observation and licentious profanation" of the appointed holy days of Christmas, Good Friday, Easter, Ascension Day, and Whitsuntide. Nevertheless both the "choice" and the "framing" were to be freely "conceived."

The other element in Scottish Protestantism's resistance to liturgical order was that it gave de facto recognition to the hated prelatic rule of that hierarchically defined church, now spitefully termed "the Devil." With free "conception" logically came the principle of egalitarianism whereby each preacher was to be deemed equal to every other. Just as the feisty Covenanters claimed to be fearless in "bearding [standing up] to [the] face" of James VI, so they would "beard" to any prelate and certainly to that "Romane [sic] Antichrist" the Pope. Sentiment against all things papistical ran high. The so-called Negative Confession of 1581, which was later to form part of the 1638 National Covenant, sets the "kyrk of Scotland" against "all contrarie religion and doctrine, but cheifly [sic] all kynd of papistrie in generall and perticular headis [sic] even as they are now damned and confuted by the worde of God and kyrk of Scotland. . . ." Against "all his tyrannous lawes," against the multitude of abominations from "worshiping of imagrie and crocecs" to "vane allegories, ritis, signes and traditioneis" [sic], the Kirk pitted its own stern "discipline" and canons of "obedience." The Negative Confession makes clear that "Godis [sic] good creatures" owe allegiance only to the "words of God," to "Christ our head," to the incorruptible and unsubverted "true religion within the kirk."

Within that same kirk no one was to go wanting, either of care (provided that the person had "honestly fallen into decay") or of education, more specifically, a "virtuous education and godly upbringing," either at the hands of an appointed schoolmaster or, in rural areas, of a kirk reader or the minister himself. The yearly election of elders and deacons, "by common and free election," would ensure the democracy of the faithful, while at the same time adding moral impetus to the task of assisting the minister in "all public affairs of the Church; to wit, in judging and decerning [sic] causes; in giving of admonition to the licentious liver; [and] in having respect to the manners and conversation of all men within their charge." Democracy also worked to sharpen the attentiveness of the faithful to all that was going on around them, but more particularly, to the "life, manners, diligence and study" of the ministers themselves. The power to admonish, to correct, and, if necessary, to depose was ever to be with the people.

A Free Disruption

In part, it was to recover that very freedom, the power to elect or not to elect, that Chalmers, McCosh, Thomas Guthrie, David Welsh, and other "Free Churchmen" packed the halls of the General Assembly being held at Edinburgh in 1843 and brought about disruption, secession (several minor "secessions" had already occurred in 1690, 1733, and 1761), and the Free Church of Scotland. (It was not until 1929 that the breach between the Free Church and the Church of Scotland was healed, and even then not for all Free Churchmen.) The disciplines of the seventeenth century had fallen prey to the lure of patronage, to cultural and intellectual pretension, and to unconceived prayers and sermons, as appointed ministers gave scant notice to their congregations and even left the preparation of their sermons to some of the now classic texts of other minds. The Second Book of Discipline of 1578, fashioned by the energetic Andrew Melville after his return to Scotland from Geneva, made it clear that discipline was something actively, not passively, to be engaged. By the beginning of the nineteenth century Moderatism had obviously allowed the Kirk to drift too far in the direction of a passive sense of what it means to be the "disciplined" elect.

Ironically, the Free Churchmen identified as the root causes of that failure of discipline many of the ills against which the two Books of Discipline, effectively the legacies of Knox and Melville, had been conceived. Scottish Protestantism had always opposed any usurpation of the true "Headship" of the church by any form of civil authority, whether king or lord or, as largely became the case in the secularizing eighteenth century, the magistrate. The "licentious liver," as we recall, had been the concern of an ever-vigilant elect, elders, deacons, ministers. Now, the perennial drunkard, McCosh complained, could go to the magistrate and gain license to drink at the communion table itself, the disciplinary restraints of the parishioners notwithstanding. Likewise, position and privilege had been eroding the democratic spirit of free election, such that clerical appointments were frequently in civil or influential hands rather than in the hands of congregations, often of far humbler station in society. McCosh openly wondered whether, in the shifting sands of history, trust in privileges had taken the place of trusting in God. Above all perhaps, in what has to be seen as a presentiment of the social upheavals of the nineteenth and twentieth centuries, the work of moral, social, and even cultural improvement, the necessary accompaniment of any rights of discipline, was being lifted out of the hands of the religious elect and placed in the allegedly more capable and more responsible hands of the politically elect. The very measures of modernity that one would otherwise herald, the very steps to humanity's improvement and progress, had become as a sty not in the "devil's" but in the kirk's own eye.

Polite Protestantism

The institution of parish schools throughout the country, which the Church of Scotland had regarded with the utmost seriousness from its very inception, had indeed served to project the role of EDUCATION on to center stage. As the *First Book of Discipline* had enjoined, the "Grammar and the Latin tongue" taught by the parish schoolmaster would enable the "children and youth of the parish" not only to read the catechism, "as we have it now translated in the Book of Common Order, called the Order of Geneva," but also, at a later stage, the arts of "Logic and Rhetoric, together with the Tongues," as taught at the colleges, then at least, of St. Andrews, Glasgow, and Aberdeen. In short, religious discipline was to be directed toward such improvements, of mind as much as of manners, as might be furnished by ever higher levels and broader compasses of education. If the duty to improvement would later sow religious dissension, if it would serve to revolutionize Scottish society itself, ushering in a greater role for secular as opposed to sacred interests, then Protestantism in Scotland would have to live with the consequences.

One of those consequences was that Presbyterianism in Scotland inevitably went the way of social division. As the historian Christopher Hill has argued, even the theology of PREDESTINATION was made subject to the revolutionary changes wrought within British society as a whole during the seventeenth century. Predestination theories were particularly susceptible to moods of social and economic insecurity that, with the rise and fall of kings and Cromwellians, were unsettling to the English and aggravating to the Scots,

of both higher and lower social orders. Somewhat brought to heel by the Act of Union, the Scottish nobility nevertheless reestablished itself with enough security that it could begin the long process of extricating itself from the clutches of predestination theory. If not wholly in the company of the "elected" ones, they could still be confident of their position as the "selected" ones in society. Hence Presbyterians of this "higher social group" could afford to "abandon Calvinism in the eighteenth century," observes Hill, although not as easily or as thoroughly as this might suggest.

The situation for the "meaner sort," the middling and lower middling classes, was manifestly more "beleaguered," less secure, at times even precarious. Presbyterianism in Scotland finds itself reflected in this division as the eighteenth century wears on. Unlike the socially selected ones, the elected members of Scottish society had little with which to defend themselves, except a stern, no doubt also proud, sense of their religious superiority over the reprobate of the world, whether above or beneath them. Although their erstwhile Calvinist countrymen of the higher orders might enjoy the fruit of their cultural and intellectual improvement (Alexander "Jupiter" Carlyle best epitomized this trend), they themselves relished strict discipline of self and others. This cultivated monitoring of lives positively feasted on capabilities of attentiveness and reflection that were truly peculiar to the Scots. Ironically, their counterparts of a more polite Calvinism also came to appreciate the "art" of attentive reflection, indeed making it one of the mainstays of Scottish HIGHER EDUCATION. Prelectors in the four Scottish universities (Edinburgh being now the fourth), especially those charged with not only the philosophy of the human mind, but also its cultivation, from rudimentary sense experience to the refinements of rhetorical discourse in the public forum, were truly masters of this "art." Key to the philosophy as to the culture of the mind was the instrument of attentive reflection, long a Calvinist virtue and one instilled in the minds of the young as early as their assiduous learning of the Catechism.

A Very Scottish Blend

McCosh always held firmly to the view that, whatever distortions the Kirk might have suffered at the hands of Crown and government in the eighteenth century, distortions that essentially deprived the church of its critical prerogative of election, there was no necessary antagonism between the philosophy that Scotland evolved in that century and "true theology." There were indeed "new lights" everywhere, "moderates" who tended to put the interests of patronage and their high moral seriousness before the strict obedience required of the elect who, by rule, were to lend themselves to be governed at "God's good pleasure." It is also quite true that the very reason in which the age was to bask did not always "yield and withdraw, to give place to the Holy Spirit." It was never intended that new lights of any sort should play the moon to that divine Light that was the sun itself holding it, as it were, in a long eclipse. Yet far from denying that moral power, McCosh chose instead to endorse it.

What George Davie later saw as the peculiar "democratic intellect" of Scotland was precisely constituted of both an egalitarian principle of freedom and an equally egalitarian, but also highly cultured intellect. McCosh knew the power of education (he went on to become the president of Princeton University) as well, and he was grateful for that surge of "intelligence and love of freedom" that he thought any "spiritually-minded observer" (not, apparently, one of H. T. Buckle's strengths) would recognize in what Scotland had brought to pass in its "new light" age. The Calvinist theology was firmly there in the seeds that the Scots had planted during that century: "in the schools and colleges planted throughout the land; in the love of education instilled into the minds of the people; and, above all, in their acquaintance with the Bible, and in their determined adherence to what they believed to be the truth of God" (McCosh 1875:20). How had Buckle seen so much of darkness in Scottish Protestantism when the same theology had clearly produced so much of light? More to the point perhaps, could thinkers such as McCosh be grateful on the one hand for all that the age had bestowed on the nation and ungrateful on the other for the age's polite shifting of the Headship from Christ to reason, or worse, to its governing patrons? Had the nation paid too high a price?

Virtue and Gratitude

If Protestantism in Scotland was indeed forever changed by the social and intellectual upheavals of the eighteenth century, far supplanting the tortured political ones of the previous century; if not even the evangelical fervor of the Disruption in the next century could halt the force of that movement or dampen its own brand of enthusiasm; perhaps the highly articulate Hugh Blair might serve as a final measure of the extent of the damage or, perchance, improvement to Protestantism. As minister of Knox's own St. Giles, on the High Street in Edinburgh, he forms a significant bridge between discipline and cultivation, between the rule of religious piety and the rule of secular morality. With Blair, one steps both backward and forward.

Somewhere on the arch of that bridge, one may perhaps discover flowing beneath the living waters of Scottish Protestantism.

For all his literary flare, and perhaps pride therein, Blair never confused, except to deepen their relationship, piety and morality. In a sermon entitled, "On the Union of Piety and Morality" Blair sought to dispel any concerns that Protestantism in Scotland had deserted the sacred in favor of the secular. He made it abundantly clear that any morality not "seconded by piety" was "mere morality," a morality not merely answering only to the voice of Reason, but suffering from "irregularity and defect." As Knox had urged on the Scots a "care of the poor," so Blair reiterates that when piety is joined "with active virtue," it issues in the "honourable [as opposed to "irregular"] discharge of the duties of the active life," not a life dark, hateful, and cringing with violent fears, but a life of "true worth," noble and free, in which honorable duty follows naturally on the heels of "Charity to men." Subtly playing on the motif of the stranger, made famous in his countryman Hume's *Dialogues concerning Natural Religion,* Blair exposes the vital weakness of the Scotsman without religion, of the secular attempt to create a national society without the earnest discipline of pious reflection. All the disciplines of the attentive mind cannot aspire to any completeness, nor can they ever broaden life's circle, unless they are "touched," stirred as it were out of virtue's complacency, by "gratitude to him for all his goodness."

The ineffectualness of morality, of the secular, of life itself, without that tincture of "gratitude to him," and the discipline arising from it, was ever the theme of Protestantism in Scotland. "The man of mere morality," admonished Blair from the pulpit, "is a stranger to all the delicate and refined pleasures of devotion. In works of beneficence and mercy, he may enjoy satisfaction. But his satisfaction is destitute of that glow of affection, which enlivens the feelings of one who lifts his heart at the same time to the Father of the Universe, and considers himself as imitating God . . . when beneficence and devotion are united, they pour upon the man in whom they meet, the full pleasures of a good and pure heart. His alms connected him with men; his prayers with God. . . ." Scottish culture and its active virtues have indeed been no stranger to Protestantism, but therein lie not grounds for contempt, but rather appreciation of its very strength.

See also Catholicism, Protestant Reactions; Church Discipline

References and Further Reading

Beveridge, Craig, and Ronald Turnbull. *The Eclipse of Scottish Culture*. Edinburgh: Polygon, 1989.

Blair, Hugh. *Sermons for the Use of Families*. London, 1808.

Buckle, H. T. *On Scotland and the Scotch Intellect*. Chicago: University of Chicago Press, 1970.

Cowan, Ian B. *The Scottish Reformation*. London: Weidenfeld and Nicolson, 1982.

Davie, George E. *The Democratic Intellect*. Edinburgh: Edinburgh University Press, 1961.

Donaldson, Gordon. *Scottish Historical Documents*. Edinburgh: Scottish Academic Press, 1970.

Gerard, Alexander. *The Pastoral Care*. London, 1799.

Hill, Christopher. *A Turbulent, Seditious, and Factious People: John Bunyan and his Church*. Oxford: Oxford University Press, 1988.

Hoeveler, J. David Jr. *James McCosh and the Scottish Intellectual Tradition*. Princeton, NJ: Princeton University Press, 1981.

Lang, Andrew. *A History of Scotland from the Roman Occupation*. 3 vols. Edinburgh: William Blackwood & Sons, 1904.

McCosh, James. *The Scottish Philosophy, Biographical, Expository, Critical, from Hutcheson to Hamilton*. London: Macmillan, 1875.

Muir, Edwin. *Scottish Journey*. London: William Heinemann Ltd., 1935.

J. CHARLES STEWART-ROBERTSON

SCOTTISH COMMON SENSE REALISM

In the wake of FRANCIS BACON's "augmentation" of learned experience (1623) the Scottish mind felt increasingly at home in a world of real things, cultivated minds, and progressive human and civic advantages. Even the skeptical DAVID HUME had a firm grip on what the mind does "naturally," if not rationally, believe. The "common sense" philosophy that emerged in SCOTLAND during the eighteenth century built itself on this same assurance.

Historical Challenges

Epistemologically the "Scotch School" had staked itself against Hume's skeptical conclusions, the sensationalism of Étienne Bonnot de Condillac, and the materialism of Claude-Adrien Helvétius. Morally it had accepted Francis Hutcheson's "moral sense" challenge to Hobbesian self-interest (see HOBBES, THOMAS) and the rationalism of Samuel Clarke. Religiously it credited the "Supreme Being" with "inspiring" in us the intelligence and self-consciousness to be "informed" both of the Supreme Being's works and of the mental operations by which we apprehend them. On those bases, it had established a view of the constituent "powers" of the mind, both intellectual and active, that were said to "furnish" the mind with the requisite "faculties" for reasoning inductively about, and responding virtuously to, the world.

Thinkers such as Thomas Reid, James Beattie, and James Oswald (criticized by the materialist JOSEPH PRIESTLEY), and later Dugald Stewart and Thomas Brown, resisted skeptical as well as idealist assaults on the notions of the self as existent and identical; of causal efficacy; of the veracity of objects of sense as well as of memory; and of the existence of conscious acts, whether in regulating thought or in initiating change. Our "natural" or "intuitive" judgments concerning these features of our experience, touching the interaction of the conscious subject and the world as perceived and attended to in reflection, were said to be "immediate" and "irresistible."

Main Tenets

Although not uniformly enunciated, these tenets or "axioms" of the Scottish position served as what Reid himself called "common Principles." They constituted "the Foundation of all Reasoning and all Science" and were the basis for that "common Understanding" among persons that rendered discourse and thus civic harmony possible. Not to believe our own eyes or to give regard to the testimony of our senses was to be "destitute of common Sense," he told his Glasgow students after 1764. Moreover, in questioning any of these first principles or the evidence of even the "simplest" or "most familiar" of our sensory devices, we bring "confusion" and "perplexity" to those "reflex senses" whereby we discern the morally agreeable in society and the aesthetically beautiful in NATURE. Nodding their approval once again to Bacon Scottish philosophers sought to free the mind from "prejudice" and "error" so that it might be brought into "the knowledge of those truths which tend to enlarge and elevate the mind." These in turn would ensure "habits of virtue and true goodness" consonant with the "dignity of [our] rational and immortal Nature." The common principles of sense were thus the first steps toward a worthier as well as "future" existence for humankind.

The Credible Real

Scottish theories of perception hinged on the factor of belief. Although conception engages our consciousness in attending to an object (attention being the key to any reflective activity of the mind), it does so without passing judgment, without any feeling of the object's pastness (Brown broke ranks somewhat on this point), but above all without any belief in its existence. In perception, however, not only is the object made present to consciousness, but it is given credence as existing in the world. Acts of consciousness are granted no less credibility. Together, the objects of outer and inner sense constitute the real, that which is intuitively known, as McCosh later rephrased it.

The credible real did admit of some uncertainties, such as the underlying physical causes that generate expectations of consequent effects. However, if Scottish thinkers sometimes held back, largely for religious reasons, from penetrating too deeply into the nature of things, both physical and mental, they were unreserved in their application of the rule of belief, founded as that was on "common sense." (This "modest" skepticism later appeared as a poor cousin to the strictures of critical philosophy in limiting the human understanding.) Always carefully distinguished from their Aristotelian predecessor, the principles of common sense arose as a considered response to the shifting epistemological ground of the early eighteenth century. They affirmed that there were modes of evidence, of testimony, and of human self-assurance that met the highest standards of reason as well as religious humility.

In Retrospect

Scottish common sense realism was judged by many post-Kantian readers as an "intellectual monstrosity," parading ordinary opinions of human beings as, in William Hamilton's approving words, a priori principles. Few appreciated that Scottish philosophers had been intent to stem the tide of various forms of "superficial" empiricism in the interests of a more "profound" one. Common sense realism was not the philosophy of the "common man," but a highly "technical" attempt to counter conflicting theories about our apprehension of the "worlds" of mind and body.

Joseph Priestley had damned the Scottish movement as "dogmatic" and "arbitrary." In the next century, Hamilton, James Frederick Ferrier, James Mc-Cosh, and Victor Cousin tried to articulate and, in doing so, to reshape its principles. Ferrier came closest to identifying its (and Reid's) real weakness. It had failed, he maintained, to get its "facts" straight. It was not the object that was "real" (the primary fact) nor the act of consciousness entertaining it, but the "consciousness of the object." His criticism highlights the seriousness with which Scottish philosophy wrestled with the problem of the real or, in another vein, with Berkeleian idealism. In 1853 J. P. Alison, a student of Dugald Stewart, summed up the tenor of that Scottish philosophy that he had inherited, but he did so rather by citing Cousin: "Our perception of simple and primary truths may be separated . . . from the fallible reason of man, and referred to that Reason which is Universal, Absolute, Infallible, and Eternal, beyond the limits of Space and time, above all contact with error or disorder . . . to that Mind, pure and incorruptible, of which ours is only the reflection."

References and Further Reading

Davie, George. *The Scottish Enlightenment and Other Essays.* Edinburgh: Polygon, 1991.

Marcil-Lacoste, L. *Claude Buffier and Thomas Reid: Two Common-Sense Philosophers.* Kingston, Canada: McGill-Queen's Press, 1982.

McCosh, James. *The Scottish Philosophy* (1875). Bristol, UK: Thoemmes, 1990 (reprint).

Norton, D. F. "David Hume." In *Common-Sense Moralist, Sceptical Metaphysician.* Princeton, NJ: Princeton University Press, 1982.

Reid, Thomas. *Philosophical Works.* Edited by Sir William Hamilton. Introduction by H. M. Bracken. Hildesheim, Germany: Georg Olms Verlag, 1983.

———. *The Birkwood Collection.* Aberdeen, Scotland: Aberdeen University Library, Unpublished manuscripts.

Stewart-Robertson, J. Charles. " 'Georgica Animi': A Compendium of Thomas Reid's Lectures on the Culture of the Mind." *Rivista di storia della filosofia* no. 1 (1990): 113–156.

———. "A Bacon-Facing Generation: Scottish Philosophy in the Early Nineteenth Century." *Journal of the History of Ideas* 14 no. 1 (1976): 37–49.

J. CHARLES STEWART-ROBERTSON

SEABURY, SAMUEL (1729–1796)

North American theologian and first American Episcopal bishop. Seabury was born in Groton, Connecticut on November 30, 1729. He was educated privately, at Yale (B.A., 1748) and at the University of Edinburgh (1752–1753), where he studied medicine. In 1753 he was ordained into the CHURCH OF ENGLAND, being appointed a missionary for the SOCIETY FOR THE PROPAGATION OF THE GOSPEL (SPG) to New Brunswick, New Jersey. In 1757 he moved to Jamaica, Long Island, where he served as an SPG missionary and as rector of the parish. In 1766 he served in a similar arrangement at Westchester, New York.

Before the American Revolutionary War, Seabury engaged in a pamphlet attack on the proposed measures of the first Continental Congress. This led to his brief imprisonment at New Haven in 1775. At the commencement of the Long Island campaign in 1776, Seabury fled for safety behind the British lines, where he served as a chaplain and supplied General Howe's army with logistical information. For the remainder of the war, he lived in British-controlled New York City, where he practiced medicine, wrote political pamphlets, and served in a variety of clerical positions. At the conclusion of hostilities Seabury supervised the exodus of Loyalists to Nova Scotia. After abandoning his opposition to American independence, he wrote a prayer for Congress. He was elected bishop by Connecticut clergy in 1783. He died in New London, Connecticut on February 25, 1796 and was buried at St. James' Church. More than anyone else, Seabury was responsible for shaping the character of the Episcopal Church along sacramental, liturgical, and historic lines, in keeping with the beliefs and practices of the wider Anglican Communion.

Career in the Church

After his ordination in the Church of England, Seabury had served in a succession of minor clerical positions in New Jersey and New York. As the Revolutionary War drew nearer, he began to be drawn into the leadership of the clergy in the northern colonies and was among the first to recognize the potential threat to the church posed by Independence. After his election as bishop Seabury sailed for ENGLAND, hoping to persuade the bishops to consecrate him for service in America, although—despite both patience and intense effort on his part—this proved unsuccessful: Parliament refused to withdraw the loyalty oath, which Seabury refused to take. Seabury also refused (despite his high church convictions) to submit to the crown's authority. He thus traveled north where, on November 14, 1784, at Aberdeen, he was consecrated by three bishops of the Non-juring Scottish Episcopal Church (see EPISCOPAL CHURCH, SCOTLAND). No oath of loyalty was required. On his return to America he served as rector of St. James' New London, bishop of Connecticut, and (after 1790) bishop of Rhode Island.

Seabury was a gifted leader of the CLERGY during difficult times, and an able and hard-working administrator. He held regular visitations of his parishes, preached frequently before his clergy, ordained numerous new deacons and priests, consecrated a number of new churches, and confirmed over ten thousand people. Implementing a "high" ECCLESIOLOGY, he governed his diocese through a series of convocations, which effectively limited lay influence; he thus circumvented the aims of WILLIAM HALE WHITE and those from Pennsylvania southward for the reorganization of the church along democratic lines.

Despite Seabury's rigid adherence to high church principles, a series of compromises allowed the delegates from Connecticut and Massachusetts to attend the General Convention of 1789, meeting in Philadelphia, where Seabury's consecration was recognized (he thus became the first presiding bishop in the church), a constitution for the new Episcopal Church was completed, a system of canon law was estab-

lished, and an American version of the BOOK OF COMMON PRAYER was adopted. The division between the northern and southern dioceses had effectively been healed, as had the division between the Scottish and English successions in America. (White and a colleague had recently been consecrated by the English bishops, without the necessity of a loyalty oath.)

Seabury was the first bishop of the EPISCOPAL CHURCH in the United States. The Church of England in America, the forerunner of the Episcopal Church, made an important contribution to Colonial religious history, although its influence was limited by the absence of a local episcopate: those seeking ordination were required to travel to England to be ordained by an English bishop. The church also suffered from the outbreak of hostilities between the colonies and Britain. Internally both clergy and LAITY were divided over the war. Externally many Patriots abandoned the church because of its close constitutional ties to the English crown. Moreover, after the cessation of hostilities, many Loyalists (including a number of clergy from the Episcopal Church) fled to CANADA or returned to England, thus diminishing the ranks of the church still further. Those who remained behind, however, soon began to formulate various proposals for the reorganization of the church in the new Republic.

A serious impediment stood in the way, however: there were no bishops in America, and, moreover, those seeking ordination in England were required to take an oath of loyalty to the British crown. To address this, in 1782 William White, the Latitudinarian rector of Christ Church, Philadelphia, proposed a series of principles that would have reorganized the church without its historic episcopate, or, in essence, as a voluntary association of clergy and laity. Until the church could secure its own bishops from England, a temporary form of presbyterian ordination would be implemented. These proposals provoked sharp debate among both clergy and laity, with those in New England objecting most strenuously to White's proposal. Consequently in 1783 ten clergy from Connecticut met secretly in Woodbury and elected Seabury as their first bishop.

See also Bishop and Episcopacy; Latitudinarianism

References and Further Reading

Primary Sources:

Seabury, Samuel. *Samuel Seabury's Ungathered Imprints: Historical Perspectives of the Early National Years,* edited by Kenneth Walter Cameron. Hartford, CT: Transcendental Books, 1978.
———. *Discourses on Several Subjects.* Hudson, NY: William E. Norman, 1815.

Secondary Sources:

Beardsley, William Agur. *Life and Correspondence of the Right Reverend Samuel Seabury, D.D.* Boston: Houghton, Mifflin and Company, 1881.

———. *Samuel Seabury, the Man and the Bishop.* Hartford, CT: Church Missions Publishing Company, 1935.

Cameron, Kenneth Walker, ed. *Samuel Seabury Among His Contemporaries.* Hartford, CT: Transcendental Books, 1980.

———. *Connecticut's First Diocesan.* Hartford, CT: Transcendental Books, 1985.

Carroon, Robert G., ed. *New Heart, A New Spirit.* Wilton, CT: Morehouse-Barlow, 1988.

Rowthorn, Anne W. *Samuel Seabury, A Bicentenary Biography.* New York: Seabury Press, 1983.

Steiner, Bruce E. *Samuel Seabury 1729–1796: A Study in the High Church Tradition.* Athens: Ohio University Press, 1972.

Thoms, Herbert. *Samuel Seabury; Priest and Physician, Bishop of Connecticut.* Hamden, CT: Shoe String Press, 1963.

GRAYSON CARTER

SECTARIANISM

Sectarianism is the process whereby new religious communities develop as alternatives to a prevailing sacred TRADITION or cultural regime. These new communities, called "sects," often form as protests against traditional religious or cultural AUTHORITY. They typically claim to embody the true or purified form of a religious tradition, or to have discovered a new form of religious truth and life altogether. Accordingly, their beliefs and practices frequently express particular religious themes such as healing or predictions about the end of the world. Sects usually gather around charismatic leaders, but their institutions tend to emphasize the equality and mutual responsibility of members. Their tightly knit communities characteristically take radical stances toward traditional religious and political authority that range from extreme separatism to revolutionary action. Sects have occurred in all of the world's major religions, but they have had perhaps the most profound influence on Christianity and especially on Protestantism, which has spawned sectarian movements continuously from the REFORMATION to the present day.

Sectarianism as a Theoretical Category

While sectarianism is a long-standing religious phenomenon, its theoretical definition and interpretation are distinctly modern developments created by social scientists using data drawn primarily from Protestant sects. During the Reformation, the term "sect" acquired pejorative connotations that dominant European churches and political regimes continued to use against dissenting religious groups during three centuries of religious violence. These tensions abated by

1900, and in the early twentieth century historians and sociologists brought the history of Protestant sects to the forefront of social theory. In his landmark study *The Protestant Ethic and the Spirit of Capitalism* (1904–1905), German sociologist MAX WEBER argued that the early Protestant sects possessed distinctive organizational and intellectual characteristics fundamentally different from those of Catholicism and the Lutheran and Calvinist state churches of Western Europe. According to Weber, the voluntary membership and strict moral discipline of Protestant sects during the sixteenth, seventeenth, and eighteenth centuries created an ethical standard of "worldly ASCETICISM" that mandated economic productivity for the glory of God while forbidding excessive consumption as sinful. Weber interpreted the INDIVIDUALISM and activism of this "Protestant ethic" as the spiritual and moral underpinning of capitalist ECONOMICS, and thereby located Protestant sectarianism as an essential element of modernity.

At the same moment, French historian Elie Halévy was researching the influence of Methodist sects on eighteenth-century English society. In two 1906 essays later published as *The Birth of Methodism in England,* Halévy presented the controversial thesis that METHODISM had played a major role in preventing revolution in eighteenth-century English society. Halévy based this judgment on the comparative claim that while INDUSTRIALIZATION had produced more revolutionary potential in ENGLAND than in FRANCE, something specific to English CULTURE had prevented the middle and lower classes from resorting to political violence. That element, he argued, was Methodism, JOHN WESLEY's sectarian movement that channeled social discontent into a quest for moral perfection and religious community while enjoining strict loyalty to the English crown.

While Weber and Halévy used historical evidence from Protestant sectarian movements to show the social, economic, and political influence of religion in the modern West, German sociologist ERNST TROELTSCH developed a theoretical distinction between sectarian and churchly forms of the Christian religion itself. In *The Social Teachings of the Christian Churches* (1912), Troeltsch presented models of the church and the sect as polar opposite forms of Christianity extending back to the very beginnings of Christian history. In Troeltch's typology, the church was a universal compulsory religious institution, closely aligned with the state, which was governed hierarchically and transmitted its doctrines and sacramental rituals through an elite priesthood. The sect was everything the church was not: a voluntary religious institution, separated from the state, governed democratically by an elected ministry, and imparting its truths through spiritual experience and moral discipline.

Troeltsch used this series of opposing traits to explain what he took to be the most basic church–sect polarity of all, that of "social teaching" or social ETHICS *(soziallehren)*. In his view, Christianity's political triumph under Constantine committed it to embracing the Stoic NATURAL LAW philosophy of the Roman elite and conferring moral legitimacy on the secular social order, thereby producing the conservative, hierarchical social teaching of the church type that dominated medieval Europe. Sects, on the other hand, insisted on what Troeltsch called the "pure divine law" ethics of individual obedience to otherworldly standards of behavior, which entailed rejection of traditional institutions and criticism of human failure to follow biblical commands. Troeltch devoted half of *Social Teaching* to interpreting all of the Reformation churches and movements through his church-sect typology, but his treatment gave far less attention to eighteenth- and nineteenth-century Protestant sects than Weber's had.

During the mid–twentieth century, many scholars debated the sectarian theories of Weber, Halévy, and Troeltsch, especially their association of sects with the rise of capitalism. R. H. Tawney reversed Weber's argument in his 1926 book *Religion and the Rise of Capitalism,* asserting that instead of causing capitalism Protestant churches and sects had actually accommodated themselves to it by legitimizing the worldly success of their followers. In the American context, H. RICHARD NIEBUHR offered a similar class analysis in his 1929 book *The Social Sources of Denominationalism,* arguing that while Protestant sects began among the poor as otherworldly "religions of the dispossessed," their aptitude for capitalistic discipline fostered material prosperity and an adjustment of their social teaching from radicalism to conservatism.

Since 1960, a new wave of sectarian studies has provided historical and empirical evidence and theoretical formulations that carry challenging implications for understanding Protestantism. Preeminent among these studies was George Huntston Williams's 1962 book *The Radical Reformation,* a masterly reconstruction of sixteenth-century Anabaptist and Spiritualist groupings on the Continent. In addition, an important series of historical studies of seventeenth-century English sects appeared, some of which followed Weber in emphasizing their religious ideologies of social radicalism and political revolution, most notably Michael Walzer's *The Revolution of the Saints* (1965) and Christopher Hill's *The World Turned Upside Down* (1972). On the other hand, E. P. Thompson's *The Making of the English Working Class* (1963) and Eric Hobsbawm's *Primitive Rebels* (1963)

reaffirmed Halévy's judgment that religious sectarianism inhibited political radicalism in eighteenth- and nineteenth-century Europe.

American Catholic sociologist Werner Stark synthesized many of these historical studies into a major new theoretical statement in his three-volume 1967 work *The Sociology of Religion: A Study of Christendom.* Stark placed heavy stress on evidence that Protestant and Russian Orthodox sects were led by discontented class groups like peasants, weavers, and merchants. He concluded that the major social cause of sects was not religious difference, but rather status discontent. He cast Christian sects into three binary categories: "retrogressive" or "progressive" movements based on social programs, "rigoristic" or "antinomian" sects defined by their internal legal codes, and "violent" or "nonviolent" groups distinguished by their teachings on the use of coercion. These defining characteristics reflected Stark's reversal of the relationship between religion and culture that Weber, Halévy, and Troeltsch had proposed, seeing religion as a dependent cultural variable that follows rather than leads the process of social, economic, and political change.

The most important recent response to classical theories, however, has been to abandon the Christian church–sect distinction altogether and to redefine of sectarianism as a fundamental type of religion found in all the world's major traditions. Many scholars have contributed to this new formulation, none more than English sociologist Bryan R. Wilson. In his 1970 book *Religious Sects: A Sociological Study,* Wilson proposed an approach to sectarianism based on many of Troeltch's attributes, but he added a new defining element of sectarianism that he called "deviant responses to the world." Rather than concentrating exclusively on religious beliefs and social mechanisms to explain sectarianism, Wilson argued that in the modern world sects come into being because their leaders and members are alienated from the world. This alienation takes a number of major forms, each of which acquires its own characteristic religious formulation. Wilson identified seven such responses and their corresponding sectarian type: conversionist, revolutionist, introversionist, manipulationist, thaumaturgical, reformist, and utopian. In *Religious Sects,* Wilson illustrated these types with examples drawn from the Euro-American Christian tradition, especially Protestant sects. Three years later, in *Magic and the Millennium,* he applied his typology to a global range of non-Christian religious movements, freeing the theory of sectarianism from its Christian derivation and inviting many provocative comparisons across the world's religions.

Theoretical work on sectarianism has continued through the 1980s and 1990s, but it is fair to say that over the past decade scholarly attention has shifted from historic Protestant sectarian movements to the sectarian qualities of contemporary worldwide religious FUNDAMENTALISM. In the American context, Nancy Tatom Ammerman has contributed the most notable study of Protestant fundamentalism and sectarianism in *Baptist Battles: Social Change and Religious Conflict in the Southern Baptist Convention* (1990). The most significant examination of global fundamentalism and sectarianism to date is *The Fundamentalism Project* (1991–1995), a five-volume comparative study of Christianity, JUDAISM, Islam, and Hinduism edited by Martin E. Marty and R. Scott Appleby. Sectarian theory has thus gained a new relevancy for interpreting the contemporary religious world, but it remains essential to any critical understanding of the history and nature of Protestantism.

While the definition and causes of sectarianism continue to be debated, there can be little doubt that it has been a primary shaping force in Protestantism. Indeed, there are good reasons to regard Protestantism itself as a sectarian movement. MARTIN LUTHER's own protest certainly had sectarian implications. His critiques of the SACRAMENTS and papal authority attacked Catholic religious culture at its ritual and institutional foundations, while his formulation of the salvific process located it in an irreducibly individual experience of GRACE through FAITH in the scriptures. H. RICHARD NIEBUHR called this "the Protestant protest," capturing in that phrase not only Luther's challenge to Catholic tradition, but also Protestantism's subsequent tendency to foment protest, even against fellow Protestants. In this sense, Protestantism has always contained an element of DISSENT ready to explode into sectarian radicalism. The immense history of Protestant sectarianism demonstrates this enduring quality. Indeed, at the outset of the twenty-first century there are more Protestants worldwide whose traditions lie in sectarian origins than in the mainstream Reformation communions of Luther, JOHN CALVIN, and ANGLICANISM. To explain how this circumstance came about over the past five centuries is the task of this article.

The Reformation

The earliest Reformation sectarians appeared almost immediately after the publication of Luther's three great Reformation tracts of 1521. They were a group subsequently called the Zwickau Prophets, men from a small city in Saxony who believed that they had experienced direct revelations from the Holy Spirit, rejected infant BAPTISM, and proclaimed Christ's imminent return to destroy the ANTICHRIST, whom they identified as the ascendant Ottoman Turks. With Luther absent in the Wartburg, the Prophets visited Wittenberg on December 27, 1521, where they urged ANDREAS RUDOLPH BODENSTEIN KARLSTADT and PHILIPP MELANCHTHON to endorse their claims. Melanchthon hesitated, while Karlstadt embraced some of their teachings on the LORD'S SUPPER, then broke with the Prophets after they fomented iconoclastic riots in the city during January and February of 1522. Luther returned on March 6, restored most of the Latin Mass, and condemned the Prophets as "fanatics" (*schwärmer*).

Radical Protestants like the Zwickau Prophets have been called "spiritualists," because of their fundamental assertion that the same Holy Spirit that inspired the biblical prophets and the apostles also dwells in them, granting the same supernatural abilities to heal, prophesy, and interpret the Word of God. The earliest Spiritualists also held radical political views based on their demand that all secular and ecclesiastical institutions be remodeled according the Mosaic Law and their expectation of the imminent second coming of Christ. Chief among these Revolutionary Spiritualists was THOMAS MÜNTZER, minister of the Zwickau parish that had nurtured the Prophets. Comprehensively articulated in his remarkable *Sermon before the Princes* (1524), Müntzer's program was rejected by Duke John of Saxony but vigorously embraced by an aroused laity. Rural peasants and urban artisans throughout GERMANY soon demanded the reform of feudal arrangements, town charters, and territorial constitutions. When their demands were not met, they rebelled in the Peasants' War of 1524–1525. The war was a disaster for the rebels, however, who were slaughtered in three decisive battles during May 1525 at Böblingen, Frankenhausen, and Zabern. Müntzer himself was imprisoned and executed after Frankenhausen, and the Revolutionary Spiritualist phase of Reformation sectarianism soon collapsed.

After the Peasants' War, the sectarian impulse relocated in a new form called ANABAPTISM. Even before the Peasants' War, agitation over baptism had broken out in Zurich, where HULDRYCH ZWINGLI's sacramental theology had denied the infusion of divine grace through ritual action. Radicals there, known as the Swiss Brethren and led by Felix Mantz, CONRAD GREBEL, and George Blaurock, argued that if SALVATION indeed came by grace through faith in the scriptures, then only believing adults should be baptized. Accordingly, they began rebaptizing their followers in 1525, gaining the name Anabaptists from the Greek for "those who baptize again." The Anabaptist movement spread quickly through SWITZERLAND.

The Anabaptists convened two synods in 1527 that prefigured their subsequent development. In February,

MICHAEL SATTLER presided over a meeting of the Swiss Brethren at Schleitheim that addressed the urgent need to define the movement institutionally. The Twelve Articles of Schleitheim rejected antinomian excess; imposed excommunication ("the ban") on disobedient members as a means of purifying the community; embraced separation from the profane world; established the office of pastor as teacher, liturgist, and administrator of the ban; and refused to bear arms or take part in civil government, including the swearing of oaths before secular authorities (see SCHLEITHEIM CONFESSION). Six months later, Denck and Hut presided over the Martyr's Synod in Augsburg, a gathering of apocalyptic radicals who debated when the Kingdom of Christ would begin (they agreed on Pentecost 1528) and how to organize Anabaptist missions in the last days. The leaders of this aggressive assembly were arrested, tortured, and executed by city authorities.

After the Martyr's Synod, Radical Anabaptists took up the apocalyptic cause of preparing the world for Christ's imminent return. The most spectacular example of Radical Anabaptism was the remodeling of the Westphalian city of Münster into the New Jerusalem during 1534–1535 by JAN MATHIIS and Jan van Leiden, Dutch followers of MELCHIOR HOFMANN, an influential millennial Anabaptist whose "covenanters" also fomented an abortive insurrection in Amsterdam in March 1534. At Münster, the Anabaptists practiced community of goods, polygamy, and military defiance of secular and ecclesiastical rulers. For these excesses the city was besieged and taken in June 1535 by the army of the prince-bishop of Westphalia, and its inhabitants were slaughtered. Münster became a byword for radical extremism, and all Anabaptist movements suffered persecution after its demise.

For their part, the Anabaptists abandoned revolutionary radicalism after Münster, turning to the Schleitheim model of sectarianism to construct purified, separatist, communal, and nonviolent communities that could survive and even thrive under the most difficult cultural conditions. The most important new Anabaptist groups of this type were the MENNONITES in the NETHERLANDS, the HUTTERITES in Moravia, and the Socinians in POLAND. Named for MENNO SIMONS, the West Frisian Anabaptist leader who gathered them together after 1537, Mennonites generally followed the Schleitheim Confession's teaching on adult baptism and the covenanted community of believers. Menno added a more rigorous deployment of the ban including not only the excommunication of the disobedient, but also total avoidance, or "shunning," of them by the faithful. With the 1540 publication of Menno's *Foundation of Christian Doctrine,* the defining text of Mennonite Anabaptism, his movement

grew quickly in the Low Countries and by 1550 stretched east along the Hanseatic coast all the way to Königsberg.

In east-central Europe, a similar Anabaptist movement emerged under JAKOB HUTTER, who became leader of the Tyrolean Anabaptists in 1529. Hutter supervised the emigration of his followers from the Tyrol to Austerlitz and Auspitz in Moravia, where he organized a federation of all Moravian Anabaptists in 1531. Hutter speedily advanced a vision of apostolic community grounded in the community of goods, carefully organized economic cohesion, strict obedience to leaders, and spiritual and material preparedness for facing persecution and exile. These preparations quickly proved their value. In the spring of 1535, at the height of the Münster episode, King Ferdinand of Bohemia ordered the expulsion of all Anabaptists from Moravia. Hutter was captured, tortured, and publicly burned in 1536, but his movement survived fierce persecution under his successor Peter Riedemann, whose *Account* (1540) became the definitive formulation of Hutterite belief and practice.

Other Anabaptists fleeing Habsburg persecution in Austria migrated east into Poland and Lithuania, where they created a powerful but theologically diverse radical presence. During the 1550s and 1560s, they were molded into the Minor Reformed Church by Peter Gonesius, Francis Stancaro, and George Blandrata. These leaders were heavily influenced by the antiTrinitarian theology of the Basque physician MICHAEL SERVETUS, burned by Calvin as a heretic at Geneva in 1553. After continuing theological and political controversy, the Lithuanian Brethren in 1577 separated under Simon Budney to form a Unitarian, nonpacifist Anabaptist community, while the Minor Church embraced PACIFISM and the esoteric anti-Trinitarian theology of FAUSTO SOZZINI (Socinus).

A somewhat different pattern of Protestant sectarianism occurred in ENGLAND. HENRY VIII had effected a magisterial reform of the CHURCH OF ENGLAND during the 1530s and 1540s shaped principally by the thought of Luther and MARTIN BUCER of Strasbourg. Decades of unrest followed under Edward VI and the Catholic Mary, then a stabilizing Anglican settlement by ELIZABETH I. During Elizabeth's reign, however, English Calvinists led by THOMAS CARTWRIGHT organized the Puritan party to press for further reformation of the national church along Genevan lines. When their attempt failed, several Puritan communities, most notably Cartwright's own congregation at Middleburg, went into sectarian exile in the Calvinist NETHERLANDS.

Other English Puritans condemned the magisterial polity and liturgical practice of the Church of England altogether and organized Separatist conventicles.

Henry Barrow organized the first of these Separatist sects in London in 1587, followed by ROBERT BROWNE's Norwich community in 1581 and JOHN SMYTH's Arminian Separatist-Baptist congregation in London in 1612. The Separatists called for absolute separation of CHURCH AND STATE, a purified church of believers only, and WORSHIP restricted to PRAYER, biblical teaching, and "prophesying"—congregational testimony and dialogue with the teacher. For these beliefs and practices, they suffered persecution and martyrdom, which in turn drove other Separatists to seek asylum in the Netherlands. One of these groups, JOHN ROBINSON's Separatist congregation at Leyden, chose an even more extreme voluntary exile, emigrating in 1620 to North America where they founded the Plymouth Colony. Americans know them as the Pilgrims.

The ongoing and increasingly violent clash between Anglicans and Puritans for control of both the Church of England and the nation's government continued to be the main source of seventeenth-century English Protestant sectarianism. The controversy escalated under James I and Charles I, exacerbated by the persecution of Puritans by WILLIAM LAUD, who was named archibishop of CANTERBURY by Charles in 1633. A significant number of Puritan ministers withdrew from the Church of England to preside over Congregationalist or Independent churches. Soon (Calvinist) Particular Baptists began to break away from the Independents, beginning in 1633 with Spilsbury's Broad Street congregation in London, joined by the Seventh-Day Baptists who believed that the New Testament mandated worship on Saturday, the Jewish sabbath, not on Sunday. The most important of these early Baptists was ROGER WILLIAMS, who founded the New England colony of Rhode Island in 1647 as a refuge for all of English DISSENT.

The Anglicans, returned to power with the restoration of the monarchy under Charles II in 1660, mounted persecution of dissenters through the Clarendon Code until the GLORIOUS REVOLUTION of 1689. This protracted religious and political struggle produced a host of sectarian movements bearing extreme eschatological and political teachings but generally lacking the Continental sectarians' demand for rebaptism as a sign of true faith. Oliver Cromwell's "New Model Army" of the 1640s was the seedbed for many of them. The most notable eschatological sects during the war were the Ranters, a loose group of extreme apocalyptic and chiliastic seers reminiscent of the Zwickau Prophets; the Seekers, an equally inchoate movement of spiritual pilgrims, the most prominent of whom was the unitarian, universalist, and perfectionist preacher William Erbery; and the Fifth Monarchists, who proclaimed the imminent return of Christ to rule over earth's final era of history. Of a more political bent were two sects of the late 1640s. John Lilburne's LEVELLERS demanded that Christian government derive from the people through a universal franchise, separation of powers, and protection of inalienable rights. The Diggers, or True Levellers, led by GERRARD WINSTANLEY and William Everard, were radical pacifists and communitarians who from 1649 to 1651 occupied and farmed common lands on St. George's Hill near London.

The most important seventeenth-century English sect, however, was the Society of FRIENDS, or Quakers. Founded by Leicestershire lay preacher GEORGE FOX in 1648, the Friends taught the universalistic doctrine that all humans were born with the Inner Light of God's spirit, which, when embraced by the will, would produce apostolic gifts of revelatory experience, inspired utterance, and healing. Gaining their nickname from agitated "quaking" brought on by extreme charismatic states, the Friends gathered into semicommunal congregations characterized by severe moral discipline, an ascetic lifestyle, consensual decision making, incessant missionary activity, and a distinctive form of silent worship broken only by speech regarded as directly prompted by the Inner Light. The Friends also embraced radical social doctrines of pacifism and egalitarianism, including in the latter a categorical refusal to acknowledge their social superiors in Restoration England. Fox's movement gained thousands of converts even as it endured persecution under both the Puritan Commonwealth and the Restoration monarchy. By 1691, the year of Fox's death, the Friends had become the largest Protestant sect in England and had established important enclaves in the West Indies as well as in British North America, including Quaker WILLIAM PENN's colony of Pennsylvania.

The Eighteenth Century: Pietism and Evangelicalism

On the Continent, the end of the religious wars in 1648 ushered in a period of theological systematization in the Lutheran and Reformed churches. This "scholastic" emphasis on the rational consistency of DOCTRINE helped launch the ENLIGHTENMENT, but it also tended to devalue the importance of lived religion. Reaction came quickly with the publication of *Pious Desires* by Lutheran pastor PHILIPP JAKOB SPENER in 1675, who called for the revitalization of local congregations by creating "colleges of piety," small lay groups guided by their pastors to study the Bible, pray together, share their experience of God's grace, and assist one another in their common pursuit of the Christian life. Popular LUTHERANISM enthusiastically embraced Spener's program and it soon spread to the German Reformed churches as well. The most prominent characteristic of PIETISM was its intense emotionalism. The spiritual intimacy of Pietist societies fostered a new vocabulary of powerful personal relationships to Christ, especially a grief-stricken sense of SIN in contemplating the crucifixion and a child-like feeling of dependency on the Savior.

By 1700 Pietism had swept German-speaking Protestantism and heavily influenced Reformed communions in England and France. Pietism became the most important source of Protestant sectarianism over the next century, especially in Britain and America. One of the earliest Continental Pietist sects was the Labadists, a communal inspirationist fellowship founded by Jean de Labadie, a Jesuit from Provence who renounced Catholicism in 1650, was excommunicated from the French Reformed Church in 1670, and led his followers to Germany, where he died in 1674. Another French Pietist sect was the Cevenole Prophets, or French Prophets, a group of apocalyptic convulsionary charismatics who emerged during the persecution of Protestants in the Cevennes following the revocation of the Edict of NANTES by Louis XIV in 1685 and emigrated to England in 1703. Two German Pietist sects found permanent homes in Pennsylvania, where William Penn had welcomed Mennonites as early as 1683. In 1732 Conrad Beissel, a preacher grounded in the German Seventh-Day Baptist tradition, founded Ephrata Cloister near Reading. The Ephratans were organized into three orders of married householders, celibate men, and celibate women who practiced an ascetic life of work, meditation, and frequent worship including midnight watch services.

The most important Continental Pietist sect, however, was the Renewed United Brethren, popularly known as the Moravians. At the turn of the eighteenth century, the long-underground remnant of Jan Hus's proto-Protestant *Unitas Fratrum,* or United Brethren, began to revive in Catholic Silesia and Moravia. In 1717 one of its leaders, Christian David, began to search for a Protestant refuge for the often-persecuted sect. David encountered Count NICHOLAS LUDWIG VON ZINZENDORF, who granted the Brethren asylum on his estate in Saxony in 1722. Five years later, the community formally reorganized at HERRNHUT as the Renewed United Brethren. Meanwhile, Zinzendorf had embraced an ecumenical vision of what he called "the pure religion of Christianity of the heart" and after becoming Moravian bishop in 1737 stamped the movement with an urgent missionary zeal (see MORAVIAN CHURCH).

One of the earliest Moravian missionary groups sailed in 1736 from London to the new British colony of Georgia. Aboard the same ship were Georgia governor James Oglethorpe and two young Anglican priests, JOHN and CHARLES WESLEY, who were assigned to organize the church and government of the colony. Leaders of a Pietistic "holy club" while at Oxford in the early 1730s, the Wesleys were strongly impressed by the Moravians' fervent piety and hymn singing. Back in London after their Georgia mission, the Wesleys experienced emotionally charged assurances of personal salvation at Peter Böhler's Moravian meeting in Aldersgate Street. They soon began itinerant preaching and organizing Methodist societies, modeled on Pietist and Moravian precedents, among Anglican artisan and working class people. The Wesleys' insistence on "the necessity of the New Birth" and their advocacy of sanctified "Christian perfection" helped spark the Evangelical Revival in England during the 1740s. John Wesley authorized a separate Methodist Episcopal Church in America in 1784 but resisted schismatic tendencies in his movement at home. Shortly after his death in 1791, however, the Wesleyan Methodists seceded from the Anglican Church to create English Protestantism's largest sectarian family of the nineteenth century, which also included Alexander Kilham's Methodist New Connexion (1797), HUGH BOURNE's PRIMITIVE METHODIST CHURCH (1807), and William O'Brien's Bible Christians (1815).

The eighteenth century was also a period of sectarian proliferation elsewhere in the Anglo-Atlantic world. In SCOTLAND, John Glas and Robert Sandeman led a schismatic Presbyterian communion after 1728 that held strict predestinarian ideas of human will and observed dietary prohibitions prescribed in Acts 15. More important Scottish sects were the Associate Presbytery formed by Ebenezer Erskine in 1733 and the Reformed Presbytery gathered in 1753. Both of these movements combined evangelical theology with an imperative to restore the classical Reformed beliefs and practices of Calvin and JOHN KNOX. After 1800, another burst of British sectarianism took a more apostolic and millenarian character. In 1830 Anglican priest JOHN NELSON DARBY gathered the PLYMOUTH BRETHREN in Devon around his radical anticlericalism and advocacy of lay exhortation and spiritual gifts. Two years later Presbyterian minister EDWARD IRVING founded the Holy Catholic Apostolic Church according to his Arian Christology and millenarian interpretations of the Book of Revelation.

It was in the American colonies, however, that the most dramatic sectarian implications of EVANGELICALISM appeared. GEORGE WHITEFIELD's preaching in the Great Awakening (see AWAKENINGS) divided American Calvinists, especially Presbyterians in the South and Middle Colonies and Congregationalists in New England. Among Presbyterians, the itinerant revival preaching of GILBERT TENNENT and doctrinal controversy over the New Birth created a thirteen-year schism (1743–1757) between the evangelical New Side and the traditionalist Old Side. New England Congregationalists polarized along similar lines into New Light and Old Light parties, but the Radical Evangelical wing of Separate or Strict Congregationalists, nearly one-third of the communion, permanently withdrew during the 1740s and 1750s. The Separates endorsed itinerant preaching, absolute congregational autonomy, charismatic gifts as evidence of the New Birth, lay testimony and exhortation in worship, and separation of church and state.

The Separate Congregationalists provided the seedbed for what would eventually become the most important American Protestant sectarian movement. During the early 1750s, some of the Separates made contact with Particular Baptists in Rhode Island who persuaded them that the old Anabaptist tenet of adult baptism upon profession of faith was true. Shubael Stearns and Daniel Marshall organized new Separate Baptist congregations in Connecticut, then migrated to the North Carolina Piedmont, where they organized the Sandy Creek Association in 1755. The Separate Baptists grew into the largest Baptist group in America by 1775 and propelled the Baptists to become independent America's largest denominational family by 1790.

As a hybrid sect, however, the Separate Baptists were themselves prone to internal dispute and sectarian division. During the American Revolution, three New England sects, the SHAKERS, the Universalists, and the FREE-WILL BAPTISTS, recruited most of their members from the Separate Baptists. The Shakers were a charismatic, celibate, pacifist, and apocalyptic sect born in the Whitefieldian evangelical milieu of Manchester, England during the 1750s. ANN LEE, the most extreme of the Manchester leaders, settled with a small band of followers at Niskayuna, New York in 1776 and conducted a highly successful mission to New England during the early 1780s, preaching CELIBACY, communalism, and millennial perfectionism. In 1787 Joseph Meacham, a Separate Baptist elder from Enfield, Connecticut, was chosen to lead the fast-growing sect. Meacham organized the Shakers into twelve communal societies scattered throughout New England and New York. UNIVERSALISM first came to America from similar English sources. John Murray, convert of one of Whitefield's associate preachers James Relly, founded the first American Universalist congregation at Gloucester, Massachusetts in 1779. Universalism's main impetus, however, came from New England Separate Baptist elders Elhanan Winchester and Hosea Ballou, who embraced universal salvation and proto-Unitarian christologies during the

1780s and built lasting institutional foundations for the emerging sect. Despite their common Separate Baptist constituency, the Shakers and the Universalists did not practice adult baptism, while the FREE-WILL BAPTISTS did. Founded by New Hampshire Separate Baptist Benjamin Randel in 1779, the Free Will Baptists rejected Calvinism for the esoteric and pacifist Arminian theology of HENRY ALLINE, yet another New England Separate Baptist who gathered a large evangelical pacifist and ecumenical sect among Yankee expatriates in Nova Scotia during the 1770s and 1780s.

The Nineteenth Century: Protestant Sectarianism in the United States

The American Revolution struck down religious establishments in the southern colonies and eventually in New England as well, while the First Amendment to the United States Constitution separated church and state in the new national government. Absent the religious establishments against which it had always struggled, sectarianism came to be redefined in America exclusively as a matter of alternative religious belief and practice. One important effect was the early Republic's receptivity to refugee sectarian movements, especially radical Pietist communions fleeing persecution in Germany. These groups generally followed a common pattern of charismatic leadership, communalism, and perfectionism. The most important of these were George Rapp's celibate colonies of Harmonie (1805) and Economy (1825) in Pennsylvania and New Harmony (1814) in Indiana, the Society of Separatists or Inspirationists at Zoar, Ohio (1817), and Christian Metz's Community of True Inspiration at Ebenezer, New York (1842) and AMANA, Iowa (1855).

Among American evangelical Protestants, religious competition and denominational schism replaced political and cultural resistance as the hallmarks of sectarian movements. These new conditions produced luxuriant results fuelled by the Second Great Awakening, another wave of intense popular concern about personal salvation and correct belief and practice that swept across America from the 1790s through the 1840s. The Methodists benefited most from the Second Awakening, in part because their institutional structure of class meetings, circuits, and conferences, carefully maintained by Bishop FRANCIS ASBURY, mitigated major sectarian ruptures. The only major American Methodist schisms before 1843 were James O'Kelly's Republican Methodists in 1794 and the Methodist Protestant Church in 1830, both of which rejected Episcopal polity. Methodists also organized the first independent denominations among African

Americans, RICHARD ALLEN's AFRICAN METHODIST EPISCOPAL CHURCH in 1787 and James Varick's AFRICAN METHODIST EPISCOPAL ZION CHURCH in 1796.

Among the Reformed denominations, however, the Second Awakening proved deeply divisive. Controversies over the proper training of ministers and the use of highly emotional preaching at CAMP MEETING revivals added to the doctrinal fractures already present among Presbyterians and Baptists. Most of the early sects of the Second Awakening were regional. In 1801 Vermonters Abner Jones and Elias Smith organized the Christian Connection, an Arminian Baptist sect based on the principle of "Gospel liberty." James O'Kelly's Republican Methodists joined the Christian Connection in 1809 to create a distinctively American sect with congregations from Maine to the Carolinas. Anti-Calvinist Pietistic sects also emerged during the Second Awakening among German-speaking Pennsylvanians. The most important of these were the BRETHREN IN CHRIST (1800), founded by German Reformed minister William Otterbein; the Evangelical Association (1800), organized by Lutheran pastor Jacob Albright and Mennonite leader Martin Boehm; and the Church of God (1830), gathered by German Reformed pastor John Winebrenner.

In the West, two years after the first great camp meeting at Cane Ridge, Kentucky in 1801, the Presbytery of Springfield, Kentucky dissolved and declared all nonlocal ecclesiastical institutions unscriptural. Some of its members followed Springfield leader Richard McNemar into Shakerism after 1805, while most joined BARTON W. STONE, convener of the Cane Ridge revival, in a search for a nondenominational Christianity based on the New Testament narrative. Thomas Campbell gathered a similar sect, the Christian Association, in 1808 among Presbyterians in western Pennsylvania and Virginia, following the motto "where the Scriptures are silent, we are silent; where the Scriptures speak, we speak." In 1810 yet another group of pro-revival Presbyterians in eastern Tennessee and Kentucky broke away from the parent denomination over standards of ministerial training and creedalism to form the CUMBERLAND PRESBYTERIAN CHURCH. At the same time, some strict Calvinist Baptists, beginning in 1792 with the Kehukee Association in Virginia, resisted the revival, condemned missionary activity, and began to practice foot-washing as an ordinance of worship (see FEET, WASHING OF). These churches created a loosely organized southern sect known as Anti-Mission Baptists or PRIMITIVE BAPTISTS.

Sectarianism continued to grow in America after the War of 1812, sparked by the resurgence of the Second Awakening. The powerful doctrinal disputes of this period fostered a sectarian search for new sources of religious authority. New England Unitarians cited reason as their guide in seceding from the orthodox Congregationalists in 1824 to pursue a Christianity free from what they considered superstitious and irrational teachings such as miracles and the doctrine of the Trinity. ESCHATOLOGY and perfectionism were also important sources of authority for antebellum sects. The most extreme eschatological sect were the Adventists, whose founder WILLIAM MILLER, a Baptist minister from upstate New York, summarized their chiliastic teachings in his 1835 book *Evidences from Scripture and History of the Second Coming of Christ About the Year 1843*. Thousands embraced Miller's prediction, and when the promised apocalypse did not occur in 1843 or on the recalculated date of October 22, 1844, the movement survived through the visions of Hiram Edson and ELLEN GOULD WHITE, who saw Christ entering God's temple in heaven to begin his work of purification and judgment. White assumed leadership of the movement, which she reorganized in 1863 as the SEVENTH-DAY ADVENTISTS, introducing dietary codes and worship practices modeled on the Hebrew Bible. A smaller sectarian branch of the Millerites organized after 1863 as the rival ADVENT CHRISTIAN CHURCH.

Perfectionism, already widely diffused in American evangelicalism though Methodism, found its most spectacular sectarian expression in John Humphrey Noyes's Putney Association in Vermont (1840) and Oneida Community in upstate New York (1848). Noyes taught that Christ had returned in 70 C.E. and initiated the kingdom of millennial perfection, of which he was now the chosen leader. The most controversial features of Noyes's communal regime at Oneida involved collective sexual practices including "complex marriage," the sharing of sexual partners; "male continence," intercourse without ejaculation; "ascending fellowship," the initiation of virgins by the community's elders; and "stirpiculture," the breeding of community children by parents selected by Noyes.

The most important source of antebellum sectarianism, however, was RESTORATIONISM, the search for a "restored" nondenominational church based strictly on Scriptural standards. In western Pennsylvania and Virginia, Thomas Campbell affiliated his noncreedal Christian Association with the Baptists in 1815; his son Alexander Campbell gathered a new restorationist sect called the DISCIPLES OF CHRIST in 1827. By 1832 Barton W. Stone's Ohio Valley "Christians" had joined the Disciples, who also aligned with Elias Smith and James O'Kelly's Christian Connection in the East, establishing restorationism as a major sectarian force in early America. In 1844 John Thomas left the Disciples to form the CHRISTADELPHIANS, or Brothers of Christ, who developed an anti-Trinitarian theology and the distinctive tenet that the souls of the unredeemed would be annihilated after death while the souls of the redeemed would sleep until Jesus returns. Among Baptists in the Deep South, in 1854 J. M. Pendleton and J. R. Graves gathered the Landmark Baptists, who believed themselves part of the continual existence of Christ's true apostolic churches since his earthly ministry.

The Latter-day Saints also proclaimed a restorationist Gospel, but with a new scripture and a new prophet to proclaim and interpret it (see MORMONISM). In addition to the Bible, the Saints followed the teachings of *The Book of Mormon,* published in 1830 by JOSEPH SMITH of Palmyra, New York, as an ancient inspired text shown to him by an angel who also provided miraculous instruments for its translation. The book told the story of the Nephites, an Israelite tribe who fled the Babylonian Captivity, crossed the Atlantic, landed in Central America, gradually migrated across the North American continent, received the Gospel directly from the preaching of the risen Christ, and died at the hands of their apostate relatives called the Lamanites. Smith, regarded by his followers as the prophet of this restored Gospel, organized the Latter-Day Saints as a communal sect and led them from upstate New York to Ohio, Missouri, and eventually Nauvoo, Illinois in search of a place to build a new American Zion. Amid rumors of polygamy and military insurrection, Smith was arrested, jailed, and murdered by a mob at Carthage, Illinois in 1844. BRIGHAM YOUNG succeeded Smith as leader of the Saints, and in 1849 brought them en masse to Utah, where Mormonism has continued to flourish as one of America's most successful and distinctive sectarian movements.

While radical groups like Latter-day Saints, Adventists, and Oneidans remained on the social periphery, the culturally legitimized location of most American sects permitted them to engage in mainstream political activity. From this position they experienced serious and ultimately schismatic controversies over SLAVERY, the greatest political issue in antebellum America. From the 1830s, Alexander Campbell steered his DISCIPLES OF CHRIST toward an apolitical position on slavery, claiming that it was a civil, not a religious, question. Presbyterians, on the other hand, divided along sectional lines into New School and Old School camps in 1837. The climax of the slavery crisis in the American churches occurred in 1843–1844, when America's two largest communions broke apart explicitly over the question of whether ministers should own slaves. In 1843 Methodists divided into the proslavery Methodist Episcopal Church South, the antislavery Methodist Episcopal Church North, and the abolitionist Wesleyan Methodist Connection. A

year later the Baptists split into rival Northern and SOUTHERN BAPTIST CONVENTIONS. These slavery schisms permanently altered the religious landscape of the United States, reinforcing a sectarian sensibility of denomination conflict and confrontation. The Presbyterian and Methodist divisions did not heal until the late twentieth century; while the Southern Baptist Convention and the Northern Baptist Convention, now called the AMERICAN BAPTIST CHURCHES, remain separated. After 1845, separations continued over the slavery issue, the most important being the antislavery Free Methodist schism of 1860.

After the trauma of CIVIL WAR, the abrupt arrival of modernity in the form of industrialization, urbanization, immigration, and the rise of SCIENCE became a new source of Protestant sectarianism. Dominant liberals in the mainline American denominations accepted the new conditions and accommodated their theologies and ecclesiastical institutions to modern conditions through the SOCIAL GOSPEL movement. Evangelicals in the South, however, adhered to "the old-time religion" as a badge of traditional identity while their counterparts in the North responded to their growing cultural alienation by asserting traditional biblical authority, the imperative of spiritual rebirth, and systematic doctrine as the antidote to what they called "MODERNISM." Darwinian liberals' denial of the biblical creation account and the Social Gospel's Christian socialism were especially galling developments against which Evangelicals reacted.

During the late nineteenth century, that reaction generally took sectarian form as the reassertion of traditional evangelical beliefs and practices. Revivalism returned during the 1870s with the northern urban campaigns of Congregationalist DWIGHT LYMAN MOODY and the rural southern itinerancy of Methodist Sam Jones. Restorationist principles, applied to the BOOK OF COMMON PRAYER, informed the separation of GEORGE DAVID CUMMINS and the Reformed Episcopal Church from the Anglican communion in 1873. A renewal of adventism informed the JEHOVAH'S WITNESSES, founded in 1881 by CHARLES TAZE RUSSELL, who proclaimed that Christ would return in 1914 and instructed converts to observe biblical dietary and sumptuary rules. Increasing concern for foreign and domestic MISSIONS drove Albert B. Simpson to organize the CHRISTIAN AND MISSIONARY ALLIANCE in 1887 and prepared the way for the favorable American reception of WILLIAM and CATHERINE BOOTH's SALVATION ARMY, founded in 1878 in London.

A salient exception to these traditionalist sectarian movements was MARY BAKER EDDY's Church of Christ, Scientist, organized in Lynn, Massachusetts in 1879. Reflecting popular interest in SPIRITUALISM and her own experience of medical hypnosis, Eddy declared in her 1875 book *Science and Health* that only spirit is real and that matter is illusory. Illness, she concluded, was caused by spiritual error and could be healed by proper faith. Jesus had known this "scientific" truth, used it in his healing ministry, and proclaimed it in the gospels. CHRISTIAN SCIENCE converts, drawn principally from middle- and upper-class New Englanders, accepted *Science and Health* as a scriptural text that supplemented the Bible and sustained Eddy's absolute charismatic and institutional authority over one of the most successful sectarian movements in American history.

The largest group of postbellum sects, however, emerged from METHODISM as the result of the HOLINESS MOVEMENT. The Second Great Awakening had produced perfectionistic Methodist sects like the Wesleyan Methodists (1843), but after the war a broader popular concern for Christian perfection emerged with the organization of the National Camp Meeting Association for the Promotion of Holiness in 1867. Holiness leaders proclaimed a "second blessing" of complete SANCTIFICATION for the truly regenerate. The movement spread quickly, inducing a number of sectarian Holiness communities to separate from the Methodists. The most important of these were the CHURCH OF GOD, ANDERSON, INDIANA (1881) and the Holiness Christian Church (1889). In 1894 the Southern Methodists rejected Holiness claims, leading to the separation of more than two dozen Holiness sects, the largest of which were the CHURCH OF THE NAZARENE (1895), the Pilgrim Holiness Church (1897), and the INTERNATIONAL PENTECOSTAL HOLINESS CHURCH (1898). The Holiness movement also reached the African American Methodist mainstream, drawing off a number of sects, most importantly Charles Price Jones and Charles H. Mason's CHURCH OF GOD IN CHRIST (1897).

The Twentieth Century: Fundamentalist and Pentecostal Sects

Doctrinal tensions and conflicts over spirituality continued to escalate in American Protestantism after 1900, finally producing FUNDAMENTALISM and PENTECOSTALISM, movements carried forward primarily by sectarian and schismatic communities. Fundamentalism was originally a northern urban phenomenon, a systematic formulation of essential evangelical doctrines by leading pastors and theologians in New York, Philadelphia, and Chicago. Central to fundamentalism was its claim that the Scriptures are verbally inspired by the Holy Spirit and entirely inerrant as historical and religious narratives. From this foundation, Fundamentalists maintained traditional doctrines such as the seven days of creation, the virgin birth of Christ, and the historicity of miracles. They also produced an elaborate political and theological interpretation of the prophetic biblical texts and urgently promoted foreign and domestic missions.

Fundamentalism spread quickly to the south and west where its classic documents appeared. The SCOFIELD REFERENCE BIBLE, published in 1909 by C. I. Scofield of Dallas Theological Seminary, provided extensive running eschatological commentary on the biblical text. The definitive statement of the movement's doctrines was *The Fundamentals* (from which the movement drew its name), published in four volumes in Los Angeles between 1912 and 1915. After World War I, fundamentalists battled unsuccessfully for control of the Northern Baptists and Presbyterians, agitating heresy trials of leading liberals and campaigning for major denominational offices. In the Northern Baptist Convention, William Bell Riley of Minneapolis led the fundamentalist minority to form the BAPTIST BIBLE UNION in 1923 and the schismatic GENERAL ASSOCIATION OF REGULAR BAPTIST CHURCHES in 1932. Among Presbyterians, fundamentalist professors from Princeton Theological Seminary resisted the liberal Auburn Declaration of 1924, eventually resigning to form Westminster Theological Seminary in 1929 and the Orthodox Presbyterian Church in 1936.

Pentecostalism was a more complex phenomenon than fundamentalism, and it produced many more sectarian movements. Some of the new Holiness churches had used the term "Pentecostal" to identify themselves, claiming that Christian perfection was a spiritual promise given to the church when it received the Holy Spirit on the day of Pentecost described in Acts 2:1–13. This controversial text, however, also described the Apostles as speaking in unknown tongues (*glossolalia* in Greek), thereby opening the possibility that it might be a "third blessing" for true Christians. In 1901 Charles G. Parham began teaching glossolalia as a sign of the Spirit's presence, and shortly thereafter "the gift of tongues" appeared among his community at Topeka, Kansas. William C. Seymour, one of Parham's African-American students and tongue-speakers, took the message of glossolalia to Los Angeles, California, where in 1906 he led a protracted charismatic revival at the AZUZA STREET MISSION that launched the modern Pentecostal movement.

Over the next decade, Pentecostalism divided many American Protestant constituencies, none more than African Americans. In 1907 Charles H. Mason, cofounder of the Church of God in Christ, experienced the gift of tongues. Following an intense struggle over the legitimacy of glossolalia, Mason gained control of the denomination, driving his colleague Charles Price Jones to form a new communion called the Church of

Christ, Holiness. After World War I, African Americans moved to the urban north in great numbers, creating a host of small "storefront" Holiness and Pentecostal sects. Several of these movements, including "Father" M. J. Divine's communal Universal Peace Mission Movement (1914), Marcus Garvey's Universal Negro Improvement Association (1914), and Wali Farad and Elijah Muhammed's Nation of Islam (1930), also included non-Christian and Afrocentric elements in their beliefs and practices. Garvey's influence was particularly important, extending to AFRICA and his native Jamaica, where his Afrocentric teachings were later incorporated into Rastafarianism after the coronation of Emperor Haile Selassie I of Ethiopia in 1930, whom Rastas considered a divine embodiment of African Christianity.

A similar developmental pattern produced a number of white and interracial Pentecostal communions in the South. Beginning as a Holiness movement, Richard Spurling's Christian Union (1886) embraced Pentecostalism in 1908 and under the leadership of A. J. Tomlinson reorganized as the CHURCH OF GOD OF PROPHECY, only to suffer a schism itself in 1923 with the founding of the rival Church of God, Cleveland, Tennessee. Although Pentecostals generally embraced fundamentalism, doctrinal conflicts deeply divided them, especially the Oneness Controversy, a Trinitarian debate over whether Christ alone was God. The interracial PENTECOSTAL ASSEMBLIES OF THE WORLD emerged after 1914 as the leading Oneness sect, while its Trinitarian rival the ASSEMBLIES OF GOD, founded in the same year in Hot Springs, Arkansas, became the most successful of the early Pentecostal sects. After 1925, fundamentalists and Pentecostals proved adept at using mass media, especially radio, to gain converts. Although most of these media ministries did not develop into full-fledged sects, one of them did. The Radio Church of God (since 1968, the Worldwide Church of God), was founded in 1934 by Herbert W. Armstrong and grew through the anti-Trinitarian and eschatological teachings broadcast on his program "The World Tomorrow."

By 1935, the first wave of fundamentalist and Pentecostal sectarianism had subsided. While the media ministries of fundamentalist preacher BILLY GRAHAM and Pentecostal GRANVILLE ORAL ROBERTS sustained these movements through the 1950s and 1960s, the CIVIL RIGHTS MOVEMENT and the Vietnam War fractured several conservative denominations. The most notable example was the schism of the PROGRESSIVE NATIONAL BAPTIST CONVENTION (PNBC) from its parent the National Baptist Convention (NBC), the largest African-American denomination (1866). Protesting the NBC's fundamentalist theological bent, its leaders' refusal to observe term limits on their offices, and its rejection of MARTIN LUTHER KING, JR. and the Civil Rights Movement, the PNBC organized in Cincinnati in 1961 and now numbers 2.5 million members.

By the mid-1970s, however, fundamentalism and Pentecostalism were poised to exert worldwide Protestant influence. Triggered in America by the Catholic Charismatic Renewal and the Bicentennial Revival, new media ministries like JERRY FALWELL's MORAL MAJORITY, PAT ROBERTSON's 700 Club, and Jim and Tammy Faye Bakker's Praise the Lord Club gained enormous popularity in the decade after 1975 (see TELEVANGELISM). The characteristic sectarian expression of this recent revival, however, has been "MEGACHURCHES," exemplified by Willow Creek Community Church, a vast nondenominational congregation founded by Bill Hybels in 1975 at South Barrington, Illinois, near Chicago, with thousands of members and more than 100 ministries located on a 155-acre campus. Thousands of such megachurches now dot the United States landscape, combining eclectic beliefs with a total community environment that provides members everything from health facilities and education to economic networks and arts collaboratives.

The most spectacular and disturbing recent examples of American Protestant sectarian extremism are Jim Jones's People's Temple and David Koresh's BRANCH DAVIDIANS. Jones, a locally ordained Disciples of Christ minister, gathered a progressive interracial community in Indianapolis, Indiana during the 1950s. Over the next two decades, Jones relocated the community in California and made increasingly extreme claims, professing powers of spiritual and physical healing and teaching the doctrine of "translation" whereby the souls of believers would be transported to another planet after death. Growing instability led Jones to move the People's Temple again to Jonestown, an isolated agricultural site in tropical Guyana in South America where, after the catastrophic death of visiting Congressman Leo Ryan, Jones and nearly 1,000 of his followers committed ritual suicide.

Vernon Wayne Howell came from Seventh-Day Adventist roots in Texas. In 1981 he joined the Branch Davidians, a small adventist sect founded in 1935 by Victor Houteff near Waco, Texas. Howell took over the community in 1990, changing his name to David Koresh and claiming to be God's true prophet in the restored royal line of David. Amid reports of illegal stockpiling of firearms and child abuse, federal agents stormed the Branch Davidian compound at Mount Carmel near Waco on April 19, 1993. Mount Carmel was destroyed and eighty-six Davidians, including Koresh, were killed.

Beyond the United States, an immense upsurge in Pentecostal and fundamentalist sects has occurred since 1975, especially in LATIN AMERICA, Africa, and East Asia. Estimates of Pentecostalism's worldwide membership ranged as high as 400 million by the year 2000. Pentecostals claim nearly 20 percent of the population in Chile and El Salvador and twice as many adherents as traditional Protestant churches in Guatemala and Venezuela. BRAZIL is the center of Latin American Pentecostalism, where it has drawn an estimated 25 million converts from the Catholic Church and traditional Spiritist religions. In addition to joining American missionary denominations like the 12-million-member Asambleas de Dios (Assemblies of God), Brazilian Pentecostals have organized a host of indigenous sectarian communions. The largest of these is Edin Macedo's six-million-member Igreja Universal do Reino de Deus (Universal Church of the Reign of God), a controversial movement founded in 1977 and widely accused of promoting spiritual blessings for monetary contributions.

In Africa, Pentecostalism has followed an earlier wave of indigenous anti-colonial and charismatic Protestant sects known as the AFRICAN INSTITUTED CHURCHES. These included SIMON KIMBANGU's Church of the Lord Jesus Christ on Earth in Zaire (c. 1920), JOSIAH OLUNOWO OSHITELU's Church of the Lord (Aladura) in Nigeria (1930), JOHN MARANKE's Apostolic Church and Samuel Mutendi's Zion Christian Church in ZIMBABWE (1930s), and Alice Lenshina's Lumpa Church in Zambia (1950s). Recent African Pentecostalism has been largely dominated by the Faith Gospel movement, a sectarian form that preaches earthly success as a sign of true faith, and by Christian Zionism, the belief that the restoration of Israel is a sign of the imminent return of Christ. Among the leading new African Pentecostal communions are Nicholas Duncan-Williams's Christian Action Faith Ministries (1979) and Mensa Otabil's International Central Gospel Church (1984) in GHANA, Grace Faith Ministries (1993) and Nevers Mumba's Victory Faith Ministries (1984) in Zambia, and John Obiri Yeboah's National Fellowship of Born-Again Churches (1986) in Uganda.

Elements of the Faith Gospel have also appeared in Korean Protestant sectarianism along with a mixture of esoteric shamanistic and Buddhist elements. SUN MYUNG MOON's Holy Spirit Association for the Unification of World Christianity, popularly known as the UNIFICATION CHURCH (or "Moonies"), was founded in 1954 in Seoul. Claiming that Jesus had authorized him to unite all Christians in a new global church, Moon was excommunicated by the Presbyterian Church of KOREA in 1948, then published his manifesto *Divine Principle* (1954) and organized his own sect. Famous for its aggressive evangelism, esoteric beliefs, mass marriages, and questionable financial practices, the

Unification Church enjoyed its greatest influence in America between 1972 and 1984. The most successful Korean Protestant sect today is Paul Yonggi Cho's Yoido Full Gospel Church. Founded in Seoul as an Assemblies of God tent revival in 1958, Cho's church now numbers more than 700,000 members, making it the largest single congregation in the world and a powerful sectarian influence. Cho's controversial doctrines about the spiritual and material powers of speech and the existence of a fourth dimension, along with his practice of healing rituals drawn from traditional Korean shamanism, illustrate the strong syncretistic element associated with many of the new Pentecostal sects outside America and Europe.

Conclusion

Sectarianism has played an essential role in the shaping of Protestantism from the Reformation to the present. Once unleashed in the 1520s by Thomas Müntzer, the Zwickau Prophets, and the Anabaptists, the sectarian impulse has flowed through virtually every Protestant communion with paradoxical results. Sectarianism unquestionably disrupts the unity of any church, causing deep doctrinal and social divisions. It almost always weakens the parent body by drawing off some of its members. On the other hand, sectarianism raises questions about faith and practice that extend the intellectual reach of Protestantism and ultimately bring more members into its religious tradition. This pattern of growth through conflict has proven nothing less than endemic in Protestant history and must be accounted one of the chief sources of Protestantism's survival and continuing vigor.

Why Protestantism produces such a pattern has never been adequately explained. The century-long theoretical debate over whether sectarianism is an intrinsically religious phenomenon or a function of secular causes is an essential interpretive discourse that continues to offer fruitful insights into how Protestantism works. Both views possess undeniable merit, but from the historian's perspective the approach of Weber and Troeltsch seems to explain more evidence. It is not possible to understand Protestant sectarianism without accounting for the religious beliefs that so powerfully influenced the self-conscious attitudes and behaviors of believers. Weber and Troeltsch isolated this religious factor in the social and moral teachings of the sects.

But, as this historical survey has suggested, there seem to be other powerful religious sources for Protestant sectarianism as well. Persistent themes of sectarian identity have included ritual practice and especially believers' baptism, eschatological expectation, esoteric beliefs about the Trinity, the quest for spiritual perfectionism, and the search for a restored apostolic church. None of these themes relates as directly to secular social behavior as did the calling for seventeenth- and eighteenth-century sectarians, according to Weber, yet all of them have been more explicitly and more consistently articulated as distinguishing marks of Protestant identity by the sectarians themselves. Similarly, it is difficult to regard such themes as genuine parts of Troeltch's "social teaching"; they address quite different realms of religious experience, activity, and meaning. It is in those realms and in Protestantism's fundamental doctrinal, ritual, and institutional instabilities that further insight into the elusive sources of Protestant sectarianism is to be found.

See also Anglicanism; Antinomianism; Anti-Trinitarianism; Apocalypticism; Arminianism; Baptist Family of Churches; Campbell Family; Catholic Reactions to Protestantism; Chiliasm; Congregationalism; Covenant; Covenant Theology; Denomination; Ecumenism; Evangelicalism, Theology of; Iconoclasm; Itineracy; Liberal Protestantism and Liberalism; Millenarians and Millennialism; Plural Marriage; Presbyterianism; Puritanism; Sociology of Protestantism; Spiritualism; Statistics; Wesleyanism

References and Further Reading

Ammerman, Nancy Tatom. *Baptist Battles: Social Change and Religious Conflict in the Southern Baptist Convention.* New Brunswick, NJ: Rutgers University Press, 1990.

Bainbridge, William Sims. *The Sociology of Religious Movements.* New York: Routledge, 1997.

Bond, George, Walton Johnson, and Sheila S. Walker, eds. *African Christianity: Patterns of Religious Continuity.* New York: Academic Press, 1979.

Cleary, Edward L., and Hannah W. Stewart-Gambino, eds. *Power, Politics, and Pentecostals in Latin America.* Boulder, CO: Westview Press, 1997.

Cox, Harvey. *Fire From Heaven: The Rise of Pentecostal Spirituality and the Reshaping of Religion in the Twenty-First Century.* Reading, MA: Addison-Wesley, 1995.

Goen, C. C. *Revivalism and Separatism in New England, 1740–1800: Strict Congregationalists and Separate Baptists in the Great Awakening.* Middletown, CT: Wesleyan University Press, 1987.

Gottschalk, Stephen. *The Emergence of Christian Science in American Religious Life.* Berkeley, CA: University of California Press, 1973.

Halévy, Elie. *The Birth of Methodism in England.* Translated and edited by Bernard Semmel. Chicago, IL: University of Chicago Press, 1971.

Hatch, Nathan O. *The Democratization of American Christianity.* New Haven, CT: Yale University Press, 1989.

Hill, Christopher. *The World Turned Upside Down: Radical Ideas During the English Revolution.* New York: Viking Press, 1972.

Hobsbawn, E. J. *Primitive Rebels: Studies in Archaic Forms of Social Movement in the 19th and 20th Centuries.* New York: Praeger, 1963.

Marini, Stephen A. *Radical Sects of Revolutionary New England.* Cambridge, MA: Harvard University Press, 1982.

Marsden, George M. *Fundamentalism and American Culture: The Shaping of Twentieth-Century Evangelicalism, 1870–1925.* New York: Oxford University Press, 1980.

Marty, Martin E., and R. Scott Appleby, eds. *The Fundamentalism Project: A Study Conducted by the American Academy of Arts and Sciences.* 4 vols. Chicago, IL: University of Chicago Press, 1991–1995.

Niebuhr, H. Richard. *The Social Sources of Denominationalism.* New York: H. Holt and Company, 1929.

Numbers, Ronald L., and Jonathan M. Butler, eds. *The Disappointed: Millerism and Millenarianism in the Nineteenth Century.* Bloomington, IN: Indiana University Press, 1987.

Shipps, Jan. *Mormonism: The Story of a New Religious Tradition.* Urbana, IL: University of Illinois Press, 1985.

Stark, Werner. *The Sociology of Religion: A Study of Christendom.* 4 vols. New York: Fordham University Press, 1966.

Stein, Stephen J. *The Shaker Experience in America: A History of the United Society of Believers.* New Haven, CT: Yale University Press, 1992.

Tawney, R. H. *Religion and the Rise of Capitalism.* New York: Harcourt, Brace and Company, 1926.

Thompson, E. P. *The Making of the English Working Class.* New York: Vintage Books, 1963.

Troeltsch, Ernst. *The Social Teaching of the Christian Churches.* 2 vols. Translated by Olive Wyon. London: Allen & Unwin; New York: Macmillan, 1931.

Walzer, Michael. *The Revolution of the Saints: A Study in the Origins of Radical Politics.* Cambridge, MA: Harvard University Press, 1965.

Weber, Max. *The Protestant Ethic and the Spirit of Capitalism.* Translated by Talcott Parsons. London: G. Allen & Unwin, 1930.

Williams, George Huntston. *The Radical Reformation.* Philadelphia, PA: Westminster Press, 1962.

Wilson, Bryan R. *Magic and the Millennium; A Sociological Study of Religious Movements of Protest Among Tribal and Third-World Peoples.* New York: Harper & Row, 1973.

———. *Religious Sects: A Sociological Study.* New York: McGraw-Hill, 1970.

STEPHEN A. MARINI

SECULARIZATION

Secularization refers to the historical process in which religion loses social and cultural significance. As a result of secularization the role of religion in modern societies becomes restricted. In secularized societies faith lacks cultural authority, religious organizations have little social power, and public life proceeds without reference to the supernatural. Secularization captures a long-term societal change, but it has consequences for religion itself. In Western countries, where it has been most pronounced, it has made the connection to their Christian heritage more tenuous. Yet secularization is important beyond the formerly Christian West, given that many of the forces that first sustained it there affect other societies as well.

Before 1648 the term *secularis* had been used to denote one side of Christian distinctions between sacred and mundane. In the Catholic Church secular priests were those serving society at large rather than a religious order; secularization had referred to the dispensation of priests from their vows. After the 1648 Treaty of Westphalia ended the European wars of religion, secularization was used to describe the transfer of territories held by the church to the control of political authorities. By the end of the nineteenth century, however, it had come to refer to the shifting place of religion in society many scholars associated with modernization. Used in this way the very notion of secularization has provoked contention for more than a century. Once at the center of conflict between traditional advocates of strong public religion and secularist intellectuals striving to reduce its role, it has more recently become the subject of scholarly controversy. Although since the 1960s prominent sociologists of religion have charted the course of secularization, partly guided by the work of MAX WEBER (1864–1920), others have questioned the validity of their interpretations.

This article first conveys what secularization means and why it happened. It then addresses the reservations of scholars. It shows how critiques have enriched our understanding of secularization without refuting the best accounts of the process. These continue to capture convincingly a significant historical transformation in and of society. This transformation still reverberates across the world stage, not least because the value and viability of secular society remains the subject of global debate.

Meaning

In Paris, Sainte-Chapelle, a sanctuary built by a Catholic monarch to house Christ's crown of thorns, stands empty, its aesthetic appeal substituting for its old religious function. Across the NETHERLANDS church buildings no longer needed to serve shrinking congregations have been razed or converted into community centers. In ENGLAND majestic cathedrals that manifest in stone and glass the splendor of an old faith now often attract more tourists than believers. Where once a sense of the sacred marked the landscape itself, where social order used to be visibly embedded in sacred order, architectural relics attest to a profound change: the vanishing of the supernatural from the affairs of the world, the waning power of religion to shape society at large. In landscapes and architecture, secularization has become visible.

Secularization describes the world the West has lost. In that world faith in the supernatural was pervasive and important, indeed taken for granted. A Christian version of that faith commanded unique AUTHORITY, shaping collective understanding of the world. Its influence extended to ART and architecture,

MUSIC, and LITERATURE (see ARCHITECTURE, CHURCH). Worldviews that denied the validity of Christian DOCTRINE, let alone the existence of the supernatural, were taboo. Religious elites maintained clear standards of transcendent belief and applied them to all spheres of cultural activity. In that world every community was also a community of faith. To be a member meant identifying with that faith. Overt unbelief constituted dangerous deviance, hence cause for exclusion. Community life, its rhythm shaped by religious ceremonies and events, was tinged with the transcendent. Political authority required religious legitimation; rulers in turn were expected to sustain the cause of religion. In principle, at least, state and church had a common mission. Precisely because religion mattered greatly in public affairs, it also contributed at times to WAR or civil strife. Organized religion commanded major resources, such as valuable land, buildings, and trained staff. Supported by such resources the church long played a key role in providing EDUCATION and social services. Its worldly influence reinforced a shared sense of overarching order, in which human affairs were subject to higher forces. This world had a tangible connection with God. It was a society suffused by the sacred.

Secularization also describes the world the West has gained. In this world, CULTURE is marked by pluralism: religious faith takes many forms, and meaning has many nonreligious sources. The specifically Christian message is one among others, only one way to make sense of the world. It is there, available for individuals to choose, although turned into a preference, religion has no binding force. Conceptions of the supernatural, Christian or otherwise, carry little authority in SCIENCE, art, and literature. No church can determine society's standards of knowledge, beauty, and morality. Even when they make their way into popular culture, supernatural notions thereby lose any sacred aura. In this world citizenship requires no religious attachment, and society sets no rules for religious conformity. Secular events shape the rhythm of public life; publicly significant religious occasions tend to lose their transcendent content. Political authority derives its legitimacy from legal procedures and public support. State institutions execute policy with scant consideration of religious purposes. In modern media, education, or business, religious institutions exercise greatly diminished influence. Their resources are dwarfed by those of secular institutions. Because religious strife is less likely to spill over into the public domain, it diminishes as a cause of domestic and international conflict. Operating within such a secular environment, the nature of religion itself changes as well. Churches are organized as the voluntary effort of citizens who choose to belong; they come to terms with pluralism by giving up claims to exclusive truth; they comfort individuals more than they shape society. In this world an encompassing sacred order turns into a specialized spiritual sphere. Modern society has no sacred canopy. It makes room for religion, but operates on human terms.

This simplified before-and-after description conveys in broad strokes what happened. Secularization theories have sought to explain how and why this epochal change took place in the West.

Explanation

Secularization theories explain the process as a conjunction of cultural conditions, structural changes, and specific historical events.

The Christian tradition provided an impetus toward secularization by making a secular world conceivable. The Judaic conception of a single high God stripped the natural world of magical elements; pervasive supernatural intervention was replaced by a tradition in which ethical and legal precepts governed human affairs. The Christian church added to this incipient separation of sacred and secular by setting itself up as a distinct corporate body that was not identified with a people or community. Protestant reformers further shrank the scope of the sacred in the world by treating God as removed from ordinary life, not accessible through mediation, and by specifying only FAITH and GRACE, rather than good works, as the path to SALVATION. Protestant thought legitimated the autonomy of the secular world. Weber's classic but controversial argument supported this point by suggesting that the Calvinist doctrine of predestination produced in believers existential questions that could be resolved only by successful, methodical work in a calling. It thus put a religious premium on worldly activity, which in turn helped to set capitalist development in motion, leading to an economic system that could dispense with its originally religious underpinnings.

Christianity also contributed to secularization by breaking up as a single tradition in its European heartland. The aftermath of the REFORMATION undermined throughout Europe the broad authority of a universal church, the unquestioned truth of a single faith, and the possibility of maintaining one sacred order. Christian conscience began to make Europe secular by allowing many religions or no religion in a state. In principle, at least, no one henceforth would be pressured into accepting society's religious axioms; in principle, again, it became possible to think of society cohering despite religious difference. Emerging religious pluralism fostered decline in religious authority. In Protestant lands, the emphasis on the BIBLE as the source of truth, displacing church TRADITION, gave rise

to textual disputes that in turn furthered DISSENT and schism. When the faith came in many versions, the authority any single one could command gradually diminished. Civil conflicts precipitated by religious difference ultimately led to settlements, such as the "separation" of CHURCH AND STATE in the American Constitution, that formally limited the public role of religion (see AMERICANS UNITED FOR THE SEPARATION OF CHURCH AND STATE).

Secularization stems above all from societal rationalization. The key element in most sociological accounts of secularization is the idea that, over the last several centuries, institutions in the West have become differentiated. First state, law, market, and science, then education, media, and other institutions, increasingly operated according to formal procedures, methodically carried out by specialists, for purposes inherent to those institutions. Institutional function dispensed with transcendent faith. Secular means sufficed to reach secular ends. In modernizing societies differentiation or rationalization eroded any lingering sense of organic unity anchored in a shared conception of the transcendent. Secularization, then, came to represent the way differentiation "played out" in the religious sphere. Religion became one institution among others, operating in its own specific arena.

In many societies particular social struggles also contribute to secularization. The nature of such struggles depends mainly on the "frame," the overall structure of the religious system, with which a society enters periods of modernizing change. For example, as in the case of FRANCE, countries that long retained a religious monopoly are likely to experience more violent opposition between defenders of tradition and advocates of secular change, with religion becoming more marginalized where the latter are successful. A starker case is that of the Russian revolution, in which a deliberately secularizing elite intended to secularize the new Soviet society by extinguishing its once-organic religious tradition (see RUSSIA). By contrast, in religiously pluralistic societies conflict is less likely to pit religious against secular forces; instead, public institutions will tend to accommodate religion in its own sphere, and conflict among elites over the direction of such institutions, as was the case around 1900 in the UNITED STATES, is more likely to be piecemeal and peaceful.

Secularization can take on a life of its own. Once society is broadly defined as a secular enterprise, religious culture becomes pluralized and rationalization takes hold—the process feeds on itself. In many instances, secularization receives increasing institutional support, for example in the form of legal provisions separating church and state, as well as cultural support, for instance in the form of liberal theological currents. The secular principle of religious freedom, construed as a fundamental human right, legitimates pluralism. In debates about the future of particular societies, the burden of proof increasingly rests on those arguing for restoration of some organic order.

In sum, secularization theories account for the process by arguing that it occurred in societies where the religious culture fostered separation of the world from the transcendent, religious tradition fragmented in a manner that undermined its former authority, social institutions underwent rationalization that reduced the social role of organized religion, contingent conflicts further undermined its authority, and over time a secular societal framework became self-sustaining. This explanation entails variation because it presents secularization as the unintended consequence of the conjunction of multiple factors in particular contexts. No single country shows the way. To analyze the course of the process in any particular case, one must first ask which religion, if any, was historically dominant, how deeply the society was affected by the Reformation aftermath, how thorough has been the experience of societal rationalization, whether religion has been involved in key conflicts, and how entrenched, if at all, in law and theology the model of a pluralistic, secular society has become.

Discussion

Secularization theory is in dispute. Scholarly controversy has focused on the issues examined below.

Historical Premises. Did secularization happen? Secularization accounts assert a shift: once religion did x, now only y. Historians have objected, first, that the timing is left fuzzy: precisely when did the process start? Any date is problematic. For example, neither the Reformation nor the European settlement of 1648 alone ushered in clear-cut secularization. Its proponents would acknowledge that they rarely supply precise dates, although this is no great problem. Watershed events such as the American and FRENCH REVOLUTIONS clearly do mark advances in secularization in those societies. Precise dates also can be misleading, insofar as the timing of secularization is in fact bound to vary from case to case. Broad comparisons over many centuries, although insufficient for fine-grained historical analysis, are themselves useful to show the depth of change. A second historical criticism is aimed at an apparent assumption behind the notion of a shift: there once existed a religious golden age, in which belief was commonly held and publicly affirmed. The evidence does not seem to support such a romantic vision because even in the heyday of medieval Catholicism heterodoxy was prevalent, commitment to the church tenuous, and conflict between church and secular authority common. However, secularization accounts need not assume general ORTHODOXY, deep commitment, or a triumphant church on the part of medieval Europeans; nor do they depend exclusively on decline in Christian influence. Their key claim, more difficult to measure but supported by evidence, is about decline in significance. This claim appears valid, although the historical criticism has shown that it is also a deliberate simplification. Societies that in fact varied in the role, meaning, and practice of faith underwent a process that had common elements and a common direction, but did not produce a single result.

Role of Christian Tradition. Did Christianity serve as its own gravedigger? To the idea that elements of Christian belief contributed to the decline in its influence, one might object that leaders never contemplated such an outcome. Reformers who in retrospect appear to have played a role in secularization themselves focused on rebuilding confessional states. Cases in point are various German states, where enforcing religious discipline became a public task. Similarly, JOHN CALVIN's Geneva and William Bradford's Massachusetts attest to the concerted efforts of several Protestant communities to keep their faith whole, public, and pure. Catholic reaction to Protestant growth in the sixteenth and seventeenth centuries further tightened the bonds of church and state (see CATHOLIC REACTIONS TO PROTESTANTISM). Even as Europe was divided along religious lines in 1648, the cultural and social significance of the dominant local faith was rarely in question. Secularization proponents would acknowledge that only in hindsight did the Reformation set the stage for future decline. Attributing some causal force to the content of Christian, specifically Protestant, belief is not to argue that history proceeded as the unfolding of a Christian script. In fact Christianity could not simply cause its relative decline, for secularization only came about as the unforeseen conjunction of Christian ideas with broader cultural and social change. Secularization accounts make plausible that secularization as understood today first occurred in the Christian West, although they stress that what appears as the "natural" consequence of Christian thought from the perspective of the twenty-first century is the contingent effect of complex processes.

Rationalization as Continuous. Is rationalization as relentless as the Weberian account suggests? To the idea of rationalization as a juggernaut moving in one direction, one might object that this is implausible as a historical scenario. Change is conflictual, resistance likely, reversal possible. Case in point is the experience of Dutch Calvinists in the late nineteenth century. Led by ABRAHAM KUYPER, they resisted secularizing trends in society and government. To advance their "anti-revolutionary" cause, they built new institutions (such as a party, university, and newspaper), imbuing modern forms with faithful content. Together with Catholics, they ultimately gained public funding for religious schools. Kuyper provided a platform for such desecularizing activity with a doctrine justifying a Christian sphere within modern society. Because Catholics built a parallel "pillar" of institutions, the Netherlands in some respects was less secular in 1950 than it had been in 1850; however, secularization proponents can respond that nothing in their accounts rules out reversals. The key question is whether reversals can take hold. The case of Dutch pillarization, for example, was one of defensive action in which religious communities adopted existing rationalized institutions and accepted the legitimacy of a secular public sphere. Church control and specifically supernatural symbolism, for instance in schools, gradually dissipated. Pillarization made the religious modern rather than the modern religious. The process complete, rapid secularization within the religious communities themselves ensued. Rationalization, so secularization proponents infer, is neither smooth nor continuous, but once in motion cannot easily be turned back.

Religion as Defense. Does religion remain socially significant where it is the core of a culture under threat? On the empirical importance of this point, there is little argument. For example, throughout the twentieth century IRELAND and POLAND remained overwhelmingly Catholic. People and nation identified with the church. This was a way to preserve some autonomy, to keep a national community intact, against a stronger foe. Secularization accounts treat this as a prime instance of external conflict that heightens the social significance of religion. Critics submit, however, that stressing the causal role of such conflict becomes a large loophole in the theory. If secularization theory allows such apparently major exceptions, then it is difficult to refute. Secularization proponents in turn counter that no immunization is intended. Arguments about religion as collective cultural defense can be recast in refutable form. For instance, if the conditions, specifically the primary external conflict, that triggered such defense disappear, then ordinary secularization should occur, leading to measurably diminished collective identification with the formerly dominant religion. Surrounded by friendly neighbors, Poland should become less Catholic. Overall, secularization accounts emphasize that contingent societal conflict affects the pace and form of secularization.

Secularization as Self-sustaining. The claim that a secular framework can become embedded in culture and law, and therefore self-sustaining, is vulnerable for two reasons. First, secularization could be self-limiting: if it supplies a product in a market, and if the latent demand of consumers is constant, then any decline in the market share of old producers will create opportunity for new ones. Competition will lead to revived religious growth over time. However, such a market argument does not address key secularization claims because it says little about the social significance of growing churches. It assumes incorrectly that demand for supernatural meaning is constant, and it actually depends on the validity of secularization accounts: to "market" religion is to operate by secular standards. A second criticism would hold that secularization is reversible, as the rise of fundamentalist movements in seemingly secularized countries demonstrates (see FUNDAMENTALISM). As indicated, secularization proponents agree that reversals are possible in principle, although they also argue that bringing institutions under a previously torn canopy is always difficult, that fundamentalists in modern societies are bound to take on features of their environment, that entering the fray of social conflict often entails co-optation into secular society, and that the burden of proof is not easily shifted back to secularizing opponents. The historical record shows few, if any, instances of full-fledged reversal.

Secularization as Privatization. What happens to individual religiosity in modern society? Secularization accounts argue that modernity means choice. Individuals may believe as they see fit. One interpretation suggests that secularization trickles down into the private sphere, and hence produces less belief, commitment, and attendance. This scenario may apply to certain European countries, and it is not surprising that British scholars have made this case, although as a general rule it is questionable. In the United States a large majority of people retain some core religious beliefs and a large minority regularly attends church. In parts of LATIN AMERICA neo-Pentecostal growth has raised commitment and attendance among converts (see PENTECOSTALISM). This does not rule out private decline over the long haul, but the record does not support such an expectation. Another interpretation posits that secularization carves out a viable sphere for individual religious practice, guided by private spiritual choices. In principle, faith can flourish and churches proselytize. This view therefore does not claim that modernity spells the demise of religion. Neither the conventional description of secularization in before-and-after terms nor the factors commonly cited in secularization theories foretell the "death of

God." Yet in many instances secularization produces profound effects even in the private sphere. The place of faith is bound to change. In the case of Latin America, for example, Pentecostal growth has meant the dismantling of an older organic model of church and society, replicating the secularizing effects of earlier, similarly vibrant Protestant movements. As it turns into private choice rather than public fate, religion casts no halo throughout peoples' lives. Less collectively affirmed, it is less easily accepted. Exposed to alternative interpretations of human problems and natural events, it becomes less plausible. Even private belief is likely to lose some supernatural content. To vary a classic phrase, although individuals may still hold transcendent belief, they can no longer be held by it. On this point, however, critics insist that privatization underestimates the public consequences of private choice, as in the case of the communities and politics of Latin-American evangelicals. Made by millions, private choices cease to be private.

Exceptions

The American Exception. Does the American experience fit any secularization scenario? Many American scholars would reply that whereas secularization may be useful to describe the Western European course of societal change, it does not apply to the United States. Far from creating a secular republic, the "separation" of church and state in the late eighteenth century created opportunities for proselytizing churches to "Christianize" America. By the early twentieth century America had become far more "churched." Throughout the twentieth century Americans continued to profess faith in God and to fill the pews more than people in other industrialized countries. Their religiosity has public significance. Across the American South the landscape itself offers evidence in the variety of prominent church buildings, physical evidence of a living faith. Church influence is especially prominent in places such as Utah, home of the Church of Jesus Christ of Latter-Day Saints (see MORMONISM). Novels with a prophetic and supernatural cast often outsell the secular competition. Many congregations provide services beyond the spiritual, not least for minorities; belonging shapes the lives of the faithful in numerous ways. For immigrants religion often constitutes the core of their communities, bridging old and new societies. At times religion becomes a focal point of political activity, as illustrated by the conservative evangelicals of the so-called CHRISTIAN RIGHT in the 1980s and 1990s. Nor has the religious inspiration that gave a powerful impetus to major reform movements of the past, such as the TEMPERANCE and CIVIL RIGHTS MOVEMENTS, disappeared. Religion serves as a re-source in defining some public issues, from ABORTION to peace. Religious perspectives on natural phenomena still contend in the public sphere, as recurrent opposition to the teaching of evolution shows (see DARWINISM; CREATION SCIENCE). In public life, references to God and religious tradition are common and legitimate; the United States remains a "nation under God."

In some respects, such examples show, the United States is not a fully secularized country, although proponents of secularization would insist that it has undergone secularization. America's religious pluralism and competition constitute the form secularization has taken there. Its religious vitality is that of voluntary organizations minding their business within a secular republic. Christianization and secularization went hand in hand. Even though religion retained some and gained other public functions, for example as the key element in various subcultures, its relative significance in all sectors of society diminished over time. The most overt attempts to reassert a religiously inspired agenda in the public sphere, such as that of the Christian Right, had little effect on policy. In debates about evolution, defenders of creationism are at a legal and intellectual disadvantage. In conflicts that involve religion, the specifically supernatural elements tend to diminish over time. The way in which religion becomes a resource among others actually shows its diminished authority. In the life of the churches themselves, secular ideas, techniques, and expectations gain influence. On balance, America is not so much an exception as a variation on a theme. It has secularized without becoming fully secular.

The Islamic Exception. Does the experience of Islamic countries show that secularization is an ethnocentric Western idea? In spite of the enormous variety among Muslim countries, all treat Islam as part of their collective identity, assign some public role to precepts of the faith, and allow little religious competition. Islam is not a "private" choice, given that it helps to shape family and community life. Nor can it be merely private, for in principle its key doctrines do not recognize any basic distinction among the spheres of society, no "church" to be separated from the political realm. Even where rulers do not appeal to Islam directly for legitimation, they must work to uphold the faith. In many places Islamist movements strive to restore faith to power by reimposing Islamic law. The Iranian Revolution of 1979 actually reversed prior secularization by instituting an Islamic republic. Only in Turkey has a secular republic been imposed with success, but this was done by force, according to foreign example, and at the cost of continued strife over the place of Islam in society. Its record seems only to confirm that Islam is an exception to the presumed rule of secularization. The exception is gaining ground, as mosques dotting the urban landscape in Europe suggest.

Described in these terms, Islam does not pose a problem for secularization theories. They do not claim that any society must become secular, but rather argue that the process is contingent on several factors. Many of these do not prevail in Muslim lands. Typically, no tradition separates sacred from secular realms, little pluralism has flourished, rationalization has made few inroads as yet, defining conflicts with outside powers have reinforced the collective significance of religion, and resources to make a secular framework legitimate on its own terms are few. Under such conditions, secularization is unlikely; at the same time, these conditions are not immutable. Pluralism can grow, rationalization spread, old conflicts recede, thus making some secularization more likely. Overall it has not been shown that societies that were once pervasively religious can become "modern" without reducing the broad significance of religion. Here, though, secularization theory runs up against its limits because it assumes that secularization is a natural process, a set of events that follow from objective conditions in particular societies. In the Islamic context, however, secularization is also a political issue, a target of criticism, a model to be feared. Secularization has a reflexive quality. Islam is therefore not an exception by virtue of not being secular; rather, it provides a counterpoint by showing that becoming secular is more contentious than conventional accounts have recognized.

Neither of the exceptions refutes secularization theory, although each supplements it. The Islamic case, in particular, calls into question an old, tacit assumption: secularization was something that happened to coherent, independent societies, specifically nation-states. Instead, once secularization occurred for the first time, dramatically, in the formerly Christian orbit, it could then be incorporated elsewhere as desirable model or dangerous precedent, to be locally adapted. As a rule social change occurs not simply as a natural process within separate units. People and institutions compare their experiences; change in one society often occurs as a semiconscious response to the example set by another; some historical events or experiments are turned into models for others to follow. In modernity reflexive comparison becomes more common in world society. With regard to secularization, this means that, attuned to the way particular groups construe its meaning and respond to precedent, we must view it as a relational process. Put another way, secularization has become a societal possibility, a course to be debated. Whether, and if so, how, to become

secular is part of the ongoing struggle over how to be modern. In some societies this old issue has been settled; in many others, it has not. Secularization therefore remains subject to contestation in the real world, a phenomenon that has yet to be fully incorporated into secularization accounts.

Conclusion

As a thesis asserting the demise of religion, secularization has been discredited; in this form it points, at best, to the now-ineradicable tension between conceptions of the transcendent and ever more assertive forms of worldly human reason, conscience, and desire. As description, secularization effectively captures the long-term decline in religious (especially, but not only, Christian) influence over culture and society. As academic theory, it explains both the common pattern in the process and the different ways in which religious tradition refracts under local conditions of modernizing change. As a contested concept, it reflects scholarly dispute over the interpretation of historical change and ongoing struggle over the place of religion in world society. Secularization therefore remains vital as an idea about the past and a problem for the future.

References and Further Reading

Berger, Peter L. *The Sacred Canopy: Elements of a Sociological Theory of Religion*. Garden City, NY: Doubleday, 1967.

Bruce, Steve. *A House Divided: Protestantism, Schism, and Secularization*. London: Routledge, 1990.

Butler, Jon. *Awash in a Sea of Faith: Christianizing the American People*. Cambridge, MA: Harvard University Press, 1990.

Chadwick, Owen. *The Secularization of the European Mind in the Nineteenth Century*. Cambridge: Cambridge University Press, 1975.

Dobbelaere, Karel. "Secularization: A Multi-Dimensional Concept." *Current Sociology* 29 (1981): 1–213.

Gorski, Philip S. "Historicizing the Secularization Debate: Church, State, and Society in Late Medieval and Early Modern Europe, ca. 1300 to 1700." *American Sociological Review* 65 (2000): 138–167.

Martin, David. *A General Theory of Secularization*. New York: Harper & Row, 1978.

McLeod, Hugh. *Religion and the People of Western Europe, 1789–1970*. Oxford: Oxford University Press, 1981.

Nichols, James Hastings. *History of Christianity 1650–1950: Secularization of the West*. New York: The Ronald Press Company, 1956.

Swatos, William H., ed. "The Secularization Debate: Special Issue." *Sociology of Religion* 60 no. 3 (1999).

Wilson, Bryan. *Religion in Sociological Perspective*. Oxford: Oxford University Press, 1982.

FRANK J. LECHNER

SEEKER

The concept of seekership was introduced into the study of religious movements by John Lofland and Rodney Stark in a pioneering study of conversion mechanisms into the Unification Church ("Moonies") in 1965, with further elaboration by Lofland in his 1966 monograph, *Doomsday Cult.* The original definition was a "floundering among religious alternatives, an openness to a variety of religious views, frequently esoteric, combined with failure to embrace the specific ideology and fellowship of some set of believers" (Lofland and Stark 1965). This approach represents a *process model* of conversion in which predisposing conditions interact with situational contingencies to effect specific religious commitments. A key aspect of the model was that subjects defined themselves as seekers and take action to change through interaction with selected others that allowed affective ties to develop between them. Later work by Colin Campbell demonstrated that the seekership model was consistent with the "mysticism type" identified by Ernst Troeltsch in his *Social Teachings of the Christian Churches* (1912) as one of three manifestations of the religious impulse. Troeltsch saw it as that form most neglected by institutionalist analyses that centered solely on the churchly and sectarian alternatives that were Troeltsch's other types, the types that had been deployed in the prior half century through the analytical device of "church–sect theory." Campbell pointed out that in his mystical type Troeltsch was not simply speaking of a personal disposition, but a religion in its own right that regards religious experience as a valid expression of a universal religious consciousness that is based in an ultimate divine ground—a view that leads to an acceptance of religious relativity as well as to religious polymorphism, in which the "truth of all religions" is recognized. Subsequently seeker-type religiosity has come to be identified by religious studies scholars with the emergent spirituality of the American "boomer" generation (persons born between 1943 and 1962), most notably in Wade Clark Roof's research published in 1993 as *A Generation of Seekers.*

References and Further Reading

Campbell, Colin. "The Cult, the Cultic Milieu and Secularization." In *Sociological Yearbook of Religion in Britain,* vol. 5. London: SCM Press, 1972.

Lofland, John. *Doomsday Cult.* Englewood Cliffs, NJ: Prentice-Hall, 1966.

———, and Rodney Stark. "Becoming a World-saver." *American Sociological Review* 30 (1965): 863–874.

Roof, Wade Clark. *A Generation of Seekers.* San Francisco: Harper, 1993.

Troeltsch, Ernst. *The Social Teachings of the Christian Churches.* New York: Macmillan, 1931 [1912].

WILLIAM H. SWATOS JR.

SEEKER CHURCHES

Sometimes also termed "MEGA-CHURCHES" or "new paradigm" churches, seeker churches represent a development in late twentieth-century American evangelical Protestantism that attempted to draw boomer- and post–boomer-generation Americans (persons born since 1943) into institutional religious affiliation. Drawing on the insights of social scientific studies of changing American religious sensibilities—and major technological innovations and cultural shifts—these new congregations, usually dissociated from well-known denominational labels, replace the traditional evangelical emphasis on converting sinners with a new approach that attempts to win SEEKERS, preeminently by presenting worship and educational emphases and programs that diverge dramatically from both high and low traditional Protestant styles.

The archetypical seeker church and defining institution of the new paradigm is Willow Creek Community Church, a suburban Chicago congregation, and its founding pastor, Bill Hybels. Not only does Willow Creek minister to thousands of people each weekend in an auditorium that may be the largest in the Chicago metropolitan area, but it has also spawned the Willow Creek Association (WCA) encompassing over five thousand seeker churches worldwide.

There are theological, organizational, and practical differences between new paradigm seeker churches and old paradigm American Protestantism.

Theologically, a seeker church does not emphasize the CONVERSION of sinners. Potential members are approached as choice-making individuals who seek a better way to live, rather than as persons alienated from God and in danger of eternal damnation. Becoming an active Christian is seen as a process in which the seeker participates in a rational evaluation of life options. Christianity is presented as a lifestyle that is beneficial in the here and now, not just the beyond. Although seeker churches certainly hold many traditional evangelical beliefs, they are normally articulated as true within the context of the local setting, rather than by appeal to a theological tradition (whether denominational or more broadly creedal). Historically rooted senses of duty and conformity as constitutive of authenticity are replaced by personal experiences of good feeling.

Organizationally, the existence of the WCA notwithstanding, seeker churches uniformly eschew denominational labels and may avoid the word "church" as well—using instead such terms as "fellowship," "community," or "Christian center." Team leadership is emphasized, and a wide variety of programs are encompassed within the scope of the institution. Hierarchical and formal criteria for leadership are subordinated to competency for a task. Persons are often "set apart" for specific ministries within a congregation or are hired from the outside because of demonstrated abilities rather than denominational credentials or training.

It is in the practical realm, however, that the seeker church is most likely to be identified as "different." Music, or the musical program, in the seeker church is dramatically different. Hymnals are unknown. Instead a contemporary theatrical style emphasizing upbeat singing, in which the congregation's participation may be limited to choruses or clapping; instrumental music by live praise bands; and multimedia acoustical and lighting effects directed by competent sound technicians are the normal fare. Gone too is the traditional sermon, to be replaced by drama presentations and shorter, practical talks. Not only are there no vested clergy or choirs, but the congregation also is more likely to dress and comport itself as if it were at a concert than in a traditional Protestant worship service. Moreover, the building itself is designed intentionally to present this aspect of relative compatibility with secular experience, often in a park-like setting. A wide variety of activity programs are offered, ranging from athletics to social action/environmental programs. Counseling and child development services are especially emphasized as benefits to affiliation with a seeker congregation. Seeker church leadership staff offer weekday and weeknight study sessions that are intended to provide more traditional theological and biblical study for those who wish to "deepen their religious experience."

Seeker churches are consciously and unabashedly molding evangelical Protestantism to contemporary cultural models. Their leadership would argue that this is not new, but rather represents the continuing efflorescence of Christian truth at all times and all places. They would argue that, for example, the Protestant churches that have European REFORMATION roots molded Christianity to fit that time and place. Likewise, American frontier EVANGELICALISM structured itself to meet the sociocultural conditions of a different era, while still seeking to maintain fidelity to core DOCTRINES. This was succeeded by urban revivalism in its day, through the mass crusades of figures like BILLY SUNDAY and, later, BILLY GRAHAM.

The issues at the turn of the twenty-first century create a new context for religious outreach and organization. Whereas the debate at the turn of the twentieth century might have been over pew rents, today pews themselves are the obstacle. Group singing, once widespread through both Europe and the United States, has similarly waned, but not the desire for mass entertainment, as expressed through huge concert venues. Lecture classes were once a norm in educational

institutions; now a variety of alternative pedagogies are more likely to be employed. The new paradigm church seeks to integrate Christianity into this cultural setting as other innovations did in earlier times.

From the standpoint of the history of religious organizations, however, one can also see similar processes of restructuring and sedimentation taking place as characterized earlier innovations. In spite of eschewing "denominationalism," for example, the WCA in fact works like a DENOMINATION in many respects. It defines appropriate "liturgy," prepares materials, trains leaders and teachers, assists in hiring staff, and provides networks for the sharing of information. Hence, it is likely that in spite of the structural free-wheeling that seems to characterize the new paradigm, a more historically informed view of likely outcomes would anticipate greater formalization in succeeding decades.

References and Further Reading

Anderson, Leith. *A Church for the 21st Century*. Minneapolis, MN: Bethany House, 1992.

Miller, Donald E. *Reinventing American Protestantism: Christianity in the New Millennium*. Berkeley: University of California Press, 1997.

Roof, Wade Clark. *A Generation of Seekers*. San Francisco: Harper, 1993.

Sargeant, Kimon Howland. *Seeker Churches: Promoting Traditional Religion in a Nontraditional Way*. New Brunswick, NJ: Rutgers University Press, 2000.

WILLIAM H. SWATOS JR.

SEMINARIES

Protestantism originated during the cultural and educational excitement of the Renaissance. The new print technology made ancient texts more available and encouraged their detailed study. Because of a popular interest in preaching, the intellectual training of the clergy became more important. In GERMANY new universities were established for this purpose.

MARTIN LUTHER's career took place in a university context. His order, the Augustinian Hermits, like other mendicant orders, saw education as its most important mission. Because the need for university teachers was so great, Luther's own preparation for teaching was accelerated so that he could become professor of BIBLE at Wittenberg, a recently established school. PHILIPP MELANCHTHON, a young humanist and educational activist, joined him in 1518. Drawing on patristic and other sources the duo stressed thorough classical education as the necessary preparation for theological study. HULDRYCH ZWINGLI and JOHN CALVIN, also deeply influenced by the new thought, reached similar conclusions. Within a century the majority of European Protestant CLERGY had both classical and theological training.

The Protestant model did not, however, completely replace the older medieval ideal, rarely achieved, of the synthesis of philosophical and theological study. As the Protestant churches increasingly faced an intellectually reborn Roman Catholicism, they needed pastors with well-developed apologetic and philosophical skills.

ENGLAND and SCOTLAND developed their own style of theological education. In England, deeply influenced by Renaissance humanism, the classical bachelor of arts was transformed into a course focused on the classical languages. Although a ministerial candidate was expected to read Divinity, perhaps with the Regius professor, the faculties of THEOLOGY atrophied. The minister was thus educated in much the same way as the gentry and other public leaders, and theology in England tended to take the form of treatises directed toward the learned public. In contrast, Scotland retained the medieval philosophical model, and its theologians used a scholastic form to present their conclusions.

These basic Protestant models of theological education have proven elastic with different intellectual movements transforming (not replacing) them at different times. In the eighteenth century, for instance, European Pietists, who tended to identify "true" religion with a heartfelt experience of Christ, emphasized personal biblical study. When the king of Prussia asked AUGUST HERMANN FRANCKE to lead in the establishment of his new university at HALLE, Francke made the reading of the Bible in the original languages the heart of the theological program. Moreover Francke insisted that theological lectures be delivered in German, rather than the traditional Latin. Francke also established a number of voluntary associations near the university where ministerial students could get direct experience in ministry.

The modernization of university education, begun by Francke, continued throughout the eighteenth century. As the ideals of modern SCIENCE spread, research became an important component of the training of German professors, and the seminar was developed to help students develop advanced skills. New philosophical and scientific developments suggested that the Bible and theology needed to be studied from a different perspective. Meanwhile the professionalization of the German civil service pointed to the need for higher standards for ministry. Led by Prussia, the various German governments adopted state examinations that reviewed a candidate's academic preparation for the ministry.

Prussia's defeat by Napoleon led to the establishment of the new University of Berlin. FRIEDRICH DANIEL SCHLEIERMACHER, already well known for his epoch-making *Speeches on Religion to Its Cultured Despisers,* brought together the various reforms of the previous century, particularly the specialization of the faculty. Although theological professors continued for some time to teach different branches of theology, the ideal was for each faculty member to concentrate his research and teaching in a particular field.

Schleiermacher used the new historical critical method in his classes, setting the stage for a century of debate over the new approach's values and limits (see HIGHER CRITICISM). The new biblical studies reopened many literary questions about the Bible's composition, including the authorship and date of many books, and questioned whether many biblical events actually happened. Even scholars who resisted the new approach had to consider the issues that its practitioners raised.

Schleiermacher was also responsible for changing the basic theological agenda. He maintained that theology, rooted in religious experience, had to be reformulated in the light of contemporary knowledge. Not only did this make parts of the tradition problematical, it also required each generation of theologians to begin their work on a clean slate.

American theological education began in the British traditions with the establishment of colleges that continued either the English pattern, such as Harvard and Yale, or the Scottish tradition, such as William and Mary. The post-Revolutionary separation of CHURCH AND STATE changed this pattern. Because the government no longer maintained religious ORTHODOXY, each DENOMINATION or even party with a denomination formed its own theological "seminary" to support its understanding of Christian faith. Significantly, the first such school, Andover Seminary in Massachusetts, was only for college graduates. Although most subsequent schools adopted this same ideal, few attained it before the Second World War.

Intellectually, American Protestant theological schools developed much as their European, particularly German, counterparts. The new biblical criticism was introduced into American theological schools in the early nineteenth century and—despite a series of nasty HERESY trials—had become normative in many of the better schools by 1900. Those who dissented from the new methods, however, continued the battle by founding their own seminaries bound to an older understanding of biblical AUTHORITY. Far more than denominational background, the attitude of a school toward Scripture tends to distinguish American theological schools from each other.

Americans innovated in use of social science as part of ministerial preparation. Initially social science was introduced as part of a broad-based interest in social reform. From 1885 to 1920, SOCIAL GOSPEL theologians attempted to demonstrate that Christianity had valuable insights into labor relationships and urbanization. In time this concern led them to use social science to train ministers for specifically religious tasks. Clinical pastoral education, for instance, placed ministerial candidates in hospitals where their interaction with the sick could be observed and criticized. Although many American techniques have spread to churches in the Third World, they have not been as popular in Europe.

The separation of church and state also affected American theological education. Whereas in European countries the academic quality of theological studies continued to be guaranteed by the state, this was not true in the UNITED STATES. Consequently the various schools banded together to form The Association of Theological Schools to set appropriate voluntary standards for themselves.

See also Bible Colleges and Institutes; Education, Overview; Education, Theology: Asia; Education, Theology: Europe; Education, Theology: United States; Higher Education

References and Further Reading

Fraser, James W. *Schooling the Preachers: The Development of Protestant Theological Education in the United States, 1740–1875.* vol. xiv. Lanham, MD: University Press of America, 1988.

Hart, D. G., and R. Albert Mohler Jr., eds. *Theological Education in the Evangelical Tradition.* Grand Rapids, MI: Baker Books, 1996.

Kelly, Robert L. *Theological Education in America: A Study of One Hundred Sixty One Theological Schools in The United States and Canada.* New York: George H. Doran Company, 1924.

Kitagawa, Joseph Mitsuo. *Religious Studies, Theological Studies, and the University-Divinity School.* Atlanta, GA: Scholars Press, 1992.

McCarter, Neely Dixon. *The President As Educator: A Study of the Seminary Presidency.* Atlanta, GA: Scholars Press, 1996.

Miller, Glenn T. *Piety and Intellect: the Aims and Purposes of Ante-bellum Theological Education.* Atlanta, GA: Scholars Press, 1990.

Niebuhr, H. Richard, Daniel Day Williams, and James M. Gustafson. *The Advancement of Theological Education.* New York: Harper, 1957.

Pacala, Leon. *The Role of ATS in Theological Education, 1980–1990.* Atlanta, GA: Scholars Press, 1998.

White, Joseph Michael. *The Diocesan Seminary in the United States: A History from the 1780s to the Present.* Notre Dame, IN: University of Notre Dame Press, 1989.

GLENN T. MILLER

SEMLER, JOHANN SALOMO (1725–1791)

German historian and theologian. Noted scholar at the University of HALLE, Semler pioneered the historical critical method in the theological disciplines and challenged Protestant orthodox assumptions on canon formation, unity of the testaments, and the traditional authority of dogma.

Son of a Lutheran minister in Saalfeld, Thuringia, Semler grew up in a strong Pietist milieu but distanced himself early from its expectations of CONVERSION and intense personal piety. In 1743 he attended the University of Halle, where he became an avid student of SIEGMUND JAKOB BAUMGARTEN. Semler graduated from Halle in 1750. After a brief stint as a journalist, he became professor of history and Latin poetics at Altstedt. In 1753 he was called back to Halle, where he worked closely with Baumgarten. As professor of THEOLOGY he lectured widely across the theological disciplines including hermeneutics, biblical exegesis, dogmatics, and ETHICS.

After Baumgarten's death in 1757, Semler took a leading position within the theological faculty at Halle. Against the Pietists who emphasized the cultivation of piety and scholarly study, Semler sought to include more secular disciplines in theological studies and emphasized academic rigor. Under his leadership the theology faculty at Halle would become the foremost representative of ENLIGHTENMENT theology in GERMANY.

Semler built on Baumgarten's legacy, but he aimed to go beyond the "scientific theology" of Baumgarten and other Wolffian theologians by applying historical critical analyses to dogma, scripture, and the CHURCH. Semler argued that dogma was not immutable but developed over time in response to the exigencies of each age and was thus subject to critical investigation. Semler granted no special AUTHORITY to the early church or councils and argued that the validity of dogma should be based solely on the proper interpretation of scripture. In contrast to dogma, which was binding only on the teachers and CLERGY of the church, Semler understood the kerygma of Jesus Christ as propagating true Christianity throughout history.

Semler's criticism of the canon and the authority of the biblical texts was more controversial. In *Abhandlung von freier Untersuchung des Canon* (1771–1775), his most influential work, he argued that the Christian sacred canon was itself a historical product that took various forms as it emerged in the early church. He rejected the verbal inspiration, divinity, and equal authority of the biblical texts. Semler still held that the biblical texts contained the Word of God but that the Holy Scriptures themselves could not be identified as the Word of God.

Semler made a series of distinctions between theology and religion, dogma and kergyma, public and private, which allowed him to affirm personal religious freedom and the right of free critical inquiry while at the same time requiring clergy and professors of theology to subscribe to the church's confessions and symbols. In the controversy concerning the REIMARUS FRAGMENTS (see HERMANN SAMUEL REIMARUS) Semler openly disagreed with GOTTHOLD LESSING's decision to publish them. At the end of his life Semler's stance on this and other issues alienated him from more radical rationalist theologians. Later, Semler would be identified among the leading Neologists in Germany (see NEOLOGY). His work on textual criticism and hermeneutics was foundational for nineteenth-century biblical scholarship.

References and Further Reading

Hornig, Gottfried. *Johann Salomo Semler. Studien zu Leben und Werk der Hallenser Aufklärungstheologen.* Tübingen, Germany: Max Niemeyer Verlag, 1996.
O'Neill, J. C. "Johann Salomo Semler." In *The Bible's Authority: A Portrait Gallery of Thinkers from Lessing to Bultmann,* 39–53. Edinburgh: T & T Clark, 1991.
Reill, Peter Hanns. *The German Enlightenment and the Rise of Historicism.* Berkeley: University of California Press, 1975.

JONATHAN N. STROM

SEPARATION OF CHURCH AND STATE

See Americans United for the Separation of Church and State

SERMONS

See Preaching

SERPENT HANDLERS

The term refers to a practice carried out by a small group of independent churches in the southeastern UNITED STATES, notably North Carolina, Tennessee, and Kentucky. Occasionally, the WORSHIP of these churches includes the handling of poisonous snakes. There is, however, in these churches no requirement to "take up" snakes; those under eighteen years of age are strictly forbidden to do so. The movement has had a varied history, mainly localized in Tennessee (Grasshopper Valley). At issue is, of course, the stark reality that there are regularly victims of poisonous bites among the members of these churches.

The churches prefer to be known as "churches of God with signs following," and their origins lie in the early twentieth century among Pentecostal-Holiness churches (see PENTECOSTALISM; HOLINESS MOVEMENT). Ewent Hensley of Tennessee is generally considered the founder of the movement, whose size, although fluctuating over time, has probably never been more than a few thousand. Hensley traveled extensively as an ardent advocate of snake handling and died from snakebite in Florida on July 25, 1955 at the age of 70.

Theologically the phenomenon of serpent handlers raises the question of the literal exegesis of biblical verses and passages, which in mainstream THEOLOGY have been interpreted symbolically or allegorically. Snake handlers are given to a literal interpretation. The belief system of the churches practicing the handling of snakes or serpents accordingly is based on a literal interpretation of the BIBLE, specifically of several New Testament passages (Mark 16:17–20; Luke 10:19). "And these signs shall follow them that believe: in my name they shall cast out devils; they shall speak with new tongues: they shall take up serpents and if they drink any deadly thing, it shall not hurt them; they shall lay hands on the sick and they shall recover."

Adherents of the movement argue that these passages contain direct admonitions on the part of Jesus. They insist that, upon repentance, remission of sins, and a new life through SANCTIFICATION, the baptism of the Holy Spirit includes such gifts as speaking in tongues, casting our demons, healing the sick, and taking up serpents (see TONGUES, SPEAKING IN; FAITH HEALING). Thus, the believer goes through the three stages of salvation, sanctification, and the baptism of the Holy Spirit. The key consideration is that the new life in Christ has the same spiritual gifts of which the New Testament speaks in I Corinthians 12:8–10. In a way, therefore, "taking up serpents" is but one facet of the new life of the sanctified, Holy Spirit–baptized believer, which also finds expression in other matters as simplicity of dress and attire, disapproval of alcohol, and so forth. The snake-handling churches do not believe that the "taking up" of serpents will leave the handler immune to poison or bite. The serpents are "taken up," that is, handled in response to the Biblical command. Believers will not take up snakes unless they believe they are "anointed," or that the power of God is sufficient to protect them. There is, however, also the sense that those who take up snakes will be protected because of their faithfulness to the biblical command.

The snake-handling churches are another instance of the important legal and constitutional issue of whether government has the right to intervene with the free exercise of religion when possible deaths of members of a religious movement are involved (an issue also posed by members of the Watchtower Society/

JEHOVAH'S WITNESSES or by followers of CHRISTIAN SCIENCE). When a member of the Dolly Pond Church of God with Signs Following died from snake handling in 1945, the Tennessee legislature banned the practice because public sentiment quickly ran high. Other states, such as Kentucky (1940), Georgia (1941), Tennessee (1947), Virginia (1947), North Carolina (1949), and Georgia (1950), followed suit, raising the question of the free exercise of religion. A decision of the Tennessee Supreme Court affirming the ban appears to have settled the legal issue of constitutionality.

References and Further Reading

Burton, Thomas. *Serpent-Handling Believers.* Knoxville: University of Tennessee Press, 1993.
Kimbrough, David. *Taking Up Serpents. Snake Handlers of Eastern Kentucky.* Chapel Hill: University of North Carolina Press, 1995.
Pelton, Robert W. *Snake Handlers. God Fearers? Or Fanatics.* Nashville, TN: T. Nelson, 1974.

HANS J. HILLERBRAND

SERVETUS, MICHAEL (c.1511–1553)

Spanish anti-trinitarian. Servetus was born in Villenueva de Sijena, Spain, in either 1509 or 1511. His family social origins are vague, but it seems he came from a petty, albeit noble family and it is known that his brother was a sometimes agent for the Spanish Inquisition. Servetus left Spain for study in Toulouse in either 1528 or 1529 and subsequently traveled extensively, visiting Strasbourg, where he met MARTIN BUCER and WOLFGANG CAPITO. In Basel he lived with JOHANNES OECOLAMPADIUS for ten months. The publication of his extremely heretical treatise, *Concerning the Errors of the Trinity De Trinitatis erroribus* (1531), and *The Righteousness of Christ's Kingdom Dialogorum de Trinitate* of the following year, brought him instant notoriety.

In these writings he challenged the authenticity of the orthodox DOCTRINE of the Trinity, arguing that it was neither scriptural nor monotheistic but the result of pagan Greek thought. Ancient Greek gods, Servetus argued, possessed divine aspects. This concept was then translated back into Christian thought as separate and distinct personalities. Servetus advanced the notion that the Godhead was composed of various modes or guises that, like hats, God changed according to the specific historical context. Although Servetus cited a host of ancient heterodox Christian authorities to make his case, he was also familiar with medieval Rabbinic thought which also interpreted the different names of God mentioned in the Old Testament as various guises or attributes of a single God. Servetus's early works were universally condemned and he was declared an outlaw. As a result, from 1533 to 1538 Servetus used the alias Michel de Villenueve and studied medicine in Paris.

Eventually he made his home in Charlieu, Lyon, and Vienne, in Southern France where he practiced medicine and published a series of medical and astrological treatises under his alias. His medical writings dealt with the conflict between "Greeks" and "Arabist" interpretations and he was the first to describe the pulmonary circulation of the blood, a century before William Harvey. His geographical writings championed the cause of comparative geography and his exegetical writings advanced a historical-contextual method to interpret Scripture so that the text was interpreted both etymologically and conceptually within the context of the times and not from the vantage point of subsequent prophetic developments.

In 1552 he published his magnum opus, *The Restitution of Christianity,* a compendium of virtually every heretical idea of the late medieval and early modern period. His true identity was eventually discovered and he was tried for HERESY in Vienne, France. After a considerable trial he was condemned to death but in 1552 he escaped from prison and secretly made his way to Geneva in hopes of eventually getting to ITALY. He was found out, however, put on trial for maintaining heretical views, and was executed a year later in Geneva.

Although no church bears his name, Servetus contributed greatly to REFORMATION Age intellectual life. Unlike orthodox Protestants, Servetus did not hope to merely cleanse Christianity of an erroneous Catholic tradition, but to restore ancient Christianity in all of its vibrancy. In seeking the historical roots of Christianity, Servetus used a score of ancient heterodox religious thinkers to refabricate what he perceived as the original Christian message. He was also one of several Christian intellectuals to become familiar with medieval Jewish thought through contact with *conversos,* Jewish converts to Christianity. Like Servetus, they too sought to reinterpret both ancient religions' traditions into a new Judeo-Christianity that would better represent "what the first Christians believed." Despite an early death, Servetus greatly influenced subsequent radical religious developments in POLAND and Lithuania and his followers were among those who eventually founded Unitarianism.

Servetus was also important to the Reformation and the development of Protestantism for other reasons. His death in Geneva served as a clarion call for the cause of religious TOLERATION. Although he had committed no civil or religious offense in Geneva—indeed, was anonymously on his way to safer refuge in Italy—Servetus had not been tried by legal authorities because of any views he propagated or preached, but purely because of views he maintained within his conscience, within the privacy of his own being. JOHN CALVIN's active role in Servetus's prosecution has also proven troubling because where the town council wished merely to condemn and exile Servetus, Calvin convinced the council to condemn Servetus and have him burned at the stake. Calvin acquired the reputation for intolerance, and SEBASTIAN CASTELLIO and other advocates of liberty of conscience made Servetus's death a rallying cry for religious toleration.

References and Further Reading

Primary Sources:

Servetus, Michael. *De Trinitatis erroribus libri septum.* Frankfurt am Main, Germany: Minerva, 1965.

Servetus, Michael, and Charles Donald O'Malley. *Michael Servetus, a Translation of his Geographical, Medical, and Astrological Writings.* Philadelphia, PA: American Philosophical Society, 1953.

Servetus, Michael, and Earl Morse Wilbur. *The Two Treatises of Servetus on the Trinity.* New York: Kraus Reprint, 1969.

Servetus, Michael, Charles Donald O'Malley, and Madeline E. Stanton. *Christianismi restitution: And Other Writings.* Birmingham, AL: Classics of Medicine Library, 1989.

Secondary Sources:

Bainton, Roland H. *The Hunted Heretic. The Life and Death of Michael Servetus.* Boston: Beacon Press, 1953.

Baron, J. Fernandez. *Miguel Servet. Su vida et su obra.* Madrid, Spain: Espasa-Calpe, 1970.

Friedman, Jerome. *Michael Servetus: A Case Study in Total Heresy.* Geneva, Switzerland: Librairie Droz, 1978.

Kinder, Gordon A. *Michael Servetus.* Baden-Baden, Germany: Valentin Koerner, 1989.

Manzoni, Claudio. *Umanesimi ed Heresia. Michele Serveto.* Naples, Italy: Guida, 1974.

JEROME FRIEDMAN

SEVENTH-DAY ADVENTISTS

The Seventh-day Adventist church is an international church headquartered in Silver Spring, Maryland, with membership exceeding twelve million worldwide. The church originated in the northeastern UNITED STATES as a surviving strand of the Millerite movement. The salient teachings of Seventh-day Adventists include a belief in the biblical account of creation and mankind's fall into SIN from an originally perfect state, salvation alone through the atoning death of Jesus, the return of Jesus to earth followed by the restoration of a sinless world, and observance of the seventh-day Sabbath. Seventh-day Adventists have an organized presence in more than 200 countries and operate global networks of publishing plants, health-care institutions, and schools, ranging from elementary to tertiary schools and a variety of postbaccalaureate programs.

Organization

The Seventh-day Adventist Church organized in 1860 in Battle Creek, Michigan after emerging from the Millerite movement, named after WILLIAM MILLER, a veteran of the War of 1812 living in Low Hampton, New York. Miller concluded that biblical prophecies predicted a premillennial return of Jesus to the earth and began preaching in 1831 in New England and New York. Other students of prophecy in the United States, Europe, and LATIN AMERICA advanced these or similar beliefs (see MILLENARIANS AND MILLENNIALISM).

The Millerite movement culminated on October 22, 1844 when Jesus did not return to earth as anticipated. By that time Millerites were also called Adventists in recognition of their belief in the second advent of Jesus. After 1844 the movement faded; however, a nucleus of Adventists who continued to believe in the premillennial return of Jesus met frequently for Bible study and PRAYER. Led by Joseph Bates, a retired sea captain from Massachusetts, and James and ELLEN WHITE from Maine, they developed a body of identifying doctrines by 1850. Bates became a leading force in doctrinal development and the Whites strongly influenced organizational and institutional growth.

J. N. Andrews, who became a president of the Seventh-day Adventist Church and the first officially sponsored worker outside the United States, joined the group in 1846. Uriah Smith, who developed into a prolific writer, editor, and one of the church's leading expositors of biblical prophecy, joined in 1852, as did J. N. Loughborough, who became a prominent evangelist, administrator, and writer.

In 1860 this group numbered more than 3,000 and organized an official church, choosing the name Seventh-day Adventist. Between 1861 and 1922 the church developed a four-tiered administrative organization. In 1861 individual congregations grouped together to constitute local conferences. Two years later an overarching organization, the General Conference, was organized as the seat of AUTHORITY for the entire church. John Byington from New York state was the first president of the General Conference.

In 1901 the church underwent major reorganization. Clusters of conferences were organized into unions, a practice that Australian Adventists had followed during the 1890s. To provide constant church leadership in distant regions, in 1903 the General Conference began assigning a vice president to a large area, which in time became known as a division of the

General Conference. By 1922 the division system was finalized.

Originally conferences sent delegates to annual gatherings called General Conference sessions to transact church business and elect church officers. Since 1970 these sessions convene every five years. Delegates approximate 2,000 and include selected lay members and representatives from the conferences, unions, and thirteen divisions that embrace all regions of the world. Between sessions the General Conference Executive Committee convenes each fall and spring to handle budget and policy matters. Officers of divisions and unions also meet every five years; conferences conduct business sessions on a three-year cycle.

Between 1860 and 1901, Seventh-day Adventists developed numerous organizations, frequently called "societies," that were semi-independent units promoting church activities. EDUCATION, religious liberty, literature publication and distribution, healthful living, TEMPERANCE, and Sabbath School (the Adventist equivalent of SUNDAY SCHOOL) were among the early societies. As a part of the 1901 reorganization these societies became departments of the General Conference, each with a leader answerable to the General Conference president. New departments have since formed, and divisions, unions, and conferences have also organized corresponding departments. The numbers of departments and leaders vary among the unions and conferences, depending on needs and financial resources.

Individual churches organize according to policies set forth in *The Church Manual,* a digest of organizational instruction periodically revised and circulated throughout the Adventist community. A church board governs each congregation by establishing local operational and financial practices within the framework of conference and union policies. Congregations also control their membership by granting or withdrawing membership to individuals by general vote. Conferences rather than congregations employ pastors, and pastors are responsible to conferences for the operational integrity of their congregations.

Teachings

Seventh-day Adventist doctrine derives from a belief in a cosmic controversy between good and evil resulting from Lucifer's challenges to God's authority as the creator of a moral universe. The stage for this conflict is the earth and the human soul. The BIBLE is the revelation of God's will for humans and is the sole source of belief about God's mercy and the divine plan to save humans from evil. God created humans with the capacity to make moral choices. By choice Adam and Eve fell from their perfect state and pro-

duced a race naturally prone to sin, but each individual continues to exercise a choice in this controversy. Scripture describes the final eradication of sin and the restoration of a perfect earth.

Adventist doctrines form a systematic body of beliefs surrounding the plan of SALVATION in which Christ is central as the redeemer of a fallen human race. These beliefs begin with salvation alone through the ATONEMENT of Christ and the intercessory ministry of Jesus as part of a final judgment of humans based on the law of God. Adventists teach that Scripture foretells a specific time of final judgment; thus humans do not receive their eternal reward when they die, but remain in "sleep" until Christ's return to pronounce divine judgment. Adventists reject the doctrine of immortality of the human soul as commonly held by Christians in favor of a conditional immortality.

Among the identifying teachings of the early Adventists led by Bates and the Whites was the seventh-day Sabbath (see SABBATARIANISM). Bates introduced the Sabbath after adopting it from a Sabbath-keeping congregation in Washington, New Hampshire, which is regarded as the first Seventh-day Adventist church. Adventists first understood and continued to teach Sabbath observance to signify their allegiance to God's authority as creator and God's power to restore the world to its original sinless state.

Adventists also teach that spiritual gifts as described in I Corinthians 12 would be present in the church and that Ellen White exercised the gift of prophecy. They believe that she received visions, dreams, and other special communications from God as did biblical prophets, but neither she nor the Seventh-day Adventist Church taught that her messages shared canonical status with Scripture. She believed her role was to render advice about organization and administration, clarify understanding of biblical teachings, and promote an Adventist lifestyle through public and personal counsel.

Adventists teach that God's law defines sin because it is an unchangeable expression of divine character, but deny that humans merit salvation through obedience. Humanity is by nature sinful and totally dependent on God's forgiving GRACE made possible through Christ's atoning death and intercessory ministry. Adventist doctrine better defines obedience as a way of life consistent with God's character, voluntarily chosen as a loving demonstration of faith in and commitment to Christ rather than compliance with the law's written form for the purpose of earning salvation. Ellen White's books, *The Desire of Ages, Steps to Christ,* and *Thoughts from the Mount of Blessing,* all written after 1880, became classic Adventist statements of these beliefs.

Adventists emphasize healthful diet and teach abstinence from alcohol, tobacco, and narcotics. These teachings stem from a wholistic view of human life, that is, the human body deserves respect because it was created perfect in God's image and, although marred by sin, is still the temple of God.

Preserving the Integrity of Beliefs

Because Seventh-day Adventists believe in *sola scriptura* and a progressive understanding of Scripture they have never adopted a formal creed. Adventist doctrines are open for discussion and church leaders have issued successive official statements of beliefs. Although the wording of these statements differs to reflect updated understanding in light of continued study, the essence of fundamental beliefs has remained.

The first document, *Fundamental Principles,* published in 1872, embodied twenty-five propositions. It remained the official pronouncement of beliefs until the second version appeared in 1931. This second statement summarized the "principal features" of "fundamental beliefs," condensing the propositions to twenty-two. In 1980 the number was revised to twenty-seven, which are commonly called the "twenty-seven fundamental beliefs."

The 1980 statement places a heavier stress on the Trinity and the heavenly sanctuary, especially the intercessory ministry of Christ. Although Seventh-day Adventists have always been creationists, for the first time the biblical explanation of the origins of life became a fundamental belief. The statement also confirms the sanctity of MARRIAGE and the family, and recognizes the broad Christian community as the prophetic body of Christ.

Primarily in the United States and AUSTRALIA a debate developed in the 1970s about Adventists' traditional understanding of Ellen White's role as a fulfillment of the biblical gift of prophecy. Questions also arose about church teachings associated with final judgment and the 2,300-day prophecy of Daniel 8. Coincident with these discussions was a wave of concern about JUSTIFICATION and righteousness by FAITH. Careful study contributed to the revision of fundamental beliefs in 1980, which clarified the wording but did not alter the substance of church teaching.

Two service departments of the General Conference help to maintain the scriptural integrity of church teachings. The Biblical Research Institute concentrates on theological studies and biblical interpretations. The Geoscience Research Institute conducts ongoing research in scientific evidence to resolve conflicts between Scripture and SCIENCE (see CREATION SCIENCE).

Adventists universally accept the 1980 statement of fundamental beliefs. Guides to scriptural study for all age groups are published by the General Conference to be used in Sabbath Schools around the world. The *Seventh-day Adventist Bible Commentary,* published between 1953 and 1957 and subsequently updated, helps to standardize beliefs, although understanding of scriptural instruction affecting lifestyle and social matters may vary from region to region. At the 1990 and 1995 General Conference sessions vigorous debate about ordination of WOMEN produced a final negative vote, reflecting differences of opinion between Adventists in the Western and developing worlds (see WOMEN CLERGY).

Prospective members voluntarily commit themselves to a concise statement of fundamental beliefs that constitutes their baptismal vow. BAPTISM is by immersion. Adventists do not baptize infants because they cannot make a voluntary choice of belief, but children who show an understanding of the meaning of such a commitment may be baptized.

Institutions

In 1849 Adventists began a paper, *The Present Truth,* in which the editor James White reviewed Adventist teachings and urged unity among believers (see PUBLISHING). The following year he changed its name to *The Second Advent Review and Sabbath Herald,* published weekly. Since 1850 it has undergone several name changes, the last in 1978 to the *Adventist Review.* It has become the general paper for Seventh-day Adventists and is intended primarily for church readership. Variations of the *Review* appear in Spanish, French, and Portuguese, prepared by local editors in fields where membership in those languages exist in substantial numbers.

To facilitate Adventist publishing, White established a press in Rochester, New York, but in 1853 he moved it to Battle Creek, Michigan. This enterprise became the first centralizing institution among Adventists and Battle Creek became a *de facto* headquarters to which prominent leaders gravitated. Organizational actions between 1860 and 1863 established Battle Creek as the capital of the DENOMINATION.

A new journal, *The Signs of the Times,* appeared in 1874 edited by James White. It was the first major paper that presented Adventist views to the non-Adventist public. The next year the Whites founded the Pacific Press Publishing Association in Oakland, California, which became the home for the new publication. This periodical became a model for similar journals for non-Adventist readership around the world. Some use the title, *The Signs of the Times,* but are edited and published in divisions outside North

America. Divisions, unions, and many conferences publish periodicals for their own members. Departments of the General Conference promote their own specialized programs with magazines for both the Adventist and non-Adventist public. Better-known publications are *Liberty* (religious freedom), *Vibrant Life* (healthful living), and *Listen* (temperance).

Their wholistic view of human life led Adventists to make health one of the strongest aspects of their teachings. In 1866 the Whites founded the Western Health Reform Institute in Battle Creek. It promoted natural foods, rest, and exercise, and advocated natural remedies in treating sickness. In 1876 Dr. John Harvey Kellogg, a graduate of Bellevue Hospital Medical College in New York, became the director of the Institute. Under his leadership the center came to be known as Battle Creek Sanitarium and gained an international reputation for teaching principles of health as a lifestyle. The Sanitarium became a clinical institution for a nursing school in 1883 and a school of medicine, American Medical Missionary College, in 1895.

Kellogg's interest in diet motivated him to advocate vegetarianism and develop a line of nut-based foods and dry cereals made from grains. Following this example, Adventists established health food factories in many countries, which became known for meat analogs, cereals, and natural foods. Sanitarium Health Food Company, established in 1897 in Australia, came to be one of the most widely known food enterprises of its kind in Australia and NEW ZEALAND.

The church lost control of Battle Creek Sanitarium to Kellogg, who separated from the church in 1907. On property purchased in 1905 in southern California, Adventists reestablished their emphasis on health by equipping a new sanitarium and nursing school. In 1910 they added a school of medicine. This institution was chartered under the name of College of Medical Evangelists until 1961 when it changed to Loma Linda University. Besides offering degrees in medicine it engages in projects of academic medicine, notably in proton treatment of cancer and heart transplants among children. It operates a school of dentistry, confers doctorates in public health and selected fields of science, and offers baccalaureate and advanced degrees in other health-related fields. Adventist health-care units around the world range from small clinics to critical-care institutions and serve more than 9,000,000 outpatients annually.

In 1872 James and Ellen White encouraged the General Conference to establish an Adventist school in Battle Creek. Goodloe Harper Bell, a convert to Adventism who had attended Oberlin College, was the first teacher. Two years later the school became Battle Creek College. The purposes of the institution were to provide an education for Adventists of all ages and to train denominational employees, primarily ministers, teachers, and various lines of office workers. Through the 1880s and 1890s enrollment fluctuated from 400 to above 800, including all levels from elementary through college.

Partly as a result of reorganization in 1901, church leaders dismantled Battle Creek as the Seventh-day Adventist headquarters. In 1901 they sold Battle Creek College and moved the school to Berrien Springs in southwestern Michigan, renaming it Emmanuel Missionary College. In 1959 the Seventh-day Adventist Theological Seminary moved from Washington, D.C., where it had operated since its founding in 1936, to the Berrien Springs campus. The college changed to Andrews University and developed doctoral programs in theology, pastoral ministry, and education, and offered advanced degrees in other fields in the arts and sciences (see CHRISTIAN COLLEGES; HIGHER EDUCATION).

In 1903 the General Conference office transferred from Battle Creek to Takoma Park, Maryland, on the north side of Washington, D.C. It remained there until 1989 when it moved to Silver Spring, Maryland, still in the Greater Washington area. Simultaneously the Review and Herald Publishing Association moved from Battle Creek to new quarters adjacent to the church offices in Takoma Park. In 1983 it transferred to a new plant in Hagerstown, Maryland.

Internationalization of the Seventh-Day Adventist Church

J. N. Andrews became the first official Seventh-day Adventist worker outside North America in 1874. Under his leadership the church set up administrative offices and a press in Basel, SWITZERLAND. At the General Conference session of 1882 a Foreign Mission Board was formed to oversee missions in countries beyond the United States. Adventism also spread informally through literature exchange, emigration, and volunteer workers. M. B. Czechowski preached twelve years in Europe after 1864 without financial support from the church. By 1900 Seventh-day Adventists had spread to Scandinavia, ENGLAND, GERMANY, RUSSIA, Romania, Argentina, BRAZIL, MEXICO, Central America, the CARIBBEAN islands, AFRICA, CHINA, INDIA, Australia, New Zealand, and some Pacific islands.

Prominent Adventists participated in this movement. Ellen White spent two years in Europe, 1885–1887, advising Adventist groups from ITALY to NORWAY about evangelism and organization. From 1891 to 1900 she and her son, William C. White, lived in Australia, where they implemented organizational and evangelistic plans. A. G. Daniells was involved in church administration in New Zealand and Australia from 1889 to 1900. L. R. Conradi, a German immigrant to the United States who converted to Adventism, returned in 1886 to preach in eastern Europe. Frank Westphal, a German-speaking North American, settled in Argentina in 1894 to establish Adventism in lower South America. J. G. Matteson, a Danish-born immigrant to the United States, published the first non-English Adventist periodical in 1872, and in 1877 returned to Denmark, where he organized the first conference of churches outside North America. G. W. Caviness, formerly president of Battle Creek College, moved to Mexico in 1897 to lead general evangelistic activities.

In many of these locations workers established printing presses and schools that later developed into major institutions. The Norwegian Publishing House started in 1879. A worker-preparation school that became Avondale College near Cooranbong, Australia traces its beginnings to 1892. Buenos Aires Publishing House in Argentina started in 1896; in 1898, also in Argentina, River Plate Adventist University began as a small school to train church workers. Hamburg Publishing House in Germany began operations in 1895, and near Magdeburg, Germany, a school that became Friedensau University opened in 1899.

By 1921 Seventh-day Adventist membership totaled 198,088, slightly more than half of which was outside North America. This number grew to more than a million in 1955. In all of the world divisions Adventists operated health-care institutions, publishing enterprises to handle literature needs for both internal and external use, and schools with the dual purpose of providing an education in an Adventist setting and preparing church workers. During these years the world fields depended heavily on financial and personnel support from North America. At the same time church growth and organization either stopped or seriously declined in the Soviet Union, China, and other countries where political conditions hampered ecclesiastical activity.

Among the leading twentieth-century evangelists in the United States were J. S. Washburn and Carlyle B. Haynes before World War I; and J. L. Shuler, Fordyce Detamore, and R. Allan Anderson in the decades before and after World War II. H. M. S. Richards experimented with radio evangelism during the 1930s and in 1942 launched the *Voice of Prophecy,* the first coast-to-coast radio program by Seventh-day Adventists. W. A. Fagal started *Faith for Today,* a televised devotional program that began in New York in 1950 but by the end of the decade was available to viewers nationwide. A third Adventist telecast, *It Is Written,* first appeared in 1955, featuring George Van-

deman. *Breath of Life,* a television program designed to attract black audiences, went on the air in 1974. All of these programs represented direct EVANGELISM by conducting live meetings and offering free literature or Bible correspondence courses to listeners. Frequently the programs were exported to other countries or became models for similar programming by Adventists in other parts of the world, most notably in Latin America, where Marcio Braulio Perez pioneered with *La Voz de la Esperanza,* a Spanish version of *The Voice of Prophecy.*

Between 1955 and 1970 Adventist membership grew to more than two million and by 1978 it exceeded three million. In June 2001 it reached twelve million. For the most part, growth occurred in Latin America, the Caribbean, Africa, KOREA, and the PHILIPPINES. Big city evangelism underwent serious revision by, among others, Walter Schubert, Arturo Schmidt, and Salim Japas, all from Latin America, but church leaders attributed membership growth to witnessing by individual members more than to formal evangelism. To accommodate the expanding church, General Conference leaders repeatedly redrew territorial borders to create new administrative divisions in Africa and Asia.

At the General Conference session of 1990, president Neal Wilson and his successor, Robert Folkenberg, launched Global Mission, a movement to penetrate all unentered areas of the world with special emphasis on the so-called 10–40 Window, the heavily populated lands between ten and forty degrees north latitude. Much of the membership increase after 1990 occurred in this region.

Beginning in the 1970s Adventist schools in the world fields upgraded to degree-granting institutions, some of which also offered postbaccalaureate degrees. Adventists own ninety-five schools of higher learning, most of them outside North America. In Latin America Adventists operate schools of medicine at the University of Montemorelos (Mexico) and River Plate Adventist University (Argentina). In the Philippines Adventists maintain a campus devoted exclusively to graduate education, the Adventist International Institute of Advanced Studies. The largest Adventist school in the world, Korean Sahmyook University in Seoul, South Korea, offers doctorates in theology and pharmacy besides other graduate degrees.

From the 1970s onward it became increasingly customary to elect non–North Americans to leadership roles in the General Conference and the divisions. In the year 2001 national leaders headed all except one of the divisions, and ten of the seventeen administrative posts in the presidential wing and secretariat of the General Conference were occupied by persons from

Europe, Africa, Asia, Latin America, and the South Pacific.

References and Further Reading

Bull, Michael, and Keith Lockhart. *Seeking a Sanctuary: Seventh-day Adventism and the American Dream.* San Francisco: Harper and Row, 1989.

Douglass, Herbert E. *Messenger of the Lord.* Nampa, ID: Pacific Press Publishing Association, 1998.

Froom, L. E. *Movement of Destiny.* Washington, D.C.: Review and Herald Publishing Association, 1971.

———. *Prophetic Faith of Our Fathers.* Washington, D.C.: Review and Herald Publishing Association, 1950.

Gaustad, Edwin, ed. *The Rise of Adventism.* New York: Harper and Row, 1975.

General Conference Archives and Statistics Department. *Seventh-day Adventist Yearbook.* [Annual directory of organizations, institutions, and workers. Published since 1883.]

———. *Annual Statistical Report.* [Annual statistical summary of organizations and institutions, showing revenues, membership, and other pertinent data. Limited circulation.]

Knight, George R. *Millennial Fever and the End of the World.* Boise, ID: Pacific Press Publishing Association, 1993.

———. *A Search for Identity: the Development of Seventh-day Adventist Beliefs.* Hagerstown, MD: Review and Herald Publishing Association, 2000.

Land, Gary, ed. *Adventism in America.* Grand Rapids, MI: Wm. B. Eerdmans, 1986.

Ministerial Association, General Conference of Seventh-day Adventists. *Seventh-day Adventists Believe, a Biblical Exposition of 27 Fundamental Doctrines.* Hagerstown, MD: Review and Herald Publishing Association, 1988.

Morgan, Douglas. *Adventism and the American Republic: the Public Involvement of a Major Apocalyptic Movement.* Knoxville: University of Tennessee Press, 2001.

Numbers, Ronald L., and Jonathan M. Butler, eds. *The Disappointed: Millerism and Millenariarism in the Nineteenth Century.* Bloomington: Indiana University Press, 1987.

Schwarz, Richard W., and Floyd Greenleaf. *Light Bearers: a History of the Seventh-day Adventist Church.* Nampa, ID: Pacific Press Publishing Association, 2000.

Strand, Kenneth A., ed. *The Sabbath in Scripture and History.* Washington, D.C.: Review and Herald Publishing Association, 1982.

FLOYD GREENLEAF

SEXUALITY

All religions regulate sexual conduct and regard sexual behavior as part of a moral system. Within Christianity, Orthodox, Catholic, and Protestant teachings differ on some matters, such as clerical marriage, but agree on others, such as monogamy (see CLERGY, MARRIAGE OF). Protestants themselves have varied (and continue to vary) widely in terms of sexual attitudes and practices: leaders of the radical Anabaptists (see ANABAPTISM) at the German city of Münster in the sixteenth century practiced polygamy, or PLURAL MARRIAGE; Moravians determined marital partners by a lottery; SHAKERS saw complete chastity as the model of the Christian life for all believers; Ranters

during the English CIVIL WAR and "perfectionists" in the American Great Awakening (see AWAKENINGS) held that religious CONVERSION made anything they did free from sin, a view echoed occasionally by twentieth-century revivalists (see REVIVALS). In every group official attitudes and policies regarding sexual issues also differed from actual behavior. Variety has only increased in the last century as Protestantism has grown more diverse, so that on some issues relating to sexuality, such as HOMOSEXUALITY or ABORTION, the opinions of liberal Protestants are closer to those of liberal Catholics (and liberals in other religions), whereas conservative or fundamentalist Protestants are closer to conservative Catholics (see LIBERAL PROTESTANTISM AND LIBERALISM).

Early Christian attitudes toward sexuality were shaped by the (relatively few and somewhat complex) words of Jesus as recorded in Scripture; the writings of Paul and the early Church Fathers; especially St. Augustine; Jewish norms and traditions, and ideas and practices of Greek, Roman, Middle Eastern, and Germanic societies. By the fifteenth century, official Christian teaching held that the only permissable sexual relations were those between husbands and wives, and that even these were tainted by original sin. Virginity and CELIBACY were more worthy states than MARRIAGE, with numerous works idealizing abstinence and denigrating sexuality. Because most of these works were written by men, they are also extremely misogynist, viewing women's sexuality, personified in Eve, as the source of evil in the world. DIVORCE was not allowed, although unhappy spouses could get a legal separation or perhaps an annulment. Sexual matters were handled by a system of church courts, guided by increasingly elaborate canon law and staffed by canon lawyers trained at universities. Priests in Western Christianity could not marry, although married men could become priests in the Orthodox church (see ORTHODOXY, EASTERN).

The Reformation Period: Ideas and Institutions

Sexuality was an integral part of the Protestant REFORMATION from its beginning. One of MARTIN LUTHER's earliest treatises attacked the value of vows of celibacy, and argued that marriage was the best Christian life; Luther followed his words by deeds and in 1525 married a nun who had fled her convent, Katherine von Bora. Both HULDRYCH ZWINGLI and JOHN CALVIN regarded the regulation of sexual activities as just as important as the regulation of DOCTRINE, and established special courts to handle marriage and morals cases, which came to have wide powers. Many of the radical groups developed distinctive ideas of the proper sexual life for their members, and punished those who did not follow their rules with complete social ostracization, termed shunning or banning. Because Protestant theology expected good works as the fruit of saving faith, one's sexual activities—and those of one's neighbors—continued to be important in God's eyes, and order and morality were a mark of divine favor.

In a number of matters regarding sexuality, Protestants did not break sharply with medieval tradition. They differed little from Catholics in regard to basic concepts such as the roots and proper consequences of gender differences, or the differences between "natural" and "unnatural" sexual practices. Although Luther flamboyantly rejected canon law—publicly burning canon law books before the students of the University of Wittenberg in 1520—it eventually formed the legal basis of much Protestant law regarding marriage and sex. Breaking with TRADITION in terms of the power of the papacy or the meaning of key rituals turned out to be easier than breaking with tradition in terms of sexual and gender relations.

Luther was faithful to Augustine's idea of the link between original sin and sexual desire, but saw desire as so powerful that the truly chaste life was impossible for all but a handful of individuals. Thus the best Christian life was not one that fruitlessly attempted ascetic celibacy, but one in which sexual activity was channeled into marriage. Marriage was not a sacrament—Luther was adamant that it conferred no special grace—but it was the ideal state for almost everyone. The centrality of sex to marriage led Luther to advocate divorce in the case of impotence, adultery, desertion, absolute incompatability, or the refusal of a spouse to have sex; reconciliation was preferable, but if this could not be effected, the innocent party should be granted a divorce with the right to remarry. Although it still carried the taint of SIN, marital sex was also a positive good in itself and not simply because it led to procreation; sex increased affection between spouses, and promoted harmony in domestic life.

Calvin agreed with Luther in simultaneously rejecting the sacramentality of marriage and praising its God-given nature, although he was more guarded than Luther on the virtue of marital sex; he and later English Puritans (see PURITANISM) recommended limiting the frequency and vigor of marital sex so as not to appear "beastly." Calvin condemned those who sought to impose restrictions on marriage that had no biblical base and accepted divorce in cases of adultery (he saw desertion as a type of adultery), although he advocated attempts at reconciliation first. New England Puritans largely agreed with their English counterparts: sexual relations within marriage were a positive good, as long as they were not excessive; all sexual relations outside of marriage were unacceptable; sexual deviancy and religious HERESY were often linked.

Most reformers did not regard sexual conduct as a matter to be left up to individuals, so advocated the establishment of courts that would regulate marriage and morals, wrote ordinances regulating marriage and other matters of sexual conduct, and worked closely with the secular rulers in their area, whether city councils or princes. To make sure the ordinances were being followed and determine what other measures were necessary, church and state officials often conducted joint investigations termed visitations, in which they questioned pastors, teachers, and lay people about their religious and moral life. These institutions and activities reflected the values and aims of both religious and political elites, who both regarded marriage and moral order as essential to a stable society.

The first Protestant court was the marriage court in Zurich, established by Zwingli in 1525, which served as a model for similar courts in many other Swiss and German cities. The most famous of these courts was the CONSISTORY established in Geneva under Calvin's leadership in 1541 and made up of the city's pastors and twelve lay elders. As CALVINISM spread into FRANCE, GERMANY, SCOTLAND, the Low Countries, northern IRELAND, and eventually the New England colonies, ordinances were adopted regulating marriage for Calvinist Protestants and consistories were established to oversee doctrine and morals. These courts heard a wide range of cases and their focus varied over the years, but in general between 30 and 80 percent of their cases involved sex. Offenders were required to confess openly before the consistory, and often before their home congregations as well, and could be punished with fines or excommunication.

Among the radical reformers, marriage was generally not a sacrament—some of them rejected the idea of SACRAMENTS completely—but many of them placed more emphasis on its spiritual nature than Luther had. Marriage was a covenant—a contract—between a man and a woman based on their membership in the body of believers, and thus was linked to their redemption. Because of this the group as a whole or at least its leaders should have a say in marital choice, broadening the circle of consent far beyond the parental consent required by Luther, Calvin, and other less radical reformers. A few of the radical groups spiritualized sexuality along with marriage, emphasizing the goodness of all aspects of human sexuality, including the sexual organs and intercourse. A small German group called the Dreamers, for example, saw intercourse simply as obedience to God's command to "be fruitful and multiply," rather than linking it to disobedience and sin. In the eighteenth century the Moravians sang hymns to Jesus's penis and Mary's breasts and uterus. The leader of the Moravians, Count NIKOLAUS VON ZINZENDORF (1700–1760), defended their hymns by asserting that shame about Jesus's or Mary's sexual organs was a denial of the full humanity of Christ (see MORAVIAN CHURCH).

Although most radical groups, including the Moravians, developed stringent sexual and moral rules for their members, there were also a few who regarded the Christian message as giving them an inner light that freed them from existing religious and secular law. This position, termed ANTINOMIANISM, only very rarely led to any long-term sexual experimentation or break with traditional marriage patterns in Europe. Radical groups that developed slightly later in North America, such as the Shakers, did institute major changes, although they did not regard themselves as above the law.

The many radical Protestant groups also developed institutions to regulate the sexual and moral behavior of their members. In some cases these were bodies of elders to whom accusations were made or who ferreted out wrongdoing themselves, and in some cases the disciplinary body was the entire group or its male members. The SOCIETY OF FRIENDS (the Quakers), begun in seventeenth-century ENGLAND by GEORGE FOX, developed the most distinctive institution, a women's meeting that oversaw the readiness of candidates for marriage, upheld the maintenance of decorous standards of dress, and at times ruled on other moral issues; the first women's meetings were established in British North America in 1681.

The Reformation Period: Actual Changes

What was the impact of these new Protestant ideas and institutions? That is more difficult to trace than ideas or institutions because the sources are scattered in thousands of court records. One of the most immediately visible changes brought by the Protestant Reformation was clerical marriage. Almost all of the continental Protestant reformers married, some, such as Luther, to former nuns. Some pastors' wives were still jeered at as "priests' whores," and they had to create a respectable role for themselves, although they had no official position in the new Protestant churches. They did this largely—and quite successfully, within a generation or so—by being models of wifely obedience and Christian charity, attempting to make their households into the type of orderly "little commonwealths" that their husbands were urging on their congregations in sermons. Maintaining an orderly household was just as important for Protestant pastors as teaching and PREACHING correct doctrine, with officials investigating charges of sexual improprieties or moral laxness just as thoroughly as charges of incorrect doctrine.

Pastoral households were not the only ones scrutinized for moral failings, as church and state authorities in Europe and North America attempted to make their vision of orderly households a reality. Orderly households required a proper foundation, so consistories and courts paid great attention to the wedding ceremony, requiring it to be public and have a pastor officiating. Parental consent was another key issue, and marriage ordinances in many Protestant areas required parental consent even for children who were no longer minors. Authorities in many areas also prohibited their citizens from marrying those of different denominations, although mixed marriages continued to occur, particularly in areas where Catholics and Protestants lived in close proximity to one another. Once a marriage had taken place, the key aim of religious and political authorities was to keep the couple together. They generally did not intervene in any disputes between spouses unless they created public scandal or repeatedly disturbed the neighbors, and attempted reconciliation first for serious cases.

Accusations of adultery were taken very seriously because adultery directly challenged the central link between marriage and procreation as well as impugning male honor. Many legal codes, including the criminal code of the Holy Roman Empire of 1532, made adultery a capital offense; this law made no reference to gender differences, but in city ordinances of the 1560s in Geneva and the 1650 Adultery Act in England, adultery was made a capital offense for a married woman and her partner, but was only punished by a short imprisonment for a married man (see CAPITAL PUNISHMENT).

Following the ideas of their reformers, Swiss, German, Scottish, Scandinavian, and French Protestant marital courts allowed divorce for adultery and impotence, and sometimes for contracting a contagious disease, malicious desertion, conviction for a capital crime, or deadly assault. This dramatic change in marital law had less than dramatic results, however, at least judging by sheer numbers. In contrast to today, when divorce is a large part of all civil legal procedures, Protestant marriage courts heard very few divorce cases because marriage was the economic and social foundation of society.

The vast majority of cases involving sexual conduct actually heard by Protestant church courts in Europe and lower courts in New England were for premarital intercourse, usually termed fornication, which became evident when the woman showed signs of pregnancy. Many of the cases of fornication were actually between individuals who intended to marry, and the solution was a quick wedding. Both spouses were generally subject to punishment as well, which might include fines, public shaming rituals, and imprisonment.

If the man disputed the woman's claim that there had been an agreement, she or her father could take him to court to force him to marry her, although this often did not work, and might result in both individuals being tortured until one changed her/his story.

The consequences of having an illegitimate child with no father identified varied widely across Protestant Europe and North America, and were often related more to economic structures than to religious ideology, with areas in which there was a labor shortage being relatively tolerant. Pregnancies in which the father was the woman's married employer or was related by blood or marriage to her were especially disastrous for the woman, for this was adultery or incest rather than simple fornication and could bring great shame on the household. Women in such situations were urged to lie about the father's identity or were simply fired.

With justifications that spoke of a rising tide of infanticide, early modern governments, both Protestant and Catholic, began to require all unmarried women who discovered they were pregnant to make an official declaration of their pregnancy; if they did not and the baby subsequently died before baptism, they could be charged with infanticide even if there was no evidence that they actually did anything to cause the death. In some areas midwives were ordered to help enforce these laws by checking the breasts of women who denied giving birth to see if they had milk, and at times even checking the breasts of all unmarried women in a parish for signs of childbirth. Such examinations of the bodies of unmarried women indicate how far early modern governments were willing to go in their attempts not only to stop infanticide, but also to control the sexual activities of those who did not gain the rights to such activities through marriage.

Along with punishing those found guilty of fornication, Protestant authorities also attempted to restrict occasions that they increasingly viewed as sources of sexual temptation, such as parish festivals, spinning bees, and dances. Pastors harangued against male clothing styles in which the penis was contained in a separate codpiece, often brightly colored, stuffed to make it more prominent, and worn with a shortened doublet so that everyone could see it; municipal sumptuary laws that regulated the clothing of urban residents sometimes specifically prohibited codpieces. Dancing was attacked in great detail in laws and sermons in Calvinist cities such as Geneva and Nîmes, where along with dancing the consistories condemned low-cut necklines, cosmetics, certain hairstyles, codpieces, comic plays, games of cards and dice, masquerades, and carnival (Mardi Gras) parties. Sodomy was generally a capital crime, although the number of actual sodomy cases in the sixteenth and seventeenth centuries was very small; the Puritans who ruled England during the period 1640 to 1660 and New England in the colonial period were much more worried about blasphemy and illegitimacy than sodomy.

The Colonial World: Sex and Race

The Protestant Reformation occurred concurrently with the beginning of European colonization, which took Christianity around the world. Christian officials tried to impose European sexual patterns, including monogamous marriage and limited (or no) divorce, but where these conflicted with existing patterns they were often modified and what emerged was a blend of indigenous and imported practices. Colonial officials and missionaries generally regarded indigenous sexual practices that deviated from Christianity, including polygyny, incest, same-sex relations, concubinage, and temporary marriage, as markers of inferiority, and invoked them as a justification for European conquest and imperialism. The first wave of colonization and missionary activity in the sixteenth century primarily involved Catholic powers and personnel from Spain, Portugal, and France. Dutch Protestants were active in Southeast Asia and SOUTH AFRICA by the seventeenth century; English Protestants in AFRICA and Asia by the middle of the eighteenth century; and American Protestants in many parts of the world by the early part of the nineteenth century.

European accounts of exploration and travel almost always discuss the scanty clothing of indigenous peoples, which was viewed as a sign of their uncontrolled sexuality. Hot climate—which we would probably view as the main influence on clothing choice—was itself regarded as leading to greater sexual drive and lower inhibitions. By the eighteenth century leading European thinkers such as Adam Smith and DAVID HUME divided the world into three climatic/sexual zones: torrid, temperate, and frigid—words that still retain their double climatic/sexual meaning. They, and many other European writers and statesmen, worried about the effects of tropical climates on the morals as well as the health of soldiers and officials, and devised various schemes to keep Europeans sent to imperial posts from fully "going native," adopting indigenous dress, mores, and who knew what else. They also linked this climatic/sexual schema with the advancement of civilization; in the torrid zones, heat made people indolent and lethargic as well as lascivious, whereas a temperate climate (like Britain) encouraged productivity and discipline along with sexual restraint and respect for WOMEN. This schema was devised by northern European Protestants, who judged southern European (and Irish) Catholics to be an intermediate category: not as moral as themselves, but less lazy and lascivious than those who lived in the tropics.

The aspect of "going native" that most concerned colonial authorities was, not surprisingly, engaging in sexual relations with indigenous people, and the colonial powers all regulated such encounters. In some cases, such as the earliest Spanish, Portuguese, and Dutch colonies, sexual relations and even marriage between Europeans and indigenous peoples were encouraged as a means of making alliances, cementing colonial power, and increasing the population; rape and enforced sexual services of indigenous women were also a common part of conquest. The directors of the Dutch East India Company gave soldiers, sailors, and minor officials bonuses if they agreed to marry local women and stay in the Dutch colonies as "free-burghers." This policy was opposed by some Dutch missionaries, but accepted by others, who hoped marriage with local women would not only win converts but give missionaries access to female religious rituals. The directors of the British East India Company gave additional encouragement in 1687, decreeing that any child resulting from the marriage of any soldier and native woman be paid a small grant on the day of its christening.

There were limits to this acceptance of intermarriage, however, often explicitly along racial lines. Rijkloff von Goens, one of the Dutch governors of Sri Lanka, supported mixed marriages, but then wanted the daughters of those marriages married to Dutchmen so that the Dutch "race" would "degenerate" as little as possible. In the Dutch colony of the Cape of Good Hope (South Africa), although the races were not segregated and there was much sexual contact between European men and African women, this color hierarchy was so strong that it largely prevented interracial marriage. Until 1823 slaves in Cape Colony could not marry in a Christian ceremony; a man wanting to marry a slave had to baptize and free her first. Slaves marrying among themselves often devised their own ceremonies, or married in Muslim ceremonies even though Islam was not a recognized religion. Some of these were slaves, and by the second and third generation many of them were women of mixed race. In Dutch and English areas some of these women were Catholic, the children of marriages between Portuguese men and local women; Protestant church authorities worried about the women retaining their loyalty to Catholicism, raising their children as Catholics and perhaps even converting their husbands. Thus although they often tolerated Catholicism in general, they required marriages between a Protestant and a Catholic to be celebrated in a Protestant church and demanded a promise from the spouses that the children would be raised Protestant.

The fate of children from extramarital, interracial unions varied enormously. Some of them were legitimated by their fathers through adoption or the purchase of certificates of legitimacy, and could assume prominent positions in colonial society. For example, two of the sons of François Caron, who had worked for twenty years for the Dutch East India Company and had five children with a Japanese woman, later became well-known ministers in the Dutch church. The East India Company Council in Batavia tried to solve the issue of mixed-race children born out of wedlock by banning their fathers from returning to Europe, a policy that was counterproductive because it simply discouraged European men from recognizing or supporting their children.

Like state and company policies, church policies regarding marriage and morality were often counterproductive. In Dutch colonies, for example, marriages could be solemnized only when a pastor visited, which in remote areas might be only every several years. This did not keep people from marrying, however, but instead encouraged them to maintain traditional patterns of marriage, in which cohabitation and sexual relations began with the exchange of gifts, rather than a church wedding. Protestant missionaries advocated frequent church attendance, viewing sermons as a key way to communicate Protestant doctrine; the Asian wives of European men took this very much to heart and attended church so frequently and in such great style that sumptuary laws were soon passed restricting extravagant clothing and expenditures for church ceremonies. In the Danish Lutheran colony of Tranquebar, children of European men and local women born out of wedlock were denied baptism, but they were simply taken down the road and baptized in Portuguese Catholic churches, clearly not the intent of the Danish political or religious authorities.

Because initially almost all Europeans in colonial areas were men, interracial sexual relations generally did not upset notions of superiority. Once more women began to immigrate, official encouragement and even toleration of mixed marriages generally ceased, although informal relations ranging from prostitution through concubinage continued. The sexual activities of European women, the wives and daughters of missionaries and governors, were closely monitored, however.

In the colonial world, both sexual and racial categories were viewed as permanent moral classifications supported by unchanging religious teachings. They were not viewed as socially constructed, but as undergirded by an even more fundamental boundary, that between "natural" and "unnatural." Thus same-sex relations were defined as a "crime against nature," but then often tried in church courts. This link between natural and godly began to lessen in intensity during the eighteenth century, but the importance of nature in setting boundaries only intensified, and "nature" came to lie at the basis of modern understandings of sexuality.

The Nineteenth and Twentieth Centuries

During the nineteenth and twentieth centuries, there were two somewhat contradictory tendencies shaping the intersections between Protestantism and sexuality. On the one hand, the basic paradigm of sexuality for educated people in the West changed from religion to science, with sexual issues viewed in medical or psychological terms as part of the "natural" or material world. On the other hand, the rise of fundamentalist Christianity affirmed the strong beliefs on the part of many people that sexual ideas and practices continued to be religious issues (see FUNDAMENTALISM). These two paradigms were sometimes in opposition to one another; for example, doctors and psychologists increasingly defined certain actions as uncontrollable sexual "fetishes," whereas religious authors labeled them as (im-)moral choices. At other times they fit together. Pornographic literature, which had been a significant share of printed works in Europe since the development of the printing press in the mid–fifteenth century, was not legally banned because of its sexual content until the mid–nineteenth century with laws such as the Obscene Publications Act passed by the British Parliament in 1857. Both medical and religious leaders supported prohibitions of pornography, with the former regarding viewing pornographic literature as unhealthy and the latter as immoral. (For an additional example of such agreement, see PROSTITUTION.)

In medical terms sex was increasingly regarded as an aspect of health, with physicians, not pastors, determining what was "normal" and "abnormal." Sexual disorders were labeled and identified, and treatments suggested that involved drugs, therapy, and surgery, not prayer. Western governments sought to promote a healthy society as a way of building up national strength, and anything that detracted from this became a matter of official and often public concern.

Moral and religious attitudes clearly shaped the new science of sexology, however. This can be seen very well in the obsession with masturbation that developed in the nineteenth century and continued well into the twentieth. Doctors drew on the older idea of bodily humors to argue that men had only a limited amount of sperm—often labeled the "spermatic econ-

omy"—so that too early or too frequent spilling of sperm might cause them to become weak and feeble, incapable of serving their country. Masturbation would also weaken boys' sense of morality, argued both doctors and pastors. This fixation was shaped by notions of race and class as well as GENDER; lower-class and non-white servants were often accused of teaching white, middle-class children to masturbate. A British soldier in Kenya, Robert Baden-Powell, founded the Boy Scouts in 1908 explicitly to teach British boys what he regarded as the right sort of manly virtues and keep them from masturbation, effeminacy, physical weakness, and homosexuality. These were traits he regarded as particularly common among the non-white subjects of the British Empire, and also among the residents of British industrial cities. If they were not counteracted with a vigorous program of physical training and outdoor life, Baden-Powell and numerous other writers, physicians, politicians, and church leaders predicted an inevitable "race degeneration" or even "race suicide."

Devotion to God (and country) was an explicit part of Boy Scout teaching, both in Britain and in other parts of the world where Boy Scout groups were organized. Boy Scouts spread fastest in Protestant areas because Catholic leaders regarded them with some suspicion, although by the later twentieth century Scouts could be found in many Catholic areas as well. Belief in God remains an explicit part of the Boy Scout motto (although now this is more generic, to allow for non-Christian members), and boys can be dismissed if they publicly deny such belief, as a 2002 case involving a Washington teen-age Eagle Scout made clear. Baden-Powell's moral concerns still shape Scout policies on other matters as well because openly gay individuals are not allowed to be members or troop leaders.

Changes in ideas about sexuality shaped other quasi-religious groups as well. The Young Men's Christian Association (see YMCA, YWCA), for example, began in England in 1848 as a Christian men's movement in which young unmarried men were expected to strengthen their character and morality through passionate attachments to one another, a union of souls that would lead to greater love for God. During the nineteenth century individuals had often expressed same-sex desire in very passionate terms, but these were generally regarded as "romantic friendships," expected as a part of growing up and, especially in women, not a sign of deviancy even if they continued throughout an individual's life. Historians debate whether such friendships should be labeled "homosexual" because this was not yet a category in people's minds, but in the decades around 1900 sexologists turned their attention to same-sex desire.

They initially labeled this "inversion," although eventually the word "homosexuality," devised in 1869 by the Hungarian jurist K. M. Benkert, became the common term. The medicalization of same-sex desire as a form of sexual deviancy changed attitudes, and intimacy between girls or between boys was increasingly regarded with distrust. By the 1920s the YMCA's official statements condemned same-sex attraction and espoused a "muscular Christianity," centered on basketball (invented at a YMCA), swimming, and other sports, and on "normal" heterosexual relationships.

At about the same time as the founding of the Boy Scouts, many Protestants, particularly in the UNITED STATES, came to understand themselves as "fundamentalists," affirming orthodox dogma, downplaying more complicated issues of doctrine, and largely supporting a conservative social agenda. Fundamentalist Protestants grew in numbers throughout the twentieth century, and became increasingly vocal opponents of abortion and gay rights, while advocating what were labeled "traditional family values." Fundamentalist groups often broke from the Protestant denominations that had developed in previous centuries to form nondenominational community churches, although some denominations, such as the Southern Baptist Convention, were also largely fundamentalist. At the same time some Protestant denominations, or individual congregations within them, became increasingly embroiled in issues of gender and sexuality, focussing on the question of practicing homosexuals as members and clergy.

Fundamentalist Protestantism became an increasingly important part of Christianity throughout the entire world in the era after World War II; in 2000 nearly two-thirds of the world's Christians lived outside Europe and North America, with many of them belonging to nondenominational and fundamentalist churches rather than traditional mainstream Catholic or Protestant churches. These churches are appealing to people whose cultural values are shaped by animism, Hinduism, Buddhism, and other religions, and the norms they are establishing in regard to sexuality and gender also draw on many traditions, with churches often deciding individually how they will handle issues such as polygamy, child marriage, remarriage of widows, and other issues in which local traditions conflict with traditional Christian teachings. As Protestantism, and Christianity in general, declines in importance in Western society—except for the United States—Protestant ideas and practices about many aspects of sexuality may also change. Because of migration, these debates will be played out not only in the former colonies, but in Europe and North America as well.

References and Further Reading

Adair, Richard. *Courtship, Illegitimacy and Marriage in Early Modern England*. Manchester: Manchester University Press, 1996.

Blussé, Leonard. *Strange Company: Chinese Settlers, Mestizo Women and the Dutch in VOC Batavia*. Dordrecht, The Netherlands: Foris, 1986.

Graham, Michael F. *The Uses of Reform: "Godly Discipline" and Popular Behavior in Scotland and Beyond 1560–1610*. Leiden, The Netherlands: Brill, 1996.

Harrington, Joel F. *Reordering Marriage and Society in Reformation Germany*. Cambridge: Cambridge University Press, 1995.

Hoffer, Peter C., and N. E. H. Hull. *Murdering Mothers: Infanticide in England and New England 1558–1803*. New York: New York University Press, 1981.

Juster, Susan. *Disorderly Women: Sexual Politics and Evangelicalism in Revolutionary New England*. Ithaca, NY: Cornell University Press, 1994.

McIntosh, Marjorie Keniston. *Controlling Misbehavior in England 1370–1600*. Cambridge: Cambridge University Press, 1998.

Mentzer, Raymond A., ed. "Sin and the Calvinists: Morals Control and the Consistory in the Reformed Tradition." In *Sixteenth Century Essays and Studies*. vol. 32. Kirksville, MO: Sixteenth Century Journal Publishers, 1994.

Nye, Robert, ed. *Sexuality*. New York: Oxford University Press, 1999.

Phillips, Roderick. *Putting Asunder: A History of Divorce in Western Society*. Cambridge: Cambridge University Press, 1988.

Shell, Robert C.-H. *Children of Bondage: A Social History of the Slave Society at the Cape of Good Hope, 1652–1838*. Hanover, NH: University Press of New England, 1994.

Smith, Merril D., ed. *Sex and Sexuality in Early America*. New York: New York University Press, 1998.

Stuart, Elizabeth, and Adrian Thatcher, eds. *Christian Perspectives on Sexuality and Gender*. Leominster, UK: Gracewing, 1996.

Weeks, Jeffrey. *Sex, Politics, and Society: The Regulation of Sexuality Since 1800*. London: Longmans, 1981.

Wiesner-Hanks, Merry E. *Christianity and Sexuality in the Early Modern World: Regulating Desire, Reforming Practice*. London: Routledge, 2000.

MERRY E. WIESNER-HANKS

SHAKERS

The Shakers are a Christian sect that originated in ENGLAND in the mid-eighteenth century. In 1774 under the leadership of ANN LEE, a handful of Believers, as they were also known, emigrated to America. This community expanded and prospered during the first half of the nineteenth century, but began a steady decline thereafter. In the twenty-first century a small number of Shakers remain in one village in the UNITED STATES. The history of this dissenting community embraces inauspicious beginnings, remarkable success in antebellum America, sagging fortunes during the twentieth century, and yet astonishing cultural stature at the start of the new millennium. Over the course of two and a half centuries Shakerism has reflected certain Protestant ideas and practices, but also has departed from those religious patterns in significant and distinctive ways.

Beginnings

Eighteenth-century England gave rise to many dissenting sects (see DISSENT; NONCONFORMITY) that resisted conformity to the established CHURCH OF ENGLAND. Among such dissenters was a group of religious enthusiasts in Manchester whose ecstatic worship and spiritual activity were often accompanied by trembling. From this they were dubbed "Shakers," or sometimes "Shaking Quakers." Led by two tailors, James and Jane Wardley, this small community first emerged in the 1740s. Historical evidence from the period is sparse. Ann Lee (b. 1736), the illiterate daughter of a blacksmith, joined the group in 1758. The Shaking Quakers attracted public attention. The frenzy of their worship provoked curiosity and criticism, the latter because of the disturbances they caused when assembling in the homes of members. They also openly condemned the Anglican Church and other religious groups (see ANGLICANISM). The Shaking Quakers derived inspiration from the radical French Prophets who came to England from the Cévennes district of FRANCE. Bold and enthusiastic in style, the Shakers invaded sanctuaries during worship and denounced the clergy. For these actions they were arrested, tried, convicted, fined, and jailed. In the early 1770s Lee, the frequent recipient of visions, emerged as the prophetic leader of the sect. She was incarcerated more than once for her activities. Lee and the others proclaimed an apocalyptic message and called for separation from the churches.

In 1774, as the result of a vision, Ann Lee and eight followers left England and traveled to America, arriving in New York City, where the group disappeared from public view. Two years later they had reassembled in Niskeyuna, a rural location adjacent to Albany, New York. However, the revolutionary context in America proved hostile because the Shakers were pacifists (see PACIFISM), and colonial patriots accused them of supporting the British cause. Again Lee and several disciples found themselves in prison because of these charges.

The community began its public ministry in 1780 with the opening of the Shaker gospel to their neighbors. The first American converts came from the ranks of evangelical BAPTISTS in the region. The Believers, who lived together, soon attracted others to their new and strange religion. Lee's charisma endeared her to her followers, who called her "Mother." They credited her with miraculous gifts and powers, including prophecy and healing (see FAITH HEALING).

In 1782 Lee and several others traveled throughout eastern New York and New England in search of converts and in support of those who had already accepted the Shaker gospel. This missionary journey lasted for twenty-six months and produced more disciples throughout the region, although on this trip Lee and other Believers experienced physical harassment and persecution in several localities. In 1784, one year after returning to Niskeyuna, Lee died, and leadership passed to her English disciple, James Whittaker. He began the process of community building outside the original settlement. Under his leadership Shakers gathered on land near Lebanon, New York, a location that subsequently became the headquarters of an emerging regional society. Whittaker, however, died three years after Lee in 1787.

Nineteenth-Century Success

At this point American converts stepped into administrative roles in the society and began systematically organizing and staffing Shaker settlements at sites where Lee's travels had generated converts. Leadership in the emerging movement rested in the hands of Joseph Meacham and Lucy Wright, the former exercising influence until his death in 1796 and the latter until she died in 1821. During their combined tenure, the society gathered scattered Believers, consolidated local villages, and established uniform religious and social arrangements, the result being the formation of a national organization eventually spanning from Maine in the East to Indiana in the West. The move into the Ohio Valley in 1805, directed by Wright, resulted in both geographical and numerical expansion. By the 1820s sixteen Shaker villages were in existence containing around four thousand residents. In this period the society adopted a set of Millennial Laws governing all aspects of collective and individual activity. Leadership responsibilities were divided between men and women, elders and eldresses, who constituted the society's ministry. Economic affairs fell under the supervision of DEACONS who managed the agricultural and light manufacturing activities.

Converts who joined the society frequently came from Protestant denominations. Shakers often attended evangelical REVIVALS or CAMP MEETINGS where they conversed with potential converts, challenging them to consider a higher form of Christianity in Shakerism (see EVANGELICALISM). Individuals who accepted the Shaker gospel and the challenge of separating from the "world" sacrificed much, including former beliefs, relationships with family and friends, sexual activity, individual decision making, and economic independence. Persons who were curious about the society or potentially interested in joining were housed in separate living units—the Gathering Order—before they were admitted as full members. The latter status required Believers to leave behind their former lives, confess their sins to the ministry, accept the principle and practice of CELIBACY, obey the leaders in all things, and turn over all private property to the community. The United Society of Believers in Christ's Second Appearing, the formal name of the organization in the nineteenth century, was a communal society, practicing a form of Christian COMMUNISM.

Life in Shaker villages was carefully regimented. Residential and economic "families" were the organizational units within the villages, each presided over by male and female leaders. Believers lived in sexually segregated quarters under close supervision of the ministry. Interaction between males and females was strictly regulated. When husbands and wives joined the society, they were separated, becoming as brother and sister; children were raised communally. Spiritual values theoretically permeated all aspects of life in the villages as spelled out in the rules set down in the Millennial Laws. All able-bodied members were to contribute to the economic well-being of the society, carrying out assigned tasks without complaint. Labor was a highly sanctioned positive value, not unlike the Protestant work ethic. Even children were assigned communal responsibilities, which they carried out under supervision.

The economic result of this collective work ethic was growing financial success at most of the Shaker villages. The Believers produced agricultural surpluses and a variety of manufactured goods, both of which were sold to the outside world. Shaker peddlers traveled widely as they marketed items, from garden seeds, herbs and herbal extracts, to baskets, brooms, and buckets. The Believers also sold cattle, wool, lumber, chairs, and other furniture items. Several villages owned gristmills and sawmills for their own use and for generating income, too. The Shakers enjoyed a widespread positive reputation for the quality of their goods.

However, labor was also a spiritual term with another meaning for Believers, who spoke of WORSHIP as "labor." Shaker worship departed from prevailing Protestant patterns in several ways. Meetinghouses were plain, with no altar or pulpit, nor other traditional physical appointments except for movable benches (see ARCHITECTURE, CHURCH). Shaker meetings resembled Quaker meetings in some respect because they included periods of silence and also individual testimonies. They were, however, filled with song and exhortation, dancing and marching, and a variety of ecstatic physical "exercises" not unlike phenomena associated with camp meetings and revivals. During

the 1830s and 1840s the society experienced a burst of extraordinary religious activity known within the community as Mother Ann's Work. This outburst of spiritual "gifts" anticipated the Spiritualist movement that flourished in America during the second half of the nineteenth century (see SPIRITUALISM). Believers at every location functioned as mediums or instruments through whom gifts and messages were received from deceased members of the society, including Ann Lee, as well as from biblical, historical, and imaginary figures. Among the gifts received were songs and hymns, dances and marches, and elaborate rituals performed in mime, which the Believers identified as proof of the truth of the Shaker gospel. Not surprisingly, this outpouring of ecstatic activity was controversial and led to stress and conflict within the society as well as ridicule and criticism from the outside world.

The first half of the nineteenth century was a time of theological innovation and reflection. Shaker leaders found themselves defending the society against public criticism and seeking to clarify beliefs for potential converts. Two major publications merit special comment. In 1808 a first edition appeared of *The Testimony of Christ's Second Appearing,* a volume that rationalized the faith and practice of the community. In it Benjamin Seth Youngs, the primary author, asserted the role of Ann Lee as a Christ figure and also the nature of God as involving both male and female aspects as Father–Mother. These judgments fueled religious opponents who attacked Shaker theology as blasphemous and heretical. In 1816 the society published an edited volume entitled *Testimonies of the Life, Character, Revelations and Doctrines of Our Ever Blessed Mother Ann Lee, and the Elders with Her,* a compilation of memories and testimonies from those who had known Lee. This collection reasserted the special VOCATION of the founder and the status she continued to enjoy among members in the years after her death. This publication also provided the basis for the ongoing construction of the image of Lee as "Mother Ann."

The American CIVIL WAR was a moment of collective trauma for the society because of the Shakers' Pacifism and because the conflict spilled onto the Kentucky sites at Pleasant Hill and Union Village. Most of the male Believers conscripted refused service; some sought exemption; many were fined. The general tax levies for the war worked economic hardship, too.

Changing Fortunes

After the war the society began a slow but steady geographical retreat from locations in the Ohio Valley and elsewhere as a result of a decline in membership and the loss of economic well-being. The Shakers were increasingly unable to attract new converts, especially male members. The result was both an aging and a feminization of the membership. Agriculture and industry both suffered from this decline. By 1900 the society numbered approximately 850 Believers, a majority of whom were women. In the following years when villages both east and west closed, remaining members at those sites moved to other locations or left the society entirely.

Despite decline, signs of religious vitality still existed. A faction of progressive Shakers was active at several sites, including the North Family at Mount Lebanon, New York (formerly called New Lebanon), and at Canterbury, New Hampshire. During the decades after the war and in the opening years of the new century, these liberals seized the public initiative and were responsible for identifying the Shakers with a variety of social causes, including women's rights and animal rights, the TEMPERANCE movement and the anti-tobacco crusade, prison reform, and diet reform. Among the most prominent voices supporting such causes were Frederick W. Evans, Antoinette Doolittle, and Catherine Allen. In 1905 the Mount Lebanon Believers sponsored a Peace Conference, attended by Shakers and prominent outsiders, that attracted national attention. These same years, however, witnessed the growing influence of evangelical Protestantism in the society's ranks. At several sites Shaker worship began to reflect Protestant patterns in hymnody and devotional life. Sometimes evangelical ministers were invited to preach in Shaker meetings.

As village after village closed, the aging female leadership debated the proper course to follow. By the middle of the twentieth century some Believers, reconciling themselves to an eventual closing of the society, saw their role simply as final guardians of a spiritual and cultural legacy. Others disputed that judgment and determined that the Shakers must continue as a living religious society. By the 1980s the two remaining villages—Canterbury, New Hampshire and Sabbathday Lake, Maine—were divided in their judgments. The ministry at Canterbury formally closed the society to new members, but in open defiance of that decision the Believers at Sabbathday Lake accepted several new converts. The death of the last sister at Canterbury in 1992 proved decisive in the contest. The Shakers in Maine have carried the living tradition into the twenty-first century.

Stature in American Culture

The second half of the twentieth century witnessed two important developments with implications for the society. First, Shakerism became the object of sustained attention by persons interested in American history, religion, and CULTURE. Shaker artifacts, in particular, became favorite items for collectors and antique dealers. Shaker religion was cast as an attractive spirituality because of its work ethic and simple lifestyle. The remaining Shakers themselves became the object of great affection by patrons, friends, and well-wishers, many of whom were eager to finance Shaker causes, buy Shaker objects, and worship with the Believers. This renaissance of interest has fueled unending publications, the restoration of historic sites, and a host of commercial enterprises linked with Shakerism. Second, the Shakers themselves reached out in ecumenical fashion to other religious groups—for example, Catholic monastic orders and the Father Divine movement. Their own worship meetings now reflect the impact of liturgical influences from mainline churches even though they retain the rich Shaker heritage of song, exhortation, and testimony. The Believers have been participants in seminars on spirituality at such distinguished institutions as Yale Divinity School. These activities represent the mainstreaming of Shaker religion.

The future is less uncertain than it may have appeared in the late 1980s. The small but devoted group of Believers in Maine under the powerful leadership of Frances A. Carr are confident that they will carry the Shaker tradition forward, that it will be a leaven in the Christian world, and that the legacy of this movement will, in fact, be a living legacy. The Shakers, once the target of religious and social opponents, have now become near celebrities in American culture.

References and Further Reading

Andrews, Edward Deming. *The People Called Shakers: A Search for the Perfect Society.* New York: Oxford University Press, 1953.

Brewer, Priscilla J. *Shaker Communities, Shaker Lives.* Hanover, NH: University Press of New England, 1986.

Garrett, Clarke. *Spirit Possession and Popular Religion: From the Camisards to the Shakers.* Baltimore, MD: Johns Hopkins University Press, 1987.

Kirk, John T. *The Shaker World: Art, Life, Belief.* New York: Harry N. Abrams, 1997.

Patterson, Daniel W. *The Shaker Spiritual.* Princeton, NJ: Princeton University Press, 1979.

Promey, Sally M. *Spiritual Spectacles: Vision and Image in Mid-Nineteenth-Century Shakerism.* Bloomington: Indiana University Press, 1993.

Stein, Stephen J. *The Shaker Experience in America: A History of the United Society of Believers.* New Haven, CT: Yale University Press, 1992.

Werkin, Gerard C. *The Four Seasons of Shaker Life.* New York: Simon & Shuster, 1986.

STEPHEN J. STEIN

SHARP, GRANVILLE (1735–1813)

English philanthropist. Sharp was born in Durham, ENGLAND, March 10, 1735, and he died at Fulham, near London, on July 6, 1813. He was the son of an archdeacon and grandson of an archbishop. Being a youngest son, he was apprenticed to a draper. Later he became a clerk of Government Ordnance, but resigned rather than send weapons for use against the American revolutionaries, with whom he sympathized.

High-principled, generous, and somewhat eccentric, Sharp possessed—although self-taught—considerable biblical, historical, and legal learning. He was devoted to the interpretation of prophecy and was also tireless in humanitarian causes, above all to the abolition of SLAVERY. After a long battle, conducted in the face of conventional legal opinion, he won from a reluctant Lord chief justice the so-called Mansfield Judgment of 1772, which had the effect of negating masters' rights over slaves in England, thus undercutting the legal basis of slavery there.

Sharp was equally concerned about the distress and destitution in the African community in Britain, which he knew at first hand. He was the principal architect of the project launched in 1787 for a "Province of Freedom" in West Africa where the "Black Poor" of London could find dignity and security and build their own prosperity. His program for the settlement incorporated long-forgotten Anglo-Saxon institutions derived from his antiquarian reading.

Sharp was more a traditional churchman than an evangelical, but he worked happily with the CLAPHAM SECT abolitionists. When the Clapham-related Sierra Leone Company took over responsibility for SIERRA LEONE in 1792 after the collapse of the original settlement, Sharp continued active involvement. Although he held no public position or special status, no one did more than Sharp to make slavery a public religious and political issue in Britain.

See also Slavery, Abolition of

References and Further Reading

Anstey, Roger. *The Atlantic Slave Trade and British Abolition, 1760–1810.* London and Atlantic Heights, NJ: Macmillan, 1975.
Fyfe, Christopher. *A History of Sierra Leone.* London: Oxford University Press, 1962.
Hoare, Prince. *Memoirs of Granville Sharp.* London: Henry Colbourn, 1820.
Lascelles, E. C. P. *Granville Sharp.* London: Oxford University Press, 1928.

ANDREW F. WALLS

SHELDON, CHARLES MONROE (1857–1946)

American pastor and author. Born in Wellsville, New York on February 26, 1857, Sheldon graduated from Brown University (B.A.) and Andover Theological Seminar (B.D.) before accepting the pastorate of Central Congregational Church in Topeka, Kansas, where he served from 1889 to 1919. Thanks to his writings on SOCIAL GOSPEL issues, by 1900 he was ranked among the nation's best-known Protestant clergymen. His fame derived from two sources. In 1900 he edited the *Topeka Daily Capital* for one week "as Jesus would," wherein he printed only positive news, rejecting all lurid tales of violence and questionable advertisements. Four years earlier he had penned a novel, *In His Steps,* in which the main characters all ask themselves, "What would Jesus do?" before making any decision.

Because of a technical error, *In His Steps* entered the public domain and so many publishers reprinted it that it became known as "the second best seller to the Bible alone." It is impossible to determine actual sales figures, which range from eight to thirty-five million. Sheldon's melding of personal EVANGELISM and social concern initially bolstered the liberal wing of Protestantism, but a century later the book attracted a largely conservative readership. Still, his timeless appeal to the idealism of young people has ensured his reputation. Later, Sheldon drew on his fame to pen over fifty books and lecture widely on such issues as ECUMENISM, world peace, and especially prohibition. He died in Topeka on February 24, 1946.

See also Publishing; WWJD

References and Further Reading

Primary Source:

Sheldon, Charles M. *In His Steps.* Nashville, TN: Broadman Press, 1935.

Secondary Sources:

Miller, Timothy. *Following In His Steps: A Biography of Charles M. Sheldon.* Knoxville: The University of Tennessee Press, 1987.
Ripley, John W. "Another Look at the Rev. Mr. Charles M. Sheldon's Christian Daily Newspaper." *The Kansas Historical Quarterly* 31 (Spring 1965): 1–40.

FERENC M. SZASZ

SHEPPARD, RICHARD (1880–1937)

English clergy. Hugh Richard Lawrie, popularly, "Dick" Sheppard was the vicar of St. Martin-in-the-Fields, magazine editor, church reformer, religious radio broadcaster, and supporter of the PACIFISM movement. He was born at Windsor Castle, ENGLAND September 2, 1880 and was educated at the University of Cambridge and Cuddesdon Theological College. In 1907 Sheppard was ordained chaplain and dean of Oxford House, which was a mission to the urban poor of London's East End. In 1911 Sheppard became curate of Grosvenor Chapel of the Church of St. Georges in Hanover Square, London.

St. Martin-in-the-Fields, a large Anglican church in Trafalgar Square, received him as vicar in 1914. There he became King George V's honorary chaplain. At St. Martin's he assumed the position of editor of the *St. Martin's Review,* a monthly news commentary with an approximate circulation of 10,000. Starting in 1924 the BBC broadcast the worship services from St. Martin-in-the-Fields every month.

Sheppard became involved in ecclesiastical reform when he joined the Life and Liberty Movement in 1917. The Movement sought reform in the areas of financial accountability, appointment of ministers, and the extending of church council membership to WOMEN. His ideals for reform were recorded in *The Human Parson* (1924) and *The Impatience of a Parson* (1927).

Because of ill health Sheppard left St. Martin's in 1926. He was appointed dean of CANTERBURY (1929–1931), to be followed by service as canon of St. Paul's Anglican Church (1934–1935). In his final years he became involved in the Peace Pledge Union of London, a peace movement whose membership included Aldous Huxley, Bertrand Russell, and Rose Macaulay. Sheppard died October 31, 1937.

See also Anglicanism; Chaplaincy; Conscientious Objection; Ecclesiology; Peace Organizations

References and Further Reading

Primary Sources:

Sheppard, H. R. L. *The Impatience of a Parson: A Plea for the Recovery of Vital Christianity.* Toronto: Musson Book Co., 1927.
———. *We Say "No": The Plain Man's Guide to Pacifism.* London: J. Murray, 1935.

Secondary Sources:

Roberts, R. Ellis. *H.R.L. Sheppard, Life and Letters.* London: J. Murray, 1942.
Scott, Carolyn. *Dick Sheppard: A Biography.* London: Hodder and Stoughton, 1977.

CHRISTOPHER M. COOK

SHEPPARD, WILLIAM HENRY (1865–1921)

African American missionary. Sheppard was born into a family of freed slaves, began to attend Hampton Institute at the age of twelve, and then went on to Stillman College, where he became immersed in the missionary fervor. Initially, upon his graduation, a pastor, he determinedly attempted to receive an appointment as missionary to AFRICA under the auspices of the Presbyterian Church, South. It was not until a white missionary was found to be the official head of the mission station that Sheppard received his own appointment.

During his decades as missionary in the Congo, Sheppard both criticized the Belgium government and business interests in the land, and accepted the notion of white supremacy. Sheppard was instrumental in recruiting numerous black missionaries for Africa. Because of his scholarly pursuits in geography, the Royal Geographic Society made him a member.

References and Further Reading

Primary Source:

Sheppard, William Henry. *Pioneers in the Congo.* Louisville, KY: Pentecostal Publishing Co., 1917.

Secondary Source:

Williams, Walter. *Black Americans and the Evangelization of Africa, 1817–1900.* Madison, WI: University of Wisconsin Press, 1982.

HANS J. HILLERBRAND

SIERRA LEONE

The boundaries of the modern West African republic of Sierra Leone follow those of the former British colony and protectorate combined. Before the declaration of the protectorate in 1896, however, the term "Sierra Leone" signified a much smaller area, usually the peninsula on which Freetown, the capital, stands. During the nineteenth century its population played a determinative part in the development of African Protestantism as a whole.

Antislavery campaigners, and especially GRANVILLE SHARP, concerned about destitution among Africans in London, devised a scheme for emigration to a piece of land purchased in Sierra Leone. Sharp designed a self-governing "Province of Freedom." In 1787 four hundred "Black Poor" left ENGLAND with a clergyman, but the settlement broke up through disease, war, and maladministration. It was reconstituted in 1792 under a Sierra Leone Company whose directors held CLAPHAM SECT ideals, with Henry Thornton as chairman.

During the American Revolutionary War the British recruited soldiers from the slave population, many of them influenced by evangelical revival movements, with promises of land and liberty. Some were later transferred to Nova Scotia, where revival movements were flourishing (see REVIVALS). The promises of land not being fulfilled, THOMAS PETERS (d. 1792) came as their delegate to London. He met directors of the Sierra Leone Company, who offered land in AFRICA. Over 1,100 people from the African congregations in Nova Scotia responded. They brought to Sierra Leone their own church organization and leadership. The Baptist preacher DAVID GEORGE (d. 1810) came with his congregation, and there were congregations of Methodists (see METHODISM, ENGLAND) and the countess of Huntingdon's Connexion (see HASTINGS, LADY SELINA). These, rather than the Colony's official chapel and chaplain, were the center of religious life. Their enthusiastic, revivalistic religion represented a different style of EVANGELICALISM from the sober, churchly form displayed by the Company's directors and officials. As political differences sharpened and trust broke down, the Nova Scotian settlers increasingly rejected European church ministry.

Several early British mission agencies tried to use Sierra Leone as a base to reach the interior, mostly with disastrous results. Only a mission of the CHURCH MISSIONARY SOCIETY (CMS) among the Susu, northward of the colony, building on the work of an earlier Scottish mission, lasted more than a year or two.

Growth and Population Expansion

In 1800 the British government transported a company of "Maroons" (escaped slaves who had conducted a guerilla war in Jamaica) to Sierra Leone. Despite their slight previous contact with the Christian faith and communal tensions with the Nova Scotians, the Maroons gradually assimilated to the religious pattern of the earlier settlers.

More drastic augmentation of the population began in 1808 when the slave trade was declared illegal in Britain. The British navy became proactive in intercepting slave ships; Sierra Leone was the only feasible center to which they could be brought. The Sierra Leone Company was disbanded, and Sierra Leone became a crown colony. Year by year people from the slave ships, originating in all parts of an area stretching from Senegal to the Congo, were brought to Sierra Leone. At first they were "apprenticed" to the Nova Scotians, but the numbers were soon too great. Sir Charles MacCarthy (governor from 1816 to 1824) developed a system of villages, each with a church

and school, and looked to the missions, especially the CMS, to provide the clergy and schoolmasters. The CMS closed its Susu mission to concentrate on Sierra Leone.

Missionaries, who were mostly—like the first, Melchior Renner (d. 1822)—German Pietists, had to take charge of villages as superintendents (see PIETISM). Many died or broke down, but gradually the villages became Christian communities, marked by literacy and worship in English, there being no single language common to those from the slave ships. The most dramatic transformation was at Regent village, where W. A. B. Johnson (d. 1823) was the missionary. Similar developments took place in Freetown, where the Methodist mission was active. In both Freetown and the villages the Nova Scotians acted—sometimes to the displeasure of the missionaries—as evangelists and role models. Sometimes communal tensions led to church disruption; both Maroon and "Liberated African" churches broke away from their Nova Scotian mentors. The West African Methodist Church, which continues today, was a Liberated African breakaway from a Nova Scotian church. It amalgamated with the (British) United Methodist Free Churches in 1859.

Sierra Leone's literacy rates and school populations were often higher than those of many European countries. Church-related grammar schools (boys' and girls') produced an educated elite. The Fourah Bay Institution, established by CMS for the ablest students, was by the 1870s teaching degree courses of the University of Durham in arts and divinity. Sierra Leone was one of the earliest successes of Protestant MISSIONS in Africa, producing a community (usually called Krio, popularly Creole) for whom Protestant Christianity and English literacy and education were constituents of identity.

Reaching Beyond Borders

Liberated Africans, as prosperity increased, traded along the West African coast. Some Yoruba found their way to their homeland in what is now Western Nigeria, resettled there, and, retaining their Christian faith, called on the missions to follow them. The Niger Expedition of 1841, although failing in its immediate objectives, increased mission awareness of the vast populations in inland Africa. The mission representatives on the Expedition, JAMES FREDERICK SCHÖN and SAMUEL ADJAI CROWTHER, both Sierra Leone–based, identified Sierra Leone as a principal resource for the evangelization of West Africa. The majority of the early CMS missionaries to Yorubaland were from Sierra Leone, and even the Europeans among them had first served in Sierra Leone. Throughout the nineteenth century and into the twentieth, hundreds of

Sierra Leonean missionaries, ordained and lay, served in the territories that now make up NIGERIA and in other regions of Africa. At first most were "Liberated Africans," who often already spoke the languages in use where they worked, although later missionaries were born in the colony. Bishop Crowther once planned a Sierra Leone mission to the Congo; in the 1880s the United Methodist Free Churches sent a Sierra Leonean to the Kenya coast. Sierra Leone traders, clerks, technicians, and professionals often preceded the missions as the first contact for inland people with Christian life and worship.

Missions among the peoples of the hinterland of the colony—Temne, Bullom-Sherbro, Mende—saw little response for a long time. Here too Sierra Leoneans served in the missions, or represented African Christianity and "civilization" as traders or in other occupations. Many adopted local children who became assimilated to the Krio Christian community.

The first American missions were directed to the Mende and Sherbro. An African American Christian settlement was attempted in Sherbro in 1821, and another in Rio Pongas in 1822. The *cause célèbre* of the Amistad trial led to the formation of the interdenominational (and multiracial) AMERICAN MISSIONARY ASSOCIATION (AMA), which in 1841 inaugurated a Mendi (*sic*) Mission at the same time as repatriating survivors from the *Amistad*. The United Brethren in Christ (UBC), a church of German Pietist immigrant origin, opened a Mende mission in 1855; it took over the AMA's Mendi Mission in 1883. American missions developed practical and technical, rather than academic, education and introduced some light industries. The establishment of the Protectorate was followed by major risings of Mende and Temne. In Mendeland American and Krio missionaries suffered appallingly in a mass attack on foreigners.

Shifting Demographics

The Protectorate permanently altered the religious balance of Sierra Leone. Earlier, Gustav Warneck, the German missiologist, had declared the colony "an evangelical land." The new colonial arrangements gave it an overwhelmingly non-Christian population, with significant Muslim communities. Poro and Sande, the powerful societies into which young men and women were initiated at puberty, often saw Christianity as a threat to tradition. New missions came from the UNITED STATES, especially to the northern peoples of the Protectorate; the older Anglican and Methodist missions started new work inland. A division that took place in the United States within the United Brethren church made one section of it, the Evangelical United Brethren, the largest church and

mission in the Protectorate. (A later merger in the United States brought a change of name to UNITED METHODIST CHURCH.)

After World War II large numbers of people from the Protectorate moved into Freetown, transforming its ethnic composition. The older churches, bastions of Krio identity and using English in worship, were not usually in a position to approach them. Newer churches, especially Pentecostal (see PENTECOSTALISM), had a notable impact on certain groups, such as the Limba, who had largely resisted both Islam and Christianity in their northern homeland, but in Freetown divided between church and mosque. One result was that Freetown congregations tended to reflect ethnic identity. Since independence in 1961 the political leadership has usually lain with the hinterland peoples. Muslim influence has spread widely, but up to the beginning of the twenty-first century, despite a troubled political and military history, interfaith relations have been equable. War has led to endemic problems of uprooted and displaced populations, with the churches playing a major role in relief and resettlement of refugees.

Sierra Leone produced one of the pioneers of the new African academic theology in Harry Sawyerr (1909–1986) of Fourah Bay College. Prophet WILLIAM WADÉ HARRIS visited Sierra Leone several times in his later years and took a Sierra Leonean wife, but his preaching there did not have the electrifying effect it had elsewhere. AFRICAN INSTITUTED CHURCHES of the prophet-healing type, led by the Church of the Lord (Aladura) and Emmanuel Owoade Adeleke Adejobi, arrived from Nigeria from the 1950s. A wider and deeper effect has come from the charismatic movement, especially since the 1970s. This has affected the older Anglican and Methodist churches (and especially their young people); it has also increased the appeal of the older Pentecostal churches such as the ASSEMBLIES OF GOD; and, particularly in Freetown, it has produced a host of new churches and "ministries," large and small. Most are indigenous; some have affiliations elsewhere in West Africa or in the United States. Healing and deliverance from malevolent powers are features of their ministry. They often have multiethnic congregations, using the Krio language, Seehe, the national lingua franca.

See also Colonialism; Missiology; Missionary Organizations; Missions, British; Missions, German; Slavery, Abolition of

References and Further Reading

Fyfe, Christopher. *History of Sierra Leone*. London: Oxford University Press. 1962.

Hanciles, Jehu J. *Euthanasia of a Mission: African Church Autonomy in a Colonial Context.* Westport, CT: Praeger, 2002.

Olson, G. W. *Church Growth in Sierra Leone.* Grand Rapids, MI: Wm. B. Eerdmans, 1969.

Reeck, D. L. *Deep Mende: Religious Interactions in a Changing African Rural Society.* Leiden, The Netherlands: Brill, 1976.

Walls, Andrew F. *The Missionary Movement in Christian History.* chap. 8. Maryknoll, NY: Orbis, 1996.

ANDREW F. WALLS

SIMEON, CHARLES (1759–1836)

Anglican evangelical clergyman. Simeon was born into an aristocratic Oxfordshire family, his mother's background including two archbishops of York. He attended Eton, where he was not known as an accomplished or pious student. Nevertheless, he won a scholarship to King's College, CAMBRIDGE UNIVERSITY where he enrolled in 1779, becoming a fellow in 1782 and graduating with his B.A. a year later. During his first term at Cambridge, Simeon discovered that he was required to receive Holy Communion and this obligation became the catalyst of his CONVERSION. His subsequent interaction with Anglican evangelicals John and Henry Venn shaped his theological thinking and he became a convinced lowchurch Evangelical.

Simeon was ordained to the Anglican priesthood in 1783. Through his father's influence he was named to the prestigious living of Holy Trinity, Cambridge. Holy Trinity's parishioners opposed his appointment and Simeon was unsure at first about accepting it but did so, beginning a life-long PREACHING ministry there. Strong opposition, indeed open hostility, from parishioners, students, and faculty did not immediately abate. Slowly, however, Simeon won the grudging acceptance of his community and, eventually, he gained their genuine affection by his generous pastoral care and winsome message.

Within the established church at large Simeon ultimately became a key leader of the evangelical party. He was involved in the founding of several important evangelical organizations, including the CHURCH MISSIONARY SOCIETY (1797) and the BRITISH AND FOREIGN BIBLE SOCIETY (1804). Although a keen Evangelical, Simeon was committed to Establishment and to the BOOK OF COMMON PRAYER. He disliked theological controversy and sought to be a voice of moderation and conciliation in the then divisive debate between Arminian and Calvinist Evangelicals. Through many students and assorted younger curates Simeon proved to have a wide influence. He penned the multivolume *Horae Homileticae,* a practical expository commentary on the BIBLE (completed in 1819–1820).

When Simeon died in 1836, much of the town and university attended his funeral. After his death Simeon continued to shape the character of his CHURCH OF ENGLAND. The trust he had founded purchased advowsons and thereby ensured parish appointments for clergy of an evangelical stripe.

See also Evangelicalism

References and Further Reading

Primary Source:

Simeon, Charles. *Horae Homileticae.* London: Holdsworth, 1832/33.

Secondary Sources:

Carus, William, ed. *Memoirs of the Life of the Rev. Charles Simeon.* New York: R. Carter, 1847.

Hopkins, Hugh Evan. *Charles Simeon of Cambridge.* London: Hodder & Stoughton, 1977.

Moule, H. C. G. *Charles Simeon.* London: Metheun, 1914.

GILLIS J. HARP

SIN

In a religious sense, sin designates the human person's failure to be a properly ordered relational self. It is contrary to one's constitution as a creature of and before God and damages human relationships and community.

In the Hebrew scriptures sin is revolt against Yahweh's COVENANT (Exodus 20:1–17) and is a consequence of idolatry (Wisdom 14:22–31; cf. Romans 1:18–32). Because the Hebrew prophets insisted sin concomitantly harms one's neighbor, maintenance of the covenant required proper WORSHIP of Yahweh and the practice of justice and loving kindness with all persons, the latter dynamic serving to authenticate and ratify one's God relation (e.g., Amos 2:6–16; Micah 6:6–8). In the New Testament Paul gave to sin the character of an impotent will unable to choose righteousness (Romans 7:13–25).

Augustine (d. 430) established the parameters of a Christian THEOLOGY of sin by characterizing it as disordered loving in which one fails to love God above all things and all things through one's primary love of God. He connected sin with pride and construed it as inordinate individuation and estimation of one's capacities, a human "no" to its divine ground. In acknowledgment of the goodness of the created order (Genesis 1), sin has neither an allotted place nor intelligibility in creation. It is a privation of the good. For Augustine and MARTIN LUTHER (d. 1546), to be a sinner is to be curved in on oneself and voluntarily shut off from God and neighbor. SØREN KIERKEGAARD (d. 1855) agreed and suggested that sin is also expressed in a despairing weakness in which one has too little self or fails to be oneself before God.

In the twentieth century PAUL TILLICH (d. 1965) characterized sin as the uncentered and estranged quality of existence produced when one's ontological polarities are separated rather than integrated, the healing of which comes from the New Being in Jesus Christ. REINHOLD NIEBUHR (d. 1971) underscored collective egoism and the corporate dimension of sin, observing that sin is the only Christian DOCTRINE for which there is empirical evidence; one need only observe human beings in society for its verification. KARL BARTH (d. 1968) echoed Augustine's insistence that sin is unreal and so impermanent, and suggested GRACE negates the self-negation of sinful humanity and redetermines humanity in Jesus Christ to covenant fidelity (Romans 6), to which the appropriate human response can only be praise and gratitude.

See also Atonement; Christology; Covenant Theology; Predestination; Salvation

References and Further Reading

Primary Sources:

Augustine, *Confessions*. 399. Translated by Maria Boulding. Hyde Park, NY: New City Press, 1997.
————. *The City of God against the Pagans (416–422)*. Translated by R. W. Dyson. Cambridge: Cambridge University Press, 1998.
Barth, Karl. *Church Dogmatics. The Doctrine of Creation*. vol. III/2. Translated by G. W. Bromiley and T. F. Torrance. Edinburgh: T & T Clark, 1960.
Kierkegaard, Søren. *The Sickness Unto Death*. Translated by Alastair Hannay. London: Penguin Books, 1989.
Niebuhr, Reinhold. *The Nature and Destiny of Man. Human Nature*. vol. I. Louisville, KY: W/JK, 1996.
Tillich, Paul. *Systematic Theology. Existence and the Christ*. vol. II. Chicago: University of Chicago Press, 1957.

JOHN N. SHEVELAND

SISTERHOODS, ANGLICAN

The first sisterhood in the CHURCH OF ENGLAND was founded in 1845; by 1900 more than ninety women's religious communities had been founded within the borders of the United Kingdom, with perhaps a dozen more within ANGLICANISM and Episcopalianism worldwide. Despite the Protestant identification of the Church of England, the great majority of these sisterhoods took vows of poverty, chastity, and obedience, in forms that directly reflected the vows of Roman Catholic religious. Many evangelicals and nonconformists in Victorian Britain refused to accept the Anglicanism of these groups, accusing them instead of being Jesuits in disguise, and imagining that they were founded to lure honest Protestants into the embrace of Rome.

The social, religious, and cultural forces that led to the foundation of sisterhoods was a complicated amalgam. The women who joined (and over 10,000 British women at least tried the life in the first fifty years of the movement), seem to have been moved by a mixture of motivations, including philanthopy, religious devotion, and a desire for a life independent of the family. They effectively served as unpaid but highly disciplined social workers, nurses, teachers, and care workers in a social system that had long been content to ameliorate the suffering of the poor in an sporadic and individualistic way. The first systematic training of hospital nurses began at St. John's House (later the Community of St. John the Divine) in 1848, twelve years before Florence Nightingale founded the training school at St. Thomas's Hospital. The first creches for working-class mothers, the first baby hospital, and the first seaside convalescent hospital, were all sisterhood achievements. Teaching sisters, especially those of the Community of the Sisters of the Church, were providing thousands of school places for working-class children by the end of the century, and a number of sisterhoods, most notably St. John Baptist, Clewer, were sheltering up to 7,000 prostitutes and other deviant women a year in refuges, homes, and penitentiaries. Many more sisters simply worked as district visitors—essentially prototypical social workers—in the urban slums of ENGLAND, INDIA, SOUTH AFRICA, and the UNITED STATES.

The religious views of most sisterhoods were decidedly "high church." Virtually all women's orders aligned themselves with the Anglo-Catholic wing of the Church of England, placing great weight upon the regular reception of the sacraments, the importance of the seven daily officers of prayer, and emphasizing the duty of charitable work among the destitute. While relatively few of them were in direct contact with English cardinal JOHN HENRY NEWMAN (1801–1890) (except for Marion Hughes, founder of the Society of the Holy and Undivided Trinity), a number of early communities were directly or indirectly influenced by English cleric Edward B. PUSEY and his followers.

The dominant cultural forces that led to the establishment of women's communities in mid-Victorian Britain were largely linked to the issue of women's work and their status in society. Most sisters were middle or upper class (although working-class women could join, they did so only in small numbers), and their families and society assumed that all women who could, would marry. Spinsters were an object of pity or derision to many, and were even described as having "failed in business." Equally, it was considered inappropriate for ladies to work for pay. This meant that unmarried women of the middle and upper classes were expected to live lives without either the satisfactions of family life, or the absorbing interests of employment. They were instead expected to either devote themselves to their parents or to any sibling whose family might need assistance; if no family duty called, some trifling and amateurish philanthropic work was considered the natural sphere of the unmarried woman.

Sisterhoods upended the accepted view of unmarried women. They argued that women who did not marry might be following a higher vocation than that of family life, and that women had the right to leave their parents and siblings in order to follow this calling. The very fact of their wide-ranging programs of nursing, teaching, and caring, emphasized their insistence that such work be performed in an organized and disciplined manner. Women who entered a community could be sure they would be offered a lifetime of hard but meaningful work, both within and without the convent walls.

The mainstream Protestant reaction to these groups was mixed. On the one hand, few were willing to criticize the communities' active work: it was too widespread, too popular, and too socially useful. However, Protestants viewed the habit, the vows, and the communal life as suspiciously similar to Roman communities. Some concluded that Anglican sisters were sadly deluded in their imitation of Roman models, but that the women themselves were essentially harmless. Others, and this was the position adopted on the harder wing of Protestant opinion, saw sisters as witting or unwitting proselytizers for Rome. It was claimed in some quarters that members of women's communities were Jesuits in disguise, actively working to subvert Protestant principles and to lure unsuspecting victims into the Roman Catholic Church. Others felt that the women themselves were dupes of priestly schemes to convert England under a façade of Anglican conformity. The extreme lunatic fringe, led by the MP Charles Newdegate, saw no difference between Anglican and Roman orders at all, writing of nameless horrors awaiting the women who entered "prisons disguised as convents." Such warnings were unnecessary, as women were free to leave Anglican communities both before and after taking the vows, but such fantasies were long a stock item in extreme Protestant circles.

References and Further Reading

Allchin, Arthur M. *The Silent Rebellion: Anglican Religious Communities 1845–1900.* London: SCM Press, 1958.

Anson, Peter F. *The Call of the Cloister.* Rev. ed. A. W. Campbell. London: SPCK, 1964.

Mumm, Susan. *Stolen Daughters, Virgin Mothers: Anglican Sisterhoods in Victorian England.* London: Leicester University Press, 1999.

SUSAN MUMM

SLAVERY

The linkage between slavery and religion dates back to ancient times. Portuguese Catholics introduced African Muslim slaves into the Western world in the 1440s during religious wars against the Moors. Slavery entered British North America in 1619 when Dutch traders sold twenty Africans to English colonists at Jamestown, Virginia. Nowhere in the world is the relationship between Protestantism and racial slavery more complex than in the Southern UNITED STATES, where the institution developed between 1619 and the end of the CIVIL WAR in 1865. Although the first recorded Christian BAPTISM of an enslaved African in North America took place in 1641, widespread CONVERSIONS did not occur until the religious REVIVALS of the Great Awakening reached the Southern colonies in the middle of the eighteenth century (see AWAKENINGS). Between the mid-eighteenth and mid-nineteenth centuries, African-American slaves embraced evangelical Protestantism in large numbers, even as slavery became an increasingly divisive force among white evangelicals, whose denominations split along sectional lines in the 1840s and 1850s. As antislavery and proslavery Protestants exchanged acrimonious volleys of rhetorical fire, they prepared the moral ground for the Civil War.

I. Early Efforts to Convert Slaves to Christianity

Although there is evidence of the practice of Christianity in AFRICA as early as the first century, widespread conversions of Africans to Protestant Christianity accompanied the forced migration of 400,000 African slaves to North America. Upon arriving in the colonies most slaves practiced a traditional African religion that emphasized the appeasement of a pantheon of gods who otherwise threatened harm to humans. A Supreme Creator God presumably remained aloof from human affairs and consequently played less of a role in everyday religious practices than did lesser deities.

African religious traditions endured and even flourished among slave communities in South America and the CARIBBEAN to a greater extent and for a longer duration than among North American slaves. This difference can be explained in part by noting that the Catholicism practiced in countries such as BRAZIL, Cuba, and Haiti was more conducive than Protestantism to syncretism. African traditions such as divination, altars, charms, and worship cults found close parallels with Catholic rituals surrounding, for instance, SAINTS, candles, and crucifixes. More important, in the American context African theologies and practices quickly disappeared because of the relative absence of a continuous influx of new slaves from Africa. As first-generation immigrants became separated from traditional social structures and as second- and third-generation slave communities matured in a novel environment, they forgot many of the traditions of their ancestors. White slave-owners, moreover, sought to eradicate African CULTURE because of its power to unify slaves, thus making resistance and rebellion easier. Although historians have debated the extent to which African religions persisted in North America, most scholars agree that specific theological contents and expressions fared less well than more general styles, such as call-and-response and rhythmic cadences.

Protestant efforts to convert African slaves to Christianity proceeded slowly in Britain's North American colonies. Some slaves adopted Christianity as soon as they learned English and could understand PREACHING; many other first- and second-generation Africans remained indifferent or hostile to Christianity, even when they did receive instruction from their masters or from Protestant preachers. The first documented slave baptism in North America took place in Massachusetts in 1641. Hoping to stimulate more systematic missionary efforts, King Charles II of ENGLAND commissioned the Council for Foreign Plantations to christianize slaves in 1660. The SOCIETY FOR THE PROPAGATION OF THE GOSPEL began the first significant institutional efforts at slave conversion in 1701. Yet there were relatively few slave conversions before the Great Awakening of the mid-eighteenth century, in part because white masters feared that Christians could not be slaves. Indeed, because early justifications of slavery distinguished between heathen and Christian peoples, some converts hoped that baptism would lead to emancipation. In 1667 the Virginia Assembly set an important precedent by legislating that baptism did not grant worldly freedom to slaves. Baptized slaves did, however, often receive more lenient treatment before slave courts than did non-Christian slaves.

A number of factors impeded the progress of Christian missions among slaves in North America. Christianization worked against slave-owners' economic interests. Some masters justified working their slaves on the Sabbath by arguing that blacks were too brutish to be encompassed in biblical injunctions to rest on the seventh day. Although the Anglican church encouraged masters to instruct their slaves in Christianity, such instruction involved time-consuming memorization of the CATECHISM, a process that took time away from crop production. The exposure of slaves to Christianity was, moreover, uneven, because many lived in isolated areas where preachers seldom visited, and because some slave-owners refused to allow their slaves to hear preaching when it was available. The first recorded slave congregation, a group of BAPTISTS, was organized in 1758 on the plantation of William Byrd in Virginia.

Fear of rebellion, especially in areas where blacks outnumbered whites, further impeded missionary efforts. Christianization of blacks proceeded most slowly in the South Carolina and Georgia low country, areas densely populated by slaves. The South Carolina legislature prohibited teaching slaves to write after the Stono Rebellion (1739). After Gabriel's Rebellion (1800), an attempted insurrection in Richmond, Virginia, resistance to slave conversions deepened. Gabriel, known as the Black Sampson, used Old Testament themes to inspire his followers to revolt. Fearing that other rebellious slaves could use religious meetings as recruiting grounds and arenas for plotting, the Virginia Assembly passed a law prohibiting blacks from assembling between sunset and sunrise for religious worship or instruction.

II. The Great Awakening and Slave Conversions

The religious revivals of the Great Awakening reached the Southern colonies by the mid-eighteenth century, stimulating renewed interest in christianizing slaves (see EVANGELICALISM). The evangelists of the Great Awakening emphasized the universal need of all humans for redemption from SIN, and the equal value of all Christians as brothers and sisters in the family of God. Revivalists preached to blacks as well as whites, sometimes sidestepping questions about the morality of slavery to persuade masters to allow them to preach to their slaves. Although JOHN WESLEY spoke against the institution of slavery, GEORGE WHITEFIELD urged masters to execute their duty to provide religious instruction to their slaves. The Great Awakening's privileging of religious experience over formal theology made Christianity more accessible to slaves than did the more lengthy processes of catechismal instruction. Emphasis on an immediate "new birth" experience, moreover, paralleled African religious practices by offering more room for emotional and physical expressions of the agonies of sin and the joys of SALVATION.

"New Light" Methodist, Baptist, and Presbyterian preachers gained many of their converts from among lower and middle-class whites and black slaves. Evangelical teachings attracted such groups—and alienated many wealthy white planters—by stressing humility, mutual submission, and the equality of all people before God. During the eighteenth-century revivals, black and white converts prayed, sang, and shouted together, scorning the religious formalism of the Anglican upper classes (see ANGLICANISM). African-influenced worship practices shaped the religious expressions of both black and white revival participants, for instance in the spread of the ring shout. Evangelical preachers encouraged unordained blacks as well as WOMEN and children to exhort and preach to others across lines of race, GENDER, and age. Baptists offered greater opportunities for black participation than did other denominations, even licensing black preachers.

During the eighteenth century slaves frequently attended the churches of their masters. Influenced by the egalitarian teachings of the Awakening many Southern churches welcomed black members between 1750 and 1790, often granting slave congregants equal rights in religious instruction and communion. In 1776 evangelicals accounted for just 10 percent of the adult white Southern population, and a much smaller percentage of the black Southern population. By 1790 14 percent of Southern whites and 4 percent of Southern blacks had affiliated with evangelical churches. As of 1815, 40,000 or nearly one third of all Methodists were African American; blacks constituted a similar proportion of Baptist church adherents. Smaller numbers of enslaved African Americans joined Presbyterian, Episcopal, and Catholic churches. On the eve of the Civil War nearly half a million slaves, or roughly 12 percent of the enslaved population, had affiliated with a Protestant church.

As the number of black church members increased, so too did the concerns of white church members with distinguishing between the prerogatives of white and black Christians. The practice of evangelical CHURCH DISCIPLINE, or the "watch care" of the church, implied that all church members should be treated alike, and that slaves could accuse white members of misconduct—a dangerously egalitarian principle that threatened the patriarchal social order on which the institution of slavery depended. The mere presence of blacks in Southern churches raised questions about the morality of slavery, calling attention to the degradation of the slave family in such instances as when slave church members were accused of adultery after the sale of a spouse.

By the 1790s evangelical church fellowship had weakened. Many churches began to seat blacks in separate pews or consign them to the galleries, or designate separate services for black congregants. As such discrimination increased, black Christians more often expressed a preference for worship services free from white supervision. Some state legislatures, recognizing the empowerment and potential danger to the social order that religious practice afforded, passed laws prohibiting slaves from establishing their own places of worship. Independent black denominations developed their greatest strength in the mid-Atlantic

rather than the Southern states. First organized in 1816 the AFRICAN METHODIST EPISCOPAL CHURCH (AME) gained a total membership of more than ten thousand by 1831, the year of founder RICHARD ALLEN's death. By 1861 there were more than fifty thousand AME members. The AME ZION CHURCH organized in New York City as an independent denomination in 1821, and gained 42,000 members by the end of the Civil War. Where Southern slaves were prohibited from forming independent churches, they attended week-night meetings for PRAYER and singing, sometimes gathering illicitly in secluded places apart from the scrutiny of their masters.

III. Protestantism and the Slave Community

As AFRICAN AMERICAN PROTESTANTISM developed, religious expressions took on distinctive forms and meanings. African American worship was characterized by the call-and-response structure of sermons and of spiritual or sorrow songs, and by preaching that emphasized liberation and justice both on earth and in heaven. Black Christians more often identified with the Old Israel, whereas white Christians frequently envisioned themselves as the New Israel. Even when whites and blacks shared common texts, beliefs, and rites, they experienced religion differently, creating their own meanings in response to distinctive needs and contexts. Christianity offered enslaved African Americans emotional and psychological strength and a sense of spiritual victory and release. Christian slaves asserted their dignity by such acts as rejecting secular music, dressing up on Sundays, and placing money in the church collection plate. Black Christians particularly seized on the Bible's teachings about the deliverance of God's people from bondage and persecution. Slave preachers replaced white messages about the religious duty of obeying AUTHORITY with accounts of Moses leading the Israelite people out of bondage to the Egyptians. As slave preachers drew on the Exodus story they viewed Christ as a second Moses, rhetorically merging Moses and Jesus into a vision of a this-worldly and otherworldly deliverer.

The slave preacher played a central role in the life of the slave community as he acted in his roles as religious leader, politician, idealist, and healer. Preachers proclaimed a message of hope that sustained slave communities and developed an oratorical tradition that provided a potent mode of expression for African American activists. Black preaching emphasized oral storytelling traditions, given that many slaves, including many slave preachers, were illiterate. Like white folk preachers, black ministers frequently employed memorized verses, repetition, vivid imagery, and dramatic delivery. In the course of a sermon, a slave preacher might begin with conversational address that built to a rhythmic cadence punctuated by congregational exclamations, and that climaxed in a tonal chant accompanied by shouting, singing, and ecstatic behavior when the Holy Spirit fell upon the meeting. Spirituals, an important component of religious meetings in the slave community, made one person's joy or sorrow into a communal expression as the congregation invited the immediate presence of God's Spirit in the midst of the gathering. In addition to leading the slave community in preaching and singing, slave preachers presided over such important events in the religious life of the community as baptisms, weddings, and funerals. Religious gatherings, under the direction of slave preachers, served as a refuge from a hostile white world, and as a center for social, economic, political, and educational activities that promoted individual and collective dignity and identity.

The slave preacher's principal rival in shaping community life was the black conjurer. Although traditional African voodoo practices took firm root in New Orleans, in other areas of North America a more diffuse system of magic, divination, and herbal medicine, known as hoodoo or conjure, developed. Hoodoo was one way that slaves expressed a belief that powers other than whites intervened in their everyday affairs. When in need, slaves resorted to potions, charms, and rituals to ward off evil, cure diseases, and harm enemies. The same individuals and communities often embraced Christianity and conjure, without necessarily experiencing contradictions between belief systems that seemingly fulfilled different communal functions.

Even as conjure constituted a mode of resisting the dominance of white masters, Christian teachings held the potential to sanction either accommodation or resistance to slavery. Historians have debated whether slave religion was more a matter of resignation or implicit resistance. It is too simple to conclude, as have some scholars, that blacks passively accepted religion handed down from their masters, or that religion bred either rebellion or docility. Although some slave-owners attempted to use religion as a means of racial control, at the same time Christianity held revolutionary potential. W. E. B. DuBois claimed that slaves used religion as a weapon against captivity. Dubois argued that for more than a century slave religion consisted of a Christian veneer that masked slaves' use of African traditions to resist slavery. In Dubois's view Christianity produced more docile laborers, who were also more prone to indulgence and crime.

Yet Christian slaves actively shaped a religious culture all their own. In some circumstances, Christian slaves developed short-term resignation and fatalism, coupled with hope of eventual freedom in heaven. At other points slaves used Christian beliefs to justify their decisions to flee or revolt against their masters. Christianity produced in Nat Turner, a Baptist slave preacher and revolutionary, the determination to enact vengeance on a wicked white ruling class. Most often slave resistance accepted the limits of what was and was not politically possible. Christian slaves developed spiritual strength, and yet political weakness, as they accepted the political and social dominance of an oppressive ruling class. Protestant Christianity, as practiced by African-American slaves, did not merely compensate for worldly unfreedom in hopes of spiritual freedom and otherworldly rewards; religion allowed slaves to retain their identity as persons, as it offered them meaning, freedom, and transcendence of their circumstances. Religious practice was itself in many instances an act of rebelliousness, a way of asserting independence that sometimes involved defiance, such as in attending secret meetings. Black Christians developed a sense of being a people set apart, and through this idea, expressed through distinctive worship styles and theologies, created collective identity and communal pride. Scholars have even argued that Protestantism encouraged the development of a protonational black consciousness. Religion endowed the enslaved community's experiences of suffering and struggle with meaning and significance and gave slaves the resources to endure.

IV. Protestantism and Slavery in the Southern United States

As Southern evangelical institutions matured between the eighteenth and nineteenth centuries, white Protestants sought to control black religious practices more rigidly. Evangelicals became increasingly concerned with gaining social acceptability and respect from nonevangelicals. Many slave-owners welcomed evangelical ministers who wanted to preach to slaves, provided that they emphasized sections of the Bible that exhorted slaves to obey their masters, rather than sections that emphasized spiritual equality among all Christians. Slave-owners and the CLERGY who supported them drew selectively from Old Testament passages to argue that slavery was a divinely ordained institution. Slave-owners used religion to teach slaves morality, discipline, and respect for their superiors. Fearing the consequences of teaching slaves to read for themselves, some slave-owners read the Bible to their slaves and prayed with them in special services.

After Nat Turner's Rebellion (1831), Southerners imposed new restrictions on black preachers and used more tightly controlled plantation missions to gain greater control over slaves' religious meetings. At the same time that Southerners passed laws against black preachers and against teaching slaves to read and write, they also encouraged oral instruction of slaves in Christianity and initiated campaigns for the more humane treatment of slaves. By making slave life more bearable masters hoped to make it safer for themselves. Frequently Protestant slave-owner motives combined self-interest with genuine concern for the spiritual welfare of their slaves and themselves.

The plantation missions of the 1830s represented an attempt to demonstrate that the Bible allowed slavery and that instructing slaves constituted a religious duty for masters. In the 1830s, in addition to sending out itinerant ministers, Protestants published an unprecedented volume of sermons and essays on slave EDUCATION, emphasizing the duties of masters to give their slaves religious instruction and of servants to submit to their masters. Religious newspapers, such as the Episcopal *Gospel Messenger,* the Presbyterian *Charleston Observer,* the Baptist *Christian Index,* and the Methodist *Southern Christian Advocate,* all endorsed religious instruction of slaves. Southern clergy used slave instruction to control the religious practices of slave communities and to counter mounting abolitionist complaints about the irreligion of slaves.

V. Protestant Disputes over the Morality of Slavery

Many white Evangelicals who participated in the revivals of the Great Awakening opposed slavery as an immoral institution, spiritually and physically harmful to both masters and slaves. In 1784 the Methodist General Conference officially condemned slavery as a sin (see METHODISM, NORTH AMERICA). The highest judicatory of the Presbyterian Church made formal declarations supporting abolition of slavery no less than six times between 1787 and 1836 (see PRESBYTERIANISM; PRESBYTERIAN CHURCH U.S.A.). Early Methodists, Quakers (see FRIENDS, SOCIETY OF), and Baptists helped fugitive slaves, taught slaves to read and write, and worked through other informal channels to undermine the slave system. Most major denominations backed away from their antislavery positions by the end of the eighteenth century, as slaveholder pressure dissolved antislavery sentiments among white church members between 1790 and 1830. Many abolitionist preachers left the South voluntarily or after being expelled by proslavery majorities. A few Southern Quakers, Baptist Friends of Humanity, and urban evangelicals remained committed to the antislavery cause through the 1820s, a period when proslavery clergymen flocked to join the ranks of overseas and domestic plantation missionaries.

Slavery became an increasingly divisive issue among white Protestants between the 1830s and the onset of the Civil War. In 1844 the General Conference of the Methodist Episcopal Church passed a resolution prohibiting bishops from owning slaves. This incident led to the secession of the Methodist Episcopal Church, South. Similarly, the Baptists split along sectional lines in 1845. Old and New School Presbyterians, having already divided in 1838 in part because of the slavery question, formally split into Northern and Southern branches in 1857 and 1861, respectively.

By the 1830s increasing numbers of Northern Protestants condemned slavery as a sin that must be removed, opposing the extension of slavery into the territories or even joining an expanding movement for the immediate ABOLITION OF SLAVERY. Antislavery evangelicals argued that the institution undermined virtue and pure religion, producing a low state of morality throughout the Southwest that posed a formidable obstacle to evangelization. HARRIET BEECHER STOWE'S Uncle Tom's Cabin (1851–1852) influentially argued that genuine Christianity was incompatible with the evil institution of slavery. Stowe condemned the hypocrisy of churches that defended slavery and urged individual religious conversion as the remedy for a national sin.

In response to hardening antislavery sentiments in the North, Southern Protestants developed more sustained proslavery arguments. No longer conceding that slavery was a necessary evil, clergy began to defend slavery as a "positive good" on moral as well as practical grounds. Southern Protestants argued that slavery benefited African slaves by civilizing and christianizing them. The Baptist minister Richard Furman, writing an "Exposition of the Views of the Baptists, Relative to the Coloured Population in the United States" (1822), argued that slavery, "when tempered with humanity and justice, is a state of tolerable happiness; equal, if not superior, to that which many poor enjoy in countries reputed free." The Presbyterian James Henley Thornwell similarly articulated the doctrine of the "Spirituality of the Church," denying that the church should intervene in social institutions under the purview of the state, instead restricting itself to matters of personal morality, such as card playing, dancing, and drinking (see CHURCH AND STATE, OVERVIEW).

Some Northern Protestants joined Southerners in articulating proslavery arguments. George Washington Blagden, the pastor of Boston's Old South Church, published a sermon, *Remarks, and a Discourse on Slavery* (1847), which denied that slavery was at odds with Christian tradition or values. The foremost nineteenth-century American biblical scholar, Moses Stuart of Andover Theological Seminary, published *Conscience and the Constitution* (1850), which presented a detailed analysis of biblical passages that Stuart considered supportive of slavery.

As proslavery proponents responded to antislavery arguments using moral and biblical arguments, they prepared the way for a Civil War laden with millennialist expectations and apocalyptic imagery deployed by Northern and Southern Protestants alike.

References and Further Reading

Campbell, James T. *Songs of Zion: The African Methodist Episcopal Church in the United States and South Africa.* New York: Oxford University Press, 1995.

Dailey, David T. *Shadow on the Church: Southwestern Evangelical Religion and the Issue of Slavery, 1783–1860.* Ithaca, NY: Cornell University Press, 1985.

Dillon, Merton L. *Slavery Attacked: Southern Slaves and Their Allies 1619–1865.* Baton Rouge: Louisiana State University Press, 1990.

Genovese, Eugene. *Roll, Jordan, Roll. Roll: The World the Slaves Made.* New York: Pantheon, 1974.

Heyrman, Christine Leigh. *Southern Cross: The Beginnings of the Bible Belt.* New York: Knopf, 1997.

Kolchin, Peter. *American Slavery, 1619–1877.* New York: Hill & Wang, 1993.

Mathews, Donald G. *Religion in the Old South.* Chicago: University of Chicago Press, 1977.

Parish, Peter J. *Slavery: History and Historians.* New York: Harper & Row, 1989.

Raboteau, Albert. *Slave Religion: The "Invisible Institution" in the Antebellum South.* New York: Oxford University Press, 1978.

Smith, John David. *An Old Creed For the New South: Proslavery Ideology and Historiography, 1865–1918.* Athens: University of Georgia Press, 1991.

———. *Slavery, Race, and American History: Historical Conflict, Trends, and Method, 1866–1953.* Armonk, NY: M. E. Sharpe, 1999.

Tise, Larry E. *Proslavery: A History of the Defense of Slavery in America, 1701–1840.* Athens: University of Georgia Press, 1987.

CANDY GUNTHER BROWN

SLAVERY, ABOLITION OF

The transatlantic slave trade and the practice of SLAVERY disintegrated throughout the European colonial empires between 1792, when Denmark first denounced the trade, and the final emancipation of Brazil's slaves in 1888. Religious REVIVALS moved many antislavery advocates from a gradualist to an immediatist abolitionist position: compensation for slaveholders or any delay in emancipation represented unacceptable compromise with sin. Perfectionist theology taught that individuals were able and therefore morally obligated to adopt lifestyles of personal

and social holiness, which constituted an essential precondition for the coming millennium. Protestants played the most decisive roles in advancing abolition in Britain and the United States. Mainstream churches adopted moderate antislavery positions, but provided the membership for more radical abolitionist societies and antislavery denominations. Religious and political abolitionists joined forces in stirring U.S. antislavery sentiment in the two decades preceding the American CIVIL WAR (1861–1865), an event that destroyed one of the world's most entrenched slave systems.

Global Comparative Perspectives

Every European colonial power participated in the transatlantic slave trade between Europe, Africa, and the Americas until the nineteenth century. Abolition proceeded gradually and unevenly for the European nations and their colonies. Denmark advocated abolition of the slave trade in 1792. In 1794 France enacted the first European law abolishing slavery in its colonial possessions and granting all French subjects the rights of citizens. The French decree did not grow out of humanitarian or religious motives so much as practical necessity. It was a response to threats posed by the self-liberated West Indian slave armies of St. Domingue and an imminent British invasion. The first French emancipation was short-lived; Napoleon reinstated colonial slavery in 1802. Britain became the first country to enact enduring abolitionist legislation, outlawing the slave trade in 1807 and abolishing the practice of slavery in 1833.

Official denouncement of the transatlantic slave trade occurred before full emancipation in most countries. Britain, Denmark, and the United States all ended their support of the international slave trade in the first decade of the nineteenth century, whereas the Dutch, French, Cuban, and Brazilian trades continued until the second, fourth, sixth, and seventh decades, respectively. The European Congress of Vienna declared in 1815 that all the European powers would discourage the international transportation of slaves. Because demand for slaves in colonial plantation economies continued unabated, such resolutions and even direct legislation did not, however, end international commerce in slaves (especially in Brazil and Cuba) until the 1870s. Laws abolishing slavery were passed in the northern United States in the 1780s; in British, Swedish, Danish, and French colonies by the 1840s; and in Spanish Puerto Rico and Cuba in 1873 and 1880, respectively.

In contrast to mass-participation Anglo-American abolitionist campaigns, the French antislavery movement was dominated by elites who enjoyed state sanction. Abolitionist leaders avoided mass recruitment tactics such as the use of petitions, newspaper publishing, public meetings, and boycotts. French abolitionists maintained a gradualist approach to emancipation, insisting on property rights and financial indemnification for slaveholders. The Protestant press and some Catholic clergy became visible participants in the French abolitionism relatively late, from 1846 to 1847, when religious networks did begin to circulate petitions on a massive scale. Ultimately the February Revolution, rather than religious or humanitarian lobbying, proved the decisive factor in permanently abolishing slavery in France and its possessions in 1848.

The Netherlands was the final European nation to join the antislavery crusade. Under British pressure the Dutch ended the slave trade in 1814 and abolished slavery in 1863. The Dutch were the last of the Europeans to sign the Brussels Act of 1890, repressing the African slave trade. The Dutch case calls into question two economic models that scholars have used to explain the rise of abolitionist sentiment throughout Europe. Studies have overwhelmingly demonstrated that slavery was economically profitable during the very same decades that abolitionist campaigns undermined the institution of slavery in one country after another. According to the "market model," societies making the transition to mercantile capitalism, long-distance commerce, banking and credit networks, and participation in world markets found slave economies outmoded. In contrast, the "free labor ideology" model views abolition as legitimizing industrial wage labor by attacking traditional labor systems for their moral failings. By the market model the earlier development of Dutch mercantile capitalism should have led to more rapid abolitionism; by the free labor model Dutch industrialization should have advanced earlier than it did.

The Brazilian example similarly challenges scholarly generalizations about the relationship between economic development and abolition. Contrary to what economic theorists would have predicted, abolitionist sentiment emerged first in the geographic regions and enterprises least involved in economic growth and modernization. Importation of African slaves by Brazil reached its apogee just before the 1851 enforcement of an 1831 law banning the transatlantic recruitment of slaves. The Rio Branco law of 1871 freed slave offspring from hereditary bondage. Brazil was the last country in the Americas to emancipate all of its slaves, through the Golden Law of 1888. Only in the last decade of the abolitionist movement did its supporters employ mass participation tactics such as newspaper campaigns, rallies, and an underground railroad. Nabuco (de Ara'jo) founded the Brazilian Anti-Slavery Society and led the abolitionist campaign through the national chamber of deputies beginning in 1878. Unlike the British and American examples, churches and religious institutions played a relatively minor role in Brazilian abolition.

Paradoxically, abolition of the international slave trade encouraged the expansion of slavery in Africa. The price of slaves on the international market fell at the same time that an expansive world market heightened its demand for African agricultural commodities. African political leaders responded to the shifting economic climate by employing more slaves domestically as agricultural workers. African slavery abated, however, by 1914, by which point European nations had enforced colonial rule throughout much of Africa.

Protestant Roots of Abolition

Religion was a motivating factor for many people who became involved in campaigns to abolish the slave trade and the practice of slavery. Religious abolitionists included Quakers (see FRIENDS, SOCIETY OF), Unitarians, Methodists, Baptists, Presbyterians, and Congregationalists, as well as those with non-Christian faiths. Nevertheless a special affinity existed between the principles of abolitionism and evangelical Protestantism. Participation in religious revivals convinced many Protestants that individuals were morally accountable and that slavery was a sin that demanded immediate repentance and abandonment. By 1830 many abolitionists, especially in Britain and the United States, had turned from gradualist to immediatist philosophies and tactics. Most gradualist antislavery agendas assumed compensation for slaveowners and colonization or apprenticeship periods for newly freed slaves. If, however, slavery was a sin, abolitionists began to reason, any form of compensation or delay in acting constituted sin. Immediatists used moral suasion to argue that action to end the evil practice of slavery must begin right away, even if it might take some time to complete the emancipation process.

The reform movements that grew out of the nineteenth-century religious revivals were grounded in a theology that emphasized human ability in the salvation process and benevolent action as the fruit of genuine religious conversion. American theologians NATHANIEL WILLIAM TAYLOR, LYMAN BEECHER, and CHARLES GRANDISON FINNEY modified Calvinist theology in the direction of greater human initiative. According to the doctrine of perfectionism, which gained prominence in many Protestant circles in the 1830s, Christians could, subsequent to justification, become entirely sanctified or holy during their present lifetime. Confidence in the possibility of perfection led to an ultraist mentality, an unwillingness to compromise with sin, and an insistence that nothing short of millennial standards for perfection should be tolerated. Proponents of entire sanctification argued that both individuals and society must separate from impure institutions and establish a sanctified religious and civil order. The theology of the revivals implied social and political activism, by teaching that individuals had an ability, and therefore a moral obligation, to do good to benefit other individuals and to redeem the world. Many revivalists believed that perpetuation of the slave system would invite God's judgment, whereas the end of slavery was an essential prerequisite to the coming of the millennium.

Some abolitionists preached immediate emancipation as a way to reform both society and religious institutions that, in the evaluation of the reformers, had allowed the purity of the early church to become tainted. Such activists feared loss of moral control and found in abolitionism a moral community in the midst of an immoral society. Whereas many antislavery advocates pushed their churches to higher levels of holiness, other abolitionists left the institutional church, making antislavery crusades a surrogate for organized religion, an avenue through which they channeled their pietistic, anti-institutional, and perfectionist zeal.

Protestants and Abolition in Great Britain

The abolitionist movement in Britain merits special attention because of its priority and influence in ending the transatlantic slave trade and the practice of slavery internationally. The antislavery movement took shape in the late eighteenth century, under the leadership of evangelical Protestants, and embraced a new immediatist agenda by 1830. Methodist founder JOHN WESLEY articulated his most comprehensive condemnation of slavery in an essay "Thoughts Upon Slavery" (1783). British Quakers first presented a petition to the House of Commons seeking abolition of the slave trade in 1784. Women and African American Protestants, including the English Quaker Elizabeth Heyrick and the Anglo-African Methodist Olaudah Equiano, made significant contributions to the British antislavery movement.

GRANVILLE SHARP, first chairman of the Abolition Committee, founded in 1787, denounced slavery as violating common law, the law of reason, and the law of God. In the Somerset case Sharp convinced the Court of the King's Bench in 1771, presided over by Chief Justice William Murray, baron of Mansfield, to declare slavery incompatible with the "free air" of England. Ten to fifteen thousand blacks living in England gained their freedom as a result of this judg-

ment, which effectively abolished slavery within England. Sharp also gained Parliamentary authority to colonize a free black community named Freetown in SIERRA LEONE in 1791.

Parliamentarian WILLIAM WILBERFORCE, converted to evangelical Protestantism in 1785, took a lead in fighting for passage of the British Abolition of the Slave Trade Act in 1807, which prohibited the slave trade in the British West Indies. Wilberforce co-founded the British Society for the Mitigation and Gradual Abolition of Slavery in 1823. The Slavery Abolition Act of 1833 was passed one month after Wilberforce's death, finally accomplishing his vision of freeing all slaves in the British Empire. The law freed 800,000 slaves on a gradual and compensated basis, and set a precedent for other European imperial powers to free their slaves.

When outlawing the slave trade did not quickly end the slave labor system, British reformers attempted to use government regulation to limit the extension of slavery and, through the Canning Resolutions, to ameliorate the conditions under which slaves lived and worked. When these efforts also failed to achieve their intended results, the reformers urged the general registration of slaves to protect their rights. The failure of registration efforts led reformers to seek direct, gradual emancipation by the British crown. The resistance of planters to even such gradualist measures convinced abolitionists of the necessity of a more aggressive, immediatist strategy. British (like American) abolitionism had reached a crucial juncture by 1830. The shift in antislavery strategy resulted not only from frustration with slaveholders' intransigence, but from a transition in reformist assumptions away from a rationalist view of human history that favors step-by-step reform of complex social institutions to an evangelical view that refuses any compromise with sin.

Scholars have been quick to point out that the growth of abolitionist movements in Britain and the United States coincided with the rise of industrial capitalism. Studies have suggested that religious benevolence served as a hypocritical mask for baser economic self-interest in motivating antislavery sentiment. Abolitionists, by this view, were ideological imperialists who attacked the practices and social customs of slaveholding societies to rationalize the social and economic changes essential to the triumph of free-market capitalism. Abolitionist rhetoric allowed the British to reinforce their identity as the world's standard-bearer of liberty, while ignoring the exploitation of industrial workers, including many women and children, in English mills and mines. A variant on the economic view is that abolition arose not from the dialectic of class conflict, but from the interplay of market-fostered values that yielded a new "cognitive style" that favored efficient, disciplined labor.

Protestants and Abolition in the United States

In colonial America members of the SOCIETY OF FRIENDS, or Quakers, pioneered in opposing slavery because of its inconsistency with the Christian principles of nonviolence, equality of all people in God's sight, and the sin of ostentation. Four Pennsylvania Quakers, JOHN WOOLMAN, Anthony Benezet, William Southeby, and Benjamin Lay, signed an antislavery petition in 1688, and spoke publicly against slavery during the 1740s to 1750s. The Society of Friends prohibited slavery among its members in 1774. In 1780 Pennsylvania enacted the modern world's first gradual emancipation law. Methodist, Baptist, and Presbyterian churches all spoke out against slavery in the 1780s to 1790s, but backed away from antislavery positions for fear of alienating Southern whites and losing the ability to preach the gospel to slaves. By the 1820s most white Southerners, including church leaders, responded to Northern attacks on slavery by defending slavery as a God-ordained social system or as a civil institution irrelevant to the "spirituality of the church."

The first major U.S. antislavery society, the AMERICAN COLONIZATION SOCIETY (ACS), formed in 1816 on gradualist principles. The ACS attracted prominent politicians and even slaveholders who wanted to rid American society of free blacks. In ten years the ACS never succeeded in transporting more than two thousand blacks to the African colony of LIBERIA. In 1831 William Lloyd Garrison founded a newspaper, *The Liberator,* to advocate immediate abolition. Garrison organized the New England Anti-Slavery Society in 1832 and the American Anti-Slavery Society (AASS) in 1833. Women were excluded from the AASS's founding meeting, and only three of the sixty-two delegates were black, although both women and African Americans organized their own antislavery organizations, such as the Boston Female Anti-Slavery Society and the American Society of the Free People of Color. Women abolitionists, such as Sarah and Angelina Grimké, Maria Weston Chapman, Antoinette Brown, Lydia Maria Child, and LUCRETIA MOTT, supported the antislavery cause by speaking publicly, editing abolitionist newspapers, raising funds, and organizing petition campaigns. Former slaves, including FREDERICK DOUGLASS, Harriet Tubman, Sojourner Truth, and William Wells Brown, undertook international speaking tours on which they gave first-person accounts of slavery's abuses.

In part through the activities of women and African Americans, the AASS gained a membership of a quarter million by 1838 and a total of 1,300 auxiliaries. Admission of women to the AASS in 1839 nearly destroyed the society. Election of a woman officeholder, Abby Kelley, in 1840, did split the AASS, when the women's issue combined explosively with other tactical disputes regarding pacifism, political involvement, and Garrison's leadership. Garrison was a controversial personality who abandoned the institutional church because he considered it hopelessly corrupted by sin, and who took unconventional positions on such issues as the Sabbath, nonresistance, and women's rights. Anti-Garrisonians formed the American and Foreign Anti-Slavery Society in 1840, which forged alliances with Methodist, Baptist, and Presbyterian denominational antislavery movements.

Although most Northern states had abolished slavery by 1800, immediate abolitionism remained a minority position among Northern Protestants until the Civil War. Although some Protestants followed Garrison's lead in giving up on organized religion, many others persisted in calling churches and nondenominational reform societies to higher levels of holiness. Lewis Tappan was among the most influential church-centered abolitionists, through his leadership of the American and Foreign Anti-Slavery Society and the AMERICAN MISSIONARY ASSOCIATION. Tens of thousands of Protestants joined "come-outer" sects based on the theological argument that Christians should refuse fellowship with other professed Christians who persisted in the sin of countenancing slaveholding. Come-outers viewed their action as protecting their own souls and as pressuring older denominations to adopt stronger antislavery positions. The most important come-outer sects were the Wesleyan Methodist Connection, Free Presbyterian Church, American Baptist Free Mission Society, Franckean Evangelical Lutheran Synod, Progressive Friends, and Indiana Yearly Meeting of Anti-Slavery Friends. Abolitionists similarly tried, without success, to sway the leaders of nondenominational reform societies, such as the AMERICAN BIBLE SOCIETY, American Tract Society, American Sunday School Union, AMERICAN BOARD OF COMMISSIONERS FOR FOREIGN MISSIONS, and American Home Missionary Society, to adopt immediate abolitionism. After a decade of fruitless lobbying, in the 1840s abolitionists formed their own rival religious benevolent institutions, including the American Missionary Association and the American Reform Tract and Book Society.

The largest segment of the Northern churches might be classed as antislavery moderates who supported gradual emancipation, but objected to abolitionist characterizations of all slaveholders as sinners or demands that slaveowners be expelled from church membership, and thus be relinquished from moral accountability. Mainstream denominations contributed to emancipation by spreading a relatively vague antislavery ideology that proved more acceptable to public opinion than radical abolitionist rhetoric and tactics. In articulating antislavery principles without calling for specific, immediate action, the churches in effect practiced a highly effective form of moral suasion. The Methodist, Baptist, and Presbyterian denominations all split along sectional lines, in 1844, 1845, and 1857, respectively; even after these schisms, the Northern denominations still refused to declare slaveowning inherently sinful or to subject slaveholders to church discipline.

Scholars have widely debated the constituency, motives, and effectiveness of abolitionists in influencing emancipation. An earlier generation of scholars argued that most abolitionists were young, middle-class, New England-born heirs of declining Federalist families, who embraced abolition to restore their declining political and social authority and to gain an exhilarating sense of self-affirmation. More recent studies have revealed the prominence of artisans, shopkeepers, and rural cash-crop farmers among the antislavery rank-and-file, and questioned whether there is any statistical difference between the occupational structure of abolitionists and the general population.

Questions regarding the motives of abolitionists have similarly generated considerable controversy, with scholars debating whether religion, economics, ideology, or psychological factors best account for abolitionist leanings. The individual and collective personalities of abolitionists have been stereotyped as impractical, self-righteous, fanatical, humorless, vituperative, disturbed, and, ironically, racist. More recently, scholars have sought to rehabilitate abolitionists from accusations of mental instability resulting from the rapid social and economic transformation of the urban North, and, more generally, to challenge generalizations about the dysfunctionality of abolitionist personalities.

Abolitionists did not directly influence the passage of much legislation, nor ever gain widespread popularity. Antislavery agitation did provoke sectional animosities that hastened the Civil War. Ultimately the strategy of moral suasion convinced Northern churches, voters, and political leaders to accept many of the arguments that the abolitionists had been making for decades.

The American Civil War and the Demise of Slavery

Tensions between the Northern and Southern United States over slavery accelerated between the 1830s and 1850s. Congress's bipartisan "gag rule" prohibiting discussion of antislavery petitions in 1836, the annexation of Texas as a slave state (1845) and disposition of territory from the Mexican-American War (1846–1848), the 1854 Kansas-Nebraska Act, the Fugitive Slave Act of 1850 and HARRIET BEECHER STOWE's publication of *Uncle Tom's Cabin* in 1852, the Dred Scott decision of 1857, and John Brown's raid on Harper's Ferry in 1859 all paved the way for sectional division over conflicting views of slavery.

Religious and political antislavery leaders formed a powerful alliance in the 1840s to 1850s. Although Garrisonians rejected political action as requiring unacceptable moral compromises, evangelical abolitionists joined new, antislavery political parties. The earliest antislavery politicians denounced slaveholding as a sin and endorsed nonfellowship with slaveowners. The Liberty Party, formed in 1840, ran James G. Birney for president, on a platform of immediate abolition and repeal of racially discriminatory legislation as a moral and political duty. Birney secured only 7,000 votes in 1840, and 62,000 in 1844, indicating that the single issue of slavery was insufficient to draw a significant number of evangelical votes away from the Whigs, a party that supported other evangelical issues such as SABBATARIANISM and prohibition.

The Free Soil Party, created in 1848, attracted more voters than the Liberty Party by adopting a more moderate antislavery platform. The 1848 ticket of Martin Van Buren and Charles Francis Adams received 290,000 votes. Free Soil united a coalition of former Liberty voters with nonextensionist Whigs and Democrats, including those who opposed expansion of slavery into the territories because they feared blacks rather than hating slavery for moral reasons. Some Protestant abolitionists felt betrayed by the Free Soil Party's weakened antislavery platform and political compromises. Yet even the party's more moderate nonextensionist position encouraged Northerners to view slavery as a morally unacceptable institution.

The Republican Party attracted former adherents to the Liberty and Free Soil parties and disaffected nonextensionist Whigs and Democrats. The new party attracted a still broader constituency than its predecessor, including those primarily interested in economic development and protection against competition from black labor. Abolitionists were so effective in keeping the Republican program on track with nonextension that most political abolitionists and even some Garrisonians endorsed the 1860 election of Abraham Lincoln as a morally principled means of combating slavery.

Despite abolitionist campaigns, the institution of Southern slavery was still firmly entrenched in 1860. The Civil War began as a fight for nonextension of slavery and preservation of the Union, and became a war to destroy slavery. Although the Emancipation Proclamation of 1863 freed a relatively small number of slaves, it transformed the Union armies into a liberationist vanguard. The Northern churches came to envision the war as a sacred cause with clear millennial overtones, and to perceive slavery as the crucial moral hurdle to overcome to preserve the nation from divine judgment. Yet post-war Northern failure to end discrimination indicates the inability of abolitionists to convert Protestant churches into advocates for racial equality.

See also American Bible Society; American Board of Commissioners for Foreign Missions; American Colonization Society; American Missionary Association; Beecher, Lyman; Civil War, United States; Douglass, Frederick; Finney, Charles Grandison; Liberia; Mott, Lucretia Coffin; Revivals; Sabbatarianism; Sharp, Granville; Sierra Leone; Slavery; Society of Friends in North America; Stowe, Harriet Beecher; Taylor, Nathaniel William; Wesley, John; Wilberforce, William; Woolman, John

References and Further Reading

Auping, John A. *Religion and Social Justice: The Case of Christianity and the Abolition of Slavery in America.* Mexico: Universidad Iberoamericana, 1994.

Azevedo, Celia Maria Marinho de. *Abolitionism in the United States and Brazil: A Comparative Perspective.* New York and London: Garland, 1995.

Drescher, Seymour. "Brazilian Abolition in Comparative Perspective." *Hispanic American Historical Review* 68 no. 3 (1988): 429–460.

———. "British War, French Way: Opinion building and Revolution in the Second French Slave Emancipation." *American Historical Review* 96 no. 3 (1991): 709–734.

———. "Long Goodbye: Dutch Capitalism and Antislavery in Comparative Perspective." *American Historical Review* 99 no. 1 (1994): 44–69.

———. "Whose Abolition? Popular Pressure and the Ending of the British Slave Trade." *Past and Present 143* (1994): 136–166.

Eltis, David. "Europeans and the Rise and Fall of African Slavery in the America: An Interpretation." *American Historical Review* 98 no. 5 (1993): 1399–1423.

Howard, Victor B. *The Evangelical War Against Slavery and Caste: The Life and Times of John G. Fee.* Selinsgrove, PA: Susquehanna University Press; London: Associated University Presses, 1996.

Kriegel, Abraham D. "A Convergence of Ethics: Saints and Whigs in British Antislavery." *Journal of British Studies* 26 (1987): 423–450.

McKivigan, John R., ed. *History of the American Abolitionist Movement: A Bibliography of Scholarly Articles.* vol. 1: *Abolitionism and American Reform*; vol. 2: *Abolitionism and American Religion.* New York and London: Garland, 1999.

———, and Mitchell Snay. *Religion and the Antebellum Debate over Slavery.* Athens and London: University of Georgia Press, 1998.

Stauffer, John. *The Black Hearts of Men: Radical Abolitionists and the Transformation of Race.* Cambridge, MA: Harvard University Press, 2002.

Strong, Douglas M. *Perfectionist Politics: Abolitionism and the Religious Tensions of American Democracy.* Syracuse, NY: Syracuse University Press, 1999.

Thomas, Herman Edward. *James W. C. Pennington: African American Churchman and Abolitionist.* New York and London: Garland, 1995.

Turner, Michael J. "The Limits of Abolition: Government, Saints and the 'African Question', c. 1780–1820." *English Historical Review* 112 (1997): 319–357.

Yarak, Larry W. "West African Coastal Slavery in the Nineteenth Century: The Case of the Afro-European Slaveowners of Elmina." *Ethnohistory* 36 (1989): 44–60.

CANDY GUNTHER BROWN

SLESSOR, MARY MITCHELL (1848–1915)

Scottish missionary. Born in Aberdeen, SCOTLAND on December 2, 1848, Mary Slessor was destined to become one of the best-known missionaries of her era to her compatriots; her death at Use Ikot Nkon, NIGERIA on January 13, 1915, after thirty-eight years of service, was noted around the world.

Mary's father suffered from alcoholism and, after the family moved to Dundee, eleven-year-old Mary was obliged to seek work in a mill to help support the family. Her mother was a devout Presbyterian (see PRESBYTERIANISM), who saw that Mary and her siblings grew up hearing about the church's mission work, especially that in the Calabar district of West Africa. Slessor was accepted as a "female agent" for the United Presbyterian Church and sailed for Calabar in August 1876. During her years of service she drew criticism in some circles because of her unorthodox habits and methods. She climbed trees, dispensed with Victorian petticoats, marched barefoot and bareheaded through the jungle, cut her hair short, refused to filter drinking water, and allowed the use of a native oath in court cases.

An educator and church planter, Slessor pressured the mission to allow her to establish stations in new areas. In addition to teaching and PREACHING, she brought an element of stability in a time of social upheaval, as she advised and settled disputes. She lived like the native peoples and spoke the language so well that she won their respect and became known as *eka kpukpro owo*—everybody's mother.

Slessor was not the first to rescue unwanted twins and orphans, but she was more determined than some colleagues. Statues in Cross River and Akwa Ibom states depict her holding a baby in each arm. Many children found shelter in her home, eight of whom she adopted. She also fought to elevate the status of WOMEN and continued the missionary struggle to eliminate such practices as trial by ordeal of poison bean or boiling oil, ritual human sacrifices, killing of twins and orphans, and ethnic wars.

The British government appointed Slessor a magistrate during the colonial period (see COLONIALISM). This meant she continued to judge local court cases, as she had already been doing informally. In 1913 she was named an honorary associate of the Order of St. John of Jerusalem, the highest honor then available to a British woman commoner.

Mary Slessor's Reformed faith (see CALVINISM; REFORMATION) was an integral part of her life; she considered PRAYER central to her ministry, as she endeavored to see lives transformed.

See also Africa; Church of Scotland; Free Church; Missions, British

References and Further Reading

Primary Source:

Slessor, Mary Mitchell. *The Letters to Charles Partridge, 1905–1914.* Dundee, Scotland: Dundee Central Library, Mary Slessor Collection.
http://www.dundeecity.gov.uk/centlib/slessor/letintro.htm (Accessed March 14, 2003).

Secondary Sources:

Hardage, Jeanette. "The Legacy of Mary Slessor." *International Bulletin of Missionary Research* 26 (October 2002): 178–181.
Kalu, Ogbu, ed. *A Century and a Half of Presbyterian Witness in Nigeria, 1846–1996.* Lagos, Nigeria: IDA-Ivory Press, 1996.
Proctor, J. H. "Serving God and the Empire: Mary Slessor in South-Eastern Nigeria, 1876–1915." *Journal of Religion in Africa* 30 (2000): 45–61.

JEANETTE HARDAGE

SMITH, HANNAH WHITALL
(1832–1911)

American higher life evangelist, best-selling author, and reformer. Hannah Whitall was born a Quaker on February 7, 1832 in Philadelphia. In 1851 she married Robert Pearsall Smith. The birth in 1852 of their first child sidetracked her intellectual ambitions. That first child died in 1858, driving Smith to search the BIBLE for its "plan for salvation." She decided that, for wholly consecrated readers, the Bible functioned as a guidebook.

Smith resigned from the SOCIETY OF FRIENDS in September 1859, proclaiming "the fact of the complete and finished salvation offered to us in Christ, our *perfect* Saviour." She received baptism and Communion, and intensified her contacts with the Methodist Holiness movement. Smith published her first article in 1867 titled "How to Live a Life of Practical Holiness."

By 1871, Smith recognized her gift for public work. Her eldest son died in 1872, and she wrote of him in *Frank: The Record of a Happy Life* (1873). The loss of the son undid her husband, who sailed for Europe in early 1873 under doctors' orders. Over the next two years, Robert and then Hannah preached the Higher Life throughout Europe. Her book *The Christian's Secret of a Happy Life* (1875) emerged from this period. In 1875, however, leaders in the movement rejected Robert's ANTINOMIANISM. This break ended Robert's career and he died in 1899.

The later 1870s saw Hannah Smith active in TEMPERANCE, women's uplift, and suffrage movements. In 1888, the family moved to ENGLAND. Smith served in the front ranks of the British Women's Temperance Union. Around 1900 she retired from public work and devoted her energies to the guardianship of her granddaughters. She died in England on May 1, 1911.

See also Higher Life Movement; Temperance.

References and Further Reading

Kaylor, Earl C., Jr. "Smith, Hannah Whitall." In *Notable American Women*. Edited by Edward T. James et al. Cambridge, MA: Belknap, Harvard University Press, 1971.
Smith, Hannah Whitall. *The Christian's Secret of a Happy Life.* Boston: 1875.
———. *The Unselfishness of God and How I Discovered It: A Spiritual Autobiography.* New York: Fleming H. Revell, 1903.
Strachey, Barbara. *Remarkable Relations: The Story of the Pearsall Smith Women.* New York: Universe, 1980.

ANNE BLUE WILLS

SMITH, JOSEPH (1805–1844)

Mormon prophet and founder of the Church of Jesus Christ of Latter-Day Saints. Joseph Smith, the unlearned visionary and prophet, went beyond the bounds of normative Protestantism in establishing MORMONISM in nineteenth-century America. Unlike other reformers of his day who strove to restore the doctrines of New Testament Christianity, Smith sought to restore its powers, including direct revelation and spiritual gifts. His followers believed Smith's revelations were scripture and equal to the Bible. In the same vein, he restored priesthood authority, including the priesthood of Melchizedek, ordained twelve apostles, and sought to build a city of Zion with a temple. Although based on passages in the Bible, Smith's doctrines went to extremes that most Protestants could not tolerate.

Smith was born in Sharon, Vermont, to Joseph Smith, Sr., and Lucy Mack Smith on December 23, 1805. The Smith family farmed in Topsfield, Massachusetts, near Salem, for four generations before hard times forced Smith's grandfather Asael Smith to move to Vermont in the 1790s. In making the move, the Smiths left behind their traditional Congregational faith. Asael became a Universalist, and Smith's father a seeker who lost faith in all the churches and had prophetic dreams about the desolate condition of the religious world. Although touched by revivals in Vermont, the Smiths did not attend church until they moved to Palmyra, New York, in 1816. Lucy Smith and three of the children joined the Presbyterians, but young Joseph stayed home with his father. Confused by the division in the family and pressured by the revival preaching in upstate New York, Smith reported a vision in 1820 in which he was forgiven of his sins and told not to join any of the churches.

The Smith family was typical of many New England migrants who spun free from the traditional churches in the early nineteenth century, and yet hungered for supernatural experience. The Smiths dabbled in treasure-seeking and magic and were part of the inchoate visionary culture that was visible also in early METHODISM. While alienated from the churches, the Smith family yearned for religion. Joseph Smith came under the influence of Methodist preaching, and for a short time joined a Methodist class after marrying Emma Hale in January 1827, a woman with Methodist connections. However, instead of finding a home in any existing religions, Smith began to receive revelations that carried him away from conventional Protestantism.

The Book of Mormon

On September 22, 1823, according to Smith's report, an angel named Moroni appeared in his bedroom to tell him about golden plates on which were engraved the history of an ancient people who had once resided on the American continent. Smith was led to the location of the plates in a nearby hill, which was later called Cumorah after a name in the record. He was permitted to view the plates but not to remove them from their hiding place until he had purged himself of the desire to profit from their value as gold. On September 22, 1827, he finally obtained the thick book of thin metal sheets, and began the process of translation. According to the story, the record was written in a combination of Egyptian and Hebrew, and Joseph was expected to translate the characters with the help of "interpreters" that came with the plates. The task was completed in June 1829, and the Book of Mormon was published in March 1830.

The Book of Mormon purported to be a history of an ancient people from whom modern American Indians had descended. The main action took place between 600 B.C. and A.D. 421, and concerned a group of exiles from Jerusalem who left the city on the eve of the Babylonian captivity and voyaged to the Western Hemisphere. Although telling a novel story, the record's basic idea of Indians being lost Israelites had been hypothesized by Christian observers since shortly after European discovery of the New World. In the Book of Mormon account, the migrants divided into two nations who battled one another for a thousand years until one group, the one not keeping the record, destroyed the other, and the story came to a close. From the survivors came the Native Americans of Joseph Smith's time. One of the Book of Mormon's stated purposes was to help restore this remnant of lost Israel to a knowledge of God.

The idea of Indian Israel would not have surprised readers familiar with speculations about Indian origins, but most Protestants would have been taken aback by the thoroughly Christian nature of the writing. Book of Mormon prophets taught the standard Christian gospel much more plainly than Isaiah or Ezekiel. Long before Christ's ministry, they preached his birth and resurrection, knew the name of his mother, taught Christian baptism, and organized Christian churches. Almost no distinction between the Mosaic and Christian dispensations was evident in the Book of Mormon. According to the book, Christ appeared to these American Israelites soon after his resurrection, but his gospel confirmed the prophetic teachings of the previous six centuries.

While the Christian nature of the Book of Mormon merely surprised Protestants, they angrily protested the Book of Mormon's presumption to be scripture of equal worth with the Bible. Without learning or ecclesiastical standing of any sort, Smith claimed that the 588-page book of prophecy and historical narrative was an expansion of the Bible, and was more likely than the Bible to be authentic because it was not damaged by editorial interventions and multiple translations. In an age that lived by the principle of *sola scriptura,* the Book of Mormon could only be looked upon as an audacious fraud.

At first the Book of Mormon was thought to be a clumsy attempt to deceive people and ultimately defraud them. After the unlikelihood of an uneducated farm boy producing such an intricate narrative dawned on the critics, the book was judged to be an imitation of a lost novel by a more learned and competent writer named Solomon Spaulding. Decades later, when Spaulding's book was found and the similarity to the Book of Mormon disproved, scholars went back to the idea of the Book of Mormon as the product of Smith's own inventiveness, the general opinion of non-Mormons today.

Church Organization

Smith began to attract followers who believed in his supernatural gifts, and on April 6, 1830, he organized them into a church in Fayette, New York. Smith's revelations, given usually by inspiration rather than vision, carried a strong millenarian message. In the calamities that would precede the Second Coming of Christ, the revelations said, the only safe refuge would be Zion, a place the Lord would designate for believers to gather. Church members, termed "saints," were to locate this site and build a holy city called the New Jerusalem. Missionaries were sent to Missouri in 1830 in search of a place for Zion, and Joseph Smith followed in the summer of 1831. A revelation identified Independence, Missouri, on the edge of American settlement, as the site of the New Jerusalem and the place for a temple.

Over the next few years, Smith's followers began to collect in Missouri, and at another site in Kirtland, Ohio, near Cleveland, where missionaries had gained nearly one hundred converts. The movement grew rapidly as a result of numerous short-term proselyting tours by the male members. No sooner was a person baptized than he was ordained and sent out to preach. The missionaries taught a simple New Testament form of salvation requiring faith, repentance, baptism, and the laying on of hands for the gift of the Holy Ghost. Mormonism resembled other restoration movements of the time, such as the Campbellites, who also sought to restore a pure New Testament gospel that circumvented the strenuous emotional ordeal of evangelical conversion.

Smith's revelations, however, did not stop with these familiar New Testament principles. He also claimed to restore priesthoods that were required to perform authorized baptisms and other sacred ordinances. John the Baptist was said to have restored the Aaronic priesthood, while Peter, James, and John, Christ's original apostles, along with other angelic visitors, were reported to have restored the higher or Melchizedek priesthood. The restoration of priesthood implicitly invalidated the sacraments of other Christian churches and made Mormons the exclusive possessors of divine authority.

Within the Mormon church, the priesthood was widely distributed. Smith did not reserve it for a clerical group set off from the laity as in most denominations. Every male member was ordained to the priesthood and authorized to perform sacred ordinances. No priestly class ever developed. Each congregation was led by lay priesthood leaders who called upon members of the congregation to preach, rather than reserving that duty for a trained ministry. Women did not receive the priesthood and did not give sermons except to other women.

Smith's revelations explained that through the priesthood believers might prepare themselves to see God and receive exaltation in the afterlife. Along with the program of gathering in Zion, Smith began to focus on the construction of temples where the saints could be instructed in the mysteries of godliness and taught to know God. The elders of the church were formed into a "School of the Prophets" to learn their duties and be shown how to purify themselves. Their schooling culminated in the 1836 dedication of a temple in Kirtland, where men, women, and children enjoyed a pentecostal outpouring.

The revelations containing these doctrines were published in 1835 as The Doctrine and Covenants, the second book of scripture produced by Smith that had equal standing with the Bible. Additions were made through the years as the revelations continued to pour forth.

Opposition to Mormonism

Almost from the beginning, Mormonism aroused opposition. The astounding claims to direct revelation, the exclusiveness of the religion, and the fear of a scheme to defraud people accounted for much of the anger. Smith was dragged from his house one night in 1832, threatened with emasculation, and tarred and feathered. In 1833, local settlers drove the Mormons from their farms around Independence, and refused to let them claim their property. The underlying problem was the Mormon practice of gathering. By concentrating members in one location, they threatened to become a majority and so control elections. Non-Mormons who might tolerate a minority of religious fanatics in their midst could not accept their dominance.

Joseph Smith's effort to found a bank in Kirtland in 1837 made still more enemies. Many of his own followers came to doubt his judgment and honesty and believed him to be a fallen prophet. In 1838 he was compelled to flee to Caldwell County, Missouri, where the saints had assembled in a largely unsettled region. Their growing power led to a fight at a polling place in the late summer of 1838, and violence erupted on both sides. The governor of Missouri ordered the Mormons expelled from the state or exterminated. In November 1838 Joseph Smith was arrested and charged with treason. He spent the winter of 1839 in prison in Missouri while his followers moved eastward toward Illinois in search of a new home.

In the spring of 1839, Smith escaped his guards, perhaps with their connivance, and joined his people. He purchased land at a place on the Mississippi called Commerce and renamed it Nauvoo. The Illinois legislature granted a charter that gave the Mormons control of local courts and a city militia. Smith wanted to erect barriers that would allow him to collect his followers and continue their instruction without fear of disruption by hostile forces. Strengthened by a flow of converts from England as well as every section of the United States, Nauvoo grew to a city of ten thousand over the next five years, with another five thousand members in the surrounding regions.

During the Nauvoo years, Smith elaborated on the temple doctrines that more than anything else differentiated his teachings from Protestantism. Family and lineage came to occupy a large place in his revelations. One of them instructed the saints to perform baptism vicariously for people now gone from the earth so that the requirement of baptism could be met by everyone. Smith said the ordinance, to be done only in temples, fulfilled the prophecy of Malachi about the hearts of the children being turned to the fathers. Another revelation made marriage a prerequisite for exaltation in the celestial kingdom. Men and women had to be sealed by priesthood authority in the temple in order to reach the highest degree of heaven.

The most controversial of Smith's revelations commanded the saints to practice plural marriage, like Abraham in the Old Testament. Smith may have received this revelation as early as 1831 and held it back, knowing the furor it would cause. His wife Emma, among others, was bitterly opposed. Beginning in 1842, he told a few of his most trusted followers about the revelation and instructed them to take additional wives as he did himself—perhaps as many as thirty-three of them. Although plural marriage was not publicly taught and was even denied until an announcement in 1852 in Utah, rumors flew about the city, turning many of the leading people in the church against Smith.

Smith's teachings in the Nauvoo years went far beyond traditional Protestantism. Though every doctrine had some foundation in the Bible—as did the polygamous practices of Abraham—Smith's revelations drove biblical passages to extremes that most Protestants could not comprehend. He taught, for example, that the phrase "be ye therefore perfect as your father in heaven is perfect" was to be taken literally. Christians were to work toward the goal of becoming gods themselves. Smith told people they were to become kings and priests, a phrase from the book of Revelation, and had himself ordained a king and priest. He established "endowment" ceremonies in the temple where the saints were instructed in how to prepare to meet God.

In the winter of 1844, Joseph Smith announced his candidacy for president of the United States. He never explained his reasons for conducting this hopeless campaign, but he sent missionaries throughout the country to promote his candidacy. Before the election, however, he was killed. Smith had closed down a reformist newspaper, *The Nauvoo Expositor,* in early June, believing that accusations by his disillusioned followers in the paper's pages were incendiary. Newspaper editors and politicians in the surrounding region were already calling for his blood, fearing the rising power of the Mormons. Closing the press was the last straw. Smith was arrested and taken to the county seat at Carthage, Illinois, where a mob attacked the jail in which he had been placed for safekeeping. He was shot on June 27, 1844.

Although building on the Bible and the Christian tradition, Smith cannot be thought of as another Protestant reformer. Untrained and inexperienced, he did not set out to revise established doctrines or to purify worship. Rather than reinterpreting the Bible, he took his cues from his own revelations. His followers thought he was more like Moses and Jeremiah than MARTIN LUTHER (1483–1546) and JOHN CALVIN (1509–1564). To this day, Mormons consider themselves to be Christians, but not Protestants, and speak of Joseph Smith as "the Prophet."

References and Further Reading

Brodie, Fawn M. *No Man Knows My History: The Life of Joseph Smith.* 2nd ed. New York: Knopf, 1971.

Brooke, John L. *The Refiner's Fire: The Making of Mormon Cosmology, 1644–1844.* New York: Cambridge University Press, 1994.

Bushman, Richard L. *Joseph Smith and the Beginnings of Mormonism.* Urbana: University of Illinois Press, 1984.

Compton, Todd. *In Sacred Loneliness: The Plural Wives of Joseph Smith.* Salt Lake City: Signature Books, 1997.

Flanders, Robert Bruce. *Nauvoo: Kingdom on the Mississippi.* Urbana: University of Illinois Press, 1965.

Hill, Marvin S. *Quest for Refuge: The Mormon Flight from American Pluralism.* Salt Lake City: Signature Books, 1989.

Newell, Linda King, and Val Tippetts Avery. *Mormon Enigma: Emma Hale Smith, Prophet's Wife, "Elect Lady." and Polygamy's Foe.* Garden City, NY: Doubleday, 1984.

Ouinn, D. Michael. *Early Mormonism and the Magic World View.* Rev. ed. Salt Lake City: Signature Books, 1998.

Shipps, Jan. *Mormonism: The Story of a New Religious Tradition.* Urbana: University of Illinois Press, 1985.

Underwood, Grant. *The Millenarian World of Early Mormonism.* Urbana: University of Illinois Press, 1993.

Wood, Gordon S. "Evangelical America and Early Mormonism," *New York History* 61 (1980): 351–386.

RICHARD LYMAN BUSHMAN

SMITH, WILLIAM ROBERTSON (1846–1894)

English biblical scholar. Smith, Hebrew BIBLE and comparative religion scholar, introduced the literary-historical methods of German HIGHER CRITICISM to English-speaking Victorian Protestants. He propounded a theory of ritual sacrifice, totemism, and kinship that influenced the development of early sociological, anthropological, and psychological theorists of religion such as Emile Durkheim, James Frazer, F. B. Jevons, and Sigmund Freud.

Career

Born at Keig, Scotland, November 8, 1846 and raised in the recently formed Free Church of Scotland (see CHURCH OF SCOTLAND; FREE CHURCH), Smith entered the University of Aberdeen at age fifteen and became professor of Hebrew and Old Testament exegesis at the Free Church College, Aberdeen, nine years later.

The 1875 publication of his entry "Bible" in the *Encyclopedia Britannica* provoked intense controversy over his denial of Mosaic authorship of Deuteronomy and postexilic dating of the levitical code. A five-year HERESY battle within Free Church assemblies (1876–1881) brought Smith international acclaim as a loyal churchman willing to be an outspoken advocate of the new biblical scholarship. Although accusing him of violating his oath to uphold the WESTMINSTER CONFESSION, the Free Church General Assembly eventually dropped all formal charges. Nevertheless, it removed Smith from his academic post in 1881. He went on to become editor-in-chief of the ninth edition of the *Encyclopedia Britannica,* to which he personally contributed over 200 articles. In 1883 he moved to CAMBRIDGE UNIVERSITY, becoming professor of Arabic, fellow of Christ College, and university librarian. He returned to the University of Aberdeen from 1888 to 1891 to deliver the Burnet Lectures, published as *Lectures on the Religion of the Semites,* his most seminal work in the field of religious studies.

Smith died of tuberculosis at Cambridge, ENGLAND, on March 31, 1894.

Assessment

Robertson Smith's use of literary-critical methods to reconstruct the history of ancient Israelite religion, which he defended as consistent with REFORMATION hermeneutics, helped clear the way for English-speaking Protestant biblical scholars to break free of the constraints of literalism and doctrinarism. For Smith, Hebrew biblical history revealed the story of an unfolding understanding of God, culminating in the prophetic consciousness of pure ethical monotheism and divine GRACE. He also expanded the study of Israelite religion by embedding it in the wider Semitic cultures of the Near East, including Arabia. As a result, Protestant Old Testament scholars could no longer ignore comparative issues.

In addition Smith gave direction to the academic study of religion by stressing the theoretical priority of rituals and symbolic actions over beliefs and myths in primal societies. He maintained that sacrificial rituals were originally totemic and constitutive of kinship bonds. Rejecting a propitiatory view of early sacrificial practices, he interpreted them as communal in nature, centering on the commensality established between divine and human participants in sacrificial meals. Although not fully accepted today, his views led to the treatment of religion as a positive and universal dimension of human life and society.

As a product of his times and influenced by ALBRECHT RITSCHL and German neo-Kantians (see KANT, IMMANUEL), Smith assumed an evolutionary scheme of human religious development from "primitive," ritually materialistic social stages to more private and less ritualistic stages of pure monotheistic awareness, culminating in the theology of Protestant Christianity. Thus, despite a passion for comparative studies, the privileged status he accorded Victorian Protestantism supports what Edward Said characterized as Smith's "Orientalism," that is, hegemonic Western cultural presumption.

See also Biblical Inerrancy; Colenso, John William; Cultural Protestantism; Drummond, Henry; Lagarde, Paul de; Nonconformity; Schleiermacher, Friedrich; Sociology of Protestantism; Westminster Catechism

References and Further Reading

Primary Sources:

Smith, William Robertson. *Lectures on the Religion of the Semites.* London: A. & C. Black, 1889/1894. Rev. ed.
———. *The Old Testament in the Jewish Church: Twelve Lectures on Biblical Criticism.* London: A. & C. Black, 1881/1892, rev. edition.
———. *The Prophets of Israel and Their Place in History to the Close of the Eighth Century B.C.* London: A. & C. Black, 1882.

Secondary Source:

Beidelman, T. O. *William Robertson Smith and the Sociological Study of Religion.* Chicago: University of Chicago Press, 1974.

WILLIAM M. KING

SMYTH, JOHN (c.1572–1612)

English Baptist. Often designated "the first Baptist," John Smyth (or Smith) was successively a Puritan,

Separatist, Baptist, and Mennonite. Perhaps born in Sturton-le-Steeple, Nottinghamshire, ENGLAND, he was at Christ's College, CAMBRIDGE UNIVERSITY from 1586 to 1598, earning a B.A. in 1590 and an M.A. in 1593 and becoming a fellow in 1594, but also studying medicine along the way.

Smyth was a Puritan city lecturer in Lincoln 1600–1602, losing that position because of a local political dispute (see PURITANISM). He wrote two books displaying standard Puritan theology: *The Bright Morning Starre* (1603) and *A Paterne of True Prayer* (1605). He was a leader in a Puritan CONVENTICLE, which covenanted to become an English Separatist congregation (that is, a believers' church separate from the CHURCH OF ENGLAND) about 1606–1607. In *Principles and inferences concerning The visible Church* (1607), he defined a true CHURCH as being composed only of saints (believers) bound together in a COVENANT, and argued that such a congregation had AUTHORITY directly from Christ to appoint leaders, administer the SACRAMENTS, and exercise discipline, for example. Smyth further defended and defined Separatist churches in *Paralleles, Censures, Observations* (1608). After the congregation fled to Amsterdam in the NETHERLANDS in 1608, Smyth supported himself (and apparently assisted the poor in the congregation financially) through the practice of medicine while also leading the congregation. He wrote *The Differences of the Churches of the Separation* (1608), in opposition to the Ancient Church, another English Separatist congregation in Amsterdam; in this book Smyth argued that books, including translations of Scripture, should not be used in WORSHIP (a prohibition perhaps aimed at the Anglican BOOK OF COMMON PRAYER and at the GENEVA BIBLE, which contained many Calvinist notes and interpretations); that a congregation should be led by several equal pastors/elders/teachers assisted by DEACONS/DEACONESSES (as opposed to the Puritan/Calvinist model, which made pastor, teacher, and elders separate positions); and that a congregation should not accept donations from outsiders.

In 1609 Smyth rebaptized himself and forty to fifty members of his congregation, thus re-establishing believer's BAPTISM, reconstituting his congregation using believer's baptism as a substitute form of the Separatist covenant, and creating what might be considered the first Baptist congregation. Smyth defended believer's baptism in *The Character of the Beast* (1609) and later in *Argumenta Contra Baptismum Infantum* (an unpublished work in Latin). John Robinson led a large group out of the Smyth congregation, disagreeing with Smyth in his argument against the ancient church and with his move to a believer's baptism position; in the spring of 1609 this group moved to Leiden in the Netherlands, where they eventually formed the nucleus of the PILGRIM FATHERS and thus helped lay the foundation for American CONGREGATIONALISM. By 1610 Smyth and most of the remaining congregation made an alliance with a group of Waterlander MENNONITES, in the process accepting Mennonite positions on the incarnation (that Christ's "first flesh" was divine and did not come from Mary), free will, and separation of CHURCH AND STATE—as evidenced by two confessions issued by the congregation, *Corde Credimus* and *Propositions and conclusions* (1612), as well as a *Defense* Smyth wrote supporting a Mennonite CONFESSION written by Hans de Ries.

Regarding free will, Smyth denied original sin and argued that Christ's death on the cross freed all human beings to the point that they were able to freely choose whether to accept or reject SALVATION—a free will position derived from the Mennonites rather than from the Reformed dissenter, JACOBUS ARMINIUS. A group of about ten members of the congregation, led by Thomas Helwys, although accepting much of this Mennonite theology, refused to follow Smyth into merger with the Mennonites. Helwys did not accept Mennonite views on the incarnation, accused Smyth and the Mennonites of not keeping the Sabbath, and held to a traditional Protestant view of JUSTIFICATION by FAITH (in opposition to the Smyth/Mennonite view that salvation was by both justification by faith and regeneration). Helwys accepted the Mennonite doctrine of separation of church and state (that the state should not interfere in religion) but differed with the Mennonites in saying that true Christians could nevertheless take part in secular government. Helwys defended the Smyth congregation's reinstitution of believer's baptism, accusing the Smyth congregation of returning to a form of apostolic succession by wanting to merge with the Mennonites; Smyth denied the charge, arguing that it is permissible to reinitiate believer's baptism but that this should be done only when baptism is not available from other baptized believers. The Helwys faction returned to England by 1612 and founded the GENERAL BAPTISTS.

Smyth died of tuberculosis in Amsterdam in 1612. In his *Last Book* (1612), Smyth affirmed his final theological position but repented some of his harshness in theological debate. In a biography published with the *Last Book,* his congregation briefly described his godly life and godly death at the end of August 1612. A common feature throughout Smyth's written works is the use of Aristotelian logic. Also central to his thought, beginning with *The Differences of the Churches of the Seperation,* was a strong distinction between Old Testament and New Testament, letter and Spirit, sinners and saints, false churches and true churches. Smyth was accused by his critics of being gifted but unstable for changing his theological positions so frequently, a charge Smyth refuted on the basis of the "further light clause" in the Separatist covenant—the idea that God would progressively lead true Christians into new truth.

See also Arminianism; Baptists; Baptists, Europe; Dissent; Nonconformity

References and Further Reading

Primary Sources:

Smyth, John. *The Churches of the Separation.* New York: Da Capo Press, 1973.

Smyth, John, and William Thomas Whitley. *The Works of John Smyth, Fellow of Christ's College.* Cambridge: Cambridge University Press, 1915.

Secondary Sources:

Coggins, James R. *John Smyth's Congregation: English Separatism, Mennonite Influence, and the Elect Nation.* Scottdale, PA: Herald Press, 1991.

Whitley, W. T., ed. *The Works of John Smyth Fellow of Christ's College, 1594–8.* Cambridge: Cambridge University Press, 1915.

JAMES R. COGGINS

SOCIAL GOSPEL

The Social Gospel was a diffuse theological movement, emerging in late nineteenth- and early twentieth-century Western Protestantism, that sought to apply Christian teachings to contemporary social reform issues. Integrating evangelical and liberal theological traditions, the Social Gospel is often classified under the larger rubric of "social Christianity" associated with a number of Protestant churches and church leaders in western Europe (chiefly Great Britain) and North America in the last quarter of the nineteenth century. The term "Social Gospel" has been used with greatest regularity to define the theological and social reform initiatives undertaken by church leaders, theologians, and denominations in the United States during the Progressive Era of the early twentieth century. The Social Gospel as a theological movement focused on issues of social salvation. Whereas many Social Gospel leaders continued to emphasize the importance of personal CONVERSION, they also reinterpreted traditional Protestant understandings of soteriology, the theology of SALVATION, to emphasize how Jesus's social teachings could be applicable to questions of economic justice and social equality. Although never a unified theological tradition, Social Gospel proponents articulated an optimistic theology, stressing human potential, the imperative for social reform, and the creation of a just social order. The most influential exponents of the tradition in Western Protestantism included the American church leaders WASHINGTON GLADDEN and WALTER RAUSCHENBUSCH.

The Social Gospel served as a major catalyst for the emergence of the Protestant ecumenical movement in the twentieth century, symbolized by the founding in the United States in 1908 of the Federal Council of Churches in Christ (see ECUMENISM). Although the Social Gospel would be eclipsed by NEO-ORTHODOXY after World War I, the tradition remained influential in Western Protestantism up through World War II. Social Gospel theological themes, stressing social equality and the interrelationship between Christian theology and secular politics, were evident in many social movements and theological traditions in the latter half of the twentieth century, including the CIVIL RIGHTS MOVEMENT and genres of LIBERATION THEOLOGY.

The Rise of the Social Gospel

Scholars have identified the emergence of the Social Gospel as a response to late nineteenth-century industrialization in the United States. At the same time the Social Gospel was also a theological synthesis emerging from a variety of disparate developments impacting North America and western Europe in the late nineteenth century.

Four factors may be cited to explain the emergence of the Social Gospel as a historical and theological tradition. First, the Social Gospel's roots can be connected to American postmillennial evangelical revivalism of the early and mid-nineteenth century. Focusing on the aftermath of the Second Great AWAKENING, scholars have linked the Social Gospel's rise to the social reform crusades that emerged in the first half of the nineteenth century. Although early and mid-nineteenth century Protestant evangelicals such as CHARLES FINNEY and PHOEBE PALMER advocated an individualistic view of Christian salvation, their view of salvation emphasized the Christian's responsibility to reform society. This belief in personal salvation led many antebellum Protestants to address social issues related to temperance reform, women's rights, and the abolition of SLAVERY.

The legacy of Protestant evangelicalism spawned a number of movements in the late nineteenth century that became important conduits for the Social Gospel's emergence in Europe and North America. Organizations such as the YOUNG MEN'S CHRISTIAN ASSOCIATION (YMCA) and the Student Volunteer Movement, a Protestant ecumenical organization that recruited university students for foreign missionary service, produced many leaders who would become associated with the Social Gospel in the early twentieth century (see MISSIONARY ORGANIZATIONS). Although proponents of the Social Gospel moved beyond a solitary focus on personal salvation, the movement by and large continued to stress the importance of individual salvation as a necessary component to build a just society.

The second factor contributing to the Social Gospel, and one cited by the majority of scholars as the primary catalyst for the tradition's emergence, was the rise of liberal theology in the latter half of the nineteenth century (see LIBERAL PROTESTANTISM AND LIBERATION). Embodied by theologians and ministers like ALBRECHT BENJAMIN RITSCHL, HORACE BUSHNELL, and HENRY WARD BEECHER, liberal theology served as a transition between traditional Protestant evangelicalism of the early nineteenth century and emerging theologies of the Social Gospel by the end of that century.

As opposed to a view of God's transcendence and separateness from history, liberal theologians stressed God's imminence and involvement within historical processes. Additionally, the development of liberal theology paralleled the emergence of biblical criticism from Germany. Both movements shared similar intellectual suppositions, including a tendency to view emerging nineteenth-century developments in the natural sciences, including DARWINISM, favorably.

Although not all liberal theologians embraced what would become the Social Gospel, the majority of the Social Gospel's theological exponents emerged from the legacy of liberal Protestantism. By the end of the nineteenth century, Social Gospel liberal theologians emphasized how the prophetic witness of the Old Testament prophets and Jesus's ethical teachings in the synoptic gospels could enable churches to address contemporary social problems. Among the prominent liberal theologians associated with the Social Gospel were SHAILER MATHEWS (1863–1941), a professor of New Testament at the University of Chicago, and Francis Peabody (1847–1936), a professor of ethics at Harvard University. Mathews's *The Social Teaching of Jesus* (1897) and Peabody's *Jesus Christ and the Social Question* (1900) investigated the historical context of Jesus's ministry, relating Christ's teaching to contemporary social problems. These works highlight the way many Social Gospel leaders in the late nineteenth and early twentieth centuries applied liberal theology and emerging currents in biblical scholarship to specific questions of social reform.

The rise of liberal theology also paved the way for the emergence of several Protestant clergy whose sermons and writings in the 1880s and 1890s are often seen as marking the beginning of the Social Gospel as a historical era in Western Protestantism. The minister often identified as the first major proponent of the Social Gospel was Washington Gladden. Throughout his career as a Congregational minister, Gladden authored several books dealing with the church's relationship to labor and capital. Like many early Social Gospel leaders, his reform agenda stressed the application of Christian social teachings to the pressing problems of urbanization and INDUSTRIALIZATION. The popularity of Washington Gladden's writings in the 1880s and 1890s coincided with the emergence of other Social Gospel clerics, whose writings became popular in both North America and Europe. These clergy included American Congregationalists Theodore Munger (1830–1910), whose book *The Freedom of Faith* (1883) was considered one of the most influential studies of theological liberalism, and Lyman Abbott (1835–1922), editor of the Progressive Era periodical, *The Outlook*. In Great Britain several clergy played a major role in propagating the rise of the Social Gospel, including the Methodist leader Hugh Price Hughes (1847–1902). Although these late nineteenth-century clergy leaders were influenced strongly by liberal theology, they also emphasized a personal piety reminiscent of earlier Protestant evangelicalism.

The intersection between Protestant evangelicalism and theological liberalism was also evident in a number of popular books published in North America and Europe in the late nineteenth century, the most prominent of which was CHARLES SHELDON'S 1896 novel, *In His Steps*. Sheldon's novel closely modeled William Stead's 1894 book, *If Christ Came to Chicago!* Stead (1849–1912), a prominent British journalist, detailed Chicago economic conditions in the 1890s, calling on churches to follow the example of Christ by serving the city's poor. Sheldon's novel describes the efforts of a congregation in a fictitious midwestern American city to follow Jesus's teachings for one year, asking one another the question, "What Would Jesus Do?" He explored many themes that became theological cornerstones for the Social Gospel. First, Sheldon emphasized the synoptic model of Jesus's ministry, epitomized by the teachings of Jesus's Sermon on the Mount. Second, his novel illustrated the vision, prominent among many American Protestant church leaders of that era, of creating a unified Protestant global culture. This vision of a "Christianized" Protestant society was predicated on the cultural assumptions held by the majority of Anglo-American Social Gospel leaders in the late nineteenth century. The book that epitomized this vision of Protestant culture was Josiah Strong's 1885 book, *Our Country*. A Congregational minister, Strong (1847–1916) reflected the hope that Protestant churches in America and western Europe (primarily Great Britain) could build a Christian cooperative society. His vision of a Christian commonwealth echoed both evangelical and liberal themes characteristic of many late nineteenth-century Social Gospel leaders.

A third factor contributing to the rise of the Social Gospel was the popularity in the second half of the nineteenth century of what has been termed Christian socialism (see SOCIALISM, CHRISTIAN). Church leaders associated with this movement attempted to integrate liberal Christian teachings directly with emerging political and economic theories of nineteenth-century democratic socialism. Like other proponents of the Social Gospel, Christian socialists focused their analysis primarily on the social problems associated with nineteenth-century urbanization, stressing the importance of labor reform. In some cases, Christian socialists encouraged political mobilization and alliances with secular socialist organizations and political parties. The rise of the Social Gospel in Great Britain and the United States has been linked primarily with several clergy within the Anglican Church in Great Britain and the Protestant Episcopal Church in the United States. The popular writings of Anglican church leaders such as F. D. Maurice and CHARLES KINGSLEY created a foundation for Christian socialism in the 1840s and 1850s. A strong tradition of Christian socialism also existed within German Protestantism in the late nineteenth century, represented by church leaders such as ADOLF STOECKER (1835–1908), a pastor in the German Evangelical Church.

These currents of Christian socialism played a key role in the emergence of numerous Christian socialist societies in North American and Europe in the 1880s and 1890s that have been associated with the rise of the Social Gospel. Examples of these Social Gospel fellowships include the Christian Social Union, founded by the Anglican Church in 1889; the Church Association for the Advancement of the Interests of Labor and the Society of Christian Socialists, founded by the Protestant Episcopal Church in 1887 and 1889, respectively; and the Brotherhood of the Kingdom, founded in 1892 by a group of American Baptist clergy. Christian socialist teachings were also evident in such leaders as George Herron (1862–1925), Congregational minister and professor at Grinnell College in Iowa, and William Dwight Porter Bliss (1856–1926), Episcopal clergyman and editor of the *Encyclopedia of Social Reform* (1897), considered the first comprehensive study of nineteenth-century social Christianity. Although some Christian socialists, like Herron, argued strongly for a political model of democratic socialism, the majority of Christian socialist movements tended to be nondoctrinal, stressing social equality among the rich and poor.

The most influential figure associated with Christian socialism in the Social Gospel era was the American economist, Richard T. Ely (1854–1943). A professor of economics at Johns Hopkins University and the University of Wisconsin, Ely's writings used liberal Protestant theological themes concerning Jesus's teachings, relating them to questions of emerging socioeconomic theory. He was a founder of the American Economic Association, and his popularity in the 1880s and 1890s reflected a growing interest among British and North American church leaders in the wider application of the social sciences (especially sociology) to questions of Christian faith and practice.

A final factor that contributed to the rise of the Social Gospel was the impact of a number of women's organizations. These groups were connected to the tradition of Protestant voluntary societies in the antebellum United States. In the aftermath of the American CIVIL WAR, Protestant women established organizations that often addressed social problems associated with urban reform.

Included in the rubric of women's organizations that served as precursors to the Social Gospel were denominational home missionary and deaconess societies, founded primarily to provide a way for women to work in a variety of intercity ministries to the poor. The rise of the home missionary movement in the 1880s within American Protestantism often complemented the intercity mission work of the institutional Settlement House movement of the times. The Settlement House movement, represented by leaders like Samuel Barnett (1844–1913), Graham Taylor (1854–1938), and Jane Addams (1860–1935), was designed to offer fellowship and self-help initiatives to poor urban residents and, in the American context, to recent immigrants. The movement integrated many secular philanthropic ideals within distinctive liberal theological and Christian socialist underpinnings, becoming a main reform movement during the Progressive Era.

Another women's organization reflecting an emerging Social Gospel consciousness was the Woman's Christian Temperance Union (WCTU). Established in 1874 as an organization devoted to enacting temperance reform in North America and Great Britain, its most prominent leader was FRANCES WILLARD. As the longtime president of the WCTU, Willard's interests ranged broadly from women's suffrage to economic reform. Although American leaders like Willard reflected a distinctive piety reflective of earlier Protestant evangelicalism, many of these women also carried a strong interest in liberal theology and Christian socialism, serving as an important linkage between Social Gospel leaders in North America and Great Britain.

In the last quarter of the nineteenth century, women's organizations, Christian socialists, popular writers, ministers, and theologians were drawn to the Chautauqua Institute in western New York State. Established in the 1870s as part of the SUNDAY SCHOOL movement in the Methodist Episcopal Church, the Chautauqua Institute became a major Progressive Era arena for speakers on social questions, including many representatives of the Social Gospel. The model of the Chautauqua Institute spawned regional Chautauquas, held throughout the United States until the early twentieth century, that featured prominent spokespersons of the Social Gospel.

Although early Social Gospel church leaders advocated solidarity with the working class and poor, the movement defined itself largely around the interests of white middle-class Protestant suppositions, often neglecting issues focused on racial justice. At the same time, however, a distinctive Social Gospel legacy emerged within African American churches, producing clergy and women's organizations committed to racial justice (see AFRICAN AMERICAN PROTESTANTISM). One of the most prominent African-American leaders associated with the Social Gospel was Reverdy Ransom (1861–1952). Ransom, a minister and later bishop in the AFRICAN METHODIST EPISCOPAL CHURCH, established numerous churches that engaged in urban settlement work directed toward African Americans. Some African-American Social Gospel leaders were also instrumental in the organization in 1909 and the early leadership of the National Association for the Advancement of Colored People (NAACP), one of the major civil rights organizations of the twentieth century. Scholarly debate continues, however, as to how the social ministries of African-American Protestantism fit into the larger Social Gospel movement in the United States.

The Maturity of the Social Gospel

The individual most identified with Protestant institutional acceptance of the Social Gospel was the German-American Baptist clergyman Walter Rauschenbusch. His formative writings, written between 1907 and his death in 1918, emphasized the interconnection between the doctrine of the KINGDOM OF GOD and contemporary imperatives for Christian social reform. More critical of economic capitalism than leaders like Josiah Strong and Washington Gladden, Rauschenbusch's theology rejected purely eschatological understandings of Christianity, maintaining that the Christian imperative to build the Kingdom of God required harsh judgments against the social and economic values of Western society. He believed that Jesus's condemnation of wealth needed to be taken literally as an indictment against contemporary socioeconomic conditions and challenged Protestant churches to devote their ministries to eradicate these inequalities. His books, including *Christianity and the Social Crisis*

(1907), *Christianizing the Social Order* (1912), and *A Theology for the Social Gospel* (1917), resonated with many church leaders who identified themselves with the Social Gospel and were widely read in North America and Europe.

Rauschenbusch's popularity was a catalyst for numerous publications emphasizing similar themes, and related to the imperative of churches to engage both theologically and practically in questions of socioeconomic reform. Prominent Social Gospel authors in the first two decades of the twentieth century included Vida Scudder (1861–1954), American Episcopalian laywoman and college professor; Samuel Batten (1859–1925), American Baptist clergyman; Charles Stelzle (1869–1941), American Presbyterian minister; and George Albert Coe (1862–1951), American Methodist clergyman and professor. Some Social Gospel leaders, like Stelzle, became active in the creation of institutional churches designed to provide outreach and ministry to poor urban populations. Other leaders of the movement wrote popular Protestant hymns, including "O Master Let Me Walk With Thee" by Washington Gladden and "Where Cross The Crowded Ways of Life," written by Methodist clergyman and ecumenical leader Frank Mason North (1850–1935). The rise of the Social Gospel also paralleled a similar movement of social Christianity within the Roman Catholic Church in the United States. The most prominent exponent of the Social Gospel in American Catholicism was the economist John Ryan (1869–1945).

Rauschenbusch's popularity symbolized the apex of the Social Gospel tradition in the United States, before American entry into World War I in 1917. Although Social Gospel proponents never formed a majority of Protestant church members, the movement's leaders became associated with numerous reform efforts within churches and in wider secular reform movements in the Progressive Era. In particular the ideals of the Social Gospel were embraced by many influential denominational church leaders by the second decade of the twentieth century. Symbolic of this acceptance was the establishment in 1908 of the Federal Council of Churches in Christ in the United States (FCC). The foundation of the Federal Council coincided with the creation of a number of denominational organizations and caucuses designed to promote awareness of social questions within their traditions.

The most influential denominational Social Gospel organization in the early twentieth century was the Methodist Federation for Social Service (MFSS). Founded in 1907 by five American Methodist clergy, the work of the MFSS was instrumental in leading the Methodist Episcopal Church in 1908 to adopt the first social creed by any American Protestant denomination—a creed that formed the basis for the one adopted later that year by the Federal Council of Churches (see METHODISM, NORTH AMERICA). Among the primary issues addressed by the Methodist and Federal Council creeds were limitations on working hours, the abolition of child labor, and the assertion that the Golden Rule of Christ be applied as the primary law to govern societal conduct. For the next decade the Federal Council's Commission on Social Service conducted numerous social survey reports designed to enable Protestant churches to eradicate social problems in both urban and rural contexts. The efforts of the Federal Council were supplemented by numerous Protestant initiatives intended to promote social service efforts in denominations, ecumenical assemblies, and local churches.

The early twentieth century also witnessed the emergence of a strong Social Gospel tradition in Canadian Protestantism that included leaders such as J. S. Woodworth (1874–1942) and Charles Gordon (pseudonym, Ralph Connor) (1860–1937). Although Canadian churches and leaders developed social service and ecumenical ministries that paralleled their American counterparts, the Canadian context produced one institutional synthesis that never occurred in the United States or Great Britain: the creation of a new denomination. The growing prominence of the Social Gospel tradition in both the Presbyterian and Methodist churches in Canada was a contributing factor to the creation of the UNITED CHURCH OF CANADA in 1925.

Although the Social Gospel has been credited with giving Protestant churches in the United States a vision of theological and cultural unity, the rise of the movement also signaled a growing theological rift within Western Protestantism. The emergence of PENTECOSTALISM and FUNDAMENTALISM in the early twentieth century signified what would become a divide between Protestants who believed exclusively in individualistic views of salvation and the literal interpretation of scripture and liberals who stressed diverse modes of interpretation. In this regard the liberal imprint of the Social Gospel contributed to the fundamentalist–modernist controversy that would lead to divisions in Western Protestantism after World War I.

Decline

The Social Gospel went into decline as a theological movement in the United States after World War I. Although scholars have pointed to the deaths in 1918 of Walter Rauschenbusch and Washington Gladden as a sign of the tradition's demise, the theological idealism of the Social Gospel remained prominent in Western Protestantism in the aftermath of World War I. Two factors can be identified as contributing to the movement's decline: the theological fractioning of the tradition and the rise of the theological tradition of NEO-ORTHODOXY.

The immediate cause for the decline of the Social Gospel was the splintering of the tradition's proponents in the aftermath of World War I. In 1918 the founding of the INTERCHURCH WORLD MOVEMENT (IWM) in the United States was a symbol for many Social Gospel leaders of their longstanding hope of building a cooperative world society in which Protestant churches would play the primary role. American postwar dissent, however, characterized by a series of major labor strikes and the vitriolic reaction of the American public against the 1917 Russian Revolution, created a rift among many Social Gospel proponents. Some proponents favored more gradualist reform initiatives and viewed the Allied victory in World War I as a sign of the coming Kingdom of God in Western society. Other church leaders, however, emerged disillusioned by the war's outcome. Many Social Gospel ministers, such as HARRY EMERSON FOSDICK, had served as YMCA chaplains in western Europe at the climax of World War I. Their experiences in Europe led to the emergence of a strong movement of Christian pacifism in American Protestantism during the 1920s.

Additionally, many Protestant leaders embraced more radical visions of Christian socialism, inspired partly by the example of communism in the Soviet Union. Several Social Gospel leaders were concerned about the American government's crackdown against the civil liberties of left-wing movements after World War I and became active in the American Civil Liberties Union (ACLU). The resulting factionalism among Social Gospel leaders contributed to a disintegration of the IWM and symbolized the emerging fragmentation of the earlier Protestant vision of building a unified Protestant society based on Western cultural suppositions.

Second, the ascendency of Neo-orthodoxy in the 1920s and 1930s challenged many of the liberal theological underpinnings of the Social Gospel. The writings of the Swiss theologian KARL BARTH signaled a strong theological challenge to the liberal idealism of the Social Gospel. In the United States the writings of REINHOLD NIEBUHR were especially important in challenging the optimistic, liberal theological roots of the Social Gospel. Niebuhr's 1932 work, *Moral Man and Immoral Society,* symbolized a growing disillusionment with theological liberalism among many church leaders in the wake of America's Great Depression and the rise of international fascism.

The neo-orthodox critique of the Social Gospel centered on two primary points. First, theologians like Reinhold Niebuhr and his brother H. RICHARD NIEBUHR critiqued the Social Gospel for its failure to differentiate the message of the Gospel from historical events. In juxtaposition to the Social Gospel emphasis that God worked through human institutions, the neo-orthodox movement stressed God's transcendence and the view that salvation could not be understood as solely connected to historical processes. Second, although not dismissing the imperative to work for social justice, neo-orthodox theologians attacked the Social Gospel for what it believed was the tradition's myopic view of human progress. The movement's leaders reacted to the rise of European fascism in the 1930s and critiqued the Social Gospel for its inability to develop an adequate theology of sin. Although some neo-orthodox theologians credited a few Social Gospel leaders such as Rauschenbusch for maintaining a theology that held in tension divine sovereignty and God's involvement in history, neo-orthodoxy castigated the general tendency of the Social Gospel to overemphasize human goodness and the perfectibility of society.

At the same time, the heirs to the Social Gospel theological tradition remained prominent in both British and North American Protestantism throughout the 1920s and 1930s. WILLIAM TEMPLE, Anglican clergyman and later the archbishop of Canterbury, was a major leader of the international ecumenical movement that emerged in the aftermath of World War I. The "Life and Work Conference" held in 1925 in Stockholm, Sweden, frequently viewed as the first modern international ecumenical conference of the twentieth century, echoed many of the predominant themes and theological suppositions of the Social Gospel, especially the conference's emphasis on the Kingdom of God. In the United States, several clergy, theologians, and church leaders continued to propagate many of the reform sentiments of the Social Gospel. In addition to Fosdick, influential liberal leaders who rose to prominence in the 1920s and 1930s included Francis McConnell (1871–1953) and G. Bromley Oxnam (1891–1963), both Methodist bishops, and GEORGIA HARKNESS, the first woman to hold an academic chair of theology in a North American theological seminary.

The 1920s and 1930s also witnessed the growing popularity of the Protestant periodical *The Christian Century*. This periodical's writers and its longtime editor CHARLES CLAYTON MORRISON (1874–1966) reflected many germane theological emphases of the Social Gospel that related to theological liberalism and Christian pacifism. Distinctive themes of Social Gospel liberalism were also evident in the teachings of non-Western religious leaders in the 1930s, including Indian independence leader Mohandas Gandhi (1869–1948) and the Japanese Protestant leader TOYOHIKO KAGAWA. The writings of these leaders were very popular within Western Protestantism, contributing to the growth of pacifist movements in Western Protestantism before World War II.

Many of the practical ideals espoused by Social Gospel leaders before World War I, particularly regarding government regulation of economic practices in the private sector, were enacted legislatively in many Western nations. In America the dissemination of Social Gospel ideals was evident within the state-sponsored economic initiatives enacted during the presidential administrations of Franklin Roosevelt in the 1930s. By the beginning of World War II, however, the majority of Western Protestant leaders had rejected the earlier progressive ideology of the Social Gospel era.

Assessment

Scholarship on the Social Gospel highlights the difficulty of defining the tradition because it never embodied a coherent systematic theological tradition. However, the tendency to apply the term "Social Gospel" chiefly to Protestant developments in the United States reflects the association of the tradition with the larger history of American Protestantism. The Social Gospel was analogous to the final historical era in American Protestantism in which Protestant churches assumed a taken-for-granted hegemony over the dominant religious and cultural lives of most Americans. As a historical movement, the Social Gospel reflected many of the cultural and class biases associated with the larger movement of progressivism in western Europe and North American society. The decline of the Social Gospel movement symbolized the ultimate demise of a larger Protestant vision of religious and cultural unity.

At the same time, the Social Gospel had a major impact on the future historical and theological development of twentieth-century Protestantism. The Social Gospel theological legacy stressed the necessity that Christian faith be integrated within the social institutions of secular society. This theme was critical to the subsequent development of many twentieth-century mainline Protestant traditions whose ministries were predicated on a belief that the church needed to embrace and reform social, political, religious, and cultural institutions. The Social Gospel also contributed to a larger theological tradition that Christian belief and practice needed to work on behalf of the poor and the oppressed in society. In addition to the impact of the tradition on twentieth-century ecumenical social teachings, the theological writings of the Social Gospel have had a germane influence on many currents in late twentieth-century theology and social ethics. The American civil rights leader and Baptist minister MARTIN LUTHER KING JR. cited Walter Rauschenbusch as one of his major intellectual influences. Theological themes of many Social Gospel writers, especially the tradition's emphasis on the rights of the poor, have been evident within currents of late twentieth-century liberation theology.

The Social Gospel embodied a high optimism in human progress that accentuated many of the larger social and theological aspirations of Western Protestant churches in the late nineteenth and early twentieth centuries. At the same time, the tradition crafted a larger legacy of social activism that has been a predominant feature of many Protestant leaders and denominations throughout the twentieth century.

References and Further Reading

Allen, Richard. *The Social Passion: Religion and Social Reform in Canada, 1914–28.* Toronto and Buffalo: University of Toronto Press, 1971.

Carter, Paul. *The Decline and Revival of the Social Gospel: Social and Political Liberalism in American Protestant Churches, 1920–1940.* Ithaca, NY: Cornell University Press, 1954.

Dorrien, Gary J. *Soul in Society: The Making and Renewal of Social Christianity.* Minneapolis, MN: Fortress Press, 1995.

Evans, Christopher H., ed. *Perspectives on the Social Gospel.* Lewiston, NY: Edwin Mellen Press, 1999.

Fishburn, Janet Forsythe. *The Fatherhood of God and the Victorian Family: The Social Gospel in America.* Philadelphia: Fortress Press, 1981.

Gorrell, Donald K. *The Age of Social Responsibility: The Social Gospel in the Progressive Era, 1900–1920.* Macon, GA: Mercer University Press, 1988.

Handy, Robert T., ed. *The Social Gospel in America: 1870–1920.* New York: Oxford University Press, 1966.

Hopkins, Charles Howard. *The Rise of the Social Gospel in American Protestantism.* New Haven: Yale University Press, 1940.

Hutchison, William R. "The Americanness of the Social Gospel: An Inquiry into Contemporary History." *Church History* 44 (1975): 367–381.

King, William McGuire. " 'History as Revelation' in the Theology of the Social Gospel." *Harvard Theological Review* 76 no. 1 (1983): 109–129.

Lindley, Susan Hill. " 'Neglected Voices' and Praxis in the Social Gospel." *Journal of Religious Ethics* 18 (1990): 75–101.

Lindsey, William D. "Taking a New Look at the Social Gospel." In *Shailer Mathews's Lives of Jesus: The Search for a Theological Foundation for the Social Gospel,* 1–33. Albany: State University of New York Press, 1997.

Luker, Ralph E. *The Social Gospel in Black and White: American Racial Reform, 1885–1912.* Chapel Hill: University of North Carolina Press, 1991.

McDowell, John Patrick. *The Social Gospel in the South: The Woman's Home Mission Movement in the Methodist Episcopal Church, South, 1886–1939.* Baton Rouge: Louisiana State University Press, 1982.

Phillips, Paul T. *A Kingdom on Earth: Anglo-American Social Christianity, 1880–1940.* University Park: The Pennsylvania State University Press, 1996.

White, Ronald C., Jr., and C. Howard Hopkins. *The Social Gospel: Religion and Reform in Changing America.* Philadelphia: Temple University Press, 1976.

CHRISTOPHER H. EVANS

SOCIAL REFORMERS AND PREACHERS

See Social Gospel

SOCIALISM, CHRISTIAN

Although Socialism arose as a Continental European phenomenon, the term "Christian Socialism" is generally used to describe a particular Protestant movement that originated in ENGLAND around 1848. Led mainly by Anglican priests this movement responded to the severe economic crisis, which had created great hardship among English industrial workers, as well as to the widespread influence of capitalist economic thought that praised competitive business and self-interest. Christian Socialists sought to create a more just society in which the working class could earn fair wages, have decent standards of living and education, and share political responsibilities with the middle and upper classes. They believed that any economic order should be based on a sense of fellowship among human beings as equal children of God, and they were confident that true Christian belief would necessarily lead to socialist principles and action, including cooperation and shared ownership of certain kinds of property. Although Christian Socialism declined in England in the 1850s (with a revival in the 1880s), socialist ideals were later taken up in other countries and by other schools of Christian thought such as LIBERAL PROTESTANTISM and LIBERATION THEOLOGY. Historically, Christian Socialism as a school of thought tended to flourish most where economic and political injustice is felt most keenly, whereas it often fades into the background during times of prosperity.

Background and Context in England

In 1776 Adam Smith (1723–1790) published *Wealth of Nations,* which is generally considered to mark the beginning of political economy as a discipline (see ECONOMICS). In it he proposed that human economic behavior (like working, buying, and selling) is motivated by individual self-interest, but that even when individuals act selfishly, a force (sometimes referred to as an "invisible hand") guides their actions so as to work toward the benefit of society as a whole. Because of this faith that the economy essentially runs by itself, Smith and his successors thought the most appropriate way for governments to handle economics was through *laissez-faire* capitalism; that is, to leave people and markets alone and let them act without too many regulations. This kind of freedom would ensure the best outcome for everybody.

The trouble that many people found with this view of economics was that wealthy people who owned the means of production tended to benefit the most, whereas wage laborers tended to suffer. This was especially true when the economy was weak and there were not enough jobs to go around, as was the case in England in the mid-nineteenth century. As a result members of the working class had begun to call for government action. In the 1820s and 1830s a socialist named Robert Owen (1771–1858) had advocated trade unions for laborers as a way for them to earn better wages, but struggles and failures within the Owenite movement caused it to fail. Another movement, Chartism (named for the People's Charter of 1838), called for political reform, including voting rights for all males, although Chartism, too, lacked unified leadership, as well as being undermined by trade unionism, and this movement had also failed.

Socialism in France and Germany

As INDUSTRIALIZATION began to spread, and with it the ideals of capitalism, workers found themselves laboring under cruel conditions with little or no power to change them. A number of French thinkers began to argue for socialist ideals—such as cooperation among workers and the sharing of wealth—often with a religious flavor. Henri de Saint-Simon (1760–1825) said Jesus's golden rule of loving one's neighbor as oneself should govern both employers and laborers. Pierre Leroux (1797–1871), one of the first to use the term "socialism" in FRANCE, called Jesus the "greatest economist" and advocated making the kingdom of God a reality on earth. Hugues-Félicité Robert de Lamennais (1782–1854), a Catholic priest, undertook social reform with the idea that society would be most just under the head of the church, although he denied that he was a socialist if socialism meant the abolition of private property. Other French socialist thinkers were less overtly religious. In 1840 Pierre Joseph Proudhon (1809–1865) published his pamphlet *What is Property?*, in which he declared that private property is essentially theft.

Socialism in France remained a largely intellectual movement until workers themselves began joining in. In Paris in 1848 conditions were ripe for revolt; industrial workers were concentrated in the city, but because of recent crop failures and subsequent depression, unemployment was high and living conditions were harsh. Tensions came to a head at a demonstration in June and workers began to riot, leading to the accidental death of Archbishop Denis-Auguste Affre, who had been sympathetic to the workers' cause. In addition thousands of other demonstrators were killed by government forces. With this violent revolt, the poor lost much political support from the Catholic Church. Because workers and their intellectual allies felt the church had turned against them, French socialism developed with a largely anticlerical tone and did not use the qualifier "Christian."

Socialism was moving among German-speaking people as well. Franz von Baader (1765–1841), a Catholic layperson and prolific writer who admired Lammenais, was the first to write in German of a "Christian social principle," by which he meant Jesus's command to love God and love one's neighbor as oneself. Later on, the Catholic archbishop of Mainz, Wilhelm Emmanuel von Ketteler (1811–1877), who felt a special concern for the plight of workers and the poor, would continue to seek a "third way" between unquestioned capitalism and greed on the one hand and total COMMUNISM of property on the other. Drawing largely from the writings of Thomas Aquinas, Ketteler affirmed the human right to own private property (and therefore rejected political socialism), but he qualified this right by emphasizing that all creation is ultimately God's and therefore to be used for the common good. He called on wealthy Christians not only to give alms for the poor, but also to address the actual causes of poverty; and he encouraged laborers to form associations or trade unions to improve their wages and working conditions. There were a small number of Protestants who also aligned themselves with the Catholic social movement in GERMANY, such as Victor Aimé Huber (1800–1869) and Lutheran pastor JOHANN HEINRICH WICHERN (1808–1881), although political hostility between Catholics and Protestants at the time prevented widespread collaboration. German-speaking Protestants, including LEONHARD RAGAZ (1868–1945) and Swiss theologian KARL BARTH (1886–1968), would become more prominent in the religious socialism of the twentieth century.

Although socialist causes in Germany enjoyed greater support from Catholics than in France, not all German-speaking socialists were open to Christian influences. A group of German exiles who called themselves the Communist League gathered in Brussels in 1847. Among them were Karl Marx (1818–1883) and Friedrich Engels (1820–1895) who would publish the *Communist Manifesto* in London in 1848. Marx believed religion was little more than an "opiate" for the poor, a tool to keep them resigned to their low status in life, and he wanted his movement to have nothing to do with Christian ideas of any kind. He referred to Ketteler as a "dog," and attacked one of his predecessors in the socialist movement, Wilhelm Weitling (1808–1871), who portrayed Jesus as a revolutionary communist and favored the abolition of private property as the means to fight poverty. Steeped in the tradition of Adam Smith, Marx believed economics should be treated scientifically rather than morally, and he sought to create a nonreligious basis for socialism that relied less on ethical norms and more on social science.

The Christian Socialist Movement in England, 1848–1854

Conditions in England in 1848 seem to have provided the fertile ground necessary for the birth of an explicitly Christian Socialism. England had observed the bloody revolts in France with horror, and fears arose that a similar violent revolt would break out among British workers who were likewise suffering under industrialization. A lawyer, John Malcolm Forbes Ludlow (1821–1911), who had been educated in France, wanted to Christianize the socialism he saw being imported to England from the Continent. He wrote to Anglican vicar FREDERICK DENISON MAURICE (1805–1872) of his idea to start a movement, and together with another clergyman, CHARLES KINGSLEY (1819–1875), they wrote a proclamation for the workers of London telling them that the Anglican Church sympathized with them but encouraged them not to riot (see ANGLICANISM). The group then briefly published a newspaper for workers called *Politics for the People,* which upheld the ideals of socialism but presented them as Christian, rather than as political, concepts. They redefined "liberty, equality, and fraternity," watchwords of the FRENCH REVOLUTION, in Christian terms of human connection and fellowship, appealing to common humanity under God rather than precise political or economic equality.

The Christian Socialists also taught against the doctrine of self-interest that had taken hold of politics and economic thought. They were not against the possibility of capitalism in principle, nor against the idea that some people must labor while others own property. Rather than self-interest and competition being the inherent laws of economics, however, Christian Socialism preached that cooperation was God's plan, serving the common good rather than the selfish individual good.

None of those who began this Christian Socialist movement was a member of the working class. To diversify their group, the founders began a BIBLE study

under Maurice's leading to which they invited some leaders of the workers' movement. At the same time Maurice began teaching at conferences for workers to bridge the chasm between workers and the church, which workers tended to associate with the wealthy. He also taught to educate the bourgeoisie, who (because of what they had seen in Europe) associated the term "socialism" with atheism and general immorality. Maurice believed that the CHURCH—which was "communist in principle"—was the only body in which all were included and equal; but he believed strongly that the state was not meant to be communist. Although all are equals in the sight of God, the state rests on the need for diversity and even inequality.

The Christian Socialist movement was thus more Christian than socialist in 1848. This changed somewhat when the group came into contact with a French socialist, Jules St. Andre le Chevalier (1806–1862), who helped to politicize the movement. They learned from him more about the socialist principles of Saint-Simon, Charles Fourier (1772–1837), Proudhon, and others; and he learned from them to believe that the church was the true embodiment of the socialist principles of fellowship or "association." The task of Christian Socialism was thus laid out more clearly: to challenge the theory of political economy that glorified competition, and to set good examples of Christian production, distribution, and consumption. With this, Christian Socialism moved out of the realm of ideas toward a policy of action. They began setting up workers' associations that divided profits on labor, as a way of protesting against competition and demonstrating that cooperation could work.

Maurice began publishing *Tracts on Christian Socialism* in 1850 to make the movement's objectives clear to the public. He wrote that the only true foundation for socialism was Christianity, and that Christianity would necessarily lead to socialism. He rejected any socialism that did not have its basis in religion (this would include Marxism) and also blamed church leaders for not teaching Christianity properly. Fellowship was God's natural order for humankind, but competition was a creation of human sinfulness. Socialism was thus not a threat to social order nor was it even a political agenda, but was a way of organizing society on Christian principles.

As Maurice sought to educate the upper classes, Ludlow began to publish another newspaper in 1850, *The Christian Socialist,* to correct what he considered wrong socialist views among workers. He emphasized that socialism was primarily spiritual, a church movement seeking to realize itself in the world of industry. Any economic system not based on the teachings of Christ was wrong; thus the "laws" of economics as seen by political economy were false. Unlike Maurice,

Ludlow was in favor of common property, given that he believed Christian principles left no room for class distinctions. He approved of a democracy in which all members have equal rights and duties, and this led him to call also for reform in the Anglican Church itself, which he believed was too hierarchical.

As the movement grew it established a board to administer what it now called the "Society for Promoting Working Men's Associations" (SPWMA). Whereas Ludlow and others focused mainly on producer-based cooperation (e.g., the Working Tailors' Association), some in the group, such as Edward Neale, began to focus on consumer-based cooperation, setting up the Central Co-operative Agency. Ludlow feared consumer associations (for purposes of acquiring goods) were not as spiritual as producer associations. Ludlow and Neale also clashed on whether members of the movement should necessarily be Christian; Neale felt it was more important to include as many people as possible than to insist on Christian doctrines. Maurice sided with Neale; he also believed (against Ludlow) that Christian Socialism should not seek to become a political party. The name of *The Christian Socialist* was changed in 1852 to the *Journal of Association,* and because of Maurice's fame, Christian Socialism under his leadership gained much sympathy among workers and wealthy alike. Association was seen as being good for the poor and workers and it helped revive England's social conscience. It opened the door among politicians for serious thought about socialism and cooperation, which had previously seemed too threatening. Christian Socialism also stimulated a new tone in trade unionism, eventually leading to legislation that protected workers' cooperatives.

Nevertheless, the movement had begun its decline. The *Journal of Association* ceased printing, leading to a loss in profile for the movement. In 1853 Maurice was fired from his teaching position and decided to found a Working Men's College (1854), which would educate workers to make them fit for greater social responsibility. This model was widely imitated across England. When Maurice shifted his attention and energy from associative movements to EDUCATION, the movement followed, including a disillusioned Ludlow. This marked the end of the first wave of Christian Socialism in England.

Revival and Legacy of Christian Socialism

England enjoyed relative prosperity in the 1860s and 1870s, providing little impetus for workers' movements, although in the latter 1800s the Fabian Society and trade unions carried on socialist ideals. When recessions hit in the 1880s Christian Socialism found a wide audience again. In 1888 the LAMBETH CONFERENCE of Anglican bishops declared its sympathy for the state taking an active role in improving the workers' conditions, believing that to be compatible with Christian morals, and by 1900 Christian Socialism had become a prominent political force in England. Christian Socialism encouraged critique of English society and helped to create communication between the church and workers. Thus workers in England did not feel obligated to become either atheists or revolutionary communists, and instead were able to use the tools of democracy to further their objectives. In 1893 a number of Christian Socialists were influential in the formation of the Independent Labour Party.

The great change in the situation between 1848–54 and the 1880s and 1890s must be properly understood. At the former time, Socialism was just beginning. It had no generally accepted definition and little political influence. By the latter time, the working class had grown massively in numbers and political influence, not the least because of the extensions of the franchise. A Socialist party was a major force not only in England but most European countries. Karl Marx had emerged as the most influential Socialist thinker, against whom other Socialists had to define themselves, even if (as in the case of most Christian Socialists) they rejected many of his ideas. Clergymen were now seldom in a position to take a lead in the way Maurice and his colleagues had done in 1848, and the influence of Christian Socialism was exercised mainly through those individuals who became active in trade unions and Socialist parties.

Socialism also caught on in the UNITED STATES. In 1872 the Christian Labor Union formed to promote just wages and just prices; Marxists organized the Socialist Labor Party in 1877; and in 1889 the Society of Christian Socialists was founded. By 1912 the Socialist Party had 120,000 members, 1,200 elected officials, and 300 periodicals, including *The Christian Socialist,* which had 20,000 readers. What they shared in common was a rejection of the economic principles of competition and INDIVIDUALISM, and a desire to foster a just society through a sense of cooperation and fellowship. American churches were also sympathetic to the movement, and a Protestant theological movement known as the SOCIAL GOSPEL became prominent around the turn of the twentieth century, led by such preachers as WASHINGTON GLADDEN and WALTER RAUSCHENBUSCH. These Christians rejected any use of religion as an "opiate of the people" and sought ways to make the KINGDOM OF GOD a reality on earth, not only within the church but also in the realms of politics and economics. The belief that Christianity must include active involvement in the fostering of justice had a deep impact on twentieth-century American theology, and was furthered by such key figures as MARTIN LUTHER KING JR. and JAMES HAL CONE.

The prominence of Christian socialism in England and the United States stood in contrast to Continental Europe, where socialism still had a largely anticlerical tone arising from a persistent sense that the Catholic Church was unsympathetic to workers. Historically the Catholic Church was against socialism because of the church's belief that private property is in accordance with NATURAL LAW (MARTIN LUTHER and JOHN CALVIN likewise protected the right to private property against the Anabaptists of their time who promoted common property; see HUTTERITES), as well as because of socialism's frequent association with atheism and Marxism. In 1891 Pope Leo XIII (who referred to Archbishop Ketteler as "our great predecessor") sought to address the divide between the church and the poor. After commissioning a number of social and economic study groups in Rome and elsewhere, he wrote his papal encyclical *Rerum Novarum* ("New Things" or *On the Condition of Workers*). In it he advocated for workers' rights, encouraged the formation of Christian labor unions, and called for industrial reforms to improve working conditions. At the same time, however, he still rejected socialism (including Christian socialism) because of its call to abolish private property, as well as because of its previous tendencies toward revolution. Many workers and socialists at the time felt that Leo's encyclical was too mild in its criticism of capitalism and merely supported the status quo. Nevertheless, the pope's boldness in directly addressing economic matters encouraged Christians to become more engaged in politics. Catholic popes after Leo, including John XXIII and John Paul II, took seriously the need to protect workers from the more extreme consequences of capitalism. They rejected the idea that humans were merely instruments of production and, although they did not embrace socialism, they affirmed that much of what was good in socialist principles could be found in Christianity. Christian Socialism in the late twentieth century, although not calling itself socialism, thus found one of its most persuasive voices in Catholic Liberation Theology. Advocated by such Latin American thinkers as Peruvian priest Gustavo Gutierrez (*A Theology of Liberation*, 1973), Liberation Theology sought to reconcile Marxist social ideas with Christian theology and ETHICS.

In Germany, an Association of Religious Socialists (*Bund Religiöser Sozialisten Deutschlands*) was formed after World War I. Small in size, this association consisted of both those who sought to combine Marxian socialism with Christianity and those who were concerned about a proper Christian response to the various social issues and problems of the day. In a way, the pioneering efforts in this regard had come from SWITZERLAND already, late in the nineteenth century, with such figures as HERMANN KUTTER and Leonhard Ragaz. At issue was their conviction that Christianity had not succeeded in dealing with the social issues of the late nineteenth century.

In many European countries, the restructuring of political life after World War II brought the formation of political parties, which combined the terms "Christian" and "Social" or "Socialist" in their names, for example the *Christlich Soziale Union* in Bavaria. Though mainly supported by Catholics, these parties were a major political force for decades; at this time, however, only in Germany does this legacy continue to exist.

See also Oxford Movement

References and Further Reading

Christensen, Torben. *Origin and History of Christian Socialism 1848–54.* Aarhus, Denmark: Universitetsforlaget, 1962.

The Columbia Encyclopedia. Sixth edition. New York: Columbia University Press, 2002. http://www.bartleby.com/65/ch/Christ-soc.html (Accessed March 30, 2003).

Cort, John C. *Christian Socialism: An Informal History.* Maryknoll, NY: Orbis Books, 1988.

Dorrien, Gary. *Reconstructing the Common Good: Theology and the Social Order.* Maryknoll, NY: Orbis Books, 1990.

Jones, Peter D. *The Christian Socialist Revival 1877–1914: Religion, Class, and Social Conscience in Late-Victorian England.* Princeton, NJ: Princeton University Press, 1968.

Kaufmann, M. *Christian Socialism.* London: Kegan Paul, Trench & Co., 1888.

Raven, Charles E. *Christian Socialism 1848–1854.* London: Macmillan & Co., 1920.

Stauffer, John L. *Socialism in the Light of Scripture.* Altoona, PA: John L. Stauffer, 1959.

Wilkinson, Alan. *Christian Socialism: Scott Holland to Tony Blair.* London: SCM Press, 1998.

KATHRYN D. BLANCHARD

THE SOCIETY FOR PROMOTING CHRISTIAN KNOWLEDGE

The Society for Promoting Christian Knowledge (S.P.C.K.) was founded in 1699 by a CHURCH OF ENGLAND priest, THOMAS BRAY (1656–1730), and four lay associates, supported by the archbishop of Canterbury. Its purpose was to promote "Religion and Learning in any part of His Majesty's Plantations abroad, and to provide Catechetical Libraries and free Schools in the parishes at home."

The context in Britain was the GLORIOUS REVOLUTION of 1688, which had secured an unequivocally Protestant monarchy. Here, "at home," there was need for catechetical and general education for the impoverished mass of children, and provision of theological and general libraries for the poorer clergy. The context "abroad" was the emergent British empire, competing with the imperialism of the Roman Catholic nations, FRANCE and Spain. Bray's appointment as the bishop of London's commissary for Maryland alerted him to the needs of the church among settlers, indigenes, and slaves in North America. This appointment also prompted his other great creative achievement in 1701, the SOCIETY FOR THE PROPAGATION OF THE GOSPEL (S.P.G.), to recruit and send missionaries. These two societies inaugurated Protestant mission from Britain and Ireland, their work largely complementary. They represented a High Church form of Protestantism, exemplified in S.P.C.K.'s provision of bibles bound with the BOOK OF COMMON PRAYER. As societies dependent on voluntary support, they were characteristic creations of the golden age of philanthropy in Britain.

There have been various aspects to S.P.C.K.'s work in Britain. The commitment to "free Schools" was realized in the eighteenth century through support for the Charity Schools, which catechized and gave extremely basic education to poor children. For similar schools in WALES, S.P.C.K. published books, chiefly religious, in Welsh. The nineteenth century saw the state beginning to assume responsibility for schools, although the Church of England continued to educate large numbers with S.P.C.K. funding teacher training, school inspection, and publishing. Publishing in support of children's religious education and general theological publishing continued through the twentieth century. Bray's support for the large number of poor clergy in poor parishes was by the provision of parish libraries, work that S.P.C.K. sustained through the nineteenth and twentieth centuries, adding book grants for ordinands.

Initially S.P.C.K.'s work in the "Plantations" was through the provision of libraries, although S.P.G. became increasingly responsible for this in North America. Tens of thousands of books were sent there during the eighteenth century, these having a significant impact on religious and cultural developments. An unexpected but important role for S.P.C.K. came with a request in 1709 to support Lutheran missionaries beginning work then in South India, a role more appropriate to S.P.G. but precluded by its constitution until 1826, when this task was devolved to it. With the extension of British colonial rule S.P.C.K. translation, publishing, and distribution work became virtually global throughout the Anglican Communion. The society entered the third millennium with such work in 120 countries and autonomous sister S.P.C.K. organizations in INDIA, AUSTRALIA, NEW ZEALAND, and the UNITED STATES.

References and Further Reading

Clarke, W. K. L. *History of the S.P.C.K.* London: S.P.C.K., 1959.

Thompson, H. P. *Thomas Bray.* London: S.P.C.K., 1954.

DANIEL O'CONNOR

THE SOCIETY FOR THE PROPAGATION OF THE GOSPEL

Founded by Royal Charter in 1701, the Society for the Propagation of the Gospel (SPG) was the CHURCH OF ENGLAND's response to the Roman Catholic Propaganda Fide (1622). The founder was THOMAS BRAY, previously creator of the SOCIETY FOR PROMOTING CHRISTIAN KNOWLEDGE (SPCK). Continental Protestants were co-opted. The charter authorized the Society to send missionaries to work among settlers, indigenes, and slaves in areas under British sovereignty, although its range was later widened. More than 400 missionaries, including a number of WOMEN, were sent to North and Central America, the CARIBBEAN and AUSTRALIA in the eighteenth century, and thousands were sent into Asia, South America, the Pacific, and AFRICA in the nineteenth and twentieth centuries, laying the foundations of the Anglican Communion of Churches.

Nineteenth-century developments of the Evangelical Revival and the OXFORD MOVEMENT had the effect of fragmenting the Church of England's missionary endeavors, although the SPG continued to seek to serve the whole church. In 1965, amalgamation with the Universities Mission to Central Africa, and subsequently with other, smaller agencies, led to the SPG becoming the United Society for the Propagation of the Gospel.

Educational and medical initiatives accompanied the SPG's evangelizing efforts, with hundreds of schools, colleges, and hospitals established. In the nineteenth and twentieth centuries, some SPG missionaries (e.g., ROLAND ALLEN, Mark Trollope, and J. C. Winslow) effectively promoted inculturation of church and belief, whereas a small number, including Krishna Mohan Banerjea, CHARLES FREER ANDREWS, and A. S. Cripps, bravely opposed COLONIALISM. In the later twentieth century, the Society was vigorous in opposition to apartheid in SOUTH AFRICA, and, into the twenty-first century, was doing effective medical work in the field of AIDS as well as advocating solutions to global indebtedness.

See also Missions; Missionary Organizations

References and Further Reading

O'Connor, D. *Three Centuries of Mission. The United Society for the Propagation of the Gospel 1701–2000.* London and New York: Continuum, 2000.

DANIEL O'CONNOR

SOCIETY OF BROTHERS (BRUDERHOF)

In early twentieth century Germany, Eberhard Arnold began a search for "true Christian community" that led him, his family, and a few disciples to establish a small Christian communitarian settlement in the 1920s, later called the Society of Brothers or Bruderhof. University studies in church history acquainted him with Anabaptist Writings (see ANABAPTISM), the most attractive of which were those of the sixteenth-century HUTTERITES, with whom he came to share views of community of goods. Only later did he discover that the Hutterites were not extinct but maintained a vibrant existence in the United States and Canada, still following the centuries-old customs and traditions he had read about. After a lengthy correspondence and a personal visit by Arnold, the Bruderhof in Germany united with the American and Canadian Hutterites in 1931.

The rise of National Socialism and the death of Arnold in 1935 created havoc for the Bruderhof church. Eventually forced out of Germany, the members settled briefly in England. However, with the outbreak of war, English society was uncomfortable with a strange, largely German group in their midst, and again they were forced to leave. They found refuge in Paraguay and Uruguay, where they struggled to survive while holding on to their Christian communitarian outlook and practice. Socioeconomic difficulties and internal strife in South America and the promise of a more suitable situation caused them to migrate en masse in 1961 to the United States where they established settlements in New York, Pennsylvania, and Connecticut. There were later efforts to establish settlements in Germany and Nigeria.

From the beginning of the union of Arnold's group with the "Western Hutterites" (whose settlements were primarily in the U.S. Midwest and central plains of Canada), distance and circumstance plagued the concerted efforts of both to enrich the relationship. Despite significant ideological and theological similarities, differences in historical background, socioeconomic perspectives, and especially views of what constitutes true Christian discipleship created considerable tension. The "Western Hutterites" share a much narrower, homogeneous Germanic genealogy dating to the mass migration from Hutterite settlements in Russia in the 1880s, and they maintain almost exclusively an agricultural economy. The continued intermarriage within this group over the decades reinforced social homogeneity and their numerical growth was through a high birth rate rather than "outside" converts. On the other hand, the "Eastern Hutterites" (now called Society of Brothers) settled in the northeast United States and developed a small industry economy. Their membership is largely made up of converts from the outside, although a few trace their heritage to the Arnold family and early disciples. They are much more aggressive in EVANGELISM, largely centered on promoting PACIFISM and activism against such practices as capital punishment, and many have joined them from other types of communitarian endeavors. Tensions between the Western Hutterites and the Society have led to periods of estrangement from 1955 to 1974 and from 1995 to the present.

References and Further Reading

Arnold, Emmy. *Torches Together: The Beginning and Early Years of the Bruderhof Communities.* Rifton, NY: Plough Publishing House, 1984.

Bohlken-Zumpe, Elizabeth. *Torches Extinguished: Memories of a Communal Bruderhof Childhood in Paraguay, Europe and the USA.* San Francisco: Carrier Pigeon Press–The Peregrine Foundation, 1993.

Brothers Unite: An Account of the Uniting of Eberhard Arnold and the Rhoen Bruderhof with the Hutterian Church. Edited by Hutterian Brethren in America. Rifton, NY: Plough Publishing House, 1979.

Mow, Merrill. *Torches Rekindled: The Bruderhof's Struggle for Renewal.* Rifton, NY: Plough Publishing House, 1989.

WES HARRISON

SOCIETY OF FRIENDS IN NORTH AMERICA

From its English origins in the seventeenth century, the Society of Friends in North America has evolved and splintered to encompass broad diversity, ranging from fundamentalists to devotees of New Age spirituality.

Beginnings

The roots of Quakerism lie in ENGLAND, with GEORGE FOX (1624–1691). Seeking the true church among the competing sects of the English revolution, between 1647 and 1652 Fox had a series of what he called "openings" in which he was convinced that God had spoken directly to him. Among Fox's teachings were the existence of an "Inward Light" of Christ in all people; direct revelation from God without priestly intermediaries; worship based on silent waiting, with all worshipers theoretically able to preach if led by the Holy Spirit; pacifism; the equality of men and women in the ministry and most religious affairs; and a series of peculiarities, such as a refusal to swear oaths or to use the titles of social superiors. The popular impression that Fox's followers quaked when under the influence of the Holy Spirit led to the pejorative nickname "Quaker," one which Friends began to use themselves.

In 1656 several English Quakers, women prominent among them, visited New England, New Netherland, Maryland, and Virginia. Only in Rhode Island did they find toleration. Persecution was worst in Massachusetts; between 1659 and 1661 Massachusetts authorities hanged three men and one woman.

Persecution in England in the 1660s led Friends to establish colonies in North America as havens. The major Quaker colony was Pennsylvania, granted to WILLIAM PENN (1644–1718) in 1681. Penn's government was a curious amalgam of Quaker liberalism and medieval lordship; he guaranteed toleration to all Christians, provided for an elected assembly, and tried to deal fairly with Native Americans, while at the same time reserving ultimate authority to himself.

In the mid-eighteenth century, a feeling of spiritual deterioration developed. Quaker leaders, most notably JOHN WOOLMAN (1720–1772), led a reform movement designed to return Friends to spiritual fervor and disciplinary rigor. Through rigid enforcement of church discipline, especially rules against marriage with non-Quakers, this movement was responsible for the loss of thousands of members. On the other hand, while attempting to build up Quaker defenses against "the world," it made Quakers leaders in various humanitarian movements, particularly those involving American Indians and African Americans. Friends became public opponents of slavery. By 1784 all of the American yearly meetings had ruled that members who owned slaves must free them unconditionally.

The nineteenth century witnessed the splintering of American Quakerism in a series of schisms whose impact is still visible. At their center was an influential minister from Long Island, Elias Hicks (1748–1830). Hicks saw himself as a defender of traditional Quakerism. He emphasized the power and authority of the Inward Light over that of the written Scriptures. He also defined the divinity of Christ in Sabelian terms: Christ had become divine, the Son of God, through His perfect obedience to the Inward Light. Hicks encountered opposition especially among the leaders of Philadelphia Yearly Meeting, whose views on Christ and the Bible were similar to those of non-Quaker evangelicals. Their attempts to silence Hicks and his supporters led to a split in 1827 and 1828, with the orthodox emerging as the majority.

Quaker fractiousness continued after this schism. In the 1840s and 1850s Hicksite Friends found themselves badly divided over how they should respond to the abolitionist, women's rights, and nonresistance movements. Some Hicksites, most notably LUCRETIA COFFIN MOTT (1793–1880), championed Quaker participation. A majority of Hicksites were more conservative, denouncing ties with non-Friends as threatening Quaker peculiarity. Many of the radical Hicksite reformers split off to form what they called Congregational or Progressive Friends meetings.

Orthodox Friends also experienced tensions between 1830 and 1860. An English Quaker minister, Joseph John Gurney (1788–1847) championed an evangelical vision of Quakerism, including the necessity for an instantaneous conversion experience, the superiority of the Bible to the Inner Light, and the desirability of joining with non-Quaker evangelicals in good works, such as temperance, education, prison reform, and SUNDAY SCHOOL movements. Gurney traveled in the United States between 1837 and 1840, winning considerable support among a majority of Orthodox Friends, but some Orthodox Friends criticized Gurney as compromising Quaker distinctiveness, most notably Rhode Island Friend John Wilbur (1774–1856).

These gaps widened after the CIVIL WAR. Hicksite Friends became more self-consciously liberal. They also developed or adapted new institutions, like Sunday Schools (First Day Schools for Hicksites), and opened the third Quaker college in the world, Swarthmore in Philadelphia, in 1869. In 1900 the Hicksite yearly meetings merged biennial conferences on education and reform under an umbrella organization, Friends General Conference.

Orthodox Friends changed more radically. After 1870, most Gurneyite Friends meetings were swept up in a wave of revivalism imported largely from the interdenominational second-experience holiness movement. Under its influence, pastors were hired, music and choirs became part of worship, the Peace Testimony was abandoned, and in many places meetings were renamed the "Friends Church." Such Friends also championed Quaker work in foreign missions, laying the groundwork for the growth of Quakerism in AFRICA, LATIN AMERICA, the CARIBBEAN, and Asia. This movement brought in thousands of new members, but also led to a new round of splits between 1877 and 1904.

The 1890s saw a reaction develop among Gurneyites. This movement found its leader in Haverford College professor RUFUS M. JONES (1863–1948), who tried to meld Quaker doctrine with the modernist movement. But his work, especially his editorship of the periodical, the *American Friend,* aroused considerable opposition from other Gurneyites, who embraced views that were similar to those of the emerging Fundamentalist movement. Modernist and Fundamentalist Friends battled for control of the central Gurneyite organization, the Five Years Meeting, formed in 1902, culminating in the formation in 1947 of the Association of Evangelical Friends, now known as Evangelical Friends International (EFI).

The most visible Quaker activities in twentieth-century America involved social activism. Best known has been the American Friends Service Committee, formed by Friends of all persuasions in 1917 as a vehicle for Quaker nonviolent service during World War I.

American Quakerism today spans the spectrum of Christianity and beyond. Many pastoral Friends are allied with the most conservative elements of American EVANGELICALISM. Many in the unprogrammed yearly meetings embrace a Universalist outlook that argues that Quakerism is not necessarily Christian or even theistic. Total membership is now about 90,000.

References and Further Reading

Bacon, Margaret Hope. *Mothers of Feminism: The Story of Quaker Women in America.* San Francisco: Harpers' Row, 1986.

Barbour, Hugh, and J. William Frost. *The Quakers.* Westport, CT: Greenwood, 1988.

Punshon, John. *Portrait in Grey: A Short History of the Quakers.* London: Quaker Home Service, 1984.

THOMAS D. HAMM

SOCINIANISM

Socinianism refers to a number of Antitrinitarian churches in POLAND, Lithuania, and elsewhere shaped by the thought of FAUSTO PAOLO SOZZINI (see ANTI-TRINITARIANISM). Several groups and religious entities fall within the definition of eighteenth-century Socinianism. The term itself was created by Protestant theologians in the seventeenth century and was rejected by Socinians. Although "Socinianism" was meant to describe them, they preferred to be called "Christians," "Polish Brethren," or "Unitarians."

History of Socinianism in Poland

Socinianism is considered to be a continuation of sixteenth-century Antitrinitarianism, despite the fact that reforms by Augusto Sozzini changed its doctrinal shape. Between 1601 and 1602 Sozzini worked as a tutor in Rakow, a town that soon became a capital of the movement, which it remained until 1638. In 1606–1609 and 1619 Sozzini's favored successor Valentius Smalcius continued the work of his teacher. Even though the name of the famous theologian from Siena was remembered, believers themselves opposed being called Socinians.

Rakow was also the place where a Socinian educational institution was founded in 1601. Excellent teaching made this academic institution (the first students arrived in 1603) extremely challenging. No wonder it attracted many Protestant and even Catholic students. The school in Rakow also included a modest theological faculty for future Socinianic clergy. It never regained its former glamour after it was closed in 1638 and moved to Kisielin in the Wolyn district.

Rakow was also the place of Sebastian Sternicki's print shop that published some 250–300 books in Polish, German, Flemish, and Latin, a great majority of which were in theology (for example, the *Racovian Catechism* [first Polish edition, 1605; first German edition, 1608; first Latin edition, 1609]). A vast number of books from the Rakow press were secretly distributed throughout the whole of Europe. Many of the Socinians in the Polish–Lithuanian Commonwealth were German. Together with the Poles they formed the administrative and intellectual elites of the movement. This included such names as Johann Volker (d. 1658), author of the basic Socinian doctrinal work entitled *De vera religione* ("Concerning true religion," 1630); Johann Crell (1590–1633), an intellectual and biblical scholar; and Joachim Stegman, senior (1592–1633), mathematician and theologian. The vast majority of German Socinians—for example, Valentius Smalcius—were Polish citizens who adapted to the new culture. On the other hand, German presence in the community allowed the church to maintain its missions in areas where German was a native language.

Although Socinianism enjoyed relatively good conditions during its early development, subsequent years brought problems and defeats caused by the Catholic Counter-Reformation, which considered Socinianism its greatest enemy.

An act of the Polish Senate in 1638, passed after schoolboys were allegedly seen throwing stones at a wayside cross, ordered the closing of schools and the printing office in Rakow. The seminary was moved to Wolyn, where it did not manage to regain its former importance and reputation. In 1647 Socinians were refused the right to any pedagogical or PUBLISHING activity in the territory of the Commonwealth. Finally in 1648 Catholics excluded Socinianism from the so-called Warsaw Confederation (1573), an act that had been the guarantee of freedom of religion to all.

Nevertheless, the main blow to Polish–Lithuanian Socinianism came after the Swedish War, during which part of the non-Catholic gentry and leaders declared their support for SWEDEN. This caused an increase of reluctance skillfully fomented by Catholic propaganda. On July 10, 1658 Parliament ordered the expulsion within three years of the "Arians" (Socinians) under the penalty of death or confiscation of all property. This, however, was only binding for those Socinians who refused to convert to Catholicism. In

1659 Parliament decided not to delay any longer and enforced the earlier law. Socinians were refused protection, and their religion was found unlawful in 1660.

Socinian Emigration

Probably only a couple of thousand Socinians decided to leave the country. Not only did the rest stay and officially agree to practice the religion of the majority, but also supplied the outlawed Socinians with financial aid. This phenomenon, which existed until the end of the eighteenth century, is known as Crypto-Socinianism. Despite the draconian law, none of the Socinians was sentenced to death. However, cases of expulsion from the country or fines for delays in converting to Catholicism were common.

Intensified Socinian emigration from Poland took place in the fall of 1660, when a couple hundred Socinians were forced to Transylvania. Robbed of the last penny along the way, Socinians were hospitably welcomed by the Hungarian Unitarians. The refugees established local religious communities that managed to preserve the national identity of their members. They lasted until 1784. Years of Hungarian influence on the younger generations weakened differences and enabled Socinians to join the national church of HUNGARY.

The situation of emigrants in East Prussia and Neumark was worse. Despite being constantly attacked by Lutheran CLERGY, the small community managed to survive until the beginning of the nineteenth century.

A third group, led by a historian and astronomer Stanislaw Lubieniecki, unsuccessfully looked for protection in North GERMANY and the Palatinate, but the influence of the Lutherans was too strong. Therefore a part of the group decided to settle in the NETHERLANDS with their famous leader Anrzej Wiszowaty (1608–1678), the author of the masterpiece *Religio rationalis* ("Rational religion"). He and his son Benedict (who died after 1704 as a pastor of exiles) tried to preserve the heritage and history of Socinianism. Thus between 1665 and 1668 Andrzej Wiszowaty published the eight-volume work called *Bibliotheca a Fretrum Polonorum (Library of Polish Brethren)* consisting of pieces written by F. Sozzini, J. Crell, J. Szichling, and J. L. Wolzogen. (An incomplete collection of works by Samuel Przypkowski titled *Cognitationes sacra* published in 1692 was a ninth volume.) New editions of "the Racovian Catechism" (1665, 1680, 1681, 1684), *Bibliotheca Antitrinitariorum (Antitrinitarian Library)* (1684) by Christoph Sondius, and *Historia reformationis Polonicae (History of Polish Reformation)* (1685) by Stanislaw Lubieniowski were issued thanks to Wiszowaty's devotion and persistence.

The Socinian diaspora remained in continuous contact among themselves. This contact was lost in the eighteenth century when local churches absorbed emigration. Until this time Transylvania and Prussia were the places where regular synods met. The latter also included representatives of Crypto-Socinianism from the Polish–Lithuanian Commonwealth. Leaders of emigration churches—Stanislaw Lubieniowski, Samuel Przypkowski, and Andrzej Wiszowaty—endeavored often to encourage their English and Dutch brethren to be generous. They also sought to return to Poland through fruitless efforts to obtain the repeal of the act that declared Socinians outlaws.

The Spread of Socinianism in Europe

Fausto Sozzini and his successors had made promoting religion one of their top priorities. Books printed in Rakow were dispersed all over Europe. Traveling Socinians, who were sometimes specially trained for that kind of mission, soon became the main instruments of propaganda.

German universities, attended by Polish students and tutors who were Socinian activists, also became an extremely important terrain for missionary activity. The reputation of Ernst Solar, a philosopher popular among students, was one of the greatest Socinian successes at the University at Altdorf. This center of Crypto-Socinianism (from 1605 to 1616) that had remained in close relations with Rakow was closed after an intervention of University activists.

The dissent of Rakow occasioned a great concern and a brisk polemics among Lutheran clergy. Earl M. Wilbur suggested that in seventeenth- and eighteenth-century Germany some 700 proceedings against Socinians took place.

Before that time, as early as 1598, there were signs of Socinian activity in the Netherlands. That is the time when Andrzej Wojowski and Christoph Ostrorodt appeared there. However, they were soon dismissed from the country and the books from Rakow they brought with them were burned. Although their ideas were treated with reserve, Socinians maintained close relations with the Remonstrants in the Netherlands. They never managed to attract their friends with Trinitarian and soteriological notions. Nevertheless, the influence of Socinianism on two representatives of the "left wing" of the Remonstrants, also known as Collegiants, was significant. Two leaders of this stream, Johannes Geestteranus (1586–1622) and Dirk Camphuysen (1586–1622), were in a close contact with Rakow while translating biographies of F. Sozzini and V. Smalcius into Dutch.

Socinian propaganda found a fertile ground in ENGLAND as well. Two editions of the Racovian Catechism in 1614 and 1624 (with a false issue date of 1609) initiated the process. The real expansion of the movement began in the thirties of the seventeenth century. Theologians from the so-called Tew Circle, John Hales (1584–1654) and Wiliam Chillingworth (1602–1644) seemed to be interested in Socinianism. Both had a significant influence on English religious thought, including JOHN LOCKE, who was familiar with Socinianism. John Biddle (1615–1662), also known as a father of English Unitarianism, translated the works of Samuel Przypkowski and Joachim Stegmann. Nevertheless, he had a separate view of the role of the Holy Spirit. Socinianism seemed to have interested ISAAC NEWTON as well.

The Doctrines of Socinianism

Although Fausto Sozzini was a source of the vital part of concepts that became Socinian doctrine, his successors enriched it with new ideas or modified some important issues.

The function of the Holy Trinity is the most important part of Socinian belief. It was also the main subject of Socinian literature. Nevertheless, Socinian thought produced no new argumentation beyond what is already found in early works of Antitrinitarians from ITALY, Poland, or Transylvania. The reflection on God, on the other hand, was without doubt deepened by seventeenth-century philosophy. Socinians believed God to be the only creator of the world and an eternally existing matter. According to Socinians, God is a substance localized in HEAVEN, acting gradually *(per gradus)* over time in the world. He is immutable and his decisions do not belong to his substance.

Christ is a human being *(purus homo)* born without SIN from the VIRGIN MARY. However, he is not everlasting. According to F. Sozzini and other Socinian theologians, Jesus was in heaven where he received instructions from his Father before he was sent on a mission to earth.

Socinianism—just like Sozzini—rejected the redemptive role of the crucified Christ, claiming that his main aim was to teach people the way to SALVATION. They also rejected the dogma of original SIN, insisting that it never destroyed the perceptive abilities or moral dispositions of humankind. Humans must have a full disposition of their free will, otherwise any good deed would be impossible and God would be responsible for sin.

Humans are mortal. Immortality is a gift only to those who believe in Christ and fulfill his commandments. The souls of unbelievers will be annihilated.

Elements of religious rationalism are an important part of Sozzini's thought. Sozzini pointed out that religion must be in conformity with the intellect. In his opinion it is impossible for humans to discover the nature of God because revealed truth is partial. Sozzini's position was questioned by other theologians who proposed the idea of natural religion, giving an important role to the senses as a source of perception. Such notions were a substantial part of Joachim Stegmann and Samuel Przypkowski's already mentioned treatises *Religio rationalis* ("Rational Religion") published by Andrzej Wiszowaty. The mind is the highest judge on earth; therefore the Bible must be interpreted according to rational rules. The Holy Gospel is a source of truth *(supra rationem)* existing above the mind. This means that, even though the teachings of the Gospel cannot be fully understood, they are not contrary to reason *(contra rationem)*.

The social and political doctrines of Socinianism in its early stage were not much different from the views of Sozzini. As a source of the new approach he tried to find a connection between the radical ideas of the first Antitrinitarians and everyday life. He was not against possession of goods, feudalism, or holding offices, but was against CAPITAL PUNISHMENT and the active participation of believers in WAR (see PACIFISM).

The discussion over the state and wars was open by a Dutch Collegiant Daniel Brenius (1594–1664). His negative approach was expressed in *De qualitate regni Christi* ("About the Quality of Christ's Kingdom") (1641), a first statement of disapproval of both the state and its institutions. It became the catalyst of a long dispute between Socinian thinkers: Johann Ludwig Wolzoen (c. 1599–1661), Joachim Stegmann, Jr. (c. 1618–1678), Daniel Zwicker (1612–1678), Jonasz Szlichtyng (1592–1661), and Samuel Przypkowski (1592–1670). Wolzoen, Stegmann, and Zwicker declared their unambiguous opposition to supporting the state, whereas Szychtyng and Przypkowski sought to defend the old order. Treatises by Przypkowski played a most important role: *Animadversiones in bellum cui titulus est De qualitate regni Christi* ("Remarks on a Book with the title The Quality of Christ's Kingdom"), c. 1650; *De iure Christiani magistratu* ("About the Right of Christian Office"); *Apologia prolixior de iure Christiani magistratu* ("The Extended Apology about the Right of the Christian Magistracy"); *Vindiciae tractatus de magistratu* ("The Defense of the Treaty of the Magistracy"). In these works the author argued that because the spheres of the two institutions are not contradictory, state and church should cooperate for the sake of the citizens' best interest (see CHURCH AND STATE, OVERVIEW). Whereas the clergy is meant to use spiritual power with all those who voluntarily obey their orders, the state uses force to maintain order. Only cooperation of both organizations is a guarantee for a proper spiritual and secular life of communities. Przypkowki criticized Sozzini's argumentation, which closed the way of political participation for the members of the Socinian Church.

During the late phase of Socinian activity, both tendencies—the sectarian one close to ANABAPTISM and the civil one proposing Christians' full participation in the social and political life—coexisted. Nevertheless, emigrants seemed to appreciate the first more.

Socinian doctrine fascinated many eighteenth-century philosophers. Those with Protestant roots tended to overestimate the meaning and reach of Socinianism and saw it as a major danger for Catholicism. At the same time Western European Catholic thinkers seemed to be far less interested in it.

A majority of positive and moderate attitudes existed among philosophers who appreciated tolerance and the high level of morals in Socinian communities, although this should not imply the lack of any critique. The Socinian attempts to create a rational religion were disapproved by French philosopher PIERRE BAYLE (1647–1706). In his opinion any religion was irrational by its very nature. Another famous philosopher, Voltaire (1694–1778), sympathized with Socinians but considered their actions anachronistic— they should not attempt to attract new members in times indifferent to religion.

See also Unitarian Universalist Association

References and Further Reading

Balazs, Mihaly, and Gizella Keser, eds. *Gy rgy enyedi and Central European Unitarianism in the 16th–17th Century Countries.* Budapest, Hungary: Balessi Kiado, 2000.

Florida, Robert E. "Voltaire and the Socinians." In *Studies on Voltaire and the Eighteenth Century,* 122. Banbury, UK: Voltaire Foundation, 1974.

Kot, Stanislas. *Socinianism in Poland. The Social and Political Ideas of the Polish Antitrinitarians in the Sixteenth and Seventeenth Centuries.* Translated by Earl Morse Wilbur. Boston: Starr King Press, 1957.

Lubieniecki, Stanislas. *History of the Polish Reformation.* Translated and interpreted by George Hunston Williams. Minneapolis, MN: Fortress Press, 1995.

McLachlan, Herbert John. *Socinianism in Seventeenth Century England.* Oxford: Oxford University Press, 1952.

Ogonowski, Zbigniew. *Socinianism vs. Enlightenment. Studies on Philosophical-Religious Thought of Arians in Seventeenth Century Poland.* Warsaw: PWN Polish Scientific Publisher, 1966.

———, ed. *Arian's Thought in Seventeenth Century Poland. Anthology of Texts.* Wroclaw, Poland: Ossolineum, 1991.

Szczucki, Lech ed. *Socinianism and its Role in the Culture of Sixteenth to Seventeenth Centuries.* Warsaw: PWN Polish Scientific Publisher, 1983.

Tazbir, Janusz. *Polish Brothers on Exile. Studies on Arian's Emigration Times.* Warsaw: PWN Polish Scientific Publisher, 1977.

Wilbur, Earl Morse. *A History of Unitarianism. Socinianism and its Antecedents.* Cambridge, MA: Harvard University Press, 1946.

———. *A History of Unitarianism. In Transylvania, England, America.* Cambridge, MA: Harvard University Press, 1952.

Williams, George Hunston. "The Polish Brethren. Documentation of the History and Thought of Unitarianism in the Polish–Lithuanian Commonwealth and in the Diaspora 1601–1685." In *Harvard Theological Studies,* parts I–II, 30. Missoula, MT: Scholar Press 1980.

LECH SZCZUCKI

SOCIOLOGY OF PROTESTANTISM

Since its emergence, the discipline of sociology has concerned itself with an analysis of the role of religion in society. Beginning with Auguste Comte, the father of the discipline of sociology, and continuing in the works of the classical pioneers of the discipline, Emile Durkheim and MAX WEBER, sociology was intensely interested in the role of religion in society. The interest in religion was strongly linked to the rise of the modern world and changes brought about by INDUSTRIALIZATION and political transformation. In the midst of these social changes, the perception emerged that modern societies were moving from social orders dominated by religion and tradition to modes of social life dominated by bureaucracy and instrumental rationality. Weber devoted special attention to Protestantism, because he saw in it a key contributing factor to the emergence of the modern economic order. Durkheim, in *Suicide* (1897), considered Protestantism to be a more modern form of religion than JUDAISM or Catholicism, and a form that was less effective in creating social cohesion and integration than they were.

This article considers a number of perennial issues in the sociological study of Protestantism, beginning with the discussion of Durkheim and Weber. One issue raised by Durkheim is the question of the relationship between voluntaristic Protestantism and INDIVIDUALISM. Weber's study *The Protestant Ethic and the Spirit of Capitalism* (1905) addressed the impact of Protestant forms of religiosity on economic life. Closely related to this issue is the question of the political impact of Protestantism. One of the most fruitful perspectives in the social analysis of religion, sect–church typology, emerged from Max Weber's and ERNST TROELTSCH's considerations of the various social forms of Protestantism. Finally, this article considers the ongoing sociological debate about SECULARIZATION and Protestantism and the importance of the globalization of Protestantism, especially in its evangelical and Pentecostal forms.

The Consideration of Protestantism in Early Sociology

Emile Durkheim, the central figure in early French sociology, was concerned throughout his career with the problem of social order in modern society. His first work, *The Division of Labor* (1893), proposed that in traditional society, social order and cohesiveness were maintained by the homogeneity of the population. Because the diversity of occupations and social roles was limited, the beliefs and perspectives of the populace tended to be relatively uniform and unified. This traditional social order contrasts with modern, urban, industrial society, which has a highly developed division of labor and tremendous diversity of occupation, outlook, and interest. Here social order and cohesiveness are maintained by the functional interdependence of people engaged in specialized occupations.

Durkheim formulated the concept of the "collective conscience" to describe what he believed to be a vital component of a unified society. He defined the collective conscience as the "totality of beliefs and sentiments common to average citizens of the same society" (Durkheim 1933:79). In traditional society, the collective conscience was strong and extensive; that is, most people were in substantial agreement about the essential truths and moral values of their society. Unity and solidarity in traditional society rested on the homogeneity of the population.

In modern society, however, the collective conscience was less extensive in scope, and its hold on the population was weaker. This idea concerning the collective conscience becomes central to Durkheim's later theorizing, which serves to demonstrate the validity of this concept and clarify its nature. Increasingly, he comes to view the basis of the collective conscience as religious and also to regard it as having continued vital importance even in modern society.

In the bulk of his work, Durkheim does not give full attention to an analysis of Protestantism. His definitive work on the sociology of religion, *The Elementary Forms of Religious Life* (1912), focuses on the religious life of the Australian aborigines as an example of what is most basic to all religious life, even in more complex societies. However, Durkheim's important statistical study of suicide rates in Europe, titled *Suicide*, focuses on contrasts between Protestantism, Catholicism, and Judaism. Durkheim compared suicide rates in different regions of Europe, particularly France and Germany, in an effort to understand the causes of the variations in rates. He found that provinces and regions with predominantly Protestant populations tended to have higher suicide rates than did regions where Catholicism predominated. By conclusively demonstrating a religious in-

fluence on suicide rates, Durkheim supported the notion of a collective conscience exerting a profound influence on social behavior. He inferred that Protestantism produced a weaker collective conscience than did Catholicism. As a result, individuals were less socially integrated in Protestant regions than in Catholic regions and experienced weaker forms of social control. Under these circumstances, anomie and egoism were less thoroughly checked, and the incidence of suicide increased. Durkheim suggested that Protestantism, because of its insistence on individual assent on matters of FAITH and conscience, created a more individualistic society with weaker social integration and cohesion than a more corporate Catholic society. Protestantism here was viewed as being related to those changes of modernity that opened the way to free inquiry and undermined medieval, traditional society. This connection between Protestantism and individualism continues to be important in present-day sociological considerations of Protestantism.

Weber's study, *The Protestant Ethic and the Spirit of Capitalism,* was a defining work in his understanding of the emergence of the modern economic order. The central concept in much of Weber's writing was the idea of rationalization. Weber argued that history had progressed in such a way that rational thought and rationalized procedures increasingly dominate social existence. He sought to show in this study that Protestantism had been a key factor in this process of rationalization. A significant transformation of social existence occurred in the modern world in the shift from a limited economy of agriculture, craft production, and localized trade in the medieval period to the new capitalist economy of continuous investment, manufacturing, and global trade that characterizes the modern era. Marx's dialectical materialism claimed that ideas and beliefs were ultimately rooted in the social arrangements of economic life. Weber, on the other hand, argued that ideas and beliefs could have a profound effect in shaping the social and economic order.

Weber argued that the spirit of modern capitalism was more than simply the quest for economic gain, which, he said, has always been a part of the world's history. Rather, modern capitalism is based on the rational, methodical organization of economic life in the pursuit of gain. Whereas merchants in previous eras certainly sought to get rich, modern capitalism is characterized by the continuous investment and reinvestment of earnings to create more profit. This disciplined and rationally organized economic system is something new on the scene of world history.

Weber argues that to some degree Protestantism has provided a stimulus to the development of this new economic order. He begins by pointing out the relative importance of Protestant regions in the development of the capitalist system. He also finds a preponderance of Protestants among businessman and skilled tradesman in Germany in his time. Weber argues that Protestantism altered the ETHICS of medieval Christianity in such a way as to promote capitalist enterprise. He labels this new behavioral and ethical orientation inner-worldly ASCETICISM.

Weber argues that MARTIN LUTHER's contribution to the Protestant economic ethic was the doctrine of VOCATION (*beruf* in German). In his polemic against MONASTICISM, Luther argued that people could serve God best not by abandoning the life of the world by entering a monastery or convent, but rather by serving God in the context of their everyday life and work. As Luther put it, a milkmaid faithfully milking and caring for the cows with trust in Christ in her heart served God better than a monk who sought to please God through a self-chosen righteousness of works. Weber stated that Luther's emphasis on godly labor in a vocation gave a new positive valuation to earthly economic activity that differed from the characteristic medieval attitude, where mundane economic activity was considered to be inferior to contemplation and otherworldly religious activity.

However, Weber argues that LUTHERANISM's focus on passive acceptance of God's GRACE through Word and Sacrament did not provide the powerful inducement to the rational discipline of economic life that other forms of Protestantism, especially CALVINISM, did. Thus Lutheranism, although it provides an ethical impulse toward economic activity as a means to serve God (it is "inner-worldly" as opposed to monasticism and the medieval ethic), is not ascetic because of its emphasis on objective grace, and so it does not induce a high level of discipline in its adherents.

Calvinism, on the other hand, is ascetic in that it promotes a disciplined and consistent ethical discipline to a degree not found in Lutheranism or in Catholicism outside the monastery. The Calvinistic emphasis on the doctrine of PREDESTINATION as the inscrutable decree of God, in the absence of a strong sacramental emphasis, left the believer with the question, "How do I know I am one of the elect?" Whereas Lutheranism directed the believer to the written Word of God, the SACRAMENTS and confession, and Catholicism also directed the believer to the sacraments, Calvinism emphasized an unmediated relationship between the individual and God. Although both Calvinism and Lutheranism vigorously asserted the doctrine of justification by grace through faith, Calvinism in practice directed individuals to confirm the reality of their election through faithfulness in Christian living. One could be assured of one's ELECTION by the reality of one's renewed Christian life. Although one was not saved by works, one could produce the evidence of SALVATION by one's works. As Weber put it:

> The Calvinist . . . creates his own salvation, or, as would be more correct, the conviction of it. But this creation cannot, as in Catholicism, consist in gradual accumulation of individual good works to one's credit, but rather in a systematic self-control which at every moment stands before the inexorable alternative, chosen or damned (Weber 1998:115)

For the Calvinist, to prove one's election, one must display a systematically consistent Christian life, while for the Lutheran or Catholic, Weber says, daily Christian ethics are more a matter of living from hand to mouth. When one sins, one returns to the sacrament and confession for grace or the promise of grace.

So where Luther provided the religious impulse toward inner-worldly economic activity, Calvinism provided the ascetic impulse that led to the transformation of Europe's economic traditionalism into capitalism. For the Calvinist, the best way in which one can live out one's Christian life is by consistent and disciplined work in one's calling. This is to be combined with an avoidance of worldly pleasure and frivolous expenditure. The result is an economic ethic of hard work, savings, and careful accounting of all that one has to the glory of God.

Weber sees this as a matter of unintended consequences. Certainly, Calvin was no supporter of a worldly orientation toward life, but Weber sees a gradual drifting from the rigorous and otherworldly Calvinism of the REFORMATION to a more worldly form that sees material prosperity as a sign of God's favor. Weber sees the ideal type of the secular form of the Protestant ethic in Benjamin Franklin with his worldly maxims encouraging hard work and savings.

Weber's thesis concerning Protestantism and the spirit of capitalism, although not without its opponents, has had wide influence in sociology and other fields and continues to shape debates today about economic development and the globalization of Protestantism.

Sect–Church Typology

In contrast with Durkheim, who viewed religion primarily as a force promoting social unity, Weber was much more interested in the divisions of society by groups and interests that are in conflict. In his analysis of religious groups and their social orientation, he came up with a distinction that has since been very fruitfully used as a typology for the analysis of Protestant, as well as other, religious orientations to the world. In Weber's essay "The Protestant Sects and the Spirit of Capitalism," he describes the *church* as a "compulsory association for the administration of grace" and the *sect* as a "voluntary association of religiously qualified individuals." This fundamental distinction has been worked and reworked by a number of sociologists of religion since that time. The basic contrast in church–sect typology comes from the emergence of voluntary religious groups in the context of European Christendom where one religious organization exercises a religious monopoly, but it has proven to be a typology that can be applied more broadly to examine the orientations of various religious groups to the wider society. Weber's basic idea is to contrast those groups in which membership is voluntary and which one must be religiously qualified to enter (sects), and those groups where membership is presumed to be coterminous with society and is given at birth (churches).

The most influential proponents of this typology have in fact been not professional sociologists, but rather theologians. Troeltsch took Weber's basic distinction and fleshed it out both theologically and sociologically in the context of Christian churches in his *The Social Teachings of the Christian Churches.* Troeltsch views the two sociological types, church and sect, as being rooted in the New Testament. The church type is based theologically on the Pauline emphasis of universal grace. The church type develops sociologically after Constantine's CONVERSION, as the church becomes an institution that embraces all of society. People are born into the church (membership is ascribed rather than achieved), and this is best demonstrated by the practice of infant BAPTISM. From a sociological standpoint, it is important to note that Troeltsch stresses that the church type tends to have a professional CLERGY and to ally itself with the ruling powers and upper classes.

Troeltsch relates the sect type theologically to Jesus's call to radical repentance as found in the Gospels. "Come out from among them and be separate" (II Corinthians 6:17) would be the text that perhaps best describes the orientation of the sect to the wider society. Whereas people are born into the church, they enter the sect voluntarily. Adult baptism symbolizes this commitment to voluntary membership.

Troeltsch's development of sect–church typology looks at each type as having a series of paired contrasting characteristics. Whereas the church emphasizes grace, the sect tends toward legalism. Whereas the church embraces all of society, the sect is exclusive. Lay participation and a strong fellowship are social characteristics that describe the internal functioning of the sect type. Professional clergy and a view of the church as more of an institution and less of a community characterize the church. The sect tends to

be associated with the poor. In contrast, the church tends to be allied with the ruling classes. The sect stands in opposition to society and in rebellion against it; the church seeks to direct and incorporate society. The medieval Roman Catholic Church epitomizes the church type and the Anabaptists (see ANABAPTISM) of the sixteenth century, the early Quakers (see FRIENDS, SOCIETY OF) of the seventeenth century, and the early Pentecostals (see PENTECOSTALISM) would be good examples of the sect type. The Protestant state churches following the Reformation in Europe would be good examples of the church type as well.

The second theologian who developed and popularized church–sect typology, especially within the context of the UNITED STATES, is H. RICHARD NIEBUHR in two of his best-known works, *Christ and Culture* and *The Social Sources of Denominationalism.* For theologians and ethicists, the first work has been more significant, but for sociology of religion, the second is the more interesting work. In *The Social Sources of Denominationalism,* Niebuhr built on Troeltsch's basic scheme, applying it to the American context. He developed the idea of the DENOMINATION as a third type mediating between the sect and church types. In the American context of disestablished religion, the denomination combines the voluntarism of the sect with a more relaxed attitude toward the world and other religious groups. Niebuhr is also very interested in the development and change of religious groups and in their relationship to the social class structure. In this regard, his analysis benefits from a post-Marxian understanding and interest in social stratification.

Niebuhr discusses the development of certain sect-like groups that he refers to as the "churches of the disinherited." He describes how the theology and practice of these churches were related to the social status and situation of their adherents. He suggests that churches of the poor often emphasized emotion and informality in WORSHIP, while churches among more prosperous sectors of the population emphasized formality and more abstract thought. Churches of the disinherited, in keeping with the sect type, also tended to be more lay oriented than the churches of the prosperous with their professional and highly educated clergy. Because of a greater inconformity with existing social arrangements, the church of the disinherited had a higher tension with the world and tended to be more legalistic.

However, Niebuhr points out that groups that at one time were very sectarian in orientation evolve toward a more churchly type as their social status changes. Churches that began as movements of the disinherited evolve into middle-class denominations as they rise socially. Niebuhr points to METHODISM as an excellent example of this process. In ENGLAND, JOHN WESLEY appealed to the working classes, and Methodism was particularly successful among them. In the United States, Methodism expanded on the frontier, often among people of little education. Its REVIVALS and CAMP MEETINGS were emotional and unsophisticated. The movement depended on strong lay leadership operating in organized classes. Adherents were warned against worldliness. However, as time went on, Methodists became an established presence on the American scene. Methodists prospered and rose into the middle class. With these social changes came a demand for more social respectability. Methodists began to expect and develop an educated professional clergy. Sectarian tension with the world diminished. In his own time, Wesley noted that as his converts prospered they seemed to become less zealous. Niebuhr sees this as a continuing trend in American denominationalism. Sect-like churches of the disinherited become transformed into church-like denominations as their adherents move up in the social class system.

Protestantism, Secularization, and the Modern World

When Martin Luther stood at the DIET OF WORMS, refused to retract, and appealed to Scripture and reason, a challenge was issued to the medieval principle of religious AUTHORITY. Henceforth, in Protestantism, TRADITION and constituted religious authority in a hierarchy no longer held sway over the conscience of the individual. With this challenge to traditional religious authority came a new relationship of the individual both to the hierarchy of the church and to the religious community. The old idea of Christendom would soon break down under the strain, and a new relationship between religion and the social order would emerge. Protestantism also brought a new view of the LAITY. No longer passive recipients of a religion administered and controlled by the clergy and religious bureaucracy, they were called to understand the doctrines of the church and their foundation in Scripture. They were also called to act themselves to preserve and extend the church. Luther's "Address to the Christian Nobility" called the German princes to act independently from the church hierarchy to defend and support biblical faith. The social consequences of these ideas would be profound.

The immediate consequence of Luther's Reformation was to establish state churches where the relationship between CHURCH AND STATE was similar to that between the Catholic church and the empire. As the power of the state grew in the modern era, the state's power over religious life grew in both Protestant and Catholic societies. Yet, Luther had clearly taught a distinction between the two kingdoms, the left-hand kingdom of secular power and the right-hand kingdom of God's proper work, the proclamation of the Gospel. Where the Pope had claimed authority in both temporal and spiritual matters, the Protestant Reformation led to a distinction and a separation between two spheres, the secular and the religious. In addition, the rise of new sects and quarreling among Protestants led to an even greater disintegration of the old medieval unity of society and faith.

Although in most European countries, state churches were established that attempted to maintain religious monopolies within their territories, the seeds of the political principle of separation of church and state had been sown. In the United States, these seeds led to fully disestablished religion after the American Revolution. Rather than disestablishment leading to religious decline, it led in the United States to more vigorous and lay-oriented religious life.

Classical sociology assumed that secularization was an inevitable process of the modern world. Most sociologists argued that religion was destined to shrink under the assault of reason, SCIENCE, and marginalization from influence over political and economic life. Its influence was to be confined to private life, and even there it was viewed as an anachronism that would slowly fade away.

From the perspective of Durkheimian sociology, Protestantism was a part of this weakening of religious life in society. In traditional society, religion was largely unchallenged, because it held a central role in integrating social life and was uniformly adhered to by all. Protestantism, however, appealed to the individual conscience. It required individual assent. No longer did all in a society hold the same religious views. Rather, everyone examined religious convictions for themselves. The collective conscience was weakened. The increasing pluralism and individualism of modern life, of which Protestantism was a part, would lead to a diminishing plausibility of religious belief, which depended on social affirmation and collective ritual. Peter Berger's *The Sacred Canopy* (1967) makes this Durkheimian argument that secularization is a phenomenon brought about by religious pluralism.

However, many sociologists of religion, including Berger, no longer hold this secularization paradigm. On closer examination, various scholars have argued that there is in fact insufficient evidence to conclude that religion is disappearing from the modern world. There *is* a separation of spheres in modern society, where political, economic and other institutions operate free of direct religious influence and control. However, it is not at all clear that religion is destined to diminish in influence or be restricted to the private sphere.

Although in Europe state-supported churches seem to have sapped the vitality from Christian faith, in the United States, where churches have operated free from direct state support and control, religion has maintained a strong position in the culture. A number of historians and sociologists of religion have indeed argued that religious influence in the United States, rather than shrinking, has actually grown since colonial times. Certainly, church membership as a percentage of population has grown since then.

It is important to note, however, the trends in growth within Protestant denominations in the United States. Researchers following Kelley (*Why Conservative Churches Are Growing*) have found that it is the more conservative churches, those that resist the trends of secular society, that grow in numbers, while those churches that most clearly accommodate themselves to secularism are shrinking. Kelley argued that people are looking for clear authoritative religious answers. Churches that supply those answers attract and hold on to adherents, while those that do not dwindle in numbers and influence. Thus, the traditional mainline denominations in American society, such as the Methodists and Episcopalians, are declining, while the conservative evangelical church bodies are growing.

The strongest challenges to the secularization paradigm have argued that a free market for religion and religious pluralism, rather than undermining the plausibility of religion, actually strengthen its practice and influence and mobilize greater participation from the population. Europe, with its highly secularized population and state-supported churches, rather than representing the trend of modernity, is a particular response to a unique history and social organization of religious life. Protestantism, because it allows for religious competition and pluralism, can maintain its vigor also in modern societies.

The Globalization of Protestantism

Some of the greatest challenges to be faced in the sociological study of Protestantism are being raised by the globalization of Protestantism. Historically Protestantism arose and developed in the countries of northern Europe and was taken by immigrants to the United States and the countries of the British Commonwealth. The growth of Christianity worldwide, however, has shifted the demographic balance of the Christian church in general and Protestantism in particular. LATIN AMERICA has experienced tremendous growth in Protestant, especially Pentecostal, adherents in the twentieth century. Sub-Saharan AFRICA has had great increases in numbers of both Protestant and Catholic Christians. In CHINA, Christianity, both Prot-

estant and Catholic, has grown since the Communist revolution in 1949 (see COMMUNISM). Estimates of the current number of Christians run as high as 100 million (Jenkins 2002:70). Most of this growth has been in the underground church, which is mostly Protestant and evangelical (Martin 2002:155). South Korea (see KOREA) has experienced high rates of Christian growth and Protestants have become a significant part of the population there. Understanding the sociological dimensions of the worldwide growth of Protestantism and its implications for the world's societies and for the future of Christianity is a major task for sociologists of religion.

The most important sociological studies of global Protestantism have focused on the rise of Pentecostalism. Protestant growth worldwide has been most notable among Pentecostal and Pentecostalized Christian movements, particularly among the poor of the Third World. Since its beginnings in the AZUSA STREET REVIVAL in 1906 in Los Angeles, California, Pentecostalism has been a religious movement that carries some of the same social characteristics earlier associated with Methodism. It has had great success among the poor and disenfranchised. Its roots in the United States are associated with the African-American community and the poor white community. As it has grown, Pentecostalism and Pentecostal influences have become important and significant among the middle classes as well. Like Methodism in its early stages, Pentecostalism is grassroots religion; it is responsive to the religious needs of the masses and gives a voice to the LAITY. Its leaders are not primarily seminary trained, but rather rise up from the ranks of the membership because of their demonstrated charismatic qualities. Among the urban poor in squatter settlements around the world, Pentecostalism provides community and moral discipline for people who are uprooted from their old traditions and living in an economically hostile environment.

David Martin calls Pentecostalism "the Christian equivalent of Islamic revivalism" (Martin 2002:167). It is comparable to Islamic revivalism in its global scope and in its dynamism among the urban poor. However, Martin points out that its political logic is much different. Because Christianity conceives of two distinct spheres of authority, church and state, based on Jesus's words "Render unto Caesar the things that are Caesar's and to God the things that are God's," Pentecostalism represents a religious revolution that is voluntaristic and not directly political. In fact, as Martin points out, Pentecostalism thrives as previous religious monopolies begin to break down, as is the case in Latin America. Pentecostalism represents a break with the past but at the same time, because it concerns itself with issues of spiritual power, healing, exorcisms, and spiritual warfare, it addresses itself directly to issues of concern to peoples emerging from animistic religions concerned with shamanism and the power of spirits.

Due to the dramatic growth of Pentecostalism in Latin America, the most detailed sociological studies of its growth in the developing world have been done there. A brief outline of the various sociological interpretations offered for the global rise of Pentecostalism would include the following: (1) a Weberian, developmental understanding of Pentecostalism as being tied to processes of modernization and the expansion of capitalism; (2) a Marxian critique of Pentecostalism that sees it as a form of false consciousness brought on by the expansion of that same global capitalism; (3) a perspective that links Pentecostal growth to its responsiveness to the needs of WOMEN and its reformulation of domestic morality; and (4) an interpretation that seeks to explain Pentecostal growth in terms of its responsiveness to concerns about healing and spiritual power.

Martin's work is a good example of the first perspective. He sees Pentecostalism and Protestant growth in the developing world in the context of life-long work on secularization processes. Pentecostalism grows when religious monopolies begin to decay. It both benefits from the social free space that is created when these monopolies weaken, and at the same time works to create a cultural free space for voluntaristic religious DISSENT and expression. Martin suggests that though Pentecostalism is apolitical, it can nevertheless impact political life by working in the sphere of culture. While proponents of LIBERATION THEOLOGY often criticize Pentecostalism as a form of false consciousness, Martin and others point out that it meets the felt needs of the poor and does indeed bring helpful change into their lives.

The Marxian interpretation popular among a number of Latin American interpreters of Pentecostalism focuses on this issue of false consciousness. As global capitalist markets penetrate third-world societies, these societies are transformed in ways that break down traditional social relationships and economic patterns. The resulting alienation in the lives of the poor leads them to Pentecostal religiosity as a form of escape, an "opiate of the masses." This interpretation, whether in the hands of secular critics or liberation theologians, tends to view Pentecostalism as inauthentic and often charges that Pentecostalism is a cultural import from the United States. Martin and others counter that though Pentecostalism did originate in the United States, it has become thoroughly indigenous in other parts of the world and reproduces itself through local, rather than foreign, leadership and cultural forms.

Elizabeth Brusco, in a work titled *The Reformation of Machismo,* provided the most complete exposition of the third point of view, that Pentecostalism is successful because of its appeal to women. Brusco argues that women are attracted to evangelical Protestantism because it transforms the ethic of their husbands. Although Pentecostalism generally affirms biblical injunctions in favor of patriarchy, at the same time it succeeds in enforcing a domestic morality of marital fidelity, abstinence from alcohol, and an investment of the families' limited income in the home. This is a powerful attraction for the urban poor, whose lives are often devastated by the vices and temptations of the city.

Finally, some researchers (e.g., Chesnut 1997) have focused on Pentecostal responsiveness to concerns about healing and spiritual power. They have found that belief in divine healing plays a major role in Pentecostal conversion and growth. This is due in part to the fact that the poor often have little access to adequate medical care and suffer from health problems related to poor sanitation and malnutrition. In addition, traditional belief systems focus on the power of spirits, SAINTS, and magic to effect healing or to cause illness or trouble. While Pentecostalism challenges these traditional beliefs, it does so in a way that takes the concerns about spiritual power and threats seriously. Thus, there is both continuity and a break with traditional belief systems.

Weber linked Protestantism to the rise of the modern world. Studies of global Protestantism are influenced by many of Weber's ideas. Protestantism is proving to be adaptable in many cultures even (or perhaps especially) in the face of modernity. Given the social and political importance of religion in today's world, an understanding of the global growth and dynamism of Protestantism today makes the sociology of Protestantism as important as it was a century ago.

See also Culture; Economics; Evangelicalism; Methodism, England; Methodism, North America; Modernism; Politics; Sectarianism

References and Further Reading

Berger, Peter L. *The Sacred Canopy.* Garden City, NY: Doubleday, 1967.

Brusco, Elizabeth. *The Reformation of Machismo.* Austin, TX: University of Texas Press, 1995.

Chesnut, R. Andrew. *Born Again in Brazil: The Pentecostal Boom and the Pathogens of Poverty.* New Brunswick, NJ: Rutgers University Press, 1997.

Durkheim, Emile. *The Division of Labor in Society.* Glencoe, IL: Free Press, 1933.

———. *Suicide: A Study in Sociology.* New York: Free Press, 1951.

Jenkins, Philip. *The Next Christendom: The Coming of Global Christianity.* Oxford, UK: Oxford University Press, 2002.

Kelley, Dean. *Why Conservative Churches Are Growing.* New York: Harper and Row, 1972.

Martin, David. *Pentecostalism: The World Their Parish.* Oxford, UK: Blackwell, 2002.

Niebuhr, H. Richard. *The Social Sources of Denominationalism.* New York: The World Publishing, 1957.

Troeltsch, Ernst. *The Social Teachings of the Christian Churches. Vol. II.* Translated by Olive Wyon. London: Allen & Unwin, 1931.

Weber, Max. *The Protestant Ethic and the Spirit of Capitalism.* Translated by Talcott Parsons. Los Angeles, CA: Roxbury Publishing, 1998.

ERIC MOELLER

SÖDERBLOM, NATHAN (1866–1931)

Swedish Lutheran archbishop and pioneer in ecumenism. Söderblom was born January 15, 1866, at Trönö, Hälsingland, Sweden, and died February 12, 1931, at Uppsala, Sweden. After his ordination to the priesthood in 1893, Söderblom became the rector of the Swedish Church in Paris. He studied the ancient religions of Iran and received his doctorate in history of religions in 1901 at the Sorbonne. While in Paris he made a significant friend in AUGUSTE SABATIER. After Söderblom's disputation, he was immediately made professor of the history and philosophy of religions at the University of Uppsala. That post was linked to that of vicar of one of the parishes at Uppsala. As a priest as well as a professor, he made strong impressions on an entire generation of students. From his own years as a student onward, he was influenced by the theology of A. RITSCHL and J. Wellhausen, and he counts as a "modern" theologian. In his work *Uppenbarelsereligion* (The Religion of Revelation, 1903), he distinguished between natural-cultural religion and prophetic religion, and also between the non-Christian mysticism of indefiniteness and the specifically Christian mysticism of personality. This work marks the declaration of his theological program. Between the years 1912 and 1914 he was professor of the history of religions at the University of Leipzig. During that period he wrote *Gudstrons uppkomst* (The Emergence of Belief in God, 1914). As a summary of his research into the history of religions, his Gifford Lectures—*The Living God. Basal Forms of Personal Religion*—were posthumously published in 1933 (Swedish translation in 1932).

In 1914 Söderblom was appointed archbishop of Uppsala and thus became the head of the Church of Sweden. Already as a student, his interests had extended to the international scene. He took part in the YMCA World Congress in 1888 and again in 1891, and in the Christian Student Movement International Assembly at Northfield, Massachusetts in 1890. At Northfield the experience of the universality and unity of the Church became overwhelming and DWIGHT L. MOODY made a great impression. Thanks to his extensive and lifelong international contacts, Söderblom considered the First World War a challenge for the worldwide Christian churches to seek closer interconfessional and ecumenical relations. Immediately after his appointment as archbishop, he became a public critic of the political leaders of the nations at war, challenging them to work "for peace and Christian fellowship." In 1925 he issued the invitation to The Universal Conference on Life and Work in Stockholm, which gathered representatives, not only for the churches and denominations of the Reformation, but also for the Orthodox churches. The invitation had also been issued to the Holy See. Söderblom is thus the founder of the current Life-and-Work Movement as well as the inspiration behind it. This marks him as a portal figure of modern ecclesiastical ecumenism (see ECUMENISM). Inspired by Sabatier, Söderblom's ecumenical program was determined by the conflict he perceived between what he called the body and the soul of the Swedish Church (*Svenska kyrkans kropp och själ,* 1915), that is, between the temporary organization, confessions, and forms of services on the one hand and, on the other, the abiding prophetic calling of the church throughout the ages. He summarized his view on the nature of the church in the concept of "evangelical catholicity," thus clearly demarcating his position against both the Roman Catholic claim to universality and the liberal catholicity championed by some Anglicans. The church is "the one and only holy catholic and apostolic church," the global Christian community of "all honest souls in every specific denomination." As archbishop, he emphasized the historic ministry of episcopacy as well as the apostolic succession of the Church of Sweden, and he also consecrated bishops for the Evangelical Lutheran Churches in Estonia, Lithuania, and Slovakia. As an ecumenist, Söderblom, more than any other Swede, made an active contribution to international ecclesiastical developments. In 1930 he was awarded the Nobel Peace Price in acknowledgment of his ecumenical achievements.

In 1941, on the seventy-fifth anniversary of Söderblom's birth, Nathan Söderblom-Sällskapet (Societas Soederblomiana Upsaliensis) was established in Uppsala, as a learned society of scholars, chiefly in history of religions and in exegetics; its yearbook is entitled *Religion och Bibel (Religion and Bible).*

See also Sweden

References and Further Reading

Brodd, S.-E. "A Swedish Archbishop between American and German Lutheranism. American Influences on the Ecumenical Strategies of Nathan Söderblom." *Tro & Tanke* (Uppsala) no. 3 (1997).

———. *Evangelisk katolicitet. Ett studium av innehåll och funktion under 1800- och 1900-talen.* [Summary: Evangelical Catholicity: A Study of Content and Function during the 19th and 20th Century]. Lund, Sweden: CWK Gleerup, 1982.

Curtis, C. J. *Nathan Söderblom, Theologian of Revelation.* Chicago: Convenant Press, 1966.

Dahlgren, S. "Nathan Söderblom as European." *Tro & Tanke* (Uppsala) no. 7 (1993).

Nathan Söderblom in memoriam [with bibliography by S Ågren]. Stockholm: Svenska kykans diakonistyrelses bokförlag, 1931.

Sharpe, E. J. *Nathan Söderblom and the Study of Religion.* Chapel Hill: University of North Carolina Press, 1990.

Sundkler, B. *Nathan Söderblom. His Life and Work.* Lund, Sweden: Gleerups, 1968.

OLOPH BEXELL

SOUTH AFRICA

Throughout history, religion has played a major role in the South African context. This is equally true of Roman Catholicism, Eastern Orthodoxy, and Protestantism. In a historical overview, attention is given to the origin and rise of Protestantism in three major periods in South African history. Aspects such as the sociopolitical context and theological developments also receive necessary focus.

The Seventeenth and Eighteenth Centuries

The original inhabitants of South Africa consisted primarily of the indigenous Khoikhoi (Hottentot) herdsmen and San (Bushmen) hunters, together known as the Khoisan. Elsewhere in southern Africa there dwelt various Bantu-speaking peoples. Although the Khoisan and black groups had a common origin, thousands of years of separated development resulted in widely different lifestyles, languages, and cultures. With the permanent settlement of Europeans, beginning at the Cape in 1652 and reaching toward the interior, came radical changes to the structure and nature of South African society.

Europe made first contact with indigenous South Africans in 1488 when Bartholomeu Diaz (d. 1500) rounded the Cape of Good Hope. The period between 1488 and 1652 saw intermittent contact between the Khoisan and the Portuguese, English, and Dutch navigators. The temporary nature of the European visits to the Cape allayed any fears the Khoisan might have had that the visitors would establish themselves permanently at the Cape and subdue them, creating a false sense of security among the Khoisan.

In the periods of European imperialism (1500–1800) and Western neo-imperialism (1880–1920), the establishment of overseas colonies took a variety of forms. The colony at the Cape was originally established by Jan van Riebeeck (1619–1677) as a replenishment station. The Reformed tradition in South Africa had its beginnings with the arrival of the Dutch in 1652, the early German settlers in the 1660s, and the French Huguenots in 1688. Except for a few cases, these settlers were Protestants. The Dutch and French settlers were Calvinists.

On April 6, 1652 Jan van Riebeeck arrived in Table Bay. For the first few months his company of some ninety people lived in tents. Work immediately commenced on the erection of a fort, and on June 4 the first "sick-comforter," Willem Wylant, and his family moved in. The sick-comforters were initially responsible for the spiritual welfare of the settlers. Before any man could be appointed sick-comforter, he had to furnish a testimonial to his life and beliefs, pass an examination in doctrine, and prove his competence in reading aloud and in leading in singing. A commission of the *classis* (PRESBYTERY) of Amsterdam was charged with the task of examining and recommending sick-comforters to the directors of the company.

Although a number of Khoikhoi became economically involved in the establishment of the replenishment station at the Cape, there was little involvement on their part in the church. No Khoikhoi was, for instance, baptized before 1662.

The first thirteen years of the settlement at the Cape can be seen as the period when the church was incompletely constituted. Although there was no established church, it existed nonetheless: the faithful gathered for public worship and the sacraments were administered.

The ideas of European ENLIGHTENMENT had only a limited influence on the colony. Bearers of enlightened ideas to the Cape were chiefly travelers on the ships that called regularly at the Cape. They were mainly representatives of political movements, students who traveled to Europe to study, correspondents between the two continents, and adventurers and retired sailors who sometimes acted as teachers. Colonists at the Cape were also influenced by the Eighty Years War (1568–1648) in Europe and the patriotic movement in the NETHERLANDS. As a consequence of the FRENCH REVOLUTION (1789), the rights and freedom of citizens became subjects of intense discussion. It was a stormy period, concerned to some extent with righteousness, justice, and freedom. There was a widespread spirit of distrust in and opposition to the government.

The year 1688 saw the population of the Cape considerably increased, and Protestantism (more specifically the DUTCH REFORMED CHURCH) further strengthened with the arrival of the French Huguenots. The Edict of Nantes, which had granted the Huguenots a certain degree of religious freedom, was revoked in

October 1685, resulting in a great number of Huguenots fleeing from France. Many emigrated to the Netherlands, where French-speaking Protestant communities already existed. These "Walloon" congregations dated from the period when French-speaking Reformed Church members fled from the southern Netherlands (the present Belgium), to escape Spanish domination.

In the course of the next decades the Dutch colonists gradually trekked further into the hinterland. The great distances prevented them from attending church services regularly. At times ministers journeyed to their members in the remote districts to conduct services and administer the sacraments. Governor General van Imhoff (1705–1750) undertook a journey through the colony in 1743. On his return he made Governor Swellengrebel (1700–1760) aware of the need to create two new congregations with a schoolmaster for each.

Shortly after the first Dutch Reformed minister, Van Arckel's, arrival in 1665, the church council decided that Lutherans of good standing would be permitted to partake of the Lord's Supper, but a letter written by the church council to the *classis* of Amsterdam in 1714 indicates that by that date this provision had been set aside. The classis replied that if they held to a correct doctrine of justification, Lutherans might certainly be admitted to the sacrament. As a result several Lutherans presented themselves at the Lord's table. These people had been in the habit of attending divine worship, and they already constituted a considerable section of the population.

In 1742 a petition signed by sixty-nine people was presented to the Council of Policy, asking for permission to request from the Dutch Council of Seventeen a minister for the local Lutherans and to be allowed to hold public worship. The Council of Policy rejected the petition on the grounds that it was ill timed. In the course of the next years various further requests for permission were submitted.

Eventually, in 1780, the first Lutheran minister, Andrew Kolver, landed at the Cape. On December 10 the warehouse built by Martin Melck and the grounds on which it stood were granted to the congregation and formally consecrated as a church. The Dutch Reformed church council of Cape Town now had to accept the inevitable.

To begin with, a good understanding prevailed between the two congregations, though the departure of the Lutherans from the Dutch Reformed Church had the immediate effect of decreasing the number of young people coming forward to profess their faith. This led the church council to take what steps it could to ensure that the Lutherans did not expand at the expense of the Dutch Reformed Church.

The Lutherans were granted freedom of worship on the same basis as their fellow-Lutherans in Batavia. One of the stipulations was that in the case of parents belonging to different churches, the boys were to be baptized in the father's church, the girls in the mother's church. These parents were also permitted to have all their children, boys as well as girls, baptized in the Dutch Reformed Church, if they so desired.

The Nineteenth Century

The British settlers of 1820 were to have a considerable influence on developments in South Africa. These settlers came from Europe and Britain which, after the French Revolution and the following Napoleonic wars, faced serious political, economic, and social problems. Although the influx of English people to the eastern Cape was small in comparison to their emigration to other parts of the world, the approximately 4,000 settlers were strongly resolved in their determination to improve the quality of their lives. This goal was not to be realized in the short term; the climatic conditions to which they had to adapt and various disturbances on the eastern border were serious setbacks. Accustomed as they were to the rule of law and a parliamentary government, the settlers were critical of the authoritarian style of government at the Cape. After 1825 the process of constitutional government and the development of the legal system gradually took place.

The Great Trek was not "great" because of the numbers participating in it, but rather because of the far-reaching sociopolitical implications it was to have. By the middle of the nineteenth century the interior had been transformed into an interdependent multiracial society characterized by both cooperation and conflict. With the passage of time, the Great Trek was regarded as an Afrikaner national movement, and the great majority of the Afrikaner people were later to identify themselves with its ideals.

The discovery of gold and diamonds had explosive economic, social, and political results for the subcontinent of South Africa, beginning in the second half of the nineteenth century. This was to become the heartbeat of the South African economy, ushering in the industrial period and giving rise to a new capitalist society. The process of urbanization, especially in the diamond city of Kimberley and the gold city of Johannesburg, brought about radical changes in South African demography. Dramatic political developments left their mark on relations both within and outside the country. For the black community, all these events brought about the disintegration of their traditional socioeconomic structures.

The Church Order of de Mist, formally known as the "Provisional Ecclesiastical Decree of the Batavian Settlement at the Cape of Good Hope," appeared on July 25, 1804. It was an important watershed in South African church history, particularly because of its implications for the relationship between church and state and for wider religious freedom at the Cape.

The second half of the nineteenth century saw a split among Afrikaans churches into three churches: the larger Dutch Reformed Church (*Nederduitse Gereformeerde Kerk*), the *Nederduitsch Hervormde Kerk van Afrika,* and the *Gereformeerde Kerk.* Theological issues and ecclesiastic and political differences played a role. (Because it is virtually impossible to translate the names of these churches into English and still to be able to differentiate between them, the Afrikaans names are used.) The *Nederduitse Gereformeerde* was born in South Africa as a historical continuation of the Reformed Church in the Netherlands. The *Nederduitsch Hervormde Kerk van Afrika* also lays claim to this continuation, but was in fact a new church that originated in the Transvaal with the arrival of the Reverend Dirk van der Hoff (1814–1881) in 1853. The *Gereformeerde Kerk* was founded in 1859 by Reverend Dirk Postma (1818–1890). The *Gereformeerde Kerk* objected to hymns sung in the *Nederduitse Gereformeerde Kerk* at the Cape.

The missionary calling of the *Nederduitse Gereformeerde* Kerk in the late nineteenth century seems to have receded into the background in the face of problems of institutional consolidation. Pastoral care in the new situations created by the diamond mining and slums seems to have been neglected. One generation later, Pentecostal services on the Rand drew huge crowds of poor whites, including many *Nederduitse Gereformeerde* members.

One of the key reasons why British missionaries came to South Africa was the great missionary thrust of European Protestant churches during the nineteenth century. Also, when British rule was established for the second time (1806), soldiers from different British denominations came looking for fellowship and a spiritual home. At the time, the CHURCH OF ENGLAND based at the Cape thought of itself as an outstation of Canterbury, with all the rights of the establishment, only to find out inadvertently (in the Colenso litigation) that legally this was not the case. Although the first bishop, Robert Gray, had been appointed in 1847, the diocese was only given the status of an Anglican Province in 1866.

Missionary work was undertaken by the Anglican Church, though missionaries reported directly to the bishop and were therefore in a different position than other clergy; thus the organizational unity of the church was not jettisoned. This work continued qui-

etly, with the result that the church of the province was able to create the dioceses of St. John's (Transkei, 1873; and Zululand, 1870). Concern for the welfare of members on the goldfields prompted the bishop of Zululand to proclaim the diocese of the Transvaal—a fine example of the give and take between outreach to the heathen and the unchurched.

Long before a Methodist minister could be sent to the Cape, the initiative was taken by laypeople to gather members of this confession into a fellowship. Even when Barnabas (1788–1857) and William Shaw (1798–1872) arrived in their far-flung parishes, their call to minister to the needs of the white settlers could not stifle their concern for the salvation of the local people, work that was undertaken almost from the start, true to the spirit of the founder of this denomination. Work proceeded in Namaqualand, Caffraria, and Bechuanaland and a chain of mission stations was established from Caffraria to Natal. Frontier warfare not only destroyed mission buildings, but also greatly affected the evangelism. Lack of funds necessitated the transfer of some of the mission stations north of the Orange River, respectively, to the Rhenish Mission, to the *Nederduitse Gereformeerde Kerk,* and to the Anglicans from the late 1860s. This purposeful mission to black South Africans ensured that the Methodist Church would eventually have more black members than any of the other mainline denominations.

The work to convert whites had already commenced in Cape Town, as well as by the 1820 Settlers. By 1860 there were 132 Methodist missionaries/ministers in the eastern Cape and Natal, and their flock numbered 5,000. English immigration swelled the number of whites, particularly in the Kimberley and Reef areas, and the Methodist Church became the largest of the English-speaking churches in South Africa. The whole church was divided into different geographical circuits. The Methodist missionaries were more sympathetic to the colonists' point of view regarding the frontier situation in the Ciskei, most probably because they worked among white settlers as well as with the black tribes beyond the frontier. Though John Philip regarded the Methodists as traitors to black people, they did much to restore the image of the missionary among the colonists.

By 1829, when the Presbyterians erected their first church, St. Andrew's in Cape Town, Presbyterian services had already been started by Thomas Pringle in the Eastern Province, John Brownlee was working at Chumie, and Lovedale had also been established. Lovedale produced not only indigenous ministers but provided artisan and academic education on an interdenominational and nonracial basis. It was rated as one of the foremost educational centers in South Africa. Missionary outreach, especially by the Glasgow Mission Society, London Mission Society (LMS), Free Church of Scotland, and expansion of the work to convert whites to Natal in the Orange Free State (OFS), and later to Kimberley and the goldfields continued. Adams, Grout, and Lindley did pioneer work among the Zulus in Natal.

The beginnings of the Baptist Church in South Africa were modest, and were primarily concerned with finding members and establishing fellowship groups among the 1820 settlers. The first Baptist service was held by William Miller in the Albany district. Baptists, too, had a passion for reaching the unconverted, something they shared with the Methodists, in contrast to the complacent Anglican attitude toward mission work at the time. Their numbers were appreciably swelled with the arrival of co-religionists among the German Legion settlers (1857), who settled in the King William's Town area.

The Baptists were the first of the Protestant English-speaking churches to begin conversion of Afrikaans-speaking people (Vrede). Once white congregations had been started in Durban and Pietermaritzburg, work began with the Zulu by the Swedish Baptists. The Baptist Union of 1877 evidenced the determination of this small and relatively poor denomination to live out its commission faithfully. Like the Anglican, Methodist, and Presbyterian churches (the last until the 1920s), the Baptists became a multiracial union with separate congregations and work.

Early in the nineteenth century, the LUTHERAN CHURCH was shaken by theological controversies over baptism and missionary work among the slaves at the Cape, a most emotive issue in those pre-abolition days. This led to a split in the congregation. An Afrikaner, who had served as interim minister, was not appointed as third minister to cater to the Dutch-speaking members of the congregation, and a German-speaking congregation seceded from the parent body, in which services were held regularly in both Low German and Dutch. This struggle between mission-consciousness and culture-oriented churchmanship stunted further expansion.

The missionary outreach, which the local white Lutheran congregation seemed to lack, was imported, so to speak, in the form of the Rhenish and Berlin Missions. They were located within the settled areas, Wuppertal, Stellenbosch, and the eastern frontier, but also far away in Namaqualand-Bethanie in the Orange Free State. Not only did their workers occasionally serve the dispersed white settlers in their jurisdictions, but sometimes they were also called to serve a white community, such as Sachs in Pretoria. Some even left mission work for this new calling (e.g., Döhne in Pietermaritzburg).

The Norwegian Mission Society workers served the Scandinavian community in Natal, just as the Hermannsburg missionaries served the small German communities in the Transvaal. The image of constant enmity and mutual accusations and suspicion between all missionary bodies and white settlers, especially in the Afrikaans Republics, seems to be a distortion.

During the period 1652 to 1795 the Dutch Reformed Church (*Nederduitse Gereformeerde Kerk*) was the state church in the Cape Colony. In the period of English rule from 1806 to 1875, both the *Nederduitse Gereformeerde* Kerk and the Anglican Church were subordinated to the Cape government. After the introduction of the Voluntary Bill in 1875, these churches were allowed a far greater measure of freedom and independence. During this period both the Anglican and the Dutch Reformed churches experienced difficult heresy trials (the Colenso, Kotzé, and Burgers trials), after which they became increasingly unhappy about too close a relationship with the state. In both these cases, after an appeal by the accused to the state, the latter upheld the appeals. Disestablishment seemed the only option open to the churches. Therefore, contrary to their usual position on church–state relations, they supported Saul Solomon, a member of both Parliament and the CONGREGATIONAL CHURCH, who tried for some time to convince Parliament to withdraw state aid to the churches. Finally in 1875, the Voluntary Bill was passed, and there has been no officially established church in South Africa since that time. All the churches in the Cape henceforth became free churches; free to pursue their affairs in their own way. The year 1875, therefore, is an important watershed in South African church history.

The Twentieth Century

Among the English-speaking Protestant churches, the Methodist Church has the second largest number of white members, and the largest number of black members. The Methodist Church in South Africa, which was started by Sergeant Kendrick, gradually spread throughout South Africa. At the local level, most congregations were still segregated according to race, while the multiracial character of the church was expressed in the highest of its church bodies, the conference. That multiracial character has also become increasingly expressed in district synods, and from January 1980 congregations became multiracial.

The United Congregational Church of Southern Africa was formed in 1967. It was a merger of three groups: the Congregational Union, which consisted of a union of separate congregations after the London Missionary Society withdrew from the Cape Colony in 1859; the London Missionary Society Church of

Botswana and Zimbabwe; and the Bantu Congregational Church, which was a product of the labors of the American Board of Missions in Natal. Ecclesiastical authority is centered in the local church meeting, although each region holds a yearly meeting. An annual assembly is also held consisting of representatives of churches throughout South Africa.

The Presbyterian Church of Southern Africa traces its history at the Cape to 1806, when a Scottish regiment founded a Calvinist association. In 1812 the first Presbyterian congregation was founded, with the Reverend George Thom (1789–1842) as its minister. From Cape Town the work spread over the entire country. In 1897 the Presbyterian Church accepted as its doctrinal standard the Twenty-four Articles of the Faith, which were drawn up in 1890 by the Presbyterian Church of Britain. At the general assembly level the races are united, but they are divided on a congregational level.

It could be agreed that various theological, and some other factors, helped to influence developments in the English-speaking churches: The English-speaking churches came to South Africa during or shortly after European upheavals and the rise of British movements such as the Enlightenment, the Industrial Revolution, and the Methodist revival. This means that they were in varying degrees under the influence of biblical and theological criticism, scientific optimism, liberal and pietistic evangelicalism, and deeply aware of and influenced by the struggle against slavery, child labor, and in the case of the nonconformists, the struggle against the established church itself.

The Lutheran Church, and in particular the German, Norwegian, Swedish, Finnish, and American Lutheran missionary societies, made a major contribution to the evangelization of South Africa. The Moravian, Rhenish, Berlin, and Hermannsburg missionary societies were among the first to pioneer missionary work in South Africa. The missionary activities of the Lutheran churches fall into three clear phases: a pioneering period (1829–1889), a period of cooperation (1889–1959), and a period of consolidation (since 1959).

Various attempts were made during the late nineteenth and twentieth centuries toward greater understanding between the churches in South Africa. Movements were launched from various quarters, either to promote Christian and church unity, or to protect the churches against deviant teachings. One of these was the Evangelical Alliance, which, for instance, the *Nederduitse Gereformeede Kerk* joined as far back as 1857. The emphasis was on Christian unity in and through prayer. The alliance played a prominent role for many years with Dr. Andrew Murray as one of the leading figures.

The Presbyterian Alliance, which was founded in 1875, was very significant for the South African churches that followed the Presbyterian Church order. Contacts are still maintained between these churches. Delegates from the English-speaking churches and from the *Nederduitse Gereformeede Kerk* have regularly attended the alliance's international congresses. Even during the turbulent years of the Anglo-Boer War, a delegation of the *Nederduitsch Hervormde* or *Gereformeerde Church of the Transvaal* (the present *Nederduitse Gereformeerde Kerk*) attended the alliance's conference overseas. The former Presbyterian Alliance is now known as the WORLD ALLIANCE OF REFORMED CHURCHES, to which several South African churches still belong.

The Methodist Church of South Africa, as well as the Lutheran, Baptist, and Anglican Churches, all participated in the great international gatherings of their respective denominations (the Anglican Lambeth conferences are particularly well known). This worldwide interaction between churches of the same confession or church order helped to promote ecumenism, albeit in a restricted sense.

There have also been various attempts to bring about unity between the English-speaking churches. In 1928 the Presbyterian, Congregational, and Methodist churches sought closer cooperation because, in their view, a divided church in South Africa could not effectively uphold the principles of evangelical religion. After the Methodists withdrew, the matter was taken up again in 1934. After various fruitless attempts to unite, the attempted union was abandoned in 1947. After the instigation of the Lambeth Conference in 1958, the Anglican Church initiated discussions with the Presbyterian Church in 1960. These talks were extended to include the Tsonga Presbyterian Church, the three Congregational Churches, and the Methodist Church. Talks between the three Presbyterian churches and the Congregationalists have shown the most progress. However, this was checked in 1976 when the Presbyterian Church of Southern Africa advocated a federation, while the other three churches supported organic union. The Church Unity Commission has, nontheless, continued to work for unity between the Anglicans, Presbyterians, Methodists, and Congregationalists, and several united churches have already been formed.

The South African Council of Churches (SACC) remains one of the few comprehensive ecumenical organizations in South Africa. Its weakness is that it does not represent all the churches and missions in the country. At first, all the Afrikaans churches and the majority of Evangelical churches remained outside its organization. Nonetheless, it has created a fellowship for dialogue among a wide and representative group of churches. At present the SACC is undoubtedly the most comprehensive and ecumenical church organization in South Africa, embracing churches of all racial groups and almost all languages. Its aim is to promote church unity, coordinate church and missionary endeavors, and undertake joint enterprises.

The strained situation experienced in South Africa during the 1950s and 1960s acquired a fresh dimension with the Soweto riots in 1976, when black youth demonstrated their dissatisfaction with the state's education policy and the existence of certain laws, which broke up homes, families, and ordinary life. In 1976 there was widespread unrest that assumed far greater dimensions than the events following the Sharpeville uprising in 1960. Young people were no longer prepared to accept the situation in which they found themselves. Soweto gradually became a national symbol of a new generation of nationally and politically conscious black people in South Africa.

Meanwhile, the Afrikaans-speaking churches followed the national government in the crucial matter of racial discrimination. However, some South African churches (including the Afrikaans-speaking churches), were part of the rapid developments in social and political reforms. They have expressed their concern and involvement through discussions, talks, conferences, and concrete action.

During the 1980s events in the church were in continued flux and change: the *Nederduitsch Hervormde Kerk* resigned from the World Alliance of Reformed Churches, the banning order on Dutch Reformed Church Clergyman and anti-apartheid activist Beyers Naudé was lifted, Bishop *Desmond Tutu* received the Nobel peace prize, and documents like "Church and Society," "Evangelical Witness," and the "Kairos Document" were published.

At the beginning of the 1990s, the progress of ecumenical relations in South Africa remained uncertain. Within South Africa the gulf between the so-called evangelical churches on the one hand and members of the SACC on the other remained, and there were few signs of reconciliation or greater mutual understanding.

The political situation in South Africa was charged with a desire for negotiations between the major political players, and a spirit of uncertainty and expectancy emerged in broader society. In this connection, the consultation of Christian Churches at Rustenburg in November 1990, where leaders of different churches gathered to discuss their Christian witness, proved historically significant, because it was the largest and most representative gathering of Christian churches ever held in South Africa.

In the critical period of negotiations and transition toward a new South Africa in the last decade of the twentieth century, church and religion in general, and Protestantism more specifically, played a decisive and formative role. Naturally, not all the positive developments during these years can be attributed to either the direct or indirect role of the churches. It can, however, be stated that without the presence, witness, and involvement of the Protestant Churches, South Africa may have advanced further along the road to violence and possibly civil war. Without the churches, the uncertain process of transition would have been far more difficult and much more dangerous.

Involvement in church life and church affairs in South Africa is still at a high level, both in rural and urban areas. The different Protestant churches are well served by ministers, officials, and laity. Ministers of churches are still respected members of the community, and apart from the ministry, they serve in various other spheres as well. The church enjoys freedom of worship and is therefore free to fulfill its prophetic task toward governmental institutions. By and large, the importance of religion in South Africa cannot be overemphasized, and Protestantism plays a major role in the consolidation, expansion, and development of church and society.

In the global context of the twenty-first century, issues such as democratization, high moral values, non-racism, justice, reconciliation, reconstruction, and development will probably be the order of the day. In some ways South African society, particularly because of the Protestant churches' involvement, is showing the way to that future.

References and Further Reading

Balia, D. *Black Methodists and White Supremacy in South Africa.* Durban: Madiba Publications, 1991.

Bredekamp, H., and R. Ross, eds. *Missions and Christianity in South African History.* Johannesburg: Witwatersrand University Press, 1995.

Cochrane, J. *Servants of Power: The Role of the English-speaking Churches, 1903–1930.* Johannesburg: Ravan Press, 1987.

Davenport, T. R. H. *South Africa: A Modern History.* Bergvlei: Southern Book Publishers, 1987.

De Gruchy, J. W. *The Church Struggle in South Africa.* Cape Town: David Philip, 1979.

Elphick, R., and R. Davenport, eds. *Christianity in South Africa: A Political, Social and Cultured History.* Cape Town: David Philip, 1997.

Hofmeyr, J. W., and G. J. Pillay, eds. *A History of Christianity in South Africa. Vol. 1.* Pretoria: Haum, 1994.

Prozesky, M., ed. *Christianity in South Africa.* Bergvlei: Southern Publishers, 1990.

J. W. HOFMEYR

SOUTH INDIA, CHURCH OF

On September 27, 1947, the same year in which INDIA achieved her independence, the Church of South India was inaugurated. This event concluded nearly thirty years of negotiations, which concerned matters of DOCTRINE, LITURGY, ordination, and SACRAMENT. The Church of South India united the Anglican dioceses of India, Myanmar (Burma), and Ceylon (Sri Lanka) with the Methodist Church of South India and the South Indian United Church (SIUC). The SIUC itself was established in 1908 and included Presbyterian, Reformed, and Congregational churches. The South Indian union scheme sought to preserve distinctive features of each of its historic traditions, while tailoring them to the Indian context.

The formation of the Church of South India was the product of two distinct, but overlapping processes: movement toward ecumenical cooperation between Western-based churches and missionary societies, and the rise of Indian NATIONALISM. To a great extent, this spirit of cooperation was prompted by the imperatives of missionary work in societies where Christians were in a small minority. Limited resources in the field, conflicts over spheres of influence, and a growing need for churches to accommodate local converts from wide-ranging ethnic and denominational backgrounds all prompted ecumenical dialogue.

Since the mid-nineteenth century, mission societies in India established regular conferences to discuss their common objectives. Local or provincial conferences during the 1850s and 1860s were followed by a General Missionary Conference held in Allahabad in 1872, consisting of 136 missionaries who were predominantly European. In 1900, the South Indian Missionary Conference in Madras drew nearly 150 missionaries representing forty-five missionary organizations. Among these were the London Missionary Society, CHURCH MISSIONARY SOCIETY, American Baptist Mission, and SOCIETY FOR THE PROPAGATION OF THE GOSPEL. Subsequently, missionaries in the main Christian centers of South India, Madras, and Bangalore organized themselves into missionary conferences. Organizations such as the Christian Literature Society, the YMCA (see YMCA, YWCA), and the Christian Endeavor Convention, along with the leadership of Madras Christian College were instrumental in bringing European and Indian church leaders together in dialogue. This climate of ecumenical dialogue helped prepare the way for the formal union of churches embodied the Church of South India.

In 1919, delegates from Anglican and SIUC churches met in Tranquebar to explore a scheme that would lay the groundwork for the formation of the Church of South India. G. Sherwood Eddy, H. A. Popely, V. Santiago, Meshach Peter, and V. S. AZARIAH drafted a manifesto that stressed the importance of church unity. This manifesto sought to reconcile the Anglican emphasis on the historical episcopate with

the SIUC's emphasis on the spiritual equality of all believers. The delegates proposed a union on the basis of a common regard for the Old and New Testaments, belief in the Apostle's and Nicene Creeds, the sacraments of BAPTISM and the LORD'S SUPPER, and the historic episcopate, "locally adapted" (Sundkler 1954: 102). At the Lambeth Conference of Anglican bishops the following year, questions of "reordination" and "rebaptism" for members of the united church and intercommunion were discussed at length.

Since the deliberations of 1919, the relationship between the "Church of England in India" and the colonial government weighed heavily on those involved in negotiations for church union. Leaders of free churches insisted that they would enter a union only with a disestablished church. In response to such concerns, a decision was made in December 1927 to replace the designation "Church of England in India" with "Church of India, Burma, and Ceylon." Anglican leaders were willing to regard the same as a "disestablished Anglican province" (Sundkler 1954:157). This decision significantly raised hopes that ecumenical union between Anglican and non-Anglican churches could be realized in India.

Influence of Nationalism

The disestablished character of the envisioned church union was particularly significant in light of the rise of Indian nationalism. Into the 1920s and 1930s, Mohandas K. Gandhi led Indians in a campaign of nonviolent civil disobedience against the British *raj* in India. An important aspect of Indian nationalism was *swadeshi*, a doctrine of economic, political, and cultural self-reliance. Under the influence of this ideology, Indian Christian leaders stressed the need to "Indianize" Christianity.

For some, Indianization involved efforts to make the church more "Hindu" or Sanskritic in its LITURGY, hymnody (see HYMNS AND HYMNALS), and ARCHITECTURE. For others, Indianization called for greater representation of Indians within the ranks of Christian institutions. At a time when the British *raj* itself was implementing policies of devolution, which increased Indian representation within every branch of government, ecumenical circles stressed the need to implement ideas of the former Church Missionary Society secretary, Henry Venn. Known today as the father of the "indigenous church" principle, Venn advocated the rapid transfer of influence and responsibility of church administration into indigenous hands.

Since the late nineteenth century, several key indigenizing projects emerged: Pulny Andy's National Church, Sadhu Sunder Singh's Christo Samaj, and the Christian Ashram Movement. Together, these movements envisioned an Indianized Christianity that was to be free from the denominational divisions that afflicted the Western church. Some advocates of this vision expressed their views through the evolving Christian press of South India, most notably the newspaper *The Guardian*.

In 1938, a group of Indian Christian intellectuals published *Rethinking Christianity in India*, which among other things took objection to the South Indian union scheme. According to theologian Vengal Chakkarai, the union scheme was a Western invention that addressed Western denominational illnesses more than it did Indian realities. Another member of the Rethinking Group, P. Chenchiah, contended that the debates over the church union scheme were steeped in Western ecclesiastical history. As such, they were irrelevant to the masses of illiterate Indian laypersons far removed from that history. Attitudes of the Rethinking Group downplayed the church as a visible, dogmatic institution, drawing attention to its "inner core" of spirituality that suited the Indian ethos.

Such criticisms show how participants in the debate over church union were able to view it either as a genuinely Indian project or as a Western one that was being foisted on Indians. J. E. LESSLIE NEWBIGIN, former Church of South India Bishop in Madura and Ramnad and an ardent ecumenist, advocated the union precisely because it addressed the heterogeneous character of Indian congregations and provided a more effective means for EVANGELISM. Alternative perspectives were put forth not only by advocates of a more "Indianized" Christianity, but also by those who would later embrace Donald MacGavran's principles of church growth, which emphasized the value of segregating congregations on the basis of caste.

See also Dialogue, Interconfessional; Ecumenism; Missions; Missionary Organizations

References and Further Reading

Job, G. V., et. Al: *Rethinking Christianity in India*. Madras, India: A. N. Sudarisanam, 1938.

Harper, Susan Billington: *In the Shadow of the Mahatma: Bishop V. S. Azariah and the Travails of Christianity in British India*. Grand Rapids, MI: Eerdmans and Richmond, Surrey, UK: Curzon Press, 2000.

Hollis, Michael. *The Significance of South India*. Richmond, VA: John Knox Press, 1966.

Neill, Stephen C. *Men of Unity*. London: SCM, 1960.

Newbigin, J.E. Lesslie. *The Reunion of the Church: A Defense of the South India Scheme*. New York: Harper & Brothers, 1948.

Paton, David M., "Ecumenism in Action: A Historical Survey of the Church of South India," *Ecumenical Review*, 25 (1973), 375–376.

Rajaiah, D. Paul. *Ecumenism in Action: Church of South India, An Assessment* Madras, India: Christian Literature Society, 1972.

Samartha, Stanley., "Vision and Reality: Reflections on the Church of South India, 1947–1997," *Lexington Theological Quarterly*, 33 (1998), 47–60.

Stackhouse, Max L., "Tensions Beset the Church of South India," *Christian Century*, 104, no. 25, S 9–16, 1987, 743–744.

Sundkler, Bengt. *Church of South India: The Movement Towards Union, 1900–1947*. London: Lutterworth Press, 1954.

Webster, John B., "The Church of South India Golden Jubilee," *International Bulletin of Missionary Research*, 22 (1998), 50–54.

CHANDRA MALLAMPALLI

SOUTHERN BAPTIST CONVENTION

This is the largest Protestant denomination in the United States, numbering some 17 million members in 38,000 congregations. While its largest constituency remains primarily in the American South, the convention includes churches that are located throughout the United States and Canada. Its missionary task force at home and abroad is also one of the largest in the world.

The Southern Baptist Convention (SBC) was founded at First Baptist Church, Augusta, Georgia in May 1845, as a result of a schism with Baptists in the north regarding the appointment of slaveholding missionaries by the General Missionary Convention of the Baptist Denomination in the United States for Foreign Missions (Triennial Convention). The Baptist missionary society, founded in 1814 as a means of promoting and funding the mission enterprise, was the first national organization of BAPTISTS in the United States. After years of remaining neutral on the slave question, the Triennial Convention was confronted with a test case when Georgia Baptists demanded the appointment of James Reeve, a southern slaveholder, as a home missionary. When the mission board denied the appointment, declaring "we can never be a party to any arrangement which would imply approbation of slavery," Baptists in the South formed a new convention to promote their own missionary cause.

Convention Organization

The SBC soon established a convention system that was much more connected than the earlier society method of forming Baptist organizations. Societies were autonomous, freestanding agencies funded by churches, associations of churches, and individuals to carry out specific functions such as home and foreign missions, publishing, and education. The convention system linked those agencies in a more centralized, connected organization. While boards and agencies retained their own boards of trustees, they were not completely autonomous, but agencies of the entire convention. Trustees were appointed by the convention, not by self-perpetuating boards. Nonetheless, local Baptist churches retained their autonomy and could unite with local associations of churches, state Baptist conventions, and the national Southern Baptist Convention. State conventions, many formed before the SBC itself, maintained their own regional organizations and programs. They founded and supported state Baptist colleges and universities, hospitals, and other regional endeavors. Many Baptist colleges in the South were founded before the beginning of the SBC. These include what is now the University of Richmond, Virginia (1832); Wake Forest University, North Carolina (1834); Furman University, South Carolina (1826); Samford University, Alabama (1841); and Baylor University, Texas (1846).

Associations of churches were formed for fellowship, ministry, and mutual encouragement by churches in a given geographic area, roughly paralleling townships or counties. Associations extended the work of local congregations within a more proximate region. All these connections meant that individual churches could maintain connections on local, regional, national, and (through the mission boards) international, operations.

This system encouraged the development of elaborate denominational programs for education, missions, publications, and evangelism. Home and foreign mission boards were established almost immediately. The first Southern Baptist foreign missionaries were appointed to China in 1846. In 1847 and 1848 the board also appointed two African Americans, John Day and B. J. Drayton, as missionaries to the African colony of LIBERIA.

The Domestic Mission Board, later called the Home Mission Board, was founded in Marion, Alabama in 1845. Russell Holman (1812–1879), a northerner, served as its first executive secretary, encouraging work with blacks, native Americans, and immigrants. Conflicts with Northern Baptist home missionaries after the CIVIL WAR and difficulties in raising funds made Southern Baptist efforts difficult until the 1880s, when I. T. Tichner (1825–1902) assumed leadership and put the organization on more solid financial and organizational foundations.

In 1859 the Southern Baptist Theological Seminary was founded in Greenville, South Carolina, to provide ministerial education for the new denomination. Its first faculty was composed of four prominent educators: John A. Broadus (1827–1895), James P. Boyce (1827–1888), Basil Manley, Jr. (1825–1892), and William Williams (1804–1895). Following the Civil War the school was relocated in Louisville, Kentucky in 1877.

Southern Baptists supported the Confederacy during the Civil War and experienced the desolation of defeat and Reconstruction. After the war, the denomination became one of the primary vehicles for perpetuating the "religion of the lost cause," a reassertion of Southern morality and idealism amid the devastation of Northern conquest. Programmatic organization, evangelical zeal, and loyalty to the South combined to create a powerful denominational system and identity for Southern Baptists from Virginia to Texas. It is impossible to understand the development of the SBC apart from the relationship between Southern Baptist denominational programs and Southern culture that characterized the convention throughout the first 150 years of its history. The Foreign Missions Board was located in Richmond, Virginia. In 1882 the Home Missions Board was moved from Marion, Alabama, to Atlanta, Georgia. The Sunday School Board was founded in 1891 with headquarters in Nashville, Tennessee. It was charged with publishing monographs, denominational literature, and other resource materials for use in churches and schools. Concerns for the financial needs of ministers led to the founding of a relief and annuity board in 1918. In 1925 the SBC developed a cooperative program of collective funding whereby local church monies were sent to state Baptist conventions that retained a portion and then sent a percentage on to the national denomination, which then funded specific boards and agencies. Also in 1925, the convention established an executive committee to oversee denominational administration. A full-time president of the executive committee of the SBC is the chief administrative agent of that committee.

The Woman's Missionary Union (WMU) was founded as an auxiliary to the Southern Baptist Convention in 1888. Many of the males who led the convention were not sure that women should be included in the operations of the convention, and thus it began as a freestanding body alongside the official denominational organization. Its purpose was to raise support for women missionaries, to provide programs in mission education for youth, and to raise offerings for support of home and foreign missions. In 1907 the WMU founded a missionary training center for women in Louisville, Kentucky, a school that ultimately merged with the Southern Baptist Seminary in 1962 as the Carver School of Missions and Social Work. The school was closed in the 1990s.

The Women's Missionary Union sponsors two annual offerings for foreign and home mission programs, which raise millions of dollars for the support of Southern Baptist missionary activity. The Lottie

Moon Christmas Offering, begun in 1888, honors the work of Charlotte Diggs (Lottie) Moon (1840–1912), one of the Southern Baptists' first single female missionaries in China. The Annie Armstrong Easter Offering for home missions is named for Annie Walker Armstrong (1850–1938), a founder of the WMU.

The Laymen's Missionary Movement of the Southern Baptist Convention was formed in 1907 for the purpose of educating and enlisting men in the church's missionary calling. It later became the Brotherhood Commission and is currently known as Baptist Men.

The Southern Baptist Convention meets annually, usually in mid-June, to elect officers, approve the annual budget, and conduct other matters of business. Worship services include elaborate music and a "convention sermon." The president of the convention is elected annually, and may serve two one-year terms. The president has primary responsibility for appointing nominating committees that name trustees to convention boards and agencies. Decision making at the annual meeting is vested in messengers sent from member congregations. To this day, congregational size and a minimal amount of financial support determine the number of representatives from each church. Southern Baptists distinguish delegates who might speak officially for congregations from messengers whose votes do not necessarily reflect the consensus of opinion in their specific church. No church may send more than ten messengers. A resolution admitting women as messengers was approved in 1918. Messengers are required to provide information regarding church contributions to the convention, and sign a statement that neither they nor the church they represent supports or affirms homosexuality in any way.

In 1919 Southern Baptists instituted the Seventy-five Million Campaign, an effort to raise $75,000,000 to alleviate debt and move the convention into a new era of denominational solvency. While the goal was not met, the convention did receive over $58,000,000.

The Sunday School Board of the Southern Baptist Convention publishes books on Baptist history, polity and doctrines, devotional works, and wide variety of materials for use in church educational programs. Its Sunday school materials, which include weekly lessons, provide Bible study guides for millions of Southern Baptists from Sunday to Sunday across the United States and throughout the world. Throughout much of the twentieth century, Sunday evening programs known variously as the Baptist Young People's Union (BYPU), Training Union, and Church Training, provided study courses in church history, Baptist studies, ethics, and Christian discipleship. While it continues in various forms, these evening events have declined steadily during the last two decades.

During the 1990s the names of many of the denominational agencies were changed. The Foreign Mission Board became the International Mission Board of the SBC, and the Home Mission Board became the North American Mission Board of the SBC. The Sunday School Board was renamed Lifeway Christian Resources of the Southern Baptist Convention.

By the 1950s the SBC had established six theological seminaries, funded by the denomination, and offering ministerial training at locations spread across the continent. These included the Southern Baptist Theological Seminary, Louisville, Kentucky (1859); Southwestern Baptist Theological Seminary, Fort Worth, Texas (1905); New Orleans Baptist Theological Seminary, New Orleans, Louisiana (1918); Golden Gate Baptist Theological Seminary, Mill Valley, California (1950); Southeastern Baptist Theological Seminary, Wake Forest, North Carolina, (1956); and Midwestern Baptist Theological Seminary, Kansas City, Missouri (1957). During the latter decades of the twentieth century, one out of five seminarians in the United States was registered in one of these schools. Southwestern Baptist Seminary, with an enrollment of several thousand students, remains the largest Protestant theological seminary in the world.

Evangelism

Evangelical zeal has long characterized the Southern Baptist Convention and its churches. One of the reasons for its dramatic increase in size following the war was its efforts to convert persons to faith and bring them into Baptist churches. Revival services were scheduled seasonally in most Baptist churches well into the twentieth century. These evangelical campaigns often ran for weeks at a time with calls for sinners to be converted, Christians to be renewed, and young people to surrender for full-time Christian service as ministers, missionaries, or other Christian workers. By the twenty-first century one- or two-week revivals were shortened to three or four days. Some churches, particularly in the southwest, continued the practice, while others gave it up all together, promoting abbreviated "renewal" services, "deeper life" conferences, or "preaching" series.

Many Southern Baptist churches and individuals place great emphasis on personal evangelism, or "soul winning," the direct, one-on-one presentation of the "plan of salvation" culminating in an invitation to "trust Christ as Savior." In many congregations, members are taught how to "witness" and encouraged to do so at every opportunity. Southern Baptist church members often testify to their conversion and entrance into Christian faith. At the same time, Southern Baptists also give serious attention to the nurturing of children to faith. The average age of baptism in most Southern Baptist churches is somewhere between nine and twelve years of age. Thus some members describe dramatic conversions while others testify to gradual nurturing into Christian faith.

Baptist Distinctives

Southern Baptists identified themselves with the broader Baptist movement, a tradition that began in 1608 in Holland when a group of Puritan Separatists, exiled from England, renounced their earlier infant baptism and received baptism on the basis of a profession of faith. A portion of the group returned to England in 1612, constituting a church in Spitalfields, just outside the walls of London. These were called General Baptists and were Arminian in their theology, affirming Christ's death for all persons, the role of human free will in salvation, the need for all persons to repent and believe in Jesus Christ, that God's grace could be accepted or resisted, and the possibility that believing individuals could fall from grace, thereby rejecting an earlier salvation. By the 1630s another group of Baptists had appeared in England, affirming the basic tenets of Calvinism or reformed theology. These Particular Baptists insisted that Christ died only for the elect, a number chosen unconditionally by God before the foundation of the world. Grace was irresistible to the elect and would ultimately claim them before they departed this world. Those who received grace could not reject it and would persevere to the end.

The first Baptist church in America was founded in Providence, Rhode Island, around 1639 by Roger Williams (1603–1683), the quintessential colonial dissenter. Baptists came into the south in the late 1690s when a Baptist congregation from Kittery, Maine, moved to Charleston, South Carolina, founding the first Baptist church there.

Baptists in the south were influenced by numerous Baptist traditions. These included the Regular Baptists, who came to Charleston and emphasized classic Calvinist doctrines, preferred ordered worship, and sang the Psalms, not "man-made" hymns. They were evangelicals in their concern that the elect be brought to salvation, but were often suspicious of revivalistic methods as too "enthusiastical" (overly emotional). Regulars encouraged their ministers to seek formal education. Revivals and awakenings throughout the colonies in the 1740s and 50s influenced the development of Separate Baptist churches that encouraged emotionalism in conversion and worship, permitted women to preach, and were suspicious of written creeds or confessions. Separate Baptists disparaged an educated or paid ministry. Separate Baptist presence

in the South began in North Carolina in 1755 with the founding of the Sandy Creek Baptist Church by Shubal Stearns (1706–1771) and Daniel Marshall (1706–1784), popular preachers and church planters. As revivalism came to permeate Southern evangelicalism, many Southern Baptists softened their original Calvinism and placed greater emphasis on the general atonement of Christ and the possibility that all persons might freely choose salvation through repentance and faith.

From their beginnings in 1845, Southern Baptists were heirs of certain basic Baptist "distinctives," common to the tradition worldwide. These included:

1. The authority of the Bible as the guide for faith and practice.
2. Freedom of conscience in matters of religious faith and practice.
3. A regenerate church membership. Each congregation was to be composed of believers only.
4. The autonomy of each local congregation.
5. Associational relationships between congregations.
6. Congregational polity.
7. The priesthood of the laity.
8. An ordained clergy to provide ministry in the churches.
9. Religious liberty in the church and the state.
10. Immersion baptism and the Lord's Supper as "ordinances" of the church.
11. A strong concern for evangelism and the missionary enterprise.

While Southern Baptists share these distinctives, they have not hesitated to disagree over the nature and meaning of each characteristic. The autonomy of the Southern Baptist system at almost every level insured differences of opinion, debate, and even schism, especially in local congregations. Indeed, denominational controversies and church splits have been so prevalent as to reinforce the saying: "Baptist churches multiply by dividing."

Throughout their history, Southern Baptists have differed on questions of doctrinal uniformity and denominational participation. Some insist that a basic doctrinal consensus is necessary for cooperation, while others suggest that Baptists may disagree on doctrinal definitions and work together in ministry. Freedom of conscience and autonomy of the local congregation are often promoted as allowing churches and individuals room for interpretation and disagreement. The need for orthodoxy and doctrinal consistency are viewed as essential for denominational stability and order. Those differences, long present in the

SBC, became more pronounced in the late twentieth and early twenty-first centuries.

Worship Practices

Southern Baptists also reflect a variety of styles in the practice of public worship. Heirs of both the Regular and Separate Baptist traditions, Southern Baptist churches could be formal and orderly, as well as informal and spontaneous in their orders of worship. Heirs of a strong evangelical, revivalistic ethos, most placed great emphasis on preaching, calls to conversion, and opportunities for public commitment usually known as "invitations," or "altar calls," in which persons were invited to come forward in public professions of faith. In the nineteenth and twentieth centuries, shouts of "amen" or "hallelujah" were not uncommon in certain congregations across the South. HYMNS, usually sung to the accompaniment of organ or piano, included traditional English hymnody as well as frontier revival songs, and, more recently, simple praise choruses. The standard worship service incorporates prayers, hymns, Bible readings, an offering, musical selections from choirs or ensembles, and a sermon. Services generally conclude with an "invitation," or "call to Christian discipleship." The sermon remains the central element of Southern Baptist Sunday worship. It involves an extended commentary on specific texts of scripture in an effort to expound biblical teachings, encourage ethical behavior, and address pastoral needs of the worshiping congregation.

In the nineteenth and early twentieth centuries some Southern Baptist clergy wore black "frock coats" (tails) in the pulpit. In some the ministers now wear pulpit robes. In certain contemporary worship services, the ministers were casual clothing in an effort to promote a less formal style. Most, however, conduct worship in business attire. Choirs in most Southern Baptist churches generally wear matching robes. In the nineteenth and much of the twentieth centuries, Southern Baptists generally held services on both Sunday and Sunday night, with a mid-week prayer meeting on Wednesdays. While that remains the norm in many congregations, other, particularly urban, congregations have given up Sunday evening services. Some have added two or three services on Sunday morning both to accommodate crowds and the schedules of their parishioners.

During the waning years of the twentieth century and the beginning of the twenty-first, a growing number of Southern Baptist churches developed what is sometimes known as contemporary worship services, aimed at younger audiences or at "seekers" who have little background or interest in traditional worship. These services promote informality in dress and content, utilize skits, videotapes, film, and drama along with sermons and praise choruses projected on screens above the congregation. Some of these services reveal the influence of the charismatic movement as practitioners lift their hands heavenward in prayer, clap and shout in worship services, and, perhaps, even speak in tongues. Debates over this more folksy, contemporary style have resulted in a variety of "worship wars" among Southern Baptists. At the beginning of the twenty-first century, Southern Baptist worship practices are increasingly varied and demonstrate significant diversity in theology and practice.

Controversies

Controversy has been a hallmark of Southern Baptist life since the beginning of the convention. Begun in schism and racism, the SBC struggled throughout its history with issues of race, generally supporting the institution of slavery before and during the Civil War, cooperating or at least acquiescing to Southern segregationists, and dividing over the CIVIL RIGHTS MOVEMENT. For example, Richard Furman (1755–1825), pastor of the First Baptist Church in Charleston, South Caroline, and one of the South's most prominent ministers, articulated one of the most famous Biblical defenses of slavery (1822) produced in America. Although there were significant exceptions, most Southern Baptists participated in or remained silent about Jim Crow laws and other segregationist policies throughout most of the twentieth century. During the Civil Rights movement in the South, the SBC passed various resolutions calling for peaceful responses from blacks and whites, and urging an end to segregationist legislation. Nonetheless, innumerable churches debated and divided over the integration of schools and churches. In some cases church deacons stood at the doors of church buildings in an effort to obstruct the entry of African Americans and even Africans seeking a place to worship. MARTIN LUTHER KING, JR. (1929–1968) was invited to speak in the chapels of only two Baptist-related schools in the South, the Southern Baptist Theological Seminary and Wake Forest University. In 2000 the denomination officially apologized for its participation in the support of slavery and all that accompanied it. While the number of people of color was increasing significantly in the SBC in the late twentieth and early twenty-first centuries, the SBC remains an overwhelmingly Anglo-Saxon denomination.

Another enduring controversy involved the Old Landmark Movement that began around 1859 in Tennessee and Kentucky. Initiated by J. R. Graves (1820–1893), Nashville Baptist preacher and editor, it involved the question of whether non-immersed ministers could officiate in Baptist churches. Graves's colleague, J. M. Pendleton, pastor of First Baptist Church in Bowling Green, Kentucky, concluded that they could not because their "pedobaptism" (infant baptism) was invalid. Landmarkists took their name from Proverbs 22:28, "Remove not the ancient Landmark, which thy fathers have set." They insisted that Baptist churches were the only true churches of Christ because they alone could trace their history in a succession of dissenting churches all the way back to Jesus's baptism by John the Baptist in the River Jordan. Landmark Baptists required the immersion of all those not baptized in Baptist churches and practiced "close" communion, limiting the participation in the Lord's Supper only to members of the congregation where it was being celebrated. While the SBC resisted Landmark attempts to impose their interpretations on the entire denomination, the Landmark legacy shaped baptismal and communion practices in many churches into the twenty-first century. Likewise, Landmark concern for the absolute autonomy of the local congregation led them to oppose denominationally-based mission agencies, financial programs, and general operations as too "hierarchical."

Anti-denominationalism was also a facet of the fundamentalist movement that developed in America in general and Baptist life in particular in the early twentieth century. Fundamentalism called the church to reassert the basic doctrines of Christianity, such as biblical inerrancy, Christ's virgin birth, his sacrificial atonement, his bodily resurrection, his second coming, and literal miracles. While Southern Baptists were theologically conservative and generally affirming of these dogmas, they resisted efforts to impose them on the entire convention. J. Frank Norris (1887–1952), pastor of First Baptist Church in Fort Worth, Texas, was a strong proponent of fundamentalism who denounced the denominational "machine," and charged that liberalism was present in many Baptist seminaries and universities in the south. His efforts were unsuccessful and he ultimately distanced himself from the SBC, helping to form the independent Baptist movement.

Largely in response to the fundamentalist–modernist controversy, the SBC approved its first official confession of faith known as the Baptist Faith and Message in 1925. Taken largely from the nineteenth-century New Hampshire Confession of Faith, it contained basic statements on biblical authority, the need for conversion, baptism by immersion, local church autonomy, and other doctrines. The confession was revised in 1963 and in 2000 and remains the denomination's doctrinal standard.

During the 1960s the denomination confronted two controversies regarding biblical authority and the use of historical/critical methods of biblical studies. In 1961 Broadman Press, the denominational publishing house, released a book entitled *The Message of Genesis*, written by Ralph Elliott, professor at the Midwestern Baptist Theological Seminary in Kansas City, Missouri. Elliott's use of critical methods of biblical scholarship provoked an immediate response from Southern Baptist conservatives who felt that the book undermined the authority of the Scriptures. In response to the controversy, Broadman Press ceased publication of the book and Elliott was dismissed from his teaching position, not for his scholarly views, but for insubordination when he resisted a mandate from the seminary that he not republish the book.

In 1969 another controversy over biblical authority developed with the publication of a commentary on the book of Genesis in *The Broadman Bible Commentary*, a series published by Broadman Press. Written by British Baptist professor G. Henton Davies, the commentary also made use of critical methods of biblical study, with attention to the JEDP theories of multiple compilers of the Hebrew Torah. Convention conservatives again demanded that the book be rejected. Broadman Press editors responded by discontinuing publication of the volume and contracting with Southern Baptist Seminary professor Clyde Francisco for a new edition.

These controversies highlighted increasing division between convention conservatives and moderates over the theological underpinnings and leadership of the denominations. Conservatives insisted that the denomination was perched on a slippery slope that would lead to liberalism and the loss of orthodoxy. They were particularly concerned that professors in SBC seminaries did not adhere to the doctrine of biblical inerrancy, the belief that the Bible is totally without error in its original manuscripts on every subject it addresses.

In 1979 conservatives, led by Houston Appeals Court Judge Paul Presslar and conservative educator Paige Patterson, began a concerted effort to elect a series of SBC presidents who would use the appointive powers of that office to add trustees to convention boards who would promote inerrancy and other conservative agendas. At the annual SBC meeting in Houston, Texas they succeeded in electing Adrian Rogers, pastor of Bellevue Baptist Church in Memphis, Tennessee (a conservative), to the convention presidency. Conservatives declared that they were simply offering a "course correction" that would return the SBC to its orthodox origins. Moderates charged that the conservatives were attempting a takeover in order to gain political control of America's largest Protestant denomination. For a decade, conservative and moderate Southern Baptists confronted each other every June in an effort to elect presidents sympathetic to their vision for the convention. Conservatives won every election and succeeded in changing the denominational boards enough to gain complete control of the national convention structure. So intense were the divisions that the 1985 SBC meeting in Dallas, Texas attracted some 45,000 messengers, the largest such gathering in the denomination's history.

Biblical inerrancy was not the only divisive issue between the two groups. One significant debate involved the role of women in the church, particularly focused on the ordination of women to the Baptist ministry. The first ordination of a Southern Baptist woman occurred in 1964 when Addie Davis was ordained by the Watts Street Baptist Church in Durham, North Carolina. Others soon followed, and conservatives challenged such actions as a violation of biblical mandates that they believed limited the pastoral office only to males. In 1984 conservatives at the annual SBC meeting approved a (nonbinding) resolution stating that women should be excluded from the pastoral office on the basis of 1 Timothy 2:12ff in order "to preserve a submission God requires because the man was first in creation and a woman was first in the Edenic fall." In 2000 the revision of the Baptist Faith and Message (the denomination's confession of faith) declared officially that women were not to serve as pastors.

The controversy between conservatives and moderates had significant long-term effects on the nature and organization of the SBC. It produced a variety of divisions, even formal schisms, throughout the old SBC system. During the 1980s and 1990s, numerous Baptist colleges and universities chose to distance themselves from the state Baptist conventions that controlled them and appointed their trustees. The University of Richmond, along with Wake Forest, Furman, Samford, and Baylor Universities were among the schools that renegotiated their relationships with their parent bodies and asserted the right to appoint their own trustees while retaining varying Baptist connections. Likewise, as the six Southern Baptist seminaries came under complete control of the conservatives, new Baptist-related seminaries and divinity schools appeared. These included Beeson Divinity School at Samford University; Baptist Theological Seminary, Richmond, Virginia; George Truett Seminary at Baylor University; Logston School of Theology at Hardin-Simmons University, Abilene, Texas; McAffee School of Theology at Mercer University, Atlanta, Georgia; Christopher White School of Divinity at Gardner-Webb University, Boiling Springs, North Carolina; Campbell University Divinity School in Buies Creek, North Carolina; and Wake Forest University Divinity School in Winston-Salem, North Carolina. Baptist houses of study were also established at Duke Divinity School, Durham, North Carolina; Candler School of Theology at Emory University, Atlanta, Georgia; and Brite Divinity School at Texas Christian University, Fort Worth, Texas.

State Baptist conventions also reexamined their relationship with the national denomination. Baptist conventions in Georgia, Florida, and South Carolina generally affirmed the conservative directions of the convention, while the state conventions in Virginia and Texas reflected more moderate sentiments. In Texas and Virginia, conservatives formed their own state conventions, creating formal schisms with the traditional state organizations. The Baptist General Convention of Texas not only developed its own denomination-like programs, but also invited moderates from throughout the nation to join them. In other southern states moderates and conservatives maintained an uneasy coalition, often by permitting a variety of alternative funding possibilities for churches, thereby enabling them to designate money to conservative or moderate causes.

New Baptist organizations also developed out of the controversy in the Southern Baptist Convention. The Alliance of Baptists was founded in 1986 as a moderate/liberal "conscience" within the convention. Its member churches moved away from the denomination more rapidly than other moderate congregations. The alliance affirmed women's ordination, academic freedom, and freedom of conscience.

The Cooperative Baptist Fellowship, founded in 1991, became a clearinghouse for moderate Baptist missionary, educational, and benevolent endeavors. Based in Atlanta, Georgia, it sends out missionaries, funds theological education, and provides resources for churches in areas of Christian education, Baptist identity, and church leadership. Many of its member churches retain their affiliation with the SBC.

In the year 2000 the denomination's revision of its confession of faith, the Baptist Faith and Message, delineated more specific doctrinal and ethical concerns of the conservatives and further delineated the differences with the moderates. The revised document included additions regarding the "total truthfulness" of Scripture; opposition to abortion, adultery, and homosexuality; and the denial of the pastoral role to women. In their public statements on the role of the denomination in the "public square," SBC leaders often believe themselves to be a counterculture movement, at odds with an increasingly secular society and churches that have sold out to the culture. All this makes it more difficult for moderate churches to continue formal association with the SBC.

The Southern Baptist denominational system was one of the most elaborate and enduring religious organizations in American religious history. Continued controversy between conservatives and moderates has led to significant restructuring of the denomination, the redefining of the nature of the convention, and the realignment of institutions and individuals connected with it. These changes make the Southern Baptist Convention an important case study in transitions in American denominational life, theology, and practice.

References and Further Reading

Ammerman, Nancy Tatom. *Baptist Battles.* New Brunswick, NJ: Rutgers, 1990.

Baker, Robert A. *The Southern Baptist Convention and Its People, 1607–1972.* Nashville: Broadman Press, 1972.

Cothen, Grady C. *What Happened to the Southern Baptist Convention?* Macon, GA: Smyth & Helwys Publishers, 1993.

Eighmy, John Lee. *Churches in Cultural Captivity.* Knoxville, TN: University of Tennessee Press, 1974.

Encyclopedia of Southern Baptists. Nashville, TN: Broadman Press, 1958.

Fletcher, Jesse C. *The Southern Baptist Convention, A Sesquicentennial History.* Nashville, TN: Broadman & Holman Publishers, 1994.

James, Robison B., and David S. Dockery. *Beyond the Impasse? Scripture, Interpretation, and Theology in Baptist Life.* Nashville, TN: Broadman Press, 1992.

Leonard, Bill J. *God's Last and Only Hope: The Fragmentation of the Southern Baptist Convention.* Grand Rapids, MI: William B. Eerdmans Publishing, 1990.

Wills, Gregory A. *Democratic Religion, Freedom, Authority, and Church Discipline in the Baptist South.* New York: Oxford University Press, 1988.

Wilson, Charles Reagan. *Baptized in Blood: The Religion of the Lost Cause.* Athens, GA: University of Georgia Press, 1980.

BILL J. LEONARD

SOUTHERN PROTESTANTISM

The Southern United States, popularly called the Bible Belt, has long been a bastion of an evangelical Protestantism inclined toward ORTHODOXY in belief. Historical reality undergirds that perception, although there has also consistently been a substratum of diversity even within Southern Protestantism. This complex story has roots in the earliest English colonial settlements in the region.

English immigrants who made their first permanent settlement in Virginia in 1607 were decidedly Protestant, by birth members of the CHURCH OF ENGLAND, by inclination attracted to Puritan ways. In each Southern colony, although the timetable differed, the Church of England in time became legally established, supported by tax monies and often the only recognized form of Christianity. Throughout the colonial period Anglican churches in the South had too few CLERGY to make this tradition vital and dynamic and had to rely on the bishop of London for episcopal oversight (see BISHOP AND EPISCOPALY). In addition, when the first Africans forced to migrate as slaves arrived in 1619, Anglicans were ambivalent about whether to seek slave CONVERSIONS; they were also ignorant of how African tribal sensibilities continued to provide a substratum of religious meaning for the slave population. White Anglican laymen assumed greater control over parish life than was the case in ENGLAND, and, for many, religion was more an expression of rational gentility than of deep piety.

Before the era of independence, however, other Protestant currents were undermining Anglican dominance. Evangelist GEORGE WHITEFIELD in the mid-eighteenth century preached a more enthusiastic style of the gospel, whereas the steadily increasing migration of Scots-Irish into the Southern upcountry along the eastern slopes of the Appalachian mountain chain also brought a decidedly more evangelical cast to Southern religious life. By the time of independence, which left the Church of England in disarray, EVANGELICALISM was poised to dominate Southern Protestantism.

Evangelicalism's penetration into the South owed much to itinerant Methodist CIRCUIT RIDERS and Separate Baptists preachers whose mobility enabled them to reach people where they were (see BAPTISTS, UNITED STATES; METHODISM; METHODISM, NORTH AMERICA). With a more emotionally charged emphasis on personal conversion, evangelicals appealed especially to WOMEN and to African Americans. The evangelical message offered spiritual power to those on the margins of the larger society. In addition, by stressing experience over intellectual formulation, Evangelicals shunned the formal education for preachers thought necessary for Episcopal priests or even Presbyterian clergy. Powerful African-American preachers, often unable to read Scripture but with an ability to speak dynamically about their own experience of conversion, attracted a biracial audience. The disorganization independence brought to the Church of England also aided evangelical growth; in many areas Anglican women found spiritual needs better met by Evangelicals, especially when parishes lacked priests.

The Impact of Frontier Camp Meetings

After independence, as Euro-Americans migrated west of the Appalachians, the frontier CAMP MEETING further secured evangelicalism's dominance of Southern Protestantism. The date and location of the first camp meeting are lost to history, but the notable revival at Cane Ridge in Kentucky in 1801 became a model for those that followed along much of the

Southern frontier. Attracting preachers from different denominations, the REVIVALS lasted two weeks or so, during the time between the maturing of crops and their harvest. The revivals drew thousands, providing opportunities not only for spiritual experience but for socializing with neighbors who lived so great a distance away that the camp meeting was the only time for coming together. The revivals also drew African Americans into their orbit, furthering the biracial character of much Southern Protestant life.

With dramatic manifestations of the Spirit as individuals were seized by the jerks or began to bark like animals, frontier camp meetings were also times of emotional excess. Yet they had a more somber cast, with a celebration of the LORD'S SUPPER often closing the gathering. This sacramental dimension most likely reflected the influence of the Scots-Irish; similar celebrations were part of Scottish religious culture in the eighteenth century. In the camp meetings, too, lie some forerunners of Southern gospel as a musical genre, for camp meetings songs added distinctive rhythmic patterns and refrains to familiar HYMNS.

Among the organizers of the Cane Ridge camp meeting was BARTON W. STONE, who with Alexander Campbell (see CAMPBELL FAMILY) sought to restore Christian practice to patterns thought to prevail in New Testament times. Abandoning the notion of denominations, these Christians saw themselves reconstituting the church according to apostolic models. In time the movement spawned several divisions; the Churches of Christ, which retain pockets of strength in parts of Tennessee and Texas, originated in the Stone–Campbell movement (see CHRISTIAN CHURCHES, CHURCHES OF CHRIST). Linked today by colleges, lectureships, and a variety of publications, the Churches of Christ continue to eschew denominational structures. The other major body rooted in Stone–Campbell RESTORATIONISM, but stronger outside the South, is the DISCIPLES OF CHRIST.

The frontier experience made revivalism a hallmark of Southern Protestant life. In the twentieth century, for example, the nation's most well known evangelist was BILLY GRAHAM, a native North Carolinian.

Controversy over Slavery

The early nineteenth century not only cemented the hold of the evangelical denominations on Southern Protestantism, but also led to increasing concerns over chattel SLAVERY and the moral issues involved. Debates over slavery were not limited to the South, nor were concerns over race regionally exclusive. As antislavery sentiment mounted in the North, Southern Protestants became more strident in efforts to support slavery on biblical grounds and to resist moves toward abolition (see SLAVERY, ABOLITION OF). Among Presbyterians in the South there developed the idea of the "spirituality of the church," articulated forcefully by James Henley Thornwell and Benjamin Morgan Palmer. This notion insisted that only spiritual matters like SALVATION were the proper concern of the church; on political issues, like slavery, the church should remain silent. Such thinking allowed Southern Protestants formally to avoid the moral dilemma posed by slavery. It also elevated an individual ethic over a social ethic in much popular thinking, such that social matters became issues of political concern, not religious; in time, this narrower ethical perspective would almost restrict ethical concern to the realm of personal behavior, although some, even among Evangelicals, always called for a gospel with ramifications for the social order.

Within the churches, increasing angst over slavery led to the introduction of balconies where African Americans would be required to sit, although most Southern worship remained biracial. This move paralleled moves in the North that followed on the ejection of RICHARD ALLEN and a few others during worship at Philadelphia's St. George's Methodist Church in 1787 for refusing to move to the balcony. That episode spurred the organization of separate congregations and also of separate denominations for African Americans. In the South there were already a few congregations that were entirely or predominantly African American, with Silver Bluff Baptist Church near Augusta, Georgia, among the oldest. However, in the South, creating racially separate congregations and denominations was largely a post–Civil War phenomenon.

As regional tensions over slavery increased, the major evangelical denominations eventually split, foreshadowing the national schism that came when the Confederate States of America formed after South Carolina seceded from the Union in 1860. The Methodists divided in 1844, not reuniting until 1939; the Baptist division in 1845 still endures, with the SOUTHERN BAPTIST CONVENTION by the later twentieth century becoming the largest Protestant group in the nation. Among major Protestant bodies, only the Episcopal Church did not divide over slavery, although during the war, separate conventions were held in the South and in the North. Ironically, the CIVIL WAR years furthered the evangelical grip on Southern Protestantism. Revivals spread among the Confederate army from time to time, leading many soldiers to reaffirm their commitment to an evangelical understanding of Protestant Christianity.

After the war, Northern-based groups like the AFRICAN METHODIST EPISCOPAL and AFRICAN METHODIST

EPISCOPAL ZION churches made inroads among former slaves in the South, as did the Christian (formerly Colored) Methodist Episcopal church that emerged from Southern Methodism in 1870 and various Baptists denominations (see BLACK METHODISTS; NATIONAL BAPTIST CONVENTION OF AMERICA; NATIONAL BAPTIST CONVENTION, U.S.A.). The result was that race continued to mark Southern Protestantism. The white denominations, in an effort to seize victory out of defeat, helped promote a civil religion that glorified a mythic past and celebrated presumed Confederate virtue, whereas the African-American denominations became centers of social life for the free black population that had to contend with a virulent racism that replaced slavery.

African-American churches kept alive profound ways African religious sensibilities buttressed Southern Protestantism, by fashioning an underlying foundation in theology and practice that drew on both the African and the slave experience (see AFRICAN-AMERICAN PROTESTANTISM). For example, for a time the African-American pastor was as much conjurer and root doctor as educated cleric, fusing roles and moving freely from one to the other. In addition, the black church became and remained a center of social and political life, providing opportunities for leadership, recreation, and expression of social welfare concern that white Protestantism readily yielded to other cultural institutions. Thus, when the CIVIL RIGHTS MOVEMENT erupted with the Montgomery, Alabama, bus boycott in 1955, a pastor, MARTIN LUTHER KING JR., became its acknowledged spokesman and the churches became cradles of leadership and support.

Holiness and Pentecostal Expressions

Not all who came into the Appalachian mountains in the late eighteenth and nineteenth centuries moved on to the Southern frontier. Some who remained developed distinctive styles of Protestantism, many influenced by currents of Holiness that took the BIBLE very seriously and greatly emphasized how the Holy Spirit empowered personal behavior and experience. Many churches scattered through the mountains lack denominational affiliation, although most major denominations are represented. Among the unaffiliated congregations are those that look to the Gospel of Mark, chapter 16, for signs that accompany faith. Since the early twentieth century, these signs have often included handling serpents and ingesting strychnine (see SERPENT HANDLERS). Several Southern states tried to outlaw such practices, but freedom of religion ideals prevailed. Serpent handling churches rarely proselytize. Handlers usually come from families where several generations have engaged in the practice, but most children born of handlers eventually affiliate with nonhandling groups.

In the mountains, too, came the first Southern stirrings of PENTECOSTALISM, although the modern American Pentecostal movement tracks its roots to the 1906 AZUSA STREET REVIVALS in Los Angeles. A decade earlier Pentecostal experiences were reported around Camp Creek, North Carolina. Pentecostals accept "gifts of the Spirit" such as glossolalia (see TONGUES, SPEAKING IN). At first biracial, in time most Pentecostal congregations divided along racial lines. Several groups, such as the CHURCH OF GOD and the Church of God of Prophecy, maintain headquarters in Cleveland, Tennessee, whereas the largest African American Pentecostal body, the CHURCH OF GOD IN CHRIST, is based in Memphis, Tennessee. By the twenty-first century the growth of Southern Pentecostal groups outpaced that of other evangelical denominations, spurred by immigration of Hispanic Pentecostals into the South as well as by the appeal of Pentecostal experience. As well, the enthusiasm characteristic of Pentecostalism was influencing WORSHIP in congregations affiliated with most Protestant denominations.

The South has also been fertile ground for many smaller religious groups. Groups as diverse as Quakers (see FRIENDS, SOCIETY OF) and Unitarians (see UNITARIAN UNIVERSALIST ASSOCIATION) have found a place in the South. There are also a variety of smaller Baptist bodies, such as Old Regular Baptists, Seventh-Day Baptists, and PRIMITIVE BAPTISTS. Alongside larger denominations are smaller ones that represent offshoots, often over matters of DOCTRINE, POLITY, or social policies. Among them are the Southern Methodist Church and the Presbyterian Church of America. Groups popularly identified as more sectarian, such as the SEVENTH-DAY ADVENTISTS, have likewise flourished in the region. Even so, their combined presence only modestly challenges the continuing dominance of the Southern Baptist Convention and the UNITED METHODIST CHURCH among the region's Protestants.

The Impact of Fundamentalism

By the second decade of the twentieth century, FUNDAMENTALISM had made inroads into the South, although its primary impact had first been among northern Baptists and Presbyterians. In 1925 in Dayton, Tennessee, the conviction of John Scopes on charges of teaching evolution in a public school signaled that fundamentalism or an extreme Protestant orthodoxy had come to the South. Until then most Southern Protestants believed that MODERNISM had only a small following in the South and that most remained consistently orthodox in belief and practice. Aided by the long history of evangelistic revivals and camp meetings, linked by a network of BIBLE COLLEGES AND INSTITUTES (including Bob Jones University), and adept at using the most advanced communications media, fundamentalists became a force within most Southern Protestant denominations by the middle of the twentieth century. The rise of Southern fundamentalism also reinforced the evangelical emphasis on a personal ethic, although groups like the FELLOWSHIP OF SOUTHERN CHURCHMEN represented an alternative perspective that sought to promote a SOCIAL GOSPEL in the region.

When the Civil Rights movement challenged the racism long taken for granted in the South and U.S. courts moved to eliminate prayer and Bible reading from the public schools, fundamentalists perceived that the religious substratum of the region was crumbling. Many congregations started private schools, both to maintain racially segregated educational opportunities and to ensure that children would receive instruction in traditional evangelical moral values. Televangelists like JERRY FALWELL and PAT ROBERTSON sought to translate fundamentalist leanings into political power through organizations such as the MORAL MAJORITY and other so-called CHRISTIAN RIGHT groups (see TELEVANGELISM). Such political organizations represented a significant break with earlier understanding that had seen religion's role almost exclusively concerned with the SALVATION of individuals, not with political matters.

Within the Southern Baptist Convention, similar concerns over a perceived erosion of traditional faith and practice by the late 1960s led more conservatively inclined leaders to launch a campaign to wrest control of the denomination's bureaucracy and affiliated institutions, such as colleges and SEMINARIES, from those thought too moderate or liberal. Although the effort was successful, the internal controversy left the region's largest Protestant body deeply divided, with many institutions and local congregations forming a parallel network through the Cooperative Baptist Fellowship to keep a less conservative presence flourishing.

At the dawn of the twenty-first century, Southern Protestantism remained predominantly evangelical in style and orthodox in belief. However, there were increasing challenges to that hegemony, many from other Protestant bodies whose approach was different, and the Protestant landscape was becoming decidedly more diverse. Ethnicity continued to signal some of that diversity, with a growing Hispanic population joining people of African descent in offering alternatives to the white evangelical style. As well, Pentecostal groups were growing at a faster rate than had been the case a half century before. Protestants also had to confront a rapidly increasing proportion of

Southerners who were not Protestant or even Christian. Roman Catholicism and JUDAISM both had a distinguished history in the region, and, after immigration laws changed in 1965, Hinduism, Buddhism, and Islam also took their place in Southern religious culture.

References and Further Reading

Bruce, Dickson D. Jr. *And They All Sang Hallelujah: Plain-Folk Camp-Meeting Religion, 1800–1845*. Knoxville: University of Tennessee Press, 1974.

Frey, Sylvia R., and Betty Wood. *Come Shouting to Zion: African American Protestantism in the American South and British Caribbean to 1830*. Chapel Hill: University of North Carolina Press, 1998.

Glass, William R. *Strangers in Zion: Fundamentalists in the South, 1900–1950*. Macon, GA: Mercer University Press, 2001.

Harvey, Paul. *Redeeming the South: Religious Cultures and Racial Identities among Southern Baptists, 1865–1925*. Chapel Hill: University of North Carolina Press, 1997.

Heyrman, Christine Leigh. *Southern Cross: The Beginnings of the Bible Belt*. Chapel Hill: University of North Carolina Press, 1997.

Hill, Samuel S. *Southern Churches in Crisis Revisited*. Tuscaloosa: University of Alabama Press, 1999.

———, and Charles H. Lippy, eds. *Encyclopedia of Religion in the South*. 2nd ed. Macon, GA: Mercer University Press, 2004.

Kimbrough, David L. *Taking Up Serpents: Snake Handlers in Eastern Kentucky*. Chapel Hill: University of North Carolina Press, 1995.

Leonard, Bill J., ed. *Christianity in Appalachia: Profiles in Regional Pluralism*. Knoxville: University of Tennessee Press, 1999.

Lyerly, Cynthia Lynn. *Methodism and the Southern Mind, 1770–1870*. New York: Oxford University Press, 1998.

Mathews, Donald G. *Religion in the Old South*. Chicago: University of Chicago Press, 1977.

McCauley, Deborah Vansau. *Appalachian Mountain Religion: A History*. Urbana: University of Illinois Press, 1995.

Morgan, David T. *New Crusades, New Holy Land: Conflict in the Southern Baptist Convention, 1969–1991*. Tuscaloosa: University of Alabama Press, 1996.

Raboteau, Albert J. *Slave Religion: The "Invisible Institution" in the Antebellum South*. New York: Oxford University Press, 1978.

Wilson, Charles Reagan. *Baptized in Blood: The Religion of the Lost Cause, 1865–1920*. Athens: University of Georgia Press, 1980.

———, ed. *Religion in the South*. Jackson: University Press of Mississippi, 1985.

CHARLES H. LIPPY

SOZZINI, FAUSTO PAOLO (SOCINUS, FAUSTUS) (1539–1604)

Italian reformer. Born in Siena, ITALY on December 5, 1539 to a famous family of lawyers, Sozzini spent his childhood in Siena, Bologna, and Scopeto. He planned for a career as a lawyer, traditional for his family, but in his studies he only marginally dealt with jurisprudence and instead concentrated on humanist studies and writing poetry in Italian and Latin. He became a member of the Accademia degli Intronati in Siena, the intellectual salon of the city. He soon became expert in the organization of various games and plays that were popular in Siena.

He also developed an interest in religious issues at a very young age. His family was under the influence of reform ideas very early. Sozzini's cousins Camillo, Celso, Cornelio, but above all Lelio (1525–1562) were supporters of reform. From 1547 on Lelio Sozzini, who had left Italy, proved to be a skeptic intellectual and convinced Antitrinitarian linked to radical REFORMATION circles. He also enjoyed warm and even friendly relations with many leaders of the Reformed Church.

The anti-Catholic sentiment of the Sozzini family, including Fausto, was closely observed by the Catholic Inquisition, which arrested a few of its members in November 1560. Alerted in time, Fausto managed first to hide out in the Siena area but then to leave for Lyon in FRANCE in April 1561. He represented his family's interests there, corresponding with his friends. Religious issues became of even greater interest to him, and when he learned about the death of his uncle Lelio in Zurich, he immediately left for that city to secure Lelio's manuscripts. He later often noted that Lelio's works highly influenced his own religious convictions. Fausto's commentary on the first chapter of St. John's Gospel, *Expliatio primi capitis Ioannis* ("Explication of the first chapter of John"), an interpretation of this passage in the spirit of radical ANTITRINITARIANISM with his rejection of Christ's eternity, is an example of Lelio's influence. During his stay in SWITZERLAND, Sozzini came to know SEBASTIAN CASTELLIO, whose thought also shaped his religious beliefs.

Return to Italy

Toward the end of 1563 Sozzini returned to Italy. His stay, presumably with the intent to take care of inheritance matters, was supposed to be short, and he planned to return to Switzerland quickly to undertake theological studies. Nevertheless, he remained in Italy almost twelve years. This is an enigmatic period of Sozzini's life. Sozzini was in Rome between 1565 and 1568, probably as secretary of the auditor of the Roman Rote Serafin Razzali. Between 1569 and 1575 he entered the service of Isabelle de' Medici and her husband Paolo Giordano Orisini. Socinius later described these years as lost in unproductive activities. At the same time he had secret contacts with Italian religious dissenters in Switzerland (see DISSENT). In

1568 Sozzini's commentary appeared in Alba Julia, Transylvania, and shortly thereafter the Polish version was published in Krakow by Grzegorz Pawel from Brzeziny.

At the end of 1575 Sozzini left Italy for good and moved to Switzerland, where he spent three years. This stay was characterized by intensive writing and numerous debates during which Sozzini defined the main lines of his theological system. Presumably he had developed most of these ideas while in Italy.

The first important debate, in which Jacques Covet—a Huguenot theologian—was his main opponent, touched on soteriological, or SALVATION, issues (see HUGUENOTS). Sozzini rejected the redemptive character of Christ's DEATH on the cross, claiming that Christ's saving mission consisted of showing the right way of life. This debate led him to write the important work *De Iesu Christo Servatore* ("About Christ the Savior"), published in 1594 in POLAND. The second debate with Italian religious emigrant Francesco Pucci included anthropological problems—the state of the first human before original SIN. Sozzini claimed that human beings were mortal by nature. This debate, *De statu primi hominis ante lapsum* ("About the state of the first man before the fall"), was published after his death in 1610.

Move to Poland

In June 1579 Sozzini moved to Krakow, where he established close relations with the Polish Antitrinitarian Church known as the "Minor"—that is, "smaller"—church. While stressing his desire to join this church, he did not hide his own views on numerous matters. BAPTISM by immersion practiced in the Minor Church represented the main point of disagreement. He rejected this practice, stating that it was not relevant for Christians. This position, as well as his ideas about eternity, JUSTIFICATION, and Christ's sacrifice on the cross, prevented the synod in 1580 from accepting him into the church. Nevertheless, he quickly gained a high informal position within the church.

At the end of the 1580s Sozzini fought for leadership in the Polish Antitrinitarian Church, putting forward his soteriological concepts, defending his belief about the symbolic character of the LORD'S SUPPER. A prolific writer, he answered vigorous Jesuit attacks against Antitrinitarians. The treaties against Jacob Wujek, *Refutatio libelli, quem Iacobus Vyjekus Iesuita edidit* ("Refutation of the books published by the Jesuit Jacob Wujek"), in 1595 and the Calvinist Andrzej Wolan, *De Iesu Christi Filii dei natura* ("About the nature of Jesus Christ son of God") in 1588 are the culmination of these efforts.

At the Lublin synod (May and June 1593) he imposed his positions on redemption, justification, and the Lord's Supper on the Minor Church. In political and social issues he was not that successful. The synod agreed to welcome lay rulers but did not enable its members to take part in court proceedings. From the synod in Lublin (1598) on, Sozzini occupied a leading spiritual role among Polish Antitrinitarians.

Sozzini married Elzbieta Morsztyn in May 1586. In May 1587 his daughter Agnieszka (mother of the Socinian thinker Andrzej Wiszowaty) was born. In September of that year his wife died, and in October his Tuscan protector Ferdinando de' Medici also died. The new ruler, Cardinal Ferdinando de' Medici, had no friendly feelings toward Sozzini and did not prevent the Inquisition from charging him with HERESY on February 3, 1591. He was sentenced to death but was burned in effigy because of his absence. This, however, put an end to his income from the property in Italy. He had to lead a very modest life, relying on the help of his friends and cobelievers.

Final Years

On April 29, 1598 Sozzini was attacked by Catholic students in Krakow, who managed to get into his apartment and destroy his manuscripts and books. They intended to drown him in the Vistula River. Already sick at the time, he was saved by several professors from the University of Krakow. He could not overcome the loss of his manuscripts and books, particularly his treaty against atheism. He left Krakow on April 30 and spent the remainder of his life at various places. Works including *Commentarius in Epistolam Ioannis Apostoli prima* (*Commentary to the First Letter of St John the Apostle*) (1614) and the unfinished *Lectiones sacra* (*Sacred lectures*) were published after his death. Troubled with failing eyesight, Sozzini dictated both works. He did not finish another work against Jesuits and a CATECHISM, which were important to him. The treaty to Reformed Evangelicals asking them to join the Antitrinitarians (*Manifestation . . .* , 1600) was his only work published in Lutoslawce. He died in Lutoslawce on March 3, 1604 and was buried there.

Despite his long stay in Poland, Sozzini did not learn to speak Polish (he had a passive understanding of the language). He remained a patrician from Tuscany, dreaming of a return to his native country. At the same time he understood that Poland was the only country where he could develop his program of radical Christian reform.

Sozzini influenced Polish Antitrinitarianism of the sixteenth and seventeenth centuries and European SOCINIANISM. Many of his works have also been published (in the original language or translated) in other countries, mainly ENGLAND, Holland, and GERMANY. His grandson Andrzej Wiszowaty prepared a collection of his works, including some unedited ones. It appeared in Amsterdam in 1688 as t. I and t. II *Bibliotheca Fratrum Polonorum*.

References and Further Reading

Cantimori, Delio. *Eretici italiani del Cinquecento e altri scritti.* Edited by Adriano Prosperi, 146–148, 331–360, 365–368, 400–417. Torino, Italy: Giulio Einaudi editore, 1992.

Chmaj, Ludwik. *Faust Socyn (1539–1604).* Warsaw, Poland: Książka i Wiedza, 1963.

Godbey, John. "Fiducia. A Basic Concept in Fausto Sozzini's Theology." In *Socinianism and Its Role in the Culture of XVI-th to XVIII-th Centuries.* Edited by Lech Szczucki, 59–67. Warszawa-Łódź, Poland: PWN, 1983.

Lubienieki, Stanislaw. *History of the Polish Reformation.* Minneapolis, MN: Fortress Press, 1995.

Marchetti, Valerio. *I simulacri delle parole e il lavoro dell'eresia.Ricerca sulle origini del socinianesimo.* Bologna, Italy: CISEC, 1999.

Ogonowski, Zbigniew. "Faustus Socinus." In *Shapers of Religious Traditions in Germany, Switzerland, and Poland 1560–1600.* Edited, with an Introduction by Jill Raitt, 195–209. New Haven and London: Yale University Press, 1981.

Wilbur, Earl Morse. *A History of Unitarianism: Socinianism and Its Antecedents.* 384–407. Cambridge, MA: Harvard University Press, 1946.

Williams, George Huntston. "The Christological Issues between Francis Dávid and Faustus Socinus during the Disputation on the Invocation of Christ." In *Antitrinitarianism in the Second Half of the 16th Century.* Edited by Róbert Dán and Antál Pirnát, 287–321. Budapest, Hungary: Akadémiai Kiadó-Leiden/E. J. Brill, 1982.

———. *The Radical Reformation.* 3rd rev. ed. 978–989, 1162–1175. Kirksville, MO: Sixteenth Century Publishers, 1992.

LECH SZCZUCKI

SPALDING, JOHANN JOACHIM (1714–1804)

German theologian. This leading personality of the religious ENLIGHTENMENT was born on November 11, 1714 in Tribsees, at that time a part of Swedish Pomerania, and died on May 22, 1804 in Berlin. His father was the principal of the municipal school in Tribsees. After studying THEOLOGY in Rostock and Greifswald and receiving his doctorate in 1736, Spalding worked as a tutor and then as a parish minister in Pomerania. He moved to Berlin, where his responsibilities included not only those of a parish clergy but also the position of provost and membership on the supreme CONSISTORY council for Prussia.

Spalding is considered the main representative of NEOLOGY, the new theology of the eighteenth century. This "modern theology" sought to overcome Protestant ORTHODOXY and PIETISM. The optimistic view of this theology understood God as a loving father whose wisdom and providence worked to lead humanity to its moral perfection. Ethics played a central role in this theology.

Much of what new theologians advocated was taken from English theologians. Spalding was one of the most important purveyors of moderate antideist literature, made famous through his translations. These included Joseph Butler's *Analogy of Religion,* an apologetic work that weaves together Christian creed, scientific knowledge, and the fundamental principles of the Enlightenment.

In 1748 Spalding won literary fame and significant ecclesiastical influence with his *Gedanken über die Bestimmung des Menschen (Thoughts on the Human Destiny).* In this work he opposed the French philosophical materialism of the court of the Prussian king Frederick II. Among his other successful publications were *Gedanken über den Wert der Gefühle im Christentum (Thoughts on the Value of Emotion in Christianity,* 1761; 5th ed., 1784); *Über die Nutzbarkeit des Predigtamtes und deren Beförderung (On the Usefulness of the Preaching Office and its Enhancement,* 1772; 3rd ed., 1791), in which he opposed the dogmatic doctrines broadcast from the pulpit; and a kind of bequest, *Religion, eine Angelegenheit des Menschen (Religion, a Human Affair,* 1797; 4th ed., 1806).

In Berlin and beyond, Spalding maintained a vigorous correspondence with many important personalities, including J. F. W. Jerusalem, JOHANN SALOMO SEMLER, Johann Wilhelm Ludwig Gleim, Christoph Friedrich Nicolai, FRIEDRICH ERNST DANIEL SCHLEIERMACHER, Moses Mendelssohn, and IMMANUEL KANT. In protest against the religious edict of Johann Christoph Wöllner, which required CLERGY in Prussia to teach only officially recognized DOCTRINE, Spalding resigned his leadership positions in the church in 1788.

References and Further Reading

Primary Sources:

Religion, eine Angelegenheit des Menschen. vol. 1. [First volume in a critical edition of Spalding's works]. Tübingen, Germany: Mohr Siebeck, 2001.
———. *Ueber die Nutzbarkeit des Predigtamtes und deren Beförderung. 1772.* Tobias Jersak, ed. Kritische Ausgabe. Johann Joachim Spalding. Albrecht Beutel, ed. Abt. 1. Schriften, Bd. 3. Tübingen, Germany: Mohr Siebeck, 2002.

Secondary Sources:

Schollmeier, Joseph. *Johann Joachim Spalding: ein Beitrag zur Theologie der Aufklärung.* Gütersloh, Germany: Mohn, 1967.
Nordmann, Hans. *Johann Joachim Spalding: Ein Bild aus dem geistigen Ringen der deutschen Aufklärung.* Naumburg, Germany: Sieling, 1929.

MARTIN GRESCHAT

SPCK

See Society for Promoting Christian Knowledge

SPENER, PHILIPP JAKOB (1635–1705)

German Pietist. Spener is known for having spearheaded a movement of moral and religious renewal within German LUTHERANISM known as PIETISM, which blossomed in the aftermath of the destructive Thirty Years War (1618–1648).

Early Life and Education

Born in Alsace, the son of a councilor to the duke of Rappolstein, Spener was influenced in his youth by his reading of JOHANN ARNDT's *Wahres Christentum (True Christianity),* which countered a formalized system of orthodox Lutheran DOCTRINE with an emphasis on a new birth, understood in terms of the categories of late medieval German mysticism. His reading of Puritan literature (see PURITANISM), especially RICHARD BAXTER and Lewis Bayly, also heightened his interest in self-examination and predisposed him to theological study at the University of Strasbourg, where, under Johann Conrad Dannhauer's influence (1603–1666), he was led to value the role of the LAITY, the vernacular reading of Scripture, and a casuistic approach to personal ETHICS and Sabbath observance. As was customary for theological students, he spent two years as a traveling scholar in SWITZERLAND, FRANCE, and GERMANY. In Geneva he fell under the influence of the radical HUGUENOT preacher, Jean de Labadie (1610–1674).

Ministry in Frankfurt am Main (1666–1686)

After completing a doctorate in theology at Strasbourg, and marrying, Spener was called at the age of thirty-one to become senior of the Lutheran CLERGY at Frankfurt/Main. Here he gave emphasis to reviving the rite of confirmation through a program of catechization of the youth, as well as befriending the youthful GOTTFRIED LEIBNIZ. He also instituted his method of activating the laity to assist the clergy in renewing parish life, by means of the *collegia pietatis,* private gatherings of "earnest" laity, first held biweekly in his home, where the sermon of the previous Sunday was discussed. In time, other devotional literature was studied, and the central focus eventually became BIBLE Study.

A prolific writer, Spener's most noted work, which was highly acclaimed throughout Germany, was his *Pia Desideria* (1675). It appeared as the preface to a new edition of Arndt's *True Christianity,* but it created such a sensation that it was soon published separately. It was organized in three parts: an account of the shortcomings of the church of the day, the possibility of reform, and a program of specific proposals for effecting that end. These proposals were intended to address such abuses as churches controlled by the absolute pretensions of local princes, the rigid observance of class and ecclesiological distinctions, and the duplicity implicit in a church life that was outwardly flourishing but which appeared to yield little evidence of producing genuine Christian life. Spener's response to these conditions included a call for a more extensive use of Scripture, charity when engaged in controversy, PREACHING for purposes of edification, and the reform of schools, especially theological education (see EDUCATION, THEOLOGY: EUROPE).

Spener's book reflected his efforts to activate the universal Christian priesthood, as announced in a sermon in 1669, which called for committed members of the congregation to serve with the clergy in reforming parish life. There was a tendency for the *collegia pietatis* to be regarded as the heart of the church, as an *ecclesiolae in ecclesia,* a church within the church, although this was not Spener's intention. To avoid charges of Donatism and to circumvent rumors of raging ANTINOMIANISM in the *collegiae,* he attempted to forestall the unchecked proliferation of conventicles, the small Bible study groups, by letters and tracts, and by requiring that they be held in the church, under the pastor's leadership, rather than in private homes. They were to be vehicles for parish reform and renewal, although they also precipitated withdrawal from the church on the part of the Frankfurt separatist leader Johann Jakob Schutz (1640–1690).

Although Spener wrote against the separatists, he did not regret forming the *collegium,* particularly because it represented the only place where all three social classes (the clergy, nobility, and general laity) could meet and strategize in the work of the CHURCH. Nonetheless, despite his initial enthusiasm for this structure, that Spener refrained from instituting CONVENTICLES in his later parish appointments.

Service in Dresden (1686–1691) and Berlin (1691–1705)

After twenty years in Frankfurt, Spener accepted the post of first court chaplain to the elector of Saxony in Dresden (1686–1691). Here he found some respite from controversy, with more leisure for serious theological writing. He also became acquainted with a younger teacher at Leipzig, AUGUST HERMANN FRANCKE (1663–1727), whom he helped to obtain a post at the new Saxon university of HALLE. Spener's final post was as inspector of churches and preacher in the Church of St. Nicholas in Berlin (1691–1705).

Here he became more involved in the controversies of the Pietist movement, including several doctrinal and moral charges leveled against it by the theological faculty of the University of Wittenberg, the hotbed of Lutheran Orthodoxy. In his latter years, he consented to publish his voluminous letters and papers. He also served as sponsor at the baptism of NIKOLAUS VON ZINZENDORF (1700–1760), providing a link with that renovator of the MORAVIAN CHURCH.

Conclusion

Spener differed from those Orthodox Lutherans who placed the doctrinal content of the Lutheran symbolical books on a par with Scripture. He balanced the Lutheran concern for the inspiration of Scripture with an emphasis on the effects of the Bible on persons, through the activity of the Holy Spirit. There was also an implicit doctrinal shift from the centrality of forensic JUSTIFICATION to the biological metaphor of regeneration.

With an eschatological interest grounded in his doctoral dissertation on the Revelation of John, he held out hope for "better times" for the church on earth, and regarded Christian existence from the standpoint of its goal, its perfection in Christ. Spener's devout, modest, and even cautious style belie the extent to which he became a central figure for church renewal in seventeenth-century Germany.

References and Further Reading

Primary Source:

Tappert, Theodore, ed. *Pia Desideria, by Philip Jacob Spener.* Philadelphia, PA: Fortress, 1964.

Secondary Sources:

Brown, Dale. *Understanding Pietism.* Grand Rapids, MI: Wm. B. Eerdmans, 1978.
Erb, Peter, ed. *Pietists: Selected Writings.* New York: Paulist Press, 1983.
Stein, K. James. *Philipp Jakob Spener; Pietist Patriarch.* Chicago, IL: Covenant Press, 1986.

J. STEVEN O'MALLEY

SPEYER, DIETS OF

Two imperial diets, or legislative assemblies, met in Speyer, GERMANY in 1526 and again in 1529 primarily for the purpose of dealing with the religious controversy that had arisen within the Holy Roman Empire because of the theological teachings of MARTIN LUTHER. The first diet resulted in a unanimous agreement among the estates to suspend in effect the EDICT OF WORMS (1521), which had outlawed Luther's teachings, until a general ecumenical council could be called. Three years later a council had not convened, so a second diet was held to decide the issue. Here the Catholic majority voted to rescind the 1526 Recess and to enforce the Edict of Worms. The evangelical minority formally protested the decision, but was disregarded. Their objection revealed a new corporate character of the REFORMATION and led to a new designation for followers of reform—Protestants.

The Diet of Speyer, 1526

In February 1525, Emperor Charles V achieved a decisive military victory over the French, allowing him to deal with the religious controversy within the German estates at an imperial diet. The diet was to convene in Speyer in the spring of 1526, but by March it was apparent Charles would be unable to attend because of renewed conflict with the French, the papacy, and the Turks, so he sent his brother, Ferdinand, instead. The business of the diet opened on June 25 with the proposition sent by Charles instructing those assembled to resolve the religious issue by prohibiting liturgical innovation and requiring enforcement of the Edict of Worms. The Emperor also sent secret instructions to Ferdinand informing him to cease all business if the discussion of the diet proceeded in a contrary direction. When the proceedings diverged, however, Ferdinand revealed Charles's instructions.

The estates were forced to delineate the nature of their AUTHORITY in relation to the emperor's. From recent conflicts, particularly the Peasants War of 1525, they had learned they could maintain their authority without Charles's assistance through the formation of alliances, even transconfessional alliances. Thus, the estates stood together in unanimous agreement. On August 27 they resolved in the Recess that, with respect to the Edict of Worms, each ruler along with his subjects would "live, govern, and carry himself as he hopes and trusts to answer to God and His Imperial Majesty" until a general council convened. This agreement was meant as a temporary solution to the question of the enforceability of the Edict of Worms. Many of the estates insisted that the edict could simply not be enforced. The Recess, supported by the Catholic estates, was meant to petrify the status quo. As time passed and a general council was not convened, the temporary solution became more permanent, especially since the reform-minded estates proceeded to undertake reform.

The Diet of Speyer, 1529

Two years later, as Charles continued his struggle against FRANCE and its new English allies, Ferdinand, recently crowned king of both Bohemia and HUNGARY, also confronted political problems. First was the prospect of violence among the opposing religious parties in the German lands. Additionally he faced possible war with the Turks, which would require financial support from these same estates. Hoping to resolve these difficulties, Ferdinand, as the emperor's representative, called for a diet to convene in the spring of 1527. It was postponed twice, first when Ferdinand was unable to attend and then because of Charles's objections. Realizing the inevitability of such a meeting, Charles called for a diet to meet in Speyer in February 1529, again with Ferdinand as his representative.

To Ferdinand's benefit, the imperial messengers were delayed, allowing him to modify the Proposition read to open the business of the diet on March 15. The proposition called for the revocation of the 1526 Recess of Speyer as well as the enforcement of the Edict of Worms. A committee drafted several new provisions: estates observing the Edict of Worms should continue to do so; evangelical estates in which the new teaching could not be abandoned without considerable trouble should discontinue all innovations; the mass could not be outlawed; communion in one kind could not be forbidden; those convicted of practicing rebaptism would be sentenced to death; CLERGY were forbidden to preach against the church's standard teachings; and the confiscation of property was outlawed. All provisions would be obligatory until a general council would make a final decision.

On April 19 the Catholic majority voted to approve the committee's proposal while simultaneously rejecting the evangelical opposition. The next day the evangelical estates submitted an official protest to the majority's action. Appealing to the constitutional *protestatio* principle, they argued that the unanimous decision of the 1526 Recess could not be overturned by a majority decision. They contended further that in matters concerning God's honor and the SALVATION of souls they were bound by conscience not to concede to the majority. Ferdinand and the Catholic majority rejected the protest. The Recess, approved on April 22, included only the majority decision.

With their communal stand the newly dubbed "Protestants"—John of Electoral Saxony, Philipp of Hesse, George of Brandenburg-Ansbach, Wolfgang of Anhalt, Ernst and Franz of Braunschweig-Lüneburg, and the cities of Strasburg, Nuremberg, Heilbronn, Ulm, Constance, Lindau, Memmingen, Kempten, Nördlingen, Reutligen, Isny, Saint Gall, Weissenburg, and Windesheim—achieved a new corporate character for the evangelical movement. Although they remained in Speyer, some took steps to form a defensive alliance should the dispute turn violent, but this was later hindered by theological disagreements. Many of these Protestants, however, would come together again in 1530 to make a theological defense of the evangelical movement with the AUGSBURG CONFESSION.

See also Lutheranism; Lutheranism, Germany

References and Further Reading

Friedensburg, Walter. *Der Reichstag zu Speier 1526 in Zusammenhang der politischen und kirchlichen Entwicklung Deutschlands im Reformationszeitalter.* Reprint (1887), Nieuwkoop, The Netherlands: B. de Graaf, 1970.

Kidd, B. J., ed. *Documents Illustrative of the Continental Reformation.* Oxford, UK: Clarendon Press, 1911. [Especially chapters 29 and 32.]

Kühn, Johannes. *Die Geschichte des Speyrer Reichstags 1529.* Leipzig, Germany: M. Heinsius Nachfolger, Eger & Sievers, 1929.

Ney, Julisus, ed. *Die Appellation und Protestation der evangelischen Stände auf dem Reichstage zu Speier 1529.* Reprint (1906), Darmstadt, Germany: Wissenschaftliche Buchgesellschaft, 1967.

MARY ELIZABETH ANDERSON

SPIRITUALISM

Spiritualism is described as a theological tendency and religious movement that seeks direct spiritual communication with God, while minimizing or rejecting external, material media, for example, SACRAMENTS, CLERGY, and Scripture. Spiritualism derives ultimately from the BIBLE and the Platonic tradition. In the early church the impact of both can be seen in pneumatic movements such as Montanism and theologians such as Origen and Augustine. Although the elements of spiritualism were pervasive in THEOLOGY thereafter, the mass of the population adhered to a materialist approach in the cult of the SAINTS, the sacraments, and the clergy. That is, because they imagined spirit as a fine material substance, they readily accepted its presence in and transmission by material objects.

Beginning in the eleventh and twelfth centuries spiritualism became much more prominent both among the orthodox and the heterodox (heretics) as a reaction to growing clerical power and increased emphasis on the objective sacrality of the CHURCH, the clergy, the sacraments, and other holy objects. The REFORMATION is the result and heir to these concerns. All Protestant theologies were spiritualist as compared to Catholic DOCTRINE and practice. The Radical Spiritualists (e.g., THOMAS MÜNTZER, SEBASTIAN FRANCK, CASPAR SCHWENCKFELD) went beyond the Magisterial Reformers (e.g., MARTIN LUTHER and JOHN CALVIN). They denied the need for any visible church, clergy, or sacraments. The erection of state churches made Spiritualism attractive to those who resisted the legal imposition of belief and who complained of the lack of fervor that they decried in the established churches. Spiritualism provided thinkers like JOHN LOCKE with arguments for religious TOLERATION. A pervasive non-aggressive spiritualism allows Western societies to escape the cycle of religious conflict and WAR seen elsewhere.

At the root of "Spiritualism" is the "Spirit." Christian Spirit derives from two quite different sources: Platonic "Mind" and biblical "Spirit." Both Platonic "Mind" and Ideas are immaterial—the Ideas exist apart from Mind and physical reality in a superior realm of which the physical universe is an inferior reflection. The Ideas are eternal, unchanging, and absolute. SALVATION for the human is achieved by looking within and ascending to this higher reality through use of the rational powers of the intellect. The mind "turns its back" on the external, material world and the physical desires and emotions (which Platonists associated with the body) that it provokes. The goal is eternal rest in the static perfection of the Ideal realm. Platonism accepts a stark dualism between mind and body, immaterial and material, with the latter incapable of containing or conveying the former. Rather, material reality, the world of bodies, is a distraction and obstacle to be avoided.

By contrast, biblical Spirit, in both the Old and New Testaments, is a force that shakes NATURE, transforms humans, and drives them to do God's will. The Bible does not describe the Spirit as immaterial and Spirit's behavior suggests physical power and presence. Its effects on humans can include a quiet wisdom, but more often involve heightened states of faith, fear, hope, love, anger, and the full range of human emotions. Spirit is an active force that works upon humans, not a crystalline perfection toward which humans strive. Although Spirit sometimes made use of an initial period of withdrawal to remake the human into a fitting instrument of God's will, Spirit normally propels humans to work in the world, not to flee it. Unlike the INDIVIDUALISM often associated with Platonism, biblical Spirit created community—the People of God or the church. Biblical Spirit could dwell in, be conveyed by, and make use of bodies and physical objects, although it also worked directly. Its effects ranged from military victory, to miracle, to prophecy, to individual enlightenment. Spirit was often associated with resistance to injustice, the rescue of the weak, and the punishment of the powerful. Biblical Spirit's dualism was not mind and matter, but spirit (reliance on God) and flesh (reliance on self or other humans).

Early movements like Montanism continued the biblical tradition. They appealed to prophecy against a growing clericalism, increasing reliance on the written Word, and marginalization of the pneumatic elements so characteristic of New Testament Christianity. Although structure eventually won out over spirit, biblical Spiritualism remained an option wherever the Bible was known. Radically dualist Gnosticism drew on Platonism. Within the institutional church, however, Christian thinkers trained in classical philosophy planted the seeds of Platonic Spiritualism. Already visible in Clement of Alexandria and Origen, Platonism was pervasive after the CONVERSION of the emperor Constantine when the learned elites joined the church and created sophisticated theological systems using Greek philosophy. Neoplatonists like Augustine produced a Christian understanding of the Spirit and of God by equating Platonic immaterial mind with biblical spirit. The implications for the Eucharist or LORD'S SUPPER were apparent in Augustine's famous line "Why do you prepare your teeth, if you have faith you have already eaten." Protestant reformers cited that passage repeatedly.

The fall of the Roman Empire, the decay of education, and the reduction of the learned elite to a few scattered clerics prevented the spread of Platonic Spiritualism to the church as a whole. A materialist understanding of Spirit remained common for the mass of the population and clergy. The theological defense of a real presence (see TRANSUBSTANTIATION) of Christ in the bread and wine of the Eucharist resulted.

The revival of Europe in the eleventh and twelfth centuries established a spiritualistic trajectory leading to the sixteenth-century Protestant Reformation. The weight of new bureaucracies in church and state provoked popular resistance and HERESY that drew on the biblical Spirit for its authorization. Monastic (see MONASTICISM) and university cultures produced mysticism (direct ecstatic union with God) and further elaborated immaterialist theologies. New religious orders (e.g., Franciscans and Dominicans) spread both intellectual/religious currents in the wider culture, primarily through PREACHING. Joachim of Fiore predicted a new Age of the Spirit; rigorist Franciscans who rebelled against the church were labeled the Spirituals; and the spiritual human *(homo spiritualis)* became the goal of ascetic and devotional regimens. By the beginning of the sixteenth century, "spiritual" had become a term that was promiscuously used to describe any form of piety or practice of which one approved, a meaning that it retains to this day.

A Neoplatonist revival on the eve of the Reformation caused the rediscovery and publication of the entire surviving corpus of Platonic and Platonist writings. Erasmus of Rotterdam, who influenced many first-generation Protestant reformers, recast Neoplatonic thought into a Christian vision marked by simplicity, inwardness, and lack of interest in the outward trappings of medieval Catholicism.

The Reformation

Every form of sixteenth-century Protestantism embraced a more "spiritualized" Christianity than did medieval Catholicism. The number, frequency, and sacrality of the sacraments were drastically reduced. Popular piety was curtailed or eliminated. The cult of the saints was outlawed. The clergy were denied a superior sacral status. All post-biblical miracles were viewed with suspicion or rejected. After a brief flirtation with late medieval mysticism, however, Luther was little affected by Platonism as his retention of a real presence in the Lord's Supper shows. His core teachings of JUSTIFICATION by FAITH alone and Scripture alone also owed little or nothing to that spiritualistic tradition. Reformed Protestantism (e.g., HULDRYCH ZWINGLI and Calvin), by contrast, owes much to the Platonic tradition, as its arguments against a real presence and its hostility toward religious art make manifest. The Radical Spiritualists drew the logical, if unacceptable to the other Protestant reformers, conclusions.

Radical Spiritualism assumed three identifiable forms whose differences derive from their ultimate biblical and Platonic sources. Müntzer is the purest representative of the biblical spirit among the Radicals and, perhaps, in the Reformation as a whole. Assuming the role of an Old Testament prophet, he thundered against secular rulers and clergy, both Catholic and Protestant, as enemies and oppressors of the people of God who corrupted God's Word and practiced "idolatry." He emphasized God's continuing revelation to Christians, the need for inspiration to understand Scripture, and the direct implantation of faith by God, that is, not through the Bible. Müntzer denied the real presence and criticized infant BAPTISM, but he retained both the Lord's Supper and infant baptism. Franck offered the most thoroughgoing Platonic Spiritualism. He dismissed all the sacraments as toys that God had given to the earliest Christians in their childish weakness. They were no longer necessary or useful. Rather, they were an impediment. The clergy were also superfluous, but dangerous, because they sought to impose their fantasies on others. Franck found no use for the church as a body of believers. His was an intensely individual appropriation of the Christian message. As for the Bible he found it a dark and contradictory book whose obscurity forced Christians to look elsewhere—inward—for the true Word of God. He and Schwenckfeld were two of the most consistent defenders of religious toleration in the Reformation. Schwenckfeld's Spiritualism owed much to medieval Catholic Eucharistic piety. Medieval theologians had overcome the spirit/matter dualism by arguing that material objects, including the flesh and blood of Christ, could in fact "contain" and "convey" Spirit, despite the manifest contradiction involved. Schwenckfeld retained that mystery, but internalized and "spiritualized" it so that the entire interchange took place within the believer. An Inner Word, Inner Baptism, and Inner Supper replaced the outer Bible and sacraments. Christ, the inner teacher, replaced the clergy. Schwenckfeld's rejection of the outward or visible church was less thoroughgoing than Franck's. Although the church had vanished with the Apostles, it would return with Christ at the end of time. The outward Eucharist and baptism would also be reinstituted, but as mere symbols of the true inner rites.

Although Spiritualism became pervasive during the Reformation and thereafter, it is impossible to determine exactly the extent of its influence. Müntzer had imitators, but the violence that they ignited quickly consumed them. We know of many other writers from the sixteenth century whose thinking was Spiritualist or at least spiritualizing in the way of Franck or Schwenckfeld (e.g., Valentin Crautwald, Hans Bünderlin, Christian Entfelder, Johannes Campanus, VALENTIN WEIGEL, Dirk Volketszoon Coornhert). Schwenckfeld had a popular following in Silesia whose descendants now live in the UNITED STATES. However, the vast majority of practicing Spiritualists were Christians who maintained a silent resistance where state churches ruled (see CONFESSIONALIZATION), or an independence of all churches (called "libertinism" by Calvin) in areas where membership in the official church was not legally required, as in the NETHERLANDS. In the seventeenth century PIETISM's call for a more heartfelt faith continued the Spiritualist tradition, although so did a Rationalism that led to DEISM and beyond. John Locke drew on Spiritualist arguments to advocate religious toleration and that has reshaped the religious landscape in Anglo-Saxon countries.

In the modern West the Spiritualist conviction that each believer has direct access to the divine Spirit, that no person or institution can or should impose a faith on another, and that external rites—"empty rituals"—are inessential has become a new ORTHODOXY for many and, perhaps, most Christians.

References and Further Reading

Hegler, Alfred. *Geist und Schrift bei Sebastian Franck: Eine Studie zur Geschichte der Spiritualismus in der Reformationszeit.* Freiburg, Germany: J.C.B. Mohr, 1892.
Jones, Rufus M. *Spiritual Reformers in the 16th and 17th Centuries.* London: Macmillan, 1914.
Klaassen, Walther, "Spiritualization in the Reformation." *Mennonite Quarterly Review* 37 (1963): 67–77.
Ozment, Steven E. *Mysticism and Dissent: Religious Ideology and Social Protest in the Sixteenth Century.* New Haven, CT: Yale University Press, 1973.
Rupp, Gordon. "Word and Spirit in the First Years of the Reformation." *Archive for Reformation History* 49 (1958): 13–26.
Troeltsch, Ernst. *Social Teachings of the Christian Churches.* Translated by Olive Wyon. Louisville, KY: Westminster/John Knox Press, 1992.
Williams, George H. *Spiritual and Anabaptist Writers.* Philadelphia, PA: Westminster Press, 1957.
———. *Radical Reformation.* 3rd ed. Kirksville, MO: Sixteenth Century Journal Publishers, 1992.

R. EMMET MCLAUGHLIN

SPORTS

Overview

Serious academic study of the relationship between Protestantism and sports has been a product of the new interest in social history that began in the 1960s. Despite a great deal of detailed historical research, no one overarching theory that convincingly explains the interaction between the two has achieved widespread assent. This is partly because of the diversity of Protestant denominational attitudes to sports, but also because the nature of sports has changed considerably over time. For this reason it is helpful to begin by looking at sports and Protestantism in preindustrial society.

In the period from 1500 to 1800, sporting activities were largely local in character and formed part of a wider and predominantly rural pattern of leisure that could include religious festivals, fairs, and holidays that were governed by the rhythms of the agricultural year. Protestants viewed many of these traditional kinds of sporting activity with suspicion, but we need to be careful not to caricature Protestant and particularly Puritan attitudes to sports as entirely negative.

The period from 1800 to about 1880 can be characterized as the formative period in the creation of modern sport. Seen by historians as intimately connected with the growth of INDUSTRIALIZATION and urbanization, sports became more national in character and more governed by explicit rules. Protestant attitudes to sports underwent significant changes in this period. Beginning in ENGLAND, what was called "muscular Christianity" emphasized the links between sporting and spiritual prowess. This ideal assumed that sports were participant and amateur activities. Finally, the late nineteenth century saw the advent of modern professional sports as forms of mass entertainment. Although many professional teams owed their beginnings to Protestant initiatives aimed at EVANGELISM, in the twentieth century sports came to seem more of a rival than an aid to Protestant Christianity. Sport in this period was often described as a new form of religion. Nevertheless, among some evangelical Protestant groups attempts to convert men to Christianity continued to associate the gospel with sportsmen and with sporting achievement, although as a form of consumerist entertainment modern sport is less closely identified with Protestant theology and practice than in the nineteenth century.

Protestantism and Sports: Theorizing the Relationship

The new forms of social history that emerged in the 1960s stimulated interest in this subject from two different directions. On the one hand, historians of religion were encouraged to move beyond a theological and institutional focus in their studies of Protestantism and of the REFORMATION and to study the interaction between these movements and elite and popular CULTURE. Although much of this work has concentrated on topics such as SEXUALITY, MARRIAGE, and GENDER, some work has been done on the impact of Protestantism on other aspects of culture including sports. On the other hand, social historians began to study the history of sport in its social and cultural context, although much of this work has emphasized the relationship between modernization and sports, and has tended to neglect religion. One notable earlier pioneering thinker who attempted to combine these approaches was MAX WEBER in his 1904–1905 work *The Protestant Ethic and the Spirit of Capitalism*. Weber argued that what he called Protestantism's doctrine of worldly ASCETICISM, in which work became part of the Christian's calling, created a hostility to traditional forms of recreation and sports. Weber's insights remain valuable and still inform our understanding of the relationship between PURITANISM and sports. However, attempts to build on his work and to create a coherent theoretical perspective for understanding the relationship between sports and Protestantism have remained problematic because many researchers have noted not only hostility between the two, but also notable affinities. Jay Coakley has suggested that this contradiction may be more apparent than real, given that the Weberian Protestant ethic—with its emphasis on rationality, organization, self-discipline, hard work, and success in one's calling—is compatible with, and may well have contributed to, the development of modern forms of sports. However, because interest in sports has not been limited to Protestant cultures, and because Protestantism has been an exceptionally diverse form of religious belief and practice, it seems more helpful to regard such theoretical perspectives as stimuli to thought and re-

search and to proceed by adopting a more historically based approach to this subject.

Sports and Protestantism in Preindustrial Society

On the eve of the Reformation, sporting activities were very different in form and social significance from the kinds of professional codified sports that we now associate with the term sport. Upper-class pursuits included hunting, hawking, jousting, and tennis. Archery, an important form of military training, and horse racing tended to transcend class distinctions. There also existed a range of more exclusively popular activities such as football, bowling, wrestling, animal baiting, and cockfighting. The latter were often conducted according to local rules and took place on the great religious holidays such as Christmas, Epiphany, Shrove Tuesday, and Pentecost, or on the feast days of the patron SAINTS of particular parishes or guilds. Such events were also marked by more general communal celebrations that might include mystery plays, dancing, and beer drinking.

Like their medieval Catholic predecessors, early Protestant reformers were often hostile to popular sports because they linked them to what they regarded as dangerous and immoral habits including drinking, gambling, sexual license, and failure to attend church. However, Protestants had two further distinctive theological reasons of their own for suspicion of sports. First, they associated them with a Catholic way of life that they rejected as superstitious. Second, LUTHERANISM sought to emphasize the PRIESTHOOD OF ALL BELIEVERS within the Christian scheme of SALVATION. This was in reaction to what Protestants believed had been the false dichotomy within medieval Catholicism between the priestly and monastic religious life of the elite and that of the rest of the population. One result of this change was to endow work, along with all other aspects of secular life, with a new kind of importance. One's worldly occupation and recreations became part of one's calling as a Christian. Although this meant that sports could be engaged in as a means of maintaining physical health or as part of a regime of military training, without such justifications, sports appeared to be forms of idleness that hindered the Christian's struggle to lead a godly life and thereby attain eternal salvation.

MARTIN LUTHER exemplifies this attitude in his 1523 work, *On Temporal Authority: To What Extent it Should be Obeyed*. After stressing the high calling of the Christian prince to lead a life of devoted service to the needs of the people, Luther considered the objection that this would leave no time "for princely amusements—dancing, hunting, racing, gaming and similar worldly pleasures." His reply was that, "We are not here teaching how a temporal prince is to live, but how a temporal prince is to be a Christian, such that he may reach heaven." Nevertheless, such rigorism was combined with a sense of proportion. In his 1524 program for the education of boys who were not destined to be scholars, Luther advocated one to two hours of schooling each day. This was to be combined with teaching at home or learning a trade to limit, but not eliminate, the amount of time that boys would otherwise spend in "ball playing, racing, and tussling." The Zurich reformer HULDRICH ZWINGLI took a similarly balanced, but cautious view. Games with educational value, such as chess—which taught mathematics and strategy—were permissible, but only in moderation, "since there are some who neglect the serious business of life and devote themselves to this alone." Dicing and card playing were to be banned. Games such as "running, jumping, throwing, fighting and wrestling" were, Zwingli acknowledged, prevalent among almost all nations, but especially among the Swiss who found them "useful in many different circumstances." Wrestling, however, was to be engaged in only with moderation, and Zwingli found no great value in swimming, although he admitted that it was on occasion "pleasurable to immerse our limbs in water and become a fish."

In the draft of Ecclesiastical Ordinances that he drew up for the city of Geneva in 1541, JOHN CALVIN made a similar distinction between different kinds of sports, decreeing that "no one is to play at games played for gold or silver or at excessive expense." In practice Calvinist authorities were more diligent than their Lutheran counterparts in their attempts to regulate the lives of Christian citizens through the religious sanctions imposed by CONSISTORY courts. The same was true of Puritans in England in the seventeenth century, although their efforts did not go uncontested. In 1618 King James I issued a declaration that came to be known as *The King's Book of Sports,* which was written in response to disputes in Lancashire between Puritans on the one hand, and Anglicans and Roman Catholics on the other, as to the morality of traditional sports. Conservative Protestant Anglican opinion rejected the Puritan case (see ANGLICANISM). The declaration stated that it was the king's wish that after the end of divine service, activities such as "archery for men, leaping, vaulting, or any other such harmless recreation" were not to be prohibited. During the English CIVIL WAR, when Puritan influence was in the ascendant, Parliament in 1644 issued an ordinance stating that "no person or persons shall hereafter upon the Lord's Day use exercise, keep, maintain, or be present at any wrestlings, shootings, bowling, ringing of bells for pleasure or pastime, masque, wake, oth-

erwise called feasts, Church-ale, dancing, games, sport, or pastime whatsoever." Again, we should notice that sports were viewed here as part of a much wider range of suspect activities and that the thrust of the legislation was aimed at Sabbath-breaking rather than at sports as such. When in 1647 Parliament abolished the traditional church festivals of Christmas, Easter, and Whitsuntide, it decreed that alternative days for recreations should be established on the second Tuesday of each month. The same pattern of a Puritan attempt to limit what were deemed to be unsuitable types of sporting activities, tempered by Protestant denominational variety, was exported to colonial America. For example, Puritans in Massachusetts Bay, although conceding what the first governor of the Massachusetts Bay Company, John Winthrop, called the need to "recreate the mind with some outward recreation," were far from accepting the passion for horse racing that characterized the plantation society of Anglican-dominated Virginia.

Protestantism and Sports in the Era of Industrialization

During the nineteenth century profound changes began to occur in the nature of sporting activities. As a result of industrialization, urbanization, and the revolution in communications, sports such as football and cricket began to be organized on a national rather than a local basis. Agreed systems of rules and new forms of record keeping of results and of sporting achievements also contributed to this change. The modernization of sports was also, however, partly created by a revolution in Protestant attitudes to such activities that, as we have seen, had hitherto been at best ambivalent. This change began in the great English private boarding schools in which the playing of organized sports came to be associated with team spirit, masculinity, and Christian virtue.

This revolution has come to be associated with the reforms of the Anglican Liberal Protestant clergyman, THOMAS ARNOLD, at Rugby school after he became its headmaster in 1828. In fact Arnold saw the organized playing of games such as rugby, football, and cricket as only one of many methods designed to instill new standards of discipline into the hitherto often violent and unruly world of boys' boarding schools. The equation of sporting activity with Christian holiness was popularized much more effectively by another Liberal Protestant clergyman and novelist, CHARLES KINGSLEY, to whose writings the term "muscular Christianity" was first applied (see LIBERAL PROTESTANTISM AND LIBERALISM). Although Kingsley repudiated this label, arguing that he did not seek to exalt physical qualities above spiritual ones, many of his heroes are characterized as engaging in sports. Even more important, Kingsley identified participation in sporting activities with English Protestantism and with English nationalism. By contrast, he depicted Catholicism as characterized by a foreign, unhealthy, and ascetic rejection of the body and of sporting activities (see CATHOLICISM, PROTESTANT REACTIONS). For example, in Kingsley's 1851 novel *Yeast* the hero may be a "poor wild uneducated sportsman," but in contrast to his unflattering portrait of the sickly Roman Catholic priest, Kingsley depicts him as "full of manhood." Rightly in Kingsley's view, his ideal Christian prefers the physical discomforts of duck shooting to the false asceticism of wearing hair shirts. The belief that the battle of Waterloo was won on the playing fields of Eton can thus be seen as a product of Kingsley's heady blend of English Protestantism, sports, and NATIONALISM. Kingsley's identification of Protestantism, not Catholicism, with sporting achievement was of course a myth, although it was one that could influence the reality. Partly because of the association between sports, Protestantism, and nationalism, in the nineteenth century major Catholic boarding schools, such as Stonyhurst, were slower to adopt the cult of athleticism that characterized schools such as Eton and Harrow. When they did so, however, there is no evidence that their pupils were any less accomplished sportsmen.

Muscular Christianity and its sporting ethos found a ready reception among many American Protestants. The incorporation of organized sports into elite colleges paralleled English developments. Yale inaugurated the first rowing club in 1843 and baseball, football, and athletics followed in the 1860s and 1870s. American advocates for the new cult of sports and Christianity were as persuasive as their English counterparts. For example, in the 1861 edition of his widely read book *Christian Nurture,* the Congregationalist minister HORACE BUSHNELL was highly critical of the puritanical strain within American culture and with what he saw as its overemphasis on work. Sport and recreation were, he argued, fully compatible with faith. A major vehicle for the practical outworking of these ideas was the Young Men's Christian Association (see YMCA, YWCA), which had been founded in London in 1844 and first appeared in America in Boston in 1851. Branches created gymnasiums for physical training and promoted sports such as basketball and volleyball. By 1915 it seemed a commonplace for the Association's Bible Study secretary, Fred Goodman, to comment that "the risen Jesus is a member of every gymnasium class, of every athletic team in which there are Christians." The benefits of such activities could also be extended to women, although Protestant writers drew the line at

their engaging in competitive sports because this, they feared, would encourage qualities deemed to be unfeminine.

Scandinavian and German Protestants developed similar ideas about the beneficial role of sports in Christian EDUCATION, although they tended to place less emphasis than in America and Britain on the role of competitive team games and more on gymnastic training in the curriculum. German Protestantism had its own native tradition of Christian athleticism exemplified by the eighteenth-century Pietist JOHANN KASPAR LAVATER, who regarded efforts to perfect the human body as following on naturally from the Christian doctrine of the incarnation. By the end of the nineteenth century, Protestant advocates of sports and gymnastics struck much the same tone as their muscular Christian counterparts in Britain. Thus the Protestant school teacher Konrad Koch, in his 1900 work *Education for Courage through Gymnastics, Games and Sport,* identified the development of willpower and character with sports, Christianity, and patriotism.

The further spread of these ideals across the globe was one of the consequences of nineteenth-century COLONIALISM. Protestants who believed in their God-given role to disseminate Christian civilization often saw sports as one of its essential elements as well as being a useful means of its dissemination. The best-known example of sporting missionary enterprise was the Cambridge and England cricketer C. T. STUDD. A devout Evangelical, Studd became famous as one of "the Cambridge Seven," a group of sportsmen who joined JAMES HUDSON TAYLOR's CHINA INLAND MISSION in 1885. The effect of Studd on a group of university students encapsulated the ideals and hopes of the muscular Christian movement. According to one observer he soon dispelled the then prevalent idea that Christians were "unfit for the river or cricket field, and only good for Psalm-singing and pulling a long face." The spread of sports such as cricket and rugby throughout the British empire was one result of such enthusiasm.

Protestantism and Modern Sport

The latter part of the nineteenth century saw the creation of modern sport as an activity characterized not only by participation by large numbers of people for health and recreation, but also by the existence of large-scale professional sports organizations that exist primarily to provide forms of mass entertainment. The role of Protestantism in this change was a complex one. Muscular Christians envisaged sporting activities as forms of character building through self-discipline and not as means to financial gain. For this reason the ideal of amateurism was deeply ingrained in school and university institutions. In Britain, for example, the playing of football or soccer as it was often called was shunned by most private schools, especially after it became associated with the creation of a predominantly professional league in the 1880s. Rugby football was preferred because it retained its amateur status. For similar reasons in America, the YMCA's Athletic League stressed the virtues of amateurism in sport and in 1911 severed its ties with the Amateur Athletic Union when it proposed to field professional teams.

Despite these reservations, Protestant churches contributed significantly, if often unwittingly, to the development of sports as forms of professional entertainment. This was partly because of their belief that the spiritual benefits of sports should be spread to not just the middle, but also to the working classes. Sports were also seen as a form of EVANGELISM, as a means of making the Christian gospel attractive to what the churches saw as the alarmingly large numbers of the working class who had no contact with Christianity. One result of this in Britain was that a number of football clubs that went on to become the backbone of the professional football league owed their origins to the initiative of local churches. This was true, for example, of Aston Villa in Birmingham, which was formed by young men associated with the local Methodist chapel. In the industrial town of Sheffield in 1879 the local newspaper recorded the fortunes of eight church or chapel clubs. More of a pointer to the future was the outcome in Bolton where the football club was formed by a local CHURCH OF ENGLAND school in 1872 with the support of the local vicar. In 1877 it changed its name from Christ Church to Bolton Wanderers after a dispute with the vicar, thereby becoming a purely secular organization.

The growth of mass sports as a form of entertainment that threatened to compete with, rather than support, religion was part of a much wider crisis that befell the movement to associate sports with Protestant Christianity in the early twentieth century. There were a number of reasons for this. Despite the enthusiasm of a generation of propagandists, not all Protestant leaders ever accepted that there was a beneficial link of this kind. More seriously, many facets of the cult of athleticism and games had causes that either had no logical links with Christianity or were antithetical to Christian beliefs and practices. These included fears over the supposedly declining virility of the white Anglo-Saxon male transported from the morally bracing atmosphere of rural life to the sickly environment of the city; alarm over levels of teenage delinquency; and an often negative response to feminism and the supposed feminization of the churches. The First World War also dealt a severe blow to the concept of heroic Christian sportsmanship. If it had been believed that the battle of Waterloo was the result of prowess on the games field, then the slaughter of millions of young men in the trenches of Europe could be said to have had similar ideological roots. Denominational rivalry proved to be another unintended consequence of linking sports and religion. A notable example of this was the identification of Scotland's two principal football teams, Celtic and Rangers, with Catholicism and Protestantism, respectively. Finally, despite the assertions of Charles Kingsley, it became increasingly apparent that Protestantism had no convincing claims to a monopoly of interest in sport. As Pope Pius XII explained near the end of the Second World War, the Catholic Church regarded sport as a form of education and one that was closely related to morality.

Yet interestingly, the symbiotic relationship between Protestantism and sports still continues, particularly in America. The belief that sports can be a means of evangelism has not disappeared. For example, the television evangelist JERRY FALWELL argued at the inauguration of the sports program at his Liberty University in the 1970s that Christian witness to young people worked better when Christians proved themselves to be their equal on the playing field. The evangelical men's organization The Promise Keepers, founded by a football coach at the University of Colorado, also enlists sport in its outreach to men, associating it with traditional models of MASCULINITY. Successful Christian sportsmen and women continue, as in the past, to be enlisted as potentially attractive exemplars of the Protestant Christian lifestyle. According to the National Basketball Association player David Robinson, playing sports provides "a great opportunity to model Christ in front of a lot of people by the way I play and the way I conduct myself." The belief in the character-building effects of sports is also still in evidence. For instance, the evangelist BILLY GRAHAM argued in 1971 that "The Bible says leisure and lying around are morally dangerous for us. Sports keeps us busy; athletes, you notice, don't take drugs."

Graham's mention of drugs and sport does in some respects have an unintentionally ironic ring given their misuse as performance enhancers in modern competitive sports. This is one of a number of factors that suggest that the relationship between sports and Protestantism has become, for very different reasons, as problematic in the twenty-first century as it was in the fifteenth. Although the examples of individual Christian sporting heroes and heroines can be presented as part of a gospel of self-discipline and success, the aggression and naked materialism that surround much of modern sport as a form of mass entertainment make this connection difficult to sustain. Whether this heralds the end of the long, complex, and changing relationship between Protestantism and sports remains to be seen.

References and Further Reading

Burke, Peter, ed. *Popular Culture in Early Modern Europe.* London: Temple Smith, 1978.

Coakley, Jay. "Sports and Religion. Is it a promising combination?" In *Sport in Society: Issue and Controversies,* by Coakley Jay, 475– 500. Boston, MA: Irwin McGraw-Hill, 1998.

Higgs, R. J. *God in the Stadium: Sports and Religion in America.* Lexington: The University of Kentucky Press, 1995.

Hoffman, Shirl J., ed. *Sport and Religion.* Champaign, IL: Human Kinetics Books, 1992.

Mangan, J. A. *Athleticism in the Victorian and Edwardian Public School: The Emergence and Consolidation of an Educational Ideology.* Cambridge: Cambridge University Press, 1981.

Putney, Clifford. *Muscular Christianity: Manhood and Sports in Protestant America, 1880–1920.* Cambridge, MA: Harvard University Press, 2001.

Riess, Steven A. *Major Problems in American Sport History.* Boston: Houghton Mifflin Company, 1997.

Vance, Norman. *The Sinews of the Spirit: The Ideal of Christian Manliness in Victorian Literature and Religious Thought.* Cambridge: Cambridge University Press, 1985.

SEAN GILL

SPURGEON, CHARLES HADDON (1834–1892)

English revival preacher. The greatest preacher of the later nineteenth century in the English-speaking world was Charles Haddon Spurgeon. Born in Kelvedon, Essex, ENGLAND, on June 19, 1834, he was converted and baptized as a believer in 1850 and, before he was twenty, he became minister of the prestigious New Park Street Baptist Church in London. When the congregation outgrew the premises, in 1861 Spurgeon started to preach in the purpose-built Metropolitan Tabernacle. He established a college to train pastors, issued weekly sermons, and wrote popular religious works. In 1887–1888 he criticized other members of the Baptist Union in the "Down-Grade Controversy" for drifting into theological liberalism (see LIBERAL PROTESTANTISM AND LIBERALISM) and withdrew from his DENOMINATION. He maintained his ministry, although with increasing bouts of ill health, until his death at Mentone in FRANCE on January 31, 1892.

Early Life

Spurgeon was molded by the powerful Puritan (see PURITANISM) tradition of East Anglia. His father, John Spurgeon, was Independent minister at Tollesbury near Colchester in Essex and also worked as a coal-yard clerk, while his grandfather James served as another Independent minister in the same county, at Stambourne. There Charles spent part of his childhood, devouring the works in the library that had been assembled by successive ministers since the seventeenth century. In January 1850, at the age of fifteen, he was converted to a personal faith after hearing a sermon by a PRIMITIVE METHODIST local preacher in Colchester. In May, as a matter of personal conviction, he was baptized as a believer at Isleham in Cambridgeshire and, moving to Cambridge to teach, became the pastor of the small church in the nearby village of Waterbeach in 1851. His PREACHING was so remarkable that in 1854 he was called to the ministry of New Park Street Baptist Church in Southwark, London, which had previously been the congregation of John Gill and John Rippon, leading Baptist theologians.

London Ministry

Spurgeon rapidly became a pulpit sensation. Seemingly uncouth and certainly very young, he nevertheless possessed a self-command, a mastery of evangelical theology and a directness of address that deeply stirred his hearers and brought many CONVERSIONS (see EVANGELICALISM; EVANGELICALISM, THEOLOGY OF). He was censured for vulgarity, but the criticism only enhanced his celebrity. While his chapel was being extended, he preached in the Exeter Hall, the meeting place of the great evangelical societies, but it soon became necessary to secure an even larger building. To the disgust of his critics, he hired the Surrey Gardens Music Hall, a place of secular amusement, for evening services. On the first day there, October 19, 1856, there was a malicious cry of fire, the crowd panicked, and, to Spurgeon's great distress, seven people died. Yet his ministry continued to attract thousands. To accommodate them permanently, a vast new church, the Metropolitan Tabernacle, was opened in 1861. There, for the next thirty years, Spurgeon became one of the sights of London. His church grew from 232 members in 1854 to 5,311 at the end of 1891. He added a series of institutions to the church—prayer meetings, evening classes, almshouses, and even an orphanage. The church magazine, called *The Sword and the Trowel,* a Colportage Society for distributing Christian literature, and a Book Fund for poorer ministers run by Spurgeon's wife, Susanna, extended the influence of his ministry. Most significant among Spurgeon's creations was the Pastor's College, designed to train candidates for the ministry without regard for their financial circumstances or their educational qualifications. The theology taught in the college, like that of the founder, was distinctly

Calvinistic (see CALVINISM). Spurgeon often supported his students in pioneering EVANGELISM and church planting. By the end of his lifetime over a fifth of the Baptist ministers in England and WALES had been trained at his college (see BAPTISTS).

Spurgeon remained an outspoken Baptist and conservative Evangelical all his life. In 1864 he denounced Anglican Evangelicals for remaining in a church that taught baptismal regeneration, and he became increasingly restive about the growth of liberal opinion in NONCONFORMITY. In 1887 *The Sword and the Trowel* carried a series of articles warning of doctrinal downgrading, and Spurgeon withdrew from the Baptist Union. He was not opposing ARMINIANISM, as has sometimes been supposed, for he had a Methodist preach for him in the aftermath of the "Down-Grade Controversy." Rather he was concerned that younger men were lax in their views on the ATONEMENT, biblical inspiration, and JUSTIFICATION by FAITH. He was disappointed, however, that few of even his own trainees followed him in severing denominational links. His sense of isolation was accentuated by separation from the Liberal Party that he had previously strongly supported when, in 1886, he could not accept its policy of Home Rule for IRELAND. Rheumatic gout had brought on Bright's disease, and in his last years he often traveled to recuperate in Mentone in the south of France, where he died in 1892. His writings, many of which remain in print, constitute a lasting memorial. They include the popular and witty *John Ploughman's Talk* (1868) and a multivolume extended commentary on the Psalms, *The Treasury of David* (1870–1886). His sermons, published weekly until 1917, continued to enjoy a huge international sale.

References and Further Reading

Primary Sources:

Spurgeon, Charles Haddon. *The Early Years, 1834–1859.* London: Banner of Truth Trust, 1962.
———. *The Full Harvest, 1860–1892.* Edinburgh: Banner of Truth Trust, 1973.
———. *John Ploughman's Talk.* London: n.p., [1868].
———. *The Treasury of David.* 7 vols. London: Passmore & Alabaster, 1870–1886.

Secondary Sources:

Bebbington, David W. "Spurgeon and British Evangelical Theological Education." In *Theological Education in the Evangelical Tradition*, edited by D. G. Hart and R. Albert Mohler, Jr. Grand Rapids, MI: Baker Books, 1996.
Hopkins, Mark Thomas Eugene. "Baptists, Congregationalists and Theological Change: Some Late Nineteenth Century Leaders and Controversies." Ph.D. dissertation, University of Oxford, 1988.
Kruppa, P. S. *Charles Haddon Spurgeon: A Preacher's Progress.* New York: Garland Publishing, 1982.
Payne, Ernest A. "The Down Grade Controversy: A Postscript." *Baptist Quarterly* 28 no. 4 (1979): 146–158.

D. W. BEBBINGTON

STAHL, FRIEDRICH JULIUS (1802–1861)

German political theorist. The influential legal theorist and ecclesiastical policy maker was born on January 16, 1802 in Würzburg as Julius Jolson and died on August 10, 1861 in Bad Brückenau. Stahl grew up in an orthodox Jewish merchant family, but, inspired by Protestant neohumanism, he converted in 1819 to LUTHERANISM and took the new name for which he is known.

Stahl studied law and graduated in 1827. In 1832 he became professor of the philosophy of law in Würzburg, and in 1834 he moved to Erlangen, where he came under the influence of Lutheranism. The Prussian king Friedrich Wilhelm IV, shortly after his coronation, saw to Stahl's appointment as a professor in Berlin, with the expectation of finding in him a sharp, convincing advocate who shared his understanding of the state during the period of German restoration. Stahl did not disappoint the king's expectations, and his reputation and influence in politics and church policy grew accordingly.

The two-volume *Philosophie des Rechts (Philosophy of Law)* that appeared in 1830 (vol. 1) and 1837 (vol. 2) is Stahl's greatest work. Influenced by FRIEDRICH WILHELM JOSEPH VON SCHELLING, Stahl formulated the foundation of the state not in liberal or romantic terms but in terms of divine right, which consequently laid the foundation for the Christian state. According to Stahl any form of popular sovereignty was the same as revolution, something he considered a continuous threat whose only cure was the Christian state. To establish such a state, the idea of nation needed a theory that reasserted the duty of the throne, the state, and the CHURCH. With this intention Stahl wrote *Die Kirchenverfassung nach Lehre und Recht der Protestanten (The Constitution of the Church according to Protestant Doctrine and Law,* 2nd ed., 1862) and *Über das monarchische Prinzip (On the Principle of Monarchy)* in 1846. In 1853 he gave his idea its most pointed conception in the work *Der Protestantismus als politisches Prinzip (Protestantism as Political Principle).*

Stahl was a brilliant speaker who had a tremendous impact not only as a professor but also as a popular writer and politician. In 1848 he helped found the Conservative Party in Prussia and its main newspaper, the *Neue Preussische Zeitung.* Because of the iron cross on the title page, it was generally known as

"Kreuzzeitung." The end of the period of restoration (1858–1861) also brought an end to his influence. His conception of the Christian state had a lasting impact, however, not only in Prussia and GERMANY but also beyond.

See also Church and State, Overview

References and Further Reading

Primary Source:

Stahl, F. J. *What is the Revolution?* State College, PA: Penn State University Press, 1977.

Secondary Source:

Nabrings, Arie. *Friedrich Julius Stahl: Rechtsphilosophie und Kirchen-politik.* Bielefeld, Germany: Lutherverlag, 1983.
MARTIN GRESCHAT

STANTON, ELIZABETH CADY (1815–1902)

U.S. women's rights leader. Born in Jonestown, New York, into a prominent Presbyterian family (see PRESBYTERIANISM), Elizabeth Cady married attorney Henry Stanton in 1840; they raised seven children. Active in the abolitionist movement, Stanton and her husband spent their honeymoon at the World's Anti-Slavery Convention in London (see SLAVERY; SLAVERY, ABOLITION OF). There she, LUCRETIA COFFIN MOTT, and other women delegates were prohibited from being seated because of their sex.

This discrimination prompted Stanton and Mott to organize the first U.S. women's rights convention in 1848 in Seneca Falls, New York. Stanton wrote the convention's Declaration of Sentiments modeled after the Declaration of Independence, stating that "all men and women are created equal." For the next fifty years, she was the leading theorist of the women's rights movement. In 1866 Stanton established the American Equal Rights Association with Mott and Lucy Stone; founded the National Woman Suffrage Association with Susan B. Anthony in 1869, serving as its president until 1890; coedited *The History of Woman Suffrage* (1881–1886) with Anthony and Matilda Joslyn Gage; and wrote numerous articles on women's right to vote, equal wages, fair DIVORCE laws, access to EDUCATION, and property ownership.

Stanton devoted her final decades to attacking women's oppression by organized Christianity. In 1895 and 1898 she published *The Woman's Bible,* two volumes of seething critiques of women's roles in the Old and New Testaments. Although a committee was credited with the work, Stanton wrote over half the commentaries herself. She lauded uppity biblical women like Eve, Jael, and Esther, and vilified contemporary Christian women who obeyed clerical injunctions to submission. This radical work alienated her from many suffragists. Stanton died in 1902 in New York City. Her legacy is an indomitable faith that women can think and live for themselves apart from men, church, or state.

See also: Women; Women Clergy; Feminist Theology; Womanist Theology

References and Further Reading

Primary Sources:

Stanton, Elizabeth Cady. *Eighty Years and More: Reminiscences 1815–1897.* Introduction by Ellen Carol DuBois; Afterword by Ann D. Gordon. Boston: Northeastern University Press, 1993.
———, and the Revising Committee. *The Woman's Bible.* New York: European Publishing, 1895, 1898; reprint, Seattle, WA: Ayer, 1974.

Secondary Source:

Griffith, Elisabeth. *In Her Own Right: The Life of Elizabeth Cady Stanton.* New York: Oxford University Press, 1984.
EVELYN A. KIRKLEY

STATISTICS

This article outlines the quantification of Protestant affiliation in the context of global Christianity and world religions. Every year, virtually all of the world's 8,600 Protestant denominations conduct an in-house census asking clergy and lay leaders a wide variety of statistical questions. These cover in aggregate 180 major religious subjects and number more than 1,000 different variables. This whole exercise costs the churches $600 million annually. Its long-established purposes are threefold: to assist the churches in analyzing their past, in deploying their resources for the present, and in planning for the future. Table 1 summarizes the results of these censuses worldwide and across the years 1900–2050, the latter being conservative future predictions based on current long-term trends.

Origin of the Term "Protestant"

In the year 1529 in Germany, the Second DIET OF SPEYER voted to rescind previously agreed-upon Lutheran geographical expansion. A minority of five German princes of the Holy Roman Empire and fourteen free cities then issued a formal "Protestation" (Latin, *protestatio*). Thereafter, supporters of Lu-

Table 1. The Pilgrimage of Protestantism and its Affiliated Church Members in the Context of Global Christianity and World Religions, 1900–2050

Year: Religion	1900 Adherents	%	1970 Adherents	%	Mid-1990 Adherents	%	Annual change, 1990–2000 Natural	Conversion	Total	Trend	Mid-2000 Adherents	%	Mid-2025 Adherents	%	Mid-2050 Adherents	%	Countries in 2000
Christians	558,131,000	34.5	1,236,374,000	33.5	1,747,462,000	33.2	22,709,000	2,501,000	25,210,000	1.36	1,999,564,000	33.0	2,616,670,000	33.5	3,051,564,000	34.3	238
Unaffiliated Christians	36,489,000	2.3	106,268,000	2.9	101,889,000	1.9	1,305,000	-382,000	924,000	0.87	111,125,000	1.8	125,712,000	1.6	124,655,000	1.4	232
Affiliated Christians	521,642,000	32.2	1,130,106,000	30.6	1,645,573,000	31.3	21,404,000	2,883,000	24,287,000	1.39	1,888,439,000	31.2	2,490,958,000	31.8	2,926,909,000	32.9	238
Roman Catholics	266,547,000	16.5	665,954,000	18.0	929,702,000	17.7	13,118,000	-355,000	12,763,000	1.29	1,057,328,000	17.5	1,361,965,000	17.4	1,564,603,000	17.6	235
Independents	**7,931,000**	**0.5**	**95,605,000**	**2.6**	**301,536,000**	**5.7**	**4,496,000**	**3,925,000**	**8,421,000**	**2.49**	**385,745,000**	**6.4**	**581,642,000**	**7.4**	**752,842,000**	**8.5**	**221**
Protestants	**103,024,000**	**6.4**	**210,759,000**	**5.7**	**296,349,000**	**5.6**	**4,224,000**	**341,000**	**4,565,000**	**1.44**	**342,002,000**	**5.7**	**468,633,000**	**6.0**	**574,419,000**	**6.5**	**232**
Orthodox	115,844,000	7.2	139,662,000	3.8	203,766,000	3.9	751,000	386,000	1,136,000	0.54	215,129,000	3.6	252,716,000	3.2	266,806,000	3.0	134
Anglicans	**30,571,000**	**1.9**	**47,501,000**	**1.3**	**68,196,000**	**1.3**	**1,072,000**	**74,000**	**1,145,000**	**1.56**	**79,650,000**	**1.3**	**113,746,000**	**1.5**	**145,984,000**	**1.6**	**163**
Marginal Christians	**928,000**	**0.1**	**11,100,000**	**0.3**	**21,833,000**	**0.4**	**269,000**	**153,000**	**423,000**	**1.79**	**26,060,000**	**0.4**	**45,555,000**	**0.6**	**62,201,000**	**0.7**	**215**
Doubly affiliated	-2,609,000	-0.2	-29,781,000	-0.8	-154,615,000	-2.9	-2,458,000	-1,558,000	-4,016,000	2.34	-194,780,000	-3.2	-308,402,000	-3.9	-413,844,000	-4.7	93
Disaffiliated	-592,000	0.0	-10,694,000	-0.3	-21,193,000	-0.4	-68,000	-82,000	-150,000	0.69	-22,695,000	-0.4	-24,897,000	-0.3	-26,102,000	-0.3	11
Non-Christians	1,061,495,000	65.5	2,459,774,000	66.6	3,518,980,000	66.8	56,152,000	-2,501,000	53,651,000	1.43	4,055,485,000	67.0	5,207,033,000	66.6	5,857,531,000	65.8	238
Muslims	199,941,000	12.3	553,528,000	15.0	962,357,000	18.3	21,723,000	865,000	22,589,000	2.13	1,188,243,000	19.6	1,784,876,000	22.8	2,229,282,000	25.0	204
Hindus	203,003,000	12.5	462,598,000	12.5	685,999,000	13.0	13,194,000	-660,000	12,534,000	1.69	811,336,000	13.4	1,049,231,000	13.4	1,175,298,000	13.2	114
Nonreligious	3,024,000	0.2	532,096,000	14.4	707,118,000	13.4	6,639,000	-535,000	6,104,000	0.83	768,159,000	12.7	875,121,000	11.2	887,995,000	10.0	236
Chinese universists	380,006,000	23.5	231,865,000	6.3	347,651,000	6.6	3,801,000	-86,000	3,716,000	1.02	384,807,000	6.4	448,843,000	5.7	454,333,000	5.1	89
Buddhists	127,077,000	7.9	233,424,000	6.3	323,107,000	6.1	3,531,000	157,000	3,688,000	1.09	359,982,000	6.0	418,345,000	5.4	424,607,000	4.8	126
Ethnoreligionists	117,558,000	7.3	160,278,000	4.3	200,035,000	3.8	4,098,000	-1,265,000	2,833,000	1.33	228,367,000	3.8	277,247,000	3.5	303,599,000	3.4	140
Atheists	226,000	0.0	165,400,000	4.5	145,719,000	2.8	1,315,000	-878,000	437,000	0.30	150,090,000	2.5	159,544,000	2.0	169,150,000	1.9	161
New-Religionists	5,910,000	0.4	77,762,000	2.1	92,396,000	1.8	1,032,000	-36,000	996,000	1.03	102,356,000	1.7	114,720,000	1.5	118,845,000	1.3	60
Sikhs	2,962,000	0.2	10,618,000	0.3	19,332,000	0.4	364,000	29,000	393,000	1.87	23,258,000	0.4	31,378,000	0.4	37,059,000	0.4	34
Jews	12,292,000	0.8	14,763,000	0.4	13,189,000	0.3	195,000	-70,000	125,000	0.91	14,434,000	0.2	16,053,000	0.2	16,695,000	0.2	134
Spiritists	269,000	0.0	4,603,000	0.1	10,155,000	0.2	137,000	81,000	218,000	1.96	12,334,000	0.2	16,212,000	0.2	20,709,000	0.2	55
Baha'is	10,000	0.0	2,657,000	0.1	5,672,000	0.1	117,000	26,000	143,000	2.28	7,106,000	0.1	12,062,000	0.1	18,001,000	0.2	218
Confucianists	640,000	0.0	4,759,000	0.1	5,856,000	0.1	56,000	-11,000	44,000	0.73	6,299,000	0.1	6,818,000	0.1	6,953,000	0.1	15
Jains	1,323,000	0.1	2,618,000	0.1	3,868,000	0.1	75,000	-40,000	35,000	0.87	4,218,000	0.1	6,116,000	0.1	6,733,000	0.1	10
Shintoists	6,720,000	0.4	4,175,000	0.1	3,082,000	0.1	9,000	-41,000	-32,000	-1.09	2,762,000	0.1	2,123,000	0.0	1,655,000	0.0	8
Taoists	375,000	0.0	1,734,000	0.0	2,402,000	0.1	25,000	0	25,000	1.00	2,655,000	0.0	3,066,000	0.0	3,272,000	0.0	5
Zoroastrians	108,000	0.0	122,000	0.0	1,959,000	0.0	45,000	13,000	58,000	2.65	2,544,000	0.0	4,440,000	0.1	6,965,000	0.1	22
Other religionists	49,000	0.0	784,000	0.0	964,000	0.0	10,000	0	10,000	1.03	1,067,000	0.0	1,500,000	0.0	1,938,000	0.0	78
Doubly-counted religionists	0	0.0	-4,000,000	-0.1	-11,879,000	-0.2	-215,000	-50,000	-265,000	2.04	-14,531,000	-0.2	-20,665,000	-0.3	-25,516,000	-0.3	24
Global population	1,619,626,000	100.0	3,696,148,000	100.0	5,266,442,000	100.0	78,861,000	0	78,861,000	1.41	6,055,049,000	100.0	7,823,703,000	100.0	8,909,095,000	100.0	238

Notes.

1. The six columns headed "%" give the size of adherents as a percentage of world population.

2. Christian megablocs are ranked by size in 2000; Non-Christians also by size in 2000. For definitions of terms, see *World Christian Trends*, 2001.

3. The four lines in **bold** type across the page make up the category of Wider Protestants. The line labeled "Protestants" is called and explained in the accompanying article as Core Protestants.

4. The main category "affiliated Christians" refers to church members. "Unaffiliated Christians" are those professing to be Christians but without affiliation or contact with the churches.

5. Under the heading "Annual change," "Natural" means births minus deaths per year, "Conversion" means converts (the newly baptized or initiated) minus defectors, and "Trend" gives each line's rate of change as a percent.

theran doctrines on the European continent began to be called, and to call themselves, "Protestants." After 1600, Calvinists, who up to this point were termed "Reformed," began to be included in the term Protestants. Two distinct applications of the term then gradually arose, resulting in widely differing statistics, as follows and as systematized in Table 2.

Core Protestants. This term is used here to depict the original Lutheran and Reformed churches of Europe together with the vast number of denominations linearly descended from them, holding to the basic REFORMATION doctrines and calling themselves (and called by others) by the same term "Protestants" (in German, *evangelischen;* in French, *evangéliques;* in Spanish, Portuguese, and Italian, *evangelicos*). Major dictionaries agree with this definition; thus Protestant churches are "Christian churches separating from the Roman Catholic Church in the Reformation of the 16th century or from another Protestant church to defend beliefs and practices held vital" *(Webster's Third New International Dictionary of the English Language [WTNIDEL]).* Their numbers are represented in Table 1 by the one single line "Protestants" across the table in bold type. In the year 2000, their total of affiliated church members can be seen to have been 342,002,000, increasing at a rate of approximately 4,565,000 per year. These may be regarded as constituting the whole of mainstream historic Protestantism (in German, *Protestantismus;* in French, *Protestantisme*). As well as "historic Protestants," they could also be called "classical Protestants," "inner Protestants," and even "Protestants proper." For convenience, the term "Core Protestants" is adequately descriptive.

Wider Protestants. Dictionaries record the narrow or straightforward definition above but all add a second, wider definition. Webster's *New World Dictionary of the American Language (NWDAL)* defines "Protestant" as not only a member of German/French/Lutheran/Calvinist churches, but also as "any Christian not belonging to the Roman Catholic or ORTHODOX EASTERN church." This is a huge expansion of the definition. Many government census organizers, administrators, journalists, and even scholars follow this definition of Protestant to cover and include all other non-Catholic and non-Orthodox traditions.

This wider usage has arisen over the last five centuries, both in popular usage and in ecclesiastical parlance, as well as in those scholarly circles. It arose to meet the need for a shorter, simpler overall classification and typology of Christians for those persons working with or frustrated by the vast complex of more than 300 different varieties of Christian denominations. The most widely used such typology simplifies the nomenclature to three categories only—dividing all Christians into Catholics, Orthodox, or Protestants.

Table 1 shows the numerical implications of this enlarged definition. While Core Protestants are shown in bold on the line "Protestants," this second usage, here termed Wider Protestants, now includes all four lines in bold type—those four basic megablocs known as Protestants, Anglicans, Independents, and Marginal Christians.

A caution needs to be stated at this point. These last three additional megablocs do not normally call themselves Protestants. First, although *NWDAL* had extended its core definition of a Protestant to include "a member of any of the Christian churches as a result of the Reformation," it expanded the definition by adding the words "especially a Lutheran, Calvinist, or Anglican." Anglicans themselves preferred (and still prefer) to describe themselves not as "Protestant," but rather as "Catholic and Reformed." Since the High Church OXFORD MOVEMENT of 1833, several thousand Anglican clergy of Anglo-Catholic or Anglo-Roman persuasion overtly rejected the label "Protestant" for themselves, for the CHURCH OF ENGLAND, and for the entire Anglican Communion. Moreover, *WTNIDEL* states that to define "a member of the Anglican Church" as "Protestant" is now an "archaic" usage, invalid since the reign of Charles I. This whole subject is investigated in depth in the *Oxford Dictionary of the Christian Church* (1997:1338–1340).

Second, "Independents" are defined here as those claiming to be "independent of historic Protestant denominationalism." In most cases they do not trace their roots to the Protestant Reformation in sixteenth-century Europe—one thinks of the 75 million affiliated to the African Independent Churches, the 50 million in China's HOUSE CHURCH movement, or the 15 million nonbaptized Hindu believers in Christ. The vast majority of these 140 million indigenous believers in Christ do not understand the main languages of the Reformation—German, French, English—and hence there is little empirical sense in calling them "Protestants."

Finally, "Marginal Christians" is the self-definition of those churches rejecting both Protestantism and mainstream Trinitarian Christianity (e.g., Unitarians, JEHOVAH'S WITNESSES) although regarding themselves as still on its margins.

Having given this evidence, it is still valuable to accept this usage of "Wider Protestants," although many scholars or journalists do not indicate which usage they are using. For the credibility of the science of empirical Christianity, all quantitative use of the term "Protestants" needs to make clear what exact definition is meant. Table 1 assists in this clarification by analyzing the magnitude of its composition under

Table 2. Terminology, Usages, and Statistics of Protestantism in AD 2000
The table depicts relations between the two major statistical constructs: Core Protestants and Wider Protestants.

Column A	Column D CORE PROTESTANTS 342,002,000	Column E NON-CORE PROTESTANTS 491,455,000			Column C 833,457,000
Basic Protestant Statistics in 2000		INDEPENDENTS Column F	ANGLICANS Column G	MARGINALS Column H	
1. Affiliated to churches	342,002,000	385,745,000	79,650,000	26,060,000	833,457,000
2. Affiliated, % of world	5.7	6.4	1.3	0.4	13.8
3. Growth p.a.	4,565,000	8,421,000	1,145,000	423,000	14,554,000
4. Growth % p.a.	1.44	2.49	1.56	1.79	1.74
5. Worship centers	952,800	1,587,000	91,700	106,100	2,737,600
6. Denominations	8,600	22,100	300	1,470	32,470
7. World Communions	39	92	40	25	196
8. Countries present in	232	221	163	215	238
Relations with and Interest in Protestantism, % (0% = none, 100% = maximum)					
9. 16th-century Reformation	90	0	60	0	50
10. Subsequent heritage	80	0	40	0	40
11. Major locations	Europe	Asia, Africa	Europe	Americas	World
12. Contact with core	100	1	50	10	60
13. Use of term "Protestant"	100	0	30	0	60
14. Main autonym	Protestants	Charismatics	Anglicans	Marginal Christians	Christians
15. Subsidiary autonym	Lutherans/Reformed	Postdenominationalists	Episcopalians	Neochristians	Believers
16. Component autonym	Evangelicals	Apostolics	Catholics/Evangelicals	Unitarians	Followers
17. Official use of term	90	0	20	0	50
18. Interest in the "Protestant"	70	0	10	0	30
19. Confessionalism	90	10	60	10	60
20. Conciliarism (councils)	80	20	80	0	70
21. Church union (mergers)	70	0	60	0	40
22. Denominationalism (HQs)	100	0	80	0	60

(Table header, top: WIDER PROTESTANTS 833,457,000 Column B | Totals 833,457,000 Column C)

those four lines in bold type labeled "Protestants," "Independents," "Anglicans," and "Marginal Christians." The total shows that by mid-2000, wider Protestants numbered 833,457,000 affiliated church members, increasing at a rate of approximately 14,554,000 per year (adding the four numbers under "Annual Change, Total").

A further complexity arises because 194,780,000 Christians are doubly affiliated, which means that they are individually members of two or more Protestant denominations at the same time, or members of one Protestant and one non-Protestant body, or collectively members in congregations affiliated with two Protestant denominations. Likewise, 22,695,000 persons are disaffiliated (baptized members who have subsequently abandoned Christianity but without rescinding or notifying their old affiliation). Again, 14,530,000 persons are doubly counted religionists, these being mostly Hindus who are also followers of Christ. All of these factors enumerate Christians correctly, but their precise definitions must be stated and recognized by their users.

The relationship between core Protestants and Wider Protestants and their subcategories is set out in Table 2. The first half of the table, "Basic Protestant statistics in 2000," gives a statistical profile of the five categories of Protestants. Its eight statistical measures demonstrate how core Protestants (column D) and the three non-core Protestants (Independents in column F, Anglicans in column G, and Marginal Christians in column H) all add up to Wider Protestants (column B). Particularly noteworthy in passing is line 7, stating in column C that of the world's 196 distinct and different Christian World Communions (CWCs) of Protestant origin or character, ninety-two have been created by Independents with little or no assistance from the thirty-nine CWCs in column D or the forty CWCs in column G.

The second half of Table 2, "Relations with and Interest in Protestantism," gives a descriptive verbal profile of the five statistical varieties of Protestants. The final line (22) sums up the whole typology and its status; all Core Protestants belong to denominations characterized here as "Denominationalist," that is, controlled to some extent by strong centralized head-quarters and bureaucratic staff. Most Anglicans (80 percent) likewise belong to dioceses exercising centralized control over members and churches and finances. In strong contrast, virtually all Independents are Postdenominationalists, which means that although they have created thousands of new networks, new denominations, and new communions, they steadfastly reject all centralized denominationalist power or control over members and their local churches and finances.

The Current Situation of Protestantism

A further analysis of several aspects of Protestant phenomenology can now be made. From their humble beginnings in Central Europe in the early sixteenth century, Protestants are now found in every country of the world, in some 32,470 wider Protestant denominations with more than 2.7 million congregations claiming more than 833 million followers. Today's Protestants, like other Christians, who were more than 80 percent white in 1900, are now found mainly in AFRICA, Asia, and LATIN AMERICA. This diverse collection of cultures and denominations at first may seem difficult to enumerate. But seen in the context of global efforts of counting Christians, there is actually a remarkably consistent wealth of data to draw on. To further understand the Protestant situation, one must first outline in more detail how all Christians and other world religions enumerate their followers.

The Overall Context of Counting

Vast efforts are put into the collection of statistics relating to the 10,000 or so distinct and separate religions in today's world. The most detailed data collection and analysis is undertaken each year by some 34,000 Christian denominations and their constituent churches and congregations of believers. This massive, decentralized, and largely uncoordinated global census of Christians includes both local and global contexts. Around 10 million printed questionnaires are sent out in 3,000 different languages. This collection of data provides a year-by-year snapshot of the progress or decline of Christianity's diverse movements, offering an enormous untapped reservoir of data for the researcher to track trends and make projections. The most extensive of these inquiries is that done by the Roman Catholic Church. As with many other church leaders, all Roman Catholic bishops are required to answer, by a fixed date every year, a twenty-one-page schedule in Latin and one other language asking 140 precise statistical questions concerning their work in the previous twelve months. Results

are then published every January in *Annuario Pontificio*. The entire operation, undertaken in varying degrees by all Christian bodies and some non-Christian religions as well, is best termed the annual "religion megacensus."

Government Censuses of Religion

At the same time, the world's governments also have—since the twelfth century—collected information on religious populations and practice. A question related to religion is thus asked in more than 120 of the world's countries in their official national decennial population censuses. Until 1990, this number was slowly declining each decade as developing countries began dropping the religion question as too expensive (in many countries, each census costs well over a half a million dollars per question) and, apparently, too uninteresting. This trend appears to have reversed by 2001. Thus Britain, which produced the world's first national census of religious affiliation (the Compton Census in 1676), and later a religion question in the national census of 1851 although none thereafter, reintroduced the question in Britain's 2000 census as the best way to get firm data on each and every non-Christian minority to fairly apportion education, broadcasting, health care, and other benefits.

Analyzing and Defining

The starting point in any analysis of religious affiliation is the United Nations' 1948 *Universal Declaration of Human Rights*, Article 18: "Everyone has the right to freedom of thought, conscience and religion; this right includes freedom to change his religion or belief, and freedom, either alone or in community with others and in public or private, to manifest his religion or belief in teaching, practice, worship and observance." Since its promulgation, these phrases have been incorporated into the state constitutions of a large number of countries across the world, with many countries instructing their census personnel to observe this principle: If a person states that he or she is a Protestant, or a Catholic or other Christian (or Muslim, Hindu, Buddhist, Sikh, Jew, etc.), then no one has a right to say he or she is not. Public declaration or profession must be taken seriously. The result is a clear-cut assessment of the extent of religious profession in the world.

Resolving Apparent Contradictory Data

Meanwhile, a formidable amount of new material for each year is being collected by the religious bodies themselves. In a particular country, the results from these two methods (government censuses and religion megacensus) can be strikingly different. For example, in Egypt, where the vast majority of the population is Muslim, elaborate government censuses taken every ten years for the last 100 years show that only some 5 percent of the population declare themselves as or profess to be Christians. However, detailed church censuses reveal the number of Christians affiliated with churches to be 15 percent of the population. Why this discrepancy? The reason appears to be that due to Muslim pressure on the Christian minority, to avoid being discriminated against many Christians are recorded in censuses by enumerators, or record themselves, as Muslims. Thus, any understanding of religious affiliation must take into account precisely what is being measured by these two approaches.

A Threefold Dynamic of Change in Religious Affiliation

Both of these sources—religions and governments—must be explored to gain an understanding of the total context of religious affiliation. With this in mind, the dynamics of change in religious affiliation over time can be limited to three sets of empirical population data. Overall numerical growth among religious adherents (increase or decrease, per year) may be measured by adding three components: (1) births minus deaths, (2) converts minus defectors, and (3) immigrants minus emigrants. All future projections of religious affiliation within any subset of the global population (normally a country or region) depend on this dynamic.

Births Minus Deaths. The primary mechanism of religious change globally is births and deaths; the number of adherents goes up with the number of births and down with the number of deaths. Children are almost always counted to have the religion of their parents (this is the law in NORWAY and many other countries). This means that a religious population has a close statistical relationship to demography. The change over time in any given community is expressed most simply as the number of births into the community minus the number of deaths out of it. Many religious communities around the world experience little else in the dynamics of their growth or decline.

The impact of births and deaths on religious affiliation can change over time. For example, the recent Northern IRELAND census revealed a closing of the gap between Protestants and Catholics over the past three decades. Protestants used to make up 65 percent of the population, but by 2001 this had dropped to 53 per-

cent. Catholics, in the meantime, had grown from 35 percent to 44 percent of the population. This shift is due primarily to the higher birthrate among Catholic women. One would expect that, given time, Catholics would eventually exceed 50 percent of the population. But the census also revealed two countertrends: (1) the death rate among Protestants is falling and (2) the birth rate among Catholics is falling. Given these trends, forecasters believe that, barring any other factors, Protestants are likely to remain in the majority in the coming decades.

Converts Minus Defectors. Nonetheless, it is common observation that individuals (or even whole villages or communities) change allegiance from one religion to another (or to no religion at all). Within a specific Christian community, it should be noted that "converts per year" is often similar, or even identical, to the number of new persons baptized over the last twelve months. Defectors, in contrast, are never enumerated or recognized or even known about by each and every religion. In the twentieth century, this change was most pronounced in two general areas:

1. Tribal religionists, more precisely termed "ethnoreligionists," have converted in large numbers to Christianity, Islam, Hinduism, or Buddhism.
2. Christians in the Western world have defected to become nonreligious (agnostics) or atheists in large numbers. Both of these trends slowed considerably by the dawn of the twenty-first century, however.

Immigrants Minus Emigrants. At the national level, it is equally important to consider the movement of people across national borders. From the standpoint of religious affiliation, this can have a profound impact. In the colonial era in the nineteenth century, small groups of Europeans settled in Africa, Asia, and the Americas. In the late twentieth century, people from these regions emigrated to the Western world. Thus, in the United States, such religions as Islam, Hinduism, and Buddhism grew faster than either Christianity or the nonreligious and atheists. This growth is due almost entirely to the immigration of Asians. In Europe, massive immigration of Muslims has not only been transforming the spiritual landscape, but also has now become a major political issue, notably in FRANCE, GERMANY, Austria, and ITALY and also in plans for European Union expansion. In the Central Asian countries of the former Soviet Union, Christianity has declined significantly every year since 1990, due to the mass emigration of Russians, Germans, and Ukrainians.

Methodology

In a recent survey volume, tables have been prepared enumerating both the Christian and religious situation for each of the world's 238 countries; see Country Tables 1 (religions) and Country Tables 2 (Christian denominations) in Volume 1 of *World Christian Encyclopedia: A Comparative Survey of Churches and Religions in the Modern World (WCE)*. A further analysis of the world's 12,600 ethnic peoples and their 10,000 distinct religions has provided much additional context for these tables (*WCE* Vol. 2). Detailed descriptions of methodology explaining how the formidable technical difficulties were resolved in these tables are found in the *WCE* and *World Christian Trends, AD 30–AD 2200: Interpreting the Annual Christian Megacensus (WCT)*. Every two years since 1950, the databases have incorporated the updates of the United Nations' population database for all countries from 1950 to 2050 and for some 100 variables each. A summary global report on the religion megacensus has been published annually in *Encyclopaedia Britannica's Book of the Year* since 1987.

Christian data are more complete globally than data on other religions. These data are presented in Country Tables 2 in *WCE* Part 4, "Countries," for each of the world's 238 countries. Statistics on the world's 33,800 denominations are given for 1970 and 1995. Christian data can then be presented in the total context of other religions and demographic data. This is done in Country Tables 1 for each country in *WCE* Part 4, "Countries." Here one finds a breakdown of the population into all of its constituent pieces—religious and nonreligious for the years 1900, 1970, 1990, 1995, 2000, and 2025. The growth rates of all categories from 1990 to 2000 are presented here as well. The results of this method have for selected years been shown in Table 1.

Further Details on Protestant Trends

Table 1 illustrates the changing fortunes of Protestants over the twentieth century. First is their apparent decline in percentage of the world's population, dropping from 6.4 percent in 1900 to 5.7 percent in 2000. This decline can be explained largely by the meteoric rise of Independents in the same period from only 0.5 percent to, coincidentally, 6.4 percent. Many of these Independents are schisms from Protestants and Anglicans (thus the tendency for scholars to consider them all as Protestants). If one combines Anglicans, Independents, Protestants, and Marginal Christians, then a different picture emerges. Together, these represented 8.8 percent of the world's population in 1900, but had

risen to 13.4 percent by 2000. Nonetheless, the fastest-growing segment remains the Independents.

Second, as noted earlier, another significant trend is the changing ethnic and cultural mosaic of the Protestant world. What was largely a white church 100 years ago is now largely nonwhite. These "new Protestants" have emerged largely from three phenomena:

a. The CONVERSION of Roman Catholics in Latin America has been so pronounced that a major study was recently published with the title "Is Latin America turning Protestant?"

b. The conversion of ethnoreligionists in Africa has meant that since 1900, thousands of tribal groups have been penetrated by Protestant missionaries in sub-Saharan Africa. Although many of these new Protestants later split off and became Independents, most have remained within the Protestant denominations.

c. To a lesser extent, Protestant MISSIONS among world religions, such as Islam or Hinduism, have begun to make more progress in recent years. Most of these are found in Asia.

Third, Protestants across the world have been impacted by the Postdenominationalist movement. Many churches no longer identify their denominations in their titles. Leadership structures have become less hierarchical. WORSHIP has become less formal. What Protestants have to offer amidst the fast-growing Postdenominationalist world, ironically, may be its continuity with historic Christianity. Many Independent Christian leaders are studying the lives and writings of MARTIN LUTHER and JOHN CALVIN in an attempt to find theological moorings for their movements. It is likely that Core Protestants will remain in a unique position to thus guide their Independent neighbors.

Protestants and Catholics Each Reach 1.5 Billion

Table 1 extends its statistical coverage into the future by cautious extrapolation from existing long-term trends. Four columns near the right edge depict the situation in 2025 and 2050. One startling finding is that Core Protestants in 1900 and in 2050 both show a percentage of global population unchanged at 6.7 percent. Wider Protestantism, in contrast, is expanding unabated, to become 17.2 percent of the world by 2050. Observers carefully comparing all these figures in the total context will have observed the even more startling finding that for the first time ever in the history of Protestantism, Wider Protestants will by 2050 have become almost exactly as numerous as Roman Catholics—each with just over 1.5 billion followers, or 17 percent of the world, with Protestants growing considerably faster than Catholics each year. Many believers born in the twentieth century will be the church leaders guiding both constituencies at that time.

The Long-Term Future of Protestantism

The future of the Protestant enterprise may be found in its growth outside of its European and American homelands. One hundred years from now, while continuing its traditions and doctrines, its cultural forms may be largely unrecognizable to Western Protestants. That may be an unintended consequence of its commitment to world evangelization, but it augurs well for its richness of cultural and linguistic diversity that Luther advocated for German Christians nearly 500 years ago.

See also Anglicanism; Anglo-Catholicism; Calvinism; Denominations; Lutheranism; Sectarianism

References and Further Reading

Annuario Pontificio. Citta del Vaticano: Tipografia Poliglotta Vaticana, annual.

Barrett, D. B., and T. M. Johnson. *World Christian Trends, AD 30–AD 2200: Interpreting the Annual Christian Megacensus.* Pasadena, CA: William Carey Library, 2001.

Barrett, D. B., G. T. Kurian, and T. M. Johnson. *World Christian Encyclopedia: A Comparative Survey of Churches and Religions in the Modern World.* 2nd ed. New York: Oxford University Press, 2001.

Cross, F. L., and E. A. Livingstone, eds. *The Oxford Dictionary of the Christian Church.* 3rd ed. London: Oxford University Press, 1997.

Eliade, M., et al., eds. *The Encyclopedia of Religion.* New York: Macmillan, 1986.

Encyclopaedia Britannica Book of the Year. Chicago: Encyclopaedia Britannica, annual.

"Protestantism" in *The New Encyclopaedia Britannica.* 15th ed., vol. 26, 206–267, 1995.

Statistical Yearbook of the Church. Citta del Vaticano: Secretaria Status, biennial.

Stoll, David. *Is Latin America Turning Protestant?: The Politics of Evangelical Growth.* Berkeley, CA: University of California Press, 1990.

World Population Projections to 2150. New York: United Nations, 1998.

World Population Prospects. New York: United Nations, 2001.

TODD M. JOHNSON AND DAVID B. BARRETT

STOECKER, ADOLF (1835–1909)

German theologian. Stoecker is remembered as a Christian socialist, anti-Semite, ardent German nationalist, outspoken critic of Marxist socialism, prolific journalist, controversial court preacher in Berlin, member of the Reichstag, the German parliament, for twenty years, and leader of the *Freie Volkskirche* movement. He was born in Halberstadt in northern GERMANY in 1835 and studied for the ministry at the universities of HALLE and Berlin. In 1874 Stoecker was appointed by Emperor Wilhelm I to be a court preacher in Berlin, where he preached sermons based on biblical Christianity, patriotism, and social reform until he was dismissed by Bismarck in 1890.

Stoecker became convinced that the traditional methods of pastoral care and charitable activities were inadequate responses to the needs of impoverished people and the challenges of social problems. In addition, he realized that the Social Democrats, with their Marxist-oriented revolutionary and atheistic agenda, would alienate the disestablished classes from both the church and the state. Therefore, in 1878 Stoecker organized the Central Association for Social Reform and founded the Christian Socialist Workers Party based on Christian and nationalistic principles as an alternative and competing political and social movement for the purpose of renewing and reforming society. After the party failed to elect any candidates, Stoecker reorganized it as the Christian Social Party and added ANTI-SEMITISM to its platform because he had become convinced that the *Judenfrage* was one of the key elements of the social problem. In 1880 Stoecker was elected to the Reichstag, where he served until 1893, and then again from 1891 to 1908.

In spite of his anti-Semitism and his linking of German NATIONALISM with Christianity, Stoecker made a significant contribution to German Protestantism by reinterpreting individualistic and private faith (see INDIVIDUALISM) into a politically and socially oriented Christianity. For Stoecker, the gospel was not just evangelical but a significant force that belonged in the everyday lives of people and the nation. Although not a blueprint, the gospel, claimed Stoecker, provided the necessary impetus and appropriate grounding for social change. Understanding human existence in historical terms, he argued that social change must be evolutionary because revolutionary attempts to sever humans from their past were alienating and dehumanizing. Stoecker supported shaping social structures by the gospel vision of the KINGDOM OF GOD, although he recognized that this very vision always relativized any human effort to create it. Rejecting both individualized CHARITY and revolutionary approaches, he advocated the alternative of CHRISTIAN SOCIALISM. Adopting the human-in-community perspective, Stoecker argued for the dual approach of religious-ethical renewal (a change in individual human consciousness) and structural reform (an evolutionary change in the social, political, and economic structures of life and living). Although unsuccessful relative to the church and nation at large, Stoecker along with other Christian socialists injected a significant perspective and alternative for those Protestants concerned with the plight of people marginalized by industrialized society.

See also Industrialization

References and Further Reading

Primary Sources:

Stoecker, Adolf. *Christlich-sozial: Reden und Aufsätze.* Leipzig: Velhagen und Klasing, 1885; 2nd ed. Berlin: Verlag der Buchhandlung der Berliner Stadtmission, 1890.

Stoecker, Adolf. *Reden und Aufsätze.* Edited by Reinhold Seeberg. Leipzig, Germany: A. Deichert, 1913.

RONALD L. MASSANARI

STONE, BARTON (1772–1844)

American church leader and theologian. Born on December 24, 1772, at Port Tobacco, Maryland, Stone became a New Light Presbyterian pastor in Kentucky in 1793 and hosted the Cane Ridge (Kentucky) REVIVAL of 1801, before founding a movement of churches that embraced what they understood to be New Testament Christianity and took the name Christian. An advocate of Christian unity, Stone led his churches into a relationship with the DISCIPLES OF CHRIST movement of Thomas and Alexander Campbell in 1832.

Stone had broken with the Presbyterians over doctrinal matters in 1804. Unable to reconcile Calvinist understandings of PREDESTINATION, the Trinity and substitutionary atonement found in the WESTMINSTER CONFESSION of Faith, with his understanding of the New Testament, Stone joined fellow ministers in dissolving the Springfield Presbytery of Kentucky with the "Last Will and Testament of the Springfield Presbytery." In 1805 Stone became embroiled in a debate over the ATONEMENT and published a pamphlet entitled *Atonement,* in which Stone argued that Christ's DEATH served not to appease God's wrath but to lead all humans to repentance by demonstrating the nature of human SIN. Stone's advocacy of unity and simple biblical Christianity gave birth to a movement of churches called CHRISTIAN CHURCHES, which adopted both a noncreedal form of Christianity and BAPTISM by immersion. By 1830 the Christians had more than sixteen thousand members in at least five states. In 1826 Stone began publishing the *Christian Messenger,* a monthly journal, as a way of communicating with the growing network of Christian Churches and to advance his vision of Christian unity. After the 1832 merger Stone continued to publish the *Christian Messenger,* pushing his vision of Christian unity until his death on November 9, 1844.

See also Calvinism; Presbyterianism; Salvation

References and Further Reading

Dunnavant, Anthony, ed. *Cane Ridge in Context: Perspectives on Barton W. Stone and the Revival.* Nashville, TN: Disciples of Christ Historical Society, 1992.

Williams, D. Newell. *Barton Stone: A Spiritual Biography.* St. Louis, MO: Chalice Press, 2000.

R. D. CORNWALL

STOWE, HARRIET BEECHER (1811–1896)

American author. Harriet Beecher was born June 14, 1811 at Litchfield, Connecticut, the seventh child of Roxana Foote and the Congregationalist minister LYMAN BEECHER. She was educated at her sister Catharine's Hartford Female Seminary, where she became a teacher in 1827. In 1832 she moved with the family to Cincinnati when Beecher became the president of Lane Theological Seminary and the pastor of a Presbyterian church there. At Cincinnati she again taught in a school headed by Catharine, until her marriage in 1836 to the recently widowed Calvin Stowe of the seminary faculty. The Stowes moved to Bowdoin College in Maine in 1850, and to Andover Theological Seminary in Massachusetts in 1852. Beginning in 1867 they divided their time between homes in New England and in Florida. Mentally incompetent during the last years of her life, Stowe died July 1, 1896.

Although she authored over thirty books, Stowe is usually remembered for her epic antislavery novel, *Uncle Tom's Cabin: or, Life among the Lowly* (1852). Angered by the Fugitive Slave Law of 1850, Stowe—already a published author—wrote this novel (first serialized in the *National Era*) to expose the systemic evils of SLAVERY, and to indict Northerners and Southerners who countenanced its continuance. Although the Beecher family was antislavery without being abolitionist (see SLAVERY, ABOLITION OF), there was little in Harriet's education or previously expressed sentiments to indicate that she would become "the little woman who wrote the book that made this great war," as ABRAHAM LINCOLN is said to have quipped upon meeting Stowe in 1862. *Uncle Tom's Cabin* was an immediate commercial success; over 300,000 copies were sold in the year after its publication, and millions have been sold since. Indeed, it is often described as the best-selling novel of all time. That it helped galvanize antislavery sentiment in the North in the years leading up to the CIVIL WAR is unquestioned.

The critical reaction to *Uncle Tom's Cabin* was immediate and diverse. Southerners attacked it for inaccuracies in its description of slavery, for its overly generous estimation of the capabilities and character of African Americans, and for its clarion call for active resistance to the Fugitive Slave Law. In the

South, distribution of the book was often forbidden. Northern critics debated its portrayal of slavery, its radicalism, and its artistry; the critical reception in the North was, however, mainly positive. The book was also popular overseas, where it was critically acclaimed; within a few years it had been translated into over twenty languages. In response to questions about its portrayal of slave life, Stowe documented her knowledge of slavery in *A Key to Uncle Tom's Cabin* (1853). She also wrote another, less successful, antislavery novel, *Dred: A Tale of the Great Dismal Swamp* (1856). After the Civil War, plays based on *Uncle Tom's Cabin,* which often severely distorted the original message, remained popular with the general public. The book itself was little read, however, and critics became increasingly negative in their estimation of its artistry, calling it "popular" and "sentimental," a work by one of that mid-nineteenth century "mob of scribbling women" (the dismissive words with which Nathaniel Hawthorne had described his female rivals). By 1900 Stowe and *Uncle Tom's Cabin* were largely ignored in literary history and theory.

Critical rediscovery of Stowe came in the mid-twentieth century, initially under the impetus of attacks on her alleged racism. James Baldwin pilloried *Uncle Tom's Cabin* in a 1949 article, accusing Stowe of racism (for her frequent use of racial stereotypes), "theological terror" (for her threatened divine retribution against slaveholders), and for robbing the central character of the book of his manliness (by making him a longsuffering and forgiving Christ-figure). Baldwin's provocative criticism was followed by that of J. C. Furnas, in his book *Goodbye to Uncle Tom* (1956). Although recognizing the truth in these critiques, especially that Stowe's racial stereotyping (even when intended to be benevolent) could be destructive, critics soon began to enunciate more nuanced interpretations. The ensuing discussion of not only her antislavery books, but of the larger corpus of her work—especially that portion focusing on life in New England, and her controversial *Lady Byron Vindicated* (1870)—has continued to the present. Feminist, and to a lesser extent African-American, scholars have taken the lead in examining a wide range of religious, racial, political, economic, and social issues in her books, as they attempt to understand her within the context of her own time.

As a result of this reexamination of her work, Stowe has reappeared within the canon of American literature from which she was ejected in the late nineteenth century. Her racial attitudes, her feminism (she supported women's suffrage and equal pay for equal work, but rejected some ideas and programs of the more radical feminists), her friendships with other women writers and reformers, her reaction to personal tragedies (especially the deaths of three of her children), and her religious views (she significantly altered her inherited Calvinist theology, becoming an Episcopalian in her later years) all continue to be widely discussed.

Many critics, from her time to ours, have noted that much of Stowe's writing was essentially sermonic. As the daughter of a Protestant minister, and the sister of several others, including the famous HENRY WARD BEECHER, this is hardly surprising. Her own self-understanding was primarily religious and moral; she struggled creatively all her life with the theological ideas and ethical convictions that she had learned from her New England Puritan upbringing.

See also Calvinism; Congregationalism; Episcopal Church, United States; Presbyterianism; Puritanism; Weld, Theodore Dwight

References and Further Reading

Primary Sources:

Stowe, Harriet Beecher. *Uncle Tom's Cabin, or, Life Among the Lowly.* New York: Literary Classics, 1982.
Stowe, Harriet Beecher, and Joan D. Hedrick. *The Oxford Harriet Beecher Stowe Reader.* New York: Oxford University Press, 1999.

Secondary Sources:

Ammons, Elizabeth, ed. *Uncle Tom's Cabin: Authoritative Text, Backgrounds and Contexts, Criticism.* New York: W. W. Norton and Co., 1994.
Foster, Charles H. *The Rungless Ladder: Harriet Beecher Stowe and New England Puritanism.* New York: Cooper Square Publishers, 1970.
Gossett, Thomas F. *Uncle Tom's Cabin and American Culture.* Dallas: Southern Methodist University Press, 1985.
Hedrick, Joan D. *Harriet Beecher Stowe: A Life.* New York: Oxford University Press, 1994.
Hildreth, Margaret Holbrook. *Harriet Beecher Stowe: A Bibliography.* Hamden, CT: Archon Books, 1976.

DONALD L. HUBER

STRAUSS, DAVID FRIEDRICH (1808–1874)

German theologian. Born in Ludwigsburg, GERMANY, in 1808, David Friedrich Strauss produced one of the most important theological and historical works of the nineteenth century. His landmark volume *The Life of Jesus, Critically Examined,* first published in 1835, was revised and edited again through several successive (and very different) volumes. Strauss's 1,400-page masterpiece, written in just one feverish year, was originally translated into English by the British novelist GEORGE ELIOT in 1846, introducing Strauss's revolutionary ideas to the English-speaking world. Strauss's major contribution was to place the life of Jesus in a broader mytho-historical context and pioneer in the techniques that eventually came to be known as the HIGHER CRITICISM of the BIBLE. Rejecting both the rationalist approach to biblical study, which attempted to dismiss biblical stories as fairy tales that could be attributed to natural explanation, and the supernaturalist approach, which held to the direct miraculous intervention of God in history through the life of his son Jesus, Strauss proposed that the life of Jesus as recounted in the various gospels was best explained through setting the biblical literature in the context of Judaic myths about the coming of the Messiah on earth. Strauss meant by myth "the representation of an event or idea in a historical form but characterized by the pictorial and imaginative thought and expression of primitive ages" (Lawler 1986:42). Strauss's influence was far-reaching because his work set the stage for the revolution in the historical-critical study of the Bible that was developed in nineteenth-century German academic institutions and soon spread through Christendom. Although some of Strauss's ideas are dated, and some of his historical research long since surpassed, Strauss's notion of understanding Jesus within the messianic Jewish thought of his own time is now accepted as a commonplace in biblical studies, even among biblical conservatives.

The Life of Strauss

Born to a Protestant German family, Strauss was clearly destined for a ministerial and theological role in life from his early days. However, his revolutionary study of the biblical literature on Jesus's life blocked his career opportunities both in academia and in the church world, leaving him a mostly frustrated and bitter man from the time of the publication of *The Life of Jesus,* when he was just twenty-seven and recently graduated from theological seminary, until his painful death from an ulcer in February of 1874. After publication of his work on Jesus, Strauss lost his post as a college lecturer, and was blackballed as well from any pastoral positions in German Protestant parishes. He subsequently lived in Stuttgart, Germany, where he carried on an extensive correspondence with both supporters of and detractors from his work. In 1839, after much local controversy, Strauss was offered a professorship in dogmatics and church history in Zurich, SWITZERLAND. Local reaction in the strongly Protestant hamlet was intense; and when put to the vote of the citizenry, the Swiss citizens overwhelmingly rejected use of their tax money to pay the notorious professor. From the early 1840s forward, with money from the Swiss government that bought out his con-

tract as well as a family inheritance, Strauss spent his remaining thirty-four years as an author, short-term politician, avid suitor but failed husband of a troubled opera singer, biographer, journalist, book reviewer, prolific and dyspeptic correspondent, and polemicist with and against the "Young Hegelians" in German academia. In his last decade he authored a failed popular work, *The Life of Jesus for the German People,* a kind of biography that would set the stage for countless other "Jesus Life" books to come in the twentieth century. In 1873 he left instructions to his son for his very secular funeral; by that time his youthful dream to deepen the Christian faith through his landmark scholarship and engagement with the ideas of the likes of FRIEDRICH SCHLEIERMACHER and GEORG WILHELM FRIEDRICH HEGEL had long since died.

The Life of Jesus: Background Preparation

As a young man, from 1821 to 1825, Strauss studied with the historian FERDINAND CHRISTIAN BAUR at a preparatory seminary in Blaubeuren, Germany. From there he moved on to university studies at Tübingen. From 1827 to 1830 he continued advanced theological studies and came under the influence of the famous German theologian Schleiermacher, as well as Hegel. He also completed a Ph.D. dissertation, his only substantial piece of writing before *The Life of Jesus.* Entranced by the Hegelian dialectic, Strauss came to Berlin in October of 1831 to study further with the philosopher-king, although Hegel died of cholera a few weeks later. Strauss expressed his dismay at the news in front of the proud theologian Schleiermacher, who normally expected more deference from his students. Strauss later wrote: "Schleiermacher has greatly stimulated me and I owe him a lot; but the man has still not satisfied me. He only goes half way; he doesn't pronounce the final word." Strauss determined to go intellectually where Schleiermacher, and no man, had gone before (Harris 1973:35).

Strauss decided to put before the public a life of Jesus that would deconstruct the older but no longer satisfactory ways of understanding the Gospels and the life of Jesus. He would strip away the accretion of false DOCTRINE and rationalistic simplicities that had distorted biblical study, and in doing so "re-establish dogmatically that which has been destroyed critically" (Strauss 1840:757).

What he soon learned was that "what has been destroyed critically" was about all the shocked and horrified reading public could talk about; and that Strauss as a thinker and writer was simply better at annihilation than at creation. The results of his work were that the foundations for the doctrines of the Christian faith were undermined, and Christian THE-

OLOGY could never again be the same. Point by point, incident by incident, Strauss ruthlessly dissected the Gospel stories, showing again and again how little real knowledge could come from them, and how many of the supposed sayings and doings of Jesus fulfilled and arose out of older Jewish traditions and rabbinic literature. Jesus's DEATH, although real in Strauss's mind, could not have been followed by a literal physical resurrection. Older myths and legends, he contended, were recast into reports on the ostensibly empty tomb, whereas Jesus's later appearances to the disciples were clearly hallucinatory; Jesus's final ascension into HEAVEN capped the story with the ultimate messianic denouement.

In his younger years Strauss innocently believed he could carry on his work but that the essential faith would remain pristine; that the virgin birth, the miracles, and the death and resurrection would remain deep truths even if one might question their exact historicism. However, once doubt was cast on them as historical facts—and doubts coming *not* from known infidels such as Voltaire and DAVID HUME, but rather from a sturdy German Protestant scholar and parish minister whose intent was to deepen and enrich contemporary understanding of the Christian faith—the revolution was on. Strauss's own happiness was to be a casualty of the German culture wars of the mid-nineteenth century.

The Life of Jesus: Major Ideas

"Our standpoint," Strauss announced in his major work, "allows the same laws to hold sway in every sphere of being and activity; and, therefore, where a narrative runs contrary to the laws of nature, it must be regarded as unhistorical" (Harris 1973:42). With that dictum in mind Strauss calmly picked apart what could be known truly about the historical Jesus. The result, as he himself put it, was that "the boundless treasure of truth and life, on which humanity has been nurtured for eighteen centuries, now seems to have been destroyed . . . God divested of his GRACE, man of his dignity, the bond between heaven and earth rent asunder" (Harris 1973:51). As he told a friend, however, all this destruction to "partly shake the infinite significance which faith attributes to this life," was in the service of restoring it again "in a higher way." This reconstruction would begin by "showing first, the crudity of supernaturalism; secondly the emptiness of rationalism, and thirdly the truth of SCIENCE" (Harris 1973:33–34).

By "science" Strauss meant that

"which sees in the life of Jesus the consciousness which the Church has of the human spirit objectified as divine spirit; this consciousness is not projected into particular features, into miracles which are then allotted their significance; in the history of Jesus' death and resurrection, however, that idea in its whole process sums itself up systematically and shows that the Spirit attains the true positivity, the divine life . . . only through the negation of the negation" (Harris 1973:34).

The Hegelian influence is obvious: supernaturalism was the historic *thesis,* the truth that had comforted Christians for centuries (the notion that the Gospels record history accurately and nothing can be discarded, as Strauss summarized it); rationalism was its *antithesis,* the crude village atheist rejection of the supernatural (such as the notion that Jesus did not really walk on water but must have been stepping on rocks submerged just beneath the surface, and other like trivializations of the profound stories of the Bible). Strauss used the Hegelian method of using the thesis and antithesis positions to refute one another; the truths of supernaturalism refuted the trivial empiricism of rationalism, whereas the historical investigation of the rationalists undermined the simplistic faith of the supernaturalists. Strauss's view—the mythical approach—would provide the majestic *synthesis,* by proposing the new interpretation of Jesus's life as the representation of the Infinite Spirit in finite form, expressed in the Bible in the poetic and mythological language of the Jewish messianic authors of the Gospel (with the notable exception of the Gospel of John, which Strauss, at least in the first edition of his work, denied as too untrustworthy and internally fallacious to bear up under study).

Most radically, Strauss proposed that the essential truth was the unity of God and man, with Jesus being the individual physical representative of that unity for the ancient mind that needed a concrete symbol of that unity, although modern man could understand the idea philosophically. The fructifying contact of the Infinite Spirit of God with the finite being of man no longer needed the mythological props of the quasi-historical Jesus. The union of the divine and the human transcended the historic Jesus; the union was realized in the spirit of the human race as a whole. Indeed, Strauss saw Jesus himself as given to dubious and time-bound forms of a fanatical messianism, hardly an appropriate symbol for the more profound ideas of the modern age. Through the various editions of the work Strauss wavered somewhat on his opinion of Jesus the person, but even in his most positive readings he found Jesus the individual to be a shaky symbol for the more profound immanence of God as Spirit in Man.

Strauss's use (and, in the analyses of many critics, *abuse*) of Hegelianism in an attempt to wrest the deeper truths of religious thought from the time-bound conventions of the Gospels was the least successful portion of his work. As explained by scholar Peter Hodgson, "instead of a *hermeneutics* of symbols and religious myths, he proposed to *destroy* them, together with the historical tradition in which they were imbedded. It is no wonder that his constructive program remained barren and unfruitful" (Hodgson 1972: xxxvi).

Impact of Strauss's Work

Strauss put out three versions of his work in the late 1830s, during a time in which he remained intensely religious and sought to help his critics understand that he was not the devilish infidel that was quickly becoming his public persona. At one point, nearly pleading with the public, he proclaimed that "to this historical, personal Christ belongs everything from his life in which his religious perfection is portrayed: his discourses, his moral actions and his suffering." That was as close as Strauss came to endorsing Protestant ORTHODOXY. In later editions he drew back from such forms of apologia. His efforts were without much success. After his rejection by the seminary in Zurich, the jobless Strauss, unable to fulfill his dream of being an august university professor and exiled from the church that had raised him, grew increasingly bitter. By that point he was inclined to be the very ogre to the faithful that he had been (falsely) reputed to be in his more pious years in the 1830s.

Strauss grew less concerned about defending the Christian faith, but as the years progressed was more agitated by the Hegelian left, notably LUDWIG FEUERBACH. The young Hegelians, picking up where Strauss left off, turned the idea of God itself into a projection of human desire; rather than God creating man, it was instead the case that man created God in his own image, they insisted. It was the beginnings of what would later be called the DEATH OF GOD theology. By that time Strauss was no longer truly a revolutionary, for the young Hegelians had surpassed him. Strauss despised them, in part because they had stolen his thunder. By that time he was the object of hatred from the traditionalist Christian right, and of scorn from the revolutionary left. Perhaps for this reason Strauss grew more conservative and conventional in his own political views.

Whatever its faults and limitations, whatever its own time-bound and abstruse Hegelian formulations, Strauss's work revolutionized theology by introducing into it the anthropological concept of myth and symbol. Since that time thousands of theologians and writers have grappled with the life of Jesus; none has come close in intellectual impact and international controversy to the work of David Friedrich Strauss.

See also Jesus, Lives of; Liberal Protestantism and Liberalism

References and Further Reading

Primary Source:

Strauss, David Friedrich. *The Life of Jesus Critically Examined.* 4th ed., 1840. Edited by Peter Hodgson. Translated by George Eliot. Philadelphia, PA: Fortress Press, 1972.

Secondary Sources:

Harris, Horton. *David Friedrich Strauss and His Theology.* Cambridge: Cambridge University Press, 1973.

Hodgson, Peter C. "Editor's Introduction: Strauss's Theological Development from 1825 to 1840." In David Friedrich Strauss, *The Life of Jesus Critically Examined.* Repr. ed. Philadelphia, PA: Fortress Press, 1972.

Kim, Jee Ho. "David Friedrich Strauss (1808–1874)." http://people.bu.edu/wwildman/WeirdWildWeb/courses/mwt/dictionary/mwt_themes_475_strauss.htm (December 1998).

Lawler, Edwina G. *David Friedrich Strauss and His Critics: The Life of Jesus Debate in Early Nineteenth-Century German Journals.* New York: Peter Lang Publishing, 1986.

Massey, Marilyn Chapin. *Christ Unmasked: The Meaning of The Life of Jesus in German Politics.* Chapel Hill: The University of North Carolina Press, 1983.

PAUL HARVEY

STRONG, JOSIAH (1847–1916)

American clergy. Strong was born in Naperville, Illinois on January 19, 1847. After studying at Lane Theological Seminary between 1869 and 1871, he assumed pastorates in various Congregational churches in Ohio. In 1886 he became the general secretary of the American branch of the EVANGELICAL ALLIANCE, which had been founded in ENGLAND in 1846 as a reaction to the OXFORD MOVEMENT. This gave Strong a national platform and position of considerable importance. Strong's commitment to Christian solutions to contemporary social problems found expression in his editorship of the journal *The Kingdom and Social Service,* in which the ideals of the SOCIAL GOSPEL movement were reiterated incessantly. All the same, his efforts to commit the Evangelical Alliance to the approach of the Social Gospel proved not overly successful.

More important was Strong's commitment to American imperialist expansion. In his numerous books—all in all, Strong published eleven books, alongside countless articles—he sought to make the case not only for the superiority of the Anglo-Saxon, that is, English-speaking race (which would forever retain its superiority because of its growing numbers) but also for American expansion. This argument was embedded in the moral dicta of Christianity and is found in such books as *Our Country* (1886), which sold over 25,000 copies, and *Expansion: Under New World Conditions* (1900).

References and Further Reading

Primary Sources:

Strong, Josiah. *The New Era. Or, The Coming Kingdom.* New York: Baker and Taylor, 1893.
———. *Expansion under New World Conditions.* New York: Garland, 1971 [1900].
———. *Our Country.* Cambridge, MA: Belknap, 1963.

Secondary Sources:

Deichmann Edwards, Wendy J. "Manifest Destiny, the Social Gospel and the Coming Kingdom: Josiah Strong's Program of Global Reform, 1885–1916." In Wendy J. Deichmann Edwards, ed. *Perspectives on the Social Gospel,* 81–116. Lewiston, NY: Edwin Mellen Press, 1999.
Jordan, Philip D. "Josiah Strong and a Scientific Social Gospel." *Iliff Review* 42 (1985): 21–31.
Muller, Dorothea R. "Josiah Strong and the Social Gospel: a Christian's Response to the Challenge of the City." *Journal of the Presbyterian Historical Society* 39 (1961): 150–175.

HANS J. HILLERBRAND

STUDD, CHARLES THOMAS (1860–1931)

English missionary. Studd was born near Andover, ENGLAND in 1860, and he died in Ibambi, Belgian Congo July 16, 1931. Both missionary and mission advocate, he was the son of a wealthy retired tea planter who had been converted through DWIGHT L. MOODY's campaigns. At Eton and Trinity College, Cambridge, Studd became one of the leading cricketers in England and toured Australia with the Test team of 1882–1883 that regained the Ashes.

Studd was the best known, although not the moving spirit, of the small group of CAMBRIDGE UNIVERSITY students and army officers known as the Cambridge Seven who volunteered for service with the CHINA INLAND MISSION in 1885. The Seven—who between them represented wealth, social standing, and athletic fame—made a deep public impression. Their evident spirit of sacrifice (Studd gave up a considerable inheritance) promoted the idea of missionary service among English university students and the upper classes generally, sectors not previously noted as major sources of missionary recruits. In 1894 Studd left CHINA, sick, and engaged in missionary advocacy for the Student Volunteer Missionary movement. In 1900 he returned to mission service, this time in INDIA, until 1906 when, again ill, he resumed mission advocacy and home EVANGELISM.

In 1910 he went to the south Sudan, and in 1911 established the nondenominational Heart of Africa

Mission for the evangelization of the African interior, leading it himself from the Belgian Congo from 1913. He spent the rest of his life there. His charismatic presence and eloquence in person and in print moved many, but his eccentric behavior, dictatorial style, and increasing dependency on drugs brought controversy and disruption to the mission. His abiding monument is the large and international Worldwide Evangelization Crusade, embodying his principles without his eccentricities, and shaped by his son-in-law, Norman P. Grubb. Studd's brother Kynaston (1858–1944), lord mayor of London from 1928 to 1929, was also a prominent spokesman for MISSIONS and evangelism.

Studd was a leading representative of one important strand in the Protestant missionary movement during the later nineteenth and early twentieth centuries. Its features included energetic verbal evangelism, a spirituality based on "a blessed interior life of peace and triumph"; a call to consecration and sacrifice; and a strong premillennial ESCHATOLOGY. It displayed little interest in THEOLOGY or intellectual activity. The missionary movement of the period accommodated other strands of thought, outlook, and activity. The Cambridge Seven, of which Studd was a vital component, gave impetus to the founding of the Student Volunteer Missionary Union. This in turn, with the support of the university Christian unions, especially at Cambridge and Oxford, gave rise to the Student Christian Movement and thereafter to the INTERVARSITY CHRISTIAN FELLOWSHIP. Between them these organizations reflected most of the determinative forces in twentieth-century Anglo-Saxon Protestantism and affected ecumenical thought and action.

See also Africa; Ecumenism; Missionary Organizations; Missions, British

References and Further Reading

Buxton, Edith. *Reluctant Missionary.* London: Lutterworth, 1968.
Grubb, Norman P. *CT Studd, Famous Cricketer and Pioneer.* London: Lutterworth, 1933.
Pollock, J. C. *A Cambridge Movement.* London: Murray, 1953.
———. *The Cambridge Seven.* London: Inter-Varsity Press, 1955.

ANDREW F. WALLS

SUDAN INTERIOR MISSION

The Sudan Interior Mission (SIM) began with the vision of three young men: Canadians Walter Gowans and Rowland Bingham, and Thomas Kent of the UNITED STATES. In 1893 they banded together to carry the Gospel to the "Soudan," a vast expanse stretching eastward from the Niger river across the central tier of sub-Saharan AFRICA. They landed at Lagos in late

1893 and made their way into the interior. Within a year Gowans and Kent had died of malaria. Bingham was stricken, and returned to CANADA gravely ill, but unbroken. After being driven back by illness on his second attempt, Bingham returned home and committed his life to recruiting and funding others for the task. By 1902 the first party of missionaries had established a base in the interior, and the Sudan Interior Mission was born.

Although the first decade of work was not particularly fruitful, two of the first wave of missionaries would make a considerable impact on the breadth and depth of the work. A. W. Banfield established Niger Press, which would evolve into a wide-ranging translation and Christian publication service. Dr. Andrew Stirrett came in the first decade of the new century, and would serve for over fifty years, establishing clinics and hospitals throughout Africa. SIM quickly developed into a general mission, with work in translation, education, publication, medicine, and social ministry. However, the focus always remained centered on EVANGELISM and church planting.

In the early 1920s several candidates from AUSTRALIA and NEW ZEALAND entered service with SIM. Mr. Bingham traveled "round the world" to establish offices in those locations, and in the process his vision for the work of SIM was considerably broadened. Ethiopia was the first field outside the "Soudan," and in time SIM missionaries were at work in many other fields throughout the world.

Ministry Characteristics

Four characteristics have marked out SIM from the beginning: evangelical, interdenominational, international, and church centered. All SIM personnel must affirm the doctrinal statement of the organization, which places it squarely within the conservative evangelical tradition of nineteenth- and twentieth-century Euro-American Protestantism. The statement affirms the BIBLE as the "inerrant and authoritative Word of God," the Trinity, the lost estate of the race, SALVATION by GRACE through FAITH in Jesus Christ, and a commitment to fulfill the Great Commission.

Although the statement is clear, it is narrowly drawn, omitting such issues such as BAPTISM, the LORD'S SUPPER, church offices, gifts of the spirit, church government, PREDESTINATION, or ESCHATOLOGY. This is consistent with the firm commitment to be an interdenominational mission, open to a wide range of Christian believers. This was so from the beginning: Walter Gowans was a Presbyterian, Thomas Kent a Congregationalist, and Rowland Bingham was an Anglican who joined the SALVATION ARMY and was ordained by the BAPTISTS. SIM has opened its ranks to

missionaries from a wide range of denominational backgrounds and has consistently opposed the introduction of denominational "distinctives," tensions, or hostility into its varied ministries, or into the host of churches spawned from its endeavors. However, in some areas those churches have joined together in indigenous bodies that have many of the marks of a DENOMINATION. The Evangelical Church of West Africa (ECWA) is the clearest example, a faith community of several thousand churches that sits most comfortably in the broad evangelical Wesleyan tradition.

SIM is also international is scope. From the beginning the mission looked to the United States, Canada, SCOTLAND, and ENGLAND for funds and personnel. This base soon expanded to Australia, New Zealand, then to other "sending" nations.

Finally, SIM is church centered. From the initial vision of the founder down to the present, SIM has remained convinced that the church is God's primary agent for transforming the world. The mission works closely with local churches for the purpose of starting churches where none exist, and then building up and strengthening those churches so that they might fulfill their part in the Great Commission. Again, the Evangelical Church of West Africa stands as a clear example of that goal. In 1976 ECWA assumed responsibility for most of the social, medical, literature, educational, and church expansion ministries of SIM in NIGERIA. Today ECWA has over 1,200 missionaries, working primarily with unreached people in Nigeria and other West African nations.

In the early 1980s the International Christian Fellowship (a mission working primarily in INDIA) and the Andes Evangelical Mission merged with the Sudan Interior Mission to form the new SIM, the Society for International Ministries. Currently SIM assists local churches in over forty different nations to send out some sixteen hundred cross-cultural missionaries to over fifty fields, ranging from Togo to Ecuador to India to Italy.

See also Anglicanism; Biblical Inerrancy; Congregationalism; Missionary Organizations; Missions; Presbyterianism

References and Further Reading

Adeyemi, E. A. *From Seven to Seven Thousand: The Story of the Birth and Growth of SIM/ECWA Church in Ilorin.* Lagos, Nigeria: Okinbaloye Commercial Press, 1995.

Bingham, Roland V. *Seven Sevens of Years and a Jubilee: The Story of the Sudan Interior Mission.* Grand Rapids, MI: Zondervan, 1943.

Carpenter, Joel A., ed. *Missionary Innovation and Expansion.* New York: Garland Publishing, 1988.

Turaki, Yusufu. *An Introduction to the History of SIM/ECWA in Nigeria 1893–1993*. Lagos, Nigeria: Self-published under a grant from the PEW Charitable Trust, 1993.

JAMES D. CHANCELLOR

SUN YAT-SEN (1866–1925)

Chinese nationalist politician. Sun Yat-sen (1866–1925) was born in Guangdong province in south CHINA, but raised and schooled in Hawaii and Hong Kong. He was actively dedicated to the overthrow of the Qing (Manchu) government from the 1890s until the Revolution of 1911. Sun was first president of the provisional government of the Republic of China in early 1912, but was outmaneuvered politically and relegated to an outsider's role, although after 1912 he became leader of the new Kuomintang (Guomindang, Chinese Nationalist Party).

Relatively powerless for a number of years, Sun's fortunes skyrocketed in the 1920s when his Kuomintang became the beneficiary of strong new nationalistic currents among urban Chinese. Sun also allied himself and his movement with the Comintern and the Soviet Union, which provided advisors as well as military and material assistance for the small but dynamic Kuomintang power base around Canton, as well as brokering an alliance with the Chinese Communists. At this point Sun died, leaving his protégé Chiang Kai-shek to inherit his leadership role in the Nationalist Party. Sun is known as the "father of the country," and is claimed as a hero by both Communists and Nationalists today.

Sun's Christian identity is hard to pin down. He attended an Anglican school in Hawaii (see ANGLICAN-ISM), and studied medicine at missionary hospitals in Hong Kong and Canton. He was baptized by the American missionary Charles Hager in 1884, the same year he had an arranged marriage that produced three children. Sun's Christianity, although well known, does not seem to have strongly colored his political career. In 1914, however, in a second marriage that scandalized Protestant circles, he wed Soong Ch'ing-ling (Song Qingling), daughter of Charles Jones Soong, patriarch of the large and well-connected Soong clan, the single most politically influential Chinese Protestant family of the twentieth century. This association alone makes Sun an important figure in Chinese Protestant history.

See also Communism

References and Further Reading

Bergere, Marie-Claire. *Sun Yat-sen*. Stanford: Stanford University Press, 1998.
Chang, Sidney H., and Leonard H. D. Gordon. *Bibliography of Sun Yat-sen in China's Republican Revolution, 1885–1925*. Lanham, MD: University Press of America, 1998.

DANIEL H. BAYS

SUNDAY SCHOOL

Sunday School is a form of religious instruction undertaken as a supplement to Sunday worship for children. ROBERT RAIKES is conventionally recognized as the founder of the Sunday School, a "ragged school" set up for the poor in the English city of Gloucester in 1783. There were in fact a number of Sunday Schools in existence before Raikes's experiment, the earliest of which may have been set up by Hannah Ball in 1763. The Charity School Movement of the early eighteenth century had sought to transform the lives of the poor in WALES, and then in ENGLAND by the use of "dame schools" to teach the children to read. The use of Sunday for education was the result of a pragmatic recognition by the 1780s that weekday schools were ineffective for children who were already employed. Raikes's description of the school in the *Gloucester Journal* created widespread interest in other towns. The experiment was not confined to one DENOMINATION and was often organized by community committees quite separate from any local church. They had among their goals the preservation of society from social anarchy, rather than just religious knowledge.

These early schools taught reading and used the BIBLE as their primary text. They were always envisaged as catering primarily to the children of the poor. By 1787 some 250,000 children were enrolled and by 1831 some 37 percent of all children—and a much higher proportion of factory children—were attending. Conservatives sometimes feared the scale of the organization involved and its potential for giving the poor ideas above their station. However, the British Sunday School Union, founded in 1803, continued to exert significant influence.

The schools slowly became located in local churches and came under the control of the religious bodies. In 1800 the large Manchester Sunday School split up into Anglican and nonconformist schools (see ANGLICANISM; NONCONFORMITY), with the Methodists particularly successful in their efforts (see METHODISM, ENGLAND). A building spree resulted to house the classes in the urban districts. The growth of child employment in the factories meant that the Sunday School remained a vital social instrument, while Sunday School teachers were often former successful students. The Sunday School gained huge popularity in the working class community, and its festivals—awarding prizes, picnics, and church parades—could attract a huge attendance. There were fierce debates about the place of reading in the curriculum, and this led to some splits and the establishment of radical Sunday Schools with an amended curriculum.

Sunday Schools in the United States

Americans adopted the vision of religious instruction in Sunday Schools soon after the War of Independence. A broadly based First Day school was organized in Philadelphia about 1790. However, there was less urgency while America remained predominantly rural. Two New York women sought to establish a Sunday School in their city in 1816, but the major breakthrough came when the prominent minister LYMAN BEECHER moved a resolution in 1828 creating the American Sunday School Union, "eminently adapted to promote the intellectual and moral culture of the nation, to perpetuate our republican and religious institutions, and to reconcile eminent national prosperity with moral purity and future blessedness." In the urban crisis of the 1830s and 1840s, concern about the "street arabs" led to fresh attempts to plant Sunday Schools in the cites, led by followers of CHARLES G. FINNEY, who idealized the Sunday School as a critical social instrument.

American schools soon developed a broader scope and the Sunday School became a symbol of republican inclusiveness. Theological debates about the legitimacy of childhood CONVERSION made the curriculum of the school controversial. HORACE BUSHNELL urged that conversion be seen as a process in which education should not be coercive. In 1872 what became the International Sunday School Lesson plan was commenced by the Sunday School Union, and this was subsequently widely adopted by liberal schools in many countries. Meanwhile the American Sunday School expanded to a period of religious instruction for adults as well as children. In contrast, in Britain and British countries Sunday Schools became the last link of the masses with the church.

After the 1960s the scope of Sunday Schools declined dramatically. They have largely catered to the children of church members and been run parallel with the main morning church service. Moreover, a declining sense of the value of voluntary education for the young has taken away the value of the Sunday School. Its efficacy is being questioned.

The Sunday School has often been viewed as a key instrument used by middle-class interests to redirect the leisure and radicalism of the working class. Thomas Laqueur offered another explanation, that the Sunday School helped the formation of working class identity by giving them literacy and entrusting them with their own education.

References and Further Reading

Lynn, Robert W., and Elliott Wright. *The Big Little School: 200 Years of the Sunday School*. 2nd ed. Nashville, TN: Abingdon Press, 1980.

Laqueur, W. T. *Religion and Respectability: Sunday Schools and Working Class Culture 1780–1850*. New Haven, CT: Yale University Press, 1976.

PETER LINEHAM

SUNDAY, BILLY (1862–1935)

American evangelist and prohibition advocate. Born William Ashley Sunday on November 19, 1862 in a log cabin near Ames, Iowa, the evangelist frequently spoke of his hardscrabble childhood. A promising small-town baseball player, he was recruited by the Chicago Whitestockings in 1883, converted to evangelical Christianity at Chicago's Pacific Garden Mission in 1886, and married Helen Amelia Thompson (1868–1957), the daughter of a prosperous Chicago ice cream–manufacturing family, in 1888. Sunday continued to play professionally for various teams until 1890; thereafter he worked full-time for the YMCA and then became an assistant to J. Wilbur Chapman (1859–1918), a well-known traveling evangelist. In 1896 Sunday struck out on his own, assisted by his wife, and continued in full-time evangelistic work until he died of heart failure in Chicago at age 72 on November 6, 1935.

Sunday's distinctive pulpit manner, marked by athletic gestures, liberal use of slang, and excoriation of his opponents, won him wide popularity as he preached in cities across the northern United States. He was famous for exhorting converts to "hit the sawdust trail" at his upbeat urban revival meetings. Music was also an important component of Sunday's revival meetings; from 1909 to 1927 song leader Homer A. Rodeheaver (1880–1955) accompanied him, warming up audiences with stirring gospel choruses and trombone solos and coordinating performances by visiting ensembles.

By World War I, Sunday was the most recognized American preacher, but thereafter his popularity declined, due partly to his increasingly strident tone and partly to theological fissures within American Protestantism that made organizing citywide crusades increasingly difficult.

References and Further Reading

Brown, Elijah P. *The Real Billy Sunday*. Dayton, OH: Otterbein Press, 1914.

Dorsett, Lyle W. *Billy Sunday and the Redemption of Urban America*. Grand Rapids, MI: Eerdmans, 1991.

McLoughlin, William G., Jr. *Billy Sunday Was His Real Name*. Chicago: University of Chicago Press, 1955.

JAY BLOSSOM

SUNG, JOHN (SUNG SHANGJIE) (1901–1944)

Chinese revival preacher. Sung was born in Fujian, CHINA on September 27, 1901 into the family of a Methodist pastor, Sung Xue Lien. When he was very young he began to imitate his father, both in PREACHING and in handing out tracts. Because of his alert mind and Christian commitment, Shangjie ("noble and frugal one") was sent, with the support of Methodist missionaries, to the UNITED STATES to study for pastoral leadership. In 1920 Sung began his studies at Ohio Wesleyan College, where he completed a bachelor's degree in three years. He then went on to complete a master's and Ph.D. in chemistry at Ohio State University by the summer of 1926.

Remembering his reason for studying in the United States, Sung turned down lucrative offers in chemistry (including an offer to help develop explosives for GERMANY) and turned to study THEOLOGY at Union Seminary in New York. In his first semester at Union, Sung heard a fifteen-year-old girl evangelist at Calvary Baptist Church. His CONVERSION or awakening was remarkable. Sung began evangelizing his fellow seminary students, and he would sing HYMNS until late into the evening. His behavior was understood to be caused by mental problems, so Sung was placed in a mental asylum for 193 days. During this time he read through the BIBLE, according to his account, forty times, tracing different themes with each reading. This would become the foundation for his seventeen years of preaching in East Asia.

Sung then returned to China in 1927, married (Yu Chin Hua), and began teaching chemistry three days a week at the Methodist Christian High School in Fujian. His heart, though, was in preaching and so the bulk of his time was spent as an apostolic preacher in South China. He came into contact with Andrew Gih, an evangelist of the Bethel Worldwide Evangelistic Band, and cooperated with this group from 1931 to 1933. The Band was short-lived but very influential. Their doctrine of eradication of all SIN was not accepted by Sung, but their methods of organization and itineration were adopted. By 1934 Sung was on his own and he was widely known in most of south and east China. He did not approve of the work of most missionaries because of their emphasis on nonessentials (i.e., not focused solely on the Bible) and their liberal theology (see LIBERAL PROTESTANTISM AND LIBERALISM).

From 1935 to December 1939 Sung traveled to preach to Chinese communities throughout Southeast Asia: TAIWAN, PHILIPPINES, Malaya, Singapore, Thailand, and INDONESIA. His impact was great as he brought together Chinese from many denominations and dialects, and he also organized the converts in "evangelistic bands" reminiscent of the Bethel Worldwide Evangelistic Band. These local bands of ten or twelve would meet weekly to study the Bible, pray, and go out to evangelize their communities. His impact was so great that in some towns local shops would close for the week of Sung's meetings.

Sung's preaching style was full of emotion; he preached from all of the Bible and he often confronted people directly with sins of gambling, sexual affairs, or stealing. Sung lived a very simple life, prayed for great lengths of time, and held meetings for healings (see FAITH HEALING). Although not strictly speaking Pentecostal, Sung emphasized the role of the Holy Spirit in personal transformation and healing, which brought him into conflict with most missionaries (see PENTECOSTALISM). Sung, along with WANG MINGDAO, Andrew Gih, and others, pioneered an indigenous form of Chinese Christianity that has had much success among the Chinese masses both in China and overseas.

Sung and his wife had five children, but after years of preaching with great pain, John Sung died August 18, 1944 of tuberculosis (and probably cancer) at the early age of forty-three.

See also Asian Theology; Evangelism, Overview; Missions

References and Further Reading

Lyall, Leslie T. *John Sung*. Chicago: Moody Press, 1964.
Schubert, William E. *I Remember John Sung*. Singapore: Far Eastern Bible College Press, 1976.
Tow, Timothy. *John Sung, My Teacher*. Singapore: Christian Life Publishers, 1985.

SCOTT W. SUNQUIST

SWABIAN SYNGRAMMA

The Swabian Syngramma was an antisacramental treatise written by fourteen Lutheran theologians, advocating the real presence of Christ in the elements of bread and wine in the LORD'S SUPPER.

All the reformers rejected the Catholic position of TRANSUBSTANTIATION. However, HULDRYCH ZWINGLI took the further view that the Lord's Supper was a thanksgiving in which Jesus was spiritually present. JOHANNES OECOLAMPADIUS published an attack on MARTIN LUTHER's position, which held for the real presence of body and blood in the elements of bread and wine. Arguing for Christ's being only figuratively present at the Eucharist, Oecolampadius dedicated his book to the "beloved brethren" in Schwabia, his former students, intending to win them over. The region was strategically important as the reformers continued to compete for the spiritual and political allegiance of southern GERMANY.

However, Luther's influence was strong, and under the leadership of JOHANNES BRENZ some fourteen theologians responded by drafting a statement—the Syngramma Suevicum—on October 14, 1525 in support of Luther. Meant as a document to be sent to Oecolampadius, it was published with an introduction by Luther and given its title by the printer. It offered a positive affirmation of Christ's actual presence in the sacrament. The document argued that as the word of peace from Christ confers peace, and saying that sins are forgiven gives pardon, so the word of Christ imparts into the bread and wine the very body and blood of Christ. When the sacrament is consumed the believer is sanctified by the body and given the creative power of the word, whereas the unbeliever is condemned.

MARTIN BUCER responded to the document, arguing that the real presence in the Lord's Supper produces no benefit for the Christian, whereas Oecolampadius composed his Anti-syngramma noting that the Swabians had erred in an un-Lutheran spiritual activity by denying that the body of Christ is broken by hands and chewed by teeth. The ensuing controversy between Zwingli and Luther promptly overshadowed any significance the Syngramma may have had.

See also Catholicism, Protestant Reactions; Sacraments

References and Further Reading

Primary Source:

Brenz, Johannes. *Frühschriften.* Edited by M. Brecht. vol. 1, 222ff. Tübingen, Germany: Mohr Siebeck, 1970.

Secondary Source:

Sasse, Hermann. *This is My Body.* Rev. ed. Adelaide: Lutheran Publishing House, 1977.

JAMES CHAPMAN

SWEDEN

One of the Scandinavian countries located in northern Europe. Sweden has a population of 8,847,625 (1998), of whom 7,907,189 are Protestants (90 percent). Roman Catholics number 165,691 (1.5 percent); Eastern Orthodox, 68,260 (0.5 percent); and the Oriental denominations (Monophysite), 37,282 (0.25 percent). Non-Christian religious groups total 152,766 members (1998), of whom one-third are Muslims. Six percent of the total population or 546,656 people (1998) have declared that they have no religious affiliation.

Out of the 90 percent who are Protestant, 86 percent of the population belongs to the Lutheran Church of Sweden, leaving 4 percent as adherents of non-Lutheran Protestant churches. Until the latter part of the nineteenth century, when the so-called Dissenter Law was passed, it was illegal to belong to any other church other than the Lutheran State Church of Sweden. The twentieth century witnessed a marked religious pluralization of Swedish society.

Medieval Background

Protestantism was ushered into Sweden in the sixteenth century when the Protestant Reformation swept across Europe during that era. Unlike the craving for church reform that welled up in GERMANY, Swedish people were, by and large, content with the ministrations of the medieval Roman Catholic Church.

To understand the rise of Protestantism in what is today called Sweden, it is necessary to remember that three southern provinces of Sweden (Skane, Halland, and Blekinge) were actually a part of DENMARK until 1658. Thus Protestantism in Sweden is intimately intertwined with the Protestant Reformation in Denmark as well. It is also necessary to remember that Scandinavia in the sixteenth century was not composed of five separate, independent countries as it is today, but actually one. This was the result of the Kalmar Union of 1397, which united Denmark, NORWAY, and Sweden under Queen Margaret of Denmark, who ruled with a firm hand. Under her weak successor, Erik of Pomerania, Swedish NATIONALISM erupted in 1433 under Engelbrekt Engelbrektsson, who sought a strong, native Swedish rule. After the death of Engelbrekt in 1436, Karl Knutsson rallied the lower classes and was elected king on three occasions, only to be deposed by a union king from Denmark.

Much of the fifteenth century in Sweden therefore witnessed a struggle for a strong, indigenous ruler championed by the Swedish lower classes as opposed to the Swedish *Riksrad* (Council) composed of nobles and bishops who were pro-union and pro-Danish in their sympathies. By the mid-fifteenth century, nobles and bishops had become so internationalized through intermarriage that they had no real national ties to either Sweden or Denmark. People like Archbishop Gustav Trolle of Uppsala, who was actually Danish, owned property in both Sweden and Denmark. This tended to minimize national loyalties to either country.

During the latter part of the fifteenth century, Sten Sture the Elder became the Regent of Sweden and frustrated the Danish rulers' efforts to effectively gain control of Sweden. Svante Sture and Sten Sture the Younger continued this policy by deposing the Regent, Erik Trolle, but in 1515, Erik's son was elected archbishop of Uppsala. Two years later, Sten Sture the Younger succeeded in getting the *Riksdag* (Parliament) to depose Gustav Trolle. This took place before October 31, when MARTIN LUTHER (1483–1546) nailed *The Ninety-five Theses* on the door of the Castle Church in Wittenberg. It signified a significant breach with Rome because Leo X had just recently appointed and recognized Gustav Trolle as archbishop of Uppsala. Family feuding between the Sture and Trolle families had been going on for some time and there was no love lost between them.

The new Danish king (Christian II, 1513–1523) was determined to bring the unruly Swedes and Sten Sture the Younger under control. Upon the death of Sten Sture in battle (1520), Christian II was crowned king of Sweden on November 4. As a goodwill gesture, the Danish king invited the leading Swedish nobles and two Swedish bishops to a sumptuous reconciliation banquet. After dinner, instead of dessert and toasts to future cooperation, goodwill, and amnesty as had been expected, Danish soldiers barred the exit doors and the infamous Stockholm Bloodbath took place, in which over eighty of Sweden's leading noblemen were beheaded, including two Swedish Catholic bishops. Historians have long debated the identity of the instigator of the bloodbath. Fledgling history students are often assigned the task of wading through the sources in their introductory historiography courses. The blame has usually been assigned to the archbishop, Gustav Trolle, or to Christian II, referred to as "The Tyrant" by patriotic Swedes.

Instead of the Swedish unrest subsiding, the Stockholm massacre caused Sweden to erupt in rebellion under the leadership of Gustav Vasa, son of one of the beheaded Swedish noblemen. After struggling for three years, Sweden won its independence and Gustav Vasa was crowned king of Sweden in 1523.

Initial Stirrings of Protestantism

The election of Gustav as king of Sweden took place in the city of Strengnas, where a young Swedish disciple of Luther by the name of OLAUS PETRI (1493–1552) had been preaching for five years. Often called the "Luther of Sweden," Olaus Petri returned from Wittenberg in the summer of 1518 after having studied there for two years. When Petri arrived at Wittenberg in 1516, the German reformer was just beginning his lectures on Galatians. Petri soon joined his mentor in strong opposition to indulgences, and was present during the eventful days when *The Ninety-five Theses* were published. Late in 1518, after Luther had expounded his theology of the cross at the Heidelberg Disputation before his Augustinian brothers, Petri returned to Sweden aglow with his new evangelical

insights. However, there was no thought of leaving the Roman Catholic Church. John Eck would not raise the "Saxon Hus" label until the next year at Leipzig. The REFORMATION treatises of 1520 and the famous "Here I stand" declaration at the DIET OF WORMS in 1521 were still in the distant future. Thus the evangelical theology that inspired Olaus Petri was very conservative and was to remain so all his life.

Olaus Petri also had a younger brother, Laurentius Petri (1499–1573), who studied at Wittenberg some years later. Upon his return to Sweden in 1527, Laurentius was ordained as the first evangelical (Protestant) archbishop of Uppsala in 1531 by two Erasmian reform-minded Catholic bishops, thus preserving the historic episcopate in what was to become the Lutheran State Church of Sweden. Together, the two Petri brothers introduced a gradual transformation of the medieval Catholic Church in Sweden along evangelical (Protestant) lines.

It was not the intention of the Petris to break with Rome, introduce a Lutheran confessional subscription, or establish a "Protestant" church. Rather they were convinced that the pure Word of God was all that was needed to recall the Catholic Church from the error of her ways. Holy Scripture was the Word of God and upon this rock the church could prevail against the gates of hell itself. All one needed for salvation was *sola scriptura* (the Word alone).

There was little pressure to adopt any particular confessional creed. The ancient ecumenical creeds (Apostles, Nicene, and Athanasian) were seen as aids in the preparation of sermons and as guides for a faithful interpretation of Scripture for those who could not understand the message of Scripture as a whole, but they had no confessional validity as such. A corollary to the doctrine of the all-sufficiency of Scripture would negate the necessity for any formal confession. Any human attempt at writing a confession endangered the *sola scriptura* principle of the evangelical reform movement within the Catholic Church.

The Protestant Reformation

During the 1520s Gustav Vasa, the Swedish king, was hard-pressed to maintain political stability and unite his followers, who had become divided on the religious issue. Many who favored the "old faith" supported the 1527 uprising in Dalarna. In desperation, Gustav Vasa turned to the pope and asked what could be done to reform the Swedish church.

This was a golden opportunity for the pope (Clement VII) to heal the breach that was developing between Rome and the Swedish church, but instead of proposing reforms of significance, Clement VII ordered the reinstatement of Gustav Trolle as archbishop of Uppsala. This was something no Swede could contemplate after the Stockholm Bloodbath of 1520. Thus an opportunity for a throne-and-altar alliance to reform the church in Sweden was lost. In the midst of all this, burdened with a huge debt to Lübeck for its help in overthrowing the yoke of the Danish king with no hope of raising the necessary funds, struggling to suppress the revolt in Darlana, and with no encouragement from Rome, Gustav Vasa resigned in 1527. This action galvanized Sweden into supporting Gustav Vasa because no one could contemplate a return to the political domination of Denmark or the suzerainty of Lübeck.

At a hastily called meeting at Vesteras, the estates prevailed upon Gustav Vasa to continue as king and promised to crush the rebellion in Dalarna. With no hope of reform coming from Rome, the Diet of Vesteras (1527) also effectively severed the Swedish church from obedience to the Roman pontiff and established a national Catholic Church in Sweden. From that time forward, the CLERGY came under the jurisdiction of civil law. The king received the church's income in order to repay the Lubeck debt. All material goods given to the church before 1454 were returned to the legal heirs, and all complaints against the "new faith" were to stop provided that the Word of God was preached in its purity. Bishops were instructed to see that their parishes were staffed with preachers of ability, otherwise the king was empowered to intervene. There was no Lutheran or Protestant confession enunciated except "to teach and preach according to the Word of God."

In the decades that followed the Diet of Vesteras, there was very little discussion or explicit mention of Lutheran confessional subscription. The Church of Sweden was becoming an evangelical Protestant church without any formal confessional subscription. Nevertheless, the Petri brothers maintained a consistent, though conservative, Lutheran stance as seen in the HYMNAL (1526), the pastors' manual (1529), and the Swedish Mass (1531), which came from the pen of Olaus Petri.

It was not until the reign of Erik XIV (1560–1568) that confessional subscription became a problem. The new king leaned toward CALVINISM and was very sympathetic toward the many Calvinist refugees who fled to Sweden. In 1564 some Calvinists drew up a confession of faith that they claimed was Lutheran, but it was quickly seen to be a Swedish translation of the Calvinistic GALLICAN CONFESSION of 1559. For the first time, the AUGSBURG CONFESSION of 1530 was invoked to define what was authentically Lutheran. Laurentius Petri, as archbishop of Uppsala, also effectively thwarted Erik XIV from introducing Calvinism into Sweden by royal decree while at the same time

quietly withdrawing his own *Church Ordinance* for a more opportune time.

The long life of Laurentius Petri, his faithful service under three kings, and his conservative but consistent Lutheran theological principles gradually came to the forefront. Slowly but surely, and in the absence of any official Lutheran confessional subscription, popular religious loyalty slowly swung from a Roman Catholic to an evangelical and increasingly Lutheran theological position. Ten years after his failed attempt to introduce his *Church Ordinance,* Laurentius Petri placed the capstone on his career when he persuaded the new king John III (1568–1592), the younger brother of the Calvinist Erik XIV, to adopt it as the law of the land in 1571. There was no confessional subscription espoused in this ordinance, nor was there any in the oath pastors took upon their ordination. Instead, the tried and true formula that everything was to be judged by the Word of God was reiterated. Ordinands were asked if they would "at all times remain steadfast in the pure Word of God and flee all false and heretical doctrines." Clergy were admonished to "preach the Word with all freedom" so it might grow in the hearts of people and be fruitful (see PREACHING). To proclaim the Word meant that the archbishop preached repentance and forgiveness of sin through Jesus Christ. Two years later (1573), Laurentius Petri died after having served as the first Protestant archbishop of Uppsala for forty-two years.

The Counter-Reformation

After the death of the archbishop, the theological battlefield shifted from Calvinism to Roman Catholicism. The new king had a decided predilection in that direction. Shortly after Laurentius Petri's death, John III, who saw himself as a liturgical scholar, issued his *Red Book* (named after the color of the covers), which manifested his leanings toward Rome. It has been much debated whether John III actually converted to Roman Catholicism, but it is known that he was greatly influenced by his Polish wife's Jesuit chaplains and his own father confessor, the Norwegian Jesuit Laurentius Norvegus (Lars the Norwegian).

Though the Peace of Augsburg (1555) had no legal validity in Sweden, it was nevertheless conceivable that if the king of Sweden became Roman Catholic, the principle of *cuius regio eius religio* (whoever the king, his religion) enunciated at the close of the Smalcald War (1555), could be extended to Sweden also. Thus it was that Pope Gregory XIII launched Operation Sweden *(Missio suetica)* under the direction of Laurentius Norvegus and the secretary of the Society of Jesus, Antonio Possevino. The plan of the Jesuits was to establish a rival "high church" theological school in Stockholm to counter the "anti-liturgical" Lutheran theological faculty at Uppsala. With the king's acquiescence, the Jesuits established the Royal Stockholm College under the pretext of educating a new generation of theological students who were more in agreement with the king's high-church predilections. In reality, it was a front for the secret Jesuit mission to turn Sweden back to Rome.

On the verge of success in 1580, Operation Sweden suddenly soured when John III insisted on three concessions before he would publicly announce his conversion to Roman Catholicism. The post-Tridentine papacy was not, however, inclined to compromise on the issues of clerical CELIBACY, vernacular WORSHIP, and communion in both kinds (communicants received both bread and wine). Against the strong counsel of Laurentius Norvegus, Possevino tried to force the hand of John III by publicly announcing the king's CONVERSION.

Instead of the intended effect, John III immediately renounced Roman Catholicism and ordered the Jesuit mission out of Sweden. As a result of Operation Sweden, the Swedish people had become thoroughly aware of the dangers of the COUNTER-REFORMATION, but Rome needed only to bide her time because Sigismund III, the Roman Catholic son of John III who had just recently been elected king of POLAND, stood ready to become king of Sweden as well upon the death of his father. When John III died in 1592, it was just too much for the clergy and people of Sweden to contemplate. "Bloody" Mary's reign in England, the "Reign of Terror" in the Lowlands, and the St. Bartholomew Day Massacre in France had all occurred during the lives of most Swedes living in the 1590s.

Triumph of Lutheranism

At a hastily called church assembly gathered at Uppsala in 1593 (only the king could convene the *Riksdag*), the unaltered Augsburg Confession became the legal confessional basis for the Church of Sweden for the first time. From that time forward, one could speak of the Lutheran State Church of Sweden. All Swedish sovereigns had to be Lutheran in the future. As a result, Sigismund III was never able to gain his Swedish throne, though he tried to regain Sweden by a military assault that was repulsed by his uncle, Duke Charles of FINLAND. For all practical purposes, the Protestant Reformation and LUTHERANISM had become synonymous in Sweden in spite of the Calvinist leanings of Duke Charles, who became Carl IX in 1599.

Southern Sweden (Eastern Denmark)

The three southern provinces of what is today Sweden, as was said, were controlled by Denmark in the sixteenth century. Unlike Sweden, where Lutheranism was introduced through a century-long process of ecclesiastical transformation led by the clergy and people who often opposed the wishes of the king, the Protestant Reformation in Denmark was introduced by a royal decree of Christian III (1536–1559). Here it was definitely a case of *cuius regio eius religio,* with LUTHERANISM being the order of the day. The decree of 1536 also applied to the three southern provinces of Skaane, Blekinge, and Halland.

It was not as though there had not been a grass roots reform movement in Denmark and southern Sweden. Indeed there had. Under HANS TAUSEN (1494–1564) and Jens Sadolin, a strong evangelical movement had arisen in Jutland, which was brought to Copenhagen by the sympathetic Danish king Fredrik I (1523–1533). Another center of reform was in eastern Denmark (what today is southern Sweden) centered around the city of Malmo. Here was the hotbed of an Erasmian-type of Christian humanism that clamored for reform. The leaders were disciples of the "Erasmus of Scandinavia," Paul Helie, who remained within the Roman Catholic Church to the end of his life. However, his followers, Claus Mortensen, Frants Vormordsen, Peder Lauritzsen, and Oluf Chrysostomus, went beyond their mentor and embraced Protestantism and Lutheranism in particular. With their theological leadership and the support of the Danish king, Christian III, Lutheranism swept across eastern Denmark and by 1658, when this part of Denmark came under the political control of Sweden, all of what is today the country of Sweden was found to be firmly within the fold of Protestantism and the Lutheran State Church of Sweden.

The Seventeenth and Eighteenth Centuries

During the next two centuries, Protestantism and Lutheranism in Sweden were one and the same. Both people and king had to be Lutheran; no other choice was allowed. The seventeenth century saw Sweden reach the height of political greatness during the reign of GUSTAVUS II ADOLPHUS (1612–1632). During the Thirty Years War, the "Lion of the North" was credited with saving Protestantism. It was also during his reign that plans were laid for a colonial venture in the New World that resulted in the founding of New Sweden along the Delaware River in 1638. Though taken over by the Dutch and in 1664 by the English, the settlement continued to be supplied by Swedish pastors into the nineteenth century, when the Swedish language died out and the congregations migrated to the EPISCOPAL CHURCH. One lasting legacy of the Swedish colony was the preservation of the Delaware Indian language through the translation of Luther's Small Catechism by Johan Campanius, the first translation into an American Indian language by a European.

After the successful struggle to preserve Protestantism in the latter part of the sixteenth century, the next century witnessed the dominance of Lutheran ORTHODOXY in Sweden. The Lutheran confessional writings were stressed, as was correct doctrine. It is interesting to note that in Campanius's work with the Delaware Indians, he did not translate the BIBLE into their language as might have been expected, but instead chose to translate Luther's Small Catechism. The leading exponent of Lutheran orthodoxy in Sweden at this time was Johannes Rudbeckius (1581–1646), bishop of Vesteras.

During the years following the Great Northern War (1700–1721), a conservative churchly PIETISM grew (see also FRANCKE, A. H.; and SPENER, P. J.). Regeneration, conversion, the new life in Christ, and assurance of salvation were stressed. A decade later, a more radical Pietism arose similar to that championed by Gottfried Arnold in Germany as well as Moravian Pietism under the leadership of NIKOLAUS ZINZENDORF (1200–1260). Devotional literature came to play a dominant role in the Pietist movement and its adherents were often known as "Readers." Toward the latter part of the eighteenth century, the theological rationalism of CHRISTIAN WOLFF (1679–1754) of HALLE made its presence felt in Sweden.

Spiritual Awakenings in the Nineteenth Century

In 1809, in the midst of the Napoleonic Wars, Sweden lost Finland to RUSSIA. This caused a great deal of soul searching on the part of clergy and laity alike. Religious freedom, which had been experimented with during the era of the ENLIGHTENMENT, though still on the books, was for all practical purposes abrogated. Censorship was imposed, and rationalism with its internationalism was found wanting. In its place arose a strong nationalistic and religious AWAKENING. In the old Danish archbishopric of Lund, Henrik Schartau (1757–1825) labored for forty years to bring about a spiritual awakening along Lutheran orthodox lines, while to the north in Stockholm, a Pietist-type revival broke out under the leadership of George Scott and Carl O. Rosenius (d. 1868). Scott was actually a Methodist pastor stationed in Stockholm (1826–1842) to minister to English sailors and other English-speaking people in Sweden. Through his work, the Methodist Church came into being in Sweden (see METHODISM, EUROPE). Rosenius, on the other hand, was a Lutheran theological student who never chose to be ordained but who worked closely with Scott. Through their partnership and especially through the prolific writings of Rosenius, which have been translated into over twenty different languages, a spiritual renewal swept across Sweden. Rosenius stressed the objective grace of God coupled with a strong emphasis on sanctification. Far to the north, LARS L. LAESTADIUS (d. 1861), spearheaded a REVIVAL movement that bears his name to this very day and has spread across to Norway and especially Finland. Much of the awakening was inspired by the hymns of Johan Wallin (d. 1830). These were brought to America in the latter half of the nineteenth century by Swedish immigrants and sung into the hearts of the people by the renowned "Nightingale of Sweden," Jenny Lind, much like "How Great Thou Art" (another Swedish hymn) was sung by George Beverly Shea during the Billy Graham Crusades.

As an outgrowth of the spiritual awakenings, many VOLUNTARY SOCIETIES were founded such as the Swedish Missionary Society (1835), the Lund Missionary Society (1845), and various Bible and tract societies. In 1856 the *Evangeliska Fosterlands-Stiftelse* (Evangelical National Society) was founded by Rosenius, which sought to reach all of Sweden through evangelistic activity. Five years later it expanded its scope worldwide.

Rise of Non-Lutheran Protestantism

In the wake of the revolutions of 1848 throughout Europe, the new religious impulses welling up in Sweden, the writings of SOREN KIERKEGAARD (1813–1855), and the example of Norway and Denmark, the old CONVENTICLE Law of 1726 was abolished in 1858 in spite of high church Lutheran opposition. This allowed Lutheran laymen to gather and lead devotional meetings and religious assemblies. Two years later, the Dissenter Law was passed, allowing non-Lutherans freedom of religion and worship.

It did not take long before various "free churches" or "dissenter churches" came into being. The first were the BAPTISTS, who trace their beginnings back to 1848 when it was still illegal to be a non-Lutheran. F. O. Nilsson, a Swedish seaman who had been converted in America, returned to Sweden as a lay preacher and championed the cause of adult BAPTISM, but the real leader of the Baptist movement in Sweden, until his death in 1887, was Anders Wiberg. He had been an ordained pastor in the Lutheran State Church of Sweden for nine years when he resigned his position in 1851. The following year F. O. Nilsson, the lay preacher, rebaptized him. The same year (1852) Wiberg published *Vilken bor dopas och varuti bestar dopet? (Who Should Be Baptized and What Is Baptism?)*. This was the first exposition of the Baptist DOCTRINE of baptism ever written in Swedish. Also in 1852, Bethel Seminary was founded to train Swedish pastors and evangelists for the new church. A church newspaper and a foreign mission society followed in quick order. By 1889 the Baptist Church in Sweden numbered some 33,500 members, but the movement splintered thereafter, and in the year 2000 numbered only 18,631 members.

The Methodist Church also came into being in Sweden through the work of Swedish seamen who had been converted while in America. The initial Methodist work had been done by the English Methodist pastor, George Scott, in the 1830s but congregations made up of Swedish citizens had not been allowed. With enactment of the Dissenter Law, Methodist work resumed in 1868. In 1876 the Methodist Church in Sweden was uniquely and legally recognized as an independent faith community with the right to perform marriages and burials. This lasted until 1951, when other churches obtained the same right. In the year 2000, there were 5,177 members in the Methodist Church.

Another religious impulse from England led to the founding of the SALVATION ARMY in 1882. As it had in several other countries, the leadership fell to a woman, Hanna Ouchterlony. Under her ten-year leadership, the Salvation Army grew to 10,000 soldiers (members) and 500 officers. In 1905, having deteriorated under the centralized generalship of WILLIAM BOOTH (1829–1912), a schism occurred in the Salvation Army in Sweden which, since 1988, has become a nongeographical district within the Mission Covenant Church. In the last decade of the twentieth century, the Salvation Army membership declined thirty percent to 18,789.

The Mission Covenant Church (MCC) grew out of a theological dispute over the doctrine of ATONEMENT. Its members had been part of the Evangelical National Society (ENS) founded by Rosenius, which sought to evangelize, among others, the new proletariat in the urban centers created by the Industrial Revolution. Unlike Rosenius, the leader of this more radical wing of the ENS, Paul P. Waldenstrom (1838–1917), urged his followers to withdraw from the Lutheran State Church, which they did in 1878. Waldenstrom taught a subjective doctrine of the atonement as opposed to the traditional forensic (or objective) doctrine, which stated in effect that a person was justified (see JUSTIFICATION) by Christ because Christ died "for you" and not because Christ dwelled "in you" as Waldenstrom taught. This theological position of Waldenstrom, who

had been a Lutheran pastor up until that time, not only caused a rupture within the Lutheran State Church of Sweden, but caused the other free churches and societies like the Swedish Mission Alliance to distance themselves from Waldenstrom and the MCC. In the year 2000, the MCC had some 70,000 members in Sweden. Much of its membership emigrated to the United States in the early twentieth century and founded a DENOMINATION by the same name. The Swedish Baptists followed a similar path.

PENTECOSTALISM developed in Sweden when the Norwegian Methodist pastor, T. B. Barratt, who had experienced "the baptism of the Holy Spirit" while in the United States, drew a young twenty-three-year-old Swedish Baptist pastor from Linkoping into his orbit. The young pastor, Lewi Pethrus, became the pastor of the famous Pentecostal congregation in Stockholm (Filadelfia) and the leader of the Swedish Pentecostal movement. When he retired in 1958 after a forty-seven-year pastorate, the congregation numbered 6,500 members. At the outset of the twenty-first century, Swedish Pentecostals number some 91,000.

Secularism and Modernity

The rise of the free churches following the passage of the Dissenter Law in 1860 and the accompanying spiritual awakenings can be misleading and paint too rosy a picture of religious life in Sweden at this time. Swedish society was actually bifurcating and going in two different directions. At the time Protestantism was experiencing religious revivals, the inroads of modernity were coming into play. The Industrial Revolution was having its debilitating effect on huge segments of Swedish people, alienating them from the church. Marxist philosophy (see MARXISM), secular materialism, political liberalism, biblical higher criticism, and the teachings of Darwinian evolution (see DARWINISM) all combined to form a modern schism in which the masses of Swedish society became accustomed to ordering their lives without much need for the ministrations of the church.

Ecumenism and Lundensian Theology

In the twentieth century, Swedish Protestants (Lutherans) made a huge contribution to the modern Ecumenical Movement (see ECUMENISM). After the WORLD MISSIONARY CONFERENCE at Edinburgh in 1910 and the Armistice had been signed ending World War I, many Christians around the world longed to work together to help solve the horrendous human problems caused by the war. Under the leadership and inspiration of NATHAN SODERBLOM (1866–1931), archbishop of the Lutheran State Church of Sweden, the first meeting of the Life and Work Conference was held in Stockholm in 1925 seeking to relate the Christian faith to social issues, POLITICS, and ECONOMICS without first having to arrive at a theological consensus. During these years Swedish theologians also made a major theological contribution to what has been called "Lundensian Theology," with its motif methodology as epitomized by ANDERS NYGREN's (1890–1978) *Agape and Eros* (1930) and Gustav Aulen's study on the atonement (*Christus Victor,* 1930).

Pluralization of Swedish Society

After World War II, Swedish Protestants and especially the Lutheran State Church of Sweden continued to be challenged by the ever-increasing SECULARIZATION of Swedish society. At the same time, Swedish society was becoming much more pluralistic as a result of its liberal political asylum policy, its generous attitude toward providing a haven for world refugees, and the influx of workers from southern Europe. This accounts for the increase in the non-Protestant churches mentioned at the outset of this article, as well as for the increased number of Muslims from Bosnia, Kosovo, and Turkey. During the last decade of the twentieth century, JEHOVAH'S WITNESSES grew to 23,393 members and the Mormons to 8,817, while the historic free churches from the nineteenth century leveled off in their membership growth.

Separation of Church and State

With the increased pluralization of Swedish society during the latter half of the twentieth century and the ongoing pressure from the free churches and those who had voluntarily withdrawn from the Lutheran State Church of Sweden and declared themselves to be without religious affiliation, legislation was set in motion during the 1990s to separate church and state. This legislation took effect on January 1, 2000. Today the Lutheran Church of Sweden is no longer a state church. It is legally recognized as one church among several. The state now collects the church tax for those churches that so desire on a proportionate basis and not for the Lutheran Church alone. Every Swedish citizen in the future, however, will have to pay a cultural tax for the maintenance of historic Swedish church buildings as well as a cemetery tax.

Facing the Twenty-first Century

New challenges in the twenty-first century facing Swedish Protestantism (and not just the Lutheran Church of Sweden) include the need for an ongoing spiritual revitalization of its church life, bold evangel-ical initiatives to reach the unchurched people of Sweden, and outreach to the non-Protestant Christian churches as well as to the non-Christian faith communities.

See also Bible; Book of Concord; Christology; Colonialism; Confession; Darwinism; Dissent; Ecumenism; Francke, August Hermann; Herrnhut; Justification; Marriage; Marxism; Methodism, Europe; Missionary Organizations; Missions; Mormonism; Preaching; Spener, Philipp Jakob; Theology; Universities.

References and Further Reading

Aulen, Gustav. *Christus Victor.* Translated by Arthur G. Herbert. London: SPCK, 1931.
Bergendoff, Conrad. *Olavus Petri and the Ecclesiastical Transformation in Sweden.* Philadelphia: Fortress Press, 1965.
Ekstrom, Soren. *Svenska kyrkan i utveckling.* Stockholm: Verbum Forlag, 1999.
Ferre, Nels. *Swedish Contributions to Modern Theology.* New York: Harper Torchbooks, 1967.
Garstein, Oskar. *Rome and the Counter-Reformation in Scandinavia.* 3 vols. Oslo: Universitetsforlaget, 1963–1992.
Grell, Ole, ed. *The Scandinavian Reformation.* Cambridge: Cambridge University Press, 1995.
Hofgren, Allan, ed. *Svenska trossamfund.* Uppsala: EFS Forlaget, 1990.
Kyrkoordning for Svenska kyrkan faststalld av Kyrkomotet 1999. Stockholm: Verbum Forlag, 1999.
Lindhardt, P. G. *Den Nordiske Kirkes Historie.* Copenhagen: Nyt Nordisk Forlag, 1945.
Nygren, Anders. *Agape and Eros.* 2 vols. Translated by Philip S. Watson. London: SPCK, 1932–1939.
Scott, Franklin D. *Sweden: The Nation's History.* Minneapolis: University of Minnesota Press, 1977.
Skog, Margareta, ed. *En salig blandning.* Stockholm: Svenska kyrkans forskningsrad, 1998. (*Tro og Tanke* 1997:3).
Straarup, Jorgen, ed. *Perspektiv pa Svenska kyrkans statistik 1997.* Stockholm: Svenska Kyrkans forskningsrad, 1998. (*Tro og Tanke* 1998:8).

TRYGVE R. SKARSTEN

SWEDENBORG, EMANUEL (1688–1772)

Swedish reformer. Born on January 29, 1688 in Stockholm, SWEDEN as the second son of Jesper Svedberg, court chaplain and later professor and bishop of Skara, Svedberg studied in Uppsala from 1699 and devoted himself intensively to studies both in the humanities and natural sciences. Having gained his doctorate in 1709 he traveled to Holland, ENGLAND, FRANCE, and GERMANY until 1715 in connection with his studies, before joining the civil service. In 1719 he was ennobled together with his brother and took the name Swedenborg. In 1747 he gave up his position as a Swedish civil servant to work as an independent researcher and live alternately in France, ENGLAND, Sweden, and Germany. Swedenborg died on March 29, 1772 in London.

Swedenborg's writings and his impact can be divided into two sections: 1745 was the decisive year dividing these two periods. As can be gleaned from Swedenborg's record of his dreams (which was not published within his lifetime), he experienced a deep religious crisis in 1743/44. At the end of this crisis Swedenborg felt himself called as a prophet to bring a religious message to the people.

In his first creative period, before 1745, Swedenborg made a name for himself as a natural scientist whose work attracted much attention. From 1716 to 1718 he published Sweden's first scientific journal (*Daedalus Hyperboraeus*). In addition, he published popular works on mineralogy (*Opera philosophica et mineralica*, 1734) and anatomy (*Oeconomia regni animalis in transactiones divisa*, 1740/41; *Regnum animale, anatomice, physice et philosophice perlustratum*, 1744/45).

His second creative phase began after 1745 and constituted a complete break in terms of methodology. After his sudden CONVERSION, which signified a rejection of DEISM and mechanistic natural philosophy, Swedenborg made clear in his first theological work *De cultu et amore dei* (1745) that he had not given up the search for a synopsis, an all-embracing synthesis. However, the paths of discovery were entirely different. He left the analytic method of the natural sciences behind and searched along spiritual paths for religious certainty, which was expressed in an exegetic interpretation of the story of the Creation in Genesis. For Swedenborg it became clear that the Book of Genesis contains a teaching of correspondences. He believed that everything has its natural, spiritual, and divine significance. He held on to the outer form of the written Word, but considered the inner meaning to be definitive. Chosen by God to interpret the spiritual meaning of the Scripture and to establish contact with the spiritual world, which he saw as corresponding to the earthly world, Swedenborg believed he was able to give an insight into the divine secrets in his *De cultu et amore dei,* an interpretation of the books of Genesis and Exodus. This was Swedenborg's principal theological work.

Adjusting the Canon

Taking his teaching of correspondences as a basis, he removed all biblical books from the canon that do not fit in with this theory. Thus the entire writings of Paul are discarded, as Swedenborg strictly rejected Paul's teaching of JUSTIFICATION. He maintained that it is not the literal but rather the spiritual sense that is decisive for an understanding of the Scriptures. Swedenborg summarized his THEOLOGY in *Summaria expositio doctrinae novae ecclesiae* (1769). In this he rejected a Christian concept of the Trinity. God is regarded as a person who is differentiated within Godself. God is the spiritual original being in whose image we are formed. However, only the spiritual person in us is the image of God, which means that our goal lies in shedding the natural and being taken up in the spiritual kingdom. Reconciliation with God takes place not in God's acquittal of humans but rather through rebirth and revival in the spiritual world.

Swedenborg's conviction that the Last Judgment had already taken place in 1757 and the parousia of the Lord had already occurred are of great significance for his ECCLESIOLOGY. This parousia, Swedenborg maintained in his interpretation of St. John's Apocalypse *Apocalypsis revelata* (1766), was not the physical appearance of the Lord but synonymous with the disclosure of the inner meaning of the Apocalypse. Swedenborg's interpretation of the Apocalypse testified to the parousia of the Lord. A new era had come, he said, a new church had been born—a new church that, according to Swedenborg's optimistic conviction, all believers would join as soon as they had been told of its teaching.

Swedenborg's ideas on correspondences between this and the heavenly world prompted comment from IMMANUEL KANT and Friedrich Christoph Oetinger as well as JOHANN WOLFGANG VON GOETHE, WILLIAM BLAKE, Honore de Balzac, Charles Baudelaire, Ralph Waldo Emerson, William Butler Yeats, and Jorge Luis Borges.

Within a relatively short space of time after his death, the first Swedenborg followings were formed (London 1787, Baltimore 1792). In 1810 the first society was founded under the name of "The Swedenborg Society in London," which saw its most important task in translating and printing his writings. In the Anglo-Saxon sphere, in particular in the UNITED STATES, further followings were rapidly established ("General Convention of the New Jerusalem," Philadelphia 1817; since 1980 "Swedenborgian Church of North America"). In 1897 a group strongly emphasizing the priesthood split off and formed the "General Church of the New Jerusalem," centered around Bryn Athyn in Pennsylvania. In Europe groups who felt committed to Swedenborg's interpretation of the BIBLE did not develop until after the liberalization of religious laws in the mid-nineteenth century. Today there are a large number of groups in Europe, in JAPAN, KOREA, AUSTRALIA, NEW ZEALAND, BRAZIL, and CANADA, as well as in over twenty states in the United States.

References and Further Reading

Primary Sources:

Swedenborg, Emanuel. *The Apocalypse Revealed.* New York: Swedenborg Foundation, 1968.

———. *The Four Leading Doctrines of the New Church, Signified by the New Jerusalem in the Revelation.* New York: AMS Press, 1971.

———. *The Four Doctrines: The Lord, Sacred Scripture, Life, Faith.* New York: Swedenborg Foundation, 1976.

———. *Swedenborg's Journal of Dreams, 1743–1744.* New York: Swedenborg Foundation, 1977.

Swedenborg, Emanuel, and John Curtis Ager. *True Christian Religion.* New York: Swedenborg Foundation, 1981.

Swedenborg, Emanuel, and Frank Bayley. *The True Christian Religion Containing the Universal Theology of the New Church.* New York: E. P. Dutton, 1933.

Swedenborg, Emanuel, and George F. Dole. *The Universal Human and Soul-body Interaction.* New York: Paulist Press, 1984.

———. *Heaven and Hell.* New York: Swedenborg Foundation, Inc., 1984.

Swedenborg, Emanuel, and Michael Stanley. *Emanuel Swedenborg: Essential Readings.* New York: Sterling, 1988.

Swedenborg, Emanuel, and John Whitehead. *Posthumous Theological Works of Emanuel Swedenborg.* New York: Swedenborg Foundation, 1928.

Warren, Samuel M. *A Compendium of the Theological Writings of Emanuel Swedenborg.* New York: Swedenborg Foundation, 1979.

Woofenden, William Ross. *Swedenborg Researcher's Manual.* Bryn Athyn, PA: Swedenborg Scientific Association, 1988.

Secondary Sources:

Block, Marguerite Beck. *The New Church in the New World: A Study of Swedenborgianism in America.* New York: Swedenborg Publishing Association, 1984.

Brock, Erland J., ed. *Swedenborg and His Influence.* Bryn Athyn, PA: Academy of the New Church, 1988.

Jonsson, Inge. *Emanuel Swedenborg.* New York: Twayne, 1971.

Larsen, Robin, and Stephen Larsen, eds. *Emanuel Swedenborg: A Continuing Vision.* New York: Swedenborg Foundation, 1988.

Lenhammar, Harry. "Swedenborg, Swedenborgianer." *TRE* 32 (2001) Berlin: Walter de Gruyter, 472–476.

ANDREAS MÜHLING

SWIFT, JONATHAN (1667–1745)

Irish essayist. Swift was born in Dublin of English parents on November 30, 1667. He was educated in IRELAND, graduating from Trinity College, Dublin, in 1686, and was ordained a priest in the Church of Ireland in 1695. Early in his career he played a significant role in obtaining the remission of certain Crown taxes to the Irish church. As its agent in London he negotiated with Robert Harley, leader of the Tory ministry, and following the success of his mission in 1710, he accepted Harley's offer to lend his pen in support of the ministry's efforts to end the war with FRANCE. For his services he was appointed dean of St. Patrick's Cathedral in Dublin in 1713. With the fall of the Tory government in 1714 he returned to Dublin to take up his duties as dean. Although for much of the remainder of his active life his opposition to ENGLAND's political and economic domination of Ireland frequently involved him in public controversy, he discharged his decanal duties conscientiously and effectively until 1742, when a series of strokes incapacitated him. He died on October 19, 1745.

In a collection of aphorisms, *Thoughts on Various Subjects* (1711), Swift wrote that "We have just Religion enough to make us *hate,* but not enough to make us *love* one another." The pertinence of this observation to conditions in eighteenth-century Ireland is borne out by Swift himself. He shared the bias held by most English Protestants against Roman Catholicism and that held by many Anglicans against Protestant DISSENT. He approved of the Penal Laws, which deprived Irish Catholics of virtually all their rights, and of the Sacramental Test Act, which effectively excluded dissenters from holding civil and military posts. Swift's endorsement of this measure was grounded in his belief that episcopacy (see BISHOP AND EPISCOPACY) was closer to the primitive church than were other ecclesiastical institutions, and that as the established religion, ANGLICANISM should be maintained to preserve stability in the state. Protestant dissent, on the other hand, he associated with the English CIVIL WAR, the execution of Charles I, and the military dictatorship of OLIVER CROMWELL. To Swift the growing economic and political strength of the ULSTER Presbyterians and their increasing agitation for the repeal of the Test Act represented a serious threat to the Church of Ireland. Throughout his career he wrote pamphlets opposing efforts to repeal, including *The Sentiments of a Church-of-England Man* (1711), *The Presbyterians Plea of Merit* (1733), and, most notably, the ironic masterpiece *An Argument against Abolishing Christianity* (1711). Swift's implacable antipathy to both Protestant and Roman Catholic dissenters informs one of his major secular writings, *A Tale of a Tub* (1704), a brilliant satire on these and other targets.

The available evidence suggests that Swift was a competent, although not inspiring, preacher. In *A Letter to a Young Gentleman, Lately enter'd into Holy Orders* (1720), he cautioned against highly rhetorical sermons and speculations on abstruse theological points. The aim of PREACHING should be "to tell the People what is their Duty; and then to convince them that it is so." This prosaic conception of homiletics is illustrated by his eleven extant sermons. They are commonsensical rather than profound, and their topics more often treat temporal than spiritual concerns. The most emotionally charged of them, *Upon the Martyrdom of King Charles I* (published 1765), is principally an intemperate attack on the Puritans, who beheaded Charles, and on their successors, "our present dissenters." The sermon that deals most centrally with DOCTRINE is *On the Trinity* (published 1744), a conventional defense of the Christian mysteries against those "who are Enemies to all Revealed Religion." The doctrine of the Trinity is beyond the comprehension of human reason and must therefore be accepted on implicit FAITH. A telling statement occurs in a collection of Swift's miscellaneous remarks, published posthumously as *Thoughts on Religion* (1765): "I am not answerable to God for the doubts that arise in my own breast, since they are the consequence of that reason which he hath planted in me, if I take care to conceal those doubts from others, if I use my best endeavors to subdue them, and if they have no influence on the conduct of my life."

The sermon *On Mutual Subjection* (published 1744) urges the duty of believers to practice CHARITY, a virtue Swift performed both privately and publicly. In addition to gifts to the needy, he established an alms house for destitute widows and regularly extended small loans at low interest to distressed tradesmen. He served on various philanthropic committees, was active in the charity-school movement, was a charter member of the Incorporated Society in Dublin for Promoting English Protestant Schools in Ireland, and was a trustee of Dr. Steevens' Hospital. His most noteworthy benefaction was St. Patrick's Hospital, established and endowed by him as an asylum "for Idiots, Lunaticks and Incurables."

No assessment of Swift's place in the history of Irish Protestantism can ignore the narrow range of his influence. His loyalty was exclusively to the Established Church. Granting this limitation, his contributions to the Church of Ireland were substantial. Although Swift is best known as the author of *Gulliver's Travels* (1726), he had in his own day a distinguished reputation as a clergyman as well. According to contemporary accounts, large crowds attended his sermons—evidence not only of his renown as a secular writer but also of the public's recognition of his conspicuous services to his church.

See also Catholicism, Protestant Reactions

References and Further Reading

Primary Source:

Swift, Jonathan. *The Prose Works of Jonathan Swift*. Edited by Herbert Davis et al. 14 vols. Oxford, UK: Basil Blackwell, 1939–1968.

Secondary Sources:

Beckett, J. C. *Protestant Dissent in Ireland, 1687–1780*. London: Faber & Faber, 1948.

Ehrenpreis, Irvin. *Swift, the Man, His Works, and the Age*. 3 vols. Volumes 1 and 2, Cambridge, MA: Harvard University Press, 1962, 1967; volume 3, London: Methuen, 1983.

Ferguson, Oliver W. *Jonathan Swift and Ireland*. Urbana: University of Illinois Press, 1962.

Landa, Louis A. "Jonathan Swift and Charity." *The Journal of English and Germanic Philology* 44 (1945): 337–350.

———. *Swift and the Church of Ireland*. Oxford, UK: Clarendon Press, 1954.

OLIVER W. FERGUSON

SWITZERLAND

The late-medieval development of the Swiss Confederation is crucial to understanding the course of the REFORMATION in Switzerland. The Confederation was in many ways a relic of the older Germanic CULTURE in which valley communities came together in alliances of mutual support. Founded by three states (Uri, Schwyz, and Unterwalden) in 1291, the Swiss Confederation grew during the next two centuries to thirteen by 1501, along with a collection of associated and communal territories. The importance of the Swiss Confederation to Europe was primarily attributed to the trade routes from ITALY over the Alpine passes to the Rhine. During the fourteenth and fifteenth centuries, however, the Confederates won a series of major battles against their principal enemies, the Habsburgs and Burgundy, securing for themselves a formidable reputation as soldiers. Foreign rulers were quick to take advantage of the young men from these poor lands, and the history of the Swiss quickly became closely intertwined with mercenary service. There were various attempts to draw the members of the Confederation into a closer bond, but essentially each of the Confederates remained autonomous, able to conclude alliances with whomever it chose. The fragility of this arrangement was demonstrated in the Old Zurich War of 1439–1450, when Zurich made a serious attempt to gain hegemonic control of the Confederation. By the start of the sixteenth century the Confederation was an unequal mixture of wealthy urban members (Zurich, Berne, Basel [older Basle], Schaffhausen, Lucerne, Fribourg, and Solothurn) and the poorer, largely rural states (Uri, Schwyz, Unterwalden, Zug, Appenzell, and Glarus).

Although victory in the Swabian War of 1501 had essentially guaranteed independence of the Confederation from the Holy Roman Empire, the Swiss were still closely bound by language, trade, and religion to the southern German world. The cities of Berne, Basel, and Zurich belonged to the civic culture of the Imperial cities of the southwest, and this was crucial for the Reformation. There was only one university in the Confederation, Basel, so Swiss students regularly crossed the Rhine to the north to study in GERMANY. Basel was itself key to the Reformation. A cosmopolitan center, it had a flourishing printing industry and it was here that MARTIN LUTHER's works were printed in the crucial years of the early Reformation. Also, Basel had been the residence of Erasmus, who had developed a circle of reform-minded humanists around him in the city. HULDRYCH ZWINGLI had studied in Basel, knew Erasmus personally, and was drawn into this world. Basel University was a crucial point of contact for many who would lead the Reformation in the Confederation.

Role of Zwingli

It was, however, the work of Zwingli in Zurich that was the beginning point. From his arrival in 1519 as stipendiary priest in the Grossmünster, Zwingli began a program of *lecto continua* PREACHING—sermons on the whole book and not simply selected passages. These sermons were the catalyst for reform, and from the pulpit Zwingli attacked the venality of the hierarchical church and the profiteering of the mercenary service, and he inveighed against idolatrous worship and moral turpitude. God, Zwingli argued, is pure and demands that his people be pure. There was a strong ethical dimension to Zwingli's message—men and women should lead lives of moral rectitude. Drawing on a mixture of St. Paul, Augustine, late-medieval scholasticism, Luther, and Erasmus, Zwingli emphasized both the sovereignty of God and the complete separation of the spiritual and material. God who is spirit must be worshipped in spirit, and true religion, therefore, must be purged of all attempts to reduce the divine to material representations (i.e., the mass and religious images). The role of the Holy Spirit is central to Zwingli's thought because it was the means by which men and women, as well as the world in which they lived, could be transformed into the new reality of the Christian life.

Zwingli's preaching brought him notoriety and infamy. His denunciation of established religion and mercenary service jarred with influential elements of Zurich society, and there were protests from other parts of the Confederation. The influence of Luther's teachings, particularly in the cities of Berne and Basel, was creating unrest along the lines found in Germany. For his part Zwingli saw little difference between what he was preaching and what he read by Luther. The crucial year was 1523, when two disputations were held in Zurich resulting in the *de facto* establishment of the new faith. The result of Zwingli's alliance with sympathetic magistrates was a new POLITY that envisaged a central role for the political rulers.

Zwingli developed the model of Christian government based on the Old Testament monarchy. The kings (magistrates) were to govern with laws and the sword, and the prophets (essentially Zwingli) were to convey to them God's message. Thus by 1523 Zwingli had a new vision of the CHURCH as the gathering of those united by the spirit. He had essentially rejected the medieval church, but to realize this new church he was dependent on the good will of the political masters in Zurich. The immediate consequence of this, however, was the alienation of those who had been attracted to Zwingli's more radical message articulated in his early sermons. This group around CONRAD GREBEL broke away at the start of 1524, focusing their opposition on the issue of infant BAPTISM.

Reformation Unrest

By the middle of the 1520s the evangelical movement was present in both urban and rural areas and the Swiss found themselves caught up in the vicissitudes of the Peasants' War. The tumults made the magistrates extremely nervous about the effects of evangelical preaching, and in Berne and Basel there were attempts to control what was taught from the pulpits. Catholic opposition, however, was weak and disorganized, and evangelical sympathizers, most of whom were friends of Zwingli, made progress. In Zurich, however, opposition remained considerable and the Reformation Mandate of spring 1525 was only narrowly passed by the Council at a poorly attended session. Zwingli was very much in charge, but he worked with close colleagues such as Leo Jud and the printer Froschauer. The first reforms pertained to worship and a new order for celebration of the LORD'S SUPPER was introduced on Maundy Thursday 1525. Other key institutional reforms included morals mandates, a new marriage court, and the Prophezei, the foundation of higher education. The nature of reform in Zurich was fairly conservative: the parochial system was retained and virtually all of the urban and rural clergy remained in post. The main inspiration for the institutional reforms was drawn from the decrees of the Council of Basel.

In Berne and Basel evangelical movements were struggling, and these movements lacked a person with the authority and charisma of Zwingli, although the crucial role of the writings of JOHANNES OECOLAMPADIUS in Basel in formulating the theological character of the Swiss Reformation has been recently recognized. Nevertheless, in contrast to Zurich, the LAITY played a much more significant role in the implementation of the Reformation in Berne and Basel. The guilds gave decisive weight to the movement, forcing the hesitant Councils in the cities to act. In Berne, however, one must also acknowledge the pivotal role played by Niklaus Manuel, the painter and politician. The Disputation of Berne in 1528, which led to the implementation of the Reformation in the city, was the most important gathering of Swiss reformers and a decisive stage in the formation of Swiss Reformed theology. In Basel revolutionary activity among the lower guilds succeeded in strengthening the Council's hand to introduce the new faith in early 1529.

By the end of 1529, Zurich, Berne, Basel, and Schaffhausen had adopted the Reformation. Furthermore, the movement had made stunning gains in the eastern part of the Confederation in St. Gall, Appenzell, and Glarus. Zwingli was the dominant figure, but his authority must not be overstated. Both Basel and Berne had their own traditions and they were not prepared to follow Zurich. This became very clear in the years 1529 to 1531, when Zurich under Zwingli led a campaign to force the remaining parts of the Confederation to accept the new religion. The focus for hostilities between Catholics and Reformed was the Mandated Territories (lands jointly governed by the Confederates), where numerous local conflicts inflamed passions. Zwingli came to the conclusion that only war could overcome Catholic resistance, although Berne and Basel disagreed. The First Kappel War of 1529 saw virtually no military conflict, but it stirred bad memories of Zurich's previous attempts at domination of the Confederation. Particularism in the Confederation overrode confessional solidarity, and Zwingli was dismayed by the lack of support from the other Reformed states. Relations between Zurich, Berne, and Basel were fragile and the failure to find common purpose led to the rash attempt by Zurich to force the matter in 1531, when an army was sent out and defeated at a surprise battle at Kappel in the night of October 11. It was more of an ambush than a battle, but it left Zwingli and a good number of Zurich ministers dead.

Zwingli's death brought to an end a period of rapid reform and great conflict. During his ten years as a reformer he had given shape to a reform movement that focused on the creation of a new form of church. In so doing he had incurred the wrath of Catholics, Anabaptists (see ANABAPTISM), and—most famously—Luther, with whom he fell out so disastrously and venomously over the LORD'S SUPPER. In connecting the reform movement so closely to Zurich he had also alienated the other Swiss states, which feared that the Reformation was simply a renewed form of hegemony by Zurich. It is also important to note that the reform movement under Zwingli was almost entirely guided by an urban core that had little time for the rural population, who in turn became disenchanted with the Reformation.

New Unity, New Tension

The result of Kappel was the fragmentation of the Swiss Reformation. It was the work of Zwingli's successor, HEINRICH BULLINGER, which eventually succeeded in restoring unity to the Swiss Reformed churches. Bullinger, in his forty years as head of the Zurich church, established a new relationship with the political authorities, gave the Swiss Reformation a clearer theological profile through his leadership, international influence, and writings (in particular the SECOND HELVETIC CONFESSION of 1566), and became a father figure to reform movements across Europe, from HUNGARY to ENGLAND. Under Bullinger and men like Konrad Pellikan and Theodor Bibliander, Zurich remained the theological center of the Swiss Reformation. Of particular importance was the ongoing work on the Zurich BIBLE, which first appeared in 1531. Zurich also became a center for religious refugees, particularly from Italy and England, and this did much to spread the influence of Bullinger's ideas across Europe. Bullinger also played a key role in securing the position of JOHN CALVIN in Geneva. Although the two men were not especially close, Bullinger was Calvin's key ally among the Swiss and their agreement on the Lord's Supper (Consensus Tigurinus) in 1549 marked an important stage in the development of Reformed thought.

In both Berne and Basel the Reformed tradition of Zwingli and Oecolampadius was locked in a struggle with Lutheran influences, and during the 1530s and 1540s both saw rancorous theological struggles that led to the clampdown by the magistrates on the churches. Although Bullinger's status as the leading churchman was recognized, neither Berne nor Basel saw itself as subordinate to Zurich. Basel had extensive contacts with the Empire and was involved in the network of southern German cities, whereas Berne was preoccupied with the conquest of the Pays du Vaud and the expansion toward Geneva after 1536. Berne's influence was in the French-speaking west, whereas Basel regained its place as a center of learning and culture, and like Zurich attracted many refugees who helped to create a diverse religious culture. Until the end of the sixteenth century Basel retained a distinct theological character and refused to sign the Second Helvetic Confession of 1566, which was the key theological document of the Swiss Reformation.

For about a century after Bullinger's death in 1575 the SECOND HELVETIC CONFESSION and Calvin's Genevan CATECHISMS remained the theological standards of the Swiss Reformed churches. To this must be added the Canons of the Synod of Dordrecht, or Dort (see DORT, CANONS OF), which were officially adopted by the Swiss churches. Theologically, the Swiss were greatly influenced by the Dutch Reformed churches. The period 1575 through the middle of the seventeenth century did not produce theologians of great distinction among the Swiss. There were, however, some notable figures, such as Johann Jakob Grynäus in Basel, Johan Jakob Breitinger in Zurich, and THEODORE BEZA and then Theodor Tronchin in Geneva. Basel, so often the renegade in the sixteenth century, had, under Grynäus, become a bastion of Reformed ORTHODOXY. The Swiss churches felt extremely vulnerable during the Thirty Years War. They remained unreconciled with German Lutherans, and they were surrounded by the Catholic forces of FRANCE, the Spanish Habsburgs, and the Austrians. There was considerable instability within the Confederation as numerous confessional disputes, particularly in the Grisons, threatened to upend the precarious Peace of Kappel of 1531. The most dramatic, or infamous, even, was the massacre by Catholics of six hundred Protestants in the Veltelina on July 23, 1620. The Grisons saw the only major confessional change of the seventeenth century, as many of the areas which had adopted the Protestant Reformation were forcibly re-Catholicized. At the same time there was trouble in the west as the Waldensian communities were being persecuted by Savoy.

Although the Swiss formally received their independence from the Holy Roman Empire with the Peace of Westphalia in 1648, confessional dissonance remained. The third religious war (after the First and Second Kappel Wars of 1529–1531) was the First Villmerger War of 1656, which was a defeat for the Reformed Confederates, above all Zurich, and led to the Peace of 1656. Swiss Protestantism was largely on the defensive during the period from 1650 to 1750 as Baroque Catholicism seemed to prevail everywhere. The Formula Consensus of 1675 was issued as a response to doctrinal controversies and was the principal articulation of late-orthodox Swiss theology. It enshrined a strict understanding of the doctrines of verbal inspiration and double PREDESTINATION and was meant to be binding on all the Swiss Protestant churches, but already there was considerable opposition to the imposition of Reformed creeds.

Influence of Pietism, the Enlightenment

With the emergence of PIETISM and the ENLIGHTENMENT in the seventeenth and eighteenth centuries), confessions lost much of their credibility. Opposition to the form of Protestantism which arose out of the state churches of the Reformation took the form of Pietism, which flourished in Swiss lands from the second half of the seventeenth century. Many of the first members of the Pietist movement were HUGUENOTS fleeing France. The Pietist awakenings took place in Berne and Zurich, and the state churches responded aggressively against these movements, which they regarded as heterodox. During the eighteenth century there was a strong movement among the Pietists to separate from the established Protestant churches. At the same time, the eighteenth century saw the rise of "rational orthodoxy," an accommodation with ideas of the Enlightenment. What both of these movements shared was a rejection of the religion of theological confessions, and by the late eighteenth century the formal obligation to the traditional confessions of faith was gradually abolished. The eighteenth century also saw the last religious war, the Second Villmerger War of 1712, which was a victory for the Protestants over the Catholics, shifting political weight decisively towards the Protestant Confederates in the Swiss Confederation, where it would remain.

During the seventeenth and eighteenth centuries the Swiss Protestant churches developed their own unique structures and traditions, but to preserve a sense of unity they continued to meet regularly at Aarau. In each case the church was a part of the state, and the clergy were officials of the ruling government (see CHURCH AND STATE, OVERVIEW). These institutions would remain intact until the end of the old regime following 1789.

The rise of liberal theology in the nineteenth century led to further conflict (see LIBERAL PROTESTANTISM AND LIBERALISM). Perhaps the most significant theologian of the nineteenth century was FRANZ OVERBECK (1837–1905), professor of church history in Basel and close friend of FRIEDRICH NIETZSCHE. The protest against liberal theology and governmental interference in church life (e.g., the abolition by decree of the traditional confessions of faith) as well as the general impulses of the Revival Movement led to secessions of Reformed free churches: 1846 in Vaud, 1849 in Geneva, 1873 in Neuchâtel. The Geneva Free Church still exists today, but the free churches in Neuchâtel and Vaud reunited with the official Reformed Church in 1966 and 1943 (see FREE CHURCH). In addition to these Reformed free churches, a number of pietistic associations were formed following the Revival in the nineteenth century. They were organized as groups within the Reformed churches; e.g., Evangelical Societies (the first in Berne in 1831) or the Pilgrim's Mission St. Chrischona (beginning in 1869). The Swiss Reformed churches owe much to Pietism and the Revival Movement. Most of the church-related social service and missionary organizations go back to the initiative of Revival groups. Although structurally independent, these organizations have spiritual ties to the churches. Basel was the center for most of these organizations with the most significant being the BASEL MISSION, which was founded in 1815. The social and pastoral orientation of the Swiss churches was reflected in the dominant theological figures of the twentieth century, so-called neo-orthodox EMIL BRUNNER (1889–1966) and KARL BARTH (1886–1968), both of whom had enormous international audiences, above all in the UNITED STATES.

Until the nineteenth century the Swiss Reformed churches remained dependent on the political authorities of the cantons. This changed during the twentieth century so that the churches were regulated separately in each canton, resulting in major variations among the cantons. Basel (since 1905), Geneva (since 1907), and Neuchâtel (since 1943) separated church and state, while Berne, Zurich, Vaud, and also Basel-Land have retained the close relationships forged at the Reformation.

The Swiss Reformed churches have no central AUTHORITY. In 1858, following the foundation of the Swiss Confederation (1848), the churches founded a Swiss Church Conference, which met annually, as the Reformation churches had done. After World War I, partly in response to the American Federal Council of Churches, which sought a partner to coordinate reconstruction help for war-damaged Europe, the Federation of Swiss Protestant Churches was founded in 1920. The Federation is not itself a church but an alliance of autonomous churches.

In addition, the Swiss Reformed churches have created a series of organizations for specific tasks. In the French-speaking area of Switzerland the *Département missionnaire des Eglises protestantes de la Suisse romande* (DM) and in German-speaking Switzerland the *Kooperation evangelischer Kirchen und Missionen* (KEM) are responsible for church partnerships. The *Hilfswerk der evangelischen Kirchen der Schweiz* was founded to do relief work, while *Brot für alle* is the Reformed churches' agency for development work.

Conclusion

A brief summary does little justice to the complexities of the Swiss Reformation. In character it was created by a small network of humanist-minded reformers who drew their inspiration from Erasmus, Luther, and Zwingli. Zurich was the dominant force and without the Reformation in Zurich there would have been no Swiss Reformation. However, there were crucial differences between the states reflecting the manner in which the Confederation had evolved historically. Zwingli had created a dynamic reform movement that was closely enmeshed in the political and cultural realities of the Confederation, yet his ideas concerning God, the SACRAMENTS, and WORSHIP spread across Europe. Heinrich Bullinger turned the Swiss Reformation into an event of profound importance for the sixteenth century, and for a period of decades in the sixteenth century this backward Confederation was a

center of religious and intellectual development. After his death in 1575 the Swiss churches became part of the international Reformed world but in the shadow of those areas, such as England, the NETHERLANDS, France, and SCOTLAND, they had once influenced.

See also Calvinism; Catholic Reactions to Protestantism; Catholicism, Protestant Reactions; Lutheranism

References and Further Reading

Brady, Thomas A. *Turning Swiss. Cities and Empire 1450–1550.* Cambridge: Cambridge University Press, 1985.

Brecht, Martin. *Der Pietismus vom siebzehnten bis zum frühen achtzehnten Jahrhundert.* Göttingen, Germany: Vandenhoeck & Ruprecht, 1993.

Gordon, Bruce. *The Swiss Reformation.* Manchester, UK: Manchester University Press, 2002.

Gossmann, Lionel. *Basel in the Age of Burckhardt. A Study in Unseasonable Ideas.* Chicago: Chicago University Press, 2000.

Guggisberg, Hans. *Basel in the Sixteenth Century: Aspects of the City Republic before, during and after the Reformation.* St. Louis, MO: Sixteenth Century Studies, 1982.

Locher, Gottfried. *Die zwinglische Reformation im Rahmen der europaeischen Kirchengestchichte.* Göttingen, Germany: Vandenhoech & Ruprecht, 1979.

Pfister, Rudolf. *Kirchengeschichte der Schweiz.* 2 vols. Zurich, Switzerland: Theologischer Verlag Zurich, 1974.

Potter, George. *Zwingli.* Cambridge: Cambridge University Press, 1976.

Wernle, Paul. *Der schweizerische Protestantismus im XVIII. Jahrhundert.* Tübingen, Germany, 1923–24.

F. BRUCE GORDON

SYNOD

The word "synod" comes from the Greek *synodos,* which means "a group of people traveling together," a "gathering," an "assembly," "a meeting," "together on the way," and "going the same way." A synod is a meeting of the CLERGY, and sometimes the LAITY, of a particular CHURCH, nation, province, or diocese to discuss ecclesiastical matters, make decisions, and promulgate regulations related to issues of DOCTRINE, LITURGY, ethical concerns, and discipline (see CHURCH DISCIPLINE). In the early church the terms "synod" and "council" were interchangeable. Sometimes a meeting covering a large area was called a council and one covering a smaller region was called a synod. Gradually, the ecumenical councils were called councils and not synods, and synod was used for regional meetings.

The earliest synods were those held in Asia Minor in response to Montanism and those held in the East and the West to settle the quartodeciman (date of Easter) controversy. Possibly the first official synod, the calling together of the clergy of a diocese, was held by Bishop Siricius of Rome in 387. Later Pope Benedict XIV (1758–1769) ruled that a synod was a convocation of the diocese, and the meeting of all the bishops was to be called a council. The major synod in Roman Catholicism is the Synod of Bishops, sometimes called the World Synod of Bishops, which was mandated by the Second Vatican Council's Decree on the Bishops' Pastoral Office in the Church, and established by Pope Paul VI on September 15, 1965, in the document *Apostolica Sollicitudo* (Apostolic Solicitude). The Synod of Bishops meets every few years at the call of the pope, and is an opportunity for bishops from around the world to discuss issues with the bishop of Rome.

The Synod in Protestantism

In Protestantism, synod has been used in a variety of ways. At the time of the REFORMATION, the Reformed/Presbyterian tradition introduced synodical structures of church government (see PRESBYTERIANISM). The first synod of the canton of Zurich was held in April 1528, and consisted of the pastor and two lay deputies from each parish. It was primarily a means of maintaining standards for the ministry. In late May 1559, in Calvinistic FRANCE, representatives of about fifty churches met in Paris and adopted a form of discipline and the GALLICAN CONFESSION. It established a synodical form of church government. At the local level was the CONSISTORY and above that was the colloquy, composed of the pastor and one elder from each congregation. The colloquy was subject to the provincial synod, which was attended by each pastor and two elders. The supreme AUTHORITY was the annual national synod, which consisted of two ministers and two elders from each of the provincial synods. A similar system was arranged in the NETHERLANDS, which had three synods meeting annually, and at the top, biennial national synods.

The CHURCH OF ENGLAND replaced the General Assembly with the General Synod in 1969. It consists of the CONVOCATIONS OF CANTERBURY AND YORK joined together in a House of Bishops and a House of Clergy joined by a House of Laity. It is the highest authority in the Church of England.

In the American colonies, synods were used in New England CONGREGATIONALISM as early as 1637. One of the most important of the colonial synods was the Cambridge Synod, which met on September 1, 1646. At the request of the General Court of the Bay Colony, Massachusetts, a synod consisting of elders (ministers) and messengers (laymen) from the four Puritan (see PURITANISM) colonies—Bay Colony, New Haven, Plymouth, and Connecticut—met to discuss issues of ECCLESIOLOGY. Chapter xvi of the CAMBRIDGE PLATFORM was "Of Synods." It noted that Acts 15 referred to a synod, so synods are the ordinance of Christ, but not absolutely necessary to the being of the church. Synods are necessary for the well-being of the church

because of the iniquity of men and the perverseness of the times. Synods could be called to debate and determine controversies of faith, cases of conscience, directions for the public worship of God, and the good government of the church. It gave synods strong advisory and admonitory powers, but not legal coercive authority. The first synod of the Presbyterians in the American colonies met at Philadelphia in 1717.

The EPISCOPAL CHURCH in the United States is organized into nine provinces. Each province has a synod consisting of a House of Bishops and a House of Deputies. The Provincial Synod has a president who may be a bishop, presbyter, deacon, or lay person in the Province.

LUTHERANISM also uses the term synod. In 1807 FRIEDRICH SCHLEIERMACHER made a proposal for a new constitution for the Protestant Church in Prussia, which included the adoption of a synodical system. Gradually this synodical system dominated European Lutheranism. Synods became very important after World War I. Participation of pastors and laymen in synods during the *Kirchencampf* increased the prestige of synods. The first synod of the CONFESSING CHURCH at Barmen, May 29–30, 1934, drew up the BARMEN DECLARATION in response to the Nazi GERMAN CHRISTIANS.

In American Lutheranism, synod has been used in several ways. One is as a national label, such as the LUTHERAN CHURCH–MISSOURI SYNOD and the WISCONSIN EVANGELICAL LUTHERAN SYNOD. The primary use of synod in American Lutheranism has been as a geographical area. The first Lutheran synod was held in Philadelphia in 1748. The EVANGELICAL LUTHERAN CHURCH IN AMERICA has sixty-five synods. There are two small bodies in the UNITED STATES that use the word synod in their titles—the Evangelical Lutheran Synod and the Lutheran Ministerium and Synod–United States of America.

The MORAVIAN CHURCH in America (Unitas Fratrum) is divided into three provinces. The highest administrative body in each is the provincial synod, which is composed of ministers and laypersons, and meets every three or four years.

References and Further Reading

Church of England, National Assembly, Synodical Government Commission. *Synodical Government in the Church of England: Being a Report of a Commission Appointed by the Archbishops of Canterbury and York.* London: Church Information Office, 1966.

Hauck, Albert. "Councils and Synods." In *The New Schaff-Herzog Encyclopedia of Religious Knowledge,* edited by Samuel Macauley Jackson, vol. 3, 279–284. Grand Rapids, MI: Baker Book House, 1950.

Margull, Hans, ed. *The Councils of the Church.* Philadelphia, PA: Fortress Press, 1961.

DONALD S. ARMENTROUT

T

TAIT, ARCHIBALD CAMPBELL (1811–1882)

Archbishop of Canterbury. Tait was born and educated in Edinburgh. He moved from Edinburgh High School to the University of Glasgow in 1827. Although born into a Presbyterian family, he decided to enter the ministry of the CHURCH OF ENGLAND. He joined Balliol College, Oxford in 1829 and was confirmed in the Church of England in 1830. After securing a first-class degree in classics in 1833, he taught in the university as a fellow and tutor of Balliol College and became one of the most respected tutors in the university, lecturing in logic and ethics. Tait was not drawn to the OXFORD MOVEMENT of the time and contributed to a public protest against Tract 90, in which JOHN HENRY NEWMAN attempted to show that the Calvinist THIRTY-NINE ARTICLES of the Church of England were compatible with Roman Catholic teaching. In 1842 Tait was appointed headmaster of Rugby School in succession to THOMAS ARNOLD, and in 1849 he became dean of Carlisle.

In 1856 family tragedy overtook Tait. In one month, from March 10 to April 10, the Taits lost five daughters to scarlet fever. In the same year he was appointed bishop of London. Here he was prepared to be innovative, preaching in public places like transportation depots and encouraging popular services in Westminster Abbey and in London theaters. He was active in the cholera epidemic of 1866.

In 1869 he became archbishop of CANTERBURY. He attempted to curb the excesses of the Anglo-Catholic ritualists through the Public Worship Regulation Act of 1874. He incurred much criticism by adopting a liberal attitude to the use of non-Anglican forms by nonconformists who exercised their right to burial in Anglican churchyards (see NONCONFORMITY). Tait was judged to have had greater influence in the House of Lords than any other archbishop since the REFORMATION and was an able and persuasive speaker. During his tenure the LAMBETH CONFERENCE, begun in 1867, was consolidated as a meeting for Anglican bishops from overseas, thus changing the role of archbishop into a leader of a worldwide communion.

References and Further Reading

Davidson, R. T., and W. Benham. *The Life of Archibald Campbell Tait.* 2 vols. London: Macmillan and Co., 1891.

Edwards, David L. *Leaders of the Church of England 1828–1944.* Cambridge: Cambridge University Press, 1971.

Fremantle, W. H. *Dictionary of National Biography.* vol. 55. London: Oxford University Press, 1898.

Marsh, P. T. *The Victorian Church in Decline: Archbishop Tait and the Church of England 1868–1882.* London: Routledge & Kegan Paul, 1969.

TIMOTHY E. YATES

TAIWAN

The island of Formosa ("beautiful [island]") was inhabited solely by aboriginal peoples of uncertain origins until the modern period. Less than a century after Japanese and Chinese established communities on the island, the Dutch arrived (1626) and occupied a southern region of Formosa in 1642. The Dutch came not as missionaries, but as a multinational corporation known as the Dutch East India Company (VOC) to protect their spice trade from the north. The rule of the VOC in the south lasted only thirty-eight years. When the Dutch were expelled (1662), a long period of Chinese domination began that included a long and steady exodus of Han Chinese from the mainland to Taiwan. This Chinese domination of the island was ended only by the newer imperial power of Japan (1895–1945). Upon the defeat of the Japanese, and then the victory of the Communists in China, in 1949,

Taiwan became the refuge of great numbers of Nationalists from CHINA.

The earliest Christian presence on Formosa began in the 1620s with Dutch Reformed ministers who were funded by the VOC. Thirty-two ministers came to serve the Dutch community but also with the clear purpose to evangelize the Aboriginal population. During their brief stay, over 17,000 local people were baptized, and a good amount of catechetical material was translated into the local tongue.

The next Protestant phase in Taiwan began in 1860, after the signing of the Tien-chin Treaty (1858), an agreement between Qing China and a number of Western powers that opened various treaty ports for evangelization. In September 1860 Carstairs Douglas and H. L. Mackenzie, English Presbyterians who had been working in South China, made an exploratory trip to the island. Thus begins a long tradition of Christian development in Taiwan being closely linked with China. The first resident missionary to Taiwan was a physician, Dr. James L. Maxwell, who arrived from Amoy, China with three Chinese assistants. For the next half-century, church work in Taiwan was dominated by Presbyterians from the United Kingdom, CANADA, and later the UNITED STATES. Most notable of the early missionaries was Canadian George Leslie Mackay (1844–1901). His work, mostly with the Han Chinese, helped to establish the first hospital, first college (Oxford), and established the first Presbytery in the North (1914). Antiforeign persecution, as in China, periodically cropped up on Taiwan, aimed both at missionaries and at Christian converts. Other institutions founded in the nineteenth century include the Taiwan Theological Seminary (1876), the first Presbytery (1896), and the Taiwan Church Press (1884).

In 1915 another turn occurred when Japanese rule was established in Taiwan. This meant a greater encouragement to self-support as well as greater cooperation among churches, enforced by the Japanese. Still there was a close relationship with mainland China. In the 1920s the recently formed True Jesus Church (TJC, 1918; Beijing), an indigenous Chinese Pentecostal Church, began work in Taiwan. The TJC became an important church on the island, having its greatest influence among the poor and less educated. Also during this time of Japanese occupation, the aboriginal work went forward. Although the impetus to this growth came from both Western mission and Japanese mission leadership, the growth in the work was mostly the work of indigenous Christian leaders like Loh Sian-chhun, Kho Iu-chai, and others.

Another great shift in the Christian presence and Christian influence occurred at the close of the Pacific War. The Japanese influence ended, but very quickly the island was dominated by Guomindang personnel under the leadership of Chiang Kai-shek. Along with the various refugees fleeing Maoist rule were a number of Christians. This marks the end of the Presbyterian and Reformed domination of Protestant MISSIONS in Taiwan. Soon both Chinese Christians and missionaries were arriving from Methodist, Baptist, Lutheran, and other churches. Numerous smaller churches sent missionaries to evangelize the mainland Chinese, adding further to the church diversity. Some of these missionaries came from China, already speaking certain dialects of Chinese, but few spoke Taiwanese. Thus the division between ministry to Han Chinese and local Taiwanese and aboriginal peoples increased.

After nearly four centuries of often interrupted Christian witness, Taiwan is still less than 7 percent Christian. More Taiwanese are members of newer, non-Christian, religious groups than are members of Christian churches. One of the ongoing themes in Christianity in Taiwan is the appropriate role of political involvement. For some, independence from the People's Republic of China is a central concern, but for others the main issue is the domination of political life by "foreign" Nationalist elements from China. The Presbyterian Church in Taiwan is the largest Protestant church, although it is still only half the size of the Roman Catholic Church. PENTECOSTALISM, even though it arrived very late in Taiwan, is followed by about one-third of the Christian population. It seems that indigenous forms of Christianity such as the True Jesus Church and the Little Flock will continue to have influence, but that overall Protestant Christians will remain a significant but small minority of the population.

References and Further Reading

Band, Edward. *The History of the English Presbyterian Mission: 1847–1847.* London: Publishing Office of the Presbyterian Church of England, n.d. (reprinted. Taipei: Ch'eng Wen Publishing Company, 1972).

Moffett, Samuel A. *A History of Christianity in Asia.* vols. 1 and 2. Maryknoll, NY: Orbis Press, 1998/2004.

Rubenstein, M. A. "Taiwan." In *The New International Dictionary of Pentecostal and Charismatic Movements,* edited by Stanley M. Burgess. Grand Rapids, MI: Zondervan, 2002.

Tong, Hollington K. *Christianity in Taiwan: A History.* Taipei: China Post, 1961.

SCOTT W. SUNQUIST

TAUSEN, HANS (1494–1561)

Danish Lutheran reformer. Tausen was born in Birkende on the island of Fyn in 1494. Little is known of his early childhood. As a young monk in the Order of

St. John in Antvorskov, he was sent in 1516 to study theology at Rostock. Upon his return to Copenhagen in 1521, he came under the influence of Paul Helie, the leading Christian Humanist in Scandinavia and a disciple of Erasmus. Tausen continued his theological studies at the University of Wittenberg, where he was strongly influenced by MARTIN LUTHER.

Upon his return to DENMARK in 1525 Tausen began to preach in Viborg (Jutland), where an evangelical, grassroots awakening broke out. Imprisoned for his preaching and expelled from his order, Tausen came under the personal protection of Frederik I who appointed him to be his personal chaplain in 1526. A printing press set up in Viborg in 1528 greatly aided the dissemination of Tausen's views. By 1529 when Tausen was called to be the pastor of St. Nicholas Church in Copenhagen, a popular evangelical renewal movement had spread throughout Jutland.

In July 1530 Tausen led a group of like-minded evangelical preachers in presenting Forty-three Articles *(Confessio Hafniensis)* to the Danish National Assembly. This Copenhagen Confession was avowedly Lutheran and more polemical in tone than the AUGSBURG CONFESSION. However, in 1537 when JOHANNES BUGENHAGEN drew up the Danish Church Ordinance, the Augsburg Confession came to overshadow the *Confessio Hafniensis* as a confessional statement of the Lutheran Church of Denmark.

In 1538 Tausen was appointed lecturer at the Cathedral School in Roskilde, one of the last Roman Catholic strongholds in Denmark. As "superintendent" (bishop) of Ribe (1542), Tausen spent the rest of his life introducing the vernacular into congregational hymn singing and worship while augmenting his influential collection of *Sermons (Postil).*

See also Evangelicalism; Hymns and Hymnals; Lutheranism, Scandinavia

References and Further Reading

Primary Sources:

Andersen, Niels K. *Confessio Hafniensis.* Diss. Copenhagen: 1954.
Tausen, Hans. *Postille.* Edited by Bjoern Kornerup. Facs. edition, 2 vols. Copenhagen: Levin & Munksgaard, 1934.

Secondary Sources:

Bugge, Knud E. *Tro og Tale: Studier over Hans Tausens Postil.* Copenhagen: Gad, 1963.
Christensen, Marie. *Hans Tausen.* Copenhagen: 1942.
Rordam, Holger F., ed. *Smaaskrifter af Hans Tausen.* Copenhagen: 1870.

TRYGVE R. SKARSTEN

TAYLOR, JAMES HUDSON (1832–1905)

English missionary to China. Taylor was born on May 21, 1832 in Barnsley, ENGLAND. He was a pioneer Protestant missionary to inland CHINA and the founder of the interdenominational CHINA INLAND MISSION (CIM). He raised funds for missionary work and served as a recruiter of missionaries to China. By the time of his death, on June 3, 1905, the CIM had sponsored over 800 missionaries to China. Throughout his missionary work Taylor traveled on eleven journeys.

Early Years as a Missionary

Taylor received his calling to serve as a missionary at age seventeen. His first missionary work was with the Chinese Evangelization Society. This Society paid for him to undergo medical training in London. He arrived in China for the first time in 1854 at Shanghai aboard the ship the *Dumfries.* Shanghai was one of five port cities opened to foreign trade through the signing of the Treaty of Nanking (1842), which also gave control of Hong Kong to Great Britain.

At the time of Taylor's arrival, China was in the middle of the Taiping rebellion (1850–1864), a revolt against the Chinese emperor Xian Feng led by a pseudo-Christian religious fanatic. The rebellion was reported initially to have the effect of opening up China to foreign missionaries.

South of Shanghai, Taylor worked in the missionary hospital at Ningpo. In 1857 Taylor resigned from the Chinese Evangelization Society. He had objected to being supported by borrowed money. It was Taylor's conviction that a Christian should not be indebted to anyone. Taylor instead believed that monetary support for MISSIONS work should come from God, asked for in PRAYER. He continued to work as an independent missionary in China after his work with the Society.

Hudson Taylor differed from other missionaries of his time. He adapted himself cross-culturally throughout his work in order to fit in more easily with the Chinese people. Having won the affections of Maria Dyer, a missionary daughter, Taylor married her in 1858. He gave up Western attire and wore Chinese robes, dyed his hair black, and attached a queue, resembling a pigtail, to his hair. Taylor later required all missionaries serving with the CIM who traveled into the Chinese interior to do likewise.

Returning to England in 1860 on account of ill health, Taylor asked for additional missionaries to China. Before he returned to China in 1865 he revised the translation of the New Testament in the Ningpo dialect. His book *China: Its Spiritual Needs and*

Claims (1865) motivated many to consider missionary work to China.

Work with the China Inland Mission

Missionaries usually remained near the shore provinces of China. Taylor, however, intended to travel inland with the gospel message. This shift in Protestant Chinese missionary work resulted in the establishment of the China Inland Mission in 1865 in London. Taylor returned to China under the auspices of the CIM. The CIM was to be a "faith mission," in which the missionaries would rely on God's help to finance their labors. The CIM was an international organization, represented by England, SWEDEN, the UNITED STATES, CANADA, and others. Taylor had brought sixteen missionaries on his second voyage. Arriving at Shanghai in 1866, the missionaries spread the gospel message into interior China.

Taylor's wife, Maria, died in July 1870 at age thirty-three. She had borne eight children. In 1871 Taylor married Jennie Faulding in England. One year later, the whole family returned to China.

China's Millions, the monthly journal of the CIM, was first published in 1875. This journal continued being published until 1952, when the CIM was renamed the Overseas Missionary Fellowship. Taylor had contributed numerous articles to the journal, including "To Every Creature" (1889). In that article Taylor outlined an ambitious plan to evangelize the whole of China. The article was inspired by the Conference of Missionaries, held in Shanghai in 1887.

The Chefoo Convention, signed between Great Britain and China in 1876, had the effect of allowing missionaries to travel into inland China. For the next two years Taylor traveled over thirty thousand miles in the nine interior provinces of China. He was accompanied by eighteen missionaries, who Taylor believed were an answer to many prayers. Against criticism by other MISSIONARY ORGANIZATIONS, Taylor brought single female missionaries to work in teams to inland China in 1878. They served an important role with the CIM, establishing mission settlements in the Chinese interior. He was the first to involve single women in missionary work to China.

Among the missionaries traveling to China with Taylor in 1885 were the "Cambridge Seven." They were a group educated at the University of Cambridge who gave up careers in England for the missionary work in China and sparked a student movement.

Taylor left China for SWITZERLAND in 1900 because of his failing health, and entered into semiretirement. While Taylor was convalescing, the Boxer Rebellion, (1900), directed against foreigners in China, took the lives of over a hundred CIM missionaries—men, women, and their children.

James Hudson Taylor lost his second wife (1904) in Switzerland, a year before his own death. He undertook what was to become his final journey to China in 1905. That year Taylor took ill and died in Changsha, Hunan Province. He was buried near the Yangtze River. Taylor is remembered as a man of faith who had a pioneering missionary spirit that opened inland China to foreign missions.

See also Bible Translation; Cambridge University; Missions, British; Studd, C. T.

References and Further Reading

Primary Source:

Taylor, James Hudson. *Hudson Taylor*. Minneapolis, MN: Bethany House, 1987.

Secondary Sources:

Cromarty, Jim. *It is not Death to Die: A New Biography of Hudson Taylor*. Sevenoaks, UK: Hodder & Stoughton, 2001.
Steer, Roger. *J. Hudson Taylor: A Man in Christ (An OMF Book)*. Wheaton, IL: H. Shaw Publishers, 1993.
Taylor, Howard, and Geraldine Taylor. *Spiritual Secret of Hudson Taylor*. New Kensington, PA: Whitaker House, 1996.
———. *Hudson Taylor: Two-Volume Biography*. 2 vols. Littleton, CO: OMF Books, 1998.

CHRISTOPHER M. COOK

TAYLOR, JEREMY (1613–1667)

English theologian. Jeremy Taylor was born on August 15, 1613, at Cambridge, and died on August 13, 1667, at Lisburn, Ireland. He studied at Gonville and Gaius College, CAMBRIDGE UNIVERSITY. Taylor lectured at St. Paul's, London, and attracted the attention of WILLIAM LAUD, archbishop of Canterbury. He served at rector of Uppingham and then chaplain in the Royalist army. After imprisonment for a short time he retired in 1645 to WALES, where he lived as a chaplain and where he wrote many of his best works. On January 27, 1661, he was consecrated bishop of Down and Connor, to which the small adjacent diocese of Dromore was later added, in IRELAND.

Taylor's fame rests almost entirely on his devotional writings. In 1646 he published *Theologia eklektike; a Discourse of the Liberty of Prophesying,* in which he asked that deprived CHURCH OF ENGLAND clergy be allowed to function. It is a plea for TOLERATION that advocated a more liberal attitude to religious differences. It had an impact on the American colonies and was highly regarded by ROGER WILLIAMS.

An Apology for Authorized and Set Forms of Liturgy (1646) was an attack on the *Directory of Public Worship,* which was opposed to all forms of written prayers including the Lord's Prayer. *Doctor Dubitantium, or the Rule of Conscience* (1660) was a treatise on moral theology. *A Dissuasive from Popery* (1664) was an attack on Roman Catholicism in which he argued that councils are not infallible, that Scripture is sufficient for understanding SALVATION, and that indulgences were a Roman innovation.

Taylor's two major devotional writings were *The Rule and Exercises of Holy Living* (1650) and *The Rule and Exercises of Holy Dying* (1651). These are probably the most widely known writings of any seventeenth-century Anglican divine. Both volumes describe how a Christian can live a holy life and die a holy death. Both volumes had an impact on JOHN WESLEY and influenced his understanding of perfection and sanctification.

Because he lived through the chaotic period of the Commonwealth, Taylor had a great fear of ANTINOMIANISM and moral chaos. Justification by GRACE through FAITH should not weaken insistence of living a good life. For Taylor JUSTIFICATION was a process, and holy living was a matter of constant repentance. He argued that Christ is the medium to God, but obedience is the medium to Christ. Before one receives Holy Communion (see LORD'S SUPPER) there must be the complete removal of any known sin or desire to sin as well as an earnest belief never to commit sin again.

Taylor was a great prose stylist and he has been called the prose Shakespeare, the English Chrysostom, and the Anglican Bossuet. He was a pre-Tractarian High Churchman.

References and Further Reading

Bolton, Frederick Rothwell. *The Caroline Tradition of the Church of Ireland, with Particular Reference to Bishop Jeremy Taylor.* London: S.P.C.K., 1958.

McAdoo, H. R. *The Eucharistic Theology of Jeremy Taylor Today.* Norfolk, UK: Canterbury Press Norwich, 1988.

Scott, David A. *Christian Character: Jeremy Taylor and Christian Ethics Today.* Oxford, UK: Latimer House, 1991.

Williamson, Hugh Ross. *Jeremy Taylor.* Norwood, PA: Norwood Editions, 1975.

DONALD S. ARMENTROUT

TAYLOR, NATHANIEL WILLIAM (1786–1858)

American theologian and educator. Born in Connecticut June 23, 1786, Taylor graduated from Yale in 1807, where he studied theology under TIMOTHY DWIGHT, and became his amanuensis. In 1812 he was ordained and became the pastor of the First Church of New Haven. He was handsome and dignified, and a powerful preacher. Taylor was called to be Dwight professor of didactic theology in 1822 at Yale Divinity School, where he remained until his death on March 10, 1858.

The theology of JONATHAN EDWARDS, modified by SAMUEL HOPKINS, Bellamy, and Dwight, was the orthodox belief held in most New England churches. It taught that man's only freedom of choice is liberty to obey the strongest motive. Taylor disagreed, denying the doctrines of total depravity and original SIN. He stated that no one is depraved but by his own acts because the sinfulness of the human race does not pertain to human nature as such. "Sin is in the sinning," he declared, and therefore it is "original" only in being universal. Humans always had, in his famous phrase, "power to the contrary." Fully in accord with the AWAKENINGS of the time, his intention was to formulate a revival theology that could prosper in the democratic ethos of Jacksonian America, and prevent the feeling of inability in people. Taylor taught that preachers must confront sinners with their state, and demand immediate response to the gospel. He regarded human beings as free and rational, and therefore fully responsible for everything they did.

In 1828 Taylor presented his New Haven Theology in his *Concio ad Clerum* address before the Congregational clergy of Connecticut, shocking many and dividing the churches into "Taylorites and Tylerites," the latter following his chief opponent, Bennet Tyler. The controversy among Congregationalists became so heated that a more orthodox and Calvinistic seminary was formed in 1833, with Tyler as president. Taylor's influence soon passed beyond the borders of New England and was a factor in the Presbyterian Church schism of 1838, with the New School faction generally accepting his views. Taylor's works include *Practical Sermons* (1858), *Lectures on the Moral Government of God* (1859), and *Essays . . . upon Selected Topics in Revealed Theology* (1859).

See also Congregationalism; Presbyterianism

References and Further Reading

Ahlstrom, Sydney E. *A Religious History of the American People.* New Haven, CT: Yale University Press, 1972.

Foster, Frank H. *A Genetic History of the New England Theology.* Chicago: University of Chicago Press, 1907.

Haroutunian, Joseph. *Piety versus Moralism: The Passing of the New England Theology.* New York: Henry Holt and Company, 1932. Reprint. Introduction by Sydney H. Ahlstrom. New York: Harper and Row, Torchbooks, 1970.

Mead, Sidney E. *Nathaniel William Taylor, 1786–1858: A Connecticut Liberal.* Chicago: University of Chicago Press, 1942.

KEITH J. HARDMAN

TELEMANN, GEORG PHILIPP
(1681–1767)

German composer. Telemann, born March 14, 1681, was GERMANY'S most eminent and prolific composer during the first half of the eighteenth century. A musically precocious child, he began formal study of singing in 1691 and claimed to have learned to play several instruments—organ, violin, and zither, and later, flute, oboe, chalumeau, viola da gamba, double bass, and trombone—with little or no instruction. Two years later, at the age of twelve, he wrote his first opera, *Sigismundus,* and began writing a motet almost every week for the church choir at his school in Zellerfeld.

In 1701, apparently giving in to the wishes of his family that he not follow a musical career, he began to study law at Leipzig University. Even so, he was soon commissioned to write music for both the Thomaskirche and Nikolaikirche. He also founded a student Collegium Musicum, became director of the Opernhaus (writing four operas before leaving Leipzig), and was appointed (in 1704) to the posts of organist and music director at the Neukirche. Telemann left Leipzig in 1705 to take up the post of Kappellmeister at the court of Count Erdmann II of Promnitz in Sorau (now Zary in Poland).

During these early years, he wrote most of his motets, masses, and psalm settings. In 1708 Telemann left Sorau to take up the appointment of *Konzertmeister* to Duke Johann Wilhelm of Saxony-Eisenach, and was promoted Kapellmeister the following year. He married Amalie Louise Juliane Eberin, a musician's daughter and a lady-in-waiting to the countess of Promnitz, who died in 1711 giving birth to their daughter. The child's godfather was Erdmann Neumeister (poet-theologian and court chaplain at Sorau), whose texts Telemann set the same year for an annual cycle of cantatas; these pieces helped establish the "mixed" style of cantata, in which operatic arias and recitative were interspersed with chorales.

The death of Telemann's wife and a dissatisfaction with court politics may have contributed to what Telemann described as a religious awakening that led him to seek church employment. In 1712 he took the post of city director of music and Kapellmeister of the Barfüsserkirche in Frankfurt, where, among other duties, he was responsible for providing music for two city churches and for civic gatherings. Over the following three years he started a public concert series with a revived Frankfurt Collegium Musicum, married Maria Catharina Textor (the sixteen-year-old daughter of the council clerk, who in subsequent years bore eights sons and one daughter), and began publishing his instrumental works. In 1716 he performed his setting of the Hamburg poet B. H. Brockes's passion-oratorio, which was to become a favorite Lenten piece in Germany even up to the early nineteenth century. During the same year he visited the Eisenach and Gotha courts and was installed as the nonresident Kapellmeister to the former. He was offered a resident position at the Gotha court, which he declined after negotiating a salary increase from the city of Frankfurt. Three complete cantata cycles survive from these years (1714–15; 1716–17; 1717–18) that show Telemann's conscious attempt to master national styles and also demonstrate his lifelong interest in incorporating the styles of secular, including operatic, music into his church music.

In 1721 he left Frankfurt to become Kantor of the Johanneum Lateinschule (where he gave a Latin oration on the superiority [*excellentia*] of church music) and musical director of Hamburg's five main churches. Before settling in at Hamburg, however, he applied (in 1722) for the post of Thomaskantor at Leipzig. He was selected over six other candidates, including J. S. Bach, but negotiated a salary increase that convinced him to remain in Hamburg. His many duties there included giving music instruction four days each week at the school and providing a sacred oratorio and serenata each year for the military, two sacred cantatas each week, and a new passion each Lent. Twenty-three of these passions, which are for liturgical use—he set each Evangelist's account in turn—are still extant. In spite of such a heavy workload, Telemann found the energy to direct the weekly concerts of the Hamburg Collegium Musicum, two years later expanding the series to two concerts each week. He also became director of the Gänsemarkttoper, where he performed his own, Handel's, and Keiser's operas.

In 1725 he began to concentrate on publishing his music, bringing out forty-three publications (not counting second editions) over the next fifteen years. Telemann's published cantata cycles from these years [1725–26; 1726–27; 1731–32] consist of practical music for fairly small scorings, suitable for domestic as well as small church settings. In 1736 his marriage (which had deteriorated twelve years earlier) ended when his wife left home, possibly to stay in a convent. Although by 1740 he had effectively retired, the death of his eldest son, Andreas, in 1755, led to Telemann's taking responsibility for his musically gifted seven-year-old grandson, Georg Michael. This seems to have rejuvenated him, ushering in his last phase of creative activity, during which he concentrated on writing sacred oratorios; one of his finest, *Der Tag des Gerichts,* dates from 1765. Telemann died June 25, 1767, at the age of eighty-six, having produced over 3,000 works, including 1,700 cantatas (1,400 of which are still extant). His popularity (attributed to his native talent for melody and to his dramatic sense) and the freedom that he found in church employment enabled him to bring music of a quality generally reserved for the most wealthy courts to a new urban and middle-class concert-going public.

References and Further Reading

Menke, Werner. *Thematisches Verzeichnis der Vokalwerke von Georg Philipp Telemann.* 2 vols. Frankfurt: Klostermann, 1988 (vol. 1), 1983 (vol. 2).

Ruhnke, Martin, and Wolf Hobohm, eds. *Georg Philipp Telemann: Musikalische Werke.* Kassel, Germany: Bärenreiter, 1950–.

Telemann, Georg Philipp. *Autobiographien: 1718, 1729, 1739.* Blakenburg, Germany: Konsultationsstelle, Leistungzentrum beim Telemann-Kammerorchester, 1976.

Zohn, Steven. "Telemann, Georg Philipp." In *The New Grove Dictionary of Music Online.* Edited by L. Macy. http://www.grovemusic.com.

WILLIAM T. FLYNN

TELEVANGELISM

The new communications technologies of the twentieth century challenged the Protestant, especially evangelical, understandings of the Great Commission, ultimately resulting in the massive proliferation of television ministries, often referred to collectively as the "Electronic Church." The flamboyant early twentieth-century revivalist BILLY SUNDAY, although active before the advent of television, anticipated the methods of later televangelists by measuring the economic costs of bringing souls to Christ. Television dropped the costs of God's saving GRACE, at least in the minds of televangelical pioneers, through large potential audiences. The transition from tent REVIVALS to television, however, necessitated changes in the way televangelists presented the Gospel. Driven by financial imperatives and the need to purchase broadcast time, televangelists developed styles of programming that, although individually unique, relied heavily on continuous financial appeals. Moreover, the large influx of funds combined with often secretive and careless accounting standards resulted in suggestions of corruption. Besides accountability problems and other moral improprieties, however, a group of televangelists began garnering attention for their active role in national politics beginning in the late 1970s. Despite the mostly unfavorable attention televangelism has received, it has survived, albeit with a changing cast of characters. Finally, although its potential audience of regular viewers and contributors appears finite, its cultural and political influence appears disproportionate to its numerical base because of both its own media strength and the sense of panic its activities trigger among its secular detractors.

The Rise of the Electronic Church: Historical Elements

Evangelists have typically used new methods and technologies as quickly as these could be harnessed, despite the occasional reservations of evangelical laypersons and critics within the mainline churches. The Second Great AWAKENING (c. 1800–1860), for example, witnessed the rise of a phenomenon known as urban revivalism, which allowed talented evangelists to reach larger audiences. The first of these, CHARLES GRANDISON FINNEY (1792–1875), introduced *new measures,* or techniques designed to win converts more effectively. Finney also organized his revivals to an extent previously unknown, especially through his use of advance publicity. Finney's successors, DWIGHT L. MOODY (1837–1899) and Billy Sunday (1862–1935), further augmented Finney's techniques with musical performances, vaudeville entertainment, and an urgent sense of "the soon coming of Christ." Sunday further rationalized Moody's methods, actually organizing his ministry around the belief that it cost $2 to save a soul. Such rational calculation in business matters, combined with emotional and dramatic presentations of the Gospel, prepared the stage for broadcast ministries.

Evangelical broadcasters, however, met with resistance from regulatory agencies and mainline churches. The government's initial reluctance to provide time for evangelical broadcasts can be traced to several factors, although two personalities had much to do with federal decisions. AIMEE SEMPLE MCPHERSON, the famed INTERNATIONAL CHURCH OF THE FOURSQUARE GOSPEL revivalist, dominated the airwaves with her radio broadcasts and even refused orders from secretary of commerce Herbert Hoover to desist from broadcasting because of her unregulated use of radio bandwidth. Hoover, however, lacked sufficient authority to implement his directive. McPherson's defiance, along with the increasingly radical political statements of another broadcaster, Father Charles Coughlin, necessitated tighter control of the airwaves by the Federal Communications Commission (FCC). Established by the Communications Act of 1934, the FCC created a special category of broadcast time for edifying programming called "sustaining," or "free time." Stations and networks allotted this time through the mainline Federal, later NATIONAL COUNCIL OF CHURCHES (NCC) to mainline broadcasters who provided inoffensive programming to fill the required slots, continuing a tradition begun in 1928 with the relationship between the NBC network and mainline churches. Most stations also proved reluctant to sell time outright; thus evangelical broadcasters found themselves scrambling for airtime.

The first religious television broadcasts occurred on Easter Sunday 1940, with the airing of Catholic and Protestant services. In 1952 Bishop Fulton J. Sheen, who officiated the Catholic broadcast, became the first religious figure to offer a regular program, the Emmy-award winning "Life is Worth Living." Although Bishop Sheen benefited from network sponsorship, evangelical broadcasters required more startup capital and advocacy. To help obtain the necessary airtime evangelical broadcasters formed the National Religious Broadcasters (NRB) in 1944, a group that gained increasing clout as a Washington lobby. By 1953 televangelist Rex Humbard began broadcasting to local stations in Ohio, and ORAL ROBERTS interrupted his tent revivals to broadcast on January 10, 1954. JERRY FALWELL rounded out the triumvirate of evangelical broadcast pioneers in 1957, and his "Old Time Gospel Hour" helped launch Liberty University along with his later political ambitions.

Several landmark changes beginning in the 1960s marked the end of the NCC's dominance of religious broadcasting. First, the FCC ruled in 1960 that no difference existed between "paid-time" and "sustaining-time," at least as required by FCC regulations for edifying programming. This meant, in practice, that networks could sell their allotments of sustaining time at significant profit while still fulfilling FCC requirements. Mainline denominations could not afford such luxuries; but televangelists, relying on extensive donor support, could. Second, the development of tape in the early 1960s allowed broadcast distribution and syndication. Finally, by the 1970s satellite and cable distribution became possible, which further allowed the proliferation of the Gospel over the nation's airwaves.

Televangelism: Personalities, Messages, and Audiences

Among the televangelical superstars, BILLY GRAHAM stands most prominent, although his crusades appear only irregularly as media events. Nevertheless, he typically appears in prime time, a practice few televangelists can afford. The next tier includes the other pioneers of the 1950s: Falwell, Humbard, and Roberts. PAT ROBERTSON joined this group with the purchase of a defunct UHF station in 1959 in Portsmouth, Virginia for far less than its market value. His flagship program, "The 700 Club," although initiated by Jim Bakker, became a staple of religious programming, helping Robertson build a cable television empire, Regent University, and, ultimately, the Christian Coalition. Jim and Tammy Faye Bakker launched their own cable network in the 1970s, and their "Praise the Lord" program regularly drew hundreds of thousands

of viewers until the Bakkers' scandalous collapse in 1987. Much the same could be said of Jimmy Swaggart, whose rise in the 1970s was equaled by his rapid decline after a series of sex scandals. Robert Schuller completed the list of early heavyweights with his message of positive thinking gleaned from noted optimist NORMAN VINCENT PEALE of the Marble Collegiate Church in New York City. The only mainline televangelist with a significant following, Schuller is best known for his "Crystal Cathedral" in Garden Grove, California, an all-glass edifice complete with drive-in stalls for cars, hearkening back to Schuller's humble beginnings preaching on the roof of a snack bar at a drive-in theater.

Current celebrities include Paul and Jan Crouch, whose own cable and satellite ministry, the Trinity Broadcasting Network (TBN), has grown into a televangelical empire, providing airtime for almost every major televangelist. TBN has also moved aggressively into international markets, buying stations and beaming broadcasts to an ever-expanding list of countries. Benny Hinn appears frequently on TBN, broadcasting miracle crusades from across the country that feature Hinn's healing powers. Kenneth Copeland, also a noted healer and former pilot of Oral Roberts, appears often on TBN's only rival, the DayStar Network founded in 1997 by Marcus and Joni Lamb.

Among the multitude of programs, one can trace five basic formats, excepting church broadcasts that remain mostly local phenomena: revival crusades that often feature live music and healing, talk-show formats modeled after "The Tonight Show," prophecy programs that highlight current events as "signs of the times," newsmagazines that resemble major network morning news programs, and a fifth category characterized by its familiarity and "living room" feel. Billy Graham and Jimmy Swaggart have both used the crusade format with great success. Jim Bakker's defunct "Praise the Lord" program featured him as an evangelical Johnny Carson, mixing in the country-gospel melodies of Tammy Faye. Jack van Impe's weekly broadcasts interpret news headlines in light of his eschatological perspectives. Pat Robertson's "700 Club" has perfected the newsmagazine format, featuring a slick newscast that leads off the program before the anchorperson turns to Robertson for his interpretation of world events. Co-hosted by Terry Meeuwson, the "700 Club" also spotlights testimonials of CONVERSION and miraculous deliverance from sickness and debt, along with "soft" segments that deal with mundane topics such as cooking and investment strategies. TBN's "Praise the Lord" program best typifies the fifth format, as guests make themselves at home amid an elaborate, *nouveau riche* rococo backdrop that suggests material success, with participants alternating between PRAYER, prophecy, discussions of current events, and an occasional country-gospel performance.

Despite the diversity of formats, however, the program content remains somewhat homogeneous. Most, with the exception of Graham and Swaggart, suggest that Christians ought to have abundant success in *this* world. Kenneth Copeland claims the believer can be freed from the demons of disease, whereas Oral Roberts, to name just one example, believes in "seed faith" and "giving out of one's need." That is, if one lacks sufficient material success, one ought to give to the televangelist who will ensure that God will provide a positive turn on the "seed," or investment. A second pervasive theme of televangelism is its conservative political content. Although not all ministries adopt such political tones, Pat Robertson, Jerry Falwell, and James Robison, especially, have acted centrally in the development of the so-called Religious or CHRISTIAN RIGHT.

Program audiences tend to be disproportionately female. Jimmy Swaggart did best among male viewers, at least before his departure, despite a two-to-one female-to-male ratio. The elderly are also overrepresented, tuning in especially to Jimmy Swaggart, along with prosperity programs like those of Oral Roberts, and, more recently, TBN. Pat Robertson's "700 Club" reverses the age trend somewhat, attracting many younger viewers, attributed in part to the high production values and content geared toward working professionals. Minorities are also overrepresented, along with those on the economic and social margins. Finally, viewers tend to concentrate in the South. Robert Schuller, whose "Hour of Power" has done reasonably well on the West Coast and in the Midwest, provides a notable exception.

Controversies

Televangelism has been an object of controversy from its earliest days. Its heavy reliance on financial appeals has raised suspicions and many critics have suspected, and occasionally found, widespread fraud. The criticism of the Electronic Church seems at least partially validated by the embarrassing financial and sex scandals of Jim Bakker and Jimmy Swaggart in the late 1980s. Moreover the same period also witnessed Oral Roberts's increasingly intense appeals for funds, including his vision in 1980 of a 900-foot Jesus who commanded him to raise funds for a new hospital, along with his 1987 claim that God would "call him home" if he failed to raise $8 million for the project. Combined with the high-profile scandals of lesser figures like Robert Tilton, whose ministry collapsed

after the 1991 airing of a *Prime Time Live* expose, audience shares fell dramatically by 1992.

The entry of televangelists into national POLITICS in 1980 proved even more alarming to its critics. After James Robison and a consortium of televangelists unofficially blessed the presidential candidacy of Ronald Reagan at the National Affairs Briefing in Dallas, Texas, critics became shrill in their assaults on the Electronic Church. Jerry Falwell's MORAL MAJORITY helped consolidate a cross section of conservative Protestantism to further their mutual political interests, intensifying the anxieties of many on the left. Even Pat Robertson's failed bid for the Republican nomination in 1988 led to a more powerful political entity, the Christian Coalition, which by 1992 became a major force within the Republican Party.

Beyond money and politics, however, some critics have charged that the Electronic Church has not only failed to follow the Great Commission but, through its application of a rational, businesslike calculus to spiritual matters, has cheapened the grace it purports to dispense. Critic Quentin J. Schultze, who has conducted extensive studies of the Electronic Church from both sociological and theological perspectives, has also questioned whether the mere presence of the Electronic Church has weakened the creedal emphasis and theological gravity of nonbroadcast ministries. Noting the increasing de-emphasis of THEOLOGY in evangelical churches in favor of entertainment ministries, Schultze fears that new generations of Evangelicals, raised at least partially on TV PREACHING, will demand less substance and more style, mirroring the inherent limitations of the televisual format. Such claims will require time to evaluate as cultural trends develop. Nevertheless, Schultze's charges seem more apt than the cynical observations of those who perceive rampant hucksterism. On the contrary, as Schultze notes, televangelists for the most part are probably sincere in their beliefs, which may, ironically, intensify the allegedly harmful effects they have on more traditional theologies and styles of WORSHIP.

Conclusions

Despite aggressive international expansion, televangelism persists as a distinctly American phenomenon, enduring despite periodic scandals. New figures continue to emerge, and even veterans like Pat Robertson strive to reinvent themselves, adapting to ever-changing audience demands. This audience, however, appears finite. Although it is inconclusive whether electronic ministries siphon funds from brick-and-mortar ministries, televangelists do seem to compete against each other for a limited supply of potential donors. Nevertheless, the electronic church perseveres because, in spite of its critics, it does appear to provide a service to some that brick-and-mortar churches either cannot or will not provide. In a spiritual economy the donations flow to those who best meet the needs of consumers; and televangelism, built on a business ethos, rapidly perceives and adapts to those needs. This is both its strength and a major source of its criticisms. Nevertheless, like its revivalist forebears who rankled the sensibilities of established churches, televangelism will continue as a unique blend of American pragmatism and popular entertainment, combined with the Gospel of Jesus Christ. Thus while critics may decry it as fraudulent or even idolatrous, it will likely endure so long as pious viewers find benefit in its programming. Whether it furthers the Great Commission and preaches to more than the choir, however, remains unclear.

See also Evangelicalism; Evangelism, Overview; Faith Healing; Mass Media

References and Further Reading

Frankl, Razelle. *Televangelism: The Marketing of Popular Religion.* Carbondale: Southern Illinois University Press, 1987.

Hadden, Jeffrey K. "The Rise and Fall of American Televangelism." *The Annals of the American Academy of Political and Social Science* 527 (May 1993): 113–130.

———, and Anson Shupe. *Televangelism: Power and Politics on God's Frontier.* New York: Henry Holt, 1988.

———, and Charles E. Swann. *Prime Time Preachers: The Rising Power of Televangelism.* Reading, MA: Addison-Wesley, 1981.

Harding, Susan Friend. *The Book of Jerry Falwell: Fundamentalist Language and Politics.* Princeton: Princeton University Press, 2000.

Horsfield, Peter G. *Religious Television: The American Experience.* New York: Longman, 1984.

Martin, William. *With God on Our Side: The Rise of the Religious Right in America.* New York: Broadway Books, 1996.

Melton, J. Gordon, Phillip Charles Lucas, and Jon R. Stone. *Prime-Time Religion: An Encyclopedia of Religious Broadcasting.* Phoenix, AZ: Oryx Press, 1997.

Peck, Janice. *The Gods of Televangelism: The Crisis of Meaning and the Appeal of Religious Television.* Cresskill, NJ: Hampton Press, 1993.

Schultze, Quentin J. *Televangelism and American Culture: The Business of Popular Religion.* Grand Rapids, MI: Baker, 1991.

GLENN W. SHUCK

TEMPERANCE

When the ship *Arabella* came into port in the Massachusetts Colony in 1630, the new settlers unloaded 10,000 gallons of beer and 12 gallons of distilled spirits, and this was only the communal supply. Each family had packed its own liquor and home-brewing equipment. Although a few of the Puritan colonial governments passed laws against excessive drinking, colonial New Englanders in general tranquilly imbibed their rum in moderation. Kentucky and Pennsylvania frontier settlers swilled their corn and bourbon whiskey, the latter, supposedly, first produced by a minister. Although the Quakers (see FRIENDS, SOCIETY OF) had taken an early temperance stand (seen in minister Elizabeth Levis's temperance pamphlet of 1761), churched and unchurched Americans generally viewed alcohol as essential as bread and safer than water. Men, women, and even children downed their "toddies" at breakfast, had "eleveners" at mid-day instead of tea, and sipped their afternoon whiskey "drams." In the mid-1800s, after the arrival of hundreds of thousands of German immigrants and major technological advances in mechanical refrigeration and integrated transportation, beer became the all-American drink of choice, especially lager beer.

After the Revolutionary War, some elites in the newly established nation feared that the people lacked the self-control necessary to handle an experiment in democracy. Religious, political, and economic leaders feared the fine line between democracy and anarchy. For "rule by the people" to work, the people had to be self-restrained, disciplined, educated, and focused. A little alcohol-induced pleasure was good—even necessary—when the colonials faced British oppression, but a keen mind and strong body would be needed to keep the fledgling democracy afloat.

Changing Attitudes

Medical authorities provided the theoretical grounding for this shift in attitude toward alcohol, but it was evangelical CLERGY who launched the "temperance" movement into a major reform crusade. In his pamphlet *An Inquiry into the Effects of Ardent Spirits Upon the Human Body and Mind* (1784), Dr. Benjamin Rush reversed conventional wisdom by pronouncing distilled liquor bad for human health. Protestant clergy carried this torch of medical discovery into the moral and political sphere. About the time of the Second Great Awakening (see AWAKENINGS), with its perfectionist message that humans could hasten the coming millennium by improving themselves morally, well-known preachers like LYMAN BEECHER gave sermons on the biblical basis for temperance. Evangelical clergymen led the way in forming organizations to promote temperance, the most widespread being the American Temperance Society (ATS), founded in 1826. Basing its organization closely on evangelical tract and missionary societies, the ATS spread its gospel of temperance via the spoken and written word. It sent out itinerant temperance speakers to organize local auxiliaries and deluged the country with temperance tracts and a weekly newspaper. Temperance as an issue transcended doctrinal infighting, bringing white Protestants together around their common interest in moral reformation and national prosperity. By 1835, the ATS reached a peak of 1.5 million members, possibly as many as one in five free adults. The membership was varied in age and gender, with about 50 percent female and a significant contingent of young men in college as a result of campus REVIVALS that combined Christianity and abstinence in the call to CONVERSION.

In the 1830s, the ATS became a largely middle-class movement when it changed its abstinence pledge from a focus on distilled liquors (aimed at the poor) to include a pledge against wine (aimed at the upper classes). Members from the upper classes rejected this new "teetotalism" of the renamed American Temperance Union (ATU), and a significant number of clergy and lay people also rejected teetotalism, but for a different reason: its impact on their communion, or LORD'S SUPPER, service. For example, although the Methodist Episcopal Church strongly advocated temperance, it did not accept the substitution of unfermented wine in communion until fifty years later, in 1880.

Teetotalism caused the Protestant-initiated movement to fragment during the 1840s, but a new type of temperance group emerged to renew enthusiasm. In 1840, six working-class, unchurched tavern drinkers founded the Washingtonians, the first temperance group among the poor and working classes. Most of the Protestants who joined the Washingtonian societies came from Methodist and Baptist churches; conspicuously absent were the Congregational, Unitarian, and Presbyterian clergymen who had led the early temperance movement.

Cultural Weapons

Almost all of the temperance efforts until the 1850s focused on moral suasion. In addition to formal societies, the temperance message spread through popular culture, usually according to heavily Protestant plots and narratives that positioned conversion and piety as the solutions to intemperance. Temperance literature hit the print market as popular authors like Timothy Shay Arthur, Louisa May Alcott, E. D. E. N. Southworth, and others gave the country heroes and heroines who eschewed booze or courageously recovered from it. Arthur's "Ten Nights in a Barroom" (1854) sold millions of copies and was a Broadway blockbuster even in the early 1900s. In this pathos-packed story, Joe Morgan's life is ruined because evil saloonkeeper Simon Slade gets him hooked on booze. Joe finally turns his life around after Slade accidently kills

Joe's daughter, little Mary Morgan, in a saloon brawl. There were visual images as well: "Drunkard's Progress" (1846) by Nathaniel Currier etched into people's minds the steps of degeneration from "first glass to drunkard's grave." The well-dressed man sips a glass of whiskey with a friend in the first frame and by the last frame, he has suffered jail (for robbery and rioting), disease, unemployment, humiliation of his family, loss of friends, poverty, and suicide.

This massive cultural assault against liquor, combined with the influx of Italian, German, and Russian immigrants, convinced many native-born Protestants that moral suasion alone would never solve the problem of intemperance. In 1851, Maine was the first state to make the sale of liquor illegal, and several other states followed with similar laws. The temperance movement's shift from moral suasion to legal coercion provoked thousands of evangelical Protestant women to join, and eventually take over, the temperance movement.

Although the male temperance fraternities (the Sons of Temperance, founded in 1842, and the Independent Order of Good Templars, founded in 1851) revived after the CIVIL WAR, it was female temperance activism that flourished between 1873 and 1901. Protestant women, including Annie Wittenmyer (first president of the Woman's Christian Temperance Union) and Mother Eliza Stewart (leader of the Woman's Temperance Crusade), served as federally appointed "sanitation" leaders during the Civil War and found they liked public leadership. Temperance work, they discovered, was an "acceptable" arena for them to continue their public advocacy. Because evangelical Protestantism had pedestalized WOMEN as the morally superior sex, women in the Northeast and Midwest used this to their own advantage when critics accused them of moving out of their "proper" sphere. Temperance, they replied, was a moral problem requiring legal action, and the best solution lay in the work of the morally superior sex.

A Women's Movement

In the Woman's Crusade of 1873–1874, hundreds of thousands of women in thirty-one states marched in bands to pray and sing in front of local saloons. Women usually sought to avoid saloons by crossing the street or detouring for blocks. When they had to enter a saloon to purchase milk or other items, they would use the discreet "ladies' entrance." But the Woman's Crusade marchers went right to the front doors. They had an axe to grind (sometimes literally) with saloons, because women tended to suffer the most from excessive drinking. An alcoholic husband had the legal right to liquidate all communally held property, as well as his and his wife's wages in the saloons. Drunken men frequently beat or abandoned their wives and, because of the saloon's reliance on prostitution as a drawing card to clients, they also passed on syphilis and gonorrhea to their wives. If not threatened at home by a violent or negligent alcoholic male, women faced the threat in streets where they were often physically and verbally harassed. Drunken rowdies even disrupted church services by making commotion in the aisles or hurling bottles through the windows. Women were virtually powerless over the quality of their own and their children's lives, and they were barred by law or custom from divorcing inebriate husbands. Without the ballot, they could not vote against the liquor industry either. Women were eyewitnesses to the way that saloons, as they believed, caused the irreversible degeneration of men and boys. Saloon-smasher Carry Nation saw her first husband go to an early grave, leaving her in poverty, because of a saloon in her hometown's Masonic lodge. Eliza Thompson, the revered leader of the Woman's Crusade of 1873, grieved the loss of her minister son, who died in an asylum for "inebriates."

The saloons, in addition to ruining their lives and livelihoods, reinscribed women's political marginalization, because they served as clearinghouses for underground exchanges of money and favors to which women did not have access. They were bastions of male privilege. Saloons also were often used as polling stations, where unknowing wanderers enticed inside for a drink could be persuaded to vote a certain way. In New York City during the late nineteenth century, more than one-half of the nominating conventions held by major parties occurred in saloons. The saloons also symbolized the rise of male leisure and a growing commercialism that tapped into it. Already alienated from the market economy and lagging behind men in "leisure" consumption, women were angry at the saloons for further cordoning off spaces of male privilege and taking the men (and their money) away from the family.

The greatest contribution of the 1873–1874 Woman's Crusade was its galvanization of women into the first mass organization of women, the Woman's Christian Temperance Union (WCTU). The WCTU was founded in 1874 by Protestant women, many of them connected through the Methodst-initiated summer Chautauqua program. By the late nineteenth century, the WCTU outnumbered all other women's politically oriented organizations, including all of the various national suffrage associations combined. Unlike the suffrage organizations, the WCTU did not permit male sympathizers or affiliates to vote; it was an organization run by women for women. Under the leadership of President FRANCES WILLARD (1879–

1898) and her "do everything" policy, the WCTU added many other reforms to its temperance agenda, including suffrage—an agenda that further made it impossible for conservative Protestant Southern women to join. The WCTU functioned as a political training school where women learned about constitutional law, petitioning, lobbying, partisan politics, public speaking, organizing marches, planning large meetings, labor issues, infrastructure, public education, advertising, and more. The WCTU paper admonished members to own three books: "the Bible, a copy of the state laws, and a copy of the city laws."

Most women entered the WCTU because it was a religiously inspired effort to promote the moral virtues of temperance and purity. But once in the WCTU, many initially conservative women began to work for progressive reforms like suffrage, welfare, sanitation, and child labor laws. Historians debate whether the WCTU ultimately liberated women or simply reinforced conventional GENDER roles, but clearly in many cases, the WCTU empowered women to assert policy and legislation that they believed would liberate their sex from the clutches of liquor-lubricated oppression. Without a doubt, the organization never lost its original religious inspiration. Even though efforts were made to include Catholic women and unchurched women, the WCTU remained an "arm" of the Protestant churches. Significantly, whereas most Protestant denominations did not ordain women into the preaching ministry until the mid–twentieth century, the WCTU gave those with an aptitude and desire to preach the opportunity to have a career as an "evangelist" or "lecturer," and many women discovered their aptitude for PREACHING through lecturing on temperance. Mabel Madeline Southard, for example, was the only female member of the ministerial association at her college. But when she graduated and realized that she would not be given a Methodist Episcopal pastorate like all of her male colleagues, she entered the WCTU to work as an "evangelist."

Drive to Prohibition

The WCTU was at the forefront of temperance advocacy during the 1880s, joining other organizations, including the Prohibition Party, to fight for national prohibition. But the prohibition movement became divided over procedure and goals, especially in the 1890s. Some activists were "abolitionists," whose goal was immediate abolishment of the entire liquor industry because it was seen as a moral and social evil and the main cause of other problems such as poverty, disease, and corruption. These radical reformers also tended to be "broad gaugers," uniting around a constellation of reforms like women's suffrage and progressive taxation. They expressed impatience with the "regulationists" like the Anti-Saloon League (ASL), who sought to work within existing political structures to regulate liquor consumption and keep the liquor industry in check through licensing. Unlike all of the other temperance organizations, the ASL had a single goal: prohibition. Founded in 1893 by Congregationalist minister Howard Hyde Russell, the ASL rose to dominate the temperance movement in the early 1900s. Most historians credit the ASL's lobbying, single-mindedness, and local-option gradualism with achieving the Eighteenth Amendment, which was finally ratified in 1919. The Protestant churches played a key role in the success of the ASL. Whereas the Prohibition Party had become so alienated from the Protestant denominations that it formed its own "prohibition churches" during the 1890s, the ASL aligned itself with the Protestant churches, describing itself as "the Church in Action Against the Saloon." Three-fifths of the ASL leadership was composed of Protestant clergymen, and they relied on local pastors to build up the League's grassroots organization. Cooperating churches set aside one Sunday each month for an ASL "field day" at which representatives solicited pledges and gave reports on the progress of the movement.

After a successful campaign effort to have Republican Herbert Hoover elected over the "wet" Democratic (and Catholic) candidate Al Smith in 1928, the ASL lost influence. The economic crisis shifted attention away from alcohol as the burning issue. Americans voted in Franklin D. Roosevelt, a wet, for the economic recovery he promised, knowing that he favored repealing national prohibition. The Twenty-First Amendment was ratified in 1933.

New Methods

Thereafter, the most influential efforts to address drinking steered away from both moral suasion and legal coercion, focusing instead on a fusion of self-improvement and loosely defined spirituality. Certainly many Pentecostal, Fundamentalist, and Evangelical Protestant churches preached abstinence throughout the twentieth century; however, they usually limited their preachments about alcohol to their own members. As with many aspects of social and political life in an increasingly religiously diverse society, Protestants had to give up their custodial role regarding American drinking habits. Secularized "experts" in a burgeoning treatment industry took over the mantle of alcohol awareness and recovery; nonetheless, segments of this industry bore the marks of the spiritual origins of temperance concerns.

Alcoholics Anonymous (AA) invites people with drinking problems to rely on their "higher power" for help in overcoming addiction, as well as faithfully attend meetings and be accountable to another person who has achieved sobriety. AA was founded in 1935 by Wall Street businessman Bill Wilson and Dr. Robert Smith after Wilson had experienced a spiritual awakening in a hospital for alcoholics. The founders drew heavily from the evangelical Protestant movement called the Oxford Group (later called MORAL REARMAMENT). For example, Wilson and Smith incorporated several of the Oxford Group's practices: the self-survey, confession, amends to those harmed by one's actions, service to others, and sense of group support. But Wilson and Smith avoided those aspects that turned people off, such as the pressure to make a religious commitment and the requirement to identify oneself. By the late 1970s, AA claimed some 1 million active members worldwide, including 350,000 in the United States.

The popularity of AA rose at the same time that drinking became more and more widespread, with abstinence decreasing from 45 percent of the adult population in 1959 to 29 percent in 1977. In previous times, Protestants would have blamed such low abstinence rates for social chaos, family breakdown, and economic malaise. The failure of national prohibition changed this. However, although late twentieth-century Protestants rarely mentioned alcohol, they did carry on the temperance crusade's legacy of political and legal coercion to advance their position on a variety of moral issues, from ABORTION to same-sex marriage to the legalization of drugs. The issue changed, but the strategy of legislating morality remained.

See also Evangelism

References and Further Reading

Bader, Robert Smith. *Prohibition in Kansas*. Lawrence, KS: University of Kansas Press, 1986.

Blocker, Jack Jr. *"Give to the Winds Thy Fears": Woman's Temperance Crusade, 1873–1874*. Westport, CT: Greenwood Press, 1985.

———. *American Temperance Movements: Cycles of Reform*. Boston, MA: Twayne Publishers, 1989.

Bordin, Ruth. *Woman and Temperance: The Quest for Power and Liberty, 1873–1900*. Philadelphia, PA: Temple University Press, 1981.

Crowley, John, ed. *Drunkard's Progress: Narratives of Addiction, Despair, and Recovery*. Baltimore, MD: Johns Hopkins University Press, 1999.

Fahey, David. *Temperance and Racism: John Bull, Johnny Reb, and the Good Templars*. Lexington, KY: University Press of Kentucky, 1996.

Grace, Fran. *Carry A. Nation: Retelling the Life*. Bloomington, IN: Indiana University Press, 2001.

Gusfield, James. *Status Politics and the American Temperance Movement.* Urbana, IL: University of Illinois Press, 1963.

Kerr, Austin. *Organized for Reform: A New History of the Anti-Saloon League.* New Haven, CT: Yale University Press, 1985.

Parker, Alison M. *Purifying America: Women, Cultural Reform, and Pro Censorship Activism, 1873–1933.* Urbana, IL: University of Illinois Press, 1997.

Pegram, Thomas. *Battling Demon Rum: The Struggle for a Dry America, 1800–1933.* Chicago, IL: Ivan Dee, 1998.

FRAN GRACE

TEMPLE, FREDERICK (1821–1902)

Archbishop of Canterbury. Noted for his involvement in some of the most controversial issues facing the Victorian Church, Frederick Temple was born on November 30, 1821 in Santa Maura (Lefkada) in the Greek Ionian Islands. He was educated at Balliol College, Oxford and ordained to the Anglican priesthood in 1847. His early career as an educational reformer culminated with his appointment as headmaster of the prestigious public school at Rugby in 1857.

Temple contributed the lead article to the controversial *Essays and Reviews,* a collection of works by noted Anglican liberals published in 1860 to the dismay of traditional churchmen. The article gained Temple a reputation as a liberal and caused some public embarrassment when he was elevated to the bishopric of Exeter in 1869. As bishop he supported the Education Act of 1870 and, in 1884, delivered the Bampton Lectures at Oxford on religion and science, an attempt to reconcile orthodox Christian beliefs with DARWINISM. In 1885 Temple was consecrated bishop of London and, in 1897, was elevated to the archbishopric of CANTERBURY, where he served until his death on December 22, 1902. Frederick Temple married Beatrice Blanche in 1876 and had two sons, including WILLIAM (b. 1881), who was also archbishop of Canterbury from 1942 to 1944 and was one of the most prominent Anglican churchmen of the twentieth century.

Frederick Temple's active career spanned an important period in the history of the English Church when Christianity was confronted with the challenges of modernization and unbelief. He participated in debates over such issues as the relationship between religion and science, the role of the Christian churches in public education, the relationship between the CHURCH OF ENGLAND and the Roman Catholic Church, and the nature of Anglican ritual. Temple was essentially a moderate who attempted to reconcile modernist trends in Victorian CULTURE with orthodox ANGLICANISM and a conservative acceptance of ecclesiastical AUTHORITY.

See also Liberal Protestantism and Liberalism; Modernism

References and Further Reading

Primary Source:

Temple, Frederick. *The Relations between Religion and Science.* New York: Macmillan, 1884.

Secondary Sources:

Hinchliff, Peter. *Frederick Temple, Archbishop of Canterbury.* Oxford: Oxford University Press, 1998.

Sandford, E. G., ed. *Memoirs of Archbishop Temple by Seven Friends.* London: Macmillan, 1906.

RICHARD J. JANET

TEMPLE, WILLIAM (1881–1944)

Archbishop of Canterbury. Of all the archbishops of Canterbury, William Temple has been described as the most distinguished successor to St. Anselm. He was born in the Bishop's Palace in Exeter on October 15, 1881; and apart from brief terms as fellow and lecturer in Queen's College, headmaster of Repton School, as rector of St. James, Piccadilly, and head of the Life and Liberty Movement, he lived most of his life in bishop's palaces. In 1916 he and Frances Anson were married. After a brief canonry at Westminster he was consecrated bishop of Manchester in 1921, and enthroned as archbishop of York in 1929. At the time of his death on October 26, 1944, he was archbishop of Canterbury. He is buried alongside his father, FREDERICK TEMPLE, in the cloisters of Canterbury Cathedral; they are the only father and son to sit on St. Augustine's throne.

Natively brilliant and classically trained, he was the author of more than fifty books and a vastly larger number of essays. The master influences on his life, he said, were Plato, St. John, and ROBERT BROWNING. His lifelong socialist convictions were developed while an Oxford undergraduate in Balliol College, and his philosophical theology begins with a view "far nearer to Materialism than Idealism."

In the nineteenth century "natural theology" consisted of thought about God conducted without reference to the BIBLE, whereas "revealed religion" was human response to the self-disclosure of God as contained in the Bible. By the 1930s, when Temple delivered his Gifford Lectures, this distinction had been changed, and concern had shifted from the "content" of particular beliefs to the "method" that underwrote and supported them. Is the Bible itself the revelation, or the record of revelation? Is revelation in the book or the events recorded in the book? Temple's answer was succinct: plainly revelation cannot be in the book unless first in the events recorded in the book. Revelation, in his view, does not consist in propositional truths about God; instead, it is the "coincidence of divine event and human appreciation," and must incorporate both communication and apprehension. What is offered, therefore, in any specific revelation is not a truth concerning the subject, but the living subject him/herself.

Temple held that philosophy attempts a problem—to construct a conception of God (or "Mind") equal to the universe, whereas THEOLOGY attempts a theorem—to show that God is equal to the universe. Were philosophy able to achieve its goal of a single system, explanatory of the world, we would have a theistic worldview. However, philosophy cannot achieve its goal because it confronts a world over whose destiny we appear to have little control. The most important question, therefore, inquires about the nature and character of that AUTHORITY that does order and control the world process.

Yielding that question to sheer *ratio,* Temple believed, results in frustration and uncertainty because we cannot comprehend the full range of experience and fact. Lacking that comprehensiveness and clarity, the philosophical method of intellection is driven back on itself and readied, through despair, for the answer that Christian theism posits. While at Repton School Temple wrote in *Religious Experience and Other Essays and Addresses* (1913): "The whole of my theology is an attempt to understand and verify the words, 'He that hath seen me hath seen the Father' " (p. 21); and four years later the first book of the trilogy that would define his theology was published.

Mens Creatrix (1917) was Temple's response to Henri Bergson's *Creative Evolution.* It was his philosophical attempt to show that the Christian Incarnation supplies the central point: actual belief in a living God rests primarily on religious experience, but it finds intellectual support because it is a belief that is capable of supplying an explanation of purpose in the universe, which no other hypothesis available to us offers any hope of doing. Temple's theism is dialectical, resting on a convergence of both philosophy and religious experience, rationality, and faith.

Temple's CHRISTOLOGY is more concerned about the character of God than the identity of the historical Jesus. In *Christus Veritas* (1924), the theological companion to *Mens Creatrix,* he argued that the human search for meaning finds its answer only in the central event of Incarnation. Although rejecting any form of external compulsion, Temple nevertheless believed that the miracle of Incarnation—because it offers persons a reference for meaning, purpose, and value that is other than themselves—is (almost!) irresistibly at-

tractive. One does not worship a principle, and Jesus Christ's "human personality is actually the self-expression of the Eternal Son" (pp. 150–151). Temple graphically represented the many points of human experience as on the circumference of a circle, all of which point inward in search of a unifying core postulate that, in turn, points outward to embrace the entire circumference of the circle. That core postulate is Jesus Christ who emancipates us from failed attempts to discover for ourselves our own *raison d'être:* "You could not cure yourself; but God has offered the means of your cure in Christ."

Temple's Gifford Lectures, *Nature, Man and God* (1934) laid out his "dialectical realism." In it he argued for personal theism by beginning with the world as offered by science and, thereafter, showing how only a special revelation of the God who is both immanent and transcendent makes it finally intelligible. Reality exists in a series of ascending and descending grades or strata; and he employed a Platonic motif to describe a perceptible scale of reality that ranged "from mere inorganic matter at one end, through organic matter, vegetable life, animal life, to personality as we know it in human life" (Muirhead 1925:214).

"Matter, life, mind, and spirit" were his abbreviated categories for this continuous whole. In his scheme the lower forms are necessary to the actualization of the higher ones, whereas, coincidentally, the lower forms find their purpose and meaning only when employed by a higher one as the instrument of its self-expression. These strata were presided over by what he called "personality" or "intelligent purpose," which provides the "governing principle" of the world process. Mind is purposive when it no longer merely adjusts itself to its environment but adjusts its environment to its own ends.

Experience is thus always of the real world; and mind, when conscious, is always engaged directly in apprehending reality. This basic correspondence of mind with reality is the core postulate for value inasmuch as it is good to know the real. Things do not possess value as an extended attribute of a knowing mind; value in real objects is primarily in the object. Still, value *qua* value is latent until actualized by an appreciating subject, and value only becomes actual in and through subjective appreciation of the value of an object. Value is a relational category that signifies that what is given to us in experience is the value *of* an object and a value *for* the subject.

A further clue from this ontology, epistemology, and axiology is what Temple calls the "sacramental universe," in which the apparent good is also the real good and where the "material" has been made a vehicle for the "spiritual." On these terms "inward and spiritual grace" is conveyed only through matter, and the sacraments are "real" because they are not dependent on psychological verification or validation for their efficacy.

References and Further Reading

Primary Sources:

Temple, William. *Basic Convictions*. London: Harper Brothers, 1936.
———. *Christianity and Social Order*. New York: Penguin Books, 1942.
———. *Christus Veritas*. London: Macmillan and Company, Ltd., 1924.
———. *Mens Creatrix*. London: Macmillan and Company, Ltd., 1917.
———. *Nature, Man and God*. London: Macmillan and Company, 1935.
———. *Nazi Massacres of the Jews and Others*. London: V. Gallancz, 1943.
———. *Readings in St. John's Gospel*. 2 vols. London: Macmillan and Company, 1949.
———. *Religious Experience and Other Essays and Addresses*. 1913.

Secondary Sources:

Baker, A. E., ed. *William Temple's Teaching*. Philadelphia: Westminster Press, 1951.
Iremonger, F. I. *William Temple, Archbishop of Canterbury: His Life and Letters*. London: Oxford University Press, 1948.
Muirhead, J. H. *Contemporary British Philosophy*. London: Allen & Unwin; New York: Macmillan, 1924–1925.

HARMON L. SMITH

TENNENT, GILBERT (1703–1764)

Presbyterian minister and Great Awakening evangelist. Tennent was born in IRELAND, the oldest, most gifted son of a Scotch-Irish minister who immigrated to Pennsylvania. Educated in his father's "log college," Gilbert received his M.A. from Yale and entered the Presbyterian ministry in 1725. The Scottish tradition of promoting REVIVALS through prolonged LORD'S SUPPER celebrations bore fruit in his New Jersey parish. Tennent led a minority group in the Philadelphia Presbytery, called the New Lights or New Side, which supported the AWAKENINGS and assessed ministerial candidates on personal piety rather than education.

Interaction with GEORGE WHITEFIELD further emboldened Tennent's demand for revival. The mounting tensions in the presbytery increased with Tennent's famous sermon of 1740 on "The Danger of an Unconverted Ministry," which derisively likened antirevival ministers to a "Man who would learn others to swim, before he has learn'd it himself." In 1741 Old Side pastors responded, enacting seven protestations expelling the New Lights. The Tennents and their supporters formed the conjoint presbyteries of New Brunswick and Londonberry, which later joined with the New York Presbytery to form the Synod of New York.

The Old Side/New Side schism lasted until 1758 with Tennent laying the groundwork for reunion and serving as the first moderator of the reunited synod. The fervor of the revivals waning, he backed off the extreme characterizations of his opponents, and in 1749 Tennent passionately argued for Christian union in "Irenicum Ecclesiasticum." Seeking middle ground, Tennent combined education with piety in the training of ministers. He left an institutional legacy in Princeton College, for which he and the Rev. SAMUEL DAVIES solicited the initial financial support in Great Britain.

See also Presbyterianism

References and Further Reading

Coalter, Milton J. *Gilbert Tennent, Son of Thunder*. New York: Greenwood Press, 1986.
Fishburn, Janet F. "Gilbert Tennent, Established Dissenter." *Church History* 63 no. 1 (1994): 31–49.

STEPHEN R. BERRY

TENNYSON, ALFRED (1809–1892)

English poet. More than any other Victorian poet, Tennyson is remembered for struggles with religious FAITH and doubt. The son of an Anglican priest, Tennyson's Christianity was more intuitional and practical than doctrinal. He was only twenty-four when his closest friend from Cambridge, Arthur Hallam, a young man of brilliant promise, died in 1833. For the next seventeen years Tennyson, who shared the depressive tendencies of many of his family, fought to reconcile his grief with some kind of Christian belief. The result, *In Memoriam*, a series of over 100 short lyrics meditating on Hallam's death, his memory, the meaning of life, and the possibility of immortality in the light of new scientific discoveries in geology and paleontology, was an instant popular success. The tightly controlled verse form, combined with memorable and pithy phrases, produced some of the finest poetry of the period. Many of his lines, "'Tis better to have loved and lost/Than never to have loved at all" and "Nature red in tooth and claw," have passed into the language.

Although it provided few answers, *In Memoriam* caught the then-current mood of metaphysical insecurity, as none of his other works, such as the Arthurian *Idylls of the King,* were to do; and its conclusion, that Hallam was a forerunner of a higher evolutionary type of humanity, seemed to offer a solution that was both scientifically and religiously satisfactory. In retrospect, after Darwin's *Origin of Species* (1859) had made Tennyson's Lamarckian evolution seem facilely optimistic, and the definition of "faith" as "believing where we cannot prove" was questioned, many saw the poems more in terms of expressive doubt than triumphant faith. Nevertheless, it gave Queen Victoria "inexpressible comfort" after the death of Prince Albert, and fame and royal patronage were assured—Tennyson reluctantly accepted both poet laureateship and, eventually, a peerage.

See also Darwinism; Death and Dying; Literature

References and Further Reading

Henderson, Philip. *Tennyson, Poet and Prophet*. London: Routledge & K. Paul, 1978.
Levi, Peter. *Tennyson*. London: Macmillan, 1993.
Marshall, George O. *A Tennyson Handbook*. New York: Twayne Publishers, 1963.

STEPHEN PRICKETT

TETRAPOLITAN CONFESSION

The Tetrapolitan Confession *(Confessio Tetrapolitana),* or "Confession of the Four Cities (Strasbourg, Constance, Memmingen, and Lindau)," was written by MARTIN BUCER and WOLFGANG CAPITO during the 1530 Augsburg Diet.

Emperor Charles V had convened the Augsburg Diet to deal with the REFORMATION controversy besetting the empire, pledging to "hear everybody's opinion" in the matter. This prompted the various Protestant parties to consider drafting statements of their beliefs. MARTIN LUTHER and his Wittenberg colleagues prepared, at the request of Elector John of Saxony, a brief statement but quickly found (because of Johannes Eck's *404 Theses*) that they had to write a more lengthy Confession (the AUGSBURG CONFESSION). The delegates from Strasbourg, in an attempt to unite the Protestant free imperial cities in South Germany with the northern Protestant princes, hoped to secure their signatures to the Augsburg Confession. Because of political complications and distrust between the two factions over Holy Communion (see MARBURG, COLLOQUY OF), this proved impossible. Jacob Sturm, the lead Strasbourg delegate to the diet, hoped to overcome theological disagreement and called on Bucer and Capito in hopes that they might convince the princes to allow Strasbourg to sign the Augsburg Confession.

Bucer was an ideal candidate. Converted to the notion of theological reform by Luther in 1518 and a close theological ally of HULDRYCH ZWINGLI's for a time, Bucer believed that unity was of the utmost importance and dedicated himself to its pursuit. Failing in their attempts to persuade the Lutheran theologians and forbidden by Elector John to sign the Augsburg Confession, the Strasbourg delegates were forced into writing their own confession. Bucer and Capito drafted the Tetrapolitan Confession, which purposefully mimicked PHILIPP MELANCHTHON's Augsburg Confession. Even the article on Holy Communion (Article XVIII) was written in an attempt to persuade the Lutherans of the essential agreement of the Strasbourg position with their own. Ultimately only three other South German cities joined in their support of the Tetrapolitana; the Lutherans rejected it completely. Because it ultimately satisfied no one it was later replaced by other more specific Reformed Confessions.

References and Further Reading

Primary Sources:

Cochrane, Arthur C., ed. *Reformed Confessions of the 16th Century*. Philadelphia: Westminster Press, 1966.
Stupperich, Robert et al., eds. *Martin Bucers Deutsche Schriften*. Vol. 3, 13–185. Gütersloh, Germany: Gütersloher Verlagshaus, 1969.

DAVID M. WHITFORD

THEOLOGY

Protestant theology is faith seeking understanding, *fides quaerens intellectum*. It is a way of speaking of God that arises naturally from the biblical witness to God's saving presence in the world, and which thereby has as its ultimate origin God's Word, the crucified Christ. FAITH in this sense is God's gift of God's Son, in which gift lies the meaning of creation and of ourselves as God's creatures.

Faith seeking understanding is a definition of theology that was made famous by its appearance in the work of Anselm of CANTERBURY, but which comes to characterize most appositely those changes in European thought that occur in the sixteenth century and which have come to be recognized as the Protestant REFORMATION. By understanding faith as something that comes from God, rather than human discovery or ingenuity, the first reformers were able to identify the single most important aspect of how human beings understand their relationship with God. That quality is the way in which humans live *coram deo,* before God. "Living before God," properly understood biblically as a relationship with Jesus of Nazareth, is the starting point of any deeper understanding of Protestant theology.

The biblical origin of this way of thinking about theology can be recognized if one considers the sophisticated interpretation of *coram deo* in MARTIN

LUTHER's early career. Luther, teaching the exegesis of Scripture in Wittenberg 1513–1515 and reacting against the received conventions of several versions of scholasticism, was involved in the study of the Psalms. His work was characterized by a strong emphasis on the fallen nature of human existence as a consequence of SIN, and in particular by the abject unworthiness of human beings in God's eyes. For Luther this reality was constantly in evidence through the manifold temptations that confront humanity, and which humanity constantly fails to resist. Luther's word here for temptation—*Anfechtung*—is vitally important for any understanding of the origins of Protestant theology because of its ability to characterize humanity's fallen nature.

The notion of *Anfechtung* remains with Luther throughout his career, so that not only his own work up until his death in 1546, but also the work of his successors, is best understood in its immediate light. It is, as Gordon Rupp so memorably named it, "that unremitting spiritual conflict which never ends until death" (Rupp 1953:105), and which crucially is nothing less than humanity's just deserts for its sinful nature. Or, better expressed: *Anfechtung* is the manifestation of not only humanity's sinfulness, but also God's righteous anger when faced by that same sin. God's righteousness, therefore, is for the early Luther God's justified condemnation of our sinful lives, and the fear and collapse we feel as a result is the necessary consequence of our realization that we stand condemned before God—*coram deo*.

Anfechtung has another popular translation in Luther's Bible: the wrath of God. For Luther the Psalms are replete with evidence of humanity's dereliction before this same divine anger. Here one recognizes again and again Luther's acknowledgment of this situation and, as significantly, his confirmation of the theology that binds humanity's fate to the outcome of this condemnation. Out of this apparently hopeless predicament, however, arises a deeper and more positive understanding of God's love, and ultimately an insight that comes to characterize all true Protestant theology, both Lutheran and Reformed. Stated simply, Luther began to realize in 1514–1515 that the most profound manifestation of our temptation is the *"tentatio cogitationum de securitate,"* that temptation to seek and believe that one has obtained the security of holding faith beyond all doubt; namely, spiritual certainty. Such an understanding does violence to faith, argues Luther, because it fails to recognize that faith is always in the balance; faith is never secure, but must always be delivered by God. That faith comes from God, and that God freely gives it to the repentant sinner not because of anything he/she has done, but in spite of everything he/she is.

When Luther starts to understand the fragile character of humanity's grip on faith, and yet the sovereign immortality of faith itself as God's gift to the world, then he begins to understand that faith as a gift is not the product of a righteous anger and condemnation—however justified this might be—but rather of a divine love that cannot be constrained but that must be freely given. The resolution of humanity's *Anfechtung,* consequently, is to be found not in a doctrine of justification by endless religious observation, but rather in Luther's famous doctrine of JUSTIFICATION by faith alone, which Luther identifies by working through the depth of humanity's rejection of God, and God's insistent overcoming of that same rejection.

There is a consistent logic at work in Luther's theology after this primary discovery. Luther understands after 1515 that faith is about love, and love is about God's embrace of the world, not its rejection. Although it is true to say for Luther therefore that sin always remains a visceral reality in a man's life, nevertheless the meaning of his faith, and the true origin of Protestant theology, is to bring people before God, so that they might hear the Word, repent, and slowly learn to follow lives of Christian discipleship. It is this quality, rather than the more melodramatic images of Luther nailing theses to a church door in 1517, or before the DIET OF WORMS in 1521, that characterizes Luther's deepest insights. It is why Protestant theology, at its outset, is about God's love of people and where those same people discover that love, rather than being about the church. It is this very practical emphasis, rather than a rejection of mediation, that brings Luther to his split with the Catholic Church in 1517–1521.

The clearest example of this development in Luther's theology came in 1522 in his famous Wittenberg sermons, which were delivered over eight consecutive days and in which Luther gives his first sustained exposition of his theology. The occasion was Luther's return from the Wartburg, and the anxieties caused by the overly accelerated rate of reform in Wittenberg effected by other figures there, most notably ANDREAS BODENSTEIN VON KARLSTADT. What makes these sermons so significant is the way in which they establish those same principles that will inform not only the development of the German Reformation in the 1520s and 1530s, but also the consistent development of Protestant theology ever since.

The first sermon was preached on March 9, 1522, Invocavit Sunday. Luther admonishes Wittenberg for its sins, judging the reformers' conduct in the light of God's will, rather than their own ecclesial aspirations. In so doing he clearly outlines the basis of his belief and theology:

Dear friends, the kingdom of God—and we are that kingdom—does not consist in talk or words, but in activity, in deeds, in works and exercises. God does not want hearers and repeaters of words, but followers and doers, and this occurs in faith through love. For a faith without love is not enough—rather it is not faith at all, but a counterfeit of faith, just as a face seen in a mirror is not a real face, but merely the reflection of a face. (LW 51:68)

Luther returns to this theme again and again throughout the sermons, reiterating constantly his main theme that the BIBLE teaches the faithful to be justified before God, to understand this justified faith as the basis of all Christian practice, and to support each other in building up God's people on earth. Such, Luther states, is the heart of the Gospel, and all other questions, concerning images, the sacraments, and CONFESSION and absolution, are secondary to this principal doctrine. As Luther concludes, at the end of this same first sermon: "If we do not earnestly pray to God and act rightly in this matter, it looks to me as if all the misery which we have begun to heap upon the papists will fall upon us" (LW 51:70).

There are five key themes that arise naturally from Luther's Wittenberg sermons, and that characterize orthodox Protestant theology: the authority of the Bible as the proclaimed Word of God; human existence before God, which embraces repentance and justification by faith alone; the relationship between faith and reason; the pastoral emphases of Protestant theology, which includes questions of church–state relations and theological education; pietism as the mark of the true congregation. In what follows, an understanding of these central themes will be developed in conjunction with an interpretation of the evolution of Protestant theology.

The Authority of the Bible

For Protestantism the Bible is the proclaimed word of God, identified in its theological meaning with the revealed Word of God, Jesus Christ. The Bible's authority rests on its unique status as the divinely inspired witness to God's act of self-disclosure. That uniqueness is not to be understood contingently, as if the Bible were unique because it just happens to be the only record to what took place in the first Christian communities. Rather, the Bible is unique because it, like Christ himself, is God's gift of God to creation. In the Bible we receive God as God speaks to us, its words resonant with God's Word.

The origin of such a reading of biblical authority lies in the development of Luther's understanding of the doctrine of justification by faith alone, meaning also that the distinctively Protestant sense of biblical authority is linked with Luther's rejection of scholasticism. This fact is significant, not because it implies that scholastic theologies were uninterested in the Bible (which would be erroneous), but because it identifies a tension with other forms of AUTHORITY that, for Protestantism, must always be resolved in favor of the Bible. For Protestantism, scholasticism's emphasis on the power of reason to resolve questions of divine being must always be secondary to the disclosure of revealed knowledge in the Bible. Thus, although it is undoubtedly true that many Protestant theologians have sought to place reason (and other cognate authorities) within their work, nevertheless such attempts must always give way to the Bible in a genuinely Protestant theology.

This requirement has not always been met without tension. Although it was true, therefore, that the primacy of biblical authority was largely unchallenged during the sixteenth and seventeenth centuries, the advent of biblical criticism in the eighteenth century, founded on a developing appreciation of the significance of scientific reasoning, presented important challenges. Similarly, FRIEDRICH SCHLEIERMACHER'S Reformed theology constituted a diminution of biblical authority in favor of more philosophical arguments derived from IMMANUEL KANT, which was certainly how KARL BARTH responded to Schleiermacher's work in the early part of the twentieth century. Notwithstanding Barth's great significance in that period, however, nineteenth-century neo-Kantianism continued to exert an influence on Protestant theology into the 1950s, a situation that one finds in the background to the work of such figures as JÜRGEN MOLTMANN, WOLFHART PANNENBERG, and Eberhard Jüngel.

Such challenges are significant because they make Protestantism think again about the role of the authority of the Bible in its understanding of faith. The Bible is not authoritative because it is old; rather, the Bible is authoritative because it is God's. In this respect neither philosophies, nor social theories, nor cultural and aesthetic achievements are in the same way God's. They are humanity's achievements, and as such are of necessity secondary to the Bible. None of this requires human reflection to avoid attempting to make sense of the Bible, and none of it vitiates the significance of biblical exegesis and theological interpretation. The simple given of the authority of the Bible, however, is the origin of all Protestant theology. Everything else flows from it.

Coram Deo

If one asks why the Bible has this authority, moving on from the simple fact of its being given by God, one recognizes that in the Bible one stands before God;

that *coram deo,* as Luther had it, is the defining characteristic of biblical humanity. Again, if one contrasts that with, say, philosophy or social theory, then one would say that standing before philosophy is standing before a human construct; or at best, standing before certain principles of indeterminate status. The best philosophers, GEORG W. F. HEGEL and Martin Heidegger for example, are clearly aware of this distinction and do not understand their philosophies as functioning in the same way, or with the same character, as faith. This fact did not stop theologians like RUDOLF BULTMANN from attempting to draw together certain methodological and conceptual parallels with, for example, Heidegger's historical phenomenology. It must be acknowledged, however, that the attempt was not always successful, and certainly not universally popular with Protestant churches, both Lutheran and, particularly, Reformed.

The same comments about the authority of the Bible, therefore, also apply to the doctrine of *coram deo,* with the qualification that certain theologians, for example Schleiermacher, have taken the *coram deo* argument seriously, without necessarily positioning the Bible as its sole medium. Schleiermacher's idea of religion's "sense and taste for the infinite," for example, could be argued to take very seriously a notion of standing before God. Schleiermacher would not be willing to limit it to the Bible, however, preferring instead to position the idea as something akin to a universal opportunity for the individual, which is clearly problematic for orthodox Protestantism. The idea of *coram deo* itself can be problematic for Protestantism, if it is so closely restricted to the Bible that it does not leave sufficient room for the DOCTRINE of the church. One might argue, under such circumstances, that a fundamental distinction between Lutheran and Reformed Protestantism is in their doctrine of the church, and the mediating role the church plays in communicating God's presence to believers. If orthodox LUTHERANISM has rather more of an emphasis on Word and People, therefore, it is probably true to say that Reformed Protestantism understands "Church and People" as being as key a component as "Bible and People." Certainly, that would be the sense emerging from figures like HULDRYCH ZWINGLI, MARTIN BUCER, and JOHN CALVIN in the Swiss Reformed Churches in the sixteenth century.

If the question is about *coram deo,* therefore, it is also about mediation, and indeed immediation, an issue that has always been problematic for Protestantism because of the close historic ties between mainstream and radical (often Anabaptist) Reformations. There is a radicalism in Protestantism, evident today in the many conservative evangelical movements (see EVANGELICALISM), that wants to think in terms of a Pentecostal and immediate inspiration for the Christian life, imbued with the Spirit and independent of mediation by church and sacrament and even, arguably, the Bible. Although it is undoubtedly wrong to suggest simply that such positions constitute bad theology, nevertheless it is more plausible to argue that, properly understood, orthodox Protestantism is as much a religion of mediation in principle as Catholicism—the principle being, however, mediation through the Bible, *coram deo.*

Faith and Reason

Because of its historical origins in the sixteenth century, and particularly the intellectual shift from medieval to modern mindsets, Protestant theology has generally been coincidental with the development of scientific reasoning, something that particularly came to characterize Protestant exegesis of the Bible from the early eighteenth century onward. This coincidence can be understood in terms of the relationship between faith and reason that to a great degree becomes in modernity the relative tension between epistemology in general, and theological epistemology in particular. Or, stated differently: the tension is between general theories of how we know things, which are commonly the domain of philosophy or science, and theological theories of how we know things, which for Christianity are theories of how God makes God known in the world. As has been demonstrated, for Protestantism the latter questions are ones of biblical authority.

The shift from medieval to modern here is informative because the various schools of scholastic theology, against which Luther struggled, were concerned with understanding how reason could be employed to demonstrate the will or mind or being of God, often in terms of how, by analogy, theology could reason itself philosophically back toward the divine by starting from the natural. To turn Luther's thoughts around, for certain strands of scholasticism it was not so much *coram deo* as *coram mundo*—the latter allowing us to demonstrate how and why God created the world, including humanity. For Protestantism, by contrast—both Lutheran and Reformed traditions—God's creative will/being/mind allows of no demonstration: it is axiomatic that God wills to create, because—as the Bible states—God is love. So as God is love is axiomatic, so also is the medium by which God communicates this will to the world; that is, the Word and the word, Jesus and the Bible. One thereby arrives at a very arresting view of the relationship between faith and reason, established in the confessed authority of the Bible: we know things because God tells us things, a proposition that cannot be demonstrated, but rather only confessed as Word and Gospel.

This understanding of the relationship between faith and reason has dominated Protestant theology ever since Luther and Calvin, both positively and negatively. Positively, it has allowed generations of theologians, from GOTTHOLD LESSING through to SØREN KIERKEGAARD and on to FRANZ OVERBECK and Barth and then Moltmann, to return to biblical first principles, certain in the conviction that their Protestantism is determined by the axiomatic character of the Protestant witness to truth. Negatively, however, it has also provoked generations of Protestant thinkers, from Kant and Schleiermacher through neo-Kantianism and ADOLF VON HARNACK to Bultmann and Pannenberg, to struggle with the precise role of general or philosophical reflection in relation to Christian belief. It is probably best not to understand these tensions as either right or wrong *per se,* but rather as indicative *per accidens* of the Protestant struggle with Luther's doctrine of *coram deo.* It is more a matter of understanding—and then teaching—something of what it is to be human, to understand axiomatically what it is to be divine, as hearers and Speaker of the Word, respectively. Orthodox Protestant doctrine, however, argues that the relationship between faith and reason is one in which the former always conditions the latter, not vice versa.

Theology's Pastoral Character

The Protestant understanding of the relationship between faith and reason helps to make sense of theology's pastoral character, which otherwise can too often be reduced to an echo of biblical images of the Good Shepherd that, although not insignificant, are perhaps too open to naïve interpretation. Protestant theology's pastoral character, as exemplified by Luther's Wittenberg sermons, is really a matter of lay education. The pastoral quality of Protestant theology consists in leading the People of God to a deeper understanding of their position *coram deo,* and a better understanding of their faithful responsibilities to God in the light of Christ's saving death on the cross. Gerald Strauss characterized this initiative in the 1520s as "Luther's House of Learning" (Strauss 1978), and the early Reformation's commitment to the provision of new CATECHISMS, family Bibles, village pastors, and public confessions, was evidence not so much of the desire to build a new church, as to make the ordinary people understand and own their responsibilities to God. To a large extent similar initiatives were followed by Zwingli in Zurich and Bucer in Strasbourg, and slightly later Calvin in Geneva, who codified these protestant pastoral concerns into a more systematic understanding of what it was to be a Reformed Christian.

The important features of this turn in Protestant theology, and why it is best described as "pastoral," can be enumerated quite straightforwardly. First, Protestant theology originates in the conviction that there is a right relationship with God, as realized in Jesus Christ, and as proclaimed in the Gospels and the Letters of St. Paul. Properly understood, therefore, the role of the pastor is to teach people how to return to this right relationship with God, something that God achieves in peoples' hearts and which is known in repentance and confession. This in turn leads, second, to the need to keep people together as the People of God, which means avoiding fragmentation and individualization by teaching people as communities, and equipping them with the means to remain together; that is, Bible and WORSHIP, or better, Word and the SACRAMENTS of baptism and Eucharist (see LORD'S SUPPER). Only in this way, third, can the People of God realize its moral commitments to God, commitments that are better realized as the cost of discipleship.

Even today these central features of Protestant theology's pastoral character are realized in countless congregations in very straightforward terms. The difficulty with modernity, however, has been in the way that this pastoral character has been replaced on occasions by a more secular understanding of the therapeutic role of religion, which has tended historically to work against the communal character of Protestantism, toward a more individualized notion of what it is to be saved. As with faith and reason the tension here is chronic, something that remains always a major part of being a modern religion. At its worst, however, arguably in many Western, outwardly Protestant denominations, this tendency has produced religious movements that are not really Protestant congregations in any orthodox sense, but rather collections of amorphously religious individuals.

Pietism

One might argue that the tendency toward such individualization is an inherent weakness in Protestantism, as with the relationship between faith and reason, stemming from its peculiar historical origins. On such a reading, one might argue that it is Protestantism's inherent PIETISM that is both its greatest strength and its greatest weakness, if that same pietism is defined as Protestantism's instinct for life before God, in the light of Word and sacraments. On such a reading there is something almost inevitably human in the desire or need to understand standing before God as something pious individuals must own for themselves, just as the same pious individuals must repent for themselves, and indeed confess for themselves. In these terms the question of the right response to God, which characterizes so much of Protestantism's heart and soul, is inevitably for most people going to be an individual response to God. It is the way human beings relate to others, and therefore The Other: as individuals.

Here one arrives at the heart of the matter. In keeping with what has been said about the relationship between faith and reason, one might acknowledge that it is intrinsically human to behave as individuals, and that this tendency is something sciences like anthropology and psychology can elucidate for theology. Nevertheless, this is not the same thing as saying that this is the way in which human beings should behave, and certainly not the same thing as saying that this is how they should behave *coram deo*. Protestantism teaches that human beings before God are called to return to the People of God, which means they are called to return to being together one with the Lord (to state it devotionally). This is why all of the essential structures of Protestant theology—the authority of the Bible, standing before God, the tension between faith and reason, and Protestant theology's pastoral character—are properly understood as communal realities, as principles that are true because they are shared, with each other and, most important, with God. Properly understood, the principles of Protestant theology pull people back toward the Protestant understanding of Trinitarian Incarnationalism, the central doctrines of the Christian faith that are only intelligible as the actions of the communal God.

The historical origins of the Protestant Reformation demonstrate this reality clearly enough, so that it is justified to speak of pietism as a shared practice of devotion that arose as early communities, orthodox and Anabaptist (see ANABAPTISM), were placed under considerable duress by Catholic and secular authorities in the sixteenth century. The Hutterite Communities (see HUTTERITES), which later evolved to include the Moravian Brethren and which in turn profoundly influenced Schleiermacher and subsequently Karl Barth, typify this pietistic tendency. Pietism, on this reading, is a distinctive feature of Protestantism not simply because it reflects the essential characteristics of its theology, but also because it was the historical lived experience of generations of Protestant Christians in Europe and subsequently around the world. As such it is exemplified in the many social and cultural achievements that Protestantism has given the world, from the integration of civil and religious understandings of shared authority through to the great traditions of hymnody and chorales that are often the best-known features of Protestantism, and arguably some of its finest theologies (see HYMNS AND HYMNALS; MUSIC).

If this analysis comes close to speaking of Protestant theology as the elucidation of first principles in the tense relationship between the KINGDOM OF GOD and the kingdom of the world, then that is simply to state the case in Luther's explicit terms. The key point for Protestant theology then becomes how to teach people fidelity to these first principles, all the time being sensitive to the fact that those same people are called to become one in the midst of a world that pulls them away from God and each other, toward a misguided sense of themselves as free agents. To refer to this conviction as "Pietism" is not to trivialize Protestant religiosity as emotive or sentimental, but rather to identify Protestantism as a religion of observation and devotion, one in which the taught praxis of discipleship is as important as the theological sense of the confessed Word.

Protestant Theology Today

Even though these historic strands remain normative for orthodox Protestant theology, contemporary social and cultural pressures obtain. Although the question of justification remains central to Protestantism, therefore, as the recent dialogue with Rome demonstrates, Protestant theology has also to come to terms with a very wide range of issues, including human SEXUALITY, HIV/AIDS, interfaith Dialogue, ECOLOGY, and so forth (see DIALOGUE, INTERCONFESSIONAL). These pressures mean that the tension between theological consistency, on the one hand, and theological relevance, on the other, are probably more heightened than at any time since the sixteenth century. The differing theologies of Pannenberg and Moltmann, for example—the former inherently conservative, pursuing the classical themes of Protestant thought, the latter far more attentive to contemporary issues, albeit within an orthodox framework—highlight the kind of tension that now exists. This is to reckon without the very many practicing theologians who would regard themselves as Protestant, and who would yet be generally identified far more with one particular issue, as is the case, for example, with various feminist theologians (see FEMINIST THEOLOGY).

In a world where there are now literally thousands of Protestant denominations, many of them taking a profoundly conservative view of the evangelical character of the Christian faith, particularly in relation to social issues, it would seem likely that any defining sense of orthodox Protestant theology is doomed to increasing fragmentation. The possibilities, however, are more promising, particularly if one returns to an authentic sense of the origins of faith itself. If Christian BAPTISM functions for Protestantism as the entry into a new creation, therefore (II Corinthians 5:17), binding all believers together into one People of God, then the requirement to address the salvation of the old creation becomes a religious responsibility identifiable with the gift of the Spirit at Pentecost. If there is one consistency in Protestant theology that holds together Lutheran and Reformed Churches, it is the conviction that the eschatological character of revelation marks human existence out in a unique way, and that that uniqueness is really a oneness of which many aspects are but reflections and refractions.

The apparent fragmentation of contemporary Protestant theology, consequently, albeit a symptom of the identity crisis of contemporary society, is also implicitly acknowledged in the original understanding of the Christian faith itself. No one believed that resolving the tension between old and new was ever straightforward. Paul and Luther did say, however, that it would be necessary, if the Word of God were to be genuinely confessed to souls in need of redemption. Such was the gist of Luther's sermons to the Wittenberg congregation in 1522: that the path would be rocky because the needs of the faithful were many and the Word of God was One.

References and Further Reading

Brecht, Martin. *Martin Luther.* 3 vols. Minneapolis, MN: Fortress Press, 1985–1993.

Bruce, Steve. *A House Divided: Protestantism, Schism and Secularization.* London: Routledge, 1990.

Jones, Gareth. *Christian Theology: A Brief Introduction.* Cambridge, MA: Polity Press, 1999.

Oberman, Heiko. *The Dawn of the Reformation: Essays in Late Medieval and Early Reformation Thought.* Edinburgh: T.&T. Clark, 1986.

Pauck, Wilhelm. *The Heritage of the Reformation.* London: Oxford University Press, 1968.

Rupp, Gordon. *The Righteousness of God: Luther Studies.* London: Hodder and Stoughton, 1953.

Strauss, Gerald. *Luther's House of Learning. Indoctrination of the Young in the German Reformation.* Baltimore, MD: Johns Hopkins University Press, 1978.

Wagner, Falk. *Zur gegenwärtigen Lage des Protestantismus.* Gütersloh, Germany: Gütersloher Verlagshaus, 1995.

GARETH JONES

THEOLOGY, AFRICAN

See African Theology

THEOLOGY, ASIAN

See Asian Theology

THEOLOGY, BLACK

See Black Theology

THEOLOGY, COVENANT

See Covenant Theology

THEOLOGY EDUCATION: ASIA

In the earliest centuries of Christianity in Asia, theological education was very much linked with the theological developments in the West. Although Antioch is technically in West Asia, we usually speak of early Asian Christianity as Christian communities east of the Roman Empire, in Persia and thus east of Antioch. Some of the themes of theological education from this early period—close relations with the West, contextualization of theology in Asia, and languages used in theological education—continue throughout the history of Christianity in Asia. Before the advent of Protestant churches in Asia, theological education was generally monastic, focused on memorization of scripture and learning to follow the exegesis of the "great teachers." In the School of Nisibis, for example, the basic curriculum was the BIBLE, taught in Syriac, following the teaching of the great Nestorian doctors. The theology of this school was determined by its relationship with the West.

Protestant theological education came to each new region with the earliest resident missionaries. Protestants pioneered most all of the BIBLE TRANSLATION work in Asia, and this meant that people needed to learn to read. Thus, the normal progression would be from a small group of language helpers studying the Bible in a missionary's home, to a small class of recent converts to a "school" taught by one or two missionaries, to a more formal "Bible college." Some of the early Protestant missionaries saw the need to establish seminaries, but little was done until the nineteenth century. In the East Indies, for example, Dutch chaplains working mostly with Dutch, but with a concern for training Ambonese pastors, proposed in the 1630s that a seminary be established in the East Indies. The Dutch could not yet envision theological education anywhere except in Europe, so these ideas were never carried out. For a brief period of one decade in the middle of the eighteenth century (1745–1755), the first Protestant seminary was established in the East Indies, but in its 10 years it graduated only two students. The Dutch seemed to have more commitment to Asian theological education in Ceylon. After rooting out the Portuguese, they imitated the Iberians by starting two SEMINARIES, one in Colombo (1685) and another in Jaffna (1690). And yet Europeans, both Roman Catholic and Protestants, still sent most of their candidates for ministry to Europe to get a "proper" theological education. Only in the later part of the nineteenth century can we talk about seminary education carried out by Europeans in Asia with the confidence that future pastors could be educated for ministry without going to Europe. The very earliest Protestant missionaries (as opposed to chaplains) in Asia, the Danish-Pietist mission in Tranquebar, South India, began to teach catechists who were to be ordained as the first Protestant pastors in INDIA. Until the development of the Baptist college at Serampore, this method of private tutoring was the standard used.

Developments in the Nineteenth Century

In the nineteenth century, most of the pioneering Protestant theological centers were established from the Mediterranean to the Pacific. Virtually all countries in Asia, excluding KOREA, Vietnam, JAPAN and Nepal, had developed some type of Protestant Bible colleges or institutes for preparing local pastors in the nineteenth century. One of the first countries that developed schools for training pastors was India. In 1818 the Serampore Trio of WILLIAM CAREY, Joshua Marshman, and William Ward established Serampore as the first Protestant college in India. As with many Christian colleges in Asia, Serampore began with the dual mission of reaching out to the non-Christian elite and providing theological training for the young Christians. It was not until 1910 that higher theological education was added, and in 1918 a consortium of Christian schools under the "Serampore Senate" was established. By this time, BIBLE COLLEGES and seminaries were being established in most other regions of Asia. For the most part, schools established in the nineteenth century were started by MISSIONS or denominations and reflected the particular theological outlook of the mission. In the twentieth century, with the rising tide of the ecumenical movement, many union or ecumenical schools were established.

In Burma, formal theological education began with the Baptist school started by E. L. Abbot in Thandwe in 1840. Originally founded to educate converts in the faith, this school developed into a seminary for training Baptist clergy. The first Protestant seminary in Thailand was the Evangelistic Training School, founded by the Laos Mission of the Presbyterian Church in 1889. After various starts and stops, the school was finally named after the great Protestant pioneer in northern Thailand, Daniel McGilvary. The McGilvary Theological Seminary taught advanced courses in English beginning in 1926, but soon added the Thai medium. In Pakistan, the Punjab Synod of the Presbyterian Church of North America established the first seminary for the region. Immediately, other churches (including Scotch Presbyterians, Methodists, Anglicans, and others) began to establish their own schools. In Korea, the first resident Methodist missionary in Korea, Henry Appenzeller, began training three Korean Christians in his home. This group became the core of a theological class that in time became Methodist Theological Seminary in Seoul.

Theological Education Comes of Age in Asia

In northern Korea, a Presbyterian pioneer, Samuel A. Moffett, also began teaching young pastors in his home in Pyongyang in 1901. Classes were held during the off seasons for farmers and those in rhythm with the agricultural calendar. Students were taught for three or four weeks, and then they returned to their villages and passed on what they had learned during their planting or harvesting seasons. This became what today is one of the largest seminaries in the world, The Presbyterian College and Theological Seminary, now based in Seoul.

In CHINA, the basic strategy of the Protestant denominational missions was to reach China through education. Thus, colleges and universities providing Christian perspectives on the sciences were as much of a priority as theological seminaries. By 1876, there were a reported 20 training centers for Christian leaders with 231 students. By 1906, this had increased to 68 schools with 772 men and 543 women enrolled. It is clear from these last statistics that from the very beginning in China, the training of both WOMEN and men was important to the effort to reach all of the society. Women were generally educated to be "Bible women," passing out Bibles and engaging local households and villages in the study of the Bible. Some of the theological education for women however, was on par with the education given to men, requiring courses in church history and theological studies, as well as in the Bible.

Although new seminaries were being started in CHINA, as in other countries in Asia, there was also a movement to consolidate or combine efforts in larger institutional work such as seminaries, colleges, and hospitals. In 1910, for example, Nanking became a Union Bible School by combining three older schools from four missions. In the first decades of the twentieth century, with the rapid increase in Christian college graduates, there developed in China as much as anywhere in Asia a two-tiered type of theological education. Some students received a four-year certificate after completing a basic theological education. These students had little or no previous formal education. Other students had graduated from the new "Western-style" colleges and would follow the more traditional three-year Bachelor of Divinity or Masters of Divinity program from the West.

In Vietnam, the Nhatrang Bible and Theological Institute was founded in 1921 by missionaries of the CHRISTIAN AND MISSIONARY ALLIANCE (CMA) Church.

The seminary (first called the Tourane Bible College) grew from eight students that first year to sixty-six students in 1927. The CMA later started Bible colleges in Cambodia in 1925, Thailand in 1936, and then Laos in 1957. With the Communist victory in Vietnam, the Institute was closed in 1976, with 264 students studying at the time. All Protestant theological education in Vietnam had found its home in this important school.

Along with the rapid development of theological education in the twentieth century came movements of NATIONALISM and contextualization. As more and more pastors are taught in their local contexts, in their own language, a pool of indigenous theologians has begun to develop. Christian leaders are often among the better-educated people in Asian countries, and they often respond to social and political issues with greater understanding. Although we see the results of this theological development in such movements as the Korean Independence Movement (1919) and the number of theological leaders supporting the end of the Qing Dynasty in China, it was not until after the Pacific War and the ensuing independence movements that indigenous Christian leaders began to make a national and continent-wide impact.

During the height of Japanese imperialism, it became most clear that theological education is both shaped by and shapes cultures and countries. In Japan, the rise of Japanese imperialism brought with it state-directed reordering of Christian institutions. To ensure close supervision by the Japanese government, church institutions were forced to combine efforts and organizations. As a result, the fifteen seminaries and departments of theology started by various denominations in Japan during the first half of the twentieth century were merged to form three seminaries in 1941. After the war, these merged into Tokyo Union Theological seminary. A similar development occurred with the Communist victories in China. During the late nineteenth and early twentieth centuries, a number of regional seminaries were started in China (such as the Sheng Dao Guan [Methodist]), and other theological schools were attached to the Protestant colleges (such as at Shanghai Baptist College). However, after 1951, these regional schools were again consolidated. Yenching Union Theological Seminary, for example, was the merger of thirteen Protestant seminaries from northern China and Nanjing ("Jinling") seminary was the product of a merger of twelve Protestant Bible schools and seminaries in East China directed by the Three-Self Patriotic Movement Committee in 1952. In 1961 these two seminaries were merged to form Nanjing Union Theological Seminary, the one national seminary of the China Christian Council in China. The other regional seminaries were also organized through the CCC as approved by the government.

Diversification and Growth After Independence Movements

In the last half of the twentieth century, theological education in Asia exploded, both in terms of increased diversity and in terms of the number of schools and organizations for overseeing theological education. A number of trends deserve mention for this most recent period. First, newer missions and churches began to establish their own schools for training pastors. The day of the ecumenical cooperation ended and the day of free-market proliferation of seminaries had begun. Many missions and churches, in both Asia and the West, became critical of the liberal orientation of established seminaries. Thus, schools like Union Biblical Seminary (originally in Yeotmal) were founded to provide an alternative to the more liberal education of Serampore or United Theological College. Union, in fact, was started by eleven church and mission groups, including the Evangelical Fellowship of India. In Singapore, the ecumenical or union seminary, Trinity Theological College, was founded in 1948 (English medium) and Singapore Theological Seminary (now Singapore Bible College) was founded four years later (Chinese medium). Two other theological divisions from the West, fundamentalism and pentecostalism, promoted the founding of other seminaries supporting these particular theologies. In Nepal, one of the earliest theological schools after Nepal opened up to Christian worship was an ASSEMBLIES OF GOD institute established in 1980 as a nine-month training program for pentecostal pastors. Pentecostal schools are now the fastest-growing schools in Asia.

In the 1950s and 1960s, these newer seminaries and Bible colleges were mostly founded by Western leaders. By the 1970s, however, an increasing number were being founded by Asian leaders. Most of the theological schools founded since 1980 in Asia were started by Asians who felt constrained by the older seminaries built on Western models. Indians have founded schools in Nepal, Singaporeans have started schools in Cambodia, and Koreans are founding schools all over Asia.

A second trend since World War II is the development of Asian forms of theological education. In south Asia, this has meant using the pattern of the Ashram or "retreat" center for theological education. The Nepal Bible Ashram, for example, was founded on May 14, 1981 in the village of Jorpati, east of Kathmandu. The first group of 11 students were all converts from Hinduism. This Ashram, like many others, has developed a local curriculum (including reading through the whole Bible, because most of the students would not have done so), health care, agricultural studies, and adult literacy.

A third trend worth noting is the development of associations for the standardization of theological education in Asia. These associations help coordinate theological education, and they usually provide some type of accrediting for seminaries and Bible schools. Most of these associations had some type of relationship with theological education in the West, either as a reaction to other developments or as an extension of these developments. In 1968 the Philippine Association of Bible and Theological Schools (PABATS) was formed to bring together in cooperation Philippine schools that shared a common evangelical heritage. At its founding it included 17 schools, but by the twenty-first century more than one-half of the Protestant schools had been involved in someway in PABATS. The ecumenical Association for Theological Schools in Southeast Asia was formed in 1957 in Singapore, with 16 schools in the original membership. This is one of the most active associations (now called the Association for Theological Education in Southeast Asia), accrediting theological schools in Southeast Asia, publishing the *Asia Journal of Theology,* as well as operating the Southeast Asia Graduate School of Theology (SEAGAST). Like the Serampore Senate in India, SEAGAST pools the faculty and libraries of member schools in the region to provide advanced training in theological studies. A parallel organization, the Asia Theological Association, does the same thing for schools that are more evangelical in theology. There are some schools that have dual membership, demonstrating that the divisions in Asia are not always the same as those in the West.

A fourth trend in Asian theological education is the contextualizing of the curriculum and the courses themselves. In most Asian seminaries, a general course in church history, as well as a course in national or regional church history, is required. Most seminaries also are teaching in a local language (with India the major exception to this), but another research language, like English, is required. Thus, in most seminaries modern languages are being taught along with biblical languages. Theological studies in seminaries often include required courses such as "Asian theologies" and "Minjung theology," as these movements continue to develop. Most Asian seminaries also require courses in other Asian religions (e.g. Buddhism, Hinduism, Islam). These three subtrends (local languages, local theologies, and local religions) are mutually enhancing to theological formation in Asia.

A fifth trend would have to be the rapid increase in Asian publications that are available and are being used in theological education. This is related to the fourth trend just mentioned, but it also has an economic cause: Books and periodicals printed in Asia are much more affordable for Asian students. For example, in 1973, supported by the German East Asia Mission Society, the Korea Theological Institute was formed, with the express purpose of promoting the best of modern, especially Korean, theological thinking. Its journal, *Shinhak Sasang (Theological Thought)*, as well as its translations of contemporary theological works, provides material for Korean seminaries and Bible colleges. Newer publications, like the *Asian Journal of Pentecostal Studies,* are beginning to express global movements from an Asian perspective. Larger projects, such as the Church History Association of India's multivolume history of Christianity in India, are giving greater credibility and honor to Christianity as an Indian religion.

Finally, the last trend is the increasing number of women in theological education. Women entered theological education in Asia later than men, although from early in the nineteenth century, women were involved in ministries of teaching, EVANGELISM, and (later) medical work. Not until late in the twentieth century were women involved in higher theological education as both students and teachers. Through such regional organizations as the Christian Conference in Asia, as well as at national levels, women-supported networks and conferences were developed to meet the special needs of women in theological education. In 1978, for example, the Association of Women in Theology (AWIT) was formed in the Philippines with the purpose of supporting women's movements in theology. The AWIT was supported in part by the Asian Christian Women's Association. In some countries, including China, women are the backbone of theological education.

References and Further Reading

Allen, Yorke, Jr. *A Seminary Survey.* New York: Harper and Brothers, Publishers, 1960.

Hunt, Robert, Lee Kam Hing, and John Roxborogh, eds. *Christianity in Malaysia: A Denominational History.* Selangor, Malaysia: Pelanduk Publications, 1992.

Latourette, Kenneth Scott. *A History of Christian Missions in China.* New York: McMillian, 1949.

Sugirtharajah, R. S., ed. *Asian Faces of Jesus.* Maryknoll, NY: Orbis Books, 1993.

Wilson, L. F. "Bible Institutes, Colleges, Universities." In *The New International Dictionary of Pentecostal and Charismatic Movements.* Edited by Stanley M. Burgess. Grand Rapids, MI: Zondervan, 2002.

SCOTT W. SUNQUIST

THEOLOGY, EVANGELICAL

See Evangelicalism, Theology of

THEOLOGY, FEMINIST

Origins and Agenda

Feminist theology may be said to have appeared in the nineteenth century in the context of women's struggles in Europe and North America to better their legal, social, and economic condition, following on from the attempts of women in the period of the American and European revolutions in the eighteenth century to improve their lot. That early phase is classically represented by Mary Wollstonecraft's *A Vindication of the Rights of Woman* (1792), which remained influential through the next century as women assimilated its arguments. Feminism and feminist theology has always been a "protest" movement, and North American Protestant women launched feminist theology on its way.

Although she was by no means the first to struggle with the biblical texts and their connections with women's position in church and society, ELIZABETH CADY STANTON, a veteran campaigner for women's voting rights and for the abolition of slavery, coordinated a team of female collaborators to produce a best-seller, *The Woman's Bible* (1895–1898). This work attempted critically to evaluate what the Bible did and did not say about women, from the perspective of women. This was the first serious attempt to dislodge an exclusively male-centered (androcentric) perspective in biblical criticism and exposition. So from the beginning, feminist theology has been concerned with what is nowadays refered to as "gender," that is, relationships between the sexes, as these vary over time in different social and cultural conditions, and, crucially, the interaction of gender with how human beings respond to and understand God. Feminist theology has always been engaged with questions about how the use and interpretation of the Bible impacts on women's lives, and inevitably, therefore, also on their relationships to men. From this perspective, a central conviction is that women's perspectives are to be taken with utter seriousness in theology, because being female is just as important a dimension of being human as being male. A male-only focused understanding of reality is a distortion, and the Christian tradition needs to come to terms with the insights of feminist theology if it is to be reinvigorated and not to be seen to be yet one more religious tradition that does not unequivocally uphold the full human dignity of women. Feminist theology rejoices in complexity, readily acknowledging the need for much sensitivity to the complications of race and class, "grass roots" experience, and the legacies of colonialism, as well as working to have an impact on church and the academic world. No one group of feminist theologians presumes to speak for another, and learning to appreciate the perspectives of feminist theologians across the globe is an important dimension of theological reflection. The names of Chung Hyun-Kyung, Ada Maria Isasi-Diaz, Mercy Amba Oduyoye, and Delores Williams are key here.

Feminist Biblical Theology

Feminist theologians endeavor to explore the riches and the limitations of biblical and related literature, even as many factors will affect the weight still to be given to biblical perspectives. Biblical texts have been used to argue for the submission of women to men and women's incapacity to represent God or Christ, since they have not seen to bear the image of God independently of men. Of particular interest to Feminist theologians are "feminine" images for God found in Biblical texts, especially the association of "Sophia," divine wisdom, with the dignity and intelligence of the human female/feminine. Related has been the complexity of allowing women to gain access to theological education, and to the linguistic and critical tools of biblical scholarship as it developed in the course of the twentieth century. Feminist theology has found common cause with feminist perspectives on biblical material from a whole range of other academic disciplines.

Outstanding work has been done, by Phyllis Trible for example, in her re-reading of texts from Genesis and the Song of Songs in her *God and the Rhetoric of Sexuality* (1978). Here she finds resources to challenge convictions about women's inferiority and thus necessary subordination to men, and explores the way in which the "love-story gone wrong" is redeemed in the love lyrics of the Song of Songs. Trible tracks down overlooked female/feminine-related language for God in the Bible, language that is as reality-depicting as much as any language for God may be. Her *Texts of Terror: Literary-Feminist Readings of Biblical Narratives* (1984) explored appalling cases of violence to women in the Bible, prompting questions about the connections between the devaluation of women and their abuse, as well as the abuse of dependent children, which continues to be a live issue even in Christian contexts.

The most outstanding contribution to feminist theological interpretation of the New Testament is that of Elisabeth Schussler Fiorenza, first woman President of the Society of Biblical Literature in 1987, almost a century after the publication of *The Woman's Bible*. Fiorenza's book *In Memory of Her. A Feminist Theo-*

logical Reconstruction of Christian Origins (1983) was a Feminist landmark study. Central to this book is the conviction that women may claim Jesus and indeed the habits and practices of the earliest Christian communities as a prototype (not a blueprint) of their own history. The point here is that by taking clues from the beginnings of Christianity, with a future-orientated perspective rather than a backward-look, Christianity remains open to future transformation as it did in the first centuries of its existence. The implications are considerable, not only for the ways by which human beings understand God, but also for the structures of ecclesiology and ministry—sore points in many devout women's lives. By paying attention to what was at stake in the movement initiated by Jesus of Nazareth, the women and men associated with him, and the way they and later generations came to understand him, we can find resources to shift toward mutual acknowledgement of the full dignity and worth of all individuals. Some of her critics have insisted that Fiorenza is too generous in her evaluation of early Christianity painting an idealized picture. Important, however, is Fiorenza's argument that faithful representation of the discipleship and apostolic leadership of women supports women in their efforts to appropriate Jesus' notion of love and service, so that they too may be seen as the image and body of Christ.

In another monograph, *Miriam's Child, Sophia's Prophet* (1994) Fiorenza turns her attention to Jesus' execution and the theology of the cross. This relates to Phyllis Trible's perspective in *Texts of Terror,* for feminist theology is suspicious of texts and traditions of interpretation which urge the willing suffering of violence, even when such suffering is allegedly redemptive, since such suffering makes the dominated serve the interests of the dominant. Rather, in the New Testament is evidence of the way in which the earliest Christians struggled to make sense of the disaster of Jesus' death, with the presence of women ascribed a leading role in the stories of his suffering, death and resurrection. At the center of these narratives is the future-orientated empty-tomb proclamation of Jesus as the vindicated, resurrected one, who is always ahead to summon a new future. Thus the challenge to believers, and to women especially, is to position themselves, as it were, within the "open space" of the empty tomb and the open road to Galilee, to experience and proclaim divine and life-enhancing transformation and empowerment.

Assessment and Further Agenda

Apart from the interests of feminist biblical theologians, attention to the texts of the Bible has char-

acterized other fields of feminist study, such as archaeology, linguistics, social history, economics, literature, history, and anthropology. The interests of feminism have ensured that biblical criticism and biblical theology did not remain only the concerns of faculty of Religion and Theology in the academic world or institutions concerned with the training of future clergy, into which women have moved in large numbers in the latter half of the twentieth century. In turn, the insights of faculty in Religion and Theology that have an interest in "gender matters" help refresh biblical theology, and, not gender in relation to women, but also in relation to men.

One of the weaknesses of feminist theology in some of its modes, has been its indifference to the materials from the pens of historians, which illuminate the lives of women in the churches through the centuries. The legacy of the Reformation era deserves particular attention. There is much to be learned here, for the interpretation and evaluation of biblical texts and doctrines has never been a simple matter, not least where the lives of women have been concerned.

Feminist Doctrinal Theology

Doctrinal or systematic theology has been the central feature of the theological discipline, as the study of the first millennium alone reveals. In these times, creeds, doctrinal reflection, and the Bible interrelated with one another, not least as the New Testament writings came into being, and were gradually established as an authorized list of readings. It is important to remember that one of the long-term aims of feminist theology is the reintegration of areas of theology too long and too often kept apart in the interests of habits of "academic" theology as that developed in universities over the last three centuries. At times neglected are sacramental theology, liturgy, pastoral practice, ethics, and popular piety. The reintegration of different areas of theology could have a major impact on the way not merely these disciplines, but also the topics within them, are to be treated. For instance, "liturgical theology," that is, the context of worship in which most people learn their theology, has been engaging the attention of Protestant as well as Roman Catholic theologians for half a century, and it concerns itself with the work of poets and hymn-writers, as the work of Teresa Berger exemplifies. Feminist theology has only begun to engage with this area, or with inter-faith dialogue. The prospects are promising, however, because of the range of theological approaches both East and West, though feminist theology as yet has few interpreters from within the Orthodox family of churches, except on the issue of ordination, a touchstone for many women of how they are regarded within their churches.

Key Developments

In the aftermath of the Second Vatican Council of the Roman Catholic Church, two books by Mary Daly were the major catalyst for reappraisal of Christian doctrine. What Elizabeth Cady Stanton was to the nineteenth century, Mary Daly was for the twentieth. Defending her tradition in *The Church and the Second Sex* (1968), Daly wrote herself out of it. A ground-breaking book by Rosemary Radford Ruether, *Sexism and God-Talk: Towards a Feminist Theology* (1983), recalled a fundamental principle that an understanding of Christ must be adequate for the salvation of women as well as men. The Incarnation reverses and under-mines claims to privilege and status as Jesus undoes all claims to male dominance in his very vulnerability, thus revealing God to us. Ruether has become one of the most significant of recent voices in theology in the course of her career.

The most important writer of feminist doctrinal theology at the present time, however, is Elizabeth A. Johnson, not least in Roman Catholic–Lutheran inter-church discussion in the United States. She has tack-led the issue of language for God, both biblical and non-biblical. Given the theological principle that God transcends both sex and gender, and the hope that God is given to us and we respond to God in humanly inclusive ways, we may name God in a variety of ways, each of which acts as a corrective to every other, reminding us of the mystery of God. To over-come the unease in formal expressions of belief about the association of the "feminine" with the divine, however, we need to go further than that and say that the "feminine" can of and by itself represent God in as full and in as limited a way as God is represented by the "masculine": "She Who Is." All of our language for God is inadequate, but it may be feminist theolog-ical insight that will revitalize the Trinitarian tradition and enable the praise of God in many ways. The use of the doctrines and liturgies of the past for the in-sights they preserve, should be enriched. Johnson also wrote a major book on the "Communion of Saints," taking the cue for her book title ("friends of God, and prophets") from Wisdom 7.27. At once biblical and feminist, attending to the insights of ecological theol-ogy as well as to those of the Reformation and JOHN and CHARLES WESLEY, her work is a major example of feminist ecumenical theology, exploring a credal doc-trine and enlightening it for our time.

At this juncture, many women from different ec-clesiastical backgrounds are contributing to the re-shaping of theology, and it may be helpful to think of a theological schema based on the traditional pattern given by the creeds developed in the early period of the Church's formation. One re-appreciation of a creed as a whole is the book by Elizabeth Rankin Geitz, and we may follow that with attention to new understandings of creation written by Celia Deane-Drummond, based on "wisdom theology." A book by Shannon Shrein discussing two contrasting Christolo-gies (those of Sallie McFague and Elizabeth Johnson) is illuminating, since these represent two approaches to Rosemary Radford Ruether's perceptive question, "Can a male saviour save women?" The latter's most recent book discusses the many ways in which women past and present have engaged with Christianity. The most pungent critique of sentimentality about women in some feminist theology is that by Angela West; and the most profound exploration of the experience of evil is Melissa Raphael's book about women in Ausch-witz, a feminist study of the meaning of holiness. Elina Vuola's book tackles the limiations of liberation theology in dealing with the suffering and death of women in Latin America; Denise Ackerman's book raises acute questions about "redemption" from South Africa. Serene Jones has written on the reconfigura-tion of the Church, tackling such central topics as "sanctification and justification," and Susan Ross writes on the renewal of sacramental theology. And since some men are now feminist theologicans, in addition to Elizabeth Johnson's book on the Trinity, the work of Gavin D'Costa is much to be recom-mended.

See also Gender; Theology; Women; Women Clergy

References and Further Reading

Ackermann, Denise M. *After the Locusts. Letters from a Land-scape of Faith.* Grand Rapids, MI: Eerdmans, 2003.

Bauckham, Richard. *Gospel Women. Studies of the Named Women in the Gospels.* New York: Continuum, 2002.

Behr-Sigel, Elisabeth. *The Ministry of Women in the Church.* Redondo Beach, CA: Oakwood, 1991.

Berger, Teresa. *Theology in Hymns? A Study of the Relation-ship of Doxology and Theology According to A Collection of Hymns for the Use of the People Called Methodists (1780).* Nashville, TN: Abingdon, 1995.

Chopp, Rebecca S. "Feminist and Womanist Theologies" in Ford, David, ed. *The Modern Theologians.* Oxford: Black-well, 1997, 389–404.

Deane-Drummond, Celia. *Creation Through Wisdom.* Edin-burgh: T.&T. Clark, 2003.

D'Costa, Gavin. *Sexing the Trinity. Gender, Culture and the Divine.* London: SCM, 2000.

Fiorenza, Elisabeth Schussler, ed. *Searching the Scriptures. A Feminist Introduction; A Feminist Commentary.* New York: Crossroads, 1993/1994; London: SCM, 1994/1995.

———. *The Power of Naming: A Concilium Reader in Fem-inist Liberation Theology.* Maryknoll, NY: Orbis; London: SCM, 1996.

Geitz, Elizabeth Rankin. *Gender and the Nicene Creed.* Harrisburg, PA: Morehouse, 1995.

Graff, Ann O'Hara, ed. *In the Embrace of God. Feminist Approaches to Theological Anthropology.* Maryknoll: Orbis, 1995.

Hilkert, Mary Catherine. "Current Theology. Feminist Theology: A Review of Literature." *Theological Studies* 56 (1995): 327–352.

Johnson, Elizabeth A. *Friends of God and Prophets. A Feminist Theological Reading of the Communion of Saints.* London: SCM, 1998.

———. *She Who Is. The Mystery of God in Feminist Theological Discourse.* New York: Crossroad, 1993.

Jones, Serene. *Feminist Theory and Christian Theology. Cartographies of Grace.* Minneapolis: Fortress, 2000.

Karant-Nunn, Susan, and Merry Wiesner-Hanks, ed. *Lutheran Women.* Cambridge/New York: Cambridge University Press, 2003.

King, Ursula, ed. *Feminist Theology from the Third World: A Reader.* Maryknoll: Orbis, 1994.

Loades, Ann. *Feminist Theology: Voices from the Past.* Oxford, U.K.: Blackwell, 2001.

McFague, Sallie. *Models of God. Theology for an Ecological, Nuclear Age.* Philadelphia: Fortress, 1987. Important for re-thinking divine creativity and Christology.

Mowry LaCugna, Catherine. *Freeing Theology. The Essentials of Theology in Feminist Perspective.* New York: Harper San Francisco, 1993.

Newsom, Carol A., and Sharon H. Ringe, eds. *The Women's Bible Commentary.* Louisville, KY: Westminster/John Knox, 1992; London: SPCK, 1992.

Parsons, Susan Frank, ed. *The Cambridge Companion to Feminist Theology.* Cambridge, U.K.: Cambridge University Press, 2002.

Raphael, Melissa. *The Female Face of God in Auschwitz: a Jewish Feminist Theology of the Holocaust.* London/New York: Routledge, 2002.

Ramshaw, Gail, and Jennifer Walton. *God Beyond Gender: Feminist Christian God-Language.* Minneapolis: Fortress, 1995.

Ross, Susan A. *Extravagant Affections. A Feminist Sacramental Theology.* New York: Continuum, 1998.

Ruether, Rosemary Radford. *Women and Redemption: A Theological History.* London: SCM, 1998.

Sawyer, Deborah F. *God, Gender and the Bible.* London: Routledge, 2002.

Schrein, Shannon. *Quilting and Braiding. The Feminist Christologies of Sallie McFague and Elizabeth A. Johnson in Conversation.* Collegeville, MN: Liturgical Press, 1998.

Vuola, Elina. *Limits of Liberation. Feminist Theology and the Ethics of Poverty and Reproduction.* Sheffield/New York: Sheffield Academic Press, 2002.

Watson, Natalie K. *Introducing Feminist Ecclesiology.* Sheffield, U.K.: Sheffield Academic, 2002.

———. *Feminist Theology.* Grand Rapids: Eerdmans, 2003.

ANN LOADES

THEOLOGY, LIBERATION

See Liberation Theology

THEOLOGY, PROCESS

See Process Theology

THEOLOGY, TWENTIETH-CENTURY

The twentieth century began with great confidence in the powers of Western civilization. Europe was still in control of many of its colonies, and industrial and economic progress was celebrated in the United States. Nevertheless, the two World Wars, the HOLOCAUST, and the Depression of the U.S. economy soon changed this confidence and raised new questions that would have a deep impact on the future of theology. In this context, Protestant theology found itself in an ongoing struggle between adaptation and resistance.

Early Developments in Mainline Theology in Europe and North America

In the early decades of the twentieth century, academic Protestant theology was concentrated in Europe and the UNITED STATES, with German theology occupying one of the most prominent positions. Theologians in training from all over the world would spend time at German universities. Most theological discourse outside of Europe and the United States was shaped by the debates at the theology centers.

At the beginning of the twentieth century, the most prominent manifestations of Protestant theology developed in close relationship with the interests and concerns of Western CULTURE. What was not seen as clearly at the time, however, was that this also implied a close relationship with political and economic developments.

The theologians of what has become known as "culture Protestantism" (see CULTURAL PROTESTANTISM) in GERMANY, for instance, were interested in showing the relevance of Christian theology in a culture that did not expect much from Christianity, and they sought to reestablish the place of Protestantism as a major force of civilization. In the very last decades of the nineteenth century, ALBRECHT RITSCHL (1822–1889), seeking to leave behind metaphysics as a premodern discipline, grounds the theological enterprise in "the particular structures of revealed religion" and the "actuality of those structures in the founder and in the community" (Ritschl 1972: 210). Here theology becomes a practical matter, embedded in history. Following in these footsteps, the project of ERNST TROELTSCH (1865–1923) is summarized in the foreword to his *The Social Teaching of Christian Churches* (1960) as "think[ing] through and formulat[ing] the world of Christian thought and life in frank relation to the modern world." In these approaches, the ethical aspect of Christianity is central—"Christianity is first and foremost a matter of praxis"—and theology needs to make use of other disciplines, including history, philosophy of religion, and sociology to create a harmony with state and society "in such a way that together they will form a unity of civilization." (Troeltsch 1960:19, 32)

In the United States, similar efforts took shape. The work of SHAILER MATHEWS (1863–1941), a prominent representative of the liberal Chicago school of theology, is interested in the embeddedness of Christianity in the world. Christian belief in God is belief not in a force removed from the universe, but rather in a cosmic force that produces individual and social relationships. In this context, the work of WALTER RAUSCHEN-BUSCH (1861–1918) introduces a different note. Rauschenbusch, like most other theologians of the early decades of the twentieth century, emphasizes the immanence of God and the social implications of Christianity. But Rauschenbusch opts for CHRISTIAN SOCIALISM rather than the liberal capitalism promoted by Mathews or the liberal state promoted by Troeltsch. Rauschenbusch, more aware than most theologians of his day of the devastating underside of industrial society (see INDUSTRIALIZATION), particularly in the lives of the workers and the unemployed of the inner cities, turned the attention of theology to the internal limits of Western culture and set out to "christianize" it. While he saw the failures of the modern world in sharper relief than most of his contemporaries in Europe and the United States and thus was less interested in adapting his theology to it, he did not give up the fundamental optimism of the liberal perspective and continued to believe in the possibility of reform (see LIBERAL PROTESTANTISM AND LIBERALISM).

Theology and the World Wars

While the major theme in the early decades of the twentieth century was adaptation and in some cases reform, new voices after the end of World War I refused to adapt and introduced themes of resistance. Sensing that things have gone wrong in liberal society and in the liberal theology that catered to it, the most prominent voice of resistance was that of Swiss theologian KARL BARTH (1886–1968), who would emerge to be the most prominent theologian of the twentieth century. Barth critiqued the synthesis between Christianity and society of his predecessors and introduced a sharp contrast. Already early on, as pastor of blue-collar workers in Safenwil, SWITZERLAND, Barth picked up a new theological theme when he began to address God's otherness. God is not with the powers that be, but rather where we usually do not expect Him: on the underside, with those who suffer.

The contrast between God and humanity emphasized by Barth has been developed in different ways by other members of what has been called "dialectical theology," or NEO-ORTHODOXY, including Swiss theologian EMIL BRUNNER (1889–1966) and the German theologians FRIEDRICH GOGARTEN (1887–1967) and RUDOLF BULTMANN (1884–1976). While, under the shock of World War I, these theologians saw the shortcoming of liberal theology in focusing too strongly on humanity and not enough on God, they refused to sever the relation of God and humanity in their theological thinking. Brunner, in contradistinction to Barth, continued the search for a "point of connection" between humanity and God, and Gogarten tried to identify God in the midst of human history to such an extent that in 1933 he united with the so-called "GERMAN CHRISTIANS" who found God at work in National Socialism (Gogarten, nevertheless, maintained a certain level of resistance when he rejected their racist ideology). Bultmann's later efforts at demythologizing the Gospel to make it more understandable and useful for modern humanity show not only his efforts to adapt to the modern world (the remaining challenge of Christianity, where it must not adapt, has to do with the fact that God's GRACE is given without merit), but also another aspect characteristic of this group of theologians: Humanity is seen by and large in terms of the modern middle class, with little awareness of the lower classes (except for the early Barth) and relatively little awareness of non-Western and non-European humanity. This is the case also in the work of the German-American theologian PAUL TILLICH (1886–1965) and his attempt to develop a "method of correlation" that brings together theological answers and existential human questions. Tillich's questions identify the Western middle class's anxiety, meaninglessness, and despair as universal human questions.

In this regard, the theology of DIETRICH BONHOEF-FER (1906–1945), a theologian who was executed at the end of World War II for his resistance to Adolf Hitler and National Socialism, introduced a new element. In agreement with the new theological focus on the reality of God, Bonhoeffer argued for theology's need to follow God where God has preceded us—not only out of the church into the world in general, but also to the underside of history—and to see things from that perspective. "Our relation to God is a new life in 'existence for others', through participation in the being of Jesus" (Bonhoeffer 1971:381). Bonhoeffer, whose life ended on the underside of Western culture and in persecution and imprisonment, provided new theological impulses without being able to pursue them to the next level.

In the United States, resistance took a different shape. Theologians like REINHOLD NIEBUHR (1892–1971) and his brother H. RICHARD NIEBUHR (1894–1962) began in their own ways to question the adaptation of the cultural characteristics of liberal theology. The central theological theme in their work and in a broader movement of that time known as neo-orthodoxy is, as in continental dialectical theology, the sovereignty of God. In these approaches, however, this theme is connected with a stronger focus on the nature of human sinfulness. This leads to what is often seen as a more realistic assessment of the human predicament, picked up by so-called "Christian realism." Against liberal optimism, these theologians seek to develop a view of God and the world that takes into account our limitations. H. Richard Niebuhr's reflections on Christ and culture, for instance, expanded Troeltsch's "historical relativism in the light of theological and theo-centric relativism" (Niebuhr 1951: xii). Niebuhr did not advocate relating Christ and culture either in terms of a synthesis (here he resisted liberal theology) or in terms of a contradiction (here he resisted more radical theologies of resistance). His sympathies tended to be closer to his final model, according to which Christ transforms culture. One of the achievements of these approaches is that they reintroduce concerns about sociopolitical developments into theological reflection. Reinhold Niebuhr's assessment of colonialism is a case in point that demonstrates both the broad perspective of his work and the principles of Christian realism. Niebuhr is one of the few theologians to deal with the moral ambiguity of COLONIALISM. At the same time, however, Niebuhr defends U.S. imperialism by economic means as a more advanced model that provides a service to the world. The European sense of ethnic and cultural superiority, in his opinion, was much worse and caused much more harm.

The Second Half of the Twentieth Century

The second half of the twentieth century was heavily influenced by the events of the first half. Theologians from both Jewish and Christian traditions have raised questions as to how theology can still be done in light of the murder of six million Jews in the Holocaust and in light of the two World Wars. Such questions have been taken up by German Protestant theologians like JÜRGEN MOLTMANN (1926–) and Dorothee Sölle (1929–2003), and American Protestant theologian Frederick Herzog (1925–1995). In an effort to inspire Christianity's engagement with its Jewish heritage, Moltmann's work developed to a significant degree in dialogue with Jewish theological themes, including fresh research on messianic and apocalyptic traditions.

Other mainline theologians went back to the basic tenets of liberal theology to develop them further. In the United States of the 1970s, John Macquarrie announced that the star of FRIEDRICH SCHLEIERMACHER

(1768–1834), the father of liberal Protestant theology, was rising once again. The work of Schubert M. Ogden (1928–) builds on the foundations laid by the work of Rudolf Bultmann and tries, in conversation with other contemporary perspectives, to be "at once appropriate" to Christian witness "and credible to men and women today" (Ogden 1992:19). John B. Cobb, Jr. (1925–), one of the founders of PROCESS THEOLOGY, seeks to develop another natural theology (one of the classic concerns of liberal theology) on the basis of the process philosophy of Alfred North Whitehead (1861–1947). In Germany, WOLFHART PANNENBERG (1928–) is attempting to connect theology with a future-directed universal history.

In the United States, resistance to this new liberal theology, sometimes called "revisionist theology," emerged in postliberal theology. George Lindbeck (1923–) questions liberal theological approaches that are based on general religious experience and proposes an approach to theology built on the texts of the CHURCH and the cultures that are based on those texts. Postliberal theology aims at reshaping the world in terms of the texts of the church. This agenda shares various parallels with certain strands of so-called "evangelical theology," particularly in its emphasis on the BIBLE as represented in the work of theologians like Donald Bloesch (1928–) and others, and in similar critiques of what is seen as the "secular culture" of modernity. Nevertheless, evangelicals generally prefer a more realist view of the biblical texts than postliberals. Despite significant differences, however, liberal, postliberal, and evangelical paradigms share in common a focus on cultural phenomena and a focus on the Western world. There is little awareness of political and economic horizons and virtually no discussion of questions of power. Of the theologians that belong to these groups, only John B. Cobb in his later work breaks the mold in significant ways by dealing with economic and ecological issues and by introducing themes of resistance.

The second half of the twentieth century also gave birth to a strong ecumenical theology movement, closely related to the WORLD COUNCIL OF CHURCHES. This movement significantly extends the narrow focus on the Western world that characterizes much of twentieth-century theology. Often overlooked by "first-world" Protestant theology is the work of such theologians as D. T. Niles (1908–1970) from Sri Lanka and M. M. Thomas (1916–1996) from INDIA. Thomas's reflections on SALVATION as "humanization" pushes beyond Western anthropocentrism, and Niles reminds theology of the significance of the presence of the Holy Spirit outside of traditionally Christian contexts.

Transitions Into the Twenty-first Century

It might be argued that twentieth-century theology ends not with a particular date. The themes of mainline twentieth-century theology are interrupted by new themes and issues raised in Protestant theology in the final decades of the century that come from voices that have not traditionally been part of academic theological discussions. These voices include various political theologies and liberation theologies as well as feminist and African-American theologies in the United States. In these contexts, the horizon of theology is expanded to include questions of POLITICS and ECONOMICS and the lives of people crushed by these powers. In the process, the notion of culture is broadened significantly to include not only popular cultures, but also many other expressions and struggles that have not been part of mainline Protestant theology. Academic theology is thus no longer centered solely in the middle classes in the United States and Europe, even though these affiliations continue. Some of the most prominent newer names in Protestant theology at the end of the twentieth century include José Míguez Bonino (1924–) from Argentina, C. S. Song (1929–) from Taiwan, and Elsa Tamez (1950–) from Costa Rica. This diversity in theology has led to a wealth of new theological insights that complement some of the mainline twentieth-century debates that are still with us and that continue to be addressed by such European thinkers as Moltmann and Pannenberg as well as Rowan Williams, John Milbank, Sarah Coakley, Miroslav Volf, and Michael Welker. Add to these voices those of the evangelical Protestant theologians and this diversity has also led to concerns that theology is becoming more fragmented and fractured. Nevertheless, new forms of unity emerge in the midst of this diversity where theologians address God's responses to human suffering and where they come up once again with theological forms of resistance rooted in their own experiences of the power of God.

See also African Theology; Asian Theology; Black Theology; Dialogue, Interconfessional; Ecumenism; Evangelicalism, Theology of; Feminist Theology; Theology, Twentieth Century British; Theology, Twentieth Century, North American; Womanist Theology.

References and Further Reading

Barth, Karl. *Protestant Theology in the Nineteenth Century: Its Background and History*. Valley Forge, PA: Judson, 1973.
Bloesch, Donald G. *A Theology of Word and Spirit: Authority and Method in Theology*. Downers Grove, IL: InterVarsity, 1992.
Bonhoeffer, Dietrich. *Letters and Papers from Prison*. The enlarged edition. Edited by Eberhard Bethge. New York: Touchstone, 1997.
Bultmann, Rudolf. *Faith and Understanding*. Edited with an introduction by Robert W. Funk. Translated by Louise Pettibone Smith. Philadelphia, PA: Fortress Press, 1987.
Lindbeck, George A. *The Nature of Doctrine: Religion and Theology in a Postliberal Age*. Philadelphia, PA: Westminster Press, 1984.
Moltmann, Jürgen. *The Way of Jesus Christ: Christology in Messianic Dimensions*. Translated by Margaret Kohl. Minneapolis, MN: Fortress Press, 1993.
Niebuhr, H. Richard. *Christ and Culture*. New York: Harper, 1951.
Niebuhr, Reinhold. *The Structure of Nations and Empires: A Study of the Recurring Patters and Problems of the Political Order in Relation to the Unique Problems of the Nuclear Age*. New York: Charles Scribner's Sons, 1959.
Ogden, Schubert M. *The Point of Christology*. Dallas, TX: Southern Methodist University Press, 1992.
Pannenberg, Wolfhart. *Systematische Theologie*. 3 vols. Göttingen: Vandenhoeck & Ruprecht, 1988 ff. (Systematic Theology. Edinburgh: T.&T. Clark, 1991ff.)
Rauschenbusch, Walter. *A Theology for the Social Gospel*. New York: Macmillan, 1917.
Rieger, Joerg. *God and the Excluded: Visions and Blindspots in Contemporary Theology*. Minneapolis, MN: Fortress Press, 2001.
Ritschl, Albrecht. *Three Essays*. Translated and with an introduction by Philip Hefner. Philadelphia, PA: Fortress Press, 1972.
Thomas, M. M. *Salvation and Humanisation: Some Crucial Issues of the Theology of Mission in Contemporary India*. Madras, India: Christian Literature Society, 1971.
Troeltsch, Ernst. *The Social Teaching of the Christian Churches*. Translated by Olive Wyon, with an introduction by H. Richard Niebuhr. New York: Harper, 1960.

JOERG RIEGER

THEOLOGY, TWENTIETH-CENTURY, BRITISH

Since the English Reformation, theology in Britain has had a significant impact on the character and direction of Protestant theology throughout the world. Its primary contribution to twentieth-century Protestant theology has arguably been its dialogue concerning Incarnational CHRISTOLOGY, its appropriation of KARL BARTH in giving new impetus to Trinitarian thought, discussions on SCIENCE and THEOLOGY, studies on the ATONEMENT, and developments in the field of New Testament.

Twentieth-century British theology must be understood through several historical factors shaping its direction, including the Elizabethan Act of Uniformity (1559) which proposed a *via media* between Catholic and REFORMATION Theology for ANGLICANISM, the development of nonconformist churches (see NONCONFORMITY), the influence of Cambridge and Oxford Universities as centers of theological education (see CAMBRIDGE UNIVERSITY), two World Wars, Britain's geographical and consequently theological role as an interface for North American and continental theology, the attack of logical positivism on theology, the liberal–fundamentalist debate, and particularly the ENLIGHTENMENT.

David Ford (1997; 2000c) contends that British theology is best understood not by tracking doctrinal tendencies, but rather through interaction with various disciplines. He opts for a taxonomy of: (1) theology through history, (2) theology through philosophy, and (3) theology and society. The advantage of this approach is that it highlights that British theology has never been performed in a vacuum. Nevertheless, it tends to omit several important areas of theological contention. The approach herein highlights the general tripartite Protestant "parties" and provides an overview of several significant areas of theological discussion in Britain.

Theologies in Conflict: Liberalism, Anglo-Catholicism, and Evangelicalism

Broadly speaking, theological positions in Britain can be divided into liberalism, ANGLO-CATHOLICISM, and EVANGELICALISM, with numerous variations and intersections between them. Theological liberalism (see LIBERAL PROTESTANTISM AND LIBERALISM) arose in Britain from the Enlightenment critique of supernatural religion and was expressed in LATITUDINARIANISM. Old liberalism (i.e., pre–World War I) was characterized by a perception of the BIBLE as historically fallible, a denial of the miraculous, and a reinterpretation of biblical doctrines such as creation, incarnation, and atonement. Liberalism was also distinguished by social action (see SOCIAL GOSPEL) and the development of an ethical spirituality. R. J. Campbell's work *The New Theology* (1907) made a forthright case for liberal theology but amounted to virtual pantheism. World War I had a cataclysmic effect on liberal theology, destroying its optimism about human benevolence and the immanence of the KINGDOM OF GOD in human society. Yet it did not wane completely in Britain, with the Modern Churchmen's Union founded in 1928. It was revived further by such scholars as John Macquarrie, who incorporated existential philosophy into their liberal tendency. In the post–World War II setting, the "DEATH OF GOD" debate reached ENGLAND with Bishop JOHN A. T. ROBINSON's *Honest to God* (1963), which drew heavily from PAUL TILLICH, for whom God was "the ground of being." Don Cupitt advocated similar ideas in *Sea of Faith* (1984), couching Christianity in postmodern terms and promoting theological antirealism. D. E. Nineham represented the liberal wing of biblical scholarship and popularized form criticism and RUDOLF BULT-MANN's demythologization. The introduction of comparative religion in Britain had far-reaching consequences, chiefly through John Hick and Maurice Wiles, who vigorously attacked Christian exclusivism.

Anglo-Catholicism is predominantly, but not exclusively, an Anglican phenomenon. Its heritage lies in the Tractarians, especially JOHN HENRY NEWMAN and E. B. Busey, as well as the OXFORD MOVEMENT. It stresses the encounter of God through LITURGY, the need for community, the visible nature of the church, continuity with Roman Catholicism, the centrality of the episcopacy, and a synthesis of scripture, reason, and TRADITION. It reached prominence in the 1920s and 1930s and attracted well-known converts such as authors T. S. ELIOT and C. S. LEWIS. Two notable archbishops of Canterbury, A. M. RAMSAY and Rowan Williams, have given scholarly support to Anglo-Catholicism. Rowan Williams's *On Christian Theology* (1999) has granted Anglo-Catholic theology arguably its most succinct and cogent theological expression to date. He avers that theology operates in three domains: the celebratory, the communicative and the critical. In a work titled *Radical Orthodoxy* (1999), Anglo-Catholic scholars such as John Milbank, Catherine Pickstock, and Graham Ward have endeavored to engage postmodernism (see POSTMODERNITY) from an Anglo-Catholic perspective and yet retain their essentially orthodox beliefs.

British evangelicalism is a transdenominational phenomenon that owes its roots to PURITANISM, PIETISM, and Revivalism (see REVIVALS), and emerged more fully from the liberal–fundamentalist debate. The overarching agenda was to maintain biblical AUTHORITY, an emphasis on personal CONVERSION, and a focus on the atonement. The movement has had several prominent preachers and theologians. J. I. Packer has been a leading evangelical exponent, with works such as *Fundamentalism and the Word of God* (1958). John Stott is another evangelical voice known for Bible exposition as well as his concern for evangelical unity and social action. G. Campbell Morgan and Martin Lloyd Jones were prominent preachers, with Lloyd Jones even calling for evangelicals to leave their liberal-run denominations. The Tyndale Fellowship for Biblical Research has attempted to promote evangelical biblical scholarship. Gordon Wenham, F. F. Bruce, and I. Howard Marshall are examples of evangelicals who made in-roads into biblical scholarship. Alister McGrath has endeavored to help evangelicalism recapture its reformed heritage. A charismatic stream of evangelicalism has also emerged in figures such as Michael Green (see PENTECOSTALISM). The tension in evangelical theology has been one of defense against liberalism, the quandary of relating to other Christian groups, self-definition, and balancing evangelistic zeal with social action.

Significant Areas of Theological Discourse

An important development in British Christology began with Charles Gore in an edited work *Lux Mundi* (1889), which attempted to reconcile chalcedonic christology with the conclusion of critical scholarship. The solution was a Kenotic theology that emphasized Jesus's self-emptying of his divine attributes to participate fully in humanity. The view found prominent defenders in H. R. Mackintosh and PETER TAYLOR FORSYTH. JOHN BAILLIE represented a synthesis of NEO-ORTHODOXY, liberalism, and mysticism that saw revelation given uniquely in Christ but not exclusively to Christianity. His brother Donald Baillie, in *God Was in Christ* (1948), reaffirmed the humanness of Christ and defended the liberal view that Jesus was a man who fully discovered God and in whom God dwelt. The incarnation is understood as a paradox of GRACE wherein God dwells in Christ, who ascribes all goodness to God. John Macquarrie used existentialism as a matrix for christology. John Hick advocated a pluralistic framework for christology and a view of the incarnation in terms of myth and metaphor. Historical treatments of christological origins were published by C. F. D. Moule and I. Howard Marshall. James D. G. Dunn, in *Christology in the Making* (1981), examined the development of christology from its Jewish framework, alleging that Jesus did not think of himself as pre-existent and neither did Paul, who instead used Adam and wisdom motifs to express Christ's cosmic significance. In contrast, Richard Bauckham, in *God Crucified* (1998), advocated that second-temple Jewish was indeed a "strict monotheism," but the concept of God was constituted in such a way as to make it possible for Jesus to be incorporated into the divine identity. N. T. Wright has argued similarly that early Christianity redefined God so as to accommodate their belief in Christ. This suggests (contra Macquarrie 1990:327) that British christological discussion is more than a commentary and criticism of Continental ideas.

In contrast to the liberal view of ESCHATOLOGY that saw the Kingdom of God progressing immanently through human society and the wholly futurist eschatology of ALBERT SCHWEITZER, C. H. Dodd set forth a "realized eschatology" that saw the kingdom as present and manifested in Jesus's ministry dislocating futuristic hopes of the kingdom. Popular as Dodd's thesis was, it has been eclipsed by a more balanced approach to biblical eschatology that stresses the kingdom as being both a present reality and a future event. Such a view was arguably foreshadowed in the work

of JOSEPH B. LIGHTFOOT. JOHN A. T. ROBINSON attempted to revive the idea of a nonapocalyptic eschatology by focusing on the Gospel of John as being indicative of Jesus's eschatology. The parousia of Christ is a symbolic presentation of what happens when Christ comes in love. Richard Bauckham popularized JÜRGEN MOLTMANN's "Theology of Hope," making it more widely known in Britain. G. B. Caird questioned the nature and function of apocalyptic language in the Bible, contending that attempts to invest political events with cosmic meaning were problematic.

In terms of the doctrine of God, the most vigorous discussion centered on the Trinity. Heavily indebted to KARL BARTH, Thomas Torrance and Colin Gunton were the vanguard of a resurgence of Trinitarian thought in the British academy. For Gunton, the Trinity is not a mathematical enigma, but rather encapsulates the heart of the Christian gospel. Ultimately, it is Christ who makes the Trinity visible and accessible to us. Moreover, the church is an institution called to reflect on earth the eternal divine community of the Trinity.

British theology has been the battleground for competing interpretations of Christ's death. The view of penal substitution was attacked by liberalism on the grounds that it rested on the unacceptable notion of original sin and the idea of vicarious sacrifice was morally reprehensible. H. Rashdall, in *The Idea of Atonement* (1919), launched a barrage of criticism against the historical doctrine, instead arguing for a moral improvement theory. According to Donald Baillie and John Macquarrie, the atonement is not a once-for-all activity, but rather illustrates God's continuing reconciliation with creation and constitutes a continual or eternal event. P. T. FORSYTH wrote several works on the atonement, including *The Cruciality of the Cross* (1909) and *The Justification of God* (1916). In conjunction to his defense of penal sacrifice, Forsyth suggested that the cross is God's means of restoring justice in the cosmos. His emphasis on christology and grace largely foreshadowed Karl Barth. Similar apologies for substitionary atonement were offered by James Denney, Vincent Taylor, John Stott, J. I. Packer, and I. Howard Marshall. Alister McGrath's study of justification represents an effort to restore the doctrine back to centrality in evangelicalism. Richard Swinburne's *Responsibility and Atonement* (1989) put forward the notion that Jesus's sacrifice is a gift of utmost value to God that humans may plead upon. Colin Gunton in *The Actuality of Atonement* (1988) and Vernon White in *Atonement and Incarnation* (1991) have defended an objective approach to the atonement, contending that genuine reconciliation is contingent on a real, extrinsic action by God in the cross that confronts SIN and moral evil.

The tradition of British biblical scholarship that commenced with F. J. A. Hort, B. F. Westcott, and J. B. Lightfoot continued on in the twentieth century. The *International Critical Commentary* series has provided an outlet to express the finest of British biblical scholarship. The Biblical theology movement evolving out of GERMANY gained a foothold in Britain through H. Wheeler Robinson, H. H. Rowley, F. V. Wilson, and Vincent Taylor. Several glaring criticisms were leveled at the movement by James Barr, which significantly diminished its influence. Anthony Thiselton sought to awaken biblical scholarship to the challenges posed by hermeneutics. Postmodern reading strategies have received support on various fronts, particularly from John Barton. James D. G. Dunn coined the term "the New Perspective on Paul," which asserts that Paul's problem with Judaism was not over Jewish legalism, but rather over Jewish exclusivism. Patristics studies have also been furthered by Hendry Chadwick, Rowan Williams, Maurice Wiles, and Frances Young advocating their significance for the modern church.

Since the publication of Charles Darwin's *The Origin of the Species* (1859), theologians have had to wrestle with scientific theories and their relationship to theological doctrines (see DARWINISM). The relationship between the two disciplines has been explicated by Arthur Peacocke, T. F. Torrance, John Polkinghorne, and Alister McGrath. Keith Ward, in *God, Chance and Necessity* (1996), attempted to expose the scientific and philosophical inadequacies of scientific atheism. An integration of philosophy and theology was attempted by Richard Swinburne and Donald MacKinnon. The former attempted to demonstrate the philosophical coherence of Christian doctrine, while the later studiously engaged metaphysics, evil, and Marxism in relation to Christian doctrines such as christology and the Trinity. Logical positivism made a strong challenge to theology in Britain by asserting that theological language was unverifiable and therefore meaningless. Several responses followed, including that of John Hick, who saw religious belief as eschatologically verifiable. Others tried to legitimize God-talk through Wittgensteinian philosophy.

ECUMENISM gained a strong following in Britain in the twentieth century. Advances were made at the WORLD MISSIONARY CONFERENCE of 1910 in Edinburgh, the 1920 LAMBETH CONFERENCE, and from the Faith and Order Movement. JOHN R. MOTT, John Baillie, and WILLIAM TEMPLE were instrumental in providing the theological rationale behind ecumenism and formation of the WORLD COUNCIL OF CHURCHES. This coincided with several studies on the church by British scholars such as L. Thornton, A. M. Ramsay, R. N. Flew, and J. E. LESSLIE NEWBIGIN. However, ECCLESIOLOGY has generally been eclipsed by other doctrinal discussions, and publications in Continental Europe by Barth, Karl Rahner, Hans Küng, and Jürgen Moltmann have dominated debate. The Anglican-Roman Catholic International Commission has maintained steady contact between CANTERBURY and ROME, dialoguing on such issues as authority, CHURCH, eucharist, ETHICS, justification, and ministry.

LIBERATION THEOLOGY found expression in urban theology, the "Radical Evangelicals," the British Jubilee group, and a scholarly voice in Christopher Rowland. Feminist, black, and gay theologies likewise have respectively emerged since the 1970s with the formation of such journals as *Theology and Sexuality* stimulating thought in adjacent areas (see FEMINIST THEOLOGY; HOMOSEXUALITY; BLACK THEOLOGY; WOMANIST THEOLOGY). Despite the critique of Barth, the British tradition of natural theology that started with WILLIAM PALEY was continued by F. R. Tennant, Basil Mitchell, John Hick, and Richard Swinburne and publicized through the Gifford lectures.

Conclusion

A distinguishing feature of British twentieth-century theology is that it has never been dominated by one school or figure. Although significant inroads were made by Barth, Tillich, and Bultmann, various philosophies such as existentialism and logical positivism, and theological movements like death of God theology and neo-orthodoxy, none came to dominate Britain's theological landscape. This is perhaps attributable to the emergence of a significant breadth of theological diversification in Britain, further enhanced by the fact that since the Reformation the British have never taken to religious excesses and have always preferred the *via media*.

Whereas in the twentieth century British theologians had to grapple with Christianity and MODERNISM, it appears that in the twenty-first century a similar struggle will be waged over Postmodernity. The gradual de-Christianization of Britain through an increasingly secularized and multifaith population, the rise of relativistic epistemologies, and religious pluralism will present their own unique challenges to British theology in the future.

See also Catholicism, Protestant Reactions; Education, Overview; Evangelicalism, Theology of; Secularization; Theology, Twentieth-Century; Theology, Twentieth-Century, Global

References and Further Reading

Ford, David F., ed. *The Modern Theologians: An Introduction to Christian Theology in the Twentieth Century.* 2nd ed. 225–305. Blackwell, UK: Oxford, 1997.

———. "Theological Wisdom, British Style." *The Christian Century* 117 no.11 (2000a): 388–391.

———. "British Theology After a Trauma: Divisions and Conversations." *The Christian Century* 117 no. 12 (2000b): 425–431.

———. "British Theology: Movements and Churches," *The Christian Century* 117 no. 13 (2000c): 467–473.

Gunton, Colin. "An English Systematic Theology?" *Scottish Journal of Theology* 46 (1993): 479–496.

Hastings, A. *A History of English Christianity 1920–1990.* 2nd ed. London: SCM, 1991.

Macquarrie, John. *Jesus Christ in Modern Thought.* London: SCM, 1990.

Worrall, B. G. *The Making of the Modern Church: Christianity in England Since 1800.* London: SPCK, 1988.

MICHAEL BIRD

THEOLOGY, TWENTIETH-CENTURY, GLOBAL

Theology is reflection on God; for Christians, it is "faith-seeking understanding." It may also include fundamental theology or natural theology, which are attempts to provide rational support to belief in God and God's self-revelation that faith grasps. Christian theology began with the second-century church fathers; Protestant theology arose in the sixteenth century with the reforming movements led by MARTIN LUTHER, HULDRYCH ZWINGLI, and JOHN CALVIN. The nineteenth century was a particularly successful one for Protestant theology, in that it flourished and underwent several renewals. During that century, Protestant theology in Europe began to come to terms with the ENLIGHTENMENT and scientific revolutions. FRIEDRICH SCHLEIERMACHER and ALBRECHT RITSCHL gave great impetus to the progressive movements in Protestant theology during the nineteenth century. They sought to do theology in a manner consistent with modern philosophy's "turn to the subject"; their theologies took seriously universal human experience as a source and norm for Christian theological reflection. Also during the nineteenth century, Protestant ORTHODOXY underwent a revival, especially in North America, where a dynasty of conservative Protestant thinkers at Princeton Theological Seminary influenced generations of Protestant ministers and theologians for a theology of Reformed retrieval ("back to the sources") that opposed accommodation to the modern thought world.

Divergent Directions

As the twentieth century dawned, two opposing forces of Protestant theology threatened to tear it apart. On the one hand, the heirs of Schleiermacher and followers of Ritschl developed various forms of liberal Protestant theology, which was labeled "MODERNISM" by its more conservative critics (see LIBERAL PROTESTANTISM AND LIBERALISM). On the other hand, the followers of the Old Princeton School theologians Charles Hodge and Benjamin Warfield joined forces with revivalists influenced by evangelist DWIGHT L. MOODY to form the fundamentalist movement to oppose liberal theology. Fundamentalists emphasized the AUTHORITY of Scripture interpreted relatively literally and promoted what they regarded as "traditional Christianity." They condemned any deviation from what they considered the "fundamentals" of the true Protestant Christian faith. Among their fundamentals were the verbal inspiration of Scripture, the virgin birth of Jesus Christ, and the substitutionary ATONEMENT. Some added the "premillennial return of Christ" to the list of Christian fundamentals. FUNDAMENTALISM came in many variations, all of which opposed progressive Protestantism's tendency to accommodate to the spirit of modernity. The most influential fundamentalist theologian was the last representative of the Old Princeton School of Protestant theology, J. GRESHAM MACHEN, whose book *Christianity and Liberalism* (1923) declared the theology being developed by Schleiermacher's and Ritschl's progressive heirs not authentically Christian but a different religion altogether.

Liberal Protestant theology's leading defender and expositor at the opening of the twentieth century was German church historian ADOLPH VON HARNACK, whose *What Is Christianity?* (*Das Wesen des Christentums*) was published in 1900. Interpreting his mentor Ritschl's revisionist approach to Protestant theology, Harnack summed up Christianity with three basic principles: the KINGDOM OF GOD and its coming, God the father and the infinite value of the human soul, and the higher righteousness and the commandment of love. According to Harnack and most other progressive Protestants, the essence of Christianity has little or nothing to do with supernatural events or the traditional dogmas of the person of Jesus Christ; rather, it has to do with the message proclaimed by Jesus Christ about the historical kingdom of God as a real possibility within history. In the UNITED STATES, Baptist theologian and church historian WALTER RAUSCHENBUSCH and other progressives formed a type of liberal theology known as the SOCIAL GOSPEL that blended the liberal emphasis on the historical kingdom of God with evangelical themes of CONVERSION and transformation. Rauschenbusch's influential manifesto, published in 1917 as *A Theology for the Social Gospel,* proclaims the essence of Christianity as the kingdom of God as a society organized according to love. Whereas liberal theology revolved around an optimistic vision of human nature and history, fundamentalist theology was pessimistic about humanity and the future. It stressed humanity's sinfulness and incapacity for good apart from supernatural transformation by God; liberal theology viewed God's transforming activity as in and through human social progress. Liberal theology encouraged a spirit of free inquiry and nondogmatic theology within the churches, whereas fundamentalist theology promoted commitment to what it saw as Protestant Christianity's foundational beliefs even against the allegedly assured results of modern SCIENCE and philosophy. By the 1920s, fundamentalism and liberal thought were locked in mortal combat over the souls of most mainline Protestant denominations, many of which experienced divisions over the issues raised in the fundamentalist–modernist strife.

Dialectical Theology

Many commentators believe that twentieth-century theology was actually born in 1919 with the publication of Swiss Protestant theologian KARL BARTH's *Der Römerbrief (The Epistle to the Romans),* a theological commentary on Romans. According to one historian, the book "fell like a bombshell on the playground of the theologians." A new school of Protestant theology that would indelibly place its stamp on twentieth-century theology was being born that would be known popularly as NEO-ORTHODOXY and as dialectical theology by most scholars. Its two main early representatives were Barth in Basel, SWITZERLAND and EMIL BRUNNER, who taught theology in Zurich, Switzerland. Barth's magnum opus, the multivolume *Church Dogmatics* (1932–1967), is the classic of the movement, whereas Brunner's smaller three-volume *Dogmatics* (1946–1960) and other writings first introduced neo-orthodoxy to English-speaking audiences. In *Der Römerbrief,* Barth countered liberal Protestant theology with a strong emphasis on the transcendence of God and God's Word and a stress on humanity's sinfulness and need for obedience to the Word that is foreign to its own thinking. Although many liberals—including Barth's teacher Harnack—regarded the first soundings of neo-orthodoxy as little more than a sophisticated version of fundamentalism, it was in actuality far from fundamentalistic.

Neither Barth nor Brunner, nor any other dialectical theologian, affirmed the verbal inspiration and inerrancy of Scripture (see BIBLICAL INERRANCY). Brunner denied the virgin birth (although not because of anti-supernatural bias) and raised questions about many of the Bible's miracle stories. Both Swiss theologians and their followers decried liberal theology's per-

ceived maximal acknowledgment of the claims of modernity and fundamentalism's perceived slavish adherence to its own "paper pope," the BIBLE. For neo-orthodox thinkers, the Bible "becomes the Word of God" in the moment when God chooses to speak through it; the Word of God is event and not propositions. Nevertheless, they averred, the Word of God in and through Jesus Christ, Scripture and the proclamation of the CHURCH, contradicts every human ideology and *zeitgeist* (spirit of the age) and invites people into crisis with God, where they are judged and called to repent. Against both liberal theology and fundamentalism, neo-orthodoxy embraced paradox as a necessary form of theological expression. Lurking behind dialectical theology was the figure of nineteenth-century Protestant philosophical prophet SÖREN KIERKEGAARD OF DENMARK, who embraced the incarnation as the "absolute paradox" and eschewed attempts to achieve a synthesis of truth based on human reasoning.

Twentieth-century Protestant theology can be understood largely in terms of these three major movements of thought and their permutations: liberal Protestantism, Protestant fundamentalism, and neo-orthodoxy. In 1959 Protestant publisher Westminster Press presented three volumes by proponents of these three general theological movements with the intention of summarizing twentieth-century theology under this rubric: *The Case for Orthodox Theology* by EDWARD JOHN CARNELL, *The Case for a New Reformation Theology* by William Hordern, and *The Case for Theology in Liberal Perspective* by L. Harold DeWolf. Carnell, who was president of Fuller Theological Seminary, was not representative of the militant wing of fundamentalism; his book was influenced by the Protestant orthodoxy of the Old Princeton School of Hodge and Warfield. Hordern preferred "new Reformation theology" to "neo-orthodoxy," but his volume presented dialectical theology. However, these three types of Protestant theology hardly exhaust the range of theological opinion in the twentieth century.

Two of the century's most influential Protestant thinkers cannot be comfortably categorized by them. REINHOLD NIEBUHR (1892–1971) and PAUL TILLICH (1886–1965) broke out of the molds of liberal Protestant theology without becoming neo-orthodox. Neither was fundamentalist. Niebuhr's magnum opus *The Nature and Destiny of Man* (1941–1949) represented a manifesto for "Christian realism" that blended elements of neo-orthodox pessimism about humanity with liberal elements of accommodation to modern CULTURE. Niebuhr also affirmed the traditional symbols of Protestant orthodoxy even if he did not interpret them literally. According to Niebuhr, liberal theology overestimated the human potential for perfection and underestimated human depravity as pride. He retrieved the classical Augustinian doctrine of original SIN from its neglect by liberal Protestantism while leaving behind the literalism of the fall of humanity in the primeval garden. He interpreted the kingdom of God as an impossible ideal that is always coming but never arriving, and warned against eschewing harsh justice because it falls short of the perfection of love. Tillich's three-volume *Systematic Theology* (1951–1963) presented a chastened liberalism heavily influenced by existentialist philosophy with its tragic sense of the human condition. According to Tillich, God is not to be thought of anthropomorphically as "person" but ontologically as "Being Itself" or "the Ground of Being," and humanity is not infinitely perfectible, but rather is caught in the polarities of a predicament that leads inevitably to sin. Nevertheless, human beings can come to accept that they are accepted by Being Itself and thereby achieve the "courage to be" in the face of the threat of non-being.

Other Theologies

The 1960s witnessed the fragmentation of Protestant theology with the rise of secular and radical theology, the theology of Christian atheism, PROCESS THEOLOGY, theology of hope, and the beginnings of LIBERATION THEOLOGY. Conservative theology also experienced a renewal as it emerged out of militant fundamentalism into a less restrictive and separatistic "new evangelical theology." One of the most influential Protestant voices in the 1960s was that of one who died in a German concentration camp in 1945—DIETRICH BON-HOEFFER. His *Letters and Papers from Prison* was published by one of his students in the 1950s and 1960s (it appeared in several editions containing different collections of letters and papers) and aroused a great deal of excitement, especially among so-called secular and radical Protestants who hailed the arrival of "religionless Christianity" in a "world come of age." Precisely what Bonhoeffer meant by these and other enigmatic phrases is a matter of debate, but many radical Protestant theologians interpreted them as promoting a secularized church that allows the world to set its agenda. A few more radical Protestant thinkers proclaimed the "DEATH OF GOD" in modern culture and promoted the "gospel of Christian atheism," which was a message about the way of Jesus Christ devoid of a transcendent divine being. In GERMANY, JÜRGEN MOLTMANN published *A Theology of Hope* (1964) and *The Crucified God* (1968), in which he expounded an alternative theological vision to secular and radical theology that placed God in the future and traced the arrival of God out of the future in the

promises of God and in the life, death, and resurrection of Jesus Christ. WOLFHART PANNENBERG also created an eschatological theology that defined God as the God of history whose full deity would appear and be finally established only at the end of history. History itself is divine revelation, and God is realizing or actualizing Godself in and through humanity's discovery of God. For all their differences, the two German theologians presented a way of thinking about God and the world that took with utmost seriousness the secularity of the world and the evil within history without discarding God or the sacred.

The 1960s also witnessed the rise of "POLITICAL THEOLOGY" within both Roman Catholic and Protestant theological communities. In Germany, Johannes Baptist Metz, Dorothee Sölle, and Jürgen Moltmann called for greater application of the Gospel to the creation of a just society of equal persons; they decried the continuing tendency of some theologians to focus attention on questions of secularity and atheism while the poor became poorer and the rich became richer. In LATIN AMERICA, various liberation theologies arose beginning in the late 1960s and gained strength throughout the 1970s and into the 1980s. Argentinian Methodist theologian Jose Miguez Bonino joined Catholic theologian Gustavo Gutierrez of Peru and other Catholic and Protestant thinkers in calling for *Doing Theology in a Revolutionary Situation* (1975). For liberationists, theology must recognize God's preferential option for the poor and the privileged insight into God provided by poverty. It must also side with the poor in their struggle for liberation from all that dehumanizes and oppresses them. In North America, Presbyterian feminist theologian Letty Russell attempted to do liberation theology from a feminist perspective and joined with Catholic feminists Rosemary Radford Ruether and Elizabeth Schüssler Fiorenza in calling for a radical revision in Christian theological categories and language to rid them of patriarchy and misogyny. The second half of the century saw Protestants of various theological orientations entering into positive dialogue and alliances with Roman Catholic thinkers, overcoming many, if not most, of the hostilities that separated Protestant and Catholic communities of scholars before the Second Vatican Council (1962–1965).

Non-Western Protestant theologians increasingly weighed in to the theological conversations during the second half of the twentieth century. One of the first Asian Protestant theologians to gain worldwide notice was Japanese Lutheran thinker Kazoh Kitamori, whose 1946 *Theology of the Pain of God* went through many editions and translations. Kitamori reflected on the suffering of God in the tragedies of history against the background of his own country's defeat at the end of World War II. He questioned the traditional doctrines of God's immutability and impassibility and brought resources from his own culture to bear on reconstructing the doctrine of God's transcendence and immanence. About a year before Kitamori's book was published, Dietrich Bonhoeffer wrote that "only the suffering God can help." Their dual influence led to a vast reconsideration of God's involvement in the historical travail of humanity.

During the last few decades of the century, other Asian theologians contributed to the ongoing discussions about contextualization of the Gospel and the nature of theological reflection. Kosuke Koyama, a Japanese theologian working in Thailand and Singapore, drew on South Asian cultural resources to shape a new Christian theology specifically for Asian Christians. His best-known and most influential volume of Asian theology is *Waterbuffalo Theology* (1974). A Chinese theologian, Choan-Seng Song of Taiwan, published several volumes of theology that sought to integrate Christianity with traditional and modern Chinese culture. His *Third-Eye Theology* (1979) argued for the development of a new vision for Christian theologians that incorporates Asian culture with its mystical insights into Christian theology shaped by the more rational West.

The continent of AFRICA contributed a number of fresh Christian approaches to theology during the 1970s through the 1990s. Among them was a creative new interpretation of the doctrine of the Trinity based on African tribal and family structures titled *On Communitarian Divinity: An African Interpretation of the Trinity* (1994). In North America, Puerto Rican Methodist church historian and theologian Justo González helped create a Christian theology from a Hispanic perspective in his *Mañana: Christian Theology from a Hispanic Perspective* (1990). There he argued for greater attention by theologians of all ethnic and denominational background to the plights of powerless minorities in cultures dominated by powerful majorities and sought to show that such powerless minorities have the right and the responsibility to develop their own forms of Christian life, worship, and theology.

As the twentieth century drew to a close, Protestant theology was more fragmented than ever. Many Protestant theologians were less concerned about carrying the torch for Protestantism and its distinctive themes than about developing contextual theologies that cross traditional boundaries.

See also Catholicism, Protestant Reactions; Evangelicalism, Theology of; Theology; Theology, Twentieth-Century; Theology, Twentieth Century, British.

References and Further Reading

González, Justo. *Out of Every Tribe and Nation: Christian Theology at the Ethnic Roundtable.* Nashville, TN: Abingdon Press, 1992.

Grenz, Stanley J., and Roger E. Olson. *20th Century Theology: God and the World in a Transitional Age.* Downers Grove, IL: InterVarsity Press, 1992.

Livingston, James, and Francis Schüssler Fiorenza, eds. *Modern Christian Thought, Volume II: The Twentieth Century.* Rev. ed. Upper Saddle River, NJ: Prentice-Hall, 2000.

ROGER E. OLSON

THEOLOGY, TWENTIETH-CENTURY, NORTH AMERICAN

The great majority of North American Protestant Christians in the twentieth century was influenced by theologies of the Reformed and Evangelical traditions. The First Great AWAKENING, typified by North America's preeminent theologian, JONATHAN EDWARDS, and the revivals of the nineteenth-century Second Great Awakening, set the general terms of North American theological thought and practice. It was liberal theology, however, that became the prominent antagonist in twentieth century theological schools and mainline denominations (see LIBERAL PROTESTANTISM AND LIBERALISM).

The European ENLIGHTENMENT's disruption of orthodox Christianity arrived in full force in North America only after the CIVIL WAR. Devastating dismissals of Christianity and theology by the doubt and atheism of the modern intellectual world led to the enduring twentieth-century conundrum: how to reestablish theology's integrity as a discipline. Five crises have confronted twentieth-century American theology, and at least the first four have their roots in the Enlightenment. The first crisis is epistemological, that is, the problem of knowledge, introduced classically by JOHN LOCKE and IMMANUEL KANT. If we become clear about the limits of human knowledge, then theology must press the question: Can God really be known, and if so, how?

The second crisis is one of AUTHORITY. The modern dedication to the new criteria of historical reliability was eventually applied to the BIBLE and the Christian TRADITION. This led to questions that are still current: To what extent must theology recover the Christian past, or can theology do without the "house of authority"? If we are conditioned by many factors in our context as we seek to interpret the past, what would constitute true interpretation of scripture and tradition? Should the primary task of theology be establishing the identity of the Christian faith or demonstrating its relevance to MODERNITY?

A third crisis was prompted by the application of scientific approaches, such as historical critical methods, to religion itself. Modern thinkers such as Karl Marx, Charles Darwin (see DARWINISM), and Sigmund Freud offered alternatives to the traditional story of Christianity (embracing creation and new creation) and in the process gave alternative, reductionist explanations of religion. Can theology describe religion in such a limited way as to protect it from the "science" of history, or does theology need an altogether new overarching conception of history? A fourth crisis stems from the violence, oppression, and suffering of the twentieth century, which was dubbed at its beginning "the Christian century" but, as it unfolded, mocked the Enlightenment visions of eternal peace, freedom, and justice. Two World Wars, Fascism, state COMMUNISM, the nuclear threat, the massive growth of technology, and the global market with the attendant degradation of the environment, recalcitrant forms of racism, GENDER oppression, and neocolonialism were negations that contradicted everything modernity stood for. Theology in the twentieth century ended with a final crisis, that is, the collapse of modernity itself. How could theology proceed without its failed modernist partners?

North American theologies in the twentieth century, whether in the Reformed/Evangelical strands or in the "liberal" strands, can be categorized according to their responses to these pressing questions of "modernity." At the turn of the century liberal theology on both sides of the Atlantic was thriving. It was recognizable by its attempt to rehabilitate theology in the face of modernity by stressing practical reason, subjectivity, ethical/moral content, the immanence of God, and the centrality of freedom. It recommended abandoning doctrines that seemed clearly antimodern, such as original sin, and reinterpreting other doctrines according to the spirit of the age, for example, jettisoning the divinity of Jesus in favor of his ethical teachings. It grounded theology in immediate human experience, following the lead of the first "liberal" theologian, FRIEDRICH SCHLEIERMACHER, thus obviating the problem of mediating God through scripture or tradition.

A second skein of liberal theology shaping much of American theology through the 1930s sprang from what some scholars call the "Third Great Awakening" or the SOCIAL GOSPEL. Informed by the theology of ALBRECHT BENJAMIN RITSCHL, it was inspired by a vision of human progress. The "KINGDOM OF GOD" was interpreted as a realm of static values guiding society toward perfection. WALTER RAUSCHENBUSCH and SHAILER MATHEWS provided the theological framework for the radical criticism of the unjust economic conditions produced by unregulated industrial giants and the first modern economic globalization. An old

theological motif of the coming of the kingdom of God in America was revived.

There were three strands of North American theology that radically broke off from liberal and modernist theology during the first three decades of the twentieth century. The initial torrid enemy of liberal theology arose in the form of FUNDAMENTALISM and extreme EVANGELICALISM, movements that thoroughly resisted modernity, although it is widely recognized that in their opposition to modernity these thought forms took on modern characteristics. Fundamentalists used doctrines like biblical inerrancy and the premillennial return of Christ as barriers to separate themselves from secular culture. It is generally thought that fundamentalism as a major force ended with the Scopes "monkey" trial of 1925, but its temper continued to influence some evangelicals until it was repudiated by the "new" evangelicalism after World War II.

A second type of theological criticism of liberal secular culture uses a thought system of modernity (such as idealist, empiricist, or historicist philosophies or a combination of them) to overcome the challenges of modernity, but in so doing assumes that Christianity has validity only insofar as it fits into a modern philosophical framework. Out of this approach arose the first peculiarly American theologies of the twentieth century based on the empirical philosophies of WILLIAM JAMES and John Dewey, the idealist philosophy of JOSIAH ROYCE, and the pragmatist philosophy of Charles Pierce. These theologies, eschewing liberal subjectivism and romanticism, prized reason and scientific enquiry above all. The vanguard of these movements was concentrated in what was known as the "Chicago School" and was best exemplified by the empirical theology of Henry Nelson Wieman.

A third general criticism of liberalism characterizes the middle third of the twentieth-century North American theology and, in part, is given various patterns by the different directions taken by the so-called German "dialectical" theologians of the 1920s (KARL BARTH, PAUL TILLICH, RUDOLF BULTMANN, and FRIEDRICH GOGARTEN), who were united in their criticism of a liberalism that foundered on the concussions of World War I but who later disagreed about how and what to retrieve from the best of nineteenth-century theology.

Barth, perhaps the most generative theologian of the twentieth century, has been called on by a wide spectrum of American theologians who are primarily concerned to protect Christian identity over against what they consider modernity's pretensions. Christianity must develop its own framework of interpretation and verification, although it must responsibly engage modernity in all its promises and threats. Although Barth came into vogue again in the last third of the twentieth century, in large part through the sway of Postliberal Theology, in the 1930s the main thrust of North American theology appreciated Barth's cautions but wanted to maintain the questions and some answers of nineteenth-century theology, especially as summarized in the thought of ERNST TROELTSCH, whose work provided a framework for much of liberal theology in the remainder of the twentieth century.

The brothers REINHOLD NIEBUHR and H. RICHARD NIEBUHR were prominent in setting the North American theological agenda in the middle third of the twentieth century and, in their quite distinctive ways, cast the largest shadows over American theology in the last fifty years of the twentieth century through their teaching of two generations of theologians, Reinhold at Union Theological Seminary in New York and Richard at Yale. Reinhold's experience as a pastor among the families of automobile workers in Detroit led to his thoroughgoing criticism of liberal theology as ineffective in dealing with the new situation of industrial democracy because of its naive doctrines of human perfectibility and progress. His theology tended to be largely anthropological and his social criticism benefited from a recovery of the doctrine of SIN, but his thought left much to be desired in terms of CHRISTOLOGY, ESCHATOLOGY, and ecclesiology.

In the theology of H. Richard Niebuhr is found both an appreciation of the radical insights of Barth and SØREN KIERKEGAARD, but also a loyalty to the liberal tradition, especially the Schleiermacherian experiential root of theological reflection and a Troeltschian historical and sociological orientation. In the former he found a radical monotheism that replaced liberal anthropomorphism with the sovereignty of God's being and action over the human. From the latter he learned that theology cannot escape its locus in the historical relativity of the language and experience of the believing community. He dealt with the problem of revelation and history by describing the way each human being, even a scientist, expresses faith in Being's peculiar revelation of itself to him or her.

The revolt against a superficial modernity took yet another form in the theology of Paul Tillich, who in effect became an "American" theologian after leaving Nazi Germany. Tillich developed a theological method of "correlation," which was devoted to both the relevance and identity of the Christian faith. It does not claim an overarching integration that would obviate either the essence of Christianity or modernity but juxtaposes them in a variety of dialogical patterns. Basic existential questions are raised through philosophical analysis in expectation of answers in the form of the reinterpretation of various Christian symbols, especially of Jesus as the Christ.

North American theology in the middle third of twentieth century was also deeply affected by the theology of Rudolf Bultmann and his philosophical mentor, Martin Heidegger. Bultmann joined the most extreme conclusions of the History of Religions School with Heideggerian existentialism for an answer to the question of history. He demythologized those elements of the New Testament that did not fit the modern consciousness. This left an isolated kerygma of Jesus, which can be proclaimed as an offer of freedom, without the necessity of historical mediation, to the individual conscience in the present.

The 1960s represent a watershed in North American theology, which now seemed to be declaring independence from European theology in a new age of diverse, more global theological conversation. A veritable explosion of novel theological options was tendered in the academic marketplace in response to a new pluralist context for theology and a growing crisis of modern secularism. The Vietnam War, the CIVIL RIGHTS struggle, the nuclear threat of a blistering Cold War, a growing inequality in wealth, feminist and youth revolts, the sexual revolution, and novel forms of popular culture created a new sense of historical threat.

In the early 1960s PROCESS THEOLOGY appeared as another distinctively North American theology. It attempted to deal with a deficit in modern liberal theology with regard to the doctrine of God and attracted deep interest as a new endeavor to conceive God in relation to the modern world. It provided a radical critique of many God concepts in the Christian tradition, but did not discard the best of the classical tradition. Depending on the metaphysics of Alfred North Whitehead, in which neither being nor self but rather "events" or "actual occasions" in a purposive, living cosmos are primary, Charles Hartshorne, John B. Cobb Jr., and Schubert Ogden, the main proponents of Process Theology, set out to depict God as the unifier and envisioner of all possibilities. As the one who gives direction to reality, God experiences all and surpasses all. In experiencing all, God changes, and yet in God's purpose, God remains immutable. Whereas Process Theology often gained a new relevance to modern dynamic views of NATURE, it showed a deficit in the appropriation of the tradition for dealing with evil and suffering.

Revived interest in the theologies of Friedrich Gogarten and DIETRICH BONHOEFFER and a new focus on history and eschatology in the theologies of JÜRGEN MOLTMANN and WOLFHART PANNENBERG gave rise to a theological turn from the individual self to concrete history, society, and politics. North American theology was suddenly focused on the questions of concrete suffering among specific people, and "liberation" emerged as a common theme among many different theologies. In the late 1960s, just about the time Latin American LIBERATION THEOLOGY began, BLACK THEOLOGY arose out of the long struggle of African-American people against the inhumanity of SLAVERY and the ensuing bitterness of racism in all its forms. Working from the new historical context created by the civil rights movement of MARTIN LUTHER KING JR., and the black power movement of Malcolm X, black theologians JAMES CONE, Gayraud Wilmore, and J. Deotis Roberts created a theology that made the suffering of black people the subject of theology. In Cone's theology a Barthian emphasis on God's self-disclosure was now identified with God's revelation within the liberation of blacks, and the identity of Jesus was inseparable from the fate of the humiliated within an inhuman society.

FEMINIST THEOLOGIES also began to emerge in the 1960s in response to the peculiar denigration and subordination of WOMEN in North American society. These theologies took up the several North American feminist movements of the nineteenth and twentieth centuries and many global intellectual developments that work for the well-being and participation of women in family, church, and society. Some feminist scholars held that the maleness of the Christian symbol-system inevitably named women as inferior and subjected, and should therefore be rejected. Other feminist theologians, such as Rosemary Radford Ruether, Elisabeth Schüssler Fiorenza, Letty Russell, and SALLIE MCFAGUE attempted, in very different ways, to deconstruct and reconstruct the Christian traditions, texts, or symbols/metaphors for their use in the service of women's liberation.

By the 1980s a new theological movement termed "womanist" sought to show that African-American women suffered a kind of oppression that had not been dealt with by either Black Theology or feminist theologies (see WOMANIST THEOLOGY). Jacquelyn Grant, Kelly Brown Douglas, and Delores S. Williams produced new readings of the Bible, Jesus, and atonement in the context of African-American women. Other theologies of freedom that played major roles in the last third of the twentieth century centered on the specific contexts of oppression among NATIVE AMERICANS, the Hispanic/Latino and Asian-American communities, and gay and lesbian communities (see HOMOSEXUALITY).

Another new horizon for encountering modernity begins in the 1960s with a reconceived hermeneutical theology dealing with the old themes of history, tradition, and interpretation. In depending on the hermeneutic theories of Hans-Georg Gadamer and Paul Ricoeur, these theologians move beyond the perceived devaluation of history and individualism in the Bultmannian approach.

In the last third of the twentieth century there was a growing sense that modernity itself was breaking down and that the liberal tradition did not serve theology well. Postliberal theology and various forms of postmodern theologies radically distinguished themselves from the Schleiermacherian liberal tradition. Postliberal theology is identified with Hans Frei and George Lindbeck of Yale. Following the philosophies of Ludwig Wittgenstein and Alasdair MacIntyre, postliberal theologians developed a view of religion as historical and tradition-shaped. They eschewed unmediated religious experience common to all human beings or any other universal foundation for theology. For them, becoming religious means interpreting the narrative, the language of faith, of a community and entering into the peculiar practices of that tradition's way of life. Stanley Hauerwas developed these perspectives in an ethic of virtue in a community loyal to the fundamental commitments of the Christian tradition.

The Constructive Theology of Gordon Kaufman and others may be mentioned as a late twentieth-century theology that went in the opposite direction of postliberal theology by obviating scripture and tradition in favor of the construction of the doctrine of God out of the best current scientific and moral attempt to confront the life and death questions of our time, such as nuclear armaments and the survival of the environment.

The 1980s and 1990s produced a widespread postmodern consciousness, reflected in the philosophies of Michel Foucault and Jacques Derrida, in the North American intellectual setting. A number of new theological impetuses thrived in this context, including a wide variety of new, invigorated evangelical theologies (that went well beyond the postwar "new evangelicalism" of CARL F. H. HENRY), the Reformed epistemological theology of Alvin Plantinga and Nicolas Wolterstorff, and the "Radical Orthodoxy," led by the Cambridge theologian John Milbank, now transplanted to the United States.

A mainstay of the twentieth century was the theology created in the ecumenical movement, in which the American JOHN RALEIGH MOTT was a prime mover as president of the WORLD MISSIONARY CONFERENCE in Edinburgh in 1910. Ecumenical theology increasingly found its focus in various theologies of mission, and as Western MISSIONS came under more intense criticism, the *oikoumene* by the end of the century found its bearings mostly in liberation, postcolonial (see POST-COLONIALISM), and Third World theologies.

Ecumenical and mission theology made way for a significant increase of theologies of world religions during the last three decades of the century. Unmistakable at the end of the century was the rebirth of the "religious." Many commentators pointed out that, despite the predictions of secularism at the beginning of the twentieth century, at its end the world was more religious than ever, and, as is ever the case, religion was full of promise and threat for the future of the globe.

References and Further Reading

Braaten, Carl E., and Robert W. Jenson, eds. *A Map of Twentieth-Century Theology*. Minneapolis: Fortress Press, 1995.

Ford, David S. *The Modern Theologians*. 2nd ed. Oxford: Blackwell, 1997.

Frei, Hans. *Types of Modern Theology*. New Haven: Yale University Press, 1992.

Grenz, Stanley J., and Roger E. Olson. *20th-Century Theology: God and the World in a Transitional Age*. Downers Grove, IL: InterVarsity Press, 1992.

Hodgson, Peter, and Robert H. King, eds. *Christian Theology: An Introduction to Its Traditions and Tasks*. Minneapolis: Fortress Press, 1994.

Küng, Hans. *Great Christian Thinkers*. London: SCM Press, 1994.

Livingston, James C., et al. *Modern Christian Thought: Vol II, The Twentieth Century*. 2nd ed. Upper Saddle River, NJ: Prentice-Hall, 2000.

Macquarrie, John. *Twentieth Century Religious Thought*. 4th ed. London: SCM Press, 1988.

Nicholls, William. *Systematic and Philosophical Theology, Vol. III: Pelican Guide to Modern Theology*. London: Penguin, 1971.

Zahrnt, Heinz. *The Question of God: Protestant Theology in the Twentieth Century*. New York: Harcourt Brace & World, 1969.

M. DOUGLAS MEEKS

THEOLOGY, WOMANIST

See Womanist Theology

THIRTY-NINE ARTICLES OF RELIGION

Implemented for dynastic reasons intended to secure the Tudor Succession, HENRY VIII's celebrated breach with Rome inevitably had doctrinal repercussions. Yet if isolated in Catholic Europe at a time when the Protestant princes who had staged the SPEYER "walk out" would have provided natural allies, the vulnerable English king chose only to flirt with the Lutherans; a commitment to orthodoxy (papal sovereignty only excepted) kept him loyal to the traditional religion of the Western Church.

This observation is fundamental to the historian's consideration of the English articles, if only because it illustrates the diplomatic and political backdrop against which the high drama of doctrinal debate was to play. MARTIN LUTHER's teaching had secured a considerable following in continental Europe, and carefully codified in the AUGSBURG CONFESSION (1530) by the irenic scholarship of PHILIPP MELANCHTHON, much of the Wittenberg manifesto influenced England's Ten Articles when they were drafted in 1536. However, the Bishops' Book (1537) first set out the beliefs reforming prelates pressed on Henry VIII. When treating of justification, the sacraments, and the subordination of church tradition to the authority of the BIBLE, they argued in tones more Protestant than the Ten Articles. Failing to ride Court faction, however, any advantage was short-lived, traditional counselors soon securing the Six Articles; and "the whip with six strings" Henry's regime wielded on heretics at home, the king used to impress rulers abroad as he faced new threats from Pope Paul III. With the accession of that young Josiah, EDWARD VI, the tables turned again, despite the fact that diplomatic considerations still impeded progress toward an English CONFESSION of faith. THOMAS CRANMER's ecumenical vision had convinced the primate that a "godly synod" would provide the REFORMATION with a real alternative to the resurgence of Roman DOCTRINE urged on the faithful by the COUNCIL OF TRENT. The archbishop thus sought to enlist Melanchthon, JOHN CALVIN, and HEINRICH BULLINGER for the cause while taking great care not to jump the gun with any confessional statements that might conflict with the singular achievement of Augsburg and alienate the Lutherans rather than bringing unity to the cause as a whole. When idealism was obliged to give way to reality and his much cherished solution proved abortive—how could Melanchthon or Calvin possibly be expected to put Reformation itself at risk by traveling to England?—Cranmer tried to regain lost time and make amends. In short, the affirmation of Forty-two Articles, and their subsequent recension as the Thirty-nine Articles set forth under ELIZABETH I, were the result of some twenty-five years of theological uncertainty. However highly prized their biblical and patristic pedigree, the Articles were something of a rushed job.

Forty-two Articles

Altogether different in tone from the Tridentine decisions, Cranmer's Forty-two Articles, with a CATECHISM set out in both Latin and English, were published "by the King's Majesty's authority" (but without the backing of Convocation as was claimed) in June 1553. They constitute a cautious, even idiosyncratic, commitment to present in places a bland kind of Protestantism, as if diplomatic pragmatism still conditioned the king's mind; because if Rome is certainly ridiculed and ANABAPTIST SECTS repeatedly attacked, the evidence suggests that Cranmer took good care to chart a course between Wittenberg and Geneva, particularly in the focus he placed on the key issues "Of the Justification of Man" (XI), "Of Predestination, and Election" (XVII), and "Of the Lord's Supper" (XXIX).

At the same time Cranmer's work showed a clear sense of priorities in framing an English formulary that, if it set forth "the new religion" of Reformation, also consciously chose to counter any charge of innovation. This he achieved by immediate concentration (I–IV) on key clauses of orthodoxy so regularly rehearsed in the creed. As if to dispel any lingering doubts too, Article VII stated that all three creeds—"Nicene . . . Athanasius . . . and that . . . commonlie called the Apostles"—should be "thoroughly received." If there was a lapse, this concerned extended reference to the Spirit of God, an omission Archbishop MATTHEW PARKER later made good (following the Württemberg Confession, 1552) in Article V ("Of the Holy Ghost") in the Thirty-nine Articles.

The Church of Rome, which "hath erred, not only in . . . living, but also in . . . faith" (XX), Cranmer indicted in a range of Articles (XII, XIII, XXIII, XXVI, XXIX, and XXXI). Just as the Litany prayed that the Lord deliver his people "from the tyranny of the bishoppe of Rome and all his detestable enormities," so Article XXXVI denied the pope "jurisdiction in this realm of England." Treating "Of Civil magistrates," the same Article is unique to the XLII for its reference to "The King of England" as "Supreme head in earth, next under Christ, of the Church of England, and Ireland." Article XXXVII of Elizabeth's XXXIX simply afforded "The Queen's Majesty . . . chief power." As for Cranmer's other *bêtes noires* the Anabaptists or "Heretics called Millenarii" (XLI) who do "boast themselves continually of the Spirit" (XIX), they were targeted in as many as eighteen of the Forty-two Articles (II, III, IV, VI, VIII, IX, X, XV, XVIII, XIX, XXIV, and XXXVI–XLII), a sure indication that such sectaries were regarded as a menace to lawful authority in mid-Tudor times.

The Thirty-nine Articles

With the death of Edward VI on July 6, 1553, less than a month after the Forty-two Articles had been promulgated, it seemed that Cranmer's work on both that formulary and Prayer Book revision would die too. For the accession of Mary the Catholic meant not only the restoration of the "Old Religion" but the martyrdom of the Protestant reformers such as HUGH LATIMER, Nicholas Ridley, John Hooper, and above all Cranmer himself. However, like that of Edward, the new regime was itself to have a limited life, and with the accession of Queen Mary's half sister as ELIZABETH I in November 1558, it was soon clear that England would return again to Reformation faith and

order. It was equally evident that any new settlement could not be achieved overnight, just as precedent itself dictated that, granted Henry VIII's constitutional revolution, religion must be "by law established." Determined to be independent too, Elizabeth declined marriage to Philip of Spain, an act that united Catholic Europe against her in a way that demanded she proceed with particular caution in matters like Prayer Book revision and any reissue of the Articles. Nevertheless, to profess faith and inform the clergy, the new primate set out Eleven Articles for subscription in 1559. Archbishop Parker's document, credal in content, thus simply confirmed Trinitarian belief, affirmed the importance of Scripture, the sacraments, and ecclesiastical discipline, and in due deference to royal prerogative, repudiated the bishop of Rome.

By 1562 it was time for Convocation to deal with the issues, and the following year, "for the avoidance of diversities of opinions, and for establishing of consent touching True Religion," the Thirty-nine Articles made their *debut* as a preliminary revision (set out in Latin) of the Edwardian Articles. Sensitivity toward German Lutheran princes suspended Article XXIX as if to respect *manducatio impiorum* ("of the wicked who do not eat") because Luther's REAL PRESENCE belief had clearly held the reverse to be the case with the result that some critics had even ridiculed the Wittenberg Reformer as but a "new papist." Then too, in a key half sentence, Article XX recognized that Elizabeth's "Church hath power to decree Rites or Ceremonies, and authority in controversies of faith." Unknown to the "Supreme Governor," a parallel bill had been promoted in Parliament, but because of royal fury had been rapidly withdrawn. Accordingly it was not until 1571 that the Thirty-nine Articles (in Latin and English) were finally approved by both Convocation and Parliament to stand as a duly authorized part of the religious settlement and a specifically English confession of Protestant faith.

Matthew Parker's revision dropped seven of Cranmer's original Articles and added four, but the final meticulous and at times ingenious trimming is no mere compromise. After a specifically credal introit resonating well with Cranmer's collect for Advent II in the BOOK OF COMMON PRAYER, Article VI ("Of the sufficiency of the Holy Scriptures for salvation") provides a Protestant bedrock for the formulary as a whole. By providing the "names and numbers of the Canonical Books" too, Parker and his Convocation colleagues not only went beyond Cranmer in spelling out detail, but also followed Jerome's respect for the Apocrypha as "books . . . the Church doth read for example of life and instruction of manners." In similar vein, respecting the conscientious application of JOHN JEWEL, bishop of Salisbury, who widened the range of

Cranmer's Homilies, Article XXXV lists "the several titles" the clergy were convinced "contain a godly and wholesome doctrine . . . necessary for these times." Homilies 3 and 6, treating respectively "Of repairing and keeping clean of Churches" and "Against excess of apparel" certainly cast rare shafts of light for the social historian.

In their firm biblical base the Thirty-nine Articles constituted a full spectrum of Reformation orthodoxy in both faith and order. Carefully sourced from Protestant confessions like those of Augsburg and Württemberg, roughly a third were drafted in sensitive style that made them at least patient of different interpretations. Down the centuries critics have caricatured this approach with extremist labels, but the fine line between ambiguity and irenicism endowed the formulary with an enduring quality and no mean respect, before JOHN HENRY NEWMAN started to demolish them in nineteenth-century Oxford. Parker shared Cranmer's zeal for patristic scholarship, as second only to Scripture; this is highlighted in the way the creeds are described as "proved by most certain warrants of Holy Scripture" (VIII). Various Articles devoted to man's sin and Christ's loving righteousness (IX, XIII, XIV, XV, XVI) deal in language reminiscent of Luther's "rediscovery" of the Gospel, and the wording of Article XI—"We are accompted righteous before God, only for the merit of our Lord and Saviour Jesus Christ, by faith, and not for our own works or deservings"—is no deviation from the Wittenberg party line. Quite the contrary, given that that same Article made abundantly clear how justification "by faith only, is a most wholesome doctrine, and very full of comfort as more largely expressed in the Homilie."

Following St. Paul, Protestant orthodoxy so embraced the idea of PREDESTINATION that every theologian and all formularies had to gloss over difficult and divisive doctrines. (Calvin's legacy is accordingly to be found in Article XVII, albeit without the "double take" of those Calvinists who distorted the balanced teaching of Geneva's patriarch on the sovereignty of God by directing the elect to life and the reprobate to damnation.) For in language decidedly urbane with every approximation to the scriptural statements of apostolic letters to the young churches at Rome (Romans 8 and 9) and Ephesus (Ephesians 1), the faithful are to take "sweet, pleasant and unspeakable comfort" in the "purpose of God" by whose mercy "they attain to everlasting felicity." To believe otherwise "is a most dangerous downfall" and the work of "the devyll." In short, and especially in an embattled sixteenth-century setting, Article XVII was indebted to Melanchthon as much as to Calvin, and extended reference to Articles IX, X, and XI confirm a biblical

reference, just as Articles II and XXXI clearly state that Christ died "for all actual sins of men."

Parker sustained the two-pronged attack on the sects and on Rome, a prominent feature of Cranmer's Articles, in the Articles of 1571. Zealots were thus checked (cf. especially Articles IV, VII, VIII, IX, XVI, XVIII, XXXVII–XXXIX) on the one hand, and popery abused on the other. In any case, by the Bull *Regnans in Excelsis* (February 1570), Pius V had formally excommunicated and deposed Gloriana. As far as the papal see was concerned, any diplomatic deference was now pointless, and the royal "heretic and favourer of heretics" no longer felt the need to tread warily. Governed by the kind of biblical and patristic principles Jewel had rehearsed in his celebrated *Apology* (1562), Rome was singled out for leading the Catholic Church astray, a criticism that fell short of Calvin's denunciation of it as an entirely "false church." Article XIV drew attention to the "arrogance and impiety" of works of supererogation; Article XIX indicated that "the Church of Rome hath erred," but in Article XXI it was also made clear that "General Counselles" may err "and sometime have erred." If Cranmer had condemned purgatory as an invention of the "Scholeaucthoures," Article XXII held such doctrine "Romishe" and, like pardons, the adoration of images and relics, "a fond thing" not merely "vainly invented" but altogether repugnant to the word of God. Convinced that they had "grown partly of the corrupt following of the Apostles," Article XXV denied the sacramental status of "Confirmation, Penance, Orders, Matrimony and extreme Unction"; and "Transubstantiation," with reservation and any procession or adoration of the consecrated eucharistic elements, with the "sacrifice of Masses" were all roundly condemned in Articles XXVIII and XXXI.

By contrast, seen as a bond of unity, the Eucharist was afforded pride of place in a Protestant revision that prized the sacrament of the LORD'S SUPPER "given, taken, and eaten . . . only after an heavenly and spiritual manner . . . received and eaten" by "faith" (Article XXVIII). Then too, omitted in 1566, as much to appease Rome as the Lutherans, Elizabeth no longer found Article XXIX (a denial of *manducatio impiorum*) politically inconvenient, and in 1571 consented to its restoration. In all, eleven Articles (IX, XV, XVI, XXIII, XXIV, XXV, XXVI, XXVII, XXVIII, XXIX, and XXX) relate to sacramental doctrines, "Baptism and the Supper of the Lord" being "not only badges or tokens of Christian men's profession: but rather . . . certain sure witnesses and effectual signs of grace" (XXV).

From Cranmer's day, the Articles of Religion provided a litmus test to determine orthodoxy, and an Act of 1571 required the clergy, schoolmasters, and later those entering the universities to subscribe to it. The force of those Articles dealing with consecration and ordination (XXXVI), Civil Magistrates (XXXVII), and the "Christian man's oath" (XXXIX) proved relevant here. Only in the nineteenth century, largely as a result of Tractarian caricature, was the formulary recognized to be not timeless, but itself very much a tract of Reformation times. Nowadays diluted from a "Form of Assent" to a simple affirmation of the "inheritance of faith," whence clerks in Holy Orders should find "inspiration and guidance under God," many Anglican clergy poke fun at "reading in." Not so the remarkable evangelist Reverend J. R. W. Stott, who as rector of All Souls', Langham Place, London, publicly read the Articles annually to remind his congregation of their Protestant heritage. His letter to *The Times* (May 30, 1963) is significant for the conviction he expressed that "the widespread ignorance of the reformed doctrines of the CHURCH OF ENGLAND is one of the major causes of its weakness today."

In the United States, the clergy of the Protestant EPISCOPAL CHURCH have never been required to subscribe to the Articles of Religion, although a revised version of the formulary was published in 1801. In this, Article VIII omits mention of the Athanasian creed; Article XXI ("Of the Authority of General Councils") was dropped; Article XXXV ("Of Homilies") suspended until such a time as "obsolete words and phrases" are removed; and Articles XXXVI and XXXVII amended to avoid references to the English Crown, capital punishment, and, strangely, the propriety of bearing arms.

It was WILLIAM WORDSWORTH's "Solitary Reaper" who sang of "... old, unhappy, far-off things," and although the Thirty-nine Articles are very much a period compilation, the literary quality of their expression surely affords the formulary a significant place among Christian Confessions. Appropriately paired with the *Book of Common Prayer* itself, the Articles remain a key primary source of the English Reformation and as such a valuable heritage document of the Protestant faith.

See also Anabaptism; Augsburg Confession; Bible; Book of Common Prayer; Bullinger, Heinrich; Calvin, John; Catechism; Church of England; Confession; Cranmer, Thomas; Doctrine; Elizabeth I; Episcopal Church; Henry VIII; Jewel, John; Latimer, Hugh; Lord's Supper; Luther, Martin; Melanchthon, Philipp; Newman, John Henry; Parker, Matthew; Predestination; Wordsworth, William

References and Further Reading

The Book of Common Prayer (as Revised and Settled at the Savoy Conference, 1662). Edited by D. MacCulloch. London: Everyman, 1999. [Contains Charles I's reprint of Articles agreed by Convocation in 1562 (pp. 443–461).]

Bicknell, E. J. *A Theological Introduction to the Thirty-Nine Articles of the Church of England.* Revised by H. J. Carpenter. London: Longmans, Green and Co., 1955.

Browne, E. H. *An Exposition of the Thirty-Nine Articles, Historical and Doctrinal.* Edited by J. Williams. Houston, TX: Classical Anglican Press, 1998.

Dickens, A. G. *The English Reformation.* London: Batsford, 1964. [The first edition of this classic work includes a most sensitive analysis of the Articles of Religion (pp. 249–254).]

Hardwick, C. *A History of the Articles of Religion.* Cambridge, UK: Deighton, 1851. [Useful for the texts of both XLII and XXXIX Articles.]

Ketley, J. *Liturgies of Edward VI.* Cambridge, UK: For the Parker Society, 1844. [Contains the Latin text of Cranmer's XLII Articles (pp. 572–582).]

O'Donovan, O. *On the Thirty Nine Articles. A Conversation with Tudor Christianity.* Exeter, UK: Paternoster Press, 1986.

PETER NEWMAN BROOKS

THOLUCK, FRIEDRICH AUGUST GOTTREU (1799–1877)

German theologian. Born in Breslau, Tholuck first studied philology, then THEOLOGY in Berlin. As a student he was influenced by Pietistic-revivalistic circles. Although FRIEDRICH SCHLEIERMACHER opposed his appointment, he taught Old Testament in Berlin (1820–1826). There he published his best-known work, *Guido und Julius. Die Lehre von der Sünde und vom Versöhner* (1823). A revivalistic tract in the form of correspondence between two young men, it countered an earlier tract by de Wette that criticized the notion that recognition of one's sinfulness was necessary for a theologian. In 1826 Tholuck became professor at HALLE where, with interruptions for travel and a year as preacher in Rome, he remained until his death. Martin Kähler was his most famous student.

Tholuck was a major figure of the nineteenth-century German REVIVALS. His theology stressed SIN and redemption. He was Lutheran, although he approved the union of Lutheran and Reformed churches and distrusted the growing confessionalism of the time. He also opposed theological and social liberalism. Tholuck's influential biblical commentaries, reprinted many times, sought to counter rationalistic approaches to scriptural interpretation. He affirmed that historical-critical interpretation did not negate biblical truths. In opposition to DAVID F. STRAUSS's *Life of Jesus* (1835) he maintained the historical authenticity of the gospels. Less well known is his sympathetic scholarly work on the history of rationalism. A gifted linguist, Tholuck's influence extended abroad. He had many international contacts and was active in the Evangelical Alliance.

See also Ecumenism; Evangelicalism; Higher Criticism; Liberal Protestantism and Libiralism; Pietism

References and Further Reading

Primary Sources:

Tholuck, Fredrich A. G. *Der sittliche Character des Heidenthumus.* 1867.
———. *Calvin as an Interpreter of the Holy Scriptures.* Edinburgh: [s.n.], 1854.

Secondary Sources:

Bainton, Roland H. "Yale and German Theology in the Middle of the Nineteenth Century." *Zeitschrift für Kirchengeschichte* 66 (1954/55): 294–302.
Krumwiede, Hans-Walter. "August G. Tholuck." In *Gestalten der Kirchengeschte,* edited by Martin Greschat, vol. 9.1, *Die neueste Zeit I,* 281–291. Stuttgart: Kohlhammer, 1985.
Schaff, Philip. "Tholuck." In *Germany: its Universities, Theology, and Religion,* 278–294. Edinburgh: T & T Clark, 1857.

MARY JANE HAEMIG

THOMASIUS, CHRISTIAN (1655–1728)

German jurist. Born into a respected academic family in Leipzig, GERMANY, and raised in Lutheran ORTHODOXY, Thomasius studied philosophy in Leipzig and law in Frankfurt/Oder. In 1680 he started practicing law in Leipzig and lecturing at the university. A nonconformist, he lectured (1687) in German rather than in Latin, a step toward the breakdown of unified European academic culture. In Leipzig, a center of Lutheran orthodoxy and Aristotelian thought, Thomasius defended the NATURAL LAW theories of SAMUEL PUFENDORF among jurists and the PIETISM of AUGUST HERMANN FRANCKE among theologians. These stances and his acerbic manner led to his move to HALLE (1690), a center of Pietism and the ENLIGHTENMENT.

Thomasius soon was combating what he saw as the authoritarian tendencies of Pietism. His ethical teachings, holding that no pietistic CONVERSION was necessary to practice love toward one's neighbors, led to an edict forbidding him to teach anything but law (1702). Known as an advocate of religious TOLERATION, Thomasius thought true religion was an inner, private matter, not subject to state direction. The state could regulate the outward cult, but uniformity of religion was not necessary in a state. Thomasius opposed witch trials (see WITCHCRAZE) because he believed the state had no right to punish heretics (see HERESY). He believed that individual insight took precedence over received AUTHORITY; law and matters of state were subjects for human reason, not religious authority. Thomasius was concerned with the practical application of juristic and philosophical thought. His teach-ings led to the separation of law and morality as areas of inquiry.

References and Further Reading

Primary Sources:

Thomasius, Christian. *Uber die Hexenprozesse.* Weimar, Germany: H. Bohlaus Nachfolger, 1967.
———. *Auserlesene deutsche Schriften.* Hildesheim, Germany: G. Olms, 1705.
———. *Ausgewahlte Werke.* Hildesheim: G. Olms, 1705.
———. *Über die Folter.* Weimar, Germany: H. Bohlaus Nachfolger, 1960.

Secondary Sources:

Hattenhauer, Hans. "Christian Thomasius." In *Gestalten der Kirchengeschte,* edited by Martin Greschat, vol. 8, *Die Aufklaerung.* Stuttgart, Germany: Kohlhammer, 1983.
Schroeder, Peter. "Thomas Hobbes, Christian Thomasius and the Seventeenth-Century Debate on the Church and State." *History of European Ideas* 23 (1997): 59–79.

MARY JANE HAEMIG

TILLICH, PAUL (1886–1965)

German theologian. Tillich was one of the most influential Protestant theologians of the twentieth century. Born and educated in GERMANY, he fled the Nazi regime and established himself as a seminary professor and religion scholar in the United States, becoming a bridge between European theological currents and the English-speaking world. He became a major spokesman for Protestant progressivism in the public arena and published a number of widely read theological works, most notably the three-volume *Systematic Theology.*

Life and Work

Paul Tillich was born in 1886 in the village of Starzeddel in eastern Germany (now in POLAND), the son of a minister and high official of the Evangelical Union Church of Prussia. Tillich understood his deepest theological roots to be in the Lutheran Tradition (see LUTHERANISM), and he reaffirmed characteristic Lutheran emphases throughout his life. After undergraduate and graduate studies that focused on theology and philosophy at several German universities, Tillich entered the Christian ministry. At the outbreak of World War I he became a chaplain in the German army. After the war—for him a traumatic and transforming experience—he became a professor of philosophy and theology first in Berlin, then Marburg, Dresden, and finally Frankfurt. In the 1920s he was a leading figure in a movement called "religious socialism," which attempted to offer an ideological alternative to traditionalism and fascism. This affiliation, plus his close association with Jewish scholars and students, brought about his dismissal from his academic post when the Nazis came to power in 1933. Shortly thereafter he and his family emigrated to the United States. After the war he became a professor successively at three distinguished American universities: Union Theological Seminary at Columbia University (1933–1955); Harvard University (1955–1962); and The University of Chicago (1962–1965).

Although Tillich became known principally as a scholar of religion rather than as a churchman, his sermons—often preached in university chapels—were warmly received. During World War II Tillich delivered a large number of antifascist speeches that were broadcast over the Voice of America. After the war he became increasingly influential as an interpreter of the religious dimension of CULTURE, termed by Tillich "the depth dimension." In the 1950s Tillich gave more attention to psychological and existentialist analyses of the human predicament and to the completion of his systematic theology (see especially *The Courage To Be* and *Systematic Theology*, vols. 1–3). In the late 1950s Tillich turned from dialogue with Western secularity to dialogue with non-Western religions, an interest brought into focus by his visit to JAPAN in 1960, at which time he engaged in conversations with Buddhist scholars (see *Christianity and the Encounter of the World Religions*).

Thought

Tillich gave considerable attention to the history of Protestantism and to its fate in the twentieth century (see *The Protestant Era*). He criticized the pre–Vatican II Roman Catholic Church for a strain of authoritarianism, while valuing much in Catholic thought and experience (see CATHOLICISM, PROTESTANT REACTION TO). This breadth of perspective is captured in his distinction between "Catholic substance" and "Protestant principle." For Tillich, Catholic sacramentalism reflects the "holiness of being," the presence of the divine within the world. Without some religious "substance"—some sense of divine presence—Protestantism becomes sterile and empty, but the Protestant principle represents the protest against any tendency toward absolutizing finite symbols of holiness. Without this protest, religion—whether Protestant or Catholic—becomes "heteronomous." Both emphases are needed for what Tillich called "theonomous" Christianity, which expresses its religious substance but is self-critical of any absolutizing of its own finite forms.

Tillich viewed the Protestant principle as an expression of the REFORMATION Doctrine of "justification by grace through faith." This DOCTRINE, which criti-

cizes dependency on all humanly devised assurances, was extended by Tillich to apply to intellectual "works" of religious belief as well as to works of moral or sacramental practice. One cannot be justified before God by right belief, said Tillich, any more than by right behavior or right ritual observance. Even while doubting, one can be in a state of reconciliation with God.

Tillich displayed his Protestant personalism by finding his theological starting point in something subjective, in what he called "ultimate concern." In this he followed the nineteenth-century Protestant theologian, FRIEDRICH SCHLEIERMACHER, for whom religion begins with the "feeling of absolute dependence" rather than with a claim of truth content or revelation. God is understood to be the correlate of this feeling. Tillich attempted to counter the charge of subjectivism by asserting that one is "grasped by the power of an ultimate concern"; faith is received ecstatically (in the strict sense of standing beyond one's ordinary self). All religion is revelatory in this sense.

The philosophical side of Tillich's thought was nourished by his reading of the nineteenth-century German idealists, who sought to revive metaphysics on Protestant soil after IMMANUEL KANT's critique. Tillich agreed with Kant that morality is constitutive of human individuality, autonomy, and freedom. Indeed, Tillich put metaphysical as well as moral weight on human freedom (and, linked with freedom, creativity). Following F. W. J. Schelling, Tillich saw freedom as the point where the completion of creation and the "fall" coincide. Tillich thought there was no rational necessity for humanity's existential predicament (here countering rationalism, but in accord with Schelling's existentialist successor, SØREN KIERKEGAARD). Nor is there any rational path to SALVATION (or human fulfillment). Human existence rests on incalculable freedom, and all paths to salvation involve the "risk of faith." However, there is for Tillich a power that makes for salvation and reconciliation. The power that reunites is love; in all its forms love *is* reunion, and—as G. W. F. HEGEL taught in his early theological writings—ultimately it is the divine power in all things.

The Christian faith affirms the presence of this reconciling power in "the New Testament picture of Jesus as the Christ" (in Tillich's auspicious phrase). All religions employ symbols that claim to mediate divine power; the distinctiveness of the Christ symbol is that Jesus sacrifices that which is finite in himself that he might point beyond himself to the ultimate power of reconciliation. Herein lies a criterion for a valid religious symbol—that it points beyond itself without making claims of ultimacy for itself. Although rooted in the Jesus of history, the New Testament picture includes mythic elements. Instead of "demythologizing" in the manner of the New Testament theologian RUDOLF BULTMANN, Tillich favored acknowledging the necessary presence of mythic expression. The doctrine of Christ's incarnation is viewed by Tillich as "broken" (that is, acknowledged) myth, subject to interpretation but not to replacement by rationalizing categories.

In embracing the "apologetic" role for Christian theology, reformulating itself so as to provide answers to contemporary culture's most pressing questions, Tillich differed sharply from his Swiss Protestant contemporary, KARL BARTH. Barth rejected all efforts toward a "natural theology" (a theology based on reason, science, or general human experience). Tillich on the contrary reached back to the apologetic tradition found in the early church and in St. Augustine; here Christianity is seen as fulfilling human culture's passionate quest for ultimacy. Tillich contended that different issues become the focus of concern in different cultural epochs. The predominant problem of contemporary life, he asserted, is not finitude and DEATH, or sin and guilt, but emptiness and meaninglessness—this theme derived from much twentieth-century literature. In the face of doubt about the meaning-giving qualities of the traditional symbols (including the theistic, personal God), Tillich reflected on "the God beyond the God of theism." To ground our affirmations of the meaningfulness of finite being, he argued, we are in a time of quest for new symbols.

In his social ethics Tillich can be seen as a precursor of the LIBERATION THEOLOGIES that have come into prominence since the 1960s. Tillich backed away from explicit commitment to socialism in his American years, although he remained a steadfast critic of the excesses of capitalism and of the individualist culture of "self-sufficient finitude." The social ideal of the KINGDOM OF GOD—Christianity's key symbol for the goal of human history—in his view captures the affirmation of the goodness of finite existence along with criticism of the injustices of present societies.

References and Further Reading

Primary Sources:

Tillich, Paul. *The Protestant Era*. Chicago: University of Chicago Press, 1948.
———. *Systematic Theology*. 3 vols. Chicago: University of Chicago Press, 1951, 1957, 1963.
———. *The Courage to Be*. New Haven: Yale University Press, 1952.
———. *Dynamics of Faith*. New York: Harper & Row, 1957.
———. *Christianity and the Encounter of the World Religions*. New York: Columbia University Press, 1963.

———. *Main Works/Hauptwerke*. 6 vols. Edited by C. H. Ratschow. Berlin and New York: Evangelisches Verlag and de Gruyter, 1987–1993.

Secondary Sources:

Adams, James Luther, Wilhelm Pauck, and Roger L. Shinn, eds. *The Thought of Paul Tillich*. San Francisco: Harper & Row, 1985.
Pauck, Wilhelm, and Marion Pauck. *Paul Tillich: His Life and Thought*, vol. 1: *Life*. New York: Harper & Row, 1976.

GUYTON B. HAMMOND

TILLOTSON, JOHN (1630–1694)

Archbishop of Canterbury. Tillotson was born in Sowerby, Yorkshire, ENGLAND in 1630. After a CAMBRIDGE UNIVERSITY education, where the CAMBRIDGE PLATONISTS taught him tolerance, Tillotson served in PRESBYTERIANISM but conformed to the episcopally ordered CHURCH OF ENGLAND at the Restoration. He served parishes in rural Hertfordshire and London and became well known as a preacher.

Although his vigorous advocacy of Protestantism (*The Rule of Faith*, 1666) irritated Charles II, he was made dean of CANTERBURY in 1672. When the Roman Catholic James II was replaced in 1688 by his Protestant daughter Mary II and her husband William III, Tillotson helped to secure TOLERATION for Protestant Dissenters. He was appointed dean of St. Paul's, London, November 1689. The archbishop of Canterbury, Sancroft, was finally deposed for nonacceptance of the new reign. Reluctantly, Tillotson consented to succeed him in May 1691. He died in November 1694 in London.

Tillotson wrote against SOCINIANISM (1693), and he has often been called Latitudinarian, both for his preference for morals over doctrinal strife and his appeal to reasonable self-interest and natural inclination as motives for CONVERSION. More positively, he called for holiness: "To see God is to be happy; but, unless we be like him, we cannot see him. The sight and presence of God himself would be no happiness to that man who is not like to God in the temper and disposition of his mind" (Sermon VII).

See also Latitudinarianism

References and Further Reading

Primary Source:

Tillotson, John. *The Works of Dr. John Tillotson, late Archbishop of Canterbury, with the Life of the Author, by Tho. Birch, M.A., . . .* [1759, later edition] *. . . in Ten Volumes*. London: Richard Priestley, 1820.

Secondary Sources:

Gordon, Alexander. "Tillotson, John." in *Dictionary of National Biography*, vol. XIX, 872–878. Reprinted Oxford: Oxford University Press, 1921–1922.

Reedy, Gerard. "Interpreting Tillotson." *Harvard Theological Review* 86 no. 1 (January 1993): 81–103.

DAVID TRIPP

TINDAL, MATTHEW (1657–1733)

English deist. Born in 1657 in Devonshire, ENGLAND, Tindal is best known for his apology for natural religion, *Christianity as Old as the Creation* (1730). Son of a High-Church minister, Tindal studied at Lincoln College at Oxford and later at Exeter College. He became a law fellow at All Souls' College in 1678 and earned his doctor of civil law in 1685. Religiously, he moved from the High-Church tradition to a temporary interest in Catholicism to Unitarianism to a later self-professed Christian DEISM.

His early works—for example, *An Essay Concerning Obedience to Supreme Powers* (1693), *The Liberty of the Press* (1698), and *The Rights of the Christian Church Asserted* (1706)—are characteristically anti-authoritarian and anticlerical in tone. Tindal aimed, as found in *Christianity as Old as the Creation,* to demonstrate that the "Religion of Nature" is the original and perfect religion to which revelation has nothing to add or subtract. Tindal taught that true religion is natural, universal, and innate within the human soul and that morality is its essence. According to Tindal, natural and revealed religion (i.e., Christianity) have a common source, but the ideas given by reason are more certain than those given by TRADITION or "revelation." Thus, what is true in Christianity must be "as old as the creation," and all else is false. Tindal attacked "absurdities" and inconsistencies in the BIBLE (e.g., miracles, immoral stories, anthropomorphisms, and arbitrariness of God) and insisted that the Bible should be read like any other book.

After his death on August 6, 1733, *Christianity as Old as the Creation* came to be known as the "Deists' Bible." Tindal's emphasis on the primacy and universality of reason, avenues into biblical criticism, and advocacy for natural religion had significant influence on the ENLIGHTENMENT in both GERMANY and FRANCE.

See also Higher Criticism

References and Further Reading

Primary Sources:

Tindal, Matthew. *Christianity as old as the creation*. Edited and translated by Günter Gawlick. Stuttgart-Bad Cannstatt, Germany: Frommann-Holzboog, 1967–.

———. *Christianity as old as the creation: or, The gospel, a republication of the religion of nature*. London: [s.n.], 1730.

———. A defence of the rights of the Christian church: against a late visitation sermon, intitled, The rights of the clergy in the Christian church asserted; preach'd at Newport Pagnell in the county of Bucks, by W. Wotton, B.D., and made publick at the command and desire of the Bishop of Lincoln, and the clergy of the deaneries of Buckingham and Newport. London: [s.n.], Printed in the year 1707.

———. A letter to the reverend the clergy of both universities, concerning the Trinity and the Athanasian creed [microform]: with reflections on all the late hypotheses, particularly Dr. W's, Dr. S–th's, the Trinity placed in its due light, The 28 propositions, The calm discourse of a Trinity in the Godhead, and the defence of Dr. Sherlock's notions: with a short discourse concerning mysteries. [London: s.n.], 1694.

———. The nation vindicated, from the aspersions cast on it in a late pamphlet, inititled, A Representation of the present state of religion, with regard to the late excessive growth of infidelity, heresy and profaneness, as it pass'd the Lower house of convocation. London: Printed for A. Baldwin, 1711–1712.

Secondary Sources:

Herrick, James A. *The Rhetoric of the English Deists*. Columbia: University of South Carolina Press, 1997.

Kavcic, John Andrew. *English Deism and Natural Law: The Case of Matthew Tindal*. Ottawa: National Library of Canada, 1999.

Leland, John (1691–1766). *A View of the Principal Deistical Writers, 1755–1757*. vol. 1. New York: Garland, 1978.

G. SUJIN PAK

TING, K. H. (DING GUANGXUN) (1915–)

Chinese theologian. Born in Shanghai, CHINA, K. H. Ting has been China's foremost Protestant leader and theologian since the reopening of churches after the end of the Cultural Revolution era in the late 1970s. He became principal of Nanjing Union Theological Seminary at its founding in 1953, a position that he still holds. He was chair of the Chinese Christian Three-Self Patriotic Movement Committee (TSPM) and president of the China Christian Council (CCC) from 1981 until his retirement in 1997. Ting continues to serve as vice-chair of the Chinese People's Political Consultative Conference, in which capacity he seeks to promote openness and reform in the religious policy of the government.

Ting grew up in a comfortable Christian home, the third of four children. His maternal grandfather was one of China's first Anglican priests, and his father a banker. The greatest influence in his early life was his mother, a devout Christian, who encouraged her son to enter the ministry. Ting received a B.A. from St. John's University in Shanghai in 1937 and a B.D. from its school of theology in 1942. In 1948 he received an M.A. in religious education from Union Theological Seminary in New York. In 1942 he was ordained to the Anglican diaconate and priesthood, and in the same year, he married Siu-may Kuo (d. 1995). They had two sons. In 1955 he was consecrated bishop of the Anglican diocese of Chekiang (Zhejiang).

Ting's experience as a student and priest in Japanese-occupied Shanghai (1937–1945) convinced him of the need to be involved in the struggle for national salvation and freedom from foreign domination. He became one of the many YMCA student workers inspired by Y. T. Wu (1893–1979). Later he served as curate of the Church of Our Savior, and then as pastor of Shanghai's Community Church. In 1945 the Tings went to CANADA, where K.H. had been appointed mission secretary for the Student Christian Movement. In 1948 Ting moved to Geneva to work for the World Student Christian Federation. In this capacity he traveled widely and got to know many men and women in the ecumenical movement and the WORLD COUNCIL OF CHURCHES.

In 1951, against the advice of many friends and colleagues in Geneva, the Tings returned to China with their young son. They were committed to the newly established People's Republic of China, and K.H. became associated with the TSPM. This was the time of the Korean War, when foreign missionaries were being expelled and Chinese churches were severing their connections with Christians overseas. Ting served for a brief time as general secretary of the Christian Literature Society (1952–1953) in Shanghai, before moving to Nanjing where he became principal of Nanjing Union Theological Seminary.

In the 1950s and early 1960s Ting was active in the TSPM, and became a well-known interpreter of the Chinese revolution in the West. He was convinced that Christians should work together with socialists, and in his writings, he attempted to provide Christians with a convincing theological rationale. Conservative and evangelical Christians in China and in the West tended to disagree with Ting's approach, but he was widely respected among Protestants and Anglicans in the ecumenical movement.

With the intensification of radical political movements in the China of the late 1950s and early 1960s Ting's position became increasingly difficult. He was removed from all his church and political posts at the start of the Cultural Revolution in 1966. He again came into public view in the early 1970s, and over the next few years met with many overseas visitors.

At the end of the Cultural Revolution era, K. H. Ting emerged as the preeminent leader of China's Protestant Christians and headed both the newly organized CCC (1981) and the reestablished TSPM. He promoted the reopening of churches and other religious institutions, the printing of the BIBLE and reli-

gious literature, and increasing contacts with churches in other parts of the world. In 1991 he led the CCC delegation to Canberra when it joined the World Council of Churches. By this time Ting had become a significant voice for the interests of the church on a national level, using his government positions to promote both religious freedom and the rebirth of theology and religious studies.

As China's best-known Protestant theologian, Ting's central theological concern has been love as God's primary attribute, and the importance for Christians to practice love in their ETHICS and in society. His writings have stressed the continuity between creation and redemption; the Cosmic Christ who presides over all human history; and a deemphasis on "justification by faith" in Chinese Protestantism, insofar as it divides Christians from non-Christians. Since retirement Ting has promoted "theological reconstruction" in the Chinese Church, which implies the broadening and opening of Christian faith to the changes taking place in society.

K. H. Ting's contributions to the reemergence of Chinese church life, Protestant THEOLOGY, and the opening of China to the outside world are widely recognized. His views on "theological reconstruction" and the need for working in concert with the government continue to be criticized in some conservative church circles. However, under Ting's leadership, Christianity in China has assumed a higher profile than at any time in its history. He has promoted reconciliation between church and society, Christian and non-Christian, China and the world, and this continues to be K. H. Ting's enduring legacy to Christians in China and to the church universal.

See also Ecumenism; YMCA, YWCA

References and Further Reading

Primary Sources:

Ting, K. H. *No Longer Strangers: Selected Writings of K. H. Ting.* Edited by Ray Whitehead. Maryknoll, NY: Orbis, 1989.
———. *Love Never Ends: Papers by K. H. Ting.* Edited by Janice Wickeri. Nanjing: Yilin Press, 2000.
Wickeri, Janice, and Philip Wickeri, eds. *A Chinese Contribution to Ecumenical Theology: Selected Writings of K. H. Ting.* Geneva: WCC Books, 2002.

Secondary Source:

"A Tribute to K. H. Ting on His Eightieth Birthday." *The Chinese Theological Review* 10 (1995).

PHILIP WICKERI

TOCQUEVILLE, ALEXIS DE (1805–1859)

French writer. De Tocqueville's fame rests on a single work. For nine months, beginning in May 1831, the young French aristocrat studied the emergent democratic culture in the United States. His classic work *Democracy in America* continues to be seen as a most insightful analysis of American society. In it, he devotes considerable attention to the cultural significance of American Protestantism.

De Tocqueville described Americans as deeply religious and credited their faith for creating a bulwark of republican freedom. Although Catholic by birth and elusive about his own religious beliefs, he applauded the fact that political liberty had multiplied ways of believing in America but had not led to religious skepticism as predicted by ENLIGHTENMENT Philosophers. Such divisions provoked heated theological debates, he admitted, but they could not undermine a prevailing harmony of Christian social purpose.

Harboring deep concerns about the centrifugal tendencies of unbridled DEMOCRACY, de Tocqueville assigned particular importance to the ways Protestants balanced personal spiritual devotion with equal commitment to moral reform, political freedom, and material improvement. Such earthly applications enabled religion to control popular passions and preserve republican order without benefit of formal political power. His sanguine expectations met a far different reality in the 1840s, however, when the SLAVERY issue divided BAPTISTS and METHODISTS along sectional lines, aggravating social tensions that led to the CIVIL WAR in 1861.

Finally, the absence of a clerical establishment in America led de Tocqueville to give WOMEN particular prominence in American political culture. He concluded that this most vitally religious segment of the population made the home a private reservoir of Christian morality indispensable to training citizens committed to the public good.

References and Further Reading

Tocqueville, Alexis de. *Democracy in America.* vol. 1 originally published 1835; vol. 2 originally published 1840. Edited by J. P. Mayer. Translated by George Lawrence. New York: Harper and Row, 1968.

Mitchell, Joshua. *The Fragility of Freedom: Tocqueville on Religion, Democracy, and the American Future.* Chicago: University of Chicago Press, 1995.

MARK Y. HANLEY

TOLAND, JOHN (1670–1721)

English theologian. Toland was born in Londonderry, Ireland, on November 30, 1670, of Roman Catholic parents, and died in Putney, near London, on March 11, 1721. He studied at the University of Glasgow and then at Leiden in the NETHERLANDS. In 1694 he went to Oxford and two years later, in 1696, published his first and most important book, *Christianity Not Mysterious, or a Treatise Showing That There is Nothing in the Gospel Contrary to Reason Nor Above It, And That No Christian Doctrine Can Properly Be Called a Mystery.* In this volume, in the Deist tradition of his time, Toland rejected such external authorities as TRADITION, the Scriptures, and the church. Reason is the only principle of AUTHORITY for the Christian. The criterion for making all religious decisions and for formulating all Christian DOCTRINE must be unimpaired reason. Although the Christian may get information from revelation, that is, Scripture, that information must be confirmed by reason. Therefore, in Christianity there is nothing that is mysterious. Here Toland goes beyond some Deist writers who (see DEISM) taught that there were truths of reason, truths of revelation that agree with reason, and truths above reason. Toland insists that there are not truths above reason, such as the resurrection and the virgin birth. The argument that there are truths above reason is the source of all absurdities in Christianity, usually promulgated by the CLERGY, such as TRANSUBSTANTIATION.

Toland insists that what can be known by revelation must as well be understood as any other matter in the world. In this regard reason is superior to revelation, just as a *Greek Grammar* is superior to the *New Testament,* for we make use of the grammar to understand the language and of reason to understand the sense of the BIBLE. Reason is no less from God than revelation; indeed, reason is the candle, the guide within each person. Revelation is never mysterious nor incomprehensible once it is known. There cannot even be the appearance of a conflict between revelation and the gospel. Toland wanted to prove that the essence of Christianity is found in natural religion that all peoples and races have in common. In a sense, Christianity is "sectarian," that is, a special branch of the real, natural religion.

Toland was convinced that a special revelation was limited to a particular time and a particular people; thus it lacks universality. True religion is universally available and is equally available to all peoples in all times. In *Nazarenus* (1718) he argued that the original simple moral precepts of Christianity as found in the synoptic gospels were corrupted by priests and philosophers.

References and Further Reading

Cragg, G. R. *Reason and Authority in the Eighteenth Century.* Cambridge, UK: Cambridge University Press, 1964.

Stephen, Leslie. *English Thought in the Eighteenth Century.* vol. I. New York: G. P. Putnam's Sons, 1927.

Sullivan, Robert E. *John Toland and the Deist Controversy: A Study In Adaptations.* Cambridge, MA: Harvard University Press, 1982.

DONALD S. ARMENTROUT

TOLERATION

Toleration, *tolerantia,* is taken by many to be an overwhelmingly modern virtue. Most associate the idea with the separation of church and state as embodied, paradigmatically, in the constitution of the United States of America. Most look to English philosopher John Stuart Mill's (1806–1873) *On Liberty* (1859) or, at the earliest, to philosopher JOHN LOCKE's (1632–1704) *A Letter Concerning Toleration* (1689) for its intellectual antecedents. Toleration is, furthermore, taken to be a positive virtue, indicating an acceptance of pluralism and diverse behaviors and beliefs. It is variously interpreted as referring to an array of different acts, individuals, or claims of truth, and a refusal to judge any one position, individual, or claim as beyond the boundaries of a common humanity. Often, as can be perceived, such a position can easily shade off into a shallow relativism, indifference, or alternatively into a skepticism toward all truth-claims and normative desiderata. On the other hand, an attitude of toleration is deemed central to the working of a pluralistic, democratic polity—the prerequisite to any idea of universal human rights. As such, it is central to the changing world order at the turn of the twenty-first century.

The Problem of Toleration

The idea of toleration has a much longer history and is both conceptually and historically a more elusive concept than is commonly held. Taken today as a positive trait, *tolerantia* was, historically, understood as a negative one, a necessity, the lesser of two evils, but not as a positive good. Tolerance, in the medieval period in Europe was understood as restraint, forbearance, and as the ability to suffer and endure what was unacceptable but could not, for all that, be eradicated. In medieval canon law the two primary examples of this restraint involved Jews and prostitutes. In both cases the toleration demanded was a restraint of hatred rather than a command to love. The existence of both in society was taken as a necessary evil rather than as a positive good. The move from treating tolerance as the lesser of two evils to treating it as a normatively desirable state is, in fact, one of the chief differences between medieval and modern positions.

This changing valuation of toleration does, however, enormously complicate many of the problematic and contradictory aspects of the term. Any attitude of toleration immediately raises the question of the limits of toleration, And if, in the modern world, we do not accept the position that any individual can be beyond the boundaries of a shared humanity, certain forms of behavior most certainly can. What then are the limits of tolerance? Can these be framed in a universal language, shared by all societies and peoples? How can the limits be justified in terms that would benefit from worldwide compliance—if such is indeed a goal. Or, would such a goal in itself be intolerant toward myriad local traditions and practices?

Viewing toleration in a positive light returns us to the very contradictory meaning of the term. Tolerance implies endurance of something we reject as wrong (otherwise we would not need to be tolerant of it). Tolerance is clearly relative to practices and beliefs whose validity or normative status we reject as somehow incorrect, unreasonable, or undesirable. Tolerance does not, moreover, involve coming to accept these beliefs as correct or somehow less wrong. Rather it involves the ability to abide by, to live with those beliefs we continue to think of as wrong or misguided.

Moreover, if one group of people simply hated another we would not demand tolerance of them, but rather that they lose their hatred. We do not ask the racial bigot to tolerate the black, but to lose his hatred of him, or of the anti-Semite to tolerate the Jew (as in the Middle Ages). We do not, furthermore, consider the bigot who, through a vast expenditure of psychological energy refrains from acting on his prejudice, tolerant. This is not to say that toleration does not involve restraint, but it is a restraint of more than action; it is a restraint of thought and a restraint, quite possibly, of judgment. Thus, toleration involves some tension between commitment to one's own set of values and principles or religious edicts, and a willingness to abide by those of others who adhere to beliefs we believe are wrong. Again, the question of boundaries or limits to tolerance arises.

One way modern societies have posited these boundaries has been through the liberal distinction between public and private realms, which thus becomes a distinction in realms and types of toleration; certain beliefs and/or practices are deemed private and so, almost by definition, are to be tolerated. Here then, tolerance is not quite indifference *simpliciter,* but more a principled indifference, for one has no right to intervene in private matters, or even to judge them. In this reading, all conflicting views are reduced to an almost aesthetic realm of different matters of taste (or what are often termed lifestyles). One could, however, query if this is tolerance at all. Principled indifference is not tolerance. The much-vaunted toleration of modern societies may well be more complicated and problematic than we often take it to be, tending, in fact, to constantly be in danger of slipping into indifference and relativism.

Within the experience of most Western European and North Atlantic societies, the development of toleration has been marked by a retreat of religion from the public arena, its privatization, and the general growth of secularization as the defining context of public life. Toleration has come to be associated with pluralism, which, when accepted as a value, implies the ability to exist together with other, competing visions of society and of the cosmos. Pluralism implies tolerance, not solely the toleration of error (what can perhaps be termed tolerance with a small "t"), but tolerance of alternative and competing civilizational visions (tolerance with a capital "T") with their own claims to the public sphere and the organization of communal life.

In Western Europe the development of this form of tolerance has taken a very particular form—that of secularization. That is to say, as society secularized and religion retreated from the public domain, reducing its claims on the public sphere and becoming more and more a matter of the congregant's internal value disposition, there developed, concomitantly, a growing tolerance of other faiths. This change has generally been identified with the ENLIGHTENMENT and the influence of the FRENCH REVOLUTION. Within Europe, the test case of this type of toleration has been in attitudes toward the Jewish people, from which we also learn that privatized belief in itself is far from sufficient for the development of toleration toward the other. The HOLOCAUST was perpetrated less than one hundred years after Jews were granted full civic emancipation in Western European countries.

Tolerance and Protestantism

The privatization of religious belief as a basis for toleration is very much rooted in the institutionalization of Protestant religiosity. The very circumscription of religious truth claims to the realm of the private rather than that of shared, public culture has much to do with the way sectarian Protestantism developed in England and New England in the seventeenth and early eighteenth centuries. The epistemological foundations of this orientation were, in part, laid by John Locke, who claimed that because religion was a matter of belief, any coercion of the will would simply not work in enforcing religious conformity, for the structures of belief were not subject to the workings of the will.

While true, such an approach indicates its own particular religious assumptions in its stress on belief as standing at the center of religious consciousness, reflecting, that is, a very particular type of Protestant religiosity. For while belief cannot indeed be coerced, practice, and most especially public practice, certainly can. There are religions where public practices are a good deal more central than the structure of individual belief systems. If we look to Hinduism, Islam, or JUDAISM we immediately see this to be so. No small number of people continue to be engaged in violent, illegal, and often repressive behavior in many parts of the world over issues of religious practice, such as whether coffee houses can be open in Jerusalem on the Sabbath and whether women must go veiled in public or can attend university, and so on.

The path of toleration that eventually led to modern positions on the privatization of belief, freedom of thought, and individual rights is nevertheless rooted in Protestant beliefs in the privatization of grace and the internalization of conscience that developed most saliently among groups of sectarian Protestants—MORAVIANS (see Moravian Church), QUAKERS, BAPTISTS, ANABAPTISTS (see Anabaptism), Collegiants, Socinians (see Socinian Church)—in the late sixteenth and seventeenth centuries. Such religious thinkers as Hans Denck (1500–1527) and SEBASTIAN FRANCK (1499–1542) played an important role in developing an attitude of toleration, not just of different Christian sects to one another, but to all of humankind. Sebastian Franck's belief in religious freedom, the opaqueness of all ultimate truths, and the common nature of the human predicament continued to be influential much beyond his own lifetime.

The writings of thinkers such as Jean Bodin (1529–1596) and Pierre Bayle (1647–1706) developed less explicitly religious bases for toleration and provided a critical bridge between the explicitly religious discourse of the sixteenth century and the arguments of the late seventeenth and early eighteenth centuries, increasingly based on natural law. Pierre Bayle, who himself converted to Catholicism in 1668 and back to Protestantism less than two years later, was exceptional for his time, extending toleration even to atheists, which neither Jean Bodin nor, later, John Locke was to do. (Locke also refused toleration to Catholics.) Bayle, indeed, anticipated a very modern approach to toleration predicted on individual liberty and freedom of expression. Samuel Pufendorf's (1623–1694) writings on toleration within the context of the early modern natural law tradition (though less radical than Bayle) must also be noted in this context.

Belief in the unmediated access of the believer to the deity, the importance of faith, and the freedom of conscience all contributed to the growth of toleration in early modern Europe. Eventually these beliefs led to the secularization of the ideas of inner light or Holy Spirit, the internalization of the idea of grace and, by the eighteenth century, its secularization into more contemporary notions of morality, civic virtue, and often romantic nationalism as well. Critical here were developments in the thirteen colonies of what became the United States of America. The unique nature of individual rights as expressed in the bills of rights of the different states was the perceived source of these rights in godly dictates rather than in any tradition or customary ideas of inherited privileges. Individual rights and the tolerance that accompanied them were deemed sacred and rooted in the words of the Gospel rather than in the positive law of the state. A direct inheritance of the Puritan migration of the 1630s, it is not clear that such an attitude can be generalized to other religious traditions and cultures.

Toleration and Skepticism

There has, historically, been another foundation posited for toleration, one that for a period shared the stage with what became the modern argument for individual rights, but then retreated to the background; this was an argument based on *skepticism.* Both arguments—that predicated on individual rights and the freedom of conscience, and that predicted on skepticism—emerged out of the Protestant REFORMATION and the wars of religion and the challenge that the Reformation posited for the faith, practices, and criteria of justification of Catholic Europe.

The history of skepticism has been less studied outside the history of science. Here too, though, the Protestant Reformation was critical, most especially in challenging the church's infallibility. For in so doing, Protestant thought challenged existing ideas of certitude as well as the veracity of received truth as proclaimed by church authorities. Consequently, in the debates between Catholics and Protestants over sufficient evidence, the problems of knowledge and faith were joined and ultimately characterized by the failure to justify faith on the basis of knowledge. This led, in turn, to pure fideism on one hand (that is, belief by faith alone) and on the other a sort of mitigated skepticism. It was this latter position that was taken by Sebastian Castellio (1515–1563) in his condemnation of the burning of Miguel Servetus (1511–1553) in the Geneva of JOHN CALVIN (1509–1564)—a reasonable belief that because we cannot be sure of truth, we cannot be sure of the nature of HERESY and hence cannot go to extremes such as the burning of heretics. Tolerance came to be based on a skepticism toward our ability to know ultimate truth.

The debate between Castellio and Calvin took place in an atmosphere characterized by the revival of classical Pyrrhonism (i.e., the doubting of all propositions including those of doubt itself), which was itself called up by the search for justification of an infallible truth via a self-evident criteria. While the Protestants contested papal authority, the Catholics vigorously attacked Protestant belief in the work of inner conscience. Francois Veron (c. 1575–1625) was one of the masters of the Counter-Reformation polemic that showed how (1) the Protestant claim that Scripture was self-evidently clear was manifestly false and in need of interpretation, and (2) predicating interpretation on individual conscience opened the floodgates to endless sectarianism and antinomian potentialities.

One side claimed that the Catholic demand for infallible knowledge led to the discovery that no such knowledge exists and hence to complete doubt and Pyrrhonism, while the other claimed that the very proliferation of opinions that Protestantism led to, ended in compete uncertainty in religious belief and hence to total doubt. That such a position could also be the basis of a deeply felt humanism and widely practiced toleration is best evinced in the life and writings of Michael de Montaigne (1533–1592).

Criticism of biblical narrative in the writings of Baruch Spinoza (1632–1677) and others also contributed to an increasing skepticism of religious truth-claims and a tolerance toward different interpretations of godly edicts and divine commandments. Together with a growing realization of the magnitude of human suffering caused by religious persecution, this contributed to a growing, albeit mitigated, toleration in societies such as Holland and, in the late seventeenth century, in England and New England as well. (In England for example, the Toleration Act of 1689 granted freedom of religion to dissenting Protestant sects but not to Roman Catholics nor to those who denied the Trinity).

Historically, in the countries of Western Europe, the argument for a tolerance based on skepticism was overtaken by two developments: (1) the liberal argument for individual autonomy, and (2) the process of secularization itself, which obviated the very need for religious tolerance. To these was added the Cartesian revolution, which reoriented the whole issue of certitude as well as the position of the knowing subject.

Conclusion

A principled toleration based on skepticism is a difficult position to maintain as it would seem that people have a marked preference for certitude, even if it is of a tremendously circumscribed horizon. To maintain a position of belief while at the same time maintaining a position of skepticism as to its truth-claims—indeed a skepticism so great that one is tolerant of other such claims—is a truly stoic position, but it is one that, first and foremost, rests on some belief, otherwise the whole issue of tolerance becomes moot.

Religious beliefs that have, throughout history, been the cause of persecution and intolerance, have been important sources of toleration as well. From Israelite injunctions of the stranger and fellow-human, to the Sermon on the Mount, to Islamic edicts on the *zakat* (poor-rate), religion has universally provided an openness to the other and an idiom within which to discuss and mediate differences in a tolerant manner. As societies throughout the world become more diverse and pluralistic, both types of religious attitudes—of intolerance and of tolerance—are surfacing and playing an increasingly important role in the politics of different countries. From Hindu nationalists in India to evangelical Christians in the United States of America and Shi'ite Muslims in Iran, religion has reemerged as a major factor in world politics. With this global reemergence of religious identities and commitments, the problem of tolerance is also reemerging as one of the defining problems of the twenty-first century. Engagement with this challenge demands mobilizing the resources of many idioms and a wide range of traditions: not only the United Nations Universal Declaration on Human Rights of 1948, but also the pluralism of Islamic Sufi thought, the Second Vatican Council's Declaration on Religious Freedom (*Dignitatis Humanae),* the theology of KARL BARTH (1886–1968), and the injunction of the Torah on the stranger in our midst. All are part of the global language of toleration.

References and Further Reading

Bejczy, Istvan. "Tolerantia: A Medieval Concept." *Journal of the History of Ideas* 58 (1997): 365–384.

Grell, Ole, and Bob Scribner, eds. *Tolerance and Intolerance in the European Reformation.* Cambridge: Cambridge University Press, 1996.

Heyd, David, ed. *Toleration: An Elusive Virtue.* Princeton, NJ: Princeton University Press, 1996.

Laursen, John, and Cary Nederman, eds. *Beyond the Persecuting Society: Religious Toleration Before the Enlightenment.* Philadelphia: University of Pennsylvania Press, 1998.

Lecler, Joseph. *Toleration and the Reformation.* New York: New York Association Press, 1960.

Locke, John. *A Letter Concerning Toleration.* Indianapolis, IN: Bobbs-Merrill, 1955.

Mendus, Susan, ed. *Justifying Toleration: Conceptual and Historical Perspectives.* Cambridge: Cambridge University Press, 1988.

Mill, John Stuart. *On Liberty and Consideration on Representative Government.* Oxford: Basil Blackwell, 1948.

Moore, R. I. *The Formation of a Persecuting Society. Power and Deviance in Western Europe, 950–1250.* New York, NY: Blackwell, 1987.

Nederman, Cary, and John Laursen, eds. *Difference and Dissent: Theories of Tolerance in Medieval and Modern Europe.* New York, London: Rowman and Littlefield, 1996.

Remer, Gary. *Humanism and the Rhetoric of Toleration.* University Park, PA: Pennsylvania State University Press, 1996.

Seligman, Adam. "Tolerance and Tradition." *Society* 36 (1999): 47–53.

Stanton, Graham, and Guy Stoumsa, eds. *Tolerance and Intolerance in Early Judaism and Christianity.* Cambridge: Cambridge University Press, 1998.

Walzer, Michael. *On Toleration.* New Haven: Yale University Press, 1997.

ADAM B. SELIGMAN

TONGUES, SPEAKING IN

Tongues in the New Testament

"Speak in tongues" is a phrase based on three passages in the New Testament: Mark 16:17, Acts 2, and I Corinthians 12–13 as found in the Authorized (King James) Version of the BIBLE of 1611 and in some other more recent English translations. *Tongues* renders the Greek word *glossa,* used in the New Testament for both tongue (in one's mouth) and language, but in the English version of the epistle it may reflect the translators' compromise in dealing with a phenomenon that appeared different from speaking natural languages. Although some interpreters of Paul's words maintain that he was writing about real languages—but ones that were not known to the participants in a religious event—others believe that the speech was fundamentally different from human language. Translations, therefore, have reflected these two views, based partly on philological and partly on theological grounds: for example, *new, unknown,* and *ecstatic* languages.

The linguistic issue is not problematic in Acts 2. The miracle that took place in Jerusalem on the Day of Pentecost, as reported, was that the apostles were able to speak "different languages" that the audience recognized as "their own [ethnic] languages" and were able to understand what was being said about "the wondrous works of God." This alleged phenomenon—being able to speak in a language one has never learned or even heard—is known as *xenoglossia,* and has been reported in contexts that are not religious at all, being used to defend the belief that there are paranormal phenomena that SCIENCE has not yet been able to account for.

In Corinth, by contrast, it would appear that the speech events were of common occurrence in Christian gatherings, some of which were unruly enough to be criticized by Paul. The speech, moreover, according to some interpretations of the text, was incomprehensible. The utterances were nonetheless considered by Paul in this pastoral letter to be languages in the common sense and the ability to speak in them one of the "gifts" granted by the Holy Spirit. What was more important than uttering something incomprehensible, however, was for it to have meaning, either for oneself or for other believers as well. One was advised, therefore, to pray for understanding of what one had said, but there were also in a fellowship persons gifted in providing the meaning of an otherwise incomprehensible utterance.

The Corinthian speech events have been explained by non-Christians and even by some Christians as having an origin in Greek or eastern cults in which participants sought ecstatic, out-of-this-world (dissociative, altered) states of being, explanations that are considered speculative by serious historians.

Subsequent History

Very little is known—but much speculated—of the subsequent history of the occurrence and distribution of the use of "unknown" languages in Christian communities. Although there are some reports of unusual behavior—sometimes accompanied by gibberish— among fringe groups of Christians, that may in some cases have been concurrent with dissociation (see some of the patristic writings, Montanism, the prophets of Cevennes, and *Les convulsionnaires,* for example), nothing credible can be said about what people were doing from the perspective of scientific linguistics, given the wide range of possibilities for articulatory, psychological, and cultural reasons. These occurrences in any case have been occasional, revealing no continuity whatsoever throughout the centuries, and cannot be corroborated with samples of what was actually uttered, as one must in linguistics. People may have exclaimed in gibberish or produced anything in a rather wide range of verbal (or just oral) phenomena but incomprehensible without having produced pseudolanguage of the recent and contemporary kind. There has, indeed, been no uninterrupted tradition of charismatic religion in canonical and popular Christianity in any of its varieties.

Although emotional behavior is better documented in Protestantism since disestablishmentarianism, the proliferation of denominations and sects, and the emergence of mass popular EVANGELISM, again nothing can be said about the use of speech except that it might be exclamatory or allegedly incomprehensible. In any case, such behavior apparently was idiosyncratic: it had not become part of a community's TRADITION or dogma; it was not theologized.

Tongues and the Pentecostal and Neo-Pentecostal Movements

Speaking in tongues did not emerge as behavior of religious significance until it was associated with the revivalist "second blessing" that had been preached as an advanced stage in one's Christian maturity: one had to be born again first, and then one had to be filled with the Holy Spirit (although the two experiences might occur concurrently). Although profound piety had been preached since at least the seventeenth century in English-speaking communities, and although seeking it and ostensibly achieving it were frequently emotional in public meetings, it was not until the dogmatization of tongues as the experiential, necessary evidence of being filled with the Holy Spirit that this linguistic phenomenon acquired supreme importance in new communities of Protestants.

Tongues, the phrase now being abbreviated, arose in the UNITED STATES early in the nineteenth century and very soon became the hallmark of the Pentecostal movement, which was most successful at first in rural and lower-class North America. It was preached that one should seek the filling of the Holy Spirit and that one could have it. Large meetings to facilitate this experience were emotional and so frequently characterized by dissociative behavior that the people were called "holy rollers" because of their falling to the floor, "slain" by the Holy Spirit. For many leaders in the movement such behavior was not sufficient evidence: one had to speak in tongues. Moreover, because of the belief that these were real languages and that languages could be prayed for, Pentecostalists of various kinds joined the modern missionary movement with the confidence that they would be able to preach the Gospel in any language.

Reports from the last century by believers and by critics about tongues, although considerable, are too vague to allow a scientific linguist to characterize what must have been a wide range of vocal behavior. It is not until the rise of the neo-Pentecostal (or charismatic) movement, once again in the United States, in the 1960s that we can attest empirically to a single phenomenon that could be studied as one would any unknown language of the world, thanks to the availability of tape recorders. It is not unreasonable to suppose that, given (1) the lively existence of old-fashioned Pentecostalists and (2) the doctrinal similarity between the old and the new believers, the new tongues were modeled on the pattern of the old. At the apogee of the charismatic movement internationally, when Roman Catholic and Orthodox Christians became involved in large numbers in the 1960s and 1970s, there undoubtedly were several millions of glossolalists—and, of course, many more Pentecostalists and charismatists who are not tongues speakers. The number has most certainly decreased because of the waning of the movement and, among glossolalists themselves, disillusionment, disbelief, or disuse.

However, the beliefs of the new charismatics were not exactly like those of the old, partly because many arrived at their own appreciation and critique of their lingual experience. Many, if not most, people believed—as had their predecessors—that they were speaking in real languages (demonic ones, their critics declared). Indeed, reports of a tongue's having been identified as "classic" Hebrew or "perfect" Hawaiian by a native speaker in the assembly spread by word-of-mouth, were proclaimed from the pulpit, or published in the literature. These alleged miracles would be instances of xenoglossia. No reports have been scientifically authenticated. Other neocharismatics, coming from conservative (and even anti-Pentecostalist) traditions and being better educated than their predecessors, considered their tongues to be divine gifts for personal use in private events of worship, praise, and intercession. From glossolalists in the ecumenical charismatic movement also came the belief that speaking in tongues was just one of the gifts of the Holy Spirit, not the very one that validated a new and better religious experience. Many others believed that they were engaging in "expressive language," alluding to nonrealistic art.

Tongues as a Linguistic Phenomenon

The serious discussion of glossolalia is facilitated by recognizing all utterances or discourse that fail to meet the criteria posited for natural languages. The fundamental one is that there be a systematic correlation between, on the one hand, phonological units, and, on the other hand, cognitive units (i.e., units of meaning). It follows from this characterization of human language that even before knowing what the meaning of a stretch of language might be, one will identify (a) a restricted set of sounds and (b) sequences of sounds that are distributed in a patterned way, the latter assumed to be carriers of meaning, like roots, affixes, and words. (Even ancient Mayan hieroglyphics have been decoded on this premise with help from contemporary Mayan languages.)

Although samples of glossolalia can be transcribed from tape recordings as all languages can be, they are exotic (a) in having a limited number of consonants and vowels, which are (b) almost always sounds borrowed from the speaker's native language. Here is one sample simplified of phonetic details, including stress (or accent), typical of standard North American English, pauses being real:

kolamasiando, labokatohoriamasi, lamosiando, labokatahandoria

Words of different lengths could be created with these strings of syllables, but they would be subjective and arbitrary, not being correlated with units of meaning. Also illustrated in this sample is (c) repetition—syl-

lables, for example, being rearranged linearly as if they were blocks of sound: *labo/lamo* and *kato/kata*.

It has been argued linguistically that these characteristics of glossolalia make it possible for a person to improvise a stream of sound that resembles language in superficial ways, drawn profoundly, however, from material learned early in childhood. Everyone who has acquired a language (even—perhaps, especially—children), according to this argument, can produce glossolalic utterances, depending on a willingness or ability to do something out of the ordinary, the reasons for doing so, and the contexts. In this sense, therefore, glossolalia is a perfectly natural linguistic phenomenon while being culturally uncommon in the world through time. (The word "natural" is used as in scientific discourse; theologians might quibble about what is and is not "natural.")

Learning to Speak in Tongues

Ignoring the linguistic data themselves, others have speculatively suggested different explanations. (1) Only certain kinds of people are able to speak in tongues: (a) the intellectually and socially deprived, and (b) those who are susceptible to the influence of an authority figure. (2) Glossolalia is always an effect of an altered state of consciousness (dissociation, trance, etc.). Such explanations do not satisfy linguists because they fail to demonstrate that these independent variables are necessary (i.e., causal). With respect to these views, critics have demonstrated that some glossolalists learn from each other: many will have heard short or long stretches of tongues in public meetings even before they are "filled with the Holy Spirit." (There have even been manuals and tape recordings to teach people to speak in tongues.) Many others subsequently and unconsciously adopt bits of what they hear, a regularly meeting prayer group thereby producing its own "dialect." A favored word has been found in different locations in North America and Europe in slightly varying forms: *shanda,* possibly derived from *santa.*

Tongues Defined

Glossolalia, now, can be narrowly defined as a vocal act believed by the speaker to be language and showing rudimentary languagelike structure but no consistent word-meaning correspondences recognizable by either speaker or hearers, attributed in Christianity to the Holy Spirit (the human being just a channel of communication), who can intervene in its interpretation. Used loosely, however, even by psychologists, anthropologists, and others, the word is synonymous with gibberish, but contemporary glossolalists do not consider poorly articulated vocalizations authentic tongues. Although a wide range of speech that is not typical of human language is found in different cultures, usually in a religious context, contemporary glossolalia is different in kind. In play or pretense, of course, people are at liberty to say what they want of their glossolalic utterances.

Glossolalia, however, is fundamentally similar to certain kinds of vocalizations that appear in English and other languages, as in song, play, spells, chants, and so forth. Thus, *abracadabra* (or *abra ka dabra*) is glossolalic in nature, easily becoming the source of *kabra dabra kakada brakada adaka.*

Because Christians believe that what they utter is a real language, glossolalia is used for different purposes: in PRAYER, song (in a group, each person producing different lyrics), exorcism, and "prophecy," the latter meaning a "word from the Lord"—at which time a speaker brings a message from God to the gathering, and is considered authentic only if its meaning is given to the others in the human language they have in common.

See also Bible, King James Version; Evangelicalism; Pentecostalism; Revivals

References and Further Reading

Forbes, Christopher B. *Prophecy and Inspired Speech in Early Christianity and its Hellenistic Environment.* Peabody, MA: Hendrickson, 1997.

Goodman, Felicitas D. *Speaking in Tongues: A Cross-Cultural Study of Glossolalia.* Chicago: University of Chicago Press, 1972.

Kildahl, John P. *The Psychology of Speaking in Tongues.* New York: Harper & Row, 1972.

Malony, H. Newton, and A. Adams Lovekin, eds. *Glossolalia: Behavioral Science Perspectives on Speaking in Tongues.* New York: Oxford University Press, 1985.

Mills, Watson E. *Glossolalia: A Bibliography.* New York: E. Mellen Press, 1985.

Samarin, W. J. "Glossolalia as Learned Behavior." *Canadian Journal of Theology* 50 (1969): 60–64.

———. "Evolution in Glossolalic Private Language." *Anthropological Linguistics* 13 (1971): 55–67.

———. *Tongues of Men and Angels: The Religious Language of Pentecostalism.* New York: Macmillan, 1972.

———. "Review of Kildahl 1972." *Sisters Today* (St. John's Abbey, Collegeville, MN) 44 (1972): 41–44.

———. "Variation and Variables in Religious Glossolalia." *Language in Society* 1 (1972): 121–130.

———. "Sociolinguistic vs. Neurophysiological Explanations for Glossolalia." *Journal for the Scientific Study of Religion* 11 (1972): 293–296.

———. "Religious Motives in Religious Movements." *International Yearbook for the Sociology of Religion* 8 (1973): 163–174.

———. "Glossolalia as Regressive Speech." *Language and Speech* 16 (1973): 77–89.

———. "The Language of Religion." In *Language in Religious Practice,* edited by W. J. Samarin, 3–13. Rowley, MA: Newbury House Publishers, 1976.

———. "The Functions of Glossolalic Nonsense." In *L'analyse du Discours/Discourse Analysis,* edited by Pierre R. Léon and Henri Mitterand, 37–47. Montreal, Quebec: Centre Éducatif et Culturel, 1976.

———. "Making Sense of Glossolalic Nonsense." *Social Research* 46 (1979): 88–105.

Stevenson, Ian. *Unlearned Languages: New Studies in Xenoglossy.* Charlottesville: University Press of Virginia, 1984.

Williams, Cyril G. *Tongues of the Spirit: A study of Pentecostal Glossolalia and Related Phenomena.* Cardiff: University of Wales Press, 1981.

WILLIAM J. SAMARIN

TORREY, REUBEN ARCHER (1856–1928)

American congregationalist minister. Torrey, born in Hoboken, New Jersey, played a pivotal role in the development of FUNDAMENTALISM and DISPENSATIONALISM. After graduating from Yale College (1875) and Yale Divinity School (1878) and gaining an introduction to what he considered the troubling field of HIGHER CRITICISM at Leipzig and Erlangen universities in Germany (1882–1883), Torrey pastored several churches and served as superintendent of the Chicago Evangelization Society and the MOODY BIBLE INSTITUTE (1889–1908), and as dean of the Los Angeles Bible Institute (1912–1924). One of Torrey's foremost concerns was training students for "soul winning service," and especially for urban missionary work. He supported the HIGHER LIFE MOVEMENT, believing that after CONVERSION inbred sin was progressively subjugated but never eradicated. He interpreted baptism with the Holy Spirit as a distinct second experience that endowed the Christian with power for witness, sacrifice, and service. He wrote more than a dozen books and conducted worldwide evangelistic campaigns, sometimes in conjunction with DWIGHT L. MOODY, in Europe, North America, Asia, and Australia. Torrey supported conservative theology against what he considered the "infidelity" of LIBERAL PROTESTANTISM, MODERNISM, and the SOCIAL GOSPEL, most influentially through his coeditorship of *The Fundamentals,* a twelve-volume series of ninety tracts that championed Biblical inerrancy, the divinity of Jesus Christ, the virgin birth, substitutionary atonement, and the bodily, physical second coming of Christ.

References and Further Reading

Primary Source:

Torrey, Reuben Archer, ed. *The Fundamentals: A Testimony to the Truth.* vols. 11–12. Chicago: Testimony, 1910–1915.

Secondary Sources:

Harkness, Robert. *Reuben Archer Torrey: The Man, His Message*. Chicago: Bible Institute Colportage Association, 1929.

Martin, Roger. *R. A. Torrey: Apostle of Certainty*. Murphreesboro, TN: Sword of the Lord, 1976.

Staggers, Kermit L. "Reuben A. Torrey: American Fundamentalist, 1856–1928." Ph.D. dissertation, Claremont Graduate School, 1986.

CANDY GUNTHER BROWN

TOTALITARIANISM

The term *totalitarian* first appeared in 1923, when Benito Mussolini refused to allow his political opponents to present election lists for that year. The term has helped focus debate in Europe and the UNITED STATES on the central issues of the twentieth century. The logic of totalitarianism is designed to counter the modern ideal of emancipation as well as the Protestant concept of freedom.

Totalitarianism is rule by force rather than by consent and has as its goal the eradication of political freedom, democratic process, and legality. Pronouncements of the political leader and party theoretically exercise control over all the institutions of the state and society. Totalitarians also violate freedom of conscience and attempt to politicize all aspects of life, including those that liberalism and Christianity would relegate to the private sphere. Thus totalitarianism can be viewed as an outgrowth of modernity (see MODERNISM) and as countering the anomie that is occasioned by the critical process of emancipation, by the modern rationalization and instrumentalization of culture and society, by the democratization of society (see DEMOCRACY), and by the secularization of daily life.

Totalitarians historically have tried to restore a world of meaning, but have created a dilemma. On the one hand, alienated persons seem temporarily to find a degree of comfort in a totalitarian response. On the other, meaning cannot be restored without reneging on the modern commitment to the freedom and self-determination of the individual in matters of conscience. The political and religious predicament emerging since the FRENCH REVOLUTION revolves around how to establish a sense of spiritual value and of meaningfulness to the world without succumbing to totalitarian tendencies.

Religion and Identity

The persuasiveness of a theological system also hinges on its ability to provide a broad system of relationships to as many as possible in a given community. Religion is supposed to provide an explanation of reality and to establish coherent relationships among the varied elements of human experience. Religion is not exclusively about happiness, but rather about constructing an understanding of diverse realities. In one sense religion and totalitarianism have the same identical goal of creating relationships on a level larger than that of the family. For religion the key task is to provide a satisfactory resolution to the essential problems of the human condition by responding to issues of self-identity and place. Similar to community identity, religion strives to maintain a continuity between the past and present as well as to develop an interrelationship among those within the religious belief system.

Both religious and political ideologies historically have striven to organize the human world around unifying ideals (see AUTHORITY). NATIONALISM has tried to cement large groups together socially, culturally, and politically, and religious worldviews have also strenuously tried to construct their own integrated worlds. In the twentieth century Protestantism has had to negotiate identity and alienation issues as it has confronted Nazism and COMMUNISM. German Protestantism offers one example of how the church has engaged totalitarianism.

Protestantism and National Socialism

In modern GERMANY, at least until 1945, Protestants continued their ongoing agenda of freeing the "German spirit" from Rome. From this perspective, to be Protestant was to be German. In its anti-ultramontane version, German Protestantism was seen as reinforcing national identity by appealing to an exclusive and marginalizing vision of what it meant to be German. Such Protestant spokespersons as Willibald Beyschlag, for example, imagined German history to be the history of Protestantism and Germany's future destiny to be the completion of the REFORMATION.

The Nazi Reich and its relationship to Protestantism must be placed in the context of the tension existing between religion and nationalism in the twentieth century. The record of how the churches attempted to use their theological doctrines (see CHRISTOLOGY) to justify political practices is replete with instances of contradiction and ambivalence. Theology itself was all too frequently employed to provide ideological justifications that could nurture the dominant political stances toward societal issues. German Protestant churches were not unique. From the beginning of the twentieth century virtually all of the Christian churches became caught up in organizational and spiritual crises that exerted an impact on how the churches in Germany and elsewhere could respond to the rise of populist totalitarian dictatorships. Protestant theology, for example, had justified nationalistic war efforts in 1914–1918. The theologians depicted the war in spiritual terms and insisted that personal sacrifice could be seen as moral regeneration. The spiritual leadership of Protestants as they demonized their enemies had already been so gravely compromised that the Nazi years really brought few surprises. The teachings of Jesus and the hideous message from the battlefields produced a widespread disillusion that warped European church life for decades (see KARL BARTH).

Facing the chaos in Europe after 1918, the wounded Protestant message could not counter the hatred that kept Europe in turmoil for decades. At least until 1945 the churches lacked a theology potent enough to support a critical stance toward totalitarianism. Christians adapted to Nazism, convinced by the arguments that political cooperation was crucial. Protestants accepted a dualistic worldview, in which "good" could be equated with the völkisch-nationalist agenda and "evil" with JUDAISM, materialism, and liberal internationalism.

Hitler appealed to national unity as well as self-sacrifice and service. He was hostile toward Bolshevism and launched a campaign against political corruption and vice, while promising to uphold Christianity. Through his German Christian Movement (see GERMAN CHRISTIANS), he hoped to create one Reichskirche. Almost immediately, however, a surprising opposition emerged. The CONFESSING CHURCH worked to create its own parallel arrangements, that is, councils of brethren. The BARMEN DECLARATION (1934) reaffirmed that there can exist nothing higher than the power of God, a view that would be foundational for any real resistance against totalitarianism. After 1934 several Lutheran bishops, including Hans Meiser in Munich and Theophil Wurm in Stuttgart, added a more institutional dimension to the controversy. Even though the totalitarian state restricted options, these men and the ecclesial forces that they represented negotiated with and at various levels confronted the regime on the local and national level until 1945. Although some resistance arose, the Protestant churches were not really prepared to prevent or even meaningfully to mitigate the criminal acts of war and the genocidal policies of the Third Reich. Under the Nazi assault the failure of the Protestant churches to articulate standards of moral responsibility became a serious obstacle to Christianity's credibility in the postwar world.

Despite the heroism of MARTIN NIEMÖLLER and DIETRICH BONHOEFFER as well as others in the Pastors' Emergency League, the lack of effective resistance was rooted in the euphoria of 1933, when members of the Protestant churches rejoiced in the expectations for national renewal and regeneration offered by Nazi promises. Protestant theological dissent was often combined with fervent approval of the regime's secular goals of anti-Bolshevism. National renewal and ANTI-SEMITISM can be seen, for example, in the theological work of Emanuel Hirsch. Basically, Protestant church leaders were reluctant to oppose the regime on issues beyond the impinging church struggle that revolved around state interference in church affairs (see CHURCH AND STATE, OVERVIEW). Except for such leaders as Bonhoeffer, their nationalism generally trumped their Christianity. Bonhoeffer, for example, drew attention to the church's adaptations to the nationalist, authoritarian, and militaristic conditioning of the German people.

Even when the ecclesial leaders saw the dangers of accommodation, they possessed no credible theological criteria to deal with politically oppressive policies. They assumed, therefore, a defensive stance resting on an irrelevant past, and could not critically address totalitarianism while trying to preserve the purity of the gospel. This retreat into Protestantism's core milieu was deadly. By limiting those in their community of obligation, Protestants abandoned others, especially the Jews (see HOLOCAUST), to the brutalization of Nazi terror and racist ideology. Such adaptation weakened the Protestant churches that now had to confront communism.

Protestantism and the German Democratic Republic

After its establishment in 1949, the Communist-dominated Socialist Unity Party clearly expressed its atheistic hostility to the churches, which were perceived as the outmoded pawns of both capitalism and Nazism. Communist propaganda and persecution seemed to be a repetition of the oppression that Protestants had suffered under the Nazis. By the end of the 1950s, however, the regime had begun to appreciate that the persecution of the churches was counterproductive and that strategies would have to be changed. Governmental contacts were established with "friendly" churchmen, which were designed to mobilize support for the regime's goal of the international recognition of the German Democratic Republic.

For their part, church leaders tried to accommodate to the communist regime in different fashions. Minimal support existed for the idea that the churches should assume the role of watchdogs in the state as they had unsuccessfully attempted during the Third Reich. One attractive approach, therefore, was political neutrality with a commitment to avoiding confrontation with the state, a practice particularly successful in Saxony, and very much in the Lutheran tradition of the Two Kingdoms. Albrecht Schoenherr, bishop of

Berlin (1972–1981), supported this notion of the "churches in Socialism." Some ecclesial leaders appealed for a carefully defined level of critical solidarity with the Democratic Republic. They hoped to integrate Christianity with socialism. The chief exponent of this approach was Heino Falcke, the Lutheran Dean of Erfurt. Impressed by Karl Barth's reflections, Falcke developed the idea of "improvable socialism." Other church leaders in East Germany in the 1960s began to seek a more constructive relationship to the Communist state. They rejected giving the state limited and critical support and tried to avoid being enlisted into a Western-sponsored anti-Communist crusade. They adopted a perspective more akin to Bonhoeffer's theology. Protestantism should relinquish, they insisted, its traditional privileges and its theological justification for militarism and nationalism. The church, they were convinced, should become the "church for others" as a community of service and witness within socialist society, not beside it, and not against it, while avoiding the risk of legitimating the regime.

The events in POLAND, perestroika in the Soviet Union, and economic problems in the German Democratic Republic (GDR, or East Germany) produced in the second half of the 1980s an expansion of the social role of the churches as they mediated between nonreligious groups and the state. Increasingly the CLERGY courageously now concerned themselves with a whole range of HUMAN RIGHTS issues. When Protestantism supported the service of civil society and its concerns, it did so within the accepted framework of socialist reality. It was not the Protestants, however, who spearheaded the peaceful revolutionary movement that would lead to the collapse of the GDR. The sociopolitical forces of society used the church's means of communication to realize their goal.

The church had sought to serve God in a Marxist land. To do so Protestant leaders had to deal with an ambivalence in modern communist theory as to whether the CHURCH should be seen as an ideological opponent or as a potential partner in building a socialist society. "Progressive" churchmen hoped to construct a theologically attractive CHRISTIAN SOCIALISM. More radical leaders sought the freedoms enjoyed by their colleagues in the West. Pragmatic church leaders, however, sought to enlarge the "free space" theoretically guaranteed by the constitution. In the process they also sought to repudiate the long Lutheran tradition of subordination to the state, nationalism, and the capitulation to authoritarian political leaders. Even though in the religious sphere the churches lost membership and support, they paradoxically attracted adherents because they were the only ideological and political alternative to the regime. By finally seeking to define themselves as "within socialism," the churches tried to adopt a position of "critical solidarity" toward Communism. The churches upheld a theology powered by democratic impulses and provided a potent support network for opposition groups. They played a pivotal role in the 1989 end of Communism in Europe.

At the time of the *Wende* (1989–1990) the role the Protestant leaders played in the development of democratization and their influence on the masses seemed to suggest that they were the leaders in this upheaval. Within two years, however, revisionist interpretations were introduced. Members of the opposition to the communist state complained that they had not been really supported enough by the church. The opening of the Stasi (State Security Office) archives also convincingly illustrated that the "free" space of the churches was not as extensive as many had thought. Protestant leaders were accused after 1990 of having been co-opted by the regime because their ecclesial offices had been extensively infiltrated by the Stasi. Almost immediately the churches lost the prestige gained in 1990 and were accused of collaboration as well as collusion with the regime. The tentacles of the Stasi had penetrated the church with scores of informers. The churches' heroic opposition to the regime had to be rethought. Critics thought that the church leaders may even have prolonged the nefarious hold of the regime.

Why did Protestants in the German Democratic Republic seem to learn nothing from the Nazi experiences of their church? What happened to the Protestant tradition of prophetic witness? What conclusions should be drawn about the character of German theology in light of these traumatic experiences? Such questions revolving around the proper relationship between Christianity and totalitarianism have delayed dealing with the Nazi past and critiquing the communist regime in East Germany. The debates on the controversial issue of which political values (see POLITICAL THEOLOGY) are theologically sustainable as Christians face regimes powered by brutalizing and/or secularizing ideologies continue. Protestantism's former claim to being the sole agent for moral guidance in political and social affairs may no longer be tenable, unless a sensitivity to human dignity as such can now be grounded on a theological foundation capable of engaging the political aspirations that are shaping the political order in the new millennium.

References and Further Reading

Chandler, Andrew. *The Moral Imperative: New Essays on the Ethics of Resistance in National Socialist Germany, 1933–1945.* Boulder, CO: Westview Press, 1998.

Conway, John. "Coming to Terms with the Past: Interpreting the German Church Struggles, 1933–1990." *German History* 16 (1998): 377–396.

Eckardt, Alice. "How Are the Protestant Churches Responding 50+ Years After?" In *Remembering for the Future: The Holocaust in an Age of Genocide,* edited by John K. Roth and Elisabeth Maxwell. vol. 2, 533–543. New York: Palgrave, 2001.

Halberstam, Michael. *Totalitarianism and the Modern Conception of Politics.* New Haven, CT: Yale University Press, 1999.

Smith, Helmut Walser. *German Nationalism and Religious Conflict: Culture, Ideology and Politics, 1870–1914.* Princeton: Princeton University Press, 1995.

DONALD J. DIETRICH

TRACTARIAN MOVEMENT

See Oxford Movement

TRACTARIANISM

See Oxford Movement

TRADITION

The place and role of tradition in the life and teaching of the church is crucial to the question of AUTHORITY. Few issues come closer to the heart of Protestantism than that of authority. Authority was ultimately at stake in MARTIN LUTHER's reform and was endlessly debated in Roman Catholic–Protestant polemic in the centuries that followed the REFORMATION.

Authority questions fall into three groups: dynamics, structures, and sources. The Reformation was concerned with all three. The reformers challenged the way that authority was exercised in the Church (dynamics): they believed that it should be pastoral and fraternal, not dictatorial and oppressive. The Reformers made changes (not always intended) to the structures that mediated authority in the Church. Notably they rejected the jurisdiction of the pope and in some cases awarded oversight of the church to civil rulers (the prince or magistrate). They regarded episcopacy (see BISHOP) as dispensable if the gospel was at stake. More profoundly, the reformers reconstructed the sources of authority—scripture, tradition, and reason—to give uncompromising priority to scripture, to critique tradition in the light of scripture, and to bring the new scholarly methods of Renaissance humanism to bear on both (reason). Our concern here is with Protestant attitudes to tradition, and our main focus is on the magisterial reformers of the sixteenth century (this enables us to include Anglican theology within the category of Protestantism).

Sixteenth-Century Presuppositions

It is important not to read back into the sixteenth century modern concepts of tradition. The reformers did not operate explicitly with the distinctions that have passed into the ecumenical consensus between three senses of the word: "Tradition" as the essential faith or gospel; "tradition" as the living stream of belief, worship, and spirituality that conveys Tradition and elucidates it in the history of the church; and "traditions" as diverse specific practices on which churches differ. The reformers did not use the modern ecumenical language of tradition. This may explain why some standard expositions of Luther's theology have no index entry for tradition.

Some of the animus that the Reformers evinced against tradition should be attributed to the scholar's contempt for outmoded academic methods. The Aristotelian logic-chopping of the universities and the layers of interpretation typical of the *Sentences* of Peter Lombard, a widely used textbook approach, were equally repugnant to men who had imbibed Erasmus's Greek New Testament and worked with what they believed to be authentic texts of St. Augustine and other Fathers. Even here, however, we should note that the reformers invoked authentic (original) tradition against more recent corruptions.

Against Oppressive Human Traditions

When the reformers spoke of tradition, the overtones were generally pejorative. Tradition was suspect for them and called for a hermeneutic of suspicion. Matthew 15:6 was ringing in their ears: "for the sake of your tradition you make void the word of God." The negative tone that the Reformers adopted with respect to tradition should not mislead us: the reference was specific and limited. What they had in mind was certainly not everything that they shared with the Latin church: the canon of scripture, the Our Father, the creeds, and other teachings of the early councils (Luther and the reformers generally insisted that councils could err and had done so), the ordered ministry, the need for structures of worship, and oversight and for church law.

The magisterial reformers (as opposed to the radicals including the ANABAPTISTS) honored the Fathers of the early Church and studied them assiduously, appealing to their authority in confirmation of scriptural arguments or where Scripture was reticent. They regarded them as biblical theologians *par excellence,* as the witnesses who stood closest to the revelation inscribed in Scripture. At the least, as in the case of HULDRYCH ZWINGLI, they employed their authority *ad hominem,* against opponents who relied on them.

The reformers' polemic against "tradition" or "traditions" is directed at particular human practices ("human traditions") that the late medieval Roman church had made binding on the faithful. What roused the reformers' indignation was not the fact that church authorities (such as the pope) made laws or insisted on certain practices: the church was bound to do this in the interests of good order and unity. What they objected to was the imposition of rules on the consciences of the faithful and as necessary to SALVATION. What belonged to human right was elevated to divine right. What belonged in the earthly forum was falsely situated *coram deo* (before the face of God), and what belonged to "things indifferent" (*adiaphora*—making no difference to one's salvation) was made necessary to salvation.

For the reformers all things necessary to salvation were to be found expressed clearly in the text of Scripture, and the Bible did not need the assistance of tradition to convey its saving message. It nowhere stated that auricular confession to a priest, confirmation, indulgences, obedience to the papacy, and so forth were conditions of salvation. (Luther's generation did not have to contend with the Council of Trent's decree of 1546 that appeared to place unwritten traditions on a par with Scripture, twin channels of divine revelation, although JOHN CALVIN among others later attacked it.)

The criterion the reformers applied in this context as elsewhere was that of JUSTIFICATION. The keeping of human rules, rites, and ceremonies could never justify the sinner in the sight of God. On the contrary, some of these requirements could not be kept without committing sin (AUGSBURG CONFESSION XXVIII). In his *Apology of the Augsburg Confession* (XV, 20–21) PHILIPP MELANCHTHON made this distinction abundantly clear:

> Although the holy Fathers themselves had rites and traditions, they did not regard them as useful or necessary for justification. They did not obscure the glory or work of Christ but taught that we are justified by faith for Christ's sake, not for the sake of these human rites. They observed these human rites because they were profitable for good order, because they gave the people a set time to assemble, because they provided an example of how things could be done decently and in order in the churches, and finally because they helped instruct the common folk. . . . For these reasons the Fathers kept ceremonies, and for the same reasons we also believe in keeping traditions. We are amazed when our opponents maintain that traditions have another purpose, namely to merit the forgiveness of sins, grace and justification.

Melanchthon added on behalf of the churches of the reform in Germany: "We gladly keep the old traditions set up in the church because they are useful and promote tranquillity, and we interpret them in an evangelical way, excluding the opinion that holds that they justify" (38). Such opinions were "doctrines of demons."

Similarly in the INSTITUTES OF THE CHRISTIAN RELIGION (IV, X) Calvin attacked as "human traditions" various decrees regarding forms of worship that lacked biblical authority, but he made it clear that he supported lawful, useful church constitutions. Where liberty of conscience was flouted and human regulations were made necessary to salvation, "a kind of Judaism" had been introduced. The same point occurs, for example, in Calvin's *The Necessity of Reforming the Church* (1544).

Ambivalence about Tradition

Tradition in its etymological New Testament sense (*paradosis*) means the act of handing on from one person to another for safekeeping, not the act of handing down from one generation or one century to another, like passing on the baton in a relay race. This distinction suggests that the reformers' relation to tradition was marked by a certain ambivalence about historical continuity.

On the one hand, the driving force of the Reformation was the attempt to retrieve in its integrity what had been handed on to the church by Christ and the Apostles. The true gospel in the true church had been rediscovered. It was the true treasure, the pearl of great price, the one thing needful. To safeguard it one must be willing to die a martyr's death. The act of rediscovering, safeguarding, and handing on to faithful men leapfrogged the centuries and had little to do with ideas of succession (although some of the more radical Protestants elaborated an alternative apostolic succession, located in the dissident movements of late medieval Europe). Unbroken continuity was not a virtue in itself. The received historical structures of papacy, episcopacy, and canon law were dispensable. Saving faith was a timeless moment, so to speak.

On the other hand, the reformers found themselves necessarily involved with matters concerning the handing down of truth, of authority, of forms of church life. They were adamant that they were not setting up a new church. Their aim, on the contrary, was to renew the face of the one church (as Calvin put it). They were not, they insisted, inventing new doctrines, but rather reinstating the apostolic teaching that had been held since the beginning but had become obscured. In sacramental theology and practice they were clear that they were not innovating. In reforming the mass (e.g., giving communion in both kinds: the wine as well as the bread) they were restoring ancient practice. They insisted that authority to minister word and sacrament was not be seized by the individual but had to be given by constituted authority.

In defending infant baptism the magisterial reformers were of course perpetuating long-standing tradition. Luther and Melanchthon claimed that it came down from the Apostles, from the pure time of the church, before the rise of heresies. If infant baptism had not been true BAPTISM, there would have been no church for all those centuries because the church always remains, by the promise of God, and without baptism there is no church. On their own premises Zwingli and Calvin could not appeal to tradition for something as vitally connected with salvation as infant baptism, but found sophisticated biblical warrants for it.

The English Reformation

Like their continental counterparts, from whom they tended to take their lead theologically, the English reformers (whose views are embodied in the THIRTY-NINE ARTICLES) held that Scripture contained all things necessary to salvation and that those human traditions that innovated against the teaching of Scripture were to be abolished. Other practices could be maintained on their merits provided they were not imposed on the conscience or made necessary to salvation. These practices need not be the same everywhere; particular (i.e., national) churches had authority to legislate for themselves, but not for others, in rites and ceremonies.

The approach that is typical of the English Reformers is clearly seen in JOHN JEWEL's *Apologia Ecclesiae Anglicanae* (1562) and in his extensive *Defence* of the *Apology*. Jewel's chosen field of battle, on which he prevailed, was the testimony of the early church to scriptural truth. English reformers such as Jewel felt themselves at one with the primitive church, appealed to the consent of the Fathers, and claimed that the Romanists had forsaken the fellowship of the holy Fathers and blessed martyrs.

ANGLICANISM gives early tradition a place in deciding matters concerning the outward ordering or POLITY of the church, provided that they are "not repugnant" to Scripture. This distinctive theme becomes pronounced in RICHARD HOOKER (1554–1600). Hooker attacked the contention of the PURITANS in the CHURCH OF ENGLAND that nothing could be done in worship and church government that did not enjoy explicit biblical warrant (therefore, e.g., no surplices and no bishops). In place of "things indifferent" Hooker spoke of "things accessory" (i.e., to salvation). Although what was necessary to salvation was revealed only in Scripture, nothing in the life of the church was entirely neutral.

The role of tradition is only one element in Hooker's argument: sanctified reason and a sense of what is appropriate to the circumstances also play a part in clarifying God's will where Scripture does not inform us. Tradition is a rather crude term for what Hooker has in mind: collective practice and experience and the expressed mind of the church together with the consent of its members are all involved. Hooker's balanced, integrated approach was distorted by some Anglican divines of the next century who took the appeal to "antiquity" to an extreme.

The uniformitarian assumptions of Western culture, unchallenged until the Romantic and historical movements of the late eighteenth and early nineteenth centuries and common to Protestants and Roman Catholics, are evident in these debates. What enjoyed universal consent was right for all times and places. Oldest was best. The golden age lay in the remote past. Therefore Hooker has a prejudice against change, which should always be contemplated reluctantly and only when urgently called for. One could not improve on ancient wisdom and well-tried practice. In his thinking on the scope of tradition, Hooker is not far removed from Luther's "freedom of a Christian man," although it is a more urbane, sapiential approach to the considerable area where God has placed responsibility for ordering its own life firmly in the hands of the church itself.

References and Further Reading

Avis, Paul. *Authority in the Church: An Anglican and Ecumenical Approach.* Edinburgh: T. & T. Clark/Continuum, 2004.

Fraenkel, Peter. *Testimonia Patrum: The Function of the Patristic Argument in the Theology of Philipp Melanchthon.* Geneva: Librairie E. Droz, 1961.

McAdoo, Henry R. *The Spirit of Anglicanism.* London: A. & C. Black, 1965.

McGrath, Alister E. *The Intellectual Origins of the European Reformation,* ch. 5. Oxford, UK: Blackwell, 1987.

Middleton, Arthur. *Fathers and Anglicans: The Limits of Orthodoxy,* part 1. Leominster Herefordshire, UK: Gracewing, 2001.

Oberman, Heiko. *The Dawn of the Reformation,* 269–296. Edinburgh: T. & T. Clark, 1986.

Pelikan, Jaroslav. *Obedient Rebels: Catholic Substance and Protestant Principle in Luther's Reformation.* London: SCM Press, 1964.

Tavard, George H. *Holy Writ or Holy Church: The Crisis of the Protestant Reformation.* London: Burns & Oates, 1959.

PAUL AVIS

TRANSCENDENTALISM

Transcendentalism was an intellectual reform movement, centered in the Boston area, during the 1830s and 1840s. Although the term covered a wide range of diverse thought, its fundamental idea was a belief in the superiority of intuitive knowledge over sensory knowledge (the empiricism of the ENLIGHTENMENT). Looking to Plato, IMMANUEL KANT, and ROMANTICISM as spiritual ancestors, transcendentalism began to formalize in 1836 when RALPH WALDO EMERSON published his manifesto of the movement, *Nature,* and ORESTES BROWNSON wrote his social critique, *New Views of Christianity, Society and the Church.* In addition to Emerson and Brownson, the names belonging to this group constitute a hall of fame in U.S. intellectual, cultural, and reform history: WILLIAM ELLERY CHANNING, Charles Dana, MARGARET FULLER, Nathaniel Hawthorne, THEODORE PARKER, Elizabeth and Sophia Peabody, George Ripley, Henry David Thoreau, and many others.

Many of those who played leading roles in the transcendental movement were Unitarian clergymen who believed that the source of religious truth was not to be found in the BIBLE, the CHURCH, Jesus, or TRADITION, but rather in intuition, which they deemed to be the internal voice of an immanent God. Some of these Unitarian ministers, such as Emerson and Ripley, left the church because they believed the institution was incapable of reform. Others, however, such as Channing and Parker, remained in the church and became instrumental in ecclesiastical change. At first most Unitarians considered Parker to be heretical, although 3,000 people each week came to hear the gifted and controversial preacher. Over time, however, Unitarianism became what Parker advocated, and he is often credited as marking the emancipation of Unitarianism from all semblance of Christian ORTHODOXY.

Because all people were capable of receiving intuitive revelation, all people, regardless of race, ethnic background (see ETHNICITY), or station in life, were to be valued. This caused the transcendentalists to be heavily involved in social reform, opposed to anything in society that devalued human worth and impeded human potentiality. Various transcendentalists emphasized different reforms, which included opposition to intemperance, PROSTITUTION, WAR (especially the Mexican War, which was perceived as an attempt to extend the boundaries of SLAVERY), a corrupt judicial system, and unjust economic practices that caused the rich to become richer and the poor to become poorer. Many transcendentalists were in the forefront to make EDUCATION available to all. The greatest contribution to social reform was the transcendentalists' opposition to slavery. Parker, one of the early American preachers to take an uncompromising stand against slavery, toured many of the northern states addressing the evils of slavery. Thoreau went to jail rather than pay taxes to support the Mexican War and wrote his still famous treatise, "On the Duty of Civil Disobedience." Intuition for the transcendentalists was "higher law," a standard that eclipsed judicial and ecclesiastical laws, even the U.S. Constitution.

Although short in duration as a formal movement, transcendentalism has had an enormous impact on American thought. Individuals such as Walt Whitman, EMILY DICKINSON, Charles William Eliot, John Dewey, MARY BAKER EDDY, and MARTIN LUTHER KING JR. have all acknowledged their indebtedness to various transcendentalists.

See also Slavery, Abolition of; Unitarian Universalist Association

References and Further Reading

Hutchinson, William R. *The Transcendental Ministers: Church Reform in the New England Renaissance.* New Haven, CT: Yale University Press, 1959.
Miller, Perry, ed. *The Transcendentalists: An Anthology.* Cambridge, MA: Harvard University Press, 1950.

DAVID B. CHESEBROUGH

TRANSUBSTANTIATION

According to the Agreed Statement on Eucharistic Doctrine issued by the Anglican–Roman Catholic International Commission (1971), communion with Christ in the Eucharist "presupposes his true presence, effectually signified by the bread and wine which, in this mystery, become his body and blood" (paragraph 6). The word *transubstantiation* occurs only in a footnote: "The word *transubstantiation* is commonly used in the Roman Catholic Church to indicate that God acting in the eucharist effects a change in the inner reality of the elements. The term should be seen as affirming the *fact* of Christ's presence and of the mysterious and radical change which takes place. In contemporary Roman Catholic theology it is not understood as explaining *how* the change takes place."

Paschasius Radbertus (c. 790–c. 860) composed the first surviving Latin monograph on the Eucharist: the real presence of the flesh born of Mary, which suffered on the cross and rose from the dead, is miraculously multiplied by divine power, in a spiritual mode, at each consecration. His colleague Ratramnus in the ninth century introduced a distinction between presence *in figura* and *in veritate.*

Berengar of Tours (c. 1010–1088) emphasized the fact of the real presence, acknowledging no physical change in the bread and wine. Lanfranc of Bec (c. 1010–1089) maintained the presence of the invisible body of Christ, identical with the body born of Mary, but hidden under the *species* of bread and wine. Between 1073 and 1078 Guitmond of Aversa wrote of the elements being "substantially transmuted" (PL 149:1467).

An anonymous treatise dated to about 1140, originating probably in Paris and perhaps by the Oxford master Robert Pullen (d. 1146), contains what reads like an innovation: "not a transformation of a quality but, if I may say so, a transubstantio [sic] or transmutatio of one substance into another" (cf. Goering). By 1170 the word is widely used, as a noun as well as in verbal and adverbial forms.

The word first appears in a conciliar text at Lateran IV (1215), in the verbal form: "by divine power bread and wine having been transubstantiated, *transsubstantiatis,* into the body and blood." This is not, and was not intended to be, a dogmatic definition. Three different understandings of the concept continued to be regarded as orthodox (cf. Jorissen): the substances of the bread and wine *coexist* with the substances of Christ's body and blood; they are *annihilated;* and they are *converted* into the substances of Christ's body and blood.

By the 1260s Thomas Aquinas was arguing that the third of these meanings is the only acceptable one. He wanted to secure the presence of Christ's body and blood in the sacrament *secundum veritatem,* not solely *secundum figuram* or *sicut in signo* (*Summa Theologiae* 3.75.1). He knows that some have held the coexistence position, but argues that it should be avoided "as heretical": none of his four arguments involves Aristotelian philosophy (75.2). He knows that others held that the substances of the bread and wine are annihilated and replaced by those of Christ's body and blood: this view is "false," he says, because it depends on a mistaken analogy with local motion (75.3). Citing Eusebius of Emesa (as he thinks), Ambrose, and John Chrysostom, thus deliberately reaching back to patristic authorities, he holds that this *conversio,* unlike all "natural changes," is "totally supernatural, effected by God's power alone"; "can be called by a name proper to itself: transubstantiation" (75.4). In his study of Lateran IV for Giffredus of Anagni (Vives 27:424–438), Aquinas holds that the first view was condemned and the third (his own) defined by the Council.

In 1306/07, in his *Opus Oxoniense,* John Duns Scotus, contending that coexistence and substitution made better sense, concluded nevertheless that Lateran IV had defined the less "reasonable" position: God, after all, was free to effect the eucharistic presence as he willed. Invoking Lateran IV, the Council of Trent upheld transubstantiation against what was understood as MARTIN LUTHER's doctrine of consubstantiation. Whether this left Aquinas's view as the only alternative is unclear; the substitution view seems to have remained the preferred option for many (cf. Wohlmuth). Luther himself seems not to have objected to any one else holding Aquinas's view, stupid as he thought it was.

Elucidating the miracle of the eucharistic change, Aquinas argues that, after the consecration, the *accidents* of the bread and wine remain (75.5), with no subject in which to inhere (77.1–2). This is Aristotelian terminology; yet Aquinas bases his theory on the first theorem of the Neoplatonist *Liber de Causis:* the first cause can suspend a second cause, and thus keep accidents in existence in the absence of the substance of which they were the accidents (cf. Imbach).

Although John Wycliffe (c. 1330–1384) certainly taught a version of the coexistence view ("true bread naturally and Christ's body figuratively"), his principal objection was to the "madness" of the "accidents without a subject" thesis. Again, in article 28 of the THIRTY-NINE ARTICLES of the CHURCH OF ENGLAND (1563), the word *transubstantiation* is rejected because it is taken to mean a metaphysical explanation in terms of the separability of accidents from substance.

In the seventeenth century and since, Descartes, Malebranche, and others sought to account for the eucharistic change in terms of natural SCIENCE. Such efforts continued in the twentieth century (M. M. De Munynck, A. Mitterer, and B. Krempel since 1928; F. Selvaggi and C. Colombo since 1948). In the 1960s, turning to phenomenology, linguistic philosophy, and so forth, theologians reinterpreted transubstantiation in such terms as transfinalization and transignification (J. de Baciocchi, P. Schoonenberg, E. Schillebeeckx).

According to the authoritative Catechism of the Catholic Church (1992), the mode of Christ's eucharistic presence is "real" inasmuch as it is "a substantial presence by which Christ, God and man, makes himself wholly and entirely present" (§1374). This involves a "conversion of the bread and wine into Christ's body and blood," as attested by John Chrysostom and Ambrose of Milan (§1375). Finally, recalling the Council of Trent, "this change the holy Catholic Church has fittingly and properly called transubstantiation" (§1376). In effect philosophical explanations are tacitly set aside, and the word transubstantiation is equated with its patristic antecedents.

See also Catholicism, Protestant Reactions; Lord's Supper

References and Further Reading

Armogathe, J. R. *Theologia Cartesiana: L'explication physique de l'eucharistie chez Descartes et dom Desgabets.* The Hague: Martinus Nijhoff, 1977.

Clark, J. T. "Physics, Philosophy, Transubstantiation, Theology." *Theological Studies* 12 (1951): 24–51.

Goering, J. "The Invention of Transubstantiation." *Traditio* 46 (1991): 147–170.

Imbach, R. "Le traits de l'eucharistie de Thomas d'Aquin et les averroistes." *Revue des Sciences Philosophiques et Theologiques* 77 (1993): 175–194.

Jorissen, Hans. *Die Entfaltung der Transsubstantiationslehre bis zum Beginn der Hochscholastik.* Münster: Müsterische Beiträge zur Theologie, 1965.

Kidd, B. J. *The Thirty-nine Articles: Their History and Explanation.* London: Rivingtons, 1899.

Macy, Gary. *Treasures from the Storeroom: Medieval Religion and the Eucharist.* Collegeville, MN: The Liturgical Press, 1999.

Wohlmuth, Josef. *Realprasenz und Transubstantiation im Konzil von Trient.* Frankfurt: Peter Lang, 1975.

FERGUS KERR

TRAVELS AND PILGRIMAGES

Travels and pilgrimages have taken many forms in the history of Protestantism, and have often involved varied combinations of missionary activity, cultivation of personal piety, and spiritually motivated use of leisure time. While travel has been viewed as a means of self-improvement, Protestants have tended to be wary of treating particular places as especially holy. Pilgrimage practices carried out by Roman Catholic or Orthodox Christians are sometimes criticized as being idolatrous because they are said to involve worship of specific objects as opposed to submission to an omnipresent and omnipotent God. Sacred journeys are likely to be seen by Protestants as means of cultivating both personally meaningful religious experience and deeper engagement with Scriptures. Pilgrimage has also been viewed in metaphorical ways as symbolizing movement towards salvation and union with the divine.

Reformed and Puritan Origins

Opposition to pilgrimage was an important part of the Protestant Reformation in the sixteenth century. Reformers objected to offering prayers to dead saints or going on pilgrimages in order to gain miraculous cures and salvation. These forms of worship appeared to mix the spiritual and the material in ways that were considered to be misdirected, not least because they attempted to confine an infinite God within finite and humanly constructed forms. MARTIN LUTHER (1483–1546) felt that indulgences (grants of remission of sin), often gained through pilgrimage, reflected the corruption of the church and the papacy. JOHN CALVIN (1509–1564) claimed that miracles had ceased at the end of the time of the Apostles. As the scholar Erasmus (c. 1466–1536) had done before him, Calvin attempted to expose the worship of relics and images as both superstitious and naïve. Part of his aim was to move religious focus from physical objects toward the development of an inner piety, thus allowing the Holy Spirit to operate through the Word. The REFORMATION in Europe frequently led to iconoclasm, abandonment

of old sites of worship, and even the outlawing of pilgrimage.

Nonetheless, the notion of the spiritual journey took hold as an influential part of Protestant thought. JOHN BUNYAN'S (1628–1688) *Pilgrim's Progress,* first published in 1678, became a classic text for Puritans and has remained an important source of inspiration for Protestants (and other Christians) ever since. Bunyan wrote at a time of personal and political turbulence, in an ENGLAND marked by civil war as well as persecution against nonconformists. His book documents the search for truth and salvation by the central character, called Christian, who overcomes worldly temptation, doubt, and despair on the long road from a city of destruction to a celestial city. Bunyan drew on biblical and Calvinist imagery, including the constant battle between forces of light and darkness. He combined realistic details of everyday life with religious allegory as he depicted the lonely Puritan struggle with the self as well as the external world. The linking of salvation with sacrifice and self-denial is also emphasized, with Christian running away from his family at the beginning of the story as he cries out his longing for "Life, life, eternal life."

Similar themes were evident in the thinking of Puritans and Pietists in the early years of settlement in North America. The whole of life could be seen as a symbolic journey, an exile in the wilderness that might ultimately lead to dwelling permanently with God. Existence in the world involved much toil, but was also an inner quest of the individual (located within the church) toward death or perhaps potential salvation. Pioneers learned to view their situation through language and metaphor derived from both the New and the Old Testaments. They sometimes saw themselves as akin to Israelites, close to Zion—the hill where Israel's altar had been placed, which came in Christian thought to represent the church and the route toward salvation for God's people. INCREASE MATHER (1639–1723), the leading Puritan theologian of the late seventeenth century, licensed the first American reprint of *Pilgrim's Progress,* and indeed talked of his own life as a pilgrimage on earth. A folk image of pilgrimage was linked to travel across the new land, and pioneers frequently gave the name Zion to newly founded settlements.

From Mission to Tourism

The sense of Christianizing and domesticating the wilderness was also evident in the actions of sectarian groups such as the Mormons as they moved westward across the landscape in the nineteenth century. Followers of this movement likened themselves to Pilgrims crossing the Atlantic in the Mayflower. They gave the name of Jordan to a river flowing near Salt Lake in Utah, and that of Zion to a nearby canyon. In addition, the pilgrimage metaphor could be adapted for the purposes of missionaries who played an important part in European colonialism. Such evangelical travelers again invoked Bunyan's text (as well as the wandering imagery derived from Exodus) as they constructed narratives of their own journeys into the wilderness. Thus the apparent savagery of local people in AFRICA, the so-called "Dark Continent," was juxtaposed with the enlightenment of imperial mission, just as the African landscape could be seen as akin to a biblical desert. Eventually, dissenting black Christians would themselves appropriate biblical imagery of wandering toward a Promised Land as a symbol of potential liberation from colonial bonds.

Improvements in systems of communication and transport evident in the nineteenth century proved to be of benefit to many types of travelers. They were instrumental in the emergence of new forms of leisure associated with journeying, at least among those who could afford to pay for passage by rail or steamship. Often, travel was perceived to be self-improving as well as an opportunity for pleasure, reflecting influences from the European Grand Tour as well as a characteristically Protestant mistrust of mere idleness. An example of the combining of secular enjoyment with spiritual edification was provided by the development of Laurel Hill Cemetery by the Quaker John Smith (1798–1881). The site not only provided a final resting place for notable figures in the Protestant world, but was also a semirural location, suitable for excursions from nearby Philadelphia. Contemporary guidebooks to the cemetery suggested that visitors might see themselves as pilgrims, and in the absence of a Catholic cult of the saints, the place could prompt meditations on the achievements and exemplary character of those who had passed away.

For more ambitious travelers, the Victorian era saw the development of the package tour and the beginnings of organized movement around the globe. Thomas Cook (1808–1892) had been a preacher and secretary of a temperance society in England before he started to arrange group tours on a commercial basis. Among his many activities, he provided the opportunity for thousands of travelers to visit the HOLY LAND as part of a more extensive tour around the Middle East. Increased British presence in the area, prompted by the weakness of the Ottoman Empire and the desire to maintain a Western presence in important trade routes, meant that access to Palestine was much easier than before. Cook's illustrious customers included Mark Twain and, in 1890, Kaiser Wilhelm, grandson of Queen Victoria, but his main achievement was to

provide reliable, safe transport to people of varying economic means.

Many Victorian visitors to the Holy Land were evangelical in outlook. On their journeys they would bring BIBLES and hymn books in order to hold services at holy spots. Visits often confirmed such pious tourists in their assumption that Western culture and Protestantism were superior to other forms of belief, and at times the journey was seen as an opportunity to convert the local populace and even redeem the Holy Land itself. Their visits reflected their religious convictions in other ways. In Jerusalem, Protestants might walk along the Via Dolorosa but would not incorporate the Stations of the Cross as would Roman Catholics. In addition, Protestants were frequently highly suspicious of certain sites as mere tourist traps and fraudulent representations of the Bible. They attempted to avoid any tendency to see special grace or sanctity as being inherent in particular places. The Holy Land was ideally regarded not as holy in and of itself, but as a powerful catalyst for the cultivation of spiritually powerful experiences rooted in the interaction between believer and Bible. Thus the Sea of Galilee was a favorite spot for Protestant visitors, not only because Christ had taught and preached there, but because the site constituted a landscape rather than a church or monastery that had been filled with alien religious paraphernalia. Similarly, the rocky topography of the Garden Tomb allowed evangelicals to imagine that they were viewing a biblical place uncluttered by later distractions. Conviction in the lasting truth of the Bible was reinforced by such visits at a time when the historical validity of Scripture was being placed under question by new techniques of textual analysis and wider forces of secularization evident in the Western world.

The Present

Despite many predictions of the end of religion that have been made since the nineteenth century, both Protestantism and pilgrimage continue to flourish. Volume of travel in general has of course increased dramatically. Although many shrines of medieval devotion did not survive the ravages of the Reformation in Europe, they were often restored in the nineteenth and early twentieth centuries. Today, such sites frequently reflect the ecumenical relations between faiths that are a feature of modern spirituality. Thus in England, the site of Walsingham provides a good example of the complex pluralism evident in much contemporary religion. Situated in the rural county of Norfolk, in eastern England, it contains both an ANGLO-CATHOLIC and a Roman Catholic shrine as well as an Orthodox presence. The site has mythic origins in pre-Norman, eleventh-century England, and the modern restoration of pilgrimage is a revival of links with a past spirituality that was evident before the Reformation. In common with many pilgrimage shrines, a connection is made with the landscape of the Holy Land, as the village is sometimes called England's Nazareth. Visitors include tourists as well as devout representatives of a variety of Christian denominations, while on occasion the site plays host to vocal demonstrations from Protestant evangelicals who accuse high Anglicans of idolatry. The site of Glastonbury in southwest England is equally complex in its historical and contemporary associations. It has become the site of a revival of medieval Christianity alongside the flourishing of New Age spirituality. Pilgrimage badges have been reintroduced by local clergy in an effort to echo ancient tradition, and since 1986 the main Anglican and Roman Catholic pilgrimages have been held simultaneously in order to express unity. As at Walsingham and many other pilgrimage sites around the world, the boundaries between tourism and pilgrimage, secular and sacred travel, have become hard to define. For Mormons, who have spread throughout the world since the nineteenth century, visits to the American "homeland," and Utah in particular, represent the opportunity to combine holiday travel with overtly religious activity.

Protestant evangelicals may shy from the associations of the word pilgrimage, yet they have continued to engage in travel for sacred purposes. Africa and LATIN AMERICA in particular have proved to be fertile missionary fields over the past century and more, and in many cases Protestants have competed with Islamic and Catholic presences in contexts that have received waves of missionary activity over hundreds of years. In addition, travel closer to the pilgrimage model has been evident among such Christians. Pilgrimage motifs can be discerned in North American Protestant rural and kinship-based revivalist gatherings and prayer meetings, as well as annual evangelical gatherings such as "Spring Harvest" in England. Primitive Baptists in the United States have maintained the Calvinist tradition of seeing themselves as pilgrims and strangers in a barren land. The image of the traveling pilgrim fits the actual movements of elders and laity as they move from one church to another. It echoes in many Protestant hymns, including the famous lines "Guide me, O thou great Jehovah, Pilgrim through this barren land." Meanwhile, the Christian Zionist movement has refocused attention on Jerusalem as a key location for millenarian and apocalyptic predictions of Christ's Second Coming. The International Christian Embassy, based in Jerusalem, organizes annual Feast of Tabernacles pilgrimages to Jerusalem. These occasions are meant to enact the "coming up of the nations to Jerusalem" as described in Leviticus. Drawn from around the globe, Christian Zionists not only visit the sites of Christ's historical life and death, but also see their actions as contributing to the divine redemptive plan for the future of the world.

Other developments in the Protestant world reflect contemporary processes of globalization as well as the ability of Christians to take advantage of new communications technologies. During the 1990s the "Toronto Blessing" entailed many thousands of Protestant charismatics visiting Toronto Airport Christian Fellowship in the hope of gaining access to a large-scale manifestation of the Holy Spirit. The phenomenon of the blessing itself spread through ministries and congregations around the world, and news of its diffusion was relayed by word of mouth, television images, faxes, and the Internet. Some devotees described the journey to Toronto as akin to a pilgrimage experience. Although apparently highly contemporary and specific to a certain branch of Protestantism, the Toronto Blessing revealed characteristics evident in much of the history of Protestant travel and pilgrimage. Specific objects were not deployed as the focus of worship and the locale of the Toronto Fellowship was not considered to be special or holy in itself.

Despite frequently voiced overt opposition to pilgrimage, both literal and metaphorical travel have proved to be important aspects of many forms of Protestantism throughout the centuries since the Reformation. Journeying for pious purposes has provided opportunities for sacrifice as well as spiritual development, spreading of the Word to the unconverted, and furthering personal union with God. In common with many forms of pilgrimage and travel carried out by people of different cultures and faiths, moving temporarily away from home can be seen as a rite of passage that has important effects on individual and collective identity.

References and Further Reading:

Coleman, Simon, and John Elsner. *Pilgrimage Past and Present in the World Religions.* Cambridge: Harvard University Press, 1995.

Comaroff, Jean, and John Comaroff. *Of Revelation and Revolution: Christianity, Colonialism, and Consciousness in South Africa.* Vol. 1. Chicago: Chicago University Press, 1991.

Covey, Cyclone. *The American Pilgrimage: The Roots of American History, Religion and Culture.* New York: Collier Books, 1961.

Eire, Carlos. *War Against the Idols: The Reformation of Worship from Erasmus to Calvin.* New York: Cambridge University Press, 1986.

Hummel, Ruth, and Thomas Hummel. *Patterns of the Sacred: English Protestant and Russian Orthodox Pilgrims of the Nineteenth Century.* London: Scorpion Cavendish, 1995.

Neville, Grace. *Kinship and Pilgrimage: Rituals of Reunion in American Protestant Culture.* New York: Oxford University Press, 1987.

Peacock, James L., and Ruel W. Tyson. *Pilgrims of Paradox: Calvinism and Experience Among the Primitive Baptists of the Blue Ridge.* Washington: Smithsonian Institution Press, 1989.

Percy, Martyn. "The Morphology of Pilgrimage in the 'Toronto Blessing'." *Religion* 28 (1998): 281–288.

SIMON M. COLEMAN

TRIBAL MOVEMENTS (INDIA)

The great majority of Christians in INDIA (90 percent at the time of the 1991 census) were equally divided among three groups: the ancient community of St. Thomas Christians in the southwestern state of Kerala, the dalits (the people formerly identified as outcastes or untouchables) found throughout the country, and the tribals found everywhere in the country but concentrated in the central, eastern, and northeastern regions. The great majority of St. Thomas Christians belong to the Oriental Orthodox and Roman Catholic traditions. The earliest numerically significant responses to the Protestant missionaries who began working in India came from among the dalit peoples of Tamil Nadu and Andhra Pradesh in the mid-nineteenth century. The scale of this response led to a new MISSIOLOGY. Instead of prioritizing work among the higher caste peoples on the theory that they would then be responsible for the evangelization of the lower classes, Protestant missions began to emphasize work among the marginalized groups. By the end of the nineteenth century this had come to include the tribal peoples. At the beginning of the twenty-first century Christianity was growing more rapidly among the tribal peoples than any other group. Although they represent only 8 percent of the Indian population, they now constitute one third of the Christians.

The first historically significant movement of tribal peoples to Christianity took place in Jharkhand. The Gossner Evangelical Lutheran Mission began work there among the Munda and Oraon tribes in 1850. The legal aid provided by the missionaries to the people who were being dispossessed of their ancestral lands by outsiders led to large-scale movements to Christianity. By the end of the century there were over 50,000 Protestant Christians in this area. At that time they were divided among Lutheran and Anglican churches. A later movement to Christianity led by Belgian Jesuits resulted in the emergence of a large tribal Christian community. The tribes of Jharkhand represent those Indian tribals collectively referred to as "adivasis" (original inhabitants). These tribes are concentrated in an area stretching across the center of India from Orissa in the east to Maharashtra in the west.

Although there are many adivasi Christians, the great majority (approximately 75 percent) of tribal Christians belongs to the Indo-Mongolian tribes of North East India (NEI). Tribals are either in the majority or are significant minorities in the eight states of the region. The Christian movement there was begun by American Baptist and Welsh Presbyterian missionaries in the 1830s and 1840s, first in the Assam plains and then in the hills of what is today Meghalaya. During the nineteenth century Christian communities began to be established by them in Nagaland, Manipur, and Mizoram. There were also significant migrations of Lutherans from Jharkhand. They came to work as contract laborers in the tea gardens of Assam and stayed on as permanent settlers.

The largest church in the region is the Council of Baptist Churches in North East India (CBCNEI), with some 900,000 communicant members distributed through the states of Assam, Meghalaya, Nagaland, Manipur, and Arunachal Pradesh. The second largest Protestant church is the Presbyterian Church of India (PCI) with congregations in Meghalaya, Mizoram, Assam, and Manipur. A constituent member of the PCI, the Presbyterian Church of Mizoram, spends half of its annual income on missionary work outside its own area—including missions in Nepal and Taiwan. These and the smaller Protestant denominations work cooperatively in the North East India Christian Council. The Roman Catholic church began significant work in the region in the third decade of the twentieth century. It began to grow rapidly after the constraints imposed by the British government were removed after Indian Independence in 1947.

Although the rapid growth of Christianity among the tribal peoples of Northeast India is the result of the convergence of a number of different historical developments, the free church Protestantism of the pioneer MISSIONS was an important contributing factor. It was relatively easy to adapt the traditional lay- and village-based polities of the tribes to the Christianity that these missionaries introduced. The Protestant emphasis on the centrality of the BIBLE in the language of the people coupled with the evangelical emphasis on EDUCATION as a means of bringing about religious and social change created effective means for the people to maintain their distinctive identities in the modern world to which they were increasingly exposed. Because the tribal languages had no written form, a written language had to be created for them. Protestants were responsible for putting the languages of over fifty different tribes into written form. The creation of a standard language for an entire tribe, the introduction of the first literature of which first portions and then the whole of the Bible was the most important part, the opening of schools, and the establishment of ecclesiastical organizations brought into existence a new POLITY through which distinctive tribal identities could continue to be expressed.

See also Baptists; Bible Translation; Lutheranism; Missionary Organizations; Presbyterianism

References and Further Reading

Downs, Frederick S. *History of Christianity in India: North East India in the Nineteenth and Twentieth Centuries.* vol. 5, part 5. Bangalore, India: Church History Association of India, 1992.

———. *Essays on Christianity in North-East India.* Edited by M. S. Sangma and D. R. Syiemlieh. New Delhi, India: Indus Publishing Co., 1994.

———. "Christian Conversion Movements among the Hills Tribes of North East India." In *Religion in South Asia,* edited by G. A. Oddie. 2nd rev. ed. New Delhi, India: Manohar Publications, 1991.

Sa, Fidelis de. *Crisis in Chota Nagpur.* Bangalore, India: Redemptorist Publications, 1975.

Swavely, C. H., ed. *The Lutheran Enterprise in India.* Madras, India: Federation of Evangelical Lutheran Churches in India, 1952. [Useful for both Jharkhand and Assam.]

FREDERICK S. DOWNS

TRIBULATIONISM

Generally, "tribulation" refers to the suffering of God's people during life on earth. The basic Christian confessions of faith look forward to the return of Christ to judge the living and the dead, bringing an end to this period of suffering, persecution, distress, and trouble.

A more specific use of "tribulation" is found within some Protestant eschatological positions. Jesus's reference to "great tribulation" (Matthew 24:21; cf. Revelation 7:14) is interpreted by some as a reference to a specific period of time. Perspectives on the tribulation generally are connected to millennial views (see MILLENARIANS AND MILLENNIALISM). Amillennialists and postmillennialists tend to interpret even this language of "tribulation" as a description of the suffering characterizing the present age, perhaps with an escalation in intensity as the return of Christ approaches.

Although agreeing that people of God have always endured suffering, premillennialists expect a period of severe and unparalleled tribulation immediately before the return of Christ. For some this period is of indeterminate length. For others, particularly evangelical Protestant premillennialists, the length of this period is delineated in Daniel's vision of "seventy weeks" (Daniel 9:24–27). The "weeks" or "sevens" in this vision are interpreted as weeks of years, thus the "seventy weeks" are 490 years. The first sixty-nine years conclude with the death of the Messiah. Then there is an indeterminate gap of time until the fulfillment of the seventieth week, the seven years of great tribulation. Many of these premillennialists take a futurist approach to the Apocalypse described by John, also interpreting Revelation 4–19 as describing this tribulation period.

Evangelical Protestant premillennial eschatological perspectives can also be delineated according to belief in the RAPTURE of the CHURCH in connection with the tribulation. Primarily on the basis of I Thessalonians 4:13–18, many believe that the second coming of Christ occurs in two stages. According to the pretribulation rapture view, before the seven years of tribulation the church will be "caught up" (raptured) to escape this period of divine judgment because God has promised believers deliverance from wrath (I Thessalonians 1:10; 5:9). Other premillennialists hold to a post-tribulation rapture, believing that the rapture occurs after the tribulation, immediately before the second coming of Christ. A variety of mediating views are found among premillennialists, some seeing the rapture at the midpoint of the rapture or at some other point before the end.

Although differences exist among premillennialists concerning the rapture of the church and the tribulation, all agree that the church age is marked by persecution and suffering and that the blessed hope of all Christians is the return of Christ to establish an eternal kingdom of righteousness and peace (Titus 2:13).

See also Eschatology; Evangelicalism

References and Further Reading

Archer, Gleason L. Jr., et al. *Three Views on the Rapture: Pre-. Mid-, or Post-Tribulational?* Grand Rapids, MI: Zondervan Publishing House, 1996.

Gundry, Robert H. *The Church and the Tribulation.* Grand Rapids, MI: Zondervan Publishing House, 1976.

Ladd, George Eldon. *The Blessed Hope.* Grand Rapids, MI: Wm. B. Eerdmans, 1956.

Walvoord, John F. *The Rapture Question.* Revised and enlarged edition. Grand Rapids, MI: Zondervan Publishing House, 1979.

G. R. KREIDER

TROELTSCH, ERNST (1865–1923)

German sociologist and theologian. Troeltsch was born near Augsburg in 1865 and studied THEOLOGY in Erlangen, Berlin, and Göttingen. At Göttingen he was impressed by the teachings of ALBRECHT RITSCHL and his attempt to conceptualize Protestantism in terms of modernity. No sooner had he begun to study theology then Troeltsch asked how one could justify adherence to the Christian faith in a world marked by the scientific discourse. Troeltsch taught systematic theology in

Bonn from 1892 to 1894 and then in Heidelberg from 1894 to 1915. In 1910 he began teaching in the Arts and Sciences faculty as well. There he encountered MAX WEBER, with whom he developed a true intellectual kinship, and Heinrich Rickert who, after Wilhelm Dilthey, helped to establish the scientific character of cultural studies. Noted theologian, philosopher, sociologist, and intellectual, Troeltsch died in Berlin in 1923.

In 1915 Troelstch received the professorial chair of philosophy at the University of Berlin, considered at the time the most important professorship in GERMANY. This chair allowed him to pursue his work free of any ecclesiastic constraint. Considered the "theologian of the history of religions school," one fundamental question permeated his entire work, which is how to reconcile the relativism of historical research with the absoluteness of Christianity. Troeltsch, who was politically and culturally active in the Germany of his time, was a member of the German Democratic Party. As a parliamentary undersecretary of state in the Prussian ministry of culture from 1919 to 1920 he contributed to the formulation of Prussia's ecclesiastical policy upon the reorganization of Germany in 1919.

The scope of his work went beyond the field of Protestant theology and dealt with the philosophy of history and the sociology of religion. This is why his work involved the social and cultural sciences. Today his thoughts on the confrontation between Christianity and the modern world offer the opportunity to rediscover his ideas. By pointing out that the "European world is made up of Antiquity and modernity" and that Christianity, while setting them apart, unites both legacies, Troeltsch invites the attention of anyone thinking about European culture and the role of Christianity.

In 1912 Troeltsch published a socio-history of Christianity as the account of the social doctrines of Christian churches: *Die Soziallehren der christlichen Kirchen und Gruppen* (The Social Teachings of the Christian Churches). According to him, no Christian era can be considered as normative. Each one has its own relationship with the proclamation of Jesus, which can itself be considered as the first typical period of Christianity. Next came Pauline Christianity, ancient Christianity, medieval Christianity, LUTHERANISM, CALVINISM, and ascetic Protestantism. These typical periods themselves must be linked with three main types of religious organizations: the *Church,* the *Sect,* and the *Mystical.* The *Church* type is an institution that precedes its members and integrates all the faithful, no matter the degree or quality of their religiosity. The religious organization of the *Church* type, established worldwide, maintains positive relations with its sociocultural environment. The *Sect* type corresponds to the voluntary grouping of believers who are said to be breaking away from society, while the *Mystical* type corresponds to the fluid network of individuals who are sharing their direct religious experience, beyond ritual mediations and dogma. Troeltsch's Christianity itself, by taking the shape of free and pure individual religiosity that fully partakes in the questions of its time, approximates the latter type. His theology may be spiritualistic, as he himself admitted, but his attention to the history and types of religious organizations made him acknowledge the importance of the organization for religious transmission. This typology, similar to the Church/Sect typology of Max Weber, was debated by many sociologists of religions who speak of "Weber-Troeltschian" typology. H. RICHARD NIEBUHR drew from it in his famous study, *The Social Sources of Denominationalism* (1929). Besides his interest in the *Mystical* type, Troeltsch's originality is found in his insistence on a "Free-Church" model, an intermediary religious organization that, although having the sectarian characteristics of voluntary groupings of converts, is nonetheless strongly integrated and involved in society.

Troeltsch, like Weber, believed that Protestantism contributed to the rise of the modern world's ideals. While pointing out the great differences between LUTHERANISM and CALVINISM in this relation to modernity, he especially insisted on the ruptures between what he called "old Protestantism" (Lutheran and Calvinist Protestantism at the beginning, which he perceived as still very much limited by medieval culture) and "modern Protestantism." Since the end of the eighteenth century the latter had given up trying to subordinate state and CULTURE to the criteria of revelation. It accepted the existence of an autonomous secular world by its side, thus making religion a matter of personal conviction and personal initiative. According to Troeltsch ascetic Protestantism practiced by Puritans and BAPTISTS embodies this modern Protestantism (see PURITANISM). Along those lines he pointed out its historical importance as creator of civilization as he compared its impact to that of medieval Catholicism.

While demonstrating that, similar to other religions, Christianity was at different times in its history a purely historical and conditioned phenomenon, Troeltsch sought to explain that because it was the "strongest and most intense revelation of a personalist religiosity," it represented the "highest religious truth that we know."

See also Liberal Protestantism and Liberalism; Sociology of Protestantism

References and Further Reading

Primary Sources:

Troeltsch, Ernst. *Gesammelte Schriften.* 4 vols. Tübingen: J.C.B. Mohr, 1912–1915. Reprinted Aalen, Germany: Scientia Verlag, 1961–1966.

———. *The Social Teaching of the Christian Churches.* New York and Evanston, IL: Harper Torchbooks, 1960 (Midway reprint paperback, 2 vol. Chicago: University of Chicago Press, 1976).

———. *Protestantism and Progress.* Boston: Beacon Paperback/Beacon Press, 1958.

———. *The Absoluteness of Christianity and the History of Religions.* Richmond, VA: John Knox Press, 1971.

Secondary Sources:

"Bibliographical Focus: Ernst Troeltsch." *Journal for the Scientific Study of Religion* I no. 1/2 (1961–1962).

"Ernst Troeltsch ou la religión dans les limites de la conscience historique." *Revue de l'Histoire des Religions* 214 no. 2 (1997): 131–266.

Coakley, Sarah. *Christ without Absolutes.* Oxford: Oxford University Press, 1988.

Drescher, Hans-Georg. *Ernst Troeltsch.* Minneapolis, MN: Fortress Press, 1993.

Morgan, Robert, and Michael Pye. *Ernst Troeltsch: Writings on Theology and Religion.* London: Duckworth, 1977.

Pauck, Wilhelm. *Harnack and Troeltsch.* Oxford: Oxford University Press, 1968.

Smart, Ninian. *Nineteenth Century Religious Thought in the West.* Cambridge: Cambridge University Press, 1985.

Steeman, Theodore M. "Church, Sect, Mysticism, Denomination." *Sociological Analysis* 36 no. 3 (1975): 181–204.

JEAN-PAUL WILLAIME

TUTU, DESMOND MPILO (1931–)

South African churchman and statesman. Tutu was born in Klerksdorp, Transvaal (now Gautheng), SOUTH AFRICA on October 7, 1931. The son of a teacher, he was greatly influenced as a boy by the missionary priest TREVOR HUDDLESTON. Tutu became a teacher and, while so working, studied for the B.A. degree at the University of South Africa. Thereafter he entered St Peter's College, Rosettenville, to study for the Anglican ministry, being ordained deacon in 1960 and priest in 1961. Further theological study in Britain brought the B.D. and M.Th. of the University of London and parish experience in ENGLAND. He returned to South Africa to teach at the Federal (i.e., ecumenical) Theological Seminary, and then to Lesotho to teach at the University of Botswana, Lesotho, and Swaziland from 1970 to 1972.

From 1972 to 1975 he was associate director of the Theological Education Fund of the WORLD COUNCIL OF CHURCHES and responsible for grants to universities and SEMINARIES in AFRICA to improve their theological education resources. Before his term with the fund was complete, he was back in South Africa as dean of Johannesburg. He now became one of the most prominent voices in the country raised against the suffering created by the policy of apartheid. This prominence was briefly interrupted by his election as bishop of Lesotho in 1976. By 1978, however, he was back as general secretary of the South African Council of Churches. Under his leadership the Council became one of the most effective legal organs of opposition to government policy. Although trenchant and outspoken, Tutu always spoke in Christian terms and from Christian premises, with emphasis on the meaning of the Cross, never advocating violence, so that it was hard to find grounds to silence him. His public activity continued after his election as bishop of Johannesburg in 1985 and as archbishop of Cape Town and metropolitan of the Church of the Province of South Africa the following year. His reputation abroad, his eloquence, and charismatic presence gave potency to his calls for boycotts of South African exports to Europe and North America and for a ban on investments in South Africa. The personal impact he had was indicated in the award of the Nobel Peace Prize in 1984.

As apartheid and white minority rule crumbled, Tutu became a mediating figure; the meeting between F. W. de Klerk and Nelson Mandela that inaugurated the new South Africa in 1994 took place in the archbishop's garden. He called for reconciliation based on full acknowledgment of past horrors, repentance, and forgiveness. Before he retired as archbishop in 1996, he had secured the embodiment of these ideas in a national Truth and Reconciliation Commission, which he chaired, taking evidence from those who had suffered and those who had inflicted suffering, and "opening wounds to cleanse them." It is one of the most striking modern examples of the application of Christian thinking in the public sphere. It has been imitated in other areas of endemic violence, but not usually with such rigor or such coherent Christian thinking.

References and Further Reading

Primary Sources:

Tutu, Desmond. *Crying in the Wilderness: The Struggle for Justice in South Africa.* London: Collins, and Grand Rapids, MI: Wm. B. Eerdmans 1982.

———. *Hope and Suffering: Sermons and Speeches.* London: Collins, and Grand Rapids, MI: Wm. B. Eerdmans, 1983.

———. *Rainbow People of God: The Making of a Peaceful Evolution.* New York and London: Doubleday, 1994.

———. *No Future without Forgiveness.* New York and London: Doubleday, 1999.

Secondary Sources:

Du Boulay, S. *Tutu, Voice of the Voiceless.* Grand Rapids, MI: Doubleday, 1988.

Thlagale, B., and I. J. Mosala. *Swords into Ploughshares: Essays in Honor of Archbishop Desmond Tutu.* Grand Rapids, MI: Wm. B. Eerdmans, 1986.

ANDREW F. WALLS

TYNDALE, WILLIAM (c. 1494–1536)

English reformer. Tyndale can justly be said to be the founder of the REFORMATION in England among the people. In the early sixteenth century the church continued to forbid the reading of even a few words of the BIBLE in English, under the direst penalties (including that of being burned alive). Tyndale set out to give all English-speaking people the whole Bible printed in English, from the original languages of Greek for the New Testament and Hebrew for the Old Testament, instead of the Church's Latin. He did it at the cost of his life.

Initiated by him, the complete English Bible, in various versions owing almost everything to his work, became the most widely read and studied text in the English language. Such new knowledge rapidly revolutionized national religious thinking, removing many of the church's practices and doctrines (such as Purgatory), which were not found in the Bible, and allowing each believer to meet God without any intermediary priest or hierarchy—guided by the entire Gospels and Epistles of St. Paul.

Eighty-three percent of the New Testament in the famous King James Version of 1611 is pure Tyndale, and only a little less in the Old Testament. The global effect of that version is incalculable.

Life

Tyndale was born around 1494 in Gloucestershire, England. As a schoolchild he learned the *new, good Humanist Latin*. He attended the University of Oxford where, after his B.A. and M.A., he learned Greek, then beginning to be taught more widely. He may have gone on to Cambridge, where Desiderius Erasmus had been teaching Greek.

Back in Gloucestershire, as tutor to the children of Sir John and Lady Walsh, he recognized his life's vocation, to translate and print the Bible in English. An ignorant cleric at the Walsh's table had remarked that "we were better without God's law than the Pope's." To this Tyndale famously replied that if God spared his life he would "cause the boy that driveth the plough to know more of Scripture than thou dost."

In 1516 the original Greek New Testament had been printed for the first time by Erasmus. Tyndale in around 1522 sought permission of the bishop of London, Cuthbert Tunstall (a friend of Erasmus), to translate it into English and print it. Tunstall snubbed him, and Tyndale soon left for Germany, where in 1523

MARTIN LUTHER's first German New Testament (from the Greek) was already a bestseller. In Cologne Tyndale worked with a good local printer, but he was betrayed and fled up the Rhine to the safe Lutheran city of Worms. There in 1526 he produced one of the great treasures of Western culture, his first English New Testament. Pocket-size, it was smuggled down the Rhine in bales of cloth, and into English and Scottish ports. Within eight years nearly 20,000 copies (with piracies from Antwerp printers) had been bought. Only two of the original survive.

Antwerp

Somewhere in Germany, Tyndale learned Hebrew, which was virtually unknown in England. He moved to Antwerp, a port with thriving trade with England and many printers. In 1530, copies, also pocket-size, of his translation of the Pentateuch (the first time that Hebrew had ever been translated into English) reached English ports and were snapped up. At Creation God was seen and heard to say not *Fiat lux et lux erat,* but "Let there be light: and there was light."

His printer in Antwerp, Marten de Keyser, produced four or five other books by Tyndale, notably his *Obedience of a Christian Man* (1528). This, also smuggled into England, was, like his New Testament and Pentateuch, immediately banned, with copies hunted by the English bishops, and the owners punished (sometimes with death). In *Obedience,* Tyndale countered the lie being put about (principally by Thomas More) that reformers (such as Luther) preached sedition and bloody rebellion. Tyndale showed from the New Testament that a Christian's obedience was to the ruler, who had also to be obedient to God. King Henry VIII himself, shown a copy by his wife-to-be, Anne Boleyn, approved.

Tyndale revised his New Testament in 1534, this time with prologues to the books (especially Paul's Epistle to the Romans) and a few explanatory notes. This was also widely read (Queen Anne's personal copy has survived). He also at this time translated the second quarter of the Old Testament, again the first time the Hebrew text was translated into English.

Tyndale's enemies were led apparently by the new bishop of London, the ruthless John Stokesley, and were under the banner of the gross attacks on "heretics" by Thomas More (whose treatment of them makes an ugly blot on his reputation) at first in Latin, and then by permission in English. Attacked in print at length by More, Tyndale was again betrayed. He was arrested, charged with heresy, and imprisoned in a dark, dank cell in Vilvoorde Castle, outside Brussels, for sixteen months, without proper clothing or a light. On October 6, 1536, before a large self-congratulatory assembly of churchmen, he was taken out and burned.

Because he was a scholar, he was allowed to be strangled as the fire was lit.

Tyndale died ignorant of his tremendous influence. First, the language he had created (unusual for the time) fed into English-speaking consciousness forever after, so that many of his phrases are still in common speech (e.g., "the spirit is willing" and "the powers that be"). Second, his friend John Rogers completed publication of his work, and within twelve months of his death it was licensed by King Henry VIII: this went on to be the basis of all the great English Bible translations that followed, even until today. Third, what he opened has never been shut up.

See also Bible Translation; Bible and Literature; Bible Societies

References and Further Reading

Primary Sources:

Tyndale, William. *The Obedience of a Christian Man*. London: Penguin Classics, 2000.
———. *Tyndale's New Testament*. New Haven and London: Yale University Press, 1989.
———. *Tyndale's Old Testament*. New Haven and London: Yale University Press, 1992.

Secondary Source:

Daniell, David. *William Tyndale: A Biography*. New Haven and London: Yale University Press, 1994.
DAVID DANIELL

U

ULSTER

Ulster is the most northern of Ireland's four provinces and the only province in which a majority of the population has ever been Protestant. This was attributed to colonization from Britain, chiefly in the seventeenth century, differentiating Ulster from the rest of Ireland and leading to partition in 1921 when six of Ulster's nine counties remained part of the United Kingdom as Northern Ireland, but with a hostile Catholic and Irish nationalist minority. The identification of religious and political loyalties spawned violent sectarian conflict, and whereas the main churches are committed to reconciliation, popular Protestantism remains notoriously anti-Catholic.

The Reformation in Ireland

Protestantism was never an indigenous growth in IRELAND but a transplant from ENGLAND. Ireland was an English colony from the twelfth century, and the Irish Reformation, establishing the Church of Ireland on the model of the CHURCH OF ENGLAND, was an act of state without popular support. It was perceived as an aspect of English colonization, resisted by Gaelic Ireland which was claiming religious legitimacy in the name of Catholicism, supported by the pope and Counter-Reformation Spain. In the last decade of ELIZABETH I's reign, Ulster's Gaelic chieftains led a nine-year rebellion ending in defeat, leaving Ulster devastated and depopulated, ripe for fresh colonization.

Protestantism in Ulster

Colonists from SCOTLAND and England brought Protestantism to Ulster in the seventeenth century. Many of the Scots were Presbyterians and a religious revival, anticipating similar REVIVALS in colonial America a century later, strengthened their PRESBYTERIANISM. Originally Presbyterians were accommodated within the established Church of Ireland but when CHURCH AND STATE combined to bring the Irish church into closer conformity with the Laudian Church of England, Presbyterians were expelled as nonconformists. NONCONFORMITY was illegal but a Scots army came to Ulster in 1642 in response to a Catholic rebellion in 1641, and its chaplains formed a presbytery in Carrickfergus, beginning the institutional history of Ulster Presbyterianism. During the subsequent Cromwellian interregnum, other Dissenters, including Independents, BAPTISTS, and Quakers (see FRIENDS, SOCIETY OF), arrived in Ireland, although their numbers remained small. The restoration of monarchy and of the established Church of Ireland after 1660 brought difficulties for Dissenters as well as Catholics but the Irish colonial government could not afford to alienate Ulster's Scots settlers completely and TOLERATION was gradually extended to Presbyterians who joined with their fellow Protestants in supporting William III against James II and Catholic Ireland in 1689. From 1690 onward a Synod of Ulster met annually as the Presbyterians' governing body but in the eighteenth century they suffered fresh disabilities under penal legislation aimed primarily at Catholics.

The Eighteenth Century

Presbyterians also suffered conflicts in the eighteenth century between conservative Calvinists (Old Lights) and liberals (New Lights), and the successful advance of New Light brought Presbyterian dissenters from Scotland, Seceders and Covenanters who established congregations and presbyteries in Ulster. Large numbers of Presbyterians, suffering economic hardship as tenant farmers, as well as religious disabilities, emigrated to colonial America in the eighteenth century in the footsteps of Francis Makemie, the Ulster Presbyterian minister who is honored as the Father of American Presbyterianism.

Inspired by the American and FRENCH REVOLUTIONS, Ulster Presbyterians were in the vanguard of a movement to unite Protestant, Catholic, and Dissenter in Ireland to establish an independent nonsectarian Irish state. The disastrous failure of their rebellion in 1798 led to the Act of Union in 1801, which replaced the Irish parliament and government by direct rule from Westminster.

The Nineteenth and Twentieth Centuries

Conflict came in the nineteenth century when the restoration of the Irish parliament, Home Rule, became the political objective of Catholic Ireland and Protestants resisted, insisting the Home Rule would be Rome Rule, following the concession of full civil rights to Catholics. Political tensions were exacerbated by religious friction as EVANGELICALISM inspired a Protestant crusade to evangelize Roman Catholics, provoking their resentment as they experienced their own renewal movement in Ultramontanism, emphasizing papal AUTHORITY and devotion to Mary. In Ulster evangelicalism exploded in the revival of 1859, intensifying Protestant anti-Catholicism, with Baptists and PLYMOUTH BRETHREN growing in numbers and mission halls and evangelical agencies proliferating.

When Home Rule became an imminent prospect in 1912 Ulster Protestants prepared to resist in arms, with the result that Ireland was partitioned in 1921. The Catholic and nationalist minority in Northern Ireland resented partition and their subjection to its Protestant and Unionist parliament, which regarded them as subversive and discriminated against them in various ways. A Catholic civil rights movement in the 1960s increased tension, which erupted in violence by extremists on both sides. Protestants and Catholics have been involved in ventures for reconciliation like the Corrymeela Community and Protestant and Catholic Encounter (P.A.C.E.), whereas the Orange Order, founded in 1795, institutionalizes Protestant Unionism and anti-Catholicism. The wide spectrum of Ulster Protestantism ranges from what are called the main churches, Presbyterian (336,891); Church of Ireland, a member of the Anglican family (279,280); and Methodists (59,517), to the Rev Ian Paisley's fundamentalist Free Presbyterian Church (12,363), with a growing but still small number of charismatic churches and fellowships. (Numbers are from the 1991 census.) One Pentecostal church, the Elim church, originated in Ulster in 1915. Although Protestant churches remain strong and influential in Ulster, SECULARIZATION is advancing rapidly, particularly in the twenty to forty-five age group.

References and Further Reading

Bowen, Desmond. *History and Shaping of Irish Protestantism.* New York: Peter Lang Publishing, 1995.

Ford, A., J. McGuire, and K. Milne, eds. *As by Law Established. The Church of Ireland since the Reformation.* Dublin: Lilliput Press, 1995.

Hempton, David, and Myrtle Hill. *Evangelical Protestantism in Ulster Society, 1740–1890.* New York: Routledge, 1992.

Holmes, Finlay. *The Presbyterian Church in Ireland. A Popular History.* Dublin: Columba Press, 2000.

Livingstone, David N., and Ronald A. Wells. *Ulster-American Religion.* Notre Dame, IN: University of Notre Dame Press, 1999.

Richardson, Norman, ed. *A Tapestry of Belief. Church Traditions in Northern Ireland.* Belfast: Blackstaff Press, 1998.

Westerkamp, Marilyn J. *Triumph of the Laity: Scots–Irish Piety and the Great Awakening.* New York: Oxford University Press, 1988.

FINLAY HOLMES

UNDERHILL, EVELYN (1875–1941)

English theologian. Born December 6, 1875 and died June 15, 1941, Underhill was based in London throughout her life. She married Hubert Stuart Moore in 1907, and they had no children. As an adult Underhill studied in the "Ladies" department of King's College, University of London, which made her their first woman "Fellow" in 1927. Although baptized and confirmed, it was not until 1921 that she publicly identified herself as a member of the CHURCH OF ENGLAND, by which time she had established herself as an independent thinker and writer. She was the first woman to lecture in religion under the auspices of the University of Oxford faculty of theology, and was offered an honorary degree of doctor of divinity by the University of Aberdeen in 1938, a very rare honor for a woman, but which she was too ill to travel to receive. She became a semiprofessional conductor of retreats, to CLERGY as well as LAITY, breaking through ecclesiastical tradition against women's speaking and teaching theology to do so. She published two major books, both of them now considered classics.

Rather unusually for a Protestant she became an expert on the lives and work of the mystics of the church, prompting much further research in the twentieth century. *Mysticism* (1911; many reprintings) explains her view of the evidence that many persons have experienced such a depth of intimacy with God that they were transformed into persons of exemplary effectiveness. In *Worship* (1936) she revealed her profound appreciation of what was at stake in different forms of WORSHIP. By World War II she had become a pacifist, and exemplified her own high expectations for the laity's life of PRAYER, especially prayer of intercession. Significant here are such works as *The Golden Sequence* (1932), *The School of Charity* (1934), *The Mystery of Sacrifice* (1938), and *Abba. Meditations on the Lord's Prayer* (1940).

References and Further Reading

Greene, Dana. *Evelyn Underhill. Artist of the Infinite Life*. London: Mowbrays, 1991 [includes extensive bibliography].

Loades, Ann. *Evelyn Underhill*. London: Fount, 1997.

Underhill, Evelyn, and Thomas Samuel Kepler. *The Evelyn Underhill Reader*. New York: Abingdon Press, 1962.

Underhill, Evelyn. *The House of the Soul; Concerning the Inner Life*. Minneapolis, MN: Seabury Press, 1984.

Underhill, Evelyn. *The Fruits of the Spirit. Light of Christ, with a Memoir by Lucy Menzies. Abba: Mediations Based on the Lord's Prayer*. London and New York: Longmans, Green, 1956.

Underhill, Evelyn. *Worship*. Westport, CT: Hyperion Press, 1979.

ANN LOADES

UNIFICATION CHURCH

The Unification Church can be grouped under the rubric of New Religious Movements. It is thus not altogether clear if it is properly subsumed under the heading of a Protestant tradition. The Unification Church has gone through several incarnations and telling transformations. In spite of vociferous vilifications from many circles, the religious movement continues to be the harbinger of the good news for millions of people all over the world. The Unification Church has been mired in controversy since it was founded by SUN MYUNG MOON in 1954 in Seoul, KOREA. He was born on January 6, 1920 in North Korea. Christianity was practiced in deep secrecy during the Japanese occupation of Korea. Christians met underground for fear of persecution by Japanese authorities. Moon's parents eventually converted to Christianity. Moon claims that in 1935, while he was fervently praying in the mountains, Jesus appeared to him in a vision. Jesus gave him a divine injunction: to complete the assignment of establishing God's kingdom on earth. Moon later developed the "Unification Principle," according to which God established the universe to manifest true love.

According to the Unification Principle, Adam and Eve were meant to develop into a level of perfection. Then they would have been blessed by God in Holy Matrimony and established what is known as the Four Position Foundation of the Ideal Family. In this setting they would have a loving relationship with God, with each other, and as True Parents, with their children. This wonderful vision did not come into fruition because of the diabolical activities of archangel Lucifer. Rev. Moon was given the divine injunction to restore the world to the pristine model originally designed by God.

Moon traces the human predicament to the story of the fall of Adam and Eve. In Moon's theological analysis Eve lost her position and purity because of an unlawful relationship with Lucifer, symbolized as a serpent, and she subsequently seduced Adam. They never achieved the spiritual maturity whereby they could have attained true love. The story will even turn more devastating: their son Cain killed his brother Abel because he inherited a bogus and self-centered form of love from his parents. According to Moon this was how false love has been passed down from one generation to the other. This problem has infected the entire human race.

The family is seen as the basic institution for the growth of God's love in the world. The spiritual and moral teachings within the family structure must prepare people to live for the sake of all others in all situations. However, according to Moon, people do not live according to God's design; personal aggrandizement prevails in interpersonal relationships and in relationships between ethnic groups and nations. Moon proclaims that God commanded him to teach in North Korea, where communist leaders were against all forms of religious organizations. He has survived many arrests, incarcerations, and unsavory conditions. In the 1970s there was a rapid global growth in membership in the Unification Church. Young people put aside their careers, gave up all their possessions, left their families, and dedicated themselves to activities and mission of the Unification Church. They saw their new religious calling as a blatant rejection of the materialistic worldview, especially in the West.

The Unification Principle of one human family and world peace has been spread through massive international activities reportedly engineered to change the world. Through conferences, seminars, consultations, service projects, and publications the Unification Church has left an indelible mark on the global religious landscape.

An interesting aspect within the Unification Church is the massive wedding ceremonies in which people from all over the world are "matched" by the church or already married couples seeking to dedicate themselves to "live for the sake of others" and ultimately create an ideal world family are blessed by Moon and his wife. Millions of couples have been blessed in public weddings all over the world. Unificationists see these mass weddings as an ideal way to create one human family, with couples from all races and nationalities being incorporated into God's plan of true love. Unificationists also believe that couples who are blessed by Moon through the Holy Wine ceremony that precedes the blessing ritual have been purified and cleansed of original SIN and, as a result of this act, their children are free from the burden of original sin.

The entire human history, according to the *Divine Principle,* has been a passionate attempt by God and certain important people to reinstate the world to the state originally designed by God. To accomplish this task, the sins that have been committed in the past need to be "worked backwards" so that bad actions are cancelled out by good actions. These acts of "indemnity" are carried out as a preparation for the only definitive solution to human sin: the coming of a Messiah who will accomplish the role that Adam should have finished by not succumbing to sin. Jesus came as the Messiah, and he lived a great and sinless life. The *Divine Principle* claims that the death of Jesus was not planned by God, but through this ultimate sacrifice, Jesus was able to offer redemption and SALVATION to humankind.

The Unification Church is a movement with a robust theology, philosophy, and social theory. A litany of accusations has been leveled against Moon and his followers. Some of these accusations have been documented by John Biermans in *The Odyssey of New Religious Movements: A Case Study of the Unification Church.* Biermans's extensive study examines the persecution and struggles of the members of the Unification Church, although young people are still attracted to Moon's message of love and world peace. One of the central issues that will affect the future of the Unification Church is how the church continues to respond to what Moon describes as "three major headaches of God": inter-religious conflicts, increasing immorality, and the rise of atheism. The Unification Church has endeavored to address some of these issues through its programs and global outreach.

See also Moon, Sun Myung

References and Further Reading

Biermans, John T. *The Odyssey of New Religious Movements.* Lewiston, NY/Queenston, Canada: The Edwin Mellen Press, 1986.
Fitcher, Joseph H. *The Holy Family of Father Moon.* Kansas City, MO: Leaven Press, 1985.
Grace, James H. *Sex and Marriage in the Unification Movement: A Sociological Study.* New York: Edwin Mellen, 1984.
Matczak, Sebastian A. *Unificationism: A New Philosophy and Worldview.* New York: Learned Publications, 1982.
Sontag, Frederick. *Sun Myung Moon and the Unification Church.* Nashville, TN: Abingdon, 1977.

AKINTUNDE E. AKINADE

UNITARIAN UNIVERSALIST ASSOCIATION

Unitarian Universalist churches claim their origin in theological and doctrinal disputes of early Christianity. Unitarians find an early affinity with Arians and others who resisted the doctrine of the Trinity as it developed in the West after the Council of Nicaea in 325 C.E. Universalists trace their origin to early debates concerning the ultimate destiny of humanity. Universalists affirmed that the love of God is irresistible, that it is not God's will that any should perish and therefore, in the end, all of creation will be restored to harmony with God because an eternity of punishment in hell would constitute an unthinkable frustration and defeat of God's plan.

Although both movements have roots in European religious thought, the Unitarian Universalist movement is largely a North American phenomenon, the result of the 1961 merger of the AMERICAN UNITARIAN ASSOCIATION (founded in 1825) and the Universalist Church of America (founded in 1793). The Unitarian Universalist Association maintains close relations with indigenous Unitarian movements in Romania, Great Britain, and the Kassai Hills of INDIA, with an indigenous Universalist movement in the Philippine Islands and with scattered Unitarian movements in such varied parts of the world as The Czech Republic, AUSTRALIA, NEW ZEALAND, and SOUTH AFRICA. Recently the Canadian Unitarian Council established itself as independent of, although allied with, the Unitarian Universalist Association, headquartered in Boston, Massachusetts.

Unitarian Universalist churches are creedless and congregational in polity. This has produced a movement theologically diverse, varied in its WORSHIP practices, and significantly distanced from much of Protestantism. Thinking of themselves as religious liberals, Unitarian Universalists are frequently to be found engaged in liberal social and political causes and identify this stance as a religious imperative.

Sociologically Unitarian Universalist churches in the UNITED STATES largely consist of suburban well-educated, middle- and upper-middle-class Euro-American professionals. In recent years the Unitarian Universalist Association has sought ways to break out of this limited demographic and welcome racial, economic, and social diversity.

European Unitarianism

Although Unitarians trace their origins to the Arian CHRISTOLOGY that was rejected by the Council of Nicaea, specific Unitarian churches emerged as a consequence of anti-Trinitarian thought that was part of the left wing of the Protestant REFORMATION. In the years after the Northern European rebellion against the Roman Church religious thinkers used their new freedom to examine scripture to evaluate and judge the teachings and practices of the CHURCH. This attempt resulted in rejection of infant baptism, the doctrine of the Trinity, and the concept of a state church, thus producing a Protestantism far more radical than that of mainstream reformers.

Unitarians trace themselves to the work of MICHAEL SERVETUS (1511–1533), Spanish theologian, physician, and reformer. While studying law in Toulouse Servetus began a secret study of the New Testament and the writings of the early Church Fathers. He hoped to find a convincing way to explain the doctrine of the Trinity so that Jews and Moors in his homeland might embrace the essential truth of Christianity and escape the persecution of the Inquisition. In the process of his study Servetus became convinced that the doctrine of the Trinity has no real basis in the scriptures or in the writings of the early Church Fathers. Failing to persuade major figures in the Reformation of the accuracy or the importance of his conviction, Servetus produced a book entitled *On the Errors of the Trinity*. The work was received with such hostility that Servetus went into exile, living quietly under an assumed name in FRANCE. Goaded by the publication of JOHN CALVIN's INSTITUTES OF THE CHRISTIAN RELIGION, Servetus produced a second work, *Christianismus Reinstitutio* (*The Restoration of Christianity*). His identity discovered, Servetus fled France, was recognized in Geneva, arrested, tried for HERESY, and, in 1553, burned at the stake in Calvin's Protestant Geneva.

Although Servetus did not convince the major reformers, he deeply influenced a number of the radical reformers. As a consequence of his writings three major Unitarian (or proto-Unitarian) movements came into existence on the continent. The shortest-lived of these emerged in Northern ITALY, in and around Venice. By 1550 there were some sixty secret congregations where anti-Trinitarian and Anabaptist views predominated (see ANABAPTISM). Two years later the movement was betrayed to the Inquisition and its members scattered—some to Eastern Europe, some to Protestant Geneva, some to the Moslem East.

A major haven for Italian refugees was the kingdom of POLAND. A large, liberal nation with a weak central government and church, Poland provided a refuge for religious radicals from all over Europe. LUTHERANISM had penetrated the kingdom early and was soon followed by Calvin's Reformed Church. Within the reformed church there was substantial theological fluidity—a situation that provided significant opportunity for refugees from Northern Italy to pursue their anti-Trinitarian agenda. Among them was

Georgeo Biandrata (c. 1515–1588), physician to the Italian queen Bona of Poland. Biandrata, a religious radical, invited other Italian radical reformers to Poland and thus moved the Reformed Church in a more radical direction. Eventually the Reformed Church of Poland split over the doctrine of the Trinity.

The anti-Trinitarians were known as the Minor Reformed Church of Poland, or more simply, The Polish Brethren. They are better known to history as the Socinian Church, taking its name from its most influential theologian, FAUSTO SOZZINI (Socinus) (1539–1604), an Italian refugee who had fled to Poland from Italy to escape the Inquisition. Socinus developed a theological system that viewed Christ as an exemplar and denied the traditional doctrines of the Trinity and of ATONEMENT, insisting that SALVATION comes as a consequence of following the example of Jesus. Therefore correctness of doctrine is less important than correct living. Socinus taught that, although the scriptures contained a revelation from God, those scriptures must be read and interpreted by human reason. Like many groups in the radical reformation, the Minor Church of Poland advocated separation of CHURCH AND STATE, questioned the validity of infant baptism, and placed great emphasis on pious living. Under Socinus's leadership the Minor Church embraced tolerance as a religious value, insisting that people ought not be persecuted because of disputed doctrines.

At its height the Minor Church of Poland counted more than 300 congregations. It had established a press that produced more than 500 titles by 1600, and a school at Rakow, its principal city, that drew students from all over the continent. Shortly before his death Socinus held several synods in which the teachings of the church were consolidated and reaffirmed. In 1605 the church issued the Racovian Catechism, a concise statement of its faith, and began publishing the works of Socinus.

However, a Catholic resurgence in Poland, and the failure of the various Protestant bodies to unite in their own defense resulted in the destruction of the Minor Church and, eventually, of the Protestant movement in Poland. In 1660 the Minor Church of Poland was banned and its adherents forced to convert or go into exile. Many fled to Transylvania, Prussia, or Holland. For several generations some observed their faith in secret, ministered to by clergy who made secret returns to the country. The history of the Minor Church of Poland, however, had come to an end.

Concurrently with the events in Poland a similar movement was emerging independently in Transylvania. About two-thirds the size of the state of Maine, in the sixteenth century Transylvania consisted of the eastern quarter of the kingdom of HUNGARY. After the

Turks defeated the Hungarians at the battle of Mohacs (1526), killing much of the Hungarian nobility, a struggle for the Hungarian throne resulted in an independent Transylvania. For a century the Transylvanians maintained independence by exploiting the conflict between neighboring world powers—the Moslem East and the Christian West.

John Zapolya, the first independent ruler of Transylvania, married Isabella, daughter of the queen and king of Poland. Shortly after the birth of their son, John Sigismund (1540–1571), Zapolya died, leaving the throne to his infant son, with Isabella as queen regent. During a period of turmoil after the death of her husband Isabella fled with her son to Poland. When she returned to Transylvania in 1555 she found a nation now predominantly Protestant. In an effort to avoid religious conflict, Queen Isabella issued a decree of religious TOLERATION in 1557, in which she affirmed the right of individuals to follow the faith of their choosing, provided that they bring no harm or injury to others because of differing religious opinion.

Lutheranism had been imported into Transylvania by Saxon elements in the Transylvanian society as early as 1520. The Calvinist Reformed church also established itself in Transylvania and became a focus of theological debate and dispute, particularly around the doctrine of the Trinity.

Two men played a major role in the emergence of Unitarianism in Transylvania. Georgio Biandrata, physician to Queen Bona of Poland, was sent to Transylvania to serve as physician to Bona's daughter Isabella and the young prince John Sigismund. In Transylvania Biandrata quickly became a trusted advisor to the royal family, and once more resumed his work in advocating a radical religious agenda. He found an accomplice in the person of FERENC DAVID (1510–1579). David, a native of Transylvania, was educated at Wittenberg. He returned to Transylvania and accepted a position as rector of a Catholic school and later as a parish priest. In 1553 he embraced Lutheranism, and by 1557 had been chosen bishop of the Hungarian section of the Lutheran Church. After a series of debates between the Lutherans and the Reformed, David resigned his position and cast his lot with the Reformed Church. Soon after, David was chosen superintendent, or bishop, of the Reformed Churches and was named court preacher by King John Sigismund, who had assumed the throne upon the death of his mother.

In 1563 John Sigismund reissued and extended the original edict of religious toleration. In this tolerant climate Biandrata and David began to examine the doctrine of the Trinity. David, influenced by Servetus's writings, had questioned the traditional teachings while still a Lutheran. He now began to raise questions publicly, both as court preacher and from his pulpit in the Great Church in Kolozsvar (Cluj Napoca) and through printed works produced by a press given to David and Biandrata by the king. As the nature of his questions became public the Reformed church was threatened with dissension and schism. King John Sigismund called for a series of public debates. In March 1558, after ten days of debate, David triumphed over his theological opponents. The king, the court, and the majority of the country embraced David's Unitarian theology. In 1571 the king and the Diet provided legal recognition to Unitarianism, proclaiming Unitarianism, CALVINISM, Lutheranism, and Catholicism the four received faiths of the kingdom.

Two months later John Sigismund died, leaving no heirs to his throne. The subsequent rulers of Transylvania were not favorably inclined to the Unitarian faith. As a condition of their elevation to the throne they were required to swear to abide by the edict of toleration. However, toleration was defined as the religious situation as it existed in 1571. Any deviation from that standard was to be dealt with harshly.

David was dismissed as court preacher, but he was elected superintendent, or bishop, of the Unitarian Churches. A restless spirit, David was not yet finished with reforming the church. He began to preach publicly that prayers to Christ and adoration of Christ were inappropriate because only God is entitled to that devotion. He abandoned infant BAPTISM and the LORD'S SUPPER. He was charged with innovation, tried, and condemned to perpetual imprisonment. He died in the dungeon at Deva in 1579.

Georgio Bindrata continued as a royal counselor for John Sigismund's successor. He engineered a conservative statement of faith for the Unitarian Church and the selection of an administrator as bishop. Although he may have secured the survival of the church, he earned the contempt of his fellow Unitarians, who saw him as a traitor to the memory and faith of Ferenc David.

Unitarianism continued to exist in Transylvania, despite hostility, pressure, and outright persecution by Catholic, Protestant, Nazi, and Communist rulers. Most of Transylvania is now within the borders of modern ROMANIA, and the oldest Unitarian Churches in the world are to be found there. These churches still identify strongly with their historic Hungarian culture. After the fall of COMMUNISM a new and vital relationship was created between these churches and the Unitarian Universalist Churches in the West. A Partner Church Council arranges relationships between North American congregations and Transylvanian congregations, and facilitates the flow of financial aid and mutual interaction. In recent years the Transylvania Church has revised its constitution, making its structure more democratic. New leadership, including a significant number of women ministers, has reinvigorated the movement (see WOMEN CLERGY).

Western Europe was influenced by Socinian works from the press at Rakow and to a lesser degree by books from Transylvanian Unitarians. Much of this influence came to focus in Holland after the expulsion of the Socinians from Poland. Earlier the Polish Brethren had provided refuge for Dutch radicals fleeing persecution. The Dutch returned the favor when the Polish Church was exiled. Although no Socinian movement, as such, was established in Holland, it was there that the definitive collection of Socinian works was published—the *Biblioteca Fratrum Polonorum* (*The Library of the Polish Brethren*)—in 1668. Socinian thought was part of the ferment of ideas that ultimately made Holland one of the most religiously tolerant countries in Europe. It was from Holland that Socinian thought entered ENGLAND.

The Reformation in England was originally a political rather than doctrinal issue, as HENRY VIII sought to secure the Tudor dynasty by producing a legitimate male heir to the throne. Henry thought of himself as "defender of the faith," a title bestowed on him by the pope, rather than as reformer. However, the politics of the situation drove England into alliances with Protestant states, making the island nation a haven for Protestant scholars and refugees and opening it to divergent theological positions, including ANTI-TRINITARIANISM.

One source of theological diversity was The Strangers' Church, established by Henry VIII in 1550 to serve the religious needs of the more than 3,000 Protestant refugees in London. Despite its theological heterodoxy, the church survived until the reign of Queen Mary. In her effort to return the nation to the Catholic faith, Mary disbanded the Strangers' Church, although ELIZABETH I reestablished the church in 1560. This institution became a vector through which Socinian influence flowed quietly into England.

This Socinian influence may have "prepared the ground," although the "father of British Unitarianism" had no direct contact with continental SOCINIANISM. John Biddle (1615–1662), the son of a tailor, was educated at Magdalen Hall, Oxford. His study of Scripture convinced him that the doctrine of the Trinity was unsupported by Scripture or reason. These views brought him into conflict with the authorities. Biddle spent much of his adult life in prison for his heretical convictions. He spent the time in jail writing tracts and treatises outlining his faith and arguing its scriptural and rational basis. In those intervals when he was not in prison Biddle gathered a congregation of like-minded followers for worship and the study of scriptures. After Biddle died, after another lengthy imprisonment, his followers scattered.

Theophilus Lindsey (1723–1808) founded the first permanent Unitarian Church in England, the Essex Street Chapel in London in 1774. Unable to accept the creeds of the CHURCH OF ENGLAND, Lindsey had resigned his position as an Anglican priest. Although many sympathized with Lindsey and shared his discomfort with the creeds, few followed his example and the leadership of the nascent Unitarian movement fell to liberal Dissenters. Here and there, across England, congregations of Separatists, BAPTISTS, Independents, and Non-Subscribing Presbyterians moved toward Arian, Arminian, Socinian, and Unitarian theological positions, but there was little sense of a common identity among them.

The man who welded these disparate and independent groups together was JOSEPH PRIESTLEY (1733–1804). Priestley, best known as the discoverer of oxygen, considered himself a clergyman whose hobby was natural science. Priestley served several Unitarian congregations, wrote tracts and books outlining a radical Unitarianism, and published magazines and educational materials, all of which functioned to create a sense of common identity among the dispersed and disparate Unitarian congregations in the country.

After Priestley fled England to escape persecution for his radical religious and political views, the mantle of leadership fell to Thomas Belsham (1750–1829), who continued the work Priestley had begun and gave Unitarianism an institutional form. Under his leadership the Unitarian Book Society was founded and a new version of the New Testament based on recent criticism of the Greek text was published.

In 1825 the British and Foreign Unitarian Association was organized. Bringing together several groups created to secure Unitarian interests, the new organization marked the institutional establishment of the Unitarian Church in England. Throughout its history the Unitarian movement in Great Britain has combined a liberal theological stance with a consistent concern for liberal social causes. Unitarians were instrumental in establishing schools and academies, were active in efforts to abolish SLAVERY, were concerned with women's rights and with the conditions of the poor and the destitute—seeing all of these as religious imperatives. Many of these concerns are reflected in the writing of Charles Dickens, perhaps the best known of the British Unitarians.

As the name of the organization created in 1825 implies, Unitarians in Great Britain maintained relationships with Unitarians in New Zealand, CANADA, and especially in India. The British Unitarian movement continues to be a small but vital part of the religious life of Great Britain.

Unitarianism in North America

In Poland, Transylvania, and England, Unitarianism emerged independently, shaped by the needs and circumstances of specific times and places. The same can be said of Unitarianism in the United States. With the exception of one congregation in upstate New York, which was founded under Socinian influence; and the two congregations founded by Joseph Priestley in Pennsylvania; and Kings Chapel, an Anglican congregation in Boston that became Unitarian in 1785, Unitarianism in the United States is the outgrowth of developments within the Congregational churches of New England. (It should be noted that Canadian Unitarianism, although closely tied to Unitarianism south of its borders, has always maintained a closer identification with British Unitarianism.)

In 1648 the churches of New England, seeking a formal structure of governance, created the CAMBRIDGE PLATFORM—a plan that protected the independence of each local congregation, while offering a vision of interdependence in which autonomous congregations might support and strengthen each other. The Platform was programmatic rather than creedal in purpose. Most of the congregations in New England were defined by local covenants rather than by adherence to specific creedal or doctrinal statements. With no episcopal structure to define, monitor, or enforce ORTHODOXY, congregations—under the leadership of strong and long-serving ministers—often drifted into local variations of the PURITANISM that had brought them to New England. These differences provoked occasional concern over growing laxity from religious leaders, but there was little to be done to halt the perceived drift toward Arianism, ARMINIANISM, and various other forms of heterodoxy.

Theological differences between various churches became a matter of public concern after the Great Awakening of the 1730s and 1740s (see AWAKENINGS). The emergence of a highly emotional, evangelical religious movement served to make visible the chasm between the conservative and liberal wings of the Congregational churches of New England. Liberal churches and their ministers found the practices of the Awakening to be little more than emotionalism and fanaticism run rampant. They refused to participate in the groundswell of religious enthusiasm and often closed their doors to itinerant preachers who carried the revival from place to place (see REVIVALS). The itinerants responded by denouncing the settled clergy as "dumb dogs, half devils and half beasts, spiritually blind and leading people to hell."

The Great Awakening created two self-conscious parties within the Standing Order of Congregational Churches in Massachusetts and throughout New England. The conservative party saw itself as defending the faith from forces that would erode it from within and attack it from without. The liberal party argued for latitude in matters of belief—especially doctrines not well supported in scripture like the doctrine of the Trinity—and for a more optimistic view of human potential than the doctrine of original sin would allow.

These two wings of the Congregational Church remained in uneasy relationship through the remainder of the eighteenth century. The final separation came in 1805, in a struggle over whether a liberal or a conservative would be appointed to the chair of divinity at Harvard College and be given responsibility for the education of future ministers. The liberal candidate, Henry Ware, was elected. The conservatives withdrew from Harvard, founded a seminary in Andover, and the Unitarian Schism was under way. In time most of the oldest, wealthiest congregations in eastern Massachusetts became Unitarian.

Early Unitarians were reluctant to adopt a sectarian mantle, preferring to think of themselves as Liberal Christians. In 1819, however, WILLIAM ELLERY CHANNING (1780–1842), minister of the Federal Street Church in Boston, and the acknowledged leader of the liberal churches preached an ordination sermon entitled "Unitarian Christianity." This "Baltimore sermon," quickly reprinted and widely distributed, became the program for the Unitarian Movement in the United States. Unitarian Churches were founded in Baltimore, New York, Washington, D.C., Charleston, South Carolina, and in the new cities of the Midwest. In 1825 the American Unitarian Association was founded for the purpose of publishing Unitarian works and spreading Unitarianism by way of the printed word. From this institution has evolved subsequent denominational structures.

Channing's Unitarianism was based on a strong faith in reason and the ability of reason to interpret scripture and apply it to a continuous process of self-perfection. This biblically based Unitarianism was challenged by the next generation of Unitarians. In 1838 RALPH WALDO EMERSON (1803–1882) addressed the Harvard Divinity School, challenging his listeners to free themselves from slavery to the BIBLE and to explore the sources of revelation in their own lives. Their task, Emerson insisted, was to show that God lives, not lived; speaks, not spake. Reliance on scripture and its miracles blinded people to the living miracles of their own lives. Emerson's Divinity School Address would echo throughout subsequent Unitarian history. In 1841 THEODORE PARKER, one of those who had listened to Emerson at Harvard, delivered an ordination sermon entitled "The Permanent and the Transient in Christianity," in which he suggested that Christianity is but one of the transient forms assumed by Eternal Truth and that true religion consists in serving that eternal truth rather than the forms it takes from time to time.

Over time Emerson's and Parker's influence moved Unitarianism beyond liberal Christianity and toward a radical religious reconstruction. Over the course of the next century Unitarianism would reconceive itself as a religious alternative, centered on ETHICS and moral living rather than on scripture or DOCTRINE. It would open its doors to non-Christians and eventually to nontheists, insisting that unity of spirit and a desire to live an ethical and moral life were more important than unity of doctrine.

This shift would produce a religious body tolerant and diverse in matters of religious faith, and committed to a liberal social vision. Unitarians became strong advocates for public education, child labor laws, prison reform, civil rights, and women's rights.

Universalism in America

Although faith in universal SALVATION was an early element in Christian thought, and was frequently present among radical reformers of the sixteenth century, except for a few sporadic efforts in England, UNIVERSALISM would first take institutional form in the United States in the late eighteenth century. A number of Protestant groups had brought universalist convictions with them to the new world, especially the German Pietists who emigrated to Pennsylvania in the mid-eighteenth century. Dr. George DeBenneville (1703–1790) preached universalism among the German settlers and the indigenous peoples from his arrival in 1741 until his death. Although he influenced many, he left no institutional legacy.

The man who is known as the father of Universalism was John Murray (1741–1815), who became convinced of the truth of Universal Salvation while still a Methodist lay preacher in England. In 1770 Murray came to North America and took up a career as itinerant preacher of the "greater gospel" of Universal Salvation. A sympathetic group in Gloucester, Massachusetts established a church in 1779 and invited Murray to become the settled minister. This was the first permanent Universalist church in the United States, perhaps the world.

Murray served congregations in Gloucester and in Boston, strongly supported by his wife, Judith Sargent Murray, a member of the original congregation, a writer, and strong advocate for Universalism and for women's rights. Under his leadership the movement grew rapidly. In 1793 in Oxford, Massachusetts the New England Universalist Convention was organized—a body that, with several name changes, would continue to exist until it consolidated with the Amer-

ican Unitarian Association to form the Unitarian Universalist Association in 1961.

Murray's theology was conservative in most aspects, including acceptance of the doctrines of original sin and of the Trinity. More radical ministers who had found Universalism in the frontier country of Vermont and New Hampshire and who were strongly influenced by the rationalism of Ethan Allen challenged his leadership of the movement. The leader who emerged from this group was Hosea Ballou (1771–1852), who published *A Treatise on Atonement* in 1805. This work set forth a consistent Universalist theology that affirmed the key role of reason in interpretation of scripture, that subjected the doctrines of eternal punishment, predestination, and atonement to scornful analysis and presented a unitarian understanding of the relation of Jesus to God. Within a decade Ballou's theology had replaced Murray's more conservative views.

Universalism was, from the start, an evangelical faith. Lacking formal education, its itinerant preachers were filled with zeal. They carried the Universalist Gospel to the frontier, establishing hundreds of churches and preaching posts in New York state, and west into the Northwest Territories (see FRONTIER RELIGION). So rapid was its expansion that Universalism was labeled "the reigning heresy of the day."

Universalists eagerly engaged in theological and ethical debate throughout the nineteenth century. In some ways they were so successful that it proved the movement's undoing. By the early twentieth century much of mainline Protestantism had dropped its insistence on the existence of a literal hell and had embraced much of the Universalist gospel (see HEAVEN AND HELL). As a consequence Universalism lost the monopoly on its central message. As demographic shifts brought decline to small-town and rural America—the center of Universalist strength—Universalism began a serious decline.

In reponse the Universalists began a theological reconstruction, reconceiving their movement as more than a corrective of Christian error, but as a religion for one world—with a message that was larger than Christianity and addressed to a larger audience. They adopted a new symbol for the movement—a off-center cross in a circle, symbolizing that although recognizing their Christian roots, they no longer thought Christianity central to what was being called "the larger Universalism."

Universalism, from its beginnings in the 1790s, combined its wider gospel with a strong social vision. As early as 1790 Universalists in Philadelphia had opposed slavery. Massachusetts Universalists were among the early advocates for separation of church and state. Believing that God never gave up on any of his children, Universalists became early and persistent advocates for prison reform and for the end of CAPITAL PUNISHMENT. They established academies and colleges across the continent, and published a number of papers, magazines, and journals. Universalists were the first to ordain WOMEN with full denominational authority, when Lydia Jenkins was ordained in 1860 and Olympia Brown in 1863. Whitney Cross has said that the impact of Universalists "on reform movements and upon the growth of modern religious attitudes might prove to be greater than that of either the Unitarians or the freethinkers. And their . . . warfare upon the forces fettering the American mind might be demonstrated to have equaled the influence of the transcendentalist philosophers" (Cross 1957:27).

In 1961, after decades of negotiation, the Universalist Church of America and the American Unitarian Association consolidated into the Unitarian Universalist Association. In subsequent years the movement has continued the heritage of the two preceding bodies—a commitment to freedom, reason, and tolerance within an open and diverse community, and a strong social justice witness. Unitarian Universalists were strongly represented in the CIVIL RIGHTS and antiwar movements of the mid-twentieth century, in the struggle for women's rights, in the struggle for gay, lesbian, and transgendered people (see HOMOSEXUALITY), and in issues of ecological and economic justice.

References and Further Reading

Bumbaugh, David E. *Unitarian Universalism, A Narrative History.* Chicago: Meadville Lombard Press, 2000.

Cassara, Ernest. *Universalism in America, A Documentary History.* Boston: Beacon Press, 1971.

Cross, Whitney. *The Burned Over District.* Ithaca, NY: Cornell University Press, 1957.

Howe, Charles A. *The Larger Faith.* Boston: Skinner House, 1993.

Hughes, Peter, ed. "Dictionary of Unitarian Universalist Biography." Unitarian Universalist Historical Society, http://www.uua.org/uuhs/duub/

Miller, Russell. *The Larger Hope.* 2 vols. Boston: Unitarian Universalist Association, 1979, 1985.

Parke, David. *The Epic of Unitarianism.* Boston: Beacon Press, 1957.

Robinson, David. *The Unitarians and the Universalists.* Westport, CT: Greenwood Press, 1985.

Wilbur, Earl Morse. *A History of Unitarianism, Socinianism and its Antecedents.* Cambridge, MA: Harvard University Press, 1945.

———. *History of Unitarianism in Transylvania, England, and America.* Cambridge, MA: Harvard University Press, 1952.

Wright, C. Conrad, ed. *Three Prophets of Religious Liberalism: Channing, Emerson and Parker.* Boston: Beacon Press, 1964.

DAVID E. BUMBAUGH

UNITED CHURCH OF CANADA

The founding of the United Church of Canada stands as one of the most important and controversial episodes in Canadian religious history. The inaugural ceremony in Toronto on June 10, 1925 brought together the Methodist Church (of Canada, Newfoundland, and Bermuda), the Congregational Union of Canada, and all but one-third of the Presbyterian Church in Canada. A number of local congregations already operating as union churches, most of them in western Canada, were also formally received into the new organization. The United Church of Canada began with approximately 8,000 congregations, 600,000 members, and 3,800 ministers. Since then it has remained the largest Protestant denomination in CANADA.

By bringing together METHODISM and two varieties of the Reformed tradition (Presbyterians and Congregationalists; see PRESBYTERIANISM, CONGREGATIONALISM), the United Church of Canada was the first modern experiment in union across confessional lines in western Christianity. Despite much enthusiasm for Christian unity in the nineteenth and twentieth centuries, this "organic" type of union was rarely consummated in other places. However, it was a model well suited to the Canadian context. Divisions were easier to overcome than in many other countries because the uniting parties had already succeeded in consolidating along denominational lines by the time serious union discussions were underway. The prospect of creating a church that would relate in a special way to the young nation of Canada, which had been confederated in 1867, was an alluring one at a time when national identity was fragile. Church leaders also saw union as the most effective way to take care of the religious needs of new immigrants who were arriving in large numbers. Western Canada was a particular challenge; attempts to reach new settlements in the prairies stretched competing denominational resources.

Even under these propitious circumstances, church union was accomplished only after a long and bitter round of negotiations drawn out over a period of nearly three decades. After hearing exhortations from denominational leaders urging greater cooperation for over a decade, representatives of the three traditions began work on a "Basis of Union" in 1904. Four years later it was ready for consideration by the courts of the three churches and their members.

Support for union among Methodists and Congregationalists was solid, and approval was quickly secured, with only Methodists in Newfoundland voting to reject it. The story was different in the Presbyterian Church, which saw the organization of an effective resistance movement to oppose union at the local level after the General Assembly approved it. Under the provisions of legislation passed in federal parliament in 1924, a congregational vote was held in each Presbyterian congregation to determine whether it would join the new church. A commission was appointed to distribute the general denominational assets. Dissenting congregations who rejected the recommendation of the General Assembly to enter union thus continued to hold property as the "Presbyterian Church in Canada." The issue of whether the dissenters could legally carry that name was contested until it was resolved by the Supreme Court of Canada in their favor in 1939.

Religious life in Canada was thus left less united than the founders had hoped. Their anticipation of the 1925 union, as the first of more to follow, has also gone largely unrealized, although the Evangelical United Brethren became part of the United Church of Canada in 1968. Over the years other denominations, notably the Anglicans (see ANGLICANISM), BAPTISTS, and Christian Church (DISCIPLES OF CHRIST) have considered amalgamation, but no such discussions are currently underway. Particularly disappointing was the termination in 1975 of discussions with the Anglicans to create the Church of Christ in Canada. However, the United Church of Canada remains a leader in ecumenical activity (see ECUMENISM), with mutual recognition of ministries emerging as the main expression of its commitment to Christian unity. It provides leadership in ecumenical affairs nationally as well as at the international level. It was instrumental in organizing the Canadian Council of Churches in 1944 and was a charter member of the WORLD COUNCIL OF CHURCHES in 1948. It retains its relationship with the WORLD ALLIANCE OF REFORMED CHURCHES and the WORLD METHODIST COUNCIL.

Characteristics

During the controversy over church union, those who objected to forming the United Church of Canada claimed that it was liberal to the point of being apostate and more interested in politics than spirituality. Such charges obscured the importance of its evangelical heritage and the commitment to transformation of both individuals and institutions, which was central to the evangelical piety of the founding traditions.

The articles of faith adopted in 1925 as part of the Basis of Union reflected the liberal evangelical perspective of its early twentieth-century formulation. Those who prepared it regarded it as a statement of the "common faith" of the uniting denominations and an articulation of the theological convictions of their own generation. Because formulation of a CONFESSION of faith in meaningful language for the times was viewed as the ongoing task of each generation, a committee

soon began work on the Statement of Faith, approved in 1940. What is referred to as the New Creed has been in use since 1968, with a few modifications over the years. In response to calls for a new confession of faith, the General Council requested in 2000 that the Committee on Theology and Faith begin work on a document that would honor the church's theological diversity and acknowledge its place in a pluralistic world.

The church also proudly celebrates the influence of the SOCIAL GOSPEL, which was evidenced in its impulse to serve as the "conscience of the nation." It has claimed that aspect of its heritage when taking positions on political and social issues viewed at the time as risky or controversial. Its theological schools and congregations have been receptive to biblical criticism, an openness reflected in PREACHING and educational projects, notably the New Curriculum introduced in the 1960s. Some decisions, such as its positions on remarriage of divorced persons in the early 1960s (see DIVORCE) and ordination of gay and lesbian persons in 1988 (see HOMOSEXUALITY), generated controversy at the time but later have been adopted with less fanfare by other denominations. It continues to study, issue statements, and make efforts to influence governments and other agencies responsible for shaping policy on issues such as ABORTION, CAPITAL PUNISHMENT, racial equality, land use, refugees, and poverty.

Being the "conscience of the nation" has not always been a comfortable role. The apology to native peoples issued by the denomination in 1986 was accompanied by an experiment to provide their congregations with greater autonomy and responsibility through creation of the All Native Circle Conference in 1988. The church continues to wrestle with the financial and moral implications of the residential schools set up and supported by those who saw assimilation of native children to mainstream CULTURE as their best hope of inclusion in modern industrial society. This proved to be an experiment with tragic consequences for many native families. The church's involvement in helping the federal government to operate the schools was an entanglement for which the General Council apologized in 1998.

Leadership

The church's leaders have set the tone for its work from the outset. One of the memorable moments of the first General Council in 1925 came when former Methodist general superintendent S. D. Chown (1872–1991), the architect of church union and considered the leading candidate for the moderator's position, stepped aside in favor of George Pidgeon (1892–1971), the principal spokesperson for the uniting Presbyterians. The position of moderator has since recognized the gifts of distinguished men and women in the church, while providing the church with a way to highlight its mission and ideals in the selection.

Other executive positions have provided the incumbent with opportunities to put the social and spiritual agenda of the church before the public. James Endicott, a missionary to China, caught the attention of the public and gained notoriety as a "public enemy" for his outspoken support for the Communist Revolution. In the early years, the secretaries of the Board of Evangelism and Social Service were particularly effective in using press and pulpit. In the 1950s James R. Mutchmor opposed the three B's: "betting, beer, and bingo," while in the 1960s Ray Hord's condemnation of the Vietnam War and support for draft dodgers created headlines. Medical missionary Robert McClure was an effective public spokesperson for overseas work, and in 1968 became the first lay member to serve as moderator.

The United Church of Canada was the first DENOMINATION in Canada to ordain women (Lydia Gruchy in 1936) and has since elected WOMEN to other prominent positions (see WOMEN CLERGY). In 1980, Lois Wilson became the first woman to serve as moderator, and in 1994, Virginia Coleman was elected as secretary of General Council, the denomination's chief administrative office.

Structure, Key Organizations, and Publications

The United Church of Canada is organized at four levels: local congregations or pastoral charges; ninety-one district Presbyteries, which exercise oversight of twenty to fifty pastoral charges; thirteen regional conferences that meet annually; and the national General Council, which meets on a biennial or triennial basis to make decisions in areas of program and administration concerning the whole church. The work of the divisions of General Council is supported through contributions from local congregations through the Mission and Service Fund. The four-court structure of the church was reviewed in 2000. The General Council approved a restructuring plan that will be voted on by all presbyteries and pastoral charges and the results considered by the next General Council. The proposed changes would combine the responsibilities and powers of current presbyteries and conferences into a single entity.

The United Church of Canada relates to a variety of educational institutions including thirteen theological schools and programs, five educational centers, and six liberal arts colleges and universities. The educational work of the denomination is also carried on in congregations through organizations for children, youth, and gender-specific associations for adults. Centralized coordination at the national level was evident in the 1940s and 1950s in organizations such as Canadian Girls in Training, which began in 1915 and continued after union, Trail Rangers for boys twelve to fourteen, Tuxis Boys for fifteen and up, an Older Boys Parliament, and the Young People's Society. "As One That Serves" was an idea for a Methodist men's club in Vancouver just before church union, which then spread across Canada. At the time of church union, the VOLUNTARY SOCIETIES organized by women in the nineteenth century emerged as the Woman's Missionary Society and the Woman's Association, which in turn amalgamated in 1962 as the United Church Women (UCW).

Since the 1970s the church's special-purpose groups have experienced loss of membership and dwindling support for volunteer activities. This has spurred a number of efforts to loosen national coordinating structures to see what new forms emerge. The most striking move was a decision in 2000 to adopt the name "Women of the United Church of Canada" to refer collectively to the church's programming for women. Whereas the focus of United Church Women was fundraising, hospitality, and study, the new organization will incorporate UCW units as well as spirituality and support groups that have emerged as alternatives.

The publication of *The Hymnary* (1930) and *The Book of Common Order* (1932) gave definition to the worship traditions of uniting congregations. A new *Service Book* was published in 1969. The *Hymn Book*, published jointly with the Anglican Church of Canada in 1971, was followed a generation later by *Voices United* in 1996, a work that has received a more enthusiastic reception than its predecessor (see HYMNS AND HYMNALS). *The United Church Observer* is the official publication of the denomination.

Places It Was and Is Practiced

The United Church of Canada operates primarily in Canada, although a few Methodist congregations in Bermuda comprise a presbytery related to the Maritime Conference. The denomination has also been involved in overseas missions since its founding (see MISSIONS). The churches joined to form the denomination had established missions in such places as Angola, CHINA, INDIA, JAPAN, KOREA, and Trinidad. This work continued and at first expanded after union. The largest mission in the whole of China before the Communist Revolution was its West China Mission. Reflecting a changed concept of world outreach from foreign missions to an emphasis on working with ecumenical partners around the world, the United Church of Canada now works under the direction of indigenous ecumenical partners in overseas countries at the request of churches and agencies, providing funding and personnel for projects.

Expansion or Decline

Since its founding, the United Church of Canada has followed a trajectory similar to mainstream churches in the United States during the same period: it enjoyed something of the status of a voluntary (though never legal) establishment for the first few decades; suffered a decline in membership and financial resources during the depression years; experienced a postwar revival of religious interest that included new congregational development in the suburbs; and has recently seen lower rates of membership and participation with the first reported loss of membership in 1966. Although in 1999 it reported the number of confirmed members as 668,549, the most recent census data (1991) indicate that 3,093,120 Canadians consider themselves to be affiliated with the denomination.

See also Dialogue, Interconfessional

References and Further Reading

Airhart, Phyllis D., and Roger C. Hutchinson, eds. *Christianizing the Social Order: A Founding Vision of the United Church* [special issue]. *Toronto Journal of Theology* 12, no. 2 (1996).

Anderson, Daphne J., and Terence R. Anderson. "United Church of Canada: Kingdom Symbol or Lifestyle Choice." In *Faith Traditions and the Family.* Edited by Phyllis D. Airhart and Margaret Lamberts Bendroth. Louisville, KY: WJKP, 1996.

Chalmers, Randolph Carleton. *See the Christ Stand: A Study in Doctrine in the United Church of Canada.* Toronto: Ryerson Press, 1945.

Chambers, Steven. *This Is Your Church: A Guide to the Beliefs, Practices and Positions of the United Church of Canada.* 3rd ed. Toronto: United Church Publishing House, 1993.

Clifford, N. K. *The Resistance to Church Union in Canada.* Vancouver: University of British Columbia Press, 1985.

Grant, John Webster. *The Canadian Experience of Church Union.* London: Lutterworth Press, 1967.

Manson, Ian. "'Fighting the Good Fight': Salvation, Social Reform, and Service in the United Church of Canada's Board of Evangelism and Social Service." Th.D. dissertation, Emmanuel College of Victoria University, University of Toronto, 1999.

Silcox, C. E. *Church Union in Canada: Its Causes and Consequences.* New York: Institute of Social and Religious Research, 1933.

The United Church of Canada. http//:www.uccan.org (November 5, 2001).

White, Peter Gordon, ed. *Voices and Visions: Sixty-Five Years of the United Church of Canada.* Toronto: United Church Publishing House, 1990.

PHYLLIS D. AIRHART

UNITED CHURCH OF CHRIST

Established in 1957 as the organic union of the Congregational Christian Churches and the EVANGELICAL AND REFORMED CHURCH, each itself the product of an earlier merger, the United Church of Christ (UCC) is widely recognized as the most theologically and socially progressive among those American denominations historically called "mainline." The heritage of the UCC is essentially orthodox: its trinitarian presuppositions, its claiming "as its own" the ancient creeds and the reformulations of the Protestant Reformation, its reliance on Scripture, and its recognition of two SACRAMENTS—all affirmed in the denomination's *Constitution and Bylaws*—place the UCC firmly in the tradition of historic Protestantism.

There are several denominations worldwide that are called "United Church of Christ," for example, in those in JAPAN and the PHILIPPINES. These groups are not, however, organically related. The United Church of Christ (USA) is not an international body, although it has numerous ecumenical partnerships worldwide.

Multiple Traditions

Congregationalism

The largest and oldest of the UCC's four constituting traditions is CONGREGATIONALISM, which arose in the late 1500s as a movement of protest against perceived abuses and limitations, both theological and structural, within the CHURCH OF ENGLAND. The Pilgrims, who advocated total separation from the Anglican Church, and the Puritans, who hoped to change and purify it, migrated to New England in the first part of the seventeenth century and there established autonomous, local bodies of believers (see PILGRIM FATHERS; PURITANISM). Gathered by consent and covenant among the presumed regenerate, these congregations—rather than any national or regional body—were understood to define the true church.

Both Pilgrim and Puritan Congregationalists looked to the teachings of Genevan reformer JOHN CALVIN, adapting his ideas to the American environment. In particular, Massachusetts Bay Puritans developed and elaborated a "COVENANT" THEOLOGY, in which (1) the covenant of GRACE was understood as the means by which God works in the human heart and enables saving FAITH; (2) a careful balance between local church autonomy and regional church interdependence was maintained; (3) God was assumed to be in COVENANT not only with individuals, but with the group as a whole; (4) religious homogeneity in church and community was considered essential. Under the leadership of layman John Winthrop, the MATHER FAMILY, John Cotton, and others, the Puritans anticipated forming a unique godly commonwealth—a "city on a hill"—that would be imitated elsewhere.

Revivals, migration, pressure from other religious bodies, political changes in ENGLAND and America, and, in the early 1800s, a schism that resulted in formation of the AMERICAN UNITARIAN ASSOCIATION: all these gradually altered the nature of historic Congregationalism. Although New England continued to be the primary locus of Congregational churches, post-Revolutionary settlers gathered new congregations in the upper midwest and, eventually, in California and the far west. Between 1865 and 1913 three national gatherings produced a basic denominational structure—albeit one that recognized local autonomy as fundamental—for churches that had previously been essentially unrelated. Theologically, although some members continued to self-identify as Calvinists until the end of the nineteenth century, Congregationalism as a whole had become vastly more liberal. The broadly ecumenical Burial Hill Declaration of 1863 eliminated references to CALVINISM, affirmed the need for social amelioration, and asserted the fellowship of all those who hold "one faith, one Lord, one baptism."

The Christians

Smallest of the UCC's four traditions, the Christian Churches (sometimes called the "Christian Connexion") emerged as an indigenous, populist movement in the early 1800s in rural and frontier America. Arriving at similar conclusions about the nature of church and faith, defectors from three distinct groups—BAPTISTS in New England, Methodists in Virginia, and Presbyterians in Kentucky—gathered small churches of the like-minded. Eschewing creeds, confessions, and the formalities of both church life and traditional theology, they held to the BIBLE alone as the rule of right faith and practice, rejected the divisiveness caused by "sectarian" denominationalism (hence their preference for the simple name "Christian"), and insisted that right action, rather than right belief, is the most important factor in a Christian's life. These ideas resulted in a widely diverse—and often misunderstood—fellowship that embraced theological positions ranging from unitarian to evangelical. The Christians' beliefs—and their initial discomfort with the idea of ordination—led them as early as 1815 to accept the validity of women's preaching and evangelistic activities.

Although the Christian founders had no desire to become a DENOMINATION, renegade ministers and disorders in newly gathered frontier churches quickly led to the establishment of annual conferences for mutual support. Some Christians in the south eventually aligned themselves with Thomas and Alexander Campbell (see CAMPBELL FAMILY), whose similar ideas produced today's Christian Church (DISCIPLES OF CHRIST), with which the UCC has a formal ecumenical partnership. Divided by the issue of SLAVERY in 1850, other northern and southern Christians eventually came together at the end of the century to form a unified, congregationally structured national body that included a number of black churches from the old Afro-Christian Convention of the south (now the largest regional body of African American churches within the United Church of Christ). An early antipathy toward creeds, confessions, and all rules and regulations that might abridge the right of private judgment continued throughout the century, and as a group Christians remained committed to the ideal of tolerance for theological diversity. Drawn together by POLITY as well as by common commitments to church unity and theological openness, the General Convention of Christian Churches merged with the National Council of Congregational Churches in 1931 to become the Congregational Christian Churches.

The German Reformed Church

The Reformed Church, second largest tradition in the United Church of Christ, had its origins in the Palatinate area of GERMANY, and was transplanted to America's southeastern and mid-Atlantic region, especially Pennsylvania, as early as 1710. A second wave of immigrants in the 1830s settled primarily in the Midwest. Unlike the Puritans, the Reformed came not for religious reasons nor to undertake a social experiment, but to escape war, poverty, and social unrest in their homeland.

Nurtured in an area where both Reformed and Lutheran influences prevailed, the German Reformed were a people whose lives were shaped by the HEIDELBERG CATECHISM of 1563, with its distinctive ecumenical thrust. Along with the Bible this devotional and educational document enabled them initially to sustain their faith in the absence of formal pastoral leadership, a lack that was not addressed until church planter John Philip Boehm was ordained by the DUTCH REFORMED CHURCH in 1728. By this act the Reformed initiated an organizational and supervisory relationship with the Dutch church that lasted until 1793, when the American body became independent.

During the nineteenth century new immigration, as well as issues of ETHNICITY and Americanization, language, and revivalism, caused tensions within the Reformed fellowship, although these continued to be mitigated by the unifying influence of the Heidelberg Catechism. Under the leadership of JOHN WILLIAMSON NEVIN and PHILIP SCHAFF the influential Mercersburg movement stressed the centrality of LITURGY and sacrament in devotional life, critiqued the prevailing American ethos of revivalistic individualism, and asserted the essential unity of the Christian Church across history, the latter a "Romanizing" view that was both prescient and, at the time, highly controversial.

Structurally the German Reformed Church was connectional. Governed internally by ministers and "consistories" of elected elders and deacons, congregations were united in regional *classes,* and eventually in larger synods; a national General Synod was formed in 1863, when the name "German" was dropped from the denomination's title. Unlike Congregationalists, the Reformed understood "church" to be most perfectly defined not by individual local congregations, but by the aggregate of many congregations, unified by common worship, practice, and organizing structure.

The German Evangelicals

Youngest of the four traditions, the Evangelical Church represents a second wave of German immigration to America. Beginning in the third decade of the nineteenth century, settlers from northern Germany migrated to the midwestern frontier of Missouri and southern Illinois, bringing with them a tradition of "unionistic" Protestantism that had flourished in their homeland. Finding neither Reformed nor Lutheran churches in America to their taste, the Evangelicals were influenced not only by their isolation in a frontier setting, but also by Swiss missionaries whose PIETISM emphasized the importance of religious experience rather than acceptance of a confession as the foundation of church membership. With the latter's help the German Evangelical Church Society of the West (*Der Deutsche Evangelische Kirchenverein des Westens*) was formed in 1840. Reflecting the independent and antiauthoritarian stance of these Evangelicals, the Church Society was at first a loosely organized pastors' conference, with minimal ecclesiastical authority. By the end of the century basic denominational structure was in place, with a national German Evangelical Synod that united churches in the West, Midwest, and Northwest.

Theologically, Evangelicals were independent and open-minded, and like the Christians, they were often indifferent to doctrinal particularities, believing that creeds are "testimonies, not tests" of faith. Nevertheless both a CATECHISM—used with liberty of conscience regarding interpretation—and a CONFESSION were quickly developed, and a seminary was founded by 1850. The motto of that school—now Eden Theological Seminary—articulates the Evangelical perspective, as well as that of today's United Church of Christ: "In essentials, unity; in non-essentials, liberty; in all things, charity." Strong ecumenical commitments and ties of history and ethnicity among both Evangelicals and Reformed led the General Convention of the Evangelical Synod to unite with the Reformed Church in 1934, becoming the Evangelical and Reformed Church.

Other Traditions

In addition to these four constituting strands, other regional and ethnic traditions significantly inform and influence the contemporary United Church of Christ. These include Armenian Evangelical, German Congregational, African American, Hispanic, Native American, Hungarian Reformed, and various Asian and Pacific Island traditions. Although numerically none of these traditions is large, the commitment of the United Church of Christ to become a "multicultural, multi-racial" denomination is evidenced in the highly visible role members of these groups play in leadership.

A New Denomination

Beginning with informal conversations in 1937 the union of the Congregational Christian Churches and the Evangelical and Reformed Church took twenty years to complete. Although the "Basis of Union with Interpretations" was approved in 1949, a lawsuit filed by the Cadman Memorial (Congregational) Church of Brooklyn, New York questioned the right of the General Council to take such action. At issue were matters of Congregational polity that continue to be debated in the UCC: are agencies of the wider church (such as the General Council or today's General Synod) accountable to and under the control of local churches, or are they accountable only to themselves? A court decision in 1953 removed barriers to union, and the merger was consummated June 25, 1957, in Cleveland, Ohio, now the site of denominational headquarters. Two years later a trinitarian Statement of Faith, understood as "testimony rather than creed" and emphasizing God's saving acts and the church's call to mission, was adopted. In 1961, four years after merger, a *Constitution and Bylaws* was finalized. Both have been revised and amended regularly. An "inclusive language" version of the Statement of Faith and a doxological version are also official.

The polity of the United Church of Christ contains both congregational and connectional elements. At the insistence of denominational founders from the Congregational tradition, the *Constitution and Bylaws* ensures that "the autonomy of the local church is inherent and modifiable only by its own action." Thus local congregations are the "basic unit" of the Church, possessing all those things necessary for both spiritual needs and good order: ministry, the Word, sacraments, and structure, as well as property, fiduciary responsibilities, and other legal rights and privileges. Local churches, however—even in the traditions of Congregationalism—were historically bound together, both formally and informally, in relationships of mutual accountability for matters of order, discipline, and mutual nurture. In the United Church of Christ these churches are grouped in presbytery-like Associations, with responsibilities for ordaining, installing, and disciplining CLERGY; receiving (and dismissing) churches; and caring generally for the welfare of local congregations in the area.

Associations are subunits of Conferences, which meet annually and provide services, counsel, and administrative support to churches and Associations within their boundaries. The General Synod, the national representative body, meets biennially. Although it sets missional and financial priorities for the denomination and issues pronouncements about matters of broad social concern, it is understood to speak "to, not for" the churches: it "recommends" and "urges," rather than "directs." A major denominational restructure in 2000 changed the composition of the General Synod to include not only elected conference delegates, but also voting members of four "covenanted ministries" (the Office of General Ministries, Local Church Ministries, Wider Church Ministries, and Justice and Witness Ministries), which serve both internal needs and mission. The Executive Council, meeting semiannually, serves as Synod *ad interim.* Use of "covenantal" language in the restructure was deliberate, implying the voluntary but important task of each setting of the church—local, regional, and national—to attend prayerfully to the concerns, actions, and pronouncements of the others. (Internally, the UCC's polity itself is often described as "covenantal.") In keeping with the denomination's commitment to inclusivity, each of the several governance or mission instrumentalities is mandated to include "underrepresented constituencies," including racial and ethnic minorities, WOMEN, persons under 30, and gays and lesbians (see HOMOSEXUALITY).

Defining Theological and Other Characteristics

Paragraph 2 of the United Church of Christ's *Constitution and Bylaws* reads:

> The United Church of Christ acknowledges as its Head, Jesus Christ, Son of God and Savior. It acknowledges as kindred in Christ all who share in this confession. It looks to the Word of God in the Scriptures, and to the presence and power of the Holy Spirit, to prosper its creative and redemptive work in the world. It claims as its own the faith of the historic Church expressed in the ancient creeds and reclaimed in the basic insights of the Protestant Reformers. It affirms the responsibility of the Church in each generation to make the faith its own in reality of worship, in honesty of thought and expression, and in purity of heart before God. In keeping with the teaching of our Lord and the practice prevailing among evangelical Christians, it recognizes two sacraments: Baptism and the Lord's Supper or Holy Communion.

This brief statement indicates the denomination's theological ORTHODOXY as well as its liberalism. No other doctrinal test or universally held dogma exists, no systematic or comprehensive theology, nor is there a magisterium from which theological pronouncements are issued. Theological perspectives—often lively and varying widely across the spectrum from evangelical to neo-orthodox—may be found in the widely used Statement of Faith, in occasional papers sponsored by denominational initiatives, in pronouncements of Conferences and Synod, in scholarly writings, on the denominational website, and in the pages of *Prism,* the seminary-sponsored theological journal for the denomination. This theological freedom is a function both of the original need to mediate differences among the four constituent traditions and of existing convictions within these traditions and their inheritors. Commitment to theological openness and diversity is today a widely held and defining conviction for the United Church of Christ.

The United Church of Christ has no "official" ecclesiological statement, and, as with doctrinal matters, perspectives about the essential nature of the church vary widely. However, members generally understand that the church is founded on the acts of God named in the Scriptures and interpreted through the ancient creeds, the writings of the Protestant reformers, and the inspired understandings of each new generation. By confessing Jesus Christ as sole head of the church, they affirm, first, that all human leadership is radically equal, and second, that all who confess Christ are bound covenantally, sharing common Christian experience and responsibility for mission in the world. The church's basic purposes are four: to proclaim the gospel through scripture, sacrament, and witness; to gather and support communities of faithful men and women for celebration and mission; to manifest more fully the unity of church, humankind, and the whole creation; and to work for the furtherance of God's realm of justice, peace, and love.

The latter two purposes are especially significant. Born out of the passionate desire for church unity among its founders, and formed in an era of massive social upheaval that included the struggle of African Americans for civil rights (see CIVIL RIGHTS MOVEMENT) and the Vietnam War, the United Church of Christ is distinctively animated by concerns for the wider church and world. An early commitment to church unity led founders to choose a broadly inclusive name, without historical antecedent—"United Church of Christ"—that signaled their willingness for the denomination "if need be, to die" for the sake of future unions. Today the UCC participates widely in both national and international ecumenical discussions (including the National and World Councils of Churches, Churches Uniting in Christ, and the WORLD ALLIANCE OF REFORMED CHURCHES), and has numerous ecumenical relationships globally. A full communion partnership with the Christian Church (Disciples of Christ) since 1985 includes periodic joint synodical meetings and the sharing of staff for global ministries. The UCC also is part of a full-communion agreement with the PRESBYTERIAN CHURCH, USA; the REFORMED CHURCH IN AMERICA; and the EVANGELICAL LUTHERAN CHURCH IN AMERICA.

The UCC is widely known as one of the most socially active among American Protestant churches, with an unwavering commitment to pursue justice and peace for all persons. Believing that "the love of God in Christ cannot ever be expressed except in a just society," the denomination has taken strong and often controversial stands and actions against numerous perceived injustices, in particular racism, WAR (the UCC understands itself as a "just peace church"), and economic oppression in its various forms. The General Synod, as well as individual Conferences and local churches, regularly takes action and issues formal pronouncements about dozens of social issues, ranging from accessibility for "differently abled" persons to equitable taxation and the civil rights of all, regardless of sexual orientation. The United Church of Christ is the only Protestant denomination that routinely, if not universally, accepts gays and lesbians into the ordained ministry and other leadership positions. Because ordination is handled by regional Associations, in some areas gays and lesbians may not be accepted for ordination; however, the church in its national setting has strongly advocated regarding this matter, and all seven denominational SEMINARIES admit homosexual persons without reservation into the ordination track. Members typically summarize the warrant for "prophetic" stands that challenge existing practices with the words of Pilgrim pastor JOHN ROBINSON, nearly 400 years ago: "God has yet more light and truth to break forth from his holy Word."

Like other historically "mainline" denominations, the United Church of Christ suffered significant membership losses in the late twentieth century. Presently it consists of roughly 1.4 million members.

See also Dialogue, Interconfessional; Ecumenism

References and Further Reading

Book of Worship. New York: United Church of Christ Office for Church Life and Leadership, 1986.

Dunn, David, ed. *A History of the Evangelical and Reformed Church.* Philadelphia: The Christian Education Press, 1961.

Gunnemann, Louis H. *The Shaping of the United Church of Christ: An Essay in the History of American Christianity.* New York: Pilgrim Press, 1977.

———. *United and Uniting: The Meaning of an Ecclesial Journey.* New York: United Church Press, 1987.

Horton, Douglas. *The United Church of Christ: its origins, organizations, and rate in the world today.* New York: Thomas Nelson & Sons, 1962.

Johnson, Daniel L., and Charles E. Hambrick-Stowe. *Theology and Identity: Traditions, Movements, and Polity in the United Church of Christ.* New York: Pilgrim Press, 1990.

Morrill, Milo True. *A History of the Christian Denomination in America 1794–1911 A.D.* Dayton, Ohio: Christian Publishing Association, 1912.

Newman, William M. "The Meanings of Merger: Denominational Identity in the United Church of Christ" In *Beyond Establishment: Protestant Identity in a Post-Protestant Age,* J.W. Carroll, ed. Louisville, KY: Westminister/John Knox, 1993.

Nordbeck, Elizabeth C., and Clyde J. Steckel. *The Unfinished Church: Theology and Polity in the United Church of Christ.* Cleveland, Ohio: United Church Press, 2003 (forthcoming).

Rohr, John von. *The Shaping of American Congregationalism 1620–1957.* Cleveland, Ohio: Pilgrim Press, 1992.

Shinn, Roger L. *Confessing Our Faith: An Interpretation of the Statement of Faith of the United Church of Christ.* New York: Pilgrim Press, 1990.

Zikmund, Barbara Brown, ed. *Hidden Histories in the United Church of Christ.* vols. 1 and 2. New York: United Church Press, 1984, 1987.

———, series ed. *The Living Theological Heritage of the United Church of Christ.* Vols 1–7 (*Ancient and Medieval Legacies, Reformation Roots, Colonial and National Beginnings, Consolidation and Expansion, Outreach and Diversity, Growing Toward Unity, United and Uniting*). Cleveland, Ohio: Pilgrim Press, various dates.

ELIZABETH C. NORDBECK

UNITED CHURCH OF INDIA

see North India, Church of; South India, Church of

UNITED METHODIST CHURCH

The United Methodist Church (UMC) was created on April 23, 1968 in Dallas, Texas, when The Methodist Church (MC) and the EVANGELICAL UNITED BRETHREN CHURCH (EUB) united. Both churches were products of predecessor unions. The MC was formed in 1939 by a merger of the Methodist Episcopal Church, the Methodist Episcopal Church South, and the Methodist Protestant Church. In 1946 the Evangelical Church and the Church of the United Brethren in Christ consolidated to become the Evangelical United Brethren Church. At the time of union, the UMC had approximately 11,000,000 members, 40,000 local churches, and 35,000 clergy, making it the largest Protestant DENOMINATION in the UNITED STATES. It also had congregations in AFRICA, Asia, INDIA, and Europe.

The MC and the EUB had historic ties reaching back to their predecessors' earlier years. Jacob Albright (1759–1808), the founder of the Evangelical Association (later Evangelical Church) had a high regard for METHODISM, and following his conversion in 1791 was nurtured in a ME class meeting. Philip William Otterbein (1726–1813), German Reformed pastor and co-founder of the United Brethren, along with a reformed Mennonite, Martin Boehm (1725–1812), assisted at the ordination of FRANCIS ASBURY (1745–1816) at the celebrated Christmas Conference in Baltimore in December 1784 (see BALTIMORE CONFERENCE). Although there were Reformed elements in the theology of both churches, the Evangelicals and United Brethren before their union were heavily influenced by Wesleyan thought and Methodist polity.

Theology

The UMC is basically Wesleyan in its theology although within this broad framework there is considerable theological diversity in the denomination (see WESLEYANISM). At the time of union it was agreed that the denomination's official theological position would include four documents referred to as "doctrinal standards." They include JOHN WESLEY's (1703–1791) standard sermons, his *Explanatory Notes Upon the New Testament*, Articles of Religion sent by Wesley to America in 1784 and based on the Church of England's THIRTY-NINE ARTICLES of Religion, and the Confession of Faith of the EUBC. The complete texts of the Articles and Confession are published in the denomination's *Book of Discipline*.

At the 1972 UMC General Conference, the church adopted a document titled "Our Theological Task," the chief architect of which was Albert C. Outler (1908–1989), theologian, ecumenist, and Wesley scholar. The document emphasizes John Wesley's use of scripture, TRADITION, reason, and experience (referred to by some as the "Wesleyan quadrilateral") as sources for understanding and practicing the faith. It urges United Methodists to use these sources for their theological reflection. The document is published in the UMC *Discipline*, its principal ecclesiological guide, and has appeared in every *Discipline* since 1972 (although it was revised substantially in 1988). The revised document makes clear that the BIBLE is the primary source for Christian belief and life.

United Methodism has been a leading force in renewing interest in the life and thought of John Wesley, Methodism's founder, who more than anyone has left his imprint on the theology, structure, and mission of the denomination. The United Methodist Publishing House has regularly published interpretive studies of Wesley's theology and ministry, and is publishing a critical and authoritative 35-volume edition of Wesley's works.

Polity

The UMC is governed by a constitution and is organized as a connectional system maintained by a system of conferences. Every congregation is affiliated with a local charge conference. Charge conferences elect delegates to a regional annual conference. Every four years annual conferences choose delegates to attend the denomination's Jurisdictional (U.S.) or Central (outside the U.S.) conferences and the church's General Conference.

The General Conference is the supreme legislative body of the church and is the only entity that may speak officially for the church. The General Conference meets every four years and is composed of approximately 1,000 lay and clergy delegates in equal numbers representing various nations, but mostly from the United States. It revises *The Book of Discipline*, which describes the church's mission and structure, and adopts a number of positions on social issues that are published as "Social Principles" in the *Discipline* and in *The Book of Resolutions*. Legislation adopted by the General Conference provides direction for every level of the connectional structure.

The denomination has an Episcopal form of government in which bishops, elected and assigned by Jurisdictional or Central Conferences, ordain men and women as deacons and elders and generally superintend the church's work. They preside at the sessions of annual, Jurisdictional or Central, and General Conferences. UMC pastors serve in an itinerant system in which they are annually appointed by a bishop to serve local churches or other ministries. Bishops are assisted in administration and receive advice on appointments from district superintendents who supervise groups of churches in the annual conference.

General agencies composed of several councils, boards, and commissions amenable to the General Conference are an important feature of the connectional system. They provide services and ministries beyond the local church and annual conference in such areas as EVANGELISM, stewardship, social issues, global mission, finance, HIGHER EDUCATION, publishing, and communications. Each agency has voting members who represent the wider church and who employ staff to do the agency's work.

The UMC uses a carefully defined system of judicial administration described in its *Discipline*. A Judicial Council, constitutionally created, is the denomination's highest judicial body. It determines the constitutionality of legislation and rules on the legality of actions taken by any entity created or authorized by the General Conference.

Worship and Liturgy

Worship practices in local UMC churches vary. Almost all local churches have Sunday services, though they may also have other gatherings for WORSHIP during the week. Some congregations prefer a more formal LITURGY that does not vary much from week to week. Others choose more spontaneous worship allowing for liturgical freedom. In almost all congregations, however, the elements of worship include hymns, prayers, scripture readings, and a sermon. United Methodism recognizes two sacraments, BAPTISM and holy communion, or the LORD'S SUPPER. Baptisms of infants and adults are held occasionally in congregational worship as is needed. Baptism is required for church membership. Celebrations of Holy Communion are usually held monthly, but in some churches weekly.

Worship is guided by hymn books (see HYMNS AND HYMNALS), including *The United Methodist Hymnal*, which was last revised in 1989, and *The United Methodist Book of Worship* (1992), although these resources are not utilized in every congregation. Supplemental collections of hymns and worship materials have also been published, including the African American *Songs of Zion* (1981), the Asian American *Hymns from the Four Winds* (1983), the Hispanic American *Celebremos* (1983), and the Native American *Voices* (1992).

Ministries and Institutions

A wide variety of ministries and institutions are supported by the UMC. Local churches support denominational work in their annual conferences and other parts of the world through a system of giving known as "apportionments." In addition to their apportionment giving, many congregations sponsor scouting programs, soup kitchens, clothing banks, and other ministries pertinent to their local communities. Among the denomination's most important ministries are health and welfare institutions, including hospitals, retirement homes, agencies to aid children and families, and shelters for the homeless.

The UMC and its predecessor denominations have been at the forefront of Protestant educational endeavors. Every local church is expected to have a SUNDAY SCHOOL for training children, youth, and adults. United Methodist Women, the church's principal women's organization, carries on an effective mission education

program in local churches and annual conferences. The church is also involved in secondary and higher education. A network of colleges and universities, including several black colleges, is related to the church. In 1992 the denomination opened Africa University in ZIMBABWE for the education of students across that continent. UMC theological schools in the United States and Europe train its CLERGY and also enroll students from other denominations.

The UMC is a vigorous supporter of ecumenical institutions. At the denominational level it is an active member of the WORLD COUNCIL OF CHURCHES and the NATIONAL COUNCIL OF CHURCHES, two of the world's principal ecumenical organizations. United Methodism also provides substantial financial and organizational support to the WORLD METHODIST COUNCIL, which links the family of Methodist and related United Churches in more than 100 countries.

Caucuses

UMC denominational life has been significantly influenced by a number of unofficial caucuses, some of which were formed in the years immediately following the church's inception. Among them are four racial/ethnic caucuses that have been effective advocates for racial inclusiveness in the leadership of the denomination (see ETHNICITY). Black Methodists for Church Renewal (BMCR), a national forum of black United Methodists, was founded in 1968. BMCR was especially successful in promoting the establishment of a general agency, the General Commission on Religion and Race, in 1968 to advance the goal of a racially inclusive church. In 1970 the Native American International Caucus was formed, and that same year Hispanics began to form Methodists Associated Representing the Cause of Hispanic Americans (MARCHA). The National Federation of Asian American United Methodists was founded in 1975. Racial/ethnic people are significantly represented in the membership of the UMC in the United States, and their caucuses have been powerful forces in the choice of denominational leaders, including bishops.

Other caucuses have been voices on theological and social issues. The Methodist Federation for Social Action, which had its origins in the Methodist Episcopal Church in 1907, has been an advocate for liberal social change, including racial and GENDER inclusiveness and the complete acceptance of gay and homosexual people in the denomination. Its counterpart, Good News, formed in 1966, is a representative of the evangelical party in the church and advances a conservative theological agenda (see EVANGELICALISM). A caucus of gay and lesbian United Methodists, Affirmation, was organized in 1975. United Methodist charismatics formed United Methodist Renewal Services in 1977. The caucuses, racial/ethnic or otherwise, are well organized and publish newsletters or magazines on a more or less regular basis. Their lobbying efforts are especially visible at the sites of the General Conference.

Issues and Controversies

The UMC struggles with a number of issues that have occupied its attention since its creation. Among these issues are sexism, racism, HOMOSEXUALITY, membership decline, and the global nature of the church.

WOMEN have always been prominent in the life of the denomination. But although women have represented much more than half its membership, it took a considerable time for them to be regularly chosen as delegates to conferences, to serve as clergy in local churches, and to become leaders in the connectional structure (see WOMEN CLERGY). Their situation has changed considerably. In 1972 there were fewer than 300 active female clergy, but by 2000 their numbers had grown to approximately 8,000. In 1980 the UMC elected its first female bishop, Marjorie Swank Matthews (1916-1986). While increasing numbers of women occupy leadership positions in the local church, annual conference, and other levels of the denomination, they still wrestle with gender bias in many areas of denominational life.

Racial diversity has been an issue in the UMC since its inception. While the church affirms commitment to racial inclusiveness, this remains an unfulfilled goal in many areas of denominational life. Racial/ethnic diversity is often represented in annual conference and general church leadership. However, local church memberships generally do not reflect racial diversity, even in communities where the population is multiracial. The denomination has a general agency, the General Commission on Religion and Race, which monitors and advocates racial inclusiveness.

Homosexuality has been a very controversial issue in the denomination. UMC General Conferences have discussed the issue since 1972. Although the church affirms the civil rights of homosexuals, it declares homosexuality incompatible with Christian teaching and prohibits avowed and practicing homosexual people to be ordained and appointed to its ministries. At the 2000 General Conference, the church also took a position that its clergy may not perform ceremonies that celebrate homosexual unions. Many believe that changing the church's position on homosexuality may cause a schism in the denomination.

Declining membership in the United States and Europe has been troubling. In its first three decades UMC membership in the United States decreased approximately 25 percent, dropping it from the first to the second-largest Protestant denomination in the United States. Meanwhile, the church's membership in Africa and the PHILIPPINES, its two other geographical regions increased steadily during the same period. For this reason, African and Filipino United Methodists have asked for a larger role in the denomination's life and ministry. As it becomes more conscious of its international character, the church is working on ways to insure that it does not understand itself as simply a North American denomination.

See also Bishop and Episcopacy; Methodism, North America

References and Further Reading

Behney, J. Bruce, and Paul H. Eller. *The History of the Evangelical United Brethren Church.* Nashville, TN: Abingdon Press, 1979. *The Book of Discipline of the United Methodist Church.* Nashville, TN: The United Methodist Publishing House, 1968–. *The Book of Resolutions of The United Methodist Church.* Nashville, TN: The United Methodist Publishing House, 1968– .
Frank, Thomas E. *Polity, Practice, and the Mission of The United Methodist Church.* Nashville, TN: Abingdon Press, 1997.
McEllhenney, John G. *United Methodism in America: A Compact History.* Nashville, TN: Abingdon Press, 1992.
Richey, Russell E., William B. Lawrence, and Dennis M. Campbell, eds. *Questions for the Twenty-First Century Church.* United Methodism and American Culture, vol. 3. Nashville, TN: Abingdon Press, 1999.
Richey, Russell E., Kenneth E. Rowe, and Jean Miller Schmidt, eds. *The Methodist Experience in America: A Sourcebook.* Nashville, TN: Abingdon Press, 2000.
Yrigoyen, Charles Jr. *Belief Matters: United Methodism's Doctrinal Standards.* Nashville, TN: Abingdon Press, 2001.

CHARLES YRIGOYEN, JR.

UNITED STATES OF AMERICA

So closely was Protestantism identified with the early years of America's history that the country was regarded as manifestly a Protestant one in the minds of many. This was particularly true through roughly the first half of the nineteenth century. When immigration patterns shifted dramatically from northern to southern and eastern Europe, heroic efforts to "convert" newly arriving immigrants to Protestantism revealed the depth of the earnest conviction that this was a Protestant nation—and must remain so. By the early years of the twenty-first century, however—and indeed well before—this article of faith could no longer be maintained as pluralism dethroned the Protestant hegemony in virtually every part of the country, although for more than two centuries, Protestant spokesmen saw their denominational and their political loyalties as calling them toward a common goal.

Colonial Foundations

The first permanent English settlement on American soil, Jamestown (1607), saw itself as a mere extension of the mother country and of her political structures and religious institutions. Naming the tiny settlement in honor of the reigning monarch, King James I, pointed to this unquestioned orientation. Where England's flag flew, England's church (ANGLICANISM) must take root. Not until 1619 was the CHURCH OF ENGLAND officially established in Virginia, not because of any hesitation or doubt, but because only then was any legislative body in a position to declare what all had been intended from the beginning.

Bold intentions, however, had a way of running aground onto geopolitical realities that often mocked the earlier visions. The first legislators conceived a Virginia that would re-create modest English towns and cohesive English parishes. A local church would be established (that is, officially supported by tax monies) and a proper clergyman would be imported from ENGLAND. His salary would be paid by the colonial government just as all Anglican clergymen back home drew their income from the state. Then settlers would naturally erect their primitive homes near the church; the town would grow; schools would be built; and soon an English village—hardly distinguishable from one left behind—would miraculously appear.

It simply never happened this way. Virginians, desperately searching for some means of survival and some source of income, found their economic salvation in tobacco. Tobacco, however, required land, large quantities of land, so plantations arose alongside such major rivers as the James and the Rappahannock. These plantations might be only two or three miles in width, back from the river, but they could be twenty or thirty miles in length. Among such widely scattered plantations, where could one build the town—and the church? In fact, colonial Virginia never had towns of any significant size, and colonial churches there never drew large congregations.

Anglican CLERGY of necessity became itinerants, traveling to outlying plantations, along impassible roads or on the river to be pestered by sudden storms and ever-present mosquitoes. Religious services, particularly christenings, weddings, and funerals, were more often held in homes than in the rural churches, thus giving a special sanctity to the plantation manor and even to the land. So far did the religious life of early Virginia differ from that of the English village that attracting clergy to the colony proved difficult. Some who did come, escaping a troublesome debt or a nagging wife, did Anglicanism no great favor. Nonetheless Anglicanism grew more powerfully in Virginia than anywhere else in America. As it spread well beyond the borders of that one colony, the Church of England by the end of the colonial period had emerged as one of the two great denominational powers in early America.

The other and even more powerful denomination found its base in New England, especially in Massachusetts and Connecticut. Here CONGREGATIONALISM (earlier known as PURITANISM) took deep root, and towns and schools and parish churches did look more like the English villages left behind. The churches were locally "owned and operated" (which is the force of the word "congregational"), but with the blessing and support of the colonial governments. Tax monies built churches and paid salaries for the Congregational churches in Massachusetts just as tax monies did for the Anglican churches in Virginia. In both instances government did all that it could to preserve a religious monopoly for its respective established churches: that is, it actively discouraged any competing DENOMINATION, even resorting to persecution (whips, jails, fines, executions) where deemed necessary.

Not dependent on England for its supply of ministers (Harvard and Yale early served as ministerial training grounds), Congregationalism grew with a steadiness that resulted in New England's being the most thickly churched area of America by the end of the colonial period. Each parish church provided real cohesion in the town, but beyond that, a theological rigor provided unity in the region as a whole. One can speak of a "New England way" that gave distinctive intellectual character to all the institutions of the area: educational, political, social, and of course ecclesiastical. This cohesion endured not only through the colonial period but well beyond; and as westward migrations later moved across the country, it shaped a good deal of institutional life all the way to the West Coast.

However, Anglicanism and Congregationalism did not divide all of early America between them. Despite efforts to keep all alternative religious options far away, other denominations managed to infiltrate, even in the seventeenth century. BAPTISTS found refuge in Rhode Island, a colony created in reaction against the cozy church–state alliance elsewhere in New England. The SOCIETY OF FRIENDS (Quakers) also flourished initially in Rhode Island, but even more dramatically in Pennsylvania, founded in 1682 (so much so that Pennsylvania even came to be called the "Quaker State"). Swedish Lutherans established a tiny and precarious foothold along the shores of the Delaware River, near the present site of Wilmington, Delaware. New York and New Jersey, for two generations under Dutch control (New Amsterdam), was dominated to a fair degree by the national church of Holland, the DUTCH REFORMED. Even after the English conquered the Dutch in 1664 the national church of the latter continued to give a distinctive cultural coloration to that area. Presbyterians from Scotland, later from northern Ireland ("Scotch-Irish"), migrated to America where they settled chiefly in the middle colonies of New York, New Jersey, and Pennsylvania.

In their earliest years all these Protestant groups concentrated on their own survival. Nevertheless some efforts to reach out to the NATIVE AMERICANS and the African Americans can be seen. Although tiny in number, Swedish Lutherans translated the catechism of MARTIN LUTHER into the "American-Virginian" tongue to evangelize the Delaware Indians. Much larger in number, Congregationalists in New England established mission stations for the Indians on Martha's Vineyard and elsewhere; one missionary, JOHN ELIOT, won enduring fame by producing an Indian Bible in 1663 in the Algonkian tongue (see BIBLE TRANSLATION). Hostility often frustrated missionary efforts among the Native Americans, just as SLAVERY limited evangelical inroads among colonial blacks. Some argued on the one hand that "gospel liberty" might undermine the institution of slavery itself, whereas others argued that slaves were subhuman, beyond the reach of Christianity. Not until blacks assumed a major role themselves in the propagation of the Christian religion did African Americans flock in large numbers to the religion of their masters.

Denominational Development

In the eighteenth century Anglicanism had one element working in its favor, but a second element working against it. The SOCIETY FOR THE PROPAGATION OF THE GOSPEL, founded by THOMAS BRAY in 1702, greatly assisted the Anglican Church in its spread throughout the American colonies. Missionaries sent out from London established their preaching stations with particular force in the middle colonies and in New England, where they met much resistance. The Society paid the salaries, provided books, and offered advice if not assistance in the building of churches. The correspondence flowing back and forth between America and England offers eloquent testimony to the vigor and effect of the Society's labors.

The missionary labors had their downside as well. The men sent out from London remained English in their loyalties and their affections. They did not normally bring families with them and did not normally set down deep roots in the communities where they lived. In short, they did not become Americans. When tensions began to grow between the mother country and her colonies, notably in the second half of the eighteenth century, the Society's employees remained largely Loyalist, often vociferously so. By 1776 the

position of the missionaries had become intolerable, as Thomas Barton reported from Lancaster, Pennsylvania: "Every clergyman of the Church of England who dared to act on proper principles was marked out for infamy and insult; in consequence of which the Missionaries have suffered greatly."

One issue in particular roiled the Anglican waters: that is, the matter of Bishops (see BISHOP AND EPISCOPACY). Anglican church polity, of course, required the presence of bishops—bishops to ordain, to confirm, to maintain discipline in the church. So why did England decline to send bishops to America? The answer lay in the deep distrust of many Americans, including some Anglicans themselves (especially in the South), of what powerful bishops might do to disrupt the religious scene in America. Memories were too fresh of persecuting bishops and archbishops of the WILLIAM LAUD stripe. Such men, it was widely assumed, would bring not peace but a sword, if allowed to settle on American soil. So inflamed did this issue of episcopacy become that it can be reasonably argued that the anxieties and fears associated with it helped to bring about the American Revolution.

Congregationalism in the eighteenth century continued to solidify its position in New England, although that position had been shaken by the witchcraft episode in and around Salem, Massachusetts, at the end of the previous century (see WITCHCRAZE). It had also been enraged, though not seriously shaken, by the forced introduction of Anglicanism into Boston in 1689. This action was so clearly political and intrusive that it initially made Congregationalism even stronger. Other religious bodies, notably Baptists and Quakers, made slow but steady inroads into New England, although none of these encroachments seriously threatened the strong alliance between church and state in Massachusetts, Connecticut, and New Hampshire. Of more concern to the Congregational churches were their internal difficulties in polity or dilutions of piety.

So far as the governance of these churches was concerned, theory called for each church to be autonomous, each congregation invested with the full authority to hire and fire its clergy, to receive or expel its members. This theory when put into practice raised some concerns. Autonomy began to look too much like anarchy, as each local parish ran its affairs indifferent to the interests of the colony as a whole. So in 1705 several ministerial associations in Massachusetts met to consider proposals for tightening the connections between the churches, to create a standing committee "which shall consult, advise and determine all affairs that shall be proper matter for the consideration of an Ecclesiastical Council." These steps, widely interpreted as a "presbyterianizing" of pure Congregational polity, were successfully resisted in Massachusetts, but more closely followed by Connecticut's Saybrook Platform adopted in 1708.

On the matter of personal piety, successive generations in New England kept comparing themselves unfavorably with their forebears in the first generation of settlers. A Reforming Synod in 1680, for example, complained of the "visible decay in the power of godliness," of "sinful hearts and hatreds," and of a general decline in "public spirit." Then, in the following century, what came to be called the Half-Way Covenant made it easier for persons to become members of the church without necessarily being able to relate their own experience of divine grace. The denomination's (and the country's) greatest colonial theologian, JONATHAN EDWARDS, helped recall New England to a deeper piety. Despite internal quarrels or compromises, Congregationalism continued to thrive and in 1750 had more churches (465) by far than any other denomination in America.

By that same year PRESBYTERIANISM had become a major denominational force, in third place after Congregationalism and Anglicanism. This Calvinist body was especially powerful in Pennsylvania and New Jersey, but it also had a significant presence in New York. The creation of the College of New Jersey (later Princeton) in 1746 was one measure of this denomination's growing influence and vigor. Its rapid rise resulted chiefly from immigrants leaving Ulster and landing at the port of Philadelphia—some 200,000 in the half-century between 1710 and 1760. In this same time period, other immigrants, now from Germany, swelled the ranks of LUTHERANISM and GERMAN REFORMED. Pennsylvania offered these two groups, as it had the Presbyterians, the most fertile soil for settling and maturing.

Two major events of the eighteenth century require notice here: the upheaval of religious revivalism known as the Great Awakening (1720–1770) (see AWAKENINGS), and the outbreak of political passion known as the American Revolution. The Awakening was largely a Calvinist affair, at least in its initial stages. It pervaded the parishes of the Congregationalists, the Presbyterians, and the Dutch Reformed. Baptists, drawn to it in large numbers, turned Calvinist in their theological orientation. Indeed, the great growth of the Baptists dates from roughly the middle of the eighteenth century forward; before that time Baptists were withdrawn, introverted, and not conspicuously evangelistic. After 1750, however, this picture changed dramatically.

The Church of England held itself aloof from the Awakening, this despite the fact that the most powerful preacher of the movement, GEORGE WHITEFIELD, was himself an Anglican. However, the Church of England was being reborn or revitalized from within. Small reforming societies and Bible study groups, associated with the names of JOHN and CHARLES WESLEY, strove to bring a higher level of personal piety into England's national church. The Wesleys did not initially envision a rupture with that church, but when the break came, it gave America yet another denomination, METHODISM. This body, not formally organized until 1784, proved to be a powerful evangelistic engine. Methodists, together with Baptists, would in the next century radically change the face of American religion.

The other great public event of the eighteenth century, the Revolution, did not produce new denominations, but it did shift the relative strengths of the religious bodies already present. Some Protestant bodies prospered, some suffered. Anglicanism suffered most. A long American war against the nation of England could not but bring harm to England's church. As noted earlier, Anglican missionaries returned home in droves; those who remained found churches locked against them and liturgies—especially if they included prayers for the king—rudely interrupted. Moves to disestablish this national church began as early as 1776 in Virginia, and soon thereafter elsewhere. By the time the Church of England could reorganize itself in 1789 into the Protestant Episcopal Church of the United States of America, this denomination was in total disarray and near collapse (see EPISCOPAL CHURCH, UNITED STATES). It would take decades for it to regain some of its footing, although it would never again enjoy the numerical superiority of an earlier day.

Congregationalists and Presbyterians, who shared a close theological connection, supported the Revolution in overwhelming numbers. An American victory was their victory. Despite serious schisms introduced during the Great Awakening, both denominations continued to prosper, with Presbyterians gaining an edge. Profiting particularly from schisms among the Congregationalists, Baptists flourished, even though a good deal of Baptist loyalty could be found in the middle colonies. Pacifist groups (Quakers, MENNONITES, Moravians, and others) suffered some public disdain, especially in Pennsylvania where they were so numerous. In an effort to ameliorate the situation Benjamin Franklin encouraged the pacifists to be conspicuous in their noncombatant duties: evacuating aged men, women, and children, digging trenches, and carrying "off wounded men to places where they may receive assistance." The greatest impact of the Revolution, however, lay in the charting of a broad new path to religious liberty.

The New Nation

Delegates from the thirteen colonies, now states, gathered in Philadelphia in the summer of 1787 to draw up a new constitution. By 1789 a sufficient number of states had voted (often by quite narrow margins) to ratify the document and bring a new form of government into being. The Constitution itself said virtually nothing about religion, only asserting that "no religious test shall ever be required as qualification to any office or public trust under the United States." This single declaration about religion reassured some that religious tests would not play the kind of role in America that they continued to play in much of Europe. However, the assertion alarmed others who thought that the office of President, for example, should certainly be limited to Christians, and most likely to Protestants. Still others—a majority, as it turned out—worried that the Constitution carried no guarantee of religious liberty, so they hedged their ratification of the document until receiving assurance that the First Congress would remedy this oversight.

That Congress, gathered in 1789, did just that when it drew up the first ten amendments to the Constitution, these collectively known as America's BILL OF RIGHTS. The first clause of the First Amendment stipulated that "Congress shall make no law respecting an establishment of religion, or prohibiting the free exercise thereof." It would be too much to declare that these sixteen words made everything perfectly clear in the intersections between CHURCH AND STATE, but it would not be too much to observe that a wide door had been opened to religious liberty on the national level.

What was immediately clear to some denominations, and only gradually became clear to others, was that religion now entered the free market place. Competition would henceforth determine the winners, not state patronage or social position. In that competition, newly invigorated Baptists and newly organized Methodists proved to be the most successful market managers. Neither denomination concerned itself too much over formal educational qualifications or rigorous theological precision; rather, each concerned itself with reaching the people, wherever they were and of whatever background. The chief requisite for the preacher was a "call," a sense that God had chosen one for the ministry and, if chosen by God, that minister would certainly be blessed by God. With this call came a spiritual certainty and passionate excitement that made the gospel come alive to thousands, then to millions.

On the rapidly expanding western frontiers, Baptists employed, as much by accident as by design, the farmer-preacher model. In any given locality, where neither church nor school might be found, one farmer might feel God's call. This could result in little more than his taking the initiative to gather a few neighbors together for Bible study, WORSHIP, or some modest homily. Because Baptist POLITY was strictly congregational, no outside AUTHORITY had to approve or oversee or regulate this activity. This was grass roots religion, and it grew as plentifully as the grasses themselves. African Americans were among those attracted in large numbers to a denomination that demanded no supervising authority, white or black, and to a mode of worship that could be as spontaneous and joyous as one wished. Religious liberty meant not only the freedom to propagate one's faith, but also, within Baptist confines, the freedom to worship largely as one pleased—and it worked. Between 1750 and 1850 the number of Baptist churches in America spurted from 132 to nearly 10,000.

Methodists had a tighter organizational structure, at least in theory. Bishops (or superintendents) did ordain and appoint, but often on the basis of little more than a warm heart. These bishops employed the technique of the circuit rider, with the young nation's most vital Methodist leader, FRANCIS ASBURY, setting the pattern. Methodist CIRCUIT RIDERS covered great expanses of territory, lived with hardship and deprivation, but often were the very first voices of comfort and instruction to be heard on the frontiers. The number of miles traveled, the number of sermons preached, the number of souls touched by the circuit riders stagger the imagination. One might well question the reports as exaggerations or boasts, except that the results cannot be denied. In 1750 Methodists had no churches, but by 1850 they had well over 13,000, surpassing even the Baptists. Although phenomenally successful on the frontier, Methodists also had a major impact back East—notably in Delaware and Maryland. Methodism adapted marvelously to the frontier and its CAMP MEETINGS, but it also adapted successfully to the urban centers, filling any spiritual vacuum that might momentarily appear.

In sparsely settled western lands, new denominations arose, conspicuously the DISCIPLES OF CHRIST (see CAMPBELL FAMILY) and the CHRISTIAN CHURCHES (BARTON STONE). These two groups, merging in 1833, could reach the west because they were of the west. Ohio and Kentucky were early strongholds, but soon the message of a restored New Testament church reached Tennessee, Missouri, Illinois, Indiana, and beyond. Restoring primitive Christianity was the vision, adopting only the New Testament and rejecting all man-made creeds was the method. The fond hope, to move beyond all denominational labels and to become simply "disciples," struck responsive chords on the frontier (see FRONTIER RELIGION). However, the movement ended, ironically, in contributing even more denominational diversity to an already crowded American field.

Religious liberty meant, among other things, a freedom to experiment, to create something fresh and new. Utopian adventures sprang up in the first half of the nineteenth century: for example, John Humphrey Noyes and his Oneida Community. Far more successful was MORMONISM, which under the leadership of JOSEPH SMITH moved from a tiny knot of believers in upstate New York to a larger group in Nauvoo, Illinois, and then, under the leadership of BRIGHAM YOUNG, to a utopian success story in Salt Lake City, Utah. Mormons, officially the Church of Jesus Christ of Latter-Day Saints, took seriously the millennial teachings of a second coming of Christ, and in this regard, they were far from alone. WILLIAM MILLER, lecturing to large, eager audiences, predicted the end of the world in 1843. When this did not occur, those surviving the Great Disappointment regrouped, none more successfully than the SEVENTH-DAY ADVENTISTS who made a name for themselves in medical missions and in the promotion of healthy foods and healthy habits.

Meanwhile, back East, what of the two colonial powerhouses, Anglicanism (now Episcopalians) and Congregationalism? The Episcopalians, still recovering from the weakness resulting from abrupt disestablishment, found themselves losing out to the Methodists, even in such strong centers as Virginia and South Carolina. Congregationalists held on to their establishments, in Connecticut until 1813 and in Massachusetts until 1833. However, they suffered from internal schism in the form of Unitarianism, which divided churches and parishes, especially in eastern Massachusetts. If the American ENLIGHTENMENT had a denominational expression, it would be Unitarianism, a religion that emphasized the role of reason and minimized the place of miracles and mystery. THOMAS JEFFERSON at one point thought that Unitarianism would become the prevailing religion of the new nation. This, of course, did not happen because powerful countervailing forces were at work.

If the Enlightenment seemed to challenge many of the assumptions on which Protestantism rested, the defenders of a "Protestant empire" were not ready to surrender. What has come to be called the Second Great Awakening (1810–1860) constituted the counteroffensive. Its warriors fought back with new agencies, new educational institutions, and new techniques of recruitment.

In the early decades of the nineteenth century, a host of voluntary organizations arose to provide whatever was required to Protestantize America. The AMERICAN BIBLE SOCIETY, formed in 1818, provided inexpensive Bibles for a growing population, east and west. Where necessary, it would also undertake translations for Native Americans and for newly arriving immigrants. In 1824 the American Sunday School Union reached children as well as adults, offering Christian instruction and, where required, the fundamentals of reading and writing. As lay institutions, SUNDAY SCHOOLS did not require an ordained ministry; it could therefore utilize the talents of men and women, especially the latter, to be a valued adjunct to the church and, on occasion, an outpost before the church arrived. So also the American Tract Society (1825), the American Education Society (1826), and a plethora of other Protestant voluntary efforts would turn back the tide of French infidelity and frontier barbarism (see VOLUNTARY SOCIETIES).

Although states were taking major steps to provide HIGHER EDUCATION to their citizens, the churches still saw education as falling very much in their domain. Protestant clergymen still served as college presidents, even of state institutions. Denominations such as the Congregationalists and Presbyterians that long had an interest in an educated clergy worked together in a Plan of Union (1801) to create several colleges in the opening West: Western Reserve (1826) in Ohio, Knox (1837) in Illinois, Grinnell (1847) in Iowa, and Ripon (1851) in Wisconsin. Baptists and Methodists, who placed less emphasis on formal ministerial preparation, also busied themselves in founding many schools: the Methodists, with McKendree (1835) and De Pauw (1837) in Indiana, and Ohio Wesleyan (1842); the Baptists, with Denison (1832) in Ohio, Shurtleff (1835) in Illinois, and Baylor (1845) in Texas. These four denominations accounted for about one half of all colleges established before 1860, although such smaller Protestant bodies as Quakers, German Reformed, and Lutherans also founded new institutions. The education of American youth would not be left to the enemies of religion (see CHRISTIAN COLLEGES).

The Second Great Awakening also utilized revivalism as a recruiting technique for new members and a revitalization program for current members CHARLES GRANDISON FINNEY of Oberlin College (1833), another of those "presbygational" institutions, emerged in the years before the CIVIL WAR as the leading practitioner of and apologist for revivalism. Revivals worked on the frontiers of the West, but they also worked in the cities of the East. Said Finney: one need not passively wait for a revival to come, like dew falling on the grass. One could labor to promote REVIVALS and reap a harvest of saved souls, just as surely as through appropriate efforts one could reap a harvest of corn. Churches had lost sight of the simple connection between cause and effect, he argued, with the result that "more than five thousand million have gone down to hell, while the church has been dreaming, and waiting for God to save them."

All of these instruments—the societies, the colleges, the revivals—illustrated what had come to be the guiding characteristic of religion in America: the voluntary principle. In an early treatment of American religion, designed principally for foreign consumption, Presbyterian minister Robert Baird in 1843 rhapsodized about the voluntary principle. By means of this principle, one could defeat immorality, promote TEMPERANCE, abolish slavery (see SLAVERY, ABOLITION OF), even turn away the gods of war. This principle, he wrote, "seems to extend itself in every direction with an all-powerful influence." For Baird voluntarism stood forth as the essence of evangelical religion, and evangelical Protestantism was, for him, the essence of America.

Protestantism Torn and Challenged

In the 1830s and 1840s two issues threatened the unity of Baird's evangelical Protestantism: first, the growing presence of Roman Catholicism; second, the intensifying discord over slavery. Immigration chiefly from Ireland swelled the ranks of Catholics in America, so much so that by 1850 America had more Roman Catholics than either Baptists or Methodists. If this trend continued, what would become of the evangelical empire? The Protestant response to this influx of Catholic immigrants was first alarm, then organized resistance and hostility (see CATHOLICISM, PROTESTANT REACTIONS).

In 1840, for example, the "American Society to Promote the Principles of the Protestant Reformation" took shape in New York City, its stated purpose being to call attention to the dangers of "popery" and "to arouse Protestants to a proper sense of their duty in reference to the Romanists." For members of this society, and for many other Protestants of that era, the principles of the U.S. Constitution and of the Vatican were irreconcilable; if a citizen believed in the first, he or she must in good conscience strongly resist the second. In the 1850s this religious NATIVISM took a political turn in the creation of the Know-Nothing Party whose aim was to elect only Protestants to public office. Although that party was short-lived, the anti-Catholic sentiment on which it was based lasted well into the twentieth century.

Evangelical Protestants could unite in their dread of Catholicism, but they could not unite in their positions regarding slavery. Indeed, the deep and bitter divisions in such denominations as Methodists, Baptists, and Presbyterians in the 1840s and 1850s pointed to the inevitable divisions in the nation itself that resulted in the tragedy of the Civil War. In 1844 the Method-

ists were the first to divide into two halves: the Methodist Episcopal Church, and the Methodist Episcopal Church, South. Both sides accused the other of having abandoned the gospel of Christ, the Northerners arguing that slavery was "a great evil" to be eradicated as soon as possible, the Southerners denouncing those who substituted POLITICS for theology and social reform for DOCTRINE.

The very next year the Baptists followed suit, with Baptists in the north arrayed against a SOUTHERN BAPTIST CONVENTION. When the Baptist Board of Foreign Missions refused to appoint an Alabama clergyman and a slaveholder as a missionary, Baptists in the south resolved to withdraw from the national body to form their own mission society and, ultimately, their own agencies of every kind. As with the Methodists, both sides appealed for patience and understanding, thinking that once slavery was no longer the issue, the two sides could come together again; however, that proved a false hope. Recriminations and even denunciations made reunion impossible for the Methodists for nearly one hundred years, and for Baptists far beyond that.

Last of the large denominations to divide, the Presbyterians in 1857 separated along lines not theological but geographical. Both sides appealed to the Bible, of course. The North argued that to use the Bible in defense of slavery was to bring ridicule and calamity to Christianity itself; the South argued that to turn the Bible into an antislavery tract was to pervert it beyond recognition. Not only did these denominational divisions anticipate the brutal war to come, they also weakened Protestantism's public voice. Protestant clergy appealed to the same Bible and prayed to the same God but somehow ended up on opposite sides of the most urgent moral issue of the time. How could this be? Did Protestantism guide the CULTURE, or did the culture determine the direction that the Protestant witness would take?

Protestantism presented no united front on other critical questions in the nineteenth century. Charles Darwin's *Origin of the Species,* published in 1859, shook both the theological and the scientific worlds on both sides of the Atlantic. Evolution was not a new idea, but evolution as a credible theory if not a scientific proposition was new. The Protestant responses were now not geographical but theological. An eastern journalist and Congregational clergyman Lyman Abbott saw evolution as compatible with Christian understandings. Creation was a process, not a "once upon a time" event of the past. God's method was growth, development, progress—"What Jesus was, humanity is becoming." On the other hand, Princeton theologian and professor Charles Hodge saw in Darwin's hypotheses a direct challenge to everything that

Christianity stood for. If chance is king, God no longer sits on his throne. If SCIENCE is the source of all truth, then we might as well, thought Hodge, shelve our Bibles and scuttle our creeds. If the war over evolution seemed noisiest in the nineteenth century, all the smoke of battle had by no means cleared in the twentieth.

Both the institution of slavery and DARWINISM raised questions about how one reads the Bible and what authority the Bible has—not just in religion, but in politics, science, and history. The questions grew more intense as Protestant scholars, first in GERMANY, then in England and America, examined the biblical manuscripts as to authorship, date, editorial revision, and mutual agreement. They also looked to the manuscript traditions to see whether, for example, the King James Version of the Bible was based on the best and most authentic manuscripts. It was not, and this led to new scholarly translations and biblical editions, the English Revised Version of 1885 being the first in a long line of "modern" Bibles. If Protestantism had cast its lot in the sixteenth century very much on the side of Scripture as opposed to Tradition, then any challenge to the biblical foundation was bound to shake the institutional superstructure—as it did.

Protestant churches also reacted with something less than unanimity to the growing leadership roles exercised by WOMEN. Antoinette Brown Blackwell was ordained as a Congregational minister in 1853, although this was hardly the first rumble of a grand tidal wave. FRANCIS E. WILLARD directed the fortunes of the Women's Christian Temperance Union, organized in Ohio in 1874, giving her and her followers more visibility in public life than women in America had heretofore enjoyed. ELIZABETH CADY STANTON, who in 1848 joined with Quaker preacher LUCRETIA MOTT in organizing the famous Seneca Falls gathering on behalf of women's rights, turned her talents a half century later to the production of *The Woman's Bible.* All of these nineteenth century efforts did little more than suggest what in the succeeding century would more fully capture the attention of Protestant and political institutions.

Meanwhile, the country continued to grow, with much immigration from eastern and central Europe (Catholic and Jewish), as well as with some immigration from Scandinavia (Lutheran). The country gradually moved from a predominantly rural population to a heavily urban one. Major cities, long a feature of the Atlantic coast, now sprang up in the Midwest: Chicago, Detroit, Milwaukee, Minneapolis, Cleveland, Kansas City, and Omaha. Urbanization together with its close companion, INDUSTRIALIZATION, presented Protestant leaders with new circumstances for which their earlier and simpler piety now seemed inadequate, if not irrelevant.

Especially in the northern half of the country, where industrialization had advanced further, Protestant clergy searched for fresh answers to growing problems of slums, poverty, crime, child labor, economic exploitation, rootlessness, and hunger. Protestants developed new institutions, notably the Young Men's and Young Women's Christian Associations (YMCA, YWCA) to address some of these concerns, whereas another Protestant entity, the SALVATION ARMY, found its special ministry among the urban destitute and demoralized. Pastors and theologians constructed what came to be called the SOCIAL GOSPEL in an effort to move beyond the issue of personal redemption and personal SALVATION: was it perhaps possible to redeem the social order itself?

Congregational clergyman WASHINGTON GLADDEN of Columbus, Ohio, spoke and wrote widely on behalf of a gospel relevant to labor and capital, civic corruption, and municipal reform. Baptist WALTER RAUSCHENBUSCH of Rochester, New York, took his cue from ancient prophets of Israel who overthrew dynasties, condemned SIN in high places, fomented rebellion, and "rebuked to their faces kings who had robbed the plain man of his wife or tricked him out of his ancestral holdings." Academician Richard T. Ely, first Presbyterian and then Episcopalian, declared that the church must turn its attention from the world to come to the world at hand. "I take this as my thesis," he wrote in 1899, that "Christianity is primarily concerned with this world, and it is the mission of Christianity to bring to pass here a kingdom of righteousness and . . . redeem all our social relations."

In the face of radically new circumstances and inescapable new challenges, Protestantism spoke in different tones and addressed different issues. Protestants also saw before them a disturbingly different country. When Congregationalist Josiah Strong in 1885 published his *Our Country,* the "our" referred to an Anglo-Saxon way of life and predominantly Protestant culture that he saw rapidly disappearing. He intended to raise enough alarms and order enough redirection to set "our country" again on its proper course, but Protestantism in the decades ahead had even more turbulent waters to navigate.

Protestant Advances, Protestant Retreats

For American Protestantism the twentieth century opened on a daringly optimistic note. Methodist layman and visionary organizer, JOHN R. MOTT, published a book in 1900 whose title spoke to and further invigorated that optimistic spirit: *The Evangelization of the World in This Generation.* The dream was breathtaking, but it was more than an idle dream. Mott himself had organized thousands of college students in the Student Volunteer Movement, starting in 1886, which in the space of only a dozen or so years had, in Mott's words, "spread from land to land, until it has now assumed an organized form in all Protestant countries." By the time of World War I, Mott's organization had sent out more than five thousand volunteers.

The mission dream was even broader than that, however. Congregationalist, Presbyterian, Methodist, and Baptist churches all had their own mission boards, and the role of women in each case had increased dramatically over the years. Again, by the time of World War I something more than three million American women were involved in the missionary enterprise: as fund raisers, as publicity agents, and often themselves as volunteers abroad in the role of teachers, nurses, doctors, and selfless spouses of officially appointed missionaries. Although World War I interrupted some of these efforts, that international conflict only drove others to greater labors in bringing healing and understanding to injured nations.

In 1919 Presbyterian missionary executive Robert E. Speer sounded every bit as urgent as Mott had in 1900. In his book, *The New Opportunity of the Church,* Speer urged a redoubled effort on the part of the missionary movement, "an agency of righteousness." Western civilization, Speer readily conceded, had been guilty of great crimes against humanity: the slave trade, the traffic in alcohol and opium, and many others. Against all this, however, the one element in the West protesting man's inhumanity to man was the missionary enterprise. "As the years have gone by," Speer wrote, "it alone has represented in many non-Christian lands the inner moral character of the Western world." Newer denominations such as the Mormons, the Seventh-day Adventists, and JEHOVAH'S WITNESSES displayed equal if not greater vigor in taking their messages to lands far beyond America's borders.

Of course the "world" was not evangelized in Mott's generation or in any other. By the 1930s some in the mainline denominations began to question the emphasis on personal conversions, seeing more justification for the enterprise in the educational and medical benefits it brought to needy countries. Some missionaries, notably Methodist E. Stanley Jones, even spoke of MISSIONS as a two-way street: one learned from the host country (India, in his case) no less than one gave to that country. In a major reevaluation of the whole ambitious effort, WILLIAM E. HOCKING, professor of philosophy at Harvard, chaired a "Layman's Inquiry" into the previous hundred years of Protestant missions. His report concluded that it was appropriate to give even greater emphasis to Christian service in the form of hospitals, schools, tractors, inoculations, and the like. Personal EVANGELISM was not to be

forgotten, Hocking wrote in 1932, but neither should it stand alone.

At least from the time of John Mott, missionaries recognized that denominational labels had little meaning abroad. Often, in fact, they became obstacles to the spread of Christianity. In the first half of the twentieth century, many Protestant clergy concluded that the same was true at home: denominational divisions had become a scandal and a stumbling block. In an effort to reverse the trends toward schism—so evident in American Protestantism—the ecumenical movement got under way in 1908 with the creation of the Federal Council of Churches. Some thirty denominations joined together to give Protestantism a stronger voice, especially when confronted with opposition forces so much better organized than the churches were. Our enemies, said the Federal Council, "so confidently faced a derided Church . . . because they faced a divided one." A NATIONAL ASSOCIATION OF EVANGELICALS was born in 1942, bringing greater cooperation among conservative elements not in the Federal Council, and in 1948 the WORLD COUNCIL OF CHURCHES appeared on the international scene.

In 1950 the Federal Council was superseded by an even stronger NATIONAL COUNCIL OF CHURCHES OF CHRIST IN THE USA, an agency that spoke for a membership of some forty million, although this "speaking" often represented the pulpits more faithfully than the pews. Although largely a Protestant entity, the National Council included some Eastern Orthodox bodies (see ORTHODOXY, EASTERN), and invited Roman Catholics to join in its deliberations as "observers." Then in 1960 a CONSULTATION ON CHURCH UNION explored the possibility of actual union among such Protestant bodies as Presbyterians, Congregationalists, Methodists (all branches), Disciples, and Episcopalians. By the end of the twentieth century a good deal of steam had gone out of both of these engines of ECUMENISM; nonetheless, denominational families executed some of the broader ideals of the bodies named above.

The northern and southern halves of Methodism had managed to reunite as early as 1939. This body then absorbed a German Methodist group to become in 1968 the UNITED METHODIST CHURCH. Congregationalism had united with a small entity in 1931 to become the Congregational Christian Church, then merged with an EVANGELICAL AND REFORMED CHURCH in 1957 to form the UNITED CHURCH OF CHRIST. In 1983 the two segments of Presbyterians, divided over slavery, joined to create the PRESBYTERIAN CHURCH, USA. Lutheranism, badly separated into national groups—for example, German, Swedish, Norwegian, Finnish—began to transcend those national labels in the 1960s; by 1988 this ecumenical evolution led to the EVAN-

GELICAL LUTHERAN CHURCH IN AMERICA, by far the largest Lutheran body in the United States. Besides all this merger activity within single denominational families, many serious conversations explored unions that transcended specific ecclesiastical traditions.

Some observers interpreted all of this ecumenical busyness as a sign of weakness rather than of strength, and it is true that among many of these older denominational families membership in the final decades of the twentieth century had declined. For centuries it had appeared that Protestantism in America knew only one direction in which to move: that is, up—to ever larger memberships, ever expanding budgets, ever more impressive architectural achievements. In many elements of the Protestant community that steady upswing had by the year 2000 clearly changed. Yet other Protestant groups showed no signs of waning energies. Pentecostal and Holiness bodies, for example, continued to surge. Southern Baptists, years after others experienced a decline, also peaked in their steady growth. African American denominations generally did better than their white counterparts, whereas the "electronic church" through TELEVANGELISM introduced another element in church growth that is difficult to measure. Whatever the final figures in any given year, Protestants do not speak as confidently as they once did of "our country."

In the public square Protestants compete with other religious entities, and even more with secular forces, for their share of attention or influence. Protestant clergy no longer serve as presidents of the major educational institutions of the country, nor do they regularly rate as opinion makers on the national scene, as once men like HARRY EMERSON FOSDICK or REINHOLD NIEBUHR did. In the evangelical community BILLY GRAHAM occupies a unique niche, but it is difficult to see a replacement for him on the horizon.

In the political realm, the conservative religious right received much notice for its active involvement in the final decades of the twentieth century. Earlier, in the bruising and brutal battles between FUNDAMENTALISM and MODERNISM of the 1920s and 1930s, the more conservative forces withdrew from political participation. Thus the "religious right" dropped from public view, only to reemerge rather dramatically one-half century later. Of course the Protestant "religious left" had been much in evidence through most of the twentieth century, although it did not arouse the kind of anxieties and fears often associated, legitimately or not, with the "right." In the twenty-first century some signs appeared that the "right" was once more reverting to its earlier status of a withdrawn, inward-looking, personal purifying spiritual force.

In the new millennium Protestant churches in America found themselves divided on such major questions as vouchers in private schools, prayers in public schools, women in the pulpit (see WOMEN CLERGY), HOMOSEXUALITY, pluralism, PACIFISM, CREATION SCIENCE, BIBLICAL INERRANCY, LITURGY, ecstasy, and the delicate balance between proselytizing and TOLERATION. Protestants no longer thought of empire, but of witness; they no longer spoke with one voice (if they ever did), but with many voices, sometimes in harmony, sometimes in discord.

References and Further Reading

Baird, Robert. *Religion in America.* [A critical abridgment with Introduction by Henry Warner Bowden.] New York: Harper & Row, 1970.

Balmer, Randall. *Grant Us Courage: Travels Along the Mainline of American Protestantism.* New York: Oxford University Press, 1996.

Bonomi, Patricia U. *Under the Cope of Heaven: Religion, Society, and Politics in Colonial America.* New York: Oxford University Press, 1986.

Gaustad, Edwin S., and Philip L. Barlow. *New Historical Atlas of Religion in America.* New York: Oxford University Press, 2000.

Goen, C. C. *Broken Churches, Broken Nation.* Macon, GA: Mercer University Press, 1985.

Handy, Robert T. *A Christian America: Protestant Hopes and Historical Realities.* New York: Oxford University Press, 1971.

Hatch, Nathan O. *The Democratization of American Christianity.* New Haven, CT: Yale University Press, 1989.

Hudson, Winthrop S. *The Great Tradition of the American Churches.* New York: Harper & Brothers, 1953.

Hutchison, William R. *The Modernist Impulse in American Protestantism.* Cambridge, MA: Harvard University Press, 1976.

Marsden, George M. *Fundamentalism and American Culture.* New York: Oxford University Press, 1980.

Marty, Martin E. *Second Chance for American Protestants.* New York: Harper & Row, 1963.

May, Henry L. *Protestant Churches and Industrial America.* New York: Harper & Row, 1949.

Noll, Mark A. *Between Faith and Criticism: Evangelicals, Scholarship, and the Bible in America.* San Francisco: Harper & Row, 1986.

Schmidt, Leigh E. *Consumer Rites: The Buying and Selling of American Holidays.* Princeton, NJ: Princeton University Press, 1995.

Stout, Harry S. *The New England Soul: Preaching and Religious Culture in Colonial New England.* New York: Oxford University Press, 1986.

EDWIN S. GAUSTAD

UNITING CHURCH IN AUSTRALIA

The Uniting Church in Australia was inaugurated in 1977, the result of nearly a century of ecumenical reunion plans among Protestant churches in AUSTRALIA, and the direct result of a variety of renewal emphases that swept through those churches from 1940 to 1970. It combined Methodist, Congregational, and many Presbyterians in Australia into a "uniting" ecumenical church structure that seeks to bring about a larger "united" Church of Australia.

Early twentieth-century Church Union efforts in Australia reflected that country's involvement in larger globalizing movements for international postal, economic, imperial, and other forms of federation. At the same time as the various Presbyterian churches in Australia were negotiating Federation in the 1880s political federation of the various colonies was also being planned. Models were provided for the union by (to name only the models influential on Australia) GERMANY, IRELAND, INDIA (1947), and Presbyterians had also united in SCOTLAND (1929). Missions work on a cooperative basis was occurring around the world, laying the basis for the global strategies of the WORLD MISSIONARY CONFERENCE in Edinburgh in 1910, and the rise of formal ECUMENISM in the International Missionary Committee (1921), the Faith and Order (1927), and Life and Work (1925) movements, and eventually the WORLD COUNCIL OF CHURCHES (1948). For postmillennialists, union seemed the prerequisite for the last great push that would see the world evangelized in this generation. For premillennialists the darkening situation in European and North American cities indicated the need for common action, particularly in the light of the human disaster that was World War I and the rapidity of moral, theological, and cultural change through the 1920s. Close links to the Canadian churches provided models for both negotiation and successful Union and anti-Union activities. The bitterness of the Canadian division inspired Australian Christians to wait for a more auspicious day, and so Union negotiations failed in 1924.

Another Attempt

A number of causes underlay the recommencement of negotiations for Union after World War II: the need for strong church participation in postwar reconstruction; the relativization of denominational differences through common war experiences, declining ethnic homogeneity (see ETHNICITY), and church affiliation, under the pluralizing effects of mass postwar migration; the "moral and spiritual condition of Australia"; and declining public influence of the churches in a period marked by supradenominational problems (the Cold War, the Korean War, political and economic crises in former missionary-receiving countries, Australia's engagement with Asia, etc.). With the rise of neo-orthodox theology (see NEO-ORTHODOXY) defusing the liberal–modernist debates of the 1920s and 1930s, and Vatican II undermining Catholic–Protestant differences, united action in an urbanizing, pluralizing secular Australia seemed increasingly plausi-

ble. "Mission" was the consistent theme amid a plethora of more particular reasons as to why the churches should unite, "the hermeneutical key to the Basis of Union and the most important pointer to the Uniting Church's way of being Reformed" (Dutney 1996:32). Issues of social justice (poverty, women's rights, indigenous rights, human identity, etc.) seemed more important than DOCTRINE or even form. A number of institutions gave form to these ecumenical aspirations: the long-standing Australian Student Christian movement; foundation of a national council of churches in Sydney (1946) mediating the continuing international pressure for increased unity of action through the World Council of Churches (1948); a variety of interdenominational agencies such as the Christian Youth Conference, the Australian Commission for Inter-Church Aid, and Australian Frontier; and the United Nations Organization and its various branches, all provided training grounds for future ecumenical leaders, including people such as K. T. Henderson, Malcolm McKay, Gordon Dicker, Davis McCaughey, Alan Walker, and others.

In the increasingly difficult postwar atmosphere, formal negotiations began again in 1954 leading to the appointment of a Joint Commission on Church Unity (JCCU, 1957), including representatives from all three churches. Negotiations were slowed by divergent traditions and theologies. The Presbyterians were a more strongly doctrinal and polity-based church, and negotiators knew that bringing the various state assemblies into the Union would require carryover of this content at least in name, and a strong Basis of Union. Presbyterian objections to "weak theology" in the JCCU's first report (*The Faith of the Church*, 1961) and proposed episcopacy (see BISHOP AND EPISCOPACY) in its second (*The Church—Its Nature, Function and Ordering*, 1963) slowed the process. After much wrangling a final version of the Basis of Union was published in 1971, which acted as the basis for voting, by congregation in the Congregational Union (about 90 percent for adherence to Union); in the General Conference of the Methodist Church of Australasia (a majority vote requiring 100 percent adherence); and in state assemblies and the general assembly of the Presbyterian Church of Australia (leading to a more divided vote, approximately 64 percent of congregations and 69 percent of the membership, choosing to go into Union). The Presbyterian Church of Australia legally reaffirmed its continued existence, and a small number of Congregational churches remained out of the Union in "The Congregational Fellowship." At Union the "new church" (an appellation it denied) and its constituents represented some 12.5 percent of the Australian population. Although figures are difficult to ascertain, census returns suggest that church membership has continued to decline by between 2 and 4 percent every five years, and in 1996 stood at 1,334,900 (7.5 percent of the population). Despite its ethnic congregations, it remains one of the most highly Anglo-Celtic of all denominations, has one of the highest defection rates of youth, and has a comparatively high percentage of its membership over the age of 60 (Bentley and Hughes 1996:ca. 55). Nevertheless there is some evidence that this post-Union shakeout is now stabilizing.

Living with Union

Most partners to union had issues to work through once it was achieved. Property wrangles continued with the PCA for more than a decade, and considerable feeling was generated between old friends and former fellow Congregationalists. It was only with the rise of a post-Union generation that self-definitions that did not rotate around "not being Presbyterian" or "not being Methodist" have begun to arise. The UCA recognized eldership, although not entirely in the form developed among Presbyterians, and the SACRAMENTS of BAPTISM and Communion (see LORD'S SUPPER). Most DEACONESSES of the constituent traditions chose to unite, but access to ordained ministry has since made this order obsolete (see WOMEN CLERGY). The UCA is trinitarian, and the Basis of Union recognized the ancient creeds and the reformational confessions as "instructive," although not legally binding. It has encouraged equal opportunity at all levels of ministry, as well as supporting links to large Korean, Melanesian, Polynesian, and other ethnic constituencies, and a semiautonomous Aboriginal and Islander Christian Congress (from 1985).

Although adopting the polities of its constituent denominations (hence its executive Standing Committee and triennial national Assembly, based on synodal, presbytery, and parish underpinnings) the UCA has worked hard to shift decision making away from parliamentary procedures toward consensus forums developing out of discussion documents. This has been possible only by the establishment of a significant ecclesial bureaucracy, consisting of more than twenty different agencies (commissions, committees, boards, etc.) of Assembly. Membership consists of adherents, baptized members, members in association, and confirmed members, and ministry consists of "ministers of the Word" and "deacons" ordained by the regional presbytery. Ministers are trained at or through state colleges, the largest of which is the United Theological College in North Parramatta, Sydney, and the Uniting Church Theological Hall at Ormond College,

Melbourne. Distance education occurs through Coolamon College in Brisbane, and indigenous training through Nungalinya College (Darwin). It has a very large welfare and community services arm, being perhaps the largest provider of nongovernment community and welfare programs in Australia, operating more than 1,000 property centers in operations ranging from Aged Care to schools to drug rehabilitation and community hospitals.

With other ageing denominations, the UCA has wrestled with identity, a state of flux endemic to an open church that some constituents have felt is better at posing questions than answering them. The UCA was designed as an interim structure in which the old traditions would "die to live again" so that all Australian Christian churches might eventually join in a single Catholic church. Dutney points out that there are no doctrines peculiar to the Uniting Church. Its theology has not essentially been doctrinal but an inevitably conciliar process of dialog (captured in the phrase "A Pilgrim People") over particular issues mediated by the continuance of older traditions (Wesleyan, Calvinist, evangelical, liberal, etc.) within the church at the local level. The emphasis is on the trajectory from the past rather than on the doctrines established by the (particularly Reformed) past of the church's traditions. This was a "new way of being Church." "Doctrine divides" was the old catchcry, "service unites," and subsequently the UCA has found it easier to provide social services than to come to common understandings on critical issues such as homosexual clergy (see HOMOSEXUALITY), drug policy, and other moral issues. Inevitably the teaching ministry of the church has been in tension with its membership, which was described by the Assembly Commission for Mission in 1994 as "largely pre-critical [and] semi-literalist." The conclusion reflects considerable disillusion within an intellectualist leadership over their "inflexible" constituency, or the "anti-intellectualism" of Australians (McCaughey 1997:7). These are not issues isolated to the UCA, however, and in 2001 the church reentered negotiations toward union with the Anglican Church in Australia, indicating the pivotal role the UCA continues to play in Christian reunion in Australia.

See also Congregationalism; Dialogue, Interconfessional; Methodism; Presbyterianism

References and Further Reading

Bentley, P., and P. J. Hughes. *The Uniting Church in Australia.* Canberra, Australia: AGPS, 1996.

Breward, I. "Evangelicals in the Uniting Church." *Uniting Church Studies* 2 no. 2 (August 1996): 1–7.

Dutney, A. "Is there a Uniting Church Theology?" *Uniting Church Studies* 2 no. 1 (March 1996): 17–35.

Engel, F. *Times of Change, 1918–1978: Christians in Australia.* vol. 2. Melbourne, Australia: Joint Board of Christian Education, 1993.

Joint Constitution Commission. *The Uniting Church in Australia: constitution and regulations (interim) including the Basis of Union.* Melbourne, Australia: Joint Board of Christian Education, 1976.

McCaughey, Davis. "If I had known then what I know now." In *Marking Twenty Years: The Uniting Church in Australia, 1977–1997,* edited by W. Emilsen and S. Emilsen. North Parramatta, Australia: UTC Publications, 1997.

Owen, M., ed. *Witness of Faith: Historic Documents of the Uniting Church in Australia.* Melbourne, Australia: Uniting Church Press, 1984.

Being an Elder in the Uniting Church of Australia: A Study Paper. Sydney, Australia: UCA, 1977.

Faith and Renewal. Melbourne, Australia: Joint Board of Christian Education, 1985.

Synod of South Australia. *Charismatic Renewal: A Theological Statement.* Adelaide, Australia: UCASA, 1986.

MARK HUTCHINSON

UNIVERSALISM

Universalism, "the belief or the hope that the consummation of all things will be the restoration of all intelligent beings to the image and favour of God[,] has found advocates in every age" (according to William Burt Pope, Wesleyan Methodist theologian, in his *Compendium of Theology*, revised edition, 1880, Vol. III, p. 129). Origen of Alexandria in the third century hoped that even Satan would be finally converted, and thus "God will be all in all" would be entirely true. Usually, the issue is confined to the final salvation of human beings.

Although there were Universalist congregations in ENGLAND by 1750, there was no DENOMINATION as such professing universalism until the end of the eighteenth century in the UNITED STATES. Universalist churches, growing out of Congregational and Baptist roots, were committed to the independence of local congregations. Local Associations were loose federations, and the Conventions, which began in 1790 at Philadelphia, were consultative rather than regulatory gatherings, although they developed conditions of association and even Articles of Religion. These Articles underwent continuing adaptation. Universalist declarations increasingly expressed sympathy with humanism. The Universalist Church of America elected as its president in 1951 and its General Superintendent in 1953 Brainard F. F. Gibbons, who in 1949 had addressed the General Convention to the effect that Universalism had now passed beyond Christianity and had disavowed many essential Christian doctrines. Having joined with other liberal churches in the 1935 Free Church Fellowship, and then the 1955 Council of Liberal Churches (Universalist-Unitarian), the Uni-

versalist Church of America united with the Unitarians in 1961 to form the UNITARIAN UNIVERSALIST ASSOCIATION.

The Universalist theology, in its variant forms, is probably influential far beyond any church. The Universalist question confronts every person responsible for funerals at least throughout the English-speaking world: in the majority of cases of funerals for the unchurched, the mourners expect to be assured, unconditionally, that the deceased is eternally safe.

The first classic of universalist theology is Chauncey's *Salvation of All Men* (its later popular title). He begins (Proof 1) with admitting the reality of Original Sin in Adam, but adds that in the New Adam, Christ, all may attain eternal happiness. In Proofs 2 and 3, Christ's perfect obedience includes his dying for all. For Proof 4, Chauncey argues from the New Testament, especially Romans 5 and Colossians 1, that God's will is for the full salvation of all creation. Therefore (Proof 5), either in this present state of existence or in the following state, God will finally reduce all things to obedient subjection to the divine will. In Proof 6, Christ's "mediatory interposition" is all comprehending. This scheme of argument is clearly still markedly biblical, and leans heavily on a Protestant understanding of SIN and redemption. With succeeding writers, especially Hosea Ballou, Universalists move away from any Trinitarian concept of ATONEMENT or of traditional Protestant or Roman Catholic assumptions about original sin or depravity.

The Universalist issue presents Protestantism with several problems that are inherent in the very essence of classical Protestant tenets: GRACE, freedom, FAITH, salvation, witness. The subject may be set out in a series of questions.

Is there a SALVATION? And a salvation from what? Although Balzac was wrong in saying of Protestantism that it "examines beliefs and kills them," it is true that the questioning of TRADITION on which Protestantism insists does for some lead to skepticism—for example, doubt whether there is a need for salvation, for anything more than decency and toleration. Such a view is a sort of universalism, because these ideals might be thought to be equally open to all humanity. Classical Protestant ORTHODOXY sees humankind as fallen and in need of redemption, and finds the key to that salvation in divine forgiveness to which access is opened by the sacrifice of Christ.

But how universal is that salvation, and on what terms is it available? The controversy between extreme predestinarianism (that God from eternity created some humans who would be granted saving faith and the rest of humanity, who would not believe and be eternally lost), and ARMINIANISM (that God created all humankind able freely to choose to believe and knew from eternity who would freely believe and who would not) is not dead, even if most specialist theologians avoid it. Classic Protestantism is found in KARL BARTH's suggestion that in the first archetypal human (Adam), all humans are under condemnation, and that in the second Adam (Christ), all are accepted by God.

If salvation (as Protestantism has classically taught) is by means of faith, is this only faith in the Jesus of Nazareth as found in the Gospels? And what degree of knowledge of the historical or scriptural Jesus is required in such faith? Universalism raises the question of whether all religions are the same, or of the same value? It argues that Christianity is absolute only for Christians. The traditional Protestant exposition of revelation, CHRISTOLOGY, and redemption is challenged by the reality of all religious traditions, although this requirement does not entail any assumption that these are all equal in truth or insight. Some theologians have suggested that in Christianity, in its proclamation of a divine-human Savior, we see a fulfillment of both those religions that center on deity and those that center on the self-realization of humanity. Vernon White and others maintain that all of these concerns are brought together by understanding the work of Christ as the core of a universal restorative work of God.

Universalism is also concerned with the question of whether there can be repentance and CONVERSION after DEATH. Thought on these matters is in the end reflection on the moral character of God; that reflection is in turn informed by human self-perception. A major factor in Universalism is the need not to be selfish about "our" salvation.

References and Further Reading

Cameron, Nigel M. de S., ed. *Universalism and the Doctrine of Hell: Papers presented at the Fourth Edinburgh Conference in Christian Dogmatics 1991.* Carlisle, U.K.: Paternoster Press and Grand Rapids, MI: Baker Book House, 1992.

Cassara, Ernest, ed. *Universalism in America: A Documentary History,* Boston, MA: Beacon Press and Toronto, Canada: Saunders, 1971.

Chauncy, Charles. *The Mystery Hid from Ages and Generations, made manifest by the Gospel-Revelation: or, The Salvation of All Men, the Grand Thing aimed at in the Scheme of God; As opened in the New Testament Writings, and entrusted with Jesus Christ to bring into Effect* (originally published in London, 1784). New York: Arno Press, 1969.

Farrer, Frederic W. *Eternal Hope: Five Sermons preached in Westminster Abbey, November and December, 1877.* London: Macmillan, 1883 (and other editions).

Punt, Neal. *Unconditional Good News: Toward an Understanding of Biblical Universalism,* Grand Rapids, MI: Eerdmans, 1980.

White, Vernon. *Atonement and Incarnation: An Essay in Universalism and Particularity.* Cambridge: Cambridge University Press, 1991.

DAVID H. TRIPP

UNIVERSITIES

See Higher Education; Seminaries

V

VAN DER KEMP, JOHANNES THEODORUS (1747–1811)

Dutch missionary. A pioneering missionary to the Khoikhoi (Hottentot people) of SOUTH AFRICA, van der Kemp was born in Rotterdam on May 7, 1747. After fourteen years in the Dutch Dragoon Guards he decided to study medicine in Edinburgh, graduating in 1782. In 1791, after the accidental death of his first wife and daughter, van der Kemp underwent a CONVERSION experience. Contact with a MORAVIAN CHURCH congregation aroused his interest in MISSIONS and he was sent by the London Missionary Society to South Africa in 1799. In Cape Town he founded the South African Missionary Society and after moving to Graff Reinet began work among the Khoikhoi population.

A land grant from the governor of the Batavian Republic in 1803 enabled van der Kemp to establish a missionary settlement called Bethelsdorp. Conflict with the Boers and later, the Batavian government, was precipitated by van der Kemp's antislavery views (see SLAVERY, ABOLITION OF), his critique of colonial policy, and his illegal education of Khoikhoi and Xhosa children. In 1804 van der Kemp compiled and printed a Khoikhoi CATECHISM—the earliest work printed in an indigenous South African language. Van der Kemp's relationship with the white community deteriorated further upon his marriage in 1806 to Sara van de Kaap, a fourteen-year-old ex-slave.

In 1811 van der Kemp traveled to Cape Town to provide evidence concerning the abuse of the Khoikhoi by white settlers and government administrators. He died there on December 15 after a brief illness, while awaiting the results of the government investigation.

See also Colonialism; Missionary Organizations; Missions, British; Philip, John

References and Further Reading

Enklaar, Ido H. *Life and Work of Dr. J. Th. Van der Kemp 1747–1811: Missionary Pioneer and Protagonist of Racial Equality in South Africa.* Capetown, South Africa and Rotterdam, The Netherlands: A. A. Balkema, 1988.
Freund, William M. "The Career of Johannes Theodorus van der Kemp and his Role in the History of South Africa." *Tijdschrift Voor Geschiedenis* 86 no. 3 (1973): 376–390.

JEFF CROCOMBE

VAN DUSEN, HENRY PITNEY (1897–1975)

North American educator. Born in Philadelphia, Pennsylvania in 1897, "Pit" Van Dusen received a B.A. from Princeton University in 1919, a B.D. from Union Theological Seminary in 1924, and a Ph.D. from Edinburgh University in 1932. After completing seminary he worked in the student department of the YMCA and was ordained to the ministry by the Presbytery of New York in 1924, after surviving a challenge based on his unwillingness as a life-long member of the Episcopal Church to affirm or deny the Virgin Birth, thanks in large part to a statement on his behalf by John Foster Dulles, later to become a member of Union's board of directors and U.S. secretary of state. After traveling the country for two years to visit and study the practices of other schools, Van Dusen began teaching at Union as an instructor in 1926, became dean of students in 1931, Roosevelt professor of systematic theology in 1936, and was elected Union's tenth president in 1945. He retired in 1963 at the age of 65.

Leader and Educator

Van Dusen was considered one of the major leaders in theological education in the twentieth century. Under his presidency, Union Theological Seminary experienced unprecedented growth and the greatest expansion in its history. Beginning with a faculty of twenty-two, the school had fifty-four faculty members when he retired, and the student body doubled from 300 to 600. The school's budget quadrupled, and a number of major building projects were undertaken. Even more significantly, Union attained worldwide significance as a center for theological study, with a faculty that included such seminal twentieth-century theologians as REINHOLD NIEBUHR, JOHN BENNETT, and PAUL TILLICH. Van Dusen's contributions were praised by Union's faculty and board of directors in their final tributes. "In the long history of the Seminary," the Faculty declared, "Van Dusen's presidency stands out as the high-water mark of its achievement. He . . . enlarged not only the personal and physical resources of the Seminary, but above all, its spirit and its outreach." He was described by the Board as "one of the first World Churchmen of our era, a scholar, a statesman, a leader, and—not least—a friend."

Van Dusen also made contributions to theological education through a two-year presidency of the American Association of Theological Schools and by founding the Boston Institute of Theology after his retirement from Union. He also led the Union Settlement Association. His commitment to general education was reflected in his service as trustee of many institutions, including Princeton University, Vassar College, Smith College, and The Rockefeller Foundation. His book *God in Education* contributed to the debate on religion and the schools. He received honorary degrees from twenty universities, including Edinburgh University.

In 1953 a new kind of scholarship program for theological education was developed by Van Dusen and Nathan Pusey, president of Harvard University, who believed that the quality of those entering the Christian ministry was declining. To remedy the problem they obtained a grant from the Rockefeller Brothers Fund to support a program offering an exploratory year of theological studies for qualified college graduates considering but undecided on a ministerial career. Created in close cooperation with the American Association of Theological Schools, the Rockefeller Brothers Theological Fellowship (also known as the "Trial Year" program) offered five scholarships for the 1954–1955 academic year and forty-six awards the following year. This was the initial program of the Fund for Theological Education (FTE). Scholarships to help African American doctoral students intending to teach in seminaries and other scholarships followed in the years to come.

As one of the driving forces in the ecumenical movement of the early to mid-twentieth century, Van Dusen played a dominant role in the formation of the WORLD COUNCIL OF CHURCHES, in particular in paving the way for the union of the International Missionary Council with that body. His impact also was felt through his leadership of the United Board for Christian Higher Education in Asia and the Foundation for Theological Education in South East Asia (Dong nan Ya shen xue jiao yu ji jin hui), which was established in 1963 as the successor organization to the Board of Founders of Nanking Theological Seminary, founded in 1937. Van Dusen served as the president of that seminary's Board of Founders and was the first president of the Foundation from 1952 to 1970.

A Liberal Theology

Van Dusen's theology was liberal. A student of William Adams Brown, he followed Brown's christocentric liberal theology. Explaining his belief in the necessity of the Incarnation in an article in *Liberal Theology*, he stated that

> if God be thought of in abstract metaphysical categories—infinity, immutability, impassability, substance, essence—incarnation is impossible. But if God be thought of as intelligent, holy, purposeful Personality, he [sic] may become incarnate within the persons of men [sic]. . . . This is the highest if not the only proper meaning of the immanence of God, incarnation. . . . In Jesus of Nazareth, God himself was present, as fully present as it is possible for him to be present in a truly human life. The identity of Jesus with God was of outlook, of purpose, of will, of compassion. The Christ of Christian history and of present experience should never be thought of except through the clear lineaments of the words, deeds, mind, spirit, [and] faith of the man, Jesus of Nazareth [who] ever afresh lays constraint upon his Movement in the world, holding it more or less true to his mind and faith, and impelling it to new advances for fulfillment of his purposes. This is the most important fact about the Christian religion as an historic reality.

Van Dusen's personal journey of faith was shaped by a number of influences: the evangelical fervor of his early days with the YMCA, his early interest in the fledgling field of Clinical Pastoral Education (he was a close associate of its founder, Helen Flanders Dunbar), his deep commitment to the ecumenical movement, and in his daily devotions in the chapel services of Union Seminary.

One of Van Dusen's lesser-known but nonetheless highly influential contributions was his indirect role in the development of the Twelve Steps of Alcoholics Anonymous (A.A.), written in 1938 by the cofounder of A.A., Bill Wilson, based on Wilson's earlier A.A. "Six Steps." Historians of the recovery movement suggest that these Six Steps were themselves based on six points outlined in a 1934 *Atlantic Monthly* article by Van Dusen, where he synthesized the findings of thirty Canadian church leaders who had studied and identified six central assumptions of the Rev. Frank N. D. Buchman's Oxford Group movement (later renamed MORAL REARMAMENT), of which A.A. was the major outgrowth. (Van Dusen's exposure to Buchman came through the work of Van Dusen's Princeton mentor, Dr. Samuel Shoemaker, who worked closely with Buchman from the 1920s through the 1930s and was the primary theological guiding force in the formation of Alcoholics Anonymous.) The six assumptions of the Oxford Group were:

- Men are sinners
- Men can be changed
- Confession is a prerequisite to change
- The changed soul has direct access to God
- The Age of Miracles has returned
- Those who have been changed must change others.

To these six Van Dusen added a seventh point, that "the greatest single secret of the Movement's effectiveness [is] the absolutely central place which 'the Group' holds in its mediation of religion."

Death

Ill since 1970 after a stroke, Van Dusen entered into a suicide pact with his wife, Betty (Elizabeth Coghill Bartholomew Van Dusen), who herself suffered from increasingly painful arthritis. Although neither had a terminal illness, both felt themselves to be on a downward course of increasingly poor quality of life. The suicide ended Mrs. Van Dusen's life immediately and Van Dusen's two weeks later due to a sudden, unexpected, acute cardiac arrest, after he had been physically improving. He died on February 13, 1975 at the age of 77. In a letter the Van Dusens left for their three sons and other relatives and friends, they wrote: "Nowadays it is becoming more difficult to die. We feel that the way we're taking will become more acceptable as the years pass." They concluded with this prayer: "O Lamb of God, that takest away the sins of the world, have mercy upon us. O Lamb of God, that takest away the sins of the world, grant us Thy peace." After the couple's deaths Dr. Cyril Richardson eulogized Van Dusen at Union Seminary as "a man of strong personality and inexhaustible energy" who had "what the Germans call 'Unternehmungsgeist,' the spirit, that is, to engage in large enterprises and never to flag in his devotion to them. . . . [who] gave himself to causes with unstinted vigor, and had an unbending

sense of duty, but these were mellowed by a rich heart of Christian compassion and forgiveness."

See also Bennett, John; Liberal Protestantism and Liberalism; Moral Rearmament; Niebuhr, Reinhold; Seminaries; Temperance; Tillich, Paul; World Council of Churches; YMCA

References and Further Reading

Primary Sources:

Van Dusen, Henry P. *God in These Times*. New York: Charles Scribner's Sons, 1935.

————. *For the Healing of the Nation: Impressions of Christianity Around the World*. New York: Charles Scribner's Sons, 1940.

————. *What is the Church Doing?* New York: Charles Scribner's Sons, 1943.

————. *World Christianity: Yesterday and Tomorrow*. Nashville, TN: Abingdon-Cokesbury Press, 1947.

————. *Life's Meaning: The Why and How of Christian Living*. New York: Association Press (Haddam House), 1951.

————. *God in Education: A Tract for the Times*. New York: Scribner's, 1951.

————. *Spirit, Son and Father: Christian Faith in the Light of the Holy Spirit*. New York: Charles Scribner's Sons, 1958.

————. *One Great Ground of Hope: Christian Missions and Christian Unity*. Philadelphia, PA: Westminster Press, 1961.

————. *The Vindication of Liberal Theology*. New York: Scribner's, 1963.

Van Dusen, Henry P., Robert Lowry Calhoun, Joseph Perkins Chamberlain, et al. *Church and State in the Modern World*. New York: Harper & Brothers, 1937.

Van Dusen, Henry P. and David E. Roberts, eds. "The Significance of Jesus Christ." In *Liberal Theology: An Appraisal*. New York: Charles Scribner's Sons, 1942.

Secondary Sources:

Brown, Robert McAfee. "Robert McAfee Brown remembers Henry Pitney Van Dusen." *Journal of Presbyterian History*, 56 (1978): 62–78.

Hammar, George. *Christian Realism in Contemporary American Theology; a Study of Reinhold Niebuhr, W. M. Horton, and H. P. Van Dusen*. Uppsala, Sweden, Lundequistska bokhandeln, 1940.

Leitch, Alexander. *A Princeton Companion*. Princeton, NJ: Princeton University Press, 1978.

Pass It On: The Story of Bill Wilson and How the AA Message Reached the World. New York: Alcoholics Anonymous World Services, 1984.

Thompson, Dean K. *Henry Pitney Van Dusen: Ecumenical Statesman*. Thesis. Richmond, VA: Union Theological Seminary, 1974.

————. "Henry Pitney Van Dusen and the Ecumenical Crossroads at Union Theological Seminary in New York." *Affirmation* 6 (1993): 147–164.

PAUL WILLIAM BRADLEY

VAUGHAN WILLIAMS, RALPH (1872–1958)

English composer. Vaughan Williams is generally regarded as England's greatest composer of the twentieth century. Of mixed English and Welsh ancestry, he was born October 12, 1872 in the village of Down Ampney, Gloucestershire, where his father, Arthur, was vicar of the parish church. His mother, Margaret, was related to the Wedgwood and Darwin families. Ralph (he pronounced the name Rāfe) studied at the Royal College of Music and CAMBRIDGE UNIVERSITY, where he studied history. His teachers included some of the finest musicians of his time: Sir Hubert Parry, Sir Charles Villiers Stanford, Charles Wood, and Alan Gray. He also spent some time in Berlin working with Max Bruch and in Paris, where he became a close friend of Maurice Ravel. In 1897 he married Adeline Fisher, the daughter of a prominent lawyer and tutor to the prince of Wales.

After service in World War I, Vaughan Williams was appointed professor of composition at the Royal College of Music. From 1921 to 1928 he was director of the London Bach Choir. The earliest of his several symphonies, *A Sea Symphony,* was first performed in 1910. *A London Symphony* followed in 1914 and *A Pastoral Symphony* in 1922. The 1930s and 1940s were his most prolific decades and saw the premier of a number of symphonies and works for the stage. In 1935 he was appointed to the Order of Merit, the highest honor bestowed by the British monarchy. His wife died in 1951 and two years later he married Ursula Wood, daughter of Major General Sir Robert Lock and widow of Lt. Col. Michael Forrester Wood. His last symphony, No. 9, was completed in 1958. He died in his sleep, without any long illness, on August 16, 1958.

During his school days at the Charterhouse Vaughan Williams had insisted that he was an atheist. Later, as his second wife said, he drifted into a cheerful agnosticism. He was never a professing Christian, and he left an early position as organist of St. Barnabas church in Lambeth because he was unwilling to comply with the vicar's demand that he receive communion (see LORD'S SUPPER). Nevertheless much of his finest work is religious in character. This includes the "Five Mystical Songs" setting of poems by George Herbert (1911); the "Fantasia on Christmas Carols" (1915); a Mass in G Minor (1922); "Sancta Civitas," a choral work based on texts from the Book of Revelation (1926); a Te Deum (1928) and Magnificat (1932); the anthem "O how amiable" (1934); and a Christmas cantata, "Hodie" (1954). He was active in collecting English folk songs and carols, some of which were incorporated in his choral works, and in the compilation of the *English Hymnal* (1905), *Songs of Praise* (1924), and the *Oxford Book of Carols* (1928). His hymn tunes include "Sine nomine" ("For all the saints"), "Down Ampney" ("Come down, O Love divine"), and "King's Weston" ("At the name of Jesus"). Works for organ include "Preludes on Three Welsh Hymn Tunes," one of which is the popular "Rhosymedre." His compositions were frequently performed at the Three Choirs Festival and were often directed by the composer himself.

See also Hymns and Hymnals; Music; Music, English Church

References and Further Reading

Foss, Hubert. *Ralph Vaughan Williams: A Study.* London: Harrap & Co., 1950.

Kennedy, Michael. *The Works of Ralph Vaughan Williams.* Oxford, UK: Oxford University Press, 1964.

Vaughan Williams, Ursula. *R. V. W.: A Biography of Ralph Vaughan Williams.* Oxford, UK: Clarendon Press, 1964.

STANFORD LEHMBERG

VESTMENTS

Vestments are special clothes worn by religious leaders and liturgical ministers that designate their status in the community and their role in the liturgical assembly. Protestants inherited the clerical garb and liturgical vestments that had evolved in the Western Church during the Middle Ages and had to decide whether to retain this vesture. This article traces the development and types of liturgical vestments in the ancient and medieval church, and reviews which vestments were retained or discarded in the Reformation churches. In the course of subsequent Protestant history further decisions were made by churches with regard to clerical garb and liturgical vestments in response to changing tastes and expectations.

Clerical Attire and Liturgical Vestments in the Ancient and Medieval Church

Dress for Worship

As the offices of BISHOP, presbyter, and DEACON developed in the early church, the bearers of these offices were not at first distinguished from other Christians either in everyday dress or in the liturgical assembly other than their social rank. The first pronouncements in the writings of the church fathers on what to wear to worship applied to all Christians. Clement of Alexandria (d. c. 215) called for clothes that are clean and bright. Jerome (d. 420) stated that "We ought not to enter into the holy of holies in our everyday garments, just as we please, when they have become defiled from the use of ordinary life, but with a clean conscience and in clean garments hold in our hands the sacraments of the Lord" (*Commentary on Ezekiel* 44:17ff.).

The wearing of one's "Sunday best" applied especially to the newly baptized who were to be vested in a clean white garment when they emerged from the pool. The Letter of John the Deacon to Senarius (c. 500) reported that the newly baptized "wear white garments so that, although the ragged dress of ancient error has darkened the infancy of their first birth, the garment of the second birth may symbolize the garment of glory, so that attired in a wedding garment the [newly baptized] may approach the table of the heavenly bridegroom as a new person" (7). In addition to the white garment (*alba*) the newly baptized wore a linen cloth over their heads to symbolize their priesthood in Christ (the later amice). By the fifth century they wore these baptismal robes during the week of white robes after Easter Day when they attended the mystagogical homilies given by the bishops. Augustine of Hippo (d. 430) admonished the newly baptized on the Octave of Easter not to revert to the old way of the life when they removed their baptismal robes and blended into the congregation.

Clerical Attire

What applied to the LAITY applied all the more to the CLERGY. Origen (d. 253) advised the bishop to wear one set of clothes when performing "the ministry of the sacrifices" and another when going out among the people (*Homily on Leviticus* 4:6). Jerome added that it does not dishonor God if the clergy wear white tunics at the LITURGY more handsome than the rest (*Against Pelagius* 1:4). The Canons of Hippolytus prescribe that clergy and lectors "be dressed in white vestments more beautiful than the rest of the people" (Canon 37).

Two factors affected the development of special clerical garb and liturgical vestments. The first was the legalization of Christianity by the emperor Constantine in the fourth century when the emperor honored the bishops with the status and insignia of civil magistrates. Senatorial sandals, the dalmatic (a sleeved coat worn over the tunic), and the ceremonial pallium (a kind of scarf or stole draped over the left shoulder, around and under the right arm, crossed over the breast and then laid over the left arm, leaving the right arm free) became signs of their office. Second, there was a dramatic shift in the style of men's clothing during the fifth and sixth centuries when the trousers and short tunics of the Germanic peoples replaced the long, flowing tunics of the Romans. Clergy adapted to the changing styles in their everyday dress but retained the older clothing to wear for the liturgies. As a matter of convenience it became the custom to wear the liturgical vestments over one's street clothing.

A basic clerical garment worn on the streets, but over which the liturgical vestments were donned, is the cassock. It seems to have derived from the barbarian tunic or coat, open in the front but secured with clasps and reaching down to the knees. As emperors wore longer coats reaching to their ankles, clergy followed suit. Although black remained a basic color of clergy cassocks, they could be in other colors as well. Some colors designated ecclesiastical rank: white for the pope, purple for bishops, red for cardinals. Cathedrals and prominent churches sometimes chose their own color for cassocks. Cassocks were worn by lay choir members, vergers, sacristans, and acolytes as well as clergy.

Over the cassock, clergy of the late Middle Ages who were scholars wore an academic gown. These gowns could function as an overcoat and were often fur-lined. They were worn not only by clergy but by scholars, lawyers, magistrates, and other public functionaries. As universities adopted distinctive academic hoods and scarves, these were also worn with the gown on ceremonial occasions, especially in ENGLAND.

Bishops who rode horses when making visitations of parishes adopted a sleeveless cloak called a chimere (perhaps derived from the Spanish *zamarra*), which would also be worn over the cassock and, in time, over the white tunic also. Doctors of divinity could wear a red chimere, and bishops were usually awarded a doctor of divinity degree because they were teachers of the faith. Hence, the color of the episcopal chimere was red.

Clergy also acquired distinctive headgear for outdoor wear. By the eleventh century the mitre had emerged as the distinctive hat of the bishop. It is so called because of its mitred shape, although it may have originally been a conical cap. Two lappets or fanons hang down the back. Clergy who wore academic gowns on the streets also wore academic caps. Although hats may have been worn indoors for ceremonial purposes, they were removed for prayer.

Liturgical Vestments

The basic liturgical vestment remained the white Roman tunic, or alb. By the eleventh century two developments occurred with the alb. One was that it ceased to be plain and was embroidered with rich apparel around the collar of the amice or neckerchief and on the bottom hem. Second, the wearing of fur or wool cassocks in northern countries required a larger neck opening and slits or billowy sleeves so that it could be donned over the cassock. This style of alb came to be called the surplice, from *superpelliceus* ("over the fur"). It was worn without an amice or girdle (cincture). A still further variant on the alb was the rochet, which was a sleeveless, ankle-length tunic worn up until the thirteenth century by choristers, sacristans, and servers who had to have their arms free. After that it was designated for bishops, cardinals, and canons regular, and the sleeves were added but gathered at the wrist. The close-fitting alb continued to be worn for the celebration of the Eucharist or mass, whereas the surplice or rochet was used as a choir vestment for the prayer offices or occasional services.

The other major item of clothing that survived from Roman times is the chasuble, which originated from the Roman *paenula*. This was a poncholike outdoor cloak actually favored by the lower classes that was made of skins or wools and reached down to the calves. Conically shaped, its folds had to be gathered up over the arms when moving about. The nearly universal wearing of this garment by the clergy reflects the places of liturgical assembly: in the catacombs and cemeteries at night, in processions through the streets, and in the cold churches in the lands north of the Alps. As time went on the folds that would have to be gathered over the arms were cut away to allow the arms to be free for handing books, vessels, and other objects. The chasuble became heavily decorated with a large cross embroidered on the back. The cope was a variation on the chasuble in which the conical shape was retained but cut from the neck to the foot and closed in the front with a clasp. Because it was like a cape worn for ceremonial functions, the cope became heavily embroidered and the hood became a kind of shield hung on the back. Chasubles were worn by the celebrant at the Eucharist or Mass, whereas copes were worn by officiants at solemn prayer offices, in processions, and for occasional services. Whereas any officiant, clergy or lay, could wear the cope, only priests and bishops wore the chasuble. Deacons continued to wear the dalmatic and subdeacons wore a slight variation of the dalmatic called a tunicle.

The origin of the stole is uncertain. It probably derives from the Roman *orarium*, a long towel worn over the left shoulder. The Council of Braga (Spain, 563) associated it with deacons who wore it like a waiter's towel when preparing gifts for the Eucharist. The Fourth Council of Toledo (633) prescribed the stole to be worn around the neck by bishops just as archbishops would wear the pallium. The Council of Mainz (813) extended the wearing of the stole to the priests. A similar vestment with a practical origin that

acquired a symbolic significance was the maniple (*mappula*), which originated as a ceremonial napkin or hand towel worn over the wrist by officials. It was worn by deacons from the fourth century on to cover their hands when handling eucharistic gifts and vessels. During the early Middle Ages the wearing of the maniple was extended to all major orders of clergy, to be worn from the left wrist only when celebrating the Eucharist.

By the high Middle Ages chasubles and copes, stoles, and maniples were made in various matching colors to symbolically reflect the days and seasons of the church year. A color system was codified for the local Church of Rome by Pope Innocent III (1198–1216) that exerted great influence on later liturgical color schemes: white for feasts of the Lord and saints; red for Pentecost, Holy Cross Day, and feasts of apostles and martyrs; black or purple for penitential seasons (Advent and Lent); and green for ordinary days.

Vestments in the Reformation Churches

The Attitude of the Reformers

MARTIN LUTHER (1483–1546) expressed an indifference toward vestments. In his *German Mass and Order of Service* (1526) he wrote: "Here we retain the vestments, altar, and candles until they are used up or we are pleased to make a change." In a humorous letter to George Spalatin, the chaplain to the Elector Joachim II of Brandenburg, who wanted to retain albs and chasubles and processions, Luther wrote that if the elector would allow the gospel and put away superstitious practices, "then in God's Name, go along in the procession, and carry a silver or golden cross, and a chasuble or an alb of velvet, silk, or linen. And if one chasuble or alb is not enough for your lord the elector, put on three of them, as Aaron the high priest put on three, one over the other. . . . For such matters, if free from abuses, take from or give to the gospel nothing: only they must not be thought necessary to salvation, and the conscience dare not be bound to them. . . ." In the Lutheran tradition vestments came under the category of ADIAPHORA, or "indifferent things," matters not of the substance of faith, that could be left free as long as the conscience was not constrained by a required use of them.

The Reformed tradition, on the other hand, took a much more negative attitude toward liturgical vestments and abandoned them entirely, especially those associated with the sacrifice of the Mass. Such vestments were regarded not merely as an object of superstition but had been associated with a sacrilege. In the summer of 1524, partly under pressure from the Anabaptists (see ANABAPTISM), HULDRYCH ZWINGLI

(1484–1531) had vestments, along with other costly ornaments, service books, and vessels removed from the churches of Zurich. These iconoclastic actions were replicated in other places where a more radical REFORMATION was implemented, including in England during the Edwardian Reformation.

The Black Gown, Cap, and Scarf

Luther's own practice, when PREACHING, was to wear his doctor's gown (*Talar*). Although much has been made of the fact that he and other reformers were preaching in their street clothes, given that the gown was not a liturgical vestment, it should be remembered that friars and monks in the late Middle Ages customarily preached in their habits. The only change Luther's practice represents, therefore, is from his monk's habit to the university attire. It is likely that when Luther went to the altar he donned liturgical vestments.

At first both Lutheran and Reformed pastors wore the cassock under the gown, which would have been the conventional street attire of the clergy. In the course of time Reformed pastors abandoned the cassock for ordinary lay clothing, but the gown was still worn in the pulpit. In a process similar to that of the ancient church, therefore, ordinary clothing became a vestment. The academic gown emphasized the concern of the Reformation churches for an educated clergy who were capable of studying the Scriptures and church fathers in Hebrew, Greek, and Latin.

Lutheran clergy did not at first give up wearing the cassock, but during the seventeenth century it was combined with the gown as one vestment in northern GERMANY, DENMARK, and NORWAY. In the seventeenth century it became customary for public officials to wear ruffled collars, and this included clergy. These collars remained a part of clerical attire in Denmark and Norway into the twentieth century. During the eighteenth century in other places, the elaborate ruffs gave way to simpler bands of two strips of white linen (*Beffchen*) hanging from the neck. The bands were worn by all members of learned professions, not only clergy. King Friedrich Wilhelm I of Prussia made the gown with bands the uniform of Protestant clergy in his realm in 1733 and abolished the chasuble and cope. The combination of cassock and gown with bands, three-cornered hat (*chapeau*), scarf (tippet), and buckled shoes became the formal court dress of priests and deacons in the CHURCH OF ENGLAND.

The academic cap went with the academic gown and varied in style from place to place. In Germany it took the style of a circular *beret*. In SWEDEN it took the form of a low-crowned cylindrical cap. In England it was a square cap (the precursor to the mortarboard). Up until modern times these caps often had ear flaps for protection against the cold and could be worn in the churches as well as outdoors.

The academic scarf (tippet) was generally worn only by clergy in England and Norway. In England it was worn hanging around the neck and down the front like a stole, although it is not a stole. In Norway it became a thinner black strip that was sewn onto the cassock-gown. The 1549 BOOK OF COMMON PRAYER-recommended also the academic hood as "seemly" for preachers and the 1604 Canons ordered it for all graduate ministers.

Alb, Surplice, and Rochet

The basic liturgical vestment is a white linen tunic in the style of the alb, surplice, or rochet. The close-fitting alb, with amice-collar and secured at the waist with a cincture, was gradually displaced by the knee-length slit-sleeved surplice or the ankle-length gathered-sleeve rochet in Lutheran use during the sixteenth and seventeenth centuries. The latter was favored for use with the chasuble.

The 1552 *Book of Common Prayer* of King Edward VI of England abolished the use of chasuble and cope (permitted in the 1549 Prayer Book) but prescribed that the white linen surplice be worn by officiating clergy at all services. This directive was short-lived because of the death of Edward VI and the return of Catholicism under Queen Mary I (1553–1558), although it returned with the restoration of the *Book of Common Prayer* under ELIZABETH I in 1559. Because the queen as supreme governor of the church demanded conformity in all indifferent matters, Archbishop MATTHEW PARKER published some "Advertisements" in 1566 that were a call to strict conformity. This precipitated the Vestiarian Controversy in which nonconformists (see NONCONFORMITY) within the Church of England protested the binding of consciences by the required wearing of "outwarde apparell." The Puritans (see PURITANISM) who emigrated to New England discontinued wearing the surplice, but it remained a staple vestment of Anglican clergy worn over cassock or gown with tippet and hood. Bishops wore an ankle-length rochet with sleeves gathered at the wrist by a band over which they wore a red chimere and tippet, which has remained standard Anglican episcopal dress to this day. Cassocks and surplices continued to be worn by choirs in cathedral and collegiate churches.

Chasuble and Cope

Chasubles and copes were retained by Lutherans in northern Germany and in the Nordic countries long after the stole and maniple were allowed to fall into disuse or were officially abolished. This use of alb or surplice and chasuble for Holy Communion (LORD'S SUPPER) and cope for processions survived in northern Germany until the end of the eighteenth century in such local churches as Dresden, Leipzig, Magdeburg, and Nuremberg. In 1733 King Friedrich Wilhelm I of Prussia officially abolished both vestments in his expanded realm, which included Reformed as well as Lutheran populations. In 1740, however, the more tolerant king Frederick the Great permitted their restoration in a number of Berlin parishes, and they were used in St. Nicholas Church until after 1787. By the end of the eighteenth century these vestments were being discarded in favor of the black gown favored by the ENLIGHTENMENT. Chasubles and copes survived, however, in the Churches of Denmark, Norway, Sweden, and FINLAND. The 1685 *Rituale* of the church in the united Kingdom of Denmark and Norway directed the priest to vest in a black undergarment, a white vestment, and a chasuble at the altar when the bell tolled for the start of the service and to unvest during the closing hymn. The chasuble was to be removed whenever the pastor left the altar (e.g., to go to the font, the pulpit, or the litany desk). At Ante-Communion the priest would not resume wearing the chasuble after the sermon. The Gothic vestments in use in the fifteenth century, knee-length front and back with material on the side cut away to allow arm movement and with a large gold cross embroidered on the back, continued to be the style in Germany, Denmark, and Norway after the Reformation. The "fiddle-back" style of chasuble favored in Baroque Catholicism was introduced in Sweden by King Gustav III. Swedish and Finnish bishops continued to wear the cope with matching stole and mitre and pectoral cross as episcopal dress. They also continued to carry a crozier (shepherd's crook) in their own diocese.

In England chasubles and copes, which had been permitted in the 1549 *Book of Common Prayer,* were generally discouraged and were definitively abolished in 1552. Such vestments were either confiscated by sheriffs or remade into paraments for the new communion tables that replaced the old stone ALTARS. Copes were allowed again in 1559 because they were not associated with the Mass, and were probably worn for the Holy Communion as well as the Ante-Communion in some places. Canon XXIV in 1604 ruled that the principal minister of Holy Communion in cathedral and collegiate churches should wear a colored cope over a plain alb.

No Vestments

As a matter of principle the sixteenth-century Anabaptists and seventeenth-century BAPTISTS es-

chewed all vestments. Few Anabaptist or Baptist leaders were university educated, so not even the black gown was worn by their pastors. As a matter of practicality, those pastors and preachers who tended scattered congregations on the North American frontier on horseback seldom packed gowns or vestments in their saddlebags.

The Revival of Vestment

In Anglicanism

The neo-medievalism of the Cambridge Ecclesiological Movement in England (not to be confused with the more theological OXFORD MOVEMENT) fostered the revival of Gothic architecture as the most appropriate form of church architecture. Allied with the Victorian neo-gothic revival, Ritualists advocated the restoration of the Gothic chasuble with matching stole and maniple for the celebration of Holy Communion. The mass production of these vestments in the late nineteenth century and their marketing by church supply companies promoted their rapid acquisition in parishes as the principles of the Oxford and Cambridge movements made inroads in ANGLICANISM in Great Britain and North America. The solemn celebration of Mass in Anglo-Catholic parishes also led to the restoration of matching dalmatics and tunicles for the roles of the deacon and subdeacon. Interestingly, acolytes, crucifers, thurifers, and even choristers sometimes wore the shorter cottas of the Roman style rather than the knee- or ankle-length surplices of northern Europe.

In Lutheranism

The romantic revival did little to affect vestments in European LUTHERANISM. The alb and chasuble never made a comeback in Germany, although surplices or rochets continued to be worn over gowns in Saxony and in the Slavic countries. The chasubles retained in the Nordic Churches continued to be Gothic-style vestments, although these became more fulsome in the twentieth century and matching stoles were restored.

An interesting evolution occurred in North American Lutheranism. Where vestments were worn at all, they tended to be black clergy gowns, with ruffs or tabs (bands) in the Scandinavian synods. Where choirs were vested, they also wore academic-type black gowns. In Swedish and Finnish congregations pastors wore the knee-length frock coat with white tabs typical of the street wear of their European counterparts. In lieu of a gown they might wear the long black preaching cape also worn for non-Communion services by their European counterparts. By the beginning of the twentieth century colored stoles were being introduced that were worn over the gown, although by the 1920s cassock, surplice, and colored stole began to become popular, and by the middle of the twentieth century this combination had become the most common form of vesture in all branches of American Lutheranism (see LUTHERANISM, UNITED STATES). The use of cassocks also required the wearing of Roman collars. As in Episcopal parishes, choirs and servers in Lutheran congregations were also turning to cassocks and cottas. Albs and chasubles began to appear in a few American Lutheran congregations in the 1950s and 1960s.

In Mainline Protestantism

The conditions of church life in frontier American discouraged the wearing of vestments or even formal clergy streetwear. Still, as churches became more respectable there was an expectation that clergy would wear formal men's attire to conduct Sunday morning services. In the late nineteenth century this meant the Prince Albert coat, which was an old-fashioned cutaway coat with tails, and striped trousers. By the 1920s the black "Geneva gown" (combined cassock and gown) sometimes with tabs (attached to Roman clerical collars) was making a comeback in Presbyterian and Reformed Churches. Methodist clergy (see METHODISM) also wore a black clergy gown, but without tabs. By the middle of the twentieth century many Methodist clergy were wearing colored stoles over their gowns. This became typical also of Congregationalist pastors (see CONGREGATIONALISM), who brought such vesture into the UNITED CHURCH OF CHRIST.

The Renewal of Vestments

The most remarkable development of the late 1960s to early 1970s was the use of the cassock-alb in those churches in which clergy wore the basic white tunic. This all-purpose vestment was adopted almost overnight by Roman Catholic priests and American Lutheran pastors. A practical vestment, it is usually put on like a coat rather than over the head. The amice as such was discarded, although it survives in the collar of the alb. In an effort to recapture the long flowing character of the ancient Roman tunic, cinctures were sometimes also discarded. The next development was the chasuble-alb, which was a fulsome vestment worn in place of both with the stole placed over it. In another development, a simple, unadorned, but fulsome chasuble in a lighter version of the liturgical color was worn over the alb but with the stole in the contrasting liturgical color worn on top of it. An attempt to revive the ancient conicle chasuble proved

unsuccessful. The more prevalent and traditional use has been to wear the stole under the chasuble, held in place by being slipped through loops in the cincture. Some Methodist, Presbyterian, and United Church of Christ clergy have also adopted the cassock-alb and stole as standard vesture. It has thus acquired a kind of ecumenical appeal. In churches in which the clergy wear the cassock-alb, assisting ministers, servers, and choirs have followed suit.

The Geneva gown is still the preferred vestment in Reformed Churches, although in an age of liturgical renewal in which the celebrative character of Christian worship has been emphasized, there has been objection to its dark, somber color. As a result, it has been replaced with softer-colored academic gowns (e.g., blue or white) with hoods (usually red for a degree in theology). The use of academic hoods and gowns with doctoral bars (because of the prevalence of doctor of ministry degrees) still emphasizes the academic expectations of Reformed clergy. Sometimes in an effort to distinguish preaching gowns from regular academic gowns, crosses are stitched onto the breasts or sleeves of the garment. Choirs have also retained the use of academic-type gowns, but often in bright colors with ersatz satin hoods or stoles, especially in the African American Churches.

In many Protestant traditions the use of vestments for clergy continues to be rejected. Pastors in these churches wear a plain dark business suit in which to lead worship. In churches that offer contemporary worship or SEEKER services (see SEEKER CHURCHES), the pastor might not wear a suit at all, but casual slacks and sport shirt. Nor would the musicians be vested.

The Meaning of Vestments

In the Middle Ages there was a tendency to give an allegorical meaning to all vestments. Those worn at Mass were interpreted in the medieval commentaries on the mass (*Expositiones missae*) in the light of the overall interpretation of the Mass as a dramatic reenactment of the sacrifice of Christ on Calvary. Thus, the chasuble represented the cross, in view of the large crosses embroidered on the back of the chasuble; the alb signified the gown given to Christ after his scourging; the amice symbolized the crown of thorns. This kind of interpretation undoubtedly contributed to the Reformed rejection of all vestments associated with the Mass.

Some symbolic interpretation of vestments that survive from antiquity is inevitable. Perhaps less farfetched than the interpretations in medieval commentaries, but still allegorical, is the symbolism of the alb as the baptismal robe put on by the newly baptized to signify their putting on of Christ and being covered with his righteousness, the stole as the yoke of Christ, and the chasuble as the seamless robe of Christ. However, the basic meaning of vestments is that they signify continuity with the church down through the ages. This is why if vestments are worn they ought to be those that evoke a memory of the church in its formative age.

Vestments serve to diminish the personality of the minister and to emphasize his or her role in the assembly. This suggests different vestments for different ministers. All ministers, lay and ordained, might wear the alb as the baptismal vestment of the PRIESTHOOD OF ALL BELIEVERS, but only ordained ministers should wear the stole. Any presiding minister, lay or ordained, might wear the cope in processions or at solemn prayer offices, but only ordained ministers should wear the chasuble at the Eucharist, or Lord's Supper. On the other hand, the fact that some ministers do not wear vestments, such as those who serve as ushers or gift-bearers or communion ministers, is also significant because it witnesses to the fact that the divine liturgy remains connected with everyday life in this world. Because vestments cover personality, wearing jewelry, including pectoral crosses, is inappropriate, except for bishops for whom the pectoral cross is a symbol of office.

Vestments serve to indicate the different character of the different services. The tight-fitting alb was worn for the Eucharist or Holy Communion, which requires more preparation. The looser-fitting surplice was worn for the daily prayer offices because the ministers or choir could come from other activities and slip it on more easily than the alb. The chasuble was reserved for wear only at the Eucharist. The stole has become the sign of ordination and therefore it is appropriately worn by ordained ministers for all liturgical functions exercised by the minister of word and sacrament, such as preaching, BAPTISM, CONFESSION, and Communion as well as at MARRIAGE, ordination, and funeral liturgies. However, it need not be worn at liturgical offices that do not usually require ordained leadership, such as the daily prayer offices.

Vestments add beauty, dignity, and festivity to the liturgy. The beauty of vestments derives from their material rather than from lavish ornamentation. Natural materials such as linen, silk, and wool are preferred. Vestments themselves are symbols and do not need other symbols added to them. In view of the association of the chasuble with the mass-sacrifice in the medieval commentaries, Protestants avoid having large crosses embroidered on them—or crowns of thorns, doves, or flames of fire. The plain fabric should have a dignity of its own. The colors of the outer vestments are bold: deep blue for Advent, gold on white for Christmas and Easter, unbleached earthen color or purple for Lent, deep red for Passion Sunday and Holy Week, fire red for Pentecost, and bright green for the time after the Epiphany and after Pentecost.

References and Further Reading

Cope, Gilbert. "Vestments." In *The Westminster Dictionary of Worship,* edited by J. G. Davies, 365–383. Philadelphia, PA: Westminster Press, 1972.

Dearmer, Percy. *The Ornaments of the Ministers.* London: AR Mowbray, 1920.

Laurance, John D. S. J. "Vestments, Liturgical." In *The New Dictionary of Sacramental Worship,* edited by Peter E. Fink, S.J., 1305–1314. Collegeville, MN: Liturgical Press, 1990.

Piepkorn, Arthur Carl. *The Survival of the Historic Vestments in the Lutheran Church after 1555.* St. Louis, MO: Concordia Seminary, 1956.

Pocknee, E. E. *Liturgical Vesture.* Westminster, MD: Canterbury Press, 1960.

Reed, Luther D. *Worship,* 298–310. Philadelphia, PA: Muhlenberg Press, 1959.

FRANK C. SENN

VISSER'T HOOFT, WILLEM ADOLF (1900–1985)

Ecumenical Statesman Visser't Hooft epitomized the tensions in global religious developments during the twentieth century. Born in the Dutch town of Haarlem, Visser't Hooft earned a doctorate in theology from the University of Leiden in 1928 and contributed to the development of global ECUMENISM.

Three influences shaped Visser't Hooft's THEOLOGY. The Dutch Student Christian Movement introduced the dynamics of God's calling on individual lives; JOHN R. MOTT (1865–1955) inclined him toward MISSIONS and global evangelization; and KARL BARTH (1886–1968) contributed a foundation for truth that validated the other two influences in an increasingly relativistic era.

Between 1924 and 1966 Visser't Hooft held numerous leadership positions with the Young Men's Christian Association (YMCA), the World's Student Christian Federation, and finally the WORLD COUNCIL OF CHURCHES. As global ecumenical trends developed, his speaking, lecturing, and travels increased, and his friendship with JOSEPH H. OLDHAM (1874–1969) proved mutually beneficial.

Visser't Hooft affirmed christocentric pluralism for Christian engagement of world religions. He worked to effect a unified Christendom to produce a vital witness of Christ's uniqueness in an increasingly syncretistic world. Effective Christian communication, Visser't Hooft sensed, required Christians to excise the cultural beliefs thrust upon them by their own cultures' assimilation processes, especially in the West, and to proclaim a Christ free from imposed values who exists cosmically for the entire world. He considered this a worthy revitalization of Christian theology.

The antinomy in his thought was to affirm an absolute and unique Christ with the need for global evangelization to stem chaotic religious drift on the one hand, while adopting the dialectical and relativistic theology of contemporary neo-orthodox thinkers on the other. For Visser't Hooft, the Archimedian point of truth he affirmed when he encountered Barthian theology ironically proved to aid naturalistic assumptions regarding cultural determination of religious experience in a closed universe rather than renewing Christ's uniqueness in a syncretistic age.

References and Further Reading

Selected Primary Sources

Memoirs. London: SCM Press, 1973.
No Other Name: The Choice Between Syncretism and Christian Universalism. London: SCM Press, 1963.
None Other Gods. London: SCM Press, 1933.
The Genesis and Formation of the World Council of Churches. Geneva, Switzerland: World Council of Churches, 1982.

Secondary Sources

Gérard, François C. *The Future of the Church: The Theology of Renewal of Willem Adolf Visser't Hooft.* Pittsburgh Theological Monograph Series; Pittsburgh, PA: Pickwick Press, 1974.
Moulder, D. C. "'None Other Gods'—'No Other Name.'" *Ecumenical Review* 38 (1986): 209–215.
Visser't Hooft, Willem Adolph, and A. J. Van der Bent. *Voices of Unity: Essays In Honour of Willem Adolf Visser'T Hooft on the Occasion of His 80th Birthday.* Geneva, Switzerland: World Council of Churches, 1981.

KEITH E. EITEL

VOCATION

In Protestant belief and practice, vocation is not limited to the work of the clergy, but includes every activity that fulfills the design of God's creation. All have divine vocations that enables them to live out the calling that comes with BAPTISM.

Before the sixteenth century religious tasks of contemplation and priesthood took a privileged place in society. In the Middle Ages vocation would be ordinarily pursued in places specially set aside for that purpose, and monasteries and convents were the places where religious life was to be lived.

Protestantism expanded the perimeters of the meaning of vocation beyond the walls of religious establishments to include all pursuits of livelihood. Now all jobs came under the category of vocation, inasmuch as they participated in God's care of the created world, whether they were conducted in a bakery, a shop, or a cathedral. One was no longer called *out* to serve God, but was called *in* the world to serve God. Vocation was no longer determined by the service one rendered to the CHURCH, and came to mean whatever one did for a living. It was a way in which God provided the daily bread. Historians commonly attribute this extended meaning of the term "vocation" to MARTIN LUTHER, who formulated the theology of work in terms of the PRIESTHOOD OF ALL BELIEVERS.

The traditional notion of a higher calling in ecclesiastical duties may have enhanced the AUTHORITY of the church in medieval times, but Luther called the distinction between spiritual estate and temporal estate a church-sponsored deceit. Other Protestant leaders went as far as to caricature it as timorous flight from the world.

JOHN CALVIN added a new dimension to the democratic notion of vocation, as he redefined calling as what the believer chooses to do for the glory of God. One was not simply called to carry out a function ordained for him or her in the society; God's creature was to identify the work through which she or he could glorify God.

Vocation in Relation to Baptism and Ordination

Prior to the sixteenth century, the concept of vocation was associated with either entry into monastic life or ordination to the priesthood. Protestant theology, as it regards lay people's work as valuable in God's sight as that of the CLERGY, has shifted the liturgical context of recognizing vocation from ordination to baptism. In baptism one is called to live a life that builds up the body of Christ, and the baptized pursue their vocation for the well-being and health of the community of faith.

In the actual practice among the Protestants, however, the newly recognized value of the common people's work did not necessarily downgrade the role of religious workers. Most Protestant traditions continued celebrating ordination as a communal event in which the believing community recognized the calling of teaching, PREACHING, and preserving the purity of the church, even though none listed it as one of the traditional seven SACRAMENTS. Only a few Protestant traditions discontinued the practice of ordination of the clergy, given that the ritual seemed to communicate residual distinction between religious vocations and nonreligious tasks. The Anglican tradition maintained the clear distinction between religious priesthood and everyday work, but have embraced the Protestant notion of vocation and affirmed the value of secular jobs as equal to that of the clergy. In the

Protestant theology of work, the ordained office was no longer the only form of vocation, but the clergy's work had a special role in the sense of enabling the members of the body of Christ to fulfill their own form of serving the creator.

As one serves God's calling in what God has created him or her to do in life, LITURGY is no longer an event of the sanctuary; rather the entire world becomes the sanctuary. Interestingly enough, the Protestant emphasis of the vocation of people restores the root meaning of the word *liturgy,* which came from a Greek word *leitourgia,* meaning "the public service."

Vocational Ethics

Sociological studies have often linked the Protestant view of vocation with productivity. In the early twentieth century, MAX WEBER identified the entrepreneurial INDIVIDUALISM of Protestant ethics as a major force behind modern capitalism. Protestantism may have indeed offered an ambience in which capitalism grew in the twentieth century; however, the modern secularized form of entrepreneurialism could not be further away from the Protestant notion of vocation because it defines the value of a person in terms of how much he or she produces. The value of vocation does not lie in production, but in service.

Luther maintained that a Christian person was given freedom to serve all, while being a servant to none but God. Vocation was the context in which one put the freedom of service into practice. Luther displayed a great deal of confidence in the symbiotic relationship of the kingdom of God and the kingdom of the earth as two compatible arenas of Christian vocation, but Calvin regarded it necessary for the believer to assess the value of each work that one does in the sinful world. For Calvin, the world was a place that needed God's work of SALVATION, and human work had to be evaluated in terms of one's service for the neighbor.

Vocation in the New Millennium

Vocation in Protestantism has the potential of realizing the truly democratic world in which every form of productive lifetime work is valued as God's design and desire, instead of having a certain form of work as divinely privileged. The affirmation of all forms of labor has imparted heavenly meaning to earthly endeavors.

The Protestant THEOLOGY of vocation faces a serious challenge, however, when it is used to support the status quo, as if social locations are part of God's immutable design. PURITANISM has often been cited as an example for a strand in Protestantism that believed

each person had a preordained role in his or her post in the community. One was to make austere efforts in order to carry her or his vocation apart from how he or she may feel about it. One was required to be happy about the work God assigned for each member of the community. While the Puritan view envisioned a community of the willing under all circumstances and evoked energy and dedication to work with gladness in hardy places like wilderness, the conservative work ETHICS was not equipped to address issues of institutional exploitation in the world where labor turned into a commodity.

The tendency toward conservatism in the theology of vocation made its most crude appearance in the nineteenth-century hymn of "All Things Bright and Beautiful." Originally it had the following refrain, which has been left out in modern hymnals: "The rich in his castle, the poor at the gate, God made them high and lowly and ordered their estate." In such an interpretation of Protestant vocation one was consigned, or even condemned to his or her social location.

The historical legacy of Protestantism offers a corrective to the misunderstanding of the doctrine of vocation as an endorsement of the status quo because the theology of vocation as originally envisioned by the reformers was meant to bring down the wall of separation of the privileged religious work and the faithful life of service. JOHN CALVIN noted that the faithful practice of vocation seeks justice in God's creation. Labor that pursues God's desire for justice is to be considered in consonance with the Protestant theology of vocation.

References and Further Reading

Froehlich, Karlfried. "Luther on Vocation." *Lutheran Quarterly* 13 (Summer 1999): 195–207.

Klein, Krista R. "The Lay Vocation: At the Altar in the World." In *Being Christian Today: An American Conversation,* 197–210. Washington, D.C.: Ethics and Public Policy Center, 1992.

Kolden, Marc. "Work and Meaning: Some Theological Reflections." *Interpretation* 48 no. 3 (1994): 262–271.

Marshall, Paul A. *A Kind of Life Imposed on Man: Vocation and Social Order from Tyndale to Locke.* Toronto, Canada/Buffalo, NY: University of Toronto Press, 1996.

Volf, Miroslav. *Work in the Spirit: Toward a Theology of Work.* New York and Oxford: Oxford University Press, 1991.

JIN HEE HAN

VOLUNTARY SOCIETIES

Historians and sociologists, echoing the French politician ALEXIS DE TOCQUEVILLE's (1805–1859) observations during the 1830s, have long recognized the centrality of voluntarism in American religious and cultural life. The separation of CHURCH AND STATE inscribed religious choice in the nation's legal framework, and denominations themselves constitute essentially voluntary organizations. Almost immediately following the adoption of the Constitution, a bewildering array of voluntary societies appeared on the American landscape. Organizations dedicated to distributing Bibles and tracts, reforming morals, establishing SUNDAY SCHOOLS, encouraging TEMPERANCE, supporting missionaries, and promoting myriad other causes emerged in the nation's villages, towns, and metropolises. Although these societies flourished within the UNITED STATES, they actually owed much to a transatlantic evangelical impulse. Many American organizations explicitly modeled themselves on European predecessors, receiving their initial inspiration and funding from abroad. Several matured into enduring national institutions and continue to exert an important influence on religious life. Others rededicated themselves to more secular purposes. By the early twentieth century, voluntary societies constituted a critical component of the nation's charitable and benevolent infrastructure. These organizations increased and diversified as the twentieth century wore on. Evangelicals and fundamentalists (see EVANGELICALISM; FUNDAMENTALISM), often isolated within the established denominations, proved especially successful in establishing a broad range of parachurch agencies to promote their perspectives. Many mainliners followed suit, and some sociologists have argued that special-purpose voluntary associations remain the most important religious groupings in the late twentieth century.

Antebellum Societies

Alexis de Tocqueville's influential and shrewd analysis of American antebellum CULTURE laid much of the framework for later scholarly discussions. Writing in the 1830s, he noted the propensity for Americans of all ages, classes, and dispositions to gather themselves into associations for a variety of social and reformist purposes. De Tocqueville argued that the peculiarities of democratic life, the absence of fixed classes, and the lack of state-supported churches produced a unique environment that stimulated voluntary activity. Citizens gathered together to reform morals, monitor deviance, establish educational institutions, and dispense CHARITY. Subsequent social observers, ranging from English historian James Bryce (1838–1922) to German scientist MAX WEBER (1864–1920), have echoed these observations and characterized America as a nation of joiners. Historians have often emphasized the quintessentially Protestant aspects of voluntarism, arguing that the heterogeneous and competitive American religious milieu encouraged like-minded people to gather together in societies and denominations in

order to promote their particular views. Many studies linked voluntary religion with Protestant revivalism (see REVIVALS), noting the correspondence between intense evangelical activity and the founding of social reform agencies.

Contemporary scholarship has modified earlier assumptions about antebellum voluntary societies and broadened the discussion in several ways. First, the traditional emphasis on the uniquely American nature of voluntarism seriously understated international influences. Recent literature has underscored the extent to which antebellum American evangelicals operated within a well-defined transatlantic context, as people and ideas traveled back and forth between the European and American continents. Many of the most successful early nineteenth-century voluntary agencies explicitly modeled themselves on European precedents. The AMERICAN BIBLE SOCIETY (1816), for example, copied its constitution, administrative structure, and distribution policies virtually verbatim from the BRITISH AND FOREIGN BIBLE SOCIETY (1804). Sunday school organizers in Philadelphia and Pawtucket during the 1790s drew heavily on the work and philosophy of ROBERT RAIKES (1735–1811) and other British evangelicals. The Young Men's Christian Association (see YMCA, YWCA) actually originated in ENGLAND in 1841, and was only introduced in Boston, New York, and Montreal a decade later. A broadly cosmopolitan outlook and participation in a transatlantic world of business, benevolence, and philanthropy informed the founders and early managers of all of these new national voluntary institutions.

Second, although antebellum societies found fertile ground throughout the entire United States, they appeared especially prolific among individuals and groups affected by the Second Great Awakening (see AWAKENINGS) and its theological currents. Several community studies that have examined religious life in the evangelically charged region of upstate New York uncovered full-blown association fever in the early 1830s. Dynamic and prosperous cities like Rochester and Albany, thriving canal towns and sleepy villages in Oneida County, and country hamlets in Cortland County all boasted their share of BIBLE, tract, temperance, and moral reform societies. Larger cities proved particularly hospitable venues as well. New York City Christians established independent associations to support Protestant missionary work overseas, distribute Bibles among the poor, circulate religious tracts, combat PROSTITUTION, expose sexual immorality, promote total abstinence from alcohol, advance both the abolition of SLAVERY and the cause of African colonization in LIBERIA, mandate proper observance of the Sabbath, and advocate all manner of social causes. Individuals often participated in several organizations, but each society carefully cultivated its own autonomy. In subtle ways, the voluntary associations sometimes competed with churches for moral influence and monetary contributions, thus fragmenting religious AUTHORITY and encouraging heterogeneity in many communities.

Third, voluntary societies played an important role in the formation of an aggressively activist and increasingly self-conscious middle class. Although reformers rarely achieved all of their goals or satisfied their lofty expectations, membership in voluntary crusades often produced or reinforced transformations in the lives of the participants. Volunteers typically pledged to uphold the virtues, subscribe to the moral tenets, and exercise the self-restraint that scholars associate with modern middle-class life. Prohibitionists and teetotallers, for example, won few legislative victories in antebellum America, but members of such organizations as the American Temperance Union (1836), Washington Temperance Society (1840), and the Sons of Temperance (1843) publicly proclaimed their own virtues through parades, personal testimonies, and participation in the movement. Voluntary societies offered them the opportunity to assert their piety and institutionalize their values.

Finally, membership in these organizations ranged across the entire social spectrum, but individual societies often remained segregated by class, race, and GENDER. Some organizations catered specifically to working-class whites, while others attracted upwardly mobile country boys who recently arrived in the city. Free blacks established their own institutional infrastructure, and the AFRICAN METHODIST EPISCOPAL CHURCH (AME) promoted a full range of voluntary societies among its members. Evangelical WOMEN played an especially important role in inventing, administering, and financing many charitable and benevolent organizations. Religious societies provided a socially acceptable outlet for wealthy women wishing to exert and enhance their public influence. Some women's societies functioned merely as auxiliaries and remained subservient to male-dominated benevolent boards. Others exhibited considerable independence and challenged gender roles. In sum, an astounding array of organizations dedicated to addressing specific local problems, reforming broad societal ills, and promoting the spread of Christianity established themselves within American culture by the 1850s.

Disintegration, Institutionalization, and Change

The subsequent histories of these antebellum societies reveal widely varied patterns. Some single-issue associations died out rapidly. The New York Female Moral Reform Society, established by middle-class Christian women in 1834 and boasting auxiliaries in Boston and throughout New England, offers one example. Members organized sidewalk patrols, stationed themselves outside brothels to embarrass potential patrons, supported a Magdalen Asylum designed to rescue prostitutes and train them for work as domestics, and published the names of males who frequented bawdy houses. Despite an initial wave of publicity and popularity, the movement quickly declined and virtually suspended operations by the late 1830s. Prostitutes proved resistant to reform, some religious leaders blanched at open discussion of sexual issues, and surveillance techniques proved more effective in theory than in practice.

Other voluntary societies successfully institutionalized, becoming important and enduring presences on the Protestant landscape. The American Tract Society (ATS), for example, was founded in New York City in 1825 as a centralized federation to coordinate the work of dozens of local and regional organizations. It quickly emerged as one of the largest and most innovative publishing houses in the United States, printing and circulating a diverse product line of moral reform pamphlets, children's stories, and Christian classics. The ATS implemented the most modern printing technology, replaced volunteer local distributors with a committed corps of traveling paid colporteurs, formalized its managerial structure, centralized its operations, and carefully managed its growing endowment. Despite social strains and periodic tensions within its pandenominational coalition, the tract society survived and prospered by altering its mission at key moments. It established a close working relationship with the Freedman's Bureau and produced educational literature for emancipated slaves in the late 1860s, and revived its fortunes again in the late 1940s by forging closer ties with evangelical and fundamentalist Christians. Although its core purpose remained relatively constant, the ATS adapted its practices and procedures to thrive and prosper.

The YMCA pursued a different path, yet also successfully negotiated social change to survive and persist. Initially, the founders promoted a series of moral associations and programs designed to attract a particular audience: anonymous young men from the countryside who flocked to major urban centers in the mid-nineteenth century seeking fame and fortune. YMCA administrators hoped that reading rooms, Christian dormitories, Bible study programs, and street EVANGELISM might counteract the more dubious lures of saloons and morally disreputable boardinghouses. By the late 1860s, YMCA executives believed that they could reach young men most effectively through a structured program of wholesome leisure activity. Gymnasiums, body-building equipment, bowling alleys, and swimming pools soon became synonymous with the urban "Y." The organization founded Springfield College to train YMCA executives and secretaries, institutional theorists invented basketball to promote cooperative values and morally upright recreation, and outdoor camping became a staple of the organization's programs. Christian critics in the late twentieth century complained that institutional administrators had removed the "C" from YMCA, and that evangelicalism had taken a back seat to professionalization within the movement. Clearly, the organization did aggressively cultivate new constituencies among women and non-Protestants, downplay evangelical activities in favor of general social and recreational functions, and emphasize building programs in its effort to influence youths and young men. Some viewed this as diluting Christian intent; others saw it as broadening the institutional mission in response to altered circumstances. The conflict illustrated tensions that often surfaced within voluntary societies as they matured and responded to historical change.

New voluntary societies, often with explicitly charitable and philanthropic purposes, continued to appear throughout the late nineteenth and early twentieth centuries. Many responded explicitly to INDUSTRIALIZATION and the widening economic disparities that characterized modern American life. Important broad-based organizations often emerged from somewhat narrower religious roots. The Volunteers of America (VOA) was founded by Maud (1865–1948) and Ballington Booth (1859–1940) in 1896 as a result of familial and institutional schisms within the SALVATION ARMY. Storefront missions that dispensed warm clothes and hearty meals along with the message of personal salvation characterized early VOA relief efforts for the poor. The Booths also hoped to uplift their middle- and upper-class supporters by promoting an ethic of volunteerism and bridging their social distance from poorer Americans. Eventually, the VOA evolved into a more comprehensive agency that focused on providing quality affordable housing, advocating programs for abused and neglected children, offering services for the homeless, and operating nursing facilities and residential assisted-living complexes. Over 11,000 employees and 300,000 volunteers contributed to an agency whose budget exceeded $450,000,000 by the turn of the twenty-first century.

Recent Trends

Voluntary societies exercised an even greater influence within late twentieth-century American Protestantism. Special-purpose groups expanded in size and scope, even as many denominations contracted and struggled to maintain their traditional audiences. Several distinctive features of twentieth-century religious associational life deserve notice. First and perhaps foremost, fundamentalist and evangelical movements have established and created many of the most dynamic new societies. Beginning in the late 1920s, the modernist triumph within major mainline denominations caused many religious conservatives to look elsewhere for institutional support (see MODERNISM). Fundamentalists and evangelicals created their own networks of parachurch organizations, independent ministries, educational institutes, youth groups, and missionary agencies that transcended denominational lines. By the 1950s, distinctive evangelical and fundamentalist subcultures existed, grouped largely around these new institutions. Many contained a global focus. A few enduring examples convey the flavor of the movement. WORLD VISION (1950) developed an international evangelization program, supported child sponsorship efforts for Korean War orphans, and eventually created wide-ranging emergency relief programs in AFRICA and LATIN AMERICA. YOUTH FOR CHRIST emerged from a series of independently sponsored rallies into a tightly coordinated program that sponsored Bible clubs and evangelized young people throughout the nation. The BILLY GRAHAM Evangelistic Association (1950) drew unprecedented numbers of supporters, pioneered in developing broad-based Christian crusades, carried out wide-ranging world ministries, sponsored important international conferences, and eventually institutionalized into a powerful and enduring organization that redefined evangelicalism for many Americans.

Second, governmental policies have stimulated contemporary Christians to establish voluntary societies around single issues and crusades. School PRAYER, ABORTION rights, CREATION SCIENCE, the peace movement, environmentalism, civil rights, poverty, women's liberation, and church/state issues all mobilized Protestants. Robert Wuthnow, who has studied special purpose groups in great detail, has argued that members tend to fall into two general clusters. One set of overlapping organizations consists of healing and prison ministries, Bible study groups, charismatics, and Christians concerned with world hunger. A second cluster includes protest organizations, antinuclear coalitions, holistic health enthusiasts, positive thinking advocates, and therapy groups. As denominational loyalties have disintegrated, Protestants divide sharply into these social and spiritual groupings, thus reflecting a new and deep Christian chasm in contemporary

America. From the pacifist Fellowship of Reconciliation (1915) through Focus on the Family (1977), such groups exercised a potent political and social influence on twentieth-century American life.

Finally, the philanthropic and voluntary impulse within American Protestantism remains a key component of the nation's independent sector of nonprofit institutions. AIDS ministries, homeless advocacy, soup kitchens, shelters for battered women, substance abuse support groups, and counseling centers in local communities throughout the United States rely heavily on religiously motivated volunteers for staffing and funding. During periods of government austerity such as in the 1980s, religious organizations assumed increasing responsibility for performing vital social service functions. Many receive public funding, thus illustrating the interpenetration and close relationship between the public, corporate, and nonprofit sectors of American life. Perhaps uniquely among Western democratic cultures, Protestant voluntary societies have carved out a highly visible and generally accepted public role.

See also Missionary Organizations; Missions; Philanthropy; Social Gospel

References and Further Reading

Boyer, Paul. *Urban Masses and Moral Order in America, 1820–1920.* Cambridge, MA: Harvard University Press, 1978.

Carpenter, Joel A. *Revive Us Again: The Reawakening of American Fundamentalism.* New York: Oxford University Press, 1997.

Cherry, Conrad, and Rowland A. Sherrill, eds. *Religion, the Independent Sector, and American Culture.* Atlanta, GA: Scholars Press, 1992.

Foster, Charles I. *An Errand of Mercy: The Evangelical United Front, 1790–1837.* Chapel Hill: University of North Carolina Press, 1960.

Hewitt, Nancy A. *Women's Activism and Social Change: Rochester, New York, 1822–1872.* Ithaca, NY: Cornell University Press, 1984.

Ryan, Mary P. *Cradle of the Middle Class: The Family in Oneida County, New York, 1790–1865.* New York: Cambridge University Press, 1981.

Smith, Timothy L. *Revivalism and Social Reform: American Protestantism on the Eve of the Civil War.* New York: Harper & Row, 1957.

Wuthnow, Robert. *The Restructuring of American Religion: Society and Faith Since World War II.* Princeton, NJ: Princeton University Press, 1988.

Wuthnow, Robert, Virginia A. Hodgkinson, et al. *Faith and Philanthropy in America: Exploring the Role of Religion in America's Voluntary Sector.* San Francisco: Jossey-Bass, 1990.

PETER J. WOSH

W

WALES

Protestant emphases on the priority of scripture and SALVATION by GRACE through FAITH, filtered through Episcopalianism and, more significantly, NONCONFORMITY, have deeply influenced Welsh CULTURE and national identity. During the twentieth century, Pentecostal and charismatic expressions of Protestantism emerged, although it remains to be seen whether any of these groups can contribute to national renewal and stem the tide of decline and secularization that took hold in Welsh religious life after World War II.

Protestantism came to Wales as the result of a political policy after HENRY VIII's break with Rome. There was little zeal for the new form of faith until the reign of Henry's daughter ELIZABETH I, when legislation was passed securing devotional literature in the Welsh language. By 1567 Bishop Richard Davies (c. 1510–1581) and the renaissance scholar William Salesbury (c. 1520–1584) had translated the BOOK OF COMMON PRAYER and the New Testament into Welsh, the Welsh BIBLE becoming available in 1588 after the tireless labor of William Morgan (c. 1541–1604). Morgan's Bible, revised by Richard Parry (1560–1623) and John Davies (c. 1567–1644), was the means by which generations of Welsh people learned to read and became familiar with the Christian story (see BIBLE TRANSLATION). The result was a literate and religious populace.

During Elizabeth's reign an ultra-Protestant Puritan movement emerged. Although it did not initially penetrate Wales, one of its prominent representatives and martyrs was the Welshman John Penry (1563–1593). PURITANISM was the antecedent of religious DISSENT, which interpreted the CHURCH as a gathering of believers separate from the government of the state and from pan-ecclesiastical and geographical bureaucracy. The first Independent (Congregational) church was established in Llanfaches, southeast Wales in 1639. Others followed at Wrexham, Cardiff, and Swansea, established by zealots such as William Wroth (1576–1641), Walter Cradock (c. 1610–1659), William Erbury (1604–1654), Vavasor Powell (1617–1670), and Morgan Llwyd (1619–1659). For two generations it was difficult to differentiate between Congregationalists, Presbyterians, and free-communicating BAPTISTS because all could be found worshipping in the same congregations (see PRESBYTERIANISM; CONGREGATIONALISM). Nevertheless, the first Particular (strict) Baptist church was founded at Ilston, southwest Wales in 1649 by John Miles (1621–1683).

Although numerically modest, dissent remained a significant expression of Protestantism for almost a century. It was popularized during the eighteenth-century Evangelical Revival led by the churchmen Daniel Rowland (1713–1790), Howell Harris (1714–1773), and William Williams of Pantycelyn (1717–1791), whose legacy to Welsh hymnody is abiding. METHODISM in Wales was Calvinistic rather than Arminian and created the only indigenously Welsh DENOMINATION, the Calvinistic Methodist Connexion (later Presbyterian Church of Wales) when Thomas Charles of Bala, northwest Wales (1755–1814) ordained men to its ministry in 1811, thus seceding from the Anglican church. Wesleyan Methodism arrived in 1800.

In the Religious Census held in March 1851, 12.7 percent of the population attended the parish churches, whereas as many as 43 percent attended a chapel belonging to one or the other of the Nonconformist denominations. Protestant Nonconformity had thus become a movement of the people. Its CALVINISM was moderated under the influence of men such as the Congregationalist Edward Williams (1750–1813) and the cultured Calvinistic Methodist Lewis Edwards

(1809–1887). Its pulpit became renowned for preachers of the caliber of the Baptist Christmas Evans (1766–1838), the Calvinistic Methodist John Elias (1774–1841), and the Congregationalist William Williams of Wern (1781–1840), while a peculiarly Welsh PREACHING style, known as "*hwyl*," developed. Nonconformity became associated with the freedom of individual conscience before God and the freedom of the market to be self-regulating. Its political ally was the Liberal Party and ministers such as David Rees (1801–1869) and William Rees—"Gwilym Hiraethog"—(1802–1883) were renowned for their radicalism. Alternatively, laymen such as the Calvinistic Methodist David Davies of Llandinam, mid-Wales (1818–1890) were able to use *laissez-faire* liberalism to amass a fortune from investment in railways, coal, and in the building of Cardiff docks, and to use it in support of religious causes.

While Welsh Nonconformity was consolidating its position among the ordinary people and its political influence through the bourgeoisie of the Industrial Revolution, ANGLICANISM was also undergoing a renewal. Although ostensibly Protestant through its Prayer Book and THIRTY-NINE ARTICLES, this rejuvenation stemmed mainly from Catholic emphases and the development of Tractarianism. Its perception as a foreign imposition on a "nation of Nonconformists" gave rise to the bitter campaign to disestablish the Church in Wales, which began in earnest in 1889 and culminated in the Act that was passed on the eve of World War I in 1914, although it did not come into effect until 1920. After disestablishment the Church in Wales developed into a truly national institution whose bishops were at times able to exercise a political as well as pastoral role. Among the more prominent were Timothy Rees (1874–1939), Glyn Simon (1903–1972), and Rowan Williams (b. 1950).

The revival of 1904–1905 and its association with the charismatic, if enigmatic, Calvinistic Methodist layman Evan Roberts (1878–1951) resulted in a short-lived increase in membership of the Protestant denominations and also contributed to the long-term development of international PENTECOSTALISM, particularly in the form of the Apostolic Church whose headquarters remain at Penygroes in southwest Wales. Nevertheless, the twentieth century was marked by relentless decline in religious observance suffered by all the traditional Protestant denominations. Neither the theological liberalism of the early decades, associated with men such as Thomas Rees (1869–1926), John Morgan Jones (1873–1946), D. Miall Edwards (1873–1941), and J. Oliver Stephens (1880–1957), nor the Barthian NEO-ORTHODOXY of the middle years, associated with J. E. Daniel (1902–1962), J. D. Vernon Lewis (1879–1970), and Lewis Valentine (1893–1986), could stem the tide of SECULARIZATION and religious ambivalence. An evangelical renewal associated with the battle for Welsh cultural and linguistic survival achieved some success in the 1970s, as did the HOUSE CHURCHES and charismatic groups in the 1990s, but these were exceptions in a downward trend that has shown no signs of abating.

Protestant understanding and expression of Christian faith offer a vital key to unlocking the mysteries of Welsh history in the modern period, which gives meaning to the past and helps understand the present.

References and Further Reading

Bassett, T. M. *The Welsh Baptists*. Swansea, Wales: Ilston Press, 1977.

Evans, Eifion. *Daniel Rowland and the Great Evangelical Awakening in Wales*. Edinburgh: Banner of Truth Trust, 1985.

Jenkins, Geraint H. *Protestant Dissenters in Wales, 1639–89*. Cardiff: University of Wales Press, 1992.

Morgan, D. Densil. *The Span of the Cross: Christian Religion and Society in Wales 1914–2000*. Cardiff: University of Wales Press, 1999.

Pope, Robert. *Building Jerusalem: Nonconformity, Labour and the Social Question in Wales, 1906–39*. Cardiff: University of Wales Press, 1998.

———. *Seeking God's Kingdom: The Nonconformist Social Gospel in Wales, 1906–39*. Cardiff: University of Wales Press, 1999.

Tudur, Geraint. *Howell Harris: From Conversion to Separation, 1735–50*. Cardiff: University of Wales Press, 2000.

Williams, Glanmor. *Wales and the Reformation*. Cardiff: University of Wales Press, 1997.

ROBERT POPE

WALTHER, CARL FERDINAND WILHELM (1811–1887)

German American church leader. Walther was born October 25, 1811 in Langenchursdorf, southeast of Leipzig, GERMANY. At the University of Leipzig, where he studied theology, Walther observed the prevailing rationalism and PIETISM but instead embraced orthodox Lutheran confessionalism. Unhappy with the prevailing THEOLOGY in Germany, he emigrated to the United States in 1839 with 800 other Saxons and settled in Perry County, Missouri, 100 miles south of St. Louis. When the group's bishop, Martin Stephan, was expelled from the church on moral grounds, some questioned whether they remained a Christian church, and urged a return to Germany. Walther, however, championed the position of MARTIN LUTHER that the means of saving GRACE (Word preached and SACRAMENTS of BAPTISM and LORD'S SUPPER) were held by baptized believers as the PRIESTHOOD OF ALL BELIEVERS who themselves could put men into the ministry. The Saxons stayed, providing ministers by continuing Concordia Seminary, which they had started in 1839.

Walther was called from his Perry County congregation to St. Louis in 1841 where, along with parish duties, he began to publish *Der Lutheraner* in 1844, a periodical that rallied like-minded conservative Lutheran immigrants in Midwest America. Preliminary meetings led to the 1847 formation of the German Evangelical Lutheran Synod of Missouri, Ohio, and Other States, with Walther elected president. He is thus known for being instrumental in the founding of what became THE LUTHERAN CHURCH—MISSOURI SYNOD. When Concordia Seminary was transferred to this synod and moved to St. Louis, Walther became its president. Walther met criticism of supposed democratic tendencies in the synod's view of the ministry with the publication of *Church and Ministry,* reasserting Luther's views.

A prolific writer, Walther's major efforts included *The Proper Distinction of Law and Gospel, The Congregation's Right to Choose Its Own Pastor,* and numerous sermons and homiletical abstracts. He also edited *Lehre und Wehre (Teaching and Defense),* a periodical for laypeople.

Walther died in St. Louis May 7, 1887.

See also Lutheranism, United States

References and Further Reading

Primary Sources:

Walther, C. F. W. *Church and Ministry: Witness of the Evangelical Lutheran Church on the Question of the Church and the Ministry.* Translated by J. T. Mueller. St. Louis, MO: Concordia Publishing House, 1987.
———. *The Congregation's Right to Choose Its Pastor.* Translated by Fred Kramer. St. Louis, MO: Concordia Seminary Publications, 1997.
———. *The Proper Distinction between Law and Gospel.* Translated by W. H. T. Dau. St. Louis, MO: Concordia Publishing House, 1986.

Secondary Source:

Suelflow, August R. *Servant of the Word: The Life and Ministry of C. F. W. Walther.* St. Louis, MO: Concordia Publishing House, 2000.

ROBERT ROSIN

WALTON, ISAAC (1593–1683)

English author and biographer. Walton was born in Stafford, ENGLAND in September 1593, son of Gervase and Anne Walton. He was educated in Stafford and in his fifteenth year, he left to be apprenticed to Thomas Grinsell, a linen-draper, in the parish of St. Dunstan's-in-the-West, London. Between 1608 and 1613 he discovered poets and poetry, finding his way into a literary circle that included Ben Jonson.

In 1618 Walton became a freeman of the Ironmongers' Company, and owned "half a shop" in Chancery Lane. Sometime after 1624 he met and grew friendly with JOHN DONNE—and a number of his circle—when Donne was preferred as vicar to Walton's parish.

In 1626 he married Rachel Floud. They had several children but none survived to adulthood. In addition to these family deaths, Donne died in March 1631. Walton's intimacy with Donne is implied in his involvement with his posthumous publication. In *Poems, by J.D. . . .* (1633) appears an elegy by Walton; in its 1635 edition further verses by Walton appear.

In 1638 Walton published complimentary verses before Lewis Roberts's *Merchants Mappe of Commerce.* In 1640 he became verger at St. Dunstan's in the West, his wife died, and he published his *Life of Donne* as a preface to Donne's work. He was to revise and expand it in 1658, 1670, and 1675. In it he made extensive use of Donne's own written work, artfully juxtaposed and paraphrased to stress the post-1615 "clerical"—and thus exemplary—Donne. Yet his Donne is also passionate and changeable, figured in Walton's prominent use of Augustine in his typology—a performer in pulpit and deathbed. The "Character" with which it concludes is perhaps his finest piece of writing.

An unwavering royalist, Walton is likely to have left London in 1643, although not altogether or permanently. Walton himself says that he saw WILLIAM LAUD's execution in 1645. In 1642 his complimentary verses appeared before Edward Sparke's *Scintitllula Altaris,* and he probably wrote the preface for Francis Quarles's 1646 *Shepheards Oracles.* He married his second wife, Anne Ken, in 1647. They had three children, two of whom lived to adulthood.

In 1651 *The Life of Sir Henry Wotton* appeared, again as a preface. This is a genial memorial that stresses their common loves for Donne and for angling; it depicts an orderly life whose "Circumference" was "closed up" by a serene and exemplary death. Four more revised editions of the *Life of Wotton* were to appear in Walton's lifetime: in 1654, 1670, 1672, and 1675. He also wrote the preface for Sir John Skeffington's translation of Morales's *Heroe of Lorenzo,* which appeared in 1652.

Walton's third and most enduring work was *The Compleat Angler* of 1653. This pastoral has gone through over 400 editions since its publication in that year. In a manner reminiscent of other poets of the Commonwealth, Herrick or Marvell, the disorder of the present times received muted comment in its scenes of harmony. Walton revised *The Compleat Angler* four times in his lifetime, in 1655, 1661 (there was a second issue in 1664), 1668, and 1676. Its last edition was so much expanded from its first as to be almost a different text.

Walton celebrated the Restoration with a celebratory eclogue printed in Alexander Brome's *Songs and Other Poems* of 1661. The same year he provided verses for Christopher Hervey's *The Synagogue* and joined, belatedly, the flurry of elegists for the conservative William Cartwright (d. 1643). Much later (1676) he was to write dedicatory verses for Cartwright's nephew Jeremiah Rich, promoter of Cartwright's shorthand system.

Walton seems to have had some connection with a number of the Great Tew circle, and most intimately with Bishop George Morley of Winchester, who made Walton his steward. Walton's wife Anne died in Winchester in April 1662 and was touchingly commemorated by her husband. Morley—along with Bishop Gilbert Sheldon—also encouraged him to pen his *Life of Hooker,* which appeared first in 1665, and then in 1666 as a preface to RICHARD HOOKER's works.

This was essentially a loyalist commission to provide a conservative biographical gloss on Hooker's work. The moderate bishop of Exeter, John Gauden, had published for the first time the fiercely contentious "last three books" of Hooker's *Lawes of Ecclesiasticall Politie.* Walton accordingly wrote a biography that characterized Hooker as prophesying the "unity" of the Restoration. The backdrop against which this was drawn was a highly biased parallel picture of the squabbles of the 1580s and 1590s, seen through a filter defined by the Civil Wars (see CIVIL WAR, ENGLAND).

In 1670 the *Life of Mr George Herbert* appeared. This, too, is full of Herbertian paraphrase and quotation. Yet every word is deployed to insist on the essential nobility of the priesthood (particularly the country priesthood) as a VOCATION, and the events are transformed and marked by edifices (the churches GEORGE HERBERT is narrated as restoring, for example). This underscores Walton's belief in the beauty of holiness and transforms Herbert's own handbook, *The Country Parson,* into "factual" example and his poetry into an untroubled version of a spiritual autobiography.

The four *Lives* were issued together in 1670 and 1675, with further revisions and expansion. Walton made some notes, too, for a *Life of John Hales,* another of the Great Tew circle. He produced an anonymous piece of polemic, *Love and Truth* (1680), which in its stress on lay obedience echoed the concerns of the *Life of Hooker;* and finally he was persuaded by Morley into his last considerable work, *The Life of Dr Robert Sanderson.*

Sanderson was a stern Calvinist yet an eminent casuist; he had been chaplain to Charles I, yet was also the last preacher on PREDESTINATION at Pauls Cross in 1627. He was made bishop of Lincoln at the Restoration. Walton had known him; yet the Sanderson he narrates is a pure ceremonialist. It appeared in 1678 and was revised in 1681.

Walton continued authorial work; his letter to John Aubrey on Ben Jonson was written in 1680, and in 1683, the year of his death, he wrote the preface to a verse pastoral, *Thealma and Clearchus,* attributed to John Chalkhill. He died in Winchester on December 15, 1683.

References and Further Reading

Primary Sources:

The Compleat Angler, edited with an introduction and commentary by Jonquil Bevan. Oxford, UK: Clarendon Press, 1983.

Keynes, Geoffrey, ed. *The Compleat Walton.* London: Nonesuch Press, 1929.

"The Life of Dr. John Donne." In *John Donne, LXXX Sermons,* edited by John Donne the younger. London: 1640.

Martin, Jessica, ed. *Izaak Walton, Selected Writings.* Manchester, UK: Carcanet, 1997.

Poems, by J.D. . . . London: 1633.

Saintsbury, George, ed. *Walton's Lives.* Oxford, UK: Oxford World's Classics, 1927.

Shepherd, Richard Herne, ed. *Waltoniana: Inedited Remains in Verse and Prose of Izaak Walton.* London: Pickering, 1878.

Secondary Sources:

Lein, C. D. "Art and Structure in Walton's Life of Mr. George Herbert." *University of Toronto Quarterly* 46 (1976/7): 162–176.

Martin, Jessica. *Walton's Lives: Conformist Commemorations and the Rise of Biography.* Oxford: Oxford University Press, 2001.

Novarr, David. *The Making of Walton's Lives.* Ithaca, NY: Cornell University Press, 1958.

Stanwood, P. G. *Izaak Walton.* New York: Simon & Schuster, 1998.

JESSICA MARTIN

WANG, MING DAO (WANG MINGDAO) (1901–1991)

Chinese evangelist. An independent Chinese Protestant pastor in Beijing, a nationally acclaimed evangelist and church leader, Wang Mingdao's ministry, like that of WATCHMAN NEE, coincided with the most tumultuous years within twentieth-century CHINA history. Born in 1901, educated in missionary schools, Wang became a self-conscious believer in 1920 and received believers' BAPTISM. Beginning a prolific PREACHING career in 1923, Wang promoted the establishment of an independent Chinese Christian church, later establishing one independent congregation in

Beijing. He opposed liberal theological groups' critiques of the BIBLE, and later stood adamantly against the Communist-supported Three-Self Movement, although he remained a Chinese citizen.

Wang's teachings circulated by lengthy evangelistic tours throughout the Chinese mainland and by the *Spiritual Food Quarterly,* making him a nationally recognized conservative Christian spokesman. Like MARTIN LUTHER, whose works Wang selectively studied, he refused SECTARIANISM while seeking spiritual purity based on teachings from revealed scriptures and opposing any compromise with secularism. This principled attitude compares with KARL BARTH's attitude in opposition to Nazism, but without its theological sophistication. Wang's subsequent trials were endured with the belief that "some of God's promises" are written with "invisible ink," becoming understandable only when "placed in the flame of suffering."

Wang's teachings follow three major themes: calling seekers to repentance and CONVERSION; calling Chinese Christians to holy living; and resisting theological MODERNISM and compromised political alignments. Conversion to Christ for Wang comes only by FAITH, and holiness does not require ecstatic confirmation, but both require the miraculous inner work of God the Spirit.

Wang's uncompromising opposition to the Three-Self Movement led in 1955 to his being publicly condemned in Beijing as a counter-revolutionary. Suffering lengthy propagandistic self-criticism, Wang later recanted these as being produced under duress and untrue. Consequently he ended up spending twenty-three years in Chinese prisons. Released in 1979, Wang remained a stern opponent of Communist-attached Christian communities until his death in 1991.

See also Communism; Liberal Protestantism and Liberalism

References and Further Reading

Harvey, Thomas Alan. *Acquainted with Grief: Wang Mingdao's Stand for the Persecuted Church in China.* Grand Rapids, MI: Brazos Press, 2002.

Shi, Meiling. *Liushisan nian—yu Wang Mingdao xiansheng zhailu tongxing (Sixty-three Years—Walking Together on the Narrow Road with Mr. Wang Mingdao).* Hong Kong: Spiritual Rock Publishers, 2001.

Wang, Mingdao. *Wang Mingdao wenke (Literary Treasures of Wang Mingdao).* Edited by C. C. Wang. 7 vols. Taichung, Taiwan: Conservative Baptist Press, 1996.

Wickeri, Philip Lauri. *Seeking the Common Ground: Protestant Christianity, the Three-Self Movement and China's United Front.* Maryknoll, NY: Orbis Press, 1988.

LAUREN F. PFISTER

WAR

From its beginnings, the Christian church has had to wrestle with questions about war. Historically, Christian attitudes toward war have been classified in an ascending order of violence: PACIFISM, just-war theory, and the Crusade or Holy War. In response to the enormous destruction of World War II and the threat of nuclear war, a fourth ethic has arisen, just-peace-making theory.

Just-War Theory

Just-war theory is explicitly affirmed in several REFORMATION creeds and confessions, including the Lutheran AUGSBURG CONFESSION (1530), the CHURCH OF ENGLAND's THIRTY-NINE ARTICLES (1571), and the Presbyterian WESTMINSTER CONFESSION (1648). MARTIN LUTHER's Two-Kingdom doctrine restricted the Christian love of enemies, as commanded by Jesus in the Sermon on the Mount, to individual relations. He followed Augustine in seeing the Christian soldier as motivated by love in using force to restore civil order and peace. JOHN CALVIN presumed that Christians normally would refrain from violence, but that war is justifiable as self-defense against hostile aggression. He appealed to wars fought at God's command in the Old Testament.

As it has developed historically, just-war theory has criteria for discerning the legitimacy of a particular war *(jus ad bellum).* A just war must be fought for a *just cause*—stopping the massacre of large numbers of people, or stopping the systematic and long-term violation of the human rights of life, liberty, and community. The war must be announced by a legitimate authority, the legal authority within a given nation. The devastating nature of war with modern weapons leads many to require checks and balances by the United Nations or widespread international agreement. War must have *just intent,* ending the evil conditions that caused the war and restoring international civil order, rather than revenge, NATIONALISM, or conquest of territory. There must be a reasonable chance of success in meeting the just aims of the war. War must be the last resort after all other means of resolution have been tried.

Jus in bello provides criteria for just conduct once a war begins. *Proportionality* requires that the destruction must not be disproportionate to the good ends to be achieved. This applies to the initial decision to make war and to the tactics used within the war. *Discrimination* requires that war be waged only against military targets. Unintentional killing of noncombatants is allowed (unless the amount violates proportionality), but all reasonable efforts must be made to insure "noncombatant immunity." Torture or mistreatment of prisoners, rapes, massacres, and terrorist violence—deliberately aimed against civilians—are ruled out.

Just-war theory requires guarding against an ends-justifies-the-means ethic that focuses only on just cause. It is wrong to kill large numbers of people in the name of a just cause if another alternative, such as negotiation, international intervention, or nonviolent direct action, could bring resolution without war's destruction. War is wrong if the killing will not succeed in achieving the cause, or if it will be waged by unjust means. Churches espousing just-war theory must teach members its principles and prepare them to oppose a war if it is unjust; too few Protestant churches do this.

Crusade or Holy War

Because the medieval Crusades happened before the Protestant Reformation, many have thought the Holy War ethic has had little or no influence in Protestantism. However, Lisa Sowle Cahill has shown that the Puritan revolution in ENGLAND shared many characteristics with the earlier Crusades (see PURITANISM). The post-Reformation Wars of Religion between Catholics and Protestants, and the European colonial wars of conquest in Asia, AFRICA, and the Americas, conducted by both Catholics and Protestants, often took on Holy War characteristics, and the crusade spirit often infects contemporary Protestants.

Roland Bainton and Charles Kimball judge a war to be a "crusade" or "holy war" when it exhibits the following characteristics:

- The war is fought in God's name. In our more secularized era, war may be fought for nontheistic substitutes—DEMOCRACY, freedom, justice, or the nation's good.
- God or righteousness is viewed as completely on one side, whose sins or crimes are downplayed, denied, or excused.
- The enemy is viewed as demonic, of diminished worth, or beyond redemption—described as evil, animalistic, or less than fully human. Common ground is not recognized.
- Unjust tactics—massacres, torture, the deliberate killing of noncombatants—are condoned in order to ensure the triumph of God against the forces of darkness.

Protestants often gave explicit biblical grounding for such attitudes by appealing to Israel's wars of conquest of Canaan, as depicted in Joshua and Judges. In colonial New England, Puritan divines often referred to their colonies as a "new Israel" and to the NATIVE AMERICAN inhabitants as "Canaanites" whose idolatry must be exterminated by either CONVERSION or genocide.

At least since the end of World War II, the holy war model has been nearly universally condemned by Christian ethicists. But the attitude remains and is even preached from some Protestant pulpits (usually without openly acknowledging it), especially in authoritarian circles.

Pacifism

The early Christian Church was pacifist in the first and second centuries, and the early Christian writers taught pacifism as Christian duty. John Howard Yoder has distinguished numerous varieties of Christian pacifism. A minimal definition might be the refusal to use lethal violence against other humans or to participate in or give support to any war. During the sixteenth century, most of the Anabaptists (see ANABAPTISM) and many of the spiritualists and evangelical rationalists among the radical reformers espoused pacifism. The SCHLEITHEIM CONFESSION of 1527, for instance, relegated "the sword" to those "outside the perfection of Christ." MENNO SIMONS taught his followers to be pacifist. Later Christian leaders such as Quaker (see FRIENDS, SOCIETY OF) founder GEORGE FOX also renewed the pacifist impulse of the early church. Since the end of World War II, the dramatically increased destructiveness of war, increased knowledge about how to prevent war, and increased attention to Gospel teachings in Christian ethics, have contributed to an increase of pacifism among Protestants.

Just-Peacemaking Theory

In the midst of the nuclear buildup of the 1980s, Methodist, Presbyterian, Lutheran, UNITED CHURCH OF CHRIST, Roman Catholic, and historic peace church denominations wrote substantial official statements on war and peace, calling for a reversal of the buildup. They reaffirmed the need for either pacifism or just-war theory, but recognized their inadequacy for shaping an ethic of active peacemaking for the churches. They called for an active "theology of peace" or "just-peace theory." Accordingly, twenty-three interdisciplinary and interdenominational scholars, after extensive work and dialogue, developed a consensus on a new ethic: just-peacemaking theory. The ten practices of just peacemaking are taken to be not ideals, but practices that proved their effectiveness in history since World War II in preventing wars and building conditions of peace. They are supported both by empirical political science and by biblical teaching. These ten practices are as follows:

1. Support nonviolent direct action in movements for justice or social change.
2. In situations of tension or conflict, take independent initiatives to reduce the threat to the adversary.
3. Talk with the enemy, using methods of conflict resolution.
4. Acknowledge responsibility for conflict and injustice and seek repentance and forgiveness.
5. Advance democracy, human rights, and religious liberty. The church's push for human rights has removed causes of war and spread democracy. No democracy with HUMAN RIGHTS directly engaged in war with another democracy in the twentieth century.
6. Foster just and sustainable economic development. Economic deprivation has been demonstrated by political science to be a major cause of intrastate war, and just and sustainable economic development decreases the likelihood of war.
7. Work with emerging cooperative forces in the international system. Empirical political science has demonstrated that the dramatically growing international networks decrease the frequency of war.
8. Strengthen the United Nations and international efforts for cooperation and human rights. Empirical political science research shows that nations actively interacting with UN agencies make fewer wars than nations with unilateralist policies that disengage from UN organizations. Neglect of such international institutions promotes an anarchic international system that makes war more likely.
9. Reduce offensive weapons and the weapons trade. Arms build-ups increase the chances of war, the destructiveness of wars fought, and the economic cost devoted to military expenditures rather than to sustainable economic growth and human need.
10. Encourage grassroots peacemaking groups and voluntary associations. Grassroots groups working for justice, human rights, and peacemaking foster the things that make for peace.

The just-peacemaking ethic is gaining attention both within and beyond Protestant circles. Neither just-war theory nor pacifism can stop the momentum of a determined government to make war. Realism suggests that churches not simply oppose a war, but also point to practices of just peacemaking that have proved effective in achieving resolution without war and that are related more closely to Jesus's teaching on peacemaking. Just-peacemaking theory says that Jesus taught initiatives to prevent war more directly than he taught whether or not to make war.

Just-peacemaking theory is supported by both just-war theorists and pacifists. Just-war theory and pacifism are still needed to judge whether or not a war is moral. But without just-peacemaking theory, pacifists and just-war theorists have difficulty articulating the alternatives to war.

See also Colonialism; Ethics; Peace Organizations; Politics

References and Further Reading

Bainton, Roland. *Christian Attitudes Toward War and Peace.* New York: Abingdon, 1960.
Cahill, Lisa Sowle. *Love Your Enemies: Discipleship, Pacifism, and Just War Theory.* Minneapolis, MN: Fortress, 1994.
Gros, Jeffrey, and John D. Rempel, eds. *The Fragmentation of the Church and Its Unity in Peacemaking.* Grand Rapids, MI: Eerdmans, 2001
Kimball, Charles. *When Religion Becomes Evil.* New York: Harper, 2002.
Potter, Ralph. *War and Moral Discourse.* Atlanta, GA: John Knox, 1969.
Stassen, Glen H., ed. *Just Peacemaking: Ten Practices for Abolishing War.* Cleveland, OH: Pilgrim, 1998.
Walzer, Michael. *Just and Unjust Wars.* New York: Basic Books: 1977.
Yoder, John Howard. *Nevertheless: The Varieties of Religious Pacifism,* rev ed. Scottdale, PA: Herald, 1992.
GLEN STASSEN AND MICHAEL WESTMORELAND WHITE

WATCHTOWER SOCIETY

See Jehovah's Witnesses

WATTS, ISAAC (1674–1748)

English hymn writer. Watts was born in Southampton, ENGLAND on July 17, 1674. At the time of his birth, his father, a deacon in the Independent (Congregational) Chapel, was incarcerated for his NONCONFORMITY. The boy attended a grammar school run by the local rector, and showed such an aptitude for learning that a group of prominent gentlemen offered to underwrite an Oxford education for a career in the CHURCH OF ENGLAND.

Instead the sixteen-year-old Watts enrolled in a school at Stoke Newington, London, headed by an Independent minister, Thomas Rowe. In 1694 he returned to Southampton and over the next two years wrote the first of his hymn texts for the Independent congregation there.

In 1696 he moved back to Stoke Newington as a private tutor to the son of Sir John Hartopp. On his twenty-fourth birthday, Watts preached his first sermon and shortly thereafter was ordained assistant pastor of the Independent Chapel in Mark Lane, where

Hartopp and his family worshiped. In March of 1702 he succeeded Isaac Chauncy as pastor of that prominent congregation; however, Watts's health failed, and in 1703 Samuel Price was appointed to assist him, taking on most of his duties. When the congregation moved from Mark Lane to its new building in Bury Street in 1713, Price was named copastor, and Watts withdrew to the home of Sir Thomas Abney in Stoke Newington, where he continued to write but otherwise lived the remainder of his life as a semi-invalid. The University of Edinburgh conferred the doctor of divinity degree on him in 1728. He died November 25, 1748, at Stoke Newington.

Christian Hymns

Isaac Watts's principal historical significance rests with the approximately 600 hymn texts and psalm paraphrases he published in *Horae Lyricae* (1706), *Hymns and Spiritual Songs* (1707), *Divine Songs for Children* (1715, expanded and reissued as *Divine and Moral Songs for Children* in 1720), and *Psalms of David Imitated in the Language of the New Testament* (1719). During Watts's time, such texts were restricted to private devotions. Both the established church and most dissenting groups restricted congregational singing to metrical translations of the psalms, generally taken from the *Tate & Brady Psalter* of 1696, known as the New Version to distinguish it from the earlier Sternhold and Hopkins translation, or Old Version.

Watts's hymns reflected his conviction that congregational praise should be personal and experiential, as exemplified in such well-known texts as "When I survey the wondrous cross." Similarly, Watts considered the Old Testament psalms in literal metrical translation inadequate to the needs of New Testament faith and WORSHIP. Accordingly, he maintained that congregational psalmody should be altered to reflect a Christian context, "[in] the language of our Time and Nation [and] the Spirit of the Gospel." Hence, for example, his similarly well-known paraphrase of Psalm 98, "Joy to the world, the Lord is come."

Among the Anglicans such texts were dismissed as "Watts's whims," even though it had been an Anglican clergyman who first attempted what Watts succeeded so well in doing. As early as 1679 John Patrick had composed Christianized paraphrases of the psalms. Watts not only acknowledged his debt to Patrick, but even went so far as to incorporate passages from Patrick's work into his own lyric.

Well into the nineteenth century the official position of the established Church of England—and the EPISCOPAL CHURCH in the United States—prohibited the use in public worship of "hymns of human composure," as they were termed, including paraphrases of psalms, although among his fellow dissenters, Watts's texts, both the hymns and psalm paraphrases, quickly gained a measure of acceptance and use in public worship. The EVANGELICALISM of eighteenth-century England as well as the Great Awakening in America (see AWAKENINGS) secured many of Watts's devotional lyrics and psalm paraphrases a lasting place in Protestant hymnody.

Theological Writing

Watts also authored a number of theological and philosophical studies, as well as didactic religious works for the LAITY. Although these writings have fallen into obscurity for the most part, they were highly regarded during his lifetime and issued in a collection after his death. Watts's *Logick* (1724) went through numerous printings in England and abroad and was used as a text at English and American universities well into the nineteenth century. *Philosophical Essays* (1733) contained writings spanning some thirty years and demonstrating a clear understanding of such thinkers as JOHN LOCKE and GOTTFRIED LEIBNIZ.

Watts's theological works included such studies as the *World to Come* (1721) and *Essays toward a Proof of Separate States for Souls* (1732); however, it was his speculations on the Trinity that drew the most attention. In his *Christian Doctrine of the Trinity* (1722) Watts attempted to bridge Arianism and ORTHODOXY by speculating that the soul of Christ was created before the world and subsequently joined with the Godhead. He expanded on the position in *Dissertations* (1724), *A Faithful Inquiry* (1745), *The Glory of Christ as God-Man Unveiled* (1746), and *Useful and Important Questions* (1746). Watts also held liberal views on reprobation, maintaining that God creates and maintains the soul as a thinking entity with particular responses to objects and situations. This liberalism, together with the psalm paraphrases, of which he disapproved, provoked COTTON MATHER to dismiss Watts in a diary entry dated January 28, 1726/7 as "a very Disqualified person." Other writings included a *Catechism* (1730) and *Scripture History* (1732) for children; an *Essay toward the Encouragement of Charity Schools* (1728), and essays on other subjects that interested him, including astronomy and psychology. Watts's late papers were destroyed by his literary trustees, and comparatively little critical research on him has been published in recent years.

See also Congregationalism; Dissent; Hymns and Hymnals

References and Further Reading

Davis, Arthur P. *Isaac Watts.* London: Independent Press, 1962.

Escott, Henry. *Isaac Watts: Hymnographer.* London: Independent Press, 1962.

Fountain, David. *Isaac Watts Remembered.* Worthing: Henry E. Walter, Ltd., 1974.

Hood, Paxton. *Isaac Watts, His Life and Writings, His Homes and Friends.* London: Tract Society, 1875; reprinted as *Isaac Watts, His Life and Hymns.* Greenville, SC: Emerald House, 2001.

Manning, Bernard. *The Hymns of Wesley and Watts.* London: Epworth Press, 1942.

JOHN OGASAPIAN

WEATHERHEAD, LESLIE DIXON (1893–1976)

British Methodist minister and apologist. Weatherhead was born in 1893 in London, ENGLAND. He trained for the Wesleyan Methodist ministry at Richmond College, interrupted by war service as an army chaplain, and served in circuits in Surrey and Madras, INDIA, as a missionary. In 1922 he returned, serving three years in Manchester, where his PREACHING and engagement with students marked him out for a significant ministry. He developed an interest in psychology and its relationship with the healing ministry of the church, tackling the impact of Freudian views of religion and the self. From 1925 to 1936 he had an outstanding ministry in Leeds, where he developed a Christian counseling service. He published a groundbreaking book on *The Mastery of Sex through Psychology and Religion* (1931).

In 1936 he moved to the City Temple, a Congregational chapel (see CONGREGATIONALISM), where he became a national figure attracting vast crowds to services to hear his distinctive preaching style. He developed the ideas of his London doctoral thesis in a book *Psychology, Religion and Healing* (1951) where he addressed the paralyzing effect of guilt on individuals, stressing the unconditional unchanging love of God for all. His preaching and winsome personality won over many admirers, although aspects of his ministry and his pacifist stance in the 1930s made him a figure treated with suspicion by others. This "prodigal son of METHODISM" came home in 1955 when the Methodist Conference elected him as its president. His last great book, *The Christian Agnostic,* stirred up more controversy, including attacks on him by Dr. Ian Paisley. He died in 1976.

References and Further Reading

Primary Sources:

Weatherhead, Leslie. *After Death.* London: J. Clarke and Co., 1928.

———. *Psychology and Life.* London: Hodder and Stoughton, 1934.

Secondary Source:

Weatherhead, Kingsley. *Leslie Weatherhead: A Personal Portrait.* London: Hodder and Stoughton, 1975.

TIM MACQUIBAN

WEBER, MAX (1864–1920)

German sociologist and economist. Weber was born in 1864 in Berlin and died in 1920 in Munich. He was professor of economics at the University of Heidelberg, as well as holding other positions, including administrator of hospitals for the German army during World War I. He is considered one of the founders of sociology. *The Protestant Ethic and the Spirit of Capitalism* was part of a larger work, *Aufsätze zur Religionssoziologie.* This work attempted to show how values and psychology, derived from Calvinistic Protestantism, shaped the world, which Weber saw as an "iron cage" driven by capitalism. The Protestant Ethic, Weber argued, derived from an effort to gain some assurance that one was of the elect predestined for salvation. Evidence of such election included ascetic capitalism—that is, work for the sake of work itself as a way of demonstrating that one was serving God's purpose. Weber argued that the incessant striving and reform deriving from the Protestant Ethic transformed the Western world, in contrast to Asian religions, which either affirmed the status quo (clans in China, castes in India) or offered escape through mysticism. While this so-called Weber thesis is controversial in its specific historical argument, it is influential in diagnosing sources and directions of recent contemporary values and culture, including extensions globally.

Weber's vast spectrum of writings included a second major work, *Wirtschaft und Gesellschaft* (Economy and Society), which was more abstract than the above work and provided a framework for social and cultural analysis. This included such concepts as bureaucratic, traditional, and charismatic authority and the notion of "action" *(handlung)*, which presume that human behaviors are meaningful, hence to understand them, one must grasp what they mean to the actors. Weber developed methods (e.g., the "ideal types" and *"Verstehen"*) to grasp these, thus creating a stream of thought in social sciences and humanities viable today.

References and Further Reading

Primary Sources:

Weber, Max. *The Theory of Social and Economic Organization.* Translated by T. Parsons and A. M. Henderson. New York: Oxford University Press, 1947.

———. "The Meaning of 'Ethical Neutrality' in Sociology and Economics." In *The Methodology of the Social Sciences.* Edited by E. Shils and H. Fich. New York: The Free Press of Glencoe, 1949, 1–47.

———. *The Religion of China: Confucianism and Taoism.* Translated and edited by H. H. Gerth. Glencoe, IL: The Free Press, 1951.

———. *The Protestant Ethic and the Spirit of Capitalism.* Translated by T. Parsons. New York: Scribners, 1958.

———. *The Sociology of Religion.* Translated by E. Fischer, Boston: Beacon Press, 1964.

———. *The Religion of India: The Sociology of Hinduism and Buddhism.* Translated by H. H. Gerth and D. Martindale. Glencoe, IL: The Free Press, 1967.

———. *Economy and Society,* Translated by E. Fischoff, edited by G. Roth and C. Wittich. New York: Bedminster Press, 1968.

Secondary Sources:

Parkin, Frank. *Max Weber.* London: Routledge, 2002.

Behnegar, Nasser. *Leo Strauss, Max Weber, and the Scientific Study of Politics.* Chicago: University of Chicago Press, 2003.

Ekstrand, Thomas. *Max Weber in a Theological Perspective.* Leuven, Belgium: Peeters, 2000.

The Cambridge Companion to Weber. Cambridge, UK; New York: Cambridge University Press, 2000.

Schöllgen, Gregor. *Max Weber.* München: Beck, 1998.

Schluchter, Wolfgang. *Paradoxes of Modernity: Culture and Conduct in the Theory of Max Weber.* Stanford, CA: Stanford University Press, 1996.

Lindt, Andreas. *Friedrich Naumann und Max Weber; Theologie und Soziologie im wilhelminischen Deutschland.* München: Chr. Kaiser, 1973.

JAMES L. PEACOCK

WEIGEL, VALENTIN (1533–1588)

German radical spiritualist Lutheran pastor. Weigel was born in Naundorf in Saxony in 1533. He attended university at Leipzig and Wittenberg before being appointed pastor of Zschopau (1567), a post he held until his death. He signed the Formula of Concord (1576) but grew increasingly angry at the oppressiveness of Lutheran CONFESSIONALIZATION. Weigel owed much to late medieval mysticism; spiritualists such as THOMAS MÜNTZER, SEBASTIAN FRANCK, and CASPAR SCHWENCKFELD; and the cosmology of THEOPHRASTUS PARACELSUS. He was an important conduit of their thought into the seventeenth century, although he was also quite innovative. His pantheistic vision of the universe and his belief that Christ was to be found within all humans as a divine spark would be shared and developed by JAKOB BOEHME. He also employed a thoroughgoing allegorical interpretation of Scripture in support of his teachings. Interestingly, having read most of his sources while at university, his spiritualist vision remained fairly constant throughout his works. Weigel defended his orthodoxy in *A Booklet of the True Salvific Faith* in 1572, but the extent of his

departure from Lutheran orthodoxy became clear only with the publication of his other works after his death. His writings enjoyed a wide audience in the seventeenth century among Pietists, Rosicrucians, disciples of Jakob Boehme, and free thinkers of many stripes.

See also Pietism

References and Further Reading

Koyré, Alexandre. *Mystiques, spirituels, alchimistes du XVIe siècle allemand.* Paris: Gallimard, 1971.

Maier, Hans. *Der mystische Spiritualismus Valentin Weigels.* Gütersloh, Germany: C. Bertelsmann, 1926.

Ozment, Steven E. *Mysticism and Dissent: Religious Ideology and Social Protest in the Sixteenth Century.* New Haven, CT: Yale University Press, 1973.

Weeks, Andrew. *Valentin Weigel (1533–1588). German Religious Dissenter, Speculative Theorist, and Advocate of Tolerance.* Albany: State University of New York Press, 2000.

R. EMMET MCLAUGHLIN

WELD, THEODORE DWIGHT (1803–1895)

American abolitionist and educator. Weld, born at Hampton, Connecticut in 1803, early forsook his conservative Congregationalist origins for the tenets of the evangelical revivalist and reformer CHARLES GRANDISON FINNEY. Following Finney's advice to study for the ministry, Weld and several reform-minded friends matriculated at Lane Seminary in 1833, where they soon confronted president LYMAN BEECHER and others on the subject of immediate abolition of SLAVERY. When seminary authorities refused to countenance this radical doctrine, Weld and his followers left Lane. This "Lane Rebellion" garnered significant publicity for abolitionism, and greatly strengthened nascent Oberlin College, where many of the rebels subsequently enrolled, making it a hotbed of radical reforms.

After leaving Lane, Weld became an abolitionist orator and writer. His *The Bible Against Slavery* (1837) and *American Slavery As It Is* (1839) were widely read, the latter even providing material for HARRIET BEECHER STOWE's *Uncle Tom's Cabin.* In the early 1840s Weld labored for John Quincy Adams and his allies as they fought gag rules that prevented discussion of slavery in Congress. In 1838 he married fellow reformer Angelina Grimke, a pioneering feminist who shared his passion for immediate abolition (see WOMEN).

In 1844 the self-effacing Weld retired from abolitionist leadership. Becoming an educator in New Jersey, he promoted progressive education that featured liberal Christianity, stimulating academics, and robust physical exercise. He moved to Boston in 1863, where he occupied himself mainly with local and familial affairs, although he did speak out on Reconstruction. He died there on February 3, 1895.

See also Congregationalism; Education, Overview; Education, Theology: United States; Slavery, Abolition of

References and Further Reading

Primary Source:

Barnes, Gilbert H., and Dwight L. Dumond, eds. *Letters of Theodore Dwight Weld, Angelina Grimke Weld and Sarah Grimke, 1822–1844.* New York: D. Appleton-Century Co., 1934.

Secondary Source:

Abzug, Robert H. *Passionate Liberator: Theodore Dwight Weld and the Dilemma of Reform.* New York: Oxford University Press, 1980.

DONALD L. HUBER

WESLEY, CHARLES (1707–1788)

Methodist hymn writer. Wesley was the third surviving son of Samuel Wesley, rector of Epworth, and his wife Susanna Annesley, who was the daughter of Samuel Annesley, a noted dissenting minister (see DISSENT). Born prematurely on December 18, 1707 (O.S.), he received rigorous and disciplined training in the home from his mother, despite his somewhat frail constitution. At age eight he went to Westminster School, where his oldest brother Samuel was an usher (teacher). After five years he became a king's scholar, and during his last year in residence, 1725–1726, he was head boy. He then went up to Christ Church, Oxford, where his brother JOHN WESLEY was a fellow of Lincoln College. There Charles received his B.A. degree in 1730 and became a student (fellow) of Christ Church. Before accompanying his brother to the American colony of Georgia in the fall of 1735 he was ordained deacon and priest in two successive weeks in September by the bishop of London.

Oxford

During his early years at Oxford, Charles was, by his own admission, not a serious student, responding to his brother's entreaties with the plea, "would you have me be a saint all at once?" However, sometime in 1728, while John (then a fully ordained priest) was in Epworth assisting their father Samuel with his parish duties, Charles experienced a "reformation of character" that left him desiring to follow John's recently adopted pattern of holy living. He petitioned his brother for suggestions of books to read, habits to

develop, and methods to use (especially for diary keeping). By the spring of 1729 he was well into a pattern of study and devotion that impressed John, who returned to the university for a visit in the summer and to resume his duties as a fellow in the fall.

The combination of the two Wesley brothers and one or two other friends extended John's pattern of holy living into the germ of a movement. Within three years the group's public activities, such as visiting local jails, helping widows, and teaching poor children, brought attention to them, along with several epithets such as Supererogation Men, Holy Club, and Bible Moths. By 1732 they were known as Methodists, partly because of their "new method" of theology (a brand of ARMINIANISM) and their various "methods" for implementing Christianity in the individual and corporate existence. The name Methodist soon found its way into the national print media and eventually persisted as a denominator for the Wesleyan movement in and beyond the eighteenth century.

John Gambold, a friend of both Charles and John at Oxford, described Charles as being "deeply sensible" of John's seniority—"I never observed any person have a more real deference for another than he constantly had for his brother." Gambold felt that Charles imitated his older brother so much that, as he said, "could I describe one of them, I should describe both." In some cases, chronologically, the older brother John had precedence over his younger brother. In other matters, however, Charles preceded his older brother, such as in his evangelical spiritual experience and his marriage.

Georgia and London

Charles was appointed as secretary to James Oglethorp, founder and governor of the American colony of Georgia. His ordination was intended to allow him to assist his brother John with the priestly duties in Savannah and Frederica. In preparation for his duties Charles copied several of his brother's sermons while the brothers were sailing to America. Once there, however, Charles appears not to have fared well with either the colonists or their leaders, and within five months of his arrival he returned to ENGLAND, purportedly to recruit help for the religious enterprise in the colony. In that, he was somewhat successful, helping to recruit his friend and younger Oxford colleague, GEORGE WHITEFIELD, who eventually replaced John Wesley in Savannah, beginning in 1738.

Having encountered German Pietists in Georgia, Charles fell under their continuing tutelage in London, especially that of Peter Böhler and John Bray, both Moravians (see PIETISM; MORAVIAN CHURCH). Although Charles was not fully inclined toward their perspective, he experienced a sense of spiritual assurance on Whitsunday, May 21, 1738, which has at times been described as his "CONVERSION." His description of the moment, "I felt a strange palpitation of heart," presages his brother's comment three days later that his heart was "strangely warmed."

Charles's experience seems to have inspired his poetic muse. Within days, brother John went through a similar experience and, to mark the occasion, the brothers sang a new hymn that Charles had written to celebrate his newfound faith (either "Where Shall my Wondering Soul Begin" or "And Can it Be that I Should Gain"). Charles noted the first anniversary of this experience by writing one of his most beloved hymns, "Oh for a Thousand Tongues to Sing." This outpouring of the spirit represented the beginnings of a lifelong habit of letting his spirit sing through his pen.

Hymns and Poems

Charles's output of poems over the following years is estimated at nearly nine thousand, including some of the most familiar hymns in Christendom, such as "Hark! the Herald Angels Sing," "Love Divine All Loves Excelling," and "Christ the Lord is Risen Today." Of Charles's hymn "Wrestling Jacob" (sometimes known by its first line, "Come, O Thou Traveler Unknown"), ISAAC WATTS reputedly felt that "that single poem was worth all the verses he himself had written." The Wesleyan hymns remain favorites in most Christian denominations and appear throughout their hymnals.

Most of Charles's poetry was never set to music. His published collections include verses that paraphrase every chapter in the BIBLE, works on the Trinity, and poems for nearly every special occasion in the church year. Many of the publications he jointly produced with his brother John, who usually had the final editorial word. John was not a totally uncritical admirer of his brother's work. He refused to print the now-familiar "Jesus, Lover of my Soul" in the Methodist collection of hymns in 1780 because it leaned too much in the direction of Moravian sentimentality. On several occasions Charles produced hymn pamphlets independently to avoid his brother's editorial pen.

Charles's writings unpublished during his lifetime included poetry that criticized the British military effort during the American Rebellion. A special target was General William Howe, whose actions were summarized in the lines, "His Sovereign basely disobey'd; / His trust perfidiously betray'd; / His Country sold, his duty slighted." Charles also produced a series of poems that castigated the American "patriots" and defended the colonists who remained loyal to the king. This collection is typified by the poem "Written in October 1782, For the Loyal Americans," in which Charles gave high praise to those martyrs who "lost their all from Principle" in a place "where Treason and Rebellion reign."

Methodist Revival and Theology

As the Methodist revival gained momentum in the late 1730s, Charles continued to work with John in spreading the gospel. In fact he also continued to preach some of his brother's earlier sermons for several years, as his own theology developed. By mid-1739 both Wesley brothers were PREACHING at times to thousands of people: Charles saw this as God having "set his seal on my ministry."

Although not identical, the THEOLOGY of the Wesley brothers was similar: during this early period John unhesitatingly included Charles's sermon, "Awake, Thou that Sleepest" (1742) in his own first collection of published sermons (1746). Minor differences on ideas and approaches did arise over the years. In 1766 John suggested to Charles that "in connection, I beat you" but that Charles was better in "strong, short, pointed sentences." John also encouraged Charles to proceed in the directions that God had "peculiarly" called him: to "press the instantaneous blessings" while John enforced "the gradual work." As for the process of SALVATION, Charles seems to have had an earlier sense that the "almost Christian," the one who is struggling with the faith, should be taken seriously as having the "faith of a servant." John seems to have persisted longer in the sense that the "almost Christian" was no Christian at all. The focus and goal of their messages was in both cases essentially the same—to spread scriptural holiness across the land.

As the movement grew in size and John began to use more lay preachers to provide leadership in the Methodist societies, Charles became concerned about this practice. By the 1750s he tried to force John to rely less on the lay preachers and to be more selective in his choice of who was "set apart" to preach. In the ongoing dispute over this matter Charles tended to emphasize the need for gifts of intelligence and oratory in preaching, whereas John was more concerned about whether the preachers evidenced the GRACE of God. During the 1750s John appointed Charles as the monitor and examiner of the preachers. Charles took his job seriously, ferreting out the "counterfeiters and slackers" and sending several preachers back to their earlier trades.

Marriage and Family

In the mid-1740s Charles became enamored of Sarah Gwynne, a Welsh woman from a prominent family. Their marriage in 1749, somewhat grudgingly approved by brother John, included an arrangement whereby Charles would receive £100 per annum from the proceeds of the Methodist book trade. In spite of some beginning tensions between the brothers over the matter, Charles and Sally maintained a happy marriage throughout their years together. They survived the sadness of losing several children in childbirth and infancy, holding to the joys that their surviving daughter (also named Sarah) and two sons brought them. Charles Jr. and Samuel (who brought Bach's music back into view) both became trained musicians and perpetuated the musical heritage of the family into the successive generations (including another Charles Wesley and Samuel Sebastian Wesley, noted organist and composer).

When John decided to marry Grace Murray, Charles intervened in a manner that has often been considered inappropriate and unkind: he hurried his brother's fiancée off to Newcastle and married her to John Bennett, who was both a previous suitor and one of Wesley's preachers. Although the brothers were quickly reconciled, the matter left a scar on their relationship that never quite seemed to heal.

The Wesley home in Bristol became a haven to which Charles happily returned at the end of his preaching tours, which became less frequent as time went on. In 1771 Charles moved his family to London, partly to be closer to the headquarters of the movement, partly to enjoy the culture of urban life. He traveled very little around the Methodist connection after this move, but continued to preach in and around London.

Tensions with John

Charles also continued to disagree with his brother over matters that seemed to increase the strain between Methodists and the CHURCH OF ENGLAND. Charles once said that his brother was a "Methodist first" and then a Church of England man; Charles himself claimed to be a "Church of England man first" and then a Methodist. He banded with other "Church Methodists" and Anglican CLERGY to keep his brother from taking irregular actions such as registering chapels as dissenting, allowing lay administration of the SACRAMENTS, ordaining unqualified preachers, and engaging in other actions that would bring separation from the church. Charles was not simply a footdragger, but he represented the loyal opposition to some of John's actions that seemed to many to compromise the Methodists' position within the Church of England. At the same time Charles was always the younger brother. John at times exercised a grating control over some of Charles's actions. Nevertheless, Charles was frequently able to forestall several of John's less fortunate inclinations. They constantly inspired and assisted each other in many crucial ways.

When John Wesley took the decisive step after the American Revolution of ordaining ministers for the new Methodist body in the UNITED STATES, Charles considered that John had gone beyond the prerogatives of an Anglican priest, and also blamed THOMAS COKE for wrongly influencing John. He expressed his sentiments about this "pretended Episcopal action" in a couplet that has become a familiar epithet on this matter: "Wesley his hands on Coke hath laid, / but who laid hands on him?"

As a result of the many tensions between the Wesley brothers, Charles became less active in the leadership of the Methodist movement. After 1765 Charles did not even attend the annual conference of preachers, in spite of the rhetoric about the conference being those preachers in connection with "the Rev. Messrs. John and Charles Wesley," as the title of the document continued to state for several years. In 1785 John Wesley wrote a wrenching letter to him, pleading for at least a show of unity: "Do not hinder me if you will not help," the older brother scolded. "Perhaps, if you had kept close to me, I might have done better. However, with or without help, I creep on."

Death

When Charles contracted what became his final illness John was traveling in the North country. At first, not realizing the seriousness of the illness, John suggested that Charles get more outdoor exercise: "You must go out every day or die." By that time Charles was unable and, in fact, died on March 29, 1788, before John could return to London. In the days immediately after hearing of his brother's death, John was moved to silence and tears when singing his brother's hymn, "Come, O Thou Traveler Unknown" when he came to the words of the third and fourth lines, "My company before is gone, and I am left alone with thee."

Charles was buried in the churchyard at Marylebone Church, his parish church. John, who had established a nonconsecrated cemetery behind the Methodist preaching house on City Road, had earlier mocked Charles's concern about "proper" burial, asking how deep the ground was consecrated and what would happen to the souls of those who might be buried deeper. In spite of the tensions between the brothers during their later years, John missed his brother, who at one point he had assumed would succeed him in the leadership of the Methodist movement.

Why Charles was not more involved in the social mission of the Methodist movement, especially in his later years, is something of a mystery. Nevertheless, his lasting contribution to the hymnody of the age carried these concerns on the wings of music composed by others. He therefore helped to fix the message and mission of the Wesleyan movement in the consciousness of believers in all ages.

See also Hymns and Hymnals; Methodism; Methodism, England; Methodism, North America; Wesleyan Church; Wesleyanism

References and Further Reading

Primary Sources:

Baker, Frank. *Charles Wesley's Verse: An Introduction.* London: Epworth Press, 1988.
———. *Charles Wesley as Revealed in his Letters.* Madison, NJ: Charles Wesley Society, 1995.
Beckerlegge, Oliver, and S. T. Kimbrough. *The Unpublished Poetry of Charles Wesley.* 3 vols. Nashville, TN: Kingswood Books, 1988–1992.
Osborn, George. *The Poetical Works of John and Charles Wesley.* 13 vols. London: Wesleyan Methodist Conference Office, 1868–1872.
Tyson, John. *Charles Wesley; A Reader.* Oxford: Oxford University Press, 2000.

Secondary Sources:

Berger, Teresa. *Theology in Hymns.* Nashville, TN: Kingswood Books, 1995.
Kimbrough, S. T., ed. *Charles Wesley, Poet and Theologian.* Nashville, TN: Kingswood Books, 1992.
Newport, Kenneth. *The Sermons of Charles Wesley.* Oxford: Oxford University Press, 2001.
Tyson, John. *Charles Wesley on Sanctification.* Grand Rapids, MI: Asbury Press, 1986.

RICHARD P. HEITZENRATER

WESLEY, JOHN (1703–1791)

Founder of the Methodist movement. John was the fourteenth or fifteenth child and second surviving son of Samuel Wesley, rector of Epworth, and his wife Susanna Annesley, who was the daughter of Samuel Annesley, a noted dissenting minister. His early training in the home was a combination of Puritan discipline (see PURITANISM), high-Church religion, and academic rigor. At age ten he went to Charterhouse School, London (1713–1720), after which he matriculated at Christ Church, Oxford University. He received his B.A. degree in 1724 and pursued an academic career, taking the requisite steps in the following four years by being ordained DEACON, re-

ceiving a fellowship at Lincoln College, graduating M.A., and being ordained priest.

Oxford

While studying for his ordination exam Wesley embraced holy living in the tradition of Thomas à Kempis, JEREMY TAYLOR, and WILLIAM LAW. His life took on a style that could best be described as a "meditative piety" that focused on the virtues in an attempt to imitate the life of Christ. In this approach he measured his developing spirituality through disciplined self-examination and diary keeping, similar to the method prescribed by Ignatius Loyola in the introduction to his *Spiritual Exercises.* In 1729, upon his return to the university from a short period of service as curate for his father in Epworth, John was joined in this venture by his brother CHARLES WESLEY and two other friends. Within a year one of the friends, William Morgan, suggested adding to their agenda of study and piety a more public program of social service, such as schooling orphans and visiting prisoners. This program of social concern was visible in the town and earned the group a variety of nicknames, including "Godly Club," "Holy Club," and "Supererogation Men." At this point Wesley's Arminian theology was viewed by some critics, especially Calvinists, as a "new method" of doing theology, and combined with his living strictly by method and rule (there was a method for everything from reading to visiting), his followers became known as "Methodists." This name became fixed on them by the publication of a descriptive pamphlet, *The Oxford Methodists,* in early 1733.

By the following year the Methodists numbered about four dozen (including Benjamin Ingham and GEORGE WHITEFIELD), in a network of small groups throughout several colleges of the university. At least one associated group met in the town and was led by a woman, Miss Potter. The groups took their pattern of life and thought from the small group of six or eight students that met with John Wesley. This structure of small groups, with subdivisions into even smaller bands, follows the pattern set by his father's religious society at Epworth at the turn of the century and prefigures the basic pattern of Methodist organization later.

Wesley's sermons and other writings from this period illustrate his own theological journey, strongly grounded in his Anglican background but influenced by the teachings of the Early Church, the thinking of the Puritans, the discipline of the late medieval and English Pietists (see PIETISM), and the introspection of the mystics. His voracious reading during this period set the pattern for his subsequent theological development; a large proportion of works that he quotes during his later years come from works that he read at Oxford. Some of his distinctive theological ideas, such as prevenient GRACE and Christian perfection (see SANCTIFICATION), have their roots in his thinking and writing during this period. Given the similarities between the organization, theology, and mission of the Oxford Methodists and the characteristics of his later movement, it is not surprising that, in his later historical reflections on the movement, Wesley referred to this Oxford period as "the first rise of METHODISM."

Georgia

In 1732 Wesley, like his father Samuel earlier, had become a corresponding member of the SOCIETY FOR PROMOTING CHRISTIAN KNOWLEDGE. When his father died in 1735, John answered the Society's invitation to become a volunteer missionary to the new North American colony of Georgia, recently founded by his father's friend, colonel James Oglethorpe. Subsequently assigned by the Georgia Trustees and supported by the SOCIETY FOR THE PROPAGATION OF THE GOSPEL, Wesley became parish priest of Savannah, where he served with some limited success. Attendance at Morning Prayers and Communion increased during his tenure, which was marked by a strict adherence to the rubrics of the church. While serving the diverse membership of his parish he also sharpened his language skills in German, Italian, French, and Spanish. In 1737 he published in Charleston *A Collection of Psalms and Hymns,* the first English hymn book printed in America.

In April 1736 Wesley discovered from one of his fellow missionaries, Benjamin Ingham, that a small religious society was meeting in Savannah, having begun the previous summer under the leadership of the parish clerk, Robert Hows. Although they agreed to support the work of that group, such assistance did not begin until half a year later. In the meantime, in June 1737, Wesley himself began a small society in Frederica along Methodist lines (meeting extracurricular to the church services). Combined with his subsequent association with the growing Savannah religious society, Wesley looked back on this period as "the second rise of Methodism."

Very early in his Georgia venture, Wesley fell in love with Sophey Hopkey, eighteen-year-old niece of the chief magistrate, Thomas Causton. Wesley's High Church inclinations, combined with an inept courtship of Sophey, served to sharpen the edge of his criticism of Causton and Oglethorpe for mismanagement. Accusations flew in both directions. The magistrate finally seated a biased grand jury that indicted Wesley on ten trumped-up charges that led to his hasty departure from Georgia in 1737.

England

Back in ENGLAND, Wesley reported his Georgia experience to the trustees of the colony. He resumed his activities within the religious society movement, especially in London and Oxford. He also continued to pursue his spiritual search for assurance of SALVATION, which had been spurred by his acquaintance with the German Pietists in Georgia, especially August Hermann Spangenberg. His quest was heightened in London by his friendship with a Moravian, Peter Böhler (see MORAVIAN CHURCH), with whom he formed a society in Fetter Lane in May 1738, an event that he later called the "third rise of Methodism." Although he was indeed present on that occasion, in his recounting of the events he tended to portray himself as having a more central role than is evident from other accounts. Nevertheless, with Böhler's departure from London, Wesley soon assumed more of a leadership role within the group.

On Pentecost Sunday of that year, John's brother Charles had an experience of the assurance of faith that the Moravians had been emphasizing as prerequisite to salvation or calling oneself Christian. Charles characterized the moment as causing a "strange palpitation of heart." Three days later, on May 24, John Wesley had a similar experience in a society meeting in Aldersgate Street. In his journal account of the event he claimed that his "heart was strangely warmed" and that he felt "an assurance that Christ had died for me." He then adopted the Moravian stance of saying that he was now a Christian, "justified by FAITH alone," whereas previously he had been trusting in his own righteousness. Although he had been preaching "salvation by faith" since March 1738 at Peter Böhler's suggestion, his PREACHING now took on a new sense of confidence. Little changed in the response to his ministry, however, until a self-proclaimed "new era" in his life began the following year. In response to George Whitefield's suggestion, he started preaching this theology of "faith alone" and "free grace" in the out-of-doors at Bristol in April 1739 to thousands of people at a time. Their positive reaction to this message, seen by him as the action of the Holy Spirit, verified his own experience and stance.

For the next several years Wesley tested and rejected many of the Moravian assumptions that had led him to see faith as the only requirement for salvation. His maturing theology embraced the necessity of both faith and ("in some sense") good works, both undergirded by a pervasive theology of grace. His emphasis on free grace, along with his espousal of the Arminian emphasis on free will, led him also to challenge directly the teaching of the "eternal decrees" (PREDESTINATION) espoused by George Whitefield and other Calvinists (see CALVINISM).

Wesleyan Revival

The Methodist revival was part of a larger "evangelical revival," in America often called the Great Awakening (see AWAKENINGS). Not all Methodists were Wesleyans; some of his early friends did not stay within his movement. Whitefield's Calvinist leanings, for instance, led him to associate with Lady Huntingdon's movement, a separate parallel Calvinist Methodist revival. Until the mid-1740s, in fact, Whitefield was the main target of most anti-Methodist literature, his notoriety growing from his exuberant preaching style. Although Wesley's preaching could not match the oratorical mastery of Whitefield, his preaching in the out-of-doors often attracted thousands of listeners. His style was apparently devoid of the bombast one might expect from an evangelist: one eyewitness even observed that Wesley might be mistaken for a talking marble statue if he had not moved one hand to turn the pages of his sermon. However, like JONATHAN EDWARDS, whose writings influenced Wesley, the content of his message moved his listeners far beyond the manner of his preaching.

The spread of the Wesleyan revival entailed in part the amalgamation of several local REVIVALS. The increasing organization of the movement beginning in the 1740s resulted from not only the wide traveling of the Wesley brothers but also the networking of local revivals, often started and led by lay preachers who wanted to associate with the Wesleyans. By the 1760s the movement had attracted over 20,000 members, and the organization had developed a local and national structure that required annual meetings (conferences) and printed handbooks of doctrine and discipline (minutes). John viewed this movement as a manifestation of divine providence and asserted that God had raised up the Methodist preachers "to reform the nation, especially the Church, and to spread Scriptural holiness across the land."

Doctrine and Discipline

Wesley felt that the proper development of the United Societies of the People Called Methodists depended on uniformity of DOCTRINE and disciplined Christian living (see CHURCH DISCIPLINE). To these ends he called the preachers together for annual conferences to promote doctrinal integrity and uniform practices. The published minutes of these meetings began to provide the handbook of Methodist thought and organization. Although the only requirement for joining a Methodist society was the desire "to flee from the wrath to come and [to be] saved from sin," Wesley's "General Rules" outlined the specific ways the members should demonstrate their desire for salvation, by (1) doing all the good they could, (2) avoiding evil of every kind (the main ones listed), and (3) attending to the means of grace. Quarterly examinations of members, with the award of "class tickets" to those who passed muster, enforced these rules. Largely because of this strict discipline, the Methodist movement in England never grew very fast during the eighteenth century. They were a noticeable but small minority: the 72,000 British members at the time of Wesley's death represented less than one percent of the population.

Unlike Whitefield, Wesley spent as much time organizing his followers into societies as he did preaching to the masses, so that the people would have spiritual fellowship and nurture, and not become "a rope of sand." The LAITY provided much of the leadership for the societies: preachers, class leaders, band leaders, stewards, trustees, visitors of the sick. For these he not only developed rules and methods for their groups, but also furnished educational and devotional publications for their edification. Wesley published over four hundred books and pamphlets for his people, including a fifty-volume *Christian Library* with abridgements and extracts of what he thought were the most important works of divinity in the history of Christian thought. His eight volumes of published sermons (1787–1788) were largely written treatises on Christian theology, nurture, and edification rather than transcripts of his more anecdotal style preaching; Sir Walter Scott remembered Wesley's preaching for the stories. His collected *Works* (1772–1774) constituted thirty-two volumes and included some abridgements of other authors. He also published textbooks for history, science, logic, languages, classics, and other subjects that he thought a well-furnished mind should master. The school he guided at Kingswood, near Bristol, provided a curriculum for children and a course of "academical learning" that he thought surpassed the quality of an Oxford or Cambridge baccalaureate degree.

Although most elements of Wesley's movement were intentionally designed to renew the CHURCH OF ENGLAND, these same developments gave the Methodists a sense of distinctive self-identification that eventually led to their separation from the church after Wesley's death. During his lifetime he constantly reiterated his intention "not to separate," but many people, including his brother Charles, read his actions as spelling *de facto* separation by the 1780s. Since mid-century the movement had spread into SCOTLAND, IRE-

LAND, and the American colonies. With the revolt of the colonies and the return to England of the Anglican clergy, Wesley ordained his own leaders to provide sacramental services and episcopal leadership for the American Methodists who became organized into a separate church, the Methodist Episcopal Church. He refused to ordain Methodist preachers in countries where the Church of England persisted.

The Methodist "connection," organized around those preachers "in connection with" John Wesley, was an identifiable phenomenon on the religious scene in the early 1740s. Their detractors included not only those, such as Calvinists and Moravians, who disagreed with some of their theology, but also satirical writers whose portrayals of Wesley's ideas and actions fed on popular distrust of religious enthusiasm and fanaticism. The shortcomings of his private life largely escaped public notice, however, especially his aborted engagement to Grace Murray in 1749 (who his brother Charles married to one of his preachers while John was out of the country), and his failed marriage to a wealthy London widow, Mary Vazeille, in 1752 (who left him after a few years out of jealousy, spite, and perhaps loneliness). His attention was always directed to the work of renewing the church to which he saw God directing him.

Practical Theology

Wesley's theology was forged in the midst of controversy and tempered by his understanding and experience of "the Scripture way of salvation." Although his theological pilgrimage took him through several spheres of influence, including Pietism, Puritanism, mysticism, and the early church, his basic theological framework persistently reflected his Church of England heritage. His attempt to hold divergent positions in tension produced a "mediating" theology, although his occasional forays into controversy led him at times to stress one or another side against a position leaning to the other side of the spectrum. Taking his mature theology as a whole, he can be seen as holding to both sacramentalism and EVANGELISM, free will and free grace, faith and good works, without any inconsistency in his stance. Although he was probably not as unchanging through his lifetime as he sometimes claimed, there is probably more continuity between the young and the old Mr. Wesley than has usually been noticed.

His preaching centered upon what he termed "the three grand scriptural doctrines—original sin, JUSTIFICATION by faith, and holiness consequent thereon." This formulation occasionally varied in its terminology, such as one instance when he refers to the main doctrines of Methodism as (1) repentance, which he called the "porch of religion"; (2) justification by grace through faith, the "door of religion"; and (3) sanctification or holiness, "religion itself." The possibility of experiencing entire sanctification, or Christian perfection, in this lifetime was an essential Wesleyan doctrine that prevented most clergy of the Established Church from joining his revival. This also distinguished him from the generality of Lutherans (see LUTHERANISM) and many Calvinists. His major theological detractors never seemed to get beyond the terminology to hear his explanation that this doctrine did not assert "perfectionism" or "works-righteousness" but simply claimed as a gift the gracious possibility in this lifetime of loving God and neighbor to the fullest. Additionally, Wesley's conviction that one could know an assurance of salvation (both forgiveness or justification, and holiness or sanctification) created tension with the clergy, even though it was a lifelong emphasis that shaped his own spiritual pilgrimage. Exaggerated perversions of his doctrines by his own preachers, such as the perfectionists Thomas Maxfield and John Bell, did not help his cause.

Wesley's use of uneducated lay preachers to supply the pulpits of his connection led him to require that they preach "no other doctrines" than those contained in his collection of published sermons and his commentary on the New Testament. These doctrines, distinctively evangelical but in accord with the Church of England standards of doctrine (THIRTY-NINE ARTICLES, BOOK OF COMMON PRAYER, and Book of Homilies), were also impressed on the people's spirits through hundreds of popular hymns written and published by the Wesley brothers (see HYMNS AND HYMNALS). The tendency of many evangelical preachers to focus entirely on CONVERSION led Wesley to criticize the popular "gospel preacher," so-called, whom he saw as but "a pert, self-sufficient animal, that has neither sense nor grace." Their habit, he pointed out, was simply to "bawl out something about Christ, or his blood, or justification by faith, and his hearers cry out, 'What a fine Gospel sermon!' " His criticism was grounded in a firm conviction that in overemphasizing grace, these preachers neglected the obligations of the law, which the grace of God in Christ has not totally obliterated but rather has helped us to fulfill. In this sense Wesley always linked justification with sanctification, faith and good works, and love of God and love of neighbor as prerequisites for the Christian life.

Christian practice typically outweighed doctrinal ORTHODOXY, both in Wesley's thought and in the Methodist ethos. True religion was summed up in the Great Commandment to love God and neighbor. Wesley felt strongly that the gospel was contrary to solitary religion, especially as exemplified in mysticism. For Wesley there is no true holiness but social holiness, manifest in the fellowship of believers. An important part of the Christian life within the committed community was the expression of a faith that works through love. He taught that works of piety and works of mercy were both necessary for the Christian and that both represented "means of grace" or channels of God's active presence and power.

Mission

On this theological base Wesley developed an array of programs to assist his people. He organized schools for both girls and boys, most prominent that at Kingswood, which still functions. At his preaching houses in London, Bristol, and Newcastle he began medical clinics for the indigent. Supported by donors with means, he provided loan funds for small business ventures and furnished subsidized housing for widows and children. He organized a system of pension funds for "tired and worn out preachers, their widows and children." For the poor of his societies he collected clothes, food, and money.

The focus of Wesley's mission remained primarily on the British Isles. When asked by THOMAS COKE in the 1780s to support a mission to the West Indies, Wesley responded that there was more to do at home than they could handle at the moment and that there was no apparent call from God in that direction. The major exception to Wesley's focus on the British work was his interest in America. In response to a request from New York he began sending preachers to the New World in 1769. For a few years he thought seriously about returning to the colonies himself to supervise the work there. Eventually the leadership of Thomas Rankin and FRANCIS ASBURY convinced him that his personal presence was not needed. The outbreak of the Revolution, which he came to deplore, sealed his inclination to stay in England. His continuing interest in and support of the work in America, providing a plan for a separate organization there after the Peace of Paris, resulted in a significant Wesleyan stamp on the continuing mission of Methodism in the new UNITED STATES.

Wesley's published *Journal* is a monument to and apologia for Methodism rather than a simple autobiography. Its pages are filled with a description of the developing organization, theology, and mission of Methodism. It is an unabashed propaganda piece for his movement, filled with accounts of pious lives and holy deaths, earthly enemies and divine retribution. Through it all, however, his personal attributes shine forth, at times somewhat exaggerated by his own pen in spite of his aversion to self-aggrandizement. The reader can see in these pages both the evolution of the movement and the growth of Wesley's own spiritual

and theological perspective, in spite of his protests of unchanging constancy. His own habit of broad reading reflects his wide range of interests from theology to poetry, science to philosophy, travel to novels, classics to best-sellers. He became of model of Christian activity; or, as one contemporary Swedish observer, Prof. J. H. Liden, noted, "He is the personification of piety."

Nevertheless, Wesley was the target of persistent attack, especially during the first generation of the Methodist revival. He did, however, outlive most of his early detractors and became somewhat of a respected phenomenon of human and spiritual energy in his old age. For over half a century he traveled the countryside for an estimated quarter million miles, preaching over 40,000 times, while publishing over 400 items. He was not afraid to challenge government explanations of poverty; he was not slow to attack English support of the slave trade. One of his last letters was to the young WILLIAM WILBERFORCE, M.P., asking him to move Parliament toward abolishing that "vile abomination," SLAVERY in America (see SLAVERY, ABOLITION OF).

Person

In his mature years Wesley became, as one obituary noted, the most famous private person in England. More than one observer during his lifetime noted a "venerableness" in his manner that was heightened in his later years. From age forty onward, he was the subject of many portrait painters, including several Fellows of Royal Academy, such as Sir Joshua Reynolds, Nathaniel Hone, and William Hamilton. Pottery busts of him were crested by Staffordshire craftsmen Enoch Wood and Josiah Wedgewood. One contemporary, Thomas Haweis, described Wesley as "of the inferior size, his visage marked with intelligence, singularly neat and plain in his dress; a little cast in his eye, observable on particular occasions; upright, graceful, and remarkably active." From an early age he saw himself as a "brand plucked out of the fire," but always disclaimed any sense of special destiny. He has often been viewed as an autocratic leader, but his friends recognized his ability to listen. One colleague noted that Wesley possessed a fund of history and anecdote that "rendered his company as entertaining as instructive."

Wesley's physical stature was diminutive: height five foot three inches and weight about fourteen stone (about 126 pounds). As a preacher, he was outshined by George Whitefield; as a hymn-writer, he was surpassed by his brother Charles. As a theologian, he was more synthetic than original; as an organizer, he shaped a movement that never included even one percent of the population of his homeland. Nevertheless, the energy that he exhibited well into his eighties, as well as the total impact of his person and message on Great Britain, has given rise to a reputation that belies his diminutive physique and often portrays his influence in nearly epic proportions.

Wesley died in his eighty-eighth year. To avoid a public commotion, his body was buried privately at 5:00 A.M. on the morning of his public funeral service. His obituary in the *Gentleman's Magazine* (1791) noted that he was "one of the few characters who outlived enmity and prejudice, and received, in his latter years, every mark of respect from every denomination," and added that "he must be considered as one of the most extraordinary characters this or any age every produced."

See also Anglicanism; Arminianism; Methodism, England; Methodism, North America; Wesleyan Church; Wesleyan Holiness Movement; Wesleyanism

References and Further Reading

Primary Source:

Wesley, John. *The Bicentennial Edition of the Works of John Wesley*. 35 vols. Nashville, TN: Abingdon Press, 1976–.

Secondary Sources:

Baker, Frank. *John Wesley and the Church of England*. London: Epworth, 2000.
———. *A Union Catalogue of the Publications of John and Charles Wesley*. Stone Mountain, GA: Zimmerman, 1991.
Campbell, Ted A. *John Wesley and Christian Antiquity; Religious Vision and Cultural Change*. Nashville, TN: Abingdon Press, 1991.
Collins, Kenneth J. *The Scripture Way of Salvation; The Heart of John Wesley's Theology*. Nashville, TN: Abingdon Press, 1997.
Heitzenrater, Richard P. *Wesley and the People Called Methodists*. Nashville, TN: Abingdon Press, 1995.
———. *The Elusive Mr. Wesley*. 2d edition. Nashville, TN: Abingdon Press, 2003.
Jennings, Theodore W. *Good News to the Poor: John Wesley's Evangelical Ethics*. Nashville, TN: Abingdon Press, 1990.
Jones, Scott J. *John Wesley's Conception and Use of Scripture*. Nashville, TN: Kingswood, 1995.
Maddox, Randy L. *Responsible Grace; John Wesley's Practical Theology*. Nashville, TN: Kingswood, 1994.
Outler, Albert O. *John Wesley*. Oxford: Oxford University Press, 1964.
———. *Theology in the Wesleyan Spirit*. Nashville, TN: Tidings, 1975.
Rack, Henry, *Reasonable Enthusiast: John Wesley and the Rise of Methodism*. 3rd ed. London: Epworth, 2002.
Weber, Theodore R. *Politics in the Order of Salvation: New Directions in Wesleyan Political Ethics*. Nashville, TN: Kingswood, 2001.

RICHARD HEITZENRATER

WESLEYAN CHURCH

The Wesleyan Church originated in a 1968 merger of the Wesleyan Methodist Church of America and the Pilgrim Holiness Church. Both the antecedent bodies had been major participants in the nineteenth-century holiness revival movement within the Protestant churches. This common history in the HOLINESS MOVEMENT became the focus of the union. The church is categorized within Protestantism as a Wesleyan/Holiness denomination (see WESLEYAN HOLINESS MOVEMENT).

The failure of METHODISM to respond favorably to the call of abolitionist pastors Orange Scott, Luther Lee, and others for the church to acknowledge the moral evil of SLAVERY and support the reformers' call for its immediate end led to the formation of the Wesleyan Methodist denomination in 1843 (see SLAVERY, ABOLITION OF). Many Presbyterian, Congregational, and Quaker abolitionists also joined the new Methodist body. After the CIVIL WAR many of the Wesleyan Methodist reformers returned to the Methodist Episcopal Church. Others remained with the newer Methodist body and turned their energies and resources more toward EVANGELISM and promotion of Christian holiness and less to continuing reform issues such as equality of the sexes, especially the ordination of WOMEN CLERGY, and prohibition.

When former Methodist Episcopal pastor Martin Wells Knapp and Quaker evangelist Seth Cook Rees founded the Apostolic Holiness Union and Prayer League in 1897, a majority of its members, like the Wesleyan Methodists before them, had deep roots in traditional Methodism. By the end of the century, however, the original nondenominational Union and Prayer League constituents consisted of significant numbers not only of members of Methodist and other established churches, but also of large numbers of nonchurched converts that the movement had garnered from its vigorous revivalism in the UNITED STATES and CANADA and its mission stations around the world. The chief loyalty of these constituents was more to the Holiness movement than to any of the established denominations. Eventually the Pilgrim Holiness Church, as the Union finally became known, became one of a number of new denominations, which provided institutional organization to the Wesleyan/Holiness revival at the turn of the twentieth century (see CHURCH OF GOD, ANDERSON, INDIANA; CHURCH OF THE NAZARENE; Free Methodist Church; BRETHREN IN CHRIST; SALVATION ARMY). Knapp and Rees had been closely associated with A. B. Simpson of the CHRISTIAN AND MISSIONARY ALLIANCE, and consequently had incorporated his doctrines of divine healing and premillennialism into their Wesleyan/Arminian theology.

The Wesleyan Church emphasizes CONVERSION, holiness of heart and life, belief in divine healing, and the imminent return of Jesus Christ, but does not explicitly define a millennial position. The Wesleyan Church's membership in the Christian Holiness Partnership (formerly the Christian Holiness Association) continues the church's commitment to the Wesleyan/Holiness movement's doctrinal and experiential understanding of Christian Perfection (see SANCTIFICATION). The Wesleyan Church's membership in the WORLD METHODIST COUNCIL acknowledges its Protestant ORTHODOXY and Wesleyan/Anglican roots. Its membership in the NATIONAL ASSOCIATION OF EVANGELICALS represents its biblical and evangelical stance.

Although Wesleyans share a conservative theological stance with other evangelical churches, the more experientially oriented Wesleyan/Arminian theology creates tensions with other evangelicals on several issues. Their expectations of GRACE with its possibilities for personal and social holiness are too optimistic for many in the Reformed tradition. Furthermore, the Wesleyan/Arminian understanding of the freedom of the human will with its implication for the nature of Christian assurance clashes sharply with the classical understanding of perseverance in the Reformed tradition. This is especially true in the Wesleyan/Holiness churches' relation to the fundamentalist movement (see FUNDAMENTALISM) within EVANGELICALISM. The former's application of theological presuppositions to the life and mission of the church often differ sharply with that of the latter. This may be seen especially in the Wesleyan emphasis on Christian experience, the centrality of the Pentecost event, and the doctrine of the Holy Spirit in salvation history and the life of the church. At this latter point, less obvious differences distinguish Wesleyan/Holiness churches from other evangelicals in the Pentecostal Movement, especially Pentecostal/Holiness churches. The understanding of life in the Spirit of both groups often runs parallel with the other, but Wesleyans' rejection of PENTECOSTALISM's affirmation of glossolalia (or speaking in TONGUES) as the unique sign of the baptism of the Holy Spirit remains the defining difference between the two movements. Wesleyan teaching also has tended to stress the power of the Spirit to produce a holy life, whereas the tendency in Pentecostalism has been to stress the Spirit's power in the spiritual gifts and miracles.

The church has a total membership of 315,000; 129,000 of these are in the United States and Canada. The North American General Conference shares with the Philippine General Conference and the Caribbean Provisional General Conference in maintaining churches, educational institutions, hospitals, and social agencies in more than forty countries.

See also Arminianism; Faith Healing; Friends, Society of; Methodism, North America; Millenarians and Millennialism; Presbyterianism, Congregationalism

References and Further Reading

Caldwell, Wayne E, ed. *Revivalists and Reformers: A History of the Wesleyan Church.* Indianapolis, IN: Wesley Press, 1992.

Dieter, Melvin E. "The Holiness Revival of the Nineteenth Century." In *Studies in Evangelicalism,* no. 1. Metuchen, NJ and London: The Scarecrow Press, 1980, 1995.

Jones, Charles E. "A Guide to the Study of the Holiness Movement." In *ATLA Bibliography Series,* no. 1. Metuchen, NJ: The Scarecrow Press, 1974.

MELVIN E. DIETER

WESLEYAN HOLINESS MOVEMENT

The Wesleyan Holiness Movement rose out of a renewed concern for the promotion of Christian holiness and social righteousness in the revivalism of the early decades of the nineteenth century. METHODISM's doctrine of Christian perfection as taught by JOHN WESLEY became the theological and experiential focus of the movement. It called all Christian believers to consecrate themselves wholly to God and, through FAITH, to seek a second crisis of God's GRACE in their hearts that would cleanse them from their innate bent toward SIN and fill them with a whole-hearted love for God and others by the power of the Holy Spirit. This call to "Christianize Christianity" quickly spread throughout revivalistic Protestantism. Many anticipated a new Pentecostal baptism and dispensation of the Holy Spirit. Toward the end of the century many holiness adherents left their churches to organize new churches and agencies more favorable to the movement's concerns. The continuing growth of these Wesleyan Holiness churches, and other movements rooted in the holiness revival, such as the HIGHER LIFE MOVEMENT, the Pentecostal, and the Charismatic movements, have significantly changed evangelical Protestantism's demographics, theology, and praxis.

History

Through her energetic lay EVANGELISM in parlor meetings, CAMP MEETINGS, and publications throughout the Northeast and Canada, Methodist PHOEBE WORRALL PALMER became the leading voice in the pre–Civil War REVIVALS. By 1839 believers in Congregational, Presbyterian, Baptist, Episcopalian, Quaker, Mennonite, and other churches also professed to be sanctified wholly. Oberlin College's CHARLES G. FINNEY and Asa Mahan accommodated the Methodist movement's

Wesleyan/Arminian understanding of a "second blessing" to their New School CALVINISM and SCOTTISH COMMON SENSE REALISM to form a companion HOLINESS MOVEMENT. In 1867 a group of Methodist pastors under John Inskip gave more organized leadership to the movement. Their National Camp Meeting Association for the Promotion of Holiness garnered thousands of supporters for the hundreds of local holiness associations and the flood of holiness publications that kept the revival flourishing throughout the century.

The Holiness Churches

By the closing decades of the nineteenth century, denominational disciplinary restrictions on holiness CLERGY became more common. In response large numbers of pastors and laypersons who supported the revival joined thousands of its unchurched converts to organize more than a dozen new Wesleyan/Holiness denominations and agencies, including several black denominations, whereas other adherents maintained their membership in the older churches but still supported the movement. Out of a series of realignments and mergers the larger of the holiness organizations and agencies are: the SALVATION ARMY, the CHURCH OF THE NAZARENE, the CHURCH OF GOD (ANDERSON, INDIANA), the WESLEYAN CHURCH, the FREE METHODIST CHURCH, the Evangelical Friends Church, and the BRETHREN IN CHRIST CHURCH. The latter two accommodated the theology and spirituality of the holiness movement revival to their respective Quaker (see FRIENDS, SOCIETY OF) and Anabaptist traditions (see ANABAPTISM) as A. T. Pierson, A. J. Gordon, and A. B. Simpson did to their revivalistic Calvinism. The revival became especially formative in the new Pentecostal and the subsequent Charismatic traditions. In spite of often severe tensions among these children of the revival as they brought the diverse forces of the revival into organized Protestantism, their historic roots in the antecedent ecumenical holiness associations that nurtured and shaped them facilitated their later cooperation in the renewal of twentieth-century EVANGELICALISM. Churches related to the Wesleyan Holiness movement, the Higher Life Movement, and PENTECOSTALISM played a significant role in the organization of the NATIONAL ASSOCIATION OF EVANGELICALS. The Wesleyan Holiness churches continue to cooperate with one another by their participation in the Christian Holiness Partnership and The Wesleyan Theological Society. Most of them also associate with the National Association of Evangelicals and some with the WORLD METHODIST COUNCIL.

Influence of the Movement

The revival not only both expanded and divided the American churches that gave it birth, but significantly influenced the churches of ENGLAND and Europe through the ministry of Robert Pearsall and HANNAH WHITALL SMITH, prominent in the KESWICK MOVEMENT. They inspired the organization of the Keswick (England) Convention for the Promotion of Holiness, which became a center for holiness adherents in both the established and free churches to reinvigorate evangelical mission agencies and student movements around the world. In GERMANY the Wesleyan holiness message revived the old pietistic centers of the REFORMATION churches and the social concerns of the Inner City Movement. Although the Wesleyan Holiness Movement has always been theologically orthodox and conservative, significant segments within it were persistent advocates for some of the more radical changes that came to the fore only much later in Protestantism in general. Two of the earliest holiness churches, the Wesleyan Methodist Church and the Free Methodist Church, wedded their perfectionism to their call for the immediate abolition of slavery (see SLAVERY, ABOLITION OF). The growing significance of the Pentecost event within the movement supported the public ministry and leadership of WOMEN such as FRANCES WILLARD, CATHERINE BOOTH, and black evangelist Amanda Smith, as well as Palmer, more than half a century before established Protestantism accepted such innovations. The movement also challenged Protestantism to reconsider its theologies of spiritual gifts and of divine healing. Its focus on life in the Spirit and personal and social holiness strongly influenced the spirituality of evangelical Protestantism. The hymns and gospel songs of FANNY CROSBY and other composers within the movement constitute a major segment of evangelical hymnody (see HYMNS AND HYMNALS). Wesleyan/Holiness devotional works such as Hannah Whitall Smith's *The Christian's Secret of a Happy Life* and Oswald Chamber's *My Utmost for His Highest* have become classics in Protestantism.

References and Further Reading

Dayton, Donald Wilber. *Discovering an Evangelical Heritage.* New York: Harper and Rowe, 1976.
Dieter, Melvin Easterday. *The Holiness Revival of the Nineteenth Century.* 2nd ed. Lanham, MD: The Scarecrow Press, 1995.
Jones, Charles Edwin. *Guide to the Study of the Holiness Movement.* Metuchen, NJ: The Scarecrow Press, 1974.
Kostlevy, William. *A Guide to the Sources of the Wesleyan Holiness Movement in the United States and Canada.* Metuchen, NJ: The Scarecrow Press, 1994.

Smith, Timothy Lawrence. *Revivalism and Reform in Mid-Nineteenth Century America.* Nashville, TN: Abingdon Press, 1957.

MELVIN E. DIETER

WESLEYANISM

Wesleyanism is the broad term referring to the overall movement that includes most traditions of METHODISM, the WESLEYAN HOLINESS MOVEMENT, and PENTECOSTALISM. Although these traditions represent varying expressions of Wesleyanism, they hold a common heritage in the life, thought, and ministry of JOHN WESLEY (1703–1791).

Although Wesley never saw himself as anything other than a staunch Anglican, he freely incorporated many different influences into his distinctive articulation of Christian faith and practice. In addition to his obvious CHURCH OF ENGLAND heritage, there were strands of inspiration from Eastern Orthodoxy (see ORTHODOXY, EASTERN), Roman Catholicism (see CATHOLICISM, PROTESTANT REACTIONS), MARTIN LUTHER, JOHN CALVIN, JACOBUS ARMINIUS, the Moravians (see MORAVIAN CHURCH), and German PIETISM. That is, Wesleyanism represents a wider range of Christian thought than was found in either the continental reformers or the English reformers. However, this is not to say Wesleyanism is simply an eclectic amalgamation of all other traditions. It is, rather, a distinct expression of Protestant EVANGELICALISM that carries certain identifying features. Wesley was willing to glean from all Christian traditions those elements of their doctrines that he understood to be clearly in keeping with scriptural teaching, but never did he see himself as adopting any position that was contrary to official CHURCH OF ENGLAND doctrine.

It is for these reasons that Wesleyanism has sometimes been rejected by a wide range of groups on the one hand, while simultaneously being embraced by an equally wide range of other groups on the other hand. It also helps to explain why there are so many different contemporary expressions of Wesleyanism, ranging from liberal sociopolitical action to holiness revivalism to Pentecostalism. Each lays valid claim to its Wesleyan heritage, although each tends to emphasize different aspects of that heritage. In spite of often contrary appearances, there is a common doctrinal core of Wesleyanism that eventually gave rise to all these expressions.

Basis of Authority

Wesleyan faith and practice are first of all grounded on a foundation of AUTHORITY known as the Wesleyan Quadrilateral. Wesley used this four-point filter to ensure that his theological understandings were thoroughly orthodox. The quadrilateral was composed of scripture, tradition, reason, and experience.

Scripture was the first and primary source of authority. Any doctrinal concept judged to be contrary to scripture in any way was immediately rejected. In spite of his Oxford education and his wide breadth of reading, Wesley considered himself a man of one book. He immersed himself in the BIBLE as the unquestioned source of divine authority. He believed the scriptures were to be read prayerfully and under the guidance of the Holy Spirit. He strove to interpret all passages within their context and in their simplest and most obvious sense, unless this approach led to absurd or self-contradictory conclusions. If a theological concept passed the test of scripture, then it was subjected to the remaining points of the quadrilateral.

The filter of TRADITION referred primarily to the first few centuries of the Christian church, which Wesley held in very high regard. He believed the historical proximity of the Early Church Fathers to the New Testament church gave them the most accurate understanding of the pure Christian faith. He also held strongly to his own Anglican heritage, which he believed to be the best representation of scriptural Christianity.

Wesley was a man of his time, and that time was the Age of Reason. He believed orthodox doctrine would always be supported by sound reason. He was aware that reason taken to its extreme was detrimental to religion, but he did not believe reason and religion were inherently incompatible. In fact, he went so far as to assert that religion void of reason was not true religion at all. He insisted that because God is a God of order and logic, religious dogma and practice must pass the scrutiny of sound reasoning.

Wesley's emphasis on reason was, however, balanced out by his emphasis on experience. They were the two sides of the same coin, each dependent on the other. Reason makes DOCTRINE lucid and guards it from abuse, but experience gives doctrine meaning and vitality. His doctrines of assurance, holiness, and lay preachers serve as examples of some of his understandings that were profoundly affected by his willingness to let experience inform reason. Wesley sought to maintain a fine balance between these two points of his quadrilateral.

Concept of Sin

The distinction between SIN as an inherited condition and sin as a personal act is kept clearly in focus in Wesleyan theology. Wesley followed the traditional Christian view that the Fall of Adam had placed within humanity an inherently corrupted nature. He was not overly concerned with exactly how this sinful nature is "inherited" or spread throughout the human family; he simply accepted its presence as fact. Being the practical theologian that he was, he was more interested in the effects of original sin than its mode of transmission. Like Augustine and Calvin before him, Wesley too understood the corruption of inherited sin in terms of total depravity. He saw that it is systemic and universal, affecting every facet of humanity's being. It instilled within humanity an abnormal egocentrism that manifests itself as an irresistible inclination against the Creator and toward evil.

Although Wesley understood that original or inherited sin was the root of humanity's problems, he also understood that it takes personal acts of sin to give shape to the true face of evil in the world. Original sin in itself does not actually cause hatred, murder, and greed. These and other sins are caused by specific actions and attitudes of people as they give expression to their inherent moral depravity. For Wesley the real problem of sin revolves around the willful decisions of people to commit individual acts of sin. He therefore defined sin as any deliberate violation of God's known law.

The Wesleyan definition of sin is generally more restrictive than the standard Reformed definition. Wesley agreed that the natural limitations of fallen humanity are examples of humanity's inability to live up to the Adamic Law of original perfection. However, he disagreed that these limitations are truly sin. Because of the systemic effects of the Fall on humanity, it is impossible for any post-Fall person to live up to the standard of perfection in which Adam was first created. However, because this state of imperfection is attributed to an inherited condition rather than a personal choice, Wesley could not reconcile himself to see this as sin in the full biblical sense. He believed the only sins for which an individual is held accountable before God are "voluntary sins" (to use his term). That is, conscious awareness and willful intent must be involved for an act or omission to be properly called sin.

Wesley did not see unintentional sins or "involuntary sins" in the same light as voluntary sins. They may be called sin in the technical sense of violating God's law, but because they lack willful intent Wesley did not believe they fulfilled the usual scriptural definition of sin.

Wesley's view of sin is sometimes criticized as being dismissive of the full reality and responsibility of sin. Nevertheless, even though Wesley saw unintentional sin quite differently than intentional sin, he still took it very seriously. He insisted that it still requires the atoning work of Christ. The difference is in how the ATONEMENT of Christ is applied. Wesley believed unintentional sins need divine mercy and intercession, but not necessarily forgiveness because there is no personal culpability attached to them.

Wesleyanism teaches that humanity enjoyed a perfect beginning and an original state of holiness. However, through the Fall of Adam the world was subjected to the universal domination of sin and the total corruption of the human race. Along with Augustinianism and CALVINISM, Wesleyanism takes a pessimistic view of humanity in its fallen state. Wesleyanism does not stop there, however, because it takes an optimistic view of God's response of GRACE.

Grace and Free Will

Wesleyanism affirms that humanity's only deliverance from sin comes from God's grace. Grace is the unmerited mercy that God grants to people. Prevenient grace refers specifically to the grace that God extends even before people ask for it. The Wesleyan understanding of prevenient grace centers on two dimensions—forgiveness and enabling.

Wesley believed God's prevenient grace provided for the forgiveness of original sin. Wesley accepted the prevailing view that the entire human race bore the guilt of Adam's sin. However, he believed this guilt was universally pardoned through God's prevenient grace. Individuals would still need to seek God's forgiveness for their personal acts of sin, but they would not need to seek forgiveness for the guilt associated with original sin. This was already gone by God's mercy. The debilitating effects of the Fall remained, but the guilt associated with it was cancelled.

The enabling aspect of prevenient grace is seen in the fact that, despite its fallen condition, humanity is now enabled by God to recognize its fallen state and to turn toward God. Wesley maintained that through God's act of prevenient grace human nature was partially renewed to the extent that individuals could hear and respond to God's call. This meant that God had enabled fallen humanity to grasp basic spiritual concepts, to respond to God, and to make a willful choice for or against God.

Wesley accepted the traditional view that sin's introduction into the human experience had rendered the human heart incapable in itself of either knowing or responding to God. He agreed with Augustine's teaching that the Fall had reduced all of humanity to a hopeless state of sin. So thorough was this corruption that humans could not even be aware of God's existence, let alone take an initial step toward God.

This understanding of total depravity, however, presented a logical dilemma. If humanity was so hopelessly lost, how could one account for the fact that some actually do turn to God and are saved? Actually, the dilemma was not that there is a way of SALVATION, but that salvation is only realized by some rather than all. If God had chosen to leave humanity in its sin, then all would remain lost. Likewise, if God had chosen to exercise divine sovereignty over the power of evil by saving the human race, then all would be saved, although Wesley, like Augustine, recognized that neither of these scenarios was the case. Instead, only some are saved and only some are lost. Augustine's solution to this problem was the doctrine of PREDESTINATION. In this he was able to affirm that some are saved while also upholding the cardinal doctrines of total depravity and divine sovereignty.

Wesley also upheld the doctrines of total depravity and divine sovereignty, but he did not believe this led inevitably to a doctrine of predestination. Rather, he looked to the thought of Arminius to bring understanding to the apparent conflict between the doctrines of total depravity and divine sovereignty. The Arminian view of predestination was not that God had chosen some individuals for salvation, but that God had predetermined that all who accept Christ would be saved. What God predestined was the means of salvation, not individual destinies. Wesley embraced the Arminian view that predestination of individuals existed only in the sense that God could foresee who would and would not believe.

Wesley's adherence to the Arminian understanding of predestination meant that he also held an Arminian view of free will. He accepted that fallen humanity had lost the capacity to choose righteousness. After the Fall humanity was capable of choosing only from the options of evil. Choices for good were beyond reach. However, Wesley's ARMINIANISM instilled within him the conviction that the restoration of free will was one of the chief benefits of God's prevenient grace. As an act of divine sovereignty God had restored to humanity the freedom to choose between good and evil, even though the corrupted human nature was still bent toward evil.

Implicit within the Arminian Wesleyan concept of predestination is the conviction that individuals can choose to move between states of belief and unbelief. In other words believers can choose to become unbelievers and thus forfeit their salvation. Wesley rejected the doctrine of perseverance of the saints as taught by Calvin. Wesleyanism does not teach that one can "lose" salvation through some unknown sin, or even a specific act of known sin, although Wesleyanism does teach that salvation can be forfeited through conscious and deliberate abandonment of faith in Christ.

The Wesleyan concepts of a partially restored human nature and free will often led to charges of Pelagianism. Wesleyanism, like Arminianism before it, has always denied this charge. Arminian Wesleyanism affirms the Augustinian understanding of divine sovereignty, original sin, and total depravity. However, it rejects the conclusion that these doctrines must result in a doctrine of individual predestination. In that sense Wesleyanism may fairly be identified as semi-Augustinian. Likewise, Arminian Wesleyanism embraces the Pelagian regard for free will, but utterly rejects the Pelagian denial of original sin. Therefore, because Wesleyanism simultaneously embraces divine sovereignty, human depravity, and human free will, it may accurately be stated that Wesleyanism in neither purely Augustinian nor Pelagian, but is in fact both semi-Augustinian and semi-Pelagian. Wesleyans do not see this as a contradiction, but as a biblical and logical balance between two extremes.

The Wesleyan concept of Christian faith and experience is rooted in its understanding of God's grace. It is this high regard for grace that allows Wesleyanism to affirm without any sense of incongruence that (1) humanity is lost in sin, (2) humanity is absolutely powerless to save itself in any way, and (3) through the gift of prevenient grace human beings are awakened to God's presence and enabled to respond.

Christian Conversion

Wesleyanism views the overall experience of Christian CONVERSION in two categories: what happens *to* the believer and what happens *in* the believer—that is, justification and regeneration. When an individual responds to God's grace by placing faith in the atoning work of Christ and repenting of sin, God extends forgiveness. The new believer is no longer judged by God as guilty of sins committed, but now stands forgiven. Therefore, guilt is removed and the consequences of judgment withdrawn. This is God's gift of grace to the believer; however, Wesleyanism believes there is more to conversion than mere forgiveness. There is also regeneration, or new birth. The new believer is made new in the image of Christ. Therefore, the new believer is not just viewed differently by God, the believer actually is different. This is the Wesleyan understanding of imparted righteousness.

Wesley did not believe the Reformed teaching of imputed righteousness went far enough. He believed in a type of imputed righteousness, but not in the same way as the reformers. He granted that human salvation was made possible through Christ's righteousness, but he denied that Christ's righteousness was merely placed over the new believer. He was not satisfied with the notion that God called the new believer righteous when in fact God knew the believer was not righteous. Wesley believed God viewed the believer as righteous because God had actually made the believer righteous. Whereas justification speaks of a relative change, regeneration speaks of a real change.

This is the sense in which Wesleyanism affirms that the righteousness of Christ is both imputed and imparted in the new believer.

Wesley thought of humanity in three states that he identified as the natural, the legal, and the evangelical. Those who live with no regard to God are in the natural state. Individuals in this state are characterized by their apathy toward God. They may hate God, deny God, or simply ignore God. The legal state refers to those who acknowledge God and have some sense of their need for God. They often desire to live for God, but have not yet realized the need to trust Christ alone for forgiveness and salvation. The evangelical state includes those who have consciously turned to Christ and now belong to him in the full sense.

The early Wesley, under the influence of Peter Bohler, did not believe saving faith existed in degrees. One either did or did not have it. However, the post-Aldersgate Wesley came to see that faith does sometimes come in degrees. He saw this most clearly in the distinction between those in the legal state and those in the evangelical state. He expressed this by indicating that those in the legal state had the faith of a servant, whereas those in the evangelical state possessed the faith of a son. Those in the natural state are unconverted. Those in the legal state may be said to be in the process of conversion. Those in the evangelical state have been fully converted.

Assurance

One of the most important features of Wesley's own spiritual life and one of his greatest contributions to eighteenth-century Christianity was his doctrine of assurance. By assurance he meant the confirmation of the Holy Spirit to the believer of God's acceptance. This sense of assurance comes both directly and indirectly.

Direct assurance is the inaudible communication from the Holy Spirit to the heart of the believer. It is the inner peace that brings confidence of one's acceptance before God. The idea of such intimacy with the Holy Spirit was strongly resisted by most people of Wesley's day. It was widely believed that such personal encounters with the Holy Spirit had ended with the New Testament era. Furthermore, if such experiences were promoted, it was feared that all manner of abuses and excesses would quickly follow. This was the charge of "enthusiasm" that was frequently levied against the early Wesleyans. Although this term was used to imply religious fanaticism or extremism, Wesley maintained that assurance of salvation should be a normal feature of the Christian life. He saw it as neither extraordinary nor extremist, but completely ordinary and biblical.

Indirect assurance comes through practical evidence and rational deductions that the believer is able to objectively evaluate. For Wesley the Fruit of the Spirit (Galatians 5:22–23) was one of the most reliable sources of indirect assurance. Others included corporate worship, private prayers, scripture reading, and the general presence of Christian qualities in daily life. The more rationalistic nature of indirect assurance rendered it much more palatable to the Christian establishment.

Wesley was passionate about the doctrine of Christian assurance. This stemmed in many ways from his own personal struggles for assurance in his earlier life. Just as the early Wesley thought there could be no degrees of faith, so he also thought there could be no degrees of assurance. He desperately longed for the assurance of God's acceptance, but he was always left disappointed and frustrated because of his faulty concept of assurance. His early expectations were unrealistic, and therefore self-defeating. However, these expectations changed after Aldersgate and Wesley came to see fluctuations in one's sense of assurance as a normal feature of spiritual development. As his understanding of the work of the Holy Spirit matured he was able to gain perspective and insight. He then came to believe that a healthy understanding of assurance was essential to spiritual vitality. So strong was his passion for this doctrine that he was convinced that the promotion of its revival was one of the primary reasons why God had raised up the Wesleyan movement.

Sanctification

The doctrine of SANCTIFICATION, or holiness, is a theological hallmark of Wesleyanism. Wesley saw the sanctification of believers as God's ultimate purpose in salvation. This means not only forgiving sins, but releasing people from the power of sin. God's plan is to free people from sin and thereby restore them to the state of fellowship with God that they were originally created to enjoy.

The specific point at which Wesley created controversy was in his insistence that the biblical commands for holiness of heart and life were intended for the present life. The fact of these commands is not disputed by the different Christian traditions. What is disputed is the exact manner and timing of when the biblical call to holiness is intended to be realized. The main point of disagreement is whether holiness is for this life or for the life to come. Wesley took the holiness mandate in the literal sense of holiness here and now. It is this emphasis on the present call to holiness that has resulted in sanctification being identified as the most distinctive doctrine of Wesleyanism.

Wesleyans readily accept that sanctification is their distinctive doctrine, but they refute any notion that it is a unique doctrine of Wesley's creation. They point to its long history of development all the way back to the Early Church Fathers. Although the focus of the early church was on issues of CHRISTOLOGY, the initial roots of the Wesleyan concept of sanctification were clearly present in such leaders as Irenaeus, Clement of Alexandria, Origen, and Gregory of Nyssa. Other views compatible with the Wesleyan understanding of the doctrine were later expressed by such varied thinkers as Thomas à Kempis, CASPER SCHWENKFELD, THOMAS MUNTZER, Arminius, PHILIPP JAKOB SPENER, GEORGE FOX, JEREMY TAYLOR, and WILLIAM LAW. Wesley abhorred the very idea of theological novelty. He insisted that Wesleyan teachings be squarely in keeping with traditional orthodox positions and official Church of England dogma. He did not see his concept of holiness to be in violation of that principle. Rather, he saw this teaching as simply a revival of one of the grand old themes of scriptural Christianity and historic Anglicanism.

Perfection

Wesley stirred further controversy through his use of the term perfection. This was a frequent point of misinterpretation among his opponents. Actually, Wesley did not like to use the word, for he fully understood the faulty connotations that could be attached to it. However, he felt compelled to retain the word for the simple reason that it was the biblical term. He thought it better to properly teach it than to ignore it.

To be certain, the Wesleyan understanding of Christian perfection has nothing to do with absolute perfection. Wesleyanism affirms that only God is absolutely perfect and only Jesus lived a perfectly sinless life. Wesley never taught that the biblical commands to be perfect were in any way commands to be what it is impossible to be. In explaining what Christian perfection is, Wesley first described what it is not. He identified five general ways in which Christians cannot be perfect. Perfection does not mean freedom from ignorance, mistakes, "infirmities" (by which he seemed to mean confusion of mind and improper judgments in thinking), temptation, or growth.

What Wesley did mean by Christian perfection was essentially freedom from the bondage of sin and freedom to love God. Freedom from sin means abandonment of the old life of willful sinning. This is made possible by the purifying and empowering presence of the Holy Spirit. This understanding assumes a Wesleyan concept of sin in which intentional and unintentional sins are clearly distinguished. Any attempt to view the Wesleyan concept of Christian perfection through the lens of a non-Wesleyan definition of sin is doomed to misunderstanding. The Wesleyan teaching of Christian perfection remains valid only if it is approached specifically from the Wesleyan understanding of sin. This is often the fundamental point of breakdown in dialogs between Wesleyans and non-Wesleyans on the doctrine of perfection.

Freedom to love is seen by Wesleyanism as essentially the fulfillment of the great command of Moses in the Old Testament (Deuteronomy 6:5; 10:12) and Jesus in the New Testament (Mark 12:30). To love God with all our heart, soul, mind, and strength; and to live out that love toward others is to fulfill the law of love. This is what Wesleyanism means by perfect love. It was also Wesley's most succinct and consistently used definition for Christian perfection, or holiness of heart and life.

Wesley's concept of Christian perfection is sometimes cited as proof that Wesleyanism teaches sinless perfection. Here again, the interpretations are largely determined by the presupposed definitions. It may be said that Wesley taught a form of sinlessness, but this is a relative concept that must be understood in the context of his intended meaning. There are two different senses in which it may accurately be stated that Wesley believed in sinless perfection.

First, it was Wesley's understanding from scripture that all believers are called to forsake the former life of sin and to take on new life in Christ. He understood freedom from willful sin to be the normal pattern for the Christian life. In that sense Wesley would acknowledge teaching sinless perfection, although he would also insist that this is a fundamental teaching of the Bible and of all Christian traditions that merited no opposition.

Second, it was Wesley's understanding that through God's work of sanctification in the believer, the sin inherited from Adam's fall is cleansed from the believer. This too Wesley understood to be scriptural teaching. This cleansing was not seen as the removal of temptation or the possibility of sin. Rather, it was understood to be the realignment of the human spirit and will back toward God. That is, although sin always remains a possibility, it is no longer a necessity. Again, however, it must be emphasized that Wesley was speaking only of conscious, willful sins. He did not teach freedom from unconscious or involuntary sin, such as "sins" of ignorance, mistake, and human limitation. This is why Wesleyanism can on the one hand embrace a doctrine of relative sinlessness, whereas on the other hand denying any teaching of absolute sinlessness.

Social Responsibility

Wesley carried a profound sense of social responsibility throughout his ministry. This commitment to the welfare of others was not benevolence merely for the sake of benevolence. It was deeply rooted in his theology. Wesley's evangelical theology was not just a theology of personal salvation; it was a theology of practical love for others. He was especially aware of the link between holiness and social ETHICS. He insisted that Christians are morally obligated to be salt and light, not just to the world as a whole, but more importantly to the particular community where they live. That meant making positive contributions to society rather than making demands of it.

As with several aspects of his theology, Wesley's true understanding took on a significantly different perspective after his Aldersgate conversion. The focus of Wesley's social action before Aldersgate was the salvation of his own soul, but after Aldersgate, when he understood the nature of personal salvation differently, he came to see social action differently as well. No longer a means of striving to earn his own salvation, benevolence then came to be an expression of love for God and others; that is, it came to be a practical expression of holiness. The Wesleyan social ethic was transformed from merely doing good to profoundly living out one's love for God and neighbor.

Throughout his life Wesley carried on a tireless campaign of compassionate ministries to prisoners, orphans, widows, the uneducated, the unemployed, and the sick. He referred to such deeds as "works of mercy." They included feeding the hungry, clothing the naked, assisting the stranger, visiting the imprisoned, comforting the sick, educating the ignorant, confronting the wicked, and encouraging the faithful. The last letter he wrote before his death was a message of encouragement to the abolitionist WILLIAM WILBERFORCE in his fight against the slave trade (see SLAVERY, ABOLITION OF).

In the two centuries since Wesley's death Wesleyanism has spread and taken on various forms. The broad spectrum of Methodist, Holiness, and Pentecostal groups that identify themselves as Wesleyan in one way or another gives some indication of the broad appeal and diversity of Wesley's legacy. Liberal expressions of the movement tend to emphasize Wesley's social and benevolent concerns. Evangelical expressions tend to emphasize his theology of Christian conversion and holiness. A revival of both scholarly and practical interest in Wesley's unique contributions to the Christian church has brought many circles of Wesleyanism back to Wesley's original position of balance between these two variant expressions.

References and Further Reading

Primary Sources:

Wesley, John. *John Wesley's Sermons: An Anthology*. Edited by Albert C. Outler and Richard P. Heitzenrater. Nashville, TN: Abingdon Press, 1991.
———. *The Works of John Wesley*. Edited by Reginald W. Ward and Richard P. Heitzenrater. Bicentennial edition. Nashville, TN: Abingdon Press, 1988.

Secondary Sources:

Baker, Frank. *John Wesley and the Church of England*. London: Epworth Press, 2000.
Collins, Kenneth J. *A Real Christian: The Life of John Wesley*. Nashville, TN: Abingdon Press, 1999.
———. *The Scripture Way of Salvation: The Heart of John Wesley's Theology*. Nashville, TN: Abingdon Press, 1997.
Coppedge, Allan. *Wesley in Theological Debate*. Wilmore, KY: Wesley Heritage Press, 1987.
Hattersley, Roy. *A Brand from the Burning: The Life of John Wesley*. London: Little Brown, 2002.
Heitzenrater, Richard P. *Wesley and the People Called Methodists*. Nashville, TN: Abingdon Press, 1995.
Lindstrom, Harald. *Wesley and Sanctification: A Study in the Doctrine of Salvation*. Nappanee, IN: Francis Asbury Press, 1996.
Maddox, Randy L. *Responsible Grace: John Wesley's Practical Theology*. Nashville, TN: Kingswood Books, 1994.
McGonigle, Herbert Boyd. *Sufficient Saving Grace: John Wesley's Evangelical Arminianism*. Carlisle: Paternoster Press, 2001.
Oden, Thomas C. *John Wesley's Scriptural Christianity: A Plain Exposition of His Teachings on Christian Doctrine*. Grand Rapids, MI: Zondervan Publishing House, 1994.
Outler, Albert C. *John Wesley*. New York: Oxford University Press, 1964.
Rack, Henry D. *Reasonable Enthusiast: John Wesley and the Rise of Methodism*. London: Epworth Press, 1992.
Stone, Ronald H. *John Wesley's Life and Ethics*. Nashville, TN: Abingdon Press, 2001.
Thorsen, Donald A. D. *The Wesleyan Quadrilateral*. Grand Rapids, MI: Zondervan Publishing House, 1990.

DANIEL L. BURNETT

WESTCOTT, BROOKE (1825–1901)

English biblical scholar. Westcott was born in Bloomsbury, Birmingham, ENGLAND on January 12, 1825. He was educated at Trinity College, Cambridge, and then served as canon of Peterborough (1869–1883) and Westminster (1883–1890). For twenty years (1870–1890) he was Regius professor of divinity at CAMBRIDGE UNIVERSITY. On May 1, 1890 Westcott was consecrated bishop of Durham and served in that position until his death. Westcott, with Fenton John Anthony Hort and JOSEPH BARBER LIGHTFOOT, were known as the Cambridge Triumvirate, the three leading Cambridge scholars of the nineteenth century who stressed the scientific study of the BIBLE, especially the New Testament.

Westcott's major biblical writings were *History of the New Testament Canon* (1855), *Introduction to the Study of the Gospels* (1860), *History of the English Bible* (1868), and with Hort, *The New Testament in Modern Greek: Being the New Testament of Our Lord and Savior Jesus Christ: Newly Translated Direct from the Accurate Greek* (1881). These volumes brought the critical study of the Bible to a higher level and helped bridge the divide between FAITH and criticism.

Westcott was also an advocate of CHRISTIAN SO-CIALISM. He helped to found and was the president of the Christian Social Union, which based its social concern on the Incarnation. His belief in the Incarnation was the basis for his desire to work for the brotherhood of man and justice for all God's creatures. He was committed to improving theological education for CLERGY and founded the Cambridge Training School, now known as Westcott House. Westcott died at Durham on July 27, 1901.

See also Higher Criticism; Modernism

References and Further Reading

Primary Sources:

Westcott, Brooke F. *A General View of the History of the English Bible.* London: Macmillan and Co., 1905.
———. *The Incarnation and Common Life.* London/New York: Macmillan, 1893.
———. *The Gospel of Life: Thoughts Introductory to the Study of Christian Doctrine.* London/New York: Macmillan, 1892.
———. *The Bible in the Church: A Popular Account of the Collection and Reception of the Holy Scriptures in the Christian Churches.* Grand Rapids, MI: Baker, 1885, 1979.

Secondary Sources:

Clayton, Joseph. *Bishop Westcott.* London: A. R. Mowbray, 1906.
Olofason, Folke. *Christus Redemptor et Consummator: A Study in the Theology of B. F. Westcott.* Translated by Neil Tomkinson. Uppsala, Sweden: University of Uppsala, 1979.

DONALD S. ARMENTROUT

WESTMINSTER ASSEMBLY

Called by Parliament on June 12, 1643, the Westminster Assembly was a gathering of theologians to address reform of the English church during the CIVIL WAR between royal and parliamentary forces, it produced documents that shaped PRESBYTERIANISM in the CHURCH OF SCOTLAND and throughout the world. These statements included the WESTMINSTER CONFESSION of Faith, WESTMINSTER CATECHISMS (Larger and Shorter), Directory for the Public Worship of God, and Form of Church Government. The thirty lay and 121 minister commissioners began by revising the THIRTY-NINE AR-TICLES of the Anglican church. Eight commissioners of the Church of Scotland were received with voice in the Assembly, after the acceptance of the Scottish Solemn League and Covenant by Parliament and Assembly (September 25, 1643). The agenda then shifted to debating a church order with Scriptural warrant, and seeking uniformity with the Church of Scotland. Civil War and national politics formed the background for a "Grand Debate" on the order and government of the church. The Assembly met for 1,163 sessions, and was never officially dismissed; the last mention of Scottish participation was on November 9, 1647.

Members represented diverse views: the majority were conservative Puritans (see PURITANISM), with a minority of Independent Puritans, some Erastians (see ERASTUS, THOMAS), and a small group of Epis-copalians who did not participate in the Assembly. The Scots insisted on their Presbyterian views, and the majority of conservative Puritans came to favor a "presbyterian" uniformity against the minority Inde-pendents' stress on gathered congregations of visible saints. Although its church standards were of little effect in ENGLAND, the Assembly had a profound con-sequence for the future of the Reformed tradition, in the refining of Presbyterian and Congregational ec-clesiologies, and by the heightening of issues of uni-formity versus tolerance and spiritual versus judicial AUTHORITY in the ministry of the church.

References and Further Reading

Carruthers, S. W. *The Everyday Work of the Westminster Assembly.* Philadelphia, PA: Presbyterian Historical Soci-ety, 1943.
Leith, John H. *Assembly at Westminster: Reformed Theology in the Making.* Atlanta, GA: John Knox Press, 1973.
Mitchell, A. F. *The Westminster Assembly.* 2nd ed. Presbyterian Board of Publication, Philadelphia, PA: 1897.
Paul, Robert S. *The Assembly of the Lord: Politics and Religion in the Westminster Assembly and the "Grand Debate."* Edinburgh: T. & T. Clark, 1985.

STANLEY R. HALL

WESTMINSTER CATECHISM

The "Longer" and "Shorter" Catechisms were com-posed by the Westminster Assembly (1643–1653) to provide theological resources for pastors and LAITY in churches of the Reformed tradition. The CATECHISMS were approved by the English Parliament on Septem-ber 15, 1648, having been completed a year before. They were part of the Westminster Standards, the documents produced by the assembly of "divines" who were initially gathered to advise the Long Par-liament about a religious settlement in ENGLAND and to revise the THIRTY-NINE ARTICLES as a doctrinal standard for the English church. A Scottish alliance with Parliament made it advisable to compose a new confession of faith, and so the Westminster Assembly produced the WESTMINSTER CONFESSION of Faith (1646), the Larger and Shorter Catechisms (1647), the Directory for the Public Worship of God with a Psalter (1644), and the Form of Government (1644).

Structure

The Larger Catechism is composed of 196 questions and answers and is basically a restatement of the Westminster Confession in a more didactic form. The catechism is partly based on James Ussher's *Body of Divinitie* (1645) and was crafted to a great degree by Anthony Tuckney (1599–1670), who was very active in the work of the Assembly. Tuckney is particularly credited with the section on the Law of God in the Larger Catechism and was also the most influential writer of the Shorter Catechism. The Larger Catechism, because of its elaborate answers, functioned especially as a resource for CLERGY in the preparation of sermons.

The Shorter Catechism enjoyed a much wider usage and functioned primarily for the instruction of children. It is composed of 107 questions with much shorter answers. Its usefulness for teaching was enhanced by its method of using answers that included the language of the question and then formed a complete sentence in itself. An example is the famous first question and answer:

> Q. 1. What is the chief end of man?
> A. Man's chief end is to glorify God, and to enjoy him forever.

This catechism has been widely used by Presbyterians as well as by Congregationalists and BAPTISTS (see PRESBYTERIANISM; CONGREGATIONALISM).

The Larger Catechism is divided into two main parts after a five-question introduction. Part One is "What Man Ought to Believe Concerning God" (qq. 6–90). Part Two is "Having Seen What the Scriptures Principally Teach Us to Believe Concerning God, It Follows to Consider What They Require as the Duty of Man" (qq. 91–196). The overall movement is from theological understanding to Christian action.

Theology

The order of the issues with which the catechisms deal follows that of the Confession of Faith. The THEOLOGY presented is a developing form of CALVINISM, influenced by JOHN CALVIN and also by continental theologians. The Westminster Standards sought to expound a generic Reformed theology that could be accepted by Reformed Christians everywhere. Yet some doctrinal emphases in the catechisms stand out (citations here refer to questions of the Shorter Catechism).

The Scriptures are where the Word of God is contained and "principally teach what man is to believe concerning God, and what duty God requires of man" (2–3). Thus the BIBLE has a theological purpose. God is defined as "a Spirit, infinite, eternal and unchangeable, in his being, wisdom, power, holiness, justice, goodness, and truth" (4). God issues "decrees" that are God's "eternal purpose, according to the counsel of his will, whereby, for his own glory, he hath foreordained whatsoever comes to pass" (7). These decrees are carried out in God's works of creation and providence (8). A strong DOCTRINE of providence emerges in the catechisms whereby God's works of providence are his "most holy, wise, and powerful preserving and governing all his creatures, and all their actions" (11). Thus God exercises a divine sovereignty over all of nature and history.

The fall into SIN brought humanity into "an estate of sin and misery" (17). This resulted in humanity's loss of communion with God and its resting under God's "wrath and curse," ultimately bringing DEATH (19). But God has established a "redeemer of God's elect," Jesus Christ (21), who through his work as prophet (24), priest (25), and king (26) brings SALVATION to those whom God has effectually called by the Holy Spirit (30–31). They are justified (33), adopted (34), and participate in SANCTIFICATION (35). These theological realities bring believers "assurance of God's love, peace of conscience, joy in the Holy Ghost, increase of grace, and perseverance therein to the end" (36), whereas through the resurrection of Christ believers are "made perfectly blessed in the full enjoying of God to all eternity" (38).

Those who receive the benefits of salvation have as their duty "obedience" to God's "revealed will" (39). God's will is revealed through the moral law, summarized in the Ten Commandments (40–41). For each of the commandments, the catechisms ask both what is "required" and what is "forbidden" (45–81). This recognition that the commandments also entail positive duties was a feature of Calvin's theology as well.

Because humans are incapable of keeping the law of God perfectly, the only path to salvation is through FAITH in Jesus Christ. This faith is "a saving grace, whereby we receive and rest upon him alone for salvation, as he is offered to us in the gospel" (86). The benefits of redemption come through "the Word, SACRAMENTS, and PRAYER, all which are made effectual to the elect for the salvation" (88). These are discussed (88–99) before questions on the Lord's

Prayer (100–107), which is "the special rule of direction" in prayer that "Christ taught his disciples" (99).

The Westminster catechisms made the theology of the CONFESSION of faith memorable and known to pastors and laity. They continue to be used as a means of instruction and a resource for understanding the Reformed faith.

References and Further Reading

Book of Catechisms: Reference Edition. Louisville, KY: Geneva Press, 2001.

Leith, John H. *Assembly at Westminster.* Richmond, VA: John Knox Press, 1973.

Rogers, Jack. *Presbyterian Creeds.* Philadelphia, PA: Westminster Press, 1985.

Torrance, Thomas F. *The School of Faith.* New York: Harper & Brothers, 1959.

DONALD K. McKIM

WESTMINSTER CONFESSION

One of the documents produced by the WESTMINSTER ASSEMBLY (1643–1653), the Westminster Confession is regarded as a sterling statement of Reformed theology. It has been used continually throughout the world by churches in the Reformed tradition. It features clarity of thought, precise use of theological language, and is a comprehensive statement of theological belief. Because of political circumstances, the Confession—although written for the English church—was never adopted by the established CHURCH OF ENGLAND. It did, however, become the official confession of Scottish PRESBYTERIANISM. Its influence in English-speaking countries has been significant and for over three hundred years it was the sole doctrinal standard of British and American Presbyterianism. It has also had a useful history among Congregational and some Baptist bodies (see CONGREGATIONALISM; BAPTISTS). It formed the basis for the Congregationalist Savoy Declaration (1658) and the Particular Baptist Confession (1677), as well as the General Baptist Orthodox Creed (1678).

Background

The Westminster Confession was written at a tumultuous time in ENGLAND. It was composed by an assembly of "divines" who were called to meet by the Long Parliament in 1643 with the mandate to revise the THIRTY-NINE ARTICLES of Religion in a more "Puritan" direction (see PURITANISM). The Westminster Assembly was composed of 121 Puritan ministers of the Church of England. The majority were Presbyterian in their views, although some Congregationalists

and a small group favoring Episcopal church government also served. Additionally, thirty lay members were present, as well as six Scottish advisors.

When the Assembly reached the sixteenth of the Thirty-nine Articles, the political situation changed with the onset of the English CIVIL WAR. Parliament was at war with King Charles I. The parliamentary forces enlisted the help of SCOTLAND. In return for their support the Scots insisted that the *Solemn League and Covenant*, which Parliament had accepted in 1643 to provide for a Presbyterian church in England, Ireland, and Scotland, be followed. Scottish commissioners were sent to London to advise the Parliament and some of these sat as commissioners to the Westminster Assembly (with the right to debate but not to vote).

For the next several years the Assembly deliberated with an average of sixty commissioners in daily attendance. Eleven men did the majority of writing on the Confession of Faith. Seven were English divines and four were Scottish clergy. The Confession was completed and presented to Parliament in December 1646. The Assembly also produced a Larger and Shorter Catechism (1647), the Directory for the Public Worship of God (1644) including a Psalter, and the Form of Government (1644). These are collectively called the Westminster Standards. Scripture proof texts were added to the Confession of Faith in 1647, the same year in which the confession was approved by the Church of Scotland. Parliament was purged by OLIVER CROMWELL in 1649, and for the next several years the members of the Assembly met to examine and license ministers. In December 1653, Cromwell was proclaimed Lord Protector and the Assembly ceased to function, although it was never officially dissolved.

Structure

The Westminster Confession was composed of thirty-three chapters. Its theological views represented the emerging Reformed tradition that looked initially to JOHN CALVIN (1509–1564) as a shaping influence. Although the influence of continental Reformed thinkers was also formative, the immediate sources of the Westminster Confession were the Irish Articles (1615) and *A Body of Divinitie* (1645), both written by James Ussher (1581–1656), archbishop of Armagh and primate of IRELAND.

The confession was structured to deal with nearly every topic of divinity. Its first chapter was on Holy Scripture and like other Reformed confessional statements featured a listing of the canonical books that serve as "the Word of God written" (chap. 1). Chapters two through five dealt with the doctrine of God as the Holy Trinity (2), as the author of divine "eternal decrees" (3), as creator of the world (4), and as involved in and with the world through divine providence (5). Chapter six speaks of humanity's fall into SIN and its punishment, whereas chapter seven expounds God's covenants with humanity—found first in a "covenant of works" and then in a "covenant of GRACE." This sets the stage for discussion of the work of Jesus Christ as "the only mediator" between God and humanity who carries out his work as prophet, priest, and king (8). Further chapters are careful expositions of the way of SALVATION in Christ for those who have lost their "free will" to choose to "will any spiritual good accompanying salvation" (9). God has "effectually called" some (10; the "elect") and has justified (11), adopted (12), and sanctifies them (13). The way of salvation in Jesus Christ is by "the grace of FAITH" through the work of God's Holy Spirit (14), which is expressed through repentance (15) and good works whereby believers "manifest their thankfulness" among other things (16). Those "effectually called and sanctified" by God's Spirit persevere in faith and are "eternally saved," (17) receiving a certain assurance in this life that they are in a "state of grace, and may rejoice in the hope of the glory of God: which hope shall never make them ashamed" (18). Believers follow the moral law of God, which informs them of God's will as the rule for their lives—not to gain salvation but to be in obedience to the way God wants them to live (19). From here the confession moves on to consider elements of the Christian life such as Christian liberty (20), WORSHIP and the Sabbath Day (21), oaths and vows (22), the civil magistrate (23), and MARRIAGE and DIVORCE (24). Theological treatments of the CHURCH (25), the communion of SAINTS (26), the SACRAMENTS: BAPTISM and the LORD'S SUPPER (27–29) are presented before the final chapters on church censures (30), synods and councils (31), the resurrection of the dead and the last judgment (32–33).

Some church bodies that adopted the Westminster Confession have added additional chapters or modified the original 1647 edition. American churches changed the chapter on the civil magistrate to reflect belief in the separation of CHURCH AND STATE. In the twentieth century the two major Presbyterian bodies in the UNITED STATES added a chapter on the Holy Spirit and "Of the Gospel of the Love of God and Missions" (1903 by the PRESBYTERIAN CHURCH in the United States of America; 1942 by the Presbyterian Church in the United States). These sought to show that the confessions' doctrine of God's sovereignty is not in conflict with God's love for all persons and thus that the church has a missionary imperative. In the 1950s both of these Presbyterian bodies amended the con-

fession's chapter on marriage and divorce to remove the prohibition of divorce and remarriage (except on grounds of adultery or desertion) and to permit remarriage of divorced persons.

Although the Confession is precise and theologically articulate, nearly two-thirds of the document deal with practical issues of the Christian life rather than speculative theological questions. This reflects the essential convictions of the Westminster divines—and Reformed theology in general—that THEOLOGY is a science focused on Christian existence in its personal and social dimensions rather than on theoretical dimensions only.

Theological Emphases

The Westminster Confession is a transitional document from the REFORMATION era to that of the highly developed scholastic theologies that marked the later seventeenth century. The writings of Calvin were frequently published in England by the end of the sixteenth century and were highly influential among the Westminster Divines. Attributed primarily to the English Civil War, the period of the scientific revolution that marked the beginnings of modern science and that had already commenced on the European continent did not begin in England until the 1660s. This meant that many of the scientific and philosophical questions affecting Continental theologians were not presenting problems to the writers of the confession. In this regard the confession may be seen as moving beyond Calvin in many of its formulations but not as reflecting the highly scholastic theology of later continental Reformed theologians, such as Francis Turretin (1623–1687) for example.

A number of important theological emphases are characteristic of the Westminster Confession as a document illustrating the Reformed theology of Calvin and his successors.

The article on Holy Scripture (1.4) indicates that the BIBLE gains its AUTHORITY from God and not from humans or from any church. Its divine authority is established by "the inward work of the Holy Spirit, bearing witness by and with the Word in our hearts" (1.6). The confession speaks of the "light of nature," which in the Reformed tradition refers to the innate knowledge of God implanted in every human but which is suppressed by sin. God's works of creation and providence serve to reinforce this knowledge of God. Because of human sin this knowledge serves only to render humans inexcusable and is "not sufficient to give that knowledge of God, and of his will, which is necessary unto salvation" (1.1).

A hallmark of the Westminster Confession is its third chapter on "God's Eternal Decree(s)." The confession states:

> God from all eternity did by the most wise and holy counsel of his own will, freely and unchangeably ordain whatsoever comes to pass; yet so as thereby neither is God the author of sin, nor is violence offered to the will of the creatures, nor is the liberty or contingency of second causes taken away, but rather established. (3.1)

God's decree is God's action, the expression of the divine will. God has willed, through the "decree," for "the manifestation of his glory, some men and angels are predestinated unto everlasting life, and others foreordained to everlasting death" (3.3). These statements are the Reformed emphasis on ELECTION and PREDESTINATION. God's election is God's free choice to save those whom God decides to save. Predestination is the expression of election in relation to salvation.

In the broader context of the confession, this decree of God is worked out through God's "effectual call" by the Word and Spirit, "out of that state of sin and death in which they are by nature, to grace and salvation by Jesus Christ" (10.1). Predestination is necessary if any are to be saved because according to the confession, humanity's fall into sin has meant that the "original righteousness and communion with God" that human beings were created to enjoy has now been lost. Humanity, through the sin of our first parents, has now become "dead in sin, and wholly defiled in all the faculties and parts of soul and body" (6.2). Humanity's original "freedom and power to will and to do that which is good and well-pleasing to God"—the human condition before the fall into sin—has been lost. This pervasive power of sin means that humans are not by their own strength able to convert themselves or prepare themselves to be converted by God (9.3).

The confession testifies that God has reached out to humans in their sin first by a "covenant of works" whereby humans could obtain life "upon condition of perfect and personal obedience" to God (7.2). Because of the fall into sin, however, humans have made themselves "incapable of life by that COVENANT" (7.3). So God was pleased to establish a "covenant of grace" whereby sinners are offered "life and salvation by Jesus Christ, requiring of them faith in him, that they may be saved, and promising to give unto all those that are ordained unto life, his Holy Spirit, to make them willing and able to believe" (7.3). This then is the reason that predestination is key for human salvation: without God's ordaining salvation, no human could ever achieve it. Sin has left humans powerless, by their own will, to turn to God in obedience and live as God desires. Through divine predestination God provides a salvation that is unattainable by human activities or achievements.

The means by which this salvation for God's elect is accomplished is through Jesus Christ. The confession affirms the early church's orthodox view of Jesus as the second person of the Trinity who is fully divine and fully human. This enables him to be the mediator of salvation. Christ fulfills the offices of prophet, priest, and king. Through his "perfect obedience and sacrifice of himself" he has satisfied divine justice and brought reconciliation between God and the sinner (8).

This redemption is applied to those whom God has effectually called through justification through which God pardons sin and accepts them "by imputing the obedience and satisfaction of Christ unto them." They receive this righteousness of Christ by faith, "which faith they have not of themselves" but as a gift of God (11.1). SANCTIFICATION is the outworking of the new heart and spirit created in believers and their growth in holiness throughout their whole lives. Believers will never be perfect in this life because there will always remain "some remnants of corruption" in them. However, the sanctifying spirit of Christ enables the saints to "grow in grace, perfecting holiness in the fear of God" (13). Good works done by believers are "the fruits and evidences of a true and lively faith" (16.2).

It is in the context of redemption and the assurance of grace and salvation (18) that the law of God is introduced (19). The confession here echoes Calvin's view that the moral law of God is given as a guide for believers, as "a rule of life, informing them of the will of God and their duty" (19.6). Obedience to the law is not a means of salvation but an expression of God's sanctifying work in believers that leads them to seek God's will and obey it.

The confession maintains the Augustinian distinction between the "visible" (outward) church and the "invisible" church (true believers, known only to God; 25). It sees the sacraments as "holy signs and seals of the covenant of grace" (27) and indicates that only baptism and the Lord's Supper are sacraments "ordained by Christ our Lord in the gospel" (27.4).

The ultimate states of humans after DEATH either are to have their souls "made perfect in holiness" and be "received into the highest heavens" or have their souls "cast into hell, where they remain in torments and utter darkness, reserved to the judgment of the great day" (22.1). Ultimate judgment belongs to God who has appointed a day wherein "he will judge the world in righteousness by Jesus Christ" (23.1).

The Westminster Confession presents a comprehensive picture of God who in divine providence "doth uphold, direct, dispose, and govern all creatures, actions, and things, from the greatest even to the least"

(5.1). Humans are responsible for their actions but in matters of salvation can only look to God's covenant of grace in Jesus Christ.

References and Further Reading

Hendry, George S. *The Westminster Confession for Today.* Richmond, VA: John Knox Press, 1960.

Leith, John H. *Assembly at Westminster.* Richmond, VA: John Knox Press, 1973.

Mitchell, A. F. *The Westminster Assembly: Its History and Standards*, 1883.

Paul, Robert S. *The Assembly of the Lord.* Edinburgh: T. & T. Clark, 1985.

Rogers, Jack. *Presbyterian Creeds.* Philadelphia, PA: Westminster Press, 1985.

———. *Scripture in the Westminster Confession.* Grand Rapids, MI: Wm. B. Eerdmans, 1967.

DONALD K. MCKIM

WHEATLEY, PHILLIS (c. 1753–1784)

African-American poet. Born in AFRICA in the early 1750s, transported to North America, and sold to John and Susannah Wheatley in Boston in colonial New England, Phillis Wheatley, a five-year-old African child of unknown origin, became a slave. In the middle to late 1750s, when she arrived in the colony, SLAVERY, although marginal to the regional economy, had become a fixed feature of the colony's labor system. Many slaves like Wheatley worked as household servants.

Wheatley learned English very quickly and benefited from the Wheatleys and their children, who taught her to read and write and exposed her to the classics. She became proficient enough in Latin that she translated Ovid as an adolescent. The family also encouraged her poetic talents and supported Wheatley's publication in 1773 of *Poems on Various Subjects.* Newspapers in both Boston and Philadelphia took note of her book and acknowledged its quality. In several public presentations in America and ENGLAND Wheatley became known and lauded as an able poetess. George Washington, Thomas Paine, John Hancock, and others in Revolutionary America became acquainted with her.

The Wheatleys later manumitted Phillis and she married John Peters, a free black. She died in 1784 in her early thirties.

Writing in the context of the American Revolution, Wheatley's poetry echoed themes that colonists used to explain their revolt against Great Britain. Similarly Wheatley's works showed the same religious influences that affected Lemuel Haynes, Absalom Jones, RICHARD ALLEN, and other black Christian contemporaries. She viewed "Almighty Providence" as the divine master of NATURE and humankind and she saw

the soul as divinely directed and free. Although nurtured in the rhetoric of liberty and in scriptural SALVATION, Wheatley still recognized that slave trading had seized her "from Afric's distant happy seat," and she prayed that "others may never feel tyrannic sway."

See also Literature

References and Further Reading

Graham, Shirley. *The Story of Phillis Wheatley: Poetess of the American Revolution.* New York: Julian Messner, 1949.

DENNIS C. DICKERSON

WHISTON, WILLIAM (1667–1752)

English anti-trinitarian theologian. Whiston was born on December 9, 1667 in Norton-Juxta-Twycross, Leicestershire. Whiston's father and maternal grandfather were clergymen, and his father left provisions in his will for his son's university training to become "an able minister of the New Testament." Whiston enrolled at Clare Hall, Cambridge in 1686, earning a B.A. in 1689 and M.A. in 1693. He became a fellow of the college in 1691. He served as chaplain to Bishop John Moore (1646–1714) from 1694 to 1698, and was parish priest at Lowestoft, Suffolk from 1698 to 1701.

In 1701 he succeeded ISAAC NEWTON (1642–1727) as Lucasian professor of mathematics at CAMBRIDGE UNIVERSITY, but was expelled from this post in October 1710 after publicizing his antitrinitarian views, which came in part from Newton. At the end of 1710 Whiston and his family relocated to London, where he endured four years of intermittent but ultimately inconclusive HERESY proceedings initiated by the Anglican Convocation of Clergy. During this period he published the manifesto of his Arian creed, the five-volume *Primitive Christianity reviv'd* (1711–1712). In London he took up a career as a public lecturer on experiment and astronomy, thereby playing a leading role in the dissemination of the new Newtonian philosophy. He also continued his prodigious output of prophetic, theological, and natural philosophical works. Objecting to the reading of the Athanasian Creed in Anglican liturgy and long an advocate of believers' BAPTISM, from 1747 Whiston worshiped with the General BAPTISTS. He died at Lyndon Hall, Rutland on August 22, 1752.

Through his numerous publications Whiston's influence was felt in several disparate areas of eighteenth-century Protestantism. His first book, *A new theory of the earth* (1696), is an early example of flood geology and one of the first attempts to reconcile the Genesis creation account with science, which for Whiston was Newtonian physics (see CREATION SCI-

ENCE). His *Essay on the Revelation* (1706) is a historicist interpretation of the Apocalypse in the tradition of Joseph Mede and was cited by prophetic exegetes into the nineteenth century. In his 1707 Boyle lectures on the fulfillment of biblical prophecy (published in 1708) and later works, Whiston advocated the use of prophecy as an argument for the divine origin of the BIBLE. Although he set his own mark on the THEOLOGY he obtained from Newton, Whiston played a pivotal part in publicizing the heterodox theology of the secret heretic Newton. He also contributed to the development of Unitarianism. A confident expression of the design argument in Newtonian terms, Whiston's *Astronomical principles of religion, natural and reveal'd* (1717) remains a milestone in natural theology. Although a controversial figure, by pushing the limits of British heresy laws, he also helped advance TOLERATION for antitrinitarian dissent. Whiston's most enduring legacy is his translation of Josephus, a translation that found its way into countless Anglo-American Protestant homes in the nineteenth and twentieth centuries and is still in print at the beginning of the twenty-first century.

See also Anti-Trinitarianism; Deism; Dissent

References and Further Reading

Primary Sources:

Whiston, William. *The accomplishment of Scripture prophecies.* Cambridge, 1708.

————. *An essay on the Revelation of St. John.* Cambridge, 1706.

————. *Astronomical principles of religion, natural and reveal'd.* London, 1717.

————. *The genuine works of Flavius Josephus, the Jewish historian.* London, 1737.

————. *Memoirs of the life and writings of Mr. William Whiston.* London, 1749, 1753.

————. *A new theory of the earth.* London, 1696.

————. *Primitive Christianity reviv'd.* n.p., 1711–1712.

Secondary Sources:

Farrell, Maureen. *William Whiston.* New York: Arno Press, 1981.

Force, James E. *William Whiston: Honest Newtonian.* Cambridge: Cambridge University Press, 1985.

STEPHEN D. SNOBELEN

WHITE, ELLEN GOULD (1827–1915)

American church founder. Ellen Gould was born in 1827 near Gorham, Maine and grew up as a Methodist in Portland. In 1840 she accepted WILLIAM MILLER'S teaching that Christ would return in 1843 or 1844. In December 1844 Gould experienced a vision, through which she learned that the Millerites must maintain their faith in Christ's imminent return. While spreading this message, she met James S. White, whom she married in 1846. Soon after, the couple began observing the seventh-day Sabbath.

Conferences in the Northeast during 1848 formulated the doctrines of Sabbatarian Adventism. With Ellen's encouragement James published papers, including the *Review and Herald* (1850), and her first pamphlet in 1851. After the Whites moved from Rochester, New York, to Battle Creek, Michigan (1855), Ellen's book *Spiritual Gifts* (1858) was published. The Whites and Joseph Bates, a former Millerite, helped form the SEVENTH-DAY ADVENTIST CHURCH (1863) with a membership of about 3,000. Ellen also promoted health reform, which led to the establishment of what became Battle Creek Sanitarium (1866), encouraged the creation of Battle Creek College (1875), and urged denominational mission activity abroad, which officially began with the arrival of John Nevins Andrews in Europe (1874).

Among Ellen White's books are *The Great Controversy* (1888), *Steps to Christ* (1892), and *The Desire of Ages* (1898). In the 1890s and early 1900s she promoted changes in the DENOMINATION's organizational structure, expansion into the American South, and continued international development of educational, health, and PUBLISHING institutions. When she died in St. Helena, California in 1915 the Seventh-day Adventist Church had about 130,000 members.

See also Sabbatarianism

References and Further Reading

Primary Sources:

White, Arthur L. *Ellen G. White.* 6 vols. Takoma Park, MD: Review and Herald Publishers Association, 1982–1986.

White, Ellen Gould. *The (New, Illustrated) Great Controversy.* De Land, FL: Laymen for Religious Liberty, 1990.

————. *The Desire of Ages.* Mountain View, CA/Portland, OR: Pacific Press Publishers Association, 1940.

————. *The Great Controversy between Christ and Satan: The Conflict of the Ages in the Christian Dispensation.* Mountain View, CA: Pacific Press Publishers Association, 1870, 1950.

————. *Steps to Christ.* Washington, D.C.: Review and Herald Publishers Association, 1921.

————. *The Triumph of God's Love: The Story of the Vindication of the Character of God and the Salvation of Mankind.* Mountain View, CA: Pacific Press Publishers Association, 1957.

————. *Counsels on Diet and Foods: A Compilation from the Writings of Ellen G. White.* Takoma Park, MD: Review and Herald Publishers Association, 1976.

————. *Health and Happiness.* Phoenix, AZ: Inspiration Books, 1973.

————. *God's Amazing Grace.* Washington, D.C.: Review and Herald Publishers Association, 1973.

Secondary Sources:

Douglass, Herbert E. *Messenger of the Lord: The Prophetic Ministry of Ellen G. White.* Mountain View, CA/Portland, OR: Pacific Press, 1998.

Numbers, Ronald L. *Prophetess of Health: Ellen G. White and the Origins of Seventh-day Adventist Health Reform.* Knoxville, TN: University of Tennessee Press, 1992.

GARY LAND

WHITE, WILLIAM HALE (ALSO MARK RUTHERFORD) (1831–1913)

Victorian writer. Also known under the pseudonym of Mark Rutherford, White was born in Bedford, ENGLAND, the son of William White, a dissenter and doorkeeper at the House of Commons (see DISSENT). He was educated at the English School, Bedford, at the Countess of Huntingdon's College, Cheshunt, and at New College, St. John's Wood. He was highly influenced by the writings of JOHN BUNYAN, and, while in Bedford, attended the Bunyan meeting as did his father before him. He originally intended to become an independent minister, but changed vocational pursuits because of increasing disillusionment and religious doubt. This decision was solidified by the fact that he was expelled from New College, St. John's Wood, for voicing doubt over the authenticity and inspired nature of the BIBLE.

In 1854 he joined the Civil Service, where he eventually established himself as assistant director of contracts at the Admiralty. Although he wrote various pieces for journals over many years, it was not until 1881 that his literary career came to fruition with the publication of his *The Autobiography of Mark Rutherford* (1881), followed a few years later by *Mark Rutherford's Deliverance* (1885). In these works one finds a penetrative insight into nineteenth-century spirituality, religious doubt, and disillusionment. Indeed, these works are in large part a record of White's own spiritual pilgrimage through the height of nineteenth-century disillusionment with religion. He never attempted to proselytize for any particular religious position, but rather aimed simply to chart his own religious experience through the life of his pseudonym.

Although it is principally for his first two books that he has earned his place in literary and religious history, he wrote several subsequent works; these include: *The Revolution in Tanner's Lane* (1887); *Miriam's Schooling* (1893); *Catherine Furze* (1893); and *Clara Hopgood* (1896).

References and Further Reading

Maclean, Catherine. *Mark Rutherford: A Biography of William Hale White.* London: MacDonald, 1955.

ALEC JARVIS

WHITEFIELD, GEORGE (1714–1770)

English revivalist. The pioneer evangelist in the Great Awakening of the eighteenth century (see AWAKENINGS), Whitefield was born at Gloucester, ENGLAND on December 16, 1714. He died at Newburyport, Maryland on September 30, 1770. The sixth child of an innkeeper, in 1732 he gained a place at Oxford University and there attended the "Holy Club" or "Oxford Methodists," led by JOHN WESLEY, and experienced evangelical CONVERSION and a sense of forgiveness in 1735. He was ordained to the Anglican diaconate in June 1736.

Whitefield's subsequent life had two sides, one in America, the other in Great Britain. His American experience began with his appointment as a chaplain to the Georgia Company and his inspiration for an orphan home in Georgia. On his second tour Whitefield's PREACHING stimulated the so-called First Evangelical (or Great) Awakening. Intense emotion and sharp criticism did not disturb him. Although an Anglican, he associated with prominent Dissenters (see DISSENT) and adopted their CALVINISM. Seven further tours of America took place, and a ritual pattern of revival preaching developed (see REVIVALS). He did much to give American religion its own sense of purpose and character. Whitefield faced huge criticism at various periods, but survived to become an American icon, inspiring even the skeptical Ben Franklin to support him.

Whitefield's British ministry was also controversial. It was his outdoor preaching near Bristol in 1739 after Anglican churches refused to invite him into the pulpit that forced METHODISM into the popular world. Yet leadership of the new movement was assumed by Wesley, who introduced to it an Arminian theology (see ARMINIANISM). As a result Whitefield led a schism and thereafter associated closely with Welsh and Scottish Calvinists, but remained in cordial contact with John Wesley. Because of his frequent absences he increasingly depended on the sponsorship of a strong-willed aristocrat, Selina, countess of Hastings (see HASTINGS, LADY SELINA). His influence in England was greatest among "New" Dissenters, although he never left the established church.

Whitefield was essentially a preacher. Typically his sermons focused on "the new birth," communicated in a dramatic preaching style, with personal anecdotes, dramatization of the biblical narrative, and theatrical bodily gestures. He excelled in open-air settings, and was much admired by actors. The journal of his experiences led to accusations of "enthusiasm," that he was controlled by the dictates of an inner spirit. As he became more Calvinist he became more cautious, but his theology remained pragmatic. Unlike Wesley his weakness was in organization, although this mattered less in America. Moreover, Whitefield evidenced some insecurity in the face of better-bred aristocrats and properly licensed CLERGY. None of these factors inhibited the work in America, where Whitefield's converts found their place in Congregational and Presbyterian churches.

Recent studies have focused on the conscious way in which Whitefield viewed religion as a commodity, "worked" his market, distributing publicity, promoting himself and his ministry, and stimulating religious debate. Whitefield reveled in opposition, although he appreciated support in high places. Although he failed to found a separate DENOMINATION, his values lie at the heart of modern EVANGELICALISM and made him known as a pioneer evangelist in the eighteenth-century Great Awakening.

See also Congregationalism; Nonconformity; Presbyterianism; Wesleyan Holiness Movement

References and Further Reading

Primary Source:

Whitefield, George. *The Works of the Reverend George Whitefield M.A.* 6 vols. London: Edward & Charles Dilly, 1771.

Secondary Sources:

Dallimore, A. A. *George Whitefield.* 2 vols. Edinburgh: Banner of Truth, 1970, 1979.
Lambert, Frank. *Pedlar in Divinity: George Whitefield and the Transatlantic Revivals 1737–1770.* Princeton, NJ: Princeton University Press, 1994.
Stout, Harry S. *The Divine Dramatist: George Whitefield and the Rise of Modern Evangelicalism.* Grand Rapids, MI: Wm. B. Eerdmans, 1991.

PETER LINEHAM

WHITGIFT, JOHN (c. 1530–1604)

Archbishop of Canterbury. Whitgift was born in Lincolnshire about 1530, and his career led him from CAMBRIDGE UNIVERSITY to Lambeth Palace where, as archbishop of CANTERBURY (1583–1604), he was one of queen ELIZABETH I's closest advisors. Whitgift's unwavering conviction that the monarch stood as the sole and rightful head of the CHURCH OF ENGLAND put him in frequent conflict with those who desired reforms beyond those stated in the Elizabethan Settlement.

Whitgift at Cambridge

Whitgift not only received his education at Cambridge University, he also spent a significant portion of his career there. Upon receiving his B.D. in 1563 he was named Lady Margaret professor of divinity, a post he held until he earned a D.D. in 1567, whereupon he was named Regious professor of divinity and master of Trinity College. In 1570 Whitgift became vice-chancellor.

Whitgift's time at Cambridge coincided with a period of religious conflict at the university, and Whitgift quickly established himself as a defender of the status quo. When Cambridge became the center of a controversy concerning prescribed clerical VESTMENTS, Whitgift saw those who objected to donning "popish dress" as unjustly challenging the AUTHORITY of the Crown and Canterbury to fix church policy. The conflict between those who supported the establishment and those who argued for limits to royal and episcopal power would prove a recurring issue in Whitgift's career.

One of the most high profile dissenters at Cambridge was THOMAS CARTWRIGHT. Cartwright's name became almost synonymous with PURITANISM, and Whitgift stood as his committed and continuing opponent. When Cartwright gave a series of lectures in which he overtly criticized the ecclesiastical polity of the church, Whitgift joined with other heads of the university to deny Cartwright his degree. Shortly thereafter Whitgift succeeded in getting Cartwright expelled from the university. The two clashed again during a literary debate known as "The Admonition Controversy." The dispute centered on "things indifferent," that is, notions of correct liturgical and ecclesiastical procedures not mentioned specifically in the BIBLE. Whitgift's writings reveal that his position stemmed not from an intrinsic antipathy for Cartwright's PRESBYTERIANISM, but from a conviction that the church's system of governance was necessarily shaped by the larger political system in which it was situated.

Bishop and Archbishop

Not surprisingly, Whitgift's views found favor with Queen Elizabeth, and in 1576 she awarded him the bishopric of Worcester. He stayed until 1583 when Elizabeth nominated him as archbishop of Canterbury. No doubt the nomination was proof of Elizabeth's enduring good opinion of Whitgift, but it also revealed Elizabeth's desire to fill the post with someone who shared her zeal for conformity. Edmund Grindal, Whitgift's predecessor, had displeased Elizabeth mightily when he refused to suppress "prophesyings," that is, meetings where CLERGY rehearsed their PREACHING skills and facility with scripture. Grindal was placed under house arrest, and for the rest of his term was prohibited from carrying out any but the most minor of tasks.

Consequently, when Whitgift became archbishop, the church had been without effective metropolitical leadership for over five years. He rose to the challenge, proving quickly he would tolerate no opposition to the order and constitutions of the church. He issued articles that prohibited prophesyings and other private religious gatherings, allowed no compromise on questions of vestments, and demanded that all ministers of the church acclaim that the BOOK OF COMMON PRAYER contained nothing contrary to the word of God. Moreover, he required that all clergy affirm Elizabeth's dominion over all persons in her realm, over and above any other temporal, ecclesiastical, or spiritual power.

Whitgift championed the royal authority and the episcopacy throughout his career as archbishop. He supported RICHARD HOOKER during Hooker's tenure at Temple Church, and helped him acquire a more quiet living when Hooker began to write *The Laws of Ecclesiastical Polity* (the fifth volume is dedicated to Whitgift). He succeeded in passing stringent anti-Puritan laws in 1593, and successfully kept those with strong presbyterian leanings from holding important office (see PURITANISM; PRESBYTERIANISM).

Whitgift's unyielding attitude combined with his predilection for the pomp and ceremony of his position earned him many detractors. The Marprelate Tracts, a series of Puritan pamphlets published during the 1590s, labeled him "John Kankerbury, the Pope of Lambeth." Interestingly, despite their disagreement over issues of church POLITY, Whitgift and the Puritans agreed on two significant issues: the need for an educated clergy and the wisdom of the doctrine of PREDESTINATION as explicated by JOHN CALVIN. As archbishop, Whitgift refined a system he had designed in Worcester to put in place a practical and efficient method by which licensed preachers tutored unlearned clergy. Concerning predestination, Whitgift once chided Cartwright for not giving proper weight to this important principle. In 1595 a controversy at Cambridge University prompted Whitgift to form a committee that produced "The Lambeth Articles," nine statements supporting Calvinist tenets. Elizabeth was not apprised of this committee, and evidently expressed her disapproval to Whitgift. The Articles were never formally adopted.

This episode notwithstanding, Whitgift and Elizabeth enjoyed a close relationship to the end. She is said to have referred to him as "her little black husband," and he attended her at her deathbed. Elizabeth died in 1603; Whitgift survived his queen by little less than a year. He lived to crown James I, and to attend the Hampton Court Conference where his protégé and successor Richard Bancroft championed the conformist position so long defended by Whitgift. Whitgift died February 29, 1604 in London and is buried in Croyden.

References and Further Reading

Primary Source:

Whitgift, John. *The Works of John Whitgift*. Edited by Rev. John Ayre, The Parker Society. 3 vols. Cambridge: Cambridge University Press, 1851–1853.

Secondary Sources:

Dawley, Powell Mills. *John Whitgift and the English Reformation*. New York: Scribner, 1954.
Lake, Peter. *Anglicans and Puritans? Presbyterianism and English Conformist Thought from Whitgift to Hooker*. London: Unwin Hyman, 1988.
Paule, George. *Life of the Most Reverend and Religious Prelate, John Whitgift*. London: 1612.
Porter, H. C. *Reformation and Reaction in Tudor Cambridge*. Cambridge: Cambridge University Press, 1958.

KAREN BRUHN

WICHERN, JOHANN HEINRICH (1808–1881)

German reformer. Wichern was born on April 21, 1808, the eldest of seven children, and died on April 7, 1881. He is generally and correctly considered "the father of the Inner Mission"—although not because he founded many diaconal institutions, but because he brought them together for the first time and because his notion of "Inner Mission" as the primary idea behind social Protestantism in GERMANY has had a substantial impact to the present day.

Wichern came from a modest home. His father was a scrivener for a notary public until he himself became a notary public in 1806 and rose to the bourgeois middle class. He sent the ten-year-old Johann to Hamburg's Johanneum School, a prominent German high school. But Johann had to leave the school before earning his diploma. His father had died suddenly in 1823 and left behind a widow and seven children without income except what the musically talented Johann could earn by giving private piano lessons and later as a teaching assistant in a Christian school. In the years 1826–1827 he joined an ecclesiastical party in Hamburg that fought against the theological rationalism to which most CLERGY in Hamburg subscribed. Influential politicians supported evangelical religious practice. They encouraged the young Wichern and eventually provided the financial support enabling him to study THEOLOGY.

Wichern completed his theological studies at Göttingen with the professor of practical theology Friedrich Lücke, and then moved to Berlin where he studied under FRIEDRICH SCHLEIERMACHER and JOHANN AUGUST NEANDER. In Hamburg in 1832 he failed his first round of exams, and being thirtieth on the list of aspiring clergy at a time when the profession was overcrowded, he had little hope of finding a position in the church. While teaching SUNDAY SCHOOL he seized the opportunity to take over the direction of a newly established Salvation House, a place that provided rootless young men a home and a practical education. Wichern formulated a concept of EDUCATION along the lines of existing models in Weimar, Germany (Johannes Falk), and Beuggen, SWITZERLAND (Samuel Zeller). These models sought to shape individuals into a family-like group structure in which youths could experience love and trust as well as religious instruction in an environment free from repression. As a matter of principle Wichern refused financial subsidies from the state to keep the institution, dubbed the "rough house," independent of political pressures. Older assistants—soon called "brothers"—led the groups, and Wichern took responsibility for their education in a "brothers' house." From this institution evolved the diaconal brotherhood: a female counterpart was established by the diaconal minister Theodor Fliedner in Kaiserswerth near Düsseldorf in 1836.

Wichern's work in Hamburg was based on his conviction that what alienated the underclasses from Christianity and from the CHURCH was rooted in their social conditions. Mass poverty in the years before the March Revolution of 1848 had resulted from the collapse of proto-industrialization in Germany and the migration from the agricultural areas of the east to the big cities (Hamburg, Berlin) and to the regions along the Rhine River, the Ruhr valley, and Upper Silesia. These upheavals severed traditional religious connections, and the church did not know how to react effectively. Wichern outlined a program of re-Christianizing the unchurched masses and made social aid for the poor a precondition for the PREACHING of the Word of God. Wichern did not trust the state church of his day to complete the double task of providing social aid based on Christian responsibility *and* of ministering the gospel to the poor. So he set up independent religious unions, which—because of their independence from the church hierarchy and the limitations of individual congregations as were found among regional churches—formed a network of socially engaged diaconic groups. He called this network the "Inner Mission." In 1848 in Wittenberg, Wichern took the opportunity to present his ideas before an assembly of German Protestantism. Those present welcomed the possibilities in Wichern's ideas and decided to establish a committee that could coordinate the work in Germany. Out of this came in 1849 the *Central-Ausschuss für Innere Mission* (Central Committee for the Inner Mission) in Berlin, which still exists today as the *Diakonisches Werk der Evangelischen Kirche in Deutschland*, with its center in Stuttgart.

Wichern was no social reformer and no promoter of state-sponsored social welfare, although the notion of cooperation in social work between state and independent religious and philanthropic groups goes back to his idea. Above all he aimed to invigorate the church and win back all those classes of society that had become increasingly alienated after the Congress of Vienna. Included among them were not only the "poor" but also the educated and the working middle class. Inner Mission, as the link between social work and the preaching of the gospel, was for him a broad cultural phenomenon that society should embrace. In 1857 he joined the Prussian Ministry of Justice with the task of reforming prisons. He undertook the first attempts toward resocializing prisoners after their release. He was also a member of the supreme council of the Protestant church, the highest administrative body in the Prussian church.

The Inner Mission and its counterpart, the Caritas Union, founded in 1897—together with the big cities and the social-welfare departments of regional states—shaped the German model of the modern social-welfare state that is characterized by a "mixed economy of welfare" (Christoph Sachsse). Independent groups, religious organizations (nongovernmental organizations or NGOs), *and* state institutions serve the social sector together and do so by mutual agreement. The Inner Mission led by Wichern and his followers had an essential role in its development. For its impact and for the reputation of German Protestantism, this remains tremendously important, even to this day.

References and Further Reading

Primary Source:

Wichern, J. H. *Sämtliche Werke I–X,* edited by P. Meinhold and G. Brakelmann. Hamburg, Berlin, and Hannover: 1958–1988.

Secondary Sources:

Gerhardt, M. *Ein Lebensbild.* 3 vols. Hamburg: *Agentur des Rauhen Hauses,* 1927–1931.

Herrmann, V., J. C. Kaiser, and Th. Strohm, eds. *Bibliographie zur Geschichte der dt. ev. Diakonie im 19. u. 20. Jh.* Stuttgart: Kohlhammer, 1997.

Kaiser, J. C., ed. in collaboration with V. Herrmann. *Handbuch zur Geschichte der deutschen Inneren Mission im 19. u. 20. Jh.* Stuttgart: Kohlhammer, 2003.

———. "Sozialer Protestantismus und 'Zweitkirche': Entstehungskontext und Entwicklungslinien der Inneren Mission," in Karl Gabriel ed., *Der herausgeforderte Sozialstaat und die kirchlichen Wohlfahrtsverbände in Deutschland.* 27–47. Berlin: 2001.

Röper, U., and C. Jüllig, eds. *Die Macht der Nächstenliebe: Einhundertfünfzig Jahre Innere Mission und Diakonie, 1848–1998: Katalog zur Ausstellung im Deutschen Historischen Museum.* Berlin: Jovis, 1998.

Sturm, S. "Sozialstaat und Christlichsozialer Gedanke: Agentur des Rauhen Hauses Sozialtheologie und ihre neuere Rezeption in system-theoretischer Perspektive." Ph.D. dissertation, Westf. Wilhelms Universität, Münster, 1999.

JOCHEN-CHRISTOPH KAISER

WILBERFORCE, SAMUEL (1805–1873)

English bishop. Wilberforce was born on September 7, 1805 at Clapham, London, the third son of WILLIAM WILBERFORCE, the emancipationist, who was at the time a leader of the CLAPHAM SECT of Evangelicals, and Barbara Anne Spooner. After a private education he was matriculated at Oriel College, University of Oxford, in 1823 as a commoner and, under the influence of his father, began to develop his considerable debating skills. He graduated in 1826 with first-class honors in mathematics and a second in classics, and on June 11, 1828 married Emily Sargent, daughter of the rector of Lavington, Sussex. In the same year he was appointed curate of Checkendon, near Henley, Oxfordshire. In 1830 his father gained him the patronage of the bishop of Winchester who presented him to the rectorship of Brightstone, Isle of Wight where he immediately began to make a name for himself as preacher and writer.

Wilberforce was throughout his career a High Churchman in the sense of holding the CHURCH OF ENGLAND central to English life, politics, and society. His early published works included *Note Book of a Country Clergyman,* an edition of the *Letters and Journals* of Henry Martyn, with his brother Robert he wrote the *Life of William Wilberforce* (1838), and in 1840 the *Correspondence.* These were joined by *Agathos and other Sunday Stories* (1839), *University Sermons* (1839), and *Rocky Island and other Parables* (1840). In 1844 he published *History of the American Church.* However, by 1838 his writing was sufficiently opposed to the Tractarians that JOHN HENRY NEWMAN refused to publish any more of his essays (see OXFORD MOVEMENT). Over the next few years his reputation and influence grew so that in 1839 Wilberforce became archdeacon of Surrey and in 1840, canon of Winchester and rector of Alverstoke, Hampshire. The following year he was made chaplain to Prince Albert and in 1843 the archbishop of York appointed him sub-almoner to the queen. In May 1845 he was made dean of Westminster and then in October 1845, bishop of Oxford, where he stayed for twenty-five years.

At Oxford Wilberforce's career was marked by a devotion to his pastoral duties, particularly the cause of improving clerical education, but was also touched by controversy. The see at Oxford, with its close connections to the university through Christ Church, was something of a poisoned chalice for someone of Wilberforce's politics, who would be attacked on the one side for being too close to the Catholics and by the Tractarians as being too conservative. He was also cordially detested by the Evangelical wing of the church. In 1843 EDWARD PUSEY had been banned by the university from preaching for two years and in 1845 he took Newman's place as leader of the Tractarians, Newman himself just having been received into the Catholic Church. Wilberforce was not helped by the fact that over the next twenty years his brother-in-law, sister-in-law and her husband, his brothers Robert and William, his own daughter, and her husband were all received into the Catholic church.

Wilberforce quickly established himself as a powerful speaker in the House of Lords and it was there that he earned the sobriquet of "Soapy Sam"—a man with a fearsome reputation for debate but almost too clever and slippery a rhetorician. He soon became embroiled in controversy when in 1847 the prime minister offered the Hereford see to Renn Dickson Hampden, Regius professor of divinity at Oxford, whose writing was considered unorthodox by the Tractarians. Pressed by JOHN KEBLE and Pusey, Wilberforce demanded Hampden's trial if he would not recant his writings, only to be accused of weakness when, a few weeks later, he withdrew the charges thinking Hampden to have been misrepresented.

The Wilberforce-Huxley Debate

SCIENCE and religion come newly into conflict in 1860, first with the publication of the liberal *Essays and Reviews,* several of the authors of which were Oxford colleagues. Wilberforce condemned the book in the *Quarterly Review* and pursued its authors as far as the House of Lords. Then came the event that fixed his name and sealed his reputation forever in the public eye: the so-called Wilberforce–Huxley debate with T.H. Huxley at the University Museum (June 30, 1860). Wilberforce was prominent among the ardent foes of the theories of evolution expounded by Robert Chambers in *Vestiges of Creation* (1844) and then by Charles Darwin in *On the Origin of Species by Means of Natural Selection* (1859). In this he had a particular ally in Richard Owen, the London zoologist (later first director of the Natural History Museum in Kensington). The University of Oxford had just completed its brand new museum as a monument to natural theology and the British Association for the Advancement of Science held its annual meeting there, with DARWINISM the topic overshadowing all others. Before the assembled who's who of British science (except for Darwin himself), Wilberforce delivered a comprehensive rebuttal of the theory (the text, showing Owen's influences, was later published anonymously in *Quarterly Review*). He famously concluded with the rhetorical flourish that he "had been informed that Professor Huxley had said that he didn't care whether or not his grandfather was an ape." The myth has been perpetuated over the years that he had demanded of Huxley whether "it was through his grandfather or his grandmother that he claimed descent from an ape" but that (particularly "grandmother") would have been far too crude a jibe. Huxley famously ended his response by turning Wilberforce's rhetoric against him: "If then the question is out to me whether I would rather have a miserable ape for a grandfather or a man highly endowed by nature and possessed of great means of influence and yet employs those faculties and that influence for the mere purpose of introducing ridicule into a grave scientific discussion, I unhesitatingly affirm my preference for the ape."

Having been passed over for London, in 1869 Wilberforce attained the bishopric of Winchester and devoted much effort to revision of the New Testament. On July 19, 1873 he was killed in a riding accident.

See also Creation Science

References and Further Reading

Primary Sources:

Wilberforce, Samuel. *A History of the Protestant Episcopal Church in America.* London: J. Burns, 1844.
———. *The Note Book of a Country Clergyman.* New York: Harper, 1979, 1833.
———. *A Reproof of the American Church.* New York: W. Harned, 1846.
Wilberforce, Samuel, R. K. Pugh, and John Frederick Arthur Mason. *The Letter-Books of Samuel Wilberforce, 1843–68.* Aylesbury: Buckinghamshire Record Society and the Oxfordshire Record Society, 1970.

Secondary Sources:

Burgon, John W. *Lives of Twelve Good Men.* London: John Murray, 1888.
Meacham, Standish. *Lord Bishop: the Life of Samuel Wilberforce.* Cambridge, MA: Harvard University Press, 1970.
Thomson, Keith W. "The Huxley, Wilberforce and the Oxford Museum." *American Scientist* 88 (2000): 209–213.
Wilberforce, Robert I. *The Life of Samuel Wilberforce.* Rev. ed. London: J. Murray, 1888.

KEITH STEWART THOMSON

WILBERFORCE, WILLIAM (1759–1833)

English politician. Wilberforce was active in Parliament from 1780 to 1825. Converted as a young man to an Evangelical faith, he dedicated himself to campaigns for the moral improvement of the country and, supremely, for the abolition of the slave trade. He was an influential supporter of the various Evangelical causes of his day.

Career

Born in Hull, Yorkshire, on August 24, 1759, Wilberforce lost his father when he was only eight and his grandfather, a wealthy merchant, when he was fifteen. Inheriting a substantial private income, the young man went up two years later to St. John's College, Cambridge, where he became a close friend of William Pitt, later prime minister. In 1780 he was elected member of Parliament (MP) for Hull, and four years later for the vast constituency of Yorkshire, which he retained for twenty-eight years. Although he gave steady support to Pitt in the House of Commons and was considered for government office, he was thought to be too slack in his attention to business. He suffered from persistent ill health and the effects of the opium prescribed for its cure, but in 1797 he married Barbara Spooner, with whom he had four sons. After Pitt's death in 1806, Wilberforce remained loyal to his friend's principles, defending the established Constitution and insisting on the enforcement of measures designed to maintain public order. Although this stance aligned him with those subsequently called Tories, he favored moderate parliamentary reform, full civil rights for Roman Catholics, and the abolition of hanging. In 1812 he left his Yorkshire parliamentary seat because of the pressures of defending it, becoming instead MP for the small borough of Bramber in Sussex until his final retirement from parliament in 1825. He died in London on July 29, 1833 and was buried in Westminster Abbey on August 5.

Evangelicalism and Its Campaigns

The fame of Wilberforce rests on his commitment to Evangelical Christianity (see EVANGELICALISM) and the causes it sponsored. While traveling on the continent during 1784 and 1785, the young politician read Philip Doddridge's *Rise and Progress of Religion in the Soul,* which was crucial in making him realize that his faith had been only nominal, and gradually he emerged from a spiritual crisis as a believer in "vital Christianity." On the advice of John Newton, the former slave trader who was now an Evangelical clergyman, Wilberforce determined to remain in politics to advance Christian causes. One major preoccupation became "the reformation of manners." In 1787 he persuaded King George III, through Pitt as prime minister, to issue a proclamation urging magistrates to enforce existing laws against blasphemy, drunkenness, and similar misdemeanors. Wilberforce was a driving force behind the subsequent creation of a Proclamation Society, which stirred supporters into calling for local action against wrongdoing. This campaign has been interpreted as an exercise in social control in the interests of the ruling classes, but Wilberforce was concerned with reform of the whole of society. His *Practical View of the Prevailing Religious System of Professed Christians* (1797) censured the upper and middle classes for neglect of their responsibilities. Diagnosing their fundamental weakness as formal rather than convinced adherence to the gospel, Wilberforce commended "real Christianity" to them. The politician's book achieved a wide readership and contributed to bringing about many conversions similar to his own.

The most celebrated campaign undertaken by Wilberforce was the effort to suppress the slave trade (see SLAVERY; SLAVERY, ABOLITION OF). Although he had shared the growing public aversion to that trade since his youth, the politician drew his inspiration for abolition from his faith. He worked in cooperation with fellow Evangelicals, many of whom formed the group that was in retrospect to be called the CLAPHAM SECT because they lived in the London suburb of that name. In 1789 Wilberforce carried a set of resolutions against the trade in the House of Commons and over the next few years, in the teeth of opposition from planters and merchants, he sustained his humanitarian pressure. In 1806 a bill for partial abolition was carried; in the next year total abolition followed. In the same year he set up an African Institution to promote civilization in the continent, to persuade other countries to suppress the slave trade, and to improve the conditions of the slaves. In 1823 Wilberforce published *An Appeal . . . on behalf of the Negro Slaves in the West Indies,* although it was not until later years that he supported a younger generation in pressing for the emancipation of the slaves. That was to be achieved in British territories in 1833, the year of Wilberforce's death.

The politician was able to promote the Evangelical cause in a variety of ways. He supported many of the burgeoning Evangelical societies of the day such as the Church Missionary Society (1799) and the BRITISH AND FOREIGN BIBLE SOCIETY (1806). He obtained posts for promising Evangelical clergy in the CHURCH OF ENGLAND. He defended the Methodists from attempts by the authorities to suppress their activities. In 1813 he led a movement to ensure freedom for missionaries to enter INDIA at the time of the renewal of the East India Company charter. Wilberforce was one of the circle of Anglican Evangelicals who contributed to their periodical, *The Christian Observer,* in the early years after its foundation in 1802, submitting, for example, a critical review of WILLIAM PALEY's classic statement of the argument from design. Theologically Wilberforce was originally a moderate Calvinist whose CALVINISM gradually became more diluted until it virtually disappeared. His life was a supreme example of the extraordinary energy in good causes unleashed by the Evangelical movement.

References and Further Reading

Primary Source:

Wilberforce, William. *A Practical View of the Prevailing Religious System of Professed Christians.* London: T. Cadell, jun., and W. Davies, 1797.

Secondary Sources:

Howse, Ernest M. *Saints in Politics: The "Clapham Sect" and the Growth of Freedom.* Toronto: University of Toronto Press, 1952.
Pollock, John. *Wilberforce.* London: Constable, 1977.
Wilberforce, Robert I., and Samuel Wilberforce. *The Life of William Wilberforce.* 5 vols. London: John Murray, 1839.

D. W. BEBBINGTON

WILLARD, FRANCES ELIZABETH CAROLINE (1839–1898)

American social reformer. Willard was a TEMPERANCE reformer, a supporter of ECUMENISM, women's suffrage, and women's rights within Protestant churches. She was born in Churchville, New York in 1839. In her youth her family joined the Methodist Episcopal Church. Willard was a teacher, an evangelist for DWIGHT L. MOODY, and a founder and the national president of the Women's Christian Temperance Union (WCTU) from 1879 until her death in 1898.

Willard was concerned with reforming the ills of society and encouraged her organization to begin the task. She advocated suffrage as the leader of WCTU and as the editor of their periodical, *Our Union.* In her *Woman in the Pulpit,* she advocated a place for WOMEN within her religious tradition by providing an exegesis of biblical passages that discussed women's religious participation. Many consider Willard the most important laywoman in the Methodist Episcopal Church of the nineteenth century. However, she also caused controversy within her denomination over a "woman's place" when she wanted to address the Methodist General Conference about WCTU, and in 1887 she became an elected delegate to this conference. Willard is an important figure in Protestantism not only because of her support of reform, but also because of her desire to find a place for women in Protestant denominations.

See also Methodism; Methodism, North America; Social Gospel; Women Clergy

References and Further Reading

Primary Sources:

Willard, Frances E. *Women and Temperance*. Hartford, CT: Park Publishing Company, 1883.
———. *Women in the Pulpit*. Chicago: Woman's Temperance Publishing Association, 1889.
———. *Writing Out My Heart: Selections From the Journal of Frances E. Willard*. Edited by Carolyn De Swarte Gifford. Urbana: University of Illinois Press, 1995.

Secondary Sources:

Bordin, Ruth. *Frances Willard: A Biography*. Chapel Hill: University of North Carolina Press, 1986.
Earhart, Mary. *Frances Willard: From Prayers to Politics*. Chicago: University of Chicago Press, 1944.

KELLY J. BAKER

WILLIAMS, ROGER (1603?–1683)

Radical puritan and founder of Rhode Island. Williams deserves to be remembered chiefly for his unflinching embrace of religious liberty.

Born in London, probably in the first year of the reign of James I, the young Williams found an invaluable patron in the person of the famed jurist, Sir Edward Coke (1552–1634). With the latter's advice and support, he finished a preparatory education that qualified him for admission to Pembroke College of Cambridge University. Receiving his Bachelor of Arts degree in 1627, Williams stayed on in Cambridge for postgraduate work, then accepted ordination in the CHURCH OF ENGLAND in 1629.

Williams quickly identified himself with the Puritan party of that national church, joining others in urging this institution to become more rigorously and consistently Protestant.

Williams and Massachusetts Bay Colony

In the midst of vigorous agitations and intense examinations of both hearts and scripture, many Cambridge graduates resolved to leave ENGLAND and its heavy-handed bishops in order to create a true and purer church in England's lands across the Atlantic Ocean. In 1630 the lawyer JOHN WINTHROP (1588–1649) led a large contingent of Englishmen, women, and children to Massachusetts Bay, where they, in faithful covenant with God, created a holy commonwealth and a New Testament church. Before the decade of the 1630s ended, thousands followed in Winthrop's wake, setting the course for much of America's religious history to come. One of the early followers, Roger Williams, set sail from Bristol late in 1630 arriving, with his new wife, off Nantasket on February 5, 1631.

Much attention had to be given to the demands of survival in a bitterly cold, barren, and unforgiving wilderness, but even in the midst of these basic human challenges, one could neither forget nor neglect the religious urgencies that brought the Puritans to the colonies in the first place. In recognition of his piety, education, and zeal, Williams was asked to lead the newly formed church in Boston. He declined the honor, however, because he recognized that the majority of the congregation still saw themselves as members of the Church of England. They intended to complete their program of reform, unhindered, until they could show England what a model New Testament church looked like. And then, they confidently believed, their mother country would see the light, purify the national church, and be a beacon of a purer Protestantism to all the Western world.

Williams was dismayed by what he regarded as hypocrisy. How could the Puritans radically reform the national church, all the while pretending to still be members of it? How can one, Williams plaintively asked, build a square house of God on the keel of a ship? The only honest and honorable course to take, Williams asserted, was to scrap all tradition and begin afresh with only the New Testament as a guide. In this way, the cause of Christ would be magnified and the true church would be made manifest.

Williams had other concerns as well that prevented him from finding complete comfort in the civil and ecclesiastical patterns of Massachusetts Bay. The Puritans had rejected bishops, but they had not rejected all mingling of the church and the state. The civil magistrates in Massachusetts continued to enforce religious duties and to punish dissent. They even required unbelievers to swear an oath in court, "so help me God," which Williams saw as a travesty and a plain violation of conscience. Beyond all this, Williams, who had early studied the languages of the Indians and sympathetically observed their culture, complained that the Massachusetts Bay Colony had done nothing to compensate NATIVE AMERICANS for lands that had suddenly been claimed as the private property of Englishmen.

In the space of a mere four years, Williams had raised enough objections and thrown down enough challenges to completely unnerve the authorities of the Bay Colony. In October 1635, the General Court of Massachusetts Bay passed a sentence of exile against

Williams for his "new and dangerous opinions." He was given six weeks to leave.

Williams and Rhode Island

Williams readily recognized that he could neither remain in Massachusetts Bay nor return to England. His alternatives were limited. The Dutch in New Amsterdam were too far away and might be even less hospitable than his own countrymen. But between the claims of the Dutch and those of Massachusetts, much empty territory lay. Williams set out, with the help of the American Indians, to create a colony of his own, with a line clearly drawn between the civil and the ecclesiastical orders, and with sensitive regard for the tender consciences of all humankind.

Making his way on foot through winter snows, Williams, after some six weeks of not knowing "what bed or bread did mean," arrived at the headwaters of the Narraganset Bay, where he created a small settlement that he called Providence—"in a sense of God's merciful Providence to me in my distress." Slowly and never too surely, the colony of Rhode Island and Providence Plantations gradually came into being. Here Williams spent most of the remainder of his life (returning to England for a time)—nearly half a century—trying to give stability to his colony and life to his vision of a full liberty in all matters of the human soul.

In 1638 Williams joined with twenty other settlers in creating a BAPTIST church, the first on American soil. The distinguishing feature of this church was its rejection of infant baptism, replaced by a "believer's baptism" extended to those who made a voluntary profession of faith. Religion was viewed as personal, and the commitment to it as necessarily wholly free. Williams did not long remain a Baptist, as he soon concluded that no church could be fully loyal to the New Testament. Williams continued to defend the Baptists as being the closest that one could come to New Testament Christianity in the present age.

By 1640, with thirty-seven families in residence, the Providence settlers drew up formal articles of agreement. One article made clear the uniqueness of this new urban experiment: "We agree, As formerly hath been the liberties of the Town, so still to hold forth Liberty of Conscience."

To insure the survival of his tiny colony, Williams went to London in 1643 to obtain a charter. This trip enabled him to get some of his writings into print, for Providence did not have a printer and Boston had no interest in promoting his radical views. His first book, *A Key into the Language of America* (1643), proved to be his most popular. A sensitive study of the language, culture, and religion of New England American Indi-

ans, this work won an immediate audience in England and an enduring one in America. The situation was otherwise with his second book, *The Bloudy Tenant of Persecution, for Cause of Conscience* (1644). This book was burned in London almost as soon as it appeared, and was widely excoriated in America, nowhere more vigorously than in Massachusetts.

The strong message of *The Bloudy Tenant* was that the church and the state must be separated for the sake of the church, for the sake of humanity, and for the cause of Christ. Williams argued that the joining of these two institutions, ever since the days of the Emperor Constantine, had resulted not in the purity of religion but in the horror of bloody persecutions and even bloodier religious wars.

Anticipating English philosopher John Locke (1632–1704), and very probably influencing him as well, Williams argued that all civil power comes from the people. The "divine right of kings" was a fiction, a costly myth. Governments "have no more power" than the people "consenting and agreeing shall betrust them with." Churches, on the other hand, had a "divine right" or at least a divine origin. Ordained by God, chartered by Christ, they have a status quite apart from that of the civil order. It therefore made no sense, according to Williams, to put this divine institution in the hands of "natural, sinful, inconstant men, and so consequently (of) Satan himself."

Because England was in the midst of a civil war and had no king, Williams abandoned hope of receiving a royal charter and instead appealed to Parliament for some legal foundation. In March 1644 the relevant Parliamentary committee voted (with two votes to spare) for a "Free Charter of Civil Incorporation and Government for the Providence Plantations in the Narragansett Bay in New England."

In the late summer of 1644, Williams arrived back home in Rhode Island, where he was soon elected "chief Officer" of the colony, a position he would retain for the next three years. Now he faced the difficult task of demonstrating how religious liberty operated. Some citizens, of course, were ready to treat liberty as a synonym for licentiousness, while others thought the logical corollary of liberty in religion was anarchy in politics. To the end of his life, Williams repeatedly contended with these perversions of a genuine "soul liberty."

Because of continuing quarrels over authority, a second trip to London became necessary. Joining with John Clarke (1609–1676), leading citizen and Baptist pastor in Newport, Williams in 1651 had to leave his family and friends to labor once more on behalf of Rhode Island. Conferring with OLIVER CROMWELL (1599–1658) on theological issues and working with Parliament on political ones, Williams returned home after two years, leaving Clarke behind to conclude the tortuous negotiations for a new charter. Because the monarchy was restored in 1660, the new charter, granted in 1663, was a royal one, more enduring, more authoritative than a mere vote of Parliament. The charter granted to the people of Rhode Island "a full liberty in religious concernments."

While in London, Williams published a tender love letter to his wife, encouraging her in her periods of melancholy or spiritual doubt. This small book, called *Experiments of Spiritual Life and Health* (1652), reveals Williams's profound and personal piety—a side of his career too often obscured or forgotten. For him, this life was a mere shadow of the glories to be revealed in the life to come. We should think of ourselves, Williams wrote, as passengers on a ship, destined for a heavenly harbor. When persecuted or defeated or despondent, we must "sometimes warm and revive our cold hearts and fainting spirits with the assured hope of those victories, those crowns, those harvests, those refreshings and fruits . . . which God hath prepared for them that love him."

In his old age, Williams rowed from Providence to Newport (about thirty miles) in order to contest against the Quakers, whose theology he rejected. Although he believed firmly in religious liberty, Williams did not advocate religious indifference. He argued for many days trying to convince the Quakers that they were wrong, but would never permit the hand of the state to be raised against them to the slightest degree.

Williams suffered many disappointments, perhaps none so severe as the "Indian uprising" of 1675, known as King Phillip's War. All of Williams's years of delicate negotiation, of careful cultivating of friendships, of scrupulous avoidance of forced conversions, came to a brutal end in the furies of New England's bloodiest war. Williams's own house went up in flames, as did his dreams of an intercultural harmony between the American Indians and the English. In his last years he also suffered the loss of his wife and one of his six children. With ever deepening sorrow he found himself writing once more to his friends and neighbors in Providence in 1682, begging them to behave as good citizens should and reminding them that "Our Charter Excels all in New England, or the World, as to the Souls of Men."

The next year, Williams died. The exact date of his death, like that of his birth, is unknown. Instead, America's commitment to a "full liberty in religious concernments" stands as his enduring monument.

References and Further Reading

Gaustad, Edwin S. *Liberty of Conscience: Roger Williams in America* Valley Forge, PA: Judson Press, 1999.
Gilpin, W. Clark. *The Millenarian Piety of Roger Williams.* Chicago: University of Chicago Press, 1979.
Hall, Timothy L. *Separating Church and State: Roger Williams and Religious Liberty.* Urbana, IL: University of Illinois Press, 1998.
LaFantasie, Glenn W. *The Correspondence of Roger Williams.* 2 vols. Hanover, NH: University Press of New England, 1988.
Morgan, Edmund S. *Roger Williams: The Church and the State.* New York: Harcourt, Brace, & World, 1967.
Williams, Roger. *The Bloudy Tenant of Persecution.* Edited by Richard Groves. Macon, GA: Mercer University Press, 2001.

EDWIN S. GAUSTAD

WILSON, THOMAS WOODROW (1856–1924)

Twenty-eighth president of the United States. Wilson, the twenty-eighth president of the United States (1913–1921), was born in a Presbyterian manse in Staunton, Virginia. Among his ancestors were Presbyterian ministers on both sides of his family, and the family of his first wife, Ellen Axson Wilson, also included Presbyterian ministers. His father, Dr. Joseph Ruggles Wilson, was one of the founders of the Presbyterian Church in the Confederate States of America in 1861, and after the CIVIL WAR he became the Stated Clerk and one of the foremost leaders of the Presbyterian Church in the United States, the southern branch of American PRESBYTERIANISM.

Wilson was raised in the South and imbued deeply the ethos of southern Presbyterianism. Many contemporaries and subsequent biographers have argued that a crucial key to understanding Wilson's personality and politics was his religious faith. "My life would not be worth living," he declared as president, "if it were not for the driving power of religion, for *faith,* pure and simple."

Wilson attended Davidson College for one year and graduated from Princeton University in 1879. He attended the University of Virginia Law School but did not receive a degree, and after briefly practicing law, entered the new Ph.D. program in politics at the Johns Hopkins University. After receiving his degree, he taught at Bryn Mawr College and Wesleyan University and then returned to Princeton. After twelve years on the faculty, he became the university's president in 1902. Amidst the theological controversies in American Presbyterianism, Wilson tried to keep Princeton above the fray, though personally he had little regard for the archconservatives in his denomination.

Wilson resigned and was elected governor of New Jersey in 1910. Quickly establishing himself as a reformer and a progressive Democrat, Wilson was elected president in 1912 and reelected in 1916. In both foreign and domestic policy, he sought to use the power of the state and the influence of the presidency to bring new order to American society and the postwar world. His speeches reflect the missionary spirit of Protestantism; for example, he said America's role in World War I was "to make the world safe for democracy." When he formulated "the Covenant of the League of Nations," the title itself revealed the impact of the covenant theological tradition in Presbyterianism. The philosophical principles of twentieth-century American foreign policy were largely forged by Wilson—with both positive and negative consequences—and the influence of his Protestant and Presbyterian heritage helped shape his assumptions about society and politics.

References and Further Reading

Cooper, John Milton. *The Warrior and the Priest: Woodrow Wilson and Theodore Roosevelt.* Cambridge: Harvard University Press, 1983.

Link, Arthur S., et al., eds. *The Papers of Woodrow Wilson.* 69 vols. Princeton: Princeton University Press, 1966–1994. [This is the definitive collection of Wilson's writings, including those on religion.]

Link, Arthur S. *The Higher Realism of Woodrow Wilson and Other Essays.* Nashville: Vanderbilt University Press, 1973.

Mulder, John M. *Woodrow Wilson: The Years of Preparation.* Princeton: Princeton University Press, 1978.

Mulder, John M., Ernest M. White, and Ethel S. White, eds., *Woodrow Wilson: A Bibliography.* Westport, CT: Greenwood Press, 1997.

JOHN M. MULDER

WINSTANLEY, GERRARD
(c. 1609–c. 1675)

English church leader. Winstanley was born near or in Wigam, Lancashire, ENGLAND in about 1609. After he completed his apprenticeship as a merchant-tailor in London in 1637 he struggled in business and went bankrupt during the Civil Wars (1643). Winstanley and his wife, Susan, tried to reestablish themselves in Cobham, Surrey during the 1640s but failed. During this period Winstanley claimed to have had a deeply spiritual experience that led to his involvement with a group called the Diggers.

Winstanley became a leader of the Digger movement in 1649–1650. Forty to fifty people tried to cultivate the common land at St. George's Hill in Walton-on-Thames and then in the neighboring parish of Cobham. Harassed by the local population at both sites, these experiments in communal living failed by Easter 1650. His life afterward is cloudy, but it seems that his first wife predeceased him; he remarried, fathered two sons, and became a corn chandler and Quaker before his death in London in 1675 (see FRIENDS, SOCIETY OF).

Like most Christians, Winstanley believed that humanity had fallen from its original state of grace. However, little else in his writings is orthodox. He thought private property as well as commerce were negative outcomes of the Fall or perhaps even the cause of the Fall. He thought that Christ would usher in a communal society upon his return, but Winstanley's millenarianism is open to interpretation: did he believe in Christ's literal return or would Christ's Spirit bring about personal and societal regeneration? Winstanley denounced the mainstream Christian churches, their CLERGY, and doctrines as a hindrance to SALVATION. He equated God the Father with Reason; God would help bring the victory of the spirit over flesh. Conversely, the DEVIL was not a separate being but was the spirit of flesh that tried to rule humanity. Winstanley thought God would ultimately save everyone.

Gerrard Winstanley was a radical religious thinker and "communist" who published prolifically from 1648 to 1652. He was heavily influenced by the radicalism of the Protestant REFORMATION and the English Revolution. However, his impact on his own day was minimal and he received little attention from scholars until the end of the nineteenth century. Since then he has increasingly been recognized as a visionary and a gifted socioeconomic theorist, although his works have yielded very different interpretations.

See also Civil War, England; Communism; Millenarians & Millennialism

References and Further Reading

Primary Source:

Hill, Christopher, ed. *Winstanley: The Law of Freedom and Other Writings.* Harmondsworth, UK: Penguin, 1973.

Secondary Sources:

Bradstock, Andrew, ed. *Winstanley and the Diggers, 1649–1999.* London: Frank Cass, 2000.

Hill, Christopher. "The Religion of Gerrard Winstanley." *Past & Present* Supplement 5 (1978).

Mulligan, Lotte, John K. Graham, and Judith Richards. "Winstanley: A Case for the Man as He Said He Was." *Journal of Ecclesiastical History* 28 (1977): 57–75.

Petegorsky, David W. *Left-Wing Democracy in the English Civil War.* London: Victor Gollancz, 1940.

CHERYL FURY

WISCONSIN EVANGELICAL LUTHERAN SYNOD

Third largest of the three major Lutheran church bodies in the United States, after the EVANGELICAL LUTHERAN CHURCH IN AMERICA (ELCA) and the Lu-

THERAN CHURCH–MISSOURI SYNOD (LCMS), the Wisconsin Evangelical Lutheran Synod (WELS) is the most conservative theologically and least involved in interconfessional dialogue. It is not a member of ecumenical organizations, such as the WORLD COUNCIL OF CHURCHES, the NATIONAL COUNCIL OF CHURCHES, or the LUTHERAN WORLD FEDERATION. Organized in 1850 by pastors with roots in the nineteenth-century German AWAKENINGS and in several German mission societies, WELS initially exhibited a relaxed Lutheranism. Influenced by C. F. W. WALTHER and the LCMS, WELS grew increasingly conservative, joining the LCMS and other conservative, confessional Lutheran synods in forming the LUTHERAN SYNODICAL CONFERENCE (LSC) in 1872. When a bitter controversy over PREDESTINATION disrupted the LSC in the 1880s, WELS remained allied with the Missouri Synod in the Conference. In 1917 WELS formally merged with several largely German conservative Lutheran synods in the upper Midwest. Where midwestern WELS and LCMS memberships overlapped, local associations were often jointly formed to create auxiliary institutions, such as high schools and homes for the elderly and for the handicapped.

In 1961 WELS severed its relationship with the LCMS, charging that by moving into closer relationships with the AMERICAN LUTHERAN CHURCH, the LCMS had changed and no longer exhibited consistency in doctrine and practice. Because worship, including prayer, with those who are not in full agreement with WELS, including other Lutherans, is proscribed as "unionism," WELS pastors may not serve as military chaplains. WELS prohibits participation in Girl Scouts, Boy Scouts, and most fraternal organizations; condemns abortion; and excludes women from the pastorate. The Bible as the inspired, inerrant Word of God and the BOOK OF CONCORD constitute WELS's doctrinal foundation. Since the 1950s WELS has channeled its energies into the development of parochial schools, secondary and postsecondary institutions, and the expansion of domestic and foreign outreach.

See also Biblical Inerrancy; Doctrine; Lutheranism

References and Further Reading

Braun, Mark. *A Tale of Two Synods: Changes within the Evangelical Lutheran Synodical Conference of North America that Led to the Exit of the Wisconsin Evangelical Lutheran Synod.* Milwaukee, WI: Northwestern Publishing House, 2003.

Fredrich, Edward C. *The Wisconsin Synod Lutherans: A History of the Single Synod, Federation, and Merger.* Milwaukee, WI: Northwestern Publishing House, 1992.

Website: http://www.WELS.net

JAMES W. ALBERS

WITCHCRAZE

Belief in witchcraft is—like magic and religion—a universal phenomenon, and so is the persecution of suspected witches. In Europe a number of clear-cut definitions have drastically challenged traditional notions of witchcraft. Each of these interpretations is rooted in a specific intellectual environment, and the starting point causes surprise even after centuries: Christian demonology equated black and white magic. Founded on the thought of the church father St. Augustine (354–430), any kind of magic, and even superstitious customs like the wearing of amulets or watching the stars for astrological purposes, was thought to rely on a contract between a human being and a demon, the DEVIL, either explicitly or implicitly, because the magician expected an effect from a ceremony or a thing that in itself could not work. In the wake of the Roman sorcery scares, and inspired by monotheism, *any* kind of magic seemed equal to witchcraft (*De doctrina christiana,* II:30–40). Magicians and witches were seen as allies of the devil; they belonged to the *civitas diaboli*. As offenders of the law, biblical (Exodus 22:18) as well as Roman, they were to be killed.

Witches: Real or Not

In contrast, for theologians of the early and high Middle Ages, like Bishop Burchard of Worms (965–1025), author of an influential penitential, whose formulations would become part of Canon Law, witches were individuals who believed they possessed powers that in reality did *not* exist. Devils were equated with pagan gods, which were not too powerful in comparison to Jesus Christ, and witches were merely considered to be deceived by devilish illusions. They were not to be killed, but corrected and educated (Corrector Burchardi, *Decretorum libri viginti,* in *Patrologia Latina* 140, cols. 491–1090). The rise of heretical movements changed the perspective. Some late medieval theologians, like the Dominican inquisitor Heinrich Kramer/Institoris (1430–1505), author of the *Malleus Maleficarum* ("The Witches' Hammer"), imagined witches to be members of a conspiracy, directed against Christian society, which was allowed by God to cause immense physical and spiritual hardship. The witches' power, although supported by the devil with God's permission, was *real*. Witches therefore had to be physically eradicated, according to both divine and secular law, hammered out by virtually any means because exceptional crimes require exceptional measures (*Malleus Maleficarum,* Speyer 1486).

Opponents of witch-hunting generally disapproved of the atrocities, and equated them with the persecution of Christians in ancient Rome, although it took

Johann Weyer (1515–1588), the court physician of duke of Jülich-Kleve, to find a nonreligious reason. The author of the most influential early modern book against witchcraft persecutions, Weyer was an Erasmian Protestant, who—like presumably his English counterpart Reginald Scot (1538–1599)—became attached to the "Family of Love" and considered so-called witches to be melancholic females who needed leniency, love, and medical care to cure their mental illness. These "witches" were not strong, but weak; not evil, but sick; and they needed help, not punishment. Their killing could not be justified under any circumstances, but was to be seen as a "massacre of the innocents" (*De Praestigiis Daemonum,* Basel 1563, preface).

The European denial of witchcraft is firmly rooted in this pre-Cartesian opposition to atrocity, adopted by the representatives of European SPIRITUALISM, rationalism, and ENLIGHTENMENT. Because they no longer believed in the existence of witchcraft, for them witch killings were an ardent injustice committed by the authorities, "judicial murder." Only a few decades later, however, when the execution of witches already had moved into the past, a completely new, postrationalist interpretation turned up, inspired by ROMANTICISM. Witches were reinterpreted as personifications of popular CULTURE, or even of popular resistance, emphasizing the important role of WOMEN. Jacob Grimm (1785–1809), the godfather of language and folklore studies, redefined witches as *wise women,* bearers of ancient wisdom, unjustly persecuted by the Christian churches to destroy European national cultures (*Deutsche Mythologie,* Heidelberg 1835). The Romantic Paradigm culminated in the fantasies of the French historian Jules Michelet (1798–1874), who reinterpreted the witches as heroines of folk medicine, victims of feudal suppression, and predecessors of the FRENCH REVOLUTION (*La Sorciere,* Paris 1862).

Rationalism, however, remained the dominant ideology among academics during the period of INDUSTRIALIZATION. Joseph Hansen (1862–1943), the most influential protagonist of the rationalist interpretation and editor of an essential source collection, considered witchcraft to be a *nonexistent crime,* and his interpretation has molded historical research up to the present day. Nevertheless, it must have been evident for everyone reading the trial records that some of the accused had indeed experimented with magic, worked as healers, experienced ecstasies, or even dared to invoke demons, very much like their educated male contemporaries, or witches outside Europe. The European approach to witchcraft over the last two millennia has thus been characterized by "invention of tradition." Augustine, Burchard, Kramer/Institoris, Weyer, Grimm, and Michelet were founders of distinctive

traditions, the latter two, for instance, of feminist and neo-pagan witchcraft. Because of the rise of social theory, the interpretation of witchcraft underwent a leap of abstraction around 1900. Since Sigmund Freud (1856–1939), hidden desires of omnipotence and aggression, suppressed into the subconsciousness, are seen as a driving force of witchcraft fantasies, and witches as objects of projection for anxieties and aggression. Émile Durkheim's (1858–1917) idea that societies define norms by deviance has molded social anthropology's doctrine that witchcraft should be considered to be a means of securing norms, and therefore identity. MAX WEBER's (1864–1920) historical sociology linked the process of rationalization in Europe to complex changes in mental as well as economic structures, leading to a *disenchantment of the world.* Bronislaw Malinowski (1884–1942) interpreted witch fears and antiwitchcraft movements as symptoms of a crisis in society. European rationalism generally considered magic to be a product of the imagination, a consequence of deficient technology, and lack of insight into the laws of nature in a primitive society.

Protestant Response

Keith Thomas tried to link the rise of witchcraft persecutions in the sixteenth century to the REFORMATION, with its emphasis on the gospel *(sola scriptura).* MARTIN LUTHER's teachings concerning JUSTIFICATION by FAITH alone, and the Calvinist doctrine of PREDESTINATION, devaluated and indeed forbade traditional and Catholic countermagic. This in turn led to rising fears of bewitching, and therefore to increasing witchcraft accusations. According to Thomas, Protestantism forced its adherents into the intolerable position of asserting the reality of witchcraft, yet denying the existence of an effective and legitimate form of protection or cure. However, the relationship between witchcraft and Protestantism is more complex, and yet difficult to define. Pre-Reformation persecutions, it seems now, were by far more intensive than formerly assumed. Throughout the Middle Ages we can find the burning of witches, with occasional witch panics leading to the execution of groups of evil conspirators, in archaic Northern societies as well as in urbanized centers of Europe. Because of lack of sources, the size of these prosecutions, or persecutions, remains guesswork. Clearly there was an increasing concern about witchcraft from 1400, when witchcraft and heretical conspiracy were amalgamated into a novel supercrime, probably first acknowledged in the "novas sectas," consisting of Jews, heretics, diviners, and sorcerers, mentioned in a papal bull of 1409 for a Franciscan inquisitor in Savoy (ed. Hansen 1900:16f.). During large-scale persecutions with many hundreds of victims in the late 1420s and 1430s in Savoy, the Dauphiné, and the Valais, five contemporary texts report the characteristics of the new heretical sect: apostasy, the contract with the devil, sealed by sexual intercourse between humans and demons, explaining the witches' capacity of evil sorcery (maleficium), of flying through the air, the witches' dance (labeled with Jewish terms, first as "synagogue," later as "sabbat"), shape-shifting, and other supernatural abilities. From then numerous demonologies added substance to these ideas. During a wave of persecution in the 1480s the *Malleus Maleficarum* (Speyer 1486) summarized the knowledge about witchcraft, trying to provide a convincing theological fundament and practical advice to support the hunting of witches, who were now conceived as being primarily female. The Malleus, based on Augustinian theology and Aquinas, remained an authority also for Protestant demonologists.

Renaissance opposition to witch-hunting, it is usually argued, brought the burnings to a halt. In Northern Italy the mass burnings did indeed stop in the early 1520s, and papal inquisitors disappeared from Northern Europe. The Reformation made the break definitive and contributed to the decline of witch-beliefs because Protestant theologians attacked magic and supernatural agencies in general. In the eyes of Luther, HULDRYCH ZWINGLI, or JOHN CALVIN, Catholic piety and Catholic rites—the veneration of SAINTS, the expectation of miracles, the mass, the performance of pilgrimages, and the use of sacramentals—were not really different from rural superstitions, and Protestant pamphlets employed terms like "popish sorcery." Radical reformers even denied the physical power of the devil, thus questioning the demonological concept of witchcraft altogether. The focus of the debates shifted away from witchcraft in a decade of revolutionary uprisings and world-historical decisions. The flow of demonological literature stopped. The "Malleus," best-seller of the previous generation with nineteen Latin editions in GERMANY, ITALY, and FRANCE, disappeared from the market. Some contemporaries harbored the hope that the period of witch persecutions was definitively over, and were—like Johann Weyer—appalled to find that they started anew where they had it least expected—in Protestant territories.

It was indeed the hothouses of the Reformation—Wittenberg and Geneva—that were shaken by witch panics. In Wittenberg four people were executed as witches in 1540, and these burnings were part of a first wave of witch-burnings in Saxony. Luther was not involved in any of these trials, but also felt no necessity to curb them. This attitude must have bewildered Protestants as much as similar occurrences in Geneva. Calvin's Godly City had formerly been part of the witch-ridden Duchy of Savoy, and after its secession in the 1530s, followed by religious Reformation, it remained haunted by all kinds of strange fears, particularly the idea that the plague was being spread by a hidden conspiracy of poisoners, which were gradually transformed into diabolical sorcerers, or witches. Shortly after Calvin's arrival, several men were burned, and the Reformer himself literally called for the "extirpation" of the "race" of the witches. Likewise there were witch burnings in the Protestant Swiss Cantons of Zurich, Bern, and Basle. The most surprising case was DENMARK, which had gone through a tumultuous period of civil war and rapid political and religious reforms. For the first time in a Protestant territory the panic turned into a large-scale persecution, with peasants hunting witches in the open fields "like wolves," in the approving report of Peder Palladius (1503–1560), the leading Danish churchman of his age. Neither Luther, nor Zwingli, nor Calvin denied the existence of witches, and Calvinist theologians in particular, like JOHN KNOX or Lambert Daneau, perceived the witches' pact with the devil as being diametrically opposed to the believers' covenant with God.

Resurgence of Persecution

After 1560 the large-scale persecution became the decisive new style of witch-hunting, indicating a *shift of paradigm* from medieval "leniency" to the "Malleus" point of view. But why such a sudden change of mind? Researchers have pointed to the hardening of the confessional boundaries after the impact of CALVINISM and, simultaneously, post-Tridentine Catholicism, or COUNTER-REFORMATION. Furthermore, the process of state formation or nation building was speeding up in Europe, allowing for a tighter grip on the religious or superstitious beliefs of the subjects, and state formation and confessionalism were intertwined in the process of CONFESSIONALIZATION. Concerning criminal procedure, the introduction of inquisitorial law was emphasized as one of the most important results of the reception of Roman Law. From then on, a public prosecutor would "ex officio" act on behalf of the state, with torture as a legal instrument to obtain information or confessions from the suspects. This was particularly dangerous in conjunction with the idea of a witches' sabbat because suspects were asked to name their accomplices. However, the social environment also changed dramatically, with more frequent mortality crises, which can be related to the climatic deterioration of the Little Ice Age.

It is telling that within the Lutheran camp a sharp controversy on weather and weather-making witches was conducted during the 1560s, involving major Lutheran reformers like JOHANN BRENZ, Johannes Alber, Wilhelm Bidembach, and Weyer. Full-fledged Protestant demonologies started with the hunger crisis of 1570, partly in reaction to widespread witch panics from Geneva to Zurich, partly resulting from the necessity to reshape the old teachings of the "Witches' Hammer" for Protestant purposes. Zwingli's successor HEINRICH BULLINGER (1504–1575) published the first Reformed demonological advice "On Witches" in 1571. Calvin's successor Lambert Daneau (1530–1596) followed one year later (*Les Sorciers,* 1572), as well as the leading German Calvinist THOMAS ERASTUS (1524–1583) (*Disputatio de lamiis seu strigibus,* Basel 1572). The first Danish demonology was published in 1575 by Nils Hemmingsen, who inspired the demonological writings of King James VI of SCOTLAND (*Demonologie,* Edinburgh 1598) during the king's wedding trip to Copenhagen.

Post-Reformation witch-hunting started within the Protestant camp, but from 1580 massive persecutions in the Spanish Netherlands, in Luxembourg, the Franche-Comté, in Lorraine, and in some prince-bishoprics of the Holy Roman Empire (Trier, Mainz, Cologne, Eichstätt, Würzburg, and Bamberg) clearly outstripped the Protestant territories in terms of witch burnings. All of these territories saw many hundreds of executions, and Cologne, Mainz, Lorraine, and the Spanish Netherlands as many as 2,000 in the decades between 1580 and 1630, when witch-hunting climaxed in Europe. Some Protestant authors sought to use these atrocities and branded them as popish. However promising, this perspective proved unsustainable, given that the most important Catholic countries like Spain and Portugal (including their vast colonies), the papal and other Italian States, France, Austria, and Bavaria executed only few witches. On the other hand, some Protestant countries saw massive persecutions. In Pays de Vaud, subject to the reformed Swiss Canton of Berne, no less than 970 individuals were burned for witchcraft between 1581 and 1620, scattered across ninety-one local jurisdictions. It is quite likely that more than 1,200 people were sentenced to death in the Pays de Vaud in more than 2,000 trials. The Bernese government explained in a decree that the peasantry was "driven by poverty, despair . . . envy, hatred, spirit of revenge."

Influence of Institutions

Recent surveys have narrowed down the overall numbers of suspects legally killed for witchcraft to 50,000 to 60,000 in Europe between 1400 and 1800, certainly not less, or more. This is by far less than previously assumed, but we must bear in mind that this is the tip of an iceberg, with at least twice as many people tried in court, and even more informally threatened with denunciation or slander. Recent research has arrived at the conclusion that not confession, but the strength or weakness of (political, legal, social, and religious) institutions determined the treatment of witchcraft during the crucial decades around 1600. Wealthy and powerful countries with established institutions, like ENGLAND, the NETHERLANDS, or the Palatinate, could suppress popular protest and religious zeal, with the exception of brief periods of anarchy, such as during the English CIVIL WAR. To take an example from the Holy Roman Empire, where presumably half of all European witches were killed, the government of the Electoral Palatinate (about 300,000 inhabitants) held a strong grip on the lower courts, which were threatened with immediate punishment for any irregularities. Because the privy councilors in Heidelberg did not believe in witchcraft, much like the members of the law faculty and the medical faculty at the university, they would not permit witch trials. The Palatine Privy Council strictly forbade the use of torture, and ordered the release of the prisoners if there was not sufficient circumstantial evidence—which there rarely was in witchcraft accusations. The result is striking: no witches were executed in the Palatinate.

It is an interesting question whether the Palatine attitude toward witchcraft had anything to do with Calvinism at all, given that the Calvinist clergy fiercely opposed the government's attitude. Erastus as its most eminent member pointed firmly to Geneva and asked for systematic persecutions. On the other hand, some of the staunchest Calvinist opponents of witch-hunting sought refuge in the Palatinate, such as Herman Witekind (1524–1603) and Anton Prätorius (c. 1560–1614), who both denied the existence of witches. What we can learn from the example of the Palatinate is that a number of convenient stereotypes do not really work. Certainly its subjects suffered from the usual crises, and as vine growers they were vulnerable to climatic hardship. The Electorate, politically almost as fragmented as Electoral Mainz, was surrounded by hotspots of witch-hunting. The government's determined attitude, however, made no concessions to either populace or clergy, and managed to avoid the execution of witches. Territories with weak institutions and difficulties in guaranteeing survival in years of hardship, were certainly more likely to be prone to moral entrepreneurs, or to pressure from the populace. Except for Swiss Calvinist Cantons like Vaud and Grisons, this was the case in middle-sized earldoms where state formation had failed, as for instance the various territories of the Counts of Nassau, the relatives of Maurice of Nassau-Orange (1567–1625), where 400 witches were burned. In a similar position were the related counts of Isenburg-Büdingen, with another 400 victims; the counts of Schaumburg and of Lippe, with about 300 witch burnings each; and the Landgraviate Hessen-Kassel, a larger territory with more elaborate structures, which still saw a surprising 250 victims. Scotland was politically consolidated but economically marginal. As in Central Europe, there had been a rising awareness of witchcraft from the early 1560s and a peak in the 1580s; but twice in the 1590s, again in the late 1620s, and once more in the 1660s Scotland was shaken by waves of frenzied witch persecution, with about 1,350 executed in something like 2,300 trials between 1560 and 1700, in a country of roughly 900,000 inhabitants.

If we look at Lutheran Europe, we can again find that states with rudimentary institutions saw many witch trials. The Duchy of Mecklenburg, a territory of roughly 200,000 inhabitants with fragmented jurisdiction, saw close to 4,000 witch trials between 1560 and 1700, with an estimated 2,000 victims between 1600 and 1670, as many in as in the most affected Catholic principalities. In the neighboring Duchy of Pomerania, another frequently divided territory, there were at least 1,000 trials, and maybe twice as many, with at least 600 victims. Similarly in the twin duchies of Schleswig and Holstein, the former under Danish, the latter under Imperial law, there were at least 600 victims. The persecutions in Denmark flared up in the 1570s and again in 1590, remaining endemic after 1600, apparently adding up to about 1,000 victims. For the territories in Thuringia, fragmented between dozens of Saxon lines and other counts and princes, the estimates come to between 1,000 and 1,500 trials, with at least 500 victims, distributed over dozens of independent territories. There were more than 100 burnings alone under the dukes of Saxe-Coburg, famous for their dynastic connections all over Europe. In curious debates the Lutheran clergy tried to stimulate more severe persecutions, pointing to the Franconian prince-bishops as an example, whereas the lawyers referred to Catholic Bavaria in their attempt to restrain the clerical zeal. The superintendent Johann Matthäus Meyfahrt (1590–1642) probably published the most emotional pamphlet against witch trials ever in 1635.

There are only vague suggestions about the extent of the persecutions for some major Lutheran territories, such as the Electorate of Brandenburg, whose ruler adopted Calvinism in 1613, but left the Lutheran orthodoxy intact. The territory's university at Frankfurt/Oder issued about 269 legal opinions in cases of witchcraft. Consolidated, strong Lutheran territories like Electoral Saxony had, despite its harsh laws, a surprisingly low death toll, probably because of a tight supervision of the lower courts by the central government, very much like in the Lutheran Duchy of Würt-temberg. Although Saxony and Württemberg were larger and more densely populated than other German territories, the number of victims seems to have remained under 300 in both of these states. If it is correct that 350 witches were killed in Lutheran NORWAY and another twenty-two in ICELAND, this could mean that the persecution was by far more intensive there. The persecution was less severe in SWEDEN, FINLAND, and Estonia, and generally ended by the end of the seventeenth century.

English Events

How closely witch scares were connected to extraordinary situations can be seen from the persecutions of the self-appointed *Witch Finder General,* Mathew Hopkins (?–1648), who managed to use the turmoil of the English Civil War to launch the greatest ever witch persecution in England, in a situation where apocalyptic and millennial fears and hopes were mushrooming. This son of a Calvinist minister felt disturbed by the prevalence of witches in his region in the winter of 1644–1645, and his concerns were obviously shared by others, as he outlined himself (*The Discoverie of Witches,* London 1647). The imperfect nature of the surviving records makes any reconstruction difficult, but estimates suggest that at least 250 individuals were tried, and a minimum of 100, but perhaps considerably higher numbers, were executed for witchcraft during these persecutions, which also demonstrate that fantasies of demonic witchcraft were anything but absent from England. There were earlier occasions that had the potential for a large-scale persecution—for instance, the Lancashire trials of 1633–1634, where at least nineteen witches were executed—whereas another sixty were under suspicion, and some jailed, with several dying in prison. The confessions show the fully developed fantasy of a witches' sabbat, reveal ideas about a permanent meeting point in the forest of Pendle, where the witches flew for feasting and dancing, shape-shifting and having sexual intercourse, where they adored the devil, and practiced harmful magic. This persecution, stopped by the Privy Council, brought to light a remarkable divide between Puritan zealots (see PURITANISM) and Anglican moderates (see ANGLICANISM), reminding us of the fact that all major English demonologies were published by Puritan divines (George Gifford, Henry Holland, WILLIAM PERKINS, James Mason, Alexander Roberts, Thomas Cooper, Richard Bernard), whereas those advocating moderate skepticism after the Restoration, like Joseph Glanvill (1636–1680) and Meric Casaubon (1599–1671), were Anglican ministers, inclined to restore unity and order, and more concerned about atheism than witchcraft. It may be premature to draw parallels to the differences between moderate Lutherans and zealous Calvinists in Central Europe, but it seems psychologically likely that those who aspired to a Godly Republic would be more easily tempted to adopt the role of moral entrepreneurs, whether they where Presbyterian divines like James Carmichael or Catholic zealots like Peter Canisius. For both, the devil's pact was an inversion of the covenant with God and, again for both, witch-hunting served as an instrument to raise attention for their cause.

Because of the diversity of development, it is impossible to say that witch trials stopped earlier in Protestant countries. Certainly in England and the Netherlands, however, the *general* rejection of witch beliefs as a political issue gained momentum during the second half of the seventeenth century and infested the culture of enlightenment all over Europe. Protestant debates on witchcraft, launched by radical denials in England (John Wagstaffe, *The Question of Witchcraft Debated*, London 1669), the Netherlands (Balthasar Bekker, *De Betoverde Weereld,* Amsterdam 1691), and Northern Germany (CHRISTIAN THOMASIUS, *De crimine magiae,* Halle 1701) effectively terminated witch trials in these areas, and served to curb high-flying churchmen. When witch burnings kept on in Southern Germany, Austria, and even Northern Italy, Protestants consoled themselves that all of these countries were Catholic, and therefore backward by definition. However, these stereotypes, or certainties, were fragile, given that the last legal killings of witches took place in Calvinist Swiss Cantons like the Grison and Glarus. As late as 1782 the scandalous trial of Glarus against the maidservant Anna Göldi (1734–1782) took place. Although her indictment was *veneficium,* this was clearly a witch trial, emphasizing the devil's pact and harmful magic against her employer's children, who served as accusers. Her execution took place on June 18, 1782, and triggered a storm of protest. Protestant intellectuals were horrified. The enlightened Lutheran historian August Ludwig Schlözer (1735–1809) coined the term *judicial murder (Justizmord)* on this occasion (Abermaliger Justizmord in der Schweiz, in *Stats-Anzeigen,* Bd. 2 [1783]: 273–277).

Modern Witchcraze

Disbelief in witchcraft became a marker of the European civilization. Modern skepticism can be traced back to early modern attempts to build on the medieval perception that witchcraft was illusionary. Applied to her colonies in America, AUSTRALIA, Asia, and AFRICA, this European attitude usually caused discontent among indigenous peoples because it seemed as if the colonial authorities were aiming at protecting the evildoers. Throughout the nineteenth century, illegal witch killings were conducted in RUSSIA, and among indigenous peoples in MEXICO and the UNITED STATES. Throughout the twentieth century, before and after decolonization, violent anti-witchcraft movements swept through sub-Saharan Africa, with about 10,000 victims in Tanzania alone. Only recently the "modernity of witchcraft" has been emphasized—the adaptive capacities of witch beliefs to the challenges of a globalized world. Some Protestant sects capitalize on the tremendous fears of witchcraft, as for instance the Zionist Christian Church in SOUTH AFRICA. With witchcraft and related purification rites moved to the center of its activities, "African" churches are gaining ground in the competition with traditional main currents of Protestantism, becoming the fastest growing churches in the world. Witches and witch-hunts are no closed chapter in history, and the witch craze will continue to haunt us in the future.

References and Further Reading

Bengt, Ankarloo, and Stuart Clark, eds. *The Athlone History of Witchcraft and Magic in Europe.* 6 vols. London: The Athlone Press, 1999–2002.

Behringer, Wolfgang. *Witches and Witch-Hunts.* Cambridge, UK: Polity Press, 2003.

Geschiere, Peter. *The Modernity of Witchcraft. Politics and the Occult in Postcolonial Africa.* Charlottesville: Virginia University Press, 1997.

Golden, Richard M., ed. *Encyclopaedia of Witchcraft. The Western Tradition.* 4 vols. Austin, TX: ABC-Clio, 2004.

Hansen, Joseph, ed. *Quellen und Untersuchungen zur Geschichte des Hexenwahns* [Bonn 1901]. Reprint Hildesheim, Germany: Georg Olms Verlagsbuchhandlung, 1963.

Haustein, Jörg. *Luthers Stellung zum Zauber- und Hexenwesen.* Stuttgart, Germany: Kohlhammer Verlag, 1990.

Ralushai, Victor, et al. "Report of the Commission of Inquiry into Witchcraft, Violence and Ritual Murders in the Northern Province of the Republic of South Africa." Pietersburg, South Africa: Unpublished official report, 1996.

Thomas, Keith. *Religion and the Decline of Magic.* London: Weidenfeld & Nicolson, 1971.

Walker, Deward E., and David Carrasco, eds. *Witchcraft and Sorcery of the American Native Peoples.* Moscow, ID: University of ID Press, 1989.

Watson, C. W., and Roy Ellen, eds. *Understanding Witchcraft and Sorcery in Southeast Asia.* Honolulu: University of Hawaii Press, 1993.

WOLFGANG BEHRINGER

WITHERSPOON, JOHN (1723–1794)

Scotch-American presbyterian theologian. John Witherspoon was a notable Presbyterian leader in both Scotland and the United States during the eighteenth century, but he was even more important for the history of Protestantism as an intellectual mediator—first, between ENLIGHTENMENT and Protestant forms of thought, and second, between evangelical Protestant theology and revolutionary whig politics. The complexity of Witherspoon's eventful life is suggested by the fact that he began his public career as an embattled spokesman for the marginalized "little people" of patronage-ridden Scotland, but by his death on November 15, 1794 he had become an honored founding father of the new United States of America.

Personal History

Witherspoon was born in Gifford, Scotland, a few days before February 10, 1723, the date his baptism was recorded. His father, who was the parish minister, joined his mother Anne (Walker) in training the young Witherspoon in general Christian piety as well as the specific tenets of the CHURCH OF SCOTLAND. Witherspoon was an eager learner and received an M.A. from the University of Edinburgh when he was only sixteen years old. After further theological study, he was licensed for the ministry in 1743, and in January 1745 began service as the Church of Scotland minister in Beith, Ayrshire. By the time he moved in June 1757 to the larger, more prosperous Laigh Kirk in Paisley, Witherspoon had begun to make a mark in Scottish public life as a champion of the anti-patronage faction in the Church of Scotland. Witherspoon spoke, against those who adjusted Kirk's historic Calvinism to upper-class social norms and the more secular learning of the Scottish ENLIGHTENMENT, for a "popular party" that sought veto power for local congregations when they disliked the minister selected for them by a hereditary patron. Witherspoon's best-known work on behalf of the popular party was a satire entitled *Ecclesiastical Characteristics,* which ridiculed the moderates for preferring polite respectability to Scotland's traditional people's Calvinism. Witherspoon's other noteworthy polemics included an attack on the stage, a fast-day sermon linking religious uprightness and national prosperity, and an exhortation assaulting clerical meddling in public affairs.

While he was poking fun at the moderates, Witherspoon was also publishing constructive theological works on the relationship between justification and holy living (1756) and on regeneration (1764). Printed sermons also brought him wider attention at home, and soon abroad. A 1753 contribution to *The Scots Magazine,* in which he defended the reliability of physical and moral perceptions, was the first of his writings to be read in America. In this article, Witherspoon's defense of the common perceptions of ordinary people was close enough to arguments later advanced by Thomas Reid (1710–1796) and other philosophers of "SCOTTISH COMMON SENSE REALISM" to at least partially justify Witherspoon's claim to have anticipated the major principles of their work.

When the trustees of the College of New Jersey (later Princeton University) were faced with a vacancy as president in 1766, they asked Witherspoon to fill the position. Their hope was that he might revive the fortunes of the college, but also help reunite America's Old Light and New Light Presbyterians, who had divided as a result of the colonial Great Awakening. Almost as soon as he arrived in America in 1768, Witherspoon was an immediate success as educator, churchman, politician, and thinker. At the college he reorganized instruction around lectures and placed fresh emphasis on public speaking. Witherspoon added to a rapidly expanding reputation through the fundraising tours he made to New York, Philadelphia, Virginia, and New England. Soon Princeton was attracting nearly as many students as Yale; in the five years before 1776, it produced more graduates (25 per year) than ever before in its history. The destruction of the CIVIL WAR, with Princeton itself a battle site, delivered a great setback to the college's fortunes, but Witherspoon's reputation guaranteed its survival through desperate days.

As the trustees had hoped, Witherspoon also became a leading figure in the expansion and then reorganization of the PRESBYTERIAN CHURCH. Under Witherspoon's tenure, the number of Princeton students entering the Presbyterian ministry did decline, but Witherspoon still personally trained about one-third of the ministers, who in 1789 created a new general assembly to organize Presbyterian efforts in the new country. In addition, Witherspoon's moderate evangelical theology and his reputation as a patriot won approval from New Lights and Old Lights alike. Witherspoon served on several of the committees that prepared the way for a national general assembly. When that general assembly met for the first time in 1789, he drafted several of the constituting documents and he was selected to preach the opening sermon.

Politics and Religion

For broader Protestant purposes, Witherspoon's leadership in joining Christian interests to the republican foundations of American politics was a major achievement. The Scottish minister who had spoken out against arbitrary ecclesiastical power in his native country soon became a spokesperson against arbitrary political power in his adopted land. James Madison's father, in fact, sent his son to study at Princeton because he was so impressed with Witherspoon's defense of liberty. When, in response to the perception of British tyrannical acts, New Jersey began to organize in defense of its freedoms, Witherspoon was a leader in that process, too. In 1774 he became a member of his local county's Committee of Correspondence, and on June 22, 1776, he was selected as a New Jersey delegate to the Continental Congress. Shortly after arriving in Philadelphia to take that position, he voted in favor of independence and so became the only clergyman to sign the Declaration. Witherspoon remained a representative in Congress for most of the rest of the war, during which time he served on over one hundred committees. On behalf of the Congress he wrote pamphlets attacking the inflationary use of paper money and also penned recantations for two Loyalist printers whom the Congress wanted to silence. After the war he was elected to the New Jersey legislature in 1783 and 1789, and in 1787 was a member of the New Jersey convention that approved the Constitution.

Before military conflict began with the British, Witherspoon had rallied citizens of New Jersey to the patriot cause through newspaper essays. After the start of the war, he preached a memorable sermon on May 17, 1776, which was entitled "The Dominion of Providence over the Passions of Men." This sermon praised God for turning British acts of tyranny into good for the colonies; its published version also included a powerful appeal to Witherspoon's fellow immigrants from Scotland to join the patriot cause. With such efforts, Witherspoon was among the few orthodox or evangelical Christians of the 1770s to emerge as leaders in the patriot movement. (The UNITARIANISM of THOMAS JEFFERSON [1743–1826] and John Adams [1734–1826], or the extreme reticence about expressing personal religious opinions characteristic of George Washington [1732–1799] and JAMES MADISON [1749–1812], were far more common among the major founders.) Yet in the wake of Witherspoon's efforts, many leaders in later generations would continue his work of linking traditional Christianity to the republican verities of the American founding.

Enlightenment and Theology

For the history of theology, Witherspoon's importance lay in his reorientation of intellectual activity at Princeton away from the pietistic idealism associated with earlier colonial revivalism toward the common-sense and scientific principles of the Scottish Enlightenment. One of Witherspoon's first actions as president of Princeton was to banish what he called the "immaterialism" of Irish Bishop George Berkeley (1685–1753) along with the theocentric ethics of American minister JONATHAN EDWARDS (1703–1758), both of whose books were being read at Princeton before he arrived. For his own lectures on moral philosophy and divinity, Witherspoon drew heavily on the ideas of his former moderate opponents in Scotland, especially the moral philosophy of Francis Hutcheson (1694–1746), who made the natural moral sense the keystone of his ethics.

As Witherspoon expounded it, the philosophy of common sense became the foundation for useful knowledge of many kinds. Common sense defended the reality of the physical world and so allowed a wholehearted commitment to natural philosophy (i.e., science). It defined human relationships after the model of the physical sciences and so demonstrated the rationality of politics. It drew an analogy between external and internal sensations and so facilitated a science of morals. It pictured theology as dependent upon reason and so paved the way for an apologetic of scientific respectability.

Where the leading Calvinists in colonial America had based true virtue on the workings of divine grace, Witherspoon (at least after arriving in the New World) was able to find a ground for virtuous behavior in the naturally given moral capacities (the "common moral sense") of all humanity. Witherspoon's lectures on divinity assured students that reason contained no inherent criticism of revelation, and that the positive teachings of scripture reflected both sound reason and "the state of human nature." In his formal lectures Witherspoon seemed as interested in demonstrating the reasonableness of Christianity as in exploring the standard themes of Calvinistic theology.

By providing Princeton with a philosophical basis derived from Scottish moral philosophy and by replacing a New England tradition strongly under the influence of Jonathan Edwards, Witherspoon brought Presbyterians into the mainstream of eighteenth-century British-American theology. From the newer perspective, Witherspoon could demonstrate through reason and science the truthfulness of revelation instead of presupposing revelation as the foundation for science and reason. Witherspoon's new moral philosophy lacked the harmony of theology, ethics, and epistemology that Edwards had provided, but by compensation Witherspoon avoided the taint of immaterialism carried by Edwards's intense theocentricism. The fact that Witherspoon championed both divinity and science as compatible forms of truth, and that he was a pious subscriber to the WESTMINSTER CONFESSION of faith, testified to his links with historic Calvinism. Yet beneath a common commitment to broadly Calvinistic theology, a significant move was occurring from idealism, metaphysics, and conversion to realism, ethics, and morality.

Witherspoon was a key figure in later Presbyterian theological history. His immediate successor at Princeton, Samuel Stanhope Smith (1751–1819; president 1795–1812), carried Enlightenment commitments even further in the direction of a reasonable Christianity. However, Witherspoon had other students, like the influential Philadelphia minister, Ashbel Green (1762–1848), who construed Witherspoon's influence in more traditional terms. When a faction under Green's leadership ousted Smith from the College of New Jersey and founded Princeton Theological Seminary (both in 1812), that faction made more of Witherspoon's Calvinism than of his common-sense rationality. Witherspoon's combination of commitments to the eighteenth-century Enlightenment and to historic Calvinist orthodoxy continued to shape—sometimes confusedly—American Presbyterian theology for more than a century.

Witherspoon was a complex figure. In the Scottish part of his career his piety tended to be apolitical, and his polemical interests made him an opponent of Francis Hutcheson and the era's new moral philosophy. By contrast, in America he became an eager supporter of a political revolution; in his labors as college teacher and publishing minister he also borrowed liberally from Hutcheson in building his own version of common-sense ethics. The consistency in this career was Witherspoon's resistance to power (whether the moderate direction of the Scottish church or Parliament's designs for the American colonies). Witherspoon's own religious convictions—sincere Calvinism adjusted to his era's new forms of ethical reasoning—also remained relatively stable throughout his career, even if those convictions played out somewhat differently in America than they had in Scotland. As the only clergyman among the American founding fathers, and as a leader in education, church, and theology, Witherspoon was one of the key bridging figures in a rapidly changing age.

References and Further Reading

Primary Sources:

Miller, Thomas, ed. *The Selected Writings of John Witherspoon.* Carbondale: Southern Illinois University Press, 1990.

Scott, Jack, ed. *An Annotated Edition of Lectures on Moral Philosophy by John Witherspoon.* Newark: University of Delaware Press, 1982.

The Works of the Rev. John Witherspoon. Philadelphia: William W. Woodward, 1802.

Secondary Sources:

Collins, Varnum Lansing Collins. *President Witherspoon: A Biography.* Princeton: Princeton University Press, 1925.

Landsman, Ned C. "Witherspoon and the Problem of Provincial Identity in Scottish Evangelical Culture." In *Scotland and America in the Age of Enlightenment.* Edited by Richard B. Sher and Jeffrey R. Smitten. Edinburgh: University of Edinburgh Press, 1990.

Noll, Mark A. *Princeton and the Republic, 1768–1822.* Princeton: Princeton University Press, 1989.

MARK A. NOLL

WOLFF, CHRISTIAN (1679–1754)

German theologian. Wolff was born in Breslau on January 24, 1679 and died April 9, 1754 in Halle. One of the most influential German philosophers of the eighteenth century, his literary output was immense, with extensive series of books, covering the entire range of philosophical topics in addition to the natural sciences, in both Latin and German.

Wolff studied THEOLOGY, mathematics, and philosophy in Jena beginning in 1699. With the help of GOTTFRIED WILHELM LEIBNIZ he secured a position at HALLE, then a stronghold of PIETISM, teaching first mathematics and then philosophy. Wolff was a moderate rationalist. This means that, although remaining within the bounds of theological ORTHODOXY as he perceived it, he valued the use of reason as a means of defending and elucidating truths that he believed to be amenable to rational inquiry. Although early in his career he held that revelation does not include truths that human reason can discover, eventually he adopted the strategy of separating religious truths into two classes: revealed truths that can be neither discovered nor comprehended by human reason (in his terminology, "pure" revealed truths) and revealed truths that can be discovered and comprehended by reason ("mixed" truths, the subject of natural theology). An example of the first sort is the Trinity. Wolff did not doubt that this DOCTRINE is revealed in the BIBLE; however, the philosopher cannot go beyond acknowledging it as revealed because the doctrine transcends reason's powers. The second sort of revealed truths have to do with God as creator and preserver and with our moral duties toward God.

This distinction yielded several results. First, Wolff believed firmly in the agreement of reason and revelation. As noted, this did not mean that all revealed truths could be comprehended by reason. In the case of pure revealed truths human reason must, he held, submit to revelation. Nonetheless, although revelation might transcend reason, it would never contradict reason. Pure revealed truths were not, he argued, irrational. Second, this distinction meant that the methods of philosophy and natural theology on the one hand were quite different from those of revealed theology on the other. Wolff was thus careful to establish a firm demarcation between philosophy and revealed theology.

Wolff's philosophical intent was quite conservative. He had no intention of subverting orthodox theology and in fact sought, where appropriate, to support it philosophically. Certainly many of his students believed his was the best philosophical defense of the Christian faith available. However, his conviction that reason and revelation do not conflict was inevitably taken to mean that human reason functions as the standard by which doctrines are evaluated. Further, his attempt to demarcate philosophy from theology tended to make philosophy an autonomous discipline, loosed from orthodox theological moorings. The possibility of academic philosophy free of ecclesiastical doctrine was disconcerting to many in his day.

Pietist Opposition

Wolff ran afoul of certain Pietist theologians, notably AUGUST HERMANN FRANKE (1663–1627) and Joachim Lange (1670–1744), while at Halle. There were several points of dispute. For one, Wolff understood philosophy to encompass the entire range of essences, that is, of entities insofar as they are logically possible. The Pietists felt that this made philosophy into a more comprehensive and hence more significant science than theology. They also objected to his elevating God's understanding over God's will (because the range of possible being *known* by God is more extensive than the range of actual being *created* by God). Representing God primarily as an understanding mind seemed to suggest too great a similarity between God and the human mind. They were further bothered by the fact that God's omnipotence seemed compromised, given that God's will cannot, in Wolff's view, change eternal truths and the essences of things. They were also disturbed by his view of human good as being centered in happiness instead of in the moral familiar and evangelical framework of SIN and redemption.

Controversy with the Pietist theologians at Halle broke out in earnest in 1719 on the appearance of the German version of his book on metaphysics. Students were warned against attending his lectures and were used as informants to report on his lectures. The situation came to a head in 1721 when Wolff gave a lecture on Chinese ethics. In it he asserted the agreement between the wisdom of the Chinese and his own philosophy, thus arguing for a natural and universal basis of human ETHICS and implicitly denying that ethics rests on revelation. The Pietists went on the offensive and, after a considerable amount of political maneuvering, both inside and outside the university, they persuaded the king, Friedrich Wilhelm I, in 1723 to banish Wolff on pain of death.

Wolff taught at Marburg until 1740. Here he composed a series of philosophical works in Latin parallel to his German works. As a result of his experiences in Halle he became something of a *cause célèbre* and he received numerous invitations to accept teaching positions. Meanwhile the controversy in Halle sparked a debate throughout the German universities about the merits and dangers of Wolff's philosophy. After some initial setbacks Wolff's followers began to win the war of public opinion by presenting Wolff's philosophy not only as orthodox but as a valuable apologetic tool. National pride also entered into the issue because in 1733 Wolff was made a member of the French Academy, the first German since Leibniz to be so honored. At length, after more political maneuvering and a public relations campaign to convince the king that Wolff's philosophy was an important defense against atheism, Wolff was recalled to Halle, and study of his philosophy was made virtually mandatory. In 1745 he was made a prince of the Holy Roman Empire.

Assessment

Wolff is not considered to have been a first-rate philosopher on the order of Leibniz or IMMANUEL KANT. His place in history is secured by two contributions. First, he created a vocabulary of German philosophical terms and thus contributed to the development of German philosophy. Second, he conveyed to the German academic world the importance of methodological rigor in philosophy. Consequently his importance lies more in his influence than in his ideas. As the most influential German philosopher in the period between Leibniz and Kant, Wolff's moderate rationalism issued a challenge to the assumptions and methods of orthodox theology while providing a rigorous but also conservative alternative to the destructive brand of rationalism found in FRANCE and ENGLAND.

References and Further Reading

Primary Source:

Wolff, Christian. *Gesammelte Werke*. Edited by J. École, et al. Hildesheim, Germany: Georg Olms Verlag. 1962–.

Secondary Sources:

Casula, Mario. "Die Theologia Naturalis von Christian Wolff: Vernunft und Offenbarung." In *Christian Wolff: 1679–1754. Interpretationen zu seiner Philosophie und deren Wirkung*. Edited by Werner Schneiders. Studien zum achtzehnten Jahrhundert, vol. 4, 129–138. Hamburg, Germany: Felix Meiner Verlag, 1983.

Ching, Julia, and Willard G. Oxtoby. *Moral Enlightenment: Leibniz and Wolff on China*. Monumenta Serica monograph series, no. 26. Nettetal, Germany: Steyler, 1992.

Gawlick, Günter. "Christian Wolff und der Deismus." In *Christian Wolff: 1679–1754. Interpretationen zu seiner Philosophie und deren Wirkung*. Edited by Werner Schneiders. Studien zum achtzehnten Jahrhundert, vol. 4, 139–147. Hamburg, Germany: Felix Meiner Verlag, 1983.

Hinrichs, Carl. *Preußentum und Pietismus: Der Pietismus in Brandenburg-Preußen als religiös-soziale Reformbewegung*. Göttingen, Germany: Vandenhoeck & Ruprecht, 1971.

SAMUEL M. POWELL

WOLLASTON, WILLIAM (1660–1724)

English deist. Wollaston was born on March 26, 1660, at Coton-Clanford, Staffordshire, England. He was educated at Sidney-Sussex College, Cambridge, where he took an M.A. in 1681, after which he became an Anglican priest. He married into a London merchant family and began to write on moral philosophy. By far his most significant work was *The Religion of Nature Delineated* (1722), in which he considered the relationship between morality and nature. Wollaston stated that his "fundamental maxim" was "that whoever acts as if things were so, or not so, doth by his acts declare, that they are so, or not so; as plainly as he could by words, and with more reality." Moral goodness consists in acting in a natural way, whereas immorality is out of sync with NATURAL LAW. To Wollaston, "Truth is but a conformity to nature . . ." His book was widely read in Britain and the American colonies, and reflects a broader trend in eighteenth-century ANGLICANISM toward theorizing a simpler, more moralistic Christianity that did not rely on special revelation.

Like JOHN TILLOTSON, Wollaston did not deny biblical revelation but hoped that Christians could turn toward a reasonable moralism that would defuse many of the previous century's church conflicts. Some have labeled Wollaston a deist, and although his work may seem to have deistic implications, he did not directly question any orthodox Christian precepts, nor did his failure to appeal to divine revelation imply a denial of such (see DEISM). *The Religion of Nature Delineated* was published in 1724, and Wollaston died on October 24 the same year. He was buried at Great Finborough, Suffolk, England.

References and Further Reading

Primary Source:

Wollaston, William. *The Religion of Nature Delineated*. London: B. Lintot, 1724.

Secondary Source:

Feinberg, Joel. "Wollaston and his Critics." *Journal of the History of Ideas* 38 (1977): 345–352.

THOMAS S. KIDD

WOMANIST THEOLOGY

Womanist theology articulates the reality of living in relationship with divinity and humanity as a woman and as a person of color. In broad terms, womanist theology affirms the full personhood and divine image of all humanity and combats oppression on multiple fronts in response to the presence and activity of God in the cosmos. Black LIBERATION THEOLOGY and FEMINIST THEOLOGY provide both conversation partners and earlier, formative space for womanist theology. The combination of the overwhelming majority of male black liberation theologians and predominately white feminist theologians of the 1960s and 1970s failed to consistently and coherently address the spiritual and social reality of black women in the continental UNITED STATES. Emerging in the 1980s, womanist theology is in part a response to sexism in black liberation theology and racism in the feminist movement. Womanist theologians affirm that women of color have a unique perspective of and on human experience and divine matters, which cannot be replicated and without which human consideration of the divine mystery is incomplete and inadequate. Womanist theology is particularly communal, with the primary locus the black church in North America; however, the global church also functions as a site of womanist theology. Womanist theologians are ordained pastors, preachers, and lay church leaders and members, Protestant and Catholic, as well as scholars and community activists. Womanist theologians are concerned with the health and wholeness—spiritual, social, economic, educational, and ecological—of all people of color.

"Proto-Womanism"

Religious and intellectual work of women of color negotiating the intersection of GENDER and ETHNICITY within the context of the divine–human encounter born out of the historic marginalization of women of color in history and society did not begin with the 1980s. Women of color have been reflecting on their spiritual and social circumstances in the world, in Christendom, and in the North American context before they gained regular access to the tools of literacy and eventual admission to institutions of higher education. The black church has been a sustaining shelter for women of African descent since their arrival, by whatever means, on this continent. Even as black women in the Americas and CARIBBEAN sought shelter in the church from inhumane indignities visited upon them in the slave-holding, allegedly reconstructed and Jim Crow South and the less-than-free North with its lack of occupational educational opportunities for black women, they worshipped in a context that adopted, without question in most circumstances, the gender roles of their oppressors and exploiters. Yet African-American women did not reject the religious component of their historical identity. Prior to the birth of the contemporary womanist movement, black women in America insisted on being recognized as the sole legitimate arbitrators of their knowledge and experiences. Nineteenth-century writers, speakers, and thinkers such as Maria Stewart, Anna Julia Cooper, and Ida B. Wells-Barnett, and many others, advocated forcefully for the rights and responsibility of black women to form and articulate their identity or experiences without being forced to choose between being a woman and being of African descent.

Womanist/Womanism

The term "womanist" was initially introduced in a 1980 essay "Coming Apart" by Alice Walker, who coined the term in response to the racism, classism, and elitism she found in the feminist movement. Her initial proposition was that womanism was an overarching category that included feminism, which she equated with white women. For Walker, womanists were "pro-woman," which meant that womanist discourse was intentionally antiracist, anticlassist, antielitist, antiheterosexist, and antidiscriminatory in every particularity. Walker's subsequent expansion on the definition in *In Search of Our Mother's Gardens* (1983) is perhaps the most widely cited definition of womanism. This definition has four parts:

1. A womanist is a feminist of color who is responsible and mature, "sassy" and "audacious."
2. A womanist loves women and men, irrespective of her or their sexual orientation, but has a special love for women's culture.
3. A womanist is a lover of music, dance, the Spirit, food, all things round including the moon, struggle, the entire community, and herself.
4. "Womanist is to feminist as purple is to lavender" (Walker 1983:xi).

Womanist thought in general is a broad umbrella under which womanist theology can be understood. Related disciplines include womanist discourses in LITERATURE and ETHICS that can be, but are not always, intentional theological reflections. Katie Geneva Cannon was the first scholar to articulate a theology that was specifically womanist. Her 1985 essay "The Emergence of Black Feminist Consciousness" was a contribution to an anthology on feminist interpretation of the BIBLE. In the section on "Womanist Theology," Cannon argues that womanist theology is a interpretive practice that uses the reading, writing, and reflecting of black women to engage the systemic effects of white supremacy and sexism that afflict black women in the market, institutional church, academy, and home.

The Union Theological Seminary in New York nurtured the emergence of the earliest published voices in womanist theology. Katie Cannon, Kelly D. Brown, Jacqueline Grant, and Delores Williams articulated womanist theological responses to the liberation theology of JAMES HAL CONE.

Womanist Theology and Black Liberation Theology

As a community-specific response to social, ethical, and moral dimensions of racism, particularly in the Americas, AFRICA, and the Caribbean, womanist theology formally challenged black liberation theologians to account for the inherent paradox in proclaiming divinely mandated liberation to oppressed peoples while at the same time insisting that women were subordinate to men in the home, church, and CIVIL RIGHTS MOVEMENT. Black women in the church, academy, and political movements identified with the attempts of black theologians to articulate shared understandings of blackness, as well as different and overlapping experiences of class and CULTURE within the construct of blackness. However, they found that the androcentrism of those religious leaders in the academy and the church prevented them from accurately analyzing the oppressive experiences of the entire African-American community and therefore developing inadequate and inappropriate responses to their shared experiences of oppression. Both women and men in the black church and blacks in the academy wrestled with the legacy of slave-holding Christianity as the space in which Africans in the Americas became Christian themselves and the implications for the differing construction of Christian identity that necessarily followed.

The marginalization of women in the black church was identified as a challenge to the long-standing proclamations of liberation issued from the majority of African-American congregations from slavery forward. The contradiction inherent in the vehement insistence that black men be recognized as full members of the human race while black women were required to mediate their experiences with the divine through male hierarchical leadership led some black women to the egalitarian promise of the women's rights movement.

Womanist Theology and Feminist Theology

The feminist movement in North America was rooted in the abolitionist and women's suffrage movements. A white affluent leadership characterized both of these movements; eventually the movements separated, with suffragists abandoning a platform that would have enfranchised black women and men along with white women. African-American women experienced feminist theology as class-privileged and overwhelmingly white, even as they identified with feminist discourses that battled the injustice and immorality of sexism in the Western world from the nineteenth century onward. Early womanist theologians critiqued feminist theologians for not addressing the history of race relations between black and white women. Later womanist theologians would identify the vocabulary, class, theoretical practices, and practical objectives that differed between black and white feminists and between white feminists and black womanists.

Early African-American feminists disenchanted with the white supremacist ideologies perpetuated by the feminist movement began to question the methodologies as well as the motivations of the movement. One result was that womanists inherited a wariness of using the resources of the establishment and strategies conceived in and valued by dominant culture to effect any real change in the status quo. This led to one clear point of demarcation from the feminist movement in general and feminist theology in particular—a deep valuation of ancestral, nonacademic oral discourses, knowledge, and coping skills. Another point of departure is the relationship that womanist theologians have with the institutional church; they are much more likely to critique the church from inside rather than from without.

Methodologies

There is no singular womanist theological creed, canon, or communal practice. Womanist theological thought varies as widely as do the contexts in which women of color live, work, and worship. Some generalities can however, be observed:

1. Womanist theological approaches are regularly multidimensional; they can be interdisciplinary, collaborative, and/or multicontextual.
2. They emphasize and prioritize women's experience in general and the social location of the reader/interpreter in particular.
3. A (if not the) goal of womanist theological discourse is the eradication of all forms of human oppression.
4. The fruit of womanist theological reflection must be accessible to the wider, nonspecialist, worshipping community.

In LATIN AMERICA, *muherista* theology corresponds to womanist theology on the North American and African continents, while *feminista* theology corresponds to North American feminist theology. However, each theology is also a unique response to the unique cultural context from which it emerges. Caribbean and African womanism is in active dialogue with the postcolonial legacy of missionary Christianity and empire building.

Ongoing Conversations

One topic of conversation among womanist theologians is whether or not embracing sexual plurality is a prerequisite for womanist identity. Given that the option of loving sexually or nonsexually either women or men was a key component of the definition and affirmation of womanism, and the fact that sexual diversity has been a pillar of the feminist movement embraced by many womanists, some thinkers question the insistence in many black churches that heterosexuality is the only intimate relational norm, while others celebrate the African-American communal value of monogamous heterosexual MARRIAGE. Another concern is the economic disparity among women of color in the world. Many womanist theologians are published, are tenured, and have adequate health insurance and child care, whereas the vast majority of women of color throughout the world lack the adequate nutrition, clean drinking water, basic health care, and the basic tools of literacy. There is some concern that the voices that are most frequently heard in womanist theology are not representational of the larger concerns of women of color in the so-called "third world" (better, "two-thirds world"), that those who have access to print, electronic, and digital media are careful to speak with and not for women whose voices have not been heard.

Other contemporary womanist theological concerns include WORSHIP (LITURGY, PREACHING, translation, interpretation and application of biblical texts); EDUCATION (curriculum formation, hiring and tenure-granting processes, canon formation); health and welfare of all people, particularly the destitute; economic inequity; ECOLOGY (stewardship of the environment and natural resources); POLITICS (the domestic and international policies of the United States, globalization, the digital divide, CAPITAL PUNISHMENT); and diversity (cultural, religious, sexual). Changing the world is a womanist agenda.

While Alice Walker's early definitions of the term "womanist" named all black feminists as womanists, not all black women self-identify as womanists; some, such as bell hooks and Musa Dube, preferentially identify themselves as feminists. Some identify as neither. Additionally, there are black men who center the experience of black women in their work (e.g., Randall Bailey and Peter Paris), as well as white women who privilege the readings of women of color in their work (e.g., Alice Ogden Bellis). The question of whether the term "womanist theologian" discloses personal identity or political affiliation has yet to be answered.

Katie Cannon's original womanist theology construct wrestled with the role and implication of the Bible in the life of black women. Her current work interrogates the intersection of THEOLOGY and ethics. Other contemporary scholars bringing womanist theological concerns to bear on the scriptures from the vantage of biblical studies include Cheryl Anderson, Clarice J. Martin, Madeline McClenney-Sadler, and Renita Weems. Scholars whose ongoing work claims the space of theology and ethics as the site of womanist reflection include Cheryl Townsend Gilkes and Cheryl Kirk-Duggan. Other celebrated contemporary womanist theologians include Karen Baker-Fletcher, M. Shawn Copeland, Toinette Eugene, and Diana Hayes.

Womanist theologians negotiate the tension inherent in articulating shared identity markers with white women and men of color by affirming arenas of overlapping identity while nuancing difference. Although black male sexism and white female racism and classism delineate an obvious perimeter of womanist discourse, women of color have reflected on their whole identities in relationship with men and other women, children, and adults, within and across culture, social and economic lines for as long as those distinctions have been applied. Womanist theology is one vehicle by which black women engage in "God talk" for themselves and on behalf of others.

See also African Theology; Biblical Interpretation; Education, Theology, United States; Higher Criticism; Homosexuality; Human Rights; Post-Colonialism; Prayer; Preaching; Sexuality; Theology, Twentieth Century; Theology, Twentieth Century, Global; Theology, Twentieth Century, North American; Women; Women Clergy

References and Further Reading

Brown, K. D. "God Is as Christ Does: Toward A Womanist Theology." *Journal of Religious Thought* 46 (1989):7–16.

Cannon, Katie G. "The Emergence of Black Feminist Consciousness." In *Feminist Interpretation of the Bible.* Edited by Letty M. Russell. Philadelphia, PA: Westminster Press, 1985.

Cone, James, and Gayraud Wilmore, eds. *Black Theology: A Documentary History Volume II 1980–1992.* Maryknoll, NY: Orbis, 1993.

Grant, J. "White Women's Christ and Black Women's Jesus: Feminist Christology and Womanist Response." *Harvard Divinity Bulletin* 21 no. 1 (1989):17.

Miller-McLemore, Bonnie J., and Brita L. Gill-Austern. *Feminist And Womanist Pastoral Theology.* Nashville, TN: Abingdon Press, 1999.

Mitchem, Stephanie Y. *Introducing Womanist Theology.* Maryknoll, NY: Orbis, 2002.

Sanders, Cheryl J., ed. *Living the Intersection: Womanism and Afrocentrism in Theology.* Minneapolis, MN: Fortress Press, 1995.

Townes, Emilie M., ed. *Embracing The Spirit: Womanist Perspectives On Hope, Salvation, and Transformation.* Maryknoll, NY: Orbis, 1997.

Walker, Alice. "Coming Apart." In *Take Back the Night.* Edited by Laura Lederer. New York: Morrow, 1980.

———. 1983. *In Search of Our Mother's Gardens: Womanist Prose.* San Diego, CA: Harcourt Brace Jovanovich.

Williams, D. S. *Sisters In The Wilderness: The Challenge Of Womanist God-Talk.* Maryknoll, NY: Orbis Books, 1993.

WILDA C. M. GAFNEY

WOMEN, UNITED STATES

Throughout almost four centuries of the Protestant experience in the UNITED STATES, women have pushed the boundaries to bring leadership to the churches that had been restricted to men. Women have shaped their own religious space as they moved from the constricted roles allotted them in the home to their rightful lay and clergy positions in the public spheres of religion. The evolution of women's journey in American Protestantism is revealed through an analysis of the ways they claimed their due places and voices alongside men from colonial times to the beginning of the twenty-first century.

Constriction and Liberation: Colonial and Revolutionary Beginnings

The prescriptions for white women in Protestantism throughout the seventeenth and eighteenth centuries were basically the same from New England to the middle and southern colonies. Women were given the divinely assigned social role within the home to be wives and mothers. The home was to be a little church or a little seminary in which the husband held primary authority and the wife shared with him the supervision of children, servants, and slaves. She was the primary religious educator of her husband and children, particularly to train the men of the family to be virtuous decision makers and leaders in the public sphere. It was believed that women were given qualities, set forth in scriptures by God, to especially fit them for this function: they were nurturing, sensitive, and subordinate by nature, leading them to be obedient wives, indulgent mothers, and kind and charitable mistresses to the poor and needy.

During the era of the American Revolution, this God-given role assigned to white women became defined as "republican motherhood." Training men in the family in religious and ethical precepts to be worthy public leaders became a political and patriotic function, an increasingly exalted role for women. It gave women a public purpose within the home, although they were still meant to be subordinate and submissive to CLERGY and lay male authorities both in the church and household.

From the early colonial days of the mid-seventeenth century, women began to quietly stretch the boundaries of this constricted role. They formed small groups "for women only" that met in their homes to study the BIBLE and raise money for benevolent causes in their churches and towns. By the First Great Awakening of the early eighteenth century, they were even supplying funds for foreign MISSIONS. These women became "Daughters of Liberty" during the American Revolution, gathering to make clothing and medical supplies for patriot soldiers. Besides the good these communities of women did for others, they created social outlets for themselves and became the first women's support groups.

From the initial colonial settlements, a liberating stream of women in Protestantism ran alongside this mainstream-constricting tradition. Some women read Scripture, such as Galatians 3:28, Titus 2:3–4, and Acts 2:17–18, gaining courage to speak in their own voices in church and society. The consequences were tragic for both ANNE HUTCHINSON and Mary Dyer, two bold New England Protestant women. Hutchinson was banned by church and civil authorities from the Massachusetts Bay Colony in 1630 because she claimed the AUTHORITY of the Holy Spirit to interpret scripture and teach men and women together in her home. Dyer was deported and later brought back to be hung in the Boston Commons because she sought to convert others to the Quaker faith (see FRIENDS, SOCIETY OF). However, they began a tradition of women who, over almost four centuries, have been confident in their God-given gifts and right to freedom of speech.

The revivalism of the First Great Awakening (see AWAKENINGS) also had liberating consequences for both black and white women. Little effort had been made during the seventeenth century to spread Christianity among slaves and to baptize them. White colonists feared that God did not approve of SLAVERY and that BAPTISM would grant slaves full personhood necessary for their freedom. Further, slaves clung to their native beliefs and were not so interested in joining churches that permitted slavery. However, the revivalists held that the immediate work of the Holy Spirit in one's CONVERSION gave the individual power to discern the state of her or his own soul. Intervention by the clergy was not necessary, a doctrine heretical to early PURITANISM. Black as well as white women were particularly drawn to this message that broke down the rigid boundaries constricting white and black women's public role and gave them authority to pray and witness to their faith in groups and services of both men and women.

The True Woman and the New Woman: The Nineteenth Century

During the nineteenth century, the terms "True Woman" and "New Woman" characterized the evolving constriction and expansion of women's place in the home, church, and society. The qualities defining the "True Woman" were domesticity, purity, piety, and submission to husbands and other males. Most white Protestant women continued to live out this role limiting them to the home, still divinely prescribed and grounded in the theology and experience of colonial America. The corporate nature of these qualities placed on women, holding sway during the first half of the century, was defined by the terms "the Cult of True Womanhood" or "The Cult of Domesticity."

The evangelical dominance during the first half of the nineteenth century, which was promoted by the Second Great Awakening, continued to expand the boundaries of women's lives, even of women who saw themselves faithful to the True Woman's role. Evangelical emphases of personal conversion, fruits of the spirit, religious activism, and social responsibility for the poor and oppressed provided a strong base to encourage women to pursue their own ministries beyond the spiritual nurture of men and children in their homes. Barriers were broken down, empowering them to share the gospel by going outside their homes to bring persons to Christ and to improve the lives of those in need. Separatist BAPTISTS, Methodists, and New Light Presbyterians were revivalist supporters opening doors for women (see METHODISM, NORTH AMERICA; PRESBYTERIANISM). The Baptist self-governing congregations allowed women to vote and hold positions of elderess and DEACONESS.

Religiously motivated separatist groups of women continued to bring these true women together in their local communities. Missions were the most popular cause of church women. By the 1830s peer groups, determined by age, ETHNICITY, race, and social standing, began to form. Consistent with women's maternal nature and a natural extension of the True Woman, they also provided appropriate responses to Jesus's command to go into all the world and spread the gospel. Within these separatist groups, women took their first steps outside their homes as teachers, evangelists, social workers, physicians, midwives, and nurses.

By the second half of the nineteenth century the New Woman of Protestantism began to appear, first in secular society and then in the churches. Within their denominations, these women claimed public roles, long the sole province of men, as their God-given rights as women, not simply because they possessed extraordinary gifts. The distinction between the True

Woman and the New Woman was not always apparent in practice. Most Protestant women did not overtly question their primary functions in the home, but they wanted to expand their lives to find greater purpose and service in wider fields of usefulness. They brought together the rationale of the True Woman with their Christian commitment to make socially needed and personally meaningful contributions to their churches and society.

Expansion of gender-separate societies, particularly for missions, beyond the local scene to regional and national levels was the largest movement bringing together church women outside their homes. The Women's Union Missionary Society, the first national women's mission society in the United States, was interdenominational and began in 1860. However, the interdenominational structure soon broke down, and women's societies were formed in all mainline white Protestant denominations, including the Congregationalists, Baptists, Methodists, DISCIPLES OF CHRIST, Christians, Episcopalians, Presbyterians, and Lutherans (see LUTHERANISM, UNITED STATES). African-American women formed strong societies in the AFRICAN METHODIST EPISCOPAL, AFRICAN METHODIST EPISCOPAL ZION, and NATIONAL BAPTIST CONVENTION churches, as did Hispanic women in their Baptist and Methodist churches.

Consistent with the ideology of true womanhood, the women in these missionary societies did not preach in mixed assemblies including both women and men. However, they did break down strictures placed on women's public participation. In their women's organizations, from the local congregation to national levels, thousands of women gained their first experience in leading meetings, administering programs and financial resources, and speaking and praying in public. The women's missionary outreach was designed to bring all persons, men and women, to Christ, but their special emphasis was on women's work for women and children. Their particular concern was to send female missionaries and supplies to countries they deemed heathen and benighted. The missionaries taught the native women of these countries to read the Bible, improve women's health, and educate and empower women to fight against oppressive customs. They built orphanages, hospitals, and dispensaries, both in North America and in foreign lands, and became evangelistic partners with indigenous women.

By the 1880s most Protestant denominations began to develop orders of deaconesses. The Protestant equivalent of Roman Catholic nuns, in function though not in numbers, deaconesses were single women who took vows to give full-time Christian service, usually in home and foreign mission work, as evangelists, teachers, medical personnel, and social workers. As the first professional women in churches, they were seen by some lay and clergy, who did not approve of ordination, as acceptable substitutes for women who sought a church profession alongside of men. The lines blurred between the true woman and the new woman in the deaconess movement. Lucy Rider Meyer, founder of the Chicago Training School, the first institution for the training of deaconesses in the Methodist Episcopal Church, justified the deaconesses' work by saying that the world needs mothering and her trainees were taking that function to the world's needy. She also described the deaconess as the New Woman of Protestantism, whose field was as large as the world of women and the need of that work.

That same blurring was created in the origins of colleges and SEMINARIES, providing the equivalent of high school training for women after the mid-nineteenth century. Most female schools for women were initiated by Protestant denominations and, like the deaconess institutions, provided an environment of sisterhood and support among pioneer women teaching and training in HIGHER EDUCATION. Justification for seminary and college training began with the ideology of true womanhood and republican motherhood, to give education to young women leading them to create better home environments. The ideology was easily stretched to sanction the education of the New Woman: rigorous academic study, development of leadership skills, commitment to the Christian faith, preparation to teach in SUNDAY SCHOOLS and public schools, and training to be physicians.

The religious enthusiasm of EVANGELISM in the Second Great Awakening in the first half of the nineteenth century opened the doors for the first time for women to preach at CAMP MEETINGS and REVIVALS, although not at regular worship services. Seeking to preach, but not to be ordained, they claimed that their special and extraordinary abilities given them by God granted them the freedom to do what God called them to do. By the mid-century, in 1853, Antoinette Brown became the first woman to be ordained in the Protestant tradition in the United States. She was ordained by the Congregational Church in South Butler, New York, a single congregation and not a connectional denominational system. A decade later, Olympia Brown and Augusta Chapin were the first women ordained in a connectional structure, the Unitarian Universalist Church (see UNITARIAN UNIVERSALIST ASSOCIATION). Justification began to shift to ordination as a right because of gender equality of the New Woman of Protestantism by 1880. Resistance was strong, with lone women being identified as ordained by the African Methodist Episcopal Zion, National Baptist, and Methodist Protestant churches in the 1880s and 1890s.

Finally, new women of Protestantism, motivated by their religious convictions, moved outside of church structures into social reform movements in the late nineteenth century. Some entered reform movements because they were denied the opportunity to preach and to be ordained and others because they were not permitted to work alongside men in denominational missionary organizations and other lay governing bodies. Similarly, women first sought to work with men in social reform societies, such as abolitionist and peace organizations, before the CIVIL WAR. Because they were most often denied the opportunity for shared leadership but shunted to form auxiliaries, they began to form women's separatist reform groups.

Growing out of the SOCIAL GOSPEL imperative to bring the KINGDOM OF GOD on earth, the post–Civil War era became the heyday of volunteerism in social service and social justice movements. Women's organizations advanced reforms to improve life for women and children, particularly working conditions, decreasing hours in factories and sweatshops, compulsory education, temperance, and low-income housing. The Young Women's Christian Association (see YMCA, YWCA) and settlement houses were exemplary of women's social reform movements.

The Women's Christian Temperance Union, which became the largest women's organization of the nineteenth century, was representative of the socioreligious nature of Protestant women's work for the Social Gospel. Organized in 1887 it brought women together in a sisterhood of reform to work for TEMPERANCE and a host of other reforms, including peace, the double sexual standard, women's health and dress, ordination, urban problems of poverty, and working conditions for women. Some barriers of religion, GENDER, and class were broken down, enabling women to grow in leadership skills and lay the groundwork for the next generation of women who entered professional life. Lesser gains were made in breaking down barriers of race. Many white women's societies would not admit African-American women, who, in turn, joined together to form the black women's club movement, manifest in such organizations as the National Association of Colored Women and the National Council of Negro Women.

As they worked together to improve conditions for women, children, and society at large, women's reform leaders also sought to reconstruct the ideal of womanhood. They upheld aspects of true womanhood, including their belief in women's higher moral nature and the need to expand the mothering role into society. At the same time, they groomed strong and independent women who would not accept gender

limitations to their sphere of action and who developed powerful networks of support and vocational motivation for their sisters.

Legacy for the Future: The Twentieth Century and the Beginning of the Twenty-First

Simultaneous with expansion of women's space in church and society, the late nineteenth and early twentieth centuries also brought a significant loss of women's separate societies in Protestant denominations. National women's missionary organizations were dismantled and merged into larger church agencies, justified as efficient and progressive moves to integrate women and their work into wider church bureaus. Gains by women in building autonomous networks of support, control of financial expenditures, and commissioning of their own missionaries were lost or at least receded in most denominations. The one exception among denominations was in the UNITED METHODIST CHURCH, where the Women's Division of the Board of Global Ministries maintains independence and power today.

Ordination has been the major gain for women in mainline Protestant churches in the twentieth century. By the 1950s, barriers were broken down in most denominations. However, it took longer for women to be ordained in most churches than it did for females to gain the right to vote in national elections. It took seventy-two years, from the first women's rights convention in Seneca Falls, New York in 1848 to the passage of the Nineteenth Amendment granting women the national franchise in 1920. Comparatively speaking, the first women sought to be ordained in the Methodist Episcopal Church in 1880 and did not gain ordination in the Methodist Church until seventy-six years later in 1956.

Two African-American denominations, the African Methodist Episcopal Church in 1948 and the Christian Methodist Episcopal Church in 1954, ordained women shortly before more mainline, predominantly white denominations did. The PRESBYTERIAN CHURCH USA followed in 1955, the Methodists the following year, and two Lutheran denominations, the LUTHERAN CHURCH OF AMERICA and the AMERICAN LUTHERAN CHURCH, in 1970. The EPISCOPAL CHURCH, UNITED STATES allowed diocesan bishops to ordain women at their discretion in 1976, and twenty-one years later mandated ordination in all dioceses. Increasing numbers of women have been ordained in the ten largest Protestant denominations in the last quarter of the twentieth century. However, as late as 1977, only 17 percent of the clergy in these denominations were women. Over 50 percent of the women ordained by then were in Holiness, Pentecostal, evangelical, and militarily styled denominations such as the SALVATION ARMY (see HOLINESS MOVEMENT; EVANGELICALISM).

Greater success came in decentralized denominations in which individual congregations made their own decisions to ordain women. The Congregational Church, predecessor of the UNITED CHURCH OF CHRIST, ordained the first woman in the Protestant Church in 1853. The conservative SOUTHERN BAPTIST CONVENTION granted the right to its local congregations in 1964, with over 1,000 women being ordained since then. By 1979, the DENOMINATION became increasingly fundamentalist, discouraged ordination, and refused to approve women in positions of authority.

In the Salvation Army the struggle between emancipation and constriction of women was lively in the early years of the late nineteenth and early twentieth centuries. Initially women were fully commissioned as preachers, pastors, and administrators, and sent into saloons and other settings that contradicted the traditional norms of feminine behavior. As the century progressed, the concern for continuity of the organization led the Army to restrict women to more socially acceptable scenes.

Three movements in the conservative arm of Protestantism struggled with the same tension between emancipation and constriction in the late nineteenth and early twentieth centuries. PENTECOSTALISM, founded in 1906, initially empowered women as "11th Hour Laborers" to exercise their spiritual gifts for conversion of the world and individuals. As the new denomination grew up and concerns for authority and order became predominant, women's work was constricted to the support of male pastors. Openness to women as preachers and leaders has continued in the Trinitarian branch of the Latino Pentecostal movement, whereas their role has become limited to support of male leaders in the Oneness branch. The same pattern has followed in fundamentalist churches where women were initially accepted as evangelists in the late nineteenth century. However, the antifeminist bias and belief in the divinely ordered hierarchy, prohibiting women to speak in religious assemblies and to exercise authority over men, took hold by the end of the 1920s. Finally, in the Charismatic movement, the natural legacy of Pentecostalism and FUNDAMENTALISM, women outnumbered men by a ratio of ten to one in exercising spiritual gifts of healing and speaking in tongues at its founding in the second half of the twentieth century. Today, in Aglow International, the major women's arm of the movement, women are admonished to submit to husbands and pastors through their gracious choice.

Evaluating the overall position of women at the opening of the twenty-first century, the same tensions are still present that have been at the heart of gender differences in Protestant churches since colonial times. They include spiritual equality vs. social equality, male dominance vs. female submission, and the True Woman vs. the New Woman. Overall the story is more one of breakthroughs for and by women than of constriction.

Today, women have gained their own voices even in conservative denominations such as the Disciples of Christ, where the number of WOMEN CLERGY continues to grow and one-third of the students who are training for ordination in Master of Divinity programs are women. On the far left of the spectrum, Unitarian Universalist women in ordained and lay leadership slightly surpass men and the ratio of women in denominational seminaries is three to one. Steady gains by women in mainstream Protestantism are highlighted by the election of the first female bishop in the African Methodist Episcopal Church in 2000 and a woman as moderator of the 211th General Assembly of the Presbyterian Church USA in 1999. Further, in the United Methodist Church, eleven women, three of whom are women of color, serve among the fifty-one bishops, and 36 percent of the delegates at the 2000 General Conference were female. Changing demographics in the 243 seminaries in the North American Association of Theological Schools show that 35 percent of the students are women, a gain from 10 percent in 1972. Numbers of women in top administrative positions of presidents and deans have grown slowly, but they are outpaced by greater gains of women in faculty positions.

Women have sought other ways to take responsibility for themselves and to gain support of collegial males to change long-held traditions. Among African-American and Hispanic congregations, women are creating public space to resist cultural domination by predominantly white churches and social institutions. In the radical Hispanic Protestant evangelical movement, women, along with men, are resisting ways of preaching and worship that they believe have been pressed upon them by white churches. Creative new forms of WORSHIP throughout Protestant churches are often the result of feminist interpretations. Further, women have been the strong champions of inclusive language, by transforming the use of words for God and human beings, so that women, persons of color, handicapped, gays and lesbians, and others, who have been excluded by traditional patriarchal patterns, are fully represented.

The gains of greater space and more articulate voices of women over four centuries of American history have been evolutionary, not revolutionary. Both liberation and constriction are experienced today. However, the breakthroughs have been steady and deep enough that they will not be lost, but will continue to characterize the history of Protestantism in the United States.

See also Congregationalism; Missionary Organizations; Peace Organizations; Sexuality; Tongues, Speaking in; Voluntary Societies

References and Further Reading

Andrews, William L., ed. *Sisters of the Spirit: Three Black Women's Autobiographies of the Nineteenth Century.* Bloomington: Indiana University, 1986.

Brekus, Catherine A. *Strangers and Pilgrims: Female Preaching in America, 1740–1845.* Chapel Hill: University of North Carolina Press, 1998.

Cott, Nancy F. *The Bonds of Womanhood: "Woman's Sphere" in New England, 1780–1835.* New Haven, CT: Yale University Press, 1977.

———. *The Grounding of Modern Feminism.* New Haven, CT: Yale University Press, 1987.

Lindley, Susan Hill. *"You have Stept out of your Place": A History of Women and Religion in America.* Louisville, KY: Westminster John Knox Press, 1996.

Ruether, Rosemary Radford. *Christianity and the Making of the Modern Family.* Boston: Beacon Press, 2000.

———, and Rosemary Skinner Keller, eds. *In Our Own Voices: Four Centuries of American Women's Religious Writing.* Louisville, KY: Westminster John Knox Press, 2000. [Originally published by Harper Collins, San Francisco, 1995.]

———. *Women and Religion in America: A Documentary History.* 3 vols. San Francisco: Harper & Row, 1981, 1983, 1986.

Scott, Anne Firor. *Natural Allies: Women's Associations in American History.* Urbana: University of Illinois Press, 1991.

ROSEMARY SKINNER KELLER

WOMEN CLERGY

Understandings of "clergy" differ dramatically in the history of the CHURCH. Although Protestantism radically changed the nature of priesthood and expanded opportunities for women's leadership, it was not until the mid-nineteenth century that some of the more congregationally ordered Protestant denominations, like Congregationalists (see CONGREGATIONALISM) and Universalists, began ordaining women. Not until the latter half of the twentieth century did more institutionally ordered denominations, like Methodists, Presbyterians, Lutherans, and Episcopalians/Anglicans, actually grant full clergy status to women (see ANGLICANISM; EPISCOPAL CHURCH, UNITED STATES; LUTHERANISM; PRESBYTERIANISM). During the same time period, women preachers and evangelists became common in the HOLINESS MOVEMENT, and with the rise of PENTECOSTALISM, many women leaders simply went out and founded their own churches. Arguments for and against women clergy are complex, involving biblical, historical, theological, biological, social, political, cultural, practical, and ecumenical concerns. By the late twentieth century, however, a large number of Protestant denominations affirmed the growing importance of women clergy. Although new FEMINIST THEOLOGY supports women clergy, many Christians in traditional societies continue to resist. Furthermore, as church leaders have worked to reach an ecumenical consensus about ministry, the issue of women clergy has remained a big stumbling block. In the end, Protestants on all sides have simply agreed to recognize their differences and wait for guidance from the Holy Spirit.

Traditions Around Ordination

For more than 2,000 years, Christians have argued about how and who ought to be "ordained"—younger or mature persons, well-educated or especially pious persons, married or celibate persons, males or females, heterosexuals or homosexuals. In these debates, ordination is almost always understood to be more than a functional arrangement to get the work done. Persons who are ordained (known as CLERGY) are acknowledged to be especially gifted by God. After ordination, they carry an "indelible mark" that sets them apart for life from ordinary Christians (known as LAITY). All contemporary understandings of ordained ministry are grounded in the tradition that clergy are "called" by God, as well as the church, to assume "holy" or "priestly" responsibilities, such as sharing God's message through PREACHING and officiating at the sacramental rites of the church (ministries of word and sacrament). Clergy may have different responsibilities in various denominations, but despite great diversity almost all Christians practice some rite or LITURGY that sets apart church leadership by PRAYER and laying on of hands. Most traditions call this process "ordination." It emphasizes the fact that ordained ministry is a sacred trust.

In the early Christian church, before practices and liturgies around ordination were formalized, many types of people held leadership positions. Ancient and medieval church records show that women exercised key responsibilities for oversight, discipline, liturgy, teaching, and service in the emerging Christian community. Gradually, however, as ecclesiastical power consolidated and aligned itself with political and economic forces, and theological judgments were codified around the relationship of SEXUALITY to SIN, the clergy role became the exclusive prerogative of unmarried men. There were women who were revered as leaders of nuns, or mystical visionaries, but no women clergy.

During the fourteenth and fifteenth centuries, the expanding economic and intellectual climate of western Europe generated new attitudes about women. Renaissance humanists promoted the superiority of women over traditional Christian understandings of women as the source of sin and evil. Soon thereafter, sixteenth-century Protestant reformers challenged prevailing views about ordination, arguing for married and highly educated clergy. These Protestant thinkers insisted that celibacy was actually a problem, and that married clergy were needed to minister to the needs of families. Rather quickly, MARTIN LUTHER and the other reformers, many of whom had been celibate priests, sought out wives and argued for a more holistic view of ordained ministry. They felt that God had blessed MARRIAGE and that clergy would be able to serve Christians more effectively if they were married. At that time, however, few of them even entertained the idea that women should be priests.

Initially Protestantism stressed the intellectual leadership of the clergy. Clergy were not merely sacramental functionaries, they were preachers and teachers. Protestants wore the Geneva gown, worn by professors and students in the university, rather than ornate vestments. Clergy needed to "know" the BIBLE, and only those with scholarly credentials were accepted for ordination. In Protestantism, ministry became a "learned" profession open only to those who completed a rigorous academic program.

Protestantism also changed the relationship between clergy and laity. Although most Protestant denominations continued to have clergy, Protestant theology emphasized the "PRIESTHOOD OF ALL BELIEVERS," which challenged basic assumptions about the powers of clergy. In Protestantism, ordination ceased to have some of the theological weight that it carried in the Roman Catholic Church. It was no longer a sacrament; it simply recognized gifts and determined who would carry out the functions of ministry. Among Protestants, ordained ministers were not considered more holy than the laity; rather, they were persons recognized as having certain talents and empowered to "function" as religious teachers and pastors for and on behalf of the whole community. Protestants still believed that ordination was a special or "holy" calling. Clergy, however, were accountable to the whole people of God (the priesthood of all believers). Although some denominations retained the ecclesiastical office of BISHOP, most of them did not believe that clergy AUTHORITY was literally conveyed by apostolic succession through a sequence of ceremonies (or hands) linking one ordination ritual to the next one. When Protestant clergy were ordained they made promises to carry on the collective legacy of Christian faithfulness through the ages.

By the seventeenth century, charismatic female leaders were found among many groups in the "left-wing" of the Protestant Reformation. Anabaptists (see ANABAPTISM), the English Puritans and Separatists (see PURITANISM), and later leaders within the eighteenth-century Wesleyan revival encouraged and followed women leaders. Protestant women were revered as martyrs, wives, mothers, and virgins. Grassroots Protestant piety took women very seriously.

The changing understandings of ordination in Christian history, combined with actual experiences of strong women leaders, eventually shaped and reshaped the issue of women's ordination. By the early nineteenth century, many Protestants wondered aloud: If all persons were called to ministry by their baptism, and if there is neither Jew nor Greek, male nor female in Christ Jesus (Galatians 3:28), why not ordain women? If, as the apostle Paul put it, the Christian community is a royal priesthood carrying out God's ministries, women are part of that priesthood. If Christian discipleship requires all Christians, female and male, to study the Bible and share their witness and faith with their children, women can do that as well as men. And if every Christian has received the universal promise of a "baptism of the Spirit" or a "second blessing," then women have received that promise, and therefore women may be blessed with as much power as men to lead others to SALVATION.

Contemporary Protestant denominations still argue over this legacy. Within Protestantism, especially since the 1970s, many groups have changed their practice and now ordain women. At the same time, large Protestant groups, such as the Southern Baptists in the United States (see SOUTHERN BAPTIST CONVENTION), continue to cite scripture to defend their refusal to authorize the ordination of women. Officially, the Roman Catholic church remains steadfast in its judgment that women have no claim to the priesthood.

The First Women Clergy

In colonial North America women exercised more political, social, and religious freedom than many European women. The well-known story of a seventeenth-century colonial Puritan woman named ANNE HUTCHINSON, who was tried and condemned for HERESY for holding meetings in her Boston home to discuss the sermons of her pastor, indicates that women's religious leadership was an increasingly important issue. By the late eighteenth and early nineteenth century, Protestant women in the United States discovered new talents, took on new roles, and sought more public visibility and political power. Women from many religious traditions began to challenge their churches to move beyond unexamined assumptions about the maleness of clergy.

The first Protestant groups to ordain women formally were from the so-called "FREE CHURCH" denominations—Protestants that vest a great deal of ecclesial authority in the local congregation. In these denominations, all decision making takes place in local congregations and does not require regional or national approval. Congregations may seek the fellowship and the advice of other congregations or leaders, but they do not need external permission to do what they feel God is calling them to do–such as ordaining a pastor. In many of these congregationally governed churches, women were allowed to exercise significant lay citizenship privileges by the late eighteenth and early nineteenth century. The Congregationalists (now the UNITED CHURCH OF CHRIST), the Universalists (see UNIVERSALISM), the small frontier Christian movement that eventually developed into the Christian Church (DISCIPLES OF CHRIST), and the Unitarians (see UNITARIAN UNIVERSALIST ASSOCIATION) were some of the first Protestant denominations to recognize and formally authorize the ministries of women. It was easy for them to move from recognizing female lay leaders, itinerant female preachers, and female educational or medical missionaries, to giving full ordination to women.

But even though women were preaching and teaching in colonial America throughout the eighteenth century, historians believe that the first woman formally ordained to the Christian ministry in a major Protestant denomination in the United States was Antoinette L. Brown (later Blackwell). She was ordained by the Congregationalists in a small church in upstate New York in 1853. Within the next several decades, the Universalists ordained Olympia Brown (no relation to Antoinette) in 1863, the Christian Churches (General Convention) ordained Melissa Timmons (later Terrill) in 1867, and the Unitarians ordained Celia Burleigh and Mary Graves in 1871. Many of these early women clergy were viewed as "exceptions to the general rule." There was no great support for their ministries, and most "proper women" still considered public preaching of the Gospel unseemly for women. Male clergy jokingly warned their parishioners to "beware of petticoats in the pulpit."

One of the most dramatic changes in attitudes about ordination occurred among the Society of Friends. An offshoot of English radical Protestantism, the Quakers rejected all titles and class distinctions, arguing that everyone was blessed with the Divine within, and therefore either everyone should be ordained or no one should be ordained. Women exercised major leadership in local Quaker "meetings," but because Quaker nonliturgical worship was so unusual, Quaker women preachers were usually only called "clergy" by those who were not Quakers. A very famous American Quaker woman, LUCRETIA COFFIN MOTT, was formally recorded as a Quaker minister in 1821. Despite the fact that the Quakers did not support any distinction between clergy and laity, Mott was known far and wide as a "lady minister."

Another sectarian group that refused to make distinctions between male and female leadership was the SHAKERS. Founded by an English woman named ANN LEE, who came to North America at the end of the eighteenth century, the Shakers rejected marriage for men and women alike. Officially, Shakers did not have clergy, but Elders and Eldresses ruled each community of Shakers who lived in communal fellowship waiting for Christ's second coming. During the first half of the nineteenth century, Shaker communities spread throughout the North American frontier. Many women exercised extraordinary religious freedom and leadership within the Shaker movement.

In Europe a similar pattern emerged, but more slowly. Protestant groups that were organized congregationally, such as Congregationalists and BAPTISTS in Great Britain and MENNONITES in the NETHERLANDS, began ordaining women in the nineteenth century. But most of the Protestant churches in Europe, where church and state are often intertwined, did not debate or grant ordination to women until well into the twentieth century.

Generally speaking, women in more institutionally ordered Protestant denominations like Anglicans, Episcopalians, Lutherans, Methodists, and Presbyterians did not consider the question of ordination until the end of the nineteenth century or the first half of the twentieth century. It is important to realize that the issue of women's ordination was variously understood. In those denominations where laity are ordained as elders—for example, in some Presbyterian groups—women were ordained as lay elders in 1930. Women in that same denomination, however, were not ordained as teaching elders (clergy) until 1956. Within METHODISM, one denomination actually began ordaining women clergy in 1927. These women were technically "clergy," but they were not members of the annual Methodist Conference, and therefore they did not have rights and privileges equal to those of male clergy. Full Conference membership in the Methodist Church in the United States was not gained by women until 1956.

Even as European-rooted denominations wrestled with tradition and the ministries of women, numerous new Protestant denominations that emerged out of the Holiness movement of the mid-nineteenth century, and the Pentecostal movement of the early twentieth century celebrated women's leadership and had no problem ordaining women. CATHERINE BOOTH, a key leader in the SALVATION ARMY in the United States, wrote a widely distributed pamphlet titled *Female Ministry: Woman's Right to Preach the Gospel* in 1859. In many of the Holiness denominations, such as CHURCH OF GOD (ANDERSON, INDIANA) and the CHURCH OF THE NAZARENE, there were hundreds of ordained women by the 1930s. Unfortunately, as the biblical literalism of the conservative evangelical or fundamentalist movement infiltrated these denominations, the numbers of women clergy declined. Not until the 1980s and 1990s did the ranks of ordained women in many of the Holiness denominations reach levels equal to the 1930s. Within Pentecostalism there was a similar pattern; early in Pentecostalism, women were affirmed as preachers, and even ordained, but later they were ignored.

Arguments For and Against

Arguments for and against women clergy have been debated among Protestants for well over 200 years. Yet it has only been since the mid-twentieth century that a critical mass of ordained women have been authorized by various denominations and a significant body of literature developed to defend their status. Biblical, ecclesial, and cultural issues are all intertwined in the arguments.

Those who believe that women should not be ordained appeal to the authority of biblical texts. They argue that God's creation of women and men in Scripture has made women subordinate to men. They quote the second creation story in the Bible (Genesis 2:18–23) where Eve is created second as Adam's "helper." Her secondary status is further reinforced by the story of the Fall, where Eve is cast as the weaker partner and the temptress (Genesis 3:1–6). In that text, Eve is punished and condemned to bear children in pain and be ruled over by her husband (Genesis 3:16). This dominate/subordinate ordering of creation is affirmed, goes this argument, by the apostle Paul when he writes to the early church (I Corinthians 11:3–15) that woman's role is to "glorify man." This argument supports traditional marriage and upholds historic patterns of male-only leadership in the church.

Those who believe that women should be ordained also appeal to the Bible. They reject the hierachical assumptions of many biblical texts, arguing that such primitive anthropology does not connect with modern world views. They quote from the first creation story in the Bible (Genesis 1:26–31), where women and men are created together in God's image and share the inheritance of creation. They argue that Jesus preached about a new creation and that he treated women with great respect. They furthermore note that when the apostle Paul focuses on the power of Jesus Christ to change things, Paul insists that there are no significant ethnic, racial, or gender differences in the Christian church, because "all are One in Christ Jesus." (Galatians 3:27–28).

In addition to the biblical arguments, Protestant denominations with strong links to the legacy of the medieval church and the historic defense of apostolic succession (i.e., a literal linear connection between contemporary clergy and the life and ministry of Jesus Christ) maintain that because a priest mediates the ongoing presence of Christ in worship, that priest must be male. Jesus was a man, and therefore the male gender of the priest functions as an icon of Christ, the new Adam.

Others insist that the manner in which the priest embodies Christ is through his representative humanity, not through his masculine sexuality. The "persona Christi" may be even better represented by having both women and men, rather than just men, in leadership. Still other Protestants reject the "persona Christi" argument and insist that only the whole community of the church, the gathered faithful, can mediate Christ's presence. Priesthood represents the community of the faithful and gives expression to the unity of all Christians.

Debates about women clergy sometimes get into arguments about the "nature of women." God created male and female with complimentary functions and different gifts. The role of priesthood is particularly suited for men, just as the role of motherhood is suited for women. The issue is not one of inequality between women and men, but distinct differences that are grounded in creation and God's plan for salvation.

Others insist that God has given women and men (especially Christian women and men) equal talents, making them equally capable and equally equipped for ordained ministry. There are biological differences between men and women, but there is only one human nature. Unfortunately, women have been subordinated for years and hindered from fully developing themselves. The church is the poorer. It is time for women clergy to challenge the masculine captivity of the priesthood and enable the church to benefit from the leadership of women.

Arguments about the "nature of women" may also focus on women's reproductive cycle. In ancient times, women were considered unclean during menstruation and after childbirth. Cleansing rituals were more demanding if they had a female child rather than a male child. These traditions are sometimes still used to argue that it is inappropriate for menstruating, married, or pregnant women to preside at worship.

Beyond the biblical, theological, and biological arguments, there are social, political, and cultural arguments for and against women clergy. Although those opposed are fearful that acquiescing to such arguments will lead to a further SECULARIZATION of the church—damaging tradition and corrupting the church's inner life——others insist that new so-called "secular" trends may be calling the church into a new future. Advocates for women clergy note that modern science has given us all new understandings of GENDER roles. Equality is a basic principle of justice, and the ordination of women embodies that principle. It is time for the patriarchal patterns in the church to be left behind and for Christians to embrace the radical message of the Gospel. In the past, women have been primarily the receivers, responders, and implementers of male power and decision making; now women can help the church reclaim its radical mandate.

Some arguments for women clergy are very pragmatic and practical. In certain parts of the world there is a shortage of male priests. Women are already doing most of the work, so they should be ordained. Women have many of the nurturing, healing, and peacemaking skills that the world needs. Male clergy brought their unique gifts to earlier eras—now it is time for the church to benefit from the leadership of female clergy.

The Ecumenical Movement

Finally, arguments for and against women clergy are being shaped and reshaped by the ecumenical movement (see ECUMENISM). During the early twentieth century, as various Protestant denominations sought reunion and tried to build new bridges to Orthodox and Roman Catholic churches (see ORTHODOXY, EASTERN; CATHOLICISM, PROTESTANT REACTIONS), the issue of women's ordination surfaced again and again. At the founding meeting of the Faith and Order movement in Lausanne, SWITZERLAND in 1927, there were only seven women among the 400 delegates. The women graciously argued that the place of women in the church and in the councils of the church needed to be in the "hearts and minds of all." In 1948, when the WORLD COUNCIL OF CHURCHES (WCC) was organized in Amsterdam, it was decided that the issue of women's ordination needed further study. "The churches are not agreed on the important question of the admission of women to the full ministry. Some churches for theological reasons are not prepared to consider the question of such ordination: some find no objection in principle but see administrative or social difficulties; some permit partial but not full participation in the work of the ministry; in others, women are eligible for all offices in the Church" (Parvey 1985). This judgment eventually led to the establishment of a WCC Commission on the Life and Work of Women in

the Churches and a report titled *The Service and Status of Women in the Churches* (Bliss 1952).

During the last half of the twentieth century, the ordination of women has remained a volatile issue. From the 1950s through the 1970s, many major Protestant denominations in all parts of the world officially opened the way for the ordination of women. Feminist theology provided theological support for the practice. The percentages of women in theological studies increased dramatically. At the same time, many conservative evangelical Protestants continue to reject the idea of women clergy, and social and cultural values in more traditional societies keep women in the younger churches of AFRICA, Asia, and LATIN AMERICA from serving as clergy. Yet growing numbers of women are serving the churches. Around the world, surveys and interviews of women leaders (many of whom are clergy) support this fact, even as considerable resistance remains.

Ecumenical debates keep the issue alive. Many Protestant denominations active in the WCC and members of the Faith and Order Commission (which includes an even wider range of Protestants and Roman Catholics) look deeply into the nature of all Christian ministry and conclude that Christians will continue to differ on the issue of women clergy. The *Baptism, Eucharist and Ministry* document (a product of fifty years of ecumenical work on three crucial issues that divide Christians) states that "some churches ordain both men and women, others ordain only men. Differences on this issue raise obstacles to the mutual recognition of ministries. . . . Openness to each other holds the possibility that the Spirit may well speak to one church through the insights of another. Ecumenical consideration, therefore, should encourage, not restrain, the facing of this question" (1982, par. 54). On the one hand, the ordination of women seems literally to threaten the unity of the church. Christians believe that when some churches ordain women, they diminish the possibility of Christian consensus around the mutual recognition of ministries. Others argue that any consensus about ministry that fails to embrace the fullness of male and female ministry is unacceptable anyway. Each is willing to admit, however, that the Spirit may well speak to one church through the insights of another.

References and Further Reading

Baptism, Eucharist and Ministry. Faith and Order Paper 111, Geneva, Switzerland: World Council of Churches, 1982.

Bliss, Kathleen. *The Service and Status of Women in the Churches.* London: SCM Press, 1952.

Chaves, Mark. *Ordaining Women: Culture and Conflict in Religious Organizations.* Cambridge, MA: Harvard University Press, 1997.

Lawless, Elaine. *Handmaidens of the Lord: Pentecostal Women Preachers and Traditional Religion.* Philadelphia, PA: University of Pennsylvania Press, 1988.

McKenzie, Vashti M. *Not Without a Struggle: Leadership Development for African American Women in Ministry.* Cleveland, OH: United Church Press, 1996.

Nesbitt, Paula. *The Feminization of Clergy in America: Occupational and Organizational Perspectives.* New York: Oxford University Press, 1997.

Parvey, Constance, ed. *Ordination of Women in Ecumenical Perspective.* Faith and Order Paper 105. Geneva, Switzerland: World Council of Churches, 1980.

———. "Appendix 2. Stir in the Ecumenical Movement: The Ordination of Women." In *The Force of Tradition: A Case Study of Women Priests in Sweden* by Brita Stendahl. Philadelphia, PA: Fortress Press, 1985.

Schneider, Carl J. and Dorothy Schneider. *In Their Own Right: The History of American Clergywomen.* New York: Crossroad Publishing, 1997.

Tucker, Ruth A. *Daughters of the Church: Women and Ministry From New Testament Times to the Present.* Grand Rapids, MI: Zondervan Press, 1987.

Wessinger, Catherine, ed. *Religious Institutions and Women's Leadership: New Roles Inside the Mainstream.* Columbia, SC: University of South Carolina Press, 1996.

Zikmund, Barbara Brown, Adair T. Lummis, Patricia M. Y. Chang. *Clergy Women: An Uphill Calling.* Louisville, KY: Westminster John Knox Press, 1998.

BARBARA BROWN ZIKMUND

WOOLMAN, JOHN (1720–1772)

American Quaker clergy. Born October 19, 1720, in Northampton, New Jersey, Woolman spent his early life on his family's plantation in the Delaware valley. One of thirteen children, Woolman attended Quaker school and learned to read very early "through the care" of his parents. Woolman left the plantation in 1740 to work as a store clerk and began his ministry soon afterward, making the first of many missionary trips in 1743. Often these journeys were extremely long and difficult: on one trip into the South in 1757 he rode on horseback more than 1,100 miles in two months. The difficulties were not simply physical. Woolman found himself greatly uneasy when enjoying hospitality made possible by slave labor, distressed at the way slaveholding prevented "sound uniting" between Southern Friends and himself, and appalled both at the condition of the slaves and by the institution itself.

Woolman opened his own shop in Mount Holly in 1748, and according to his *Journal*, had both an inclination for, and success in, the business. However, just as "the road to large business appeared open," he "felt a stop" in his mind. After prayer and resignation to the "holy will" of God, Woolman gave up his business, in part to avoid participating in an economy where the pursuit of superfluities by some caused a burden of labor for others that he felt was greater than God intended for his creatures. In 1761 Woolman gave up dyed clothing because he was convinced that indulgence in luxury oppresses labor and encourages the "spirit of self-exaltation and strife," a spirit Woolman links in his *Journal* specifically to war.

Woolman married Sarah Ellis in 1749, and the following year the couple had a daughter, Mary. A son, William, died in 1754 at three months of age. After the French and Indian War, Woolman became an advocate for the rights of Native Americans, whose villages he had visited in western Pennsylvania. He died of smallpox on October 7, 1772, in England where he had gone to preach.

Best known for his abolitionism and his advocacy for the poor, Woolman frequently appears in American literary studies as a precursor of the Transcendentalists or an early representative of the libertarian conscience. Such interpretations tend to obscure the scriptural and Christological emphases of Woolman's thought. Woolman's *Considerations on Pure Wisdom* (1768) grounds wisdom and what he called "the Light" clearly in Christ and the Scriptures. The pure wisdom from above derives from such "true obedience" that one comes to a "state of inward purity" in which he "may love mankind in the same love with which our Redeemer loveth us." Without singleness of eye directed to Christ, "selfish desires, and an imaginary superiority, darken the mind; hence injustice frequently proceeds; and where this is the case, to convince the judgment, is the most effective remedy." For Woolman the Light is not simply a principle of inner judgment and inspiration, roughly equal to the Transcendentalists' intuition or soul, as is too often implied by American studies that treat the Quakers as forerunners of Emerson, Thoreau, and Whitman. Inseparable from Christ, the Light, as Woolman conceives it, acts to search out our motives and strivings, revealing these, more often than not, to be the results of self-will.

The *Journal* is Woolman's account of his attempt to live in radical obedience to God. Early in the work he suggests the movement of his heart as he "lived under the cross": "While I silently ponder on that change wrought in me, I find no language equal to it nor any means to convey to another a clear idea of it. I looked upon the works of God in this visible creation and an awfulness covered me; my heart was tender and often contrite, and a universal love to my fellow creatures increased in me." Love and justice are rooted, for Woolman, in awe before creation and a sense of absolute dependency. No doubt remembering his vivid childhood experience of wantonly killing a robin, Woolman now understands "that as by [God's] breath the flame of life was kindled in all animal and sensitive creatures, to say we love God as unseen and at the same time exercise cruelty toward the least creature moving by his life, or by life derived from him, was a contradiction in itself." It is difficult not to distort Woolman's thought by addressing him through the classically American paradigm of the individual versus the collective. Woolman understands himself always as a creature living in mutual and reciprocal dependency with other creatures in a world created by God and redeemed through the cross.

Woolman's sense of humanity's shared creaturely dependency on God provides the theological basis for his abolitionism and commitment to peace. Isaiah's language of eschatological gathering and Christ's "tasting death for every man" led to a deep sense in Woolman of community with people of color as well as inspiration for prophetic criticism of social arrangements, such as slavery, so obviously at odds with the universalizing pressure of Scripture. Peace is a fruit of the regeneration of the person in Christ. For Woolman Quaker nonviolence is grounded in the work God has done "in sending his son into the world" to "repair the breach made by disobedience, to finish sin and transgression that his kingdom might come and his will be done on earth as it is in heaven." The Spirit has "set up" a "spiritual kingdom . . . which is to subdue and break in pieces all kingdoms that oppose it, and shall stand for ever." Friends, Woolman continues, should thoroughly acquaint themselves with the truth and the "safety, stability, and peace there is in it," as to "be qualified to conduct [ourselves] in all parts of our life as becomes our peaceable profession." Woolman's peace witness is a way of living out what God has accomplished in the cross and resurrection: the overcoming of the powers of the world, the logic of violence and coercion, and the need to secure and justify our own lives.

See also Peace Organizations; Slavery; Slavery, Abolition of; Society of Friends in North America; Transcendentalism

References and Further Reading

Primary Sources:

Woolman, John. *Some Considerations on the Keeping of Negroes* (Pt. 1). New York: Grossman Publishers, 1754.
———. *Considerations on Keeping Negroes* (Pt. II). New York: Grossman Publishers, 1762.
———. *A Plea for the Poor.* 1763.
———. *Considerations on Pure Wisdom and Human Policy.* 1768.
———. *Considerations on the True Harmony of Mankind.* 1770.
———. *A Journal of the Life, Gospel Labours, and Christian Experiences of That Faithful Minister of Jesus Christ, John Woolman.* Philadelphia: Joseph Crukshank, 1774.

Secondary Sources:

Cady, Edwin. *John Woolman.* New York: Twayne, 1965.
Oehlschlaeger, Fritz. "Taking John Woolman's Christianity Seriously." *Renascence* 48 (1996): 191–207.
Sox, David. *John Woolman: Quintessential Quaker.* Richmond, IN: Friends United Press, 1999.
Stewart, Margaret. "John Woolman's 'Kindness Beyond Expression': Collective Identity vs. Individualism and White Supremacy." *Early American Literature* 26 (1991): 251–275.

FRITZ OEHLSCHLAEGER

WOOLSTON, THOMAS (1670–1733)

English deist. Born in Northampton, ENGLAND in 1670, Woolston is best known for his attack on the literal reading of biblical miracles. He was educated at Sidney Sussex College, Cambridge and elected a fellow there in 1691. Ordained and known as a scholar of the early church fathers, he wrote *An Apology for the Christian Religion* (1705) in which he argued that biblical miracles should be understood allegorically rather than historically. Woolston was quickly silenced by his colleagues, but he resumed his attack on biblical literalism in 1720, which led to his dismissal from the college in 1721.

From 1720 to 1729 Woolston released numerous polemical works attacking the CLERGY (e.g., *Four Free Gifts to the Clergy,* 1722–1724), whom he held responsible for the perversion of Christianity and the historicity of biblical miracles. Woolston's *A Moderator between an Infidel and an Atheist* and *Supplements to a Moderator* (1725) provoked Bishop Edmund Gibson to bring blasphemy charges against him, but these were dropped for fear of winning him sympathy. Woolston's most notorious publication was a series of six discourses *On the Miracles of our Saviour* (1727–1729). In his characteristic scathing satire, he denounced the miracles of Jesus through his rhetorical tools of insult and ridicule. Woolston argued that one cannot use miracles as proof of the Messiahship of Jesus, which is what Jesus claimed; instead, he aimed to provide a rational foundation for Christianity independent of superstition and supernaturalism. Woolston's method advocated allegorical interpretation of biblical miracle stories, using in support the allegorical interpretations of early church fathers.

Woolston's assault on the resurrection of Christ again brought on charges of blasphemy, for which he was put on trial on March 4, 1729, and sentenced to a fine and one-year imprisonment. Thomas Woolston died of stomach cancer on January 27, 1733.

See also Deism; Higher Criticism

References and Further Reading

Primary Sources:

Woolston, Thomas. *A discourse on the miracles of Our Saviour: in view of the present controversy between infidels and apostates.* London: Printed for the author, sold by him, 1727.

———. *A fifth discourse on the miracles of Our Saviour: in view of the present controversy between infidels and apostates.* London: Printed for the author, and sold by him, 1728.

———. *A fourth discourse on the miracles of Our Saviour: in view of the present controversy between infidels and apostates.* London: Printed for the author, and sold by him, 1728.

———. *A free-gift to the clergy, or, The hireling priests of what denomination soever, challeng'd to a disputation on this question: whether the hireling preachers of this age, who are all ministers of the letter, be not worshippers of the apocalyptical beast, and ministers of Anti-Christ.* London: A. Moore, 1722.

———. *Mr. Woolston's defence of his discourses on the miracles of our Saviour: against the Bishops of St. David's and London, and his other adversaries, part I.* London: Printed for the author, and sold by him, 1729.

Secondary Sources:

Herrick, James A. *The Radical Rhetoric of the English Deists: The Discourse of Skepticism, 1680–1750.* Columbia: University of South Carolina Press, 1997.

Trapnell, William. *Thomas Woolston: Deist and Madman?* Bristol, UK: Thoemmes, 1993.

G. SUJIN PAK

WORDSWORTH, WILLIAM (1770–1850)

English poet. Few poets have been hailed as profound religious thinkers with so many misgivings as Wordsworth. For many Victorians he, above all, had shown how head and heart, science and emotion, rationality and belief could be integrated into a satisfactory personal synthesis. Yet many of those whom he had most helped—John Stuart Mill, for instance, or Matthew Arnold—were most critical and skeptical of his philosophy and the kinds of religious experience he was credited with. As Mill reveals in his *Autobiography,* it was Wordsworth who had given him back a sense of wholeness and meaning to life after his disastrous adolescent breakdown in 1828. Yet Percy Bysshe Shelley, he argued, was the greater poet because he expressed "pure feeling"—which is what a poet should do. Although the *Immortality Ode* contained some "grand imagery," it was nevertheless "bad philosophy." Arnold, although more sympathetic to Christianity, was equally unsympathetic to Wordsworth's religion *and* his philosophy: "we cannot do him justice until we dismiss his formal philosophy.... However true the doctrine may be, it has ... none of the characters of poetic truth, the kind of truth we require from a poet ..." (Arnold 1888: 149–150).

Yet for many other Victorians Wordsworth was *preeminently* a religious poet. From natural dissenters like George MacDonald and Mark Rutherford (see WILLIAM HALE WHITE); to Christian Socialists (see SOCIALISM, CHRISTIAN), like CHARLES KINGSLEY, J. M. Ludlow, or John M. F. Hughes; nonparty men like FREDERICK DENISON MAURICE; Americans like RALPH WALDO EMERSON; and through JOHN KEBLE (perhaps the greatest Wordsworthian of them all) to the whole OXFORD MOVEMENT, including EDWARD B. PUSEY and JOHN HENRY NEWMAN, Wordsworth's poetry reached out to every sector of the nineteenth century's otherwise divided religious life. If Arnold assured readers that Wordsworth's influence was already waning after his death mid-century, others repeatedly assumed that Wordsworth's great affirmations of value in NATURE also reveal a transcendent God who was all-powerful, loving, and moral.

Twentieth-century criticism has been no less contradictory. Although some have continued to find in him religious inspiration, others have seen in him at best a vague pantheism, or even little that can be described as "religious" at all. A few have even suggested that his love of Nature led not to the love of humanity, but its rejection. Wordsworth, it is darkly hinted, took refuge in the pieties of conventional ANGLICANISM only to avoid the path of the Marquis de Sade (Ferry 1959; Hartman 1964). According to this view, having *failed* to find the solace he sought in Nature, Wordsworth flees *from* it to religion in disillusion and even terror.

There is nothing new in such diverse attitudes. His greatest contemporary admirers, WILLIAM BLAKE, SAMUEL TAYLOR COLERIDGE, John Keats, or (later) MacDonald, were all uneasily aware of what seems to be curious contradictions in Wordsworth's thought. In 1826, on reading *The Influence of Natural Objects in calling forth and strengthening the Imagination ...*, Blake scribbled in the margin of his copy of *Poems 1815*: "Natural Objects always did and now do weaken, deaden and obliterate Imagination in Me. Wordsworth must know that what he Writes Valuable is Not to be found in Nature." Later he told Crabb Robinson that reading the Introduction to Wordsworth's *Excursion* had made him ill. Nevertheless, he added, Wordsworth was "the greatest poet of the age." On page one of the *Poems* he wrote "I see in Wordsworth the Natural Man rising up against the Spiritual Man Continually, & then he is No Poet but a Heathen Philosopher at Enmity against all true Poetry or Inspiration." By the concluding essay (on p. 341) he concludes wearily, "I do not know who wrote these Prefaces: they are very mischievous & direct contrary to Wordsworth's own Practise" (Blake 1966:783). If elsewhere Blake had feared Wordsworth was no

Christian but a heathen Platonist, now his fear was that he was no Platonist either, but a mere worshipper of Nature (Robinson 1938:1, 327).

Blake's puzzled reaction may stand for many. Was Wordsworth a "naturalist," finding values inherent in Nature itself? Was he a Platonist, perceiving through the fleeting appearances of Nature shadows of eternal supernatural values? Was he a Pantheist, finding not a personal God, but an impersonal divinity distributed throughout the universe? Was he an orthodox Christian, seeing even in fallen Nature vestiges of the divine love that had animated all Creation?

Relation to Church

Wordsworth himself had originally intended to become an Anglican clergyman—although never with great enthusiasm. His stay in FRANCE in the early 1790s seems to have been to learn French to become a clergyman-tutor in some wealthy family. His support for the early days of the Revolution, together with his love affair with the Catholic and royalist Annette Vallon, which resulted in an illegitimate French daughter, also meant a profound revolution in his own sense of VOCATION. After a period of near despair (later movingly memorialized in *Tintern Abbey*) Wordsworth emerged with strengthened sense of the healing power of Nature and his poetic vocation to record that recovery. His subsequent theology and even relationship with his own church was to baffle both critics and sometimes his own family. "I would die for the Church of England," he once remarked on passing Grasmere Church. His sister Dorothy replied that he would die if he ever went inside one. "That," said the poet, "is because the Curate is usually drunk." According to another authority Wordsworth's aversion to his local church was because two of his children were buried in the graveyard there.

Wordsworth himself, who was an inveterate reviser of his own work, clearly had no problems with the poem that offended Blake, incorporating it into the 1850 version of *The Prelude* unaltered:

> Wisdom and Spirit of the universe!
> Thou Soul that art the eternity of thought,
> That giv'st to forms and images a breath
> And everlasting motion, not in vain
> By day or star-light thus from my first dawn
> Of childhood dids't thou intertwine for me
> The passions that build up our human soul;
> Not with the mean and vulgar works of man,
> But with high objects, with enduring things—
> With life and nature, purifying thus
> The elements of feeling and of thought,
> And sanctifying, by such discipline,
> Both pain and fear, until we recognise
> A grandeur in the beatings of the heart.
> [*Prelude*, 1805, 1, 427–40]

The problem begins with the language itself: is the overtly religious vocabulary —"spirit," "soul," "sanctifying," and so forth—metaphorical, metonymical, or literal? Similar imagery occurs later in *The Prelude*, when Wordsworth has reached the summit of Snowdon by moonlight and stands looking out over a "sea of mist" concealing the lower part of the mountain—including the route (at once spatial and historical) to that point of vision:

> Meanwhile, the moon looked down upon this shew
> In single glory, and we stood, the mist
> Touching our very feet; and from the shore
> At distance not the third part of a mile
> Was a blue chasm, a fracture in the vapour,
> A deep and gloomy breathing-place, through which
> Mounted the roar of waters, torrents, streams
> Innumerable, roaring with one voice.
> The universal spectacle throughout
> Was shaped for admiration and delight,
> Grand in itself alone, but in that breach
> Through which the homeless voice of waters rose,
> That deep dark thoroughfare, had Nature lodged
> The soul, the imagination of the whole.
> [*Prelude*, 1805, XIII, 52–65]

The word "soul," paralleling that key Romantic word "imagination," appears to come from a very different mental set. However, what appears the loose conjunction of religious and aesthetic terms here provides something new—an image that is *neither*, but primarily *psychological*. This "image of a mighty mind" (1.69) provides one of the earliest, and certainly one of the most graphic models of the unconscious in all literature: a mountain whose summit is illuminated by moonlight but whose roots, beneath the mist, are shrouded in darkness. Even Wordsworth's own term for this, "an underpresence" (1.71), uncannily anticipates later psychoanalytic terminology.

Any apparent disjunction between "soul" and "imagination" results more from fractures in our own mental maps than from the intellectual climate of the period. It had been the total integration of the spiritual and the psychological in the scheme of Wordsworth's mentor, David Hartley, that had appealed to many Romantics. Yet the two words are not tensionless synonyms; both have semantic baggage and belong to markedly different historical contexts.

The Romantic attempt to integrate feeling and thinking was more than a quest for internal unity. Starting with human subjectivity Wordsworth believed that we actively reshape—"half-create"—our perception both of the external environment and individual identity, affecting past as much as present. Autobiography was for Wordsworth an integral part of understanding his identity as a poet. Past and present were creative acts of consciousness—expressions, as it were, of becoming "a living soul" in this new sense. Telling "the story of the man, and who he was" is not confined to the major poems, but is central in some way to all his lyrics. This new inwardness, characteristic of the Romantic idea of the soul, stressing imagination, empathy, and feeling as adjuncts to personal integration, was both distinctively Protestant and essential to the Romantic consciousness of history.

For Wordsworth the description of Snowdon completes what has amounted to nothing less than the struggle *for* his soul. Retelling his life's story through its significant "spots of time" reaches its climax with that final image of the mist-covered mountain, and only *after* that do we see the full significance of the earlier meditations:

> Oh mystery of man, from what a depth
> Proceed thy honours! I am lost, but see
> In simple childhood something of the base
> On which thy greatness stands—but this I feel,
> That from thyself it is that thou must give,
> Else never canst receive. The days gone by
> Come back upon me from the dawn almost
> Of life; the hiding-places of my power
> Seem open, I approach, and then they close;
> I see by glimpses now, when age comes on
> May scarcely see at all.
> [*Prelude*, Book XI, 1805, 328–337]

If the mountain is the self, with mist allowing only tantalizing and fragmentary glimpses of the past, the rift in those clouds, "that deep dark thoroughfare" where conscious and unconscious meet, locates the soul. But there is also a historical dimension to this retrospective survey of the psyche. As much as childhood experiences, Wordsworth's poetic consciousness had been shaped by the turmoil of the French Revolution and its aftermath. If, as he invites us, we read his story in terms of moral conflict, the experiences in France, and his subsequent despairing return to ENGLAND, provide the central conflict eventual triumph.

Perception of History

Although Wordsworth's own private sense of history was always part of a broader public sense of history-in-the-making in the Revolution, affecting in different ways Edmund Burke, Fanny Burney, William Hone, Richard Price, Charlotte Smith, and others including, later, Thomas Carlyle, what makes this passage significant is *neither* its role in the construction of Wordsworth's poetic identity, *nor* its direct relation to the world of public events, but rather the author's very Protestant sense that this "soul," whether considered as integrating power or as moral identity, is not a free-floating and autonomous faculty but (in a wholly

unconscious parallel with FRIEDRICH SCHLEIERMACHER) something related *both* to immediate perception *and* to past events—and is thus very much part of the historical process. Moreover such perceptions are at once both subjective and creative—or, to use a later terminology, the poetic process is also by its very nature a *hermeneutic* activity.

For previous generations, the meaning of history lay in past events themselves. However militantly secular DAVID HUME and Edward Gibbon might be, they, like their religious predecessors, regarded the writing of history as an exemplary activity. Whether demonstrating the just wrath of God or the complex natural laws of human behavior, history held a discoverable and universally valid meaning. For the Romantics and post-Romantics, however, including Wordsworth, history was concerned less with deducing objective meanings (whether divine or natural) from the past as with the nature of our understanding of the material itself. Wordsworth is central to this shift from an exemplary to a hermeneutic mode of understanding.

Yet there is another element to Wordsworth's vision from Snowdon that, however allied with this sense of history, seems almost to contradict it, so that he seems torn between asserting the subjectivity of his insight and simultaneously proclaiming its universality. At one moment we find Nature compelling not just the poet to understand her meaning, but even "the grossest minds must see and hear / And cannot chuse but feel" (*Prelude*, Book XIII, 1805, l.71–83). Only a few lines later, however, we find the same certainties being attributed not to "Nature" but to the creative—and even divine—subjectivity of poets themselves:

> They from their native selves can send abroad
> Like transformation, for themselves create
> A like existence, and when'er it is
> Created for them, catch it by an instinct.
> . . . They need not extraordinary calls
> To rouze them—in a world of life they live,
> By sensible impressions not enthralled,
> But quickened, rouzed, and thereby made more fit
> To hold communion with the invisible world.
> Such minds are truly from the Deity . . .
> [ll. 93–106]

This is the most overtly religious confession to be found in Wordsworth's poetry to that time. Clearly his discovery of the divine is closely associated with his perception of self, and the growth of personal self-consciousness. This, at times almost solipsistic personal religion, certainly constitutes an extreme Protestantism—although always tempered by his artistic vocation and the need to communicate. Yet Wordsworth himself often seems unsure how to square the contradictions of his own argument, and it is probably symptomatic of his dissatisfaction with it that, of all the key spots of time in *The Prelude,* this Snowdon section was the most heavily revised for the 1850 version—with increasing emphasis on its theology. Here, in its most acute form, is the classic Romantic dilemma: how to claim universal validity for perceptions that are both historically conditioned and personally subjective? This, the central problem of Protestant ROMANTICISM, was eventually to drive Newman from Anglicanism to the Catholic Church, and then to attempt to remake that institution to conform to his own answer.

References and Further Reading

Primary Source:

Wordsworth, William. *Poetical Works.* Edited By E. de Selincourt. 5 vols. Oxford: Oxford University Press, 1940–1949.

Secondary Sources:

Arnold, Matthew. "Wordsworth." In *Essays in Criticism, Second Series.* New York: Macmillan, 1888.
Blake, William. *Complete Writings.* Edited by G. Keynes. Oxford: Oxford University Press, 1966.
Ferry, David. *The Limits of Mortality.* Middletown, CT: Wesleyan University Press, 1959.
Hartley, David. *Observations on Man, his Frame, his Duties and his Expectations.* London, 1749.
Hartman, Geoffrey. *Wordsworth's Poetry 1787–1814.* New Haven, CT: Yale University Press, 1964.
MacDonald, George. "Wordsworth's Poetry." In *A Dish of Orts.* London: Sampson Low, 1893.
Mill, J. S. *Autobiography.* Oxford: Oxford University Press/World's Classics, 1924.
Prickett, Stephen. *Coleridge & Wordsworth: the Poetry of Growth.* Cambridge: Cambridge University Press, 1970.
———. *England and the French Revolution.* New York: Macmillan, 1988.
———. *Romanticism & Religion: the Tradition of Coleridge and Wordsworth in the Victorian Church.* Cambridge: Cambridge University Press, 1976.
Robinson, Henry Crabb. *Henry Crabb Robinson on Books and their Writers.* Edited by E. J. Morely. London: Dent, 1938.

STEPHEN PRICKETT

WORLD ALLIANCE OF REFORMED CHURCHES

The World Alliance of Reformed Churches (WARC) is a worldwide fellowship of over 200 national churches with roots in that part of the sixteenth-century REFORMATION that was centered in Geneva, a reforming movement led by JOHN CALVIN and his colleagues in many European countries. Most of these churches today are called Presbyterian, Reformed, or Congregational; collectively they are called the Reformed family of churches. The Alliance also includes some churches, like the Waldensians in ITALY with their daughter churches abroad and the Czech Brethren, which originated in reforming movements prior to the sixteenth century but later allied themselves with the Reformed family. Also included in the Alliance membership are many united churches stemming from unions of Reformed churches with those of other traditions, such as the CHURCH OF SOUTH INDIA. This broad Reformed family represents more than 75 million Christians in over 100 countries; about three-fourths of the member churches are located in the countries of the southern hemisphere. The WARC was formed in 1970 in Nairobi, Kenya as a union of the former Alliance of the Reformed Churches throughout the World holding the Presbyterian Order and the International Congregational Council.

General Councils of representatives of all the member churches, held about every seven years, govern the WARC. The General Councils elect an executive committee that directs the work between General Council meetings. The headquarters with the general secretariat is located in Geneva at the Ecumenical Center.

The Department of Theology fosters theological work in the Reformed tradition, reflecting on the meaning of Christian faith in the many cultural contexts in which Reformed churches live. The Department also carries responsibility for ecumenical dialogue and work for Christian unity (see ECUMENISM). Since the 1960s the Alliance has been in dialogue with all the world Christian communions and with some traditions that are not organized as world communions, seeking mutual understanding and collaborative relationships. Working relationships of the WARC with the LUTHERAN WORLD FEDERATION have become intentionally close since 1989.

The Department of Cooperation and Witness focuses on the role of the church in promoting human rights, emerging democracies and civil society, economic justice, and ecological sustainability. The Department of Partnership of Women and Men promotes full partnership in church and society and seeks to eradicate sexism in theology and practice.

There are also regional councils of the WARC in Europe, the CARIBBEAN and North America, LATIN AMERICA, Southern Africa, and Northeast Asia.

Alliance of Reformed Churches (ARC)

Irish, Scottish, and American Presbyterian initiatives brought about the formation in London in 1875 of the Alliance of the Reformed Churches throughout the World holding the Presbyterian System (later, Presbyterian Order). The first General Council met in Edinburgh in 1877 with an Alliance membership of forty-nine churches from the British Isles, America, Europe, SOUTH AFRICA, AUSTRALIA, NEW ZEALAND, Ceylon, and the New Hebrides. Beginning with that first meeting the Alliance has worked periodically on the question of a common CONFESSION of faith. The Alliance has also been concerned with world mission and Christian unity, stressing the need for cooperation, not only among Reformed churches, but with all Christian churches, and also the need to help newly established churches become truly indigenous and self-governing members of the Alliance as quickly as possible. A third constant theme is the concern for HUMAN RIGHTS. The Alliance monthly journal, *The Catholic Presbyterian,* from 1879 called for aid to Waldensian pastors and to the exploited laboring classes and protested inhumane treatment of NATIVE AMERICANS in the UNITED STATES. A general secretary, Rev. Dr. G. D. Mathews, was appointed in 1888. He traveled widely in Europe, the Middle East, RUSSIA, and South Africa, especially in support of "younger churches" and religious freedom for minority churches. These concerns continued, most notably in World Alliance's deep engagement with the movement against *apartheid* in South Africa.

Leaders of the Alliance worked for the establishment of the WORLD COUNCIL OF CHURCHES and early gave leadership in it. Since its beginnings the Alliance has tailored its structure to collaborate ecumenically wherever possible.

International Congregational Council (ICC)

From the 1870s on there were discussions among British and American Congregationalists about bringing together the whole Congregational family in an international council, including churches in the colonies and mission fields. The first Council meeting in London in 1891 and four subsequent Councils between 1899 and 1930 discussed the life and theology of CONGREGATIONALISM, its relation to the state and to social problems, its relation to other Christian traditions and the unity of the church, and its worldwide mission. Representation from ENGLAND and America was heavier than had been originally planned, with fewer delegates from the colonies and the mission fields. Beginning with the second Council meeting, a few women were present and occasionally were among the speakers. There was little activity between the meetings of the Councils.

Close cooperation between British and American Congregational churches during World War II and excitement about the planning for the inauguration of the World Council of Churches in 1948 spurred fresh thinking about the role of a confessional body like the ICC in the ecumenical movement. A planning committee decided in 1947 to establish an international office in London and to appoint as its first secretary Dr. Sidney M. Berry, acting moderator of the Council and the secretary of the Congregational Union of England and Wales. The sixth Council at Wellesley, Massachusetts in 1949 confirmed a permanent international organization with a full-time "Minister and Secretary," Dr. Berry, and adopted a constitution.

Between 1953 and 1966 four more councils were held, and the connection between the ICC and the Alliance of Reformed Churches grew steadily. In 1957 the Alliance officially proposed talks between the two world bodies about areas of agreement, leading to close working relationships and a decision in 1968 to unite. In Nairobi in 1970 both bodies voted to merge as The World Alliance of Reformed Churches (Presbyterian and Congregational), joining in an act of Covenant.

See also Calvinism; Dialogue, Interconfessional; Presbyterianism

References and Further Reading

Njoroge, Nyambura J. "Women in the World Alliance of Reformed Churches: Building an Inclusive Community." In *With Love and With Passion: Women's Life and Work in the Worldwide Church,* edited by Elisabeth Raiser and Barbara Robra, 111–114. Geneva: WCC Publications, 2001.

Peel, Albert, and Douglas Horton. *International Congregationalism.* London: Independent Press Ltd., 1949.

Pradervand, Marcel. *A Century of Service: A History of the World Alliance of Reformed Churches 1875–1975.* Grand Rapids, MI: Wm. B. Eerdmans, 1975.

Sell, Alan P. F. *A Reformed, Evangelical, Catholic Theology: The Contribution of the World Alliance of Reformed Churches, 1875–1982.* Grand Rapids, MI: Wm. B. Eerdmans, 1991.

———. "World Alliance of Reformed Churches." In *Encyclopedia of the Reformed Faith,* edited by Donald K. McKim, 403–407. Louisville, KY: Westminster/John Knox Press, 1992.

Council Proceedings of ARC, ICC, and WARC. www.arc.ch www.warc.ch

JANE DEMPSEY DOUGLASS

WORLD COUNCIL OF CHURCHES

The World Council of Churches (WCC) was formally established August 23, 1948 in Amsterdam with 351 delegates, representing 147 church bodies from forty-four countries and all continents participating. This culminated a long process to create a structure that would promote unity and cooperation among Orthodox, Anglican, and Protestant churches. A group of Roman Catholic observers was invited to this first assembly, but the Vatican forbade their attendance. From the beginning the WCC has been headquartered in Geneva, SWITZERLAND.

Background

When the WORLD MISSIONARY CONFERENCE met at Edinburgh in 1910, leaders were aware of the growing church outside the West. Unfortunately, the historical and theological divisions that marked the churches in the West were being transferred to the churches in Asia, AFRICA, and LATIN AMERICA. Bishop Charles H. Brent, Episcopal Church in the Philippines, addressed the WMC on the urgent need to mitigate these historic divisions and foster Christian unity.

World War I (1914–1918) temporarily interrupted efforts toward an ecumenical organization. The founding of the League of Nations at the urging of President WOODROW WILSON in 1919 offered a model for international cooperation. In 1919 the Holy Synod of the Church of Constantinople issued an encyclical proposing that all Christian churches form a "League of Churches" to promote Christian union. Also in 1919 Archbishop NATHAN SÖDERBLOM of Uppsala proposed that an ecumenical council be founded. In 1920 JOSEPH H. OLDHAM, secretary of the Continuation Committee of the 1910 World Missionary Conference, submitted a memorandum to a group of missionary leaders at Crans, Switzerland outlining a structure for the International Missionary Council, although he predicted that it would soon "give way to something that may represent the beginnings of a world league of Churches."

In addition to well-established international Christian organizations such as the YMCA, YWCA (see YMCA, YWCA), and World Student Christian Federation, in the 1920s new initiatives were carried forward along three lines: International Missionary Council (IMC), Faith and Order, and Life and Work. The need for an "International Christian Council" was evident but the time was not yet ripe. Gradually it became clear that these multiple parallel and overlapping organizations were impediments to structural unity. William Adams Brown of Union Theological Seminary in New York, chair of Life and Work, took the lead in 1933 to convene leaders of international Christian organizations to discuss how coordination might be achieved. An Ecumenical Consultative Group was appointed to take extensive soundings of the churches.

In July 1937 the Committee of Thirty-Five met at Westfield College, London to develop a proposal to be laid before Life and Work meeting in Oxford later that month, and Faith and Order in Edinburgh in early August, concerning the future of the ecumenical movement. Four men were delegated the task of drawing up a plan: Archbishop WILLIAM TEMPLE, Oldham, Samuel McCrae Cavert, and William Adams Brown.

Cavert, general secretary of the U.S. Federal Council of Churches, suggested the name "World Council of Churches." Life and Work, and Faith and Order would be integrated into the new structure immediately. (The relationship of the IMC to the WCC would be worked out later.) Equally important, the proposal established the principle that the WCC should not have the power to legislate for the member churches. The Council could propose, but decision making rested with member churches. The work of the Council would be conducted through a General Assembly to be held every five to seven years and a Central Committee that met annually. The Committee of Thirty-Five also recommended appointment of W.A. VISSER'T HOOFT, World Student Christian Federation, as general secretary of the new World Council of Churches.

The Oxford and Edinburgh conferences responded favorably and appointed seven members each to implement the plan. The next step was to conduct consultations with the constituent member. The main sticking point was the constitutional question of the relation of the Council to its member bodies. Archbishop Temple clarified this point: "It is not a federation as commonly understood, and its Assembly and Central Committee will have no constitutional authority whatever over its constituent churches. Any authority that it may have will consist in the weight it carries with the churches by its wisdom." Equally important was the theological basis of membership in the Council. It was agreed: "The World Council of Churches is a fellowship of Churches which accept the Lord Jesus Christ as God and Saviour." This formulation did not prove to be satisfactory and finally in 1960 was revised to say: "The World Council of Churches is a fellowship of churches which confess the Lord Jesus Christ as God and Saviour according to the Scriptures and therefore seek to fulfill together their common calling to the glory of the one God, Father, Son and Holy Spirit."

In spite of mounting international tensions, preparation for launching the WCC went forward and the first Assembly was scheduled for August 1941. The growing threat of war forced an indefinite postponement. During World War II the World Council of Churches (in Process of Formation) maintained offices in Geneva, London, and New York and its leaders played an active role on behalf of member churches throughout the war years by seeking to maintain communications with all regardless of their political situation. The end of the war brought a flood of new work. In addition to emergency relief and reconstruction in war-torn areas of Europe, the WCC was concerned with reconciliation among the churches, especially in relation to GERMANY, as well as opening the way for the churches of Asia, Africa, and Latin America to become full participants.

Nature of WCC and Basis of Membership

The provisional committee met in 1946 and 1947 to complete preparations for the inaugural assembly in 1948. One question that had to be settled was the ecclesiastical status of the Council and the basis of membership in it. It was agreed that the WCC was not a "world church" or "super church." Indeed, it was not a church; rather it was an instrument that enabled member churches to "bear witness together . . . and cooperate in matters requiring united action." It was acknowledged that unity arises from God's action in Jesus Christ rather than at the initiative of the church. Each church is bound to Jesus Christ and thus to all others who make up the body of Christ. The Amsterdam Assembly declared: "Christ has made us his own, and he is not divided. In seeking him we find one another. Here at Amsterdam we have committed ourselves afresh to him, and have covenanted with one another in constituting the World Council of Churches. We intend to stay together." The WCC Constitution states the *raison d'être* succinctly: "The primary purpose of the fellowship of churches in the World Council of Churches is to call one another to visible unity in one faith and in one eucharistic fellowship, expressed in worship and common life in Christ, through witness and service to the world, and to advance towards that unity in order that the world may believe."

The WCC understood itself to be a means by which member churches would discover and realize more fully the unity of the whole body. The first of repeated attempts to clarify the nature and role of the WCC was made by the Central Committee at Toronto, CANADA in 1950. The Toronto Statement emphasized that the WCC "deals in a provisional way" with the ecclesiastical and theological differences that exist between the churches. It is not the responsibility of the WCC to espouse any particular theory or view of the church nor "to negotiate union between churches." All such matters were to remain the responsibility of the churches.

With regard to the basis of membership, it was finally agreed that only autonomous churches were eligible for membership. National councils of churches that had been organized in various parts of the world after Edinburgh 1910 were recognized as affiliates. Similarly, organizations representing confessional families could not be members of the WCC. The WCC was to be a council of *churches*.

Organization

The WCC organization has been revised periodically to fit changing needs. In 1948 the new organization consisted of twelve departments: Faith and Order, Study, Evangelism, Laity, Youth, Women, Interchurch Aid/Refugees, International Affairs, Ecumenical Institute, Publications, Library, and Finance. At the Evanston Assembly in 1954 the structure was changed. Four divisions were established with program departments under each. Then in 1961 the International Missionary Council was integrated with the WCC and the Commission on World Mission and Evangelism (CWME) set up. In 1972 a plan systematically to internationalize the WCC staff in Geneva was instituted more adequately to reflect the constituent churches. This included a uniform pay scale.

That same year a substantial reorganization was instituted with three program units replacing the five program divisions. Each program unit was mandated to carry out specific areas of work through subunits. This pattern had the advantage of allowing new subunits to be added as new needs arose and WCC program continued to expand into the 1980s. This organizational pattern was kept intact until the 1990s when another round of restructuring was instituted.

Finance

As of the 1990s, some 75 percent of WCC income came from member churches and their mission and service agencies. However, 96 percent of these monies came from thirteen countries in the West. The Council has no fixed membership fee. Although each member church is encouraged to make an annual contribution to the WCC according to their ability, one-third of the members contribute nothing. With its support coming from various countries, the WCC is acutely affected by fluctuations in the international money markets. The continuing decline in membership of many churches in Europe and North America, traditionally strong supporters of the WCC, has meant declining revenues for these churches with adverse consequences for causes they have supported in the past.

Assemblies

WCC assemblies take place approximately every seven years. Eight have been held since Amsterdam 1948: Evanston 1954, New Delhi 1961, Uppsala 1968, Nairobi 1975, Vancouver 1983, Canberra 1991, and Harare 1998. Constitutionally the general assembly is "the supreme legislative body" of the World Council of Churches. Practically speaking such a group is too unwieldy to serve as an effective decision-making body. Much of the work of an assembly is done by sections or work groups that meet for intense deliberations of draft statements that have been prepared by unit members and staff. These drafts are then brought to the full assembly for plenary debate and approval.

At Amsterdam 1948, the 147 member churches were represented by 351 delegates. This number has grown over the past fifty years. By 1991 the number of member churches had reached 317, with 842 delegates. At the Harare 1998 Assembly the 355 member and associate member churches were represented by 991 delegates.

WCC assemblies serve an important symbolic purpose. The coming together of several thousand Christians from all over the world to spend two weeks in worship and deliberations creates a statement. Frequently WCC assemblies have been accompanied by controversy when WCC leaders have spoken out on sensitive political or social issues or interest groups have tried to bring their concern into the assembly.

In addition to general assemblies, the Commission on World Mission and Evangelism, in the tradition of the IMC, continued to hold assemblies every five to seven years. WCC program units have sponsored numerous consultations over the years.

Impact

For fifty years the WCC has been a symbol of ecumenical efforts to promote unity among Orthodox, Anglican, and Protestant churches. Since Vatican Council 2, 1962–1965, cooperation between the WCC and Roman Catholics has grown greatly.

Rather than being an instrument for negotiating church unions, the WCC's role has been to keep alive the vision of a united body of Jesus Christ. This has stimulated theological and ecclesiological explorations of the meaning of *koinonia* and how it is to be actualized in the life of the church at all levels.

The WCC has sometimes been called an "ecclesiastical United Nations." The WCC came into existence amid war and international conflict. From its beginning the WCC has taken a strong interest in social and political issues that impinge on church and society and has maintained a staff with expertise in international affairs. Throughout the Cold War the WCC had to walk a fine line. It had member churches located in the Soviet bloc as well as in the West. Many Christians in Asia, Africa, and Latin America did not want to be identified with either bloc—Western or Soviet.

J. H. Oldham, a principal architect of the WCC, insisted that the Christian movement had to enlist the help of "first-class" minds in the study and interpretation of the most important issues of the day. From the beginning the WCC has placed a priority on study and publication. This has created a climate of openness to issues and trends that will influence the future of the church as well as society. For example, the WCC created a Programme to Combat Racism in the early 1970s aimed specifically at regimes in SOUTH AFRICA and ZIMBABWE where minority white governments were denying equal rights of citizenship to black citizens. This proved to be a highly controversial initiative but was consistent with the view that Christians ought to be proactive in addressing injustice. It was during this time that the Unit on Dialogue was established to study and promote dialogue with people of other faiths.

The WCC has continued to address a range of political and social issues. At the 1998 Harare Assembly the report on "Issues of Current Global Concern" included draft sections on international debt, globalization, child soldiers, the status of Jerusalem, and a draft statement on human rights. United Nations secretary general Kofi Annan addressed the assembly by video to enlist continued support by the churches for the human rights movement.

The WCC has experienced persistent tension with two ecclesiastical traditions, the Orthodox and conservative Protestants. On the one hand, Conservative Protestants, including many from churches that are constituents of WCC as well as those that reject such membership, have criticized what they perceive as the WCC's ambivalence toward the Christian mission. Contrary to expectations in 1961 when the WCC absorbed the International Missionary Council, mission and EVANGELISM appear not to have been treated as a priority. On the other hand, the Orthodox Churches have criticized what they see as the WCC's eroding commitment to its original christological basis. In his message to the Harare 1998 Assembly, the ecumenical patriarch of Constantinople urged that the WCC address basic theological issues and return to a consideration of the meaning of *koinonia* in Christ.

See also Ecumenism

References and Further Reading

Fey, Harold E., ed. *A History of the Ecumenical Movement, 1948–1968.* vol. 2. Philadelphia, PA: Westminster Press, 1970.

Hooft, W. A. Visser 't. *The Genesis and Formation of the World Council of Churches.* Geneva, Switzerland: WCC Publications, 1982.

———. *Memoirs.* Philadelphia, PA: Westminster Press, 1973.

Kessler, Diane, ed. *Together on the Way: Official Report of the Eighth Assembly of the World Council of Churches.* Geneva, Switzerland: WCC Publications, 1999.

Rouse, Ruth, and Stephen Charles Neill, eds. *A History of the Ecumenical Movement, 1517–1948.* vol. 1, rev. ed. London: SPCK, 1967.

VanElderen, Marlin. *Introducing the World Council of Churches.* Geneva, Switzerland: WCC Publications, 1990.

WILBERT R. SHENK

WORLD METHODIST COUNCIL

Heir to the Oecumenical Methodist Conferences, which met at roughly ten-year intervals from 1881, the World Methodist Council (WMC) was founded as a permanent institution in 1951. Its membership consists of some eighty denominations of Methodist origin or, in the case of united churches, having Methodist participation; these denominations include about 70 million adherents worldwide. The Council meets in full session every five years; representation is allotted according to a combination of historical, geographical, and numerical factors. The Council has no legislative authority over the member churches, which retain an autonomy exercised through their own "conferences." It serves mutual consultation and support in theological and practical matters, with standing committees in the areas of ecumenism, education, evangelism, family life, social and international affairs, worship, and youth; it facilitates the short-term exchange of pastorates across national and cultural lines. The Oxford Institute of Methodist Theological Studies meets regularly under the Council's aegis, and other affiliated organizations are the World Federation of Methodist and Uniting Church Women and the World Methodist Historical Society.

At its Rio de Janeiro meeting in 1996, the WMC adopted a statement of "Wesleyan Essentials of Christian Faith," consisting of a concise description of "our beliefs," "our worship," "our witness," "our service," and "our common life." The Council appoints the commissions for bilateral doctrinal dialogue with other world Christian communions and receives their reports. "The Church: Community of Grace" (1984) provided a framework for Lutheran and Methodist churches in several countries to enter into fellowship of word and table. "Together in God's Grace" (1987) assured Methodists and Reformed that their theological differences were not sufficient to justify ecclesial division between them. "Sharing in the Apostolic Communion" (1996) has not so far led to unity between Methodists and Anglicans. The most sustained dialogue is that since 1967 between the WMC and the Roman Catholic Church, which has produced significant statements on the Holy Spirit (1981), the Church (1986), the Apostolic Tradition (1991), Revelation and Faith ("The Word of Life," 1996), and Teaching Authority ("Speaking the Truth in Love," 2001).

The general secretariat of the WMC, with minimal administrative staff, is housed at Lake Junaluska, North Carolina.

See also Anglicanism; Catholic Reactions to Protestantism; Dialogue, Interconfessional; Lutheranism; Methodism

References and Further Reading

Wainwright, Geoffrey. *Methodists in Dialogue.* Nashville, TN: Abingdon, 1996.
World Methodist Council Handbook of Information 2002–2006. Lake Junaluska, NC: World Methodist Council, 2002.

GEOFFREY WAINWRIGHT

WORLD MISSIONARY CONFERENCE

Commonly called the EDINBURGH MISSIONARY CONFERENCE OF 1910, the World Missionary Conference (WMC) met at Edinburgh, SCOTLAND June 12–23, 1910. It was attended by more than 1,200 delegates, including seventeen Asian representatives. Most were sent as delegates of missionary societies. The WMC was not the first such missionary conference but marks a watershed in the modern mission movement. It brought into focus issues raised by earlier conferences, took steps to address the need for more permanent structures, and set in motion actions that would shape the nature and direction of Protestant MISSIONS for much of the twentieth century. Until 1900 British missions dominated the mission movement by virtue of their experience, number of missionaries, and financial resources. Edinburgh 1910 marked the transition from British to American dominance. Around 1907 the total number of American missionaries serving overseas surpassed the British. The American missionary statesman JOHN R. MOTT was a key initiator of the conference, chaired the planning committee for Edinburgh 1910, and presided at most of the sessions.

Background

From the beginning Protestant foreign missions were characterized by a lack of centralized direction. Missionary initiative typically came from highly motivated individuals or groups without benefit of official sanction. Once they arrived in the field, missionaries quickly discovered the need to cooperate with one another, regardless of DENOMINATION. Missions therefore became a primary engine of Christian unity.

A seminal initiative was the movement called the Concert for Prayer first introduced by a group of clergy in Scotland in 1744. The American theologian JONATHAN EDWARDS took up the idea in his book, *An Humble Attempt To Promote Explicit Agreement And Visible Union Among God's People, In Extraordinary Prayer for the Revival of Religion, And the Advancement of Christ's Kingdom On Earth* (1747). Edwards's book had widespread influence on both sides of the Atlantic well into the nineteenth century. It stimulated the formation of local prayer groups in support of missions through united Christian action.

Several streams of influence came together in the WMC. First, intermission conferences began to be held on the Continent, starting in Basel in 1837, setting a pattern that would be followed elsewhere. The second stream starts with the EVANGELICAL ALLIANCE (EA) that was organized in 1846 and met periodically thereafter. The EA fostered cooperation and fellowship across denominational lines but did not advocate structural unity. The Union Missionary Conference took place in New York May 4–5, 1854 with famed Scottish missionary Alexander Duff as the main attraction. One hundred fifty-six men were present. Later that year a similar conference was held in London. The Liverpool Conference on Missions in 1860 was better prepared than the previous conferences and the proceedings led to policy recommendations that would guide the administrators of missions for the next generation. This conference laid out a comprehensive agenda concerning the missionary enterprise that future conferences largely followed.

The 1888 London "Centenary Conference" was the first truly international missionary gathering. Approximately 1,600 people attended. Two important ideas resulted. First, it was proposed that a system of comity be introduced that would govern intermission relations in the field to avoid overlap and foster cooperation. Second, the delegates urged that an international missionary conference be held every ten years; however, no mechanism was set up to implement this recommendation.

The New York Ecumenical Missionary Conference in 1900 was seen as a response to this request. It was designed, however, as a public demonstration of support for missions. Held in Carnegie Hall, New York 1900 attracted some 200,000 people between April 21 and May 1. The speakers included former U.S. President Henry Harrison, President William McKinley, and Governor Theodore Roosevelt, along with mission leaders such as John Mott, Sherwood Eddy, and Robert E. Speer. Missionary leaders from Europe participated, but Americans dominated. It was geared to promoting missions rather than grappling with the issues of the day. The Protestant international missionary movement still lacked an organization that might provide continuity by planning regular meetings, working at policy issues, and coordinating joint programs.

Field conferences held in INDIA, CHINA, JAPAN, INDONESIA, AFRICA, and LATIN AMERICA constituted the third stream. In India these conferences were held in North India starting in 1855 and from 1858 in South India. In addition, the India-wide Decennial Conferences were introduced in 1862. These field conferences stimulated awareness of the need for coordination among the missions and helped focus the theological and policy issues that missions were facing.

The fourth stream of influence was the surging Student Volunteer Movement (SVM) that was attracting young people to missionary service in North America, Europe, and Asia. Although some Europeans objected to the SVM slogan, "The Evangelization of the World in this Generation," it galvanized an entire student generation to missionary action, and Edinburgh 1910 was seen as contributing to fulfillment of this vision.

Conference Organization

The first formal proposal that a major missionary conference be held in 1910 came from William Henry Grant, secretary of the Foreign Missions Conference of North America, when he laid the proposal before British mission secretaries in late 1906. Responding with dispatch, in January 1907 the Scottish group agreed to host such an event. Mott and JOSEPH H. OLDHAM, who were already acquainted through their staff positions in the SVM, quickly became the main architects of the conference, with Mott as chairman and Oldham as secretary of the steering committee. It was agreed that this conference should not follow in the path of New York 1900. Instead, this would be a working consultation based on "masterly" documents prepared from field surveys that would become the basis of concrete action. The planners faced a Herculean task. To accomplish this goal required that a research program be launched immediately to gather data from a broad range of sources. The international steering committee agreed on eight topics and set up commissions to oversee the work of preparing a study volume for each one. A recognized authority in that particular field headed each commission. The process required canvassing widely among missionaries and scholars who possessed expert knowledge in a given topic, getting written responses, distilling key findings, and then writing a synthesis. All of this had to be completed to allow a published volume to be ready for purchase by May 1, 1910, six weeks before the start of the conference.

The eight subjects selected were: Carrying the Gospel to all the Non-Christian World; The Church in the Mission Field; Education in Relation to the Christianisation of National Life; The Missionary Message in Relation to Non-Christian Religions; The Preparation of Missionaries; The Home Base of Missions; Missions and Governments; and Co-operation and the

Promotion of Unity. These became the titles of the eight preparatory volumes of Edinburgh 1910. Although the WMC has been characterized as focusing primarily on the means of carrying out the missionary mandate, this is not an entirely fair assessment. Edinburgh 1910 put the focus on the *church* more than on *missions*. The second report declared that "The Church in the Mission Field" is "itself now the great mission to the non-Christian world." This brought a theological breadth to the theology of mission hitherto lacking. The report went on: "The whole world is the mission field, and there is no church that is not a church in the mission field." This theme would be picked up with new urgency at the International Missionary Conference (IMC) at Madras in 1938.

The fourth preparatory volume, *The Missionary Message in Relation to Non-Christian Religions,* devoted chapters to five different religious traditions: Chinese, Japanese, Islam, Hindu, and animistic religions. To treat the latter theme, replies to an extensive questionnaire from twenty-five missionaries, representing several continents, were analyzed and summarized by a committee of three experts. The replies fell into five discrete models. The quality of the material demonstrates the intellectual engagement of field missionaries with their contexts. Analysis also shows the way a missionary's ecclesiastical heritage, theological tradition, anthropological theory, facility in the language of the host culture, and intellectual interaction with cultural issues shaped theory. The general conclusions to this volume emphasized "we have here much that casts light on the New Testament period and on the early centuries of the Christian Church." Consequently, it was argued, these findings are essential to an understanding of "the inner course of the New Testament thought." In other words, the West stood in need of the insights to be gained through intercultural studies.

Three of the preparatory volumes spoke to the theme of Christian unity and contributed to the emergence of the conciliar movement. The first report emphasized the fact that the missionary mandate was as yet unfulfilled and that a united response was called for. The second report drew attention to "a growing spirit of love and unity among Christians" and the imperative to "seek fellowship with all Christians." The eighth report was devoted entirely to a review of relations among missions and churches and in the conclusion noted that the "Church in the mission field" may be leading the way in healing the divisions of the church in the West. Bishop Charles H. Brent, of the Episcopal Church in the Philippines and a delegate to Edinburgh 1910, was deeply impressed with the need to work for Christian unity and urged that a

conference on Faith and Order be convened to guide the churches toward this goal.

The outstanding quality of these reports provided, for the first time, a reliable basis for decision making concerning the future of the missionary enterprise. This accounts for the impact these reports had on the conference as well as their long-term influence. The process also established a model for future ecumenical consultation and formulation of common issues.

One hundred fifty-six mission societies from fourteen countries sent delegates to Edinburgh 1910. Fifty-nine American societies were represented. The International Committee encouraged societies to include in their delegations some of their "leading missionaries" as well as "one or two natives" if practicable. No discussion of doctrinal questions was to be allowed and the word "ecumenical" would not be used because it was subject to misinterpretation and might divert attention from the basic purpose of the conference.

Edinburgh 1910 stood in the line of missionary conferences that had been held since 1854, but it broke new ground. This conference was limited to societies that had missionaries at work in the field among non-Christian peoples. (This excluded missions sending workers to Europe, the Middle East, and Latin America.) Representation was proportional to the size of budget of each society. By this time many of the leading mission societies were either a part of their denominational structures or closely related. This gave the conference a strong ecclesiastical dimension.

One Indian delegate was present at the 1860 Liverpool Conference and made a contribution to the theme of BIBLE TRANSLATION. Several Asians attended subsequent conferences, but not as official representatives. By contrast seventeen Asians came to Edinburgh 1910 as delegates and exerted influence out of proportion to their numbers. Especially memorable was the address by Bishop V. S. Azariah, who pleaded for a new basis of relationship between the emerging churches of Asia and Africa and the Western churches.

Significance and Results of Edinburgh 1910

The World Missionary Conference was a seminal event. Earlier conferences were devoted to discussion of common issues and educating the Christian public. This conference was probably the most comprehensive ecclesiastical gathering to date. Earlier meetings had been influenced by their relationship to the Evangelical Alliance, whereas Edinburgh 1910 attracted the full spectrum of Protestants engaged in foreign missions. It was consultative and geared to formulating a possible common course of action in the future. It brought into focus themes and issues that had been raised by previous international missionary conferences, dealt with them in some depth, and then decided on further steps. The specific results fell into three groups.

First, it was agreed to establish an international coordinating council. The first step was to elect a Continuation Committee, with John Mott as chair, to develop a proposal. Significantly, three of the committee members were Christian leaders from India, China, and Japan. It was anticipated that such a council would sponsor continuing study and research into missions practice. Although the International Missionary Council was not formally organized until 1921—delayed in part by World War I—the *International Review of Missions* was launched in 1912 with Oldham as editor. Oldham was the ideal person for this role. He possessed a wide-ranging intellect, keen perception of the leading issues, and a wide network of contacts. He used the IRM to encourage scholarly exploration and discussion.

The second outcome was clarification of the principle on which such an international body would operate. It was determined that this council would serve the member bodies without requiring that they surrender their own integrity and relationships to their constituent churches. The principle, proposed by the Americans and Germans, was that a council is servant of its member bodies; and operating policies are determined by each of the members. The council's work would depend entirely on the wisdom and resources brought to it by its member bodies and reflected back in the form of policy positions and recommended actions. The council could not compel compliance; it could only commend for consideration.

A third outcome of the WMC was the important impetus Edinburgh 1910 gave to the creation of the infrastructure of the Protestant conciliar movement. Between October 1912 and May 1913 Mott traveled to Asia where he held eighteen regional and three national conferences in Burma [Myanmar], Ceylon [Sri Lanka], China, India, Japan, KOREA, and Malaya [Malaysia]. Both national church leaders and missionaries were included in these consultations. These "situation conferences" were designed to highlight the issues being faced by the churches in that nation or region, encourage indigenous responsibility, and identify issues that affected comity, cooperation, and unity among Christian groups. Although the momentum Mott's visits had generated was interrupted by World War I, ultimately he laid the groundwork for the organization of Christian councils in most of these countries. These would be indispensable in the development of the conciliar movement.

Subsequently the Life and Work (1925) and Faith and Order (1927) movements were also organized. In 1948 several of these strands were brought together in the founding of the WORLD COUNCIL OF CHURCHES. In 1961 the IMC was integrated into the WCC and renamed the Commission on World Mission and Evangelism.

References and Further Reading

Askew, Thomas A. "The 1888 London Centenary Missions Conference: Ecumenical Disappointment or American Missions Coming of Age?" *International Bulletin of Missionary Research* 18 no. 3 (1994): 113–118.

———. "The New York 1900 Ecumenical Missionary Conference: A Centennial Reflection." *International Bulletin of Missionary Research* 24 no. 4 (2000): 146–154.

Friesen, J. Stanley. *Missionary Responses to Tribal Religions at Edinburgh 1910.* New York: Peter Lang, 1996.

Gairdner, W. H. T. *"Edinburgh 1910": An Account and Interpretation of the World Missionary Conference.* Edinburgh and London: Oliphant, Anderson and Ferrier, 1910.

Hogg, W. Richey. *Ecumenical Foundations: A History of the International Missionary Council And Its Nineteenth-Century Background.* New York: Harper and Brothers, 1952.

Rouse, Ruth, and Stephen Neill, eds. *A History of the Ecumenical Movement, 1517–1948.* 2nd ed. London: SPCK, 1967.

World Missionary Conference. 8 preparatory vols.; 1 vol. of records and plenary addresses. Edinburgh and London: Oliphant, Anderson and Ferrier, 1910.

WILBERT R. SHENK

WORLD VISION

World Vision is a Christian humanitarian organization whose mission is "To call people to a life-changing commitment to serve the poor in the name of Christ." World Vision was founded in 1951 by Dr. Bob Pierce as an effort to help children abandoned in the Korean War. It was in this early stage of development in 1953 that World Vision initiated its first child sponsorship program in KOREA. The sponsorships program invited Americans to provide necessary financial support for the education, health assistance, and nutrition for the child. In the 1990s World Vision began a family sponsorship program. Both child and family sponsorships have also been operating in other Asian countries and in LATIN AMERICA and AFRICA.

World Vision also began incorporating vocational and agricultural training for families into its sponsorship efforts, and parents began learning to farm and earn money through small enterprises. These efforts to affect self-sustainable change evolved into World Vision's community development efforts. Long-term development has proven central to bringing lasting hope to the people. After meeting immediate survival needs, World Vision works with communities to help them move toward self-reliance. While communities work toward self-sufficiency World Vision often provides fresh water wells and sanitation facilities, supplemental food, farming tools and seeds, loans for small businesses, and medicine. Local leaders actively participate in determining the future of their communities. In this way dignity is restored and a new cycle of hope inspires communities in their efforts for a better future. Most of World Vision's financial support for these efforts come from the UNITED STATES. In an effort to reach more resources, and to expose more individuals to the needs of others, World Vision formed World Vision International (WVI) in 1980. Today this partnership oversees sponsorship, relief, rehabilitation, and community development projects in 103 countries.

References and Further Reading

Andrade, Susana. *Visión Mundial: Entre el Cielo y la Tierra: Religión y Desarrollo en la Sierra.* Quito, Ecuador: Ceplaes, 1990.
Paeth, Scott, Max L. Stackhouse, and Tim Dearborn, eds. *The Local Church in a Global Era: Reflections for a New Century.* Grand Rapids, MI: Eerdmans, 2000.
World Vision International–Christian Relief and Development Organization. http://worldvisioninternational.org

MAUREEN KELLY

WORLD'S PARLIAMENT OF RELIGIONS

The World's Parliament of Religions of 1893, a part of the World's Columbian Exposition in Chicago, was hailed as the greatest interreligious assembly in history. During its seventeen days, about 170 religious leaders representing some twenty-five Christian sects and denominations and ten different religious traditions presented 200 papers, sermons, and speeches, addressing philosophy and theology, race issues, the role of women in religion, the future of world missions, and the prospects for universal human progress. For several years, the parliament generated controversy as concerned parties attempted to discern in it the signs of the time. By the opening of the twentieth century, however, the event had been largely forgotten, except by those who warmly recalled the roles played there by prominent Buddhist and Hindu delegates from Asia. In the 1980s the approaching centennial of the parliament renewed interest in it, leading to a large-scale commemoration of the event, once again in Chicago, called a Parliament for the World's Religions.

Anglo-American Protestants played a key role in conceiving and organizing the original parliament. Charles Carroll Bonney, a Chicago lawyer and Swedenborgian, conceived of it as capstone of the World's Congress Auxiliary, a series of international conferences devoted to humanities, sciences, law, medicine, business, and other professions. John Henry Barrows (1847–1902), pastor at Chicago's First Presbyterian church, led the auxiliary's Department of Religion. Under his direction, fourteen local Protestant ministers, a Chicago rabbi, and the diocesan Catholic archbishop coordinated meetings for some forty denominational, interdenominational, and special interest groups, all of which were designed to culminate in the parliament.

Issues articulated by Protestants also set the tone for the gathering. Henry Harris Jessup (1832–1910), a Presbyterian missionary, succinctly expressed the ethnic, geopolitical, and theological foundations for America's domestic and global missions, a recurrent leitmotif at the Parliament. The discussion of women's contributions to religion was much noted, but of the eighteen women present, fifteen represented Protestant denominations or movements. George Dana Boardman, an American Baptist, closed the assembly on a powerful postmillennial note, capturing a progressive and visionary current that ran throughout the assembly.

Religious Liberalism Ascendant

Infused with an optimistic mood contemporaries called "the Columbian spirit," the parliament often masked conflict with consensus rhetoric. Within Protestantism itself, there was ample evidence of growing tensions between progressives and conservatives that would soon lead to the liberal–fundamentalist schism. The much-noted presence of New England celebrities such as Edward Everett Hale (1822–1909), Thomas Wentworth Higginson (1823–1911), and Julia Ward Howe (1819–1910) led some conservatives to dismiss the parliament as a Unitarian affair, but Lyman Abbott (1835–1922), Theodore Munger, and WASHINGTON GLADDEN (1836–1918; Congregational), Charles Briggs, (1841–1913; Presbyterian) and Richard T. Ely (1854–1943; Episcopalian) lent the proceedings an authority both religiously liberal and specifically Protestant Christian. Conservative Protestants, among them Joseph Cook (Congregational) and James Dennis and George Pentecost (1842–1920; Presbyterian), also gave forceful presentations, but their remarks, while warmly received in many quarters, did little to correct the impression that the parliament signaled the ascendance of Protestant liberalism.

This ascendance was underscored by presentations made by Jews and Catholics who echoed the liberalism of Protestant speakers. Emil Hirsch (1851–1923), Kaufmann Kohler (1843–1926), and Isaac Meyer Wise spoke for the progressive spirit of Reform Judaism, while Archbishop John Gibbons and Bishop John Keane, two leading "Americanizers," represented forms of Catholic liberalism that would subsequently draw criticism from Rome. While Jews, Catholics, and Protestant liberals emphasized theological and institutional propositions unique to their respective traditions, their friendly rivalry at the parliament anticipated the "triple-melting pot" popularized by Will Herberg in the 1950s.

The parliament's liberalism gained additional strength from the prominent role played by the emergent field of comparative religion. European scholars such as F. Max Müller, J. Estlin Carpenter, and Jean (1794–1861), and Albert Réville (1826–1906) sent papers promoting it as a new science and introducing a humanistic interpretation of religion into discussions at the assembly. As importantly, comparative religion was invoked by many delegates in the form of an applied science supporting the idea that Christianity was the most highly evolved of all religions and, as such, fulfilled other traditions. This "fulfillment thesis" was a powerful apologetic tool favored by liberals who scorned the more conservative, exclusionary approach that dismissed non-Christian religions outright, especially those from Asia.

An Enduring Legacy

With good reason, the parliament became identified with the well-received presentations by Asians such as Protap Chunder Majumdar and Vivekananda (1863–1902) (Hinduism) and Anagarika Dharmapala (1864–1933; Buddhism). By casting their traditions in a modernist, progressive mode, they underscored the liberal spirit of the parliament. More importantly, they set into motion the Hindu and Buddhist missions to the West, which eventually resulted in the broad interest in interreligious dialogue and in Asian religions, which marked the twentieth century.

The Asians' success, along with the prominence of Jews and Catholics at the parliament, was a source of great concern to many conservative Protestants who saw the assembly as an assault on evangelical America, one fostered by liberal coreligionists. They also saw in the parliament an incipient alliance of new forces they feared would redefine the American religious mainstream in the twentieth century. The World's Parliament of Religions was an important event in its day and remains of symbolic importance to American Protestantism and American religion generally. It marked the rise to prominence of religious liberalism and of interreligious dialogue and the growing complexity of America's religious landscape. It also recalls a time when Anglo-American Protestantism confidently defined the American religious mainstream.

References and Further Reading

Kitagawa, Joseph. "The World's Parliament of Religions and Its Legacy." Eleventh John Nuveen Lecture. Chicago: University of Chicago Divinity School, 1983.

Seager, Richard Hughes. *The Dawn of Religious Pluralism: Voices from the World's Parliament of Religions, 1893.* LaSalle, IL: Open Court Publishing Company, 1993.

———, ed. *The World's Parliament of Religions: The East/West Encounter, Chicago, 1893.* Religion in North America Series. Bloomington and Indianapolis: Indiana University Press, 1995.

Ziolkowsky, Eric J., ed. *A Museum of Faiths: Histories and Legacies of the 1893 World's Parliament of Religions.* AAR Classics in the Study of Religion Series. Atlanta, GA: Scholars Press, 1993.

RICHARD HUGHES SEAGER

WORMS, DIET OF

The most celebrated of the long series of imperial diets held at Worms, at which MARTIN LUTHER defended his teaching before emperor Charles V, took place from January 27 to May 25, 1521. After his coronation in Aachen, Charles V had announced on November 1, 1520 his first diet to be convened in Worms on January 6, 1521. The emperor arrived in Worms on November 28, 1520, but the diet did not open until January 27, 1521. At its conclusion, the imperial assembly was one of the most significant in the history of the empire in the sixteenth century.

In his announcement for the diet, the emperor proposed an agenda that included the maintenance of law and public peace, public and constitutional order, regulations for the execution of imperial affairs in times of the emperor's absence, financial assistance for the emperor's journey to Rome, and the recovery of lost imperial territories. These topics reflected, in the view of the German territorial ruler, the hope that power and responsibilities would be reallocated in the empire. The emperor, meanwhile, professed the monarchical character of his rule and endeavored to strengthen his authority and centralize power. The ensuing deliberations of the diet were affected by the growing conflict between Charles V and FRANCE, the tensions between Charles and Pope Leo X, the renewed Turkish threat, the Comunero uprisings in Spain, general considerations regarding the governance of those territories bound to Charles through personal fealty, and, finally, by the "Luther affair."

On May 26 the emperor promulgated the recess of the diet with provisions pertaining to governmental administration, judicial procedures, public order, and an imperial tax authority for financing the emperor's formal journey to Rome as well as the support of governmental administration and the courts. The new judicial procedures and the imperial taxation registration proved to be permanent institutions. Regulations pertaining to safety and public order did not come into being because no agreement could be reached on central economic questions. In its results the diet of Worms ended the imperial reform movement and strengthened the emperor's power and authority through various compromises. For example, the long-standing demand for an imperial governance structure involving the estates was honored only with respect to times when the emperor was absent; this structure, moreover, was to be presided over by the emperor's representative, the archchancellor of the empire, the archbishop of Mainz. The decisions of this Imperial Regiment *(Reichsregiment)* on key issues had to be approved by the emperor.

The papal legate Girolamo Aleander arrived at Worms on November 30, 1520 and put the case against Luther forward on February 13, 1521. The "Luther case" *(causa Lutheri)*, which originally had not been a matter for consideration, was placed on the agenda at the insistence of the Saxon Elector Frederick III (called "the Wise"), who had support from the estates. On February 19, 1521 the estate refused to approve an imperial mandate against Luther and discussions began about giving Luther a hearing before the diet. Luther was subsequently granted safe passage to Worms. The assembled members of the diet were scarcely aware that, with the official declaration of the centrality of conscience of one individual, the course was set for the division of Western Christendom into various confessions. Luther arrived in Worms on April 16. On April 18 he declared his final refusal to recant his teachings, according to an early but unreliable tradition. Charles V announced the following day his resolve to take firm measures against him. After additional discussions with him, Luther departed from Worms on April 26. Later the "EDICT OF WORMS" against Luther and his followers, dated May 8, was signed by Charles V on May 26, 1521. This edict, which was not part of the formal recess of the diet, had been drafted by the papal legate Aleander but had been reworked by the imperial court with the intent of strengthening the authority of the emperor and claiming authority for the German rulers.

Another agenda item at Worms was the discussion of grievances against Rome and the church *(gravamina nationis germanicae)* as advocated especially by Duke George of Saxony. The estates had threatened—in case these grievances were not considered—to ignore the emperor's wishes and to block the recess. The difficulty lay in the fact that the emperor's advisers, headed by Chièvres and Gattinara, were influenced mainly by foreign-policy concerns, whereas the estates were chiefly motivated by political and legal considerations regarding ecclesiastical affairs, but also by their concern over the possibility of a mass movement in support of Luther.

Luther's statement and refusal to revoke during the hearing of April 17–18 proved to be the reason that the diet took on world-historical significance. With his appearance at the diet of Worms, the question of AUTHORITY was no longer an inner ecclesiastical dispute but a question that touched the basis of late medieval church and society.

See also Lutheranism; Reformation

References and Further Reading

Primary Sources:

Balan, P., ed. *Monumenta Reformationis Lutherana ex Tabulariis S. Sedis Secretis, 1521–1525.* Ratisbonae (Regensburg), Germany, 1883.

Brieger, Theodor. *Aleander und Luther, 1521. Quellen und Forschungen zur Reformationsgeschichte 1.* Gotha, Germany, 1884.

———. *Deutsche Reichstagsakten. Jüngere Reihe 2: Deutsche Reichstagsakten unter Kaiser Karl V.* [Der Reichstag zu Worms 1521]. Edited by Adolf Wrede. Gotha, Germany: 1896 [reprint Göttingen, Germany, 1962].

Iserloh, Erwin, and Peter Fabisch, eds. *Dokumente zur Causa Lutheri (1517–1521).* 2 vols. Münster, Germany: Aschendorf, 1991.

Kohler, Alfred, ed. *Quellen zur Geschichte Karls V.* Darmstadt, Germany: Wissenschaftliche Buchgesellschaft, 1990.

Secondary Sources:

Borth, Wilhelm. "Die Luthersache *(causa Lutheri)* 1517–1524." In *Die Anfänge der Reformation als Frage von Politik und Recht.* Lübeck, Germany: Matthiesen Verlag, 1970.

Kalkoff, Paul. *Depeschen und Berichte über Luther vom Wormser Reichstage 1521.* Halle, Germany: Niemeyer, 1898.

———. *Der Wormser Reichstag von 1521. Biographische und quellenkritische Studien zur Reformationsgeschichte.* Munich, Germany, 1922.

Lutz, Heinrich. *Das Reich, Karl V. und der Beginn der Reformation. Bemerkungen zu Luther in Worms 1521.* In Heinrich Fichtenau and Erich Zöllner, eds. [Beiträge zur neueren Geschichte Österreichs.] Vienna, Austria: Böhlau, 1974.

Olivier, Daniel. *Der Fall Luther. Geschichte einer Verurteilung 1517–1521.* Stuttgart, Germany: Deutsche Verlags-Anstalt, 1972.

Reuter, F., ed. *Der Reichstag zu Worms von 1521: Reichspolitik und Luthersache.* Worms: Norberg, 1971.

Rupp, E. G. *Luther's Progress to the Diet of Worms, 1521.* New York, 1964.

MARKUS WRIEDT

WORMS, EDICT OF

With the edict of Worms, the ecclesiastical and secular process against MARTIN LUTHER formally came to an end. The papal bull "exsurge Domine" of June 15,

1520 had called on Luther to obey the church and to revoke forty-four incriminating sentences. Although the Wittenberg theologian refused to do so and publicly demonstrated his resistance by burning the papal document together with other books of ecclesiastical law and a scholastic handbook, Pope Leo X (1513–1521) excommunicated him January 3, 1521 with the bull *"Decet Romanum pontificem."* Following the routine of late medieval law against heretics, the secular authority had to step in and execute the sentence. Thus the papal legate, Girolamo Aleander, arrived at Worms on November 30, 1520 to convince the emperor and the territorial rulers to pass an edict against Luther and his followers.

The Luther case *(causa Lutheri)* originally had not been a matter for consideration of the diet. It was placed on the agenda because the ruler of Saxony, Frederick III ("the Wise" [1486–1525]) hindered the routine process and forced the emperor to give Luther a hearing at Worms, a notion supported by many German estates. On February 19, 1521 the estates refused to approve an imperial mandate against Luther. Luther was subsequently granted safe passage to Worms and arrived in Worms on April 16. On April 18 he refused to recant his teachings, unless convinced by the testimony of Scripture, and, according to an early but unreliable tradition, by the logical evidence of reason. Charles V announced on the following day his resolve to take firm measures against Luther. In a formal statement that was read in French to the rulers he offered both a pious statement of his catholic belief and a public declaration of his future politics with regard to the reform grievances. He claimed AUTHORITY for the whole of Christianity *(corpus christianorum)*, whose unity must not be destroyed by a single individual.

Luther departed from Worms on April 26. A few days later the draft of an edict against Luther and his followers, dated May 8, was introduced to the assembly in Worms by Girolamo Aleander. Because of the resistance of several German estates including Archbishop Albrecht of Mainz, this draft statement did not become part of the formal recess of the Diet. Instead it was reworked by the imperial court in the direction of strengthening the authority of the emperor and claiming authority for German rulers. Charles V signed it belatedly by May 26, 1521. In it he claimed authority as the protector of the Christian faith in the Holy Roman Empire of the German Nation and referred extensively to the history of Luther's process. Partially the edict reformulated passages of Charles's confession and the speech of the papal legate Aleander of February 13, 1521. The edict also noted the united forces of ecclesiastical and secular authorities as prescribed in medieval law against heretics.

Because many German estates did not accept the edict, it was executed only occasionally and did not thwart the reform in Wittenberg or electoral Saxony. On the contrary; even though it was the strongest means for the persecution of reformers in the German Empire for the emperor and his followers, it was not successful. The estates used their resistance to reach compromises in financing the imperial administration and the war against the Turks. Charles V did not want to battle against the estates, but the unity of the Holy Roman Empire had been disrupted. Thus the elector of Saxony asked Charles V not to bother him with the edict of Worms. It seems that the emperor heeded his request. The question of religion focusing on the edict of Worms came on the agenda of future diets. The final solution came in 1555 at the diet of Augsburg and was strengthened nearly a century later by the Peace of Osnabrück in 1648.

See also Lutheranism; Reformation

References and Further Reading

Primary Sources:

Brieger, Theodor. *Aleander und Luther.* 1521.
———. *Quellen und Forschungen zur Reformationsgeschichte.* vol. 1. Gotha, Germany: Perthes, 1884.
———. *Deutsche Reichstagsakten. Jüngere Reihe 2: Deutsche Reichstagsakten unter Kaiser Karl V. (Der Reichstag zu Worms 1521).* Edited by Adolf Wrede, 643–661. Gotha, Germany: Perthes, 1896 [reprint Göttingen, Germany, 1962].
Iserloh, Erwin, and Peter Fabisch, eds. *Dokumente zur Causa Lutheri (1517–1521).* 2 vols. Münster, Germany: Aschendorff, 1991.
Kohler, Alfred, ed. *Quellen zur Geschichte Karls V.* Darmstadt, Germany: Wissenschaftliche Buchgesellschaft, 1990.

Secondary Sources:

Borth, Wilhelm. *Die Luthersache (causa Lutheri) 1517–1524. Die Anfänge der Reformation als Frage von Politik und Recht.* Lübeck, Germany: Matthiesen Verlag, 1970.
Bäumer, Remigius, ed. *Lutherprozeß und Lutherbann.* Münster, Germany: Aschendorff, 1972.
Kalkoff, Paul. *Der Wormser Reichstag von 1521. Biographische und quellenkritische Studien zur Reformationsgeschichte.* Munich, Germany: Oldenbourg, 1922.
Lutz, Heinrich. "Das Reich, Karl V. und der Beginn der Reformation. Bemerkungen zu Luther in Worms 1521." In *Beiträge zur neueren Geschichte Österreichs,* edited by Heinrich Fichtenau and Erich Zöllner, 47–70. Vienna, Austria, 1974.
Olivier, Daniel. *Der Fall Luther. Geschichte einer Verurteilung 1517–1521.* Stuttgart, Germany: Deutsche Verlags-Anstalt, 1972.
Reuter, F., ed. *Der Reichstag zu Worms von 1521: Reichspolitik und Luthersache Worms.* 2nd ed. Cologne, Germany: Böhlau Verlag, 1981. Supplement: *Luther in Worms.* Worms, Germany, 1973.

Rupp, Gordon. *Luther's Progress to the Diet of Worms, 1521.* New York: Harper & Row, 1964.

MARKUS WRIEDT

WORSHIP

Christian worship is addressed to the triune God. It is the objective articulation in ritual form of the beliefs or confession of a particular group of Christians, and it is also the subjective enactment or embodiment of the faith that is believed. The theologies of worship of the Protestant denominations show different nuances and emphases, yet most emerge from the identifiably Christian theological markers established by the ecumenical creeds. Worship practices may vary by DENOMINATION and even within a particular denomination, because theological and confessional perspectives help shape the structure, content, and style of worship, as do, to at least some extent, cultural context and local dynamics. Even from the early days of the REFORMATION, it was clear that there would be divergences in the theologies and practice of Protestant worship: the thirteenth of the Marburg Articles (1529) acknowledged that "what is called tradition or human ordinances in spiritual or ecclesiastical matters, provided they do not plainly contradict the word of God, may be freely kept or abolished in accordance with the needs of the people. . . . " Protestants regard Scripture as the principal AUTHORITY for their worship, although a range of interpretations exist on precisely what does and does not "contradict the word of God."

What Worship Is

In reaction to what has been perceived as the human "work" of the Catholic mass, Protestants have preferred to emphasize worship as an act of faith offered in grateful response to the generous GRACE and mercy of God. God grants the gift of FAITH by which worship is made possible; and consequences of worship include the growth and strengthening of faith as well as a deeper union with God. This dialogue in worship, discernable as a pattern of "call" and "response," MARTIN LUTHER recognized in the German word for worship, *Gottesdienst,* which can simultaneously mean God's service to us and our service to God. God speaks, especially in and through scripture, but also by the entire history of SALVATION. Christians then speak to God in their common language with praise, PRAYER, and sometimes, lament, by the aid of the God's own Spirit (Romans 8:26). God is the first actor in worship, who in turn expects a reply. Worship is thus not only a conversation, but also an encounter with the living God.

By God's grace, faith is instilled in the individual and in the assembly called the CHURCH, resulting in an outpouring of worship. Indeed, some Protestants would claim that God created human beings and the church for worship, and that worship therefore is their principal reason for existence. Humanity's chief and highest end, says the Westminster Shorter Catechism (1647) (see WESTMINSTER CATECHISM), is "to glorify God and to enjoy him forever." According to JOHN CALVIN in his Commentary on Psalm 33:1, God made the church by adoption "for the express purpose that his name may be duly praised by witnesses suitable for such a work." The "more closely and diligently" God's people consider God's works, remarked Calvin on Psalm 33:3, "the more will they exert themselves in his praises." Numerous Protestant doctrinal statements and CATECHISMS over the generations have defined the church mainly in terms of worship. The AUGSBURG CONFESSION (1530/1540) that would influence Lutheran congregations and other Protestant bodies identified the church as "the congregation of saints [the assembly of all believers] in which the Gospel is rightly taught [purely preached] and the SACRAMENTS rightly administered [according to the Gospel]."

Who Is Worshipped

Protestants have regarded the first and second commandments of the Decalogue (or Ten Commandments) as definitively restricting worship to God revealed as Father, Son, and Holy Spirit. Neither worship nor invocation is to be made to angels, any other creature, or SAINTS; Christ alone is mediator and intercessor. "We love [the saints] and also honor them; yet not with any kind of worship but by an honorable opinion of them and just praises of them" (Second HELVETIC CONFESSION, 1561). Exemplary Christians who have gone on to the nearer presence of God may, however, serve as models for faith and charitable works, and in some Protestant communities, both the faithful and newcomers are explicitly invited to imitate them.

Allegiance is given to the triune God through prayer formulations, by, for example, the classical and broadly Christian offering of prayer to the Father, through the Son, and in the Holy Spirit and by trinitarian doxological ascriptions (e.g., the "Gloria Patri"). Eucharistic prayers sometimes take on a trinitarian shape and content, such as those prayers produced since the mid-twentieth century that are based on fourth-century Antiochene models. However, some denominations in their worship may give emphasis to one particular person of the Godhead. Although Protestants in general recognize that "at the name of Jesus every knee should bend" (Philippians 2:10) and that worship is made "in the name of Jesus," some independent evangelical denominations interpret that almost Christomonistically. Other groups, notably Pentecostals (see PENTECOSTALISM) and quakers (see FRIENDS, SOCIETY OF), wait on the outpouring of the Spirit as the defining feature of their worship.

Time for Worship

Like other Christians, Protestants organize their times for worship according to daily, weekly, and annual cycles. Following the instruction of the fourth commandment in the Decalogue, Protestants have determined to "remember the Sabbath day and keep it holy." The vast majority have observed the first day of the week (Sunday), the day of resurrection, as the Lord's Day or Christian Sabbath and regarded it as the primary occasion for congregational worship. To varying degrees of intensity, and less so overall among more recent generations, Protestants strove to reserve this day for the Lord alone. The fifty-sixth of the Irish Articles of Religion (1615) instructed, "the Lord's day is wholly to be dedicated unto the service of God; and therefore we are bound therein to rest from our common and daily business, and to bestow that leisure upon holy exercises, both public and private." The Church Order of the Free Reformed Churches of North America (2003) called for assembling on the Lord's Day for "at least" two worship services in which the Word of God is preached. Sabbatarians (see SABBATARIANISM) in different times and places have tried to enforce ecclesiastical and civic laws to preserve the sanctity of the Lord's day, with the Puritans of England and New England (see PURITANISM) perhaps among the best known.

A handful of denominations, among them the SEVENTH-DAY ADVENTISTS, have preferred to worship on Saturday on account of their understanding Exodus 20:8 to mean that the seventh day, not the first, is the biblical Sabbath commanded by God.

Because of the biblical injunction to pray without ceasing, and because Christians believe that they ought to avail themselves of every opportunity for meeting with God and with other faithful, Protestant Christians have always advocated worship during the course of the week in the congregation, in small groups or societies, in families, and individually in private. Some Reformation churches from their origins took up portions of the Roman Catholic LITURGY of the hours in formal rites, and, after periods of decline, rediscovered the rhythm of prayer throughout the day. THOMAS CRANMER, for his BOOK OF COMMON PRAYER, conflated five offices to produce the services of morning prayer (from Matins, Lauds, and Prime) and evening prayer (from Vespers and Compline) that became the standard for later revisions across the Anglican communion (see ANGLICANISM). As a result

of the twentieth-century liturgical renewal, new interest in structured texts for prayer at different times of day arose in denominations with no or a weak tradition of formal daily offices. Yet even in those denominations lacking authorized ritual texts for daily prayer, morning and evening prayer was strongly encouraged, particularly in families. To aid family and private devotions, guides or models or prepared texts for prayer were published by private authors and denominational presses, even in denominations that ordinarily frowned on the use of printed prayers in corporate worship and preferred instead "spirit-led" extemporaneous or spontaneous prayer.

For many Protestants, historically and more recently, weekly corporate prayer outside of the main Sunday service has often taken the shape of an informal gathering on Sunday night or midweek. Prayer meetings may be led either by CLERGY or LAITY, and can comprise all-comers or be divided by some criteria, most often age, gender, or spiritual maturity. Evangelical Protestants in particular have found great benefit from these gatherings and from extended prayer and preaching or testimony sessions called "REVIVALS" or protracted meetings. Stories abound from the American frontier on how prayer meetings helped to both Christianize and civilize an unruly population.

With the Protestant Reformation, yearly temporal calendars for the liturgical days and seasons and sanctoral (saints') calendars were either modified (e.g., Lutherans and Anglicans) or expunged (e.g., Anabaptists and some Reformed). Early Lutherans kept festivals and fasts that had a christological dimension and that highlighted persons and salvation events portrayed in Scripture. The Scottish *Book of Discipline* (1560), on the other hand, forbade the observance of "papist" and unscriptural holy days, including Christmas. Such extremes in perspective have continued across Protestantism, though some denominations that previously deplored the liturgical calendar have come (sometimes with hesitation) to embrace it. Protestants, especially Reformed and "FREE CHURCH," have been much more reticent in introducing saints' calendars, though in the twentieth century some denominations began to do so. The UNITING CHURCH IN AUSTRALIA (a union in 1977 of Presbyterians, Congregationalists, and Methodists) included in its first worship book a "Calendar of Other Commemorations" that listed nintey-five names, among them biblical figures and apostles and Christian thinkers, reformers, pioneers, and witnesses with representatives from the early church to the end of the twentieth century. Free church Protestants in some places have been more willing instead to integrate denominational or congregational observances (e.g., Bible Sunday, "blanket Sunday," or the yearly revival) as well as civic festivals (e.g., Mothers' Day) into an annual cycle.

Places for Worship

Protestants, it seems, have always been opportunists regarding places for worship, because of the conviction that the worship of God does not require a particular location or structure. Sixteenth-century Protestants did not immediately worry about church construction; they simply occupied already available ecclesiastical edifices or met in private buildings or homes. The CHURCH OF ENGLAND was confronted for the first time with a demand for buildings following the great fire of London in 1666 that destroyed sixty-seven parishes churches and St. Paul's Cathedral; the architectural skills of Sir CHRISTOPHER WREN were then engaged for reconstruction. As new Protestant denominations or communities emerge, they meet in whatever space is available to them: foundries, warehouses, storefronts, boats and docks, schoolhouses, courthouses, barns, open fields, brush arbors.

Despite the view that the worship of God cannot be limited to a particular space, the physical configuration of the place for worship is extremely important and directly shapes and gives meaning to what occurs there. Typically as a denomination becomes more established, it seeks a more "churchly" venue (however defined) set apart for its worship. A group's theology of worship plays a direct role in the configuration of a worship space: a simple meeting house and an ornate, high-ceilinged Gothic structure convey different perspectives on the human encounter with the divine. Popular architectural trends in the wider society also impact the construction of Protestant places of worship, positively and negatively. CHURCH ARCHITECTURE thus signals a definition of worship as well as a group's self-understanding within the wider culture, including its economic viability. Changes in theology of worship or self-perception may create conflicts with an already existing space and may require renovation of the premises or a completely new building. For example, the spatial location of reading desk (ambo or pulpit), altar table, and baptistery or baptismal font in relationship to each other and to the gathered congregation has changed as perspectives on worship have changed, leading sometimes to a reconfiguration of the space.

Because of the emphasis on the word of God and PREACHING, across Protestantism the reading desk has usually been given a central location within the space. The reading of the BIBLE and its exposition may occur at a single furnishing, or the two actions may be carried out at separate desks identified as pulpit (for preaching) and lectern (for scripture reading and other liturgical readings). The altar table (see ALTARS) carries the double meaning of a place of sacrifice (altaria) and place of fellowship (mensa); Protestants have differed on which meaning is to receive the most emphasis. The sacrament of the LORD'S SUPPER is celebrated at the altar table, which may be located centrally near the congregation or placed at the far end (historically the east end) of the space. The size and location of the baptistery or baptismal font depend on the theological interpretation given to BAPTISM and on the mode of baptism that is preferred. Those denominations that build an indoor facility for immersion or submersion baptism have pools long and deep enough to accommodate an adult. These pools may be located at one end of the building or, as in the case of some English Baptist structures, in the floor near or underneath the pulpit (and covered with boards when not in use). Late twentieth-century experiments with baptisteries often located them on a sight line with the reading desk and altar table, sometimes offset at the side or at the entrance to the worship space as a sign of entry into the community of faith.

The placement of the congregation in the space identifies a denomination's understanding of the role of the people in worship. Protestant buildings usually have been configured either as a single room for laity and clergy or as a divided room in which the people and the worship leaders (clergy and choir) are separated by a high barrier (e.g., the rood screen in Gothic and Gothic revival churches) or low barrier. The people may be seated in chairs, pews, or even enclosed box pews. Some denominations have a history of pew rentals by which persons paid for the privilege of sitting in a specified location, thereby generating income for church coffers. Seating may be arranged to allow the people to see one another, but more typically Protestant congregations have sat so that the eyes are directed toward the reading desk and the altar table. When choirs and musical instruments are used to assist congregational singing, their location in the space most often has been the result of visual and acoustic considerations.

Other furnishings may be used depending on the denomination and the particular congregation. In general, Protestant worship spaces have included at least one cross, more typically the bare cross rather than a crucifix. Candles may be found in communities where they are not deemed "too Catholic." Among the more well-to-do, stained glass windows may be present; the latter provide a device for teaching as well as a memorial to the faithful dead. The tablets of the law (Ten Commandments) may be posted on one wall as a reminder of the necessity of Christian obedience to God. An altar rail may surround the altar table, and it has been the preferred place of evangelicals for prayer, repentance or confession, and recommitment (see EVANGELICALISM).

Components of Protestant Worship

Protestants have disagreed on what are essentials in Christian worship and what rites or ceremonies fall into the category of ADIAPHORA or "things indifferent." The Formula of Concord (1577) was adopted as a means of resolving the Lutheran adiaphoristic controversy of 1548, and concluded in the tenth article that while churches have the right to change ceremonies for the sake of edification, taking care not to offend persons or jeopardize the consciences of the weak in faith, yet "in times of persecution, when a clear and steadfast confession is required of us, we ought not to yield to the enemies of the Gospel in things indifferent." While Lutherans were more willing to permit in worship those things both commanded and not explicitly forbidden by God in Holy Scripture, the Reformed sought to conform their worship more fully to that alone which God had provided. John Calvin, in his INSTITUTES OF THE CHRISTIAN RELIGION (IV.x.30), noted that

> because God did not will in outward discipline and ceremonies to prescribe in detail what we ought to do (because he foresaw that this depended upon the state of the times, and he did not deem one form suitable for all ages), here we must take refuge in those general rules which he has given, that whatever the necessity of the church will require for order and decorum should be tested against these.

Two of the THIRTY-NINE ARTICLES approved by the CHURCH OF ENGLAND in 1562 appear to show that church's attempt to strike a middle ground on this issue; the Twentieth Article on the church's authority states that the church has the power to decree rites and ceremonies that are not "contrary to God's Word written," and the Thirty-fourth Article concedes that because traditions and ceremonies "may be changed according to the diversities of countries, times, and men's manners, so that nothing be ordained against God's Word" and "every particular or national Church hath authority to ordain, change, and abolish, ceremonies or rites of the Church ordained only by man's authority, so that all things be done to edifying."

Echoing the WESTMINSTER CONFESSION of Faith (1646), the 1689 London Baptist Confession recorded, "the reading of the Scriptures, preaching, and hearing the Word of God, teaching and admonishing one another in psalms, hymns, and spiritual songs, singing with grace in our hearts to the Lord; as also the administration of baptism, and the Lord's supper, are

all parts of religious worship of God, to be performed in obedience to him, with understanding, faith, reverence, and godly fear." Despite the various avenues that Protestants might take to determine what is essential to worship, in practice most Protestant services will invariably include those components named in the Baptist Confession, although prayer should be added and the sacraments may not be a standard feature.

Because *sola scriptura* was the watchword of the Reformation and remained a key Protestant concept, it is not surprising that the reading of scripture has been a key component of Protestant services of worship. However, different theological understandings of Scripture's function may be operative: emphasis may be on "hearing" God's word, on the "readings" for catechesis or thoughtful reflection, or on the "text" for the sermon. The amount of Scripture read in a single service differs widely. At one end of the spectrum, selections from the Old Testament, Book of Psalms, Epistles, and Gospels all may be set forth, sometimes in accordance with the design of an established lectionary (in one-, two-, or three-year cycles) that links the readings thematically, usually based on the Gospel. Rather than a lectionary, continuous readings from beginning to end throughout a book, letter, or Gospel may be used (lectio continua). At the other end of the spectrum, some communities read a single verse preceding the sermon, most often from the Gospels; others have no separate reading, but interweave direct quotations from Scripture throughout the preaching.

In *Concerning the Order of Public Worship* (1523?), Luther claimed that the worst abuse of the medieval church was that "God's Word has been silenced," with the result that "faith disappeared." The remedy, he maintained, was that a "Christian congregation should never gather together without the preaching of God's Word and prayer." With a few exceptions, Luther's medicine has been duly applied; preaching is a staple of Protestant liturgical practice and is certainly present in the principal weekly service, although it may not appear at prayer services. The history of Protestant preaching chronicles developments in theological interpretations of the role of the sermon and the preacher, changes in biblical exegesis and hermeneutics, and trends in rhetoric and elocution. Who may preach has been a subject for debate across the years. In some evangelical groups during the eighteenth and nineteenth centuries, women were given the opportunity to preach in public; some, however, were permitted only to exhort, to give testimony, but not to "take a (Scripture) text." Women came to have a more prominent role in preaching, although in some denominations their opportunities for public speaking (and leadership) remain more circumscribed.

The reading of Scripture and the preaching thereupon are understood to be an ordinary means by which God communicates with the community of faith and offers salvation. How is God's Word effectual? According to the one hundred fifty-fifth question of the Westminster Larger Catechism (1648), the

> Spirit of God makes the reading, but especially the preaching of the Word, an effectual means of enlightening, convincing, and humbling sinners; of driving them out of themselves, and drawing them unto Christ; of conforming them to his image, and subduing them to his will; of strengthening them against temptations and corruptions; of building them up in grace, and establishing their hearts in holiness and comfort through faith unto salvation.

Although prayer has been indisputably present in services, there have been disagreements within the Protestant family about whether prayers can be scripted in advance or should be left to the immediate inspiration of the Holy Spirit. Even the Lord's Prayer, regarded as the "perfect" prayer dictated by the Lord himself and quoted regularly in services of worship, is seen by some denominations as too formulaic and hence inappropriate for recitation, although it may serve as a model for prayer. One of the reasons that the English Puritans challenged the "scriptural" quality of the *Book of Common Prayer* from 1549 onward was that the printed prayers were deemed to lack a "spiritual" quality, they were "read" rather than "prayed," and they did not reflect the changing circumstances of local congregations. In answer to Puritan objections, JOHN WESLEY's revision of the 1662 Prayer Book (*The Sunday Service of the Methodists*, 1784) allowed for both written prayers and extemporary prayer. Many Protestants before and after Wesley have embraced both these approaches to prayer.

The prayers used in a given service of worship may be of different types and may be organized in a particular sequence congruent with the desired theological and liturgical shape of the service. Prayers of adoration focus on the qualities and majesty of the triune God. Prayers of CONFESSION acknowledge the sinfulness of the one (personal confession) or ones (general confession) praying. Examples of prayers of confession abound in Scripture, and Psalm 51 often finds a place in worship as a confession, particularly during the season of Lent. Prayers of petition ask God for something that is desired. Of petitions, supplications are requests for one's self, and intercessions are for others. Corporate and personal expressions of gratitude for God's goodness are framed in prayers of thanksgiving. All of these types may be found in a single service and even in a single "long" prayer.

Following the scriptural injunction that Christians are to sing psalms, HYMNS, and spiritual songs (Ephesians 5:19; Colossians 3:16), Protestants from the time of the Reformation almost uniformly have been avid supporters of congregational singing. There has not been consensus, however, on whether harmonized singing is permissible, whether choirs may also be used in corporate worship, and whether singing may be bolstered by the accompaniment of musical instruments (and if such is possible, there is a range of opinion on which instruments may be used). Differences are also evident in regard to what may be sung in worship: most narrowly, only that which God has provided, namely, psalms and scriptural canticles set to old and new melodies associated exclusively with the church, or, most broadly, texts from Scripture and even of "human composure" sung to secular or popular tunes. Such variation in opinion and performance existed in the sixteenth century and continued into the twenty-first. Typically a Protestant service of worship includes multiple opportunities for a congregation to offer praise and proclamation in song. British Methodists of the nineteenth and early twentieth centuries structured their Sunday service, dubbed a "hymn sandwich," around five congregational hymns considered normative components for their worship.

Most Protestants celebrate baptism and the Lord's Supper or Holy Communion out of the conviction that the Lord himself established these as sacraments or ordinances. Baptism may take place in the congregation's usual location for worship if there are appropriate facilities present for the mode or method desired, and occurs as need requires. The Lord's Supper may be a regular component of a congregation's weekly service, or it may be offered less frequently according to denominational or local custom. In a unique configuration, the DISCIPLES OF CHRIST (Christian Church) from their founding have practiced believer baptism by immersion and served Holy Communion each Sunday, sometimes administered by a lay leader of the congregation. A minority of Protestants at times in their histories, among them certain BAPTISTS, BRETHREN, MENNONITES, Moravians (see MORAVIAN CHURCH), and Pentecostals, have given foot-washing (see FEET, WASHING OF) a status of ordinance or sacrament.

The giving of alms for the poor and the collection of monetary offerings for the upkeep of the congregation's building and ministries found a place in many Protestant services of worship as an ethical expression of service to God and as a practical opportunity. The action could be subtle, as with the private placement of monies in a box or vessel, or it might be dramatic and public, such as the passing of a receptacle from person to person or the procession or dance of individuals and their gifts (as in some African-American congregations) to a place where they are received.

Services of Worship

The components of worship may be shaped in myriad of ways depending on the operative theological, liturgical, evangelical, and cultural factors. Fear of formality may prompt a more spontaneous sequence of actions, although over time these may take on a stable or familiar pattern. Some denominations have sought to find an order for worship delineated within Scripture itself; Isaiah's vision in the temple (Isaiah 6) has sometimes been given as warrant for a sequence of adoration and praise, confession and pardon, the hearing of God's word, and commitment to discipleship. Others have recognized a primitive paradigm in the narrative of the Emmaus encounter (Luke 24:13-35) for the unity of word ("he interpreted to them the things about himself in all the scriptures") and sacrament ("how he had been made known to them in the breaking of the bread") and have striven for a weekly practice of preaching and communion. Orders of service and standard texts may be codified in a denomination's liturgical resource to which church law requires adherence to greater or lesser degrees, or a pastor and congregation may be free to develop a service according to local needs.

Certain occasions for worship may necessitate some variation in the standard or familiar pattern of worship. Formal and informal services (or rubrics in a worship directory) for life-cycle events may address the circumstances of infertility and stillbirth, birth and adoption, adolescence and maturity, MARRIAGE, sickness, advancing age and infirmity, and DEATH. Other events may call for special services, such as the laying of a cornerstone for a building or the installation of a new pastor.

Theological, philosophical, and ideological trends may impinge on the shape and content of worship among those groups bound up with or sensitive to the climate of the wider culture. LUTHERANISM in Europe and elsewhere during the eighteenth to twentieth centuries, for example, experienced shifts as a consequence of the successive influences of rationalism, PIETISM, revivalism, and ROMANTICISM. Not only was the substance of worship affected, but the design of the space in which worship was held was also affected. In the twentieth century, ecumenical and liturgical movements helped to widen the theological and liturgical dialogue among Protestants, but beyond that to Catholics (see CATHOLICISM, PROTESTANT REACTIONS) and Orthodox (see ORTHODOXY, EASTERN). Shared conversations and the recognition of common resources in historic and scriptural materials resulted in striking similarities within the liturgical texts of some Protestants that also showed affinities with Catholic texts produced after Vatican II.

Advances in technology impact worship as well. Protestantism from the outset reaped the benefits of moveable type, and over the years has been willing to adopt new innovations for use with worship (e.g., electric lighting, mimeograph printing on site, and multimedia equipment) while at the same time recognizing the capacity of such inventions to distract or deter persons from worship attendance. At the beginning of the twenty-first century, numerous Protestant groups experimented with electronic and Internet communications as a means of EVANGELISM to the unconverted and spiritually uniformed but technologically literate. Such methods kept the historic Protestant emphasis on faithfully proclaiming the word of God while considering the needs of the people.

References and Further Reading

Allmen, Jean Jacques von. *Worship: Its Theology and Practice.* New York: Oxford University Press, 1965.

Bradshaw, Paul, ed. *The New SCM Dictionary of Liturgy and Worship.* London: SCM, 2002. Also published as *The New Westminster Dictionary of Liturgy & Worship*, Louisville, KY: Westminster John Knox, 2002.

Brunner, Peter. *Worship in the Name of Jesus.* Translated by M. H. Bertram. St. Louis, MO: Concordia, 1968.

Cuming, G. J. *A History of Anglican Liturgy.* 2nd ed. London: Macmillan, 1982.

Davies, Horton. *Worship and Theology in England.* 3 vols. Princeton, NJ: Princeton University Press, 1961–1962.

Old, Hughes Oliphant. *Worship.* Guides to the Reformed Tradition. Atlanta, GA: John Knox, 1984.

Reed, Luther D. *The Lutheran Liturgy.* Rev. ed. Philadelphia, PA: Fortress, 1947.

Schaff, Philip. *The Creeds of Christendom.* Rev. ed., 3 vols. Grand Rapids, MI: Baker, 1985.

Senn, Frank C. *Christian Liturgy: Catholic and Evangelical.* Minneapolis, MN: Augsburg Fortress, 1997.

Thompson, Bard. *A Bibliography of Christian Worship.* ATLA Bibliography Series No. 25. Metuchen, NJ: ATLA and London: Scarecrow Press, 1989.

Vajta, Vilmos. *Luther on Worship.* Philadelphia, PA: Muhlenberg, 1958.

West, Fritz. *Scripture and Memory: The Ecumenical Hermeneutic of the Three-Year Lectionaries.* Collegeville, MN: Liturgical Press, 1997.

Wainwright, Geoffrey. *Doxology: The Praise of God in Worship, Doctrine and Life.* New York: Oxford University Press, 1980.

Webber, Robert. *The Complete Library of Christian Worship.* Nashville, TN: Star Song, 1993–1994.

White, James F. *Protestant Worship: Traditions in Transition.* Louisville, KY: Westminster John Knox, 1989.

———. *The Sacraments in Protestant Practice and Faith.* Nashville, TN: Abingdon, 1999.

KAREN WESTERFIELD-TUCKER

WREN, CHRISTOPHER (1632–1723)

Architect. Wren was born into a prominent clerical family on October 20, 1632. His father, Christopher

Sr., was rector of the parish of East Knoyle, Wiltshire, and later dean of Windsor and registrar of the Order of the Garter. His uncle Matthew also held significant positions, serving ultimately as bishop of Ely. The whole family had close contact with the court of Charles I (these Royalist, High Church associations remained with Wren, although he personally never suffered much because of them). Wren received his Bachelors degree from CAMBRIDGE UNIVERSITY in 1650. Three years later he earned his Masters and was made a Fellow of All Souls College, Oxford.

As a scholar Wren was interested in all facets of mathematics and science, and turned that fascination into practical results. He translated mathematical texts into Latin. He was a pioneer in anesthetics, blood transfusion, and intravenous injections. He devised a language for the deaf and mute using hands and fingers. He invented a device for writing with two pens at once, as well as a "way-wiser" (an early precursor to the odometer). He was fascinated by the heavens, puzzling over the problem posed by Saturn's rings. He constructed a "Lunar Sphere" for Charles II, showing the surface of the moon in relief. This work in astronomy resulted in Wren's appointment as professor of astronomy at Gresham College in 1657, and, three years later, as the Savilian professor of astronomy at Oxford. During these years Wren and many of his friends (including astronomer Seth Ward and scientist ROBERT BOYLE) formed the "Philosophical Society of Oxford," which in 1661 received its charter from the king as the Royal Society.

These years also saw Wren's interests extend to the theoretical and geometric bases of architecture, including its classical roots, of which there were few examples in England; thus in 1665 Wren went to Paris, where he met with Gian Lorenzo Bernini and, possibly, François Mansart. It was in Europe that Wren was introduced to the dome, of which there were no examples in England. Shortly after his return to England, however, came the event that possibly "made" Wren as England's preeminent architect: the Great London Fire of September 1666. The five-day conflagration destroyed the Royal Exchange and the Guild Hall, eighty-seven churches (including St. Paul's Cathedral), and 13,000 private houses; little was left except the Tower of London. Wren quickly produced a brilliant plan for rebuilding the city. The design allowed for twenty-four parish churches, each to be conspicuous, many on major thoroughfares. He clearly wanted to restore the spiritual life of a destroyed London, as well as meet the material needs of the people. Although the king favored the proposal, the City Corporation needed a quick restoration and rejected the plan as too time-consuming. Wren, however, was soon appointed Surveyor of the King's Works (1669) and was given the task of rebuilding the city's churches, including St. Paul's Cathedral.

St. Paul's (completed in 1708) was Wren's architectural masterpiece. The building process was not without controversy because the final product did not exactly match any of the original plans or models. "Deception," as some contemporaries charged, also describes some of the cathedral's most important architectural features—and Wren's most significant achievements. From the exterior, for example, the viewer is deceived into assuming that the massive walls remain vertical without the help of flying buttresses; in fact, the upper portions of the exterior walls are false, hiding the buttresses. The dome, visible for miles, appears effortlessly to support the great stone lantern at the top—it too is a deception. Within the outer thin shell is a brick cone, situated over an internal dome (visible from within the cathedral); it is the brick cone that supports the lantern.

Although St. Paul's somewhat represented Wren's thinking about a different architecture required by the CHURCH OF ENGLAND's BOOK OF COMMON PRAYER, the other fifty-two churches of rebuilt London are better examples of Wren's response to this relatively recent religious sensibility. Before the REFORMATION, worship was characterized by active participation of the CLERGY and passive participation of the LAITY; its focus was on the ALTAR. Reformed worship, on the other hand, was centered on the pulpit. *Prayer Book* worship was different still, requiring both active lay and clergy participation, and with dual foci: altar and pulpit.

What were Wren's architectural ideals? Because worshipers were expected to pay attention to the service, ensuring that everyone could both see and hear became paramount. The congregation was expected to have in hand the *Prayer Book;* light was necessary for its reading, so windows and lanterns were abundant. Ideally no one should be more than fifty feet away from the preacher; benches should replace pews if possible; pulpits should be elevated; screens, if used at all, should be very open; optimal sizes of congregations would be small (St. Paul's, as a cathedral, necessarily was an anomaly). There would be no liturgical "center." The resulting "auditories" that Wren designed conformed to two basic types, depending on the available site (oblong buildings with nave and aisles, and squarish buildings arrayed variously); beyond that, there was little structural consistency. Most of the churches were relatively small. Indeed, many were identifiable as churches only by their carefully designed spires (the walls, on the contrary, were mostly continuous masonry, not much divided by piers or columns). Those churches that have survived wars and reconstruction remain, therefore, a lasting legacy to Wren's brilliant solutions to both the constraints of site and the demands of Church of England liturgy.

Sir Christopher Wren was knighted in 1673 and died in London on February 25, 1723. He is buried in St. Paul's, where his epitaph reads (in Latin): "Reader, if you seek his monument, look around."

See also Architecture, Church

References and Further Reading

Primary Source:

Wren, Christopher (II). *Parentalia: Memoirs of the Family of Wrens.* London: 1750 (facsimile reprint London 1965).

Secondary Sources:

Downes, Kerry. *The Architecture of Wren.* Reading: Redhedge, 1988.
Fürst, Viktor. *The Architecture of Sir Christopher Wren.* London: Lund Humphries, 1956.
Whinney, Margaret. *Wren.* London: Thames and Hudson, 1971.

GARY R. BROWER

WU, Y. T. (WU YAO-TSUNG, WU YAOZONG) (1893–1979)

Chinese pastor. Born in Guangzhou (Canton) CHINA in 1893 to a non-Christian family, Wu became a Christian through his reading of the Sermon on the Mount and was baptized in Beijing in 1920. He left his lucrative job in the customs service and joined the work of the YMCA (see YMCA, YWCA). Subsequently, Wu studied at New York's Union Theological Seminary and Columbia University, where he received an M.A. degree in 1927. Upon his return to China he was active in the YMCA movement in China and internationally.

Wu gradually abandoned the PACIFISM of the Fellowship of Reconciliation and became increasingly committed to progressive and patriotic causes. In 1947 he wrote "The Present Day Tragedy of Christianity in China," an essay that foreshadowed LIBERATION THEOLOGY in its social and political critique of Christianity for its identification with capitalism and imperialism. Y. T. Wu began to advocate the support of Christians for the Chinese revolution and was the principal author of the 1950 "Christian Manifesto," which called on the Protestant churches to sever their links with Western imperialism.

Wu was the leading spirit behind the Chinese Christian Three-Self Patriotic Movement (TSPM) from its formative period in 1950. In 1954 he became the Chairman of the TSPM Committee at the First Chinese National Christian Conference and remained in the movement until his death, after the end of China's Cultural Revolution era. He died in Shanghai in 1979.

Through the power of his personality, his commitment to Christian social involvement, and his writings, Y. T. Wu inspired the men and women who were to become the core leadership of the TSPM for the next fifty years. However, he remained a controversial figure in the churches because of his unwavering support for the program of the Communist Party in China. Y. T. Wu leaves an important legacy for Christianity in China, but a thorough evaluation of his life and thought has yet to be written.

See also Asian Theology; Colonialism; Communism; Post-colonialism

References and Further Reading

Chen, Chi-rong. *Wu Yao-Tsung: ein Theologe im sozialistischen China, 1920–1960.* Münster, Germany: Lit. Verlag, 1992.
Ng, Lee-ming. "A Study of Y. T. Wu." *Ching Feng* 15 (1972).
Shen, Derong. *A Short Biography of Y. T. Wu* (in Chinese). Shanghai, China: TSPM Committee, 1989.
Yamamoto, Sumiko. *History of Protestantism in China: The Indigenization of Christianity.* Tokyo: Toho Gakkai, 2000.

PHILIP L. WICKERI

WÜNSCH, GEORG (1887–1964)

German ethicist. Wünsch was one of the first theologians of social ethics in GERMANY. From 1931 to 1945 and then from 1950 to 1955, he held the professorial chair of social ethics at Philipps University, Marburg, the first ever position in social ethics at a department of evangelical theology in Germany.

ERNST TROELTSCH and Johannes Weiß were decisive influences on Wünsch's later interest in social-ethical questions. Troeltsch focused his understanding of theology's relationship to (social) reality; Weiß and the history of religion school provided Wünsch with the principle of an eschatological hope transcending all reality that Wünsch adopted for the cause of radical change.

Beginning in 1912 Wünsch served as a Protestant minister in Baden, Germany. He understood THEOLOGY as the task of shaping the world out of a sense of ethical responsibility, and he was an advocate of unqualified support for the marginalized and weak members of society. After World War I he joined the religious socialists, gave up his position as pastor in 1921, and soon thereafter received his doctorate from the University of Marburg. In 1931 the faculty of theology at Marburg elected him to the newly created position of professor of social ethics. By the time he published *Evangelische Wirtschaftsethik (Protestant Economic Ethics)* in 1927 he had already written a significant body of work on ETHICS and values.

Although a social democrat, Wünsch fell in with the National Socialists with astonishing speed. Not without some opportunism, he began to combine socialist ideas of community taken from both left-wing and right-wing ideologies. In 1936 he published *Evangelische Ethik des Politischen (The Protestant Ethic of the Political)*, a work filled with national socialist content that led to the temporary loss of his university position after the war.

Wünsch is credited with establishing social ethics as a special discipline within theology. The question remains whether one can trace his entanglement in National Socialism to his theological ideas or whether his involvement was a result of individual error. However, the fact of his association with National Socialism did limit the impact of his work.

References and Further Reading

Kaiser, Jochen-Christoph, Andread Lippmann, and Martin Schindel, eds. *Marburger Theologie im Nationalsozialismus: Texte zur Geschichte der Evangelisch-Theologischen Fakultät im Dritten Reich.* Neukirchen-Vluyn, Germany: Neukirchener Verlag, 1998.
Wolfes, Matthias. "Wünsch." In *Biographisch-Bibliographisches Kirchenlexicon* (BBKL). vol. XIV, 103–156. 1998 [including a Wünsch bibliography and secondary literature].
Ziesche, Frank. *Evangelische Wirtschaftsethik: Eine Untersuchung zu Georg Wünschs wirtschaftsethischem Werk.* Frankfurt am Main, Germany: Peter Lang, 1996.

JOCHEN-CHRISTOPH KAISER

WWJD

WWJD—the acronym for "What Would Jesus Do?"—gained prominence after an evangelical youth group adopted it as a slogan in the 1990s. However, the underlying question predates the creation of the acronym by nearly 100 years, having been popularized in the late nineteenth century by the pastor and novelist CHARLES M. SHELDON.

Sheldon (1857–1946) was born in Wellsville, New York into the family of a respected Congregationalist minister (see CONGREGATIONALISM). After completing his education at Boston University and Andover Newton Seminary, he became a Congregationalist minister in Topeka, Kansas. Sheldon's brief novel, *In His Steps,* was written in 1896 and is most remembered for its provocative ethical question: "What would Jesus do?" In Sheldon's novel, as in his activist life, Jesus was assumed to promote the social causes of late nineteenth- and early twentieth-century progressive Christianity. Sheldon was active in the TEMPERANCE movement, antiwar campaigns, child labor issues, and struggles against racism and poverty. In spite of the novel's tremendous sales, Sheldon retained no legal rights to royalties from the book's sale because of a copyright error. (When a few publishers voluntarily paid Sheldon royalties, he donated the money to charity.) Ironically, publishers' wide-scale pirating of the book promoted both the book's sales and Sheldon's literary reputation.

Sheldon published over twenty books and edited a periodical, *The Christian Herald,* but only *In His Steps* (which sold 23 million copies in his lifetime) enjoined soaring popularity during his lifetime and in subsequent generations. After his death Sheldon's novel was "rediscovered" in 1950 when Glenn Clark published a volume on a new generation's discovery of *In His Steps.* Such rediscoveries occurred regularly throughout the twentieth century and into the twenty-first century. The most important rediscovery of Sheldon's novel occurred in the early 1990s and coincided with two other events in popular CULTURE: the emergence of the World Wide Web and the popular advertising slogan "Just do it."

A youth group at Calvary Reformed Church in Holland, Michigan read Sheldon's novel and created the acronym WWJD as a countercultural Christian alternative to the secular advertising slogan "Just do it." The youth group began producing and distributing cloth bracelets emboldened with the WWJD acronym. The bracelets were popularized through several Web sites (by 1999 over 50,000 Web sites were offering WWJD merchandise and promoting related discussions). Zondervan Publishing, an evangelical publisher in central Michigan, began promoting and extending the WWJD phenomenon with a full line of complementary products, including a study BIBLE, devotional and inspirational books, T-shirts, board games, SUNDAY SCHOOL curricula, calendars, and jewelry. By 1999 over 14 million WWJD bracelets had sold.

The evangelical WWJD movement has deemphasized the socially progressive Christian agenda promoted by Sheldon and thus incurred criticism from some non-Evangelicals for usurping Sheldon's theological agenda.

See also Evangelicalism

References and Further Reading

Clark, Glenn. *What Would Jesus Do? Wherein a New Generation Undertakes to Walk in His Steps.* St. Paul, MN: Macalester Park Publishing, 1950.
Sheldon, Charles M. *In His Steps.* New York: Hurst, 1896.
www.whatwouldjesusdo.com (Accessed March 17, 2003).
www.wwjd.com (Accessed March 17, 2003).

THOMAS E. PHILLIPS

WYCLIFFE BIBLE TRANSLATORS

Founded in 1934 by William Cameron Townsend, the Wycliffe Bible Translators (WBT), with approximately 6,000 members worldwide, is now the largest nondenominational Protestant missionary organization in the world. The WBT originated with the vision of Cameron Townsend to undertake indigenous language ministry in all the Indian tribes of LATIN AMERICA. Today the WBT is an organization of linguists dedicated to translating the Scriptures into every language of the world. The WBT and its field organization, the Summer Institute of Linguistics (SIL), have completed the translation of the New Testament into almost 500 languages with linguists working in 1,100 others. The WBT was founded as a "faith mission" that, in the twentieth century, overtook denominational boards as evangelical missions of choice. Townsend's new approaches, including indigenous language ministry, linguistic education for missionaries, contracts with host countries, and the use of airplanes in jungle travel, dramatically altered the faith mission enterprise.

Townsend in Guatemala

In 1917, bored with college and inspired by his membership in the Student Volunteer Movement, Townsend went to Guatemala as an itinerant evangelist for the Bible House of Los Angeles. Townsend spent the next fifteen years in Guatemala, first with the Bible House, but primarily with the Central American Mission (CAM). Townsend's traveling companion during his year as a colporteur was Francisco Díaz, a Cakchiquel Indian. Díaz convinced Townsend that the Indians of Central America had been overlooked by American missions, which carried on their work in Spanish, a language little understood by the Indian tribes that made up the majority of the region's population. When Townsend joined the CAM, he determined to focus his work on Díaz's tribe. He created a Cakchiquel department within the CAM complete with schools for Indian children, conducted his ministry in the Indian language, and translated the New Testament into Cakchiquel. At every point he fought established mission policy that, along with current governmental policies, sought to incorporate the Indians into the broader political life of the republic by teaching them only in Spanish.

The Founding of the Summer Institute of Linguistics

Eager to pioneer where no other missionary had gone before, Townsend soon turned his attention to the small Indian tribes deep in the jungles of Amazonia. He envisioned an "Air Crusade to the Wild Tribes" in which "hydroplanes" would fly missionaries to isolated tribes. When the CAM would not support his scheme, he left, intending to devote himself to his "Air Crusade." His project, however, also required missionaries trained in linguistics who could create written languages where none existed and then translate the Scripture. To meet this need he opened the first "Camp Wycliffe" in 1934. From a rather crude beginning Townsend's summer linguistic training camp, along with a "Jungle Camp" that provided experience in rugged frontier living, helped to revolutionize evangelical missionary training. Before the creation of Townsend's school, missionaries entered faith missions with little more than a high school education and a year or two of Bible school. Townsend, however, sent his best students to earn advanced degrees in linguistics. As they returned to teach at what became known as the SIL, they demanded more from the new recruits. Today it often requires several years beyond college for recruits to complete the rigorous training provided by SIL. Where once typical WBT recruits were fervent young missionaries who chose a linguistic focus to win converts, typical WBT recruits are now well-educated linguists who choose missionary work as an avenue for uniting their career goals with their sense of Christian calling.

The Summer Institute in Mexico

Townsend was initially deterred from his goal of an "Air Crusade" to Amazonia by the suggestion of Leonard Legters, a barnstorming preacher and crusader for Indian causes, that the Indian tribes in MEXICO were both larger and easier to reach. In 1935 Townsend took his first group of SIL translators to Mexico. (The WBT was not actually incorporated until 1942, when the SIL had grown so large that the missionaries needed an organization in the UNITED STATES to manage their home affairs.) There Townsend forged a close friendship with Mexican president Lázaro Cárdenas who, despite his own government's antireligious agenda, permitted Townsend to bring in as many workers as he could recruit. Townsend's experience with Cárdenas, as well as WBT's status as an academic missionary organization, led to the mission's unique approach to government relations, whereby WBT/SIL seeks to operate under a contract with the host country. SIL provides the host country with linguistic analysis of the languages of indigenous groups, and in turn is permitted to use its knowledge to translate the Scriptures into those languages.

To Peru and Beyond

In 1943 the Peruvian government asked the WBT to undertake linguistic work with its indigenous groups. In Peru Townsend finally realized his vision of an "Air Crusade" when he founded the Jungle Aviation and Radio Service (JAARS) in 1948. The use of airplanes bypassed weeks of hard travel through the jungle and, together with radios, made the daily life of missionaries much safer.

From Peru WBT entered Guatemala in 1952; Ecuador and the PHILIPPINES in 1953; Bolivia in 1955; then Colombia, BRAZIL, and INDONESIA in rapid succession. By the end of the twentieth century, WBT linguists operated in virtually every country of the world. In addition to attracting many members from developed countries outside the United States, the movement has spawned indigenous Bible translation organizations. In some countries WBT linguists operate only as consultants to national Bible translators.

Controversy

As a very high-profile Protestant mission in the twentieth century, the WBT has often been a lightning rod for criticism. In addition to battles with anthropologists over approaches to indigenous cultures, the mission's access to and perceived influence over isolated tribal groups has led to accusations that the mission is in league with American business interests or government organizations, such as oil companies or the Central Intelligence Agency (CIA). The organization has rejected these accusations, and no direct evidence of such complicity has come to light. Townsend, at least, supported Mexican national interests against those of the United States during the Cárdenas administration (Townsend was investigated by the FBI because of his loyalty to Cárdenas), and throughout his life insisted that the U.S. government and business not interfere in Latin American affairs.

In addition the mission has often been accused of deceiving governments about its true intent, posing as a scientific organization rather than a missionary one.

The use of two names for what is essentially one organization, and government contracts that call obliquely for the translation of "works of high moral content" have tended to support this suggestion of duplicity. There is some truth to this charge, in that before the SIL became a groundbreaking academic training organization, many WBT recruits could only marginally be called linguists. The accusation, however, assumes the ignorance of host governments, most of which investigated the WBT before extending their invitations and knew that SIL linguists entered their countries with missionary intent. The governments themselves, which, especially in Latin American countries, were often beholden to the Catholic Church, tried to slip SIL in "under Catholic radar." Ironically in the 1970s and 1980s, when several WBT contracts were severely contested by academics and nationalist groups, it was at times the Catholic Church, which over the years had grown to appreciate SIL's linguistic help as well as passage to its own mission stations on JAARS airplanes, that worked behind the scenes to preserve SIL's status.

See also Bible Translation; Missionary Organizations; Missions, North American

References and Further Reading

Colby, Gerard and Charlotte Dennett. *Thy Will Be Done, the Conquest of the Amazon: Nelson Rockefeller and Evangelism in the Age of Oil.* New York: HarperCollins, 1995.

Steven, Hugh. *Wycliffe in the Making: the Memoirs of W. Cameron Townsend, 1920–1933.* Wheaton, IL: Harold Shaw, 1995.

———. *Doorway to the World, the Mexico Years: the Memoirs of W. Cameron Townsend, 1934–1947.* Wheaton, IL: Harold Shaw, 1999.

Stoll, David. *Fishers of Men or Founders of Empire?: the Wycliffe Bible Translators in Latin America.* London: Zed Press, 1982.

Svelmoe, William L. "A New Vision for Missions: William Cameron Townsend and the Wycliffe Bible Translators in Latin America." Ph.D. dissertation, University of Notre Dame, 2001.

http://www.wycliffe.org

WILLIAM L. SVELMOE

Y

YMCA, YWCA

The Young Men's Christian Association (YMCA) and the Young Women's Christian Association (YWCA) both began in London and quickly spread internationally, both reaching their largest membership numbers in the UNITED STATES. George Williams founded the YMCA in London in 1844 as a prayer group for young men new to the city. Likewise, the YWCA resulted from the union of two London-based women's organizations, both devoted to encouraging evangelical Protestant virtues. Although the YMCA and YWCA have continued to consider their official missions to be based on Christian principles, their specific connection to Christian churches have lessened as they opened their doors to members of all religious traditions and encouraged interfaith dialogue. The missions of the YMCA and YWCA have expanded over time to include issues of human justice, racial relations, HIGHER EDUCATION, physical fitness, and war relief.

Beginnings of the YMCA

The YMCA was founded in London in 1844 by George Williams, the son of a farmer, and eleven of his friends. Williams and his friends wanted the organization to serve men who were new to the city, by helping them to feel God's GRACE. The founders of the association were evangelical Protestant and early activities included PRAYER and study of the BIBLE. To join the YMCA young men had to either belong to a Christian church or show evidence of being converted to Christianity.

Other YMCAs were quickly established throughout ENGLAND with the aim of protecting respectable young men from the vices of the city, and the movement soon began to spread internationally. By 1850 the movement had reached AUSTRALIA. In Paris in 1855 all of the national associations combined to form the World Alliance. Their headquarters are now located in Geneva, SWITZERLAND. Five thousand associations were established in twenty-four countries by 1905.

In 1851 at the World's Fair in London, Americans were first exposed to the YMCA, and the first North American club was founded in Montreal later that year. On December 29, 1851 sea captain and missionary Thomas Valentine Sullivan introduced the YMCA to the United States, forming the first U.S. YMCA in Boston at the Old South Church. By 1852 there were organizations in New York; Washington, D.C.; Buffalo; Detroit; and Springfield, Massachusetts. At these YMCAs activities included prayer meetings, Bible class, and lectures. In addition the YMCAs often provided libraries and reading rooms for their members.

As early as 1856, student YMCAs were organized at universities in Tennessee, Virginia, and Wisconsin. By 1900 there were 628 student YMCAs that served 32,000 students. In addition the YMCA founded colleges and schools throughout the United States, and by 1950 there were twenty YMCA colleges in Boston, Cleveland, Chicago, Detroit, Seattle, and other cities (see CHRISTIAN COLLEGES). For instance, Golden Gate University began in 1881 as a night school operating out of the San Francisco YMCA, and Northeastern University grew out of a series of informal law courses offered by the Boston YMCA in 1897. After World War II most of the colleges founded by the YMCA became freestanding institutions, but two universities—Springfield (Massachusetts) College and Aurora (Illinois) University—have retained their affiliation.

When the national YMCA in the United States convened in 1869 in Portland, Maine, the delegates adopted the Portland Basis/Test to establish the requirements for membership. At this time membership was extended only to members of evangelical Christian churches. Although this move upset people who felt that it was too exclusionary, it did signal that the YMCA would not attempt to establish a separate Christian church. Although the policy was not always followed by individual YMCAs, it was not officially changed until 1933, when individual YMCAs were given the freedom to open their membership as they saw fit.

Beginnings of the YWCA

The YWCA resulted from the merging of two Christian organizations in London. These organizations, both founded in 1855, were the Prayer Union, founded by Emma Roberts, and the General Female Training Institute, founded by Mary Jane Kinnaird. In 1877 Roberts and Kinnaird met over tea and combined their organizations to establish the YWCA. From the beginning, they emphasized practical social action as an outgrowth of religious belief. In 1884 the organization adopted its first constitution.

In the United States the YWCA was also a result of various movements that eventually combined under one name. The religious REVIVALS in the eastern United States in 1857–1858 helped to pave the way for these women's organizations. Women in big cities recognized the need for safe housing for single young women and by 1860 residences were set up in New York and Boston. These young women, new to the city or without family ties, often turned to churches for help, and these Christian residences were a natural solution.

In 1866 thirty women met in Boston to write the constitution for their new organization, which they called the YWCA. This group was concerned not just with women's housing, but also with job training and physical recreation. In the 1870s a YWCA in New York established the first typewriting instruction for women, the first sewing machine classes, and the first employment bureau for women. In response to the growth of student YMCAs, a student YWCA was established at Normal University in Normal, Illinois in 1873.

The YWCA encountered some problems that parallel YMCAs did not. In particular, many people were reluctant to donate money to the YWCA because they doubted the organizational skills of women. However, the YWCAs succeeded, in part because of the strong conviction by many of these women that Christian women were obligated to help others, including in their spiritual development. The YWCA acted as an outlet for women to help other women and provide whatever service was needed in the community. Part of the particularly Christian motivation of the YWCA was to win souls for Christ, but the members saw the YWCA as the "handmaiden" of the church, not as an organization directly tied to the church.

YWCAs were growing throughout the world, not just in England and the United States: 1894 saw the formation of the World YWCA. Recognizing their commonalties, the YWCAs of England, the United States, SWEDEN, and NORWAY organized in London. Their headquarters were later located in Geneva, Switzerland.

Finally, in 1906, the various local branches and student branches in the United States combined to create a national YWCA. At this time the YWCA had 186,000 members, 22 percent of whom were students. Their first president was Grace Dodge, who was also one of the founders of the Columbia Teacher's College and a member of the Women's Labor Council. The organization established a national board and hired a staff. The first executive director—then called "secretary"—was Mabel Cratty.

Urban Culture and Physical Development

From their beginnings, the YMCA and YWCA were envisioned as urban organizations, designed for the benefit of young men and young women who felt lost in the city. The industrial revolution drove people from their farms and small towns into the cities to work in factories. This transition could often be very difficult, and the YMCA and YWCA were developed to help ease this change, both by providing valuable services, such as housing and job placement, and by providing a Christian community where young adults could feel at home.

From the 1860s YMCAs in the United States offered hotel-like rooms as housing opportunities for young men who were new to the cities, until they could find more permanent housing. Chicago's Farwell Hall—the first YMCA dormitory—was erected in 1867 with forty-two rooms, although it burned down three months later. From the early twentieth century until the late 1950s dormitory rooms were designed into every YMCA building. Emergency dormitories for the unemployed and homeless were also an occasional feature of YMCAs. By 1940 YMCAs offered more rooms than any hotel chain of the era, at 100,000 rooms.

Scholars have suggested that the same conditions that provided security against corruption for young Christian men new to the city—especially the anonymity and personal freedom—also allowed for the flourishing of an underground gay culture there. The all-male culture of YMCA residences was a place of fertile sexual experimentation from the 1980s onward.

Although the YMCA's establishment as a "home away from home" was meant at least in part to protect young men from sexual immorality and encourage self-restraint and celibacy, what actually occurred in the YMCAs was at odds with that vision. Gay cruising at public places was often subject to police surveillance, but at the YMCA such regulation was relatively rare. The YMCAs may have been safe from police raid because of the public perception that such activities could not occur at a Christian institution, especially once the YMCAs expanded to suburbs and became known as catering to families. Although the YMCAs were known throughout the gay male community as an ideal place to cruise, not all of the men who participated in sexual activities at the YMCA identified as homosexual or associated themselves with gay community institutions.

In addition to their concern about the spiritual well-being of young men and women, middle-class Protestants also worried about the physical health and development of these young Christians in cities. Whereas working on farms had provided physical exercise for these young workers, their new jobs and long hours in factories prevented this exercise. By 1869 YMCA buildings with gymnasiums had opened in San Francisco, Washington, D.C., and New York. Robert J. Roberts of the Boston YMCA developed "body building" classes in 1881. By the 1890s physical fitness had been officially established as an essential component in YMCA work. This association between the YMCA and physical fitness was a response to contemporary debates over the relative benefits of "brain work" versus physical exercise. Whereas some physicians prescribed relaxation therapy to cure exhaustion, others believed that what middle-class people, especially men who were occupied in sedentary work, needed was physical exercise to complement their mental work. The YMCA took the latter view and championed a philosophy of "Muscular Christianity," wherein physical development was essential to Christian salvation. "Muscular Christianity" also developed in response to fears that muscular southern and eastern European immigrants would steal jobs from the physically weaker white Protestant middle class.

A number of SPORTS owe their existence and development to the YMCA. Among these, the most well known may be basketball. In Springfield, Massachusetts, students at the International YMCA Training School enjoyed playing rugby and football during warm months, but they were not as pleased with their indoor winter sports options, among them leapfrog and tumbling. To rectify this situation, the school's director, Luther Gulick, asked teacher and minister James Naismith to develop an indoor game for the

students to play. The resulting game was basketball, which was then played with hanging peach baskets. In January of 1892 Naismith published the rules of the game and the game quickly spread among young men and women. Naismith never made any money from his invention, even refusing compensation for his public speaking about the sport. Many inventors of other YMCA sports followed Naismith's example, giving their sport to the participants without remuneration. Other YMCA inventions include volleyball, group swimming lessons, lifesaving classes, and racquetball.

Race and Ethnicity

In 1853, just two years after the YMCA came to the United States, the first black YMCA was opened in Washington, D.C., by former slave Anthony Bowen, and the annual YMCA convention included African American delegates as early as 1867. However, it was not until 1890 that the national YMCA office opened its "Colored Men's Department" and appointed William Hunton, son of a slave, to serve the African American community. In part this delay can be explained by considering that before the CIVIL WAR many African American men were slaves and thus not free to join the YMCA. Once the slaves were liberated, they were encouraged to join on a separate-but-equal basis. Ohio black minister Jesse E. Moorland, who joined Hunton in 1898, encouraged the growing class of black businessmen to join the association and benefit from the focus on developing the body, mind, and spirit.

African American men involved in the YMCAs had a very particular understanding of how to implement racial uplift, contra Booker T. Washington and W. E. B. DuBois. History professor Nina Mjahkij has suggested in her work that black YMCA leaders stressed an ideal of "true manhood" that united Victorian gentility with muscular Christianity. Thus, these black leaders encouraged the same virtues that white Christian men at the time were espousing, with the belief that individual African Americans could advance in society by displaying masculine virtues. Urban middle-class black men who were not accepted fully as men in society could express their masculinity at the black YMCAs to which they belonged.

As was the case with the nation as a whole, the YMCA long remained segregated, but by the mid-1920s there were 128 black college chapters of the YMCA and fifty-one city YMCAs, with membership totaling 28,000. Although early black YMCAs had some difficulty raising funds, the black YMCAs in the 1920s usually cooperated with white YMCA boards and received some financial support from them. Individuals such as George Foster Peabody, John D.

Rockefeller, and Julius Rosenwald also contributed to the cause.

By 1946 YMCAs were encouraged to eliminate discrimination, and they officially desegregated in 1967. During the CIVIL RIGHTS MOVEMENT of the 1960s leaders of the movement met at black YMCAs. Leaders, such as Dr. MARTIN LUTHER KING JR., Rev. Andrew Young, Vernon Jordan, and U.S. Supreme Court justice Thurgood Marshall grew up involved with their local YMCAs.

Although the YWCA in the United States was early populated with African American women, especially in its black student organizations, the official leadership of the YWCA did not always encourage and support its black members. It was not until 1914 that a secretary for the advancement of African American women in cities was added to the YWCA structure. The cause of African American women was further advanced in 1919 when the first YWCA building designed specifically for black women was opened in New York, offering the separate-but-equal facilities that the YMCAs had been offering for men.

For the women of the YWCA the debate over whether to include African American women was theological in nature. The mission of the YWCA was specifically designed to extend to all women of the same Christian faith who wanted to provide service to other women throughout their communities. However, black women were excluded from many of the social institutions of the time, and the YWCA may have had less success in accomplishing its mission without the money and social support that could have been difficult to attain if they included black women in their organization. In some ways the separation between black and white YWCAs may reflect this difficulty.

Although the black–white divide was perhaps the most salient racial divide in both the YMCA and YWCA in the United States (perhaps because African Americans were more likely than some other racial groups to be Protestant), African Americans were by no means the only racial groups involved in the movements. NATIVE AMERICANS were one of the earliest groups to become involved in both the YMCA and the YWCA. The YMCA foray into work with Native Americans began in 1879 in the Dakota Territory. Chief Little Crow's son, Thomas Wakeman, organized the first Sioux YMCA. Eventually, there were sixty-six Sioux associations, with membership reaching 1,000. The YMCA also worked with other tribes in the United States, especially in the areas of EDUCATION, health, and Christian development.

The YWCA first began its work among Native American girls in 1897 at the Haworth Institute in Chilocco, Oklahoma, and other associations for Native American girls soon followed. At least in part the women of the YWCA wanted to help these Native American girls to adjust to new situations, especially when placed on reservations and in government schools. By 1930 the YWCA was operating in forty-one schools and serving 2,600 girls. The YWCA and YMCA worked together and closely with the government in their work with Native Americans both on the reservations and off.

Like African Americans, Chinese Americans and Japanese Americans also founded YMCAs separate from the white YMCAs, especially in San Francisco. The first Chinese American YMCA was founded in San Francisco's Chinatown in 1871, with the name *Ki-Tuk Yau Hok Ching To Ui* (Young Christians Learning Upright Doctrine Society). Because of the prevalence of gambling among the Chinese of the community, one of the most strictly enforced rules was the stricture against playing games like dominos or chess. A Japanese branch of the San Francisco YMCA opened in 1918, but because of a more dispersed population and difficulties raising money, the Japanese were never as successful in their YMCA efforts in San Francisco as were the Chinese. There were also separate "Oriental" branches of the YWCA in San Francisco and Los Angeles. The YWCA also provided services for Japanese Americans in relocation camps during World War II, which may have helped familiarize them with the YWCA.

War Relief

In 1865 the YMCA of the United States began working with soldiers of the Civil War, especially in the North. The U.S. Christian Commission, designed to aid soldiers on the battlefield, was created by the combination of fifteen northern YMCAs and eventually included 5,000 volunteers. In part these numbers reflect a recruiting effort spurred on by a meeting with President ABRAHAM LINCOLN. Volunteers in the Christian Commission, forty-three of whom lost their lives in the war, wrote letters, delivered supplies and food, and kept a record of the dead. Although the Northern YMCAs were hurt by the war, they fared better than the southern YMCAs, and only two Southern YMCAs remained after the war.

YMCA volunteers helped American soldiers from the first days of World War I. Small voluntary contributions by YMCA members to the war work totaled $235 million. Praised by U.S. Commanding General John J. Pershing, the YMCA volunteers provided morale and welfare services to the troops and operated 1,500 canteens in the United States and FRANCE. In addition the YMCA volunteers, ninety-three of whom died during their service, set up 4,000 huts—many on the front lines—for recreation and religious service. It was mainly through the efforts of these YMCA volunteers that baseball, basketball, and volleyball were first given mass exposure in Europe. The YWCA also operated canteens during World War I and mobilized women for war work.

During World War II both the YMCA and the YWCA helped the soldiers. Once President Franklin Delano Roosevelt had declared a state of emergency, six national organizations—including the YMCA and the YWCA—joined forces to form the United Services Organizations for National Defense (the USO), which was formally incorporated on February 4, 1941. YMCA volunteers also worked with six million prisoners-of-war held in thirty-six foreign countries and several thousand prisoners-of-war held in the United States. World War II brought changes to the lives of women irrespective of whether they went to the front lines to help. Many women who stayed in the United States had to leave their homes and work in factories to produce goods for the war, and the YWCA provided housing and support for women who had difficulties in the transition.

Later Developments

At the Sixth World Council of YMCAs, which met in Kampala, Uganda in 1973, one of the major concerns was to determine how best to retain the Christian character of the YMCA. The membership and leadership of YMCAs throughout the world has expanded to include a broad political and religious spectrum. The YMCA in Jerusalem, which opened in 1933, for instance, is considered to be one of the few places in that city where Christians, Jews, and Muslims are able to mingle peacefully. However, many people within the organization fear that it will be difficult to retain the Christian nature of the association if YMCA leaders, especially full-time directors, are no longer required to be committed Christians. The Kampala Principles, established during this conference, give new interpretation to the nature and mission of the World Alliance. It was decided by the delegates that, although it is important to reaffirm the Christian ideals of the 1855 "Paris Basis," open membership—regardless of faith, age, sex, class—is also a fundamental principle of the YMCA. Local YMCAs were encouraged to review their own policies in relation to this new interpretation of the ecumenical character of the YMCA.

Although the world YMCA is concerned with its Christian character, the YMCA of the United States has increasingly moved away from Christian activities. In 2001 the YMCA celebrated 150 years in the United States, and they reaffirmed that their mission, although based on Christian principles, was applicable to people of all faiths, both men and women. With half

their membership under the age of eighteen in 2001, YMCAs continued to work with youth, serving one in ten teenagers and working especially with teens in high-risk communities. The focus on youth could be seen especially in camping programs, which began in 1867. Summer camps began in the United States with a YMCA trip in 1885, and by 2001 the YMCA claimed 1,600 day camps that served 500,000 children each summer. With half their population over the age of eighteen, however, YMCAs could not focus solely on youth. With the development of Jazzercise and dance exercise classes in the late 1960s the YMCA helped to pioneer the exercise craze that served adult members. Many YMCAs even included special programming for senior citizens, focusing on serving the physical and social needs of the older members.

After delegates to the World Council of the YWCA held the annual conference in Cairo in July 1999, they released their resolutions and recommendations. Their chief issues, in keeping with the mission of the World YWCA, included justice, peace, and the environment, and the ways in which women's leadership could contribute to the solutions. At that time the key goals of the YWCA Global Campaign included encouraging the continuation of current programs, raising awareness of the YWCA movement, and establishing funds for leadership development programs for women and girls. By 2003 the World YWCA included 25 million women from at least 100 different countries.

In August of 2000 the YWCA of the United States, which then numbered 316 local associations, released a report entitled "A Century of Change." According to the report the advocacy issues on which the YWCA planned to focus included childcare, violence prevention, women's health, and voter outreach. Annual events had included a YWCA Week Without Violence, and a YWCA National Day of Commitment to Eliminate Racism, which included a Racial Justice Awards Dinner and a Race Against Racism.

See also Evangelicalism; Gender; Homosexuality; Voluntary Societies; War; Women

References and Further Reading

Binfield, Clyde. *George Williams and the Y.M.C.A.: A Study in Victorian Social Attitudes*. London: William Heineman, Ltd., 1973.

Creedy, Brooks Spivey. *Women Behind the Lines: YWCA Program with War Production Workers, 1940–1947*. New York: Women's Press, 1949.

Drury, Clifford M. *San Francisco YMCA: 100 Years by the Golden Gate, 1853–1953*. Glendale, CA: The Arthur H. Clark Company, 1963.

Hopkins, C. Howard. *History of the Y.M.C.A. in North America*. New York: Association Press, 1951.

Limbert, Paul. "World YMCA Meets in Uganda, Reaffirms its Christocentric Character." *The Christian Century* 90 no. 31 (1973): 860–862.

Mjagkij, Nina, and Margaret Spratt, eds. *Men and Women Adrift: The YMCA and the YWCA in the City*. New York: New York University Press, 1997.

Philips, Kay. "YWCA History—Highlights." *YWCA Online Manual*. September 1999. http://www.geocities.com/ywca_berkeley/historyhl.html.

Sims, Mary S. *The Natural History of a Social Institution—The Young Women's Christian Association*. New York: The Women's Press, 1936.

Wilson, Elizabeth. *Fifty Years of Association Work Among Young Women, 1866–1916: A History of Young Women's Christian Associations in the United States of America*. New York: National Board of the Young Women's Christian Association of the United States, 1916.

Winter, Thomas. *Making Men, Making Class: The YMCA and Workingmen, 1877–1920*. Chicago: The University of Chicago Press, 2002.

———. *YMCA in America, 1851–2001: A History of Accomplishment Over 150 Years*. Chicago: National Council of Young Men's Christian Associations of the United States of America, 2000.

"A Century of Change: Annual Report, September 1, 1999–August 31, 2000." YWCA of the U.S.A. July 2001. http://www.ywca.org/docs/AnnRepor.pdf.

KELLY THERESE POLLOCK

YOUNG, BRIGHAM (1801–1877)

American church leader. Young was born in Whittingham, Vermont on June 1, 1801, the eighth of eleven children of John and Abigail (Nabby) Howe. He died August 29, 1877 in Salt Lake City, Utah from an abdominal disease then called cholera morbus.

The Young family moved to Western New York in 1804 and relocated several times during Brigham's childhood. His mother died when he was 14 years old. In 1817 Brigham apprenticed himself in Auburn, New York, to learn carpentry, painting, and glazing. He did carpentry work at the local prison, the local theological seminary, and at private homes.

In 1823 Young moved to Bucksville (later called Port Byron) on the Erie Canal, where he again worked as a carpenter and helped organize the Bucksville Forensic and Oratorical Society. He married Miriam Angeline Works (1806–1832) in 1824, and they settled in Aurelius, New York until early 1828 when they moved to Oswego. Later that year they moved to Mendon, where a number of his family had already located.

Brigham grew up in a devoutly religious Methodist family. His brothers Phinehas and Joseph served as Methodist ministers. As a youth Brigham listened to the preaching of CIRCUIT RIDERS and attended Methodist CAMP MEETINGS. In 1824 Brigham and Miriam joined the Methodists, apparently attracted by their emphasis on GRACE, free will, the witness of the Spirit, Christian perfectionism, and rejection of the Calvinist doctrine of ELECTION. Local people remembered Young for his "deep piety and faith in God."

Events in 1830 changed the Youngs' lives. In 1830 JOSEPH SMITH of Palmyra, New York published the *Book of Mormon* and founded the Church of Christ, later renamed the Church of Jesus Christ of Latter-day Saints. The church is not Protestant in the narrow sense of that word, but members, who are often called Mormons or Latter-day Saints (LDS), believe their religion to be the restoration of primitive Christianity.

In April 1830 Samuel H. Smith, a brother of Joseph Smith, came to Mendon where he gave Phinehas Young a *Book of Mormon*. Phinehas read the book and passed it on to the remainder of the family. In April 1832, Brigham, Miriam, and eleven other family members were baptized into the LDS Church. Young began preaching in Western New York and in CANADA.

In MORMONISM Young and his family found answers to troubling questions. The Latter-day Saints believed in continuing revelation, Christ's ATONEMENT, universal SALVATION, and priesthood ordination for all righteous men. They rejected infant BAPTISM and original SIN.

Early in their marriage Young's wife Miriam contracted tuberculosis, from which she died in 1832. Her disability left Brigham to care for the household and children while continuing to work as a carpenter and farm laborer. In the fall of 1833 Brigham moved to Kirtland where Smith had established the LDS church's headquarters. There, Young worked as a builder, and he continued preaching. On February 18, 1834 he married Mary Ann Angell (1803–1882), who helped rear his two children by Miriam and bore six other children.

Brigham joined Zion's Camp, an expedition organized by Smith on May 5, 1834, to travel to Jackson County, Missouri to restore Mormons to homes from which mobs had driven them. The expedition failed, but participants developed a close relationship with Smith and with each other.

In February 1835, at age 34, Young was called as a member of the original Quorum of Twelve Apostles. Smith assigned the Twelve to preach throughout the world and to preside outside the seat of the First Presidency. At first Young and others in the Twelve preached in Ohio, New York, Ontario, and New England. Young also worked on the construction of the Kirtland Temple of the Latter-Day Saints, and he participated in temple ordinances and in Pentecostal experiences such as singing, prophesying, and speaking in tongues.

Shortly thereafter a number of prominent members of the Kirtland temple rebelled against Joseph Smith. Young rejected the dissenters and supported Smith, although fearful of personal injury. Young left for the Mormon settlements in Northern Missouri in late December 1837.

After most Mormons had settled in Missouri, conflicts between them and other Missourians led to the defection of a number of prominent Mormons and the killing of apostle David Patten. By late 1838 these events had made Young the senior apostle. Missouri officials imprisoned Joseph Smith, and Young helped organize the Mormon exodus from Missouri to Illinois.

Young moved his family to Montrose, Iowa in 1839, and then, with most of the Twelve, left on a mission to Great Britain. The Twelve converted hundreds of people before their return to the Mormon settlement of Nauvoo, Illinois in April 1841.

In the spring of 1844 Smith announced his candidacy for the presidency of the United States. Young and others went to the northeastern United States to proselytize and campaign. While there they learned of Smith's assassination. In a special conference in Nauvoo on August 8, 1844 the members voted to accept Young and the Twelve as their leaders.

Continued internal and external conflict led the Mormons to abandon Nauvoo early in 1846, and Young led the exodus. After wintering on the Missouri, the Mormons moved to Utah. Young arrived in the Salt Lake Valley on July 24, 1847. He designated the site for Salt Lake City on July 28, then returned to Council Bluffs, Iowa in August 1847. In a conference at Council Bluffs in December 1847 the members elected him church president and prophet, seer, and revelator. Young returned to Utah in 1848 and remained there the rest of his life.

In presiding over the church, Young recognized no division between the secular and sacred. He directed the establishment of nearly 400 settlements in Utah, Idaho, Wyoming, Arizona, Nevada, Washington, and California. To preside over ecclesiastical and secular work in the settlements Young called bishops with two counselors to lead each congregation, called a ward. Young organized the wards in each county into units called stakes, presided over by a stake president, two counselors, and a twelve-man stake high council. People in the settlements carried out normal tasks such as apportioning land and constructing irrigation works.

Young also presided over the economic development of the territory. He called people on missions to mine gold, iron, lead, and coal. He supervised the establishment of a telegraph line, cooperated in building the transcontinental railroad, directed the construction of local railroads, and founded cooperative stores. In the 1870s he supervised the organization of communitarian United Orders.

Elected governor of the provisional State of Deseret in 1849, he was appointed governor and superintendent of Indian affairs of Utah Territory in 1850. He remained in the position until his removal in 1858. As governor he directed the resistance to an invasion by federal troops in 1857–1858.

Meetinghouses were constructed in the various settlements. To provide for sacred ordinances, Young began the construction of temples in Salt Lake City, St. George, Manti, and Logan, Utah and an endowment house in Salt Lake City. He dedicated the endowment house in 1855 and the St. George Temple in 1877. In the late 1860s Young reestablished the women's Relief Society, which Joseph Smith had inaugurated in Nauvoo. He also organized an auxiliary for young women called the Young Women's Mutual Improvement Association, and he approved a general SUNDAY SCHOOL organization.

He continued the practice of plural marriage, which Joseph Smith had instituted in Nauvoo. Young married at least twenty-three women in addition to his first two wives, Works and Angell. By fourteen of them he fathered forty-nine children.

Young promoted the organization of the Salt Lake Tabernacle Choir, encouraged painting and sculpture, and supervised the erection of the Salt Lake Theater.

His principal accomplishments include extensive and successful proselytizing activity, maintaining the integrity of the LDS Church after Joseph Smith's death, supervising the settlement of a large region of the American West, and promoting Christianity, economic development, and a spirituality among the people.

References and Further Reading

Arrington, Leonard J. *Brigham Young: American Moses*. New York: Knopf, 1985.

Black, Susan Easton, and Larry C. Porter, eds. *Lion of the Lord: Essays on the Life & Service of Brigham Young*. Salt Lake City, UT: Deseret Book, 1995.

Cornwall, Rebecca, and Richard F. Palmer, "The Religious and Family Background of Brigham Young." *BYU Studies* 18 (Spring 1978): 286–310.

Palmer, Richard F., and Karl D. Butler. *Brigham Young: The New York Years*. Provo, UT: Brigham Young University Press, 1982.

THOMAS G. ALEXANDER

YOUTH FOR CHRIST

This evangelistic organization targeting teenagers emerged during World War II, when young preachers like Torrey Johnson in Chicago and Jack Wyrtzen in New York began to hold youth rallies that featured upbeat music, testimonies from servicemen, and sermons tied to current events. By the end of the War

"Victory" rallies drew 20,000 to Madison Square Garden in New York and 70,000 to Soldier Field in Chicago, prompting favorable comment in the national press. BILLY GRAHAM was associated with Youth for Christ early in his career. Leaders sold the organization to adults as the solution to juvenile delinquency. They conveyed to teenagers that CONVERSION to Christ held the secret to a fun and fulfilling life. Like their peers in the NATIONAL ASSOCIATION OF EVANGELICALS, YFC leaders worked closely with a wide variety of churches and Christian businessmen in an attempt to escape the negative reputation and charge of separatism that lingered from their roots in FUNDAMENTALISM. The organization was international from the beginning, achieving a presence in 100 countries by the early twenty-first century.

In the 1950s YFC leaders experimented with high school BIBLE clubs, Christian films, games, skits, popular music styles, talent contests, and Bible quiz competitions. In the 1960s and 1970s they added ministries to juvenile offenders, urban youth, and teen mothers. YFC provided a training ground for prominent leaders of EVANGELICALISM such as Billy Graham and Bob Pierce who founded WORLD VISION, an international relief organization. YFC pioneered the use of popular culture styles to communicate a traditional evangelistic message and helped popularize such techniques in the larger evangelical movement.

References and Further Reading

Carpenter, Joel A. *Revive Us Again: The Reawakening of American Fundamentalism*. New York: Oxford University Press, 1997.

Hefley, James C. *God Goes to High School*. Waco, TX: Word Books, 1970.

Pahl, Jon. *Youth Ministry in Modern America*. Peabody, MA: Hendrickson Publishers, 2000.

THOMAS E. BERGLER

Z

ZIMBABWE

Zimbabwe is a landlocked country located north of SOUTH AFRICA, east of Zambia and Botswana, and west of Mozambique. San hunter-gatherers, who arrived from the North c. 8000 B.C., were absorbed by Bantu invaders after 500 A.D. The Shona (Bantu) word "Zimbabwe" means "houses of stone" and dates from the fifteenth- to sixteenth-century Munhumutapa kingdom. The Great Zimbabwe, an impressive collection of stone buildings, began to rise on a site in central Zimbabwe in the eleventh century after the gold-mining, cattle-ranching Bantu groups had begun to arrive from the north. Great Zimbabwe was a trading center, fortress, and shrine to the preeminent god Mwari. In the fifteenth century Great Zimbabwe's control over the region began to decline and centers of political and economic activity became more diverse.

Before the 1890 arrival of Cecil Rhodes's British South Africa Company (BSAC), the Shona and Ndebele, a Zulu subtribe that migrated from the south, ruled Zimbabwe. Portuguese traders and Catholic missionaries visited the area from Mozambique.

British rule began in 1890 and ended in 1980. The BSAC (1890–1927) defeated the Ndebele and put down a Shona-Ndebele rising (Chimurenga) in 1896. Rhodes detested African culture and stole African land and minerals. The British government ceded political control to Rhodes. Although the BSAC came for gold, not god, Protestant MISSIONS followed the Union Jack into "Rhodesia." Rhodes allowed white farmers and miners to rule while he aggrandized wealth.

The British termed the blessings and curses they brought to Africa "Western Civilization." This included capitalism, imperial rule, and the Christian faith. As the BSAC gained wealth, Rhodes allowed missions to supply Western "Christian" culture in schools, clinics, and churches. For these purposes he provided land grants to mission societies and stipends for missionary teachers and doctors. Christian culture meant not only religion, but also Western dress, marriage customs, English language, and deference to whites. Anglo-Americans christened virtually everything African as "heathen" and referred to almost everything Western, including capitalism, as Christian, as they attempted to form a little England in the heart of Africa. The BSAC, British government, and Protestant missions married acquisition of wealth to imperialism and faith.

The London Missionary Society (LMS) was the first Protestant mission in Ndebeleland. In 1859 ROBERT MOFFATT acquired land from Ndebele King Mzilikazi. Mzilikazi's son Lobengula gave the LMS a second site, although the LMS did not make a single convert in three decades. Land acquisition and friendship with kings were the LMS's achievements. In 1885 CHURCH OF ENGLAND Bishop George W. Knight-Bruce from South Africa visited Ndebeleland and gained King Lobengula's permission to establish a mission. In 1891 South Africa's DUTCH REFORMED CHURCH set up a mission at Morgenster, and British Methodists and the SALVATION ARMY arrived at Fort Salisbury in Mashonaland. In 1893 the AMERICAN BOARD OF COMMISSIONERS FOR FOREIGN MISSIONS opened a station at Mount Selinda. SEVENTH-DAY ADVENTISTS founded a station at Solusi in 1894. In 1898 Bishop J. C. Hartzell's American Methodist Episcopal Church opened Old Umtali Mission, and the BRETHREN IN CHRIST founded Matopo Mission.

In the late 1890s other Protestants scrambled into Rhodesia, including the South African General Mission; Church of Christ; Presbyterian Church of South Africa; Free Presbyterian Church of Scotland; Church of Sweden; Swedish Free Church Mission; Free Methodist Church; and South African Baptist Missionary Society. Jesuits had set up the first Catholic mission at Empandeni in 1885.

Historian C. J. M. Zvobgo argues that Christian missions in Mashonaland and Ndebeleland shared two understandings between 1859 and 1898. First, as a result of early London Missionary Society and Jesuit experiences, they believed that success depended on breaking Ndebele power in Rhodesia by force. Second, they were indebted to Rhodes for land on which to set up their stations. By 1925 the BSAC had given missions 325,730 acres. The missions purchased an additional 71,085 acres, much of it without the permission of African chiefs or people.

No mission succeeded with the rough white South African miners whose interest was material, not spiritual gain. Thus most missions readily accepted work among Africans, especially when BSAC land grants accompanied their cooperation. Few missionaries raised issues of land confiscation and denial of franchise to Africans with European or American mission boards. Few sought advice of Africans on church policy. Paternalistic notions held that Africans were incompetent in matters of church management. On the whole, deaths of missionaries were seen as "martyrdom" with no connection to land theft or denial of rights.

In 1923 white settler government replaced BSAC rule. In 1965 the settlers declared their independence from Britain to avoid majority African rule. African guerrillas fought a twelve-year war for independence to gain one-person-one-vote democracy. United Nations sanctions, support from a WORLD COUNCIL OF CHURCHES' (WCC) Program to Combat Racism, and the work of other international humanitarian agencies, as well as weapons from Communist states, helped bring majority rule under Robert Mugabe's government in 1980.

Protestants divided over the war. The Salvation Army, Irish Presbyterians, and South Africa's Reformed Church broke with the WCC over grants to "Marxist" insurgents. The Salvation Army, Zimbabwe's fourth largest church, had ninety-eight percent African members who supported independence. However, a 1978 killing of two of its missionary teachers turned its American branch against the WCC. After a brutal war against Nkomo's Ndebele, Mugabe sealed an alliance between Shona and Ndebele that held through the late 1990s turmoil over Mugabe's increasingly autocratic rule.

Zimbabwe's population of eleven million is 71 percent Shona, 16 percent Ndebele, 11 percent other African, and 2 percent Asian and white. The predominant religion is Christian, including African Christian sects. African religions persist, led by shamans who contact ancestors for advice and healing. Christianity has an African flavor in missionary sects and those founded by Africans.

See also Africa; Colonialism

References and Further Reading

Banana, Canaan, ed. *Turmoil & Tenacity: Zimbabwe, 1890–1990.* Harare: College Press, 1989.
Beach, D. N. *War & Politics in Zimbabwe, 1840–1900.* Gweru, Zimbabwe: Mambo, 1986.
Murdoch, Norman H. "The World Council of Churches & The Salvation Army, 1978–85." *Association of Third World Studies Conference Proceedings* (1996): 68–78.
Ranger, T. O. *Revolt in Southern Rhodesia, 1896–97.* Evanston, IL: Northwestern University Press, 1967.
Samkange, Stanlake. *Origins of Rhodesia.* London: Heinemann, 1968.
Zvobgo, C. J. M. *A History of Christian Missions in Zimbabwe, 1890–1939.* Gweru, Zimbabwe: Mambo, 1996.

NORMAN H. MURDOCH

ZINZENDORF, NIKOLAUS LUDWIG VON (1700–1760)

Count Nikolaus Ludwig von Zinzendorf (1700–1760) was a theologian and leader of the renewed MORAVIAN CHURCH (*Herrnhuter Brüdergemeine*) and one of the most original thinkers in eighteenth-century German Protestantism.

Background

Born in Dresden, Saxony, as a descendent of Austrian Protestant nobility, Zinzendorf was raised by his grandmother Henriette von Gersdorf on pietistic principles, and showed early on a lively interest in religious matters. In 1710 he entered the famous *Paedagogium* of August Hermann Francke (1663–1727) at HALLE, closely observing Francke's missionary and pedagogical projects. In 1716 he was sent to the university, the center of Lutheran ORTHODOXY, to study law. His grand tour (1719–1720) took him to the NETHERLANDS and FRANCE and brought him into close contact with other confessional groups, including Roman Catholicism, through a friendly acquaintance with Cardinal Louis de Noailles. Having entered a position at the Saxon Court, he purchased the Berthelsdorf estate in Upper Lusatia in 1722 and married Erdmuth Dorothea, countess of Reuss (1700–1756).

Herrnhut

Decisive for Zinzendorf's life and theological development was his founding of HERRNHUT in 1722, when Protestant refugees from Moravia sought shelter on his estate. The growth of Herrnhut into a vibrant

Pietist colony called for his leadership and gave his evangelistic impulse a specific focus. From 1727 on, when Zinzendorf quit his government post in order to devote himself fully to the Herrnhut community, his career became closely intertwined with the colony's development as an interdenominational renewal movement and mission church. Eager to maintain his ties to the Lutheran confession, Zinzendorf passed a theological examination in 1734 at Stralsund and then assumed the status of a Lutheran minister at Tübingen. Continuing conflicts with Lutheran orthodoxy led to his banishment from Saxony from 1736 to 1747. He spent the following years organizing Moravian communities throughout Europe, was ordained a Moravian bishop in 1737, and traveled to the West Indies (1739) and to Pennsylvania (1741–1743) in order to support the Moravian missionary effort and to evangelize among the Pennsylvania Germans. The newly built Herrnhaag settlement near Frankfurt, model for all subsequent Moravian settlement congregations, became the center of Zinzendorf's activities between 1743 to 1749, and saw the most exuberant but also most controversial period of his theology. He lived in London from 1750 to 1755 and spend his last years at Herrnhut. After the death of his wife Erdmuth Dorothea in 1756, he married Anna Nitschmann (1715–1760) in 1757, the eldress of the Moravian single sisters. In 1760 he died at Herrnhut.

Living at the dawn of the modern era, Zinzendorf developed his theology in critical response to Lutheran orthodoxy, ENLIGHTENMENT rationalism, and moralistic PIETISM. The core of Christian faith, according to Zinzendorf, is to know the wounded Christ in one's heart as Lord and Savior. This view combines the emphasis on intuitive and emotional spirituality ("heart-religion") with a christocentric focus on the atonement at the cross ("blood and wounds theology"). God can only be known through the crucified Christ, who is both the creator of human souls and their heavenly bridegroom. At the same time, Zinzendorf stresses Christ's full earthly humanity and suggests that his incarnation has sanctified all human states and experiences, including sexuality, insofar as marital relations reflect and anticipate the mystical union between Christ and the church. This nuptial imagery is complemented with allegorical references to the Trinity as "divine family" and to the Holy Spirit as "mother."

While it is often said that Zinzendorf was not a systematic theologian, his purposeful way of organizing the Moravian communities suggests very precise notions at least in some areas. His concept of the church, for example, distinguishes between the heavenly Communion of Saints, the historical denominations, and the possibility for true believers to come together in interdenominational fellowship. The Moravian community is intended as just such a fellowship, uniting within itself members of many different denominational backgrounds. Denominations, for Zinzendorf, are designed to lead people to God according to their specific insights. This understanding enables him to value the established churches for their particular traditions while maintaining a vision of Christian unity beyond denominational boundaries. A second example is the Moravian mission work, which illuminates Zinzendorf's eschatological emphasis on "first fruits" (cf. Revelations 14:10). Because Christ is Lord over the whole earth, the Moravians are called to go to the most remote and neglected places and sow the seeds of the gospel in preparation for his second coming. The goal is not to convert the masses, but only to make a beginning among those whom the Holy Spirit has prepared as "first fruits" for their people.

Zinzendorf's significance for the Protestant world goes far beyond his leadership among the Moravians. His pioneering efforts in Christian MISSIONS, ECUMENISM, and EDUCATION have long been recognized, and his contributions in other areas—for example, Trinitarian theology, liturgical AESTHETICS, and biblical interpretation—are attracting increasing attention. Zinzendorf had a direct influence on English cleric JOHN WESLEY's (1703–1791) religious development and paved the way for German theologian FRIEDRICH SCHLEIERMACHER's (1768–1834) concept of religious intuition. In addition, Zinzendorf has often been regarded as a stalwart defender of MARTIN LUTHER's (1483–1546) theology of the cross against the theological dogmatism and moralism of his time. Just how much his theology really represents Luther's position, however, remains a matter of scholarly debate.

See also Herrnhut; Moravian Church; Lutheranism

References and Further Reading

Primary Sources:

Zinzendorf, Nikolaus Ludwig von. *Hauptschriften* (plus *Ergänzungsbände* and *Materialien und Dokumente*). Multivolume reprint edition of Zinzendorf's works edited by Erich Beyreuther and Gerhard Meyer. Hildesheim, Germany: Olms, 1962ff.
———. *Nine Public Lectures on Important Subjects in Religion, Preached in Fetter Land Chapel in London in the Year 1746.* Translated and edited by George W. Forell. Iowa City: University of Iowa Press, 1973.

Secondary Sources:

Beyreuther, Erich. *Die große Zinzendorf Triologie.* Marburg, Germany: Francke, 1988.
Freeman, Arthur J. *An Ecumenical Theology of the Heart: The Theology of Count Nicholas Ludwig von Zinzendorf.* Bethlehem, PA: Moravian Church in America, 1998.

Meyer, Dietrich. *Bibliographisches Handbuch zur Zinzendorf-Forschung.* Düsseldorf: Blech, 1987.

Meyer, Henry H. *Child Nature and Nurture According to Nicolaus Ludwig von Zinzendorf.* New York: Abingdon, 1928.

Lewis, Arthur J. *Zinzendorf, the Ecumenical Pioneer: A Study in the Moravian Contribution to Christian Mission and Unity.* Philadelphia: Westminster Press, 1962.

Unitätsarchiv Herrnhut. *Graf ohne Grenzen: Leben und Werk von Nikolaus Ludwig Graf von Zinzendorf.* Herrnhut, Germany: Comeniusbuchhandlung, 2000.

Weinlick, John R. *Count Zinzendorf: The Story of His Life and Leadership in the Renewed Moravian Church.* New York: Abingdon Press, 1956.

PETER VOGT

ZION CHURCHES

See African Methodist Episcopal Zion Churches

ZÖLLNER, JOHANN FRIEDRICH (1753–1804)

German theologian. Born in Neudamm/Neumark on April 24, 1753, Zöllner studied theology and philosophy in Frankfurt/Oder. He lived first as an independent scholar, becoming connected with the baron Hans Ernst von Kottwitz, who was later the leader of the *Erweckungsbewegung* (revival movement) of Berlin. In 1779 Zöllner quickly began a prominent church career. First as pastor at the Charité in Berlin and the *Marienkirche,* he was appointed in 1788 as senior pastor (*Propst*) of the *Nikolaikirche* and *Oberkonsistorialrat* by King Frederick William II. His most important fields of work, engaged on behalf of the king with whom he had close contact, dealt with questions of reform of the public educational system and of the aims of education (*Ideen über Nationalerziehung,* 1804). Zöllner died in Berlin September 12, 1804.

Two influences determined Zöllner's thinking: the ENLIGHTENMENT and the religiousness of the freemasons. In 1779 Zöllner became a member of a freemasons lodge, and he later became a grand master of the freemason movement in Berlin. Zöllner considered himself a philosopher of Enlightenment, and as a pastor and writer he promoted IMMANUEL KANT's philosophy (*Über spekulative Philosophie,* 1789). He was criticized particularly by the theologian Johann Christoph Woellner (1732–1800), whose work *Religionsedikt* in 1788 was directed against the theology of the Enlightenment.

In addition to his theological, philosophical, and educational work, Zöllner published travel descriptions and popular writing on scientific topics. In Berlin he was a member of the Academy of Sciences (*Akademie der Wissenschaften*) and the society of nature-exploring friends (*Gesellschaft der naturforschenden Freunde*).

See also Education, Overview; Freemasonry

References and Further Reading

Primary Sources:

Massey, Charles Carleton, George Stuart Fullerton, and Emma Hardinge Britten. *Zöllner: an open letter to Professor George S. Fullerton of the University of Pennsylvania, member and secretary of the Seybert Commission for Investigating Modern Spiritualism.* 1887.

Zöllner, Johann Karl Friedrich, Charles Carleton Massey, and Milton Arlanden Bridges. *Transcendental physics: an account of experimental investigations from the scientific treatises of Johann Carl Friedrich Zöllner.* Boston: Colby & Rich, 1881.

Zöllner, Johann Karl Friedrich, and Charles Carleton Massey. *Transcendental physics: an account of experimental investigations from the science treatises of Johann Carl Friedrich Zöllner.* Pomeroy, WA: Health Research, 2000.

Secondary Sources:

Allgemeine Deutsche Biographie, vol. 45, 423–425. Leipzig: Duncker & Humblot, 1900.

Maser, Peter. *Hans Ernst von Kottwitz. Studien zur Erweckungsbewegung des frühen 19. Jahrhunderts in Schlesien und Berlin.* Göttingen, Germany: Vandenhoeck & Ruprecht, 1990.

Schmidt, Valentin Heinrich, and Daniel G. G. Mehring. *Neuestes gelehrtes Berlin.* vol. 2, 280–288. Berlin: 1795.

NORBERT FRIEDRICH

ZWINGLI, HULDRYCH (1484–1531)

Swiss theologian. When Zwingli arrived in Zurich in December of 1518, he was an Erasmian humanist. Soon thereafter he came to an evangelical understanding of the Christian message and became the reformer of Zurich. Although Zwingli's fully developed THEOLOGY included similarities with MARTIN LUTHER's theology, the two men differed on several important doctrines. Zurich was the cradle of Reformed Protestantism, and Zwingli's theology was its foundation. Zwingli's theology continued to influence the Reformed tradition throughout the sixteenth century and beyond.

Early Life

Zwingli was born January 1, 1484, into a well-to-do peasant family in Wildhaus, in the high Toggenburg valley, east of Zurich, Switzerland. He began his university studies at Vienna in 1498, but transferred to the University of Basel in 1502, where he received his bachelor and master of arts degrees in 1504 and 1506. Zwingli's very traditional university education was grounded in the *via antiqua*—the Aristotelian tradition of Thomas Aquinas and Duns Scotus.

During the next decade Zwingli became an accomplished humanist. After his ordination as a priest in

September 1506 he became pastor at Glarus, not far from Wildhaus, where he taught himself Greek, read widely in the classical and patristic authors, and corresponded with humanist friends. In 1516 Zwingli met the Dutch scholar Desiderius Erasmus (c. 1466–1536), and that same year he was appointed priest at the Benedictine Abbey at Einsiedeln in Schwyz, south of Zurich. There, he continued his humanistic studies, engaging in an intensive study of the Greek New Testament and learning Hebrew.

From Humanist to Reformer

The influence of Erasmus and biblical humanism was evident when Zwingli arrived in Zurich to assume his new responsibilities as common preacher (*Leutpriester*) at the Great Minster (*Grossmünster*). In his first sermon, on January 1, 1519, he began to preach consecutively through the Gospel of Matthew, and then through Acts and Paul's epistles to Timothy. In these sermons he focused on the moral purity of the church during the early years of Christianity. However, because he suffered a severe bout with the plague and because his opponents began to criticize his preaching, Zwingli's Erasmian optimism soon began to fade. During the year 1520 Zwingli moved beyond Erasmian humanism and came to a Pauline understanding of human nature and divine grace.

Zwingli claimed that his evangelical understanding of the Christian message began to develop in 1516, but it appears that the crucial process of change from an optimistic humanist to a realistic reformer did not actually begin until late in 1519. Although Zwingli viewed Luther as a fellow humanist in attacking indulgences, tithes, and invocation of the SAINTS, he was unaware of Luther's new distinctive doctrines, such as JUSTIFICATION by faith, until late 1520. Zwingli's new evangelical theology ensued from his own study of the Gospel of John and the writings of Paul and Augustine. There is no evidence that Luther was a profound influence.

When several people broke the Lenten fast by eating sausage during the Lenten season of 1522, Zwingli made his first step toward becoming a reformer. Zwingli did not participate, but he did preach a sermon defending those who broke the fast. He proclaimed that ecclesiastical rules on fasting cannot overrule Christian freedom and that according to Scripture, Christians are free to fast or to eat. Then, in July 1522 Zwingli and ten other priests petitioned the bishop of Constance to abolish CELIBACY, asserting that the ecclesiastical rules on celibacy were fallaciously based only on ecclesiastical authority and had no basis in Scripture. Zwingli himself had already publicly married Anna Reinhard. In August Zwingli publicly rejected the authority of the hierarchy of the church over matters of DOCTRINE and church order, and he condemned the bishop for opposing reform. In September Erasmus wrote a letter to Zwingli, severely criticizing him for his attack on the authority of the church hierarchy.

In each of his attacks on ecclesiastical regulations Zwingli appealed to biblical authority; however, he did not fully explain his position on Scripture until September 1522 when he published *On the Clarity and Certainty of the Word of God,* where he affirms the exclusive authority of Scripture, which became a hallmark of Protestantism. Although he does not deny the usefulness of church fathers and councils, he clearly states that they cannot add to the authority of Scripture, but only confirm it. The BIBLE is God's word and can be understood correctly only when the believer is taught by God through the Spirit.

Late in 1522 Zwingli was accused of HERESY and treason by the Diet of the Swiss Confederation. Consequently, the Zurich council convened the First Zurich Disputation on January 29, 1523, where Zwingli summarized his theology in the *Sixty-seven Articles,* or conclusions, which he had prepared for the disputation. The council absolved Zwingli of the charge of heresy and gave him permission to continue his PREACHING from the Bible.

Zwingli the Reformer

In mid-July 1523, Zwingli published his *Exposition and Basis of the Conclusions,* which expanded on and defended his sixty-seven articles. This comprehensive statement of his reformed theology demonstrates that Zwingli was no longer an Erasmian. He clearly states that the Scripture, inspired by God, stands on its own authority and that the individual needs the Holy Spirit to interpret it. He asserts that one finds SALVATION through faith in Christ, by divine grace. He sees the Eucharist (see LORD'S SUPPER) as a memorial of Christ, a view that became a distinctive doctrine within Reformed Protestantism. In another distinctive doctrine of the Reformed tradition, Zwingli declares that the moral law is a revelation of God's will and has never been abrogated. Finally, asserting that the church exists both as a spiritual body of all the faithful and as local congregations, he contends that the civil government is sovereign over the local Christian community and that it includes everyone, even infants. This is Zwingli's doctrine of the "single sphere" that became a distinctive feature of later ZWINGLIANISM.

Two weeks later Zwingli published *On Divine and Human Righteousness* to demonstrate that his views were neither politically nor socially subversive and to justify the authority of the Christian magistracy.

Zwingli asserted that divine righteousness, as expressed by the love commandment, concerns only the inner person, because humans are incapable of fully loving their neighbors as themselves. For that reason God gave other commandments, the moral law, which is expressed in the laws of the civil magistracy. This is human righteousness, a "poor weak righteousness," which concerns only the outer person. Everyone is obliged to obey these commandments and laws of the Christian government. Nonetheless, Zwingli urged the government to bring its laws (human righteousness) into harmony with the law of God (divine righteousness) as much as possible.

In late October of 1523, because many of the LAITY were dissatisfied with the pace of reform, the council convened a Second Disputation to meet to discuss images in the churches and the essence of the Mass. The council decided to keep images in the churches and to maintain the Mass for a period of time, until it was clear what should be done. Some of Zwingli's more radical followers now began to deny that the government had any authority over the church; images should be removed and the Mass abolished immediately. Zwingli, however, true to his doctrine of the single sphere, asserted that the civil magistrate is responsible for the implementation of reform measures. Finally, in June 1524, the council ordered the removal and destruction of pictures and images from the churches, although the reformed Lord's Supper did not replace the Mass until Easter week 1525.

In March 1525 Zwingli published *A Commentary on the True and False Religion,* a crucial work in which he contends that the true religion—as opposed to the false religion of the church of Rome—is derived from Scripture. Zwingli rejects monastic vows, purgatory, and the invocation of the saints, and he denounces the pope as the ANTICHRIST. Moreover, he accepts only BAPTISM and the Eucharist as sacraments. Furthermore, he clearly states his evangelical doctrine of salvation by faith through God's grace and specifically rejects the semi-Pelagianism of Roman Catholicism. Finally, Zwingli assures the reader that the true religion does not promote civil disorder, but rather supports a godly ruler. In short, this treatise touches on all of the basic points that became an enduring part of Reformed doctrine.

During the year 1525 Zurich became a reformed city and canton, when the council secularized the monasteries and created a new marriage court to replace the bishop's court in Constance. Zwingli, now the acknowledged reformer of Zurich, defended the right of the civil government to implement the reform at every step.

The radicals, however, completely rejected the doctrine of the single sphere when they asserted that the Bible did not support infant baptism and expressed their ideal of a congregation of committed Christians, separate from the state church and free of governmental control. Baptism, they said, symbolizes the faith and commitment of adults. Early in 1525 they challenged Zwingli's status as a reformer by baptizing each other as adults and forming their own self-disciplining congregation. In May 1525 Zwingli denounced ANABAPTISM and defended his own understanding of baptism in *On Baptism, Anabaptism, and Infant Baptism.* He declares that baptism is a sign or a symbol that the infant belongs to God; it is a sacrament of the new COVENANT, which has replaced circumcision, the sacrament of the old covenant. Again, in 1527, he rebutted the Anabaptist teachings' point by point, in his *Refutation of the Tricks of the Anabaptists.* Clarifying his doctrine of the covenant, he asserts that the new covenant with Christians is simply the renewal of the old covenant that God made with Abraham. Throughout his writings against the Anabaptists, Zwingli stresses the authority of the Christian government over the Christian community. Zwingli conceived of his doctrine of the covenant in conjunction with HEINRICH BULLINGER (1509–1575), who succeed Zwingli as leader of the Zurich church. Bullinger further developed the doctrine that became an integral part of the theology of Reformed Protestantism.

In the midst of his confrontation with the Anabaptists, Zwingli also became involved in a controversy with Luther over the Eucharist. Zwingli held a symbolic view of the Eucharist: the bread and the wine signify the body and blood of Christ, but Christ is not physically present in these elements. Nor is the Eucharist itself a means of grace; rather, it is a sign pointing to salvation. In February 1526 Zwingli specifically attacked Luther's teaching of the real presence in his *Clear Explanation of the Supper of Christ.* He also explained that Christians celebrate the Lord's Supper as a communal meal in memory and thanksgiving, much as the Jews observed the Passover Feast in the old covenant. This publication resulted in a bitter controversy, waged in print, between Zwingli and Luther concerning the proper interpretation of the Eucharist. Early in October 1529 the two men met in person, for the first and only time, at the MARBURG COLLOQUY, to discuss the theological issues of the day. Although they were able to come to an agreement on fourteen doctrines, Zwingli and Luther could not resolve their differences on the Eucharist. This event marks the genesis of the Reformed tradition within Protestantism. It was the initial division of Protestantism into confessional parties.

The Final Years

After Marburg, Zwingli wrote three important treatises: *Account of the Faith* (July 1530); *On the Providence of God* (August 1530); and *Exposition of the Christian Faith* (July 1531). All of these works are intensely anti-Lutheran, particularly in their treatment of the Eucharist. Zwingli also unequivocally disagreed with Luther on the matter of gospel and law. Zwingli did not oppose gospel and law, as Luther did; nor did Zwingli believe that the moral law has been abrogated for Christians. Rather, he asserted that the moral law is the revelation of the will of God for the Christian. Zwingli included the law within the gospel; he tied faith and works together and taught that the law continues to inform the Christian of the duty to live according to God's will. The Christian, justified by faith, must evidence faith through the new works of faith. Zwingli's close connection between gospel and law informed Reformed Protestantism well into the seventeenth century.

In the treatise on providence, Zwingli dealt with PREDESTINATION, asserting that only the elect will come to Christ through faith. Faith is a sign of ELECTION; without election faith is impossible. Because children of Christians are in the covenant, they must be seen as elect persons until they evidence lack of faith. Moreover, according to Zwingli, children of believing parents who die as children are of the elect. Zwingli even included virtuous pagans—such as Socrates—among the elect because God is sovereign and his election is free. When discussing predestination Zwingli always stressed election over reprobation. He did not develop a doctrine of "double predestination"; he spoke only of the decree of election to salvation. This moderate view of single predestination was one of the doctrines that later distinguished Zwinglianism from CALVINISM within Reformed Protestantism.

Political tensions were high within the Swiss Confederation in June of 1529 when war between the Catholic and Reformed states was narrowly avoided. By that time several other Swiss states, including Bern and Basel, had joined Zurich in the Reformed faith. However, when the Catholic Swiss states did declare war on Zurich on October 9, 1531, none of the Reformed states came to Zurich's aid. The Catholic forces attacked at Kappel, south of Zurich, on October 11, and in less than an hour the Reformed forces were defeated. Five hundred Zurichers were killed, including Zwingli, himself a combatant.

Even though Zwingli died, Zwinglianism continued to thrive under the leadership of Bullinger. As Zwingli's successor at Zurich, Bullinger fostered and cultivated the Zwinglian doctrines of the single sphere, the covenant, the Eucharist, the moral law, and predestination.

References and Further Reading

Primary Sources:

Egli, Emil, and Georg Finsler. "Huldreich Zwinglis sämtliche Werke." In *Corpus Reformatorum.* Berlin: Schwetschke, 1905–.

Furcha, E. J., and H. Wayne Pipkin, translator. *Selected Writings of Huldrych Zwingli.* 2 vols. Allison Park, PA: Pickwick Publications, 1984.

Jackson, Samuel Macauley, ed. *The Latin Works and the Correspondence of Huldreich Zwingli.* 3 vols. New York: Putnam, 1912–1929.

Secondary Sources:

Gäbler, Ulrich. *Huldrych Zwingli: Eine Einführung in sein Leben und sein Werk.* Munich: C. H. Beck, 1983; translated by Ruth C. L. Gritsch as *Huldrych Zwingli: His Life and Work.* Philadelphia: Fortress Press, 1986.

Locher, Gottfried W. *Huldrych Zwingli in neuer Sicht.* Zurich: Zwingli Verlag, 1969; translated by Milton Aylor and Stuart Casson as *Zwingli's Thought: New Perspectives.* Leiden, Netherlands: E. J. Brill, 1981.

Potter, G. R. *Zwingli.* Cambridge, UK: Cambridge University Press, 1976.

Stevens, W. P. *The Theology of Huldrych Zwingli.* Oxford, UK: Clarendon Press, 1986.

Walton, Robert C. *Zwingli's Theocracy.* Toronto: Toronto University Press, 1967.

Wandel, Lee Palmer. *Always Among Us: Images of the Poor in Zwingli's Zurich.* Cambridge, UK: Cambridge University Press, 1990.

J. WAYNE BAKER

ZWINGLIANISM

Reformed Protestantism began with Zwinglianism, named after the Swiss theologian HULDRYCH ZWINGLI (1484–1531). Nevertheless, Zwingli's successor HEINRICH BULLINGER was equally responsible for the development of Zwinglian THEOLOGY. Zwinglianism spread from Zurich to other Swiss states and to most areas in Europe, but it was particularly influential in ENGLAND and the NETHERLANDS. The Zwinglian doctrines on the COVENANT, the Eucharist (or LORD'S SUPPER), and the moral law became part of the established theology of Reformed Protestantism; however, by the early seventeenth century, the Zwinglian positions on PREDESTINATION and the relationship of the church to the state were, for the most part, overshadowed by orthodox CALVINISM.

The Formation and Spread of Zwinglianism

The death of Zwingli and the defeat of Zurich in the battle of Kappel in 1531 were severe setbacks for Reformed Protestantism. However, Zwinglianism entered a second phase when Bullinger was chosen to replace Zwingli as the leader of the Zurich church. Bullinger's great influence in the spread of Zwinglianism beyond the Swiss Confederation was attributed to his voluminous correspondence (more than 12,000 extant letters) and his prodigious publications (119 separate works in German and Latin). His Second HELVETIC CONFESSION—published in Latin in 1566 and translated into German, French, English, Dutch, Italian, Polish, and Hungarian—is a manifestation of his widespread importance. However, Bullinger's most crucial work for the spread of Zwinglianism was his *Decades,* a collection of fifty didactic sermons arranged topically into five groups of ten sermons. First published in Latin from 1549 to 1551, the *Decades* went through six additional editions in Latin by the end of the century, including one published in London in 1587. Moreover, the *Decades* was published in four German, three French, three English, and ten Dutch editions. Many of Bullinger's other works were also translated into French, Dutch, and English.

In these works, Bullinger clarified the theology of Zwinglianism. One of his first endeavors as leader of the Zurich church was to defend Zwingli's orthodoxy, which was being challenged by both Catholics and Lutherans. Against them, Bullinger declared that Zwingli died as a MARTYR and a prophet, not as a heretic; military defeat did not imply false DOCTRINE. Throughout his long tenure as leader of the Zurich church, Bullinger maintained that he was continuing the work of Zwingli, but, in reality, Bullinger established his own interpretation of Zwingli. Therefore, the term Zwinglianism encompasses the thought of both Bullinger and Zwingli.

Distinctive Doctrines of Zwinglianism

Five distinctive Reformed doctrines emerged from the theology of Bullinger and Zwingli. First and foremost, the concept of the covenant became a key doctrine in Reformed Protestantism. Zwingli used the doctrine of the covenant in his writings against ANABAPTISM, but he did not develop it as thoroughly as Bullinger did. Bullinger made the covenant a pervasive doctrine in his theology; he was the father of Reformed COVENANT theology. Bullinger maintained that there is only one covenant in human history, which was first made with Adam, then renewed throughout Old Testament times, and, finally, renewed and fulfilled by Christ. This is a mutual, bilateral covenant, in which God promises to be all-sufficient. The covenant conditions for humans are faith and love of one's neighbor. For Bullinger the entire Scripture is the record of the covenant.

A carefully stated doctrine of single predestination was the second distinctive teaching of Zwinglianism. Both Zwingli and Bullinger affirmed God's ELECTION of those who will have faith, although neither of them developed a doctrine of reprobation. Bullinger taught that the offer of the gospel is universal and that those who reject God's grace do so willingly and freely. Those who have faith are the elect; they are saved by God's free grace. For Bullinger election means inclusion in the people of God, in the covenant, but it does not threaten exclusion. Bullinger never acceded to JOHN CALVIN's doctrine of "double predestination," which became the generally accepted point of view in Reformed Protestantism by the early seventeenth century.

The third distinctive doctrine of Zwinglianism was its doctrine of the Eucharist. Zwingli and Bullinger viewed the Lord's Supper as a remembrance of the sacrificed body and blood of Christ. They taught that both the Eucharist and Baptism as sacraments are visible signs of God's invisible grace and reminders to God's people of their responsibilities to fulfill the covenant conditions. BAPTISM enrolls the infant into the covenant and obligates the individual to keep the conditions of the covenant, just as circumcision did in the Old Testament. The Eucharist is a spiritual, sacramental eating, through faith, in memory of the single sacrifice of Christ, reminding the individual of the responsibility of living a pious life and loving one's neighbor. Bullinger and Calvin were initially at odds on the Eucharist, but they were eventually able to forge an agreement in the Zurich Consensus (*Consensus Tigurinus*) of 1549. There, they concurred that the Lord's Supper is not simply a simile for the spiritual meal; rather, the sacrament functions as the external sealing of an inner, invisible work. Without admitting that he had done so, Bullinger thus relinquished Zwingli's position because Zwingli never would have agreed to such a connection between the external and the internal.

The Zwinglian affirmation of the continuing importance of the moral law in the life of the Christian was its fourth distinctive doctrine. Bullinger agreed with Zwingli's teaching that the moral law is God's will for the Christian, but Bullinger made a more direct connection between the moral law and the conditions of the covenant. The moral law, as stated in the Decalogue, or Ten Commandments, is a paraphrase of those conditions; the Love Commandment is a summary of the Decalogue and thus a concise statement of the covenant conditions of faith and love of one's neighbor. Therefore, the moral law continues to play an active role in the life of a Christian. This Zwinglian emphasis on the continuing importance of the moral law became a fundamental feature of Calvin's theology and within Reformed Protestantism generally.

Finally, Bullinger built on Zwingli's doctrine of the single sphere. There is a single Christian community—the church and the civil community are coterminous. At baptism an individual becomes a member of the covenanted community, which is ruled by the civil magistracy. The pastors, like the Old Testament prophets, make the conditions of the covenant (God's will) known to the people. Similarly, the rulers, like the Old Testament kings, enforce the conditions of the covenant. Calvin, however, held to the two kingdoms theory, distinguishing between the civil and ecclesiastical jurisdictions and maintaining that CHURCH DISCIPLINE must be put in the hands of a CONSISTORY made up of pastors and elders.

The breach between Bullinger and Calvin over predestination and the nature of the Christian community ensured a rift over these issues between Zwinglianism and Calvinism throughout the sixteenth century.

The Struggle over Discipline

By the middle of the sixteenth century, the differences between the Zwinglians and the Calvinists over the nature of the Christian community began to become apparent. In 1553 the Genevan city council confronted Calvin over the role of the Consistory, insisting that only the council had the right to excommunicate and rejecting the claims of the Consistory to that right. Calvin sought Bullinger's assistance, and, despite his aversion to an independent ecclesiastical court, Bullinger came to Calvin's aid by convincing the Zurich city council to give support to Calvin. In their letter to the Genevan authorities, the Zurich magistrates judged that, given the circumstances in Geneva, Calvin's form of church discipline was not utterly improper.

The issue of church discipline soon erupted again, in the Vaud, which had been conquered by Bern in 1536. In 1558 THEODORE BEZA attempted to establish an autonomous Calvinist Consistory at Lausanne, but the Bernese magistrates, who embraced the Zwinglian doctrine of the single sphere, would not allow a discipline separate from governmental control. Consequently, Beza left Lausanne and joined Calvin in Geneva. After Calvin's death Beza remained committed to the idea of an independent church discipline in the hands of a Consistory.

One particularly important struggle over discipline involved both Bullinger and Beza. In 1563 Friedrich III, elector of the Palatinate, aligned his church with Zwinglianism with a Zwinglian type of church discipline. The Calvinists, however, agitated for a church court with independent powers of discipline, and in 1568 a public debate over the issue took place. The Calvinists were victorious when a new system of discipline, including a church court, was introduced in 1570.

During the controversy THOMAS ERASTUS (Lüber) was the leading defender of the Zwinglian doctrine of the single sphere. Erastus prepared a treatise attacking the Genevan two kingdoms theory and sent a copy both to Bullinger and to Beza. In reply, Beza defended the Calvinist two kingdoms theory. Although Bullinger fully supported Erastus, in the interest of peace he persuaded both Beza and Erastus not to publish their treatises. Nonetheless, in 1589, six years after Erastus's death, his treatise was published in London, and it continued to influence Reformed Protestantism, especially in England.

Zwinglianism in England

Zwinglianism had an early and continuing impact in England. In the early 1530s, during the reign of HENRY VIII, WILLIAM TYNDALE was among the first to be influenced by Zwingli's teaching on the Eucharist and by Bullinger's doctrine of the covenant. In 1541 MILES COVERDALE translated two of Bullinger's writings, *The old fayth* and *The Christen state of Matrimonye*, into English.

John Hooper, bishop of Gloucester and Worcester under Edward VI, spent two years in Zurich absorbing the Zwinglian doctrines of the single sphere, the covenant, and the Eucharist. Hooper's Zwinglian doctrine of the Eucharist is reflected in the *Second Book of Common Prayer* (1552). Several prominent English churchmen, including JOHN JEWEL, bishop of Salisbury under ELIZABETH I, had sought refuge in Zurich during the reign of Catholic Queen Mary. Moreover, Elizabeth's second archbishop of Canterbury, Edmund Grindal, was converted to Reformed Protestantism by the writings of Bullinger.

Hundreds of letters were exchanged between Bullinger and the leaders of the Elizabethan church, and a total of forty English editions involving twenty of Bullinger's works were published between 1538 and 1587. During the 1570s and 1580s the English version of his *Decades* (three editions: 1577, 1584, and 1587) became required reading for the theological education of many English ministers.

By the 1590s the Zwinglian view of the single sphere was well known in England, but the competing Genevan two kingdoms theory—expressed by the Presbyterians—was also a powerful factor in England by the end of the century. JOHN WHITGIFT was the principal apologist for English Erastianism against PRESBYTERIANISM. Hundreds of times in his writings, he invoked the words of Zwingli, Bullinger, and other Zwinglians to buttress his own arguments.

Whitgift was the patron of RICHARD HOOKER, whose *Laws of Ecclesiastical Polity* also show evidence of the influence of Zwinglianism. The Erastians in the

Long Parliament and the Westminster Assembly during the 1640s were similarly influenced by Zurich. Finally, THOMAS HOBBES's *Leviathan* shows that the sixteenth-century Erastians were his forebears as well, although he departs from the earlier Erastians when he states that religious truth is whatever the civil sovereign determines it to be.

Zwinglianism in the Netherlands

Zwinglianism had a profound influence in the Netherlands. Bullinger's *Decades* first appeared in Dutch in 1563 and soon became one of the most widely read devotional books in the Netherlands. The *Decades* was also used by preachers in the DUTCH REFORMED CHURCH and was even read from the pulpit along with biblical passages. Furthermore, beginning in the early seventeenth century, the chaplains on the ships of the Dutch East India Company were required to read from Bullinger's *Decades,* thus making it a basic source for Christian education in the Dutch colonies.

However, sixteenth-century Dutch thinkers—forerunners of the REMONSTRANTS, who taught a conditional covenant in tandem with either a doctrine of single predestination or outright universalism—also appealed to the *Decades.* Early in the seventeenth century, the Remonstrants declared that Bullinger was in complete agreement with them and that he disagreed with Calvin's doctrine of double predestination. However, the Counter-Remonstrants disagreed, claiming that Bullinger's doctrine of predestination was in complete accord with Calvin's doctrine. In 1618 Johann Jacob Breitinger, the leader of the Zurich church, addressed the Synod of Dort, arguing that Bullinger agreed fully with Calvin on predestination. Although Bullinger himself would not have agreed with either side at Dort, his name was nonetheless sullied by the Remonstrants and his influence in the Netherlands dwindled. Of the forty-four different editions of Bullinger's works published in the Netherlands, only seven were published after Dort—one in 1619, four in 1621 and 1622, one in 1645, and one in 1665.

The Remonstrants and Calvinists also disagreed on the relationship of the church with the government. The Calvinists insisted on an independent church discipline by a Consistory to ensure that only true Christians would partake of the Lord's Supper. The Remonstrants desired a comprehensive church, under the authority of a Christian government, with the Eucharist open to all who wished to participate. They thus followed the Zwinglian model, in keeping with the thirty-sixth article of the BELGIC CONFESSION, which gave the magistrate authority over the church. As a consequence of the Calvinists' triumph at Dort, Calvinism became the official religion and was favored politically and economically by the government. Nonetheless, the civil authorities, who argued that the Reformed church now existed under a Christian government, continued to exercise authority over the church in the Netherlands.

Conclusion

The Zwinglian doctrines on the Lord's Supper and the moral law endured as characteristic doctrines in all Reformed churches. The Zwinglian doctrine of the covenant also persisted in Reformed theology, as evidenced in the WESTMINSTER CONFESSION of Faith (1647), Scottish covenant theology, and the covenant thought of JOHANNES COCCEJUS. Moreover, the new federal political theory of JOHANNES ALTHUSIUS was founded partially on Zwinglian covenant theology. Even the Zwinglian moderate view of predestination endured as a Reformed alternative to orthodox Calvinism in the thought of such men as Moise Amyraut. However, the Zwinglian doctrine of the single sphere was replaced in the Reformed tradition by the two kingdoms theory of Presbyterianism and CONGREGATIONALISM.

References and Further Reading

Baker, J. Wayne. *Heinrich Bullinger and the Covenant: The Other Reformed Tradition.* Athens: Ohio University Press, 1980.

———. "Faces of Federalism: From Bullinger to Jefferson." *Publius: The Journal of Federalism* 30 no. 4 (2000): 25–41.

———. "Erastianism in England: The Zurich Connection." In *Die Zürcher Reformation: Ausstrahlungen und Rückwirkungen* (The Zurich Reformation: Influences and Consequences), 327–349. Bern: Peter Lang, 2001.

Duke, Alistair. *Reformation and Revolt in the Low Countries.* London: The Hambledon Press, 1990.

Gäbler, Ulrich, and Erland Herkenrath. *Heinrich Bullinger, 1504–1575: Gesammelte Aufsätze zum 400 Todestag* (Heinrich Bullinger, 1504–1575: Collected Essays for the 400th Anniversary of His Death). vol. 2. Zürich: Theologischer Verlag, 1975.

Hollweg, Walter. *Heinrich Bullingers Hausbuch* (Heinrich Bullinger's Housebook). Neukirchen, Germany: Verlag der Buchhandlung des Erziehungsvereins, 1956.

Locher, Gottfried W. *Die Zwinglishe Reformation im Rahmen der europäischen Kirchengeschichte* (The Zwinglian Reformation within the Framework of European Church History). Göttingen, Germany: Vandenhoeck & Ruprecht, 1979.

McCoy, Charles, and J. Wayne Baker. *Fountainhead of Federalism: Heinrich Bullinger and the Covenantal Tradition.* Louisville, KY: Westminster/John Knox Press, 1991.

J. WAYNE BAKER

APPENDIX

Statistics of Global Protestantism in a Variety of Contexts

Table 1. Worldwide adherents of all religions by six continental areas, mid-2000.

Table 2. Religious adherents in the United States of America, AD 1900–2000.

Table 3. Protestant-affiliated church members in the world's 238 countries and six continents, in the context of the five other major Christian traditions.

Table 4. Organized Protestantism and its core global membership ranked by its 27 ecclesiastico-cultural major traditions or families, AD 1970–2025.

Table 5. Statistics describing each of the 45 ministries of evangelism.

Sources: All data in the statistical tables are courtesy of David B. Barrett and Todd M. Johnson, Center for World Evangelization Research and Center for the Study of Global Christianity, Richmond, Virginia. Tables 1 and 2 are reprinted from the *Encyclopedia Britannica Book of the Year 2003*, with permission. All data in Table 3 may be seen in wider and fuller contexts and formats in D. B. Barrett, G. T. Kurian, and T. M. Johnson, *World Christian Encyclopedia: A Comparative Survey of Churches and Religions in the Modern World*, 2d ed. New York: Oxford University Press, 2001; and *World Christian Trends, AD 30–AD 2200: Interpreting the Annual Christian Megacensus*. Pasadena, CA: William Carey Library, 2001.

Definition of "Protestants": As explained in this Encyclopedia's article "Statistics," there are two usages of the term. (1) The more common usage accepted by most observers restricts the term "Protestants" to those denominations and confessions using the term to describe themselves. In the aforementioned article we describe them by the term "Core Protestants." (2) A less common but still widespread usage includes Anglicans, Independents, and Marginal Christians as Protestants although these three reject the term; for clarity, we describe all four as making up "Wider Protestants." The four tables in this Appendix use only this first usage of "Protestants" and for rapid access all their statistical lines and columns are given here in boldface type. Readers wanting totals of "Wider Protestants" can readily obtain them by adding all four categories (columns 3, 4, 5, and 6 in Table 3).

Table 1. Worldwide adherents of all religions by six continental areas, mid-2000

	Africa	Asia	Europe	Latin America	Northern America	Oceania	World	%	Number of Countries
Christians	360,232,000	312,849,000	559,643,000	481,102,000	260,624,000	25,110,000	1,999,560,000	33.0	238
Affiliated Christians	335,116,000	307,288,000	536,832,000	475,659,000	212,167,000	21,375,000	1,888,437,000	31.2	238
Roman Catholics	120,386,000	110,480,000	285,978,000	461,220,000	71,035,000	8,228,000	1,057,327,000	17.5	235
Protestants	**89,001,000**	**49,967,000**	**77,529,000**	**48,132,000**	**69,978,000**	**7,392,000**	**341,999,000**	**5.6**	**233**
Orthodox	35,304,000	14,113,000	158,105,000	558,000	6,342,000	706,000	215,128,000	3.6	135
Anglicans	42,542,000	727,000	26,637,000	1,090,000	3,244,000	5,409,000	79,649,000	1.3	166
Other Christians	86,268,000	157,218,000	29,288,000	46,301,000	90,769,000	1,966,000	411,810,000	6.8	223
Unaffiliated Christians	25,116,000	5,561,000	22,811,000	5,443,000	48,458,000	3,735,000	111,124,000	1.8	236
Non-Christians	424,213,000	3,369,701,000	169,244,000	38,036,000	49,007,000	5,283,000	4,055,484,000	67.0	238
Atheists	420,000	121,945,000	22,922,000	2,757,000	1,680,000	365,000	150,089,000	2.5	161
Baha'is	1,733,000	3,475,000	130,000	873,000	786,000	110,000	7,107,000	0.1	218
Buddhists	134,000	354,651,000	1,547,000	647,000	2,701,000	301,000	359,981,000	5.9	126
Chinese folk religionists	32,000	383,408,000	255,000	194,000	854,000	64,000	384,807,000	6.4	89
Confucianists	0	6,264,000	11,000	0	0	24,000	6,299,000	0.1	15
Ethnic religionists	96,805,000	128,298,000	1,263,000	1,288,000	444,000	268,000	228,366,000	3.8	142
Hindus	2,351,000	805,120,000	1,416,000	768,000	1,327,000	355,000	811,337,000	13.4	114
Jains	66,000	4,145,000	0	0	7,000	0	4,218,000	0.1	10
Jews	214,000	4,429,000	2,527,000	1,142,000	6,024,000	97,000	14,433,000	0.2	134
Mandeans	0	39,000	0	0	0	0	39,000	0.0	2
Muslims	317,374,000	832,879,000	31,566,000	1,672,000	4,450,000	301,000	1,188,242,000	19.6	204
New-Religionists	28,000	100,639,000	158,000	623,000	842,000	66,000	102,356,000	1.7	60
Shintoists	0	2,699,000	0	7,000	56,000	0	2,762,000	0.0	8
Sikhs	53,000	22,421,000	239,000	0	528,000	18,000	23,259,000	0.4	34
Spiritists	3,000	2,000	133,000	12,039,000	151,000	7,000	12,335,000	0.2	55
Zoroastrians	1,000	2,463,000	1,000	0	78,000	1,000	2,544,000	0.0	24
Other religionists	5,092,000	611,262,000	107,076,000	16,026,000	29,079,000	3,306,000	771,841,000	12.7	76
Nonreligious	5,024,000	608,594,000	106,841,000	15,928,000	28,473,000	3,298,000	768,158,000	12.7	236
Total population	**784,445,000**	**3,682,550,000**	**728,887,000**	**519,138,000**	**309,631,000**	**30,393,000**	**6,055,044,000**	**100.0**	**238**

Continents. These follow current UN demographic terminology, which now divides the world into the six major areas shown above. See United Nations, *World Population Prospects: The 1998 Revision* (New York: UN, 1999), with populations of all continents, regions, and countries covering the period 1950–2050. Note that "Asia" now includes the former Soviet Central Asian states and "Europe" now includes all of Russia extending eastward to Vladivostok, the Sea of Japan, and the Bering Strait.

Countries. The last column enumerates sovereign and nonsovereign countries in which each religion or religious grouping has a numerically significant and organized following.

Adherents. As defined in the 1948 Universal Declaration of Human Rights, a person's religion is what he or she says it is. Totals are enumerated for each of the world's 238 countries following the methodology of the *World Christian Encyclopedia,* 2nd ed. (2001), using recent censuses, polls, literature, and other data.

Christians. Followers of Jesus Christ affiliated with churches (church members, including children: 1,888,437,000) plus persons professing in censuses or polls to be Christians though not so affiliated. Figures for the subgroups of Christians do not add up to the totals in the first line because some Christians adhere to more than one denomination.

Other Christians. This term in the table denotes Catholics (non-Roman), marginal Protestants, independents, postdenominationalists, crypto-Christians, and adherents of African, Asian, Black, and Latin American indigenous churches.

Atheists. Persons professing atheism, skepticism, disbelief, or irreligion, including the antireligious (opposed to all religion).

Buddhists. 56% Mahayana, 38% Theravada (Hinayana), 6% Tantrayana (Lamaism).

Chinese folk-religionists. Followers of traditional Chinese religion (local deities, ancestor veneration, Confucian ethics, Taoism, universism, divination, and some Buddhist elements).

Confucianists. Non-Chinese followers of Confucius and Confucianism, mostly Koreans in Korea.

Ethnic religionists. Followers of local, tribal, animistic, or shamanistic religions.

Hindus. 70% Vaishnavites, 25% Shaivites, 2% neo-Hindus and reform Hindus.

Jews. Adherents of Judaism. For detailed data on "core" Jewish population, see the annual "World Jewish Populations" article in the American Jewish Committee's *American Jewish Year Book.*

Muslims. 83% Sunnites, 16% Shi'ites, 1% other schools. Until 1990 the Muslims in the former U.S.S.R. who had embraced communism were not included as Muslims in this table. After the collapse of communism in 1990–91, these Muslims were once again enumerated as Muslims if they had returned to Islamic profession and practice.

New-Religionists. Followers of Asian 20th-century New Religions, New Religious movements, radical new crisis religions, and non-Christian syncretistic mass religions, all founded since 1800 and most since 1945.

Other religionists. Including 70 minor world religions and more than 10,000 national or local religions and a large number of spiritist religions, New Age religions, quasi religions, pseudoreligions, parareligions, religious or mystic systems, and religious and semireligious brotherhoods of numerous varieties.

Nonreligious. Persons professing no religion, nonbelievers, agnostics, freethinkers, or dereligionized secularists indifferent to all religion.

Total Population. UN medium variant figures for mid-2000, as given in *World Population Prospects: The 1998 Revision.*

Table 2. Religious adherents in the United States of America, AD 1900–2000

	Year 1900	%	mid-1970	%	mid-1990	%	Annual change, 1990–1995				mid-1995	%	mid-2000	%
							Natural	Conversion	Total	Rate (%)				
Christians	**73,270,000**	**96.4**	**191,182,000**	**91.0**	**217,719,000**	**85.7**	**2,218,400**	**−245,000**	**1,973,400**	**0.89**	**227,586,000**	**85.2**	**235,742,000**	**84.6**
Affiliated Christians	54,425,000	71.6	153,299,000	73.0	175,820,000	69.2	1,791,400	−107,000	1,684,400	0.94	184,242,000	69.0	191,828,000	68.8
Roman Catholics	10,775,000	14.2	48,305,000	23.0	56,500,000	22.2	575,700	−532,700	43,000	0.08	56,715,000	21.2	58,000,000	20.8
Protestants	**35,000,000**	**46.1**	**58,568,000**	**27.9**	**60,216,000**	**23.7**	**613,500**	**−151,700**	**461,800**	**0.76**	**62,525,000**	**23.4**	**64,570,000**	**23.2**
Anglicans	1,600,000	2.1	3,196,000	1.5	2,450,000	1.0	25,000	−26,000	−1,000	−0.04	2,445,000	0.9	2,400,000	0.9
Orthodox	400,000	0.5	4,163,000	2.0	5,150,000	2.0	52,500	11,900	64,400	1.22	5,472,000	2.0	5,762,000	2.1
Independents	5,850,000	7.7	35,645,000	17.0	66,900,000	26.3	681,600	527,000	1,208,600	1.74	72,943,000	27.3	78,550,000	28.2
Marginal Christians	800,000	1.1	6,126,000	2.9	8,940,000	3.5	91,100	21,300	112,400	1.23	9,502,000	3.6	10,080,000	3.6
Multiple affiliation	0	0.0	−2,704,000	−1.3	−24,336,000	−9.6	−248,000	43,200	−204,800	0.83	−25,360,000	−9.5	−27,534,000	−9.9
Evangelicals	*32,068,000*	*42.2*	*31,516,000*	*15.0*	*37,349,000*	*14.7*	*380,600*	*12,400*	*393,000*	*1.03*	*39,314,000*	*14.7*	*40,640,000*	*14.6*
evangelicals	*11,000,000*	*14.5*	*45,500,000*	*21.7*	*87,656,000*	*34.5*	*893,100*	*267,100*	*1,160,200*	*1.29*	*93,457,000*	*35.0*	*98,662,000*	*35.4*
Unaffiliated Christians	18,845,000	24.8	37,883,000	18.0	41,899,000	16.5	426,900	−137,900	289,000	0.68	43,344,000	16.2	43,914,000	15.8
Non-Christians	**2,725,000**	**3.6**	**18,929,000**	**9.0**	**36,357,000**	**14.3**	**370,400**	**245,000**	**615,400**	**1.64**	**39,434,000**	**14.8**	**42,915,000**	**15.4**
Atheists	1,000	0.0	200,000	0.1	770,000	0.3	7,800	28,200	36,000	4.29	950,000	0.4	1,150,000	0.4
Baha'is	3,000	0.0	138,000	0.1	600,000	0.2	6,100	10,300	16,400	2.60	682,000	0.3	753,000	0.3
Buddhists	30,000	0.0	200,000	0.1	1,880,000	0.7	19,200	34,800	54,000	2.72	2,150,000	0.8	2,450,000	0.9
Chinese folk religionists	70,000	0.1	90,000	0.0	76,000	0.0	800	−600	200	0.26	77,000	0.0	78,000	0.0
Hindus	1,000	0.0	100,000	0.0	750,000	0.3	7,600	28,400	36,000	4.40	930,000	0.3	1,032,000	0.4
Jews	1,500,000	2.0	6,700,000	3.2	5,535,000	2.2	56,400	−43,400	13,000	0.23	5,600,000	2.1	5,621,000	2.0
Muslims	10,000	0.0	800,000	0.4	3,560,000	1.4	36,300	16,700	53,000	1.45	3,825,000	1.4	4,132,000	1.5
Black Muslims	0	0.0	200,000	0.1	1,250,000	0.5	12,700	17,300	30,000	2.29	1,400,000	0.5	1,650,000	0.6
New-Religionists	0	0.0	110,000	0.1	575,000	0.2	5,900	17,100	23,000	3.71	690,000	0.3	811,000	0.3
Sikhs	0	0.0	1,000	0.0	160,000	0.1	1,600	4,800	6,400	3.71	192,000	0.1	234,000	0.1
Ethnic religionists	100,000	0.1	70,000	0.0	280,000	0.1	2,900	18,500	21,400	6.69	387,000	0.1	435,000	0.2
Other religionists	10,000	0.0	450,000	0.2	757,000	0.3	7,700	1,100	8,800	1.1	801,000	0.3	1,141,000	0.4
Nonreligious	1,000,000	1.3	10,070,000	4.8	21,414,000	8.4	218,200	129,000	347,200	1.57	23,150,000	8.7	25,078,000	9.0
Total population	**75,995,000**	**100.0**	**210,111,000**	**100.0**	**254,076,000**	**100.0**	**2,807,000**	**129,000**	**2,936,000**	**1.00**	**267,020,000**	**100.0**	**278,657,000**	**100.0**

Methodology. This table extracts and analyzes a microcosm of the world religion table. It depicts the United States, the country with the largest number of adherents to Christianity, the world's largest religion. Statistics at five points in time across the 20th century are presented. Each religion's *Annual change* is also analyzed by *Natural* increase (births minus deaths, plus immigrants minus emigrants) per year and *Conversion* increase (new converts minus new defectors) per year, which together constitute the *Total* increase per year. *Rate* increase is then computed as percentage per year.

Structure. Vertically the table lists 27 major religious categories. The major religions (including nonreligion) in the U.S. are listed with largest (Christians) first and Other religionists and Nonreligious last. Indented names of groups in the "Adherents" column are subcategories of the groups above them and are also counted in these unindented totals, so they should not be added twice into the column total. Figures in italics draw adherents from all categories of Christians above and so cannot be added together with them. Figures for Christians in 1970, 1990, and 1995 are built upon detailed head counts by churches, often to the last digit. Totals are then rounded to the nearest 1,000. Because of rounding, the corresponding percentage figures may sometimes not total exactly 100%. Figures for AD 2000 are projections based on current trends.

Christians. All persons who profess publicly to follow Jesus Christ as Lord and Saviour. This category is subdivided into **Affiliated Christians** (church members) and **Unaffiliated** (nominal) **Christians** (professing Christians not affiliated with any church). *See also* the note on Christians under Table 1.

Evangelicals/evangelicals. These two designations—italicized and enumerated separately here—cut across all of the six Christian traditions listed above and should be considered separately from them. **Evangelicals** are Protestant churches, agencies, and individuals that call themselves by this term (for example, members of the National Organization of Evangelicals); they usually emphasize 5 or more of 7, 9, or 21 fundamental doctrines (salvation by faith, personal acceptance, verbal inspiration of Scripture, depravity of man, Virgin Birth, miracles of Christ, atonement, evangelism, Second Advent, et al.). The **evangelicals** are Christians from all traditions who are committed to the evangel (gospel) and involved in personal witness and mission in the world.

Independents. Members of churches and networks that regard themselves as postdenominationalist and neo-apostolic and thus independent of historic, organized, institutionalized, denominationalist Christianity.

Marginal Christians. Members of denominations on the margins of organized mainstream Christianity (Mormons, Jehovah's Witnesses, Christian Science, Religious Science).

Non-Christians. Followers of non-Christian religions or, in the case of **Nonreligious,** no religion.

Jews. Core Jewish population relating to Judaism, excluding Jewish persons professing a different religion.

Other categories. Definitions are as given above under Table 1.

Table 3. Protestant-affiliated church members in the world's 238 countries, in the context of the 5 other major Christian traditions

This table gives a worldwide overview of Protestantism in all countries of the world, arranged as follows: column 1 = *short name of country,* in English; column 2 = *population* of country in AD mid-2000; column 3 (shown in bold type) = total *Core Protestants* in country (Protestantisms' total Christian community, being total affiliated church members including their children and infants; in many cases, total baptized community; column 4 = total *Anglicans* (affiliated, including children); column 5 = total *Independents* (affiliated church members and children; including Postdenominationalists and independent Charismatics); column 6 = total *Marginal Christians* (adherents and members of nontrinitarian or antitrinitarian churches, defining themselves as outside or on the margins of mainstream Christianity); column 7 = total *Orthodox* (affiliated to Orthodox patriarchates, including their children); 8 = total *Roman Catholics* (all baptized members including children).

1 Country	2 Population 2000	3 Protestants	4 Anglicans	5 Independents	6 Marginals	7 Orthodox	8 Roman Catholics
Afghanistan	22,720,416	2,000	100	3,000	200	100	1,497
Albania	3,113,434	20,000	0	17,000	12,000	500,000	521,390
Algeria	31,471,278	3,400	200	65,000	200	1,800	20,277
American Samoa	68,089	35,800	190	1,780	8,000	0	9,470
Andorra	77,985	140	0	80	450	0	69,535
Angola	12,878,188	1,930,238	4,000	880,000	120,000	0	8,000,000
Anguilla	8,309	4,126	2,650	0	100	0	310
Antigua	67,560	21,000	22,613	1,200	1,100	0	7,800
Argentina	37,027,297	2,295,000	19,000	2,050,000	500,000	158,000	33,750,000
Armenia	3,519,569	12,000	0	28,000	1,200	2,752,493	160,000
Aruba	102,747	7,500	750	1,350	1,300	0	84,341
Australia	18,879,524	2,630,000	4,060,000	840,000	220,000	700,000	5,400,000
Austria	8,210,520	413,570	3,100	73,000	65,000	155,000	6,200,000
Azerbaijan	7,734,015	1,400	0	3,600	0	345,302	7,500
Bahamas	306,529	167,171	27,300	19,000	5,000	380	48,000
Bahrain	617,217	5,100	3,000	27,058	40	2,500	25,000
Bangladesh	129,155,152	160,490	0	536,000	90	160	235,000
Barbados	270,449	85,158	77,300	17,500	5,600	300	11,000
Belgium	10,161,164	125,000	10,800	40,000	72,000	48,500	8,222,396
Belize	240,709	39,500	10,500	5,200	5,000	0	136,939
Belorussia	10,236,181	130,000	0	110,000	8,000	4,986,077	1,350,000
Benin	6,096,559	230,000	0	175,000	13,000	0	1,266,195
Bermuda	64,590	19,500	24,200	7,000	1,650	0	10,384
Bhutan	2,123,970	3,200	0	5,849	0	0	600
Bolivia	8,328,665	530,000	1,100	145,000	135,000	3,100	7,350,000
Bosnia-Herzegovina	3,971,813	2,700	0	750	1,300	700,000	681,135
Botswana	1,622,220	178,000	10,500	498,253	4,200	120	60,000
Bougainville	198,495	22,650	0	14,000	280	0	148,401
Brazil	170,115,463	30,200,000	125,000	25,500,000	1,420,000	170,000	153,300,000
Britain	58,830,160	5,050,000	26,278,000	2,140,000	550,000	370,000	5,620,000
British Virgin Is	21,366	9,792	2,800	1,000	600	0	700
Brunei	328,080	6,000	4,592	8,300	100	0	5,600
Bulgaria	8,225,045	95,000	0	580,000	6,500	5,886,450	90,000
Burkina Faso	11,936,823	799,000	0	54,000	2,000	0	1,129,078
Burundi	6,695,001	800,000	500,000	23,000	900	1,400	3,827,541
Cambodia	11,167,719	21,500	40	74,708	150	0	22,000
Cameroon	15,084,969	3,120,000	900	590,000	60,000	1,200	3,989,401
Canada	31,146,639	5,350,000	820,000	1,680,000	450,000	580,000	13,017,945
Cape Verde	427,724	15,500	0	12,800	4,800	0	417,000
Cayman Islands	38,371	20,690	500	4,050	380	0	200
Central African Rep	3,615,266	520,800	0	418,000	5,560	0	664,639
Chad	7,650,982	782,756	0	152,000	1,100	0	502,158
Channel Islands	152,898	10,500	67,511	0	270	200	22,300
Chile	15,211,294	382,000	12,000	3,820,000	420,000	23,750	11,800,000
China	1,262,556,787	640,000	23,000	80,708,347	29,000	55,000	7,500,000
Colombia	42,321,361	1,100,000	3,600	535,000	275,000	7,200	40,670,000
Comoros	592,749	900	0	400	10	0	5,751
Congo-Brazzaville	2,943,464	500,000	0	370,000	11,300	400	1,451,178
Congo-Zaire	51,654,496	10,485,000	440,000	12,050,000	360,000	8,100	26,300,000
Cook Islands	19,522	14,200	100	60	1,650	0	3,650
Costa Rica	4,023,422	330,000	1,600	108,000	75,000	0	3,660,000
Croatia	4,472,600	26,000	0	11,386	9,000	250,000	3,960,000
Cuba	11,200,684	190,000	3,600	135,000	125,000	1,400	4,367,909
Cyprus	600,506	4,600	3,300	400	8,200	525,294	9,800
Czech Republic	10,244,177	320,000	1,200	270,000	32,000	60,000	4,135,936
Denmark	5,293,239	4,639,710	4,800	36,000	36,000	1,400	33,200
Djibouti	637,634	240	0	200	0	18,900	8,854
Dominica	70,714	11,200	1,320	2,100	750	0	56,300
Dominican Republic	8,495,338	360,000	4,400	130,000	60,000	0	7,522,305
Ecuador	12,646,068	240,000	1,600	225,000	185,000	1,800	11,900,000
Egypt	68,469,695	550,000	2,500	225,000	900	9,317,066	225,000
El Salvador	6,276,023	530,000	400	710,000	110,000	0	5,723,000
Equatorial Guinea	452,661	15,200	0	18,000	1,200	0	391,000
Eritrea	3,850,388	22,000	0	7,800	0	1,774,558	130,000
Estonia	1,396,158	240,000	0	46,000	8,000	230,000	5,875
Ethiopia	62,564,875	8,510,000	800	860,000	12,500	22,837,859	450,000
Faeroe Islands	42,749	38,860	0	400	200	0	130
Fiji	816,905	375,000	8,300	86,000	15,000	0	85,000
Finland	5,175,743	4,635,000	170	77,700	38,000	55,900	6,400
France	59,079,709	910,000	13,200	1,325,000	330,000	660,000	48,600,000
French Guiana	181,313	7,000	90	1,700	5,500	0	145,000
French Polynesia	235,061	110,000	0	4,800	25,000	0	100,000
Gabon	1,226,127	233,000	0	180,000	7,500	0	745,000
Gambia	1,305,363	3,670	2,800	8,950	90	450	31,238

Table 3. (*Continued*)

1 Country	2 Population 2000	3 **Protestants**	4 Anglicans	5 Independents	6 Marginals	7 Orthodox	8 Roman Catholics
Georgia	4,967,561	24,000	0	42,000	1,000	2,886,814	55,000
Germany	82,220,490	30,420,000	27,000	728,000	540,000	680,000	28,700,000
Ghana	20,212,495	3,360,000	250,000	2,920,376	210,000	1,600	1,925,000
Gibraltar	25,082	380	1,900	0	240	0	21,200
Greece	10,644,744	21,400	3,600	228,000	40,000	9,900,000	62,000
Greenland	56,156	38,880	0	120	240	0	110
Grenada	93,717	19,100	14,400	3,700	1,400	0	52,700
Guadeloupe	455,687	22,500	0	1,120	19,700	0	433,000
Guam	167,556	17,500	900	2,900	4,300	0	139,400
Guatemala	11,385,295	1,450,000	1,800	1,030,000	160,000	0	9,600,000
Guinea	7,430,346	69,182	1,400	43,000	740	0	117,000
Guinea-Bissau	1,213,111	9,500	280	31,000	70	0	141,000
Guyana	861,334	168,636	77,000	27,000	6,100	8,800	86,500
Haiti	8,222,025	1,440,000	105,000	430,000	50,000	0	6,520,000
Honduras	6,485,445	425,000	6,000	180,000	70,000	7,200	5,590,000
Hungary	10,035,568	2,560,000	0	165,000	40,000	90,000	6,330,000
Iceland	280,969	250,459	0	11,000	900	0	2,900
India	1,013,661,777	16,826,000	0	34,200,000	50,000	3,100,000	15,500,000
Indonesia	212,107,385	12,125,000	3,400	8,436,000	48,000	100	5,752,358
Iran	67,702,199	13,800	1,200	80,000	300	202,290	16,400
Iraq	23,114,884	1,400	200	315,547	30	139,485	268,000
Ireland	3,730,239	31,500	134,000	19,000	9,500	1,550	3,159,896
Isle of Man	79,166	11,200	33,588	210	640	0	6,800
Israel	5,121,683	19,000	2,200	85,000	1,000	46,878	140,000
Italy	57,297,886	446,000	10,600	415,000	420,000	91,000	55,680,000
Ivory Coast	14,785,832	760,000	0	1,373,000	18,000	20,000	2,182,882
Jamaica	2,582,577	643,413	103,000	232,000	30,000	3,300	110,000
Japan	126,714,220	570,881	60,000	1,600,000	720,000	26,000	460,000
Jordan	6,669,341	9,822	7,200	77,000	170	131,330	48,000
Kazakhstan	16,222,563	25,000	0	650,000	5,000	1,401,803	510,000
Kenya	30,080,372	6,375,000	3,000,000	6,607,000	30,000	740,000	7,000,000
Kirgizstan	4,699,337	30,000	0	70,500	500	363,065	1,600
Kiribati	83,387	37,000	50	1,300	1,700	0	44,100
Kuwait	1,971,634	1,100	200	64,000	50	7,000	175,185
Laos	5,433,036	34,400	200	45,613	350	0	32,000
Latvia	2,356,508	560,000	0	115,000	2,500	555,000	490,000
Lebanon	3,281,787	20,000	200	118,000	8,000	535,000	1,395,000
Lesotho	2,152,553	279,000	102,000	254,000	3,800	0	806,529
Liberia	3,154,001	430,000	34,500	538,500	8,000	0	150,000
Libya	5,604,722	4,500	150	14,000	60	106,642	45,000
Liechtenstein	32,843	2,520	0	40	110	0	24,381
Lithuania	3,670,269	44,000	0	32,000	4,300	114,000	3,105,000
Luxembourg	430,615	7,500	600	2,200	3,000	1,100	407,000
Macedonia	2,023,580	7,000	0	8,192	1,400	1,200,000	70,600
Madagascar	15,941,727	4,090,000	320,000	510,000	27,500	4,400	3,662,363
Malawi	10,925,238	2,140,000	230,000	1,830,000	130,000	4,400	2,697,860
Malaysia	22,244,062	660,000	205,000	178,000	4,000	2,300	721,889
Maldives	286,223	258	0	20	0	0	80
Mali	11,233,821	82,000	0	16,300	500	0	125,565
Malta	388,544	1,000	1,100	750	900	130	367,501
Marshall Islands	64,220	67,431	0	8,100	2,500	0	5,250
Martinique	395,362	23,700	0	4,349	8,000	0	366,000
Mauritania	2,669,547	600	0	1,700	10	0	4,216
Mauritius	1,156,498	110,000	5,000	3,400	2,500	0	310,000
Mayotte	101,621	350	0	160	100	0	1,256
Mexico	98,881,289	3,280,000	187,800	2,900,000	1,950,000	100,000	92,770,000
Micronesia	118,689	47,000	0	1,700	3,300	0	74,578
Moldavia	4,380,492	78,000	0	670,000	27,000	1,950,558	73,000
Monaco	33,597	681	330	0	0	90	30,000
Mongolia	2,662,020	21,573	0	10,000	70	1,400	350
Montserrat	10,629	5,500	3,100	1,050	130	0	1,400
Morocco	28,220,843	4,100	450	147,000	110	740	22,076
Mozambique	19,680,456	1,750,000	110,000	1,422,033	68,000	500	3,110,000
Myanmar	45,611,177	2,511,664	58,000	575,000	6,800	0	590,000
Namibia	1,725,868	820,000	31,000	187,000	5,000	0	306,211
Nauru	11,519	5,840	320	380	40	0	2,920
Nepal	23,930,490	14,561	0	551,000	1,000	2,500	7,000
Netherlands	15,785,699	4,238,853	8,600	490,000	88,000	7,400	5,450,000
Netherlands Antilles	216,775	23,000	2,550	2,100	6,400	0	150,862
New Caledonia	214,029	30,000	160	11,000	4,500	0	116,019
New Zealand	3,861,905	931,219	825,000	190,000	115,000	6,000	495,000
Nicaragua	5,074,194	590,000	8,300	155,000	51,000	0	4,320,000
Niger	10,730,102	13,000	0	25,000	600	0	19,670
Nigeria	111,506,095	14,050,000	20,070,000	23,975,000	600,000	3,100	13,400,000
North Korea	24,039,193	10,000	0	432,413	2,800	0	55,000
Northern Cyprus	185,045	0	0	2,236	0	13,870	0
Northern Mariana Is	78,356	6,500	0	6,660	1,870	0	69,300
Norway	4,461,033	4,200,000	2,000	136,000	24,000	1,600	45,000
Oman	2,541,739	5,700	2,800	43,916	0	16,500	53,000
Pakistan	156,483,155	1,796,000	0	850,000	1,245	0	1,165,000
Palau	19,426	5,600	0	4,100	650	0	8,600
Palestine	2,215,393	3,900	3,500	103,349	1,400	48,140	28,000
Panama	2,855,683	340,000	23,500	73,000	42,000	1,400	2,210,000
Papua New Guinea	4,608,145	2,610,000	308,000	270,000	15,400	400	1,380,000

Table 3. (*Continued*)

1 Country	2 Population 2000	**3** **Protestants**	4 Anglicans	5 Independents	6 Marginals	7 Orthodox	8 Roman Catholics
Paraguay	5,496,453	**200,000**	17,600	70,800	26,000	2,000	4,950,000
Peru	25,661,669	**1,480,000**	2,000	456,000	330,000	5,500	24,550,000
Philippines	75,966,500	**3,775,000**	120,000	14,330,000	670,000	0	62,570,000
Poland	38,765,085	**195,000**	0	330,000	200,000	1,030,000	35,743,059
Portugal	9,874,853	**135,000**	3,050	277,000	98,000	1,200	8,970,000
Puerto Rico	3,868,602	**505,000**	12,400	249,000	95,000	1,300	2,900,000
Qatar	599,065	**4,000**	8,000	10,235	0	1,300	36,100
Reunion	699,406	**31,500**	0	700	6,000	0	611,000
Romania	22,326,502	**2,380,000**	450	290,000	150,000	19,000,000	3,237,000
Russia	146,933,847	**1,630,000**	3,300	7,800,000	200,000	75,950,000	1,500,000
Rwanda	7,733,127	**1,619,822**	600,000	165,000	8,000	2,000	3,942,000
Sahara	293,357	**0**	0	347	0	0	140
Saint Helena	6,293	**520**	4,412	160	200	0	40
Saint Kitts & Nevis	38,473	**22,270**	9,700	1,500	510	0	4,850
Saint Lucia	154,366	**20,500**	4,400	3,239	1,400	0	116,000
Saint Pierre & Miquelon	6,567	**70**	0	0	40	0	6,465
Saint Vincent	113,954	**33,854**	19,715	13,300	1,500	70	10,000
Samoa	180,073	**128,000**	450	2,000	17,000	0	39,500
San Marino	26,514	**0**	0	0	270	0	23,509
Sao Tome & Principe	146,775	**5,450**	0	15,500	600	0	110,553
Saudi Arabia	21,606,691	**38,000**	2,000	85,000	110	36,000	625,875
Senegal	9,481,161	**9,800**	160	14,000	2,300	0	441,031
Seychelles	77,435	**1,950**	5,200	50	270	0	70,000
Sierra Leone	4,854,383	**171,000**	25,000	165,000	2,700	610	169,140
Singapore	3,566,614	**126,536**	34,000	94,000	4,000	1,400	143,000
Slovakia	5,387,191	**600,000**	0	23,000	20,000	21,000	3,660,186
Slovenia	1,985,557	**32,000**	0	31,000	2,800	12,000	1,659,006
Solomon Islands	443,643	**159,000**	169,503	22,500	4,200	0	48,000
Somalia	7,264,500	**1,100**	30	5,500	0	91,753	200
Somaliland	2,832,677	**330**	320	3,300	0	4,400	31
South Africa	40,376,579	**12,410,000**	2,660,000	18,500,000	190,000	150,000	3,350,000
South Korea	46,843,989	**8,870,000**	110,000	7,700,000	850,000	5,000	3,700,000
Spain	39,629,775	**120,000**	12,000	320,000	200,000	2,250	38,000,000
Spanish North Africa	130,000	**650**	0	800	0	0	102,874
Sri Lanka	18,827,054	**102,000**	55,000	331,120	7,000	0	1,260,000
Sudan	29,489,719	**796,000**	2,320,000	150,000	900	155,000	3,148,593
Suriname	417,130	**71,334**	800	2,800	4,400	0	93,000
Swaziland	1,007,895	**153,200**	40,000	460,000	5,500	0	54,000
Sweden	8,910,214	**8,420,000**	2,880	60,000	56,000	120,000	175,000
Switzerland	7,385,708	**3,040,000**	13,300	160,000	122,000	26,000	3,260,000
Syria	16,124,618	**30,040**	4,000	100,000	400	798,269	325,000
Taiwan	22,401,000	**400,000**	1,650	451,093	27,000	0	300,000
Tajikistan	6,188,201	**17,000**	0	15,000	200	93,000	4,412
Tanzania	33,517,014	**5,530,000**	2,650,000	638,000	18,000	12,500	8,283,000
Thailand	61,399,249	**303,000**	450	778,717	8,000	0	255,000
Timor	884,541	**47,000**	0	0	0	0	796,000
Togo	4,629,218	**480,000**	0	110,000	36,100	0	1,122,995
Tonga	98,546	**42,320**	660	20,798	14,350	0	13,900
Trinidad & Tobago	1,294,958	**179,000**	154,000	42,000	14,500	8,500	397,865
Tunisia	9,585,611	**670**	100	30,413	50	270	19,000
Turkey	66,590,940	**32,500**	2,100	78,000	2,400	227,655	30,500
Turkmenistan	4,459,293	**2,800**	0	19,000	400	74,583	2,100
Turks & Caicos Is	16,760	**8,112**	2,000	2,000	400	0	750
Tuvalu	11,719	**12,000**	0	250	290	0	95
Uganda	21,778,450	**596,000**	8,580,000	815,000	6,000	32,000	9,130,000
Ukraine	50,455,980	**1,340,000**	0	8,500,000	135,000	27,400,000	5,578,901
United Arab Emirates	2,441,436	**12,800**	8,600	47,000	0	70,000	124,345
USA	278,357,141	**64,570,000**	2,400,000	78,550,000	10,080,000	5,762,000	58,000,000
Uruguay	3,337,058	**110,000**	1,200	52,500	95,000	26,500	2,608,000
Uzbekistan	24,317,851	**44,000**	0	120,000	1,400	188,934	40,000
Vanuatu	190,417	**102,254**	34,500	16,500	1,400	0	29,400
Venezuela	24,169,722	**500,000**	600	350,000	300,000	27,000	22,816,000
Viet Nam	79,831,650	**580,000**	3,100	640,000	24,000	0	5,320,822
Virgin Is of the US	92,954	**40,000**	13,800	12,800	1,500	0	29,000
Wallis & Futuna Is	14,517	**40**	0	0	45	0	13,936
Yemen	18,112,066	**4,476**	180	8,000	0	12,000	6,000
Yugoslavia	10,640,150	**99,000**	400	185,000	8,600	6,046,000	546,557
Zambia	9,168,700	**2,705,000**	220,000	1,580,000	375,680	6,400	3,070,000
Zimbabwe	11,669,029	**1,440,000**	320,000	4,700,000	64,000	6,000	1,120,000
*11 minicountries	23,079	**5,343**	2,128	730	520	779	4,598
Africa	784,445,039	**88,999,928**	42,541,902	83,840,642	2,426,550	35,304,168	120,386,235
Antarctica	4,500	**970**	300	700	0	30	1,400
Asia	3,682,550,093	**49,969,501**	727,212	154,732,021	2,485,605	14,113,465	110,480,013
Europe	728,886,951	**77,528,973**	26,637,479	25,723,708	3,563,880	158,105,154	285,977,773
Latin America	519,138,048	**48,131,716**	1,089,611	39,706,358	6,595,300	557,500	461,220,001
Northern America	309,631,093	**69,978,450**	3,244,200	80,237,120	10,531,930	6,342,000	71,034,904
Oceania	30,393,391	**7,392,067**	5,408,938	1,504,858	456,965	706,400	8,227,767
Global Total	6,055,049,115	**342,001,605**	79,649,642	385,745,407	26,060,230	215,128,717	1,057,328,093

Notes to table.

* 11 Minicountries. Smallest countries with population each under 5,000 are: Antarctica (4,500), British Indian Ocean Territory (2,000), Christmas Island (3,424), Cocos (Keeling) Islands (726), Falkland Islands (2,255), Holy See (5,000), Niue Island (1,876), Norfolk Island (2,075), Pitcairn Islands (47), Svalbard & Jan Mayen Islands (3,676), Tokelau Islands (1,500).

Table 4. Organized Protestantism and Its Core Global Membership Ranked by 27 Ecclesiastico-Cultural Major Traditions or Families, AD 1970–AD 2025

Tradition Code 1	Name 2	Congs 1995 3	Adults 1995 4	Affiliated		Denominations				Countries Count 11
				1970 5	1995 6	1970 7	1995 8	2000 9	2025 10	
CORE PROTESTANT		947,000	195,757,000	210,037,000	318,027,000	5,621	8,844	8,973	9,490	231
P-Adv	Adventist	34,000	5,966,000	4,189,000	11,011,000	195	214	218	233	199
P-Bap	Baptist	125,400	31,520,000	27,726,000	48,133,000	266	313	322	360	163
P-CBr	Christian Brethren (Plymouth Brethren; Open only)	16,700	1,341,000	1,535,000	2,798,000	120	124	125	128	113
P-Con	Congregational, Congregationalist	11,500	1,385,000	1,893,000	2,438,000	81	85	86	89	55
P-Dis	Disciple, Restorationist, Restorationist Baptist, Christian	6,700	1,053,000	2,455,000	1,919,000	13	17	18	21	18
P-Dun	Dunker (Tunker), Dipper, German Baptist, Brethren	2,100	322,000	465,000	603,000	10	10	10	10	7
P-EBr	Exclusive Brethren (Plymouth Brethren, Closed, Strict)	2,500	107,000	175,000	211,000	20	20	20	20	18
P-Eva	Anglican Evangelical, Independent Evangelical	20,100	2,842,000	1,824,000	5,482,000	112	138	143	164	89
P-Fun	Fundamentalist	2,600	122,000	67,000	211,000	13	16	17	19	14
P-Hol	Holiness (Conservative Methodist, Wesleyan, Free Methodist)	43,600	3,978,000	4,111,000	7,387,000	283	339	350	395	117
P-LuR	Lutheran/Reformed united church or joint mission	10,800	11,626,000	18,525,000	15,041,000	23	24	24	25	22
P-Lut	Lutheran	81,900	39,853,000	54,717,000	60,696,000	231	249	253	267	122
P-Men	Mennonite, Anabaptist (Left Wing or Radical Reformation)	9,500	1,166,000	1,117,000	2,009,000	99	123	128	147	59
P-Met	Methodist (mainline Methodist, United Methodist)	89,500	13,860,000	21,933,000	22,902,000	113	121	123	129	108
P-Mor	Moravian (Continental Pietist)	1,200	302,000	478,000	582,000	27	29	29	31	27
P-Non	Nondenominational (no church or anti-church groups)	11,800	1,938,000	886,000	3,434,000	166	191	196	216	76
P-Pe1	Oneness-Pentecostal or Unitarian-Pentecostal: Jesus only	11,600	1,326,000	939,000	2,463,000	57	80	85	103	74
P-Pe2	Baptistic-Pentecostal or Keswick-Pentecostal	232,000	30,284,000	12,006,000	49,420,000	311	382	396	453	174
P-Pe3	Holiness-Pentecostal: 3-crisis-experience	28,800	3,219,000	2,322,000	5,650,000	167	233	246	299	118
P-PeA	Apostolic, or Pentecostal Apostolic (living apostles)	11,500	762,000	706,000	1,597,000	29	31	31	33	30
P-Pen	Pentecostal (pluralist)	20	1,000	0	3,000	0	1	1	2	1
P-Qua	Friends (Quaker)	4,900	222,000	348,000	403,000	50	53	54	56	43
P-Ref	Reformed, Presbyterian	97,700	26,318,000	33,121,000	43,902,000	269	295	300	321	141
P-Sal	Salvationist (Salvation Army)	14,100	1,467,000	2,910,000	2,378,000	79	85	86	91	84
P-Uni	United church (union of bodies of different traditions)	50,300	12,348,000	13,608,000	22,266,000	49	53	54	57	45
P-Wal	Waldensian	200	31,000	37,000	41,000	2	2	2	2	2
P-com	Community church or union congregation	50	12,000	19,000	20,000	20	23	24	26	18

Meaning of columns.

1–2. Each's major constituent ecclesiastical traditions, listed in their codes' alphabetical order. First comes a 4-letter code then the full name of each tradition.

3–4. Congregations (worship centers) and adult church members (all referring to the year 1995).

5–6. Affiliated church members (total Christian community) in 1970 and 1995.

7–10. Denominations. A denomination is defined as an organized aggregate of worship centers or congregations of similar ecclesiastical tradition within a specific country; i.e. as an organized Christian church or tradition or religious group or community of believers, within a specific country.

11. Countries. Number of countries (out of 238) where this tradition exists.

APPENDIX

Table 5. Statistics Describing Each of the 45 Global Ministries of Evangelism

45 Modes of Evangelism	Evangelism hours originated per year	Media factor	Total offers received per year
1. Intercession	17.2 billion	1	17.2 billion
2. Inner renewal/spirituality	19.5 billion	1	19.5 billion
3. Christian lifestyle	18.3 billion	1	18.3 billion
4. Audiovisual ministries	3 billion	25	76 billion
5. Plays/concerts/operas/shows	2.4 billion	20	48.7 billion
6. Jesus films	548 million	100	54.8 billion
7. Audio scriptures	18 million	1,000	18.3 billion
8. Scripture leaflets/selections	4.1 billion	5	20.5 billion
9. Every-home campaign visits	160 million	50	8 billion
10. New Reader Scriptures	76 million	50	8 billion
11. Braille Scripture	2 billion	5	10 billion
12. Signed/deaf Scriptures	600 million	5	3 billion
13. Christian suffering	260 million	10	2.6 billion
14. Personal evangelism	59.1 billion	3	177.4 billion
15. Martyrdoms	1.6 million	1,000	1.6 billion
16. Full-time home church workers	3.7 billion	2	7.5 billion
17. Foreign missionaries	307 million	20	6.1 billion
18. Evangelists	110.5 million	100	11.1 billion
19. Short-term missionaries	146 million	10	1.5 billion
20. Part-time evangelizers	5.8 billion	2	11.7 billion
21. Mission agencies	21 million	100	2.1 billion
22. Portions/Gospels	808 million	6	4.8 billion
23. Near-Gospels	480 million	6	2.9 billion
24. New Testaments (300 pages)	3.6 billion	8	29 billion
25. Near-New Testaments	1.4 billion	8	10.8 billion
26. Bibles (1,300 pages)	7 billion	10	69.9 billion
27. Near Bibles	1.2 billion	10	12 billion
28. Lingua franca Gospels	200 million	3	600 million
29. Lingua franca New Testaments	1.4 billion	4	5.6 billion
30. Lingua franca Bibles	3.0 billion	5	15 billion
31. Denominational materials	1.9 billion	1	1.9 billion
32. Local church output	3.8 billion	1	3.8 billion
33. Outside Christian literature	10 million	10	100 million
34. Church-planting output	58 million	10	600 million
35. Institutional ministries/records	1.8 billion	1	1.8 billion
36. Christian books (100 pages)	35 billion	2	70 billion
37. Christian periodicals (30 pages)	150 million	10	1.5 billion
38. Tracts (2 pages)	2.5 billion	1	2.5 billion
39. Other documentation	1.2 billion	1	1.2 billion
40. Programmed training	180,000	10,000	18 billion
41. Christian radio programs	1 million	50,000	50 billion
42. Christian TV programs	200,000	100,000	20 billion
43. Urban media (cable TV, etc.)	450,000	12,000	5.4 billion
44. Christian-owned computers	98.1 million	350	34.3 billion
45. Internet/networks/e-mail	2 billion	30	58.5 billion

This table provides the statistics discussed in the article "Evangelism, Overview." (Article begins on page 715.)

Contributors

Adam, Margaret B.
Evanston, Ill.
Articles contributed: HOMESCHOOLING.

Aguilar, Mario I.
Saint Mary's College, University of Saint Andrews (Scotland)
Articles contributed: AFRICA.

Airhart, Phyllis D.
University of Toronto, Canada
Articles contributed: UNITED CHURCH OF CANADA.

Akinade, Akintunde E.
High Point University, High Point, N.C.
Articles contributed: MARANKE, JOHN; UNIFICATION CHURCH.

Albers, James
Valparaiso University, Valparaiso, Ind.
Articles contributed: WISCONSIN EVANGELICAL LUTHERAN SYNOD.

Alexander, Bobby C.
The University of Texas at Dallas
Articles contributed: FALWELL, JERRY.

Alexander, J. Neil
Episcopal Diocese of Atlanta, Ga.
Articles contributed: LAMBETH CONFERENCE.

Alexander, Thomas G.
Brigham Young University, Provo, Utah
Articles contributed: YOUNG, BRIGHAM.

Ames, Frank Ritchel
Colorado Christian University, Lakewood, Colo.
Articles contributed: BENGEL, JOHANN ALBRECHT; PEDERSEN, JOHANNES PEDER EJLER.

Anderson, George M.
America Press, Inc., New York, N.Y.
Articles contributed: FRY, ELIZABETH.

Anderson, Mary
Luther Seminary, Saint Paul, Minn.
Articles contributed: SPEYER, DIETS OF.

Angell, Stephen W.
Earlham School of Religion, Richmond, Ind.
Articles contributed: FRIENDS GENERAL CONFERENCE; FRIENDS WORLD COMMITTEE.

Antonio, Edward P.
Iliff School of Theology, Denver, Colo.
Articles contributed: AFRICAN THEOLOGY.

Arand, Charles
Concordia Seminary, Saint Louis, Mo.
Articles contributed: CATECHISMS.

Ariel, Yaakov
University of North Carolina at Chapel Hill
Articles contributed: JEWS FOR JESUS; MISSIONS TO JEWS.

Armentrout, Donald
University of the South, Sewanee, Tenn.
Articles contributed: BLAIR, JAMES; BRAY, THOMAS; CAMBRIDGE PLATONISTS; JEWEL, JOHN; ROBERTSON, FREDERICK WILLIAM; SYNOD; TAYLOR, JEREMY; TOLAND, JOHN; WESTCOTT, BROOKE.

Armour, Rollin
Mercer University, Atlanta, Ga.
Articles contributed: HOFMANN, MELCHIOR.

Arseneau, Mary
University of Ottawa, Canada
Articles contributed: PRE-RAPHAELITES; ROSSETTI, CHRISTINA.

Aston, Nigel
University of Leicester (England)
Articles contributed: FRENCH REVOLUTION.

Atwood, Craig R
Moravian Theological Seminary, Bethlehem, Pa.
Articles contributed: HERRNHUT.

Aune, Kristin
King's College, University of London (England)
Articles contributed: HOUSE CHURCHES.

CONTRIBUTORS

Avis, Paul
Council for Christian Unity, Church of England
Articles contributed: ANGLICANISM; CHURCH; ECCLESIOLOGY;
  TRADITION.

Bach, Jeff
Bethany Theological Seminary, Richmond, Ind.
Articles contributed: BRETHREN, CHURCH OF THE.

Badham, Paul
University of Wales, Lampeter
Articles contributed: ABORTION.

Baker, Kelly J.
Florida State University, Tallahassee, Fla.
Articles contributed: FULLER, MARGARET; WILLARD, FRANCES
  ELIZABETH CAROLINE.

Baker, J. Wayne
University of Akron, Ohio
Articles contributed: BULLINGER, HEINRICH; ZWINGLI,
  HULDRYCH; ZWINGLIANISM.

Ball, Les
Queensland Baptist College of Ministries (Australia)
Articles contributed: BRITISH AND FOREIGN BIBLE SOCIETY.

Bangs, Jeremy
The Leiden American Pilgrim Museum (Netherlands)
Articles contributed: PILGRIM FATHERS; REMONSTRANTS.

Barrett, David B.
Center for World Evangelization Research, Richmond, Va.
Articles contributed: EVANGELISM, OVERVIEW; STATISTICS.

Bassett, Paul Merritt
Nazarene Theological Seminary, Kansas City, Mo.
Articles contributed: ARMINIANISM; CHURCH OF THE NAZARENE.

Bayer, Oswald
University of Tubingen (Germany)
Articles contributed: HAMANN, JOHANN GEORG.

Bays, Daniel H.
Calvin College, Grand Rapids, Mich.
Articles contributed: CHINA; CHINA INLAND MISSION; SUN
  YAT-SEN.

Bebbington, David W.
University of Stirling (Scotland)
Articles contributed: BAPTISTS; DISSENT; SPURGEON, CHARLES;
  WILBERFORCE, WILLIAM.

Beck, Albert R.
Baylor University, Waco, Tex.
Articles contributed: CHURCH AND STATE, OVERVIEW.

Becker, Dieter
Augustana-Hochschule Neuendettelsau (Germany)
Articles contributed: GERMANY.

Behringer, Wolfgang
University of York (England)
Articles contributed: WITCHCRAZE.

Bendroth, Margaret
Calvin College, Grand Rapids, Mich.
Articles contributed: FAMILY; GENDER.

Bergen, Doris L.
University of Notre Dame, South Bend, Ind.
Articles contributed: GERMAN CHRISTIANS; HOLOCAUST.

Bergler, Thomas E.
Huntington College, Ind.
Articles contributed: REVIVALS; YOUTH FOR CHRIST.

Berry, Stephen R.
Duke University, Durham, N.C.
Articles contributed: BLAKE, EUGENE CARSON; DELANY,
  MARTIN; HOGG, JAMES; TENNENT, GILBERT.

Bertie, David M.
Arbuthnot Museum (Scotland)
Articles contributed: EPISCOPAL CHURCH, SCOTLAND.

Bevis, Kathryn
Regent's Park College, University of Oxford (England)
Articles contributed: HARTSTHORNE, CHARLES.

Bexell, Oloph
University of Uppsala (Sweden)
Articles contributed: SÖDERBLOM, NATHAN.

Bielfeldt, Dennis
South Dakota State University, Brookings, S. Dak.
Articles contributed: BRENZ, JOHANNES; CASTELLIO,
  SEBASTIAN; KARLSTADT, ANDREAS RUDOLF BODENSTEIN.

Biggar, Nigel
University of Leeds (England)
Articles contributed: NATURAL LAW.

Binfield, Clyde
Sheffield University (England)
Articles contributed: NONCONFORMITY.

Bird, Michael
University of Queensland (Australia)
Articles contributed: MATHIIS, JAN; THEOLOGY, TWENTIETH-
  CENTURY, BRITISH.

Bireley, S. J., Robert
Loyola University, Chicago, Ill.
Articles contributed: COUNTER-REFORMATION.

Birkel, Michael L.
Earlham College, Richmond, Ind.
Articles contributed: JONES, RUFUS MATTHEW.

Blanchard, Kathryn D.
Duke University, Durham, N.C.
Articles contributed: SOCIALISM, CHRISTIAN.

Bliese, Richard H.
Lutheran School of Theology at Chicago, Ill.
Articles contributed: MISSIONARY ORGANIZATIONS.

Blossom, Jay S.F.
Duke University, Durham, N.C.
Articles contributed: BIBLE CAMPS AND CONFERENCE CENTERS;
SUNDAY, BILLY.

Blowers, Paul
Emmanuel School of Religion, Johnson City, Tenn.
Articles contributed: CHRISTIAN CHURCHES, CHURCHES OF
CHRIST.

Blumhofer, Edith
Wheaton College, Wheaton, Ill.
Articles contributed: CROSBY, FANNY; EVANGELISTIC
ORGANIZATIONS; FUNDAMENTALISM; HIGHER LIFE MOVEMENT;
INTERNATIONAL CHURCH OF THE FOURSQUARE GOSPEL;
KESWICK MOVEMENT; MCPHERSON, AIMEE SEMPLE; MOODY
BIBLE INSTITUTE; PENTECOSTALISM; RAMABAI, PANDITA.

Bolt, John
Calvin Theological Seminary, Grand Rapids, Mich.
Articles contributed: KUYPER, ABRAHAM.

Bouteneff, Peter
*Saint Vladimir's Orthodox Theological Seminary, Crestwood,
N.Y.*
Articles contributed: ORTHODOXY, EASTERN.

Bowden, Henry Warner
Rutgers University, Red Bank, N.J.
Articles contributed: AMERICAN SOCIETY OF CHURCH HISTORY;
BRAINERD, DAVID; MAYHEW, JONATHAN; SCHAFF, PHILIPP.

Boyd, Stephen
Wake Forest University, Winston-Salem, N.C.
Articles contributed: MARPECK, PILGRAM.

Boyer, Paul S.
College of William and Mary, Williamsburg, Va.
Articles contributed: ANTICHRIST; APOCALYPTICISM;
ESCHATOLOGY; NATIVISM.

Brachlow, Stephen
Baptist Theological Seminary at Richmond, Va.
Articles contributed: BROWNE, ROBERT.

Brackney, William
Baylor University, Waco, Tex.
Articles contributed: BAPTISTS, EUROPE.

Bradley, Paul William
Union Theological Seminary, New York, N.Y.
Articles contributed: BEECHER, HENRY WARD; VAN DUSEN,
HENRY P.

Brand, Eugene L.
Lutheran World Federation (retired)
Articles contributed: LUTHERAN WORLD FEDERATION;
LUTHERANISM, GLOBAL.

Brandt, James M.
Saint Paul School of Theology, Kansas City, Mo.
Articles contributed: SCHLEIERMACHER, FRIEDRICH.

Bremer, Francis J.
Millersville University of Pennsylvania
Articles contributed: MATHER, COTTON.

Breward, Ian
*Ormond College, University of Melbourne, Department of
History, University of Melbourne (Australia)*
Articles contributed: PERKINS, WILLIAM.

Brock, Peter
University of Toronto, Canada
Articles contributed: PACIFISM.

Bromley, David G.
Virginia Commonwealth University, Richmond, Va.
Articles contributed: RUSSELL, CHARLES TAZE.

Brooks, Joanna
University of Texas at Austin
Articles contributed: CIRCUIT RIDER; GEORGE, DAVID;
MARRANT, JOHN.

Brower, Gary
Berkeley Canterbury Foundation, Berkeley, Calif.
Articles contributed: ANDREWES, LANCELOT; WREN,
CHRISTOPHER.

Brown, Stewart J.
University of Edinburgh (Scotland)
Articles contributed: CHALMERS, THOMAS.

Brown, Candy Gunther
Saint Louis University, Saint Louis, Mo.
Articles contributed: SLAVERY; SLAVERY, ABOLITION OF;
TORREY, REUBEN ARCHER.

Brown Zikmund, Barbara
Doshisha University (Japan)
Articles contributed: WOMEN CLERGY.

Bruhn, Karen
Arizona State University, Tempe, Ariz.
Articles contributed: COVERDALE, MILES; WHITGIFT, JOHN.

CONTRIBUTORS

Bullock, Steven C.
Worcester Polytechnic Institute, Worcester, Mass.
Articles contributed: FREEMASONRY.

Bultmann, Christoph
University of Erfurt (Germany)
Articles contributed: HERDER, JOHANN GOTTFRIED.

Bumbaugh, David E.
Meadville Lombard Theological School, Chicago, Ill.
Articles contributed: UNITARIAN UNIVERSALIST ASSOCIATION.

Bundy, David
Fuller Theological Seminary, Pasadena, Calif.
Articles contributed: FREE METHODIST CHURCH OF AMERICA;
    MOFFATT, JAMES; PENTECOSTAL ASSEMBLIES OF THE WORLD.

Bunge, Marcia J.
Valparaiso University, Valparaiso, Ind.
Articles contributed: CHILDHOOD.

Burlein, Anne
University of North Carolina at Charlotte
Articles contributed: CHRISTIAN RIGHT.

Burnett, Daniel L.
Oxford Institute for Wesleyan Studies (England)
Articles contributed: WESLEYANISM.

Bushman, Richard Lyman
Columbia University, New York, N.Y.
Articles contributed: SMITH, JOSEPH.

Butler, Anthea
Loyola Marymount University, Los Angeles, Calif.
Articles contributed: NATIONAL BAPTIST CONVENTION OF
    AMERICA; NATIONAL BAPTIST CONVENTION, U.S.A.

Cardoza, Carlos
Columbia Theological Seminary, Decatur, Ga.
Articles contributed: MACKAY, JOHN ALEXANDER.

Carey, Patrick W.
Marquette University, Milwaukee, Wis.
Articles contributed: BROWNSON, ORESTES; EDUCATION,
    THEOLOGY: UNITED STATES.

Carrigan, Jr., Henry L.
Trinity Press / Morehouse Group, Harrisburg, Pa.
Articles contributed: BIBLE; LITERATURE, OVERVIEW;
    McFAGUE, SALLIE; PUBLISHING, MEDIA; ROYCE, JOSIAH.

Carter, Grayson
Fuller Theological Seminary, Pasadena, Calif.
Articles contributed: FORSYTH, PETER TAYLOR; SEABURY,
    SAMUEL.

Carter, David
Carshalton, Surrey, England
Articles contributed: METHODISM.

Carter, Robert Lee
North Chapel Hill Baptist Church, N.C.
Articles contributed: GOODSPEED, EDGAR JOHNSON.

Castleberry, Joseph L.
Assemblies of God Theological Seminary, Springfield, Mo.
Articles contributed: BIBLE COLLEGES AND INSTITUTES.

Cavanaugh, William T.
University of Saint Thomas, Saint Paul, Minn.
Articles contributed: LOCKE, JOHN.

Chamberlain, Ava
Wright State University, Dayton, Ohio
Articles contributed: HUTCHINSON, ANNE.

Chancellor, James D.
Southern Baptist Theological Seminary, Louisville, Ky.
Articles contributed: AMERICAN MISSIONARY ASSOCIATION;
    SUDAN INTERIOR MISSION.

Chapman, James
Regent's Park College, Oxford University (England)
Articles contributed: HUDDLESTON, TREVOR; RAMSEY, ARTHUR
    MICHAEL; SWABIAN SYNGRAMMA.

Chesebrough, David B.
Illinois State University, Normal, Ill.
Articles contributed: PARKER, THEODORE; TRANSCENDENTALISM.

Cheyne, Alexander C.
University of Edinburgh (Scotland)
Articles contributed: BAILLIE, JOHN.

Claydon, Tony
University of Wales, Bangor
Articles contributed: GLORIOUS REVOLUTION.

Clements, William M.
Arkansas State University, Jonesboro, Ark.
Articles contributed: AZUSA STREET REVIVAL; CARTWRIGHT,
    PETER; LEE, ANN; McGUFFEY READERS.

Cobb, Jr., John B.
Claremont School of Theology, Claremont, Calif.
Articles contributed: PROCESS THEOLOGY.

Coffman, Elesha
Duke University, Durham, N.C.
Articles contributed: CADBURY, GEORGE; ELIOT, GEORGE;
    JACKSON, SHELDON.

Coggins, James R.
Mennonite Brethren Herald, Canada
Articles contributed: SMYTH, JOHN.

Cohen, Charles L.
University of Wisconsin at Madison
Articles contributed: HOOKER, THOMAS.

Cohn-Sherbok, Dan
University of Wales, Lampeter
Articles contributed: JUDAISM.

Coleman, Simon M.
Durham University (England)
Articles contributed: TRAVELS AND PILGRIMAGES.

Conser, Jr., Walter H.
University of North Carolina at Wilmington
Articles contributed: NATIONAL ASSOCIATION OF
    EVANGELICALS.

Conway, John S.
University of British Columbia, Canada
Articles contributed: CONFESSING CHURCH.

Cook, Christopher M.
University of Toronto, Canada
Articles contributed: BOSCH, DAVID JACOBUS; HOLINESS
    MOVEMENT; SHEPPARD, RICHARD; TAYLOR, JAMES HUDSON.

Cornwall, Robert
First Christian Church, Santa Barbara, Calif.
Articles contributed: BLOUNT, CHARLES; HERBERT, GEORGE;
    JOWETT, BENJAMIN; STONE, BARTON W.

Corts, Thomas E.
Samford University, Birmingham, Ala.
Articles contributed: DRUMMOND, HENRY.

Crocker, Robert
University of South Australia
Articles contributed: MORE, HENRY.

Crocombe, Jeff
University of Queensland (Australia)
Articles contributed: ADVENT CHRISTIAN CHURCH; VAN DER
    KEMP, JOHANNES THEODORUS.

Crosby, Donald A.
Colorado State University, Fort Collins, Colo.
Articles contributed: BUSHNELL, HORACE.

Crouse, Eric R.
Tyndale University College, Toronto, Canada
Articles contributed: FULL GOSPEL BUSINESSMEN'S
    FELLOWSHIP.

Cusic, Don
Belmont University, Nashville, Tenn.
Articles contributed: MUSIC, POPULAR.

Daniel, William Harrison
Emory University, Atlanta, Ga.
Articles contributed: ITINERACY; METHODIST EPISCOPAL
    CHURCH CONFERENCE.

Daniell, David
Hertford College, Oxford University (England)
Articles contributed: TYNDALE, WILLIAM.

Davidson, Allan
Saint John's College (New Zealand)
Articles contributed: PACIFIC ISLANDS.

Davie, Grace
University of Exeter (England)
Articles contributed: FRANCE.

Davies, Douglas J.
University of Durham (England)
Articles contributed: MORMONISM.

Davis, Edward B.
Messiah College, Grantham, Pa.
Articles contributed: BOYLE, ROBERT.

Dean, William D.
Iliff School of Theology, Denver, Colo.
Articles contributed: EMPIRICAL THEOLOGY.

de Groot, Aart
Zeist, Netherlands
Articles contributed: NETHERLANDS.

de Gruchy, John W.
University of Cape Town (South Africa)
Articles contributed: NAUDE, CHRISTIAAN FREDERICK BEYERS.

DeNeef, A. Leigh
Duke University, Durham, N.C.
Articles contributed: DONNE, JOHN.

Dickerson, Dennis C.
Vanderbilt University, Nashville, Tenn.
Articles contributed: WHEATLEY, PHILLIS.

Dickson, Neil
Troon, Scotland
Articles contributed: PLYMOUTH BRETHREN.

Dieter, Melvin E.
Asbury Theological Seminary, Wilmore, Ky.
Articles contributed: INTERNATIONAL PENTECOSTAL HOLINESS
    CHURCH; PRIMITIVE METHODIST CHURCH; WESLEYAN
    CHURCH; WESLEYAN HOLINESS MOVEMENT.

Dietrich, Donald J.
Boston College, Chestnut Hill, Mass.
Articles contributed: TOTALITARIANISM.

Dixon, Jr., John W.
University of North Carolina at Chapel Hill
Articles contributed: HICKS, EDWARD.

CONTRIBUTORS

Doan, Ruth Alden
Hollins College, Roanoke, Va.
Articles contributed: MILLER, WILLIAM.

Donahue, Mark
University of Oregon, Eugene, Oreg.
Articles contributed: LEWIS, SIR SAMUEL.

Donnelly, Fred
University of New Brunswick, Saint John, Canada
Articles contributed: ARNOLD, THOMAS; BLAKE, WILLIAM; SALT, TITUS.

Douglass, Jane Dempsey
Princeton Theological Seminary, Princeton, N.J.
Articles contributed: WORLD ALLIANCE OF REFORMED CHURCHES.

Dowland, Seth
Duke University, Durham, N.C.
Articles contributed: MORAL MAJORITY.

Downs, Frederick S.
United Theological College (Bangalore, India)
Articles contributed: TRIBAL MOVEMENTS (INDIA).

Dreisbach, Daniel L.
American University, Washington, D.C.
Articles contributed: BILL OF RIGHTS; MADISON, JAMES.

Duke, Debra L.
Princeton Theological Seminary, Princeton, N.J.
Articles contributed: EVANGELICAL AND REFORMED CHURCH.

Duke, James
Texas Christian University, Fort Worth, Tex.
Articles contributed: COTTON, JOHN.

Durden, Robert
Duke University, Durham, N.C.
Articles contributed: DUKE UNIVERSITY.

Durnbaugh, Donald F.
Juniata College, Huntington, Pa.
Articles contributed: IONA COMMUNITY.

Dyson, Erika White
Columbia University, New York, N.Y.
Articles contributed: AMERICAN UNITARIAN ASSOCIATION; NEVIN, JOHN W.

Eire, Carlos M.N.
Yale University, New Haven, Conn.
Articles contributed: ICONOCLASM.

Eitel, Keith E.
Southeastern Baptist Theological Seminary, Wake Forest, N.C.
Articles contributed: VISSER'T HOOFT, WILLEM ADOLF.

Elliott, Mark R.
Samford University, Birmingham, Ala.
Articles contributed: ALL UNION COUNCIL OF EVANGELICAL CHRISTIANS-BAPTISTS.

Ellis, Christopher J.
Bristol Baptist College (England)
Articles contributed: BAPTIST WORLD ALLIANCE.

End, Thomas van den
Articles contributed: BATAK PROTESTANT CHRISTIAN CHURCH OF INDONESIA; INDONESIA.

Endy, Jr., Melvin B.
Saint Mary's College of Maryland
Articles contributed: PENN, WILLIAM.

England, Richard
Salisbury University, Salisbury, Md.
Articles contributed: DARWINISM.

Ericksen, Robert
Pacific Lutheran University, Tacoma, Wash.
Articles contributed: BONHOEFFER, DIETRICH.

Eslinger, Ellen
DePaul University, Chicago, Ill.
Articles contributed: FRONTIER RELIGION.

Essamuah, Casely B.
Park Street Church, Boston, Mass.
Articles contributed: AMISSAH, SAMUEL HANSON; CASELY-HAYFORD, JOSEPH EPHRAIM; OPPONG, KWAME SAMPSON.

Evans, Christopher H.
Colgate Rochester Crozer Divinity School, Rochester, N.Y.
Articles contributed: SOCIAL GOSPEL.

Fackre, Gabriel
Andover Newton Theological School, Newton Centre, Mass.
Articles contributed: BIBLICAL INERRANCY.

Farley, Helen
University of Queensland (Australia)
Articles contributed: FISHER, GEOFFREY FRANCIS; GUSTAVUS ADOLPHUS; MORRISON, CHARLES; OSHITELU, JOSIAH OLUNOWO.

Farwell, James W.
The General Theological Seminary, New York, N.Y.
Articles contributed: BISHOP AND EPISCOPACY; MAURICE, FREDERICK DENISON; SALVATION.

Faupel, D. William
Asbury Theological Seminary, Wilmore, Ky.
Articles contributed: CHURCH OF GOD, ANDERSON, INDIANA; IRVING, EDWARD; MÜLLER, GEORGE; ROBERTS, GRANVILLE ORAL.

Fensham, Charles J.
Knox College, University of Toronto, Canada
Articles contributed: CULTURE; LAUSANNE COMMITTEE ON
WORLD EVANGELIZATION; MASS MEDIA.

Ferguson, Oliver W.
Duke University, Durham, N.C.
Articles contributed: SWIFT, JONATHAN.

Ferré, John P.
University of Louisville, Ky.
Articles contributed: BEST SELLERS IN AMERICA, RELIGIOUS.

Findlay, James
University of Rhode Island, Peace Dale, R.I.
Articles contributed: MOODY, DWIGHT LYMAN; NATIONAL
COUNCIL OF CHURCHES.

Finkenbine, Roy E.
University of Detroit Mercy, Mich.
Articles contributed: PETERS, THOMAS; RUSSWURM, JOHN
BROWN.

Fishburn, Janet Forsythe
Drew University, Madison, N.J.
Articles contributed: DALE, ROBERT WILLIAM;
RAUSCHENBUSCH, WALTER.

Flipper, Joseph
University of Dallas, Tex.
Articles contributed: NIEBUHR, H. RICHARD.

Flynn, Jr., Tyler
Penn State University, University Park, Pa.
Articles contributed: MORAL REARMAMENT.

Flynn, William T.
University of Leeds (England)
Articles contributed: BRITTEN, BENJAMIN; PRAETORIUS,
MICHAEL; TELEMANN, GEORG PHILIPP.

Foster, Douglas A.
Abilene Christian University, Abilene, Tex.
Articles contributed: DISCIPLES OF CHRIST.

Frank, Thomas Edward
Emory University, Atlanta, Ga.
Articles contributed: POLITY.

Freeman, Curtis W.
Duke University, Durham, N.C.
Articles contributed: BAPTIST BIBLE UNION; BAPTISTS, UNITED
STATES; BLISS, PHILIP P.

Freston, Paul
Federal University of Sao Carlos (Brazil)
Articles contributed: BRAZIL; CHILUBA, FREDERICK; LATIN
AMERICA; POLITICAL PARTIES.

Friedman, Jerome
Kent State University, Bowling Green, Ohio
Articles contributed: SERVETUS, MICHAEL.

Friedrich, Norbert
Ruhr-Universitat Bochum (Germany)
Articles contributed: BAUMGARTEN, OTTO; KIRCHENTAG;
LAGARDE, PAUL DE; NAUMANN, FRIEDRICH; RADE, MARTIN;
ZÖLLNER, JOHANN FRIEDRICH.

Friesen, Abraham
University of California at Santa Barbara
Articles contributed: HUBMAIER, BALTHASAR; MENNONITES.

Fulop, Timothy E.
King College, Bristol, Tenn.
Articles contributed: BREECHES BIBLE; COLLINS, ANTHONY;
INDEPENDENT FUNDAMENTAL CHURCHES; KIMBANGU, SIMON.

Fulton, John
Saint Mary's College, University of Surrey (England)
Articles contributed: IRELAND.

Fury, Cheryl
University of New Brunswick, Saint John, Canada
Articles contributed: WINSTANLEY, GERRARD.

Gafney, Wilda
Duke University, Durham, N.C.
Articles contributed: WOMANIST THEOLOGY.

Galli, Mark J.
Christianity Today, Carol Stream, Ill.
Articles contributed: GIDEONS INTERNATIONAL.

Gaustad, Edwin
University of California at Riverside
Articles contributed: BERKELEY, GEORGE; JEFFERSON, THOMAS;
UNITED STATES; WILLIAMS, ROGER.

Geldbach, Erich
Ruhr-Universität Bochum (Germany)
Articles contributed: EVANGELICALS, GERMANY.

Gerrish, Brian A.
Union Theological Seminary, Richmond, Va.
Articles contributed: LORD'S SUPPER.

Gibson, Scott
*Gordon-Conwell Theological Seminary, South Hamilton,
Mass.*
Articles contributed: GORDON, ADONIRAM JUDSON.

Gill, Sean
University of Bristol (England)
Articles contributed: MASCULINITY; SPORTS.

Gill, Robin
University of Kent at Canterbury (England)
Articles contributed: EUTHANASIA.

CONTRIBUTORS

Gillespie, Michael Allen
Duke University, Durham, N.C.
Articles contributed: NIETZSCHE, FRIEDRICH.

Goff, Philip
Indiana University—Purdue University, Indianapolis, Ind.
Articles contributed: CHRISTIAN AND MISSIONARY ALLIANCE.

Gordon, Bruce
University of Saint Andrews (Scotland)
Articles contributed: SWITZERLAND.

Graber, Jennifer
Duke University, Durham, N.C.
Articles contributed: CHURCH WORLD SERVICE; PURCELL, HENRY; SANKEY, IRA DAVID.

Grace, Fran
University of Redlands, Calif.
Articles contributed: TEMPERANCE.

Granquist, Mark
Gustavus Adolphus College, Saint Peter, Minn.
Articles contributed: AUGUSTANA EVANGELICAL LUTHERAN.

Grayson, James Huntley
University of Sheffield (England)
Articles contributed: KOREA.

Greenleaf, Floyd
Independent scholar, Lake Suzy, Fla.
Articles contributed: SEVENTH-DAY ADVENTISTS.

Greschat, Martin
Giessen University (Germany)
Articles contributed: BODELSCHWINGH, FRIEDRICH C.C.; BUCER, MARTIN; CALIXT, GEORGE; DIBELIUS, FRIEDRICH KARL OTTO; HOLL, KARL; PRUSSIAN UNION; RITSCHL, ALBRECHT BENJAMIN; SPALDING, JOHANN JOACHIM; STAHL, FRIEDRICH JULIUS.

Gros, Jeffrey
US Conference of Catholic Bishops, Washington, D.C.
Articles contributed: CATHOLIC REACTIONS TO PROTESTANTISM; CATHOLICISM, PROTESTANT REACTIONS.

Grovier, Kelly
Christ Church, Oxford University (England)
Articles contributed: BOUCHER, JONATHAN; BUTLER, JOSEPH.

Guelzo, Allen
Eastern College, St. David's, Pa.
Articles contributed: LINCOLN, ABRAHAM.

Guenther, Bruce L.
Mennonite Brethren Biblical Seminary, British Columbia, Canada
Articles contributed: EVANGELICALISM.

†Gunton, Colin
King's College (London, England)
Articles contributed: ATONEMENT; CHRISTOLOGY.

Guretzki, David
Briercrest College and Seminary, Caronport, Canada
Articles contributed: CARNELL, EDWARD.

Haemig, Mary Jane
Luther Seminary, Saint Paul, Minn.
Articles contributed: DIBELIUS, MARTIN; THOLUCK, FRIEDRICH AUGUST GOTTREU; THOMASIUS, CHRISTIAN.

Hall, Amy Laura
Duke University, Durham, N.C.
Articles contributed: ETHICS.

Hall, David D.
Harvard University, Cambridge, Mass.
Articles contributed: PURITANISM.

Hall, Douglas John
McGill University, Montreal, Canada
Articles contributed: NEO-ORTHODOXY.

Hall Jr., Lloyd M.
Historian, National Association of Congregational Christian Churches, Oak Creek, Wisc.
Articles contributed: CONGREGATIONALISM.

Hall, Stanley R.
Austin Presbyterian Theological Seminary, Tex.
Articles contributed: WESTMINSTER ASSEMBLY.

Hamm, Thomas D.
Earlham College, Richmond, Ind.
Articles contributed: AMERICAN FRIENDS SERVICE COMMITTEE; SOCIETY OF FRIENDS IN NORTH AMERICA.

Hammond, Guyton B.
Virginia Polytechnic Institute, Blacksburg, Va.
Articles contributed: TILLICH, PAUL.

Han, Jin Hee
New York Theological Seminary, N.Y.
Articles contributed: ART; VOCATION.

Hanciles, Jehu J.
Fuller Theological Seminary, Pasadena, Calif.
Articles contributed: CROWTHER, ARCHDEACON DANDESON; JOHNSON, JAMES; LIVINGSTONE, DAVID.

Hanley, Mark Y.
Truman State University, Kirksville, Mo.
Articles contributed: AMERICAN BOARD OF COMMISSIONERS FOR FOREIGN MISSIONS; TOCQUEVILLE, ALEXIS DE.

Hansen, Gary Neal
University of Dubuque Theological Seminary, Iowa
Articles contributed: CUMBERLAND PRESBYTERIAN CHURCH;
INSTITUTES OF THE CHRISTIAN RELIGION; PREDESTINATION.

Hardage, Jeanette
Charleston, S.C.
Articles contributed: SLESSOR, MARY.

Hardman, Keith
Ursinus College, Collegeville, Pa.
Articles contributed: TAYLOR, NATHANIEL WILLIAM.

Harinck, George
Vrije Universiteit (Netherlands)
Articles contributed: DUTCH REFORMED CHURCH.

Harley, Jason C.
University of Queensland (Australia)
Articles contributed: FAITH.

Harp, Gillis
Grove City College, Pa.
Articles contributed: BROOKS, PHILLIPS; CUMMINS, GEORGE
DAVID; KINGSLEY, CHARLES; SIMEON, CHARLES.

Harrell, David E.
Auburn University, Auburn, Ala.
Articles contributed: ROBERTSON, PAT.

Harrison, Peter
University of Queensland (Australia)
Articles contributed: SCIENCE.

Harrison, Wes
Ohio Valley College, Vienna, W. Va.
Articles contributed: HUTTER, JAKOB; HUTTERITES; SOCIETY OF
BROTHERS.

Hart, Darryl G.
Intercollegiate Studies Institute, Wilmington, Del.
Articles contributed: MACHEN, JOHN GRESHAM.

Harvey, Paul
University of Colorado at Colorado Springs
Articles contributed: GENERAL BAPTISTS; NATIONAL PRIMITIVE
BAPTIST CONVENTION; PRIMITIVE BAPTIST CHURCHES;
STRAUSS, DAVID FRIEDRICH.

Harvey, Van A.
Stanford University, Calif.
Articles contributed: FEUERBACH, LUDWIG.

Hauschild, Wolf-Dieter
University of Muenster (Germany)
Articles contributed: BUGENHAGEN, JOHANNES.

Hawkins, Jr., Merrill M.
Carson-Newman College, Jefferson City, Tenn.
Articles contributed: FREE WILL BAPTISTS.

Hawn, C. Michael
Southern Methodist University, Dallas, Tex.
Articles contributed: MUSIC, GLOBAL.

Hedlund, Roger E.
Mylapore Institute for Indigenous Studies (India)
Articles contributed: NORTH INDIA, CHURCH OF.

Heininen, Simo
University of Helsinki (Finland)
Articles contributed: AGRICOLA, MICHAEL; FINLAND.

Heitzenrater, Richard P.
Duke University, Durham, N.C.
Articles contributed: WESLEY, CHARLES; WESLEY, JOHN.

Hensley, Jeffrey
Virginia Theological Seminary, Alexandria, Va.
Articles contributed: LIBERAL PROTESTANTISM AND LIBERALISM;
ORTHODOXY.

Hequet, Suzanne S.
Luther Seminary, St. Paul, Minn.
Articles contributed: AUGSBURG INTERIM.

Herdt, Jennifer A.
University of Notre Dame, South Bend, Ind.
Articles contributed: HUME, DAVID.

Herring, George
*University of Bradford, University of Leeds, and University
of York (England)*
Articles contributed: OXFORD MOVEMENT.

Hewitt, T. Furman
Duke University, Durham, N.C.
Articles contributed: BACKUS, ISAAC.

Hillerbrand, Hans
Duke University, Durham, N.C.
Articles contributed: ARNOLD, EBERHARD; ANTI-SEMITISM;
BAUER, BRUNO; BIBLE, KING JAMES VERSION; BRAGHT,
TIELEMAN JANSZ VAN; DAVID, FRANCIS (FERENC); DIPPEL,
JOHANN CONRAD; DISTLER, HUGO; EBERHARDT, W.;
ERASTUS, THOMAS; EVANGELICAL ALLIANCE; FELGENHAUER,
PAUL; FRANCKE, AUGUST HERMANN; GERHARDT, PAUL;
GRUNDTVIG, NICOLAJ FREDERICK SEVERIN; LAESTADIUS, LARS
LEVI; LAMBETH QUADRILATERAL; MACKENZIE, JOHN; SERPENT
HANDLERS; SHEPPARD, WILLIAM HENRY; STRONG, JOSIAH.

Hilliard, David
Flinders University (Australia)
Articles contributed: AUSTRALIA.

Hillier, H. Chad
Wycliffe College, University of Toronto, Canada
Articles contributed: BAPTIST GENERAL CONFERENCE; CHURCH
OF GOD IN CHRIST; EVANGELICAL FREE CHURCH OF AMERICA.

CONTRIBUTORS

Himes, Michael J.
Boston College, Chestnut Hill, Mass.
Articles contributed: MOHLER, JOHANN ADAM.

Hodder, Alan D.
Hampshire College, Amherst, Mass.
Articles contributed: EMERSON, RALPH WALDO.

Hofmeyr, J. W.
University of Pretoria (South Africa)
Articles contributed: SOUTH AFRICA.

Holifield, E. Brooks
Emory University, Atlanta, Ga.
Articles contributed: COVENANT THEOLOGY; EDWARDS, JONATHAN.

Holmes, Finlay
Union Theological College (Northern Ireland)
Articles contributed: COOKE, HENRY; ULSTER.

Holmes, David L.
College of William and Mary, Williamsburg, Va.
Articles contributed: EPISCOPAL CHURCH, UNITED STATES.

Homan, Roger
University of Brighton (England)
Articles contributed: FAITH HEALING.

Howes, Graham A. K.
Cambridge University (England)
Articles contributed: RICHARDSON, HENRY HOBSON.

Huber, Donald L.
Trinity Lutheran Seminary, Columbus, Ohio
Articles contributed: BEECHER, LYMAN; BURNED-OVER DISTRICT; STOWE, HARRIET BEECHER; WELD, THEODORE DWIGHT.

Hunt, Stephen
University of the West of England
Articles contributed: HUMAN RIGHTS.

Hunt, Robert
English-Speaking United Methodist Church (Austria)
Articles contributed: BIBLE TRANSLATION.

Hunter, George
Asbury Theological Seminary, Wilmore, Ky.
Articles contributed: MEGA-CHURCHES.

Hunter, Harold
International Pentecostal Holiness Church Archives and Research Center, Oklahoma City, Okla.
Articles contributed: CHURCH OF GOD OF PROPHECY.

Hutchinson, Mark
Southern Cross College (Australia)
Articles contributed: ITALY; UNITING CHURCH IN AUSTRALIA.

Ion, A. Hamish
Royal Military College of Canada, Ontario, Canada
Articles contributed: JAPAN.

Jacobsen, Douglas
Messiah College, Grantham, Pa.
Articles contributed: LATTER RAIN REVIVAL.

James III, Frank A.
Reformed Theological Seminary, Oviedo, Fla.
Articles contributed: ELECTION; JUSTIFICATION.

Janet, Richard J.
Rockhurst University, Kansas City, Mo.
Articles contributed: TEMPLE, FREDERICK.

Japinga, Lynn
Hope College, Holland, Mich.
Articles contributed: REFORMED CHURCH IN AMERICA.

Jarvis, Alec
Regent's Park College, Oxford University (England)
Articles contributed: BLOMFIELD, CHARLES; MACLEOD, NORMAN; MARTINEAU, JAMES; WHITE, WILLIAM HALE.

Jauhiainen, Peter D.
Kirkwood Community College, Cedar Rapids, Iowa
Articles contributed: HOPKINS, SAMUEL.

Jeffrey, David Lyle
Baylor University, Waco, Tex.
Articles contributed: BIBLE AND LITERATURE.

Jeyaraj, Daniel
Princeton Theological Seminary, Princeton, N.J.
Articles contributed: INDIA.

Johnson, Todd M.
Gordon Conwell Theological Seminary, South Hamilton, Mass.
Articles contributed: HOUSE CHURCHES (ASIA); STATISTICS.

Jones, Norman L.
Utah State University, Logan, Utah
Articles contributed: ELIZABETH I (ELIZABETH TUDOR).

Jones, Arun W.
Austin Presbyterian Theological Seminary, Tex.
Articles contributed: BRENT, CHARLES; INDIAN THEOLOGY.

Jones, Ken Sundet
Luther Seminary, Saint Paul, Minn.
Articles contributed: CAPITO, WOLFGANG.

Jones, Gareth
Canterbury Christ Church University College (England)
Articles contributed: BRUNNER, EMIL; THEOLOGY.

Jongeneel, Jan
Bunni, Netherlands
Articles contributed: KRAEMER, HENDRIK.

Kaiser, Jochen-Christian
Philipps-Universitaet Marburg (Germany)
Articles contributed: WICHERN, JOHANN HEINRICH; WÜNSCH, GEORG.

Kalme, Guntis
Luther Academy of the Evangelical Lutheran Church of Latvia (ELCL)
Articles contributed: LATVIA.

Kaplan, Benjamin J.
University College London (England)
Articles contributed: ARMINIUS, JACOBUS.

Karthaus, Ulrich
Giesse, Germany
Articles contributed: GOETHE, JOHANN WOLFGANG; LITERATURE, GERMAN; SCHILLER, JOHANN CHRISTOPH FRIEDRICH.

Kazin, Michael
Georgetown University, Washington, D.C.
Articles contributed: BRYAN, WILLIAM JENNINGS.

Keck, David
Duke University, Durham, N.C.
Articles contributed: PHILIPPINES.

Kee, Alistair
University of Edinburgh (Scotland)
Articles contributed: DEATH OF GOD.

Keen, Ralph
University of Iowa, Iowa City, Iowa
Articles contributed: HEIDELBERG CATECHISM OF 1563; HELVETIC CONFESSION; MELANCHTHON, PHILIPP.

Keller, Rosemary S.
Union Theological Seminary, New York, N.Y.
Articles contributed: HARKNESS, GEORGIA; WOMEN, UNITED STATES.

Kelly, Maureen
Boston College, Chestnut Hill, Mass.
Articles contributed: WORLD VISION.

Kemeny, P.C.
Grove City College, Pa.
Articles contributed: INTERVARSITY CHRISTIAN FELLOWSHIP.

Kerfoot, Donna
McMaster Divinity College, Ontario, Canada
Articles contributed: BAPTIST FAMILY OF CHURCHES.

Kerr, Fergus
Blackfriars Hall, University of Oxford (England)
Articles contributed: TRANSUBSTANTIATION.

Kerr, Nathan
Vanderbilt University, Nashville, Tenn.
Articles contributed: SACRAMENTS.

Kidd, Thomas S.
Baylor University, Waco, Tex.
Articles contributed: WOLLASTON, WILLIAM.

Kilde, Jeanne Halgren
Macalester College, Saint Paul, Minn.
Articles contributed: ALTARS; COMMUNION TABLES.

King, John N.
Ohio State University, Columbus, Ohio
Articles contributed: FOXE, JOHN.

King, William M.
Albright College, Reading, Pa.
Articles contributed: ECUMENISM; GLADDEN, WASHINGTON; INTERCHURCH WORLD MOVEMENT; SMITH, W. ROBERTSON.

Kingdon, Robert
University of Wisçonsin at Madison
Articles contributed: CALVIN, JOHN; CONSISTORY; ECCLESIASTICAL ORDINANCES.

Kirchhoff, Karl-Heinz
Münster, Germany
Articles contributed: ROTHMANN, BERNHARD.

Kirkley, Evelyn A.
University of San Diego, Calif.
Articles contributed: MOTT, LUCRETIA COFFIN; STANTON, ELIZABETH CADY.

Kittelson, James
Luther Seminary, St. Paul, Minn.
Articles contributed: AUGSBURG CONFESSION.

Klaassen, Walter
Conrad Grebel College, British Columbia, Canada
Articles contributed: GREBEL, CONRAD.

Klassen, William
University of Toronto, Canada
Articles contributed: ANABAPTISM.

Knudsen, Jon P.
Nordregio, the Nordic Centre for Spatial Development (Sweden)
Articles contributed: HAUGE, HANS NIELSEN.

CONTRIBUTORS

Kolb, Robert
Concordia Seminary, St. Louis, Mo.
Articles contributed: BOOK OF CONCORD; FLACIUS, MATTHIAS;
  LUTHER, MARTIN; LUTHERANISM; MARTYRS AND
  MARTYROLOGIES.

Koop, Karl
Canadian Mennonite University, Manitoba, Canada
Articles contributed: SCHLEITHEIM CONFESSION.

Kort, Wesley A.
Duke University, Durham, N.C.
Articles contributed: DEVRIES, PETER; LEWIS, C. S.

Kraftchick, Steve
Emory University, Atlanta, Ga.
Articles contributed: JESUS, LIVES OF.

Kraybill, Donald B.
Elizabethtown College, Pa.
Articles contributed: AMISH.

Kreider, Glenn R.
Dallas Theological Seminary, Tex.
Articles contributed: DARBY, JOHN NELSON;
  DISPENSATIONALISM; TRIBULATIONISM.

Kreitzer, Beth
Saint Vincent College, Latrobe, Pa.
Articles contributed: MARY, VIRGIN; PARACELSUS,
  THEOPHRASTUS.

Labode, Modupe
Colorado Historical Society, Denver, Colo.
Articles contributed: LIBERIA.

Lagerquist, L. DeAne
Saint Olaf College, Northfield, Minn.
Articles contributed: AMERICAN LUTHERAN CHURCH.

Lamberth, David C.
Harvard Divinity School, Cambridge, Mass.
Articles contributed: JAMES, WILLIAM.

Land, Gary
Andrews University, Berrien Springs, Mich.
Articles contributed: WHITE, ELLEN GOULD.

Landes, Richard
Boston University, Mass.
Articles contributed: MILLENARIANS AND MILLENNIALISM.

Larsen, Timothy
Wheaton College, Ill.
Articles contributed: COLENSO, JOHN WILLIAM.

Laughlin, Jay
College of Charleston, S.C.
Articles contributed: BENNETT, JOHN; PUFENDORF, SAMUEL.

Lausten, Martin Schwarz
Kobenhavns Universitet (Denmark)
Articles contributed: DENMARK.

Leaver, Robin A.
*Westminster Choir College of Rider University, Princeton,
N.J.*
Articles contributed: ANGLICAN CHANT; HYMNS AND HYMNALS;
  MUSIC, AMERICAN; MUSIC, NORTHERN EUROPEAN.

Lechner, Frank J.
Emory University, Atlanta, Ga.
Articles contributed: SECULARIZATION.

Legood, Giles
University of London (England)
Articles contributed: CHAPLAINCY.

Lehmann, Hartmut
Max-Planck-Institut Für Geschichte (Germany)
Articles contributed: ABSOLUTISM; NATIONALISM.

Lehmberg, Stanford
University of Minnesota, Minneapolis
Articles contributed: CIVIL WAR, ENGLAND; LAUD, WILLIAM;
  MUSIC, OVERVIEW; MUSIC, ENGLISH CHURCH; VAUGHAN
  WILLIAMS, RALPH.

Leonard, Bill J.
Wake Forest University, Winston-Salem, N.C.
Articles contributed: KU KLUX KLAN; SOUTHERN BAPTIST
  CONVENTION.

Lettinga, Cornelis H.
Bethel College, St. Paul, Minn.
Articles contributed: BOESAK, ALAN; DUTCH REFORMED
  CHURCH IN AFRICA.

Lewis, Bonnie Sue
University of Dubuque Theological Seminary, Iowa
Articles contributed: NATIVE AMERICANS.

Lindberg, Carter
Boston University, Mass.
Articles contributed: REFORMATION.

Lineham, Peter
Massey University at Albany (New Zealand)
Articles contributed: ANTINOMIANISM; CHILIASM; NEW
  ZEALAND; SUNDAY SCHOOL; WHITEFIELD, GEORGE.

Lippy, Charles
University of Tennessee at Chattanooga
Articles contributed: CHRISTADELPHIANS; SOUTHERN
  PROTESTANTISM.

Little, David L.
University of Queensland (Australia)
Articles contributed: GARRISON, WINFRED; HIGHER EDUCATION;
  RESTORATIONISM.

Little, Geoffrey A.
Church Mission Society, New Haven, Conn.
Articles contributed: CHURCH MISSION SOCIETY.

Liu, David U.
Duke University, Durham, N.C.
Articles contributed: CHERBURY, EDWARD LORD HERBERT OF;
FELLOWSHIP OF SOUTHERN CHURCHMEN; MODERNISM.

Loades, Ann
University of Durham (England)
Articles contributed: FEMINIST THEOLOGY; UNDERHILL,
EVELYN.

Loades, David
University of Sheffield (England)
Articles contributed: ACTS AND MONUMENTS; CRANMER,
THOMAS.

Lochman, Jan Milic
University of Basel (Switzerland)
Articles contributed: HROMADKA, JOSEF.

Long, Kimberly Bracken
Drew University, Madison, N.J.
Articles contributed: LITURGY.

Long, Thomas G.
Emory University, Atlanta, Ga.
Articles contributed: FUNERARY RITES.

Longenecker, Steve
Bridgewater College, Va.
Articles contributed: OBERLIN, JOHANN FRIEDRICH;
SCHMUCKER, SAMUEL SIMON.

Lorion, Amy E.
University of North Carolina at Chapel Hill
Articles contributed: CHRISTIAN SCIENCE.

Lotz-Heumann, Ute
Humboldt-Universität (Germany)
Articles contributed: CONFESSIONALIZATION.

Lovegrove, Deryck W.
Saint Mary's College, University of Saint Andrews (Scotland)
Articles contributed: LAITY.

Luman, Richard
Ottumwa, Iowa
Articles contributed: ICELAND.

Lund, Eric
Saint Olaf College, Northfield, Minn.
Articles contributed: BERGGRAV, EIVIND; LUTHERANISM,
GERMANY; LUTHERANISM, SCANDINAVIA; LUTHERANISM,
UNITED STATES.

Lundin, Roger
Wheaton College, Wheaton, Ill.
Articles contributed: DICKINSON, EMILY.

Macquiban, Tim
Sarum College (England)
Articles contributed: BOURNE, HUGH; CHUBB, THOMAS; COOK,
THOMAS; FISK, WILBUR; FREEMAN, THOMAS BIRCH;
GLADSTONE, WILLIAM EWART; HASTINGS, LADY SELINA;
MACLEOD, GEORGE FIELDEN; METHODISM, ENGLAND;
WEATHERHEAD, LESLIE.

Maddox, Marion
Victoria University of Wellington (New Zealand)
Articles contributed: COCCEJUS, JOHANNES.

Mallampalli, Chandra S.
Westmont College, Santa Barbara, Calif.
Articles contributed: MASS MOVEMENTS (INDIA); SOUTH INDIA,
CHURCH OF.

Malpezzi, Frances
Arkansas State University, Jonesboro, Ark.
Articles contributed: LEADE, JANE WARD.

Mamiya, Lawrence H.
Vassar College, Poughkeepsie, N.Y.
Articles contributed: AFRICAN AMERICAN PROTESTANTISM.

Manetsch, Scott M.
Trinity Evangelical Divinity School, Deerfield, Ill.
Articles contributed: BEZA, THEODORE.

Marcuse, Deborah K.
Duke University, Durham, N.C.
Articles contributed: ASCETICISM; LATIMER, HUGH; OCHINO,
BERNARDINO; POISSY, COLLOQUY OF.

Marini, Stephen
Wellesley College, Mass.
Articles contributed: AWAKENINGS; SECTARIANISM.

Marino, Gordon
St. Olaf College, Northfield, Minn.
Articles contributed: KIERKEGAARD, SOREN A.

Martin, Jessica
Cambridge University (England)
Articles contributed: WALTON, ISAAC.

Martin, Sandy
University of Georgia, Athens, Ga.
Articles contributed: AFRICAN METHODIST EPISCOPAL CHURCH;
AFRICAN METHODIST EPISCOPAL ZION CHURCH; AMERICAN
COLONIZATION SOCIETY; PROGRESSIVE NATIONAL BAPTIST
CONVENTION.

Martin, William
Rice University, Houston, Tex.
Articles contributed: GRAHAM, BILLY.

CONTRIBUTORS

Martinich, A.P.
University of Texas at Austin
Articles contributed: HOBBES, THOMAS.

Mason, Roger A.
University of St. Andrews (Scotland)
Articles contributed: KNOX, JOHN.

Massanari, Ronald L.
Alma College, Mich.
Articles contributed: STOECKER, ADOLF.

Mathers, Helen
University of Sheffield (England)
Articles contributed: BUTLER, JOSEPHINE.

Matson, Mark A.
Milligan College, Tenn.
Articles contributed: CHURCHES OF CHRIST, NON-
   INSTRUMENTAL.

Maughan, Steven S.
Albertson College, Caldwell, Idaho
Articles contributed: MISSIONS, BRITISH.

Mayer, Thomas F.
Augustana College, Rock Island, Ill.
Articles contributed: HOOKER, RICHARD.

McArver, Susan Wilds
Lutheran Theological Southern Seminary, Columbia, S.C.
Articles contributed: LUTHERAN CHURCH IN AMERICA.

McCormick, Kelley Steve
Mount Vernon Nazarene University, Mount Vernon, Ohio
Articles contributed: ASBURY, FRANCIS.

McCrossen, Alexis
Southern Methodist University, Dallas, Tex.
Articles contributed: HOLIDAYS AND FESTIVALS;
   SABBATARIANISM.

McCulloh, Gerald W.
Loyola University, Chicago, Ill.
Articles contributed: MARHEINEKE, PHILIPP KONRAD.

McDermott, Gerald R.
Roanoke College, Salem, Va.
Articles contributed: DEISM.

McGee, Gary B.
Assemblies of God Theological Seminary, Springfield, Mo.
Articles contributed: ASSEMBLIES OF GOD.

McGinnis, Scott
Samford University, Birmingham, Ala.
Articles contributed: CARTWRIGHT, THOMAS; MELVILLE,
   ANDREW.

McIntire, C. T.
University of Toronto (Canada)
Articles contributed: BUTTERFIELD, HERBERT; ROUSSEAU, JEAN-
   JACQUES; SABATIER, AUGUSTE; SABATIER, PAUL.

McKim, Donald K.
Westminster John Knox Press, Germantown, Tenn.
Articles contributed: BERKHOF, HENDRIKUS; CALVINISM;
   WESTMINSTER CATECHISM; WESTMINSTER CONFESSION.

McLaughlin, Emmet
Villanova University, Villanova, Pa.
Articles contributed: CELIBACY; CLERGY; CLERGY, MARRIAGE
   OF; FRANCK, SEBASTIAN; MÜNTZER, THOMAS;
   SCHWENCKFELD, CASPAR; SPIRITUALISM; WEIGEL, VALENTIN.

McLeod, Hugh
University of Birmingham (England)
Articles contributed: INDUSTRIALIZATION.

Meeks, M. Douglas
Vanderbilt University, Nashville, Tenn.
Articles contributed: MOLTMANN, JÜRGEN; THEOLOGY,
   TWENTIETH-CENTURY, NORTH AMERICAN.

Megivern, James J.
University of North Carolina at Wilmington
Articles contributed: CAPITAL PUNISHMENT.

Mellers, Wilfrid
Professor Emeritus, University of York (England)
Articles contributed: BACH, JOHANN SEBASTIAN.

Mentzer, Raymond A.
University of Iowa, Iowa City
Articles contributed: BELGIC CONFESSION OF 1561; COLIGNY,
   GASPARD; DORT, CANONS OF; GALLICAN CONFESSION;
   HUGUENOTS; LE NAIN DE TILLEMONT, LOUIS-SEBASTIEN;
   RESTITUTION, EDICT OF.

Michalson, Jr., Gordon E.
New College of Florida, Sarasota, Fla.
Articles contributed: KANT, IMMANUEL.

Miller, Glenn T.
Bangor Theological Seminary, Maine
Articles contributed: KINGDOM OF GOD; SEMINARIES.

Moeller, Eric
Concordia University, River Forest, Ill.
Articles contributed: SOCIOLOGY OF PROTESTANTISM.

Morgan, David
Valparaiso University, Valparaiso, Ind.
Articles contributed: AESTHETICS; ICONOGRAPHY.

Morgan, Robert
Oxford University (England)
Articles contributed: BULTMANN, RUDOLF.

Moses, Wilson J.
Penn State University, University Park, Pa.
Articles contributed: CRUMMELL, ALEXANDER.

Mühling, Andreas
Universität Bonn (Germany), Universität Trier (Germany),
and Universität Luzern (Switzerland)
Articles contributed: BARTH, HEINRICH; CONVENTICLES;
GOMAR, FRANZ; GOMARIANS; HARNACK, ADOLF VON;
SCHWEITZER, ALBERT; SWEDENBORG, EMANUEL.

Mulder, John
Louisville Seminary, Ky.
Articles contributed: WILSON, WOODROW.

Mullett, Michael Anthony
Lancaster University (England)
Articles contributed: BUNYAN, JOHN; FOX, GEORGE; FRIENDS,
SOCIETY OF.

Mullin, Robert Bruce
The General Theological Seminary, New York, N.Y.
Articles contributed: BROAD CHURCH; DENOMINATION; PUSEY,
EDWARD BOUVERIE.

Mumm, Susan
The Open University (Milton Keynes, England)
Articles contributed: SISTERHOODS, ANGLICAN.

Murdoch, Norman H.
University of Cincinnati, Ohio
Articles contributed: PHILANTHROPY; ZIMBABWE.

Murdock, Graeme
University of Birmingham (England)
Articles contributed: HUNGARY; ROMANIA.

Murray, Michael J.
Franklin and Marshall College, Lancaster, Pa.
Articles contributed: LEIBNIZ, GOTTFRIED WILHELM.

Nestingen, James Arne
Luther Seminary, Saint Paul, Minn.
Articles contributed: EVANGELICAL LUTHERAN CHURCH IN
AMERICA; GNESIO-LUTHERANS; PRIESTHOOD OF ALL
BELIEVERS.

Newberry, Warren B.
Assemblies of God Theological Seminary, Springfield, Mo.
Articles contributed: ALLEN, ROLAND; MALAWI.

Newman Brooks, Peter
Robinson College, Cambridge University (England)
Articles contributed: BOOK OF COMMON PRAYER; PARKER
SOCIETY; THIRTY-NINE ARTICLES.

Ng, Maria N.
University of Alberta, Canada
Articles contributed: KINGSLEY, MARY.

Nixon, Jude V.
Oakland University, Rochester, Mich.
Articles contributed: LIDDON, HENRY PARRY.

Noll, Mark A.
Wheaton College, Ill.
Articles contributed: BOUDINOT, ELIAS; WITHERSPOON, JOHN.

Nordbeck, Elizabeth
Andover Newton Theological School, Newton Centre, Mass.
Articles contributed: UNITED CHURCH OF CHRIST.

Oakley, Francis
Williams College, Williamstown, Mass.
Articles contributed: RICHER, EDMOND.

O'Connor, Daniel
University of Edinburgh (Scotland)
Articles contributed: ANDREWS, CHARLES FREER;
MONASTICISM; SOCIETY FOR PROMOTING CHRISTIAN
KNOWLEDGE; SOCIETY FOR THE PROPAGATION OF THE GOSPEL.

Oehlschlaeger, Fritz
Virginia Tech, Blacksburg, Va.
Articles contributed: WOOLMAN, JOHN.

Ogasapian, John
University of Massachusetts at Lowell
Articles contributed: WATTS, ISAAC.

Olbricht, Thomas H.
Pepperdine University, Malibu, Calif.
Articles contributed: CAMPBELL FAMILY; CAMPBELL, JOHN.

Olson, Jeannine E.
Rhode Island College, Providence, R.I.
Articles contributed: DEACONESS, DEACON; FAREL, GUILLAUME;
GENEVA BIBLE.

Olson, Roger E.
Baylor University, Waco, Tex.
Articles contributed: EVANGELICALISM, THEOLOGY OF;
THEOLOGY, TWENTIETH-CENTURY, GLOBAL.

O'Malley, J. Steven
Asbury Theological Seminary, Wilmore, Ky.
Articles contributed: EVANGELICAL UNITED BRETHREN CHURCH;
GERMAN GROUPS IN AMERICA; SPENER, PHILIPP JAKOB.

Omenyo, Cephas N.
University of Ghana
Articles contributed: ATTOH-AHUMA, SAMUEL RICHARD BREW;
BAËTA, CHRISTIAN GONCALVES KWAMI; BASEL MISSION;
DuBOIS, W.E.B.; REINDORF, CARL CHRISTIAN.

O'Neill, J.C.
The University of Edinburgh (Scotland)
Articles contributed: HIGHER CRITICISM; LESSING, GOTTHOLD
EPHRAIM; OVERBECK, FRANZ CAMILLE.

CONTRIBUTORS

Osborn, Robert
Duke Divinity School, Durham, N.C.
Articles contributed: BARMEN DECLARATION; DEATH AND DYING.

Ostwalt, Conrad
Appalachian State Unversity, Boone, N.C.
Articles contributed: MOVIES.

Pädam, Tiit
Eesti Evangeelne Luterlik Kirik (Estonia)
Articles contributed: ESTONIA.

Pak, G. Sujin
Garrett-Evangelical Theological Seminary, Evanston, Ill.
Articles contributed: AMSDORF, NIKOLAUS VON; MOON, SUN MYUNG; TINDAL, MATTHEW; WOOLSTON, THOMAS.

Pasquier, Michael
Florida State University, Tallahassee, Fla.
Articles contributed: CALVERT FAMILY.

Paz, D. G.
University of North Texas, Denton, Tex.
Articles contributed: ANGLO-CATHOLICISM.

Peacock, Jim
University of North Carolina, Chapel Hill
Articles contributed: WEBER, MAX.

Peay, Steven
First Congregational Church, Wauwatosa, Wisc.
Articles contributed: CONGREGATIONALISM.

Peel, J. D. Y.
University of London (England)
Articles contributed: NIGERIA.

Pember, Sherry
Wilfrid Laurier University, Ontario, Canada
Articles contributed: ADIAPHORA.

Peters, Melvin K. H.
Duke University, Durham, N.C.
Articles contributed: CARIBBEAN.

Peters, Ted
Pacific Lutheran Theological Seminary, Berkeley, Calif.
Articles contributed: NEW AGE MOVEMENTS.

Peterson, Kurt W.
North Park University, Chicago, Ill.
Articles contributed: McINTIRE, CARL.

Pfister, Lauren
Hong Kong Baptist University
Articles contributed: LEGGE, JAMES; NEE, WATCHMAN (NI TUOSHENG); WANG, MING DAO (WANG MINGDAO).

Phillips, Thomas E.
Colorado Christian University, Lakewood, Colo.
Articles contributed: COKE, THOMAS; MATHEWS, SHAILER; SANCTIFICATION; WWJD.

Pierard, Richard V.
Gordon College, Wenham, Mass.
Articles contributed: BAPTIST MISSIONS.

Pinches, Charles R.
University of Scranton, Pa.
Articles contributed: ECOLOGY.

Piper, John
Lycoming College, Williamsport, Pa.
Articles contributed: COFFIN, HENRY SLOANE; FOSDICK, HARRY EMERSON; FREE CHURCH FEDERAL COUNCIL; PEALE, NORMAN VINCENT; ROBINSON, HENRY WHEELER.

Plunkett, Stephen W.
Saint Andrew Presbyterian Church, Denton, Tex.
Articles contributed: CONVERSION.

Pointer, Richard W.
Westmont College, Santa Barbara, Calif.
Articles contributed: ELIOT, JOHN.

Pointer, Steven R.
Trinity International University, Deerfield, Ill.
Articles contributed: HENRY, CARL F. H.

Pollock, Kelly Therese
University of California at Santa Barbara
Articles contributed: YMCA, YWCA.

Pope, Robert
University of Wales, Bangor
Articles contributed: WALES.

Porter, Andrew
King's College, University of London (England)
Articles contributed: COLONIALISM.

Porterfield, Amanda
Florida State University, Tallahassee, Fla.
Articles contributed: EDDY, MARY BAKER.

Powell, Samuel M.
Point Loma Nazarene University, San Diego, Calif.
Articles contributed: HEGEL, GEORG WILHELM FRIEDRICH; NEOLOGY; SCHELLING, FRIEDRICH VON; WOLFF, CHRISTIAN.

Pratt, Dorothy O.
University of Notre Dame, South Bend, Ind.
Articles contributed: CONSCIENTIOUS OBJECTION.

Prickett, Stephen
Baylor University, Waco, Tex.
Articles contributed: BROWNING, ROBERT; COLERIDGE, SAMUEL
TAYLOR; ELIOT, T. S.; ROMANTICISM; TENNYSON, ALFRED,
LORD; WORDSWORTH, WILLIAM.

Rabin, Sheila J.
Saint Peter's College, Jersey City, N.J.
Articles contributed: KEPLER, JOHANNES; NEWTON, ISAAC.

Ramírez, Daniel
Arizona State University, Tempe, Ariz.
Articles contributed: MEXICO.

Raser, Harold E.
Nazarene Theological Seminary, Kansas City, Mo.
Articles contributed: PALMER, PHOEBE WORRALL.

Rast, Jr., Lawrence R.
Concordia Theological Seminary, Fort Wayne, Ind.
Articles contributed: LUTHERAN CHURCH—MISSOURI SYNOD,
THE.

Remillard, Arthur J.
Florida State University, Tallahassee, Fla.
Articles contributed: BENTHAM, JEREMY; CHANNING, WILLIAM
ELLERY.

Rex, Richard
Queens' College, Cambridge University (England)
Articles contributed: HENRY VIII.

Richardson, James T.
University of Nevada, Reno, Nev.
Articles contributed: JESUS MOVEMENT.

Richardson, R. C.
King Alfred's College (England)
Articles contributed: LEVELLERS.

Rieger, Joerg
Southern Methodist University, Dallas, Tex.
Articles contributed: LIBERATION THEOLOGY; POLITICAL
THEOLOGY; THEOLOGY, TWENTIETH-CENTURY.

Ringenberg, William C.
Taylor University, Upland, Ind.
Articles contributed: CHRISTIAN COLLEGES.

Robert, Dana L.
Boston University, Mass.
Articles contributed: MISSIONS; PIERSON, ARTHUR TAPPAN.

Roberts, J. Deotis
Duke University, Durham, N.C.
Articles contributed: BLACK THEOLOGY; CONE, JAMES HAL.

Rodgerson Pleasants, Phyllis
Baptist Theological Seminary at Richmond, Va.
Articles contributed: BAPTISTS, GLOBAL.

Roebuck, David
Lee University, Cleveland, Tenn.
Articles contributed: CHURCH OF GOD, CLEVELAND,
TENNESSEE; PENTECOSTAL CHURCH OF GOD; PENTECOSTAL/
CHARISMATIC CHURCHES OF NORTH AMERICA; PENTECOSTAL
WORLD FELLOWSHIP.

Rosin, Robert
Concordia Seminary, Saint Louis, Mo.
Articles contributed: KRAUTH, CHARLES PORTERFIELD;
LUTHERAN SYNODICAL CONFERENCE; OSIANDER, ANDREAS;
WALTHER, CARL FERDINAND WILHELM.

Ross, Andrew C.
University of Edinburgh (Scotland)
Articles contributed: MOFFAT, ROBERT; PHILIP, JOHN.

Ross, Kenneth R.
Church of Scotland (Edinburgh, Scotland)
Articles contributed: BOOTH, JOSEPH; CHURCH OF SCOTLAND;
ETHNICITY.

Roth, John D.
Goshen College, Ind.
Articles contributed: SATTLER, MICHAEL.

Rubinstein, William D.
University of Wales, Aberystwyth
Articles contributed: PHILO-SEMITISM.

Rumrich, John
University of Texas at Austin
Articles contributed: MILTON, JOHN.

Rumscheidt, Martin
Atlantic School of Theology, Nova Scotia, Canada
Articles contributed: GOGARTEN, FRIEDRICH; NIEMOLLER,
MARTIN; RAGAZ, LEONHARD.

Ruse, Michael
Florida State University, Tallahassee, Fla.
Articles contributed: CREATION SCIENCE.

Russell, Colin A.
The Open University (England)
Articles contributed: BACON, FRANCIS; FARADAY, MICHAEL;
NATURE; PRIESTLEY, JOSEPH.

Russell, Jeffrey Burton
University of California at Santa Barbara
Articles contributed: DEVIL; HEAVEN AND HELL.

Russell, William R.
Bethel Lutheran Church, Porter, Minn.
Articles contributed: NYGREN, ANDERS; OECOLAMPADIUS,
JOHANNES; SCHMALKALDIC ARTICLES; SCHMALKALDIC
LEAGUE.

CONTRIBUTORS

Ruth, Lester
Asbury Theological Seminary, Wilmore, Ky.
Articles contributed: CAMP MEETING.

Rylaarsdam, David
Calvin Theological Seminary, Grand Rapids, Mich.
Articles contributed: CHRISTIAN REFORMED CHURCH IN NORTH AMERICA.

Sachs, William
Episcopal Church Foundation, New York, N.Y.
Articles contributed: CAMBRIDGE PLATFORM; CROMWELL, THOMAS; KEBLE, JOHN; LAW, WILLIAM; NEILL, STEPHEN CHARLES; NEWMAN, JOHN HENRY; RAIKES, ROBERT.

Saillant, John
Western Michigan University, Kalamazoo, Mich.
Articles contributed: ALLEN, RICHARD; CARY, LOTT; DOUGLASS, FREDERICK.

Samarin, William J.
University of Toronto, Canada
Articles contributed: TONGUES, SPEAKING IN.

Sauter, Gerhard
University of Bonn (Germany)
Articles contributed: GRACE.

Schattauer, Thomas H.
Wartburg Theological Seminary, Dubuque, Iowa
Articles contributed: LOHE, WILHELM.

Scheick, William J.
University of Texas at Austin
Articles contributed: ADAMS, HANNAH; BRADSTREET, ANNE; JEREMIAD; MATHER, INCREASE.

Schildgen, Robert
Sierra Club, San Francisco, Calif.
Articles contributed: KAGAWA, TOYOHIKO.

Schilson, Arno
University of Mainz (Germany)
Articles contributed: REIMARUS, HERMANN SAMUEL.

Schmid, Alois
Universität München (Germany)
Articles contributed: MARBURG, COLLOQUY OF.

Schneider, Robert
Temple University, Philadelphia, Pa.
Articles contributed: ANDERSON, RUFUS.

Scholer, David M.
Fuller Seminary, Pasadena, Calif.
Articles contributed: AMERICAN BAPTIST CHURCHES; GENERAL ASSOCIATION OF REGULAR BAPTIST CHURCHES; JUDSON, ADONIRAM.

Schuler, Rhoda
Concordia College, Moorhead, Minn.
Articles contributed: CONFIRMATION.

Schwanke, Johannes
University of Tubingen (Germany)
Articles contributed: BAUR, FERDINAND CHRISTIAN.

Schwinge, Gerhard
Independent scholar (Durmersheim, Germany)
Articles contributed: BLUMHARDT, CHRISTOPH FRIEDRICH; JUNG-STILLING, JOHANN HEINRICH; KUTTER, HERMANN; NEANDER, JOHANN AUGUST WILHELM.

Scott, Alana Cain
Morehead State University, Morehead, Ky.
Articles contributed: CROMWELL, OLIVER.

Seager, Richard
Hamilton College, Clinton, N.Y.
Articles contributed: WORLD'S PARLIAMENT OF RELIGIONS.

Sedgwick, Peter
Board for Social Responsibility, Church of England (London, England)
Articles contributed: ECONOMICS.

Seligman, Adam B.
Boston University, Mass.
Articles contributed: TOLERATION.

Senn, Frank C.
Immanuel Lutheran Church, Evanston, Ill.
Articles contributed: PRAYER; VESTMENTS.

Shenk, Wilbert R.
Fuller Theological Seminary, Pasadena, Calif.
Articles contributed: MISSIOLOGY; MOTT, JOHN RALEIGH; WORLD COUNCIL OF CHURCHES; WORLD MISSIONARY CONFERENCE.

Sheveland, John
Boston College, Chestnut Hill, Mass.
Articles contributed: SIN.

Shore, Paul
Saint Louis University, Mo.
Articles contributed: BOEHME, JAKOB.

Shriver, George H.
Georgia Southern University, Statesboro, Ga.
Articles contributed: AMERICANS UNITED FOR THE SEPARATION OF CHURCH AND STATE; CAREY, WILLIAM; HERESY.

Shuck, Glenn W.
Rice University, Houston, Tex.
Articles contributed: TELEVANGELISM.

Shults, F. LeRon
Bethel Theological Seminary, St. Paul, Minn.
Articles contributed: PANNENBERG, WOLFHART.

Sidwell, Mark
Bob Jones University, Greenville, S.C.
Articles contributed: BIBLE CONFERENCES.

Siker, Jeffrey S.
Loyola Marymount University, Los Angeles, Calif.
Articles contributed: HOMOSEXUALITY.

Skarsten, Trygve R.
Trinity Lutheran College, Issaquah, Wash.
Articles contributed: PETRI, LAURENTIUS; PETRI, OLAUS;
SWEDEN; TAUSEN, HANS.

Smith, Harmon L.
Duke University, Durham, N.C.
Articles contributed: ETHICS, MEDICAL; TEMPLE, WILLIAM.

Smith, Ruth
Cambridge University (England)
Articles contributed: HANDEL, GEORGE FRIDERIC.

Smylie, James
*Union Theological Seminary and Presbyterian School of
Christian Education, Richmond, Va.*
Articles contributed: PRESBYTERIAN CHURCH U.S.A.;
PRESBYTERIANISM.

Snobelen, Stephen D.
University of King's College, Nova Scotia, Canada
Articles contributed: WHISTON, WILLIAM.

Snyder, Howard A.
Asbury Theological Seminary, Wilmore, Ky.
Articles contributed: MISSIONS, NORTH AMERICAN.

Sonderegger, Katherine
Virginia Theological Seminary, Alexandria,Va.
Articles contributed: BARTH, KARL.

Song, Choan-Seng
Pacific School of Religion, Berkeley, Calif.
Articles contributed: ASIAN THEOLOGY.

Spargo, Tamsin
Liverpool John Moores University (England)
Articles contributed: PILGRIM'S PROGRESS.

Sprunger, Keith L.
Bethel College, North Newton, Kans.
Articles contributed: MENNONITES, GENERAL CONFERENCE OF.

Stackhouse, Jr., John G.
Regent College, Vancouver, Canada
Articles contributed: CANADA.

Stange, Mary Zeiss
Skidmore College, Saratoga Springs, N.Y.
Articles contributed: BRANCH DAVIDIANS.

Stassen, Glen H.
Fuller Theological Seminary, Pasadena, Calif.
Articles contributed: NIEBUHR, REINHOLD; PEACE
ORGANIZATIONS; WAR.

Stein, Stephen J.
Indiana University, Bloomington, Ind.
Articles contributed: SHAKERS.

Stenmark, Mikael
Uppsala Universitet (Sweden)
Articles contributed: SCIENTISM.

Sterk, Andrea
University of Notre Dame, South Bend, Ind.
Articles contributed: COMENIUS, JOHN.

Stevenson, Kenneth
Bishop of Portsmouth, Church of England (England)
Articles contributed: CHURCH OF ENGLAND.

Stewart-Robertson, J.C.
University of New Brunswick, Saint John, Canada
Articles contributed: SCOTLAND; SCOTTISH COMMON SENSE
REALISM.

Stjerna, Kirsi
Lutheran Theological Seminary, Gettysburg, Pa.
Articles contributed: AUGSBURG CONFESSION, APOLOGY OF.

Stockdale, Nancy L.
University of Central Florida, Orlando, Fla.
Articles contributed: POST-COLONIALISM.

Stout, Harry
Yale University, New Haven, Conn.
Articles contributed: CIVIL WAR, UNITED STATES.

Streiff, Patrick
United Methodist Church Europe (Switzerland)
Articles contributed: METHODISM, EUROPE.

Strom, Jonathan
Emory University, Atlanta, Ga.
Articles contributed: HALLE; MOSHEIM, JOHANN LORENZ;
PIETISM; SEMLER, JOHANN SALOMO.

Stunt, Timothy C.F.
Wooster School, Danbury, Conn.
Articles contributed: MERLE D'AUBIGNE, JEAN HENRI; REVEIL.

Suiter, David E.
Iliff School of Theology, Denver, Colo.
Articles contributed: PERIODICALS, PROTESTANT.

CONTRIBUTORS

Sunquist, Scott W.
Pittsburgh Theological Seminary, Pa.
Articles contributed: EDUCATION, THEOLOGY: ASIA; SUNG, JOHN (SONG SHANGJIE); TAIWAN.

Sunshine, Glenn
Central Connecticut State University, New Britain, Conn.
Articles contributed: CHURCH DISCIPLINE.

Surin, Kenneth
Duke University, Durham, N.C.
Articles contributed: POSTMODERNITY.

Svelmoe, William L.
Saint Mary's College, Notre Dame, Ind.
Articles contributed: WYCLIFFE BIBLE TRANSLATORS.

Swatos Jr., William H.
Association for the Sociology of Religion, Holiday, Fla.
Articles contributed: SEEKER; SEEKER CHURCHES.

Swierenga, Robert P.
Hope College, Holland, Mich.
Articles contributed: DUTCH PROTESTANTS IN AMERICA.

Sydnor, Jon Paul
Boston College, Chestnut Hill, Mass.
Articles contributed: BAUMGARTEN, SIEGMUND JAKOB.

Szasz, Ferenc Morton
University of New Mexico, Albuquerque, N. Mex.
Articles contributed: SHELDON, CHARLES.

Szczucki, Lech
Polish Academy of Sciences (Poland)
Articles contributed: ANTI-TRINITARIANISM; KECKERMANN, BARTHOLOMEW; LASKI, JAN; MODRZEWSKI, ANDREIJ; POLAND; SOCINIANISM; SOZZINI, FAUSTO (SOCINUS).

Tait, Edwin R.
Duke University, Durham, N.C.
Articles contributed: GENEVA CATECHISM; REGENSBURG COLLOQUY.

Táíwò, Olúfémi
Seattle University, Wash.
Articles contributed: AFRICAN INSTITUTED CHURCHES.

Tamcke, Martin
Georg-August-Universität (Germany)
Articles contributed: MISSIONS, GERMAN; MOLANUS, GERHARD WOLTER.

Taylor, Eugene I.
Saybrook Institute, San Francisco, Calif. and Harvard University, Cambridge, Mass.
Articles contributed: JUNGIANISM.

Teply, Alison J.
Cambridge University (England)
Articles contributed: LATITUDINARIANISM.

Thatcher, Adrian
College of Saint Mark and Saint John (England)
Articles contributed: MARRIAGE.

Thomas, Joseph L.
Trinity Evangelical Divinity School, Deerfield, Ill.
Articles contributed: DAVIES, SAMUEL.

Thompson, David
University of Cambridge (England)
Articles contributed: BRITISH COUNCIL OF CHURCHES.

Thomson, Keith S.
Oxford University Museum (England)
Articles contributed: WILBERFORCE, SAMUEL.

Thorkildsen, Dag
University of Oslo (Norway)
Articles contributed: NORWAY.

Tinsley, Barbara Sher
Stanford University, Calif.
Articles contributed: BARNES, ROBERT; BAYLE, PIERRE; CAPPEL, LOUIS; JURIEU, PIERRE.

Tipton, Steven Michael
Emory University, Atlanta, Ga.
Articles contributed: INDIVIDUALISM.

Tripp, David H.
Rolling Prairie United Methodist Church, Rolling Prairie, Ind.
Articles contributed: ARNDT, JOHANN; BELL, GEORGE; BENTLEY, RICHARD; CHARITY; CHURCH LAW; DAVIDSON, RANDALL THOMAS; FEET, WASHING OF; FREE CHURCH; JOHNSON, SAMUEL; OBSERVANCES; PARKER, MATTHEW; TILLOTSON, JOHN; UNIVERSALISM.

Tseng, Timothy
American Baptist Seminary of the West, Berkeley, Calif.
Articles contributed: ASIAN-AMERICAN PROTESTANTISM.

Tucker, Karen Westerfield
Duke University, Durham, N.C.
Articles contributed: BUXTEHUDE, DIETRICH; DIVORCE; METHODISM, GLOBAL; WORSHIP.

Underwood, Grant
Brigham Young University, Provo, Utah
Articles contributed: PLURAL MARRIAGE.

Upson-Saia, Kristi
Duke University, Durham, N.C.
Articles contributed: COMMUNISM.

Van Die, Marguerite
Queen's University, Ontario, Canada
Articles contributed: ALLINE, HENRY.

Varvis, Stephen
Fresno Pacific University, Calif.
Articles contributed: CHILLINGWORTH, WILLIAM.

Visser, Derk
Ursinus College, Collegeville, Pa.
Articles contributed: COVENANT.

Vogt, Peter
Harvard University, Cambridge, Mass.
Articles contributed: MORAVIAN CHURCH; ZINZENDORF, NIKOLAUS LUDWIG VON.

Wainwright, Geoffrey
Duke University, Durham, N.C.
Articles contributed: BAPTISM; CONSULTATION ON CHURCH UNION (COCU); DIALOGUE, INTERCONFESSIONAL; DOCTRINE; NEWBIGIN, J. E. LESSLIE; WORLD METHODIST COUNCIL.

Waite, Gary K.
University of New Brunswick, Canada
Articles contributed: MENNO SIMONS.

Walker, Pamela J.
Carleton University, Ontario, Canada
Articles contributed: BOOTH, CATHERINE; BOOTH, WILLIAM; SALVATION ARMY.

Wallace, Jr., Dewey D.
George Washington University, Washington, D.C.
Articles contributed: AMES, WILLIAM; BAXTER, RICHARD; ROBINSON, JOHN ARTHUR THOMAS.

Walls, Andrew
Scottish Institute of Missionary Studies, University of Aberdeen (Scotland)
Articles contributed: AZARIAH, V. S.; CLAPHAM SECT; CROWTHER, SAMUEL; GHANA; HARRIS, WILLIAM WADE; INCULTURATION; JABAVU, DAVIDSON DON TENGO; KILHAM, HANNAH; KOELLE, SIGISMUND W.; LIANG A-FA (LIANG FA; LEANG A-FA); LUTHULI, ALBERT JOHN; MATTHEWS, Z. K.; PILKINGTON, GEORGE LAWRENCE; SCHON, JAMES FREDERICK; SHARP, GRANVILLE; SIERRA LEONE; STUDD, CHARLES THOMAS; TUTU, DESMOND.

Wasmuth, Jennifer
University of Erlangen (Germany)
Articles contributed: RUSSIA.

Waterman, A. M. C.
University of Manitoba, Canada
Articles contributed: CAMBRIDGE UNIVERSITY; PALEY, WILLIAM.

Weaver-Zercher, David L.
Messiah College, Grantham, Pa.
Articles contributed: AMANA; BRETHREN IN CHRIST.

Webb, Stephen H.
Wabash College, Crawfordsville, Ind.
Articles contributed: EDUCATION, OVERVIEW.

Weber, Timothy
Northern Baptist Theological Seminary, Lombard, Ill.
Articles contributed: CONSERVATIVE BAPTIST ASSOCIATION.

Weddle, David L.
Colorado College, Colorado Springs, Colo.
Articles contributed: JEHOVAH'S WITNESSES.

Weigelt, Horst
University of Bamberg (Germany)
Articles contributed: LAVATER, JOHANN KASPAR.

Welch, Thomas A.
McGill University, Quebec, Canada
Articles contributed: DU PLESSIS, DAVID JOHANNES.

Wentz, Richard
Arizona State University, Tempe, Ariz.
Articles contributed: MERCERSBURG THEOLOGY; MUHLENBERG, HENRY MELCHIOR.

Wenzke, Annabelle S.
Pennsylvania State University, York
Articles contributed: DWIGHT, TIMOTHY.

Westermeyer, Paul
Luther Seminary, St. Paul, Minn.
Articles contributed: SCHÜTZ, HEINRICH.

Westmoreland-White, Michael
Louisville, Ky.
Articles contributed: WAR.

White, James F.
Notre Dame University, South Bend, Ind.
Articles contributed: ARCHITECTURE, CHURCH.

Whitford, David M.
Claflin University, Orangeburg, S.C.
Articles contributed: CANTERBURY; CANTERBURY AND YORK, CONVOCATIONS OF; FONTAINEBLEAU, EDICT OF; GALLUS, NIKOLAUS; TETRAPOLITAN CONFESSION.

Wickeri, Philip L.
San Francisco Theological Seminary, San Anselmo, Calif.
Articles contributed: CHAO, T.C. (ZHAO ZICHEN); TING, K.H.; WU, Y.T. (WU, YAOZONG).

Wiesner-Hanks, Merry
University of Wisconsin-Milwaukee
Articles contributed: PROSTITUTION; SEXUALITY.

CONTRIBUTORS

Willaime, Jean-Paul
École pratique des hautes etudes (France)
Articles contributed: ENLIGHTENMENT; NANTES, EDICT OF; TROELTSCH, ERNST.

Williams, Howell
Florida State University, Tallahassee, Fla.
Articles contributed: FINLEY, ROBERT; KRUDENER, BARBARA.

Willimon, William H.
Duke University, Durham, N.C.
Articles contributed: PREACHING.

Willis, III, Lee L.
Florida State University, Tallahassee, Fla.
Articles contributed: FINNEY, CHARLES GRANDISON.

Wills, Anne Blue
Davidson College, N.C.
Articles contributed: SMITH, HANNAH WHITALL.

Wilson, James A.
Vorys, Sater, Seymour, and Pease LLP, Columbus, Ohio
Articles contributed: PRESBYTERIAN CHURCH GOVERNMENT.

Witte, Jr., John
Emory University, Atlanta, Ga.
Articles contributed: DEMOCRACY; POLITICS.

Woodward, Kenneth L.
Newsweek, New York, N.Y.
Articles contributed: SAINTS.

Wosh, Peter J.
New York University, N.Y.
Articles contributed: AMERICAN BIBLE SOCIETY; AMERICAN BIBLE UNION; BIBLE SOCIETIES; SCOFIELD REFERENCE BIBLE; VOLUNTARY SOCIETIES.

Wriedt, M.
Institut fuer Europaeische Geschichte (Mainz, Germany)
Articles contributed: EDUCATION, THEOLOGY: EUROPE; WORMS, DIET OF; WORMS, EDICT OF.

Wright, William J.
University of Tennessee, Chattanooga, Tenn.
Articles contributed: PHILIP OF HESSE.

Wyduckel, Dieter
der Technischen Universitat Dresden (Germany)
Articles contributed: ALTHUSIUS, JOHANNES.

Yates, Nigel
University of Wales, Lampeter
Articles contributed: ENGLAND.

Yates, Timothy
Author, lecturer, and parish priest (Derbyshire, England)
Articles contributed: LIGHTFOOT, JOSEPH BARBER; MIDDLETON, THOMAS FANSHAW; OLDHAM, JOSEPH H.; TAIT, ARCHIBALD CAMPBELL.

Yong, Amos
Bethel College, St. Paul, Minn.
Articles contributed: RAPTURE.

Yrigoyen, Jr., Charles
Drew University, Madison, N.J.
Articles contributed: CONFERENCE; METHODISM, NORTH AMERICA; UNITED METHODIST CHURCH.

Zachman, Randall C.
University of Notre Dame, South Bend, Ind.
Articles contributed: CONFESSION.

Zele, Adam
Duke University, Durham, N.C.
Articles contributed: BALTIMORE CONFERENCE; BLACK METHODISTS.

Zepp, Jr., Ira G.
McDaniel College, Westminster, Md.
Articles contributed: CIVIL RIGHTS MOVEMENT; KING, MARTIN LUTHER, JR.

Ziegler, Philip G.
Atlantic School of Theology, Nova Scotia, Canada
Articles contributed: AUTHORITY.

Ziolkowski, Eric
Lafayette College, Easton, Pa.
Articles contributed: CULTURAL PROTESTANTISM.

Index

Page numbers in **boldface** indicate entry titles.

Blavatsky, Helena Petrovna, 1389
Bliss, Philip Paul, **262–263**
Bloch, Ernst, 1031
Blomfield, Charles, **263**
Blond, Phillip, 1530
Blood of the Lamb (De Vries), 588
Blood transfusion, 736
   prohibition by Jehovah's Witnesses, 981
Bloom, Harold, 1575
   biblical influence on, 231
Bloudy Tenant of Persecution, for Cause of Conscience (Williams), 2013
Blount, Charles, **263–264**
   on deism, 570
Blow, John, compositions by, 1332
Blue laws, 345
Blumhardt, Christoph Friedrich, **264**, 1044
   Basel Mission and, 205
   influence on Karl Barth, 203
   missionary institute and, 1274
Blyden, Edward Wilmot, black nationalism and, 1095
Boardman, George Dana, 998
   missionary work, 179
Boardman, Mary, 1016
Boardman, Richard, 966
Boardman, Sarah Hall, 998
Boardman, William, 870, 877, 1016
Bob Jones University, 404
Bobrowski, Johannes, writings, 1111
Bodelschwingh, Friedrich Christian Carl, **264–266**
Bodenstein von Karlstadt, abolishment of art in religion, 105
Bodmer, Johann Jakob, writings, 1108
Boehm, John Philip, 812
Boehm, Martin, 813
   influence among Mennonites, 300
Boehme, Jakob (also Boehm, Böhm, Behme, Behmen), **266–267**
   influence on Leade, 1075
Boekbinder, Gerard, Münster Anabaptists and, 1199
Boer, Harry R., 1543
Boesak, Alan Aubrey, **267–269,** 1527
Boff, Leonardo, 990, 1031
Bogard, Ben M., American Baptist Convention and, 173
Bohemian Brethren, 908
   Comenius in, 483–484
Böhme, Jakob, 1621
Bohse, August, writings, 1107
Bolsec, Jerome, 1597
Bombay Native Christian Church, 1405
Bonhoeffer, Dietrich, **269–273,** 881, 1368
   christology of, 415
   on death of God, 565–566
   on ethics, 692
   execution of, 1140, 1170
   on faith, 735
   on Nazi regime, 1904
   Neo-Orthodoxy and, 1379, 1381
   process theology and, 1293
   on reality of God, 1873

   religionless Christianity of, 1881
   as saint, 1642
Bonino, José Míguez, 1527
   liberation theology and, 1091
Bonino, Miguez, 990
Bonn Agreement, 589
Book of Acts, Stephen martyrdom in, 1640
Book of Common Prayer, **273–278,** 335, 432, 875, 917, 1513, 1532–1533, 1578, 1584
   Anglican chant, 65–66
   Anglican spirituality, 67–68
   baptismal rite, 163–164
   Calvinism in, 668
   Cambride Platonists acceptance of, 339
   confirmation in, 501, 504–505
   Cranmer, 273, 1113
   funerary rites in, 797
   John Bunyan's views on, 320
   liturgy, 1112
   Oliver Cromwell on, 536
Book of Common Worship, liturgy, 1112
Book of Concord, **278–283,** 334, 825, 1407, 1423
   German Lutheranism and, 1131
   Lutheranism defined in, 498, 1662
Book of Martyrs. see also Acts and Monuments
   Foxe, 762–763
Book of Mormon, 1313
   Mormonism and, 1314–1315
   Smith, 1697, 1747–1748
   translations, 250
Books
   American religious best-sellers, 218–221
   Bible and Literature, 227–232
Booth, Catherine, **283–285**
Booth, Joseph, **285**
Booth, L. Venchael, 1569
Booth, William, **285–288,** 1610
   Methodism and, 1214
Booth, William and Catherine, Salvation Army founding by, 1646–1648
Borg, Marcus, 990
Borgeois family, 740–742
Born again, speaking in tongues and, 1900
Bornkamm, Gunter, 989
Bosch, David Jacobus, **288–289**
   LCWE and, 1073–1074
Bosnia, Baptist Union in, 186
Boswell, James, 900, 993
Bote, Herman, writings, 1105
Boucher, Jonathan, **289**
Boudinot, Elias, **289–290,** 1547
Bourne, Hugh, **290,** 1566
Bouwens, Leenaert, Menno and, 1201
Boxer Rebellion, 1846
Boxer Uprising, 387
Boyd, R.H. (Rev.), 174, 1349–1352
Boyd Convention, 1350
Boyesen, H. H., 1364
Boyle, Robert, **291**
   views on nature, 1369, 1371

on divorce, 604
episcopacy and, 254
preaching by, 1536
views on polygamy, 1495
Buchanan, Claudius, 938
Buchman, Frank, Moral Rearmament and, 1307
Büchner, Georg, writings, 1110
Buck, Pearl S., 1555
Buckle, H. T., 1681, 1685
Buddeus, Johann Franz, Lutheranism and, 1133
Buddhism, in movies, 1321
Bugenhagen, Johannes, **314,** 814, 1472, 1599, 1623
ecclesiastical ordinances of, 627
power of princes and, 1137
Scandinavian Reformation and, 1144
Bulgaria
Baptist Union in, 187
Methodism in, 1217, 1219
Bulkeley, Peter, 229
Bullinger, Heinrich, **314–316,** 856–857, 910, 1383, 1578, 1597
concept of justification, 1004
on covenant, 523, 526
on the Lord's Supper, 1118
on Marian devotions, 1173
preaching by, 1536
in Swiss Reformation, 1838
views on predestination, 1543
Zwinglianism leadership by, 2083–2085
Bultmann, Rudolf, 986, 989, 1012, 1021, 1029, 1030, 1378, 1388, 1441
christology of, 415
theology of, 1873
Bultmann, Rudolf Karl, **316–319**
Bunting, Jabez, mission work of, 1213
Bunyan, John, **319–321,** 928, 1036, 1493, 1534, 1574, 1580, 1620, 1911
Bible translation, 228
on healing, 736
incarceration of, 1053
Pilgrim's Progress, 1102
on sin, 779–780
Burch, Robert, creation of the AME church and, 256
Burchell, Thomas, Baptist work, 177
Bürger, Gottfried August
Sturm und Drang movement and, 1108
writings, 1110
Burial Traditions. *see* Funerary Rites
Burlamacchi, Fabrizio, 962
Burma, Baptist missions to, 179
Burned-Over District, **321–322**
Burne-Jones, Edward, 1546
Burnet, Gilbert, Latitudinarianism and, 1064, 1065
Burpee, Laleah, missionary activities, 174
Burpee, Richard E., missionary activities, 174
Burritt, Elihu, 1439
Burroughs, Nannie Helen, 1351
Bursche, Juliusz, 1504, 1505
Bush-meeting Dutch, **813**

Bushnell, Horace, **322,** 1459, 1592
on childhood nuturing, 380
on education, 648
on sports and Protestantism, 1805
Bushyhead, Jesse, 1361
Butler, Bishop Joseph, 901
Butler, Joseph, **322–323,** 1375
on deism, 571
Latitudinarianism and, 1066
Butler, Josephine Elizabeth, **323–325,** 1751
Butterfield, Herbert, **325**
Buttlar, Eva von, 1490
Buttrick, George A., 1534
Butzer, Martin. *see* Bucer, Martin
Buxtehude, Deitrich, **326**
Buxton, Thomas Fowel, humanitarian work of, 1266
Byrd, William, compositions by, 1331
Byzantine icons, 926

Cadbury, George, **327**
Caedmon, "Hymn," 1099
Cain, Richard Harvey, AME Church, South Carolina, 21
Calendar reform, 874–876
Calixt (Callisen), Georg, **327–328**
Lutheran orthodoxy and, 1132
Called to Common Mission, 2001, Episcopal Church of the USA and Evangelical Lutheran Church, 69, 705–706
Calov, Abraham, 1424
writings, 1131
Calvert family, **328**
Calvin, John, 7, **328–331,** 807, 1578, 1609
altar controversy, 30
art in religion, 105–106
atonement and, 125
on baptism, 163
on Biblical inspiration, 224
on capital punishment, 349
catechism of, 361, 380
christology of, 410–411
on church and state, 419–420
on church discipline, 424
on components of worship, 2060
concept of justification, 1001, 1003
concept of Kingdom of God, 1027
concept of Lord's Supper, 1596–1597
condemnation of Servetus by, 1714
on confirmation, 165–166, 502–503
on conversion, 519
on corruption of human mind by Fall, 1671
on divorce, 604
on doctrinal authority of scripture, 607
on double predestination, 656
ecclesiastical ordinances of, 627–628
on education, 643, 647–648
episcopacy and, 254
establishment of Geneva Academy by, 867
on ethics, 691–692
on faith, 733
on free will, 585
Geneva Catechism of, **807–809,** 855

Independent Fundamentalist Churches, **935–936**
  Mormonism and, 1314
  National Association of Evangelicals and, 1348
  sectarianism in, 1691, 1698–1700
  secularization and, 1705
  sexuality and, 1724–1725
  in Southern Protestantism, 1793–1794
  in twentieth century, 1879–1880
  in twentieth century North America, 1883
  vs. restorationism, 1608
  Wesleyan Church on, 1990
  William Jennings Bryan and, 311–312
Fundamental Principles, in Seventh-Day Adventist theology, 1716
Fundament of Christian Life (Menno), 1196
Funerary rites, **796–798,** 1418
Funk, Robert, 990
Funk, Ulrich, Colloquy of Marburg and, 1158
Fürecker, Christofer, Latvian hymns and, 1068
Furly, Benjamin, 1605
Furman, Richard, on slaveholding, 196

Gaebelein, A. C., Sea Cliff Bible Conference and, 239
Gallican Confession, **799,** 1598, 1841
  of 1559, Belgic Confession and, 213
Gallicanism, absolutism and, 3
Gallus, Nikolaus, **799–800,** 825
Galphin, Jesse, ministry, 194
Gandhi, Mohandas K., 1783
  on Christian conversions, 1180
Gano, John, ministry, 193
Gardiner, William, 916
Garrison, William Lloyd, 1439
  on slavery abolition, 1743
Garrison, Winfred, **800**
Gassendi, Pierre, 871
Gassmann, Günther, Lutheran ecumenical movement and, 1136
Gaussen, Louis, 1609
Gaustad, Edwin, 1575
Gay Christians, 882–885
Gee, Donald, 1455
Gellert, Christian Fürchtegott, writings, 1108
Gellner, Ernest, 1356
Gender, **801–804**
  homosexuality and, **882–885**
  household codes and, 1164–1165
  liberation theology and, 1090, 1091
  machismo and poor women, 1062
  Margaret Fuller on, 790
  role of the laity and, 1054
General Association of Regular Baptists, **804–805**
  formation, 172, 180
  formation of, 169
General Baptists, 770–771, **805–807**
  American (*see* American Baptist Churches (ABC-USA))
  understanding of atonement, 188
General Baptists (Arminians), beliefs, 170, 185
General Protestant Missionary Society, in China, 1275
Genesis Flood (Whitcomb and Morris), 532

Geneva
  Calvin in, 329–331
  church discipline in, 424–425
  Declaration of, 695
  as printing center, 331
Geneva Academy, 867
Geneva Bible, 247, **807,** 867, 1444, 1578
Geneva Catechism, 497, **807–809,** 855
Geneva consistory, 515
Geneva gown, 1963
Genischen, Hans-Werner, on missions, 1278
George, David, **809**
  missionary efforts, 1254
George, Henry, 1592
George Stefan, writings, 1111
Georgia Test Case, 171
Gereformeerde Kerk. *See* Dutch Reformed Church
Gerhard, Johann, 1486, 1534
  Lutheranism and, 1138
  writings, 1131
Gerhardt, Paul, **809–810,** 915, 1486
  Lutheran orthodoxy and, 1132
  songs of, 1106
German Baptist Brethren, 811
  size of, 303
German Catechism, 807
German Catholics, 813
German Christians, **810–811,** 827
  Barmen Declaration and, 497, 611
  on church and state, 421
  ethnicity and, 699
  Holocaust and, 880–881
  Nazi support by, 488–489, 497, 1873, 1903
  Protestant folk church and, 1140
  support of Hitler by, 488–489, 497, 1873, 1904
German Democratic Republic, Protestantism and, 1904–1905
German Evangelical Missionary Council (*Deutscher Evanglischer Missonsrat*), 1277
German Evangelicals, in United Church of Christ, 1935
German groups in America, 811–813
German philosophy, Wolff contribution to, 2025
German Reformed Church, 812–813
  in United Church of Christ, 1934–1935
Germany, **813–818**
  AFSC work in, 43
  Baptists in, 186
  Barmen Declaration, 199–201
  Calvinism in, 334
  civil divorce laws in, 603
  deism in, 571–572
  education system in, 641
  Enlightenment in, 673
  fifteenth century, 153
  Halle, **837–838**
  Herrnhut, **864–865**
  literature of, 1105–1111
  Lutheran church moral influence in, 576
  medical ethics in, 694
  Methodism in, 1216–1217, 1218, 1219
  nationalism in, 1356–1358, 1816